Novel & Short Story Writers Market®

includes a 1-year online subscription to
Novel & Short Story Writer's Market on WritersMarket.com

WritersMarket.com
WHERE & HOW TO SELL WHAT YOU WRITE

THE ULTIMATE MARKET RESEARCH TOOL FOR WRITERS

To register your
2010 Novel & Short Story Writer's Market book and
START YOUR 1-YEAR ONLINE GENRE ONLY SUBSCRIPTION,
scratch off the block below to reveal your activation
code, then go to www.WritersMarket.com. Click on
"Sign Up Now" and enter your contact information
and activation code. It's that easy!

UPDATED MARKET LISTINGS FOR YOUR INTEREST AREA

EASY-TO-USE SEARCHABLE DATABASE

DAILY UPDATES

RECORD KEEPING TOOLS

INDUSTRY NEWS

PROFESSIONAL TIPS AND ADVICE

Your purchase of *Novel & Short Story Writer's Market* gives you access to updated listings related to this genre of writing. For just $9.99, you can upgrade your subscription and get access to listings from all of our best-selling Market books. Visit www. WritersMarket.com for more information.

WritersMarket.com
WHERE & HOW TO SELL WHAT YOU WRITE

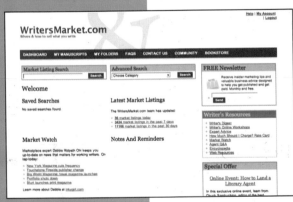

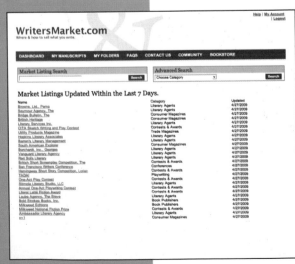

Activate your WritersMarket.com subscription to get instant access to:

- **Updated listings in your writing genre** — Find additional listings that didn't make it into the book, updated contact information and more. WritersMarket.com provides the most comprehensive database of verified markets available anywhere.

- **Easy-to-use searchable database** — Looking for a specific magazine or book publisher? Just type in its name. Or widen your prospects with the Advanced Search. You can also search for listings that have been recently updated!

- **Personalized tools** — Store your best-bet markets, and use our popular record-keeping tools to track your submissions. Plus, get new and updated market listings, query reminders, and more – every time you log in!

- **Professional tips & advice** — From pay rate charts to sample query letters, and from how-to articles to Q&A's with literary agents, we have the resources freelance writers need.

- **Industry Updates** — Debbie Ridpath Ohi's Market Watch column keeps you up-to-date on the latest publishing industry news, so you'll always be in-the-know.

YOU'LL GET ALL OF THIS
WITH YOUR INCLUDED SUBSCRIPTION TO
WritersMarket.com

To put the full power of WritersMarket.com to work for you, upgrade your subscription and get access to listings from all of our best-selling Market books. Find out more at www.WritersMarket.com

2010 29TH ANNUAL EDITION

NOVEL & SHORT STORY WRITER'S MARKET.®

Alice Pope, Editor

WRITER'S DIGEST BOOKS
CINCINNATI, OH

Complaint Procedure

If you feel you have not been treated fairly by a listing in *Novel & Short Story Writer's Market*, we advise you take the following steps:

- First try to contact the listing. Sometimes one phone call or a letter can quickly clear up the matter.

- Document all your correspondence with the listing. When you write us with a complaint, provide the details of your submission, the date of your first contact with the listing and the nature of your subsequent correspondence.

- We will enter your letter into our files and attempt to contact the listing. The number and severity of complaints will be considered in our decision whether or not to delete the listing from the next edition.

Publisher & Editorial Director, Writing Communities: Jane Friedman
Managing Editor, Writer's Digest Market Books: Alice Pope

Writer's Market Web site: www.writersmarket.com
Writer's Digest Web site: www.writersdigest.com

2010 Novel & Short Story Writer's Market. Copyright © 2009 by Writer's Digest Books. Published by F+W Media, Inc., 4700 East Galbraith Rd., Cincinnati, Ohio 45236. Printed and bound in the United States of America. All rights reserved. No part of this book may be reproduced in any form or by any electronic or mechanical means including information storage and retrieval systems without written permission from the publisher. Reviewers may quote brief passages to be printed in a magazine or newspaper.

Distributed in Canada by Fraser
Direct 100 Armstrong Avenue
Georgetown, ON, Canada L7G 5S4
Tel: (905) 877-4411

Distributed in the U.K. and Europe by David & Charles
Brunel House, Newton Abbot, Devon, TQ12 4PU, England
Tel: (+44) 1626 323200, Fax: (+44) 1626 323319
E-mail: postmaster@davidandcharles.co.uk

Distributed in Australia by Capricorn Link
P.O. Box 704, Windsor, NSW 2756 Australia
Tel: (02) 4577-3555

ISSN: 0897-9812
ISBN-13: 978-1-58297-581-8
ISBN-10: 1-58297-581-7

Cover design by Claudean Wheeler
Production coordinated by Greg Nock
Photographs © Frédéric Cirou/PhotoAlto

Attention Booksellers: This is an annual directory of F+W Media, Inc. Return deadline for this edition is December 31, 2010.

media

Contents

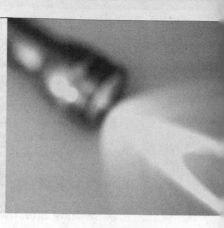

GETTING PUBLISHED

FOR MYSTERY WRITERS

FOR ROMANCE WRITERS

FOR SCIENCE FICTION, FANTASY & HORROR WRITERS

Gregory Forest

Mary Rosenblum

Brian Evenson

Patricia Briggs

MARKETS

RESOURCES

From the Editor

The book you hold in your hands is the very first edition of *Novel & Short Story Writer's Market* I edited from start to finish. For the previous edition I'd taken the helm midstream so I missed out on the really fun part of working on the book: coming up with story ideas.

So I delved into planning the 2010 edition of *Novel & Short Story Writer's Market* with a blank slate, just like all of you when you begin new writing projects. A blank page can be intimidating, sometimes even stifling. You can sit for hours staring at an empty screen hoping to be hit with some inspiration. For me, that just doesn't work. But when I stop trying, ideas flow more freely. (That's why, of course, some of our greatest creations are born in the shower or while dreaming or during a morning jog.)

When it comes to *Novel & Short Story Writer's Market*, however, the best ideas come from all you fiction writers out there. I spread the word and the queries arrive, my inbox bursting with ideas on topics I would never have conjured up myself, like Jack Smith's Writing Publishable Satire (page 41) or Janice Hussein's The Unsympathetic Protagonist (page 46).

My inbox held comedy (page 37), satire (page 41), and personal relationship fiction (page 31); romance (page 95), speculative fiction (page 109), and a bit of mystery (page 83). Writing conundrums were solved (page 23); new authors were discovered (page 17); tension was building (page 51).

It's not as easy for you, dear writers. You can't post to your blog or your Facebook page saying you need a few short story ideas or a novel plot. But that's not to say ideas aren't always around you. While sometimes the muse will simply sock it to you, she's usually more subtle. And you should make sure you're open to her voice.

When the muse is particularly fickle, take some advice from Tania Casselle's piece Reading With a Writer's Eye (page 9). She asks, How can reading other people's work practically help with your own writing? "First there's the sheer inspiration of reading wonderful fiction, the motivation it gives us to jump up from the armchair and hit the keyboard," she answers. "Then there's the osmosis factor—we absorb the art of writing just by reading widely, which emerges intuitively in our work. But when our intuition fails, when we're stuck in a project, or realize that we need to polish up a craft area, that's the time to turn our writer's eye to our favorite fiction."

Beyond reading you can follow some of I.J. Schecter's advice in Looking Skyward (page 27): eavesdrop, stargaze, write haiku… And once you get those ideas flowing onto the page, revised, polished, and ready for the world, turn to *Novel & Short Story Writer's Market* for ideas about what to do next.

Alice Pope
alice.pope@fwmedia.com
www.twitter.com/alicepope

You've Got a Story

So What Now?

To make the most of *Novel & Short Story Writer's Market*, you need to know how to use it. And with more than 600 pages of fiction publishing markets and resources, a writer could easily get lost amid the information. This quick-start guide will help you wind your way through the pages of *Novel & Short Story Writer's Market*, as well as the fiction publishing process, and emerge with your dream accomplished—to see your fiction in print.

1. Read, read, read. Read numerous magazines, fiction collections and novels to determine if your fiction compares favorably with work currently being published. If your fiction is at least the same caliber as that you're reading, then move on to step two. If not, postpone submitting your work and spend your time polishing your fiction. Writing and reading the work of others are the best ways to improve craft.

For help with craft and critique of your work:

- You'll find advice and inspiration from best-selling authors and top fiction editors in the Writing Life section, beginning on page 5.
- You'll find articles on the craft and business aspects of writing fiction in the Craft & Technique section, beginning on page 23, and in the Getting Published section, beginning on page 54.
- If you're a genre writer, you will find information in For Mystery Writers, beginning on page 83, For Romance Writers, beginning on page 95 and For Science Fiction, Fantasy & Horror Writers, beginning on page 109.
- You'll find Contest listings beginning on page 454.
- You'll find Conference & Workshop listings beginning on page 497.

2. Analyze your fiction. Determine the type of fiction you write to best target markets most suitable for your work. Do you write literary, genre, mainstream or one of many other categories of fiction? For definitions and explanations of genres and subgenres, see the Glossary beginning on page 555 and the Genre Glossary beginning on page 563. There are magazines and presses seeking specialized work in each of these areas as well as numerous others.

For editors and publishers with specialized interests, see the Category Index beginning on page 598.

3. Learn about the market. Read *Writer's Digest* magazine (F + W Media, Inc.); *Publishers Weekly*, the trade magazine of the publishing industry; and *Independent Publisher*, which contains information about small- to medium-sized independent presses. And don't forget the Internet. The number of sites for writers seems to grow daily, and among them you'll find www.writersmarket.com and www.writersdigest.com.

4. Find markets for your work. There are a variety of ways to locate markets for fiction. The periodicals sections of bookstores and libraries are great places to discover new journals and magazines that might be open to your type of short stories. Read writing-related magazines and newsletters for information about new markets and publications seeking fiction submissions. Also, frequently browse bookstore shelves to see what novels and short story collections are being published and by whom. Check acknowledgment pages for names of editors and agents, too. Online journals often have links to the Web sites of other journals that may publish fiction. And last but certainly not least, read the listings found here in *Novel & Short Story Writer's Market*.

Also, don't forget to utilize the Category Indexes at the back of this book to help you target your market for your fiction.

5. Send for guidelines. In the listings in this book, we try to include as much submission information as we can get from editors and publishers. Over the course of the year, however, editors' expectations and needs may change. Therefore, it is best to request submission guidelines by sending a self-addressed stamped envelope (SASE). You can also check each magazine's and press' Web site, which usually contains a page with guideline information. And for an even more comprehensive and continually updated online markets list, you can obtain a subscription to www.writersmarket.com.

6. Begin your publishing efforts with journals and contests open to beginners. If this is your first attempt at publishing your work, your best bet is to begin with local publications or those you know are open to beginning writers. Then, after you have built a publication history, you can try the more prestigious and nationally distributed magazines. For markets most open to beginners, look for the ☐ symbol preceding listing titles. Also, look for the ☑ symbol that identifies markets open to exceptional work from beginners as well as work from experienced, previously published writers.

7. Submit your fiction in a professional manner. Take the time to show editors that you care about your work and are serious about publishing. By following a publication's or book publisher's submission guidelines and practicing standard submission etiquette, you can increase your chances that an editor will want to take the time to read your work and consider it for publication. Remember, first impressions last, and a carelessly assembled

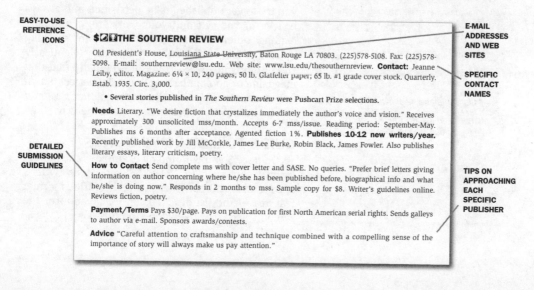

EASY-TO-USE REFERENCE ICONS

$☑☐☐**THE SOUTHERN REVIEW**

Old President's House, Louisiana State University, Baton Rouge LA 70803. (225)578-5108. Fax: (225)578-5098. E-mail: southernreview@lsu.edu. Web site: www.lsu.edu/thesouthernreview. **Contact:** Jeanne Leiby, editor. Magazine: 6¼ × 10, 240 pages, 50 lb. Glatfelter paper; 65 lb. #1 grade cover stock. Quarterly. Estab. 1935. Circ. 3,000.

• Several stories published in *The Southern Review* were Pushcart Prize selections.

Needs Literary. "We desire fiction that crystalizes immediately the author's voice and vision." Receives approximately 300 unsolicited mss/month. Accepts 6-7 mss/issue. Reading period: September-May. Publishes ms 6 months after acceptance. Agented fiction 1%. **Publishes 10-12 new writers/year.** Recently published work by Jill McCorkle, James Lee Burke, Robin Black, James Fowler. Also publishes literary essays, literary criticism, poetry.

How to Contact Send complete ms with cover letter and SASE. No queries. "Prefer brief letters giving information on author concerning where he/she has been published before, biographical info and what he/she is doing now." Responds in 2 months to mss. Sample copy for $8. Writer's guidelines online. Reviews fiction, poetry.

Payment/Terms Pays $30/page. Pays on publication for first North American serial rights. Sends galleys to author via e-mail. Sponsors awards/contests.

Advice "Careful attention to craftsmanship and technique combined with a compelling sense of the importance of story will always make us pay attention."

DETAILED SUBMISSION GUIDELINES

E-MAIL ADDRESSES AND WEB SITES

SPECIFIC CONTACT NAMES

TIPS ON APPROACHING EACH SPECIFIC PUBLISHER

2010 NOVEL & SHORT STORY WRITER'S MARKET KEY TO SYMBOLS

N market new to this edition

A publisher accepts agented submissions only

Ø market is closed to submissions

◯ actively seeking new writers

◑ seeks both new and established writers

◉ prefers working with established writers, mostly referrals

◎ only handles specific types of work

♔ award-winning market

✦ Canadian market

● market located outside of U.S. and Canada

◆ imprint, subsidiary or division of larger book publishing house (in book publishers section)

G publisher of graphic novels or comics

$ market pays (in magazine sections)

● comment from the editor of *Novel & Short Story Writer's Market*

ms, mss manuscript(s)

SASE self-addressed, stamped envelope

SAE self-addressed envelope

IRC International Reply Coupon, for use in countries other than your own

(For definitions of words and expressions relating specifically to writing and publishing, see the Glossary in the back of this book.)

submission packet can jeopardize your chances before your story or novel manuscript has had a chance to speak for itself. For help with preparing submissions read The Business of Fiction Writing, beginning on page 77.

8. Keep track of your submissions. Know when and where you have sent fiction and how long you need to wait before expecting a reply. If an editor does not respond by the time indicated in his market listing or guidelines, wait a few more months and then follow up with a letter (and SASE) asking when the editor anticipates making a decision. If you still do not receive a reply from the editor within a month or two, send a letter withdrawing your work from consideration and move on to the next market on your list.

9. Learn from rejection. Rejection is the hardest part of the publication process. Unfortunately, rejection happens to every writer, and every writer needs to learn to deal with the negativity involved. On the other hand, rejection can be valuable when used as a teaching tool rather than a reason to doubt yourself and your work. If an editor offers suggestions with his or her rejection slip, take those comments into consideration. You don't have to automatically agree with an editor's opinion of your work. It may be that the editor has a different perspective on the piece than you do. Or, you may find that the editor's suggestions give you new insight into your work and help you improve your craft.

10. Don't give up. The best advice for you as you try to get published is be persistent, and always believe in yourself and your work. By continually reading other writers' work, constantly working on the craft of fiction writing, and relentlessly submitting your work, you will eventually find that magazine or book publisher that's the perfect match for your fiction. *Novel & Short Story Writer's Market* will be here to help you every step of the way.

GUIDE TO LISTING FEATURES

On page 3 you will find an example of the market listings contained in *Novel & Short Story Writer's Market* with call-outs identifying the various format features of the listings. (For an explanation of the symbols used, see the sidebar on this page.)

Critique Groups

Should You Stay or Should You Go?

by Melissa Hart

Several years ago, I attended a 10-week fiction critique group and found myself sitting beside one man who snored audibly and another who paused in reading aloud to edit curse words from his story because there were women present. The facilitator ran the workshop in a cavalier, cut-throat style, encouraging us to savage one another's work. For this I paid $100.

Editors and literary agents are fond of telling emerging writers to find a critique group in order to workshop their prose and poetry before submitting it for possible publication. Allowing critics to review it first can mean the difference between a manuscript that finds a publisher, and one that languishes in a desk drawer. Groups may take the form of college courses, led by a professor in a classroom or online. They may be informal and cost-free, inspired by a Craigslist posting or flyer on a bookstore bulletin board, and led by a facilitator who may or may not have published work. They may include as many as 20 writers, or as few as two. A bad critique group can damage a writer irrevocably, causing him or her to throw down the pen in despair. A good one can launch a literary career.

Miriam Gershow, author of *The Local News* (Spiegel and Grau, 2009) owes at least some of her success as a novelist to a critique group. Years ago, with a B.S. in Women's Studies, she joined a formal longstanding writer's workshop in Portland, Oregon—a group so formidable that new members weren't allowed to submit their work for several weeks. "I was the lowest person on the totem pole," Gershow recounts. "In retrospect, that was a good thing because I learned so much. They taught me the basics about point of view, and about showing instead of telling. They hammered out all my bad habits as a writer."

She believes that finding a critique group can be vital if one hasn't earned a Master's degree in Creative Writing, and notes that her work with the Portland writers helped her to get into the MFA program at the University of Oregon. Still, she admits that problems can occur when people gather together to critique each other's work. "The main problem is mind-meld," she says, explaining the tendency of groups to congregate around particular criticism of a piece. "After a while, you can predict what the group will say about the work," she says. "The problem is, then you believe it's the whole truth about your writing."

Thirty years ago, environmental essayist and poet John Daniel attended workshops led by Denise Levertov and Kenneth Fields, on a Stanford Fellowship. He agrees with Gershow

MELISSA HART's newest memoir is *Gringa: A Contradictory Girlhood* (Seal, 2009). A contributing editor to *The Writer Magazine*, she teaches Journalism at the University of Oregon and Memoir Writing for U.C. Berkeley's online extension program. Visit her Web site, www.melissahart.com, and her blog for writers, http://butttochairthoughtsonthewritinglife. blogspot.com/.

about the dangers of what he terms "group think." "It can set in unconsciously," he explains, "and limit the range of comments. Group think in criticism can, over time, lead to group-write as well, as participants write, consciously or not, to suit the workshop audience. Workshoppers need to remember that writing is a solitary art and that the writer's eccentricities may well be closely tied to his genius."

I was still relatively new to writing when I discovered Daniel, whose newest book is *The Far Corner: Northwestern Views on Land, Life, and Literature* (Counterpoint, 2009). He offered a ten-week $250 workshop in memoir writing, but this time, I had to audition. "I did require writing samples," he notes, "because it's more fun to run a workshop—and for participants to take a workshop—composed of writers in the same range of experience and capability."

Daniel deemed my writing acceptable, and I met with him and seven other writers in a high-ceilinged printmaker's studio one evening a week. While red wine flowed freely and participants became friends, rules guided the group. Daniel asked us to submit writing a week ahead of time, giving participants a chance to consider each manuscript and make comments. He also asked us to refrain, when discussing a piece, from addressing the writer directly or by name.

"This author has a talent for humor writing," a woman said of my work one evening, "but this author also needs to take off the oven mitts when writing about painful subjects."

Somehow, the separation of my name from my writing helped me to see it clearly. Thanks to Daniel's perceptive leadership and his belief that writers need to know what's working about a piece, as well as what needs revision, I've continued to write memoir.

DANGERS OF CRITIQUE GROUPS

I got lucky—after one false start, I found a critique group that worked for me. But others regard them with skepticism, and even hostility. *New York Times* bestselling author and writing coach Michael Levin (www.Writer2Author.com) believes that they can be destructive to new writers. "You're getting criticism from people who generally aren't qualified to criticize writing," he explains. "Most people in groups, left to their own devices, will offer destructive rather than constructive criticism. People go to writing groups to get guidance but they really just want encouragement, and too often, they get discouraged."

Levin has taught writing at UCLA for 11 years. Many of his students have landed major book deals; five are bestselling authors themselves. One inflexible rule guides his workshops—only he is allowed to convey what doesn't work in a piece of writing. "The role of the students is to talk about what they liked," he explains. "That's because people become better writers when they learn what they're doing right, not just what they're doing wrong."

Lee Gutkind, editor of the journal *Creative Nonfiction*, believes that a successful critique group must be facilitated by a professional author and comprised of people who write as well as you, or much better. "Listening to people talk about your work can be valuable if your people are terrific readers," he allows, "but you can sabotage yourself by forcing your work to be critiqued too often. Too many people sounding off about your work can confuse you to death and make whatever insight you have turn to gloom and mud."

Like Levin, Gutkind worries that groups led by inexperienced writers may do more harm than good. He suggests that emerging writers find a mentor, instead. "I don't necessarily mean you should join an MFA program. That can cost a fortune," he says. "Just find a professional writer to work with. Sooner or later, your mentor will teach you everything he or she knows." To that end, his Creative Nonfiction Foundation pairs beginning and established authors for a fee.

"You give your work to another person whom you trust," he says, "and you don't take their criticism personally because when it comes right down to it, for people who make their living as a writer, writing is a business." He believes that critique groups don't always share this attitude—an oversight that can translate into hurt feelings when a writer feels that his or her work has been unduly criticized.

Janet Ruth Heller, a professor at Western Michigan University and the author of the award-winning children's picture book *How the Moon Regained Her Shape* (Sylvan Dell, 2006) has participated in critique groups since 1976. She recounts how her group once invited a possible new member to a meeting with disastrous results. "She spent forty minutes debating every suggestion we made about her work," Heller says. "She was overly sensitive to constructive comments for revision. We never invited her to another meeting because she wasted too much time."

Heller credits her group for helping her to spot ambiguity and contradictions in character and plot. "The key to a successful writing group is that the members need to have some knowledge of literature and give frank criticism," she notes. "Also, all members need to be able to take negative comments without falling apart."

A trustworthy critique group can also be invaluable to authors who question an agent's or editor's comments on a piece. They act as a kind of focus group. Heller notes that once an editor suggested changes on a manuscript she'd submitted. "Without labeling which was which," she explains, "I showed my critique group both my original draft and the revised version with the editor's changes. Everyone in the group liked my original version much better. This gave me the courage to tell the editor that I would not make these revisions."

QUALITIES OF A GOOD CRITIQUE GROUP

How can you find a critique group that provides constructive feedback delivered with honesty and compassion? First, identify the group you'd most like to join. Contact local organizations that serve writers, and get the names and most recent publications of facilitators. Many groups form out of flyers on a bookstore or library bulletin board. Online, venues such as Craigslist allow writers to gather by genre. Like-minded students in college writing courses may also be interested in meeting formally after the class is over.

Gershow insists that it's critical to read the work of members before you join. "Also, ask yourself how the group is run," she says, "and how often you're expected to submit work."

Interested writers should sit in on a few meetings to observe what kind of criticism is offered, and in what manner. Ask whether each member has a set time to read, and how long each meeting can expect to run. Find out small, but important details such as whether or not food and drink is allowed, and whether the writer is allowed to comment on his or her piece during the critique. "The facilitator has to take control of the group," Gutkind says. "If he or she is not in control, then bow out quickly."

I should have bowed out of my first critique group. The facilitator allowed behavior (i.e., snoring and self-editing) that wasn't conducive to workshopping manuscripts. However, I was partially at fault, as well. I hadn't read work by any of the members beforehand; if I'd done that, I would have known that it wasn't the right group for me.

Gershow, Daniel, and Gutkind no longer belong to a critique group. As professional writers with published books, they look to their editors and one or two literary friends for advice. I, too, rely on my editors for critique, but before submitting work to them, I show my memoir and essays to two other people. One is a fiction writer and a poet whom I met in a bookstore critique group shortly after finishing Daniels' workshop. Biweekly, we critique each other's writing. My other critic is a well-read professional photographer with a degree in philosophy. He's also my husband. Most anyone in the know will caution you not to seek feedback from your spouse; however, it worked for Virginia and Leonard Woolf, and it works for us.

I take the poet to lunch on occasion, and she returns the favor. We observe each other's birthdays and exchange holiday presents. I reciprocate for my husband's assessment of my work with the same careful attention to his fine-art photos.

I wouldn't dream of submitting a manuscript to an editor or agent without first showing it to both of these people. Their thoughtful, honest assessment of my work is a gift, and my most gratifying reciprocation is the privilege of thanking them both on the acknowledgements page of my latest book.

Secrets for a Successful Critique Group

- The facilitator is a professional writer with published work.
- Other participants write as well, or better, than you.
- The group meets regularly, in a quiet, private area conducive to critique.
- Writers have the opportunity to take each other's work home for thoughtful critique, rather than being expected to offer feedback on the spot.
- Critiques are respectful and well-balanced; members offer feedback on what's working, as well as what needs to be addressed in revision of a piece.
- Members refrain from commenting on the criticism they receive during the group session, except for a brief statement after the critique.
- Groups stay on task, avoiding the temptation to gossip the time away.

Reading With a Writer's Eye

Clues on Craft

by Tania Casselle

What's your best tip for new writers?" That's a question I've asked more than 50 authors in radio interviews, and they're often quick to reply: "Read! Read a lot. Read with a writer's eye."

It's advice that newer writers sometimes take with a grain of salt, perhaps suspecting that those already on the publishing ladder are just trying to sell more books. And even if we do take their advice, what does it mean to read with a writer's eye? We don't want to sound like someone else, we have our own voice and style. So how can reading other people's work practically help with our own writing?

First there's the sheer inspiration of reading wonderful fiction, the motivation it gives us to jump up from the armchair and hit the keyboard. Then there's the osmosis factor—we absorb the art of writing just by reading widely, which emerges intuitively in our work. But when our intuition fails, when we're stuck in a project, or realize that we need to polish up a craft area, that's the time to turn our writer's eye to our favorite fiction. Examining objectively what works successfully in a story, and how and why it works, helps us pick up tips, tricks, and techniques we can bring to our own writing problems, or just give a gentle nudge to open our minds to possibilities we haven't seen before.

After all, every challenge we face in fiction has already been solved by someone else. Why reinvent the wheel?

As author John Nichols says: "See how other people do it, the same way that painters go to museums and reproduce the great masters in order to understand how Rembrandt or Picasso used color and construction. The tools of the writing trade are essentially what's been written before."

DEVELOPING YOUR WRITER'S EYE

"Read the first pages of five books to see what's in common in the first pages, or the first chapters," says Lisa Tucker, whose latest novel is *The Promised World*. "This is after you've read the whole book, and you understand what the story is and you want to see how it's made, the nuts and bolts."

Study how the writer creates and establishes her characters. "A lot of new writers think

---

TANIA CASSELLE is freelance writer with nearly two decades of experience contributing to magazines and news media in the U.S. and Europe. She contributed to *Now Write! Fiction Writing Exercises from Today's Best Writers and Teachers* (Tarcher), and her fiction has appeared in lit journals including *New York Stories, The Saint Ann's Review, South Dakota Review, Bitter Oleander, Carve Magazine*, and anthologies including *Harlot Red* (Serpent's Tail Press) and *Online Writing: The Best of the First Ten Years* (Snowvigate Press, forthcoming in January 2009). She hosts the *Writers on Radio* show for NPR-affiliate KRZA in New Mexico and Colorado, also broadcast on other stations.

Word by Word

John Nichols (The Empanada Brotherhood) observes that we learn by imitation—it's how children learn language and behavior. He's taken chapters from writers he admires and typed them up, word by word. "In the process you demystify them, and you also learn a lot about how that person writes."

Lisa Tucker recalls typing out a scene from Jane Smiley's A Thousand Acres. "It helped me see how she moved from dialogue to action. I had a problem at first thinking about incorporating gestures into dialogue. Sometimes I'd have floating heads—two characters having a discussion—and I had to remember 'Oh wait, they're doing something!' It made me understand how people look away, pick things up, make expressions, and how to fit that in with dialogue in such a smooth way."

Robert Wilder typed out Ethan Canin's story The Year of Getting to Know Us when he was learning to write fiction. He liked Canin's economy, and wanted to understand the structure. "I was figuring it out from the inside out. It helped me enormously about scene and summary, and fed into my understanding of what makes a scene, dialogue, description, setting, details. And to literally feel what it's like to have those words coming out of your hands. Hopefully some of the structure of the prose and sentence-making ability will enter into your body." Wilder's two essay collections include Tales From The Teachers' Lounge, and his fiction has appeared in The Greensboro Review, Colorado Review, and Hayden's Ferry Review.

'If I kill somebody on page one, I'll really have the reader.' But you won't, unless the person you kill is somebody we already care about. You need to bring characters to life quickly, especially if you're going to murder them. Then the threat is so much more important. It's a real person that's going to be killed."

Tucker noticed how Kate Atkinson's *When Will There Be Good News?* created a vivid impression of a family in the first pages, setting up the tragedy that soon befalls them. The mother, for example, is "An artist, divorced, a sort of a wild woman. You get the feeling that she has a passionate personality, there's maybe one sentence about the painting she used to do.... and the fact that she *used* to do it... Why doesn't she do it any more? You want to give us enough about the character that we're curious about them."

Also consider how the back story is handled. "How much back story must be told? Writers feel that they have to introduce everything about their back story before they can do anything, which is not true." Tucker suggests charting out what we're told in the first pages about front story and back story, noting the interplay between them, and writing down what we're told about every character.

If your characters feel flat, Robin Romm (*The Mother Garden*) says "Look at the way Andre Dubus or Joy Williams create character. They're using very particular traits, staying consistent, and they don't say very much. It's not a list of 'blonde hair, blue eyes, six foot five.' It's more likely to be the way somebody puts a beer can on the counter."

Romm points to Flannery O'Connor's *The Life You Save May Be Your Own*, when Mr. Shiflet strikes a match. The flame creeps closer to his skin till he puts it out just before it burns him. "O'Connor never says this is a dangerous man, but the fact that he let the match burn that long, that tiny detail is all you need."

"You read a story once and it affects you, it's a great story, but you probably don't know how or why," says Antonya Nelson, whose latest story collection is *Nothing Right*. "So you read it again and again and you start to see how the writer has been manipulating your experience. How the writer has made conscious decisions about how to place its emphasis, how to inflect certain themes or moments." Nelson suggests looking at why a story ended where it did, and how motifs

First Impressions

"If you find a writer you love, go back and read their first novel. It's easier to see how they're made, they show their structure more clearly because the writer is not as good at hiding it. If you read The Song Reader, my first novel, I think it's more clear how I did it. You could make an outline and think about what I was working with, because I wasn't able to hide the bones." —Lisa Tucker.

move through it. "I was struck in an Edith Wharton novel by the patient way she described a character, and realized that I was trying short cuts with a piece I was working on."

MENTORS & MODELS

"A lot of professors in my grad program were not crazy about my work, so I found mentorship in books," says Pam Houston, who proved her profs wrong with her popular *Cowboys Are My Weakness*. Houston read Ron Carlson, Richard Ford, Lorrie Moore and Amy Bloom. "My contemporaries, but ahead of me in their careers. Writers who were doing things that seemed similar to what I was trying to do. I studied how they used metaphors, how they structured stories, how they made sentences."

When Houston started writing her novel *Sight Hound*, she was struggling with voice. Her previous books were essentially written in her own personal voice, but she couldn't see that approach working for *Sight Hound*. Yet it was a big leap to imagine it told from a different voice.

Houston laughs as she remembers. "I felt, God, I'm sick to death of this girl. Have you no range, Pam?" Then she saw *The Laramie Project* on stage, based on interviews with people around the murder of Matthew Shepard. "The bartender, the cop, the doctor, his parents, everybody, and they created monologues for all these characters. It's so moving, the idea of a choral community telling the story together." Houston bought the play that night and read it. "Seeing how a bunch of different voices could tell the story in the first person gave me permission to tiptoe into this idea of other voices. That's how *Sight Hound* wound up having 12 first person narratives."

Novels from two very different writers were helpful studies for Tara Ison's debut novel. "*The Bluest Eye* by Toni Morrison was the first time I was consciously aware of the device of multiple points of view. The texture that gave the story, to use that shifting lens so seamlessly and beautifully... It was really inspiring to me." As a teen, Ison read Stephen King's *Carrie*. "It's a narrative collage, with newspaper articles and interviews, and he takes all of these elements, and weaves them together." Both informed Ison's *A Child Out of Alcatraz*.

Ison's second novel *The List* was originally written in first person narrative voice, alternating between two characters. "It felt too claustrophobic," says Ison, so she switched gears and revisited Brian Moore's *The Lonely Passion of Judith Hearne* to see how he'd achieved a close third person voice. (So close, in fact, that on earlier readings Ison had remembered it written in first person; she'd been surprised to realize it was in third person.) "I went back to study how he was able to

Scene vs. Summary

"Pay attention to where the writer is slowing down to put us in the moment with the character, versus when the writer is doing a summarizing sweep of time, to move us along. Identify moments of discovery, confrontation, and decision making, because I think those are the moments that express character so well, and those are the moments rich in conflict, and that's when I think it's really valuable to slow down, as opposed to summarizing for the reader." —Tara Ison

make me feel so intimate to the character, yet he had the flexibility of third person. He could leave her mind when he needed to, to give us insights that the character could not have on her own."

Pamela Erens found a model structure for her first novel *The Understory* in William Trevor's *Reading Turgenev*, where chapters of past story are interspersed with chapters of current day story, and the two gradually converge.

"Trevor's book starts with a character in a bad spot, in an institution, but you don't know why. After a short chapter, you immediately jump way back in time, but the past chapters keep getting closer to the present."

Erens' character was in a different kind of institution, a Buddhist monastery, and her past story didn't sprawl back as far as Trevor's, but she immediately intuited that this was a good way to marry her material with form. "It was a very enjoyable way to bring the reader incrementally toward the present moment and explain how he got to where he was when you opened to the first page. It's reassuring to have some sort of structure to follow."

The Understory has an ominous tone which builds turn-the-page tension. Erens had already pared the writing in revisions, but during her final draft she read Camus' *The Stranger*. "It's a very short book, with a creepy sense of omission—what's being left out." Reading that made her trim back even more.

OPEN TO ENLIGHTENMENT

John Dufresne (*Requiem, Mass.*) believes that reading writers who *don't* write the way you do is especially useful to open up new vistas. "It snaps you out of your habitual way you write."

Dufresne's greatest difficulty as a writer is usually in finding his plot. "I start with characters, give them some trouble, then after 100 pages of the novel ask myself: 'Well, what's the plot?'"

In turning our writer's eye on other authors' story plots, Dufresne suggests a few questions. "The first time you read it you were surprised at everything but when you got to the end you realized it was inevitable, it had to happen this way. So how did he effect that? Do you know why the character is doing what he's doing at any moment? What does he want? Why does he want it? Why is he doing this to get it? The plot emanates from the behavior of the characters...here's where the struggle begins, here's where the character tried to get what she wanted.

"I pay attention to my own emotions. Why do I love this character so much? Why do I feel so sad at this point? The writer made me feel this way or think that way, how did she do it? When was I surprised? How did she pull that surprise off?

One way to pick up tricks of the trade is to diagram out a story you admire. You can even follow that model, using your own characters and story.

"I've done this with Alice Munro," says Dufresne. "I took a story of hers and diagrammed it out and tried to write a story in exactly the same way, as an exercise... just trying to intuit what she

Inspirations

"Dennis Cooper opened my mind on what you can actually do in a novel," says Don Waters, winner of the Iowa Short Fiction Award for his collection *Desert Gothic*. "Cooper began writing as a poet first, a novelist later. I love how in his sentences things are working! Several things can be happening in the same sentence. It's that weird thing that happens when you're striving for something, and then you see somebody else who's already done it, and something in you just physically bursts open and you think: This is it! And Cooper walks a very risky line in what he writes about. It opened my mind to what you could actually write about in terms of subject matter."

Waters recommends reading plays to study dialogue. "Like David Mamet, the master of hyper realistic dialogue. Everything happens through dialogue in a play, characterization and how to move a plot."

was thinking."

While obviously it's plagiarism to copy other writers' words, there's a difference between form and content, and everyone's techniques and approaches to craft and structure are all up for grabs.

"Hemingway and Fitzgerald, they never had workshops!" Says Robert Westbrook, whose novels include the series of Howard Moon Deer Mysteries. "They just read and read and loved books. If you do imitate, consciously or unconsciously, your own effort is going to come out different. It comes out with your own slant."

"What I discovered is the wonderful truth that it never sounds like the other writer," says Pamela Erens. "It sounds like yourself, and learning that really freed me up. While you're working on a story, things mutate so much that you end up with something that's your own. Every writer has a completely different consciousness and inflection. How else are you going to learn? It's a great resource. You have the whole library of literature to go to for help."

The Writing Life

Writers & Blogging

Creating a Presence in the Blogosphere

by Casey Quinn

The World Wide Web provides writers with an avenue of marketing that was nonexistent in the past. Before the Web, only names of writers with work published in journals or books would be recognized. The Internet changed everything. Writers now have the opportunity to stake claim and publish writing online that can be read by anyone, at any time. It is an opportunity that when done properly, can lead to writing success and increased sales. If done incorrectly, it can harm writing careers and scare away readers.

There are two options available to writers in creating their web presence. The first option—they can have a static Web site; the second option—they can create a blog.

Both options serve a different purpose. Deciding which option is best for the writer really depends on what the goals of a web presence really is. A static Web site by definition is not updated often and is a onetime information dump for readers. For a writer, it would contain a bibliography and some basic biographical information. Once a reader has found your site, there is little to keep them there or lure them back in the future. Static Web sites are the perfect solution for a writer who wants a web presence but has no desire to maintain a site.

If a writer is looking to build a readership and get their work out in front of people, this is where blogging comes into the picture. I believe blogging is the best solution for fiction writers.

Unlike static Web sites, blogs are expected to be updated often. This influx of new information keeps readers returning to check frequently. As writers, the most important thing we can have is readers, especially readers who take a genuine interest in our writing career. Even if you do not have a published book you're selling, some day you might.

There are five aspects of bogging that all writers should be aware of to make the most from their web presence.

SELECTING A BLOGGING PLATFORM

The first step is to select a host for your blog. When starting out, many writers make the most of free blogging platforms such as Blogger or WordPress. These free sites have some flexibility with how they look and are very low maintenance which is especially important for some writers who may not be to technological savvy.

The one setback with using the free software is that blogs are not portable. When you publish your writing, your posts are stored in a database wherever the blog is hosted.

CASEY QUINN is the editor and publisher for the online magazine *Short Story Library* and the publishing company, ReadMe Publishing. He has had over 1,000 pieces of writing published ranging from nonfiction, fiction to poetry. His first poetry collection *Snapshots of Life* was released in 2009 by Salvatore Publishing.

Your web address will also be defined by where you have your blog hosted for example http://caseyquinn.blogspot.com. If you chose later on to get your own web address, for example, http://caseyquinn.com, you will need to copy over all of your old posts manually into your new setup, which is a cumbersome process—and you might lose any traffic you had gained because of changing addresses.

If you are committed to writing and think a blog is the right solution for you; you might be better off buying your own web address (domain) and hosting it on your own. It's a more expensive route but provides you with more freedom and creative control over how it looks. If you are just putting your feet in the water to see if it how it feels before you jump in, try a free blog.

SELECTING A WEB ADDRESS

The second step in building a blog is to pick your web address. No matter if you go the free route or host on your own; you should have some control over what your web address ends up being. Blogs are like book covers; the first impression can make or break the sale. The selection process for your web address should take many things into account, however, in my experience the best web addresses for a writer is your pen names. You want your site to be logically named so readers can find it after hearing about your writing. If you select a random web address it makes it hard for readers to find you which is counterproductive to having a blog in the first place. Make it easy for readers to find you by sticking to your name or close to it. Exceptions to this naming rule can be made for writers with common names or with names that are difficult to spell.

CUSTOMIZING THE LOOK AND FEEL

Once you have selected your blog web address and have it hosted, you are ready for the third step which is to customize the look and feel. Your blog is the face your readers will see of you.

You want it to be professional, which can include elements of your genre or persona. For example if you are a horror writer, it's okay to have elements of horror on your site as long as they are not sloppy or low-quality. When selecting colors for your blog you need to put the readers experience in front of the coolness factor. Many people like black backgrounds with red text but it is impossible to read. As a reader, if my eyes strain to read a blog, I move on. It needs to be easy to read which means the color of the text needs to stand out clearly from the background and the font size should be large enough for anyone to read. As this is a writing blog, I would avoid having any advertisements on your site. You should be hoping to make money by selling books, not from people clicking on links from your site. Ad send the message that the blog is your means to an end, rather than the blog itself serving as the means to your writing ends.

BUILD USEFUL & WELL-WRITTEN CONTENT

The fourth part to building a blog is to build content. Blogs boil down to two things: pages and posts. Pages are static and a great place to store your biography, bibliography, reviews of your work, sample chapters, short stories or any other content you want your reader to find but you do not plan to update on a regular basis.

Posts are articles you write that get displayed on the main page of your site. The content of your posts should be kept within the goals of your Web site. If you built the Web site for your writing career then your posts should be limited to your writing career. Many times writers take far too many liberties with their blogs and post about a bad day they had or vent about something random and personal. There is a place for that type of writing but your writing blog is not it. If you can tie the post to your writing in some way, sure, post about it. Otherwise create a second blog for your personal life and post about it there. Readers want value when they come to your site and so each post should provide them with it. Value from a reader's point of view can come in the form of giving them a link to your latest published piece of writing, a writing article, a book review, tips, suggestions about the publishing process or anything writing related. Whatever you post about, it needs to have value to strangers to build a reader base; strangers generally do not care about your personal life.

In the last decade there has been an explosion in reality television and sales of nonfiction books. Why? Because people like to feel they are a part of something real. Readers like to learn about someone and how they interact in the world. Your blog is your platform to give them just that. It is your nonfiction writing about your fiction writing. Tell your readers you are querying for an agent or that you just finished your first draft of a novel. Tell them you were rejected or that you won a contest. Whatever it is, tell them about it. Get them interested in you as a writer and your career. When you get your book published, they will want to be a part of that as well which translates into buying a copy of your book.

With the content topics covered, bloggers need to focus on the writing part itself. No writer would submit a manuscript filled with errors to an editor. Blogging should be no different. In this case, you have no barrier between you and the world; you are the editor. With each post you publish, readers will form an impression of you. If your posts are filled with misspellings, grammar errors or are just poorly written, you will lose readers, not just to your blog, but to your published writing. Readers expect quality. As a writer you need your public writing to reflect quality. It should not matter if it is published in a book or on your Web site, quality should be the goal. In this case, quality means a well-edited and interesting piece of writing.

One important tip about the content you post on your blog. When you click publish, your writing becomes published. This means you no longer have first electronic rights to give away to publishers if they ask for it. Therefore before you publish anything on your blog, be sure you do not have any plans to submit it anywhere which requires first electronic publication rights.

BUILD A LOYAL READERSHIP

At this point you have a blog filled with great content that is easy to read. Now comes the harder part— you need to get people to come and read it. Finding readers and building traffic takes work and patience but in time you can build a loyal readership. Here are three great ways to build readers for your blog:

• **Social Media:** Blogging platforms have made it very easy to integrate social media "widgets" to help readers find you. Web sites like Digg or Stumble allow readers to mark Web sites as a good read. These sites then build lists of the most interesting Web sites out on the web. The more your site is tagged as interesting, the higher your Web site is ranked and read by others. Add the "widgets" to your site to make it easy for your readers to tag your site and get out there and start tagging others to promote a tagging exchange with your fellow writers. Social media also includes joining sites like Facebook and Myspace which allows you to promote your site by building a profile and networking with millions of people.

• **Build your backlinks:** Links serve as roads on the Internet where the browser is the car. The more roads out there that lead to your Web site, the more browsers will end up there. Start building backlinks by swapping links with other bloggers. Add your web address to your email signature, your profile in any forum you belong to as well as your biography for any piece of writing you get published online. Everywhere you have a presence on the web, a link to your blog should be right next to it.

• **RSS Feeds:** RSS feeds allow readers to get your updates as they occur. You can provide your readers the ability to sign up with their email and every time you post they will automatically get emailed a link to your post. A second way is that people can grab your RSS feed and plug it into an RSS reader. RSS readers allow other people to view your posts anywhere on the web. The purpose of implementing an RSS feed is that once you have driven traffic to your site, you want to give your readers no excuses to read each time you post new material. Like any of us, readers get busy and become forgetful. Getting traffic to come to your site is the hard work. Once you get it, keep it by providing an RSS feed.

Building a web presence is an important part of marketing as a writer. It provides readers a link to buy your writing, learn about you as a writer and sample your writing skills. It takes some time and dedication to create a successful blog but in the long run it will be worth it when your readers turn into buyers of your publications.

Premier Voices

Four Debut Novelists

by Travis Adkins

The debut novels featured in this year's edition of Premier Voices are an eclectic group, from a playful, genre-bending detective story to a soberly realistic depiction of one woman's struggle with Alzheimer's. The writers behind each of the novels are equally disparate.

But while their backgrounds may be different, the one thing they have in common is that each "makes sense of the world by arranging words and telling stories," as Jedediah Berry, author of *The Manual of Detection*, puts it. That urge is what drove Lisa Genova, author of *Still Alice*, to put aside her career as a Harvard-educated neuroscientist, despite the fact that her rational side told her that it was "a crazy thing for me to want to do." It kept Amy Shearn, author of *How Far Is the Ocean from Here*, going when she got to a point "where I realize I have no idea what it is I've created or where it's headed." And it inspired Rivka Galchen, author of *Atmospheric Disturbances*, to investigate the human urge to turn something "wild and strange" into something "ennobling and heroic."

Amy Shearn
How Far Is the Ocean from Here (Shaye Areheart Books)

Many first-time novelists are drawn to writing plot-driven narratives for the same reason that young children use training wheels on their first bike: it keeps them balanced and heading in a straight line while they're learning. But for Amy Shearn, author of *How Far Is the Ocean from Here*, it was character rather than plot that guided her progress through her debut novel.

How Far Is the Ocean from Here is relatively simple in its plot. Susannah Prue, a young woman who is pregnant with the surrogate child of an upper-middle-class couple from Chicago, impulsively decides to flee from her responsibilities and ends up stranded in a hotel in the desert. The barren setting of the novel doesn't allow for much in the way of page-turning action, but what it lacks in dramatic developments it more than makes up for in deeply satisfying, fully realized characters.

"*How Far Is the Ocean from Here* really all came from this central image of a young, pregnant woman driving through the desert," says Shearn. "At the time I didn't realize how much of a metaphor that is—it just seemed like an interesting, weird situation. I had the feeling that the baby wasn't hers somehow, and so my job as a writer was to figure out what that could possibly mean. The project of the book became untangling this mystery I'd set up for myself. That said, I've long been interested in the weird things the human body can do that seem almost like science fiction or myth—whether it's conjoined twins or organ transplants or hermaphrodites or just plain old pregnancy, which when you think about it is pretty insane. And for a while I'd been writing about

TRAVIS ADKINS is a freelance writer and a frequent contributor to *Novel & Short Story Writer's Market*. He lives in Brooklyn, New York.

both damaged, oddball characters and about people learning to care for each other and trying to do a good job of loving other people or creatures. In other words, many of the book's themes had been brewing, if subconsciously, for a while."

In writing the first draft, Shearn found that the middle part of the book presented the greatest difficulties. "The beginning was easy," she says. "There was so little at stake, and I was just writing for my own pleasure, not thinking anyone would ever read it. Since I write without an outline (or even a really a good idea of where the story's headed), the middle can get scary. I get to this point where I realize I have no idea what it is I've created or where it's headed or if all the strands will ever come together. With *How Far Is the Ocean from Here* I had to literally make a sort of Venn diagram, plotting out all the characters and storylines and timelines and locations, to figure out what I had gotten myself into. But then there was this wonderful moment when it all clicked. I remember realizing what the end would be, and actually gasping aloud—it seemed so obvious and inevitable."

Given the novel's character centered focus, it's no surprise that when it came time to revise, Shearn trimmed back on plot and expanded on character. "There was one stray subplot in particular that was a little too movie-of-the-week, very heavy on the coincidence and convenience, and fixing that had to be almost first thing—it was only a matter of cutting a few pages, but it had a lot of significance for the shape of the story," says Shearn. "As I worked with my editor, I actually ended up adding a lot more than I subtracted. My editor felt, quite rightly, that some of the characters were a bit thin. There was a lot of concern about whether the main character was sympathetic enough. So a great deal of my revising process involved adding back-story and lingering longer in characters' minds."

Shearn says that the decision to cut out the "wacky soap opera twist" subplot came as a result of a suggestion from her agent, P.J. Mark of the literary agency McCormick & Williams. "That was P.J.'s main input, and he was so, so, so right. He also had some very astute line notes. Other than that he felt like it was ready to go, and that whomever acquired it could take it from there." From the moment she signed with Mark, things moved quickly. "He agreed to take on the book sometime in November and told me he thought we should wait to shop it around until after the holidays. He sent it to publishers in January, and by February it had sold. I found out while sitting in my cubicle at work. It was all very surreal."

Shearn considers herself lucky to have worked with Sally Kim, then a senior editor at Shaye Areheart and now executive editor at HarperCollins. "Sally had this magical way of pointing out weaknesses in the book that I had suspected were there but couldn't quite put my finger on," Shearn says. "I think the voice was probably the first draft's strongest suit. What Sally really helped me with was developing the characters in more satisfactory ways. I can tell she did a really wonderful job, because people keep telling me that the character seemed so real to them—something no one ever said about my stories in grad school! She also worked with me on the pacing, particularly towards the beginning of the book. And she gave me wonderful, detailed line notes. I think it's unusual to get such diligent attention from an editor, and I know the book is much better for it."

"I think it helps to think of writing, if you're really serious about it, as another job—be disciplined about it, set aside time for it every day or every week," Shearn says. "Sitting around and waiting for inspiration is just another form of procrastination."

Lisa Genova
Still Alice (Pocket Books)

There are many writers who have abandoned successful careers to pursue their passion, such as Sherwood Anderson, who according to legend abruptly walked away from his job as president of a manufacturing company one day and never looked back. The ranks of these adventurous spirits now include Lisa Genova, author of *Still Alice*, who possesses a skill one doesn't often see on a first-time novelist's résumé—a Ph.D. in neuroscience from Harvard University.

Genova put her career as a strategic consultant for the biomedical industry on hold after giving birth to her daughter, fully intending at the time to get back to it. But while she was on hiatus, she started to have second thoughts. "I'd always wanted to write a novel, but at the same time, that had always seemed like a crazy thing for me to want to do," Genova says. "I was a scientist, not a writer. I've never even taken a writing class. Between thinking it was a crazy idea and being so busy in and enjoying my scientific career, I didn't pay much attention to my desire to write. Then I took a break from the career I loved when my daughter was born. When she turned four, I got divorced and was about to go back to work doing what I'd been doing. But it was a time of starting anew for me, and in that spirit, I thought, 'Hold on a second. Why do you have to go back to doing exactly what you were doing before? What if you could do anything you wanted? What do you really want to do now?' The answer came to me immediately. 'Write the book.' And so I did."

As it turned out, Genova was able to bring her training as a neuroscientist to bear on her novel, which tells the story of Alice Howland, a 50-year-old Harvard University professor who is stricken with Alzheimer's. The novel examines the ravages of the disease on Alice and her friends and family and her struggle to hold on to her identity as her memory fails. In addition to using her scientific training as a resource while writing *Still Alice*, Genova conducted extensive research to understand the emotional truth of how Alzheimer's patients feel. She corresponded with several Alzheimer's patients who were in the early stages of the disease to get a first-person glimpse into the experience, as well as shadowing neurologists at area hospitals. Her approach earned her the appreciation of the Alzheimer's Association, which praised the novel as "artfully and realistically" describing the progress of Alzheimer's.

In the course of revising the book, Genova had to make some tough choices about what to keep and what to let go. The most difficult of these choices involved entirely removing one character who played a major part in the first draft, Alice's best friend Susanna.

"Deleting Susanna was the biggest change and the biggest improvement," Genova says. "I'd been spreading out a particular impact of Alzheimer's on relationship between Susanna and Alice's daughter, Lydia. By getting rid of Susanna, I could give all her stuff to Lydia. The relationship between Alice and Lydia then became more fully realized and much more compelling. By the way, this meant I deleted a couple of well-written chapters. Once I was convinced that the story would be better served by concentrating on Lydia rather than diluting the impact between the two women, I had no trouble slashing and burning all references to Susanna. Sorry, Susanna, nothing personal!"

But writing the novel proved to be the easy part, compared to finding an agent or a publisher. "It took me a year and a half to write *Still Alice*, and I spent almost that long trying to get a literary agent to represent me," says Genova. "No one wanted it. I've still got the big pile of 'Dear Author' rejection letters. I tried going directly to editors at publishing houses, but they didn't want to talk to me without an agent. That year of rejection, sitting with a finished novel in my hands, stuck in a holding pattern, not giving myself permission to write the next book, waiting for a literary agent to tell me my book was 'good enough,' waiting to find out if I was a 'real writer,' was not a fun year."

Undeterred by the rejections, Genova decided to take matters into her own hands and self-publish *Still Alice* in 2007. Self-publication proved to be a wise course. Genova hired the book publicity firm Kelley and Hall to help her build buzz for the book, which paid off with a glowing review in the *Boston Globe*. That, combined with the novel winning the 2008 Bronte Prize for romantic fiction, got the attention of Vicky Bijur of Vicky Bijur Literary Agency. "Before she agreed to represent the book, Vicky asked me to change the ending," Genova says. "My first, knee-jerk reaction, which was thankfully spoken only inside my head was, 'No way! The ending I wrote is perfect!' My next reaction, also internal, was fear. I'd finished writing *Still Alice* almost two years ago at that point. How could I possibly go back to writing it again? And what if I did write a new ending, and it was horrible? I slept on it and decided, 'I'm a writer! Write another ending. You might love it.' Two hours later, I emailed Vicky the new ending I loved. She loved it, too and agreed to represent the book."

Soon after, Bijur sold the book in an auction to Pocket Books, which picked *Still Alice* up for a mid six-figures deal. Although her path from Harvard-educated neuroscientist to first-time author has been a long one, Genova says that her journey's only just started, and she's looking forward to taking the next step. She encourages other first-time authors to learn from her experience. "If you can't find a literary agent and you feel like your work is done and ready to be shared with the world, self-publish," she says. "Give your work to the world. Let it go. Guerrilla market. Be tenacious and generous and hopeful. And keep writing!"

Jedediah Berry
The Manual of Detection (Penguin)

"I'm someone who makes sense of the world, of myself and of the people around me, by arranging words and telling stories," says Jedediah Berry, author of *The Manual of Detection*. "I suspect this is the experience of many writers: if we're not telling stories, things stop making sense."

Making sense out of things is a quest shared by the protagonist of *The Manual of Detection*, Charles Unwin, a lowly clerk who lives in an unnamed city and works at an enigmatic detective agency cataloguing the cases of his hero, the legendary sleuth Travis Sivart. The Watson-like Unwin is pressed into becoming a detective when Sivart disappears. Aided by a narcoleptic assistant and the eponymous manual, Unwin tries to solve the mystery of Sivart's disappearance and along the way discovers some shocking truths about his hero.

Called by *Publishers Weekly* "an ambitious debut [that] reverberates with echoes of Kafka and Paul Auster," *The Manual of Detection* also echoes the works of such classic hardboiled noir writers as Raymond Chandler and Dashiell Hammett, as well as several works of Victorian detective fiction. But the influences don't end there, according to Berry. "The inspirations for *The Manual of Detection* include a series of desk jobs and the file cabinets that came with them, Edward Gorey's books, the music of Tom Waits, the record player I had when I was four years old, breakfast carts, alarm clocks, and an obsession with trains, hats, typewriters, and umbrellas," he says. "That list is by no means comprehensive, but none of those things were really what got me writing, either. I started the novel with a handful of images that came to me for no reason that I can explain. A woman waiting at a train station for someone who never arrives, two men on a rowboat sharing a single umbrella, a sleepwalker mopping floors, a bed and bedside lamp in a forest clearing: these fragments all needed a home, and the novel was an excuse to put them in the same house together."

The experience of writing the novel, Berry says, was "a haven for me—a place where I could explore a world that felt like something I understood no matter how strange it was. That's not to say there wasn't struggle and doubt, but there are struggle and doubt in most endeavors, I think. I can't say what kept me going, except the sense of dread that inevitably creeps in when I'm not writing."

In terms of technical difficulties with writing the book, Berry says that the greatest challenge was bringing the book to its end. "The hardest part to write was the bridge between the middle and the end," he says. "I knew how I wanted the book to conclude, but seeing the characters through to that conclusion was a real challenge. The novel has 18 chapters, and I wound up with three or four completely different versions of chapters 16 and 17, each with wildly dissimilar plots. In the end, it was matter of simplifying, and of letting go of certain ideas and scenes I'd been stuck on for months. A funeral, for example, that simply didn't belong in the book. I had to learn to be flexible enough to bring completely fresh ideas into a story that already felt cemented in my mind."

Berry's difficulties with the latter half of the book resurfaced during the revision process, he says. When it came time to revise the book, Berry found that the first half of the novel didn't need much work, but the second half required a great deal of revision. "An early draft of those later chapters veered deep into a backstory which, upon reflection, didn't contribute much to the novel," he says. "As one of my trusted early readers put it, I was answering questions the first part of the novel didn't ask. A lot of the revision work was aimed at pacing and focus, which I think go hand in hand. Keeping the attention on those vital details that keep the story engaging—while also knowing when to allow drifts into the unexpected—was often the key to my revision process."

Aside from making large structural changes, Berry was also keenly aware of the finer details of the novel. "I do a lot of revising as I write, and tend to obsess on the work at a sentence-by-sentence level," he says. "Precision is important to me, as is the sound and flow of each line. A book I think every writer should read is Italo Calvino's *Six Memos for the Next Millennium*. The terms Calvino used to discuss fiction—lightness, quickness, exactitude—will keep writers on their toes. Which is where we need to be."

Additional insight into shaping the novel came from Berry's agent, Esmond Harmsworth of the Zachary Shuster Harmsworth Agency, and especially from his editor at Penguin, Eamon Dolan, who Berry says is "brilliant." "For me the editorial process went something like this: Eamon would read the book, then point out anything he didn't understand. Clarity was our key concern in those final revisions. *The Manual of Detection* is a book with a lot of characters, and most of them have complicated backstories and secret agendas—some of them even have more than one identity. I wanted to keep those characters and their stories strange and mysterious, but I didn't want the book to be confusing. Eamon helped me achieve that balance."

Berry advises aspiring writers to "keep reading, keep writing, and don't give yourself too good of a backup plan. Also: If you have an idea, write it down, even if it comes to you in the middle of the night. That's the advice I give myself."

Rivka Galchen
Atmospheric Disturbances (Farrar, Straus & Giroux)

Rivka Galchen's first novel, *Atmospheric Disturbances*, might seem like an unlikely descendant of *Godzilla*. After all, the novel has at its main character not a giant fire-breathing lizard but one Dr. Leo Liebenstein, a mild-mannered New York psychiatrist who would be more at home obsessing over relationships in a Woody Allen movie than leveling Tokyo. But according to Galchen, it was the classic Japanese monster movie that inspired her acclaimed debut.

"I knew that *Atmospheric Disturbances* was going to be a novel, although I was definitely wrong about what novel it was going to be," says Galchen. "I had just seen *Godzilla* for the first time—it was being re-released 'Undubbed! Uncut!'—and I was fascinated by the way that the movie was so clearly some weird transformation of anxieties about Hiroshima and Nagasaki. That gentle fire-breathing monster awoken from her happy underwater life by nuclear testing was, well, more palatable I guess than the truth. So I wanted to have some sort of hysterical conversion like that at the center of my novel, some turning of something known and unbearably sad, into something wild and strange and so, as a consolation, somewhat ennobling and heroic."

The "hysterical conversion" that Liebenstein undergoes begins with his sudden, inexplicable conviction that his wife has been replaced by a doppelganger. As the story unfolds, it gradually becomes clear that Liebenstein is suffering from a nervous breakdown brought on by the growing estrangement between he and his wife. The novel follows Liebenstein as he transforms this "known and unbearably sad" marital rift into a paranoid fantasy land populated by mysterious meteorologists and a secret organization known as the 49 Quantum Fathers, all the while his wife tries to save him and their marriage.

Galchen took a somewhat unusual path to becoming a writer. She received an MD with a focus in psychiatry from Mount Sinai School of Medicine before getting her MFA from Columbia University, where she was a Robert Bingham fellow. Prior to publishing *Atmospheric Disturbances*, she published a short story in *The New Yorker* and received the 2006 Rona Jaffe Foundation Writers' Award.

Before she began sending *Atmospheric Disturbances* to agents, Galchen reworked the manuscript extensively, relying on her friends for ideas and advice. "I had trusted friends read the manuscript and rewrote after every round of feedback," she says. "Not necessarily following to the letter every piece of advice, but always letting myself reconsider the story in light of how it read to others. I often found that what was on the page was not what I *thought* was on the page, so I tried to at least narrow that gap in each revision." Along the way, she learned that as a writer she has "a paranoid sense of detail." "Despite having no religious streak in me—I don't think, anyway—I feel close to characters who are likely to see more significance in a small details than maybe is in fact there," she says.

All of the hard work and paranoia paid off when Galchen landed as her agent Bill Clegg of the William Morris Company. Clegg, whose client list includes film director John Waters and Nick

The Writing Life

Flynn, bestselling author of *Another Bullshit Night in Suck City,* is one of the most respected literary agents in the business, and is especially well-regarded for championing new writers. Galchen says that working with Clegg has been a great experience. "My affection and admiration of Bill turns me into some sort of fizzy teenager, making me feel stuck in phrases like *he's just totally awesome,*" she says. "I was very fortunate that a friend of mine from my MFA program at Columbia knew Bill for going on ten years, and recommended that I send my manuscript to him. At our first meeting he gave me a detailed read of the novel, after which I took a couple more months to revise and polish before we actually sent it out. Bill's a dream agent. I'd trust him with pretty much any of my life decisions."

Galchen's good fortune continued when *Atmospheric Disturbances* was bought by Eric Chinski, editor-in-chief at Farrar, Straus, and Giroux. Chinski has edited a wide range of bestselling and award-winning authors including Richard Powers, whose book *The Echo Maker* won the 2006 National Book Award for fiction. Such an impressive editor might be enough to make a first-author a little nervous, but Galchen says that Chinski proved to be "the gentlest and kindest and most self-effacing of guys." "It was easy to forget to be afraid of Eric," she says. "He's an attentive editor, incredibly smart, and I felt unbelievably lucky to work with him. Also, he helped me not rush the very last chapter of the book; I tend to be afraid of sustaining the same mood for too long, but that was the right place to hold a certain kind of note."

Atmospheric Disturbances was greeted with praise by critics including James Wood, who wrote a lengthy review of the book for *The New Yorker* and called it "original" and "affecting." (He actually called it "*sometimes* affecting," but for the notoriously difficult-to-please Wood, that's still quite a strong compliment.) The novel was named as a finalist for the Mercantile Library's 2008 John Sargent Sr. First Novel Prize, for the Canadian Writers' Trust's 2008 Fiction Prize and for the 2008 Governor General's Award, one of Canada's most prestigious literary prizes.

Galchen's advice for aspiring novelists is simple: write every day. "And don't worry about pleasing everybody," she adds. "And if you're a nerdy diagramming planner, try writing when you're either terribly sleepy or way over caffeinated. And if you're a digressive waiting for inspiration free-associating writer, try being elaborately in control of your work, and a pragmatic-minded captain of the ship. But mostly, just write lots, and read even more than you write."

Top 10 Writing Conundrums

& *Their Answers*

by I.J. Schecter

Like organizing a house from top to bottom, writing a story involves countless small choices that lead—hopefully—to a tidy, appealing result. Some of these choices are easy. They're dictated by character traits, plot direction, tone, or simple rules of language and grammar. Other choices fall into a gray area—they come down to stylistic choices, in-the-moment instincts, or, let's face it, outright guesses. Let's consider 10 of the most common dilemmas writers face during the story process and untangle them—as much as possible, anyway. You wouldn't want the process to be *too* easy, would you?

1. Will lightning strike me if I split an infinitive?

My favorite exchange in the history of television occurred on the sitcom *Frasier*. When Frasier catches his son Freddy running through the living room, he says, "What have I told you about running in the house?"

"You told me to never run in the house," Freddy replies.

Horrified, Frasier says, *"What have I told you about splitting infinitives?"*

Never mind that only fellow literary geeks laugh when I share this line—the point is that Frasier, for all his intellect, was wrong. There is no hard-and-fast rule that says splitting infinitives is a sin. Most grammarians agree, however, that keeping the "to" nice and cozy with its verb leads generally to more elegant and readable writing. As freelance writer Charmian Christie says, "This is usually a good rule of thumb to follow, but not automatically. Rhythm needs to be considered. Would you want Captain Kirk to go boldly where no one has gone before? I think not."

2. What's the deal with serial commas? I can't get a straight answer.

Comma rules are like tectonic plates, prone to shifts over time. The 1990s, for example, were characterized by a strong trend toward economy of language and, with it, punctuation. But today the serial comma seems to be making a comeback as many of those with editorial authority opt for explicit meaning over traditional usage, in which the final comma was removed in deference to the "and" or other conjunction meant to replace it.

Some instructors will tell you that if you need the serial comma, you aren't writing clearly enough. But ultimately it's up to you—and your editor—to decide how your commas affect the sound of your prose. As Lynne Truss, author of *Eats, Shoots & Leaves*, puts it, "On the

---

I.J. SCHECTER (www.ijschecter.com) is an award-winning author, essayist and interviewer. His latest release is the bestselling humor collection, *Slices: Observations from the Wrong Side of the Fairway* (John Wiley & Sons).

page, punctuation performs its grammatical function, but in the mind of the reader it does more than that. It tells the reader how to hum the tune."

3. Could you give me the straight dope on the preposition thing?

No doubt you've heard some version of Churchill's famous quote, to the effect of, "There are some things up with which I will not put." Though we don't know precisely what he said, Winston's general thrust was bang on. Nowhere is it written in stone that a sentence should not conclude with *up*, *to*, *at*, *in* or any of their cousins. Plot and characters aside, good writing depends on clarity and ease—reader-friendliness, let's say. Sentences like Churchill's facetious example are stilted and jarring, turning the reader's experience into an unpleasant one. Or, as freelancer writer Anne Borden suggests, "Clarity is your objective. Leave the hair-splitting to the fogeys."

The purpose of a preposition is to link or relate its object to some other word in the sentence—*on* a shelf, *between* us, *because* of rain. Whether the preposition precedes or follows its object is immaterial as long as the sentence sounds right. *What was he complaining about?* sounds perfectly natural. *About what was he complaining?* would make even the stuffiest Englishman cringe.

Sometimes the decision isn't so obvious, of course. *Byron expressed with great force his love of liberty* could be written with the prepositional phrase ("with great force") at the end of the sentence instead, with, arguably, better tempo. Again, what matters most is how the music of each sentence works within the overall score of your manuscript. If you don't trust me, take it from Elmore Leonard: "There's nothing wrong with ending a sentence with a preposition. I write from whoever's point of view it is, so if that's the way the character would say it, that's the way it comes out." He's sold a bunch of books, by the way.

4. Why can't I start a sentence with And or But?

You can. Sometimes a collective stylistic tendency comes to be adopted as gospel for no good reason. Not starting sentences with And or But is an example of this phenomenon. But this "rule" has no roots, now or at any other time. And and But are examples of sentence connectives—coordinating conjunctions, conjunctive adverbs or transitional expressions—which can often be put to effective use to break up long, potentially convoluted sentences or to provide contrast. Consider:

> "Transitory popularity is not proof of genius. But permanent popularity is."
> —Stephen Leacock
> "All human cultures seek to realize and protect their identity. And identity is definable only by reference to former times." —Hugh Brody

Or this:

> "The nuclei of atoms become radioactive when they absorb neutrons. That is, they decay by giving off some kind of radiation." —Robert Hofstadter

In the sentence above, "That is" falls into the same category as "And" and "But" in the previous examples. And it works just fine.

5. Whose point of view should I write from?

If you're writing a piece on assignment, say for a travel publication, this choice might already be made for you. "For example," says freelance writer Elle Andra-Warner, "there are an increasing number of travel articles now being written in the first person. The writer takes the reader with them on the journey, giving the reader the immediate experience of place."

But when it's your own project, this decision can be thornier, and you might wrestle with it for a good long while before landing on the right perspective. According to Christie, "Your plot will dictate whether first or third works best. Do you need to follow characters other than the protagonist? If so, third person is probably the right choice. Is the entire story worked around one person and their perceptions? Then first person is likely your best bet."

Second person tends to be the trickiest and least engaging perspective to write from, which is why it's usually reserved for magazine service articles—as in, "You approach the entrance of the Taj Mahal, and your breath stops." Then again, writers take chances and break rules that were thought unbreakable all the time. So write from whatever point of view you think is the most interesting one—for the reader, that is.

6. Past or present tense—what are the rules for deciding?

There are some guidelines to help you out here, but no rules—at least, none that can't be broken. For most writers, the safe choice tends to be past tense because it feels more natural to readers, and more logical, since those readers unconsciously accept that they're reading an account of events that have already occurred. Present tense can feel more contrived or forced, but it can also convey a certain mystical quality for the reader when done well. Some authors agree that, in general, perspective and tense serve each other, past tense working best with first and third person, present tense working best with first person. Most important, of course, is to be consistent, since abrupt or unnecessary shifts can obscure meaning and make for difficult reading. Second most important is not to be afraid of altering your primary point of view even if it means going back through the entire manuscript. You might not realize until page 200 that the story would be more effective if told through the eyes of the 12-year-old violin prodigy instead of his obsessively demanding father. Hey, that's part of the fun of writing! Ahem.

7. Should it always be "he said," or should I use variations?

A heated ongoing debate surrounds this question—and a rather eloquent one, since it's writers doing the debating. In one corner you've got those who insist that using any alternatives to "said" distracts from the real action, and in the other, those who insist that well-chosen verbs add flavor and impact, especially when everyone and their dog exhorts us to do away with adverbs.

Included in the former camp is Elmore Leonard again, whose view on the matter is clear: "Never use a verb other than 'said' to carry dialogue. The line of dialogue belongs to the character; the verb is the writer sticking his nose in. But said is far less intrusive than grumbled, gasped, cautioned, lied. I once noticed Mary McCarthy ending a line of dialogue with 'she asseverated,' and had to stop reading to get the dictionary."

Freelance author Lisa Bendall has a somewhat more moderate opinion. She suggests variations are acceptable as long as they aren't frequent, repetitive or unnatural-sounding. "For example, something like *'Yes,' he concurred* should never see the light of day."

A handy trick is to forego the tag altogether by referring to it in action. "Let's say Carrie from *Sex and the City* just steps in a big mud puddle," suggests Christie. "You could go with: *'Not my Manolo Blahniks!' Carrie's scream cut through the air, sharp as the stiletto heels she'd just ruined.*"

So let's bring the two camps together by agreeing on the following: However you decide to tag your dialogue, make sure it makes the writing more interesting, not less. Moving on.

8. Why do semi-colons cause such headaches?

Semi-colons are like grenades. If you know how to handle them, they can be used to great effect; if you don't, they can cause a lot of damage. Using them properly comes down to two things. The second of these is stylistic preference. The first is stone-cold knowledge of the rules governing them.

In their most frequent form, semi-colons are used to divide main clauses not linked by coordinating conjunctions. That means when you have two related parts that can work on their own as individual sentences, you can put a semi between them. Compare these two examples:

Some philosophers offer practical wisdom. Others do not. I prefer to study the former.

Some philosophers offer practical wisdom; others do not. I prefer to study the former.

While the first example isn't wrong, a semi is used to divide the two most closely related clauses in the second example, creating a more powerful result.

Often the best way to get smart about semis is to know when they should not be used. One flagrant error that makes editors nuts is the use of a semi-colon to lead off a series. That's what a colon is for. Never write, "He had three sisters; Patty, Jane and Barbara," unless you want your manuscript transferred to the circular file in a blink. Also, don't use a semi to separate two bits that are dissimilar grammatically, like a clause and a phrase: "Along came Peter; the dormitory clown." Finally, never plug a semi between a main clause and a subordinate clause that are already sufficiently connected—for example, "If this report is true; then we should act now."

Like math concepts, semi-colons can be intimidating. But with a little study and commitment, they'll cooperate, and you'll be thrilled to have them in your arsenal.

9. How do I know when my manuscript is brilliant enough to send?

Often you'll know if you've landed on just the right word. Sometimes you'll know if you've nailed a sentence. On occasion, an entire chapter might seem flawless to you. But as for being completely satisfied with an entire manuscript, well…let me defer to Anthony Burgess: "You don't say, 'I've done it!' You come, with a horrible desperation, to realize that this will do."

I have a pretty reliable test I use on myself during the course of revision. Once I start making edits back over themselves, bringing me back to the original version, I know the manuscript has reached a point where it's good enough. The other test is a more instinctive one: The voice in your head will tell you when it's ready. That voice is always worth trusting.

Of course, every writer, after deciding her manuscript is good enough, will look at it again several weeks later only to find a number of spots in which something could have been improved. Writing is dynamic, so you're just going to have to accept this. You must develop the ability to finish a manuscript, send it out and not look back or second-guess yourself. If you love your work, set it free.

10. Will I really be hung by the thumbnails if I don't follow submission guidelines?

Yes and no. When preparing a submission, you should follow them precisely, including correct spelling of the editor's name, proper margins, and whether the manuscript should be stapled, paper-clipped or loose. Use the font they ask you to use. Send it the way they want it sent. Wait the recommended amount of time before following up. The reason for all this is not to make you jump through hoops. Editors are constantly dealing with mountains of manuscripts, and the easier you can make it for them to a) read and b) find yours, the better chance it has of being given a fair shot at acceptance.

Now, the other side of the coin. Most publishers still insist on what I consider unreasonable restrictions in terms of your submitting flexibility. I might get in trouble for saying this, but with the odds of acceptance already low and response times already long, it is simply ridiculous for so many publishers to include "no simultaneous submissions" in their guidelines. They can't possibly expect every writer to wait months for a response before sending a manuscript elsewhere. Should you find yourself in the fortunate position of multiple publications or publishers wanting your story, simply decline the less attractive one and politely explain that the manuscript has been accepted elsewhere. Then give yourself a nice pat on the back and get to work on the next one.

Looking Skyward

& Other Exercises for Improving Your Craft

by I. J. Schecter

One of a writer's most important tasks is to cultivate his creative muscle memory over time. A basketball player practices dribbling endlessly and takes thousands of jump shots so that, when game time comes, those moves will be instinctive. Eventually he discovers new moves, burns them into his repertoire through the same commitment to practice, and onward the process goes. Like the athlete born with a certain gift, most writers know early on that they have an inherent facility for putting words together in agreeable ways. But this ability is like the knack for dribbling a basketball—it means little unless built upon. Both the basketball player's and the writer's range of skills can be viewed like a partially cooked bag of microwave popcorn. The fluffy, already-popped kernels represent things like spelling and simple rules of grammar—basic elements of the craft you easily master. Elsewhere in the bag there are some half-popped and un-popped kernels—skills you're in the midst of developing or haven't yet tackled. Getting every one of the kernels in your writing bag to reach its potential demands a serious, ongoing commitment. Here are some exercises you can use to get them all popping.

Listen up

While your prose is important, dialogue may be the most vital element of your work. Readers will tend to give unusual, even experimental, prose a chance to win them over. Awkward or unrealistic dialogue, on the other hand, can turn a reader off quickly, which is why it's critical that you get a handle on what your characters' words should sound like. The best way to do this is to go straight to the source: real people. Spend time listening to them. Buy a Frappuccino at Starbucks and eavesdrop for a while. Grab a hot dog from the cart in the middle of downtown and walk along the street picking up snatches of dialogue as you go. Before writing *Fast Times at Ridgemont High*, Cameron Crowe posed as a high school student for a year so he could make his characters sound authentic. And they did, right down to the unforgettable Jeff Spicoli and his nemesis, Mr. Hand.

Expand your eavesdropping

Listening in on conversations is helpful, but not if you're listening repeatedly to the same types of conversations being had by the same types of people. The people who live in your immediate area are likely to be demographically similar to you, which means they're likely to talk about similar subjects, sound approximately like you, and exhibit the same sort of

I.J. SCHECTER (www.ijschecter.com) is an award-winning author, essayist and interviewer. His latest release is the bestselling humor collection, *Slices: Observations from the Wrong Side of the Fairway* (John Wiley & Sons).

verbal inflections and tendencies. The danger with listening only to these people is that all your characters may end up sounding alike, which will make them indistinguishable from one another anytime they open their mouths. Get out there and listen to people of every stripe: different ages, different ethnicities, different personalities, different styles. Then, when you sit down to write the words coming out of your Chinese-Canadian protagonist's grandmother's mouth, you'll be able to do it with confidence.

Get some face time

Faces are like settings: one can easily fall into the trap of over-describing them for no good reason. Minimal descriptions of settings are often the most powerful ones. We don't need to know every type of flower in the garden or every feature of the cityscape. Similarly, physical descriptions of characters are usually best handled with a subtle touch, especially when it comes to their faces. It becomes tiresome when we're told about a character's eyes, ears, mouth, nose, chin, hair and lips. Most people have one feature that stands out, maybe two, and that one feature is usually all you need to focus on to give a reader the right impression. To practice, take a walk outside and, as you pass people on the street, try to describe their faces in a single sentence. Do this in your mind or under your breath, of course, otherwise you're going to draw the wrong kind of attention to yourself.

Stargaze

Head outside on a clear night and turn your eyes upward. Find some constellations you recognize: Orion, The Big Dipper, Cassiopeia. Then broaden your gaze, find an area of stars you aren't familiar with, and make up some new constellations around specific clusters, including the character inhabiting the shape you imagine, that character's nature and purpose, his friends and enemies, his dress, his idiosyncrasies, and any other backstory that occurs to you. Don't let yourself off the hook—force yourself to create at least three new constellations each time you perform this exercise. You might just get a great protagonist out of it.

Describe one thing in multiple ways

The more comfortable you get with metaphors and similes, the more diverse your writing arsenal becomes. But we're instinctively literal creatures, after all, so comparisons don't rise unbidden to the surface without a little up-front work. Practice describing everyday things with the use of metaphor and simile and the ability will come to you more naturally when you're immersed in your manuscript. The simplest and best way to practice is to walk outside, look at something—anything—and challenge yourself to come up with at least three different comparative descriptions for it.

What does that minivan seem like to you—a stealthy dinosaur, a futuristic space rover, a sleek mobile robot whose eyes emit beams of light? How about that jungle gym—a colorfully skeletal igloo, a giant's beanie, a strange volcanic formation designed just for kids and forced through the schoolyard surface? Don't worry if your comparative descriptions sound awful. The purpose of this exercise to get yourself comfortable with, and disposed toward, symbolic writing. No writer has a 100-percent hit rate on the metaphors or similes she comes up with. But all those dull or awkward-sounding ones will seem a more-than-worthwhile part of the process when you suddenly find one on the page that sparkles.

Research something you think you aren't interested in

Should you write what you know? Sure. But you have to expand what you know over time so that you don't automatically revert to the types of topics, characters, plots and settings that have made up your sum total of experience to date. The best way to force your writing horizon outward is to dive into subjects toward which you wouldn't normally gravitate.

I recently spent some time researching rodeos, since I'm completely uninterested in them. Or at least I thought I was. As it turns out, many aspects of the rodeo life are quite compelling, from the lives of the cowboys to the way the steers are trained. It's a topic I'm now interested in writing about, either in a short story or as part of something longer.

Are you habitually indifferent toward world history? Google the Boer War or Ancient Babylonia. Biology not your thing? Read up on zebrafish or honeybee navigation. If you find yourself traditionally steering away from a certain topic, do a one-eighty and dive into headlong. Do this often enough and soon there won't be any subject you don't think is potential fodder for a good story—which is how every writer should look at the world.

Write haiku

Effective writing demands two kinds of discipline: the discipline to physically write, and the discipline to use only words that are necessary for your story. Composing haiku is an excellent way to instill the latter kind because it gets you accustomed to conveying what you need to within a specific amount of space—in this case, a restricted number of syllables. Most writers will agree that the shorter the form, the less margin for error or wastefulness. A novella is harder than a novel, a short story harder than a novella, a poem harder than a short story. Which is why haiku, for all its limitations, is a fabulous tool for helping rid your writing of superfluity. If you really need convincing, do two things. First, read truly great haiku, and don't be surprised at how moved you are by these tiny gems. Second, try some haiku of your own. You may find it a serious challenge. That's good. Your manuscripts will thank you for it.

Rewrite others' work

The more you revise your own work, the more entrenched your editing habits become. To maintain your revising versatility and objectivity, open a book—any book—and rewrite a random sentence, or paragraph, or page, or chapter. Then repeat the exercise with a different book. Then do it a third time, with another book still. Making this part of your regular routine will keep you fresh as an editor and also open you up to new possibilities in your own writing. Most of all, it will help you refine and solidify your own unique voice as you consider the choices other writers have made—and those you'd have made differently.

Get back to basics

No doubt you're a writer today in part because you always showed the instincts for it. You handled grammar without a problem. You were a naturally good speller. You understood the rhythm and structure of a story without anyone formally teaching it to you. In short, you "got" language.

But those with natural talent in any area continually refresh and reinforce their fundamental skills and build upon them. Athletes, executives, technicians, artists—they all periodically revisit what in today's corporate world are referred to as "core competencies" in order to keep their basic skills honed to a fine point.

My favorite textbook I own is the grammar handbook assigned for the Introductory English class I took during freshman year of university. I love diving back into its well-worn pages and reading some of the practice exercises or boning up on transitive verbs, predicate nouns, adverb clauses—or just reminding myself where the heck to put those pesky quotation marks. Spending time with this textbook makes me feel inspired and excited about writing all over again, and even though I naturally "get" how language works, it still serves my writing well to remind myself the different between a gerund and a finite verb.

Solicit feedback—from the right sources

There are two groups of people you should always avoid giving your manuscripts to for feedback: your family and your friends. Since they want you to feel good about yourself and your writing, they're going to tell you it's brilliant even when it's not. So many writers consider their workshop groups invaluable because that's where they get the most honest and constructive responses to their work. There are plenty of writers who can pen a decent first draft of a story. It is those who flesh out and revise their stories the most thoroughly that in the end set themselves apart. To accomplish this, it's often necessary to have your story seen by fresh, objective eyes and commented on by those who care about you enough to tell you when your writing isn't as good as it could be.

Go rock climbing

Or cycling. Or do a Tone-and-Sculpt class, or a few jumping jacks, or some crunches. The point is this: When your energy and metabolism are well maintained, everything, including your brain, works better. Not only do you fire on more cylinders physically, but your creativity and stamina work at higher capacity, too. Some old-school writers might endorse a glass of scotch or two as the best creative loosener, but I disagree. Treat yourself right, and your output will increase both in volume and quality.

And here's a bonus piece of advice

As you read work by others—and I hope you do this constantly—try never to read the same type of writing more than twice in a row. Even if you love works of historical non-fiction, try to break them up now and again with, say, a little Dave Barry. You may have a steadfast devotion to turn-of-the-century short fiction, but a contemporary memoir or biography might just provide a neat new wrinkle for you. When you read the same genre or form over and over, even if it's the same type of work written by different authors, you can't help but become at least a bit imitative of that work, and you never discover the kinds of wonderful things other writers in other areas might be doing that you can learn from. The only writing you should be singularly devoted to is your own. When it comes to others, play the field.

Today's 'Personal Relationship' Fiction

by Jack Smith

P ersonal relationship story' seems as fair a synonym as I can imagine for 'literature itself,'" says Anthony Varallo, Fiction Editor of *Crazyhorse*. "If there is too much of an emphasis on personal relationship stories, surely the past 1,200 years of literature are to blame."

Indeed, what is fiction without the personal relationship story? Fiction deals with humans in relation to other humans. When we enter fictional worlds, we want to identify with real-life characters whose lives are affected by other characters and whose cases or plights we find interesting and compelling. We'd like to empathize with, sympathize with, or, better yet, root for protagonists. We want to be affected at both the emotional and intellectual level. We want an engaging prose style. What else? Expectations naturally vary from reader to reader and from editor to editor as they select work for publication from the enormous slush pile.

Some editors of literary magazines are expecting fiction to move beyond the personal/ interpersonal relationship levels. They want broader frames of reference, broader delineated contexts—social, historical, cultural, political, and philosophical—than what they're seeing. Others believe this is putting the focus in the wrong place. Fiction is not principally about this; it's about characters and their very human struggles—expressed originally and forcefully by a careful attention to craft. At literary presses, there tends to be general agreement that a novel is enhanced by taking on larger frameworks beyond the personal; still some editors insist on novels that incorporate these larger themes, while others don't.

But first, before we look at these two editorial camps on what makes serious or literary fiction, let's take up a fundamental question: Does today's fiction tend to focus on the personal level—to the exclusion of larger themes? What do editors say?

What is today's personal relationship fiction mostly about?

From one perspective, today's fiction, whether short story or novel, focuses mostly, even exclusively, on the personal level. Yet this doesn't necessarily mean that it lacks universal appeal. It may in fact reach a wide audience by exploring or illuminating various levels of the personal—if not the social, the political, etc. From another perspective, character

JACK SMITH's satirical novel Hog to Hog won the George Garrett Fiction Prize and was published by *Texas Review Press* in 2008. His stories have been published in *North American Review, The Southern Review, Texas Review, Happy, In Posse Review, X-Connect, Night Train, NEO, Southern Ocean Review, B&A: New Fiction*, and *Word Riot*. He's published reviews in *Georgia Review, Missouri Review, Texas Review, Prairie Schooner, Pleiades, Mid-American Review, X-Connect, RE:AL*, and *Environment* magazine. He's also contributed nine articles to *Novel & Short Story Writer's Market*. His co-authored nonfiction book entitled *Killing Me Softly* was published by *Monthly Review Press* in 2002. Besides his writing, he co-edits *The Green Hills Literary Lantern*, published by Truman State University.

relationships, well-handled, tend to point, by their very nature, to some of these larger spheres or contexts. Is it even possible for such relationships to be completely decontextualized? And besides, plenty of evidence suggests that writers *are* aiming at larger themes. Two sides, then, with varied conclusions on the matter. What it comes down to is how you read the fiction—it's what you see in it.

Linda Swanson-Davies, Co-Editor of *Glimmer Train*, states: "It does seem that most fiction has moved away from the philosophical/social/historical/political story to a closer, more personal story. It may be that the 'big' story seems too heavy, or it may be that our perception of the world and our places in it have shifted dramatically." Perhaps, she speculates, it's due to our complex, pluralistic world today, with any number of "legitimate perspectives," and our realization of just how informed we'd have to be to make us "feel bold enough to put out a larger statement." Even so, for Swanson-Davies, writers are producing fiction that allows readers to "empathize with each other," and in this way, are addressing "big issues, if more quietly" than classic authors such as William Faulkner, who developed social and political themes not only in his novels but also in his short stories.

What Beth Staples, Editor, *Hayden's Ferry Review*, often sees in the slush pile are "personal relationship stories that don't go much beyond that: small settings, small circumstances, small problems." Like Swanson-Davies, she finds an explanation for this in the complex world we live in: "It often feels to me that as the world gets bigger—that is, more populous, more diverse, more complicated by technology—that it gets harder and harder to generalize about big questions." At the same time, Staples believes that "*Good* relationship stories are existential, a reflection of societal trends, pointing to and commenting on some larger whole." And thus they end up commenting on issues beyond the personal after all.

Like Staples, Frederick Barthelme, novelist, short story writer, and editor of the *Mississippi Review*, holds that these themes are represented in various human relationships woven into the story—and yet more by indirection than by explicit treatment. Stories with broad themes, says Barthelme, are typically about people "moving through difficult times in their ordinary worlds, finding and facing their 'issues,' and summoning what's necessary and human in themselves and in those they travel with in order to meet the intimate challenges in their lives." From this meeting and the story's overall dramatic context, Barthelme believes, "the reader is allowed, even encouraged, perhaps even *required* to extrapolate and thus reflect upon the broader social, political, cultural, and philosophical themes." But Barthelme doesn't stop there. He views the general trend in fiction for the past 15 to 20 years to be "*away* from 'the personal level' and toward the kind of sociological, cultural, global."

Ben Barnhart, Editor of Milkweed Editions, has observed this same trend in the work he considers. "I believe a lot of fiction writers (an easy majority), write with the goal of addressing broader themes in their work." Their attempts to achieve "this tall task" through the personal story are not always successful because authors fail to develop either the characters or the story itself. Successful endeavors, says Barnhart, are clearly represented by the five 2008 National Book Award finalists. These works tell "personal stories within the context of broader social and political frameworks." For Barnhart, they constitute "literature of lasting value."

What makes fiction 'literary'?

Some literary magazine editors take the position that much of today's short fiction presently *is not*, yet *should be*, pointing to issues beyond the personal level. Too many stories, it's contended, limit their range to the romantic or the domestic relationship—with nothing universal to speak of beyond that. These stories tend not to be developed with enough breadth or depth for serious discussion. The nature of literary fiction, so goes the argument, is to provide more range of reference—to strike more universal social, political, and philosophical themes. This position is roundly disputed by those magazine editors who set different quite standards for "literary" fiction. Strong characterization, solid craft, fresh language—these are elements that make serious fiction. In the case of literary novels, perhaps the general consensus that including themes beyond the personal is of significant value is due largely to the nature of the novel form itself, with its greater capacity for a larger canvas. But if there's an agreement on this value of larger frameworks, editorial policy does vary: while some presses are quite adamant about works moving beyond the personal frame, others believe a compelling tale, well told, can trump any absolute necessity of these larger frames of reference.

Short fiction & literary magazines

Michigan Quarterly Review's listing in *Novel & Short Story Writer's Market* makes a strong plea for themes beyond the personal. For Editor Laurence Goldstein fiction "rightly focuses" on personal relationships, but in the submissions he receives, he seeks "a wider angle on the world"—that is, stories which are "not exclusively about a man and a woman of the age range from 15 to 50 who undergo romantic conflicts connected to issues of loyalty, sexuality, work, children, and tensions about extended family." These subjects and themes, says Goldstein, make up 90 percent of the fiction he receives at *MQR* and are "the standard features" of most fiction he reads in other literary magazines. What he prefers, though, are stories that "look at life from a different angle of vision and reveal more of the world hidden behind the hothouse stories of romantic attraction and repulsion." Successful "off the main line" stories published by *MQR* have dealt with such larger cultural issues as "science, war, and urban dynamism."

R.P. Burnham, Editor of *The Long Story*, is also looking for fiction that moves beyond the personal. "As a matter of fact," says Burnham, "it is exactly the (merely) personal that we dislike." Burnham wants stories that are peopled with "real characters and real situations but that connect to a wider exploration of our universal humanity—i.e. the only way to express the universal is through the individual." He attributes "merely personal" writing to "the narrow emphasis of the writing programs." Creative writing students in these programs, he states, are encouraged to write from their own subjective experiences instead of using their imaginations, a practice which leads to impoverishment of ideas. For Burnham, fiction writers need to study the humanities, "not concentrate on the merely technical and mechanical aspects of writing."

Julie Wakeman-Linn, Editor of the *Potomac Review*, takes a similar position in rejecting stories that seem, to her, to be too limited in scope. She looks for "stories that are more interesting, more complex than the usual suburban family or marriage problems." She is particularly interested in international settings, with stories that encourage readers to reflect on a variety of social, historical, and political themes. These include stories that deal with such issues as racism, traditional expectations for women, and the effects of the Vietnam War, as well as ones that "poke holes in the cult of celebrity and consumerism." The kinds of stories that Wakeman-Linn prefers are the "more textured in context than the usual domestic/relationship story." For her, "Writers should push to the heart of their stories, avoiding the safe, easy path of domestic relationship stories that lie on the surface."

Beth Staples, Editor, *Hayden's Ferry Review*, is divided on this matter of fiction needing to reach beyond the personal plane. On the one hand, she finds "the general tiredness of the slush pile" more worrisome than the subject matter itself. And yet, the subject matter *is* "worrisome" to her. She would like to see "stories that ask big questions, look at things that are hard to look at, explore social trends, etc." In fact, for Issue 39, *HFR* made a call for "Works of Witness," in which writers were invited to explore "social and political injustice on any scale." This call yielded an enormous response—"a ton of submissions"—and yet the editors didn't find the work publishable for the simple reason that ideas, not characters, were "driving" the fiction, and the ideas were simple, not complex, in development. Staples has wondered whether the essay might not be the best form for larger frameworks beyond the personal.

Like Staples, David Lenson, editor of *The Massachusetts Review*, finds the litany of conventional relationship topics he encounters in the submission pile problematic: "A running joke in our fiction slaughterhouse is that anything that mentions divorce, cancer, or grandmother on the first page is rejected—but we might make an exception for a story about grandmother's divorce." Lenson also appreciates larger themes beyond the personal, but he's not adamant about requiring them: "We tend to look for unconventional tales that begin in the weird or fanciful and wind up with universal ramifications. But the truth is that we do publish personal relationship stories as well, because human character is really an inexhaustible business and there's always a fresh way to go at it."

Frederick Barthelme provides yet another perspective—one which gets at the heart of the creative process itself. A too-conscious effort to incorporate social, political, and philosophical ideas into one's work will most likely lead to failure. It's very difficult, he says, to make one's work "more interesting, insightful, thoughtful, intriguing, informative, and engaging than what is available in the broad spectrum media." The risk is that one will simply produce a rewriting of *Newsweek*, as one of his colleagues once put it. As editor of the *Mississippi Review*, Barthelme is open to stories with broader contexts beyond the personal if they "have the richness and vitality of nonfiction while retaining the freshness and intimacy and uniqueness of the very best fiction."

This takes us to the other side of the argument—that it's simply wrongheaded to be privileging stories that move beyond the contexts of personal and interpersonal. Isn't an original voice—fresh and new—strong characterization, and felt life experiences that have the compelling ring of truth enough to make fiction "literary"? Isn't that what fiction is all about?

For Megan Sexton, editor for *Five Points*, the answer is yes. "I think about Chekhov, who I think is one of the masters of the form, and how so many of his stories deal with the web of connections that bind people within their families and society." Sexton does, then, appreciate the acknowledged master of the short story's connecting his work to a larger framework—the social. But she adds: "That said, we are open to all kinds of stories; what we hope to find in all stories is the spark of originality."

Harvard Review Editor Christina Thompson also emphasizes originality in the stories she considers. A "depressingly large number," Thompson states, "are about some kind of personal trauma usually involving a relationship of some kind: breakup stories, betrayal stories, abandonment stories, death in the family stories, and so on." Yet what makes these stories unpublishable is not the focus on interpersonal relationships; it's the predictability of sentiments, story lines, and the quality of the language itself. For Thompson, the writer must somehow get beyond "the completely conventional way these already very familiar stories are handled."

For *Berkeley Fiction Review* editors, the key to good fiction writing is strong character. Managing Editor Malia Linda Javier says "We are definitely open to social, political and philosophical stories and in the past have printed them. Specifically for me, philosophical stories are of interest." Nonetheless, Javier insists that such themes must "take second place after characterization." When stories with larger themes beyond the personal fail, they do so because the "human aspect" is missing. Assistant Editor Morgan Cotton agrees, claiming that strong characterization is what allows so-called "'genre' fiction to become 'literary.'" For Cotton, readers of serious fiction want stories to get at "greater truths" and have "some sort of direct connection to humanity." These truths, though, don't necessarily involve the social, political, or philosophical. What's more important to Cotton is the writer's adept creation of a character that "makes me feel somewhere deep in my gut."

Zeke Jarvis, Editor for *Eureka Literary Magazine*, also emphasizes strong characterization. Some of the work published by *ELM*, he notes, does include "larger frames of reference." He believes a lot of it does "in an indirect way." But this is not his focus, to seek out works that move beyond the personal level. Such works are judged along with the rest—with one key editorial standard in mind: "If a piece acknowledges the absurdity of politics while also giving us engaging characters, we're all for it."

Crazyhorse Fiction Editor Anthony Varallo categorically deemphasizes the importance of larger frames of reference beyond the personal and stresses another long-held standard for good literature—the air of reality, or believability: "Like most literary magazines, we publish the best stories we can find regardless of theme, subject matter, style, or perceived cultural relevance." The staff at *Crazyhorse*, is "glad," he points out, "to publish stories that attempt to go beyond the domestic, but we'd ask the same thing of those stories as the ones that never leave the backyard; namely, that they ring true. To write a story for any other reason—whether to explore some broader social, or philosophical theme—seems far too low an ambition to me. Truth is the only standard of excellence."

Novels & literary presses

Robert L. Giron, Editor-in-Chief for Gival Press, says that he isn't receiving enough fiction that moves beyond characters, their problems, and interpersonal relationships to establish a "larger picture." He seeks work that situates characters within a given society, but also, beyond this social level, explores philosophical ideas. "Granted many manuscripts have the social, but what is lacking in the development of many story lines is the philosophical. I don't just mean the blatant discussion of philosophical issues but having characters express, exude the dilemma of issues on the next level." Book club readers using Gival Press books "don't run out of points for discussion," says Giron. While he believes that many books selected for book clubs are well-written, there is "a lack of issues or tension to lead the book club to a meaningful discussion." What makes serious fiction, claims Giron, is what "lives on after the technique of writing."

Milkweed Editions Editor Ben Barnhart also emphasizes the importance of levels beyond the personal. The best fiction, he says, explores personal relationships within the framework of larger themes such as the social and the political. "Sacrificing either of these elements (the personal and the political) results in fiction that fails to be compelling or relevant." Barnhart values work in which "a character comes truly to life when suspended within realistic storylines that traffic in broad cultural and political themes." At the other extreme, personal fiction can become much too subjective, he says, becoming "relevant only for the author." But when that occurs, it's not the personal context itself that's at fault—it's the exclusive attention to the personal without any suggestion of the universal. Some novels like Marilynne Robinson's *Gilead* are "intensely personal novels," but, says Barnhart, they "manage to portray an inner life in such a way that the stories reach a wider audience." This novel, published in 2004, incorporates "the theme (more cogent in the 50s) of a mixed-race relationship."

Steven Gillis, Publisher and Co-Founder, Dzanc Books, is equally committed to works that go beyond the personal context. He appreciates the "themes explored in well-written personal stories," but "great works," he says, provide "an intelligent exploration of the world, an examination of all sides, an asking of questions and laying the universe bare." For Gillis, some examples of this kind of exploration include novels about war, prejudice of different kinds, and politics. The personal relationship story alone isn't enough, he claims, to achieve this kind of greatness: "A writer must be brave. There is rarely anything brave in the personal narrative." In comparison to works embodying larger themes, "it is titillation wrapped up in literary verbiage." Gillis goes so far as to say that to take on these larger themes "is what it means to be a writer."

While editors at other literary presses may definitely value these larger themes, they do not insist on them. For Algonquin Press Editor Chuck Adams, novels with larger themes will most likely reach a broader audience. As an example, he notes that "One of the formulas for writing a 'bigger' book is to take a basically intimate story and play it out against a broad canvas (think boy meets girl in Germany circa 1937, or young Oklahoma girl trying to find herself during the great Depression)." Adams says that "if a writer really wants to develop a readership and, thus, receive monetary compensation, then it's a good idea." But it's not an absolute requirement.

Lee Montgomery, Editor for Tin House Books, says that "the culture at large has gone for smaller, personal stories and conflicts," but she does look for larger social themes and is pleased with a novel Tin House will soon release on the JFK assassination and its effects on various lives surrounding Kennedy. As she sees it, when larger frameworks such as the social are included, this makes for a "better reference" in the work. Nonetheless, it's the craft, the writer's "mastery of work," that ultimately counts at Tin House, not the working out of larger social, political, and philosophical issues.

John Daniel, Editor and Publisher, John Daniel & Co., also sees the value of "fiction that tackles big issues," but he believes that "the most important issue is personal relationships." He puts it this way: "A relationship story without big issues can be good fiction, but a social issues story without human relationships is going to be a dud. Fiction is primarily about people, not ideas." It's certainly good, he says, for fiction to move beyond the personal framework, but only "if it's done gracefully and in perspective. I want fiction to be important, to deal with love and death. Aren't those ideas already big?"

Craft & Technique

As we've seen, the controversy over what current fiction is about and *should* be about depends on how one assesses the fiction being produced and how one defines serious fiction. Writers need to decide what they want to write, what their standards for good fiction are, and where they can best place their work for publication. If they believe fiction must include themes beyond the personal and interpersonal, they need to make sure their work has strong characters, the ring of truth, and originality of expression. Otherwise, they should consider expressing their ideas in nonfiction form.

Laughing Matters

The Rules for Writing Humor

by Marc Acito

I am essentially a serious person. With serious ideas. That other people laugh at.

And since I'm a serious person I've given humor some serious thought. For as with any other aspect of writing, humor is a skill you can develop: if you're not naturally funny, you can learn to be; if you are naturally funny, analyzing how it's done can help you create comedy on demand; and if you have no sense of humor whatsoever, then, in the words of Tina Fey, you can suck it.

Didn't see that last one comin', didja? You shouldn't have. That's because the number one rule of comedy is surprise. Okay, maybe it's not the number one rule because, frankly, there are no rules. But it's *my* number one rule and I'm the guy writing the article for *Novel & Short Story Writer's Market*. I've actually got four more rules but, like the Little League team where everyone gets a trophy, they're all important enough to be number one.

So, the Number One Rule of Comedy (#1): Invert Expectations.

Pretty much every comic situation reverses what you expect. In comedies, adults act like children (the Three Stooges, the Marx Brothers, every movie starring Adam Sandler) or children act like adults (the Little Rascals, *Peanuts*, *South Park*). Sophistication turns to silliness (*A Midsummer Night's Dream*, *Bringing Up Baby*), genders get bent (*Some Like it Hot*, *Tootsie*) and the private becomes public (think about the two funniest scenes in *There's Something About Mary*). In crafting something funny, you must push yourself beyond the familiar to an idea so unexpected it will make readers snort milk out of their noses.

"But Marc," you say (unless you don't know me, in which case you say, "But Mr. Acito"). "How does one craft this thing called the funny?"

"Ah—insert name here—," I reply, "you craft the funny by being a conniving, duplicitous manipulator."

Think of those old Henny Youngman one-liners: "I take my wife everywhere. But she keeps finding her way back."

Ba-doom-ching! Thank you, be sure to tip your waiter.

Old jokes like that provide a textbook illustration of how the element of surprise works.

MARC ACITO's comic debut novel, *How I Paid for College: A Novel of Sex, Theft, Friendship and Musical Theater* won the Ken Kesey Award and made the American Library Association's Top Ten Teen Book List. It was also selected as an Editors' Choice by *The New York Times* and is translated into five languages the author does not read. The eagerly anticipated sequel, *Attack of the Theater People*, was selected as a top read for 2008 by the Seattle Public Library. Marc is now a regular commentator on National Public Radio's "All Things Considered." Born in Bayonne, New Jersey, he lives in Portland, Oregon, with his long-time partner, Floyd Sklaver. The author can be contacted at www.MarcAcito.com, where he blogs about his Quixotic quest to do something new every day.

The set-up ("I take my wife everywhere…") does just that, sets up an expectation: we believe that Youngman is devoted to his wife. The punch line ("…but she keeps finding her way back") inverts the expectation: he's actually trying to lose her.

Surprise!

A variation on this model is prolonging the set-up to build the expectation before inverting it, like in this classic from Phyllis Diller: "I do dinner in three phases: serve the food, clear the table, bury the dead." Even someone as hip and contemporary as David Sedaris follows the same 1-2-3 model. In *Me Talk Pretty One Day*, he writes, "I wound up in Normandy the same way my mother ended up in North Carolina: you meet a guy, you relinquish a tiny bit of control, and, the next thing you know, you're eating a different part of the pig."

John Morreall, the religion professor and past president of the International Society for Humor Studies (yes, there is such a thing), theorizes that laughter is a relief mechanism. As far as I can understand it (which isn't very far), the dramatic tension of a joke relates to some deep-seated biological awareness of possible danger. When the danger passes, we laugh with relief.

That may sound over-analytical, but the notion of comedy as dangerous relates to the form's innate aggressiveness. Think about the stand-up comic's syntax: "I slayed 'em, I murdered 'em, I left 'em rolling in the aisles." The audience busts a gut, splits their sides, and laughs till they cry. I don't know much about biology, but apparently there's a reason why they're called "punch-lines."

As playwright Neil Simon said, "All humor is based on hostility…that's why World War II was so funny."

I learned this lesson first-hand when I was 19 years old and working as a singing waiter. My job was to make the patrons do silly things to get their desserts, then perform a floor show. After a couple of weeks of shouting I lost my voice, so I focused on the silly stunts. And what I discovered was that I had a unique gift for ridiculing others. The meaner I got, the larger my tips.

And that taught me another valuable lesson: comedy is laughing at someone else's pain.

Which leads to the Number One Rule of Comedy (#2): Misery Equals Hilarity.

Mel Brooks said, "Tragedy is when I cut my finger. Comedy is when you walk into an open sewer and die." A good example of this principle can be found in Susan Jane Gilman's hilarious memoir, *Hypocrite in a Pouffy White Dress*:

> My teacher, Estelle, was herself a genuine Sadist. This was made clear to me the very first day of nursery school, when she lead our class in a game of "Simon Says" designed to inflict flesh wounds: "Simon says: Poke yourself in the eye! Simon says: Hit yourself on the head with a Lincoln Log! Stick a crayon up your nose! Whoops. I didn't say Simon Says, now did I, Juan?"

Funny, right? And it's also about that surefire comic premise: child abuse.

"But Mister Acito—"

"Please, we've been together for almost a thousand words. Call me Marco. All my friends do."

"But Mr. Marco, how do I know if my own miserable tale of—insert disease/dysfunction/torture here—is funny?"

Unfortunately, you can't. The only way to know if something is funny is if other people laugh. That's why humor writers must workshop their material before submitting it. At the very least, have others read it. Better yet, read it in front of an audience. David Sedaris has been known to do readings with a pen in hand, noting the laughs on a work-in-progress as he goes. If I've got a line I'm not sure about, I'll drop it into cocktail party conversation just to see how it's received.

As with all writing, the key to finding misery is conflict. Basically, there are three kinds:

Inner conflict: Bridget Jones is afraid of dying alone and being found three weeks later half-eaten by an Alsatian.

Personal: Lucy always pulls the football away from Charlie Brown.

Societal: In *Catch 22*, a bombadier is considered insane if he willingly continues to fly dangerous combat missions, but if he makes the necessary formal request to be relieved of such missions, that proves he is sane and therefore ineligible to be relieved.

In other words, you've got to be willing to be a little mean to your characters.

The other key to mining life's misery for laughs is the Number One Rule of Comedy (#3): Tell the Truth.

There's a long-standing tradition of comics speaking truth to power, beginning with court jesters who got away with talking smack to the king, and continuing up to present day jesters like Jon Stewart and the staff of *The Daily Show*. Being funny is a subversive act; it's throwing a pie in the face of social norms.

George Bernard Shaw said, "When a thing is funny, search it carefully for a hidden truth." And we all know what a laugh riot he was.

In May of 2004, *Writer's Digest* reported a survey done at the University of Dayton's Erma Bombeck Writers' Workshop (yes, there is such a thing) that found that humor writers earning more than $5,000 in a year were more likely to write until they got a funny idea, while those who earned less than $500 were more likely to wait for a funny idea to hit them. The moral: Start writing what's true, it will lead you to what's funny.

Here's an example from the master, Dave Barry, reporting on the 2004 Democratic National Convention:

> BOSTON—A colorful cast of thousands...has converged on this historic city as the Democrats gather for a convention that has been carefully scripted to galvanize America's voters with the convention's Official Theme: "Four Solid Days of Talking."The highlight of Day One of the Democratic convention was the appearance of former President Bill Clinton, who gave a passionate speech on the theme "My Book Is for Sale." Hillary also gave a speech Monday, urging the delegates to support John Kerry on the grounds that "there are probably worse candidates," and adding, "I am definitely available for 2008."
>
> The star speaker Wednesday night was vice-presidential nominee John Edwards, who told the inspirational story of how he was born in a small South Carolina town where his father was a millworker who went to the mill every day and, I don't know, milled things. Senator Edwards was introduced by his wife, Mrs. John Edwards, who revealed that she supports her husband's candidacy.

Note that the six jokes in this excerpt are all formulated the same way—they tell the truth about something that everyone is thinking but dares not say. So when searching for humor, don't ask, "What's funny?" Instead, ask yourself, "What's true? What's strange, difficult or ridiculous? What's unjust, frightening or dumb?" As with all writing, think about what matters most to you, what gets you up in the morning and what keeps you awake at night.

And then follow the Number One Rule of Comedy (#4): Exaggerate the hell out of it.

Unlike memoir, where it's not okay to pretend you spent three months in jail when you actually spent only three hours, humor allows you to stretch the truth to its breaking point and call it satire. For instance, in Erma Bombeck's classic portrayal of suburban migration, *The Grass is Always Greener Over the Septic Tank*, she describes her cramped city apartment this way:

> I had to iron in the playpen. The kids were stacked in a triple bunk at night like they were awaiting burial at sea. If the phone rang, I had to stand on my husband's face to answer it. The dog slept under the oven, next to the crackers. And one day I yawned, stretched my arms and someone stored the complete works of Dr. Seuss and a pot of African violets on them.

Craft & Technique

Of course this isn't how it actually happened, but Bombeck's description not only makes us laugh (well, it makes me laugh), it makes a point. Exaggeration puts the teeth in biting humor, a principle that applies most effectively to creating comic characters. Remember what I said about the power—not to mention the fun—of ridiculing others? Well, exaggeration of human flaws is the weapon of choice.

To sustain humor in fiction, you must populate your world with funny people. That doesn't mean characters who tell jokes. It means characters who exhibit exaggerated behaviors that they are unaware are exaggerated. Comedian Mike Myers thinks of comic characters as machines: Inspector Clouseau is a SMUG machine, Pepe le Peu is a LOVE machine, Felix Unger is a CLEAN machine, Austin Powers is a SEX machine, Rebecca Bloomwood in the Shopaholic series is a BUYING machine. These comic characters are pure Id, the kind of people who will do or say anything. It's the reason Jack and Karen are funnier than Will and Grace, or Kramer and George are funnier than Jerry.

Okay, let's review: you've inverted expectations, mined your misery, told the truth and exaggerated it. What's left?

The Number One Rule of Comedy (#5): Use Your Words.

Whether you're creating comic situations and characters, writing novels, essays, screenplays, or side-splitting abuse memoirs, all a writer has is words. So use them well. Humor writers don't get the kind of respect that literary writers do, but our work is as scrupulously crafted. Instead of awards, we get laughs, which, trust me, are way better. Many of the best jokes use the best writing techniques. Like this one by Chris Rock: "If you're black, America is like the uncle who paid your way through college, but molested you." With one simile, Rock manages to be subversive while conveying misery and truth through exaggeration, all at the same time.

And don't just use words, play with them. Like Rock, George Carlin was heralded for his political commentary, but much of his material came simply from examining the English language:

Why do we say something is out of whack? What is a whack?

Why do "slow down" and "slow up" mean the same thing?

Why do we sing "Take me out to the ball game" when we are already there?

Why do we drive on a parkway, but park in a driveway?

Why is "phonics" not spelled the way it sounds?

Is it true that cannibals don't eat clowns because they taste funny?

Do infants enjoy infancy as much as adults enjoy adultery?

If one synchronized swimmer drowns, do the rest drown too?

If you try to fail, and succeed, which have you done?

And, my personal favorite: I've always wanted to be somebody, but I should have been more specific.

In comedy, every word counts. If you watch the documentary *Comedian* starring Jerry Seinfeld, you'll see how stand-up comics tinker obsessively over the most niggling of details, even contractions and prepositions. Though comics aren't recognized for it, this kind of wordsmithing is the hallmark of excellent writing. As Mark Twain said, "The difference between the right word and the almost right word is the difference between lightning and the lightning bug."

If you craft your words to continually surprise your readers, stretching both the truth and conflict as far as they will go, you won't just be funny, you will become a better writer.

And you just might get someone to snort milk out of their nose.

Writing Publishable Satire

A Difficult Form in a Tough Market

by Jack Smith

Satire had its heyday in the eighteenth-century, the Enlightenment, with famous satirists such as Voltaire, Swift, and Pope, yet there have certainly been a number of important satirists since then, among them Mark Twain, Sinclair Lewis, Nathaniel West, Evelyn Waugh, and in more recent times Terry Southern, Harry Crews, and Edward Abbey. As a form, satire certainly isn't dead, but for the most part, this is the age of the straight relationship story, calling for a strong emotional component, in which sympathetic characters with compelling needs must engage readers on a level they can identify with. These stories may well include satirical elements, but works wholly satire aren't exactly "in," though such works are certainly being published. The success of George Saunders testifies to this, and certainly the novels of Carl Hiassen and Christopher Moore are hot sellers. But these authors are more the exception than the rule. Winifred Golden of Castiglia Literary Agency says, "Satire is even harder to sell than humor." This is the case for both literary magazines and book publishers, whether commercial or small press.

Satire is very difficult to publish, but not impossible. Some editors of literary magazines are open to satire as long as it's well-handled. Now and then the commercial market will bear satire by relative unknowns, as evidenced by Phillip Jennings' debut novel, *Nam-A-Rama* (Forge Books, 2005), and independent presses will, as evidenced by David Allan Cates' *X out of Wonderland* (Steerforth Press, 2005). Most independents are not seeking satire, with two notable exceptions being Bridge Works Publishing and Kunati Books. Writers will undoubtedly continue to write satire, regardless of its marketability, and good satire will continue to be published. The key question is how do you write publishable satire? What makes it fail? What makes it successful?

Literary magazines & satirical short fiction

Some literary magazines receive very few satirical pieces and publish little to none. What they do receive they find seriously flawed: amateurish in idea, poor in execution, and thin on characterization. *Chaffin Journal* Editor Robert Witt says the typical satirical piece is "usually not well written and rather juvenile." What Phil Hey, Fiction Editor of *The Briar*

JACK SMITH's satirical novel *Hog to Hog* won the George Garrett Fiction Prize and was published by Texas Review Press in 2008. His stories have been published in *North American Review, The Southern Review, Texas Review, Happy, In Posse Review, X-Connect, Night Train, NEO, Southern Ocean Review, B&A: New Fiction,* and *Word Riot.* He's published reviews in *Georgia Review, Missouri Review, Texas Review, Prairie Schooner, Pleiades, Mid-American Review, X-Connect, RE:AL,* and *Environment* magazine. He's also contributed nine articles to *Novel & Short Story Writer's Market.* His co-authored nonfiction book entitled *Killing Me Softly* was published by *Monthly Review Press* in 2002. Besides his writing, he co-edits *The Green Hills Literary Lantern,* published by Truman State University.

Cliff Review, receives is often marked by "painful obviousness, crudity, and bad taste." What these submissions lack, he says, is what makes a story publishable: "craft and subtlety." Bayard, Editor of *Happy*, looks for work that is "well written, stylish, concise, verbose, biting, funny"—but very seldom does he discover in the slush pile satire that meets these editorial standards. For Carol Finke, Editor for *Controlled Burn*, satirical pieces are generally "cheap shots at easy targets." Characters, she says, don't necessarily need to be sympathetic, but they do need to be "compelling and three-dimensional."

The Furnace Review does receive a good amount of satire, mostly political, as much as one-fifth of the story submissions. Editor Ciara LaVelle sees this as a "reflection of the times." Even though she receives that much satire, she doesn't publish any. To begin with, satirical stories seem at odds with the journal's mission—to publish "earnest, emotional, straightforward stories." Yet if the style and tone of a satirical piece are at odds with the rest of the work in an issue, this isn't an absolute deal breaker. The main problem, for LaVelle, is the quality of the writing she encounters in a typical submission, which often "feels derivative" to her. Satire, she says, is "one of the more difficult genres to master." To write good satire, says La Valle, one must meet certain basic criteria: "The story must be subtle and ridiculous at the same time, and the author must invent innovative subjects and plot lines to channel the true subject of the satire." She finds this last part "increasingly difficult lately." The problem is that "we're exposed to so much satire in daily life, on television particularly," with TV programs like *The Daily Show*—or, says LaVelle, "from a pundit's mouth or on a snarky blog someplace."

Green Mountains Review doesn't receive "pure satire," but a number of submissions do contain "satirical and humorous elements." Like LaVelle, *GMR* Editor Leslie Daniels finds it a very difficult form: "In a world that is as close to post-irony as we have ever seen, satire is hard to achieve." If plenty of materials are out there waiting for the satirist's use, this makes an agenda-driven story more likely. Any story "in service to an agenda, whether it is political, social, sexual, or a personal neurosis" Daniels is bound to reject. "I may read the whole thing because it fits in with my own occasionally dark and satiric view of the world in its absurdity, but I am unlikely to inflict it on others."

New Letters Editor Robert Stewart also tends to receive quite a few stories that are not pure satire but instead are "satirical on some level." The satire *New Letters* publishes, however, "can be subtle and might not appear as such immediately." Satire in serious literary fiction, Stewart says, "often doesn't present itself in obvious terms, whether satire or not, as might a satire on TV or in a commercial magazine." When Stewart rejects satire, it's because it isn't "fresh, complex, or convincing." When it works, he feels drawn to *"the humor of recognition*—that is, some recognizable folly has been turned on its head in a story—in which that satirical element seems fresh and important to a bigger story." Thus, for Stewart, satire "serves as only one element of a story, and serves to complicate otherwise serious human relationships." *New Letters* has published stories that satirize such topics as commercialism, the effects of war, racial stereotyping, and historical couples having sex.

Book publishers & satirical novels

Bridge Works Publishing is one possible market for satirical novels, yet Barbara Phillips, like other editors, is quick to emphasize the difficulty of the form. Satire, she says, is one of the hardest of the writing genres because of the considerable knowledge of the subject it takes and the delicate tone it requires. "You must know the subject intimately to satirize it," she says, "which means a lot of reading." As to the tone: "It should not be done with a meat-axe approach, broad and obvious, but with a scalpel, delicate and incisive." Regardless of the difficulty, Bridge Works has been successful in finding some good satire. They have published satires that range in topic from the art scene to business to international relations. A forthcoming novel called *Chest Pains* satirizes "middle-aged angst, academia, and the human tendency to categorize people."

Kunati Books, another possible market for satire, bills itself as: "Provocative. Bold. Controversial." Five to ten percent of the submissions and queries Founder and Editor James McKinnon receives are pure satire or works containing satirical elements. To date, Kunati has published several satirical novels, taking up such issues as the world of professional golf, bureaucracy and cronyism in the U.S. Navy, and the reality TV craze. *Ruby's Humans*, to be released in 2009, is "a dog's eye view 'memoir' in which Ruby ruminates on the foibles and shortcomings of humankind."

"Deciding what to publish is a very subjective process," says McKinnon, but with satire he believes this is especially true. What one reader finds funny another finds dull; what one person finds "brilliantly insightful" another sees as "offensive or wrong." The one thing that satire must accomplish, he emphasizes, is to "ring true." This means "the feel of authenticity," and the only way for the writer to accomplish this, says McKinnon, is to have the necessary background to write with authority. The author of *Bathtub Admirals*, which satirizes the U.S. Navy from the Cold War to the mid 1990s, serves as a good example of the kind of background one needs: He is a retired commander with a full knowledge of daily life on an aircraft carrier, of the toll taken on the personal lives of the service men and women aboard, and of "the lunacy of political interference in the decision-making process and the sheer drive for power exhibited by many officers."

McKinnon warns against satire that is "a thinly disguised rant, in which the writer gets whatever is bothering him 'off his chest' in the guise of a novel." Works satirizing religion, which typically lack "focus or clarity of purpose or real knowledge of the subject, and certainly humor," are bound to be rejected. Satire, says McKinnon, must be funny "or at least surprising in some way." Otherwise, he finds it boring.

David Allan Cates: one novelist's success

It's one thing to have a list of general satirical techniques in mind. It's another to see these in action. How do you actually go about employing these techniques in a work of satirical fiction? Where do you begin? Where do you end? How do you make the work complex, not simplistic and juvenile? David Allan Cates's satire *X out of Wonderland* provides a good model of how to write successful satire.

Cates's agent, Emilie Stewart, liked the novel right away. Still it took 18 months and submissions to 20 publishers before the novel finally found an interested editor in Roland Pease at Steerforth Press. Pease accepts just two novels per year out of two hundred submissions. *X out of Wonderland* sold 3,500 copies and remains in print, unlike Cates's first novel, *Hunger in America*, and Cates considers this a success.

Landing a publisher for a satire and keeping it in print—these are certainly signs of success, the market for satire being what it is. But what makes this a successful satire, technically speaking? How does it avoid being amateurish and juvenile, merely derivative, preachy, and lacking authenticity—some of the key problems that both magazine editors and editors at publishing houses have noted.

Here's what Cates had to accomplish in order to have a successful satire:

• **Have a clear purpose**. For Cates, this began with a compelling question he had entertained since college days. "What is it in our culture that might strike people in future times as funny?" From the time he started writing, Cates wanted to satirize something funny about contemporary American life—something which contemporaries, because they're so caught up in it, might not immediately recognize. He was open to whatever would ultimately suggest itself.

• **Know what to satirize**. For Cates all literature, certainly satire, needs to deal "with a commonly held illusion—and let it play out." This "commonly held illusion" is a formula, he says, for satirical novels as well as for social novels like The Grapes of Wrath. Cates says he "glommed onto" Candide, Voltaire's famous eighteenth-century satire, for its general theme and structure. Like Candide, who is under the illusion that "This is the best of all possible worlds," X begins his journey under the illusion that the Global Free Market is a "divine creation." This topic itself would naturally fetch readers' attention with many people today concerned about the effects of a global marketplace on their lives. Like Voltaire, Cates takes his readers all around the world and back again to check out the validity of this belief in the GFM.

• **Create an appropriate world for the satire**. Satirists create different kinds of worlds. Some are fairly realistic, paralleling our own in recognizable details of setting and culture. Others seem much less realistic, more mythic in scope, closer to fantasy in a way. In many respects,

Cates's novel reads like an allegory, with its major setting "Wonderland" and its characters "X," "C," "the woman in pink lamé," "the malformed boy"—representative types, symbolic apparently, as we find in allegory. Still, Cates's novel is not an allegory on the order of Orwell's *Animal Farm*. As Cates points out, there is not an absolute one-to-one correspondence between the world he creates and the real world we see around us, though there are certainly some close parallels.

• **Manage the rug-pullings typical of satire with the right tone**. This is a tough act for any satirist. In satirizing his characters' firm belief in the Global Free Market system (its two watchwords being Choice and Mobility), Cates subjects these characters to constant rug-pullings, as the system both fails to meet their needs and nearly destroys them; now and then, when they recover, they do so only to be once again a victim. Readers might be put off, though, with a continual bloodletting of the main characters—who wants to read such as this? Effective satire, as we've been told, needs humor. We've got to find something funny, or we'll feel like we're reading a dark naturalistic novel by an author such as Émile Zola, Theodore Dreiser, or Stephen Crane. Or an exposé like Upton Sinclair's *The Jungle*. Cates's novel is much different from the grim work of these writers. It's an ingenious mix of light comedy and iconoclastic irony, a delicate balancing of optimism and despair, which Cates somehow manages to weave into a seamless whole. There are certainly very dark moments in the novel which place it in the genre of dark comedy. X is cast into prison with trumped-up charges of terrorism. As a factory laborer, he is under the tyranny of forced labor. The woman in pink lamé is gang-raped. If readers might be tempted to criticize these sections of the novel as being too dark or bleak, Cates doesn't make light of his characters' suffering. "Real pain and real pathos" make this satire, says Cates. And this is managed by an overall tone that finds humor to offset, not ridicule, the pain.

• **Know what to do when the satirizing is finished**. There is a point in X out of Wonderland when X could absolutely give up, once he realizes that he can no longer trust in the Global Free Market—because it simply no longer makes sense to him. So the question then becomes, says Cates: "How does he proceed?" This was a question not only for his protagonist but for Cates as satirist—how to proceed in his narrative, how to end things well, "when the issue being satirized is no longer an issue." The solution came out of Cates's vision of his character as a full-fledged human being with identifiable human needs, not just a cardboard character used to ridicule the system. X, he says, has to "try to find meaning and dignity when things don't pan out." X finds hope in two things: "pursuit of love" and "personal relationships." When the journey is ended, says Cates, "All we can do is hope to be fondly remembered." X has to be "okay without some grand scheme to justify his existence." This novel strikes home for readers, and this is because, as Cates himself says, it has the ring of truth: Like X at the end of the novel, we all hopefully arrive at a sense of "coming home again and being truly home."

• **Avoid cynicism**. Satire requires a fine balance: while it can't be heavy-handed, it must achieve "satirical force," as Cates calls it. To achieve this, Cates learned early on that the satirist has to avoid becoming "merely cynical." He firmly believes that good satire must be life-affirming. He ends, as we've seen, with X's optimism in what life still has to offer—on the personal, human level.

• **Make the work complex at all levels**. Besides the macro level, Cates worked carefully at the micro as well, so that his satire is not simplistic but multi-layered. "Little things should complement bigger things," he says, "the absurd tucked in with the everyday." For instance, the market X encounters after being released from prison is a veritable consumer's wonderland replete with "horrendous things for sale" right along with "rubber duckies." Consumerism in this novel is represented not only as a biological need but also as something nigh on to sacred. For Cates, the "market takes everything sacred and turns it into something banal." To show this, Cates creates wacky, humorous lists that mix these two together, with witty juxtaposition reminiscent of one of his favorite authors, Mark Twain.

• **Handle reductio ad absurdum**. This is the satirist's stock-in-trade technique—taking a matter to its logical, absurd end. In X out of Wonderland, the future of the market will probably be to sell human breath! The novel does have its surprises, many of them, and that's why we keep reading.

A final issue: the best choice of protagonist

Satire presents one special difficulty—deciding on the right narrative point of view. Which character will be the best protagonist for this work? Which character will help the writer to avoid soapboxing it, engender reader sympathy, and create interest—enough to make the reader care about what happens to the character, and to care about what's being satirized itself. X in Cates's novel, though under an illusion, is always of interest to his readers because most of us, unless we're unusually lucky, have had our share of rug-pullings, and most of us have been victimized in different ways— if not by the Global Free Market system, at least by some system, whether it's the school system, work, local government, or whatever. In Cates's hands, the Global Free Market system becomes a compelling symbol of whatever has beleaguered us at one time or another in our life—and what deserves debunking. And if we can't share the protagonist's problems in some way, we're not going to be interested in what happens to him or her.

So how does one choose the appropriate protagonist? If the character is a typical hero type, this might not work too well because it might appear that the author is self-righteously standing behind the hero, criticizing the target of the satire. This might work, however, if the writer is also planning to take the typical hero down a peg or two—to expose the folly of this "hero's" overblown belief in his own "heroism." If the character is, at the other end of the scale, completely weak, this may present a problem as well since he or she may be a victim only, with not enough to compel our interest. There are many scenarios possible, with many targets of satire and many possibilities of characters to choose from. Bottom line: Your protagonist needs to be one that is recognizably human in ways, elicits our sympathy to a degree, and above all, keeps us interested in the satire. And the satire, as we've seen, has to work without authorial intrusion—with nicely controlled authorial distance—with humor, with wit, and with enough complexity of idea that we don't find it juvenile but adult fare, completely worthy of our attention.

Craft & Technique

The Unsympathetic Protagonist

by Janice Hussein

Nearly every writer has heard about this character. From other writers, from editors, from agents. We know that editors and agents will reject a manuscript with an unsympathetic protagonist. They won't want to read the novel; they believe, rightly so, that readers won't like the protagonist, won't want to spend 400 or more pages in close association with that character.

So who is this mysterious character that invades our prose? Who is this masked entity, this unsympathetic protagonist? What is meant by this term and how can we, as writers, avoid this pitfall and create characters that are, instead, sympathetic? The answer is: By unmasking these characters, by peeling away the layers, by making them real.

'Unsympathetic' defined

First, let's unmask what is meant by "unsympathetic protagonist." Let's peel away the layers. In a novel or movie, we like and identify with the protagonist in some way—in their search for justice, for love, for escape, for growth—including their desire and efforts to reach their goals, their dreams, despite their imperfections and the odds against them. We root for them when obstacles stand in their way. Conversely, the unsympathetic protagonist is not someone we like or someone we can identify with—we can't *sympathize* with this character, with their motivations, goals and dreams. They have qualities we don't like or admire, and they don't have enough positive qualities that would balance out what we don't like. Further, they may also have *done* something we don't like or that we find reprehensible—their actions are disquieting. We can't connect with the character, and we can't empathize with them or their pursuit of goals and dreams, so we can't root for them.

Thus, if we don't like or care about the character and we don't like or care about their goals, that means we don't care about the plot, we don't care about the novel. There is nothing to keep us in the story, nothing to keep us turning those pages.

There are basically three kinds of characters who may be defined as unsympathetic: (1) the characters who we simply don't like or can't identify with, but who are not really "terrible" people; (2) the characters whose traits might seem to define them as villains or almost as villains but who escape this definition by the way they are portrayed and who actually become the protagonists of the novel; and finally (3) the actual villains. For our purposes, we will cover the first two of these.

On the spectrum of moral and likable traits, this unsympathetic protagonist lies somewhere

JANICE HUSSEIN, a freelance writer and book editor, and offers classes and workshops in fiction writing. She can be reached on the web at www.documentdriven.com.

between the normal protagonist and the villain. The normal protagonist is defined by whether he or she is sympathetic and usually whether he or she grows in a believable character arc during the course of the novel. On the other end of the spectrum, villains are defined by whether they are unsympathetic or sympathetic, and inherently evil or impelled/compelled by circumstances.

'Sympathetic' defined

So what does it mean to be sympathetic? In any novel, to be sympathetic means that a character, protagonist or villain, is multidimensional and believable—ideally both kinds of characters should have flaws as well as admirable qualities—they don't always, however. Fictional characters should be rounded, not caricatures, archetypes or stereotypes. If the antagonist is totally bad, a 2-dimensional character with no redeeming or interesting qualities, then the reader will find the character less interesting and thus, may find the story less believable, less interesting. Both the character and the novel will be less real, less believable. In the same way, if protagonists don't have flaws, the readers will not like them or find them interesting, or believe in them—the characters won't seem real. And if the protagonists have too many flaws, readers may not like them.

Ways to make this work

What can be done to change that character so that he or she is considered sympathetic? Three basic things related to characterization must occur to have the reader perceive a character as sympathetic: (1) the characters must be rounded and believable; (2) the reader must like them; thus, the author must reveal the right balance of the character's good and bad traits for the story being told; and (3) the reader must understand how and why they are how they are; the author must, therefore, make the protagonist known to the reader.

The protagonist is usually the POV character or the focus of a narrator/ POV character, and in that sense, the author has the advantage, at least temporarily, of a captive audience. Set down in that POV, the reader already views things from that character's perspective, and the author already has the advantage of being able to influence the reader more easily.

So the characters must be rounded and believable. That means the protagonist must have flaws and be a fully developed character, with a detailed biography, even if only part of that biography is used in the novel. The flaws must be consistent with who that fully developed character is, must ring true. Further, the character's actions and words must be consistent with that flaw and with who that character is. The best characters, because they reflect this aspect of real life people who aren't perfect, could be classed in the grey area that is humanity.

We've established that the protagonist should have flaws. So the question arises: How far may those flaws extend before that protagonist becomes a villain? What happens when the author and protagonist step out of this area of normalcy, of reader expectations for normal flawed characters, but are still within the boundaries of what we could define as the protagonist, but not yet as an antagonist.

The degree and extent of those flaws and admirable traits must be a balance that is a function of the dynamic among the story's main elements: the protagonists, the other characters, and the plot. The protagonist must be shown to be likeable and/or redeemable, despite any flaws; other traits that are liked and admired must be revealed as part of the character and the personality—sometimes in relation to that flaw. Ideally there should be at least one protagonist who has flaws and must change and grow over the course of the novel. The other characters are a function of the requirements of the plot, the good and bad qualities of the protagonist, the protagonist's character arc, and the setting in which the characters are placed. The plot of the story emerges from who the character is, from their choices, background, and situation.

The reader must come to understand why and how the characters are how they are. In real life, when we get to know someone and understand them better, we understand more clearly why they do the things they do, and we can, therefore, empathize with their motivations and have reasons to at least excuse behaviors we might otherwise have condemned and disliked. The more the reader knows and likes the protagonist, the more they will bond with the character and the story emotionally.

Nine techniques to use

What are the techniques needed to make the unsympathetic protagonist sympathetic? As stated above, the main way to do this is to make the reader identify with, know and like the protagonist, preferably before any revelations of wrongdoing. For some examples, I've chosen a few protagonists who might otherwise have been the villains; all are, of course, sympathetic—within the context of their stories and world—and are very good examples the techniques and of well-rounded, believable protagonists.

In *Shawshank Redemption*, the character, Andy Dufresne, has murdered his wife. If we're introduced to Andy without knowing the extenuating circumstances, then we're much less likely to try to excuse him and to like him when his good or interesting qualities are revealed. Thus, the storyteller immediately reveals that Andy was upset and drinking, that his wife was having an affair with another man, and that he tried to confront them when he was drunk. The audience can't approve, but we know why it happened, and we can excuse him more, knowing those circumstances—he didn't, for instance, murder her for the insurance, or because she drank his last beer. Normally, this kind of information needs to be presented early enough in the novel, so that the readers' sympathy and interest are aroused; ideally on the first page or within the first few pages, and definitely within the first 10 pages or the first chapter where the character is introduced. That means including some background in the first chapters, but including only just enough to tell that story.

The following are some techniques to help make your protagonist sympathetic:

1) Make the protagonist someone who is perceived as more likable and less reprehensible within that group of characters. For example, in *Pirates of the Caribbean*, Captain Jack Sparrow is not the worst character among those in the film; we see he has a better standard of behavior than the other pirates and that he's smarter. He's not perfect, but we can accept him and like him anyway. Early in the film, he saves the heroine, who we have come to like—and he's funny, rather charming and smart.

Another example is the character Andy in *The Shawshank Redemption*. First, this character is a banker and as he enters the prison, he's dressed in a conservative suit and coat. He's not someone who is hard core, but who made a mistake of passion. Right away, the narrator, "Red," observes that Andy seems different from the others by the way that he comports himself. The narrator is also made to seem more sympathetic, less reprehensible than those in the group. During the influx of new inmates, he is portrayed as more decent—quiet, thoughtful—in contrast to the other inmates who are loud, nasty, and abusive.

2) Make the antagonist less likable—someone you'd hate more and whose action/words make the audience sympathetic to the protagonist. In *Shawshank Redemption*, the protagonist Andy is brutally raped by a predatory inmate, even though he tried to quietly and firmly discourage that attention—like most of us would.

3) Show that the character is redeemable—how he or she has some redeeming qualities. You could do this by showing he cares about another character. In *Nobody's Fool*, by Richard Russo, the protagonist Sully rescues the woman with Alzheimer's when she drifts outside in the snow, and shows he is redeemable. You could also do this by showing what kind of work the protagonist performs in the community, by how he donates time or money when it is asked of him, by caring about some greater wrong in the community or in society, and so on. At the beginning of *Pirates of the Caribbean*, Captain Jack Sparrow dives in—no one else did—to save the heroine, Elizabeth Swann, despite danger or repercussions from his actions. In *Shawshank Redemption*, Andy requests the beers for his fellow prisoners as the only payment for his financial advice to the guard; the filmmakers bring out that he doesn't have any beer himself, that he gave up drinking (he was drinking when his wife's murder occurred). Another example is Don Vito Corleone in *The Godfather*. He offers a last option for justice for those who have been grievously wronged, refuses to be involved with the drug trade and believes in family, loves his own family.

4) Show that the protagonist has somewhere in his or her background been wronged, betrayed or hurt by someone—something that will get the readers' sympathy. For example, in *Bodyguard of Lies*, by Robert Doherty, the protagonist Neeley discovers she has been betrayed: "When had she finally known that the man she loved had handed her a bomb to carry onboard a plane full of people." In *Pirates of the Caribbean*, Captain Jack's ship, the Black Pearl, was stolen from him in a mutiny and he was abandoned to die on a deserted island. In *Up Close and Dangerous*, by Linda Howard, the protagonist Bailey has a trust problem because she's lived in numerous foster homes. At the beginning of *Shawshank Redemption*, when the Andy is being tried for his wife's murder, the District Attorney says: the cheating couple "obviously did something wrong, but … ." Then in a flashback, he's shown before the crime, looking obviously miserable as he drinks in his car, waiting to confront his beloved wife who is with another man. In *Ocean's Eleven*, during his parole board hearing, the protagonist Daniel Ocean is questioned about his past actions. He replies: "My wife left me, I was upset, I got into a self-destructive pattern." After he's released, he's shown wearing the wedding ring.

5) The protagonist could be funny, or say something funny. People tend to like people who make them laugh. Examples of this are protagonist Stephanie Plum in the Janet Evanovitch series, Hawkeye Pierce in the television series M.A.S.H, and Minerva Dobbs in *Bet Me*, by Jennifer Crusie.

6) The protagonists could be someone fascinating or say something fascinating. An example is Andy in *Shawshank Redemption*, when he shows how very smart he is about finances and people, while in prison. Another example is Hannibal Lecter who becomes the protagonist is *Hannibal Rising*; he is like a Sherlock Holmes who is also a serial killer.

7) The protagonist could be someone who the other sex would absolutely adore. Because of this (and usually other accompanying traits), the same sex would secretly admire and want to be like them. Women tend to like a man who has a way with women, who seems to really uncannily understand them. An example of this kind of character is Rhett Butler, who drew favor from a spectrum of women from Belle Watling to Scarlett O'Hara to Melanie Hamilton. He also becomes a hero for being a successful gunrunner, whatever his motivations. Another example of the good use of this kind of trait is the New Orleans cop Marc Chastain, Linda Howard's protagonist in *Kill and Tell*. As he pursues the heroine, it occurs to him: "There had never been a woman he'd wanted whom he hadn't gotten…"And from his partner's inner dialogue upon visiting Chastain's residence: "Man, this was the way to live. Nothing fancy, and just about everything was old as hell, but he bet Chastain drew babes like a magnet. The way he dressed, the way he lived…woman liked this stuff."

8) Show in what ways the protagonists might be admired or have them do something readers would admire. This includes doing something really well, or being a leader of some sort, having a career that is unusual—something that makes the character special. In *Pirates*, after Captain Sparrow cleverly commandeers a ship, a soldier describes him by saying: "That's got to be the best pirate I've ever seen." In *Ocean's Eleven*, Danny Ocean's team is clever, mostly likable; they are the top people in their specialties. Other examples of unusual careers: Nicole Ward, U.S. Prosecutor, in *Lone Star Surrender*, by Lisa Renee Jones; Captain J.T. Wilder, Green Beret, in *Don't Look Down*, by Jennifer Crusie and Bob Mayer; and Delilah Reese, knife and sword designer, in *Tiger Eye*, by Marjorie M. Liu.

9) Show how the protagonist is the underdog within the group of characters. Examples of this are Heathcliff in *Wuthering Heights*, by Emily Bronte; the *Titanic* hero Jack Dawson; and the protagonist Rye Forrester of *A Reason to Believe,* by Maureen McKade.

The novel is often better for having a character who verges on being a villain—as compared with the other characters—such as Capt. Jack Sparrow and Andy Dupreine, because we feel compelled to read further, watch further. We want to know how this interesting, perhaps slightly unpredictable character responds to conflict, how the story plays out. We want to know how the elaborate plan unfolds, as in the movie *Ocean's Eleven*. We want to see where the story goes, how it ends, what the fascinating characters will do and how they will end up. And their stories are often a statement about humanity and/or redemption, such as Huck Finn, Andy Dufresne (*The Shawshank Redemption*), John Sullivan (*Nobody's Fool*), and Vianne & Roux (*Chocolat*).

The above techniques should be combined. As an illustration, in *Pirates*, Captain Sparrow's flaw is that he is a pirate—he admits he steals and plunders—although he's not the worst of the bunch. He is shown as something of an underdog who has been wronged, because he lost his ship, and arrives on the scene in a sinking boat. Yet he is admirable in the way he carries this off, and by how he cleverly commandeers the ship, "The Interceptor." He is shown as redeemable when saves the heroine from drowning. He is a fascinating character, and a leader who assembles the group that sets out to recover his ship, the Black Pearl. He seems to have a way with women—just not with the heroine. And he can be amusing; for example, when he's just saved the heroine from drowning and as she's returning his possessions to him, he asks the heroine to "watch the goods," while he holds the soldiers at bay.

How does your protagonist compare with other protagonists & to real-life people

To grow in our craft, we need to be objective and learn from other writers and from life. Look at other people's work, and compare your protagonists with the protagonists that other published authors have created. Analyze why you like the protagonists. What are their flaws? What do you find endearing or interesting about them? Are there any techniques among these nine that could be applied to make your characters better? Look at the people who you like in real life. What are their flaws? Why do you like them, despite their flaws? Analyzing other protagonists will help you create better characters and increase your repertoire of narrative techniques.

Jonathan Maberry

Strategically Building Tension

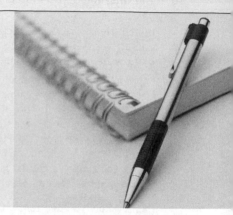

by Janice Gable Bashman

Jonathan Maberry is a master at building tension. He places strategic bits and pieces of tension throughout his work and skillfully manipulates the reader into feeling what he wants them to feel by using tension to shape the reader's experience. For Maberry, tension is not merely a single scene but rather what helps form the plot and leads the reader to a defining moment.

Maberry is the Bram Stoker award-winning author of *Ghost Road Blues*, *Dead Man's Song*, and *Bad Moon Rising*. His upcoming thriller, *Patient Zero* (St. Martin's Press, 2009), is the first in a series about Baltimore police detective Joe Ledger, who "is recruited by a secret government organization to help stop a group of terrorists from launching a weaponized plague against America that turns its citizens into zombies." The sequel, *The Dragon Factory*, will be released in 2010. Maberry also wrote the novelization of *The Wolf Man*, a remake of the classic horror film that will star Anthony Hopkins and Benicio Del Toro.

In addition to his novels, Maberry has published numerous short stories, including "Doctor Nine," which was the lead piece for the *Killers* anthology; "Pegleg and Paddy Save the World" in the *History is Dead* anthology; and "The Adventure of the Green Briar Ghost," for the *Legends of Mountain State* anthology. Maberry is a frequent speaker at writing conferences, and he provides workshops and classes for writers in all genres.

Tell us about your new book, Patient Zero, released in March 2009.
Patient Zero introduces Joe Ledger, a Baltimore cop recruited by a secret government organization—the Department of Military Sciences (DMS)—to help stop a group of terrorists armed with a plague that turns people into murderous zombies.

Though the villains have a 'zombie plague,' *Patient Zero* is not a horror novel. The pathogen used in the story isn't too far beyond the grasp of modern science, and in fact most of the science in the book is real.

Why is building tension so important to an effective story?
Tension drives all storytelling. Without it we'd know right away that the boy will get the girl, the supervillain will be stopped, and Dracula will get staked. Tension *is* the story. Storytelling is all about the race toward a goal (saving the world, etc.) and all of the complications that make the goal hard to achieve. That it is achieved should never be a given.

Tension takes a lot of different forms in fiction. It can be a simple character complication, like a misunderstanding that damages a new relationship just as it's about to blossom; or it

---

JANICE GABLE BASHMAN writes for leading publications. She is a member of the International Thriller Writers (ITW) and contributing editor of The Big Thrill (the newsletter of the ITW). Janice can be reached at janicebashman@yahoo.com

can be a group of terrorists about to release a highly infectious pathogen during a well-attended outdoor festival.

In thrillers the primary tension is the "ticking clock," which is the big bad event that will happen if the good guys don't stop it in time. This race against the clock structure allows for a very fast pace but does give elbow room for some character development. This is crucial because if the characters aren't fully drawn then the reader won't bond with them...which means the readers won't care very much about what happens to them or whether they succeed or not.

Tension is the most realistic connection between fiction and the real world, because in the real world things are seldom easy and they don't often work out. Threats are not always defeated; the guy doesn't always get the girl, and sometimes the bad guys win. When we bring that reality to fiction, the reader can't become complacent.

Explain how you use tension to draw a reader into a story and keep the reader hooked?
I like starting off with conflict. *Patient Zero* opens with these lines:

> When you have to kill the same terrorist twice in one week, then there's either something wrong with your skills or something wrong with the world. And there's nothing wrong with my skills.

The fuse is lit by establishing the nature of the conflict (the war on terrorism), the level of conflict (the hero is in direct violent conflict with the bad guys), and a tweak (he's had to kill one terrorist twice), followed by a kicker that tells us something about the hero and his abilities. Throughout the story I turn the heat up on the tension as often and in as many ways as possible.

From the beginning of the story my protagonist, Joe Ledger, is involved. He's not a passenger. I keep him constantly in motion; I don't want him to rest, because when he rests the reader rests.

A good way to heighten tension and quicken the pace is to compress the timeframe of the story. *Patient Zero* takes place over a couple of days. Every time the heroes get past one crisis there's another waiting to bite them. This puts the characters out on the ragged edge, which means I get to explore how otherwise well-trained and competent Special Ops agents would function when they were pushed way past their normal limits. It was not a nice thing to do to the characters, but who said writers should be nice to their characters? It's just the opposite: We're looking to make life as difficult as possible for our characters. That's what makes a good story.

You use bits and pieces of tension throughout your work to shape the reader's experience and lead the reader to a defining moment, rather than relying on tension within a single scene to achieve this goal. In Patient Zero this tension leads to a powerful and incredible climax. What are the key elements for building tension and sustaining it?
Tension needs to be fed. Imagine that tension in a story is like an EKG of someone as they're getting more and more excited. First you see the ordinary spikes of the rhythmic heart beating; but soon each new beat is bigger, the spike higher; and over time the spikes are both bigger and more frequent. That's the tension process in stories. We create tension early on so that we grab the reader, but along the way we need to create new spikes of tension, and each of these has to be more compelling than the last.

It's important to note, however, that tension should not always be of the same flavor throughout the book. If the hero is in a fight every other chapter, the story is going to get boring pretty quickly and the tension will deflate. Sometimes the tension is physical (a fight, a chase, etc.), sometimes emotional (memories of deaths and loss), and sometimes psychological (Joe's fractured mind and his path to balance). When Joe finally learns what the real threat is—the ticking clock—the tension is spiked again because now he's challenged with saving the whole world.

Good books have an over-arching tension (the ticking clock), set-piece tension (big moments of conflict, chase, revelation, discovery, etc.), and incidental tension (character conflict and internal conflict).

How do you incorporate these elements into your work?
I start with the high concept and ask questions. What is it that the bad guys want to accomplish?

Why? What will happen if they succeed? How far along are they by the time the hero enters the story?

Then I bring in the protagonist: Who is he and why is he the hero of this tale? What makes him larger than life? What makes him realistic? What motivates him? What are his limits? How far would he go to win? What would stop him?

When I combine the two, I have my story: When and how does the hero learn of the crisis? What will make it possible for the hero to win? What will make it difficult for the hero to win? What does the hero have to do to win?

In *Patient Zero,* the villains have weaponized a doomsday disease that it is nearly 100% communicable. If it gets out there will be no way to stop it. The terrorists are in the last stages of experimentation on the pathogen and are very close to releasing it.

That's the tension framework, and I pitch my hero, Joe Ledger, into this after the threat is already rolling forward. He has to scramble to catch up and then find a way to stop them. There isn't time to call in the cavalry or devise a sophisticated plan, so he has to think and act on the fly. That he can makes him the right hero; whether he does makes the novel a thriller.

You stated that "complex plot is the hardest because you have to both entertain the reader and keep him guessing. You can't make the puzzle too hard for them to grasp but at the same time you have to be aware that readers are smart, savvy and experienced, which means that they'll be thinking two or three steps ahead of you." Explain how that applies to shaping tension and how you address this issue.

There is a tendency in complex plotting to go overboard on exposition. Most novels have a nonfiction back-story upon which the entire story is built. However, when we research our books we often fall in love with the topic, and no one is more obsessive than a writer when it comes to devouring facts.

And yet most of what we learn does not need to be in the book. Much of it can be implied or disseminated in small bits through dialogue rather than narrative.

I like using the format of short chapters and a lot of them. I keep my characters in motion and I switch back and forth between different subplots frequently. The short chapters allow me to get each subplot moving, but prevents me from getting needlessly wordy. And the pace crackles.

It's important to remember that most readers seek out books within a range, and they read a lot of these books. Thriller readers gobble up a lot of thrillers; romance readers devour romances. That means that the reader holding your book is probably familiar with some of the tropes of your genre. Trust them. Trust that the reader is smart. They're practiced at reading novels, and they know the genre well enough so that you don't have to spoon feed everything to them.

What advice can you give to writers about building tension in their own work?

Don't try to keep your characters safe. We spend hundreds of hours alone with our characters—we're inside their heads and their hearts, we know what they feel, what they need and want, and they become real to us. That's great, but it can cause a writer to falter when it comes to breaking the hearts and bones of their characters. But we're not in the business of keeping our characters safe. Writers who are willing to introduce conflict and complications into the lives of their characters are more likely to tell a good story. Without conflict there's no opportunity for a character to rise (or fall). Without complication it's difficult to assess the value of something. When it comes to their characters, writers should be fearless and ruthless. If our characters survive all the things we throw at them then it's because they had to dig deep to find their inner strength, tap inner resources, become smarter, shake off complacency, overcome obstacles and prove that they are the hero of the story.

Can you give some quick advice to aspiring thriller authors?

Tell as realistic a story as possible, ground it safely in logic, and then give them a dollop of the fantastic. Readers will suspend their disbelief more readily (and even without realizing it) if the overall framework of the novel is realistic. That allows them to relate to the characters and situations, and when they relate the *feel.* Remember, it isn't just the characters who should feel stress and tension—it's the readers!

Writing Effective Query Letters

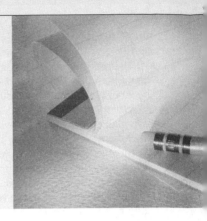

by Casey Quinn

Once a writer has a short story or novel written, edited and perfected they can begin the next stage of the publishing process—writing the query letter. The query letter is just as important as the manuscript itself. The old cliché about first impressions is true—and your letter is just that, the first impression of your writing. It is the first time you introduce yourself to an editor or agent and sets both tone and expectations. If you have a poorly written query your manuscript may never be looked at. Fiction writing is a competitive market and as writers we need every advantage we can get. Like any form of writing, a query letter is not something mastered overnight. But with some practice and revisions anyone can master it.

The reason query letters are a much needed part of the publication process is that publishers use them to determine if the story falls within the genre and style in which they publish. Instead of reading the full 80,000-word manuscript, agents read a query letter to determine if the writer has submitted a fantasy story to an agent that only works exclusively with science fiction. In this case, the agent may not read past your first paragraph before your manuscript is rejected.

There are three types of letters you should know about. The first is cover letter to accompany a short story submission to a journal. The second is a query letter asking for permission to submit work to an agent. The third is a query letter asking for permission to submit work directly to a publisher. Finding a book publisher that accepts unsolicited manuscripts is uncommon and even rarer when it comes to larger publishing houses. So how do you get your manuscript in front of a person who does not accept unsolicited manuscripts? Query letters. A well written query letter will result in a request for a partial or full manuscript or in the case of short stories; it will set the tone for your submission.

The first step in the publishing process is to identify the market in which you want to submit your manuscript. This means making lists of potential publishers, agents and journals that fit your manuscript's description. Before submitting anything to anyone, read the submission guidelines. There is no standard when it comes to submitting, only common themes. Different publishers may request that you e-mail the query, while others want paper. Some may want the query in the form of an attachment, others within the e-mail itself. Failure to follow the guidelines as written is a sure way to have your manuscript discarded without a chance of it being read.

Part of the process of knowing who to query is doing some basic research to ensure your

CASEY QUINN is the editor and publisher for the online magazine *Short Story Library* and the publishing company, ReadMe Publishing. He has had over 1,000 pieces of writing published ranging from nonfiction, fiction to poetry. His first poetry collection *Snapshots of Life* was released in 2009 by Salvatore Publishing.

query lands in front of the right person. Literary agencies have various agents who handle different genres of work. Journals have different editors for different sections. Learn what you can about where you want to send your work to before you send it. Find out the name of the agent or editor you plan on submitting to. Learn what their tastes are based on past publications or authors they have worked with. Be sure your own work lines up with what they publish to give yourself the best shot possible. Keep all of this information in one list so you can keep track of where you submit to later on.

COVER LETTERS FOR SHORT FICTION

When submitting a short story to a journal, online or print, the cover letter that accompanies your manuscript is more of an introduction and overview of you, the writer, compared to that of a novel query letter. Editors of journals can receive hundreds of submissions each day; many will ignore the cover letters all together and go right into the manuscripts while some prefer to learn about the writer beforehand. Here is a sample cover letter for short story submissions being sent to print or online journals:

Dear (Name of Editor),

Thank you for considering my submission "NAME OF SUBMISSION" for inclusion in your publication. Below is a brief biography of my writing.

Biography written in the third person should only be roughly fifty words long. It should only contain the highlights of your writing career.

Legal Name
Pen Name (Notate that it is your pen name)
E-mail address
Mailing Address

This is only a template. Most magazines provide specific requirements for what they need in the submission. Short story cover letters do not need to summarize the story. Instead they provide the publication with your biography in case they accept your work; your mailing address for sending off the check if it's a paying market; and your e-mail in case they have further questions or want revisions. If you fail to include the information they requested in their guidelines, your submission will be returned unread. Journals request certain information be in the letter for a reason—they need it for something. If they do not get it, do not expect them to ask you for it; instead they will likely reject your work.

QUERY LETTERS FOR NOVELS

If you have a novel manuscript and you are shopping for agents or publishers, your query letter will require more information than a simple cover letter would. Most of the time when contacting an agent or publisher, you will only send a query letter, no manuscript. It will be the only piece of your writing the agent or editor reads and will be used to determine if they want to see more of your work.

Query letters should be kept to one page and generally run only three paragraphs.

The first paragraph is your make or break paragraph. It is your hook and needs to tell your story in a sentence. It should not praise your book or compare it to anything else. It should act as a synopsis of your story in which you tell the reader the highlights of your story and leave them wanting to learn more. You have a word budget of roughly 50 words to do all of this. Imagine the back cover of your published book—what would it to say to get readers to pick it up and buy it? That should be your first paragraph because in a sense that is what you are doing here. You are trying to get the most important reader to buy into your book, your agent or publisher.

The second paragraph is a chance to expand on your hook and provide important details about your novel such as the title and length. Once an editor or agent is hooked in by the first paragraph, the second paragraph offers them more details on the main character, the action sequences and the twists and turns of the plot. This paragraph should run roughly 150 words.

The third paragraph is about you, the writer. Here is where you want to describe any significant publication credits you have, any contests or awards you have won and writing courses you have taken. The biography paragraph should be strictly about your writing career and nothing personal or about your professional career unless it ties very closely to your manuscript. If you have a short biography, you may want to expand your second paragraph, adding more enticing details about your novel.

John Thomas
555 Sample Street
Somewhere, NY, 11111
555-555-5555
fakee-mail@e-mail.com

(Your name and address)
January 15, 2009 (Today's date)
Mark Smith (Name and title if available)
Smith Literary Agency, LLC
(Address of publication or agency)
12 Johnson Road
Somewhere, NY, 11111

Dear Mark Smith:

When Tom Daniels moved out to the country and bought the Stevenson place, he had plans to farm, leaving the stress and bad memories of the city firmly in his past. But his hopes for a quiet, simple life are shattered when he discovers the town is haunted by a history of violence and ritual sacrifice.

BLOOD SACRIFICE is an 80,000-word horror novel which takes place in the small farming community of Clyde, Kansas. When Daniels purchased his property he had never heard of the town nor had his realtor. It was the ideal, secluded environment he had been looking for to escape his grief over the loss of his wife and child. Upon arrival he is greeted by few; most keep their distance. Daniels notes strange noises. Soon community member go missing. After following the town mayor from a local bar down into underground caverns, Daniels discovers a secret cult resides below the town, and keeps Clyde under their control with fear tactics and ritualistic killings. After watching a little girl being sacrificed, Daniels is reminded of his own deceased daughter and decides he must put a stop to the cult. As he tries to rally the locals for help, he realizes the tradition of the cult is larger than he had first thought and now fears he'll be the next to fall as a blood sacrifice.

I have been writing horror for over two decades and have had short stories published in Dark Nights Magazine, Crypt Magazine and Night Terrors Journal. I have been nominated for three pushcart prizes and for the Bram Stoker Award. I have enclosed a SASE for your convenience and I look forward to hearing from you.

Sincerely,

John Thomas

Remember that every word in your query is important—be sure it's well-edited and free of typos. The query letter should set in 12-point Times New Roman. Don't be creative with your fonts and coloring. Paragraphs should be single spaced and left aligned. You are not going to get extra credit if you try to break the mold and think outside of the box. Those are key phrases in other professions but when it comes to query letters, stick to the proven formula. You want to be taken as a professional. If you try to break out of the traditional format, you will be seen as an amateur.

Also be sure to include a formal address for the intended reader, your contact information including phone number, address and e-mail, and of course, your signature. You may think it goes without saying, but many writers forget this vital information. If your contact information is not included, it's unlikely an editor or agent is going to track you down no matter how much they are intrigued by your query letter. Here is a sample query for a novel-length manuscript. (For more sample query letters see The Business of Fiction Writing on page 77.

Once you have your query written, take your time and read it over. Have friends read it over. Treat it like you would any other piece of writing to ensure it is as perfect as you can get it. Once you're satisfied it's as good as it can be, start sending it out.

As mentioned above, read the submission guidelines for query letters and ensure that the publishers or agents you're targeting accept simultaneous submissions. As response times for queries to agents and publishers can take months, most will review queries that were also submitted elsewhere. Keep good track of your queries so you know who you've sent them to and when they were sent. Never query two agents working for the same literary agency and do not querying both agents and publishers at the same time.

By keeping track of when you sent your queries, you also will know when you can follow up with a note. Submission guidelines should generally state the turnaround time for responses. Once the time has expired, I would suggest waiting one extra week or two and then following up with a friendly and professional note. The note should just state when you submitted the original query, the name of the manuscripts you queried about, and ask for a confirmation that it was received.

Remember, completing your manuscript is only part of the process of getting published. The fact is, without a query no one will ever read your finished manuscript. Always treat your query letter with the same attention you did your story.

Submitting to Literary Journals

& Small Presses

by Mark Maynard

As a short story writer who'd amassed a thick binder full of rejection slips, I often wondered if I was doing everything to ensure that my manuscripts were being seriously considered for publication.

As the fiction editor of a small literary journal called The MeadoW, I realized that our magazine wanted to help as many burgeoning writers get published while maintaining high editorial standards.

With the help of Rob Roberge, a novelist, short story writer and editor, I contacted an esteemed group of published writers as well as literary magazine and small press editors and asked them a series of questions designed to help writers navigate the process of submitting work to literary markets and pass through the editorial gate. Their responses helped shape the following guidelines.

Changing your mindset

When sending your work out for consideration, you must plan to be published and expect to be rejected. One way to deal with this dichotomy is to change your mindset.

Author and playwright Diane Lefer says, "I don't use the term submissions. I think it was Muriel Rukeyser who said, 'A writer should never submit to anyone!' So I don't submit. I offer."

When offering your work to literary markets, it is best to have a solid plan. This includes reading as wide a variety of literary magazines as you can get your hands on. Many good publications can be found at your local bookstore and in your public library. Numerous print and online publications also feature published stories on their Web sites. And pay close attention to the "Needs" and "Advice" sections that follow each literary market listing in this book.

Send your work to publications that you enjoy reading. Find other stories that "fit" with your style, your themes and your sensibilities, but keep in mind that most editors are looking for new and different work.

Lefer offers more useful advice about which journals to send your work to. "You're always told to study the mag and see what they like, but really, every now and then they want something different; even they get bored with what they tend to publish."

MARK MAYNARD received his MFA in Creative Writing from Antioch University Los Angeles in 2007. He writes short fiction, and his work has appeared in *The Duck and Herring Pocket Field Guide, Shelf Life Magazine*, and the *Wild Things* anthology published by Outrider Press. Mark is also the fiction editor for *The Meadow*, the annual literary journal of Truckee Meadows Community College. He lives in Reno, Nevada with his wife and two sons.

Once you've developed a targeted list of five to 10 markets, make sure that you read and follow the specific submission guidelines for each. Rob Roberge says the first stories rejected are the "ones that can't ever care to be properly formatted."

Paul Mandelbaum, former managing editor of Story magazine adds "editors are inundated and looking for any excuse to put down a submission in good conscience."

But a properly formatted story will still not make it through even the first round of evaluation if it is not a well-crafted final draft.

Other Voices executive editor Gina Frangello says she rejects, "anything that is sloppy, grammatically disastrous, or just plain badly written...you don't need to read 20 pages to figure out when something is horrible or just nowhere near ready for publication. You do need to read 20 pages (or however many) to distinguish between 'good' and 'excellent'—in fact a story may need several reads and a lot of discussion to make that distinction. But it's pretty clear from page 1 or 2 when a story is a disaster."

Too much of a bad thing

Red Hen Press managing editor Kate Gale offers a useful list of things she sees too much of in rejected manuscripts: "Bad dialogue, too many brand names, too many references to television shows and too many stories about romantic entanglements (I kid you not!) between students and their writing teachers."

Frangello expands this list, adding, "Stories that are obsessed with the quaintness and quirkiness of small towns. Stories about cancer and Alzheimer's. Stories with 'punchline' surprise endings that seem clever the first time, but lose all impact on a second reading once the 'gimmick' of the story is already known," and "chick lit that doesn't know it's chick lit."

If you have a quirky, small-town story with a terminally ill character involved in a romantic entanglement with a writing instructor, that doesn't mean that your manuscript will be summarily rejected, but it must have something that makes it stand out from the crowd and a mastery of language that will grip the editor who reads it.

Other things editors see entirely too much of include stories comprised almost entirely of exposition revealed through dialogue, plots and characters that are not honest or organic but are written to shock and amaze, and current events stories that are neither compelling nor well-written.

Remember that the editors and publishers of literary magazines don't relish rejecting any manuscript. It is their job to sift through piles of submissions trying to find fresh voices, unique perspectives and, always, great writing. They want to publish your story, but you must give them a good reason to.

What makes the cut

Now that you know what will get your story buried deep in the slush pile, what traits do successful stories have?

Pushcart Prize recipient and editor Gary Amdahl says it begins with a good opening. "A good first sentence will make me look hard for evidence of its likeness elsewhere."

Roberge offers the insight that good writing is always up against length, as all print and online journals have space considerations. "A short story has a better chance than a longer one, if they are of equal quality. A 20-page story is going to bump four 5-page stories out of the magazine. That story is going to have to be four times better than each and every one of those shorter stories to justify eating up that much page count."

Some of the most difficult things to write about, when well written, can all but ensure a story's success, "both sex and humor are hard to do," says Frangello, "so what you end up with a lot is literary writing that is awfully straight-laced and humorless. If a story can do sex or humor truly well, I'm often pretty sold."

Red Hen Press' Gale looks for "great writing that, like Calvino, Marquez and Duras, is completely invested in language and in human meaning beneath the surface. Easy writing doesn't do it."

Putting the odds in your favor

All writers, especially those seeking to expand their publications, should submit their work simultaneously to several carefully selected publications. You may not emulate Tod Goldberg's prodigious offerings ("I used to carpet bomb the literary journals—like, 20 at a time—when I was starting out, but now I'll do maybe three to five,") however, "if you give anyone exclusive consideration," warns Diane Lefer, "you may end up published posthumously, if at all."

Editors understand that you are seeking to get published in any one of a number of select publications, and the knowledge that most, if not all, savvy authors simultaneously submit gives them even more incentive to get to your manuscript in a timely manner.

At The MeadoW, we publish on an annual basis, and we are sometimes informed that a piece we have selected for publication has been accepted elsewhere. As long as the writers let us know about their acceptance in another journal immediately (an absolute must when submitting to more than one market at a time), not only is it not a problem, but we are happy for the writer, and our evaluation of literary talent is reinforced by the fact that someone else thought the story was good as well.

As writer Gary Amdahl revealed about his submission process, "I would pretend to be eager to find out who would reject me first, who would reject me best, and so on. I would dream about having to say to an editor, 'sorry, you took too long; another mag has snatched that prize.'"

Embracing rejection

The most difficult part of offering a manuscript for consideration is confronting the odds that nearly every story will be rejected multiple times before it finds the right place for publication. Remember that even the best-crafted stories are evaluated subjectively by editors, each of whom is reading hundreds, maybe even thousands of stories a month. The rejection slip is a great literary equalizer that finds its way into the mailbox and inbox of every burgeoning writer and every accomplished author.

How many times can you expect to get a story rejected before it gets accepted?

"Anywhere from zero to 60 times," says accomplished short story writer Steve Almond, "Seriously."

Writer Tod Goldberg shares his daunting, yet ultimately hopeful experience sending out a manuscript: "The first story I ever sold was rejected 65 times. That's my record. That might be a world record. It ended up getting Special Mention for the Pushcart Prize that year, which tells you something about the above-noted subjective nature of things."

Leonard Chang, a novelist and short story writer, says the number of rejections varies, but the first publication is usually the hardest.

"My very first short story, one I wrote as a grad student, was rejected over 30 times before being accepted for publication. It became not only my first professional publication, but an agent read it and contacted me. Eventually he became my agent and is still my agent now. These days, most stories of mine get perhaps one to 10 rejections before finding a home."

Writers can expect to receive a number of different types of rejections, from impersonal form emails and photocopied rejection slips to the returned cover letter in a self-addressed envelope, a de facto rejection letter from yourself. The best response you can receive, besides a notice of acceptance, is the "positive rejection".

A positive rejection goes beyond an acknowledgement that your story was received and read by an editor. It is an affirmation that he or she found something memorable enough to contact you personally.

I got such a letter that read in part, "We enjoyed reading your work but decided to take a pass on this one. The piece is extremely well-crafted but just didn't fit the tone of this season's issue. That being said, we're interested in seeing more of your work. Please don't hesitate to direct any future submissions our way."

Once you have received such a personal invitation to offer another manuscript, wait a few months (and until you have something very strong to send) and then, post another story with a personal note reminding that editor of his or her earlier comments about your previous submission.

Keep track of your progress

Always keep an up-to-date list of your submissions including the markets you sent your work to, the date sent, the date you received a response and any notes (including contact information) from editors. This can be a hardcopy filing system, an electronic spreadsheet or can be tracked and updated online at WritersMarket.com.

Once a market responds, update your files (always consider any recommendations or editorial suggestions you've received before sending your work back out) and then send your manuscript out again to another five to 10 targeted publications. A writer's persistence and diligence in crafting a story must extend into the process of offering that story for publication. It will take some time and effort to get published, especially for those writers just starting out.

Remember that the editors of literary journals and online magazines want to publish your work as eagerly as you want to have it published. Give them every opportunity to say "yes" to your manuscript by offering your absolute best writing to them. Make it original, carefully crafted and thoughtfully structured while exhibiting a true mastery of language. Be willing to take constructive criticism, even in the form of a rejection letter, but stay with it, and believe in your work. If you take the time to read and understand the different markets, and if you send out your work to the publications that you enjoy reading, you will eventually find success by sharing your published story with the world.

Writing & Marketing Genre Fiction

by Jude Tulli

Genre can, in just a few words, convey perhaps more about that novel you're writing than any other shorthand. After learning this most basic of classifications, a potential reader is likely to know whether your work belongs on the night table amidst the to-be-read pile or beneath a sweaty drink as overpriced coaster of the month.

Agents often limit their searches for new clients based on preferred genres; those in which they have established connections and/or for which they hold a special place in their hearts. (It's a quantifiable fact that they do tend to have hearts, in case you were wondering, dear reader.) Large publishing houses and the editors they employ also either limit or divide their acquisitions by those little words on some corner of the back cover that in turn determine a book's shelf-mates at the store. Small presses often are born of desire to propagate one or a handful of related genres.

Yes, before a publishing entity spends a second of quality time with your characters (or even a synopsis), your submitted manuscript must be unduly categorized, and must either adhere to the limitations inherent within your chosen genre or have good reason for any deviations. Some writers view genre as a constraint only a Houdini can elude. For others, it's a welcome guide that helps shape their work and identify appropriate markets.

To help us to make sense of this (circle one: wonderful classification system/tyrannical evil/changing, changeable seascape) we have enlisted the support of authors, editors and an agent of the definitively with heart persuasion. May their perceptions and experiences help you, dear reader, to launch your work in clear waters beneath the sunniest of skies.

DONNA JO NAPOLI
On books for young readers

An award-winning and bestselling author whose works span a host of genres, Donna Jo Napoli persisted through 14 years of submitting her work before she sold her debut manuscript. Since that first easy reader found its way to print, she has built a veritable empire upon foundations that sweep across genres and readership demographics and transcend national borders and language barriers. Fit for a writer who's also a linguist, Napoli's work has been translated into a multitude of foreign languages. Her latest books The Earth Shook (picture book; Hyperion, 2009), Alligator Bayou (young adult; Random House, 2009) and Ready to

JUDE TULLI lives in the Sonoran Desert with his wonderful wife Trish, an inordinate number of indoor cats and a large goldfish aquarium that they fishlessly cycled (Google that if you have or want pet fish and don't know what it means). He is a recurring contributor to both *Novel & Short Story Writer's Market* and *Writer's Market*. He is currently trying to entice publishing type folks to read his fantasy novel manuscript. Trend-chasing though it might be, he wonders if he'd get more interest if he sprinkled in a few gratuitous vampires.

Dream (picture book which she co-authored with Elena Furrow, who happens to be her daughter; Bloomsbury, 2009) will bring her career total to 64 books.

"Before I started," Napoli says, "I didn't even know there were 'genres' so to speak. I had been reading a lot since I was a kid. And I read all the time to my own children. So I thought I knew what children's books were about. In fact, I had no idea. Somehow I had read thousands of picture books and never noticed they all had 32 pages. That seems like a trivial thing to point out, but, really, it's fundamental."

How does this apply to writing children's books for publication? "If you write what you think is a picture book, and it has thousands of words, no one is going to publish your story." Likewise, if your story "all takes place in an empty elevator there are few opportunities for interesting illustrations."

With the benefit of hindsight-tinted spectacles, Napoli says, "I wish that before I had started, I'd gotten informed about the general outlines of each market for children." Not that it should interfere with the craft: "A writer certainly does not have to work within a genre or within a format. But it helps to understand what the publishers will know how to position in the market—so that you can then decide which way you want to go (I'm talking about conscious deliberation here) rather than just bumbling around in the dark."

Napoli testifies that once you find your niche, it can easily turn out to be a pigeonhole. "Editors do not relish an author crossing over – it's much easier to keep producing in a market the author has a proven track record in than to try to introduce the author to new markets."

When her first YA novel was accepted, Naopli's editor worried "that I had started to build up a reputation as a middle-grade writer. What would happen to the unsuspecting child who reached out for another book by me and wound up with a dark, gothic, very adult-like book? So the publishing house debated whether I should be published under a different name for YA." Indeed, the adoption of a pseudonym is not uncommon practice for writers who cross over from one genre to another. For Napoli, "In the end, they decided to go ahead with me as one writer."

Napoli found one market particularly difficult to pervade. For years "I kept showing picture book manuscripts to my editor and she kept rejecting them. Then I started sending them out to other publishing houses and these new editors kept rejecting them." One lovely personalized rejection informed her "that I was 'a novelist'—why was I wasting my time with these other stories that I clearly didn't know how to write?" In all, "The first picture book I got published (Albert [Harcourt, 2001]) was rejected by nearly 30 houses before it got accepted—and then it went on to do well."

Though Napoli has "been told agents are the only way to go today," she has created her writing career without one. She also had no short story credits to include on her query letters: "I never wrote a short story," she says.

Writing Books for Young Readers

Donna Jo Napoli offers advice for a wide range of readerships:

- **Picture books:** "They're visual—keep that in mind every second." Easy readers: "Short sentences don't have to be stupid. Most of us talk in fragments all the time. Use that."
- **Chapter books:** "Try to see every chapter as a story in itself, which means have a nice, clean ending (even if it's a cliffhanger). That way the child can feel satisfaction in having read 'a whole chapter!' and can then go to sleep."
- **Middle-grade novels:** "If you want boys to keep reading, then keep the action moving. This is the hardest age to hold onto—so don't try. Make them try to hold onto you—race race race."
- **Young adult novels:** "Be careful. Younger kids pick these up. You can be as realistic as you want, but if you put a veil over certain kinds of things, you allow the older reader to deal with it without abusing the younger reader."

Getting Published

While Napoli, like many if not most authors, indulged in patches of disappointment and discouragement along the way, she still found a way to persevere far longer than those whose names never graced the cover of a book. She advises new writers "to develop thick skin and big ears. Thick skin so they can take the rejections and criticisms. Big ears so they can hear the criticisms and learn from them."

JANETTE OKE
Writing Christian fiction

With over 75 titles and more than 23 million copies in circulation, Janette Oke writes with a voice that resonates the world over. Her faith-based historical fiction has delighted a mainstream readership. Like many of her heroines, some may call Oke a pioneer.

Oke's recent release The Centurion's Wife (Bethany House, 2009), co-written with Davis Bunn, is a historical romance set in biblical times. It begins a new series entitled Acts of Faith.

"When I began writing," Oke says, "Christian fiction was not really being done. Now it is very much a part of the industry. More new fiction writers appear each year."

Oke offers some ideas about what these newer writers should expect from the industry. She encourages an awareness that "writing is not the writer's toughest job. Finding a publisher is."

An understanding of the business and a little luck never hurt, either. "It takes more than being a skilled writer to become published," Oke says. "The work must fit a need in the marketplace, be presented at the right time—to the right publishing house; be something new and fresh; connect with the editor; and appear to be able to generate a profit."

Toward that end, "There are really no short-cuts," she says. "Be willing to do the proper work. No one else can get you published. It is your job."

Even when a writer's manuscript catches an editor's eye, Oke advises, "Don't get too attached. There will be changes as your work goes through the editing process."

While this can be minimized by plotting well, before you start, Oke accepts that "Re-writes are part of the job." Still, she remains optimistic about discarded material. "Some ideas will never be used. That does not mean they are wasted. They can steer you in another direction, or lead you to something better."

Oke believes writers are in a position to aspire "beyond getting published." For her, this means seizing the "great opportunity to use writing as a ministry," and "teach spiritual truths with fictional characters."

She has found that her mission even survived the transition to film in her Love Comes Softly series. "Michael Landon, Jr. has changed the story but kept the message. An answer to my prayers." Oke believes "The printed page has great power—either positive or negative." She advises Christian fiction writers to "Seek God's help to use what you do in a positive way."

SHAWNA MCCARTHY
Agenting fantasy

Shawna McCarthy has served as editor for the likes of Isaac Asimov's Science Fiction Magazine, senior editor for Bantam and, from its debut in 1994 to its farewell April, 2009 issue, founding editor of Realms of Fantasy magazine. She also became a literary agent in 1993 and started The McCarthy Agency in June of 1999.

From her overarching view of submissions both successful and otherwise, McCarthy sees "fantasy becoming ever more folded into mainstream literature, particularly 'urban contemporary' fantasy, which is the kind that features sexy vampires, werewolves and fairies." She speculates the cause: "Because it doesn't require any specialized knowledge or a grasp of tricky scientific principles, anyone can pick up one of these books and dive right into it. I think horror may have a resurgence for the same reason."

The most notable newer subgenres for science fiction, McCarthy says, are "cyberpunk and steampunk." Since the days when "it all used to be epic fantasy," she suggests, "the cross-pollination of fantasy, romance, mystery and thriller has led to a lot of new sub and sub-sub genres."

"Before a writer writes a single word," McCarthy warns, "A lack of expertise in [spelling, grammar and punctuation] means a quick trip to the recycling bin. This is not negotiable, but you'd be surprised how many queries and stories I get from would-be writers who think it is." Got all your subjects, participles and maybe, even, commas, in all the right, places,,,? Then you're ready to sing. McCarthy suggests that "a writer should read widely and determine what sorts of books he or she likes to read—you'll probably enjoy writing what you enjoy reading."

The opposite also holds true. "Don't try to write in a genre just because you think it's selling well," McCarthy says. "Your lack of dedication will show. You should also be aware that what's selling well today was bought at least 18 months ago. Who knows what's coming down the pike 18 months from now?" According to McCarthy, this goes double for short stories: "There's no point in writing a short story that you don't feel driven to write in any genre that you don't love. There's no money in it, and very little exposure, so it's a lot of effort to very little end if you're not doing it for love."

Regarding genre-hopping, McCarthy usually advises her clients to "write out-of-genre books under a pseudonym so as not to confuse readers or mess up their sales record if the book doesn't do well. That said, I always encourage my clients to have as many irons in the fire as possible, so that if one cools down, there are others to be picked up."

McCarthy encourages all authors to "Read, read, read and read some more. Don't read for fun, read for substance. If you like a book or a scene, try to figure out what it is that worked for you and how the writer did it. Even better, if you hate something, figure out what went wrong and how it could be fixed. Then learn to apply these skills to your own writing before you send it out for publication."

GAVIN GRANT
An editor's perspective on genre

A writer, editor and publisher of Small Beer Press and Lady Churchill's Rosebud Wristlet, Gavin Grant has noticed that "Fantasy (including paranormal romance) and horror (including dark fantasy) is only getting more popular."

Grant surmises it could be because "For the last ten years, kids have grown up with the Harry Potter phenomena and publishers are still trying to find follow-ups that will do as well. In the meantime, readers have lucked out with the plethora of good work available." Consequently, "Fantasy, and young adult fantasy, seem the best genres to work on a series."

Grant says, "Science fiction has a harder row to hoe. Cinema and television rely on it whenever anyone wants to explore pushing an issue to the limit." Perhaps a detraction to some is the fact that the genre can demand "more familiarity with either science or science fiction concepts than the average reader might have."

Grant finds the question of sub-genres to be a moot point. "I'd say there are almost as many sub-genres as there are authors, or maybe as many as there are books. Whether a genre novel is called New Weird, Interstitial, New Fabulist, Dark Fantasy, Science Fantasy, or what have you, when it comes out of the box at the bookshop it will go in the science fiction, fantasy, or horror section."

Grant emphasizes the importance of craftsmanship for modern genre writers. "There is a historic misperception that craft is not important in genre fiction because it's the ideas that count. That may have been true in the 1930s, but it's not now." Concepts are essential, but it behooves authors to bear in mind that "Editors have read more bad fiction than good, and learn to very quickly discard pieces due to bad writing." This includes genius writing that masquerades as bad.

Perhaps counterintuitive for writers, Grant believes "horror is where the common adage 'show, don't tell' should be reversed. I'd much rather be told about some unthinkable horror than have it lumber on stage and think, 'Oh, I could escape that.'"

Grant suggests today's genre writers should "consider Terry Pratchett. Not the Pratchett of today whose every book is a number one in the UK and sells hundreds of thousands in the USA, but rather the Pratchett of the 1970s and 1980s: a working stiff. To work steadily as a writer is to find a balance between the kind of book you love and the kind of book readers love."

KRISTINE KATHRYN RUSCH
Crossing genres & adopting puedonyms

Kristine Kathryn Rusch is a bestselling and award-winning author of romance, mystery, science fiction and fantasy. She has published novels under her given name plus a small congress of pen names, including Kristine Grayson for romance and Kris Nelscott for mystery. She is a former editor of The Magazine of Fantasy and Science Fiction and co-founded Pulphouse Publishing.

Her newest releases include Duplicate Effort (Roc, 2009), and the upcoming Diving into the Wreck (Pyr, 2009). Both offerings bear her own name.

When writing, Rusch refuses to limit herself. "Writers should never ever write to market," she insists. "Writers should always write what moves them. Eventually the work will get published. Believe in yourself. Writing to market results in haphazard, often terrible books that usually don't get published."

Once published, how tough was it for her to break into a new genre? "Tough. It still is." But Rusch confesses that she doesn't "do well being pigeon-holed, besides, I'd get bored. So I just continued to write what I wanted." The drawback to writing a novel people adore: "Everyone wanted the same thing I had written before."

Rusch has found the adoption of pseudonyms to be a key factor in crossing over. "If I were to use the same name for each genre, eventually I would have no career. Science fiction sells at fewer numbers than mystery, which sells at fewer numbers than romance. Literary mainstream generally sells less than science fiction."

Another reason Rusch is pro-nom-de-plume is author branding. Apart from the business implications of the term, Rusch simply finds this helpful in organizing her own reading schedule. "If I read really dark/horrific work before I go to sleep, I have nightmares. So I read lighter YA or romance at that time. If a writer, like me, writes 'sweet' romances with no violence at all, and also writes horror novels or fantasy novels so dark that people's skin gets flayed off by some characters, I the reader would be upset." She's even had to boycott certain authors under artificial light: "Writers who do that under the same name—-and whose work I like—never get read at night."

In the spirit of giving her readers what she would want, Rusch has an open-book policy when it comes to her alter egos. "My readers can go to my website and find all of my pen names (except the ones that I'm legally obligated to keep secret—from the days when I did work-for-hire.)"

Rusch believes that no writer should choose any genre for the wrong reasons. If an author's latest work in progress was conceived only "'to make money' or because 'that genre's hot,' then he or she should stay far away from it. You have to read each genre you write in, and you have to love those genres."

Still, the experience gained by adapting to new genres can also provide some semblance of security against redundancy. "The genre can disappear from the bookstore shelves," Rusch says. "It happened to horror in the 1990s, and a whole bunch of writers 'lost' their careers. Simply put, they didn't read outside the genre, had no idea that other genres published horror stories as well, and often those writers refused to change their names." But the answer was simple, Rusch explains: "All they had to do was write in other genres. Mystery likes dark. Science fiction often publishes horror. And around the same time, a new genre started up called dark fantasy. What was it? Horror under a new name, with writers who took on pen names." Rusch views fluctuating genre delineations as little more cause for concern than shifting waterlines that hint at the nightly ebbing of the tide. "Genres disappear from the bookstore shelves all the time," she says, "The western busted in the 1980s, leaving few writers. Horror disappeared in the 1990s. The gothic vanished in the late 1970s." But for every recession, there is a high tide just waiting to return. "The gothic is back in some forms as paranormal romance. The western has also been adopted by romance. The cold war thriller vanished when the Berlin Wall came down, but it's back now—as a historical thriller genre. What's old is new. The key is surviving the dark times when no one buys the genre you write."

There are challenges to writing for multiple genres. "The writer who writes the same book over and over is much easier to market," Rusch says. Yet there are problems with that approach as well: "Readers often tire of the same book over and over. So what's good for the publisher in the short term is bad for everyone in the long term." Rusch's longevity in publishing is testament enough to the practical application of her perspective and philosophy.

HALLIE EPHRON
Escaping from writing ruts

Hallie Ephron is basking in the recent release of her psychological suspense novel Never Tell a Lie (William Morrow, 2009). Already well-renowned for the Dr. Peter Zak mystery series she co-created with Donald Davidoff, she has also added nonfiction books to her publishing repertoire.

"Writing crime fiction is no way to make a living," Ephron says. "I knew this early on, I just didn't want to believe it. Most crime fiction authors (as in 99 + %) do not make enough money to live off their fiction writing."

Ephron suggests "it's shortsighted to rely strictly on writing fiction. I augmented that by writing book reviews (of crime fiction), magazine pieces (about writing and writers), nonfiction (about books and writing), and marketing pieces (for corporate clients)." When she could afford to cut back, she dropped the corporate work first.

For those writers who can't resist trying to navigate the irrevocable path to noveldom, Ephron bears somewhat encouraging news. "Rejection isn't always about the book." Though, sadly, it is still rejection. The fact is simply that "editors see lots and lots of manuscripts, and often they are looking for particular kinds of books. Sometimes there isn't anything 'wrong' with the book an editor rejects; it's just not the book they were looking for."

For writers who are well-acquainted with Talent and her scruffy tagalong sister Persistence, Ephron says, "First you'll have to sell your manuscript to an agent and a publishing house. After that publishers expect you to be a partner in selling your book to readers."

If you do find your book on the bookstore shelf (and maybe even "happen" to leave a copy or two by the register) "There's no accounting for taste," Ephron says. "Some readers and reviewers will love your work, others won't. That's just the way it is." If your public opinion polls aren't where you'd like them to be, Ephron suggests, "don't keep doing the same thing. Don't be afraid to shift gears and try something new."

Fortunately, there are always shoulders to cry on: "I had no idea of the community of readers and writers that are out there until I had published my first book. Sisters in Crime and Mystery Writers of America both have national and local chapters. Attend a few of the mystery and thriller conferences each year and meet new writers, agents, editors, booksellers, and generally get a good idea of what you're getting yourself into."

Eprhon also believes it is essential to "make the book that you write uniquely your own; make it the book that you'd love to read." Writers need all the love and devotion they can harbor in their hearts to see them through the arduous process of finishing a novel, let alone selling it. Here's how Ephron solved her recent Case of the Writer's Rut:

With each book, I encounter several "what happens next?" ruts, weeks-long hiatuses that make me seriously wonder what on earth made me think I could write a novel. In Never Tell a Lie the worst "what happens next?" rut came when I'd gotten my nine-months-pregnant protagonist locked in a windowless attic with only a bed, bedding, and a straitjacket. For months I could not figure out how to get her out. It could not require "Divine Revelation, Feminine Intuition, Mumbo Jumbo, Jiggery-Pokery, Coincidence, or Act of God" (all prohibited by the Detection Club oath). No white knight (police, neighbor, husband, friend) could gallop in on horseback—she had to save herself. She couldn't scale the wall and burst through the roof because, though she was that desperate, it had to be in character and believable (remember, she's nine months pregnant). The only good news was that whatever she managed to do to escape, it was going to surprise the hell out of the reader because it was going to surprise the hell out of me. I've learned to trust the rut.

With poor Ivy waiting in the attic for me to figure out how she was going to rescue herself, I forced myself to just write pages and pages that I ended up trashing. I backed up and revised. Still I was stuck. I transferred my outline to colored index cards. I mind mapped the plot. I tortured my writing group, my friends, and my long suffering husband—if they really loved me they'd figure out how I was going to medevac Ivy out of the attic. Finally, while I was driving (a.k.a. not writing) and, for some reason, thinking about a game I loved as a kid the answer came to me. And just like that, I was out of the rut and my story was on its way…to the next rut.

Surely it must get easier with every book. Right? "It doesn't get easier," Ephron says. "It's brutally hard to write that first novel; it is still brutally hard writing my seventh."

Navigating the Online Slush Pile

by Thursday Bram

Most writers aren't fond of slush piles: if there was a sure way to get a manuscript on an editor's desk, many writers would jump at the opportunity. Most publishers don't have much love for slush piles, either. Sifting through manuscripts is a time-consuming process and if there was a way to reduce or eliminate slush piles, few editors would hesitate.

A number of publishing houses believe that they've found a solution to the slush pile problem: they're outsourcing their slush piles to the web. Companies such HarperCollins have created a variety of Web sites that allow writers to submit their manuscripts online—and to judge their peers' work. Authonomy (www.authonomy.com), operated by HarperCollins, is one of the more recent sites to launch, but it follows what has become a standard model. Writers can upload part or all of a manuscript to the site, which is then available for any of the site's users to read. Users vote for manuscripts that they particularly like and offer the occasional critique. In the case of Authonomy, the top five books, as ranked by users, will go to HarperCollins' Editorial Board for review. Other companies, like Amazon with its Breakthrough Novel Award (www.amazon.com/ABNA), also rely on users' rankings to identify winning manuscripts, but operate on a different timeline and offer a more concrete chance to get published.

On the surface, such an arrangement seems ideal. Publishers get information directly from readers about which novels they want to see in print—and therefore would be willing to buy. At the same time, editors don't have to spend as much time on reviewing manuscripts in the slush piles. Writers even get a direct shot at publication: they can get feedback on their manuscript quickly from readers and watch it throughout the process as it reaches an editor. There's no need to try to find an agent willing to take on a new writer or wait months for a response on a manuscript in a more traditional slush pile. In theory, the model of online submissions might be a way to eliminate slush piles.

While there are benefits for writers in this system, there are also drawbacks. Authors have a way to access editors through these sites, but they have to work their way through thousands of readers to do so. The prizes can be well worth the effort—the Amazon Breakthrough Novel Award includes a full publishing contract with Penguin with a $25,000 advance. Writers have more opportunity to improve their chances, as well, if they can convince more voters of their manuscripts' worth. However, such an approach can be difficult.

CAMPAIGNING FOR YOUR WORK

Trudy Schuett self-published three novels after submitting her manuscripts to agents' and

THURSDAY BRAM began freelancing in college. She has written for *WoW! Women on Writing, WHY Magazine* and numerous websites. Thursday's first book, *Working Your Way Around the World*, was published in 2009. For more information about Thursday, please visit her website, ThursdayBram.com.

Online Opportunities

AMAZON BREAKTHROUGH NOVEL AWARD
(www.amazon.com/ABNA)

Sponsored by Amazon, Penguin and Publishers Weekly, the contest for the Amazon Breakthrough Novel Award is held annually. Entrants go through a narrowing down process until only three finalists remain. Amazon customers read and vote on the finalists, choosing a winner who wins a publishing contract with Penguin, as well as a $25,000 advance. Penguin has right of first refusal on manuscripts once they reach the quarter-finalist stage until a manuscript has been eliminated from the contest. There is no entry fee.

AUTHONOMY
(www.authonomy.com)

Operated by HarperCollins, Authonomy allows writers to upload between 10,000 words and a complete manuscript. It is publicly available to readers who choose their favorite books to promote. Readers can also comment on manuscripts. Five top-ranking manuscripts are sent to the HarperCollins Editorial Board each month, who then comments on them. According to the site's FAQ, HarperCollins' policy on publishing manuscripts found on Authonomy is: "We've set up Authonomy in the hope of finding new authors for our various publishing lists, so we'll certainly be looking for promising books—as will other publishing houses and agents. We only buy books we really believe in—as such, we're not guaranteeing to publish anything submitted to us. In this way, you can be sure that any books picked off Authonomy will have been chosen because we really love them. The terms of any publication deals arising from the site would be negotiated as and when such opportunities arise—there is no fixed 'boiler-plate' offer specifically for authors who come to our attention via the site." The site is free to use.

BAEN'S BAR
(http://bar.baen.com/)

A free account is necessary to access Baen's Bar. It is a forum that offers a place to discuss fantasy and science fiction, as well as a critique group for projects in progress. Baen's Universe (http://www.baensuniverse.com), a magazine which publishes short science fiction and fantasy stories, uses Baen's Bar to find new writers. The site is also associated with Baen Books, which has published several novels found through Baen's Bar.

ZOETROPE VIRTUAL STUDIO
(www.zoetrope.com)

Began as a Web site for writers interested in submitting short stories to Zoetrope: All-Story, Zoetrope Virtual Studio now provides a place to work on a variety of creative works, including short stories, novellas and other written projects. Zoetrope: All-Story may consider stories that have been workshopped on Zoetrope Virtual Studio. Creating an account on the site is free.

publishers' slush piles. She posted her novels on Authonomy to see the responses and take a shot at getting her work read by an editor at HarperCollins. She found that the readers on Authonomy weren't exactly what she expected: "It seems like the only people visiting Authonomy are other authors, rather than readers. Authors, in my experience, tend not to give a rodent's posterior about other people's books." Schuett's experiences led her to describe Authonomy as a critique group rather than a way to get published, essentially ignoring the site's ranking system.

For a manuscript to successfully climb those rankings, the author must focus more on finding readers instead of getting useful critiques. It can require playing the system: there are plenty of techniques that can help a manuscript move up in the ranks. The quality of a manuscript is an important factor, but an author's ability to promote a manuscript to the site's readers is perhaps even more important. Playing the system is mostly limited to promotions. There is not a single particular niche or style that climbs the charts at Authonomy faster than any others. Historical romances, young adult mysteries and religious fiction have all made the top five list for Authonomy—often in the same week.

Authors can't simply upload their manuscripts and ignore them on sites that have incorporated voting to rank novels, even if they aren't interested in doing any sort of promotion. In order to convince other readers to even look at a particular manuscript, the author must promote his or her work: commenting on forums, offering comments on other writers' work and even going to other Web sites to ask for votes. Schuett said, based on her experiences on Authonomy, "You must work hard at promoting your stuff to get anyone to read it. In the end, it has very little to do with the content of the book, and it's more about how much you can promote yourself online to this group... after a while, I ran out of things to say on the forums, and found it hard to make constructive comments on other people's books." All that can translate in to hours of work, especially for authors willing to offer up critiques for other writers in hopes of a little support in return.

AUTHONOMY SUCCESS STORY

That level of promotion can pay off, however: Bill Loehfelm, a former teacher and bartender, won the Amazon Breakthrough Novel Award in 2008 with the novel, Fresh Kills. He was just one of 5,000 entrants, but Loehfelm's manuscript made it through the first cut to 800 novels. From there, his novel was posted on Amazon for readers to review. He passed the next cut to 100 readers, then to 10. At that point, Loehfelm was e-mailing everyone he could, asking for votes. Loehfelm's efforts paid off. Readers voted Fresh Kills into first place.

Fresh Kills was published through Penguin's Putnam Adult imprint in late 2008 and quickly gathered a list of impressive reviews, including comparisons to Dennis Lehane's Mystic River. Despite Amazon's success with Loehfelm, however, not all authors believe that the model of finding new manuscripts through public voting will hold up in the long-term. Questions of how much a successful manuscript depends on good writing and how much it depends on the writer's ability to network leave some dubious about such an option.

Other authors have used efforts similar to Loehfelm's in winning votes for their manuscripts. Finding readers who are willing to vote for a manuscript routinely requires going beyond those individuals who will vote on their own. Authonomy specifically recommends on its site that writers interested in increasing readership should solicit readers from outside of the site. Doing so can range from asking family to vote for a novel to requesting help on personal blogs, social networking sites and other Web sites where a writer may have built up a following.

NO END TO TRADISIONAL SLUSH PILES

Victoria Strauss is the co-founder of Writer Beware (www.writerbeware.org), an organization that tracks and publicizes literary scams and pitfalls, as well as the author of seven novels herself. She is reluctant to describe Authonomy and similar sites as the end of slush piles, in part due to the question of reader ratings. "If there are a lot of ratings—several hundred at least—and they show broad agreement on strengths/weaknesses/likes/dislikes, then maybe they might give some sense of how larger numbers of readers might respond. However, that's a different question from whether a book will sell—which depends heavily on things like packaging, publicity, distribution, and word of mouth, none of which can be gauged from readers' reactions to unpublished manuscripts," Strauss said. "I'd also be cautious of relying on reader ratings, because so many readers aren't objective (i.e., they can't distinguish between 'bad writing' and 'writing I don't like'). Just as important, the readers at sites like Authonomy are mostly going to be writers, who may not be representative of the wider reading public. Both the audience and the purpose of such sites skew the ratings system, in my opinion."

Strauss has compared Authonomy to past efforts by other publishers: "The Del Rey Digital Workshop and Time Warner's iPublish program no longer exist—the Del Rey workshop was spun off after a couple of years and become an independent writers' critique community, and iPublish never really got off the ground." While there are some sites that have provided an on-going venue for writers to promote their work to publishers, there have been several that have either closed or evolved into something else entirely.

In the end, the real value of sites like Authonomy and contests like the Amazon Breakthrough Novel Award may not be as much a chance at publication as the critiques and comments available to writers who submit their manuscripts. Information on what works in a novel, as well as what doesn't, can be difficult to come by. The fact that the majority of readers on such sites are writers themselves provides an additional benefit—a chance to build community. Strauss mentioned that if such sites were available when she was finding a publisher for her first novel, Authonomy might have appealed to her. "I think I probably would have experimented with them, largely for the chance to become involved with other writers. Writing is an isolating activity, especially if you don't know any other authors. The Internet is an amazing resource, enabling writers to connect with one another no matter where they are."

The chance to win a publishing contract is simply an added bonus, not something that should be counted on. If a writer is willing to dedicate many hours to promoting a book on Authonomy or soliciting readers for a contest, he or she will certainly have a better chance of winning. For some writers, though, those hours could be better spent on writing.

Sue Hepworth

Getting Published After 50

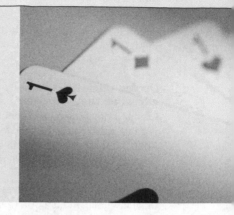

by Diane Shipley

Like the plot of a good novel, Sue Hepworth's life has undergone a few twists and turns. As an occupational psychologist, she gained valuable writing experience and insight into human nature by conducting research into other people's working practices. But she didn't realize her own true calling until her late forties, after she had survived a brief skirmish with breast cancer and her family's belongings had been burned to the ground in a storage warehouse fire. When Sue later read an article in The London Times about the value of "de-cluttering," she wrote a funny but angry rejoinder which argued for the importance of familiar objects. Her piece was published and marked the start of her writing career as she plundered her family life and especially her relationship with her husband (with his full permission) for more material. During this time, she also wrote and abandoned a couple of novels, neither of which she now considers good enough to be published.

When Hepworth attended a new writing class and got to know Jane Linfoot, a busy mother, poetry enthusiast and cycling fan, the two formed a partnership which led to the publication of a joint novel, Plotting for Beginners. ("I did about 80% of the writing but the creative work was 50-50," Hepworth says.) The book tells the story of Sally Howe, whose husband has gone to live in a cabin in the Rockies for a year, Thoreau-style, leaving her to deal with everything on the domestic front as well as trying to write her first novel. Hepworth's husband Dave may not have actually been to the Rockies but a lot of her own experiences did make it into the book—from wondering about the right hairstyle for an aspiring older author (conclusion? A long gray braid), to dealing with hot flashes and other menopausal symptoms. Her second book Zuzu's Petals is a little more serious, focusing largely on one woman's grief about the death of her father while she tries to begin a new career (and maybe a new relationship). Heavily based on Hepworth's experiences after her Dad died, it's the work she is most proud of so far, a poignant and brilliantly-crafted read that still sneaks in a few laughs.

You were 56 when Plotting for Beginners was published. Do you ever wish you had started writing when you were younger?

I don't think I had enough mental space to do it earlier. When I started getting published in The Times, my husband said "Why haven't you done this before?" But I didn't have the space to reflect on things. It was only when my two eldest children left home, my youngest

DIANE SHIPLEY, an ex-books Website editor and frequent reviewer, has written extensively about writers and writing for publications including The Guardian arts blog and women's literary magazine Mslexia. She also writes about technology, television and lifestyle for newspapers, magazines and Web sites in the U.S. and the U.K. Her Web site is www.dianeshipley.co.uk.

was at school and I was at home all day without a car that I started to be able to clear my head and think about things that were funny or that I might want to write about. So I think I had to wait until I was this age really.

Do you think it's generally better to wait; that people have more interesting things to say when they are older?

I think it depends on the person. If you're a super genius you can perhaps start at the age of 20 but it's a personal thing. If I had done it in my twenties, I don't think I would have had enough to say and I don't think I would have been able to write as well because my work writing psychology reports helped me to become confident putting words on the page.

Your books are heavily based on your own life. How do ideas come to you?

I usually have an idea or a theme that I want to explore. I think about that for a bit and then I try to find some characters to hang it on. And then I think "I've got to have a plot here somewhere!" so I work out a plot. I always work out the structure of the book before I start. I've realized that for me, the way I work best is to have it all worked out from the beginning.

Do you think you become less self-conscious as a writer when you're a bit older—less worried about offending people, for example?

Well, I'm a Quaker and there's a lady at my meeting who was really shocked by Zuzu's Petals because she thought there was a lot of swearing in it. This same lady said to a good friend of mine, "I didn't know Sue's husband had gone off to the Rockies for a year!" But I think generally, when you get into your fifties you care less about what people think. You just care less.

You used part of a bereavement journal that you wrote after your father's death in Zuzu's Petals. How did your mother feel about that?

That was quite tricky. I didn't want to publish anything that might distress her but my mom was a very strong person and was always encouraging. I did say to her "I think you might find it upsetting and you might not want to read it, and that's okay," but I knew ultimately that she would be absolutely fine with it, because that's the kind of person she was. She was very proud of me.

How does your husband feel about your books?

My biggest advantage is that Dave doesn't mind what I write. There's a lot of him in my books and he doesn't care at all and that is so liberating. He doesn't even read them and that frees me up even more.

It's really, really great to have a supportive partner. He's always thought I would get published.

So what inspired you to first put pen to paper?

I was having a drink with a friend and she said she had started going to creative writing classes. Something just clicked in my head and I thought "I want to do that." We had just moved house, and when you move to a new place, you see the world as an outsider and you observe things much more clearly, it gives you a new angle on the world. So I was having all these new experiences and more time to think about things and I started to write a few notes.

How did your collaboration with Jane Linfoot begin?

I met her at the next writing class I went to. I had this idea that I wanted to write a novel, and Jane and I would e-mail each other about our writing. Then we started e-mailing about what was happening in our family lives and I loved her dry, minimalist way of describing things.

I thought she was so funny that I wanted to have her stuff in the book. I suppose it gave me a little extra confidence as well, doing it with someone who I thought was a classy writer. It's fantastic to have someone whose opinion you trust, whose writing you think is good, to look at it and say, is this funny, is this good? Jane was very good at cutting out the boring bits. After about the fourth draft, we realized the book needed paring down and Jane cut 15,000 words in one morning.

We sold it soon after.

Did you find there was any prejudice against older authors?

I do think there was a prejudice against older authors, definitely. I don't know if it's the case now because there have been some older authors who have been very successful, such as Marina Lewycka, who wrote A Short History of Tractors in Ukrainian. But before her book took off, I read an interview where she said that her agent had told her that if she had been younger, she could have got a much bigger advance. I don't know if that's because publishers like to market you as a person so they want someone who is young and glamorous, or whether they want you to have your whole life ahead of you so they can make more money out of you. Probably both.

What advice would you give to other older authors?

I think the thing is to treat it seriously and have a very professional attitude. I get the idea that maybe people don't like older writers because they think they're just playing at it as a hobby when they're partially retired. So my advice is to show that you're really serious about it and that you're professional in everything that you do. Read books about how to approach agents, read about the literary world, read reviews, find out about different agents, and send your manuscript to the ones who are looking for your kind of work. And also have a really, really thick skin.

Which authors have influenced you?

Carol Shields inspired me a lot. When she was first published, I saw an article about her in a newspaper which said "she writes about happy marriages" and I thought that was really interesting, because if you pick up a novel about families they are almost always unhappy or awful things are happening to them. But Carol Shields wrote about ordinary people in ordinary situations. I love her writing. It's not like my writing, it's much fancier, but the topics she deals with are ones I'm very interested in. This last year I read Charlotte Mendelssohn's When We Were Bad and I thought it was excellent, the kind of book I would like to write: a comic book about a family but deeply serious as well.

And I just love Garrison Keillor because he's funny but so humane, so wise. And he's warm about his characters. I like writers who like their characters, not writers who sneer at people.

You like to write a book before you sell it and once said you 'live in dread' of a two-book deal. Why is that?

It's probably just insecurity; fear that I would have nothing to write about. But maybe it's to do with being pinned down. Writing is such fun, I don't want to make it into a "you have got to write a book by the end of next year" kind of thing. Plus if you send in a synopsis of one thing but change your mind and write a different type of book, that can cause trouble.

You wrote a journal after your father died which was then woven into Zuzu's Petals. Do you think it helps as a writer to have had difficult experiences—or can some writers just use their empathy to imagine how things feel?

I think some people can imagine it, but I have to experience things in order to understand and then write about them. I think I might try to write about something if someone close to me had been through it: my daughter has been through some difficult experiences, for example. I might write about those.

Your novels often utilize comedy, even at sad moments. Do you think it's important to laugh at life?

It's not that I have a conscious attitude that you have to laugh or you would cry, it's just that I can't keep it out. I do see the comedy in things. And when I'm writing, jokes just naturally come out in the dialogue. I think if I wrote something that was serious all the way through, it would be dull. I'm not a deep enough thinker to write seriously. But I don't like the way people don't take comedy seriously: it isn't easy. I can't imagine a comedy book getting a big literary prize, for example, but I don't see why it shouldn't.

How would you describe your work?

"Comic fiction with emotional depth" describes what I'm working on at the moment. It's another book about an older married couple who have different ideas about how they want to spend their retirement. I've written half of it and I've got the rest plotted out, I've just got to knock it into shape now. I like to take about a year a book. Plotting for Beginners took longer but when you know what you're doing you don't get lost and have to restructure things. Someone asked me the other day if it gets easier to write books and I think you just become more demanding of yourself.

The Business of Fiction Writing

It's true there are no substitutes for talent and hard work. A writer's first concern must always be attention to craft. No matter how well presented, a poorly written story or novel has little chance of being published. On the other hand, a well-written piece may be equally hard to sell in today's competitive publishing market. Talent alone is just not enough.

To be successful, writers need to study the field and pay careful attention to finding the right market. While the hours spent perfecting your writing are usually hours spent alone, you're not alone when it comes to developing your marketing plan. *Novel & Short Story Writer's Market* provides you with detailed listings containing the essential information you'll need to locate and contact the markets most suitable for your work.

Once you've determined where to send your work, you must turn your attention to presentation. We can help here, too. We've included the basics of manuscript preparation, along with information on submission procedures and how to approach markets. We also include tips on promoting your work. No matter where you're from or what level of experience you have, you'll find useful information here on everything from presentation to mailing to selling rights to promoting your work—the "business" of fiction.

APPROACHING MAGAZINE MARKETS

While it is essential for nonfiction markets, a query letter by itself is usually not needed by most magazine fiction editors. If you are approaching a magazine to find out if fiction is accepted, a query is fine, but editors looking for short fiction want to see how you write. A cover letter can be useful as a letter of introduction, but it must be accompanied by the actual piece. The key here is brevity. A successful cover letter is no more than one page (20 lb. bond paper). It should be single spaced with a double space between paragraphs, proofread carefully and neatly typed in a standard typeface (not script or italic). The writer's name, address and phone number appear at the top, and the letter is addressed, ideally, to a specific editor. (If the editor's name is unavailable, address to "Fiction Editor.")

The body of a successful cover letter contains the name and word count of the story, a brief list of previous publications if you have any, and the reason you are submitting to this particular publication. Mention that you have enclosed a self-addressed, stamped envelope or postcard for reply. Also let the editor know if you are sending a disposable manuscript that doesn't need to be returned. (More and more editors prefer disposable manuscripts that save them time and save you postage.) Finally, don't forget to thank the editor for considering your story. See the sample short story cover letter on page 55.

Note that more and more publications are open to receiving electronic submissions, both as e-mail attachments and through online submission forms. See individual listings for specific information on electronic submission requirements and always visit magazines' Web sites for up-to-date guidelines.

APPROACHING BOOK PUBLISHERS

Some book publishers do ask for queries first, but most want a query plus sample chapters or an outline or, occasionally, the complete manuscript. Again, make your letter brief. Include the essentials about yourself—name, address, phone number, e-mail and publishing experience. Include a three or four sentence "pitch" and only the personal information related to your story. Show that you have researched the market with a few sentences about why you chose this publisher. See the sample book query on page 56.

BOOK PROPOSALS

A book proposal is a package sent to a publisher that includes a cover letter and one or more of the following: sample chapters, outline, synopsis, author bio, publications list. When asked to send sample chapters, send up to three consecutive chapters. An outline covers the highlights of your book chapter by chapter. Be sure to include details on main characters, the plot and subplots. Outlines can run up to 30 pages, depending on the length of your novel. The object is to tell what happens in a concise, but clear, manner. A synopsis is a shorter summary of your novel, written in a way that expresses the emotion of the story in addition to just explaining the essential points. Evan Marshall, literary agent and author of The Marshall Plan for Getting Your Novel Published (Writer's Digest Books), suggests you aim for a page of synopsis for every 25 pages of manuscript. Marshall also advises you write the synopsis as one unified narrative, without section, subheads or chapters to break up the text. The terms synopsis and outline are sometimes used interchangeably, so be sure to find out exactly what each publisher wants.

A FEW WORDS ABOUT AGENTS

Agents are not usually needed for short fiction and most do not handle it unless they already have a working relationship with you. For novels, you may want to consider working with an agent, especially if you intend to market your book to publishers who do not look at unsolicited submissions. For more on approaching agents and to read listings of agents willing to work with beginning and established writers, see our Literary Agents section beginning on page 125 and refer to this year's edition of Guide to Literary Agents, edited by Chuck Sambuchino.

MANUSCRIPT MECHANICS

A professionally presented manuscript will not guarantee publication. But a sloppy, hard-to-read manuscript will not be read—publishers simply do not have the time. Here's a list of suggested submission techniques for polished manuscript presentation:

- **Use white, 8½×11 bond paper,** preferably 16 or 20 lb. weight. The paper should be heavy enough so it will not show pages underneath it and strong enough to take handling by several people.
- **Type your manuscript** on a computer and print it out using a laser or ink jet printer (or, if you must, use a typewriter with a new ribbon).
- **Proofread carefully.** An occasional white-out is okay, but don't send a marked-up manuscript with many typos. Keep a dictionary, thesaurus and stylebook handy and use the spellcheck function on your computer.
- **Always double space and leave a 1-inch margin** on all sides of the page.
- **For a short story manuscript,** your first page should include your name, address, phone number and e-mail address (single-spaced) in the upper left corner. In the upper right, indicate an approximate word count. Center the name of your story about one-third of the way down, skip a line and center your byline (byline is optional). Skip four lines and begin your story. On subsequent pages, put last name and page number in the upper right hand corner.
- **For book manuscripts,** use a separate title page. Put your name, address, phone number and e-mail address in the lower right corner and word count in the upper right. If you have representation, list your agent's name and address in the lower right. (This bumps your name and contact information to the upper left corner.) Center your title and byline about halfway down the

page. Start your first chapter on the next page. Center the chapter number and title (if there is one) one-third of the way down the page. Include your last name and the novel's title in all caps in the upper left and put the page number in the upper right of this page and each page to follow. Start each chapter with a new page.

• **Include a word count.** If you work on a computer, chances are your word processing program can give you a word count. (If you are using a typewriter, there are a number of ways to count the number of words in your piece. One way is to count the words in five lines and divide that number by five to find an average. Then count the number of lines and multiply to find the total words. For long pieces, you may want to count the words in the first three pages, divide by three and multiply by the number of pages you have.)

• **Always keep a copy.** Manuscripts do get lost. To avoid expensive mailing costs, send only what is required. If you are including artwork or photos but you are not positive they will be used, send photocopies. Artwork is hard to replace.

• **Suggest art where applicable.** Most publishers do not expect you to provide artwork and some insist on selecting their own illustrators, but if you have suggestions, please let them know. Magazine publishers work in a very visual field and are usually open to ideas.

• **Enclose a self-addressed, stamped envelope (SASE)** if you want a reply or if you want your manuscript returned. For most letters, a business-size (#10) envelope will do. Avoid using any envelope too small for an 8½ × 11 sheet of paper. For manuscripts, be sure to include enough postage and an envelope large enough to contain it. If you are requesting a sample copy of a magazine or a book publisher's catalog, send an envelope big enough to fit.

• **Consider sending a disposable manuscript** that saves editors time and saves you money.

• When sending electronic submissions via e-mail or online submission form, check the publisher's Web site or contact them first for specific information and follow the directions carefully.

• **Keep accurate records.** This can be done in a number of ways, but be sure to keep track of where your stories are and how long they have been "out." Write down submission dates. If you do not hear about your submission for a long time—about one to two months longer than the reporting time stated in the listing—you may want to contact the publisher. When you do, you will need an accurate record for reference.

MAILING TIPS

When mailing short correspondence or short manuscripts:

• Fold manuscripts under five pages into thirds and send in a business-size (#10) envelope.

• Mail manuscripts five pages or more unfolded in a 9×12 or 10×13 envelope.

• Mark envelopes in all caps, FIRST CLASS MAIL or SPECIAL FOURTH CLASS MANUSCRIPT RATE.

• For return envelope, fold it in half, address it to yourself and add a stamp or, if going to a foreign country, International Reply Coupons (available at the main branch of your local post office).

• Don't send by certified mail. This is a sign of an amateur and publishers do not appreciate receiving unsolicited manuscripts this way.

• For the most current postage rates, visit the United States Postal Service online at www.usps.com.

When mailing book-length manuscripts:

First Class Mail over 11 ounces (about 65 8½ × 11 20 lb.-weight pages) automatically becomes PRIORITY MAIL.

Metered Mail may be dropped in any post office box, but meter strips on SASEs should not be dated.

The Postal Service provides, free of charge, tape, boxes and envelopes to hold up to two pounds for those using PRIORITY and EXPRESS MAIL. Requirements for mailing FOURTH CLASS and PARCEL POST have not changed.

Main branches of local banks will cash foreign checks, but keep in mind payment quoted in our listings by publishers in other countries is usually payment in their currency. Also note reporting time is longer in most overseas markets. To save time and money, you may want to include a return postcard (and IRC) with your submission and forgo asking for a manuscript to be returned. If you live in Canada, see Canadian Writers Take Note on page 552.

Important note about IRCs: Foreign editors sometimes find IRCs have been stamped incorrectly by the U.S. post office when purchased. This voids the IRCs and makes it impossible for foreign editors to exchange the coupons for return postage for your manuscript. When buying IRCs, make sure yours have been stamped correctly before you leave the counter. (Each IRC should be stamped on the bottom left side of the coupon, not the right.) More information about International Reply Coupons, including an image of a correctly stamped IRC, is available on the USPS Web site (www.usps.com).

RIGHTS

The Copyright Law states that writers are selling one-time rights (in almost all cases) unless they and the publisher have agreed otherwise. A list of various rights follows. Be sure you know exactly what rights you are selling before you agree to the sale.

• **Copyright** is the legal right to exclusive publication, sale or distribution of a literary work. As the writer or creator of a written work, you need simply to include your name, date and the copyright symbol ÞCR on your piece in order to copyright it. Be aware, however, that most editors today consider placing the copyright symbol on your work the sign of an amateur and many are even offended by it.

To get specific answers to questions about copyright (but not legal advice), you can call the Copyright Public Information Office at (202)707-3000 weekdays between 8:30 a.m. and 5 p.m. EST. Publications listed in *Novel & Short Story Writer's Market* are copyrighted unless otherwise stated. In the case of magazines that are not copyrighted, be sure to keep a copy of your manuscript with your notice printed on it. For more information on copyrighting your work see *The Copyright Handbook: How to Protect & Use Written Works*, 8th edition, by Stephen Fishman (Nolo Press, 2005).

Some people are under the mistaken impression that copyright is something they have to send away for, and that their writing is not properly protected until they have "received" their copyright from the government. The fact is, you don't have to register your work with the Copyright Office in order for your work to be copyrighted; any piece of writing is copyrighted the moment it is put to paper.

Although it is generally unnecessary, registration is a matter of filling out an application form (for writers, that's Form TX) and sending the completed form, a nonreturnable copy of the work in question and a check for $45 to the Library of Congress, Copyright Office, Register of Copyrights, 101 Independence Ave. SE, Washington DC 20559-6000. If the thought of paying $45 each to register every piece you write does not appeal to you, you can cut costs by registering a group of your works with one form, under one title for one $45 fee.

Most magazines are registered with the Copyright Office as single collective entities themselves; that is, the individual works that make up the magazine are not copyrighted individually in the names of the authors. You'll need to register your article yourself if you wish to have the additional protection of copyright registration.

For more information, visit the United States Copyright Office online at www.copyright.gov.

• **First Serial Rights**—This means the writer offers a newspaper or magazine the right to publish the article, story or poem for the first time in a particular periodical. All other rights to the material remain with the writer. The qualifier ``North American'' is often added to this phrase to specify a geographical limit to the license.

When material is excerpted from a book scheduled to be published and it appears in a magazine or newspaper prior to book publication, this is also called first serial rights.

One-time Rights—A periodical that licenses one-time rights to a work (also known as simultaneous rights) buys the nonexclusive right to publish the work once. That is, there is nothing to stop the author from selling the work to other publications at the same time. Simultaneous sales would typically be to periodicals without overlapping audiences.

• **Second Serial (Reprint) Rights**—This gives a newspaper or magazine the opportunity to print an article, poem or story after it has already appeared in another newspaper or magazine. Second serial rights are nonexclusive; that is, they can be licensed to more than one market.

• **All Rights**—This is just what it sounds like. All rights means a publisher may use the manuscript anywhere and in any form, including movie and book club sales, without further payment to the writer (although such a transfer, or assignment, of rights will terminate after 35 years). If you think you'll want to use the material later, you must avoid submitting to such markets or refuse payment and withdraw your material. Ask the editor whether he is willing to buy first rights instead of all rights before you agree to an assignment or sale. Some editors will reassign rights to a writer after a given period, such as one year. It's worth an inquiry in writing.

• **Subsidiary Rights**—These are the rights, other than book publication rights, that should be covered in a book contract. These may include various serial rights; movie, television, audiotape and other electronic rights; translation rights, etc. The book contract should specify who controls these rights (author or publisher) and what percentage of sales from the licensing of these sub rights goes to the author.

Dramatic, Television and Motion Picture Rights—This means the writer is selling his material for use on the stage, in television or in the movies. Often a one-year option to buy such rights is offered (generally for 10% of the total price). The interested party then tries to sell the idea to other people—actors, directors, studios or television networks, etc. Some properties are optioned over and over again, but most fail to become dramatic productions. In such cases, the writer can sell his rights again and again—as long as there is interest in the material. Though dramatic, TV and motion picture rights are more important to the fiction writer than the nonfiction writer, producers today are increasingly interested in nonfiction material; many biographies, topical books and true stories are being dramatized.

• **Electronic Rights**—These rights cover usage in a broad range of electronic media, from online magazines and databases to CD-ROM magazine anthologies and interactive games. The editor should specify in writing if—and which—electronic rights are being requested. The presumption is that unspecified rights are kept by the writer.

Compensation for electronic rights is a major source of conflict between writers and publishers, as many book publishers seek control of them and many magazines routinely include electronic rights in the purchase of print rights, often with no additional payment. Alternative ways of handling this issue include an additional 15 percent added to the amount to purchase first rights and a royalty system based on the number of times an article is accessed from an electronic database.

MARKETING & PROMOTION

Everyone agrees writing is hard work whether you are published or not. Yet, once you achieve publication the work changes. Now, not only do you continue writing and revising your next project, you must also concern yourself with getting your book into the hands of readers. It becomes time to switch hats from artist to salesperson.

While even best-selling authors whose publishers have committed big bucks to marketing are asked to help promote their books, new authors may have to take it upon themselves to plan and initiate some of their own promotion, sometimes dipping into their own pockets. While this does not mean that every author is expected to go on tour, sometimes at their own expense, it does mean authors should be prepared to offer suggestions for promoting their books.

Depending on the time, money and personal preferences of the author and publisher, a promotional campaign could mean anything from mailing out press releases to setting up book signings to hitting the talk-show circuit. Most writers can contribute to their own promotion by providing contact names—reviewers, hometown newspapers, civic groups, organizations—that might have a special interest in the book or the writer.

Above all, when it comes to promotion, be creative. What is your book about? Try to capitalize on it. Focus on your potential audiences and how you can help them to connect with your book.

Getting Published

About Our Policies

We occasionally receive letters asking why a certain magazine, publisher or contest is not in the book. Sometimes when we contact listings, the editors do not want to be listed because they:

- do not use very much fiction.
- are overwhelmed with submissions.
- are having financial difficulty or have been recently sold.
- use only solicited material.
- accept work from a select group of writers only.
- do not have the staff or time for the many unsolicited submissions a listing may bring.

Some of the listings do not appear because we have chosen not to list them. We investigate complaints of unprofessional conduct in editors' dealings with writers and misrepresentation of information provided to us by editors and publishers. If we find these reports to be true, after a thorough investigation, we will delete the listing from future editions.

There is no charge to the companies that list in this book. Listings appearing in *Novel & Short Story Writer's Market* are compiled from detailed questionnaires, phone interviews and information provided by editors, publishers, and awards and conference directors. The publishing industry is volatile and changes of address, editor, policies and needs happen frequently. To keep up with the changes between editions of the book, we suggest you check the market information on the Writer's Market Web site at www.writersmarket.com, or on the Writer's Digest Web site at www.writersdigest.com. Many magazine and book publishers offer updated information for writers on their Web sites. Check individual listings for those Web site addresses.

Organization newsletters and small magazines devoted to helping writers also list market information. Several offer online writers' bulletin boards, message centers and chat lines with up-to-the-minute changes and happenings in the writing community.

We rely on our readers, as well, for new markets and information about market conditions. E-mail us if you have any new information or if you have suggestions on how to improve our listings to better suit your writing needs.

Important Listing Information

- Listings are not advertisements. Although the information here is as accurate as possible, the listings are not endorsed or guaranteed by the editors of *Novel & Short Story Writer's Market*.
- *Novel & Short Story Writer's Market* reserves the right to exclude any listing that does not meet its requirements.

Getting Published

Carolyn Hart

The American Agatha Christie

by Deborah Bouziden

Carolyn Hart has made her mark on the mystery genre. Her books have been published in 10 languages, with 2.7 million books in print. Her short fiction has been published in more than 20 anthologies. Her Death on Demand series, Henrie O series, and her latest Bailey Ruth Raeburn series, are read worldwide, extremely popular and have earned Hart loyal fans. In fact, her style has earned her the title, the American Agatha Christie.

Hart has been nominated nine times for the Agatha Award for Best Mystery Novel and won the award three times. She has won two Anthony Awards and two Macavitys for Best Paperback Original, received the 2001 Oklahoma Center for the Book award for fiction, 2004 Lifetime Achievement Award from the Oklahoma Center for the Book, and was the Guest of Honor at the Malice Domestic annual conference in 1997 and received its Lifetime Achievement Award in 2007.

In 2003, she was one of 10 mystery authors invited to speak at the Library of Congress National Book Festival on the Mall in Washington, D.C. Her 2003 stand-alone book, Letters from Home, won an Agatha Award, named a Publishers Weekly Best Book of the Year and was nominated for the Pulitzer Prize by the Oklahoma Center for Poets and Writers.

Born and raised in Oklahoma, Hart never imagined she would be a mystery writing icon. At age 11, she had her sights set on what she thought at the time, was a more important job.

"I grew up wanting to write, but I had no inkling I would become a novelist," Hart said. "My ambition was to be a newspaper reporter. I was a child during World War II and quickly understood the newspaper was our primary source of information. I saw that the larger and blacker the headlines, the more important the story. I was convinced there could be no more important job than providing that information."

Working toward her goal, Hart worked on school newspapers. From grade school to college she was driven to become a reporter. That work paid off when she landed a job as a reporter for The Oklahoma Daily.

After earning her journalism degree from the University of Oklahoma in 1958, she married and went to work at The Norman Transcript. It wasn't long before Hart and her husband started a family so she quit work and stayed home to focus on raising her children. As they got older, even though she missed writing, she didn't want to go back to reporting because of the long hours. It was then she first started thinking about writing fiction.

"I saw a contest in Writer's Magazine for a mystery for girls ages 8 to 12. I loved Nancy

DEBORAH BOUZIDEN has been writing and publishing articles and books since 1985. She has had hundreds of articles published in such magazines as *Woman's Day, Writer's Digest,* and *Oklahoma Today,* eight books published, and contributed to nine more. To learn more about Bouziden, visit her Web site at www.deborahbouziden.com.

Drew books and decided to try," Hart said. "I won the contest. The Secret of the Cellars was published by Dodd, Mead in 1964 and was my first published fiction."

She wrote four more books for young readers. Her first adult suspense novel, Flee from the Past, was published in 1976.

For the next 10 years, she wrote a number of mysteries. Some sold, some didn't. During one period, she wrote seven books in seven years and none sold. This was in the late '70s, when publishers weren't interested in mystery novels by American women, but Hart, with her supportive husband by her side, kept writing.

"Phil was proud of my books in the days when they didn't sell," Hart said, "and that will always mean the world to me."

So, since New York wasn't buying, Hart decided to try one more time and write the kind of book she enjoyed reading. She didn't worry about the market because she didn't think there was a market. She just wrote the book. Death on Demand, her 15th book, published in 1987, became her first bestseller.

"I taught writing for a few years and if I had one precept for students, it is this: You will never succeed unless you are willing to fail," Hart told Kathy Moad in an article for the Oklahoma Writers' Federation (OWFI) REPORT. "Whether a writer will write will be determined by the force of the compulsion to write opposed to the fear of failure or success. My suggestion is to realize there is no disgrace in failure and success is what we make of it."

With 42 books in print, Hart understand what drives writers, writers do not choose to write, they must write. Writing has been in her blood since she was a child, driving her first, to reach her goal as a reporter and now to complete book after book.

"I am not disciplined. I am compulsive," Hart continued in the REPORT interview. "Actually, I am miserable and worried and uncertain and frantic when working on a novel. I am always afraid I can't do it this time. Yet, I would be infinitely more miserable, in fact, non-functional if I did not write. Writing gives me a reason to live."

Her writing gives readers a reason to read. Her first book of a new series, Ghost on Demand, received rave reviews and was listed as a Publishers Weekly Best Book of 2008.

Two more Hart books, Merry, Merry Ghost and Dare to Die will be released this year and Hart is busy working on more.

"As long as readers read, mysteries will be read," Hart said, "and I will be writing them."

Do you think it important writers write what they are familiar with and enjoy reading? Why?

Yes, reading provides a template for writers. I have written both traditional mysteries and suspense and I continue to read both. A writer needs to have a sense of what readers expect in a particular kind of book and reading the kind of book a writer wants to write sets the groundwork.

Do you think it's easier to write series or single title books? Why?

I've written a number of stand alone novels and I currently have three series. It is harder to do series because every book limits the possibilities for later titles. However, an advantage of series is that the author knows the main characters and the setting intimately.

How much research do you recommend writers do when working on their projects?

That depends upon the book. If there is something I need to know for the writing, I will do research in advance. More often, I look for information as needed as I write. If you write historical, obviously you must know the period exceedingly well and have good research materials available.

I have a bookcase filled with material about South Carolina. Dare to Die, the 19th title in the Death on Demand series, was published in April 2009. The books are set on a sea island. I have visited there many times but I also have excellent nonfiction books about the Low Country.

When creating your characters, how do you choose traits, personality, etc.? Are your characters given your traits, friends, relatives, or are they formed from observation?

I create characters to make a particular book work. I don't know where I glean ideas for characters.

I have a shadowy sense of the characters when I start the manuscript and I learn about them as I write. Often I have to go back and revise scenes because the characters differ from my first idea. When choosing main characters they must intrigue the reader. In some fashion, they must engage the reader's interest, sympathy, displeasure, or admiration.

I often like those who are victims. Sometimes very nice people are murdered because they pose a threat to a not-so-nice person. I've never had a recurring character as a victim and would not do so. I owe the readers the return of familiar and often well-liked characters. However, recurring characters can sometimes be very engaged in the plot.

In your latest book, Ghost at Work, your main character is a ghost. How and why did you decide on a spirit?

I love cheerful, fun ghost stories. I enjoyed the Topper books by Thorne Smith. I'd often thought about having a ghost in a book. (Southern Ghost in the Death on Demand series draws on the idea of ghosts though there isn't actually a ghost involved.) I created a ghost who is wildly impetuous, well-meaning, and lively. Obviously, this provides ample opportunity to entertain the reader and complicate the plot. The late Bailey Ruth Raeburn finds it hard to follow rules. When on earth, she is supposed to honor Precepts for Heavenly Visitation. Her inability to conform also offers opportunity to entertain. I rather doubt she will ever manage to get through a visit to earth without in some way transgressing against the Precepts.

What are the benefits of setting your books locally versus exotic locations and vice versus? Which type of settings do you prefer?

I used exotic backgrounds for the Henrie O books. Henrietta O'Dwyer Collins is a retired newspaperwoman who is sophisticated and well-traveled. The exotic backgrounds suit her. Although I don't live in South Carolina, the Death on Demand books are very much a product of time I have spent on Hilton Head, South Carolina. I set a WWII stand alone, Letters from Home, in Oklahoma and it was a joy to me to do so. I love writing about Bailey Ruth Raeburn in her fictitious south central Oklahoma town. The Oklahoma books are obviously easier to write because this is my home.

How do you plot? What are your most common problems with plot and how do you handle them?

Plotting is excruciatingly difficult. I do not outline. I know these things when I start a book: the protagonist, the victim, the suspects, the identity of the murderer, the reason for the crime, and I have a working title. That is all I know on page 1. I have no idea how I will get to page 300. The choice of protagonist determines where the book will occur, what kind of mystery it will be, and whether it will be in first or third person. The identity of the victim provides the cast of characters. Those who surrounded the victim in life are the suspects after death. The murderer must have a real and valid reason for the crime. And the title gives me a sense of the reality of the book.

What advice can you give writers about first drafts?

It's fine to go back and polish and change as you are writing, but keep your main focus on finishing the first draft. Then you can see the book as a whole and make all the changes you need.

Describe what type of books you write and what readers expect from them.

I do not write cozy mysteries. I write traditional mysteries. Agatha Christie, of course, is the finest author who ever wrote traditional mysteries. Christie wrote with charm, good humor, and playfulness but she never sugar-coated evil. She believed in the existence of evil and described it with a clear, unwavering eye. In many of her books, death occurs from poison. How cozy is it for the victim to writhe in agony until dying and never to know which familiar face hid hatred?

The traditional mystery is about fractured relationships. When the detective sets out to find the killer, the detective in reality discovers what went wrong in the lives of those involved. Who succumbed to sin? The traditional mystery is one of the last bastions of admiration for goodness.

We live in a world beset by evil, but readers know that when they choose a traditional mystery, goodness will be honored and justice will be served.

Crime novels focus on the struggle of the detective to remain honorable in a corrupt world. The crime novel is essentially romantic in nature and a celebration of honor.

Readers want to be assured that goodness matters, that goodness and truth and justice will prevail. Readers want to live in a just world. They know that when they read one of my books, justice will be served.

How has the Internet changed the way you work?

The Internet has made a huge difference in reaching out to readers. More than 100,000 readers have visited my Web site, www.CarolynHart.com, and I reply to any message sent through the site. E-mail makes it very easy to be in touch with my editor and agent. And of course, Google can always turn up interesting information on any topic.

What should writers know about marketing and the publishing business today?

Publishing is changing with more emphasis on fewer titles. It is important to always provide the best book possible and to be as helpful as possible to everyone at the publishing house. A Web site is essential. For mystery writers, it is always helpful to attend meetings of mystery readers and writers.

Tell me a little about your latest projects. What are they about? When will they be released?

I have just completed Merry, Merry Ghost, a Christmas mystery featuring my redheaded ghost Bailey Ruth Raeburn. An orphan arrives at his grandmother's house just before Christmas, prompting her to change her will. Bailey Ruth is dispatched to protect the little boy and see that justice is done.

Dare to Die, the 19th in the Death on Demand series, was published in April 2009. A young woman returns to the island to seek truth, but a killer must make sure she doesn't remember one long ago foggy night.

Chelsea Cain

The Monster Is Only Scary for a Minute

by W.E. Reinka

Thriller writer Chelsea Cain posts two index cards above her desk. The first reads "Put characters in danger quickly." It's common advice. Still, the adage cannot be overstressed given how many wannabe crime fiction writers start their tales with weather reports rather than dead bodies, bloody knives or ticking time bombs.

The second reminder is that "the monster is only scary for a minute." The truth is Cain's monster, beautiful serial killer Gretchen Lowell, scares the stuffings out of readers for more than a minute. But that takes some work.

"It's all about reinvention," Cain explains. "I learned this concept from (Fight Club author) Chuck Palahniuk who's in my writers' group. Movie makers generally wait to show you the Big Space Alien until near the end because once you see the monster, it's not as scary after that. In my novel Heart Sick, when Det. Archie Sheridan first meets with serial killer Gretchen Lowell in prison—it's one of my favorite scenes—it's tense and scary and their relationship is riveting. But I can't keep going back to that same dog and pony show because every time I do, it's flatter, duller. So I had to find ways to change the dynamic and present Gretchen in different contexts. Likewise, beauty is only beautiful for a minute. When we see Gretchen's blond hair and the sparkling handcuffs against her perfect skin, we see that she's beautiful. But every time we see those things after that, they lose power. I have to keep trying to find other ways to show her beauty."

Gretchen Lowell's creepy slow torture of her victims scares readers but not her creator. "Thrillers are not unsettling for me. They're actually a lot of fun, like making up gross fairy tales. I feel absurdly safe in the world. Because of that, I can go to places in my mind without lingering there. Besides, I am in charge of what happens. Sometimes I actually giggle when I'm writing this gory stuff that I can do this for a living."

Cain's story-writing dates back to childhood. "When I was little, I would write terrible books and put them together with stapled covers made of crepe paper and wallpaper. Yet, my Bohemian mother always took my books very seriously even when I was 8 years-old. It never felt totally absurd to sit in my room and write a book. I was really fortunate to find that in my mother because writers need people who value and encourage their work and the time they must devote to it."

Despite all those crepe paper book covers, Cain had no idea how to graduate from reader to author. She went to college and got a graduate degree in journalism—that she could understand—study journalism and get a job in that field. As it turned out, a publisher picked up her masters project which became her first book, The Dharma Girls. In it, she recalls her

W.E. REINKA, who often writes about books and authors, contributes to print and electronic media nationwide.

hippie youth. She followed up with other counter-culture based books. "I put hippies in all my books," she says. In the thriller series, the mother of Susan Ward, one the focus characters, is an aging hippie.

Between her Master's degree in journalism, early counter-culture books, and working as a reporter, Cain's nonfiction roots run deep. To this day, her blog-like column for The Oregonian, Portland's largest daily, typically ruminates on her pre-school daughter, not serial killers.

While she now recognizes that her early fiction lacked originality, her imitative style proved an asset when she took on a Nancy Drew parody called Adventures of a Teen Sleuth. The tongue-in-cheek adventure remains in print, its readers never suspecting Cain's literary trysts during its creation. "While I was completing Adventures of a Teen Sleuth, I would sneak off on the side and write Heart Sick. It felt like an adulterous relationship when I was under a contract for the other novel. I developed a hotel room passion for Heart Sick because I wasn't really supposed to be doing it."

Despite her work hour dalliances, Cain still delivered the Adventures of a Teen Sleuth manuscript on time—not surprising given her writing discipline. Though she laughingly claims there are plenty of days when she only reluctantly sits down to the computer, she goes on to say, "You can't be a writer until you learn to write when you don't want to. It's really important for aspiring writers to hear that because there's this fantasy that you can wait for the muse to strike. To be a professional writer, to write for a living, you have to sit down and work at it because editing isn't always fun. I enjoy the process but I don't always love it. I sit down to work even if it's just to finish chapter five so I can get to chapter six where something interesting is going to happen."

Does she have a tip for making work easier when the muse is on vacation? "Write what you like to read. I like thrillers so I took that genre on. If you can't find something to love about your work, you'll never finish it. And finishing your work," she adds dryly, "is a key to selling it."

CREATING COMPELLING CHARACTERS

However disciplined her writing, she didn't need agent rejection letters to tell her that her early fiction wasn't very good. Her breakthrough came when she quit basing her plots on real-life events. "I kept trying to write about things in my own life or basing characters on people I knew. I'd get trapped by people I was basing the story on. I didn't assume authority over my own stories." In contrast, her thriller characters are "made from whole cloth." Though many people might consider thrillers plot-driven, she is adamant about the importance of characterization. "Good thrillers are characters studies. Get to your characters quickly and put them in an extreme situation."

What does she do when her characters take on a life of their own?

"They don't. I'm the boss. It's really important for me to control them—to make them interesting and introduce surprise. I take authority over my fiction. Gretchen and Archie are not even shadows of people I know. Writers sometimes speculate on which actors they'd like to cast in a movie version of their book. Not me. I don't cast characters. Gretchen and Archie live only in my imagination."

After Gretchen and Archie emerged from Cain's imagination, she added young Portland newspaper reporter, Susan Ward. Cain resists the notion that Ward represents "the Chelsea Cain" character. Instead she points out that Susan's profession is a matter of convenience. "I haven't been a cop or a serial killer but I know about being a 'quirky reporter.'" Rather than serve as a stand-in for the author, Ward is designed as a reliable representative for the reader "so that through her character the reader will believe all the crazy stuff that happens."

Though her "whole cloth" characters are entirely her creation, Cain readily ascribes the germination of her series to the Green River Killer who terrorized the Pacific Northwest in the 1980s and 1990s. "The story fascinated me in my youth in Bellingham, WA where we lived after we left the Iowa commune. When I saw the police video of the copy where the arresting detective interviewed serial killer Gary Ridgway who had been under suspicion for years, I was struck how convivial they were. Yet underneath they were trying to manipulate each other."

Determined not to write derivatively, she took unusual approaches to her thriller. Instead of the standard cop pursues the serial killer premise, Cain's serial killer is already behind bars. Secondly, she made her killer a woman when almost all real-life serial killers are white males. Still intrigued by that conviviality between the Green River Killer and arresting detective, she turned the relationship between Det. Archie Sheridan and psychopath Gretchen Lowell into what she calls "a twisted love story."

If it seems that it would be impossible to build a suspenseful novel based on a killer who's already in prison, the characterization in Heart Sick will convince you otherwise. (By the way, Cain's series is best read in order of printing: Heart Sick, Sweet Heart and Evil at Heart. Each novel has its own beginning, middle and end but there's an overall arc to the series, as with Anne Perry's World War I series.)

Heart Sick reveals that Det. Sheridan is the last of Gretchen Lowell's many kidnap victims, the only one she released alive after torture. (Among her predilections is performing surgery on her victims without anesthesia.) Captivity and torture leaves Sheridan physically debilitated, addicted to pain killers and estranged from his wife and kids. Yet Gretchen draws him like a siren with an unworldly, gothic-like attraction. Cain wanted to explore "the emotional fallout after the damage has occurred."

Sheridan draws Lowell, in turn. She knows that releasing him means that she will get caught. It seems that she prefers prison to giving up the magnetism that draws her to Archie. Their dynamics add sexual tension that goes way beyond standard Stockholm Syndrome victim transformation. Again, in gothic terms, it's as if Gretchen and Archie latch on to each other's souls.

As she increased her command of fiction, Cain taught herself a mechanical method for writing dialogue that is bound to help other writers. Almost any fiction writer can relate to the problem of trying to capture dialogue and mentally stopping to decide when a "he said" and "she said" are necessary or whether the character is sipping a martini or highball. Instead, Cain initially writes an entire scene of dialogue without attribution or attendant action. Her fingers fly over the keyboard as the characters speak—and only speak—the first time through. She doesn't slow down until after the characters have had their say and she has captured "the arc" of the scene. Only then does she go back and describe the room or the sweaty hand gripping the phone. "It's easy to get frozen in particulars which hinders progress. I call it my 'lasagna approach' because the novel is written in layers."

The success of Heart Sick and Sweetheart provided a soft landing for the recently-released third in the series, Evil at Heart. In it, Gretchen has attracted a devoted cadre of fans which soon grows out of control with killings of its own. For most of the novel Gretchen is at large and actually off-scene, at least in the physical sense. In truth she never strays far from Archie's thoughts, no more so than when he and Susan Ward find themselves tangled in a web of her admirers. One way Cain keeps the monster scary is by never giving point of view to Gretchen. If she allowed the reader inside Gretchen's perspective, it might make her more human and less monstrous.

Setting the series in Portland, OR where Cain lives, also keeps the scene fresh, Cain believes. It's more authoritative when the author doesn't have to look up places on MapQuest. Cain also thinks Portland ties in thematically to her books. "People live in Portland because it's beautiful out here. There's a paradox in Oregon's beauty and splendor. Along with that natural beauty come sneaker waves, avalanches and climbing deaths on Mt. Hood. Despite the danger and deaths, the natural beauty continues to challenge people. That paradox of beauty and danger is thematic to the series."

Any advice for writers hoping to make their own breakthroughs?

"Find a writing group. But you must find people whose opinions you respect. I joined one with real published literary authors and felt totally intimidated bringing in my thriller. But they were totally accepting and encouraging. Writing groups also create mini-deadlines. You have to have something for the next session. We read aloud in ours which is a tremendous help for me in pacing my thrillers, making each chapter something like a chapter in a serial—leaving the reader wanting more."

Charles Ardai

*It's a Matter of Time for This Writer/
Publisher/Editor*

by W.E. Reinka

One reason many novels don't get published is that they never get written in the first place. Time-robbing demons ranging from day jobs to grocery shopping conspire against would-be writers.

Before you decide you lack time to write, consider the accomplishments of writer/editor/ publisher Charles Ardai. After concentrating on English romantic poetry at Columbia, Ardai carried his knowledge of Coleridge and Keats out into the real world. No surprise that the business world wasn't clamoring for romantic poetry experts.

Shortly after his 1991 graduation, Ardai took an entry level job in the business world. Around that time everyone knew the burgeoning Internet was overflowing with opportunities but, other than a few techies, it seemed that most people were fumbling with how to use it, let alone looking for ways to exploit it. Where many saw confusion, Ardai saw opportunity. He struck on the idea of offering free e-mail, a service for which early Internet devotees paid monthly fees. With the backing of his employer D.E. Shaw & Company, he founded Juno. Six years later he turned over the reins of Juno when it merged with NetZero.

These days he remains Managing Director of global investment firm D.E. Shaw & Company. He is also publisher and editor of Hard Case Crime, which issues a new hard-boiled or noir novel every month and, as if that isn't enough, he has written three published novels, Fifty-to-One under his own name and Little Girl Lost and Songs of Innocence as Richard Aleas, an anagram of Charles Ardai. Sure, it helps to be a publisher when you have a manuscript. But before dismissing Ardai's novels, consider that his trophy case holds two of mysterdom's highest honors, Edgar and Shamus Awards.

TAKING THE TIME TO WRITE

While obviously a smart guy, his edge may be due more to effective time management than brains. For those of us who are still trying to work writing in around the monthly PTA meeting, Ardai advises that effective time management starts with prioritization. "If writing is something you care a great deal about and you would feel bad if your life reached its end and you had never done it, then it's something you'll make time for. It may not be a lot of time because, of course, you must pay the rent. But if it's extremely important, you will say 'This is something I'll set aside a half hour or an hour a day.' While that's not enough time to be a full-time writer, it is enough to write a book, to write short stories, and enough time to taste what it is like to write and hone your craft."

When another Edgar Award winner, S.J. Rozan, was nourishing her writing dreams while

---

W.E. REINKA, who often writes about books and authors, contributes to print and electronic publications nationwide.

working full-time as an architect, she put aside Saturday mornings for writing after she realized that most people rarely called her before noon on Saturday. Now she's a full-time writer. Similarly, Ardai uses early mornings. "Between five a.m. and 8:59 while my wife sleeps and the rest of the world slumbers, very few people call me. I use that time to write." Beneath his humorous tone, he's offering serious advice. (By the way, he extends that advice from the backseat of a New York taxi—where, rather than fritter away his commute time, he chats with us.)

He points out that the depth of writing a 300-page novel is less paralyzing when broken down into days. "Most people can get three pages written in the time it would take to watch a TV show. Is the TV show more important than your writing? The hardest part about writing should not be where will I find the time but 'what happens next?'"

EARLY SUBMISSIONS

Ardai is a rarity among writers in that he published his first-ever story submission. Just as he saw opportunity in offering free Internet access, he took a market approach in submitting his first crime story. He chose Ellery Queen's Mystery Magazine. "At the time, Ellery Queen had a Department of First Stories. Every month they had to buy a first story which meant they had to buy at least 12 first stories per year and, over the years, had to buy hundreds of first stories. So I started with them. By the way," he adds with a chuckle. "I also sold my second story to Ellery Queen's—back then they also had a Department of Second Stories."

He suggests that anthologies provide good opportunities for story writers. Writers organizations (Mystery Writers of America, Science Fiction and Fantasy Writers, etc.) often provide guidelines on pending anthologies.

No, his record isn't perfect. He's felt the sting of rejection from magazines and friends alike. "My first attempt at a novel was atrocious. It was too discursive. I gave the first 100 pages to a friend at Alfred Hitchcock for his opinion. A few days later he handed them back and said 'This isn't publishable.' At first, I was taken aback. I was offended. I thought 'How dare you say that? I'm a published author.' But he was completely right in two respects. One, it wasn't publishable. And, objectively looking at it now, I see that. Two, he was right to tell me that it wasn't publishable because that's what a friend does. You need to hear when you've written something unpublishable because when you don't you'll never improve."

He took that appreciation for his friend's honesty to his role as editor and publisher after he and a friend dreamt up the concept of Hard Case Publishing. "We were extolling the classic hard-boiled and noir novels of the '30s, '40s and '50s. 'Why doesn't anyone publish those anymore?' we asked."

WEEDING OUT HARD CASE SUBMISSIONS

That conversation led to the birth of Hard Case Crime. It does not require agented submissions and receives about 1,000 manuscripts per year. Despite publishing a new title every month, its full-time staff is zero. Ardai reviews the manuscripts personally and then a freelance typesetter and graphic designer get the books to press. Ardai takes his own advice of breaking down tasks to work down the manuscript pile. "When you think about it, 1,000 submissions breaks down to around two or three submissions per day and I only get past the first chapter in about one out of 10. In most, the quality of the language is not at the professional level."

Remembering the value of his friend's honesty on his own first novel, Ardai personally writes every Hard Case every rejection letter, giving explicit advice when possible. "When people send me submissions that aren't good enough to be published, I tell them that. Not out of a desire to be a jerk—in fact, sometimes I write, 'I don't mean to be a jerk but—.' I hope it helps them, not out of the writing profession but to become better writers."

Any submissions to Hard Case that fall outside of hard-boiled or noir crime fiction really do qualify for the baneful catchphrase of "not right for our list." Ardai cites the time someone submitted a novel where the detective relies on the help of his dead grandmother to solve crimes. "I thanked him for his submission but explained that we simply don't publish books with paranormal themes. It may be a terrific novel for all I know. Rejections really are not a reflection on you personally. Editors reject material from writers they've bought before. It's important to develop a thick skin. The answer is going to be 'no' most of the time. If you're lucky it will be 'no' less than one hundred percent of the time. But until you're an extremely good and successful writer you have to be prepared for rejection."

Another common reason Ardai rejects manuscripts is that the writers strain for a hard-boiled voice. Others seem to be well written and the jokes are funny but the scenes they depict seem all too familiar. "Please don't send me a novel that starts with a world weary detective with a bottle in his desk drawer and a blonde in his door." One reason he sees where being an editor has helped his own writing is recognizing trite scenes and expressions. "When I see an expression that 10, 20, 30 writers have used before, I don't want to use it myself."

Perhaps a finer line divides originality and pastiche in hard-boiled crime fiction than any other genre. Ardai suggests that writers wishing to learn the difference should head down to the local library. "Check out a random dozen books in your chosen genre. Read them back-to-back to back. Ninety-percent of published books are not very good. It's true in all genres. How many science-fiction plots are hoary old chestnuts? Point yourself toward fresh and natural by picking out what seems fresh and natural in those books."

As long as you're down at the library, look beyond your chosen drama. Of course those interested in crime fiction would want to read Raymond Chandler but, according to Ardai, also Coleridge, Hardy, Shakespeare and the Greeks. "You get an appreciation for the culture by reading widely. You get an appreciation for what's come before you. You understand when reading Westlake that he followed on the heels of Hammett. A generation earlier it's Hammett and Hemingway rebelling against the more ornate styles of Dickens and Tennyson. You appreciate where some of modern cynicism has its roots in the really cruel works of Thomas Hardy. If you haven't read the past you have a shallower appreciation for what you're doing. It's like being an architect and not looking at old buildings or being a chef and not learning how food was cooked in centuries past."

As for the submission process itself, Ardai offers a few other tips while wearing his editor's hat starting with "Send chapter one." For reasons unknown, people submit Chapter 17 or samples of their favorite sentences. Secondly, forget gimmicks. While sometimes clever such as the occasional writers who submit manuscripts with fake Hard Case covers, he says that gimmicks don't give a manuscript an advantage and sometimes backfire by being offensive. Multiple submissions brings another editor's gripe. "I don't mind simultaneous submissions, I understand writers have to try various houses but I get people offering me my choice of three different books. If you can't choose your best work yourself, it tells me that none are good enough." Finally, just as magazine editors will tell you that, no kidding, they really do occasionally get submissions that are handwritten on ruled paper, Ardai says it's astonishing how many manuscripts come in laden with typos. "I understand that in a 300 page manuscript, there will be a few typos. But I see submissions where typos fill almost every sentence."

The manuscripts that inch into that publishable one percent must be fit enough to pass Ardai's treadmill test. "Sometimes when I take a manuscript to read while I'm on the treadmill I get so engrossed that I keep telling myself 'one more page' as the treadmill starts going faster and faster. When the treadmill flings me off the back I know I've got a winner." From taxi cab interviews to treadmill reading, Ardai manages time well. He has another tip for new novelists on how to make the most of their time—start with a contemporary, rather than historical, setting.

"I set my first two novels, Little Girl Lost and Songs of Innocence, in present time in New York City where I've always lived. I didn't have to do additional research. By reinventing versions of myself for the hero and making him my age and size I could concentrate on the moral dilemma."

Not so with Ardai's third novel, Fifty-to-One. First, it celebrates Hard Case Crime's first fifty offerings by taking each chapter title (in order) from the previous 49 Hard Case editions. Then it's set 50 years ago. The focus character is an 18-year-old girl from South Dakota. "I had to research something on practically every page. Did they use paper towels in 1958? Were ballpoint pens around? I went down to Grand Central Station to talk to someone about trains that would have run between South Dakota in New York back then. It was fun but time consuming. Based on that, I'd tell writers, 'If you haven't written a novel before, don't make things harder for yourself by setting it in the past.'"

Resources

Where to Look for More Information

Below is a list of invaluable resources specifically for mystery writers. To order any of the Writer's Digest Books titles or to get a consumer book catalog, call (800)448-0915. You may also order Writer's Digest Books selections through www.fwbookstore.com, Amazon.com, or www.barnesandnoble.com.

MAGAZINES:

- *Mystery Readers Journal,* Mystery Readers International, P.O. Box 8116, Berkeley CA 94707. Web site: www.mysteryreaders.org.
- *Mystery News,* Black Raven Press, PMB 152, 105 E. Townline Rd., Vernon Hills IL 60061-1424. Web site: www.blackravenpress.com.
- *Mystery Scene,* 331 W. 57th St., Suite 148, New York NY 10019. Web site: www.mysteryscenemag.com.

BOOKS:

Howdunit series (Writer's Digest Books):

- *Modus Operandi: A Writer's Guide to How Criminals Work,* by Mauro V. Corvasce and Joseph R. Paglino
- *Missing Persons: A Writer's Guide to Finding the Lost, the Abducted and the Escaped,* by Fay Faron
- *Book of Poisons,* by Serita Stevens and Anne Bannon
- *Scene of the Crime: A Writer's Guide to Crime Scene Investigation,* by Anne Wingate, Ph.D.
- *Book of Police Procedure and Investigation,* by Lee Lofland

Other Writer's Digest Books for mystery writers:

- *The Criminal Mind, A Writer's Guide to Forensic Psychology,* by Katherine Ramsland
- *Writing Mysteries: A Handbook by the Mystery Writers of America,* edited by Sue Grafton
- *Writing and Selling Your Mystery Novel: How to Knock 'em Dead With Style,* by Hallie Ephron
- *You Can Write a Mystery,* by Gillian Roberts

ORGANIZATIONS & ONLINE:

- Crime Writers of Canada. Web site: www.crimewriterscanada.com.
- Crime Writers' Association. Web site: www.thecwa.co.uk.

- Mystery Writers of America, 17 E. 47th St., 6th Floor, New York NY 10017. Web site: www. mysterywriters.org
- The Private Eye Writers of America, 4342 Forest DeVille Dr., Apt. H, St. Louis MO 63129. Web site: http://hometown.aol.com/rrandisi/myhomepage/writing.html
- Sisters in Crime, P.O. Box 442124, Lawrence KS 66044-8933.   Web site: www.sistersincrime. org
- Writer's Market Web site: www.writersmarket.com.
- Writer's Digest Web site: www.writersdigest.com.

Susan Wiggs

'Every Book Feels Like a First Book to Me'

by Deborah Bouziden

Susan Wiggs penned her first bestseller at age eight. It was a story titled, A Book about Some Bad Kids, and featured Susan and her siblings. She wrote it on a Big Chief tablet, used a Number Two pencil and put it together with blunt scissors and a borrowed stapler. The volume was a complete sell out and her mother still owns the original. Due to her brother's reaction to her literary work however, Susan moved 'underground' and worked on her craft incognito for years.

While always a big reader and writer, in college Wiggs was introduced to a writer who would change the direction her life would take.

"I had a summer job at a department store fine jewelry counter," Wiggs said. "It was horrendously boring, so a coworker lent me Shanna, by Kathleen Woodiwiss, and I was a goner. I devoured the thing. I also felt that tuning fork effect—the story resounded with me on a deep level. That was how I found my genre."

Wiggs graduated from college with degrees from Stephen F. Austen State University and Harvard and a crate of "keeper" books by Woodiwiss, Roberta Gellis, Laurie McBain, Rosemary Rogers, Jennifer Blake, and Bertrice Small. She became a math teacher, just to prove to the world she did have a left brain. But numbers wouldn't take priority over words long.

Her writing career began in earnest one night when she finished the book she was reading, was wide awake and realized there was nothing in the house she wanted to read. Going back to her roots, she grabbed a Big Chief tablet and Number Two pencil and started writing A Book about Some Bad Adults.

"In reality," Wiggs said, "it was a bad book about some adults."

Through the years however, Wiggs persisted, learning her craft through trial and error. Her first book to sell, Texas Wildflower, was actually her third book written.

Since those early and humble beginnings back in 1987, Wiggs has gone on to publish over 38 books. Her books have been Publisher Weekly Starred Reviewed, chosen as Best Books of the Year by Publishers Weekly, been RITA Finalists, and won the Romance Writers of America's RITA Award. Her latest book, Just Breathe, is an Indie Next pick, selected by Independent Booksellers. But Wiggs is not keeping count, she just continues to write.

"I stopped counting how many books I'd written after 30," Wiggs said. "It was making me feel old. Every book feels like a first book to me. I never get over the excitement. I'm such a nerd."

DEBORAH BOUZIDEN has been writing and publishing articles and books since 1985. She has had hundreds of articles published in such magazines as *Woman's Day, Writer's Digest,* and *Oklahoma Today,* eight books published, and contributed to nine more. To learn more about Bouziden, visit her Web site at www.deborahbouziden.com.

Do you have a writing schedule?

Please explain how you work. Why do you think that process works for you?

What I have is a work ethic. I had it when I was a teacher and I have it as a writer. When it's time to go to work, I simply do that—go to work. Since writing is my job, I go to writing the way I would go to any other job—regularly and on a mostly-daily basis. What I love about my job is that it varies. Some days, I sit with my pen and notebook (which I discuss extensively on my blog, www.redroom.com/blog/susan-wiggs), and dream and make stuff up and write it down. Other days I'm at the computer, dictating pages (reading from the handwritten draft) or working on revisions. Or I might be listening to music and making a collage of images and objects that evoke my book-in-progress. You might even catch me creating a playlist for the book or (it has to be said) taking care of business, like responding to this interview, updating my Web site or doing whatever PR my publicist has come up with. The reason this works for me is (surprise) that I love my work.

Just an aside—many emerging writers I meet are looking for a free pass or special formula that will finally kick their asses in gear and get them to finish and publish their novel. Newsflash—and we all know this on some level—there is no mystique to this process. It's a craft. A tough one, yes, but a learnable craft. Sure, there is that element of talent that can't be taught, but that's the easy part. Craft is the hard part. If it was easy, everyone would do it. It's not easy. It's work. We love it but it's still work, still a challenge, still out of reach of anyone except those who have the passion for it.

You live in a beautiful part of the country as is evident by the pictures on your blog. Do you use it as a source of inspiration or muse? Do you think every writer needs a source of inspiration? How do you suggest writers find theirs?

I know I'm extremely lucky to be living here, at the water's edge, with Mount Rainier shining across the Sound right out my window, ferryboats and navy ships passing, sea lions barking, salmon leaping, rare and common seabirds everywhere I look...it's incredibly scenic and abundant. I've also been lucky enough to work on my writing in secluded cabins, snowed in at a
ski lodge, in a villa in Amalfi, a boutique hotel in New York, a beach house in St. Croix, on our boat...All wonderful and inspiring places.

However (you knew there was a however), all this scenery is completely superfluous to the work of a writer. If a writer waits until she has the perfect writing space, the perfect amount of time, the perfect equipment, the perfect life...she will never get anything done.

How do I suggest a writer find her source? She just needs to roll up her sleeves and write. A writer can go anywhere in her mind. It's one of a writer's gifts. I'm certainly proof of that. I wrote my first novel while living in a cramped graduate student apartment, working on a typewriter set up at a card table which also served as my kitchen table. Other novels were written in a windowless spare room in a tiny tract home in the suburbs of Houston. So the gorgeous setting is just sort of a bonus. And a reward for a job well done.

What are three or four books romance writers should have on their shelves? And why these books?

What a great question! I'm totally going to go over the limit here. All of these are books every writer should have, not just romance writers.

• Techniques of the Selling Writer, by Dwight Swain is probably out of print but well worth tracking down. It opened my mind to commercial elements in fiction, particularly pacing.

• Writing Fiction by Janet Burroway is a staple, so big and rich I find myself going back to it again and again. Don't worry about the cover price. Just hold your nose and pay it.

• The Hero's Journey, by Christopher Vogler. (Full disclosure: I'm friends with Chris and his amazing wife Alice.) Chris loves it when I say this: He is a god to me. Seriously, the memo that became this book unlocked stories for me in a way nothing else ever has. I love this book so much I annotated my own.

• *Writing the Blockbuster Novel*, by Al Zuckerman shows us how to take material apart and put it back together and why it's not insanity to do so, again and again.

• *Writing the Breakout Novel,* by Donald Maass comes with a companion workbook, and both are must-haves. Don is one of the best brainstormers and story analysts I know. He has a unique understanding of what makes fiction work.

• Anything by Michael Hauge. He's a story analyst, too, but comes at it from the perspective of screenwriting. His books and workshops are invaluable.

You've written period pieces as well as contemporary. What is your favorite time period and what advice can you give writers about research?

I tend to fall in love with whatever time period I happen to be researching for a book, be it medieval Scotland or present-day Point Reyes, California. Some writers are content to stay in their niche, with books that take place in the same setting or era, again and again. I'm too restless for that.

Research advice—learn as much as you can, as quickly as you can, any way you can. This could mean searching the Internet, making a trip, finding someone to interview, reading travel books, memoirs, how-to books, biographies, interviewing people, riding along with an EMT crew, you name it. Do whatever it takes to enable yourself to build an authentic world for your story. Readers can smell a phony a mile away. But they want to believe you know what you're doing, so do your best to fulfill that expectation. The key is to sound like you know what you're talking about so the reader feels the story's authenticity. Find the sources that will give you that authentic texture.

But there is a caution. Don't make the story a vehicle for research, to show how much you know about a particular topic. That's boring. Just because you can write 45 five pages about the flying field ambulances of Napoleon's surgeon general, Dr. Larrey, doesn't mean you should. Use only enough to flavor the story for the reader.

You've judged romance writing contests for different organizations. What mistakes do you see writers making over and over again?

Flat, ordinary writing and a lack of global knowledge. Often, the emotions don't ring true or fail to grow from an authentic place, and the conflict is missing. And maybe this is just me, but I'm a stickler for style and usage. Language is our only tool for telling a story, and too many emerging writers don't take the time to hone their craft in this area. It's inexcusable.

When creating your characters, how do you choose traits, personality, etc.?

My characters come together like pieces of a crazy quilt. I pull together colorful bits and pieces (traits, issues, background) and assemble them into a person-like creation. The bits and pieces come from people I know, but once they're assembled, they're an original creation. At the outset, I focus a lot on the character's history and the defining moments in her past that motivate her emotions and actions in the story. There are no consistent "must-have" traits for me other than being fascinating! I love the endless variety in people—and in characters.

You have such a unique sense of humor and that comes through in your books. It's a sense of humor that happens in life. Is it written into your books consciously? How difficult is it to get just right?

I'm so happy you asked this question! Many readers tell me my books make them cry—which is fair. Emotional things happen in my books and they wring a tear from me, too. But good fiction, like real life, is multifaceted. We get to have laughter and tears.

The humor in my books is organic, meaning I don't set up funny situations or laugh lines. They seem to grow out of whatever the characters seem to be doing. Even if a character is grief stricken, her spirit can shine through.

In Fireside (Feb. 2009), there's a very funny scene with the hero getting a makeover. On the surface, it's hilarious, showing him getting shined and polished for a photo shoot, but under that is a layer of seriousness and even pain. He has to change his life to fit his new circumstances.

In real life, I laugh a lot and people tell me I say funny things, so maybe some of that sneaks into the books. It's so very subjective. Sometimes I think humor comes from the reader.

How do you plot? What are your most common plot problems and how do you handle them? Have you ever had a plot disaster or crisis? How did you handle it? Do you advise outlining?

I plot like I put together characters, cobbling together shiny bits and pieces that interest me, and assembling them into a story arc. I have the common problem of not thinking things through to their logical conclusion until it's too late to change. I have a plot disaster or crisis in every f-ing book! I handle it by swearing!

Outlining can be useful at any stage. It doesn't need to be elaborate. Just list scenes and incidents and let one step grow out of the previous one.

What advice can you give to struggling romance writers?

To accept—no, embrace—the struggle. Did you think it would be easy? A smooth ride all the way? If it was easy, everyone would be a bestselling writer. Also, smack me for saying "bestselling." Every writer has the right to choose her own standard of success. For one writer, it might be a literary accomplishment. Or simply finishing a book she's been dying to write. For another, it might be a level of popularity or sales. So my advice? Define success for yourself and make sure you put your passion on the page.

What should romance writers know about marketing and the publishing business today?

Create a vibrant, user-friendly web site with a companion blog, and keep it fresh. Readers are surfers these days. Give them something great to look at on the Web.

Also, be kind to everyone you meet in the business, from the casual reader who drops by a booksigning to a book chain's vp of marketing. The first time I met Nora Roberts, she had just published her first single title novel (Hot Ice) and was at a booksigning in Houston where nobody came. She and I talked that day, and I'll never forget how genuine and kind she was to an emerging writer. Debbie Macomber is another great example. She is one of the most beloved authors around because she's genuinely kind, and very generous with advice and encouragement. Writers like that are my role models.

The romance industry has seen many sweeping changes through the years. Do you think they are for the best or detrimental to our industry? What future do you see for the romance industry?

I'm sorry to see writers exploited by some of the newer e-publishing and POD firms. Overall, the future for the industry is bright. Readers crave stories and always will, so the storytellers are safe.

Tell me a bit about your latest project. What is it about? When will it be released?

I just finished Lakeshore Christmas, a hardcover coming in October 2009. It's a nostalgic, magical love story about the town librarian charged with directing the annual Christmas pageant. Against her will, she is paired up with a bad-boy rocker who's been court-ordered to help her with the music.

Jessica Freely

On E-Pulbising & M/M Romance

by Cornelius Fortune

Sometimes the road to romance can actually be paved with space ships and time travel devices.

Anne Harris, the science fiction writer, has published such critically-acclaimed works as Accidental Creatures, The Nature of Smoke, and Inventing Memory.

Jessica Freely—her m/m writing alter ego—is on the cutting edge of e-publishing and writes romance novels featuring men in love. Her latest, Virgin, was released last August to favorable reviews and a sequel is currently in the works. As literary journeys go, few authors could have penned such a deceptively simple tale that finds itself not only gender-bending, but crossing genres.

Appropriately, Harris (no stranger to writing LGBT characters), hasn't abandoned the genre that launched her career (she still writes science fiction). But with a wider audience already growing within the m/m (commonly known as "slash") fiction community, and more publishers taking on m/m novels as "straight" romance, Freely's work, alongside others in the genre, may soon find a larger following.

True to form, her journey began with two guys…

Jay & Silent Bob strike back—again

It wasn't long ago that m/m fiction existed mainly in the crevices of the Internet, fringe entertainment for those curious enough to stumble upon it.

One night, in search of some Jay and Silent Bob material, Harris happily discovered a site unlike any she had previously encountered—this one featured the slacker duo consummating their love.

As a fan of Kevin Smith's films, this encounter—surely entertaining, certainly inspiring—served as a catalyst for the author and opened another world to her, one that she would explore as Jessica Freely.

"I have a great deal of respect for fan fiction," says Freely. "Some of it is excellent. Obviously because of copyright issues it couldn't be published (but) absolutely you are entitled to write and imagine anything that you want. Everyone should be entitled to their fantasies. Fan fiction is one form of expression."

A feminist whose own novels are representative of strong female characters, Freely believes that women don't have enough "culturally sanctioned" outlets for their fantasies. "Fan fiction has provided a wonderful outlet for many women to play, explore, and use their

CORNELIUS A. FORTUNE is the author of Stories from Arlington and a Rhysling-nominated poet. His journalism has appeared in The *Advocate, Chess Life, Metro Times, Spotlight on Recovery,* the *Pittsburgh Courier* and others. His fiction has appeared in *Nuvein, Tales of the Unanticipated, AlienSkin Magazine, Black Petals* and others.

imaginations, and I think that that's great," she says. "Ideas are not a limited resource; they are a continually renewed resource."

The lure of e-publishing

Back in the 1990s, print's position as the dominate form of publication was mostly uncontested. Today, e-publishing is growing in popularity and reach.

As more print magazines cease publication and others shift their content exclusively to the Internet, it's an interesting—if not unique—time to be an author, especially of romance.

"E-publishing is so much more direct and the turn around time is so much faster," she says. "It's very refreshing. You're not quite a supplicant at the altar as you are a partner with your publisher in e-publishing, and I really like that dynamic."

She won't prematurely forecast the death of print, but she does foresee a more specialized and limited industry in the coming years.

"There is a perception that print books are inherently of a higher quality—I don't agree with that, but it is the perception," she says. "It's been very much to my advantage to have been a print published author and be working in e-publishing now because I can lay claim to both. Nobody can say that I'm not a good enough writer for print and that's why I'm e-publishing. If you haven't been print published they may have that bias."

Freely encourages aspiring writers to do their homework about the publishers they hope to work with. Since this information is literally a Google search away, the responsibility falls upon the writer. Right now, the e-market is wide open, eagerly awaiting new voices.

Although print publishers still pay better rates, Freely admits, on average, a successful print author may only be presented with one book contract a year.

"In e-publishing you can get a contract as fast as you can write," she says. "If you are a professional fiction writer, there really is no limit to the number of contracts you can get a year. So you can, to some extent, make up in quantity what you're missing in terms of the per units amount that you get paid."

With no established print market for m/m romance, e-publishing provides a home for these specialized subjects.

"If you want to write m/m romance—any type of alternative sexuality romance, really—e-publishing is your saving grace because there is an audience for you and there hasn't been an outlet for that in print," she says.

The nuts n' bolts of love

Whether it's an electronic file downloaded to someone's desktop or a book purchased at your local bookstore, the rules of great storytelling still apply. You are duty bound, Freely advises, to give the reader what they desire above all else: escapism.

"It is important to understand the rules of the genre you're in," she says. "There are things that romance readers want and that you ignore at your peril. A happy ending is important in a romance novel. This is fiction people read to escape. They read it to get a good feeling. So a downer ending tends not to sell well in the genre."

Pleasing your audience is just one part of a romance writer's toolbox. Blogs have the potential to carry the conversation between reader and writer a step further.

Freely finds her own blog indispensable, as it helps her to keep in touch with her audience in "real time."

"I use my blog as a way to connect with my audience," she says. "I try to provide them with extra things I think they'll enjoy. I post a lot of free short stories on that blog and I think it's fun for everybody."

Freely's blog (http://friskbiskit.com) is primarily used to broaden the conversation on m/m fiction. It also includes updates on publishing trends as well as market alerts.

"If you're writing for publication, you're an entertainer," Freely says. "You're giving something to somebody else. It's not just a form of self-expression anymore—it's a dialogue in a sense. I think cultivating those relationships with your readers, making yourself accessible as a writer and being

Reading List

Books by Jessica Freely
- *Hero* (short story), *Stay* (short story), *Scars* (novella), a Torquere Books, electronic editions, 2008)
- *Virgin* (novella, Loose Id, electronic edition, 2008)—A Fallen Angels Recommended Read

Books by Anne Harris
- *The Nature of Smoke* (Tor Books, 1996)—Japanese translation made the shortlist for the Sense of Gender Award (Japanese Tiptree); Locus Recommended Reading List; Starred review, *Publishers Weekly*
- *Accidental Creatures* (Tor Books, 1998)—Winner of the first Spectrum Award in 1999
- *Inventing Memory* (Tor Books, 2004)—Booksense 76 pick; James Tiptree Jr. Award long list; Spectrum Award long list · Young adult novels: "Be careful. Younger kids pick these up. You can be as realistic as you want, but if you put a veil over certain kinds of things, you allow the older reader to deal with it without abusing the younger reader."

there for them with an online presence are important things to do once you've been published."

Freely is also involved with 25 other professional authors in a project that will make their work available to readers online. What they have found is that e-book readers want full-length works, not abridgements, which at first seemed antithetical to the fast- paced, "shorter is better" attitude that seems to exist on the Internet.

"We first approached it the same way: Do they want flash fiction or micro stories?" she says. "No: longer is better."

Writing 'Freely'

Whether writing short fiction or novel-length works, there are probably more excuses available today for not writing than ever before. In a world where information travels via Blackberrys and text messaging is the preferred method of communication for many Americans, how do you get started?

The trick, Freely says, is to give yourself room to play creatively. It won't be perfect the first time out the gate, nor should it be.

"What I tend to do in romance is a very rough outline," she adds. "I rough out the main conflicts. I try to get some idea as to what the resolution is going to be and who my major players are. A lot of beginning author's work wanders for the lack of a focused antagonist. So I get those basics down and I try to get a real feel for the characters."

Banishing the internal critic during the creative process is an important rite of passage every writer—beginners and professionals alike—must do if they are to get anything done. Otherwise, you'll just end up staring at a blank screen or page and never get past the first couple of paragraphs, let alone a sentence.

"You need to give yourself permission to make mistakes," Freely says. "Write enough so that the mistakes don't matter. If you've produced enough writing, it doesn't matter if some of it isn't great. Those are ones you stick in the drawer, but you still learn something while you're doing it."

A writer should value and own their personal writing process and write as much as possible. "I think one of the worse things you can do is look at someone else's process and try to copy it," she says. "You need to learn about yourself. In a way it all begins with self-discovery. You need to understand what you love writing about."

Read, read, read

"The other thing that I would suggest is that they read in the genre they want to write in," Freely says. "If they want to write mainstream romance they should read mainstream romance, and ideally, they should be in love with mainstream romance.

"I think that a writer works best when they're doing the kinds of stories they love, (when) the audience that you're writing for is you. The fact is—and I do believe the Internet is proof of this—there is an audience for everything."

The key, she suggests, is pinning down what kind of reader you are. Then ask yourself: What's your idea of the perfect story? Where are the other people that want to read this? Are they reading fan fiction? Are they playing computer games?

"I think it's very important to think outside the box," she says. "And don't let yourself be too tied down by what's been done in the past. I think you're much better off thinking on your feet and paying attention to what's going on around you. Some markets are not going to be in formats that we even recognize as books."

'Love is love'

Whether she's writing about women loving women or men loving men, there is no substitute for good ole fashioned love.

"I've had lesbian romances in my first two novels and I've written heterosexual romance and gay romance," Freely says. "I think it really comes down to love is love. What's important to keep in mind is to treat [your characters] as people. Really successful stories are about well-rounded people with flaws and strengths and frailties, regardless of their sexuality or their gender."

As a woman living in a male-dominated society, issues of social power and gender roles are leveled out for her when she writes. Conversely, if she were a man writing m/m romance novels, there'd be gender role baggage to contend with.

"There's something liberating about writing across gender," Freely says. "It gives you the freedom to explore things that you can get to directly, and I like that. There are different tastes even within the genre [but] I'm really into the partnership of equals."

As such, Freely loves romance, but she hates heterosexual power dynamics.

"So having two characters of the same gender in a relationship does all kinds of wonderful

About Virgin

Described as a paranormal romance, Jessica Freely's Virgin features shape-shifters, hustlers, pimps, and a main character Joam, who is unknowingly slated for a sacrifice by a cabal of dark sorcerers, lead by his employer.

Joam meets and falls for Blake, a man on the run, and doesn't stay a virgin for long. This upsets the cabal and now they want their revenge.

"The focus is on the romantic storyline but there are fantastic elements in some of the work," Freely says. "In the world that I've created, sorcery is inherently evil because it's taking natural forces and turning them to your own ends, there's a perversion in that. Joam who is a varnal (a shape-shifter with otherworldly sexual powers) was born this way. This is who he is. It's a part of nature."

The sequel will delve deeper into the magical elements of the first story, but there will definitely be romance and of course, sex.

And no, those hot scenes on the page aren't just words on paper—she really gets into it.

"I don't think that my work as a romantic romance writer would be any good if it weren't hot to me when I write it," she says. "I really don't think you can succeed with erotic writing unless you're writing the things that turn you on."

things," she says. "It evens the playing field. If there's a power differential in the relationship, it's not a societally ordained one: It's there for other reasons. I think there's also an element of seeing men be emotionally vulnerable with each other that is incredibly powerful. We have such a cultural taboo against that."

M/m also appeals to her because of its inherent simplicity.

"It's just me and the two people who are falling in love, and it's almost like I get to be outside the matriarchy for awhile," Freely says. "I'm doing what I love. I'm writing the stories that I've always wanted to write. I think it's good for the work that I really love what I'm doing."

Having grown up in a home where both her father and brother discussed science fiction books around the dinner table, it was almost inevitable that she would choose science fiction as a career path.

Interestingly enough, it was her mother who read romance novels, so her foray into romance was arguably just as inevitable. The road was paved from the very beginning.

"I think m/m is expressing something that our culture really doesn't have the tools and the words and the definitions for yet," Freely says. "It's not exploitive of gay men. It's really about women exploring all kinds of gender issues; relationship paradigms that exist outside a patriarchal context."

Kate Allan

Writing Recency Romance

by Diane Shipley

Kate Allan fell in love with romantic fiction as a bored teenager, when she searched her grandmother's bookshelves for something to read and found a stash of Harlequin novels that she re-visited many times over during the years that followed. A passionate interest in history meant that she gravitated particularly to historical romances and started trying to write a few of her own. "When I was a teenager I'd manage to get to about chapter five in various romantic novels but wouldn't go any further because I didn't really have any idea what I was doing or how to come up with a plot or anything," she admits.

After Allan graduated with a degree in History from the UK's University of York in 1997, she began writing in earnest, despite having a full-time job. In 2001, when she was 26, her first novel Fateful Deception was published and Allan is now the author of four romance novels including the Jane Austen-inspired Perfidy and Perfection. She also works as a marketing consultant and literary agent, giving her an insight into the world of publishing that can surely only encourage her career to flourish.

What makes a good romantic novel?

You need a fantastic hero who the author has to fall in love with as much as the readers do. One benefit of writing romance is that you get to fantasize about different men. The heroine has to be a strong character: she can't be a lily-livered, weak-willed little thing. She may be wrong about what she wants—I quite like female characters who think they know what they want and are proved slightly wrong—but she'll have a goal and a direction and be absolutely capable of dealing with things that are thrown at her. Up to a point, that is; everyone has flaws.

A lot of writers who are interested in writing romantic fiction seem to gravitate towards 'chick lit' these days—why didn't you?

I did consider writing chick lit because obviously I wanted to be published and chick lit is very big. But the problem is that I don't really read it. I have read some that I've quite enjoyed but it just isn't my thing. I don't identify with it, I guess.

What do you enjoy about writing historical romance?

I've got this idea that writers write what they have to write and I've been deeply interested in history for a long time. I read a lot of history books and find the past really fascinating and

DIANE SHIPLEY, an ex-books Web site editor and frequent reviewer, has written extensively about writers and writing for publications including The Guardian arts blog and women's literary magazine Mslexia. She also writes about technology, television and lifestyle for newspapers, magazines and Web sites in the U.S. and the U.K. Her Web site is www.dianeshipley.co.uk.

Allan's Favorite Online Research Resources

- **Old Bailey Online**
  The Proceedings of the Old Bailey, 1674-1913 A fully searchable edition of the largest body of texts detailing the lives of non-elite people ever published, containing 197,745 criminal trials held at London's central criminal court.
  www.oldbaileyonline.org/

- **Vision of Britain**
  A vision of Britain between 1801 and 2001. Includes maps, statistical trends and historical descriptions.
  www.visionofbritain.org.uk

- **Historical directories**
  A digital library of local and trade directories for England and Wales, from 1750 to 1919. It contains high quality reproductions of comparatively rare books, essential tools for research into local and genealogical history.
  www.historicaldirectories.org/hd/

- **Lord Byron's Letters**
  The life, letters, and poetic works of George Gordon Byron, the most prolific and controversial of the great English Romantic poets.
  http://engphil.astate.edu/gallery/byron.html

- **Greenwood's Map of London 1827**
  http://users.bathspa.ac.uk/greenwood/

For Romance Writers

always have done, so I think it was a natural thing to want to create a historical setting. The central question for me is: just because people are in a different century are they different from people today? And my answer to that is.. not necessarily. To me, writing is about exploring what people are like and although the trappings might be completely different in different historical periods, central things still matter to people. For example, my books explore romantic relationships but they also look at family relationships.

When and how did you first get published?

I managed to finish a manuscript, if you can call it that, and found the Romantic Novelists Association on the Internet. They had this New Writers scheme which you could join as an unpublished writer and send in your manuscript for a published author to read it and give you a critique. That seemed like a fabulous idea—obviously someone would read my manuscript and it would be wonderful and they would send it on to a publisher for me...That didn't happen. It got sent back with a report saying it was pretty bad. She said something like, I can see you've got some kind of storytelling ability but you have to learn about characterization, plot and structure. That's when I realized that it's not the case that you just sit down and write a novel, you actually have to learn about the craft. I took the first book away and didn't do anything for about six months because I was sort of crushed by this report. Then I realized it wasn't, "go away and never do anything again." She did say some good things like that my dialogue was good. The following year, I wrote a second book, Fateful Deception, sent that to the RNA scheme and got some feedback that it could be published. It was later shortlisted for the 2005 RNA New Writers Award.

You write on your Web site (www.kateallan.com) that it's important to have a positive attitude towards setbacks—did it take a lot of self belief to keep going?

Absolutely. Self belief is really, really important. I think there's a point when you're a serious writer where you have to "come out" and tell people what you're doing. But people can be very skeptical because you haven't got any validation that you're good so you have to believe in yourself. I left my job at a research agency in 2004 and took six months off so I could write. I had to tell my parents and my husband that even though I'd never earned a penny from my writing, I was taking six months off to finish my novel. You worry that you're destroying your résumé, but you have to take a leap of faith at some point. In fact, I finished work that February and a couple of weeks later I got a letter from publishers DC Thompson wanting to publish Fateful Deception.

How long does it take you to write a book?

Fateful Deception took me about 700 hours to write. I'm now halfway through my current novel: over the last 18 months I've written 35,000 words, writing two or three hours a week. I would like to write more, but I have to fit it in around my day job. When I had my six months off, that was fabulous because I'd start writing at 8 in the morning, go through until about one or two p.m., have a couple of hours off then get back to it and I was able to write Perfidy and Perfection in about eight weeks. It is a bit of a luxury to be a full-time writer and I think one of the problems authors have is actually earning a living. No matter what genre you're in, it's quite difficult to get to the stage where you can become a full-time writer.

A lot of aspiring authors find it hard to fit writing in alongside a job. Do you think it can be stifling creatively if a lot of your mental energy is taken up elsewhere?

Completely. From 2004-2006, I was head of marketing and communications for an Internet company and because the job was so demanding and I was doing a lot of copywriting it was very hard to get any of my own writing done at all. If you've written 1,000 words in the day for a newsletter, the last thing you want to do when you get home is switch your computer on and open up another word-processing program.

Do you do much plotting before you start writing?

No, I can't plot to save my life. I work it out as I go along. It's a romance, so I always know the hero and heroine are going to get together and I'm always trying to think of new ways to make that interesting. They realize that they really do love each other or there's a proposal scene or a wedding scene—there's going to be a pivotal moment that I try to make as interesting as possible. I got a review for Perfidy and Perfection which said it was surprisingly engaging despite the unlikely plot.. which I think was fair. Somebody said to me the other day that if you have absolutely fantastic characters you can still write a great book with a mediocre plot. But if you've got mediocre characters, the best plot in the world won't save you. That's my excuse!

Five Websites for Romance Writers

- **Romantic Novelists Association**
  www.rna-uk.org/

- **Romance Writers of America**
  www.rwanational.org/

- **The Romantic Times**
  www.romantictimes.com/

- **Romancing the Blog**
  http://www.romancingtheblog.com/blog/

- **eHarlequin Community**
  http://community.eharlequin.com/

Your books are all defined as Regency romances—what exactly does that mean, exactly?

The regency period broadly goes from about 1800 to 1830. You've probably heard of the madness of King George. George III was mad so his son George IV was given the regency [meaning he reigned in the King's absence]. The Prince Regent's set was quite profligate and did a lot of gambling and it was quite a good time. Gentlemen stopped powdering their hair and wearing makeup and young women could show their ankles and have low necklines. If you remember Pride and Prejudice, Lucy Bennet ran across the fields to see her sister when she was ill. Although that may not be the epitome of polite behavior, she doesn't wear a corset, she doesn't have a chaperone. I write heroines who aren't at the absolute top end of society but who have the freedom Lucy Bennet had. It's probably more similar to our own time than most other periods in history. That's why I think it's a popular time for people writing historical romance.

How important is it to get the historical details right?

It annoys me when I read historical fiction and it's been badly researched. To me, all historical details need to be accurate as far as possible. I've read Regencies where a chickadee wanders onto the lawn. As an English reader, that throws me out of the book. I don't think we've had chickadees in England ever. If I'm putting a bird on the lawn it will be a blackbird or a robin. Being English does give me an advantage—I can go to pretty villages and see which buildings have survived from the period, or go to the local library and pull up pictures and information. You can't always find everything out over the Internet, unfortunately—although it is getting easier.

What about getting the language right?

Much as it would be appealing, I can't write in Jane Austen's English. In dialogue I try to use appropriate words that were current at the time but I don't use anything that would make it incomprehensible to the reader. It's giving a flavor of the period rather than trying to copy.

Who do you think your typical reader is?

I hate to generalize but I imagine they're female, probably over 45 and most likely quite voracious readers who enjoy reading lots of romantic fiction. But I know I have younger readers, too. I know a girl who was about 10 who enjoyed The Lady Soldier, for example.

You're taking a university creative writing course at the moment. Why?

We're covering short stories, poetry and life writing. What I'm hoping is that it will force me to expand and try things I wouldn't normally do. I'm thinking more about my writing as a result and think there will be some benefit in my novels. In hindsight, I should have signed up for an evening class when I started writing novels. I'm now a member of a local writers circle and it's very helpful to get that critique from people. I think you're always learning.

For Romance Writers

Resources

Where to Look for More Information

Below is a list of invaluable resources specifically for romance writers. To order any of the Writer's Digest Books titles or to get a consumer book catalog, call (800)448-0915. You may also order Writer's Digest Books selections through www.fwbookstore.com, Amazon.com or www.barnesandnoble.com.

MAGAZINES:

• *Romance Writers Report*, Romance Writers of America, 16000 Stuebner Airline Rd., Suite 140, Spring TX 77379. (832)717-5200. Fax: (832)717-5201. E-mail: info@rwanational.org.

• *Romantic Times* Bookclub Magazine, 55 Bergen St., Brooklyn NY 11201. (718)237-1097. Web site: www.romantictimes.com.

BOOKS:

• *On Writing Romance: How to Craft a Novel That Sells*, by Leigh Michaels.

• *Writing Romances: A Handbook by the Romance Writers of America*, edited by Rita Clay Estrada and Rita Gallagher.

• *You Can Write a Romance*, by Rita Clay Estrada and Rita Gallagher (Writer's Digest Books)

• *Writing the Christian Romance*, by Gail Gaymer Martin

ORGANIZATIONS & ONLINE:

• Canadian Romance Authors' Network. Web site: www.canadianromanceauthors.com.

• Romance Writers of America, Inc. (RWA), 16000 Stuebner Airline Rd., Suite 140, Spring TX 77379. (832)717-5200. Fax: (832)717-5201. E-mail: info@rwanational.org. Web site: www.rwanational.org.

• Romance Writers of America regional chapters. Contact National Office (address above) for information on the chapter nearest you.

• The Romance Club. Web site: http://theromanceclub.com.

• Romance Central. Web site: www.romance-central.com. Offers workshops and forum where romance writers share ideas and exchange advice about romance writing.

• Writer's Market Web site: www.writersmarket.com.

• Writer's Digest Web site: www.writersdigest.com.

Gregory Frost

Making Fantasy Real

by Janice Gable Bashman

G regory Frost creates new worlds. He takes the ordinary and turns it into the extraordinary. For Frost, making fantasy real is about suspending reader disbelief and immersing the reader into a time and place where anything is possible. It's about making the unbelievable believable.

Frost is the author of nine books, including the recently released duology, Shadowbridge and Lord Tophet. He also has published more than 50 short stories in magazines, including The Magazine of Fantasy & Science Fiction, Isaac Asimov's Science Fiction Magazine, and Realms of Fantasy, and in anthologies such as Magic in the Mirrorstone and The Faery Reel. His story "The Final Act," is featured in Ellen Datlow's recent commemorative anthology, Poe: 19 New Tales Inspired by Edgar Allan Poe. Another of his stories, "Madonna of the Maquiladora," was a finalist for the James Tiptree, Jr. Award, the Theodore Sturgeon Memorial Award, the Hugo, and the SFWA Nebula Award. In addition to writing, Frost serves as a fiction writing workshop director at Swarthmore College.

You stated that the world you created for Shadowbridge and Lord Tophet—a world consisting of a never-ending bridge surrounded by ocean and divided by spirals and spans, each with a unique culture—is "a world that's an accretion of all of our possible myths, fairy tale elements, folk tales, oral tradition, and even the glosses on those that you can pull from Shakespeare, Blake, Byron and Rosetti." How did you create this world and what's special about it?

Well, you've just covered "what's special about it," so my work is done here.... Creating it was something of a monumental task, in that when you pour all of those possibilities into the mix, the story can go just about anywhere. Anyone and anything can show up. A trickster can appear—Monkey, or Coyote, or Spider; the Norse gods might walk in (and if they bring Loki along, you have another trickster); or a man named Burbage might create a theater and call it the Terrestre, bearing a strange similarity to the Globe Theatre of Shakespeare's world (even performing a lost play of the Bard's). The difficult part, finally, was tamping down an infinity of elements while trying to let the right ones emerge, like burls in a wood veneer. I think you do something like that anytime you're writing a work of fiction, anyway, but here it was a bit more challenging because there were so many possibilities, and because from them I was constructing stories that my character, Leodora, performs, and I wanted them to sound like stories we've heard before but not ever quite conform to those stories.

I'd been working with fairy tales for some years, writing stories for editors Terri Windling

---

JANICE GABLE BASHMAN writes for leading publications. She is a member of the International Thriller Writers (ITW) and contributing editor of *The Big Thrill* (the newsletter of the ITW). Janice can be reached at janicebashman@yahoo. com.

and Ellen Datlow (for anthologies like Snow White, Blood Red and The Faery Reel), reading books by Marina Warner, Jack Zipes, Maria Tatar, reading Navajo coyote tales, Japanese and Indian and Middle Eastern folk stories, books by Amos Tutuola...a lot of material that, in effect, was charging my battery. It was essential that cognizance be established before the time came for me to draw upon it. With material like this, I think it's best rising up out of the unconscious. I wanted to be as surprised by it as any reader. So while I had a general sense of a narrative structure, I kind of let the story lead me through it rather than me saying, "And here is where the next big thing happens."

The success of any good story lies in good storytelling; however, in fantasy, the story is rooted in an alternate world where reality is created and characters may not be human, i.e. mythical, animal, etc. Why is it so important to suspend reader disbelief?
My friend Nancy Kress would tell you that you do this with what she calls credible prose. But let's talk about suspending disbelief first. Fantasy and science fiction (and to some extent historical fiction) authors have an extra job to do on top of telling a good story. They have to create for you an entire landscape, a world that runs on its own rules, not those you're used to. In some cases those rules defy the rules of reality altogether, and at other times they've taken the laws of physics and made them into a "what might be" world—in either case, they've introduced you to a place that has never been before.

What happens then is that the world you create takes on the weight of an extra character in your fiction. Like a fictional character, it has a physical facet—the things you see; it has a sociological facet—the history and social evolution that has generated it, laws that have been passed, who invaded the country in the year 876 (and how that changed things forever), when the House of Lords filled up with vampires, etc.; and a psychological facet—is it a fascist state, or a utopia, or a dystopia. All of those sides have to agree, too. If it's a fascist state, then its social history will reflect how it got there, and its architecture will reflect this, too. If I create a world where people teleport from place to place, then there will be no traffic jams. Will there even be cars? If I have people who make their living with swords, then I'm not likely to have gunpowder, or else I'll have at most nascent and inaccurate firearms. Otherwise, we're going to have a lot of scenes out of the first Indiana Jones movie with some clown waving his scimitar about and being mowed down from across the town square by the guy with the Colt revolver.

That may sound trite, but it's extrapolative. Worlds must be organic, connective. Every feature you pick out for it has ripple effects and is the result of ripples. You as author must have some sense of these connections or your rules will be a mishmash of inconsistencies. Your reader will quickly decide this is a stupid place and will put your book or story down and pick up a book by someone who knows what the hell they're doing. And so, I think writing good science fiction and fantasy is very, very difficult.

So how do you accomplish the suspension of disbelief in your work?
The opening sentence of Shadowbridge is: "The first time Leodora spoke to a god, it was at the top of a bridge tower and she was masked." I've now in one sentence told you that we're way up on a tower above the bridge. I've introduced you to my main character, Leodora. You know she's a she. And you know that she's wearing a mask, which becomes important in this world where women are not allowed to be performers, and where because of the false identity she takes on—the persona called Jax—she inadvertently comes to attention of a force that is hunting for another shadowpuppeteer—you don't know that yet, but that's a ripple effect. The detail is an element of foreshadowing that the reader's unaware of, one that hints at a mystery and one that suggests a bit about the social order down below. You also know she's about to speak to a god, a clue here that this is not our world as such. We are someplace else, someplace new. And another mystery element.

From there it goes on with what I think is a clear, visual description of the world from her vantage high above it, further anchoring you in that world. But the mysteries of Leodora and her world have been dropped into the opening sentence, so that you're asking yourself what it means that she's going to speak to a god and why is it that she's masked? If you're busy with these questions, you will not even notice a world quickly being constructed around you. And to me that is also what Nancy means by credible prose. The narrative prose fits the story, welcomes you into the story, and maneuvers you so that you almost don't notice it being done to you. It's all a bit of prose legerdemain.

What are the key elements in creating a believable fantasy world, and what should a writer keep in mind when doing so?

First, what Gardner Dozois coined as "the ecology of the supernatural." As I said, your world has rules. Laws. If it's full of magic, then you have to know how the magic works. And it had sodding better work the same way in chapter 19 as it does in chapter one, or else you'd better have a really good excuse. You build the world, so you make the rules. The reader, once again, will soon suss out if you don't know what you're doing.

Second, and here I'm paraphrasing Jane Yolen, believe in your monsters. Whatever strangeness you create, however weird, inhuman, alien, fantastical your characters are, believe in them for the duration of this story. Because if you don't, neither will the reader. Your disbelief will translate on the page as condescension. No reader will stand for it.

Third, recognize how actual human societies work and have worked through history—what I said about the tripartite aspects of world building. Don't think "I'm going to have a world where everybody walks around armed with a handgun but nobody ever shoots anybody." Hey, good luck with that. And could you please show me the historical model of that society?

Explain how you incorporate these elements into your conception of new worlds.

One of the spans of Shadowbridge is called Hiyakiyako. The name translates roughly as "parade of monsters," and Leodora is warned almost immediately upon arriving not to stay out after dark because of the monsters on the span. It's a Japanese flavored span, and upon it Leodora meets a kitsune (a fox trickster) and a tanuki, two characters out of Japanese folklore. When she encounters them, the two are playing the Japanese board game of go.

As she is collecting stories from each span, the kitsune tells her a story about an emperor and a female kitsune. Afterwards, the kitsune offers to lead her back to the place where she is performing, but as they go, she discovers that he is leading the parade she's been warned to avoid. So the rules of the world—of this particular span—have come into play, and are internally consistent; and the strange creatures of the span are part of that internal consistency: They are expressions of the world they inhabit. That's the other thing about fantasy worlds—the people who inhabit them, however strange in our world, are expressions of that world, are as normal in that place as we are in ours. And we are pretty diverse within the confines of our own.

You stated that Shadowbridge "didn't so much change as evolve while [you were] writing it. It came more into focus." Explain why allowing a fantasy world to evolve, rather than sticking to an initial concept, is important in making fantasy real.

There are writers who stick to a form—who outline everything in detail and then stick to the outline right to the end. There are writers who, like Raymond Carver, follow a sentence down a rabbit hole and don't know where it's taking them. I fall somewhere in between. I outline to ensure that I have a story, a structure, as a point of reference, and once I'm satisfied that's the case I abandon the outline and let the story run.

In the case of Shadowbridge, I probably ended up composing five outlines by the end of the first book, because things I hadn't foreseen turned up, moving the story in new directions each time, and I had to reconsider each time. Fantasy often allows the exterior landscape, the imagined world, to reflect an inner, psychological landscape, a darkness within the writer, a disturbance in the field; and to me the best way to have that happen is not to ride roughshod over the proposed structure, but to let things emerge and see where they lead. I wouldn't do that in every book. For one thing, it takes much longer to draw upon, and you're bound to hit more dead ends. But here I felt it was essential, and if I'd written the initial outline point by point, I would have had a much less satisfying duology.

What advice would you give to writers about making fantasy real?

Remember that, whatever you're writing about, however alien your world, your culture, your people, you are, finally, writing about human beings for human beings, and you want your readers to understand, to empathize with your characters. However much extrapolation or invention you pump into the story, the book, finally you have to have some characters we care about. Frodo and Sam have some serious problems to resolve, and the harder it is for them, the more we root for them.

In The Golden Compass, Lyra has to take on an entrenched system of crypto-religious government to save her friends from spiritual annihilation. She's not entirely successful, either; but we care because she cares.

I love Michael Faber's novel Under the Skin because he presents a truly alien main character but makes her incredibly complex, interesting, and conflicted. She's dealing with questions of what makes for intelligent life and whether humans qualify, at the same time as she is helping to capture and slaughter them. It's a very fine science fiction novel with a lot of existential thought behind it. It's the characters who make the stories rich.

The better you know your people, the better the tale you're likely to tell.

Mary Rosenblum

'I Was Always a Story Maker'

by Chynna Tamara Laird

Ideas are all around. I can't help asking, 'but what if...?' and I've been doing that since I could talk," says science fiction writer Mary Rosenblum. "Drove my parents and teachers nuts, I did. Now I just let my characters ask those questions."

Rosenblum's characters have found their way to the pages of journals and books since the early 1990's. Her debut novel The Drylands (Del Rey) won the Compton Crook Award for Best First Novel from the Baltimore Science Fiction Society. Her novelette Gas Fish received the Asimov's Readers' Award and was a nominated for a Hugo. And since being touted as "one of the finest new writers to appear in the last several years," by Locus, Rosenblum has published seven novels including The Stone Garden (Del Rey) and Synthesis and Other Virtual Realities (Arkham House) and more than three dozen short stories in publications such as Asimov's and Ellery Queen. Horizons (Tor Books) is her latest novel.

In addition to her work as a writer, Rosenblum also teaches, serving as a private tutor for both adults and teens, a frequent conference speaker, and an instructor for Long Ridge Writers Group (www.longridgewritersgroup.com), for which she also serves as Web Editor and provides support to students and writers through the group's Website chat rooms, moderating live interviews, forums and After Hours discussions. Besides writing SF and mystery (under the name Mary Freeman) and teaching, Rosenblum is also a dog trainer, gardener and cheesemaker who grew all her own food while raising her two now grown boys on her own. With that sort of dedication, it's no wonder she ended up an award-winning writer.

What drew you to the to the science fiction genre?

I fell into SF when I was 12 and we vacationed for the first of several summers with my double cousins at Nag's Head, NC in a shared house. We kids had to endure a forced two-hour "rest time" every afternoon (the adults were the ones who needed it!) and I quickly ran through the books I'd brought from home. But under my bed was a box of Galaxy magazines. I was instantly hooked! My imagination always worked over time and suddenly I could contemplate museums on Mars (I remember that story vividly), crises in space, the life and death of vacuum outside a bare skin of hull, and the vastness of a universe that I

CHYNNA TAMARA LAIRD is a psychology student, freelance writer and author living in Edmonton, Alberta with her three daughters [Jaimie (six), Jordhan (four), and baby Sophie (almost one)] and baby boy, Xander (two). Her passion is helping children and families living with Sensory Processing Disorder and other special needs. You'll find her work in many online and in-print parenting, inspirational, Christian and writing publications in Canada, United States, Australia, and Britain. She's most proud of her children's picture book, *I'm Not Weird, I Have SID*, which she wrote for Jaimie. In addition, she'll have a memoir about raising a child with SPD out in August of 2009. Please visit Chynna's Web site at www.lilywolfwords.ca to get a feel for her work and what inspires her.

could by golly see by going outside at midnight and looking up!

What a way to step outside the things we have so taken for granted every day that we no longer really see and look at them with clear eyes. What a way to look at who we are and ask, "Where are we going? What are we doing?" in a way that makes people think. I fell in love with that genre and have never fallen out of love.

Yes, it is full of trashy stuff, but the good SF is, in my opinion, the most flexible and powerful genre of them all. You can make people think about big things without realizing it. (And I know it works because some readers have chided me for keeping them awake at night...thinking. Hehehe.)

When people most who aren't SF readers think about the genre, they think Star Wars, Star Trek or Close Encounters. What do you think is the definition of SF?

Science Fiction is the literature of tomorrow. Alas, it has been "pigeonholed" by Hollywood's space opera special effects movies like Star Wars, Alien, The Matrix, and so on. And of course, the gee-whiz-aren't-rockets-cool reputation of the '50s pulp fiction still lingers. But it really has come of age, and you can find very thoughtful attention to the social, technical, and ethical situations we're going to face in the near future. In my opinion it is all about thinking about tomorrow today...and having fun doing so!

Explain the different branches of the science fiction genres? What are the focuses of each?

In general, you have the "space opera" SF—fun adventures with aliens and faster than light travel to other worlds. You have military SF—wars, strategy, and battle in space. You have near future SF (my genre!) set in the near future with one foot still firmly planted in the real world of today (and reality keeps stepping on the heels of us near future folk!) And of course, within these basic divisions, you have a wide range of types of stories.

My favorite quote from you is: "Boredom and a regular day job are two things that seemed highly unappealing, even when I was a kid." Let's talk a bit more about when you got the writing bug. Your interest in SF started when you were a young girl but did you know you wanted to be a writer?

I was always a story maker. Any time I was bored and had no book nearby (or was sitting at a school desk) I made up stories to entertain myself. Sometimes they derived from stories I'd read, sometimes they were new, but stories were my way to Never Be Bored. But think of myself as a writer? No way! Writers were born, after all. They sprang full blown from the womb with scarlet "Ws" on their foreheads and if you didn't have that, you shouldn't even think about it. Such was the response to any "I want to be a writer" foolishness.

You've talked about re-telling the SF stories you'd read as a child with female protagonists. Can you describe how in doing this you decided, "Ah ha! This is my thing."?

Well, for a long time....many years....I just did it for myself because the stories really annoyed me. I wanted to play too, and they kept leaving me, and all other women, out. But then, I started publishing nonfiction and one day I just thought, "Why can't you publish the fiction, too?." I had been told by more than one English teacher that "just anybody" couldn't write publishable fiction. You had to be special. (The implication was that I was certainly not special). Hmm. I wish I had the addresses of those teachers right now. I could send them very large packing crates full of published fiction. COD!

Guess none of them will ever be in your list of dedications. Okay, let's talk about when you sit down at the keyboard. When it's time for you work on novels, how do you write? Is it difficult to get started/keep going/finish? What is your usual course of action?

I do most of my writing in my head these days. By that, I mean that I scribble notes, rough out a dramatic arc, and then play with characters, plot ideas, possible scenarios, until everything falls into place. Then I pound out that first draft. While waiting for the pieces to all line up, I generate quite the paper trail of notes scribbled in anything handy.

How do you stay motivated?

I don't think anyone can stay motivated 24/7 throughout an entire project. Well, maybe a very short one! Inevitably, my excitement flags, I start feeling like this is "so usual." Generally it's because I've had my nose pressed against this particular story for so long I've lost a sense of the larger picture. So then I go off and work on something else…another project. By the time I flag on that project, this one looks so wonderful again, and I'm off and running. I personally like to have three projects on the burners at all times.

You've participated in the Clarion West workshop (www.clarionwest.org) as both a student and an instructor. Why, in your opinion, is it such an important adventure?

Well, it is not a perfect fit for everyone. [As a student] I was simply in a place where I could make the most use of the intensive instruction and interaction that the workshop offered. I so much enjoyed teaching it this past summer. And I discovered that it's much harder to teach it than it is to participate! I was exhausted after one week!

You were a fetal endocrine researcher at one time. Do you draw upon your science background when conducting your research or actual writing? How important is the research?

I do indeed draw on my science background when I'm working on a SF story. It's very important to me to get the science right…to get all the factual details right. Otherwise you ruin your credibility with the readers. Believe me I have learned a LOT about areas of science I didn't know much about before. Research is great. I learn and the book or story is better.

One of the best pearls of wisdom I've heard you give is, "Don't ever throw anything away!" Have you ever had an experience that unearthing old material?

Never throw anything away! Just recently, searching through a bunch of very old files (more than ten years old) on my hard drive, I found a story I had written clear to the end, but couldn't make the end work. I had totally forgotten it. [When I reread it] I knew by the time I was one-third of the way through how it had to end. So I was able to add the working ending and send it out. It sold to SciFiction the top paying SF market at the time. There you go. Never throw anything away.

If a writer came to you with interest in SF, and it was a genre they'd never written in before, what advice would you give to that writer?

Don't try to market in the SF genre unless you read in the SF genre. It's very easy to reinvent the wheel, thinking that you've discovered something new and wonderful. Students who don't read SF do want to write it. My suggestion: Subscribe to Asimov's and Analog and read a year's worth of issues. Now you have a better feel for what SF is.

If one of your students had a phenomenal SF manuscript what suggestions would you give for approaching an agent or publisher with the idea? What should they do? Not do?

Get an agent if you want to sell to New York [publishers]. All the major publishers require agented material now. A way around that is to attend SF conventions and go to all the publishing panels. If you meet a SF editor, you may be able to submit something to that person later on (not at the convention, please!). When acquiring an agent, make sure that agent sells work regularly to the SF publishers and make sure, of course, that they belong to AAR.

Now you do have some very nice smaller presses who are "up and coming" in the SF universe and do not require agents (last I checked anyway). I'm thinking particularly of Nightshade, Tachyon, and Pyr. They're excellent, all three.

Did anyone hear any of those stories and encourage you to keep telling them?

Oh, gosh, I wish. That's really why I do as much support, teaching, help for novice writers as I do. Because I would have given anything to have someone take some interest in my story telling.

Brian Evenson

Truth Must Be Inflicted

by Kelcey Parker

I n Brian Evenson's 1995 book Dark Property: An Affliction, the bounty hunter Kline is interrogated by a man whose questions shift subtly but significantly from "What do you believe?" to "Do you believe?" The man writes down Kline's responses:

"I write only what you give me," said the man. "I impart only your truth."

"Truth cannot be imparted," said Kline. "It must be inflicted."

Kline proceeds to murder the man and stuff his body parts into the desk's drawers, "forc[ing] them shut until the pressed flesh was made to ooze."

It is through scenes—and language—like this that Evenson inflicts truth upon his readers, insisting on the violent power of words. On the one hand, the man in the scene is merely imparting truth by "inscrib[ing] words upon paper" while Kline seems to prove his own point about infliction by killing the man. On the other hand, the scene itself is nothing more than words inscribed upon paper; "Kline" is but a word on paper—and still the reader has an experience of violence. Evenson proves that inscription and infliction are not so very different at all.

Evenson's career began—and nearly ended—with the 1994 publication of Altmann's Tongue, a collection of stories and a novella that offended a student at Brigham Young University, where Evenson, then a practicing Mormon, was teaching at the time. The student called the book "a showcase" of violence, and when the university insisted that Evenson discontinue such writing, Evenson responded by saying, "My work offers a violence that cannot be enjoyed—it is a response to the kind of glamorization of violence that television and movies provide." Evenson resigned from his position at BYU and ultimately severed ties with the Mormon Church.

Now he is director of Brown University's Literary Arts program and has published more than a half-dozen award-winning novels and story collections that confound the distinctions between good and evil, life and death, and even literary and genre fiction. Evenson's story collection, The Wavering Knife, won an International Horror Guild award, and The Open Curtain, a novel about a Mormon teen who discovers a century-old murder case involving the grandson of Brigham Young, won a 2007 Lilly Award (Crime Fiction Category) and was a finalist for an Edgar Award. Evenson was also invited to write a book for the Aliens series, which he published as B. K. Evenson.

Here, Evenson discusses his writing process and publishing career, the pros and cons of

---

KELCEY PARKER's first book, a collection of stories, will be published by Kore Press in 2010. Her work has appeared in many literary journals, including Image, Indiana Review, Bellingham Review, Santa Monica Review, and Western Humanities Review. She has a Ph.D. from the University of Cincinnati and currently teaches creative writing and literature at Indiana University South Bend.

MFA programs, and where he thinks literature is headed. And he tells of how one fan took the idea of "inflicting truth" to a whole new level.

The Open Curtain contains a real-life murder story. Describe your process of researching the 1902 murder of Anna Pulitzer by Brigham Young's grandson, William Hooper Young, and of integrating that story into the novel's plot.

I stumbled across mention of the actual murder by accident and then everything else started to build up around it—it was the piece for a puzzle that I'd already started to make but didn't realize I was making. For research, I ended up reading a series of articles in the 1902 and 1903 New York Times, then went on to research it in other newspapers of the period. When I started, none of that stuff was available online (now a lot of it is), so I spent a lot of time with microfiche. At one point, after I'd run out of leads, I hired a research assistant to try to track down a piece William Hooper Young wrote and published called "Sunrise in Hell," but neither of us ever did manage to find it. Every once in a while some aspect of the Young case that I'd forgotten about would help me to consider what I was doing with the book as a whole.

I faced a lot of challenges writing the book, but these had more to do with learning how to structure a novel than with anything else. I went into the writing with an idea for how the novel would look and what would happen. That worked just fine for the first two sections, but when I got to the third and final section, the novel just wouldn't behave. I ended up spending several years writing and rewriting that section, and threw out probably around a thousand pages. But when I finally got it right, I knew it.

Your work is full of dopplegangers: Rudd and Lael in The Open Curtain, Theron and Aurel in "Two Brothers," and Altmann and Horst in "Altmann's Tongue," to name just a few. In most cases, the two are opposing personalities linked by brotherhood or, in "Altmann's Tongue," death. How would you describe the function of these doubles in your work?

I love doubles and doppelgangers; they're in almost everything I write, and if they're not there literally, they're there in terms of half-repeated ideas and themes or the way I use repeated syntactical and sound patterns. What I like best about doubles is that they're uncanny: There are two of them in one sense but since they're alike, they're not exactly two separate people. I like the tension of that and the confusion of something that both is and isn't individual. There's a kind of destructiveness to the pairings that you find in my work. For me, probably the uber-double story in my work is "By Halves" that probably expresses as well what I want to do with doubles as anything else.

Many critics and reviewers have quoted Kline's line in Dark Property: "Truth cannot be imparted. [...] It must be inflicted." Your fiction has a way of inflicting truth without using either force or moral commentary.

I just found out that somebody had this statement tattooed on them, half on each arm. Talk about inflicted... I like how Kafka's "In the Penal Colony" has a machine that harrows a word onto a criminal's flesh. As a reader, I think the kind of work I like best is work that stays with me, that has a permanent effect on me, that changes me, even if that change is something difficult and tough. As a writer, I'd like my readers to experience that as well. I think that's the key: making people experience the writing rather than simply being able to watch it from a distance. I like fiction that's not safe but also not gratuitous, fiction in which everything matters even if it hurts—probably partly because in life that sort of intensity and necessity so rarely happens.

How did Aliens: No Exit come about? What was it like to write for a popular series and for younger readers?

An editor at Dark Horse Comics had read my work and was interested in doing a project with me. She arranged Aliens: No Exit, but then left to start her own press, Underland. When she asked me to do it, I wasn't sure it was something I wanted to do—or even could do. She encouraged me to write a ten-page summary, which I did, and by doing that realized how much fun it could be. I grew up watching the Aliens movies, and it was fun to work in that world (though I should say that my particular book is hardly for younger readers—it's pretty intense).

Your books have been published at a variety of presses, large and small. Do you have a literary agent? Have you ever been turned down by a press you really wanted to work with?

I do have an agent, someone I've had for about six years now, and had other agents before that. My first book, Altmann's Tongue, was published by Knopf almost by sheer luck: I sent it cold to an editor there who I'd read about. He didn't like it was kind enough to pass it along to another editor who he thought would. That editor didn't take it, but was interested in working toward a story collection, which is what ended up being Altmann's Tongue. That editor left before I finished my second book. Sometimes I've been approached by presses, other times myself or my agent has found them, and often my changing presses has been due to chance or luck rather than anything else.

And yes, of course I've been turned down by presses I've wanted to work with. I've often had editors at New York presses who are very enthusiastic about the work but who run into problems with their marketing departments or trying to get approval. But all in all, I've been happy with the varied publishers I've had, and I've found that serious readers always manage to find the books.

In another interview you are quoted as saying: "I tend to throw away around half of what I write, and start a lot of stuff that doesn't work out. One has to know what not to publish, and be very strict with oneself." How do you determine what to publish and what to throw away?

I think you have to try to establish some objective distance on what you do, either through time or by reading a lot of other writers in the meantime and getting a kind of artificial distance from yourself. If I have doubts about a piece, I put it back in a drawer and let it sit for a while. Then I look at it again and try to think about it more objectively, either revising it or letting it go for good. At the same time, there are stories I've published in magazines that later I've chosen not to collect in story collections, which I felt weren't as strong as I'd hoped.

You're also a teacher a prestigious university. How do you help your students make similar determinations?

With my students, I try to make it clear that they're the only ones who can make the determination of whether to throw something away or try to submit it: I'm not there to tell them what's good; I'm there to help them to understand how they think about writing, and about their own writing.

Nathan Bransford, a literary agent at Curtis Brown who maintains a popular blog, posted an entry about the MFA program he would design, one that would "prepar[e] a writer for the writing market he/she will face upon graduation." He says, "Plot comes first. Style comes second."

I understand why that would make sense from his perspective, since his salary is based on how much he sells books for. The publishing market is quite varied, and seems to be moving away from the large houses and more toward mid-range and small presses, and most of those markets are open to work that approaches plot in a productive but non-conventional way. I do actually think plot is quite important, but I also don't think you can split things up in that way: plot and style depend on one another and influence one another and need to be seen as interconnected parts of the same narrative machine, which is driven by a particular aesthetic position.

I also think that the MFA program is one of the few times within a writer's life where they shouldn't have to think obsessively about their careers, a time where they have two years (or sometimes three) to really focus on the writing. For this reason, [at Brown] we fully fund every MFA student we accept and we fund everybody the same. Programs that have a large career component are great for the favorite student or for the student who knows how to play that game, but for every student that does well coming out of Iowa there are several who feel crippled by the process and who stop writing.

Having taught at a variety of programs, what do you think about the role of university in contemporary literature?

I think there are a lot of programs out there that have become too conservative, that are less interested in moving to new stages of contemporary literature and more interested in getting students to write a certain way or adopt a certain attitude and are still teaching writing in the way they were teaching it in the 1970s. There are some programs as well who teach their students to write toward contemporary market trends, but of course the market shifts quickly enough that by the time the student's finished a book the trends gone elsewhere.

I think potentially the universities can be the places where the next stages of contemporary literature can be formed, the places where ideas are born that start to lead us into new territories, new waters, and in my own teaching I try to take this very seriously. We read a lot of contemporary work from all over the world, talk about it a lot. We talk about structure and style, but also aesthetics and different ways of thinking about fiction and what it does. Since I feel that the workshop can often lead to a norming process that isn't useful, I try to break it up a little bit by doing what I call a diminishing workshop where we move into progressively smaller groups and speak progressively longer about each story. I try to make students conscious of the tendencies in their fiction and to teach them how to take full advantage of them in their own terms and to make them aware of both how they fit in with the writers around them and how they differ from it.

As "the next stages of contemporary literature" are forming, what do you see happening? Where do you think fiction is headed?

I see a lot of different things starting to happen right now, all of which will have some impact on the shape of fiction in the future. One is that the kinds of writers who ten years ago would have been completely rejecting genre writing are now learning from it, realizing that there are things about science fiction and fantasy and horror that are interesting and useful, that there's a great deal of very well written genre writing that cuts genuinely new ground. The categories that we thought were clear and distinct no longer are. Another similar thing is that I see a lot of fiction moving closer to poetry, concerning itself with language in a very intense way. A third thing is that I see a lot of young writers there interested in intensive or experiential fiction, fiction that makes you feel like you're undergoing an experience. I think the combination of those three things, sometimes in very different ways, points to where fiction is heading. But what further complications those trends will lead to and what other trends will develop, I don't know.

Patricia Briggs

Hitting the Heights with Urban Fantasy

by T.E. Lyons

February 2009 saw the hardcover release of Patricia Brigg's "Bone Crossed," the fourth novel of a series focusing on the world of Mercedes (Mercy) Thompson—an auto mechanic in the Pacific Northwest whose life takes some very unusual turns. Mercy has lived among packs of werewolves, she's threaded uneasy alliances with vampires…and she can turn into a coyote.

Briggs' biggest-selling titles are part of the tsunami that has swept over bookstores in recent years, placing vampires and shape-shifters and predatory demons on everything from mainstream fiction to thrillers and romances—as well as the speculative fiction genres of fantasy, science fiction and horror. The author identifies with the urban fantasy subgenre, where monster-in-the-modern world scenarios have been developed for decades in hands such as H.P. Lovecraft, Fritz Leiber, and Charles deLint. Once authors such as Laurell K. Hamilton and Charlaine Harris nudged this type of story closer to romance and brought in humor, the growth in readership was startling. As 2009 began, Briggs' publisher Ace had still not had any urban fantasy title that had failed.

Briggs' response to having her 13th novel go to hardback is typically modest: "When you're like me, where you took 15 years to become an instant overnight success, you understand that it's the 'Good Luck' Fairy that hit you." In conversation, her knowledge of her peers, inspirations, and followers borders on the encyclopedic. She clearly cares about writers at all stages.

Her own writing career began when the Montana native was adjusting to a move to Chicago. She found retreat from the faster pace and denser population in drafting a traditional fantasy story. To her own surprise, a publisher bought "Masques" (currently out of print, but under contract for an eventual revised version). That book didn't sell well, but subsequent novels, featuring "high fantasy" elements such as dragons and imaginary lands, gradually grew a significant audience as well as praise from critics and peers.

Acting on a suggestion that she try modern characters and settings, Briggs created Mercy Thompson (for "Moon Called"), and the character was a hit. After Mercy Thompson novels began reaching the New York Times Paperback Bestseller List, some of the series' characters became part of "Alpha and Omega," which was first an award-winning novella in a paranormal romance anthology but has since become its own series of novels.

The Tri-Cities area of Washington State (also the setting of the Mercy Thompson series) is home to Briggs and her family. Her husband Mike aids in her literary life in numerous ways—

T.E. LYONS' writing muse was ignited soon after he first became a father in the early 1990s. His publishing credits include more than one thousand pieces—primarily music and book reviews, previews and features, but also several dozen short stories. New Jersey born and raised, he now lives in northern Virginia.

particularly as a relentless researcher. They have appeared together at Fantasy/Sci-Fi conventions to recount one of their favorite projects: engaging metallurgists and weaponry experts to determine practical processes for producing silver bullets (the legendary means for dispatching werewolves).

Besides visiting on the nature of werewolves, Patricia Briggs talks here about her writing routine—and how her workstyle changed when she had to make an exception; how she deals with writing two novel series in the same fantasy world; and what it's like to step up from paperback to hardcover.

At a recent fantasy/science fiction convention, you passed along the following advice to aspiring authors: "Write in genres. People read genres, and [they're] looking for new authors." But some other successful authors tell writers that they shouldn't let themselves be pigeonholed.

It depends on what you want to do. If you want to earn a living writing, it is much easier to build up a career writing in genres.

You can be an awesome writer and get lucky; you can be an awesome writer and not get lucky. I know some terrific writers who write stories that don't fit into genres and can't get published. And they ought to be—they're great. I know some "okay" writers who write in genres, and build a readership. So, it's what you want out of your career. There's no wrong way, no right way…but if you want to get published, go ahead and write genre.

Fantasy is such a broad genre that you're not going to be pigeonholed: urban fantasy, traditional fantasy, you can write Sword & Sorcery, you can write a Dave Duncan "Silver Blades" kind of thing, and still do just fine. It'll still be fantasy, and you won't lose your readers from that. It's a perspective thing.

Werewolves in romance: It's a model of power and psychological exchanges in relationships, yes?

Yes, I think werewolves are very interesting psychological things, because of the beast in all of us.

It's the old Native Americans myth that says you have two wolves inside you. One of them is mean and evil and has all the wicked thoughts, and the other is good and kind…and the person you are depends on which wolf you feed. And I think that's really true.

We all have the basic inner…child that wants things that it wants, and it doesn't care about anybody else, and it's jealous and it's nasty and vindictive. And we all have what we hope is the better part of us, that takes control. And what the werewolf does, essentially, is release the wolf.

There's a lot of tragedy involved in the traditional werewolf story. You can be a great person, a loving person, give to all the right charities, see to the children…but If you get bitten by a werewolf (or however you're infected), suddenly you are a ravening sociopathic killer. In the traditional werewolf story, the werewolf has no control over what it does, it just goes out and kills. Because you have no control over it, you're damned.

Contaminated through no fault of his own, the only way he can save everybody else is to die himself. So here you have sacrifice, you have innocence and loss. This tragic theme runs through the werewolf. For the happy-ending kind of person, I've chosen to do things like give my werewolves an amount of control—but they still go out of control.

Choosing to shift perspective within the same world: First person for the Mercy Thompson series. For the Alpha & Omega stories, you're writing in the third person, but it's a little omniscient…

Yes. I head-hop. It's something that romance readers learn to deal with—hopping [between] the male and female characters' head quite often. If you're starting to write, don't head-hop! It's hard on your readers. On the other hand, as a writer it's really something to do.

The [Alpha & Omega series'] original story, from "On the Prowl," is in third person—and that's because I have parts of the story that happen with only one or the other [narrative] character in it.

Keeping this up for the novels was actually kind of a gift, because I'm alternating—writing Mercy books and then writing Alpha & Omega books. It's very easy for a writer, when you're doing two continuing series, to get the personalities of your main characters mixed up. Because after all, they're all part of you.

It's a gift to be able to write first person and then third person. I usually have a day or two of stumbling around, because I'm used to doing "I" stuff and now I have to do "she" stuff. But it gives both books a very different flavor.

Some people don't like it, saying they don't read the same—but for me that's better than if people read both books and they say they're the same.

You're not going to have a second-person novel in your future, are you?

I can't imagine it. I'm a control freak, and second-person novels spin the hair on the back of my head. Because somebody else is telling me what I'm doing!

I want the words of the story to get out of my readers' way. When you do something like second-person, you're hitting them in the face with the fact that they're reading a work of literature, because they have to pay attention to the prose.

As you write, how much do your drafts expand or contract?

The first draft comes out at whatever length it comes out. If I come to a scene that doesn't speak to me, I just go on. Sometimes I'll just say "transition scene here" as I'm going. The second time I go through, mostly it's to enrich those scenes, and add pages so they come out full and round.

The first [draft] may come out as little as 60,000 words or as many as 150,000 words. In the second draft, I'm sometimes trimming down the excess—things that I thought were really cool when I was writing them, but now as I'm reading in my editorial mode, I think, "This is really stupid. I should take it out." But most of the time I'm fleshing out in the second run-through.

And then in the final edits before I send it to my editor—or after my editor has gone through it—quite often, I'm cutting down. I refine people's speech, so they say it in fewer words or more clearly so that readers don't get bogged down.

Do you carry your entire world in your mind? No outlines, no notes?

I'm a terrible mapmaker but I've done crude maps for various and sundry books. Now I have a good friend who does maps for me.

"Raven's Shadow" I took a lot of notes for. That was my first attempt at a big fantasy, and I found that I needed them. Sometimes there were scenes that I wrote out and then would cut them up—literally. I'd print them up on paper, cut them out, and move them around to see how they worked best. Because with so many characters, from scenes happening with different people happening at the same time, and trying to figure out how to keep the story tension up while I had these events taking place. That was an interesting thing to do, for me—because usually I just write the story from beginning to end.

Outlines? Most of the time I write faster without them. If I write from an outline, I know where it's going. And then it's really hard to motivate myself to go write it, because it's not fun.

I know people who outline and do a good job; I know people who don't outline and do a good job; and when a book is well-done, I can't tell the difference. But if there are a few problems, I can tell which way they write. People who write like me have characters who tend to disappear and don't come back in; or plot points that never tie back into the story. People who write from outlines tend to have very predictable stories. As a reader, I'd rather read someone who's writing hither and yon and have a few things that don't tie back in, than read something that I can predict really well.

Is that one of the distinctions between paranormal romance and urban fantasy—that paranormals, as part of genre romance, have a greater predictability?

I haven't thought of that as a difference. Good writing is good writing—it doesn't matter the genre—and it should not be predictable. In romance you know the hero and heroine are going to get together, and I just kind of tune that out. I know that's going to happen, so what else is going on in the story?

I think the big differences are in world-building; paranormal romance readers don't care about the world; they want to read about the romance. The world is nice and good and fine, but if you spend too much time doing world-building, your readers get impatient. In urban fantasy, world-building is much more important. The world has to work: It has to have internal logic, and it has to feel real.

You wrote "Raven's Strike," the second book of a duology, under circumstances you've not had before or since. You experienced some panic and a need to increase your speed to meet an already-extended deadline. Was it a good experience, learning to push through like that? Do you recommend long hours, no sleep, or real big bursts of producing under pressure?

That was a very uncomfortable thing for me—but there were some real cool things that came out of it.

One of the real drawbacks to writing a novel over a period of months, or years, is that you have to rely on your memory a lot. Or you have to go back and reread a lot. But writing a novel in—say, from beginning to end including edits, probably about 3 months—you're more efficient. I remember the first scene, and I remember the last day I wrote—and "Raven's Strike" is the longest book I've written, at over 125,000 words. I didn't have to go back and check what I was writing, because I remembered what I'd written.

It also forced me to do the kind of "gestalt" thing, where you throw yourself into the book. Which I actually really liked. What I didn't like is that it's very hard to come out of. My real life had to go by the wayside. I didn't pay bills. I didn't make dinner for the kids. It's a little dangerous to lose yourself in a story that much.

Did your editor or agent tell you when you were moving to hardback?

"Iron Kissed" went #1 on the New York Times [Paperback Fiction List], which was really just awesome and astounding. It was a shock to all of us when "Blood Bound" hit the New York Times list—we were all dancing around and happy...but when "Iron Kissed" went to Number 1, it was just dumbfounding. Part of it was sheer dumb luck: Laurel Hamilton, for instance, didn't have a paperback coming out, and neither did Nora Roberts.

So after that, Anne [Sowards, her editor at Ace] called and said that the next Mercy [Thompson] book they'd bring out in hardback. The reason was because the publicity people said, "Once you've reached Number 1, there's no sense in keeping in paperback. You might as well go on to hardback, because you're not going to build up any more momentum than that. "

It is kind of scary, but kind of cool, too...I'm no longer just a paperback writer.

Resources

Where to Look for More Information

Below is a list of invaluable resources specifically for science fiction, fantasy and horror writers. To order any of the Writer's Digest Books titles or to get a consumer book catalog, call (800)448-0915. You may also order Writer's Digest Books selections through www.fwbookstore.com, Amazon.com, or www.barnesandnoble.com.

MAGAZINES:
- *Locus*, P.O. Box 13305, Oakland CA 94661. E-mail: locus@locusmag.com. Web site: www.locusmag.com.
- *The Horror Writer*, P.O. Box 1188, Long Beach NY 11561. Web site: www.bloodmoonrisingmagazine.com/horrorwritermag.html.
- SPECFICME! (bimonthly PDF newsletter). Web site: www.specficworld.com.

BOOKS (by Writer's Digest Books):
- *How to Write Science Fiction & Fantasy*, by Orson Scott Card
- *The Writer's Complete Fantasy Reference*, from the editors of Writer's Digest Books
- *On Writing Horror*, edited by Mort Castle

ORGANIZATIONS & ONLINE:
- Fantasy-Writers.org. Web site: www.fantasy-writers.org.
- Horror Writers Association, P.O. Box 50577, Palo Alto CA 94303. Web site: www.horror.org.
- Science Fiction & Fantasy Writers of America, Inc., P.O. Box 877, Chestertown MD 21620. E-mail: execdir@sfwa.org. Website: www.sfwa.org/.
- SF Canada, 303-2333 Scarth St., Regina SK S4P 2J8. Web site: www.sfcanada.ca.
- SpecFicWorld. Web site: www.specficworld.com. Covers all 3 speculative genres (science fiction, fantasy and horror).
- Books and Writing Online. Web site: www.interzone.com/Books/books.html.
- Writer's Market Web site: www.writersmarket.com.
- Writer's Digest Web site: www.writersdigest.com.

Literary Agents

Many publishers are willing to look at unsolicited submissions but most feel having an agent is in the writer's best interest. In this section, we include agents who specialize in or represent fiction.

The commercial fiction field is intensely competitive. Many publishers have small staffs and little time. For that reason, many book publishers rely on agents for new talent. Some publishers are even relying on agents as ``first readers'' who must wade through the deluge of submissions from writers to find the very best. For writers, a good agent can be a foot in the door—someone willing to do the necessary work to put your manuscript in the right editor's hands.

It would seem today that finding a good agent is as hard as finding a good publisher. Yet those writers who have agents say they are invaluable. Not only can a good agent help you make your work more marketable, an agent also acts as your business manager and adviser, protecting your interests during and after contract negotiations.

Still, finding an agent can be very difficult for a new writer. If you are already published in magazines, you have a better chance than someone with no publishing credits. (Some agents read periodicals searching for new writers.) Although many agents do read queries and manuscripts from unpublished authors without introduction, referrals from their writer clients can be a big help. If you don't know any published authors with agents, attending a conference is a good way to meet agents. Some agents even set aside time at conferences to meet new writers.

Almost all the agents listed here have said they are open to working with new, previously unpublished writers as well as published writers. They do not charge a fee to cover the time and effort involved in reviewing a manuscript or a synopsis and chapters, but their time is still extremely valuable. Only send an agent your work when you feel it is as complete and polished as possible.

USING THE LISTINGS

It is especially important that you read individual listings carefully before contacting these busy agents. The first information after the company name includes the address and phone, fax, e-mail address (when available) and Web site. **Member Agents** gives the names of individual agents working at that company. (Specific types of fiction an agent handles are indicated in parentheses after that agent's name). The **Represents** section lists the types of fiction the agency works with. Reading the **Recent Sales** gives you the names of writers an agent is currently working with and, very importantly, publishers the agent has placed manuscripts with. **Writers' Conferences** identifies conferences an agent attends (and where you might possibly meet that agent). **Tips** presents advice directly from the agent to authors.

Also, look closely at the openness to submissions icons that precede most listings. They will indicate how willing an agency is to take on new writers.

☑ ACACIA HOUSE PUBLISHING SERVICES, LTD.

62 Chestnut Ave., Brantford ON N3T 4C2 Canada. (519)752-0978. **Contact:** (Ms.) Frances Hanna or Bill Hanna. Represents 100 clients. Currently handles nonfiction books (30%), novels (70%).

- Ms. Hanna has been in the publishing business for 30 years, first in London as a fiction editor with Barrie & Jenkins and Pan Books, and as a senior editor with a packager of mainly illustrated books. She was condensed books editor for 6 years for *Reader's Digest* in Montreal and senior editor and foreign rights manager for William Collins & Sons (now HarperCollins) in Toronto. Mr. Hanna has more than 40 years of experience in the publishing business.

Member Agents Frances Hanna; Bill Hanna, vice president (self-help, modern history, military history).

Represents nonfiction books, novels. **Considers these nonfiction areas:** animals, biography, language, memoirs, military, music, nature, film, travel. **Considers these fiction areas:** adventure, detective, literary, mainstream, mystery, thriller. This agency specializes in contemporary fiction—literary or commercial. Actively seeking outstanding first novels with literary merit. Does not want to receive horror, occult or science fiction.

How to Contact Query with outline, SASE. *No unsolicited mss.* No phone queries. Responds in 6 weeks to queries.

Terms Agent receives 15% commission on English language sales; 20% commission on dramatic sales; 25% commission on foreign sales. Charges clients for photocopying, postage, courier.

Tips "We prefer that writers be previously published, with at least a few short stories or articles to their credit. Strongest consideration will be given to those with three or more published books. However, we would take on an unpublished writer of outstanding talent."

☑ THE AHEARN AGENCY, INC.

2021 Pine St., New Orleans LA 70118. E-mail: pahearn@aol.com. Website: www.ahearnagency.com. **Contact:** Pamela G. Ahearn. Other memberships include MWA, RWA, ITW. Represents 35 clients. 20% of clients are new/unpublished writers. Currently handles novels (100%).

- Prior to opening her agency, Ms. Ahearn was an agent for 8 years and an editor with Bantam Books.

Represents Considers these fiction areas: contemporary, glitz, psychic, adventure, detective, ethnic, family, feminist, historical, humor, literary, mainstream, mystery, regional, romance, thriller. "This agency specializes in historical romance and is also very interested in mysteries and suspense fiction. Does not want to receive category romance, science fiction or fantasy."

How to Contact Query with SASE. Accepts simultaneous submissions. Responds in 8 weeks to queries. Responds in 10 weeks to mss. Obtains most new clients through recommendations from others, solicitations, conferences.

Terms Agent receives 15% commission on domestic sales. Agent receives 20% commission on foreign sales. Offers written contract, binding for 1 year; renewable by mutual consent.

Writers Conferences Moonlight & Magnolias; RWA National Conference; Thriller Fest; Florida Romance Writers; Bouchercon; Malice Domestic.

Tips "Be professional! Always send in exactly what an agent/editor asks for—no more, no less. Keep query letters brief and to the point, giving your writing credentials and a very brief summary of your book. If one agent rejects you, keep trying—there are a lot of us out there!"

⊞ ☑ AITKEN ALEXANDER ASSOCIATES

18-21 Cavaye Place, London England SW10 9PT United Kingdom. (44)(207)373-8672. Fax: (44)(207)373-6002. E-mail: reception@aitkenalexander.co.uk. Website: www.aitkenalexander.co.uk. **Contact:** Submissions Department. Represents 300+ clients. 10% of clients are new/unpublished writers.

Member Agents Gillon Aitken, agent; Clare Alexander, agent; Andrew Kidd, agent; Lesley Thorne, film/television.

Represents nonfiction books, novels. **Considers these nonfiction areas:** current affairs, government, history, memoirs, popular culture. **Considers these fiction areas:** historical, literary. "We specialize in literary fiction and nonfiction."

How to Contact Query with SASE. Submit synopsis, first 30 pages. Responds in 6-8 weeks to queries. Obtains most new clients through recommendations from others, solicitations.

Terms Agent receives 15% commission on domestic sales. Agent receives 20% commission on foreign sales. Offers written contract; 28-day notice must be given to terminate contract. Charges for photocopying and postage.

Tips "Before submitting to us, we advise you to look at our existing client list to establish whether your work will be of interest. Equally, you should consider whether the material you have written is ready to submit to a literary agency. If you feel your work qualifies, then send us a letter introducing yourself. Keep it relevant to your writing (e.g., tell us about any previously published work, be it a short story or journalism; you may be studying or have completed a post-graduate qualification in creative writing; when it comes to nonfiction, we would want to know what qualifies you to write about the subject)."

ALIVE COMMUNICATIONS, INC.

7680 Goddard St., Suite 200, Colorado Springs CO 80920. (719)260-7080. Fax: (719)260-8223. E-mail: submissions@alivecom.com. Website: www.alivecom.com. Member of AAR. Other memberships include Authors Guild. Represents 100+ clients. 5% of clients are new/unpublished writers. Currently handles nonfiction books (50%), novels (40%), juvenile books (10%).

Member Agents Rick Christian, president (blockbusters, bestsellers); Lee Hough (popular/commercial nonfiction and fiction, thoughtful spirituality, children's); Beth Jusino (thoughtful/inspirational nonfiction, women's fiction/nonfiction, popular/commercial nonfiction & fiction); Joel Kneedler popular/commercial nonfiction and fiction, thoughtful spirituality, children's).

Represents nonfiction books, novels, short story collections, novellas. **Considers these nonfiction areas:** biography, business, child, how to, memoirs, religion, self help, womens. **Considers these fiction areas:** contemporary, adventure, detective, family, historical, humor, literary, mainstream, mystery, religious, thriller. This agency specializes in fiction, Christian living, how-to and commercial nonfiction. Actively seeking inspirational, literary and mainstream fiction, and work from authors with established track records and platforms. Does not want to receive poetry, scripts or dark themes.

How to Contact Query via e-mail. "Be advised that this agency works primarily with well-established, bestselling, and career authors." Obtains most new clients through recommendations from others.

Terms Agent receives 15% commission on domestic sales. Offers written contract; 2-month notice must be given to terminate contract.

Tips Rewrite and polish until the words on the page shine. Endorsements and great connections may help, provided you can write with power and passion. Network with publishing professionals by making contacts, joining critique groups, and attending writers' conferences in order to make personal connections and to get feedback. Alive Communications, Inc., has established itself as a premiere literary agency. We serve an elite group of authors who are critically acclaimed and commercially successful in both Christian and general markets.

AMBASSADOR LITERARY AGENCY

P.O. Box 50358, Nashville TN 37205. (615)370-4700. E-mail: Wes@AmbassadorAgency.com. Website: www.AmbassadorAgency.com. **Contact:** Wes Yoder. Represents 25-30 clients. 10% of clients are new/unpublished writers. Currently handles nonfiction books (95%), novels (5%).

- Prior to becoming an agent, Mr. Yoder founded a music artist agency in 1973; he established a speakers bureau division of the company in 1984.

Represents nonfiction books, novels. **Considers these nonfiction areas:** biography, child, current affairs, education, ethnic, government, health, history, how to, memoirs, money, popular culture, religion, self help, womens. **Considers these fiction areas:** adventure, ethnic, family, literary, mainstream, religious. "This agency specializes in religious market publishing and has excellent national media relationships, dealing primarily with A-level publishers. Actively seeking popular nonfiction themes, including the following: practical living; Christian spirituality; literary fiction. Does not want to receive short stories, children's books, screenplays or poetry."

How to Contact Query with SASE. Submit proposal package, outline, synopsis, 6 sample chapters, author bio. Accepts simultaneous submissions. Responds in 2-4 weeks to queries. Obtains most new clients through recommendations from others.

Terms Agent receives 15% commission on domestic sales. Agent receives 20% commission on foreign sales. Offers written contract.

☑ MARCIA AMSTERDAM AGENCY

41 W. 82nd St., Suite 9A, New York NY 10024-5613. (212)873-4945. **Contact:** Marcia Amsterdam. Signatory of WGA. Currently handles nonfiction books (15%), novels (70%), movie scripts (5%), TV scripts (10%).

- Prior to opening her agency, Ms. Amsterdam was an editor.

Represents novels, movie scripts, feature film, sitcom. **Considers these fiction areas:** adventure, detective, horror, mainstream, mystery, romance (contemporary, historical), science, thriller, young. **Considers these script areas:** comedy, romantic comedy.

How to Contact Query with SASE. Responds in 1 month to queries.

Terms Agent receives 15% commission on domestic sales. Agent receives 20% commission on foreign sales. Agent receives 10% commission on film sales. Offers written contract, binding for 1 year. Charges clients for extra office expenses, foreign postage, copying, legal fees (when agreed upon).

Tips "We are always looking for interesting literary voices."

☑ BETSY AMSTER LITERARY ENTERPRISES

P.O. Box 27788, Los Angeles CA 90027-0788. **Contact:** Betsy Amster. **1992**Member of AAR. Represents more than 65 clients. 35% of clients are new/unpublished writers. Currently handles nonfiction books (65%), novels (35%).

- Prior to opening her agency, Ms. Amster was an editor at Pantheon and Vintage for 10 years, and served as editorial director for the Globe Pequot Press for 2 years.

Represents nonfiction books, novels. **Considers these nonfiction areas:** art & design, biography, business, child guidance, cooking/nutrition, current affairs, ethnic, gardening, health/medicine, history, memoirs, money, parenting, popular culture, psychology, science/technology, self-help, sociology, travelogues, social issues, women's issues. **Considers these fiction areas:** ethnic, literary, quirky mysteries & thrillers, womens, high quality. "Actively seeking strong narrative nonfiction, particularly by journalists; outstanding literary fiction (the next Richard Ford or Jhumpa Lahiri); witty, intelligent commerical women's fiction (the next Elinor Lipman or Jennifer Weiner); mysteries that open new worlds to us; and high-profile self-help and psychology, preferably research based." Does not want to receive poetry, children's books, romances, Western, science fiction, action/adventure, screenplays, fantasy, techno thrillers, spy capers, apocalyptic scenarios, or political or religious arguments.

How to Contact For adult titles: b.amster.assistant@gmail.com. Submissions for children's and teen titles: b.amster.kidsbooks@gmail.com. See submission requirements online at website. The requirements have changed. Accepts simultaneous submissions. Responds in 1 month to queries. Responds in 2 months to mss. Obtains most new clients through recommendations from others, solicitations, conferences.

Terms Agent receives 15% commission on domestic sales. Agent receives 20% commission on foreign sales. Offers written contract, binding for 1 year; 3-month notice must be given to terminate contract. Charges for photocopying, postage, long distance phone calls, messengers, galleys/books used in submissions to foreign and film agents and to magazines for first serial rights.

Writers Conferences Squaw Valley Writers' Workshop; San Diego State University Writers' Conference; UCLA Extension Writers' Program; The Loft Literary Center.

EDWARD ARMSTRONG LITERARY AGENCY

fiction, PO Box 3343, Fayville MA 01745. (401)569-7099. **Contact:** Edward Armstrong. Currently handles other(100% fiction).

- Prior to becoming an agent, Mr. Armstrong was a business professional specializing in quality and regulatory compliance. **This agency is not taking submissions at this time.** Please continue to check back.

Represents novels, short story collections, novellas. **Considers these fiction areas:** mainstream, romance, science, thriller suspense. **This agency is not taking submissions at this time.** Please continue to check back. Does not want to receive nonfiction or textbooks.

How to Contact Query with SASE. Submit synopsis, 3 sample chapters, author bio. Accepts simultaneous submissions. Responds in 2-4 weeks to queries. Responds in 3 months to mss. Obtains most new clients through solicitations.

Terms Agent receives 5% commission on domestic sales. Agent receives 5% commission on foreign sales. This agency charges for photocopying and postage.

◪ ARTISTS AND ARTISANS INC.

244 Madison Ave., Suite 334, New York NY 10016. Website: www.artistsandartisans.com. **Contact:** Adam Chromy and Jamie Brenner. Represents 70 clients. 80% of clients are new/unpublished writers. Currently handles nonfiction books (50%), fiction 50%.

Member Agents Adam Chromy (fiction and narrative nonfiction); Jamie Brenner (thrillers, commercial and women's fiction, literary fiction, memoir, narrative nonfiction, books about pop culture/entertainment and YA).

Represents nonfiction books, novels. **Considers these nonfiction areas:** biography, business, child, cooking, current affairs, ethnic, health, how to, humor, language, memoirs, money, music, popular culture, religion, science, self help, sports, film, true crime, womens fashion/style. **Considers these fiction areas:** confession, family, humor, literary, mainstream. "My education and experience in the business world ensure that my clients' enterprise as authors gets as much attention and care as their writing." Working journalists for nonfiction books. No scripts.

How to Contact Query with SASE. Accepts simultaneous submissions. Responds in 2 weeks to queries. Responds in 2 weeks to mss. Obtains most new clients through recommendations from others, solicitations, conferences.

Terms Agent receives 15% commission on domestic sales. Agent receives 25% commission on foreign sales. Offers written contract; 1-month notice must be given to terminate contract. "We only charge for extraordinary expenses (e.g., client requests check via FedEx instead of regular mail)."

Writers Conferences ASJA Writers Conference.

Tips "Please make sure you are ready before approaching us or any other agent. If you write fiction, make sure it is the best work you can do and get objective criticism from a writing group. If you write nonfiction, make sure the proposal exhibits your best work and a comprehensive understanding of the market."

◻ AVENUE A LITERARY

419 Lafayette St., Second Floor, New York NY 10003. Fax: (212)228-6149. E-mail: submissions@avenuealiterary.com. Website: www.avenuealiterary.com. **Contact:** Jennifer Cayea. Represents 20 clients. 75% of clients are new/unpublished writers. Currently handles nonfiction books (40%), novels (45%), story collections (5%), juvenile books (10%).

  • Prior to opening her agency, Ms. Cayea was an agent and director of foreign rights for Nicholas Ellison, Inc., a division of Sanford J. Greenburger Associates. She was also an editor in the audio and large print divisions of Random House.

Represents nonfiction books, novels, short story collections, juvenile. **Considers these nonfiction areas:** cooking, current affairs, ethnic, health, history, memoirs, music, popular culture, self help, sports theater/film. **Considers these fiction areas:** family, feminist, historical, literary, mainstream, thriller, young women's/chick lit. "Our authors are dynamic and diverse. We seek strong new voices in fiction and nonfiction, and are fiercely dedicated to our authors."

How to Contact Query via e-mail only. Submit synopsis, publishing history, author bio, full contact info. Paste info in e-mail body. No attachments. Accepts simultaneous submissions. Responds in 8 weeks to queries. Obtains most new clients through recommendations from others, solicitations, conferences.

Terms Agent receives 15% commission on domestic sales. Agent receives 15% commission on foreign sales. Offers written contract; 30-day notice must be given to terminate contract.

Tips "Build a résumé by publishing short stories if you are a fiction writer."

◪ THE AXELROD AGENCY

55 Main St., P.O. Box 357, Chatham NY 12037. (518)392-2100. Fax: (518)392-2944. E-mail: steve@axelrodagency.com. **Contact:** Steven Axelrod. Member of AAR. Represents 15-20 clients. 1% of clients are new/unpublished writers. Currently handles nonfiction books (5%), novels (95%).

  • Prior to becoming an agent, Mr. Axelrod was a book club editor.

Represents nonfiction books, novels. **Considers these fiction areas:** mystery, romance, womens.

How to Contact Query with SASE. Accepts simultaneous submissions. Responds in 3 weeks to queries. Responds in 6 weeks to mss. Obtains most new clients through recommendations from others.

Terms Agent receives 15% commission on domestic sales. Agent receives 20% commission on foreign sales. No written contract.

Writers Conferences RWA National Conference.

☑ BAKER'S MARK LITERARY AGENCY

P.O. Box 8382, Portland OR 97207. (503)432-8170. E-mail: info@bakersmark.com. Website: www. Bakersmark.com. **Contact:** Bernadette Baker-Baughman or Gretchen Stelter. Currently handles nonfiction books (35%), novels (25%),(40% graphic novels).

Represents nonfiction books, novels, scholarly books, graphic novels. **Considers these nonfiction areas:** anthropology, art, biography, business, ethnic, gay, how-to, humor, popular culture, true crime, women's issues, women's studies comics/graphic novels. **Considers these fiction areas:** comic books, erotica, experimental, feminist, gay, historical, horror, literary, mainstream, mystery, thriller, young adult urban fantasy, magical realism. "Baker's Mark specializes in graphic novels and popular nonfiction with an extremely selective taste in commercial fiction." Actively seeking graphic novels, nonfiction, fiction (YA/Teen and magical realism in particular). Does not want to receive Westerns, poetry, sci-fi, novella, high fantasy, or children's picture books.

How to Contact Query with SASE or e-mail. "If interested, we will request representative materials from you." Accepts simultaneous submissions. Obtains most new clients through recommendations from others, solicitations.

Terms Agent receives 15% commission on domestic sales. Agent receives 20% commission on foreign sales. Offers written contract, binding for 18 months; 30-day notice must be given to terminate contract.

Writers Conferences New York Comic Convention, BookExpo of America, San Diego Comic Con, Stumptown Comics Fest, Emerald City Comic Con.

☑ BARER LITERARY, LLC

270 Lafayette St., Suite 1504, New York NY 10012. Website: www.barerliterary.com. **Contact:** Julie Barer. Member of AAR.

Represents nonfiction books, novels, short story collections. **Considers these nonfiction areas:** biography, ethnic, history, memoirs, popular culture, womens. **Considers these fiction areas:** ethnic, family, historical, literary, mainstream. This agency no longer accepts young adult submissions.

How to Contact Query with SASE.

Terms Agent receives 15% commission on domestic sales. Agent receives 20% commission on foreign sales. Offers written contract. Charges for photocopying and books ordered.

☑ LORETTA BARRETT BOOKS, INC.

fiction and non-fiction, 220 E. 23rd St., 11th Floor, New York NY 10010. (212)242-3420. Fax: (212)807-9579. E-mail: query@lorettabarrettbooks.com. Website: www.lorettabarrettbooks.com. **Contact:** Loretta A. Barrett, Nick Mullendore. Member of AAR. Currently handles nonfiction books (50%), novels (50%).

- Prior to opening her agency, Ms. Barrett was vice president and executive editor at Doubleday and editor-in-chief of Anchor Books.

Member Agents Loretta A. Barrett; Nick Mullendore; Gabriel Davis.

Represents nonfiction books, novels. **Considers these nonfiction areas:** biography, child guidance, current affairs, ethnic, government, health/nutrition, history, memoirs, money, multicultural, nature, popular culture, psychology, religion, science, self help, sociology, spirituality, sports, womens creative nonfiction. **Considers these fiction areas:** contemporary, psychic, adventure, detective, ethnic, family, historical, literary, mainstream, mystery, thriller. "The clients we represent include both fiction and non-fiction authors for the general adult trade market. The works they produce encompass a wide range of contemporary topics and themes including commercial thrillers, mysteries, romantic suspense, popular science, memoirs, narrative fiction and current affairs." No children's, juvenile, cookbooks, gardening, science fiction, fantasy novels, historical romance.

How to Contact See guidelines online. Use email or if by post, query with SASE. Accepts simultaneous submissions. Responds in 3-6 weeks to queries.

Terms Agent receives 15% commission on domestic sales. Agent receives 20% commission on foreign sales. Offers written contract. Charges clients for shipping and photocopying.

☑ BARRON'S LITERARY MANAGEMENT

4615 Rockland Drive, Arlington TX 76016. E-mail: barronsliterary@sbcglobal.net. **Contact:** Adele Brooks, president.

Represents nonfiction books, novels. **Considers these nonfiction areas:** business, cooking, economics, finance, foods, government, health, history, medicine, nutrition, psychology, science, technology, true crime business, investing, small business marketing, cook books, dating and relationships. **Considers these fiction areas:** action, adventure, detective, historical, horror, mystery, police, romance, science fiction, thriller medical and political thrillers, historical, chick lit, contemporary suspense, paranormal. Barron's Literary Management is a small Dallas/Fort Worth-based agency with good contacts in New York and London. Actively seeking tightly written, fast moving fiction, as well as authors with a significant platform or subject area expertise for nonfiction book concepts.

How to Contact Contact by e-mail initially. Send only a brief synopsis of your story or a proposal for nonfiction. Obtains most new clients through e-mail submissions.

Tips I strongly favor a e-mail queries. Have your book tightly edited, polished and ready to be seen before contacting agents. I respond quickly and if interested may request an electronic or hard copy mailing.

☑ FAYE BENDER LITERARY AGENCY

fiction and non-fiction equally., 337 W. 76th St., #E1, New York NY 10023. E-mail: info@fbliterary.com. Website: www.fbliterary.com. **Contact:** Faye Bender. Member of AAR.

Represents nonfiction books, novels, juvenile. **Considers these nonfiction areas:** young, memoirs, popular culture, womens narrative; health; biography; popular science. **Considers these fiction areas:** literary, young adult, middle-grade women's; commercial. "I choose books based on the narrative voice and strength of writing. I work with previously published and first-time authors." Does not want to receive genre fiction (Western, romance, horror, fantasy, science fiction).

How to Contact Query with SASE and 10 sample pages via mail or e-mail. Guidelines online.

Tips "Please keep your letters to the point, include all relevant information, and have a bit of patience."

☑ BENREY LITERARY

P.O. Box 812, Columbia MD 21044. (443)545-5620. Fax: (886)297-9483. E-mail: query@benreyliterary. com. Website: www.benreyliterary.com. **Contact:** Janet Benrey. Represents 35 clients. 20% of clients are new/unpublished writers. Currently handles nonfiction books (50%), novels (50%).

• Prior to her current position, Ms. Benrey was with the Hartline Literary Agency.

Represents nonfiction books, novels, scholarly, narrow focus. **Considers these nonfiction areas:** how to, religion, self help, true crime. **Considers these fiction areas:** adventure, detective, family, literary, mainstream, mystery, religious, romance, thriller, womens. This agency's specialties include romance, women's fiction, mystery, true crime, thriller (secular and Christian), as well as Christian living, church resources, inspirational. Actively seeking women's fiction, romance, mystery, suspense, Christian living, church resources. Does not want to receive fantasy, science fiction, Christian speculative fiction, erotica or paranormal.

How to Contact Query via e-mail only. Submit proposal package, synopsis, 3 sample chapters, author bio.More submission details available online Accepts simultaneous submissions. Responds in 6 weeks to queries. Responds in 3 months to mss. Obtains most new clients through recommendations from others, solicitations, conferences.

Terms Agent receives 15% commission on domestic sales. Agent receives 20% commission on foreign sales. Offers written contract; 30-day notice must be given to terminate contract. We pass on the out-of-pocket costs of copying and shipping manuscripts for new clients until we have made their first sales.

Tips Understand the market as best you can. Attend conferences and network. Don't create a new genre.

☑ MEREDITH BERNSTEIN LITERARY AGENCY

2095 Broadway, Suite 505, New York NY 10023. (212)799-1007. Fax: (212)799-1145. Member of AAR. Represents 85 clients. 20% of clients are new/unpublished writers. Currently handles nonfiction books (50%), other(50% fiction).

• Prior to opening her agency, Ms. Bernstein served at another agency for 5 years.

Represents nonfiction books, novels. **Considers these fiction areas:** literary, mystery, romance, thriller, young adult. "This agency does not specialize. It is very eclectic."

How to Contact Query with SASE. Accepts simultaneous submissions. Obtains most new clients through recommendations from others, conferences, developing/packaging ideas.

Terms Agent receives 15% commission on domestic sales. Agent receives 20% commission on foreign sales. Charges clients $75 disbursement fee/year.

Writers Conferences Southwest Writers' Conference; Rocky Mountain Fiction Writers' Colorado Gold; Pacific Northwest Writers' Conference; Willamette Writers' Conference; Surrey International Writers' Conference; San Diego State University Writers' Conference.

BLEECKER STREET ASSOCIATES, INC.

532 LaGuardia Place, #617, New York NY 10012. (212)677-4492. Fax: (212)388-0001. E-mail: bleeckerst@ hotmail.com. **Contact:** Agnes Birnbaum. Member of AAR. Other memberships include RWA, MWA. Represents 60 clients. 20% of clients are new/unpublished writers. Currently handles nonfiction books (75%), novels (25%).

- Prior to becoming an agent, Ms. Birnbaum was a senior editor at Simon & Schuster, Dutton/Signet, and other publishing houses.

Represents nonfiction books, novels. **Considers these nonfiction areas:** newage, animals, biography, business, child, computers, cooking, current affairs, ethnic, government, health, history, how to, memoirs, military, money, nature, popular culture, psychology, religion, science, self help, sociology, sports, true crime, womens. **Considers these fiction areas:** ethnic, historical, literary, mystery, romance, thriller, womens. "We're very hands-on and accessible. We try to be truly creative in our submission approaches. We've had especially good luck with first-time authors." Does not want to receive science fiction, westerns, poetry, children's books, academic/scholarly/professional books, plays, scripts, or short stories.

How to Contact Query with SASE. No email, phone, or fax queries. Accepts simultaneous submissions. Responds in 2 weeks to queries. Responds in 1 month to mss. "Obtains most new clients through recommendations from others, solicitations, conferences, plus, I will approach someone with a letter if his/her work impresses me."

Terms Agent receives 15% commission on domestic sales. Agent receives 25% commission on foreign sales. Offers written contract; 1-month notice must be given to terminate contract. Charges for postage, long distance, fax, messengers, photocopies (not to exceed $200).

Tips "Keep query letters short and to the point; include only information pertaining to the book or background as a writer. Try to avoid superlatives in description. Work needs to stand on its own, so how much editing it may have received has no place in a query letter."

BLISS LITERARY AGENCY INTERNATIONAL, INC.

1601 N. Sepulveda Blvd., #389, Manhattan Beach CA 90266. E-mail: query@blissliterary.com. Website: www.blissliterary.com. **Contact:** Jenoyne Adams.

Member Agents Prior to her current position, Ms. Adams was with Levine Greenberg Literary Agency.

Represents nonfiction books, novels, juvenile Willy Blackmore. **Considers these fiction areas:** literary, multicultural commercial. "Middle grade, YA fiction and nonfiction, young reader? Bring it on. We are interested in developing and working on projects that run the gamut—fantasy, urban/edgy, serious, bling-blingy? SURE. We love it all." "I haven't found it yet, but with a deep appreciation for anime and martial arts flicks, we are looking for the perfect graphic novel."

How to Contact Query via e-mail or snail mail. Send query, synopsis, one chapter, contact info. No attachments. Responds in 8 weeks to queries.

Tips "Non-query related matters can be addressed by e-mailing info@blissliterary.com."

✓ BOOKENDS, LLC

136 Long Hill Rd., Gillette NJ 07933. Website: www.bookends-inc.com; bookendslitagency.blogspot.com. **Contact:** Jessica Faust, Jacky Sach, Kim Lionetti. Member of AAR. RWA, MWA Represents 50+ clients. 10% of clients are new/unpublished writers. Currently handles nonfiction books (50%), novels (50%).

Member Agents Jessica Faust (fiction: romance, erotica, chick lit, women's fiction, mysterious and suspense; nonfiction: business, finance, career, parenting, psychology, women's issues, self-help, health, sex); Jacky Sach (mysteries, women's fiction, suspense, self-help, spirituality, alternative and mainstream health, business and career, addiction, chick-lit nonfiction); Kim Lionetti (women's fiction, mystery, true crime, pop science, pop culture, and all areas of romance)."

Represents nonfiction books, novels. **Considers these nonfiction areas:** newage, business, child, ethnic, gay, health, how to, money, psychology, religion, self help, sex, spirituality, true crime, womens.

Considers these fiction areas: detective, cozies, mainstream, mystery, romance, thriller, womens chick lit. "BookEnds is currently accepting queries from published and unpublished writers in the areas of romance (and all its sub-genres), erotica, mystery, suspense, women's fiction, and literary fiction. We also do a great deal of nonfiction in the areas of spirituality, new age, self-help, business, finance, health, pop science, psychology, relationships, parenting, pop culture, true crime, and general nonfiction." BookEnds does not want to receive children's books, screenplays, science fiction, poetry, or technical/military thrillers.

How to Contact Review Web site for guidelines, as they change.

☑ BOOKS & SUCH LITERARY AGENCY

52 Mission Circle, Suite 122, PMB 170, Santa Rosa CA 95409. E-mail: representation@booksandsuch. biz. Website: www.booksandsuch.biz. **Contact:** Janet Kobobel Grant, Wendy Lawton, Etta Wilson, Rachel Zurakowski. Member of AAR. Member of CBA (associate), American Christian Fiction Writers. Represents 150 clients. 5% of clients are new/unpublished writers. Currently handles nonfiction books (50%), novels (50%).

- Prior to becoming an agent, Ms. Grant was an editor for Zondervan and managing editor for *Focus on the Family*; Ms. Lawton was an author, sculptor and designer of porcelein dolls. Ms. Wilson emphasizes middle grade children's books. Ms. Zurakowski concentrates on material for 20-something or 30-something readers.

Represents nonfiction books, novels, juvenile books,. **Considers these nonfiction areas:** child, humor, religion, self help, womens. **Considers these fiction areas:** contemporary, family, historical, mainstream, religious, romance African American adult. This agency specializes in general and inspirational fiction, romance, and in the Christian booksellers market. Actively seeking well-crafted material that presents Judeo-Christian values, if only subtly.

How to Contact Query via e-mail only, no attachments. Accepts simultaneous submissions. Responds in 1 month to queries. Obtains most new clients through recommendations from others, conferences.

Terms Agent receives 15% commission on domestic sales. Agent receives 20% commission on foreign sales. Offers written contract; 2-month notice must be given to terminate contract. No additional charges.

Writers Conferences Mount Hermon Christian Writers' Conference; Society of Childrens' Writers and Illustrators Conference; Writing for the Soul; American Christian Fiction Writers' Conference; San Francisco Writers' Conference.

Tips "The heart of our agency's motivation is to develop relationships with the authors we serve, to do what we can to shine the light of success on them, and to help be a caretaker of their gifts and time."

☑ THE BARBARA BOVA LITERARY AGENCY

3951 Gulf Shore Blvd. No. PH 1-B, Naples FL 34103. (239)649-7263. Fax: (239)649-7263. E-mail: bovab4@aol.com. Website: www.barbarabovaliteraryagency.com. **Contact:** Barbara Bova, Michael Burke. Represents 30 clients. Currently handles nonfiction books (20%), novels (80%).

Represents nonfiction books, novels. **Considers these nonfiction areas:** biography, history, science, self help, true crime, womens social sciences. **Considers these fiction areas:** adventure, crime, detective, mystery, police, science fiction, suspense, thriller, women's, young adult teen lit. This agency specializes in fiction and nonfiction, hard and soft science.

How to Contact Query through website Obtains most new clients through recommendations from others.

Terms Agent receives 15% commission on domestic sales. Agent receives 20% commission on foreign sales. Charges clients for overseas postage, overseas calls, photocopying, shipping.

Tips "We also handle foreign, movie, television, and audio rights."

☑ BRADFORD LITERARY AGENCY

5694 Mission Center Road, #347, San Diego CA 92108. (619)521-1201. E-mail: laura@bradfordlit.com. Website: www.bradfordlit.com. **Contact:** Laura Bradford. Represents 50 clients. 20% of clients are new/unpublished writers. Currently handles nonfiction books (10%), novels (90%).

- Ms. Bradford started with her first literary agency straight out of college and has 14 years of experience as a bookseller in parallel.

Represents nonfiction books, novels, novellas, within a single author's collection anthology. **Considers these nonfiction areas:** business, child, current affairs, health, history, how to, memoirs, money, popular culture, psychology, self help, womens. **Considers these fiction areas:** adventure, detective, erotica, ethnic, historical, humor, mainstream, mystery, romance, thriller psychic/supernatural. Actively seeking romance (including category), romantica, women's fiction, mystery, thrillers and young adult. Does not want to receive poetry, short stories, children's books (juvenile) or screenplays.

How to Contact Query with SASE. Submit cover letter, first 30 pages of completed ms., synopsis and SASE. Send no attachments via e-mail; only send a query letter. Accepts simultaneous submissions. Responds in 10 weeks to queries. Responds in 10 weeks to mss. Obtains most new clients through solicitations.

Terms Agent receives 15% commission on domestic sales. Agent receives 20% commission on foreign sales. Offers written contract, non-binding for 2 years; 45-day notice must be given to terminate contract. Charges for photocopies, postage, extra copies of books for submissions.

Writers Conferences RWA National Conference; Romantic Times Booklovers Convention.

CURTIS BROWN, LTD.

10 Astor Place, New York NY 10003-6935. (212)473-5400. Website: www.curtisbrown.com. Alternate address: Peter Ginsberg, president at CBSF, 1750 Montgomery St., San Francisco CA 94111. (415)954-8566. Member of AAR. Signatory of WGA.

Member Agents Ginger Clark; Katherine Fausset; Holly Frederick; Emilie Jacobson, senior vice president; Elizabeth Hardin; Ginger Knowlton, vice president; Timothy Knowlton, CEO; Laura Blake Peterson; Maureen Walters, senior vice president; Mitchell Waters. San Francisco Office: Nathan Bransford, Peter Ginsberg (President)

Represents nonfiction books, novels, short story collections, juvenile. **Considers these nonfiction areas:** agriculture horticulture, americana, crafts, interior, juvenile, New Age, young, animals, anthropology, art, biography, business, child, computers, cooking, current affairs, education, ethnic, gardening, gay, government, health, history, how to, humor, language, memoirs, military, money, multicultural, music, nature, philosophy, photography, popular culture, psychology, recreation, regional, religion, science, self help, sex, sociology, software, spirituality, sports, film, translation, travel, true crime, womens creative nonfiction. **Considers these fiction areas:** contemporary, glitz, newage, psychic, adventure, comic, confession, detective, erotica, ethnic, experimental, family, fantasy, feminist, gay, gothic, hi lo, historical, horror, humor, juvenile, literary, mainstream, military, multicultural, multimedia, mystery, occult, picture books, plays, poetry, regional, religious, romance, science, short, spiritual, sports, thriller, translation, western, young, womens.

How to Contact Prefers to read materials exclusively. *No unsolicited mss.* Responds in 3 weeks to queries. Responds in 5 weeks to mss. Obtains most new clients through recommendations from others, solicitations, conferences.

Terms Offers written contract. Charges for some postage (overseas, etc.)

☑ BROWNE & MILLER LITERARY ASSOCIATES

410 S. Michigan Ave., Suite 460, Chicago IL 60605-1465. (312)922-3063. E-mail: mail@browneandmiller.com. **Contact:** Danielle Egan-Miller. Member of AAR. Other memberships include RWA, MWA, Author's Guild. Represents 150 clients. 2% % of clients are new/unpublished writers. Currently handles nonfiction books (25%), novels (75%).

Represents nonfiction books, novels. **Considers these nonfiction areas:** agriculture horticulture, crafts, animals, anthropology, biography, business, child, cooking, current affairs, ethnic, health, how to, humor, memoirs, money, nature, popular culture, psychology, religion, science, self help, sociology, sports, true crime, womens. **Considers these fiction areas:** glitz, detective, ethnic, family, historical, literary, mainstream, mystery, religious, romance, contemporary, gothic, historical, regency, sports, thriller paranormal, erotica. We are partial to talented newcomers and experienced authors who are seeking hands-on career management, highly personal representation, and who are interested in being full partners in their books' successes. We are editorially focused and work closely with our authors through the whole publishing process, from proposal to after publication. Actively seeking highly commercial mainstream fiction and nonfiction. Does not represent poetry, short stories, plays, screenplays, articles, or children's books.

How to Contact Query with SASE. *No unsolicited mss.* Prefers to read material exclusively. Put submission in the subject line. Send no attachments. Responds in 6 weeks to queries. Obtains most new clients through referrals, queries by professional/marketable authors.

Terms Agent receives 15% commission on domestic sales. Agent receives 20% commission on foreign sales. Offers written contract, binding for 2 years. Charges clients for photocopying, overseas postage.

Writers Conferences BookExpo America; Frankfurt Book Fair; RWA National Conference; ICRS; London Book Fair; Bouchercon, regional writers conferences.

Tips "If interested in agency representation, be well informed."

☑ PEMA BROWNE, LTD.

11 Tena Place, Valley Cottage NY 10989. E-mail: ppbltd@optonline.net. Website: www.pemabrowneltd. com. **Contact:** Pema Browne. Signatory of WGA. Other memberships include SCBWI, RWA. Represents 30 clients. Currently handles nonfiction books (25%), novels (50% novels/romance), juvenile books (25%).

- Prior to opening her agency, Ms. Browne was an artist and art buyer.

Represents nonfiction books, novels, juvenile reference books. **Considers these nonfiction areas:** juvenile, newage, business, child, cooking, ethnic, gay, health, how to, money, popular culture, psychology, religion, self help, spirituality, womens reference. **Considers these fiction areas:** contemporary, glitz, adventure, feminist, gay, historical, juvenile, literary, mainstream, commercial, mystery, picture books, religious, romance, contemporary, gothic, historical, regency, young. "We are not accepting any new projects or authors until further notice."

How to Contact Query with SASE. No attachments for e-mail.

Terms Agent receives 20% commission on domestic sales. Agent receives 20% commission on foreign sales.

Tips We do not review manuscripts that have been sent out to publishers. If writing romance, be sure to receive guidelines from various romance publishers. In nonfiction, one must have credentials to lend credence to a proposal. Make sure of margins, double-space, and use clean, dark type.

☑ BROWN LITERARY AGENCY

410 Seventh St. NW, Naples FL 34120. Website: www.brownliteraryagency.com. **Contact:** Roberta Brown. Member of AAR. Other memberships include RWA, Author's Guild. Represents 47 clients. 5% of clients are new/unpublished writers.

Represents novels. **Considers these fiction areas:** erotica, romance, single title and category, womens. This agency is selectively reading material at this time.

How to Contact Query via e-mail only. Response time varies.

Terms Agent receives 15% commission on domestic sales. Agent receives 20% commission on foreign sales. Offers written contract; 30-day notice must be given to terminate contract.

Writers Conferences RWA National Conference.

Tips "Polish your manuscript. Be professional."

☑ ANDREA BROWN LITERARY AGENCY, INC.

1076 Eagle Drive, Salinas CA 93905. E-mail: andrea@andreabrownlit.com. Website: www.andreabrownlit. com. **Contact:** Andrea Brown, president. 10% of clients are new/unpublished writers.

- Prior to opening her agency, Ms. Brown served as an editorial assistant at Random House and Dell Publishing and as an editor with Knopf.

Member Agents Andrea Brown; Laura Rennert (laura@andreabrownlit.com); Kelly Sonnack; Caryn Wiseman; Jennifer Rafe; Jennifer Laughran, associate agent; Jamie Weiss Chilton, associate agent, and Jennifer Mattson, associate agent.

Represents Juvenile nonfiction books, novels. **Considers these nonfiction areas:** juvenile nonfiction, memoirs, young adult narrative. **Considers these fiction areas:** juvenile, literary, picture books, young adult middle-grade, all juvenile genres.

How to Contact For picture books, submit complete ms, SASE. For fiction, submit short synopsis, SASE, first 3 chapters. For nonfiction, submit proposal, 1-2 sample chapters. For illustrations, submit 4-5 color samples (no originals). "We only accept queries via e-mail." Accepts simultaneous submissions. Obtains most new clients through referrals from editors, clients and agents. Check website for guidelines and information.

Terms Agent receives 15% commission on domestic sales. Agent receives 20% commission on foreign sales. Offers written contract.

Writers Conferences SCBWI; Asilomar; Maui Writers' Conference; Southwest Writers' Conference; San Diego State University Writers' Conference; Big Sur Children's Writing Workshop; William Saroyan Writers' Conference; Columbus Writers' Conference; Willamette Writers' Conference; La Jolla Writers' Conference; San Francisco Writers' Conference; Hilton Head Writers' Conference: Pacific Northwest Conference; Pikes Peak Conference.

☑ TRACY BROWN LITERARY AGENCY

P.O. Box 88, Scarsdale NY 10583. (914)400-4147. Fax: (914)931-1746. E-mail: tracy@brownlit.com. **Contact:** Tracy Brown. Represents 35 clients. Currently handles nonfiction books (75%), novels (25%).

• Prior to becoming an agent, Mr. Brown was a book editor for 25 years.

Represents nonfiction books, novels anthologies. **Considers these nonfiction areas:** biography, cooking, current affairs, environment, foods, health, history, how-to, humor, medicine, memoirs, money, nature, personal improvement, popular culture, psychology, religious, self-help, sports, women's issues, women's studies. **Considers these fiction areas:** literary. Specializes in thorough involvement with clients' books at every stage of the process from writing to proposals to publication. Actively seeking serious nonfiction and fiction. Does not want to receive YA, sci-fi or romance.

How to Contact Submit outline/proposal, synopsis, author bio. Accepts simultaneous submissions. Responds in 2 weeks to queries. Obtains most new clients through referrals.

Terms Agent receives 15% commission on domestic sales. Agent receives 20% commission on foreign sales. Offers written contract.

☑ SHEREE BYKOFSKY ASSOCIATES, INC.

PO Box 706, Brigantine NJ 08203. E-mail: submitbee@aol.com. Website: www.shereebee.com. **Contact:** Sheree Bykofsky. Member of AAR. Other memberships include ASJA, WNBA. Currently handles nonfiction books (80%), novels (20%).

• Prior to opening her agency, Ms. Bykofsky served as executive editor of The Stonesong Press and managing editor of Chiron Press. She is also the author or co-author of more than 20 books, including *The Complete Idiot's Guide to Getting Published.* Ms. Bykofsky teaches publishing at NYU and SEAK, Inc.

Member Agents Janet Rosen, associate.

Represents nonfiction books, novels. **Considers these nonfiction areas:** americana, crafts, interior, newage, animals, art, biography, business, child, cooking, current affairs, education, ethnic, gardening, gay, government, health, history, how to, humor, language, memoirs, military, money, personal finance, multicultural, music, nature, philosophy, photography, popular culture, psychology, recreation, regional, religion, science, self help, sex, sociology, spirituality, sports, film, translation, travel, true crime, womens anthropolgy; creative nonfiction. **Considers these fiction areas:** literary, mainstream, mystery. This agency specializes in popular reference nonfiction, commercial fiction with a literary quality, and mysteries. I have wide-ranging interests, but it really depends on quality of writing, originality, and how a particular project appeals to me (or not). I take on fiction when I completely love it - it doesn't matter what area or genre. Does not want to receive poetry, material for children, screenplays, westerns, horror, science fiction, or fantasy.

How to Contact E-mail short queries to submitbee@aol.com. Please, no attachments, snail mail, or phone calls. Accepts simultaneous submissions. Responds in 3 weeks to queries with SASE. Responds in 1 month to requested mss. Obtains most new clients through recommendations from others.

Terms Agent receives 15% commission on domestic sales. Agent receives 20% commission on foreign sales. Offers written contract, binding for 1 year. Charges for postage, photocopying, fax.

Writers Conferences ASJA Writers Conference; Asilomar; Florida Suncoast Writers' Conference; Whidbey Island Writers' Conference; Florida First Coast Writers' Festibal; Agents and Editors Conference; Columbus Writers' Conference; Southwest Writers' Conference; Willamette Writers' Conferece; Dorothy Canfield Fisher Conference; Maui Writers' Conference; Pacific Northwest Writers' Conference; IWWG.

Tips Read the agent listing carefully and comply with guidelines.

☑ MARIA CARVAINIS AGENCY, INC.

1270 Avenue of the Americas, Suite 2320, New York NY 10019. (212)245-6365. Fax: (212)245-7196. E-mail: mca@mariacarvainisagency.com. **Contact:** Maria Carvainis, Donna Bagdasarian. Member of AAR. Signatory of WGA. Other memberships include Authors Guild, Women's Media Group, ABA, MWA, RWA. Represents 75 clients. 10%% of clients are new/unpublished writers. Currently handles nonfiction books (35%), novels (65%).

• Prior to opening her agency, Ms. Carvainis spent more than 10 years in the publishing industry as a senior editor with Macmillan Publishing, Basic Books, Avon Books, and Crown Publishers. Ms. Carvainis has served as a member of the AAR Board of Directors and AAR Treasurer, as well as serving as chair of the AAR Contracts Committee. She presently serves on the AAR Royalty Committee. Ms. Bagdasarian began her career as an academic at Boston University, then spent 5 years with Addison Wesley Longman as an acquisitions editor before joining the William Morris Agency in 1998. She has represented a breadth of projects, ranging from literary fiction to celebrity memoir.

Member Agents Maria Carvainis, president/literary agent; Donna Bagdasarian, literary agent; June Renschler, literary associate/subsidiary rights manager; Jerome Murphy and Alex Slater, literary assistants.

Represents nonfiction books, novels. **Considers these nonfiction areas:** biography, business, history, memoirs, science, pop science, womens. **Considers these fiction areas:** historical, literary, mainstream, mystery, thriller, young, womens middle grade. Does not want to receive science fiction or children's picture books.

How to Contact Query with SASE. to queries. Responds in up to 3 months to mss. Obtains most new clients through recommendations from others, conferences, query letters.

Terms Agent receives 15% commission on domestic sales. Agent receives 20% commission on foreign sales. Offers written contract. Charges clients for foreign postage and bulk copying.

Writers Conferences BookExpo America; Frankfurt Book Fair; London Book Fair; Mystery Writers of America; Thrillerfest; Romance Writers of America.

☑ CASTIGLIA LITERARY AGENCY

1155 Camino Del Mar, Suite 510, Del Mar CA 92014. (858)755-8761. Fax: (858)755-7063. Website: home.earthlink.net/~mwgconference/id22.html. Member of AAR. Other memberships include PEN. Represents 50 clients. Currently handles nonfiction books (55%), novels (45%).

Member Agents Julie Castiglia; Winifred Golden; Sally Van Haitsma; Deborah Ritchken.

Represents nonfiction books, novels. **Considers these nonfiction areas:** animals, anthropology, biography, business, child, cooking, current affairs, ethnic, health, history, language, money, nature, psychology, religion, science, self help, womens. **Considers these fiction areas:** ethnic, literary, mainstream, mystery, womens. Does not want to receive horror, screenplays, poetry or academic nonfiction.

How to Contact Query with SASE. Obtains most new clients through recommendations from others, solicitations, conferences.

Terms Agent receives 15% commission on domestic sales. Agent receives 25% commission on foreign sales. Offers written contract; 6-week notice must be given to terminate contract.

Writers Conferences Santa Barbara Writers' Conference; Southern California Writers' Conference; Surrey International Writers' Conference; San Diego State University Writers' Conference; Willamette Writers' Conference.

Tips "Be professional with submissions. Attend workshops and conferences before you approach an agent."

☑ JANE CHELIUS LITERARY AGENCY

548 Second St., Brooklyn NY 11215. (718)499-0236. Fax: (718)832-7335. E-mail: queries@janechelius. com. Website: www.janechelius.com. Member of AAR.

Represents nonfiction books, novels. **Considers these nonfiction areas:** humor, womens popular science; parenting; medicine; biography; natural history; narrative. **Considers these fiction areas:** literary, mystery, womens men's adventure. Does not want to receive fantasy, science fiction, children's books, stage plays, screenplays, or poetry.

How to Contact Please see Web site for submission procedures.

☑ ELYSE CHENEY LITERARY ASSOCIATES, LLC

270 Lafayette St., Suite 1504, New York NY 10012. Website: www.cheneyliterary.com. **Contact:** Elyse Cheney, Nicole Steen.

• Prior to her current position, Ms. Cheney was an agent with Sanford J. Greenburger Associates.

Represents nonfiction books, novels. **Considers these nonfiction areas:** biography, history, multicultural, sports, womens narrative. **Considers these fiction areas:** historical, horror, literary, romance, thriller.

How to Contact Query this agency with a referral. Include SASE or IRC. No fax queries. Snail mail or e-mail (submissions@cheneyliterary.com) only.

THE CHOATE AGENCY, LLC

1320 Bolton Road, Pelham NY 10803. E-mail: mickey@thechoateagency.com. Website: www.thechoateagency.com. **Contact:** Mickey Choate. Member of AAR.

Represents nonfiction books, novels. **Considers these nonfiction areas:** history, memoirs, by journalists, military or political figures biography; cookery/food; journalism; military science; narrative; politics; general science; wine/spirits. **Considers these fiction areas:** historical, mystery, thriller select literary fiction. Does not want to receive chick lit, cozies or romance.

How to Contact Query with brief synopsis and bio. This agency prefers e-queries, but accepts snail mail queries with SASE.

☑ WM CLARK ASSOCIATES

186 Fifth Avenue, Second Floor, New York NY 10010. (212)675-2784. Fax: (646)349-1658. Website: www.wmclark.com. Member of AAR. 50% of clients are new/unpublished writers. Currently handles nonfiction books (50%), novels (50%).

• Prior to opening WCA, Mr. Clark was an agent at the William Morris Agency.

Represents nonfiction books, novels. **Considers these nonfiction areas:** art, biography, current affairs, ethnic, history, memoirs, music, popular culture, religion, Eastern philosophy only, science, sociology, film, translation. **Considers these fiction areas:** contemporary, ethnic, historical, literary, mainstream Southern fiction. "Building on a reputation for moving quickly and strategically on behalf of his clients, and offering individual focus and a global presence, William Clark practices an aggressive, innovative, and broad-ranged approach to the representation of content and the talent that creates it. His clients range from authors of first fiction and award-winning bestselling narrative nonfiction, to international authors in translation, musicians, and artists."

How to Contact Accepts queries via online form only at www.wmclark.com/queryguidelines.html. Responds in 1-2 months to queries.

Terms Agent receives 15% commission on domestic sales. Agent receives 20% commission on foreign sales. Offers written contract.

Tips "WCA works on a reciprocal basis with Ed Victor Ltd. (UK) in representing select properties to the US market and vice versa. Translation rights are sold directly in the German, Italian, Spanish, Portuguese, Latin American, French, Dutch, and Scandinavian territories in association with Andrew Nurnberg Associates Ltd. (UK); through offices in China, Bulgaria, Czech Republic, Latvia, Poland, Hungary, and Russia; and through corresponding agents in Japan, Greece, Israel, Turkey, Korea, Taiwan, and Thailand."

☑ DON CONGDON ASSOCIATES INC.

156 Fifth Ave., Suite 625, New York NY 10010-7002. (212)645-1229. Fax: (212)727-2688. E-mail: dca@doncongdon.com. **Contact:** Don Congdon, Michael Congdon, Susan Ramer, Cristina Concepcion, Maura Kye-Casella, Katie Kotchman, Katie Grimm. Member of AAR. Represents 100 clients. Currently handles nonfiction books (60%), other(40% fiction).

Represents nonfiction books fiction. **Considers these nonfiction areas:** anthropology, biography, child, cooking, current affairs, government, health, history, humor, language, memoirs, military, music, nature, popular culture, psychology, science, film, travel, true crime, womens creative nonfiction. **Considers these fiction areas:** adventure, detective, literary, mainstream, mystery, short, thriller, womens. Especially interested in narrative nonfiction and literary fiction.

How to Contact Query with SASE or via e-mail (no attachments). Responds in 3 weeks to queries. Responds in 1 month to mss. Obtains most new clients through recommendations from other authors.

Terms Agent receives 15% commission on domestic sales. Agent receives 19% commission on foreign sales. Charges client for extra shipping costs, photocopying, copyright fees, book purchases.

Tips "Writing a query letter with a self-addressed stamped envelope is a must. We cannot guarantee replies to foreign queries via standard mail. No phone calls. We never download attachments to e-mail queries for security reasons, so please copy and paste material into your e-mail."

☑ THE DOE COOVER AGENCY

P.O. Box 668, Winchester MA 01890. (781)721-6000. Fax: (781)721-6727. E-mail: info@doecooveragency. com. Website: doecooveragency.com. Represents more than 100 clients. Currently handles nonfiction books (80%), novels (20%).

Member Agents Doe Coover (general nonfiction, cooking); Colleen Mohyde (literary and commercial fiction, general and narrative nonfiction); Amanda Lewis (children's books); Frances Kennedy, associate.

Represents Considers these nonfiction areas: biography, business, cooking, gardening, health, history, science social issues, narrative nonfiction. **Considers these fiction areas:** literary commercial. This agency specializes in nonfiction, particularly books on history, popular science, biography, social issues, and narrative nonfiction, as well as cooking, gardening, and literary and commercial fiction. Does not want romance, fantasy, science fiction, poetry or screenplays.

How to Contact Query with SASE. E-mail queries are acceptable. No unsolicited mss. Accepts simultaneous submissions. Obtains most new clients through recommendations from others, solicitations.

Terms Agent receives 15% commission on domestic sales. Agent receives 10% of original advance commission on foreign sales.

☒ CRICHTON & ASSOCIATES

6940 Carroll Ave., Takoma Park MD 20912. (301)495-9663. Fax: (202)318-0050. E-mail: query@crichton-associates.com. Website: www.crichton-associates.com. **Contact:** Sha-Shana Crichton. 90% of clients are new/unpublished writers. Currently handles nonfiction books (20%), novels (80%).

• Prior to becoming an agent, Ms. Crichton did commercial litigation for a major law firm.

Represents nonfiction books, novels. **Considers these nonfiction areas:** child, ethnic, gay, government, true crime, womens Caribbean, Hispanic and Latin-American studies, African-American studies. **Considers these fiction areas:** ethnic, feminist, literary, mainstream, mystery, religious, romance. Actively seeking women's fiction, romance, and chick lit. Looking also for multicultural fiction and nonfiction. Does not want to receive poetry.

How to Contact For fiction, include short synopsis and first 3 chapters with query. Send no e-attachments. For nonfiction, send a book proposal. Responds in 3-5 weeks to queries.

Terms Agent receives 15% commission on domestic sales. Agent receives 20% commission on foreign sales. Offers written contract, binding for 45 days. Only charges fees for postage and photocopying.

Writers Conferences Silicon Valley RWA; BookExpo America.

D4EO LITERARY AGENCY

7 Indian Valley Road, Weston CT 06883. (203)544-7180. Fax: (203)544-7160. E-mail: d4eo@optonline. net. **Contact:** Bob Diforio. Represents more than 100 clients. 50% of clients are new/unpublished writers. Currently handles nonfiction books (70%), novels (25%), juvenile books (5%).

• Prior to opening his agency, Mr. Diforio was a publisher.

Represents nonfiction books, novels. **Considers these nonfiction areas:** juvenile, art, biography, business, child, current affairs, gay, health, history, how to, humor, memoirs, military, money, psychology, religion, science, self help, sports, true crime, womens. **Considers these fiction areas:** adventure, detective, erotica, historical, horror, humor, juvenile, literary, mainstream, mystery, picture books, romance, science, sports, thriller, western, young.

How to Contact Query with SASE. Accepts and prefers e-mail queries. Prefers to read material exclusively. Responds in 1 week to queries. Obtains most new clients through recommendations from others.

Terms Agent receives 15% commission on domestic sales. Agent receives 25% commission on foreign sales. Offers written contract, binding for 2 years; 60-day notice must be given to terminate contract. Charges for photocopying and submission postage.

☑ DANIEL LITERARY GROUP

1701 Kingsbury Drive, Suite 100, Nashville TN 37215. (615)730-8207. E-mail: submissions@ danielliterarygroup.com. Website: www.danielliterarygroup.com. **Contact:** Greg Daniel. Represents 45 clients. 30% of clients are new/unpublished writers. Currently handles nonfiction books (85%), novels (15%).

- Prior to becoming an agent, Mr. Daniel spent 10 years in publishing - six at the executive level at Thomas Nelson Publishers.

Represents nonfiction books, novels. **Considers these nonfiction areas:** biography, business, child, current affairs, health, history, how to, humor, memoirs, nature, popular culture, religion, self help, sports, film, womens. **Considers these fiction areas:** contemporary, adventure, detective, family, historical, humor, literary, mainstream, mystery, religious, thriller The agency currently accepts all fiction topics, except for children's, romance and sci-fi. "We take pride in our ability to come alongside our authors and help strategize about where they want their writing to take them in both the near and long term. Forging close relationships with our authors, we help them with such critical factors as editorial refinement, branding, audience, and marketing." Nonfiction. The agency is open to submissions in almost every popular category of nonfiction, especially if authors are recognized experts in their fields. No screenplays, poetry or short stories.

How to Contact Query via e-mail only. Submit publishing history, author bio, brief synopsis of work, key selling points. E-queries only. Send no attachments. For fiction, send first 5 pages pasted in e-mail. Responds in 2-3 weeks to queries.

☑ DAVIS WAGER LITERARY AGENCY

419 N. Larchmont Blvd., #317, Los Angeles CA 90004. (323)383-2974. E-mail: submissions@daviswager. com. Website: www.daviswager.com. **Contact:** Timothy Wager.

- Prior to his current position, Mr. Wager was with the Sandra Dijkstra Literary Agency, where he worked as a reader and associate agent.

Represents nonfiction books, novels. **Considers these fiction areas:** literary. Actively seeking: literary fiction and general-interest nonfiction.

How to Contact Query with SASE. Submit author bio, synopsis for fiction, book proposal or outline for nonfiction. Query via e-mail. No author queries by phone.

☑ THE JENNIFER DECHIARA LITERARY AGENCY

31 East 32nd St., Suite 300, New York NY 10016. (212)481-8484. E-mail: jenndec@aol.com. Website: www.jdlit.com. **Contact:** Jennifer DeChiara, Stephen Fraser. Represents 100 clients. 50% of clients are new/unpublished writers. Currently handles nonfiction books (25%), novels (25%), juvenile books (50%).

- Prior to becoming an agent, Ms. DeChiara was a writing consultant, freelance editor at Simon & Schuster and Random House, and a ballerina and an actress.

Represents nonfiction books, novels, juvenile. **Considers these nonfiction areas:** crafts, interior, juvenile, biography, child, cooking, current affairs, education, ethnic, gay, government, health, history, how to, humor, language, memoirs, military, money, music, nature, photography, popular culture, psychology, science, self help, sociology, sports, film, true crime, womens celebrity biography. **Considers these fiction areas:** confession, detective, ethnic, family, fantasy, feminist, gay, historical, horror, humor, juvenile, literary, mainstream, mystery, picture books, regional, sports, thriller, young chick lit; psychic/ supernatural; glitz. "We represent both children's and adult books in a wide range of ages and genres. We are a full-service agency and fulfill the potential of every book in every possible medium—stage, film, television, etc. We help writers every step of the way, from creating book ideas to editing and promotion. We are passionate about helping writers further their careers, but are just as eager to discover new talent, regardless of age or lack of prior publishing experience. This agency is committed to managing a writer's entire career. For us, it's not just about selling books, but about making dreams come true. We are especially attracted to the downtrodden, the discouraged, and the downright disgusted." Actively seeking literary fiction, chick lit, young adult fiction, self-help, pop culture, and celebrity biographies. Does not want westerns, poetry, or short stories.

How to Contact Query with SASE. Accepts simultaneous submissions. Responds in 3-6 months to queries. Responds in 3-6 months to mss. Obtains most new clients through recommendations from others, conferences, query letters.

Terms Agent receives 15% commission on domestic sales. Agent receives 20% commission on foreign sales. Offers written contract.

◙ JOELLE DELBOURGO ASSOCIATES, INC.

516 Bloomfield Ave., Suite 5, Montclair NJ 07042. (973)783-6800. Fax: (973)783-6802. E-mail: info@delbourgo.com. Website: www.delbourgo.com. **Contact:** Joelle Delbourgo, Molly Lyons. Represents more than 100 clients. Currently handles nonfiction books (75%), novels (25%).

- Prior to becoming an agent, Ms. Delbourgo was an editor and senior publishing executive at HarperCollins and Random House.

Member Agents Joelle Delbourgo (parenting, self-help, psychology, business, serious nonfiction, narrative nonfiction, quality fiction); Molly Lyons (practical and narrative nonfiction, popular culture, memoir, quality fiction).

Represents nonfiction books, novels. **Considers these nonfiction areas:** biography, business, child, cooking, current affairs, education, ethnic, gay, government, health, history, how to, money, nature, popular culture, psychology, religion, science, self help, sociology, true crime, womens New Age/metaphysics, interior design/decorating. **Considers these fiction areas:** historical, literary, mainstream, mystery. "We are former publishers and editors, with deep knowledge and an insider perspective. We have a reputation for individualized attention to clients, strategic management of authors' careers, and creating strong partnerships with publishers for our clients." Actively seeking history, narrative nonfiction, science/medicine, memoir, literary fiction, psychology, parenting, biographies, current affairs, politics, young adult fiction and nonfiction. Does not want to receive genre fiction or screenplays.

How to Contact Query with SASE. Accepts simultaneous submissions. Responds in 3 weeks to queries. Responds in 2 months to mss.

Terms Agent receives 15% commission on domestic sales. Agent receives 20% commission on foreign sales. Offers written contract. Charges clients for postage and photocopying.

Tips "Do your homework. Do not cold call. Read and follow submission guidelines before contacting us. Do not call to find out if we received your material. No e-mail queries. Treat agents with respect, as you would any other professional, such as a doctor, lawyer or financial advisor."

◙ DHS LITERARY, INC.

10711 Preston Road, Suite 100, Dallas TX 75230. (214)363-4422. Fax: (214)363-4423. Website: www.dhsliterary.com. **Contact:** David Hale Smith, president. Represents 35 clients. 15% of clients are new/unpublished writers. Currently handles nonfiction books (60%), novels (40%).

- Prior to opening his agency, Mr. Smith was an agent at Dupree/Miller & Associates.

Represents nonfiction books, novels. **Considers these nonfiction areas:** biography, business, child, cooking, current affairs, ethnic, popular culture, sports, true crime. **Considers these fiction areas:** detective, ethnic, literary, mainstream, mystery, thriller, western. This agency is not actively seeking clients and usually takes clients on by referral only.

How to Contact Only responds if interested. *No unsolicited mss.*

Terms Agent receives 15% commission on domestic sales. Agent receives 25% commission on foreign sales. Offers written contract; 10-day notice must be given to terminate contract. This agency charges for postage and photocopying.

Tips "Remember to be courteous and professional, and to treat marketing your work and approaching an agent as you would any formal business matter. If you have a referral, always query first via e-mail. Sorry, but we cannot respond to queries sent via mail, even with a SASE. Visit our Web site for more information."

◙ THE JONATHAN DOLGER AGENCY

49 E. 96th St., Suite 9B, New York NY 10128. Fax: (212)369-7118. Member of AAR.

Represents nonfiction books, novels. **Considers these nonfiction areas:** biography, history, womens cultural/social. **Considers these fiction areas:** womens commercial.

How to Contact Query with SASE. No e-mail queries.

Terms Agent receives 15% commission on domestic sales. Agent receives 25% commission on foreign sales.

Tips "Writers must have been previously published if submitting fiction. We prefer to work with published/established authors, and work with a small number of new/previously unpublished writers."

☑ JIM DONOVAN LITERARY

4515 Prentice St., Suite 109, Dallas TX 75206. E-mail: jdlqueries@sbcglobal.net. **Contact:** Melissa Shultz, agent. Represents 30 clients. 10% of clients are new/unpublished writers. Currently handles nonfiction books (75%), novels (25%).

Member Agents Jim Donovan (history—particularly American, military and Western; biography; sports; popular reference; popular culture; fiction—literary, thrillers and mystery); Melissa Shultz (chick lit, parenting, women's issues, memoir).

Represents nonfiction books, novels. **Considers these nonfiction areas:** biography, business, child, current affairs, government, health, history, how to, memoirs, military, money, music, nature, popular culture, sports, true crime, womens. **Considers these fiction areas:** adventure, detective, literary, mainstream, mystery, thriller, womens. This agency specializes in commercial fiction and nonfiction. "Does not want to receive poetry, children's, short stories, inspirational or anything else not listed above."

How to Contact For nonfiction, send query letter and SASE. For fiction, send 3 sample chapters, synopsis, SASE. Responds to e-queries only if interested. Accepts simultaneous submissions. Responds in 3 weeks to queries. Responds in 1 month to mss. Obtains most new clients through recommendations from others.

Terms Agent receives 15% commission on domestic sales. Agent receives 20% commission on foreign sales. Offers written contract, binding for 1 year; 30-day notice must be given to terminate contract. This agency charges for things such as overnight delivery and manuscript copying. Charges are discussed beforehand.

Tips "Get published in short form—magazine reviews, journals, etec.—first. This will increase your credibility considerably, and make it much easier to sell a full-length book."

☑ DOYEN LITERARY SERVICES, INC.

1931 660th St., Newell IA 50568-7613. (712)272-3300. Website: www.barbaradoyen.com. **Contact:** (Ms.) B.J. Doyen, president. Represents over 100 clients. 20% of clients are new/unpublished writers. Currently handles nonfiction books (95%), novels (5%).

- Prior to opening her agency, Ms. Doyen worked as a published author, teacher, guest speaker, and wrote and appeared in her own weekly TV show airing in 7 states. She is also the co-author of *The Everything Guide to Writing a Book Proposal* (Adams 2005) and *The Everything Guide to Getting Published* (Adams 2006).

Represents nonfiction books, novels. **Considers these nonfiction areas:** agriculture horticulture, americana, crafts, interior, newage, young, animals, anthropology, art, biography, business, child, computers, cooking, current affairs, education, ethnic, gardening, government, health, history, how to, language, memoirs, military, money, multicultural, music, nature, philosophy, photography, popular culture, psychology, recreation, regional, religion, science, self help, sex, sociology, software, spirituality, film, travel, true crime, womens creative nonfiction. **Considers these fiction areas:** family, historical, literary, mainstream. This agency specializes in nonfiction and occasionally handles mainstream fiction for adults. Actively seeking business, health, how-to, self-help—all kinds of adult nonfiction suitable for the major trade publishers. Does not want to receive pornography, children's books, or poetry.

How to Contact Query with SASE or "you can submit an e-mail via Web site as well. Include background info. Send no unsolicited samples. Accepts simultaneous submissions. Responds immediately to queries. Responds in 3 weeks to mss.

Terms Agent receives 15% commission on domestic sales. Agent receives 20% commission on foreign sales. Offers written contract, binding for 2 years.

Tips "Our authors receive personalized attention. We market aggressively, undeterred by rejection. We get the best possible publishing contracts. We are very interested in nonfiction book ideas at this time and will consider most topics. Many writers come to us from referrals, but we also get quite a few who initially approach us with query letters. Do not call us regarding queries. It is best if you do not collect editorial rejections prior to seeking an agent, but if you do, be upfront and honest about it. Do not submit your manuscript to more than 1 agent at a time—querying first can save you (and us) much time. We're open to established or beginning writers—just send us a terrific letter!"

☑ DUNHAM LITERARY, INC.

156 Fifth Ave., Suite 625, New York NY 10010-7002. (212)929-0994. Website: www.dunhamlit.com. **Contact:** Jennie Dunham. Member of AAR. Represents 50 clients. 15% of clients are new/unpublished writers. Currently handles nonfiction books (25%), novels (25%), juvenile books (50%).

> • Prior to opening her agency, Ms. Dunham worked as a literary agent for Russell & Volkening. The Rhoda Weyr Agency is now a division of Dunham Literary, Inc.

Represents nonfiction books, novels, short story collections, juvenile. **Considers these nonfiction areas:** anthropology, biography, ethnic, government, health, history, language, nature, popular culture, psychology, science, womens. **Considers these fiction areas:** ethnic, juvenile, literary, mainstream, picture books, young.

How to Contact Query with SASE. Responds in 1 week to queries. Responds in 2 months to mss. Obtains most new clients through recommendations from others, solicitations.

Terms Agent receives 15% commission on domestic sales. Agent receives 20% commission on foreign sales.

☑ DUPREE/MILLER AND ASSOCIATES INC. LITERARY

100 Highland Park Village, Suite 350, Dallas TX 75205. (214)559-BOOK. Fax: (214)559-PAGE. Website: www.dupreemiller.com. **Contact:** Submissions Department. Other memberships include ABA. Represents 200 clients. 20% of clients are new/unpublished writers. Currently handles nonfiction books (90%), novels (10%).

Member Agents Jan Miller, president/CEO; Shannon Miser-Marven, senior executive VP; Annabelle Baxter; Nena Madonia; Cheri Gillis.

Represents nonfiction books, novels, scholarly, syndicated religious.inspirational/spirituality. **Considers these nonfiction areas:** americana, crafts, interior, newage, animals, anthropology, art, biography, business, child, cooking, creative, current affairs, education, ethnic, gardening, government, health, history, how to, humor, language, memoirs, money, multicultural, music, nature, philosophy, photography, popular culture, psychology, recreation, regional, science, self help, sex, sociology, sports, film, translation, true crime, womens. **Considers these fiction areas:** glitz, psychic, adventure, detective, ethnic, experimental, family, feminist, historical, humor, literary, mainstream, mystery, picture books, religious, sports, thriller. This agency specializes in commercial fiction and nonfiction.

How to Contact Submit 1-page query, outline, SASE. Obtains most new clients through recommendations from others, conferences, lectures.

Terms Agent receives 15% commission on domestic sales. Offers written contract.

Writers Conferences Aspen Summer Words Literary Festival.

Tips If interested in agency representation, it is vital to have the material in the proper working format. As agents' policies differ, it is important to follow their guidelines. The best advice I can give is to work on establishing a strong proposal that provides sample chapters, an overall synopsis (fairly detailed), and some biographical information on yourself. Do not send your proposal in pieces; it should be complete upon submission. Remember you are trying to sell your work, and it should be in its best condition.

☑ DWYER & O'GRADY, INC.

Agents for Writers & Illustrators of Children's Books, P.O. Box 790, Cedar Key FL 32625-0790. (352)543-9307. Fax: (603)375-5373. Website: www.dwyerogrady.com. **Contact:** Elizabeth O'Grady. Other memberships include SCBWI. Represents 30 clients. Currently handles juvenile books (100%).

> • Prior to opening their agency, Mr. Dwyer and Ms. O'Grady were booksellers and publishers.

Member Agents Elizabeth O'Grady; Jeff Dwyer.

Represents juvenile. **Considers these nonfiction areas:** juvenile. **Considers these fiction areas:** juvenile, picture books, young. "We are not accepting new clients at this time. This agency represents only writers and illustrators of children's books." No juvenile books.

How to Contact *No unsolicited mss.* Obtains most new clients through recommendations from others, Direct approach by agent to writer whose work they've read.

Terms Agent receives 15% commission on domestic sales. Agent receives 20% commission on foreign sales. Offers written contract; 1-month notice must be given to terminate contract. This agency charges clients for photocopying of longer mss or mutually agreed upon marketing expenses.

Writers Conferences BookExpo America; American Library Association Annual Conference; SCBWI.

Tips "This agency previously had an address in New Hampshire. Mail all materials to the new Florida address."

☐ EAMES LITERARY SERVICES

4117 Hillsboro Road, Suite 251, Nashville TN 37215. Fax: (615)463.9361. E-mail: info@eamesliterary. com; John@eamesliterary.com; Ahna@eamesliterary.com. Website: www.eamesliterary.com. **Contact:** John Eames.

Member Agents John Eames, Jonathan Rogers.

Represents nonfiction books, novels. **Considers these nonfiction areas:** young, memoirs, religion. **Considers these fiction areas:** religious, young. This agency specializes in the Christian marketplace. Actively seeking "adult and young adult fiction that sparks the imagination, illuminates some angle of truth about the human condition, causes the reader to view the world with fresh eyes, and supports a Christian perspective on life in all its complexities. Stories might be redemptive, or tragic. Characters might be noble, or flawed. Situations might be humorous, or dark. And many manuscripts might contain some combination of all of the above. We also seek adult and young adult nonfiction that is anecdotal as well as instructional, utilizes a 'show, don't tell' philosophy of writing, and offers a unique and biblically sound perspective on a given topic. If the submission is a nonfiction narrative (e.g., memoir), the work should follow most of the same recommendations for a work of fiction, as listed above. We look for proposals that are very well written and (especially for nonfiction) are from authors with an expansive platform and processing some literary notoriety."

☑ EAST/WEST AGENCY

1158 26th St., Suite 462, Santa Monica CA 90403. (310)573-9303. Fax: (310)453-9008. E-mail: creativeideaz@roadrunner.com. **Contact:** Deborah Warren, founder. Other memberships include adheres to AAR canon of ethics. Represents 100 clients. 70% of clients are new/unpublished writers. Currently handles nonfiction books (25%), juvenile books (75%).

Member Agents Deborah Warren; Lisa Rojany Buccieri; Susan B. Katz (writers/illustrators in the Latino market, representing Spanish-speaking clients).

Represents nonfiction books, juvenile. **Considers these nonfiction areas:** crafts, interior, juvenile, art, how to, humor, language, music, photography, popular culture, religion, self help. **Considers these fiction areas:** comic, ethnic, juvenile, picture books, young. "EWA is, purposefully, a niche agency, to facilitate hands-on, personal service and attention to our authors, authorial illustrators, illustrators and their books. EWA provides career management for established and first time authors and our breadth of experience in many genres enables us to meet the demands of a diverse clientele. Understanding the in-depth process of acquisitions, sales and marketing helps Ms. Warren and her co-agents attain the stated goals for each of the agency's clients: to close the best possible deal with the best possible editor at the best possible publishing house." Actively seeking clients by referral only. This agency works with board books, illustrated picture books and bilingual (Spanish-speaking) authors frequently.

How to Contact Query with SASE. Submit first 3 sample chapters, table of contents (2 pages or fewer), synopsis (1 page).For picture books, submit entire ms. For chapter books/novels. "Send submissions to CreativeIdeaz@roadrunner.com, or snail mail to Requested Materials, EWA, 1543 Sycamore Canyon Drive, Westlake Village, CA 91361. Submit the manuscript as a Word document in Courier, 12-point, double-spaced, with 1.20 inch margin on left, ragged right text, 25 lines per page, continuously paginated, with all your contact info on the first page. Include an SASE and a manila envelope with appropriate postage to expedite our response." Responds in 2 months to mss. Obtains most new clients through recommendations from others.

Terms Agent receives 15% commission on domestic sales. Agent receives 25% commission on foreign sales. Offers written contract; 30-day notice must be given to terminate contract. Charges for out-of-pocket expenses, such as postage and copying.

☑ ANNE EDELSTEIN LITERARY AGENCY

20 W. 22nd St., Suite 1603, New York NY 10010. (212)414-4923. Fax: (212)414-2930. E-mail: info@ aeliterary.com. Website: www.aeliterary.com. Member of AAR.

Member Agents Anne Edelstein; Krista Ingebretson.

Represents nonfiction books Fiction. **Considers these nonfiction areas:** narrative history, memoirs, psychology, religion. **Considers these fiction areas:** literary. This agency specializes in fiction and narrative nonfiction.

How to Contact Query with SASE; submit 25 sample pages.

ANN ELMO AGENCY, INC.

60 E. 42nd St., New York NY 10165. (212)661-2880. Fax: (212)661-2883. **Contact:** Lettie Lee. Member of AAR. Other memberships include Authors Guild.

Member Agents Lettie Lee; Mari Cronin (plays); A.L. Abecassis (nonfiction).

Represents nonfiction books, novels. **Considers these nonfiction areas:** biography, current affairs, health, history, how to, popular culture, science. **Considers these fiction areas:** ethnic, family, mainstream, romance, contemporary, gothic, historical, regency, thriller, womens.

How to Contact Only accepts mailed queries with SASE. Do not send full ms unless requested. Responds in 3 months to queries. Obtains most new clients through recommendations from others.

Terms Agent receives 15% commission on domestic sales. Agent receives 20% commission on foreign sales. Offers written contract.

Tips "Query first, and **only** when asked send a double-spaced, readable manuscript. Include a SASE, of course."

THE ELAINE P. ENGLISH LITERARY AGENCY

4710 41st St. NW, Suite D, Washington DC 20016. (202)362-5190. Fax: (202)362-5192. E-mail: elaine@elaineenglish.com; kvn.mcadams@yahoo.com. Website: www.elaineenglish.com. **Contact:** Elaine English. Kevin McAdams, Executive V.P., 400 East 11th St., # 7, New York, NY 10009 Member of AAR. Represents 20 clients. 25% of clients are new/unpublished writers. Currently handles novels (100%).

- Ms. English has been working in publishing for more than 20 years. She is also an attorney specializing in media and publishing law.

Represents novels. **Considers these fiction areas:** historical, multicultural, mystery, romance, single title, historical, contemporary, romantic, suspense, chick lit, erotic, thriller general women's fiction. The agency is slowly but steadily acquiring in all mentioned areas. Actively seeking women's fiction, including single-title romances. Does not want to receive any science fiction, time travel, children's, or young adult.

How to Contact Prefers e-queries sent to queries@elaineenglish.com. If requested, submit synopsis, first 3 chapters, SASE. Responds in 4-8 weeks to queries; 3 months to requested submissions Obtains most new clients through recommendations from others, conferences, submissions.

Terms Agent receives 15% commission on domestic sales. Agent receives 20% commission on foreign sales. Offers written contract; 30-day notice must be given to terminate contract. Charges only for copying and postage; generally taken from proceeds.

Writers Conferences RWA National Conference; Novelists, Inc.; Malice Domestic; Washington Romance Writers Retreat, among others.

FELICIA ETH LITERARY REPRESENTATION

555 Bryant St., Suite 350, Palo Alto CA 94301-1700. (650)375-1276. Fax: (650)401-8892. E-mail: feliciaeth@aol.com. **Contact:** Felicia Eth. Member of AAR. Represents 25-35 clients. Currently handles nonfiction books (85%), novels (15% adult).

Represents nonfiction books, novels. **Considers these nonfiction areas:** animals, anthropology, biography, business, child, current affairs, ethnic, government, health, history, nature, popular culture, psychology, science, sociology, true crime, womens. **Considers these fiction areas:** literary, mainstream. This agency specializes in high-quality fiction (preferably mainstream/contemporary) and provocative, intelligent, and thoughtful nonfiction on a wide array of commercial subjects.

How to Contact Query with SASE. Accepts simultaneous submissions. Responds in 3 weeks to queries. Responds in 4-6 weeks to mss.

Terms Agent receives 15% commission on domestic sales. Agent receives 20% commission on foreign sales. Agent receives 20% commission on film sales. Charges clients for photocopying and express mail service.

Writers Conferences "Wide Array - from Squaw Valley to Mills College."

Tips "For nonfiction, established expertise is certainly a plus—as is magazine publication—though not a prerequisite. I am highly dedicated to those projects I represent, but highly selective in what I choose."

⊘ FAIRBANK LITERARY REPRESENTATION

199 Mount Auburn St., Suite 1, Cambridge MA 02138-4809. (617)576-0030. Fax: (617)576-0030. E-mail: queries@fairbankliterary.com. Website: www.fairbankliterary.com. **Contact:** Sorche Fairbank. Member of AAR. Represents 45 clients. 20% of clients are new/unpublished writers. Currently handles nonfiction books (60%), novels (22%), story collections (3%), other(15% illustrated).

Member Agents Sorche Fairbank (narrative nonfiction, commercial and literary fiction, memoir, food and wine); Matthew Frederick (scout for sports nonfiction, architecture, design).

Represents nonfiction books, novels, short story collections. **Considers these nonfiction areas:** agriculture horticulture, crafts, interior, art, biography, cooking, current affairs, ethnic, gay, government, how to, memoirs, nature, photography, popular culture, science, sociology, sports, true crime, womens. **Considers these fiction areas:** adventure, feminist, gay, literary, mainstream, mystery, sports, thriller, womens Southern voices. "I have a small agency in Harvard Square, where I tend to gravitate toward literary fiction and narrative nonfiction, with a strong interest in women's issues and women's voices, international voices, class and race issues, and projects that simply teach me something new about the greater world and society around us. We have a good reputation for working closely and developmentally with our authors and love what we do." Actively seeking literary fiction, international and culturally diverse voices, narrative nonfiction, topical subjects (politics, current affairs), history, sports, architecture/design and pop culture. Does not want to receive romance, poetry, science fiction, young adult or children's works.

How to Contact Query with SASE. Submit author bio. Accepts simultaneous submissions. Responds in 6 weeks to queries. Responds in 10 weeks to mss. Obtains most new clients through recommendations from others, solicitations, conferences, ideas generated in-house.

Terms Agent receives 15% commission on domestic sales. Agent receives 20% commission on foreign sales. Offers written contract, binding for 12 months; 45-day notice must be given to terminate contract.

Writers Conferences San Francisco Writers' Conference, Muse and the Marketplace/Grub Street Conference, Washington Independent Writers' Conference, Murder in the Grove, Surrey International Writers' Conference.

Tips "Be professional from the very first contact. There shouldn't be a single typo or grammatical flub in your query. Have a reason for contacting me about your project other than I was the next name listed on some Web site. Please do not use form query software! Believe me, we can get a dozen or so a day that look identical—we know when you are using a form. Show me that you know your audience—and your competition. Have the writing and/or proposal at the very, very best it can be before starting the querying process. Don't assume that if someone likes it enough they'll 'fix' it. The biggest mistake new writers make is starting the querying process before they—and the work—are ready. Take your time and do it right."

FARBER LITERARY AGENCY, INC.

14 E. 75th St., #2E, New York NY 10021. (212)861-7075. Fax: (212)861-7076. E-mail: farberlit@aol.com. Website: www.donaldfarber.com. **Contact:** Ann Farber, Dr. Seth Farber. Represents 40 clients. 50% of clients are new/unpublished writers. Currently handles nonfiction books (25%), novels (35%), scholarly books (15%), stage plays (25%).

Member Agents Ann Farber (novels); Seth Farber (plays, scholarly books, novels); Donald C. Farber (attorney, all entertainment media).

Represents nonfiction books, novels, juvenile, textbooks, stage plays. **Considers these nonfiction areas:** child, cooking, music, psychology, film. **Considers these fiction areas:** adventure, humor, juvenile, literary, mainstream, mystery, thriller, young.

How to Contact Submit outline, 3 sample chapters, SASE. Prefers to read materials exclusively. Responds in 1 month to queries. Responds in 2 months to mss. Obtains most new clients through recommendations from others.

Terms Agent receives 15% commission on domestic sales. Agent receives 20% commission on foreign sales. Offers written contract, binding for 1 year. Client must furnish copies of ms, treatments, and any other items for submission.

Tips "Our attorney, Donald C. Farber, is the author of many books. His services are available to the agency's clients as part of the agency service at no additional charge."

☑ FARRIS LITERARY AGENCY, INC.

P.O. Box 570069, Dallas TX 75357. (972)203-8804. E-mail: farris1@airmail.net. Website: www.farrisliterary.com. **Contact:** Mike Farris, Susan Morgan Farris. Represents 30 clients. 60% of clients are new/unpublished writers. Currently handles nonfiction books (40), novels (60).

• Both Mr. Farris and Ms. Farris are attorneys.

Represents nonfiction books, novels. **Considers these nonfiction areas:** biography, business, child, cooking, current affairs, government, health, history, how to, humor, memoirs, military, music, popular culture, religion, self help, sports, womens. **Considers these fiction areas:** adventure, detective, historical, humor, mainstream, mystery, religious, romance, sports, thriller, western. "We specialize in both fiction and nonfiction books. We are particularly interested in discovering unpublished authors. We adhere to AAR guidelines." Does not want to receive science fiction, fantasy, gay and lesbian, erotica, young adult or children's.

How to Contact Query with SASE or by e-mail. Accepts simultaneous submissions. Responds in 2-3 weeks to queries. Responds in 4-8 weeks to mss. Obtains most new clients through recommendations from others, solicitations, conferences.

Terms Agent receives 15% commission on domestic sales. Agent receives 20% commission on foreign sales. Offers written contract; 30-day notice must be given to terminate contract. Charges clients for postage and photocopying.

Writers Conferences Oklahoma Writers Federation Conference; The Screenwriting Conference in Santa Fe; Pikes Peak Writers Conference; Women Writing the West Annual Conference.

☑ DIANA FINCH LITERARY AGENCY

116 W. 23rd St., Suite 500, New York NY 10011. (646)375-2081. E-mail: diana.finch@verizon.net. **Contact:** Diana Finch. Member of AAR. Represents 40 clients. 20% of clients are new/unpublished writers. Currently handles nonfiction books (65%), novels (25%), juvenile books (5%), multimedia(5%).

• Prior to opening her agency, Ms. Finch worked at Ellen Levine Literary Agency for 18 years.

Represents nonfiction books, novels, scholarly. **Considers these nonfiction areas:** juvenile, biography, business, child, computers, current affairs, ethnic, government, health, history, how to, humor, memoirs, military, money, music, nature, photography, popular culture, psychology, science, self help, sports, film, translation, true crime, womens. **Considers these fiction areas:** adventure, detective, ethnic, historical, literary, mainstream, thriller, young. Actively seeking narrative nonfiction, popular science, and health topics. "Does not want romance, mysteries, or children's picture books."

How to Contact Query with SASE or via e-mail (no attachments). Accepts simultaneous submissions. Obtains most new clients through recommendations from others.

Terms Agent receives 15% commission on domestic sales. Agent receives 20% commission on foreign sales. Offers written contract. "I charge for photocopying, overseas postage, galleys, and books purchased, and try to recap these costs from earnings received for a client, rather than charging outright."

Tips "Do as much research as you can on agents before you query. Have someone critique your query letter before you send it. It should be only 1 page and describe your book clearly—and why you are writing it—but also demonstrate creativity and a sense of your writing style."

FINEPRINT LITERARY MANAGEMENT

240 West 35th St., Suite 500, New York NY 10001. (212)279-1282. E-mail: stephany@fineprintlit.com. Website: www.fineprintlit.com. Member of AAR.

Member Agents Peter Rubie, CEO (nonfiction interests include narrative nonfiction, popular science, spirituality, history, biography, pop culture, business, technology, parenting, health, self help, music, and food; fiction interests include literate thrillers, crime fiction, science fiction and fantasy, military fiction and literary fiction); Stephany Evans, president (nonfiction interests include health and wellness - especially women's health, spirituality, lifestyle, home renovating/decorating, entertaining, food and wine, popular reference, and narrative nonfiction; fiction interests include stories with a strong and interesting female protagonist, both literary and upmarket commercial — including chick lit, romance, mystery, and light suspense); June Clark (nonfiction: entertainment, self-help, parenting, reference/ how-to books, teen books, food and wine, style/beauty, and prescriptive business titles); Diane Freed (nonfiction: health/fitness, women's issues, memoir, baby boomer trends, parenting, popular culture, self-help, humor, young adult, and topics of New England regional interest); Meredith Hays (both fiction and nonfiction: commercial and literary; she is interested in sophisticated women's fiction such as urban chick lit, pop culture, lifestyle, animals, and absorbing nonfiction accounts); Gary Heidt (history, science, true crime, pop culture, psychology, business, military and some literary fiction); Janet Reid (mysteries and offbeat literary fiction); Amy Tipton (edgy fiction - gritty and urban, women's fiction, nonfiction/ memoir, and YA); Colleen Lindsay; Joanna Stampfel (chapter books to middle grade - covering any and all topics. If fantasy, it had better be very unique. Loves a good school story, and always looking for humorous boy reads. YA: contemporary to sci-fi and everything in between. Again, if full-out fantasy, it had better be different; Romance: historical, paranormal, multicultural; Other Adult: pop-culture, dark speculative fiction, narrative nonfiction having to do with environment, food, outdoors).

Represents nonfiction books, novels. **Considers these nonfiction areas:** interior, young, business, child, cooking, government, health, history, how to, humor, memoirs, music, psychology, science, self help, spirituality, true crime, womens narrative nonfiction, popular science. **Considers these fiction areas:** detective, fantasy, literary, military, mystery, romance, science, young, womens.

How to Contact Query with SASE. Submit synopsis and first two chapters for fiction; proposal for nonfiction. Do not send attachments or manuscripts without a request. Obtains most new clients through recommendations from others, solicitations.

Terms Agent receives 15% commission on domestic sales. Agent receives 20% commission on foreign sales.

FOUNDRY LITERARY + MEDIA

33 West 17th St., PH, New York NY 10011. (212)929-5064. Fax: (212)929-5471. Website: www. foundrymedia.com.

Member Agents Peter H. McGuigan (smart, offbeat nonfiction, particularly works of narrative nonfiction on pop culture, niche history, biography, music and science; fiction interests include commercial and literary, across all genres, especially first-time writers); Yfat Reiss Gendell (favors nonfiction books focusing on all manners of prescriptive: how-to, science, health and well-being, memoirs, adventure, travel stories and lighter titles appropriate for the gift trade genre. Yfat also looks for commercial fiction highlighting the full range of women's experiences - young and old - and also seeks science fiction, thrillers and historical fiction); Stéphanie Abou(In fiction and nonfiction alike, Stéphanie is always on the lookout for authors who are accomplished storytellers with their own distinctive voice, who develop memorable characters, and who are able to create psychological conflict with their narrative. She is an across-the-board fiction lover, attracted to both literary and smart upmarket commercial fiction. In nonfiction she leans towards projects that tackle big topics with an unusual approach. Pop culture, health, science, parenting, women's and multicultural issues are of special interest); Chris Park (memoirs, narrative nonfiction, Christian nonfiction and character-driven fiction).

Represents Considers these nonfiction areas: biography, child, health, memoirs, multicultural, music, popular culture, science. **Considers these fiction areas:** literary, religious.

How to Contact Query with SASE. Should be addressed to one agent only. Submit synopsis, 3 sample chapters, author bio, For nonfiction, submit query, proposal, sample chapter, TOC, bio. Put submisssions on your snail mail submission.

FOX LITERARY

168 Second Ave., PMB 180, New York NY 10003. (212)710-5907. E-mail: submissions@foxliterary.com. Website: www.foxliterary.com.

Represents Considers these fiction areas: erotica, fantasy, literary, romance, science historical romance. Does not want to receive screenplays, poetry, category Westerns, horror, Christian/inspirational, or children's picture books.

How to Contact E-mail query and first five pages in body of e-mail. E-mail queries preferred.

LYNN C. FRANKLIN ASSOCIATES, LTD.

1350 Broadway, Suite 2015, New York NY 10018. (212)868-6311. Fax: (212)868-6312. **Contact:** Lynn Franklin, Claudia Nys, Michelle Andelman. Other memberships include PEN America. Represents 30-35 clients. 50% of clients are new/unpublished writers. Currently handles nonfiction books (90%), novels (10%).

Represents nonfiction books, novels. **Considers these nonfiction areas:** newage, biography, current affairs, health, history, memoirs, psychology, religion, self help, spirituality. **Considers these fiction**

areas: literary, mainstream, commercial; juvenile, middle-grade, and young adult. "This agency specializes in general nonfiction with a special interest in self-help, biography/memoir, alternative health, and spirituality."

How to Contact Query via e-mail to agency@franklinandsiegal.com. No unsolicited mss. No attachments. For nonfiction, query letter with short outline and synopsis. For fiction, query letter with short synopsis and a maximum of 10 sample pages (in the body of the e-mail). Please indicate "query adult" or "query children's) in the subject line. Accepts simultaneous submissions. Responds in 2 weeks to queries. Responds in 6 weeks to mss. Obtains most new clients through recommendations from others, solicitations.

Terms Agent receives 15% commission on domestic sales. Agent receives 20% commission on foreign sales. Offers written contract. 100% of business is derived from commissions on ms. sales. Charges clients for postage, photocopying, long distance telephone (if significant).

◙ SARAH JANE FREYMANN LITERARY AGENCY

59 W. 71st St., Suite 9B, New York NY 10023. (212)362-9277. E-mail: sarah@sarahjanefreymann.com; Submissions@SarahJaneFreymann.com. Website: www.sarahjanefreymann.com. **Contact:** Sarah Jane Freymann, Steve Schwartz. Represents 100 clients. 20% of clients are new/unpublished writers. Currently handles nonfiction books (75%), novels (23%), juvenile books (2%).

Member Agents Sarah Jane Freymann; Steve Schwartz, steve@sarahjanefreymann.com (historical novels, thrillers, crime, sports, humor, food, travel); Katharine Sands.

Represents nonfiction books, novels illustrated books. **Considers these nonfiction areas:** interior, animals, anthropology, art, biography, business, child, cooking, current affairs, ethnic, health, history, memoirs, narrative, nature, psychology, religion, self help, womens lifestyle. **Considers these fiction areas:** ethnic, literary, mainstream.

How to Contact Query with SASE. Responds in 2 weeks to queries. Responds in 6 weeks to mss. Obtains most new clients through recommendations from others.

Terms Agent receives 15% commission on domestic sales. Agent receives 20% commission on foreign sales. Offers written contract. Charges clients for long distance, overseas postage, photocopying. 100% of business is derived from commissions on ms sales.

Tips "I love fresh, new, passionate works by authors who love what they are doing and have both natural talent and carefully honed skill."

☑ FREDRICA S. FRIEDMAN AND CO., INC.

136 E. 57th St., 14th Floor, New York NY 10022. (212)829-9600. Fax: (212)829-9669. E-mail: info@ fredricafriedman.com; submissions@fredricafriedman.com. Website: www.fredricafriedman.com/. **Contact:** Ms. Chandler Smith. Represents 75+ clients. 50% of clients are new/unpublished writers. Currently handles nonfiction books (95%), novels (5%).

Represents nonfiction books, novels anthologies. **Considers these nonfiction areas:** art, biography, business, child, cooking, current affairs, education, ethnic, gay, government, health, history, how to, humor, language, memoirs, money, music, photography, popular culture, psychology, self help, sociology, film, true crime, womens interior design/decorating. **Considers these fiction areas:** literary. "We represent a select group of outstanding nonfiction and fiction writers. We are particularly interested in helping writers expand their readership and develop their careers." Does not want poetry, plays, screenplays, children's books, sci-fi/fantasy, or horror.

How to Contact Submit e-query, synopsis. Accepts simultaneous submissions. Responds in 4-6 weeks to queries. Responds in 4-6 weeks to mss. Obtains most new clients through recommendations from others.

Terms Agent receives 15% commission on domestic sales. Agent receives 25% commission on foreign sales. Offers written contract. Charges for photocopying and messenger/shipping fees for proposals.

Tips "Spell the agent's name correctly on your query letter."

☑ FULL CIRCLE LITERARY, LLC

7676 Hazard Center Dr., Suite 500, San Diego CA 92108. E-mail: submissions@fullcircleliterary.com. Website: www.fullcircleliterary.com. **Contact:** Lilly Ghahremani, Stefanie Von Borstel. Represents 55 clients. 60% of clients are new/unpublished writers. Currently handles nonfiction books (70%), novels (10%), juvenile books (20%).

- Before forming Full Circle, Ms. Von Borstel worked in both marketing and editorial capacities at Penguin and Harcourt; Ms. Ghahremani received her law degree from UCLA, and has experience in representing authors on legal affairs.

Member Agents Lilly Ghahremani (young adult, pop culture, crafts, "green" living, narrative nonfiction, business, relationships, Middle Eastern interest, multicultural); Stefanie Von Borstel (Latino interest, crafts, parenting, wedding/relationships, how-to, self help, middle grade/teen fiction/YA, green living, multicultural/bilingual picture books).

Represents nonfiction books, juvenile. **Considers these nonfiction areas:** animals, biography, business, child guidance, crafts, cultural interests, current affairs, ethnic, how-to, juvenile nonfiction, parenting, personal improvement, popular culture, self-help, women's issues, women's studies. **Considers these fiction areas:** ethnic, literary, young adult. "Our full-service boutique agency, representing a range of nonfiction and children's books (limited fiction), provides a one-stop resource for authors. Our extensive experience in the realms of law and marketing provide Full Circle clients with a unique edge." "Actively seeking nonfiction by authors with a unique and strong platform, projects that offer new and diverse viewpoints, and literature with a global or multicultural perspective. We are particularly interested in books with a Latino or Middle Eastern angle and books related to pop culture." Does not want to receive "screenplays, poetry, commercial fiction or genre fiction (horror, thriller, mystery, Western, sci-fi, fantasy, romance, historical fiction)."

How to Contact Agency accepts e-queries. See Web site for fiction guidelines, as they are in flux. For nonfiction, send full proposal Accepts simultaneous submissions. Responds in 1-2 weeks to queries. Responds in 4-6 weeks to mss. Obtains most new clients through recommendations from others, solicitations, conferences.

Terms Agent receives 15% commission on domestic sales. Agent receives 20% commission on foreign sales. Offers written contract; up to 30-day notice must be given to terminate contract. Charges for copying and postage.

Tips "Put your best foot forward. Contact us when you simply can't make your project any better on your own, and please be sure your work fits with what the agent you're approaching represents. Little things count, so copyedit your work. Join a writing group and attend conferences to get objective and constructive feedback before submitting. Be active about building your platform as an author before, during, and after publication. Remember this is a business and your agent is a business partner."

DON GASTWIRTH & ASSOCIATES

265 College St., New Haven CT 06510. (203)562-7600. Fax: (203)562-4300. E-mail: Donlit@snet.net. **Contact:** Don Gastwirth. Signatory of WGA. Represents 26 clients. 10% of clients are new/unpublished writers. Currently handles nonfiction books (30%), scholarly books (60%), other(10% other).

- Prior to becoming an agent, Mr. Gastwirth was an entertainment lawyer and law professor.

Represents nonfiction books, scholarly. **Considers these nonfiction areas:** business, current affairs, history, military, money, music, nature, popular culture, psychology, translation, true crime. **Considers these fiction areas:** mystery, thriller. This is a selective agency and is rarely open to new clients that do not come through a referral.

How to Contact Query with SASE.

Terms Agent receives 15% commission on domestic sales. Agent receives 10% commission on foreign sales.

☑ GELFMAN SCHNEIDER LITERARY AGENTS, INC.

250 W. 57th St., Suite 2122, New York NY 10107. (212)245-1993. Fax: (212)245-8678. E-mail: mail@gelfmanschneider.com. **Contact:** Jane Gelfman, Deborah Schneider. Member of AAR. Represents 300+ clients. 10% of clients are new/unpublished writers.

Represents nonfiction books, novels. **Considers these fiction areas:** literary, mainstream, mystery, womens. Does not want to receive romance, science fiction, westerns, or children's books.

How to Contact Query with SASE. Send queries via snail mail only. Responds in 1 month to queries. Responds in 2 months to mss.

Terms Agent receives 15% commission on domestic sales. Agent receives 20% commission on foreign sales. Agent receives 15% commission on film sales. Offers written contract. Charges clients for photocopying and messengers/couriers.

☑ BARRY GOLDBLATT LITERARY, LLC

320 Seventh Ave., #266, Brooklyn NY 11215. Fax: (718)360-5453. Website: www.bgliterary.com/contactme.html. **Contact:** Barry Goldblatt, Joe Monti, Beth Fleisher. Member of AAR.

Represents juvenile books. **Considers these fiction areas:** picture books, young adult middle grade, all genres.

How to Contact E-mail queries query@bgliterary.com, and include the first five pages and a synopsis of the novel pasted into the text of the e-mail. No attachments or links.

☑ THE SUSAN GOLOMB LITERARY AGENCY

875 Avenue of the Americas, Suite 2302, New York NY 10001. Fax: (212)239-9503. E-mail: susan@sgolombagency.com. **Contact:** Susan Golomb. Represents 100 clients. 20% of clients are new/unpublished writers. Currently handles nonfiction books (50%), novels (40%), story collections (10%).

Represents nonfiction books, novels, short story collections, novellas. **Considers these nonfiction areas:** animals, anthropology, biography, business, current affairs, government, health, history, memoirs, military, money, nature, popular culture, psychology, science, sociology, womens. **Considers these fiction areas:** ethnic, historical, humor, literary, mainstream, thriller, young women's/chick lit. "We specialize in literary and upmarket fiction and nonfiction that is original, vibrant and of excellent quality and craft. Nonfiction should be edifying, paradigm-shifting, fresh and entertaining." Actively seeking writers with strong voices. Does not want to receive genre fiction.

How to Contact Query with SASE. Submit outline/proposal, synopsis, 1 sample chapters, author bio, SASE. Query via mail or e-mail. Responds in 2 week to queries. Responds in 8 weeks to mss. Obtains most new clients through recommendations from others, solicitations.

Terms Agent receives 15% commission on domestic sales. Agent receives 20% commission on foreign sales. Offers written contract.

☑ IRENE GOODMAN LITERARY AGENCY

27 W. 24th Street, Suite 700B, New York NY 10010. E-mail: queries@irenegoodman.com. Website: www.irenegoodman.com. **Contact:** Irene Goodman, Miriam Kriss. Member of AAR.

Member Agents Irene Goodman; Miriam Kriss; Barbara Poelle; Jon Sternfeld (intelligent literary fiction, high-end modern fiction; nonfiction and narrative nonfiction dealing with social, cultural and historical issues; an occasional memoir and current affairs book).

Represents nonfiction books, novels. **Considers these nonfiction areas:** history parenting, social issues, francophilia, anglophilia, Judaica, lifestyles, cooking, memoir. **Considers these fiction areas:** historical, literary, mystery, romance, thriller, young, womens chick lit; modern urban fantasies. "Specializes in the finest in commercial fiction and nonfiction. We have a strong background in women's voices, including mysteries, romance, women's fiction, thrillers, suspense, and chick lit. Historical fiction is one of Irene's particular passions and Miriam is fanatical about modern urban fantasies. We are also very interested in young adult fiction, both literary and those with an edgy, chick-litty voice. In nonfiction, Irene is looking for topics on narrative history, social issues and trends, education, Judaica, Francophilia, Anglophilia, other cultures, animals, food, crafts, and memoir."

How to Contact Query with SASE. Submit synopsis, first 10 pages.E-mail queries only! See the Web site submission page. No e-mail attachments. Responds in 2 months to queries.

Tips "We are receiving an unprecedented amount of e-mail queries. If you find that the mailbox is full, please try again in two weeks. E-mail queries to our personal addresses will not be answered."

☒ GOUMEN & SMIRNOVA LITERARY AGENCY

Nauki pr., 19/2 fl. 293, St. Petersburg 195220 Russia. E-mail: info@gs-agency.com. Website: www.gs-agency.com. **Contact:** Julia Goumen, Natalia Smirnova. Represents 20 clients. 10% of clients are new/unpublished writers. Currently handles nonfiction books (10%), novels (80%), story collections (5%), juvenile books (5%).

- Prior to becoming agents, both Ms. Goumen and Ms. Smirnova worked as foreign rights managers with an established Russian publisher selling translation rights for literary fiction.

Member Agents Julia Goumen (translation rights, Russian language rights, film rights); Natalia Smirnova (translation rights, Russian language rights, film rights).

Represents nonfiction books, novels, short story collections, novellas, movie, tv, tv movie, sitcom.

Considers these nonfiction areas: biography, current affairs, ethnic, humor, memoirs, music. **Considers these fiction areas:** adventure, experimental, family, historical, horror, literary, mainstream, mystery, romance, thriller, young, womens. **Considers these script areas:** action, comedy, detective, family, mainstream, romantic comedy, romantic drama, teen, thriller. "We are the first full-service agency in Russia, representing our authors in book publishing, film, television, and other areas. We are also the first agency, representing Russian authors worldwide, based in Russia. The agency also represents international authors, agents and publishers in Russia. Our philosophy is to provide an individual approach to each author, finding the right publisher both at home and across international cultural and linguistic borders, developing original marketing and promotional strategies for each title." Actively seeking manuscripts written in Russian, both literary and commercial; and foreign publishers and agents with the high-profile fiction and general nonfiction list—to represent in Russia. Does not want to receive unpublished manuscripts in languages other then Russian, or any information irrelevant to our activity.

How to Contact Query with SASE. Submit synopsis, author bio. Accepts simultaneous submissions. Responds in 14 days to mss. Obtains most new clients through recommendations from others, solicitations.

Terms Agent receives 20% commission on domestic sales. Agent receives 20% commission on foreign sales. Offers written contract, binding for 1 year; 2-month notice must be given to terminate contract.

☑ SANFORD J. GREENBURGER ASSOCIATES, INC.

55 Fifth Ave., New York NY 10003. (212)206-5600. Fax: (212)463-8718. E-mail: queryHL@sjga.com. Website: www.greenburger.com. Member of AAR. Represents 500 clients.

Member Agents Heide Lange; Faith Hamlin; Dan Mandel; Matthew Bialer; Jeremy Katz; Tricia Davey, Courtney Miller-Callihan, Michael Harriot.

Represents nonfiction books, novels. **Considers these nonfiction areas:** agriculture horticulture, americana, crafts, interior, juvenile, newage, young, animals, anthropology, art, biography, business, child, computers, cooking, current affairs, education, ethnic, gardening, gay, government, health, history, how to, humor, language, memoirs, military, money, multicultural, music, nature, philosophy, photography, popular culture, psychology, recreation, regional, religion, science, self help, sex, sociology, software, sports, film, translation, travel, true crime, womens. **Considers these fiction areas:** glitz, psychic, adventure, detective, ethnic, family, feminist, gay, historical, humor, literary, mainstream, mystery, regional, sports, thriller. No romances or Westerns.

How to Contact Submit query, first 3 chapters, synopsis, brief bio, SASE. Accepts simultaneous submissions. Responds in 2 months to queries and mss. Responds to mss. Obtains most new clients through recommendations from others.

Terms Agent receives 15% commission on domestic sales. Agent receives 20% commission on foreign sales. Charges for photocopying and books for foreign and subsidiary rights submissions.

☑ THE GREENHOUSE LITERARY AGENCY

11308 Lapham Drive, Oakton VA 22124. E-mail: submissions@greenhouseliterary.com. Website: www. greenhouseliterary.com. **Contact:** Sarah Davies. Other memberships include SCBWI. Represents 8 clients. 100% of clients are new/unpublished writers. Currently handles juvenile books (100%).

• Prior to becoming an agent, Ms. Davies was the publishing director of Macmillan Children's Books in London.

Represents juvenile. **Considers these fiction areas:** juvenile, young. "We exclusively represents authors writing fiction for children and teens. The agency has offices in both the USA and UK, and Sarah Davies (who is British) personally represents authors to both markets. The agency's commission structure reflects this – taking 15% for sales to both US and UK, thus treating both as 'domestic' market." All genres of children's and YA fiction - ages 5 +. Does not want to receive nonfiction, poetry, picture books (text or illustration) or work aimed at adults.

How to Contact E-queries only as per guidelines given on Web site. Query should contain one-paragraph synopsis, one-paragraph bio, up to 5 sample pages pasted into e-mail. Replies to submissions in which agency is interested. Responds in 6-8 weeks to requested full manuscripts. Responds in 6 week to queries. Obtains most new clients through recommendations from others, solicitations, conferences.

Terms Agent receives 15% commission on domestic sales. Agent receives 25% commission on foreign sales. Offers written contract. This agency charges for copies for overseas submissions.

Writers Conferences Bologna Children's Book Fair, SCBWI conferences, BookExpo America.

Tips "Before submitting material, authors should read the Greenhouse's 'Top 10 Tips for Authors of Children's Fiction,' which can be found on our Web site."

KATHRYN GREEN LITERARY AGENCY, LLC

250 West 57th St., Suite 2302, New York NY 10107. (212)245-2445. Fax: (212)245-2040. E-mail: query@ kgreenagency.com. **Contact:** Kathy Green. Other memberships include Women's Media Group. Represents approximately 20 clients. 50% of clients are new/unpublished writers. Currently handles nonfiction books (50%), novels (25%), juvenile books (25%).

• Prior to becoming an agent, Ms. Green was a book and magazine editor.

Represents nonfiction books, novels, short story collections, juvenile, middle grade and young adult only). **Considers these nonfiction areas:** biography, business, child, cooking, current affairs, education, history, how to, humor, memoirs, popular culture, psychology, self help, sports, true crime, womens juvenile. **Considers these fiction areas:** detective, family, historical, humor, juvenile, middle grade and young adult only, literary, mainstream, mystery, romance, thriller, young women's. Keeping the client list small means that writers receive my full attention throughout the process of getting their project published. Does not want to receive science fiction or fantasy.

How to Contact Query with SASE. Query first. Send no samples unless requested. Accepts simultaneous submissions. Responds in 1-2 months to mss. Obtains most new clients through recommendations from others, solicitations, conferences.

Terms Agent receives 15% commission on domestic sales. Agent receives 20% commission on foreign sales. No written contract.

Tips "This agency offers a written agreement."

GREGORY & CO. AUTHORS' AGENTS

3 Barb Mews, Hammersmith, London W6 7PA England. (44)(207)610-4676. Fax: (44)(207)610-4686. E-mail: info@gregoryandcompany.co.uk. Website: www.gregoryandcompany.co.uk. **Contact:** Jane Gregory. Other memberships include AAA. Represents 60 clients. Currently handles nonfiction books (10%), novels (90%).

Represents nonfiction books, novels. **Considers these nonfiction areas:** biography, history. **Considers these fiction areas:** detective, historical, literary, mainstream, thriller contemporary women's fiction. As a British agency, we do not generally take on American authors. Actively seeking well-written, accessible modern novels. Does not want to receive horror, science fiction, fantasy, mind/body/spirit, children's books, screenplays, plays, short stories or poetry.

How to Contact Query with SASE. Submit outline, first 10 pages by email or post, publishing history, author bio. Send submissions to Jane Gregory, submissions editor. Accepts simultaneous submissions. Returns materials only with SASE. Obtains most new clients through recommendations from others, conferences.

Terms Agent receives 15% commission on domestic sales. Agent receives 20% commission on foreign sales. Offers written contract; 1-month notice must be given to terminate contract. Charges clients for photocopying of whole typescripts and copies of book for submissions.

Writers Conferences CWA Conference; Bouchercon.

JILL GROSJEAN LITERARY AGENCY

1390 Millstone Road, Sag Harbor NY 11963-2214. (631)725-7419. Fax: (631)725-8632. E-mail: jill6981@ aol.com. **Contact:** Jill Grosjean. Represents 40 clients. 100% of clients are new/unpublished writers. Currently handles novels (100%).

• Prior to becoming an agent, Ms. Grosjean was manager of an independent bookstore. She has also worked in publishing and advertising.

Represents novels. **Considers these fiction areas:** historical, literary, mainstream, mystery, regional, romance. This agency offers some editorial assistance (i.e., line-by-line edits). Actively seeking literary novels and mysteries.

How to Contact E-mail queries only, no attachments. No cold calls, please. Accepts simultaneous submissions. Responds in 1 week to queries. Responds in 1 month to mss. Obtains most new clients through recommendations from others, solicitations.

Terms Agent receives 15% commission on domestic sales. Agent receives 20% commission on foreign sales. No written contract. Charges clients for photocopying and mailing expenses.

Writers Conferences Book Passage's Mystery Writers' Conference; Agents and Editors Conference; Texas Writers' and Agents' Conference.

☒ LAURA GROSS LITERARY AGENCY

P.O. Box 610326, Newton Highlands MA 02461. (617)964-2977. Fax: (617)964-3023. E-mail: query@ lauragrossliteraryagency.com. **Contact:** Laura Gross. Represents 30 clients. Currently handles nonfiction books (40%), novels (50%), scholarly books (10%).

- Prior to becoming an agent, Ms. Gross was an editor.

Represents nonfiction books, novels. **Considers these nonfiction areas:** biography, current affairs, ethnic, government, health, history, memoirs, popular culture, psychology, sports, women's issues, women's studies. **Considers these fiction areas:** historical, literary, mainstream, mystery, thriller.

How to Contact Query with SASE. Submit author bio. Responds in several days to queries. Obtains most new clients through recommendations from others.

Terms Agent receives 15% commission on domestic sales. Agent receives 20% commission on foreign sales. Offers written contract.

☒ REECE HALSEY NORTH/PARIS/NEW YORK

98 Main St., #704, Tiburon CA 94920. Fax: (415)789-9177. E-mail: info@reecehalseynorth.com. Website: www.reecehalseynorth.com. **Contact:** Kimberley Cameron. Member of AAR. 30% of clients are new/ unpublished writers. Currently handles other(50% fiction, 50% nonfiction).

- The Reece Halsey Agency has had an illustrious client list of established writers, including the estate of Aldous Huxley, and has represented Upton Sinclair, William Faulkner, and Henry Miller.

Member Agents Kimberley Cameron, Elizabeth Evans; April Eberhardt, Amy Burkhardt.

Represents nonfiction and fiction. **Considers these nonfiction areas:** biography, current affairs, history, language, popular culture, science, true crime, women's issues, women's studies. **Considers these fiction areas:** contemporary, adventure, detective, ethnic, family, historical, horror, literary, mainstream, mystery, science, thriller, women's fiction. We are looking for a unique and heartfelt voice that conveys a universal truth.

How to Contact Query via e-mail with first 50 pages of novel. Responds in 3-6 weeks to queries. Responds in 1 month to mss. Obtains most new clients through recommendations from others, solicitations.

Terms Agent receives 15% commission on domestic sales. Agent receives 10% commission on film sales. Offers written contract, binding for 1 year.

Writers Conferences Maui Writers Conference; Aspen Summer Words Literary Festival; Willamette Writers Conference, numerous others.

Tips "Please send a polite, well-written query to info@reecehalseynorth.com."

☒ HALSTON FREEMAN LITERARY AGENCY, INC.

140 Broadway, 46th Floor, New York NY 10005. E-mail: queryhalstonfreemanliterary@hotmail.com. **Contact:** Molly Freeman, Betty Halston. Currently handles nonfiction books (65%), novels (35%).

- Prior to becoming an agent, Ms. Halston was a marketing and promotion director for a local cable affiliate; Ms. Freeman was a television film editor and ad agency copywriter.

Member Agents Molly Freeman, Betty Halston.

Represents nonfiction books, novels. **Considers these nonfiction areas:** agriculture horticulture, newage, biography, business, child, current affairs, ethnic, gay, government, health, history, how to, humor, memoirs, psychology, self help, true crime, womens. **Considers these fiction areas:** adventure, detective, ethnic, feminist, historical, horror, humor, literary, mainstream, mystery, romance, science, thriller, western, womens. "We are a hands-on agency specializing in quality nonfiction and fiction. As a new agency, it is imperative that we develop relationships with good writers who are smart, hardworking and understand what's required of them to promote their books." Does not want to receive children's books, textbooks or poetry. Send no e-mail attachments.

How to Contact Query with SASE. For nonfiction, include sample chapters, synopsis, platform, bio and competitive titles. For fiction, include synopsis, bio and three sample chapters. No e-mail attachments. Accepts simultaneous submissions. Responds in 2-6 weeks to queries. Responds in 1-2 months to mss. Obtains most new clients through recommendations from others, solicitations, conferences.

Terms Agent receives 15% commission on domestic sales. Agent receives 20% commission on foreign sales. This agency charges clients for copying and postage directly related to the project.

☑ HALYARD LITERARY AGENCY

Chicago IL E-mail: submissions@halyardagency.com; agrayson@halyardagency.com (general info). Website: www.halyardagency.com. **Contact:** Alaina Grayson.
Member Agents Alaina Grayson.
Represents nonfiction books, novels. **Considers these nonfiction areas:** biography, history, science. **Considers these fiction areas:** fantasy, historical, juvenile, science, young general, paranormal. Based out of Chicago, Halyard Literary Agency is a new agency on the lookout for authors who have the same passion for innovation that we do. Halyard is small, but provides assistance through every stage of book production. We're dedicated to building relationships with our authors, not just for one book or one year, but throughout their publishing life.
How to Contact Query with SASE. E-mail queries only to submissions@halyardagency.com. Send requested materials as e-mail attachments only if requested from query.

THE MITCHELL J. HAMILBURG AGENCY

149 S. Barrington Ave., #732, Los Angeles CA 90049-2930. (310)471-4024. Fax: (310)471-9588. **Contact:** Michael Hamilburg. Signatory of WGA. Represents 70 clients. Currently handles nonfiction books (70%), novels (30%).
Represents nonfiction books, novels. **Considers these nonfiction areas:** anthropology, biography, business, child, cooking, current affairs, education, government, health, history, memoirs, military, money, psychology, recreation, regional, self help, sex, sociology, spirituality, sports, travel, womens creative nonfiction; romance; architecture; inspirational; true crime. **Considers these fiction areas:** glitz, New Age, adventure, experimental, feminist, humor, military, mystery, occult, regional, religious, romance, sports, thriller crime; mainstream; psychic.
How to Contact Query with outline, 2 sample chapters, SASE. Responds in 1 month to mss. Obtains most new clients through recommendations from others, conferences, personal search.
Terms Agent receives 10-15% commission on domestic sales.

◨ HARTLINE LITERARY AGENCY

123 Queenston Dr., Pittsburgh PA 15235-5429. (412)829-2483. Fax: (412)829-2432. E-mail: joyce@hartlineliterary.com. Website: www.hartlineliterary.com. **Contact:** Joyce A. Hart. Represents 40 clients. 20% of clients are new/unpublished writers. Currently handles nonfiction books (40%), novels (60%).
Member Agents Joyce A. Hart, principal agent; Terry Burns; Tamela Hancock Murray; Diana Flegal.
Represents nonfiction books, novels. **Considers these nonfiction areas:** business, child, cooking, money, religion, self help, womens. **Considers these fiction areas:** contemporary, adventure, family, historical, literary, mystery, amateur sleuth, cozy, regional, religious, romance, contemporary, gothic, historical, regency, thriller. This agency specializes in the Christian bookseller market. Actively seeking adult fiction, self-help, nutritional books, devotional, and business. Does not want to receive erotica, gay/lesbian, fantasy, horror, etc.
How to Contact Submit summary/outline, author bio, 3 sample chapters. Accepts simultaneous submissions. Responds in 2 months to queries. Responds in 3 months to mss. Obtains most new clients through recommendations from others.
Terms Agent receives 15% commission on domestic sales. Offers written contract.

◨ JOHN HAWKINS & ASSOCIATES, INC.

71 W. 23rd St., Suite 1600, New York NY 10010. (212)807-7040. Fax: (212)807-9555. E-mail: jha@jhalit.com. Website: www.jhalit.com. **Contact:** Moses Cardona (moses@jhalit.com). Member of AAR. Represents over 100 clients. 5-10% of clients are new/unpublished writers. Currently handles nonfiction books (40%), novels (40%), juvenile books (20%).
Member Agents Moses Cardona
Represents nonfiction books, novels young adult. **Considers these nonfiction areas:** agriculture horticulture, americana, interior, young, anthropology, art, biography, business, current affairs, education, ethnic, gardening, gay, government, health, history, how to, language, memoirs, money, multicultural, nature, philosophy, popular culture, psychology, recreation, science, self help, sex, sociology, software,

film, travel, true crime music, creative nonfiction. **Considers these fiction areas:** glitz, psychic, adventure, detective, ethnic, experimental, family, feminist, gay, gothic, hi lo, historical, literary, mainstream, military, multicultural, multimedia, mystery, religious, short, sports, thriller, translation, western, young, womens.

How to Contact Submit query, proposal package, outline, SASE. Accepts simultaneous submissions. Responds in 1 month to queries. Obtains most new clients through recommendations from others.

Terms Agent receives 15% commission on domestic sales. Agent receives 20% commission on foreign sales. Charges clients for photocopying.

☑ HIDDEN VALUE GROUP

1240 E. Ontario Ave., Ste. 102-148, Corona CA 92881. (951)549-8891. Fax: (951)549-8891. E-mail: bookquery@hiddenvaluegroup.com. Website: www.hiddenvaluegroup.com. **Contact:** Nancy Jernigan. Represents 55 clients. 10% of clients are new/unpublished writers.

Member Agents Jeff Jernigan, jjernigan@hiddenvaluegroup.com (men's nonfiction, fiction, Bible studies/curriculum, marriage and family); Nancy Jernigan, njernigan@hiddenvaluegroup.com (nonfiction, women's issues, inspiration, marriage and family, fiction).

Represents nonfiction books, novels, juvenile. **Considers these nonfiction areas:** juvenile, biography, business, child, history, how to, language, memoirs, money, psychology, religion, self help, womens. **Considers these fiction areas:** adventure, detective, fantasy, literary, religious, thriller, western, womens. "The Hidden Value Group specializes in helping authors throughout their publishing career. We believe that every author has a special message to be heard and we specialize in getting that message out." Actively seeking established fiction authors, and authors who are focusing on women's issues. Does not want to receive poetry or short stories.

How to Contact Query with SASE. Submit synopsis, 3 sample chapters, author bio. Accepts queries to bookquery@hiddenvaluegroup.com. No fax queries. Accepts simultaneous submissions. Responds in 1 month to queries. Responds in 1 month to mss. Obtains most new clients through recommendations from others, solicitations.

Terms Agent receives 15% commission on domestic sales. Agent receives 15% commission on foreign sales. Offers written contract.

Writers Conferences Glorieta Christian Writers' Conference; CLASS Publishing Conference.

HOPKINS LITERARY ASSOCIATES

2117 Buffalo Rd., Suite 327, Rochester NY 14624-1507. (585)352-6268. **Contact:** Pam Hopkins. Member of AAR. Other memberships include RWA. Represents 30 clients. 5% of clients are new/unpublished writers. Currently handles novels (100%).

Represents novels. **Considers these fiction areas:** romance, historical, contemporary, category, womens. This agency specializes in women's fiction, particularly historical, contemporary, and category romance, as well as mainstream work.

How to Contact Submit outline, 3 sample chapters. Accepts simultaneous submissions. Responds in 2 weeks to queries. Responds in 1 month to mss. Obtains most new clients through recommendations from others, solicitations, conferences.

Terms Agent receives 15% commission on domestic sales. Agent receives 20% commission on foreign sales. No written contract.

Writers Conferences RWA National Conference.

☑ ANDREA HURST LITERARY MANAGEMENT

P.O. Box 19010, Sacramento CA 95819. E-mail: (agentfirstname)@andreahurst.com. Website: www.andreahurst.com. **Contact:** Andrea Hurst, Judy Mikalonis, Amberly Finarelli. Represents 50+ clients. 50% of clients are new/unpublished writers. Currently handles nonfiction books (75%), novels (10%), juvenile books (15%).

> • Prior to becoming an agent, Ms. Hurst was an acquisitions editor as well as a freelance editor and published writer; Ms. Mikalonis was in marketing and branding consulting.

Member Agents Andrea Hurst, andrea@andreahurst.com (nonfiction—including personal growth, health and wellness, science, business, parenting, relationships, women's issues, animals, spirituality, women's issues, metaphysical, psychological, cookbooks and self help; fiction interests include adult fiction); Judy Mikalonis, judy@andreahurst.com (YA fiction, Christian fiction, Christian nonfiction); Amberly Finarelli amberly@andreahurst.com (Nonfiction: humor/gift books, crafts, how-to, Relationships/advice, Self-help, psychology, Travel writing, Narrative nonfiction. Fiction: Commercial women's fiction, Comic and cozy mysteries, Literary fiction with a focus on the arts, culture, and/or history, Contemporary young adult.

Represents nonfiction books, novels, juvenile. **Considers these nonfiction areas:** crafts, interior, juvenile, newage, animals, art, biography, business, child, cooking, education, health, how to, humor, memoirs, military, money, music, nature, photography, popular culture, psychology, religion, science, self help, sociology, true crime, womens gift books. **Considers these fiction areas:** psychic, juvenile, literary, mainstream, religious, romance, thriller, young, womens. We work directly with our signed authors to help them polish their work and their platform for optimum marketability. Our staff is always available to answer phone calls and e-mails from our authors and we stay with a project until we have exhausted all publishing avenues. Actively seeking well written nonfiction by authors with a strong platform; superbly crafted fiction with depth that touches the mind and heart and all of our listed subjects. Does not want to receive sci-fi, mystery, horror, Western, poetry or screenplays.

How to Contact Query with SASE. Submit outline/proposal, synopsis, 2 sample chapters, author bio. Accepts simultaneous submissions. Obtains most new clients through recommendations from others, solicitations, conferences.

Terms Agent receives 15% commission on domestic sales. Agent receives 20% commission on foreign sales. Offers written contract, binding for 6 to 12 months; 30-day notice must be given to terminate contract. This agency charges for postage.

Writers Conferences San Francisco Writers' Conference; Willamette Writers' Conference; PNWA; Whidbey Island Writers Conference.

Tips "Do your homework and submit a professional package. Get to know the agent you are submitting to by researching their Web site or meeting them at a conference. Perfect your craft: Write well and edit ruthlessly over and over again before submitting to an agent. Be realistic: Understand that publishing is a business and be prepared to prove why your book is marketable and how you will market it on your own. Be Persistent!"

◙ INTERNATIONAL TRANSACTIONS, INC.

P.O. Box 97, Gila NM 88038-0097. (845)373-9696. Fax: (845)373-7868. E-mail: info@intltrans.com. Website: www.intltrans.com. **Contact:** Peter Riva. Represents 40+ clients. 10% of clients are new/unpublished writers. Currently handles nonfiction books (60%), novels (25%), story collections (5%), juvenile books (5%), scholarly books (5%).

Member Agents Peter Riva (nonfiction, fiction, illustrated; television and movie rights placement); Sandra Riva (fiction, juvenile, biographies); JoAnn Collins (fiction, women's fiction, medical fiction).

Represents nonfiction books, novels, short story collections, juvenile, scholarly illustrated books, anthologies. **Considers these nonfiction areas:** anthropology, art, biography, computers, cooking, current affairs, ethnic, gay, government, health, history, humor, language, memoirs, military, music, nature, photography, science, self help, sports, translation, true crime, womens. **Considers these fiction areas:** adventure, detective, erotica, experimental, feminist, gay, historical, humor, literary, mainstream, mystery, spiritual, sports, thriller, young adult women's/chick lit. "We specialize in large and small projects, helping qualified authors perfect material for publication." Actively seeking intelligent, well-written innovative material that breaks new ground. Does not want to receive material influenced by TV (too much dialogue); a rehash of previous successful novels' themes or poorly prepared material.

How to Contact First, e-query with an outline or synopsis. E-queries only!. Responds in 3 weeks to queries. Responds in 5 weeks to mss. Obtains most new clients through recommendations from others, solicitations.

Terms Agent receives 15% (25% on illustrated books) commission on domestic sales. Agent receives 20% commission on foreign sales. Offers written contract; 120-day notice must be given to terminate contract.

Tips "'Book'—a published work of literature. That last word is the key. Not a string of words, not a book of (TV or film) 'scenes,' and never a stream of consciousness unfathomable by anyone outside of the writer's coterie. A writer should only begin to get 'interested in getting an agent' if the work is polished, literate and ready to be presented to a publishing house. Anything less is either asking for a quick rejection or is a thinly disguised plea for creative assistance—which is often given but never fiscally sound for the agents involved. Writers, even published authors, have difficulty in being objective about their own work. Friends and family are of no assistance in that process either. Writers should attempt to get their work read by the most unlikely and stern critic as part of the editing process, months before any agent is approached."

JABBERWOCKY LITERARY AGENCY

P.O. Box 4558, Sunnyside NY 11104-0558. (718)392-5985. Website: www.awfulagent.com. **Contact:** Joshua Bilmes. Other memberships include SFWA. Represents 40 clients. 15% of clients are new/unpublished writers. Currently handles nonfiction books (15%), novels (75%), scholarly books (5%), other (5% other).

Member Agents Joshua Bilmes; Eddie Schneider.

Represents nonfiction books, novels, scholarly. **Considers these nonfiction areas:** biography, business, cooking, current affairs, film, gay, government, health, history, humor, language, money, nature, popular culture, science, sociology, sports, young adult. **Considers these fiction areas:** contemporary, glitz, psychic, adventure, detective, ethnic, family, fantasy, gay, historical, horror, humor, literary, mainstream, regional, science, sports, thriller. This agency represents quite a lot of genre fiction and is actively seeking to increase the amount of nonfiction projects. It does not handle children's or picture books. Book-length material only—no poetry, articles, or short fiction.

How to Contact Query with SASE. Do not send mss unless requested. Accepts simultaneous submissions. Responds in 3 weeks to queries. Obtains most new clients through solicitations, recommendation by current clients.

Terms Agent receives 15% commission on domestic sales. Agent receives 20% commission on foreign sales. Offers written contract, binding for 1 year. Charges clients for book purchases, photocopying, international book/ms mailing.

Writers Conferences Malice Domestic (May 2009); World Sci-Fi Convention (August 2008); World Fantasy Convention (October 2009); full schedule on Web site.

Tips "In approaching with a query, the most important things to us are your credits and your biographical background to the extent it's relevant to your work. I (and most agents) will ignore the adjectives you may choose to describe your own work."

J DE S ASSOCIATES, INC.

9 Shagbark Road, Wilson Point, South Norwalk CT 06854. (203)838-7571. **Contact:** Jacques de Spoelberch. Represents 50 clients. Currently handles nonfiction books (50%), novels (50%).

• Prior to opening his agency, Mr. de Spoelberch was an editor with Houghton Mifflin.

Represents nonfiction books, novels. **Considers these nonfiction areas:** biography, business, cultural interests, current affairs, economics, ethnic, government, health, history, law, medicine, metaphysics, military, New Age, personal improvement, politics, self-help, sociology, sports, translation. **Considers these fiction areas:** crime, detective, frontier, historical, juvenile, literary, mainstream, mystery, New Age, police, suspense, westerns, young adult.

How to Contact Query with SASE. Responds in 2 months to queries. Obtains most new clients through Recommendations from authors and other clients.

Terms Agent receives 15% commission on domestic sales. Agent receives 20% commission on foreign sales. Charges clients for foreign postage and photocopying.

JET LITERARY ASSOCIATES

2570 Camino San Patricio, Santa Fe NM 87505. (505)474-9139. Fax: (505)474-9139. E-mail: etp@jetliterary.com. Website: www.jetliterary.com. **Contact:** Liz Trupin-Pulli. Represents 75 clients. 35% of clients are new/unpublished writers.

Member Agents Liz Trupin-Pulli (adult and YA fiction/nonfiction; romance, mysteries, parenting); Jim Trupin (adult fiction/nonfiction, military history, pop culture); Jessica Trupin, associate agent based in Seattle (adult fiction and nonfiction, children's and young adult, memoir, pop culture.

Represents nonfiction books, novels, short story collections. **Considers these nonfiction areas:** biography, business, child, current affairs, ethnic, gay, government, humor, memoirs, military, popular culture, sports, true crime, womens. **Considers these fiction areas:** adventure, detective, erotica, ethnic, gay, glitz, historical, humor, lesbian, literary, mainstream, mystery, romance, thriller. JET was founded in New York in 1975, so we bring a wealth of knowledge and contacts, as well as quite a bit of expertise to our representation of writers. Actively seeking women's fiction, mysteries and narrative nonfiction.

Does not want to receive sci-fi, fantasy, horror, poetry, children's or religious.

How to Contact An e-query is preferred; if sending by snail mail, include an SASE. Responds in 1 week to queries. Responds in 8 weeks to mss. Obtains most new clients through recommendations from others, solicitations, conferences.

Terms Agent receives 15% commission on domestic sales. Agent receives 10% commission on foreign sales. Offers written contract, binding for 3 years. This agency charges for reimbursement of mailing and any photocopying.

Writers Conferences Hillerman Mystery and Suspense Conference, Florida Writers Association Conference.

Tips Do not write 'cute' queries—stick to a straightforward message that includes the title and what your book is about, why you are suited to write this particular book, and what you have written in the past (if anything), along with a bit of a bio.

☑ CAREN JOHNSON LITERARY AGENCY

132 East 43rd St., No. 216, New York NY 10017. Fax: (718)228-8785. E-mail: caren@johnsonlitagency. com. Website: www.johnsonlitagency.com. **Contact:** Caren Johnson Estesen, Elana Roth. Represents 20 clients. 50% of clients are new/unpublished writers. Currently handles nonfiction books 35%, juvenile books 35%, romance/women's fiction 30%.

- Prior to her current position, Ms. Johnson was with Firebrand Literary and the Peter Rubie Agency.

Member Agents Caren Johnson Estesen, Elana Roth, Rachel Downes

Represents nonfiction books, novels. **Considers these nonfiction areas:** history, popular culture, science, women's studies, social science. **Considers these fiction areas:** detective, erotica, ethnic, romance, young adult middle grade, women's fiction. Does not want to receive poetry, plays or screenplays/scripts. Elana Roth will consider picture books but is very selective of what she takes on.

How to Contact Query via e-mail only, "directing your query to the appropriate person; responds in 12 weeks to all materials sent. Accepts simultaneous submissions. Responds in 4-6 weeks to queries. Responds in 6-8 weeks to mss. Obtains most new clients through recommendations from others.

Terms Agent receives 15% commission on domestic sales. Agent receives 20% commission on foreign sales. Offers written contract; 30-day notice must be given to terminate contract. This agency charges for postage and photocopying, though the author is consulted before any charges are incurred.

Writers Conferences RWA National; BookExpo America; SCBWI.

☑ VIRGINIA KIDD AGENCY, INC.

538 E. Harford St., P.O. Box 278, Milford PA 18337. (570)296-6205. Fax: (570)296-7266. Website: www. vk-agency.com. Other memberships include SFWA, SFRA. Represents 80 clients.

Member Agents Christine Cohen

Represents novels. **Considers these fiction areas:** fantasy, historical, mystery, science, womens speculative; mainstream. This agency specializes in science fiction and fantasy.

How to Contact Query with SASE. Submit synopsis (1-3 pages), cover letter, first chapter, SASE. Snail mail queries only. Responds in 6 weeks to queries.

Terms Agent receives 15% commission on domestic sales. Agent receives 20-25% commission on foreign sales. Agent receives 20% commission on film sales. Offers written contract; 2-month notice must be given to terminate contract. Charges clients occasionally for extraordinary expenses.

Tips "If you have a completed novel that is of extraordinary quality, please send us a query."

☑ KLEINWORKS AGENCY

2814 Brooks Ave., # 635, Missoula MT 59801. E-mail: judyklein@kleinworks.com. Website: www. kleinworks.com. **Contact:** Judy Klein. Represents 10 clients. Currently handles nonfiction books (60%), novels (40%).

- Prior to becoming an agent, Ms. Klein spent a dozen years with Farrar, Straus & Giroux; she also held the position of editor-in-chief at The Literary Guild Book Club and at Booksonline.com.

Represents nonfiction books, novels. **Considers these nonfiction areas:** biography, business, health, how to, memoirs, money, nature, popular culture, self help. **Considers these fiction areas:** ethnic, experimental, humor, literary. "Kleinworks Agency may be geographically removed from the red-hot center of New York publishing, but our credentials and connections keep us close to New York's best publishers and editors. As a publishing veteran with two decades of book experience, intimate knowledge of the industry and expertise in domestic and international negotiations, I provide my clients with an edge in getting their books published well. Kleinworks offers dedicated services to a very small, select group of writers and publishers so that we can guarantee spirited and undivided attention."

How to Contact Query with SASE. Submit proposal package, outline/proposal, synopsis, author bio, sample chapters. No phone queries. Accepts simultaneous submissions. Responds in 4 weeks to queries. Responds in 1-2 months to mss. Obtains most new clients through recommendations from others.

Terms Agent receives 15% commission on domestic sales. Agent receives 20% commission on foreign sales. Offers written contract, binding for optional, for 1 year; 3-month notice must be given to terminate contract. Charges for postage and photocopying fees after six months.

Writers Conferences Montana Festival of the Book, Yellowstone Nature Writers' Field Conference.

☑ HARVEY KLINGER, INC.

300 W. 55th St., Suite 11V, New York NY 10019. (212)581-7068. E-mail: queries@harveyklinger.com. Website: www.harveyklinger.com. **Contact:** Harvey Klinger. Member of AAR. Represents 100 clients. 25% of clients are new/unpublished writers. Currently handles nonfiction books (50%), novels (50%).

Member Agents David Dunton (popular culture, music-related books, literary fiction, young adult, fiction, and memoirs); Sara Crowe (children's and young adult authors, adult fiction and nonfiction, foreign rights sales); Andrea Somberg (literary fiction, commercial fiction, romance, sci-fi/fantasy, mysteries/thrillers, young adult, middle grade, quality narrative nonfiction, popular culture, how-to, self-help, humor, interior design, cookbooks, health/fitness)

Represents nonfiction books, novels. **Considers these nonfiction areas:** biography, cooking, health, psychology, science, self help, spirituality, sports, true crime, womens. **Considers these fiction areas:** glitz, adventure, detective, family, literary, mainstream, mystery, thriller. This agency specializes in big, mainstream, contemporary fiction and nonfiction.

How to Contact Query with SASE. No phone or fax queries. Don't send unsolicited manuscripts or e-mail attachments. Responds in 2 months to queries and mss. Obtains most new clients through recommendations from others.

Terms Agent receives 15% commission on domestic sales. Agent receives 25% commission on foreign sales. Offers written contract. Charges for photocopying mss and overseas postage for mss.

☑ ELAINE KOSTER LITERARY AGENCY, LLC

55 Central Park W., Suite 6, New York NY 10023. (212)362-9488. Fax: (212)712-0164. **Contact:** Elaine Koster, Stephanie Lehmann, Ellen Twaddell. Member of AAR. Other memberships include MWA, Author's Guild, Women's Media Group. Represents 40 clients. 10% of clients are new/unpublished writers. Currently handles nonfiction books (10%), novels (90%).

- Prior to opening her agency in 1998, Ms. Koster was president and publisher of Dutton-NAL, part of the Penguin Group.

Represents nonfiction books, novels. **Considers these nonfiction areas:** biography, business, child, cooking, current affairs, ethnic, health, history, how to, money, nature, popular culture, psychology, self help, spirituality, womens. **Considers these fiction areas:** ethnic, feminist, historical, literary, mainstream, mystery, regional, thriller chick lit. This agency specializes in quality fiction and nonfiction. Does not want to receive juvenile, screenplays, or science fiction.

How to Contact Query with SASE. Prefers to read materials exclusively. Responds in 3 weeks to queries. Responds in 1 month to mss. Obtains most new clients through recommendations from others.

Terms Agent receives 15% commission on domestic sales. Bills back specific expenses incurred doing business for a client.

Tips "We prefer exclusive submissions. Don't e-mail or fax submissions. Please include biographical information and publishing history."

☑ KRAAS LITERARY AGENCY

E-mail: irenekraas@sbcglobal.net. Website: www.kraasliteraryagency.com. **Contact:** Irene Kraas. Represents 35 clients. 75% of clients are new/unpublished writers. Currently handles nonfiction books (2%), novels (98%).

Member Agents Irene Kraas, principal.

Represents novels. **Considers these fiction areas:** literary, thriller, young. This agency is interested in working with published writers, but that does not mean self-published writers. "Actively seeking psychological thrillers, medical thrillers, some literary fiction and young adult. With each of these areas, I want something new. No Da Vinci Code or Harry Potter ripoffs. I am especially not interested in storylines that include the Mafia or government. Not interested in personal stories of growth, stories about generation hangups and stories about drugs, incest, etc." Does not want to receive short stories, plays or poetry. This agency no longer represents adult fantasy or science fiction.

How to Contact Query and e-mail the first 10 pages of a completed ms. Requires exclusive read on mss. Accepts simultaneous submissions.

Terms Offers written contract.

Tips "I am interested in material - in any genre - that is truly, truly unique."

EDITE KROLL LITERARY AGENCY, INC.

20 Cross St., Saco ME 04072. (207)283-8797. Fax: (207)283-8799. E-mail: ekroll@maine.rr.com. **Contact:** Edite Kroll. Represents 45 clients. 20% of clients are new/unpublished writers. Currently handles nonfiction books (40%), novels (5%), juvenile books (40%), scholarly books (5%), other.

• Prior to opening her agency, Ms. Kroll served as a book editor and translator.

Represents nonfiction books, novels, very selective, juvenile, scholarly. **Considers these nonfiction areas:** juvenile, selectively, biography, current affairs, ethnic, gay, government, health, no diet books, humor, memoirs, selectively, popular culture, psychology, religion, selectively, self help, selectively, womens issue-oriented nonfiction. **Considers these fiction areas:** juvenile, literary, picture books, young adult middle grade, adult. "We represent writers and writer-artists of both adult and children's books. We have a special focus on international feminist writers, women writers and artists who write their own books (including children's and humor books)." Actively seeking artists who write their own books and international feminists who write in English. Does not want to receive genre (mysteries, thrillers, diet, cookery, etc.), photography books, coffee table books, romance or commercial fiction.

How to Contact Query with SASE. Submit outline/proposal, synopsis, 1-2 sample chapters, author bio, entire ms if sending picture book.No phone queries. Responds in 2-4 weeks to queries. Responds in 4-8 weeks to mss. Obtains most new clients through recommendations from others.

Terms Agent receives 15% commission on domestic sales. Agent receives 20% commission on foreign sales. Offers written contract; 30-day notice must be given to terminate contract. Charges clients for photocopying and legal fees with prior approval from writer.

Tips "Please do your research so you won't send me books/proposals I specifically excluded."

☐ KT LITERARY, LLC

9249 S. Broadway, #200-543, Highlands Ranch CO 80129. (720)344-4728. Fax: (720)344-4728. E-mail: queries@ktliterary.com. Website: www.ktliterary.com. **Contact:** Kate Schafer Testerman. Other memberships include SCBWI. Represents 20 clients. 60% of clients are new/unpublished writers. Currently handles nonfiction books (5%), novels (5%), juvenile books (90%).

• Prior to her current position, Ms. Schafer was an agent with Janklow & Nesbit.

Represents nonfiction books, novels, juvenile books. **Considers these nonfiction areas:** popular culture. **Considers these fiction areas:** adventure, fantasy, historical, juvenile, romance, young adult. "I'm bringing my years of experience in the New York publishing scene, as well as my lifelong love of reading, to a vibrant area for writers, proving that great work can be found, and sold, from anywhere." "Actively seeking brilliant, funny, original middle grade and young adult fiction, both literary and commercial; witty women's fiction (chick lit); and pop-culture, narrative nonfiction. Quirky is good." Does not want picture books, serious nonfiction, and adult literary fiction.

How to Contact Query with SASE. Submit author bio, 2-3 sample pages.Absolutely no attachments. Paste text in e-mail body. E-mail queries only. Responds in 2 weeks to queries. Responds in 1 month to mss. Obtains most new clients through recommendations from others, solicitations, conferences.

Terms Agent receives 15% commission on domestic sales. Agent receives 20% commission on foreign sales. Offers written contract; 30-day notice must be given to terminate contract.

Writers Conferences Various SCBWI conferences, BookExpo.

Tips "If we like your query, we'll ask for (more). Continuing advice is offered regularly on my blog 'Ask Daphne', which can be accessed from my Web site."

❑ KT PUBLIC RELATIONS & LITERARY SERVICES

1905 Cricklewood Cove, Fogelsville PA 18051. (610)395-6298. Fax: (610)395-6299. Website: www.ktpublicrelations.com. **Contact:** Jon Tienstra. Represents 12 clients. 75% of clients are new/unpublished writers. Currently handles nonfiction books (50%), novels (50%).

- Prior to becoming an agent, Kae Tienstra was publicity director for Rodale, Inc. for 13 years and then founded her own publicity agency; Mr. Tienstra joined the firm in 1995 with varied corporate experience and a master's degree in library science.

Member Agents Kae Tienstra (health, parenting, psychology, how-to, crafts, foods/nutrition, beauty, women's fiction, general fiction); Jon Tienstra (nature/environment, history, cooking/foods/nutrition, war/military, automotive, health/medicine, gardening, general fiction, science fiction/contemporary fantasy, popular fiction).

Represents nonfiction books, novels. **Considers these nonfiction areas:** agriculture horticulture, crafts, animals, child, cooking, health, history, how to, military, nature, popular culture, psychology, science, self help interior design/decorating. **Considers these fiction areas:** adventure, detective, family, fantasy, contemporary - no swords or dragons, historical, literary, mainstream, mystery, romance, science, thriller. "We have worked with a variety of authors and publishers over the years and have learned what individual publishers are looking for in terms of new acquisitions. We are both mad about books and authors and we look forward to finding publishing success for all our clients. Specializes in parenting, history, cooking/foods/nutrition, crafts, beauty, war, health/medicine, psychology, how-to, gardening, science fiction, fantasy, women's fiction, and popular fiction." Does not want to see unprofessional material.

How to Contact Query with SASE. Prefers snail mail queries. Will accept e-mail queries. Responds in 3 months to chapters; 6-9 months for mss. Accepts simultaneous submissions. Responds in 2 weeks to queries.

Terms Agent receives 15% commission on domestic sales. Agent receives 20% commission on foreign sales. Offers written contract. Charges clients for long-distance phone calls, fax, postage, photocopying (only when incurred). No advance payment for these out-of-pocket expenses.

◧ THE LA LITERARY AGENCY

P.O. Box 46370, Los Angeles CA 90046. (323)654-5288. E-mail: laliteraryag@mac.com. **Contact:** Ann Cashman, Eric Lasher.

- Prior to becoming an agent, Mr. Lasher worked in publishing in New York and Los Angeles.

Represents nonfiction books, novels. **Considers these nonfiction areas:** animals, anthropology, art, biography, business, child, cooking, current affairs, ethnic, government, health, history, how to, nature, popular culture, psychology, science, self help, sociology, sports, true crime, womens narrative nonfiction. **Considers these fiction areas:** adventure, detective, family, feminist, historical, literary, mainstream, sports, thriller.

How to Contact Query with outline, 1 sample chapter. No fax or e-mail queries.

◧ PETER LAMPACK AGENCY, INC.

551 Fifth Ave., Suite 1613, New York NY 10176-0187. (212)687-9106. Fax: (212)687-9109. E-mail: alampack@verizon.net. **Contact:** Andrew Lampack. Represents 50 clients. 10% of clients are new/unpublished writers. Currently handles nonfiction books (20%), novels (80%).

Member Agents Peter Lampack (president); Rema Delanyan (foreign rights); Andrew Lampack (new writers).

Represents nonfiction books, novels. **Considers these fiction areas:** adventure, detective, family, literary, mainstream, mystery, thriller contemporary relationships. "This agency specializes in commercial fiction and nonfiction by recognized experts." Actively seeking literary and commercial fiction, thrillers, mysteries, suspense, and psychological thrillers. Does not want to receive horror, romance, science fiction, westerns, historical literary fiction or academic material.

How to Contact Query via e-mail. *No unsolicited mss.* Responds within 2 months to queries. Obtains most new clients through referrals made by clients.

Terms Agent receives 15% commission on domestic sales. Agent receives 20% commission on foreign sales.

Writers Conferences BookExpo America; Mystery Writers of America.

Tips "Submit only your best work for consideration. Have a very specific agenda of goals you wish your prospective agent to accomplish for you. Provide the agent with a comprehensive statement of your credentials - educational and professional accomplishments."

☑ LAURA LANGLIE, LITERARY AGENT

239 Carroll St., Garden Apartment, Brooklyn NY 11231. (718)855-8102. Fax: (718)855-4450. E-mail: laura@ lauralanglie.com. **Contact:** Laura Langlie. Represents 25 clients. 50% of clients are new/unpublished writers. Currently handles nonfiction books (15%), novels (58%), story collections (2%), juvenile books (25%).

- Prior to opening her agency, Ms. Langlie worked in publishing for 7 years and as an agent at Kidde, Hoyt & Picard for 6 years.

Represents nonfiction books, novels, short story collections, novellas, juvenile. **Considers these nonfiction areas:** animals, not how-to, biography, current affairs, ethnic, government, history, humor, memoirs, nature, popular culture, psychology, film, womens history of medicine and science; language/ literature. **Considers these fiction areas:** detective, ethnic, feminist, historical, humor, juvenile, literary, mystery, romance, thriller, young mainstream. "I'm very involved with and committed to my clients. I also employ a publicist to work with all my clients to make the most of each book's publication. Most of my clients come to me via recommendations from other agents, clients and editors. I've met very few at conferences. I've often sought out writers for projects, and I still find new clients via the traditional query letter." Does not want to receive children's picture books, science fiction, poetry, men's adventure or erotica.

How to Contact Query with SASE. Accepts queries via fax. Accepts simultaneous submissions. Responds in 1 week to queries. Responds in 1 month to mss. Obtains most new clients through recommendations, submissions.

Terms Agent receives 15% commission on domestic sales. Agent receives 20% commission on foreign sales. No written contract.

Tips Be complete, forthright and clear in your communications. Do your research as to what a particular agent represents.

LANGTONS INTERNATIONAL AGENCY

240 West 35th St., Suite 500, New York NY 10001. (212)929-1937. E-mail: langtonsinternational@gmail. com. Website: www.langtonsinternational.com. **Contact:** Linda Langton.

- Prior to becoming an agent, Ms. Langton was a co-founding director and publisher of the international publishing company, The Ink Group.

Represents nonfiction books, novels. **Considers these nonfiction areas:** biography, health, history, how-to, politics, self-help, true crime. **Considers these fiction areas:** literary, political thrillers, young adult and middle grade books. "Langtons International Agency is a multi-media literary and licensing agency specializing in nonfiction, thrillers and children's books as well as the the visual world of photography, illustrative art, gift books, calendars, greeting cards, posters and other related products."

How to Contact Query with SASE. Submit outline/proposal, synopsis, publishing history, author bio. Only published authors should query this agency Accepts simultaneous submissions.

☑ MICHAEL LARSEN/ELIZABETH POMADA, LITERARY AGENTS

1029 Jones St., San Francisco CA 94109-5023. (415)673-0939. E-mail: larsenpoma@aol.com. Website: www.larsen-pomada.com. **Contact:** Mike Larsen, Elizabeth Pomada. Member of AAR. Other memberships include Authors Guild, ASJA, PEN, WNBA, California Writers Club, National Speakers Association. Represents 100 clients. 40-45% of clients are new/unpublished writers. Currently handles nonfiction books (70%), novels (30%).

- Prior to opening their agency, Mr. Larsen and Ms. Pomada were promotion executives for major publishing houses. Mr. Larsen worked for Morrow, Bantam and Pyramid (now part of Berkley); Ms. Pomada worked at Holt, David McKay and The Dial Press. Mr. Larsen is the author of the third editions of *How to Write a Book Proposal* and *How to Get a Literary Agent* as well as the coauthor of *Guerilla Marketing for Writers: 100 Weapons for Selling Your Work*, which will be republished in September 2009.

Member Agents Michael Larsen (nonfiction)

Represents Considers these nonfiction areas: anthropology, art, biography, business, current affairs, ethnic, film, foods, gay, government, health, history, humor, memoirs, money, music, nature, popular culture, psychology, science, sociology, sports, travel, true crime futurism. **Considers these fiction areas:** contemporary, glitz, adventure, detective, ethnic, experimental, family, fantasy, feminist, gay, historical, humor, literary, mainstream, mystery, religious, romance, contemporary, gothic, historical chick lit. We have diverse tastes. We look for fresh voices and new ideas. We handle literary, commercial and genre fiction, and the full range of nonfiction books. Actively seeking commercial, genre and literary fiction. Does not want to receive children's books, plays, short stories, screenplays, pornography, poetry or stories of abuse.

How to Contact Query with SASE. Responds in 8 weeks to pages or submissions.

Terms Agent receives 15% commission on domestic sales. Agent receives 20% (30% for Asia) commission on foreign sales. May charge for printing, postage for multiple submissions, foreign mail, foreign phone calls, galleys, books, legal fees.

Writers Conferences This agency organizes the annual San Francisco Writers' Conference (www. sfwriters.org).

Tips "We love helping writers get the rewards and recognition they deserve. If you can write books that meet the needs of the marketplace and you can promote your books, now is the best time ever to be a writer. We must find new writers to make a living, so we are very eager to hear from new writers whose work will interest large houses, and nonfiction writers who can promote their books. For a list of recent sales, helpful info, and three ways to make yourself irresistible to any publisher, please visit our Web site."

THE STEVE LAUBE AGENCY

5025 N. Central Ave., #635, Phoenix AZ 85012. (602)336-8910. E-mail: krichards@stevelaube.com. Website: www.stevelaube.com. **Contact:** Steve Laube. Other memberships include CBA. Represents 60 + clients. 5% of clients are new/unpublished writers. Currently handles nonfiction books (48%), novels (48%), novella(2%), scholarly books (2%).

- Prior to becoming an agent, Mr. Laube worked 11 years as a Christian bookseller and 11 years as editorial director of nonfiction with Bethany House Publishers.

Represents nonfiction books, novels. **Considers these nonfiction areas:** religion. **Considers these fiction areas:** religious. We primarily serve the Christian market (CBA). Actively seeking Christian fiction and religious nonfiction. Does not want to receive children's picture books, poetry or cookbooks.

How to Contact Submit proposal package, outline, 3 sample chapters, SASE.No e-mail submissions. Consult Web site for guidelines. Accepts simultaneous submissions. Responds in 6-8 weeks to queries. Obtains most new clients through recommendations from others, solicitations, conferences.

Terms Agent receives 15% commission on domestic sales. Agent receives 20% commission on foreign sales. Offers written contract; 30-day notice must be given to terminate contract.

Writers Conferences Mount Hermon Christian Writers' Conference; American Christian Fiction Writers' Conference.

☑ LAZEAR GROUP, INC.

431 Second St., Suite 300, Hudson WI 54016. (715)531-0012. Fax: (715)531-0016. Website: www.lazear. com. **Contact:** Editorial Board. 20% of clients are new/unpublished writers. Currently handles juvenile books (5%), other(commercial fiction and nonfiction).

- The Lazear Group opened a New York office in September 1997.

Member Agents Jonathon Lazear; Christi Cardenas; Darrick Kline; Nate Roen; Anne Blackstone.

Represents nonfiction books, novels, juvenile. **Considers these nonfiction areas:** agriculture horticulture, americana, interior, juvenile, newage, young, animals, anthropology, art, biography, child, computers, cooking, creative, current affairs, ethnic, gardening, gay, government, health, history, how to, humor, language, memoirs, military, money, multicultural, music, nature, philosophy, photography, popular culture, psychology, recreation, regional, religion, science, self help, sex, sociology, software, spirituality, sports, film, travel, true crime, womens creative nonfiction. **Considers these fiction areas:** newage, psychic, adventure, confession, detective, ethnic, family, fantasy, feminist, gay, gothic, hi lo, historical, humor, juvenile, literary, mainstream, military, multicultural, multimedia, mystery, occult, picture books, plays, poetry, poetry trans, religious, romance, science, short, spiritual, sports, thriller, translation, western, young, womens. Actively seeking new voices in commercial fiction and nonfiction.

It's all about the writing, no matter the subject matter. Does not want to receive short stories, poetry, scripts and/or screenplays.

How to Contact Query with SASE. Submit outline/proposal, author bio, 1-2 page synopsis, 5-7 page sample.Query first. The agency will respond if interested. Include SASE for snail mail queries. Responds in 4 weeks to queries. Responds in 3 weeks to mss. Obtains most new clients through recommendations from others, solicitations.

Terms Agent receives 15% commission on domestic sales. Agent receives 20% commission on foreign sales. Offers written contract. Charges clients for photocopying, international express mail, bound galleys, books used for subsidiary rights sales. No fees charged if book is not sold.

Tips The writer should first view himself as a salesperson in order to obtain an agent. Sell yourself, your idea, your concept. Do your homework. Notice what is in the marketplace. Be sophisticated about the arena in which you are writing. Please note that we also have a New York office, but the primary office remains in Hudson, Wis., for the receipt of any material.

☑ ROBERT LECKER AGENCY

4055 Melrose Ave., Montreal QC H4A 2S5 Canada. (514)830-4818. Fax: (514)483-1644. E-mail: leckerlink@ aol.com. Website: www.leckeragency.com. **Contact:** Robert Lecker. Represents 20 clients. 20% of clients are new/unpublished writers. Currently handles nonfiction books (80%), novels (10%), scholarly books (10%).

- Prior to becoming an agent, Mr. Lecker was the co-founder and publisher of ECW Press and professor of English literature at McGill University. He has 30 years of experience in book and magazine publishing.

Member Agents Robert Lecker (popular culture, music); Mary Williams (travel, food, popular science).

Represents nonfiction books, novels, scholarly syndicated material. **Considers these nonfiction areas:** biography, cooking, ethnic, how to, language, music, popular culture, science, film. **Considers these fiction areas:** adventure, detective, erotica, literary, mainstream, mystery, thriller. RLA specializes in books about popular culture, popular science, music, entertainment, food and travel. The agency responds to articulate, innovative proposals within 2 weeks. Actively seeking original book mss only after receipt of outlines and proposals.

How to Contact Query first. Only responds to queries of interest. Discards the rest. Accepts simultaneous submissions. Responds in 2 weeks to queries. Responds in 1 month to mss. Obtains most new clients through recommendations from others, conferences, interest in Web site.

Terms Agent receives 15% commission on domestic sales. Agent receives 15-20% commission on foreign sales. Offers written contract, binding for 1 year; 6-month notice must be given to terminate contract.

☑ LESCHER & LESCHER, LTD.

346 E. 84th St., New York NY 10028. (212)396-1999. Fax: (212)396-1991. **Contact:** Carolyn Larson. Member of AAR. Represents 150 clients. Currently handles nonfiction books (80%), novels (20%).

Represents nonfiction books, novels. **Considers these nonfiction areas:** current affairs, history, memoirs, popular culture biography; cookbooks/wines; law; contemporary issues; narrative nonfiction. **Considers these fiction areas:** literary, mystery commercial. Does not want to receive screenplays, science fiction or romance.

How to Contact Query with SASE. Obtains most new clients through recommendations from others.

Terms Agent receives 15% commission on domestic sales. Agent receives 10% commission on foreign sales.

LEVINE GREENBERG LITERARY AGENCY, INC.

307 Seventh Ave., Suite 2407, New York NY 10001. (212)337-0934. Fax: (212)337-0948. Website: www. levinegreenberg.com. Member of AAR. Represents 250 clients. 33%% of clients are new/unpublished writers. Currently handles nonfiction books (70%), novels (30%).

- Prior to opening his agency, Mr. Levine served as vice president of the Bank Street College of Education.

Member Agents James Levine, Daniel Greenberg, Stephanie Kip Rostan, Lindsay Edgecombe, Danielle Svetcov, Elizabeth Fisher, Victoria Skurnick.

Represents nonfiction books, novels. **Considers these nonfiction areas:** New Age, animals, art, biography, business, child, computers, cooking, gardening, gay, health, money, nature, religion, science, self help, sociology, spirituality, sports, womens. **Considers these fiction areas:** literary, mainstream, mystery, thriller, psychological, womens. This agency specializes in business, psychology, parenting, health/medicine, narrative nonfiction, spirituality, religion, women's issues, and commercial fiction.

How to Contact See Web site for full submission procedure. Obtains most new clients through recommendations from others.

Terms Agent receives 15% commission on domestic sales. Agent receives 20% commission on foreign sales. Offers written contract. Charges clients for out-of-pocket expenses—telephone, fax, postage, photocopying—directly connected to the project.

Writers Conferences ASJA Writers' Conference.

Tips "We focus on editorial development, business representation, and publicity and marketing strategy."

☑ PAUL S. LEVINE LITERARY AGENCY

1054 Superba Ave., Venice CA 90291-3940. (310)450-6711. Fax: (310)450-0181. E-mail: paul@paulslevinelit. com. Website: www.paulslevinelit.com. **Contact:** Paul S. Levine. Other memberships include the State Bar of California. Represents over 100 clients. 75% of clients are new/unpublished writers. Currently handles nonfiction books (60%), novels (10%), movie scripts (10%), TV scripts (5%), juvenile books 5%.

Member Agents Paul S. Levine (children's and young adult fiction and nonfiction, adult fiction and nonfiction except sci-fi, fantasy, and horror); Loren R. Grossman (archaeology, art/photography/architecture, gardening, education, health, medicine, science).

Represents nonfiction books, novels, episodic drama, movie, TV, movie scripts, feature film, TV movie of the week, sitcom, animation, documentary, miniseries syndicated material, reality show. **Considers these nonfiction areas:** art, biography, business, computers, cooking, crafts, current affairs, education, ethnic, film, gay, government, health, history, humor, language, memoirs, military, money, music, nature, New Age, photography, popular culture, psychology, science, sociology, sports, true crime creative nonfiction,. **Considers these fiction areas:** glitz, adventure, comic, confession, detective, erotica, ethnic, experimental, family, feminist, gay, historical, humor, literary, mainstream, mystery, regional, religious, romance, sports, thriller, western. **Considers these script areas:** action, biography, cartoon, comedy, contemporary, detective, erotica, ethnic, experimental, family, feminist, gay, glitz, historical, horror, juvenile, mainstream, multimedia, mystery, religious, romantic comedy, romantic drama, sports, teen, thriller, western. Does not want to receive science fiction, fantasy, or horror.

How to Contact Query with SASE. Accepts simultaneous submissions. Responds in 1 day to queries. Responds in 6-8 weeks to mss. Obtains most new clients through conferences, referrals, listings on various websites and in directories.

Terms Agent receives 15% commission on domestic sales. Offers written contract. Charges for postage and actual, out-of-pocket costs only.

Writers Conferences Willamette Writers Conference; San Francisco Writers Conference; Santa Barbara Writers Conference and many others.

Tips "Write good, sellable books."

☑ LINDSTROM LITERARY MANAGEMENT, LLC

871 N. Greenbrier St., Arlington VA 22205. Fax: (703)527-7624. E-mail: submissions@lindstromliterary. com. Website: www.lindstromliterary.com. **Contact:** Kristin Lindstrom. Other memberships include Author's Guild. Represents 9 clients. 30% of clients are new/unpublished writers. Currently handles nonfiction books (30%), novels (70%).

- Prior to her current position, Ms. Lindstrom was an editor of a monthly magazine in the energy industry, and an independent marketing and publicity consultant.

Represents nonfiction books, novels. **Considers these nonfiction areas:** animals, biography, business, current affairs, history, memoirs, popular culture, science, true crime. **Considers these fiction areas:** adventure, detective, erotica, mainstream, mystery, religious, thriller, womens. "In 2006, I decided to add my more specific promotion/publicity skills to the mix in order to support the marketing efforts of my published clients." Actively seeking commercial fiction and narrative nonfiction. Does not want to receive juvenile or children's books.

How to Contact Query via e-mail only. Submit author bio, synopsis and first four chapters if submitting fiction. For nonfiction, send the first 4 chapters, synopsis, proposal, outline and mission statement

Accepts simultaneous submissions. Responds in 6 weeks to queries. Responds in 8 weeks to requested mss. Obtains most new clients through recommendations from others, solicitations.

Terms Agent receives 15% commission on domestic sales. Agent receives 20% commission on performance rights and foreign sales. Offers written contract. This agency charges for postage, UPS, copies and other basic office expenses.

Tips "Do your homework on accepted practices; make sure you know what kind of book the agent handles."

LINN PRENTIS LITERARY

155 East 116th St., #2F, New York NY 10029. Fax: (212)875-5565. E-mail: Linn@linnprentis.com. **Contact:** Linn Prentis, Acacia Stevens. Represents 18-20 clients. 25% of clients are new/unpublished writers. Currently handles nonfiction books (5%), novels (65%), story collections (7%), novella(10%), juvenile books (10%), scholarly books (3%).

• Prior to becoming an agent, Ms. Prentis was a nonfiction writer and editor, primarily in magazines. She also worked in book promotion in New York. Ms. Prentis then worked for and later ran the Virginia Kidd Agency. She is known particularly for her assistance with manuscript development."

Represents nonfiction books, novels, short story collections, novellas, from authors whose novels I already represent, juvenile, for older juveniles, scholarly anthology. **Considers these nonfiction areas:** juvenile, animals, art, biography, current affairs, education, ethnic, government, how to, humor, language, memoirs, music, photography, popular culture, sociology, womens. **Considers these fiction areas:** adventure, ethnic, fantasy, feminist, gay, glitz, historical, horror, humor, juvenile, lesbian, literary, mainstream, mystery, thriller. Because of the Virginia Kidd connection and the clients I brought with me at the start, I have a special interest in sci-fi and fantasy, but, really, fiction is what interests me. As for my nonfiction projects, they are books I just couldn't resist. Actively seeking hard science fiction, family saga, mystery, memoir, mainstream, literary, women's. Does not want to "receive books for little kids."

How to Contact Query with SASE. Submit synopsis. No phone or fax queries. Snail mail is best. Accepts simultaneous submissions. Obtains most new clients through recommendations from others, solicitations.

Terms Agent receives 15% commission on domestic sales. Agent receives 20% commission on foreign sales. Offers written contract; 60-day notice must be given to terminate contract.

Tips Consider query letters and synopses as writing assignments. Spell names correctly.

☑ LIPPINCOTT MASSIE MCQUILKIN

27 West 20th Street, Suite 305, New York NY 10011. Fax: (212)352-2059. E-mail: info@lmqlit.com. Website: www.lmqlit.com. **Contact:** Rachel Vogel. Represents 90 clients. 30% of clients are new/unpublished writers. Currently handles nonfiction books (40%), novels (40%), story collections (10%), scholarly books (5%), poetry(5%).

Member Agents Maria Massie (fiction, memoir, cultural criticism); Will Lippincott (politics, current affairs, history); Rob McQuilkin (fiction, history, psychology, sociology, graphic material); Jason Anthony (pop culture, memoir, true crime, and general psychology).

Represents nonfiction books, novels, short story collections, scholarly graphic novels. **Considers these nonfiction areas:** animals, anthropology, art, biography, business, child, current affairs, ethnic, gay, government, health, history, language, memoirs, military, money, music, nature, popular culture, psychology, religion, science, self help, sociology, film, true crime, womens. **Considers these fiction areas:** adventure, comic, confession, family, feminist, gay, historical, humor, literary, mainstream, regional. "LMQ focuses on bringing new voices in literary and commercial fiction to the market, as well as popularizing the ideas and arguments of scholars in the fields of history, psychology, sociology, political science, and current affairs. Actively seeking fiction writers who already have credits in magazines and quarterlies, as well as nonfiction writers who already have a media platform or some kind of a university affiliation." Does not want to receive romance, genre fiction or children's material.

How to Contact "We accepts electronic queries only. Only send additional materials if requested." Accepts simultaneous submissions. Responds in 1 week to queries. Responds in 1 month to mss. Obtains most new clients through recommendations from others, solicitations, conferences.

Terms Agent receives 15% commission on domestic sales. Agent receives 20% commission on foreign sales. Offers written contract; 30-day notice must be given to terminate contract. Only charges for reasonable business expenses upon successful sale.

✒ LITERARY AGENCY FOR SOUTHERN AUTHORS

2123 Paris Metz Road, Chattanooga TN 37421. E-mail: southernlitagent@aol.com. **Contact:** Lantz Powell. Represents 20 clients. 60% of clients are new/unpublished writers. Currently handles nonfiction books (50%), novels (50%).

* Prior to becoming an agent, Mr. Powell was in sales and contract negotiation.

Represents nonfiction books, novels, juvenile, for ages 14 and up. **Considers these nonfiction areas:** crafts, interior, newage, art, biography, business, current affairs, education, ethnic, government, history, how to, humor, language, military, photography, popular culture, religion, self help, true crime. **Considers these fiction areas:** cartoon, comic books, humor, literary, mainstream, regional, religious, satire, young adult. "We focus on authors that live in the Southern United States. We have the ability to translate and explain complexities of publishing for the Southern author." "Actively seeking quality projects by authors with a vision of where they want to be in 10 years and a plan of how to get there." Does not want to receive unfinished, unedited projects that do not follow the standard presentation conventions of the trade. No romance.

How to Contact Query via e-mail first and include a synopsis. Accepts simultaneous submissions. Responds in 2-3 days to queries. Responds in 1 week to mss. Obtains most new clients through recommendations from others.

Terms Agent receives 15% commission on domestic sales. Agent receives 25% commission on foreign sales. Offers written contract. "We charge when a publisher wants a hard copy overnight or the like. The client always knows this beforehand."

Writers Conferences Conference for Southern Literature; Tennessee Book Fair.

Tips "If you are an unpublished author, join a writers group, even if it is on the Internet. You need good honest feedback. Don't send a manuscript that has not been read by at least five people. Don't send a manuscript cold to any agent without first asking if they want it. Try to meet the agent face to face before signing. Make sure the fit is right."

✒ THE LITERARY GROUP INTERNATIONAL

51 E. 25th St., Suite 401, New York NY 10010. (212)274-1616. Fax: (212)274-9876. E-mail: fweimann@theliterarygroup.com. Website: www.theliterarygroup.com. **Contact:** Frank Weimann. 65% of clients are new/unpublished writers. Currently handles nonfiction books (50%), other(50% fiction).

Member Agents Frank Weimann; acquisitions editor Jaimee Garbacik.

Represents nonfiction books, novels graphic novels. **Considers these nonfiction areas:** animals, anthropology, biography, business, child guidance, crafts, creative nonfiction, current affairs, education, ethnic, film, government, health, history, humor, juvenile nonfiction, language, memoirs, military, multicultural, music, nature, popular culture, politics, psychology, religious, science, self-help, sociology, sports, travel, true crime, women's issues, women's studies. **Considers these fiction areas:** adventure, contemporary issues, detective, ethnic, experimental, family saga, fantasy, feminist, historical, horror, humor, literary, multicultural, mystery, psychic, romance, sports, thriller, young adult regional, graphic novels. This agency specializes in nonfiction (memoir, military, history, biography, sports, how-to).

How to Contact Query with SASE. Prefers to read materials exclusively. Only responds if interested. Obtains most new clients through referrals, writers' conferences, query letters.

Terms Agent receives 15% commission on domestic sales. Agent receives 20% commission on foreign sales. Offers written contract; 30-day notice must be given to terminate contract.

Writers Conferences San Diego State University Writers' Conference; Maui Writers' Conference; Agents and Editors Conference; NAHJ Convention in Puerto Rico, among others.

✒ JULIA LORD LITERARY MANAGEMENT

38 W. Ninth St., #4, New York NY 10011. (212)995-2333. Fax: (212)995-2332. E-mail: julialordliterary@nyc.rr.com. Member of AAR.

Member Agents Julia Lord, owner.

Represents Considers these nonfiction areas: biography, history, humor, nature, science, sports, travel, and adventure African-American; lifestyle; narrative nonfiction. **Considers these fiction areas:** adventure, historical, literary, mainstream.

How to Contact Query with SASE or via e-mail. Obtains most new clients through recommendations from others, solicitations.

☑ LOWENSTEIN-YOST ASSOCIATES

121 W. 27th St., Suite 601, New York NY 10001. (212)206-1630. Fax: (212)727-0280. Website: www. lowensteinyost.com. **Contact:** Barbara Lowenstein or Nancy Yost. Member of AAR. Represents 150 clients. 20% of clients are new/unpublished writers. Currently handles nonfiction books (60%), novels (40%).

Member Agents Barbara Lowenstein, president (nonfiction interests include narrative nonfiction, health, money, finance, travel, multicultural, popular culture and memoir; fiction interests include literary fiction and women's fiction); Nancy Yost, vice president (mainstream/contemporary fiction, mystery, suspense, contemporary/historical romance, thriller, women's fiction); Norman Kurz, business affairs; Zoe Fishman, foreign rights (young adult, literary fiction, narrative nonfiction); Natanya Wheeler (narrative nonfiction, literary fiction, historical, women's fiction, birds).

Represents nonfiction books, novels. **Considers these nonfiction areas:** animals, anthropology, biography, business, child, current affairs, education, ethnic, government, health, history, how to, language, memoirs, money, multicultural, nature, popular culture, psychology, self help, sociology, travel, womens music; narrative nonfiction; science; film. **Considers these fiction areas:** detective, erotica, ethnic, feminist, historical, literary, mainstream, mystery, romance, contemporary, historical, regency, thriller, womens fantasy, young adult. This agency specializes in health, business, creative nonfiction, literary fiction and commercial fiction—especially suspense, crime and women's issues. We are a full-service agency, handling domestic and foreign rights, film rights and audio rights to all of our books.

How to Contact Query with SASE or via electronic form on each agent's page. Submit to only one agent. Prefers to read materials exclusively. For fiction, send outline and first chapter. *No unsolicited mss.* Responds in 4 weeks to queries. Obtains most new clients through recommendations from others, solicitations, conferences.

Terms Agent receives 15% commission on domestic sales. Agent receives 20% commission on foreign sales. Offers written contract. Charges for large photocopy batches, messenger service, international postage.

Writers Conferences Malice Domestic

Tips Know the genre you are working in and read! Also, please see our Web site for details on which agent to query for your project.

☑ LYONS LITERARY, LLC

27 West 20th St., Suite 10003, New York NY 10011. (212)255-5472. Fax: (212)851-8405. E-mail: info@ lyonsliterary.com. Website: www.lyonsliterary.com. **Contact:** Jonathan Lyons. Member of AAR. Other memberships include The Author's Guild, American Bar Association, New York State Bar Associaton, New York State Intellectual Property Law Section. Represents 37 clients. 15% of clients are new/ unpublished writers. Currently handles nonfiction books (60%), novels (40%).

Represents nonfiction books, novels. **Considers these nonfiction areas:** crafts, animals, biography, cooking, current affairs, ethnic, gay, government, health, history, how to, humor, memoirs, military, money, multicultural, nature, popular culture, psychology, science, sociology, sports, translation, travel, true crime, womens. **Considers these fiction areas:** psychic, detective, fantasy, feminist, gay, historical, humor, literary, mainstream, mystery, regional, science, sports, thriller, womens chick lit. "With my legal expertise and experience selling domestic and foreign language book rights, paperback reprint rights, audio rights, film/TV rights and permissions, I am able to provide substantive and personal guidance to my clients in all areas relating to their projects. In addition, with the advent of new publishing technology, Lyons Literary, LLC is situated to address the changing nature of the industry while concurrently handling authors' more traditional needs."

How to Contact Only accepts queries through online submission form. Accepts simultaneous submissions. Responds in 8 weeks to queries. Responds in 12 weeks to mss. Obtains most new clients through recommendations from others.

Terms Agent receives 15% commission on domestic sales. Agent receives 20% commission on foreign sales. Offers written contract.

Writers Conferences Agents and Editors Conference.

Tips "Please submit electronic queries through our Web site submission form."

☑ DONALD MAASS LITERARY AGENCY

121 W. 27th St., Suite 801, New York NY 10001. (212)727-8383. E-mail: info@maassagency.com. Website:

www.maassagency.com. Member of AAR. Other memberships include SFWA, MWA, RWA. Represents more than 100 clients. 5%% of clients are new/unpublished writers. Currently handles novels (100%).

- Prior to opening his agency, Mr. Maass served as an editor at Dell Publishing (New York) and as a reader at Gollancz (London). He also served as the president of AAR.

Member Agents Donald Maass (mainstream, literary, mystery/suspense, science fiction)

Represents novels. **Considers these nonfiction areas:** narrative nonfiction (and see J.L's bio for subject interest). **Considers these fiction areas:** psychic, detective, fantasy, historical, horror, literary, mainstream, mystery, romance, historical, paranormal, time travel, science, thriller, womens. This agency specializes in commercial fiction, especially science fiction, fantasy, mystery and suspense. Actively seeking to expand in literary fiction and women's fiction. Does not want to receive nonfiction, picture books, prescriptive nonfiction, or poetry.

How to Contact Query with SASE. Returns material only with SASE. Accepts simultaneous submissions. Responds in 2 weeks to queries. Responds in 3 months to mss.

Terms Agent receives 15% commission on domestic sales. Agent receives 20% commission on foreign sales.

Writers Conferences Donald Maass: World Science Fiction Convention; Frankfurt Book Fair; Pacific Northwest Writers Conference; Bouchercon. Jennifer Jackson: World Science Fiction Convention; RWA National Conference.

Tips We are fiction specialists, also noted for our innovative approach to career planning. Few new clients are accepted, but interested authors should query with a SASE. Works with subagents in all principle foreign countries and Hollywood. No prescriptive nonfiction, picture books or poetry will be considered.

⬛ MACGREGOR LITERARY

2373 N.W. 185th Ave., Suite 165, Hillsboro OR 97214. (503)277-8308. E-mail: submissions@ macgregorliterary.com. Website: www.macgregorliterary.com. **Contact:** Chip MacGregor. Signatory of WGA. Represents 40 clients. 10% of clients are new/unpublished writers. Currently handles nonfiction books (40%), novels (60%).

- Prior to his current position, Mr. MacGregor was the senior agent with Alive Communications. Most recently, he was associate publisher for Time-Warner Book Group's Faith Division, and helped put together their Center Street imprint.

Represents nonfiction books, novels. **Considers these nonfiction areas:** business, current affairs, history, how to, humor, popular culture, religion, self help, sports marriage, parenting. **Considers these fiction areas:** detective, historical, mainstream, mystery, religious, romance, thriller women's/chick lit. "My specialty has been in career planning with authors—finding commercial ideas, then helping authors bring them to market, and in the midst of that assisting the authors as they get firmly established in their writing careers. I'm probably best known for my work with Christian books over the years, but I've done a fair amount of general market projects as well." Actively seeking authors with a Christian worldview and a growing platform. Does not want to receive fantasy, sci-fi, children's books, poetry or screenplays.

How to Contact Query with SASE. Accepts simultaneous submissions. Responds in 3 weeks to queries. Obtains most new clients through recommendations from others.

Terms Agent receives 15% commission on domestic sales. Agent receives 15% commission on foreign sales. Offers written contract; 30-day notice must be given to terminate contract. Charges for exceptional fees after receiving authors' permission.

Writers Conferences Blue Ridge Christian Writers' Conference; Write to Publish.

Tips "Seriously consider attending a good writers' conference. It will give you the chance to be face-to-face with people in the industry. Also, if you're a novelist, consider joining one of the national writers' organizations. The American Christian Fiction Writers (ACFW) is a wonderful group for new as well as established writers. And if you're a Christian writer of any kind, check into The Writers View, an online writing group. All of these have proven helpful to writers."

⬛ CAROL MANN AGENCY

55 Fifth Ave., New York NY 10003. (212)206-5635. Fax: (212)675-4809. E-mail: will@carolmannagency. com. Website: www.carolmannagency.com/. **Contact:** Nicole Bergstrom. Member of AAR. Represents

roughly 200 clients. 15% of clients are new/unpublished writers. Currently handles nonfiction books (90%), novels (10%).

Member Agents Carol Mann (health/medical, religion, spirituality, self-help, parenting, narrative nonfiction); Laura Yorke; Nicole Bergstrom; Urvashi Chakravarty.

Represents nonfiction books, novels. **Considers these nonfiction areas:** anthropology, art, biography, business, child, current affairs, ethnic, government, health, history, money, popular culture, psychology, self help, sociology, sports, womens music. **Considers these fiction areas:** literary commercial. This agency specializes in current affairs, self-help, popular culture, psychology, parenting, and history. Does not want to receive genre fiction (romance, mystery, etc.).

How to Contact Keep initial query/contact to no more than two pages. Responds in 4 weeks to queries.

Terms Agent receives 15% commission on domestic sales. Agent receives 20% commission on foreign sales. Offers written contract.

☑ MANUS & ASSOCIATES LITERARY AGENCY, INC.

425 Sherman Ave., Suite 200, Palo Alto CA 94306. (650)470-5151. Fax: (650)470-5159. E-mail: manuslit@manuslit.com. Website: www.manuslit.com. **Contact:** Jillian Manus, Jandy Nelson, Penny Nelson. Member of AAR. Represents 75 clients. 30% of clients are new/unpublished writers. Currently handles nonfiction books (70%), novels (30%).

- Prior to becoming an agent, Ms. Manus was associate publisher of two national magazines and director of development at Warner Bros. and Universal Studios; she has been a literary agent for 20 years.

Member Agents Jandy Nelson, jandy@manuslit.com (self-help, health, memoirs, narrative nonfiction, women's fiction, literary fiction, multicultural fiction, thrillers); Jillian Manus, jillian@manuslit.com (political, memoirs, self-help, history, sports, women's issues, Latin fiction and nonfiction, thrillers); Penny Nelson, penny@manuslit.com (memoirs, self-help, sports, nonfiction); Dena Fischer (literary fiction, mainstream/commercial fiction, chick lit, women's fiction, historical fiction, ethnic/cultural fiction, narrative nonfiction, parenting, relationships, pop culture, health, sociology, psychology).

Represents nonfiction books, novels. **Considers these nonfiction areas:** biography, business, child, current affairs, ethnic, health, how to, memoirs, money, nature, popular culture, psychology, science, self help, womens Gen X and Gen Y issues; creative nonfiction. **Considers these fiction areas:** literary, mainstream, multicultural, mystery, thriller, womens quirky/edgy fiction. "Our agency is unique in the way that we not only sell the material, but we edit, develop concepts, and participate in the marketing effort. We specialize in large, conceptual fiction and nonfiction, and always value a project that can be sold in the TV/feature film market." Actively seeking high-concept thrillers, commercial literary fiction, women's fiction, celebrity biographies, memoirs, multicultural fiction, popular health, women's empowerment and mysteries. No horror, romance, science fiction, fantasy, Western, young adult, children's, poetry, cookbooks or magazine articles.

How to Contact Query with SASE. If requested, submit outline, 2-3 sample chapters. All queries should be sent to the California office. Accepts simultaneous submissions. Responds in 3 months to queries. Responds in 3 months to mss. Obtains most new clients through recommendations from others, solicitations, conferences.

Terms Agent receives 15% commission on domestic sales. Agent receives 20-25% commission on foreign sales. Offers written contract, binding for 2 years; 60-day notice must be given to terminate contract. Charges for photocopying and postage/UPS.

Writers Conferences Maui Writers' Conference; San Diego State University Writers' Conference; Willamette Writers' Conference; BookExpo America; MEGA Book Marketing University.

Tips "Research agents using a variety of sources."

☑ THE EVAN MARSHALL AGENCY

Six Tristam Place, Pine Brook NJ 07058-9445. (973)882-1122. Fax: (973)882-3099. E-mail: evanmarshall@optonline.net. **Contact:** Evan Marshall. Member of AAR. Other memberships include MWA, Sisters in Crime. Currently handles novels (100%).

Represents novels. **Considers these fiction areas:** adventure, erotica, ethnic, historical, horror, humor, literary, mainstream, mystery, religious, romance, contemporary, gothic, historical, regency, science, western.

How to Contact Query first with SASE; do not enclose material. No e-mail queries. Responds in 1 week to queries. Responds in 3 months to mss. Obtains most new clients through recommendations from others.

Terms Agent receives 15% commission on domestic sales. Agent receives 20% commission on foreign sales. Offers written contract.

◙ THE MARTELL AGENCY

1350 Avenue of the Americas, Suite 1205, New York NY 10019. Fax: (212)317-2676. E-mail: afmartell@aol.com. **Contact:** Alice Martell.

Represents nonfiction books, novels. **Considers these nonfiction areas:** business, health, fitness, history, memoirs, multicultural, psychology, self help, womens. **Considers these fiction areas:** mystery, thriller, womens suspense, commercial.

How to Contact Query with SASE. Submit sample chapters. Submit via snail mail. No e-mail or fax queries.

◙ MAX AND CO., A LITERARY AGENCY AND SOCIAL CLUB

115 Hosea Ave., Cincinnati OH 45220. (201)704-2483. E-mail: mmurphy@maxlit.com. Website: www.maxliterary.org. **Contact:** Michael Murphy.

• Prior to his current position, Mr. Murphy was with Queen Literary Agency. He has been in book publishing since 1981. His first 13 years were with Random House, where he was a vice president. Later, he ran William Morrow as their publisher, up until the company's acquisition & merger into HarperCollins.

Represents Considers these nonfiction areas: humor, memoirs narrative nonfiction. **Considers these fiction areas:** literary. Actively seeking narrative nonfiction, memoir, literary fiction, humor, and visual books. Does not want to receive genre fiction nor YA and children's books.

How to Contact Submit via e-mail attachment only.

◙ MARGRET MCBRIDE LITERARY AGENCY

7744 Fay Ave., Suite 201, La Jolla CA 92037. (858)454-1550. Fax: (858)454-2156. E-mail: staff@mcbridelit.com. Website: www.mcbrideliterary.com. **Contact:** Michael Daley, submissions manager. Member of AAR. Other memberships include Authors Guild. Represents 55 clients.

• Prior to opening her agency, Ms. McBride worked at Random House, Ballantine Books, and Warner Books.

Represents nonfiction books, novels. **Considers these nonfiction areas:** biography, business, cooking, current affairs, ethnic, government, health, history, how to, money, music, popular culture, psychology, science, self help, sociology, womens style. **Considers these fiction areas:** adventure, detective, ethnic, historical, humor, literary, mainstream, mystery, thriller, western. This agency specializes in mainstream fiction and nonfiction. Does not want to receive screenplays, romance, poetry, or children's/young adult.

How to Contact Query with synopsis, bio, SASE. No e-mail or fax queries. Accepts simultaneous submissions. Responds in 4-6 weeks to queries. Responds in 6-8 weeks to mss.

Terms Agent receives 15% commission on domestic sales. Agent receives 25% commission on foreign sales. Charges for overnight delivery and photocopying.

THE MCCARTHY AGENCY, LLC

7 Allen St., Rumson NJ 07660. Phone/Fax: (732)741-3065. E-mail: mccarthylit@aol.com. **Contact:** Shawna McCarthy. Member of AAR. Currently handles nonfiction books (25%), novels (75%).

Member Agents Shawna McCarthy (New Jersey address); Nahvae Frost (Brooklyn address).

Represents nonfiction books, novels. **Considers these nonfiction areas:** biography, history, philosophy, science. **Considers these fiction areas:** fantasy, juvenile, mystery, romance, science, womens.

How to Contact Query via e-mail. Accepts simultaneous submissions.

McCARTHY CREATIVE SERVICES

625 Main St., Suite 834, New York NY 10044-0035. (212)832-3428. Fax: (212)829-9610. E-mail: PaulMccarthy@McCarthyCreative.com. Website: www.McCarthyCreative.com. **Contact:** Paul D. McCarthy. Other memberships include The Authors Guild, American Society of Journalists & Authors,

National Book Critics Circle, Authors League of America. Represents 5 clients. 0% of clients are new/unpublished writers. Currently handles nonfiction books (95%), novels (5%).

- Prior to his current position, Mr. McCarthy was a professional writer, literary agent at the Scott Meredith Literary Agency, senior editor at publishing companies (Simon & Schuster, HarperCollins and Doubleday) and a public speaker. Learn much more about Mr. McCarthy by visiting his Web site.

Member Agents Paul D. McCarthy.

Represents nonfiction books, novels. **Considers these nonfiction areas:** animals, anthropology, art, biography, business, child, current affairs, education, ethnic, gay, government, health, history, how to, humor, language, memoirs, military, money, music, nature, popular culture, psychology, religion, science, self help, sociology, sports, translation, true crime, womens. **Considers these fiction areas:** glitz, adventure, confession, detective, erotica, ethnic, family, fantasy, feminist, gay, historical, horror, humor, literary, mainstream, mystery, regional, romance, science, sports, thriller, western, young, womens. "I deliberately founded my company to be unlimited in its range. That's what I offer, and the world has responded. My agency was founded so that I could maximize and build on the value of my combined experience for my authors and other clients, in all of my capacities and more. I think it's *very* important for authors to know that because I'm so exclusive as an agent, I may not be able to offer representation on the basis of the manuscript they submit. However, if they decide to invest in their book and lifetime career as authors, by engaging my professional, near-unique editorial services, there is the possibility that at the end of the process, when they've achieved the very best, most salable and competitive book they can write, I may see sufficient potential in the book and their next books, that I do offer to be their agent. Representation is never guaranteed." Established authors of serious and popular nonfiction, who want the value of being one of MCS's very exclusive authors who receive special attention, and of being represented by a literary agent who brings such a rich diversity and depth of publishing/creative/professorial experience, and distinguished reputation. No first novels. "Novels by established novelists will be considered very selectively."

How to Contact Submit outline, one chapter (either first or best).E-queries only, with Responds in 3-4 weeks to queries. Obtains most new clients through recommendations from others.

Terms Agent receives 15% commission on domestic sales. Agent receives 20% commission on foreign sales. Offers written contract; 30-day notice must be given to terminate contract. "All reading done in deciding whether or not to offer representation is free. Editorial services are available. Mailing and postage expenses that incurred on the author's behalf are always approved by them in advance."

Tips "Always keep in mind that your query letter/proposal is only one of hundreds and thousands that are competing for the agent's attention. Therefore, your presentation of your book and yourself as author has to be immediate, intense, compelling, and concise. Make the query letter one-page, and after short, introductory paragraph, write a 150-word KEYNOTE description of your manuscript."

☑ MENDEL MEDIA GROUP, LLC

115 West 30th St., Suite 800, New York NY 10001. (646)239-9896. Fax: (212)685-4717. E-mail: scott@mendelmedia.com. Website: www.mendelmedia.com. Member of AAR. Represents 40-60 clients.

- Prior to becoming an agent, Mr. Mendel was an academic. "I taught American literature, Yiddish, Jewish studies, and literary theory at the University of Chicago and the University of Illinois at Chicago while working on my PhD in English. I also worked as a freelance technical writer and as the managing editor of a healthcare magazine. In 1998, I began working for the late Jane Jordan Browne, a long-time agent in the book publishing world."

Represents nonfiction books, novels, scholarly, with potential for broad/popular appeal. **Considers these nonfiction areas:** americana, animals, anthropology, art, biography, business, child, cooking, current affairs, education, ethnic, gardening, gay, government, health, history, how to, humor, language, memoirs, military, money, multicultural, music, nature, philosophy, popular culture, psychology, recreation, regional, religion, science, self help, sex, sociology, software, spirituality, sports, true crime, womens Jewish topics; creative nonfiction. **Considers these fiction areas:** contemporary, glitz, adventure, detective, erotica, ethnic, feminist, gay, historical, humor, juvenile, literary, mainstream, mystery, picture books, religious, romance, sports, thriller, young Jewish fiction. "I am interested in major works of history, current affairs, biography, business, politics, economics, science, major memoirs, narrative nonfiction, and other sorts of general nonfiction." Actively seeking new, major or definitive work on a subject of broad interest, or a controversial, but authoritative, new book on a subject that affects many people's lives." I also represent more light-hearted nonfiction projects, such as gift or novelty books, when they suit the market particularly well." Does not want "queries about projects written years ago that were unsuccessfully shopped to a long list of trade publishers by either the author or another agent. I am specifically not interested in reading short, category romances (regency, time travel, paranormal, etc.), horror novels, supernatural stories, poetry, original plays, or film scripts."

How to Contact Query with SASE. Do not e-mail or fax queries. For nonfiction, include a complete, fully-edited book proposal with sample chapters. For fiction, include a complete synopsis and no more than 20 pages of sample text. Responds in 2 weeks to queries. Responds in 4-6 weeks to mss. Obtains most new clients through recommendations from others.

Terms Agent receives 15% commission on domestic sales. Agent receives 20% commission on foreign sales. Charges clients for ms duplication, expedited delivery services (when necessary), any overseas shipping, telephone calls/faxes necessary for marketing the author's foreign rights.

Writers Conferences BookExpo America; Frankfurt Book Fair; London Book Fair; RWA National Conference; Modern Language Association Convention; Jerusalem Book Fair.

Tips "While I am not interested in being flattered by a prospective client, it does matter to me that she knows why she is writing to me in the first place. Is one of my clients a colleague of hers? Has she read a book by one of my clients that led her to believe I might be interested in her work? Authors of descriptive nonfiction should have real credentials and expertise in their subject areas, either as academics, journalists, or policy experts, and authors of prescriptive nonfiction should have legitimate expertise and considerable experience communicating their ideas in seminars and workshops, in a successful business, through the media, etc."

☑ HENRY MORRISON, INC.

105 S. Bedford Road, Suite 306A, Mt. Kisco NY 10549. (914)666-3500. Fax: (914)241-7846. **Contact:** Henry Morrison. Signatory of WGA. Represents 53 clients. 5% of clients are new/unpublished writers. Currently handles nonfiction books (5%), novels (95%).

Represents nonfiction books, novels. **Considers these nonfiction areas:** anthropology, biography, government, history. **Considers these fiction areas:** adventure, detective, family, historical.

How to Contact Query with SASE. Responds in 2 weeks to queries. Responds in 3 months to mss. Obtains most new clients through recommendations from others.

Terms Agent receives 15% commission on domestic sales. Agent receives 25% commission on foreign sales. Charges clients for ms copies, bound galleys, finished books for submissions to publishers, movie producers and foreign publishers.

☑ MORTIMER LITERARY AGENCY

52645 Paui Road, Aguanga CA 92536. (951)763-2600. E-mail: kmortimer@mortimerliterary.com. Website: www.mortimerliterary.com. **Contact:** Kelly L. Mortimer. Other memberships include American Christian Fiction Writers. Represents 15 clients. 70% of clients are new/unpublished writers. Currently handles nonfiction books (5%), novels (90%), juvenile books (5%).

• Prior to becoming an agent, Ms. Mortimer was a freelance writer and the CFO of Microvector, Inc. She has a degree in contract law, and was nominated for the ACGW Agent of the Year award.

Represents nonfiction books, novels, novellas, juvenile, young adult and middle grade. **Considers these nonfiction areas:** religion, self help relationship advice, finance. **Considers these fiction areas:** adventure, detective, historical, mainstream, mystery, religious, romance, thriller, young middle grade. "I keep a short client list to give my writers personal attention. I edit my clients' manuscripts as necessary. I send manuscripts out to pre-selected editors in a timely fashion, and send my clients monthly reports. I am not seeking new clients now, but will be in the future."

How to Contact Only accepting new clients through conferences or contests. Accepts simultaneous submissions. Responds in 4 months to mss. Obtains most new clients through recommendations from others, solicitations, conferences.

Terms Agent receives 15% commission on domestic sales. Agent receives 20% commission on foreign sales. Offers written contract. "I charge for postage - only the amount I pay and it comes out of the author's advance. The writer provides me with copies of their manuscripts."

Writers Conferences RWA, ACFW.

Tips "Follow submission guidelines on the Web site, submit your best work and don't query unless your manuscript is finished. Don't send material or mss that I haven't requested."

☑ DEE MURA LITERARY

269 West Shore Drive, Massapequa NY 11758-8225. (516)795-1616. Fax: (516)795-8797. E-mail: query@ deemuraliterary.com. **Contact:** Dee Mura, Karen Roberts, Bobbie Sokol, David Brozain. Signatory of WGA. 50% of clients are new/unpublished writers.

- Prior to opening her agency, Ms. Mura was a public relations executive with a roster of film and entertainment clients and worked in editorial for major weekly news magazines.

Represents Considers these nonfiction areas: animals, anthropology, biography, business, child guidance, computers, current affairs, education, ethnic, finance, gay, government, health, history, how-to, humor, juvenile nonfiction, law, lesbian, medicine, memoirs, military, money, nature, personal improvement, politics, science, self-help, sociology, sports, technology, travel, true crime, women's issues, women's studies. **Considers these fiction areas:** action, adventure, contemporary issues, crime, detective, ethnic, experimental, family saga, fantasy, feminist, gay, glitz, historical, humor, juvenile, lesbian, literary, mainstream, military, mystery, psychic, regional, romance, science fiction, sports, thriller, westerns, young adult political. **Considers these script areas:** action, cartoon, comedy, contemporary, detective, (and espionage), family, fantasy, feminist, gay/lesbian, glitz, historical, horror, juvenile, mainstream, mystery, psychic, romantic comedy, romantic drama, science, sports, teen, thriller, western. "Some of us have special interests and some of us encourage you to share your passion and work with us." Does not want to receive "ideas for sitcoms, novels, films, etc., or queries without SASEs."

How to Contact Query with SASE. Accepts e-mail queries (no attachments). If via e-mail, please include the type of query and your genre in the subject line. If via regular mail, you may include the first few chapters, outline, or proposal. No fax queries. Accepts simultaneous submissions. Only responds if interested; responds as soon as possible. Obtains most new clients through recommendations from others, queries.

Terms Agent receives 15% commission on domestic sales. Agent receives 20% commission on foreign sales. Offers written contract. Charges clients for photocopying, mailing expenses, overseas/long distance phone calls/faxes.

Tips "Please include a paragraph on your background, even if you have no literary background, and a brief synopsis of the project."

☑ MUSE LITERARY MANAGEMENT

189 Waverly Place, #4, New York NY 10014. (212)925-3721. E-mail: museliterarymgmt@aol.com. Website: www.museliterary.com/. **Contact:** Deborah Carter. Associations: AWP, NAWE, International Thriller Writers, Historical Novel Society, Associations of Booksellers for Children, The Authors Guild, National Writers Union, and American Folklore Society. Represents 5 clients. 80% of clients are new/ unpublished writers.

- Prior to starting her agency, Ms. Carter trained with an AAR literary agent and worked in the music business and as a talent scout for record companies in artist management. She has a BA in English and music from Washington Square University College at NYU.

Represents novels, short story collections, poetry books. **Considers these nonfiction areas:** narrative nonfiction (no prescriptive nonfiction), children's. **Considers these fiction areas:** adventure, detective, juvenile, mystery, picture books, suspense, thriller, young adult espionage; middle-grade novels; literary short story collections, literary fiction with popular appeal,. Specializes in manuscript development, the sale and administration of print, performance, and foreign rights to literary works, and post-publication publicity and appearances. Actively seeking "writers with formal training who bring compelling voices and a unique outlook to their manuscripts. Those who submit should be receptive to editorial feedback and willing to revise during the submission provess in order to remain competitive. " Does not want "manuscripts that have been worked over by book doctors (collaborative projects ok, but writers must have chops); category romance, chick lit, sci-fi, fantasy, horror, stories about cats and dogs, vampires or serial killers, fiction or nonfiction with religious or spiritual subject matter."

How to Contact Query with SASE. Query via e-mail (no attachments). Discards unwanted queries. Responds in 2 weeks to queries. Responds in 2-3 weeks to mss. Obtains most new clients through recommendations from others, conferences.

Terms Agent receives 15% commission on domestic sales. Agent receives 20% commission on foreign sales. One-year contract offered when writer and agent agree that the manuscript is ready for submission; manuscripts in development are not bound by contract. Sometimes charges for postage and photocopying. All expenses are preapproved by the client.

◙ JEAN V. NAGGAR LITERARY AGENCY, INC.

216 E. 75th St., Suite 1E, New York NY 10021. (212)794-1082. E-mail: jvnla@jvnla.com. Website: www. jvnla.com. **Contact:** Jean Naggar. Member of AAR. Other memberships include PEN, Women's Media Group, Women's Forum. Represents 80 clients. 20% of clients are new/unpublished writers. Currently handles nonfiction books (35%), novels (45%), juvenile books (15%), scholarly books (5%).

• Ms. Naggar has served as president of AAR.

Member Agents Jean Naggar (mainstream fiction, nonfiction); Jennifer Weltz, director (subsidiary rights, children's books); Alice Tasman, senior agent (commercial and literary fiction, thrillers, narrative nonfiction); Jessica Regel, agent (young adult fiction and nonfiction).

Represents nonfiction books, novels. **Considers these nonfiction areas:** juvenile, New Age, biography, child, current affairs, government, health, history, memoirs, psychology, religion, self help, sociology, travel, womens. **Considers these fiction areas:** psychic, adventure, detective, ethnic, family, feminist, historical, literary, mainstream, mystery, thriller. This agency specializes in mainstream fiction and nonfiction and literary fiction with commercial potential.

How to Contact Query via e-mail. Prefers to read materials exclusively. No fax queries. Responds in 1 day to queries. Responds in 2 months to mss. Obtains most new clients through recommendations from others.

Terms Agent receives 15% commission on domestic sales. Agent receives 20% commission on foreign sales. Offers written contract. Charges for overseas mailing, messenger services, book purchases, long-distance telephone, photocopying—all deductible from royalties received.

Writers Conferences Willamette Writers Conference; Pacific Northwest Writers Conference; Bread Loaf Writers Conference; Marymount Manhattan Writers Conference; SEAK Medical & Legal Fiction Writing Conference.

Tips "Use a professional presentation. Because of the avalanche of unsolicited queries that flood the agency every week, we have had to modify our policy. We will now only guarantee to read and respond to queries from writers who come recommended by someone we know. Our areas are general fiction and nonfiction—no children's books by unpublished writers, no multimedia, no screenplays, no formula fiction, and no mysteries by unpublished writers. We recommend patience and fortitude: the courage to be true to your own vision, the fortitude to finish a novel and polish it again and again before sending it out, and the patience to accept rejection gracefully and wait for the stars to align themselves appropriately for success."

◙ NAPPALAND LITERARY AGENCY

A Division of Nappaland Communications, Inc., P.O. Box 1674, Loveland CO 80539-1674. Fax: (970)635-9869. E-mail: Literary@nappaland.com. Website: www.NappalandLiterary.com. **Contact:** Mike Nappa, senior agent. Represents 8 clients. 0% of clients are new/unpublished writers. Currently handles nonfiction books (45%), novels (50%), scholarly books (5%).

• Prior to becoming an agent, Mr. Nappa served as an acquisition editor for three major Christian publishing houses.

Represents nonfiction books, novels. **Considers these nonfiction areas:** child, current affairs, popular culture, religion, womens. **Considers these fiction areas:** adventure, detective, literary, mainstream, religious, thriller. This agency will not consider any new authors unless they come with a recommendation from a current Nappaland client. All queries without such a recommendation are immediately rejected. "Interested in thoughtful, vivid, nonfiction works on religious and cultural themes. Also, fast-paced, well-crafted fiction (suspense, literary, women's) that reads like a work of art. Established authors only; broad promotional platform preferred." Does not want to receive children's books, movie or television scripts, textbooks, short stories, stage plays or poetry.

How to Contact Query with SASE. Submit author bio. Include the name of the person referring you to us. Do *not* send entire proposal unless requested. Send query and bio only. E-queries preferred and given first priority. No attachments please. Accepts simultaneous submissions. Responds in 1 month to queries. Responds in 3 months to mss.

Terms Agent receives 15% commission on domestic sales. Agent receives 20% commission on foreign sales. Offers written contract; 30-day notice must be given to terminate contract.

Writers Conferences Colorado Christian Writers' Conference in Estes Park.

☑ THE NASHVILLE AGENCY

P.O. Box 110909, Nashville TN 37222. (615)263-4143. Fax: (866)333-8663. E-mail: info@nashvilleagency. com; submissions@nashvilleagency.com. Website: www.nashvilleagency.com. **Contact:** Taylor Joseph. Represents 18 clients. 50% of clients are new/unpublished writers. Currently handles nonfiction books (40%), novels (15%), novella(5%), juvenile books (40%).

Member Agents Tim Grable (business books); Jonathan Clements (nonfiction, juvenile); Taylor Joseph (fiction, novels, memoirs).

Represents nonfiction books, novels, novellas, juvenile, scholarly, movie, documentary. **Considers these nonfiction areas:** crafts, juvenile, biography, business, child, cooking, current affairs, education, history, how to, humor, memoirs, military, music, popular culture, religion, self help, sports, true crime, womens. **Considers these fiction areas:** adventure, fantasy, historical, humor, juvenile, literary, mainstream, mystery, regional, religious, thriller, young, womens. **Considers these script areas:** action, contemporary. "Our agency looks not as much for specific genres or stylings. Rather, we look for far-reaching potentials (i.e., brands, properties) to branch outside a token specific market." Actively seeking novels, nonfiction, religious/spiritual material. Does not want to receive poetry, stage plays or textbooks.

How to Contact Query via e-mail or by mail with SASE. No fax queries. Submit proposal package, synopsis, publishing history, author bio, Description of how your relationship with The Nashville Agency was initiated. Accepts simultaneous submissions. Responds in 3 weeks to queries. Responds in 3 months to mss. Obtains most new clients through recommendations from others.

Terms Agent receives 15% commission on domestic sales. Agent receives 20% commission on foreign sales. Offers written contract, binding for 5 years; 30-day notice must be given to terminate contract. This agency charges for standard office fees.

Writers Conferences Blue Ridge Writers' Conference.

☑ NELSON LITERARY AGENCY

1732 Wazee St., Suite 207, Denver CO 80202. (303)292-2805. E-mail: query@nelsonagency.com. Website: www.nelsonagency.com. **Contact:** Kristin Nelson. Member of AAR.

- Prior to opening her own agency, Ms. Nelson worked as a literary scout and subrights agent for agent Jody Rein.

Represents novels select nonfiction. **Considers these nonfiction areas:** memoirs. **Considers these fiction areas:** literary, romance, includes fantasy with romantic elements, science fiction, fantasy, young adult, womens chick lit (includes mysteries); commercial/mainstream. NLA specializes in representing commercial fiction and high caliber literary fiction. Actively seeking Latina writers who tackle contemporary issues in a modern voice (think *Dirty Girls Social Club*). Does not want short story collections, mysteries (except chick lit), thrillers, Christian, horror, or children's picture books.

How to Contact Query by e-mail only.

☑ NORTHERN LIGHTS LITERARY SERVICES, LLC

11248 N. Boyer Rd., Sandpoint ID 83864. (888)558-4354. Fax: (208)265-1948. E-mail: agent@ northernlightsls.com. Website: www.northernlightsls.com. **Contact:** Sammie Justesen. Represents 25 clients. 35% of clients are new/unpublished writers. Currently handles nonfiction books (90%), novels (10%).

Member Agents Sammie Justesen (fiction and nonfiction); Vorris Dee Justesen (business and current affairs).

Represents nonfiction books, novels. **Considers these nonfiction areas:** crafts, newage, animals, biography, business, child, cooking, current affairs, ethnic, health, how to, memoirs, nature, popular culture, psychology, religion, self help, sports, true crime, womens. **Considers these fiction areas:** glitz, psychic, adventure, detective, ethnic, family, feminist, historical, mainstream, mystery, regional, religious, romance, thriller, womens. "Our goal is to provide personalized service to clients and create a bond that will endure throughout the writer's career. We seriously consider each query we receive and will accept hardworking new authors who are willing to develop their talents and skills. We enjoy working with healthcare professionals and writers who clearly understand their market and have a platform." Actively seeking general nonfiction—especially if the writer has a platform. Does not want to receive fantasy, horror, erotica, children's books, screenplays, poetry or short stories.

How to Contact Query with SASE. Submit outline/proposal, synopsis, 3 sample chapters, author bio.E-queries preferred. No phone queries. All queries considered, but the agency only replies if interested.

Accepts simultaneous submissions. Responds in 2 months to queries. Responds in 2 months to mss. Obtains most new clients through solicitations, conferences.

Terms Agent receives 15% commission on domestic sales. Agent receives 20% commission on foreign sales. Offers written contract; 30-day notice must be given to terminate contract.

Tips "If you're fortunate enough to find an agent who answers your query and asks for a printed manuscript, always include a letter and cover page containing your name, physical address, e-mail address and phone number. Be professional!"

◙ KATHI J. PATON LITERARY AGENCY

P.O. Box 2240 Radio City Station, New York NY 10101. (212)265-6586. E-mail: kjplitbiz@optonline.net. **Contact:** Kathi Paton. Currently handles nonfiction books (85%), novels (15%).

Represents nonfiction books, novels, short story collections book-based film rights. **Considers these nonfiction areas:** business, child, humor, money, personal investing, nature, psychology, religion personal investing. **Considers these fiction areas:** literary, mainstream, multicultural short stories. This agency specializes in adult nonfiction.

How to Contact Accepts e-mail queries only. Accepts simultaneous submissions. Obtains most new clients through recommendations from current clients.

Terms Agent receives 15% commission on domestic sales. Agent receives 20% commission on foreign sales. Offers written contract. Charges clients for photocopying.

Writers Conferences Attends major regional panels, seminars and conferences.

Ⓝ PAUL J. ZACK LITERARY AGENCY

P.O. Box 3787, Oak Brook Illinois 60522. E-mail: queries@zackliterary.com. Website: www.zackliterary. com. **Contact:** Paul J. Zack. Represents 6 clients. 25% of clients are new/unpublished writers. Currently handles nonfiction books 60%, novels 35%, story collections 5%.

- Before starting the agency, principal agent Paul Zack worked as an editor at two publishing houses. He spent several years in marketing, promotion and advertising, and he is also a published author (both fiction and nonfiction).

Member Agents Paul J. Zack

Represents nonfiction books, novels, short story collections. **Considers these nonfiction areas:** anthropology, architecture, art, autobiography, biography, business, cultural interests, current affairs, design, education, environment, ethnic, government, health, history, humor, inspirational, law, memoirs, metaphysics, military, nature, New Age, personal improvement, popular culture, politics, psychology, religious, science, self-help, sociology, technology, war, women's issues, women's studies. **Considers these fiction areas:** action, adventure, crime, detective, frontier, historical, horror, humor, inspirational, literary, mainstream, mystery, police, psychic, regional, religious, romance, satire, science fiction, short story collections, supernatural, thriller, westerns, women's. "We specialize in metaphysical, visionary, and spiritual books at the forefront of new thought, both in fiction and nonfiction; also regional literary voices in fiction, particularly Midwestern. We seriously consider every query we receive and we will accept dedicated authors willing to develop their talents. We prefer long-term partnerships with authors. If we believe in a project, we work hard to see the work accepted for publication. We offer focused, hands-on representation, including career advice, suggestions for manuscript revision, speaking coaching, and editorial guidance." Actively seeking a wide range of fiction and nonfiction. Does not want to receive children's, young adult, sports, cookbooks, true crime, poetry, or screenplays.

How to Contact "We accept regular mail and email queries. No phone calls. Send all items to the address below. Please do not send certified mail or email attachments." Please see website for additional requirements for fiction and nonfiction submissions. Accepts simultaneous submissions. Response time within several weeks. Usually obtains clients through recommendations from others, queries/submissions, and conferences.

Terms Receives 15% commission on domestic sales; 20% on foreign sales. Offers contract binding for one year; 30 day notice must be given for termination. Charges for postage, photocopying, and misc. office expenses, only after a sale is made.

Writers Conferences Book Expo America

ALISON J. PICARD, LITERARY AGENT

P.O. Box 2000, Cotuit MA 02635. Phone/Fax: (508)477-7192. E-mail: ajpicard@aol.com. **Contact:** Alison

Picard. Represents 48 clients. 30% of clients are new/unpublished writers. Currently handles nonfiction books (40%), novels (40%), juvenile books (20%).

- Prior to becoming an agent, Ms. Picard was an assistant at a literary agency in New York.

Represents nonfiction books, novels, juvenile. **Considers these nonfiction areas:** juvenile, newage, young, animals, biography, business, child, cooking, current affairs, education, ethnic, gay, government, health, history, how to, humor, memoirs, military, money, multicultural, nature, popular culture, psychology, religion, science, self help, travel, true crime, womens. **Considers these fiction areas:** contemporary, glitz, newage, psychic, adventure, detective, erotica, ethnic, family, feminist, gay, historical, horror, humor, juvenile, literary, mainstream, multicultural, mystery, picture books, romance, sports, thriller, young. "Many of my clients have come to me from big agencies, where they felt overlooked or ignored. I communicate freely with my clients and offer a lot of career advice, suggestions for revising manuscripts, etc. If I believe in a project, I will submit it to a dozen or more publishers, unlike some agents who give up after four or five rejections." No science fiction/fantasy, Western, poetry, plays or articles.

How to Contact Query with SASE. Accepts simultaneous submissions. Responds in 2 weeks to queries. Responds in 4 months to mss. Obtains most new clients through recommendations from others, solicitations.

Terms Agent receives 15% commission on domestic sales. Agent receives 20% commission on foreign sales. Offers written contract, binding for 1 year; 1-week notice must be given to terminate contract.

Tips "Please don't send material without sending a query first via mail or e-mail. I don't accept phone or fax queries. Always enclose an SASE with a query."

PROSPECT AGENCY LLC

285 Fifth Ave., PMB 445, Brooklyn NY 11215. (718)788-3217. E-mail: esk@prospectagency.com. Website: www.prospectagency.com. **Contact:** Emily Sylvan Kim. Represents 15 clients. 50% of clients are new/unpublished writers. Currently handles novels (66%), juvenile books (33%).

- Prior to starting her agency, Ms. Kim briefly attended law school and worked for another literary agency.

Member Agents Emily Sylvan Kim; Becca Stumpf (adult and YA literary, mainstream fiction; nonfiction interests include narrative nonfiction, journalistic perspectives, fashion, film studies, travel, art, and informed analysis of cultural phenomena. She has a special interest in aging in America and environmental issues); Rachel Orr (fiction and nonfiction, particularly picture books, beginning readers, chapter books, middle-grade, YA novels)

Represents nonfiction books, novels, juvenile. **Considers these nonfiction areas:** art, biography, history, juvenile nonfiction, law, memoirs, popular culture, politics, science, travel prescriptive guides. **Considers these fiction areas:** adventure, detective, erotica, ethnic, family, juvenile, literary, mainstream, mystery, picture books, romance, science, thriller, western, young. "We are currently looking for the next generation of writers to shape the literary landscape. Our clients receive professional and knowledgeable representation. We are committed to offering skilled editorial advice and advocating our clients in the marketplace." Actively seeking romance, literary fiction, and young adult submissions. Does not want to receive poetry, short stories, textbooks, or most nonfiction.

How to Contact Upload outline and 3 sample chapters to the Web site. Accepts simultaneous submissions. Responds in 3 weeks to queries. Responds in 1 month to mss. Obtains most new clients through recommendations from others, conferences, unsolicited mss.

Terms Agent receives 15% commission on domestic sales. Agent receives 20% commission on foreign sales. Offers written contract.

Writers Conferences "Please see our website for a complete list of attended conferences."

P.S Literary Agency

520 Kerr St., #20033, Oakville ON L6K 3C7 Canada. E-mail: query@psliterary.com. Website: www.psliterary.com. **Contact:** Curtis Russell. Represents 8 clients. 25% of clients are new/unpublished writers. Currently handles nonfiction books (50%), novels (50%).

Represents nonfiction books, novels, juvenile. **Considers these nonfiction areas:** biography, business, child, cooking, current affairs, government, health, how to, humor, memoirs, military, money, nature, popular culture, science, self help, sports, true crime, womens. **Considers these fiction areas:** adventure, detective, erotica, ethnic, family, historical, horror, humor, juvenile, literary, mainstream, mystery, picture books, romance, sports, thriller, young, womens. "What makes our agency distinct: We take on a small number of clients per year in order to provide focused, hands-on representation. We pride ourselves in providing industry leading client service." Does not want to receive poetry or screenplays.

How to Contact Query via mail or e-mail. Prefers e-mail. Submit synopsis, author bio. Accepts simultaneous submissions. Responds in 6 weeks to queries. Responds in 6 weeks to mss. Obtains most new clients through solicitations.

Terms Agent receives 15% commission on domestic sales. Agent receives 25% commission on foreign sales. Offers written contract; 30-day notice must be given to terminate contract. "This agency charges for postage/messenger services only if a project is sold."

Tips "Please review our Web site for the most up-to-date submission guidelines."

☑ QUICKSILVER BOOKS: LITERARY AGENTS

508 Central Park Ave., #5101, Scarsdale NY 10583. Phone/Fax: (914)722-4664. E-mail: quickbooks@optonline.net. Website: www.quicksilverbooks.com. **Contact:** Bob Silverstein. Represents 50 clients. 50% of clients are new/unpublished writers. Currently handles nonfiction books (75%), novels (25%).

- Prior to opening his agency, Mr. Silverstein served as senior editor at Bantam Books and Dell Books/ Delacorte Press.

Represents nonfiction books, novels. **Considers these nonfiction areas:** newage, anthropology, biography, business, child, cooking, current affairs, ethnic, health, history, how to, language, memoirs, nature, popular culture, psychology, religion, science, self help, sociology, sports, true crime, womens. **Considers these fiction areas:** glitz, adventure, mystery, thriller. This agency specializes in literary and commercial mainstream fiction and nonfiction, especially psychology, New Age, holistic healing, consciousness, ecology, environment, spirituality, reference, self-help, cookbooks and narrative nonfiction. Does not want to receive science fiction, pornography, poetry or single-spaced mss.

How to Contact Query with SASE. Authors are expected to supply SASE for return of ms and for query letter responses. Accepts simultaneous submissions. Responds in 2 weeks to queries. Responds in 1 month to mss. Obtains most new clients through recommendations, listings in sourcebooks, solicitations, workshop participation.

Terms Agent receives 15% commission on domestic sales. Agent receives 20% commission on foreign sales. Offers written contract.

Writers Conferences National Writers Union.

Tips "Write what you know. Write from the heart. Publishers print, authors sell."

☑ RAINES & RAINES

103 Kenyon Road, Medusa NY 12120. (518)239-8311. Fax: (518)239-6029. **Contact:** Theron Raines (member of AAR); Joan Raines; Keith Korman. Represents 100 clients.

Represents nonfiction books, novels. **Considers these fiction areas:** adventure, detective, fantasy, historical, mystery, picture books, science, thriller, western.

How to Contact Query with SASE. Responds in 2 weeks to queries.

Terms Agent receives 15% commission on domestic sales. Agent receives 20% commission on foreign sales. Charges for photocopying.

☑ THE REDWOOD AGENCY

4300 SW 34th Avenue, Portland OR 97239. (503)219-9019. E-mail: info@redwoodagency.com. Website: www.redwoodagency.com. **Contact:** Catherine Fowler, founder. Adheres to AAR canon of ethics. Currently handles nonfiction books (100%).

- Prior to becoming an agent, Ms. Fowler was an editor, subsidiary rights director and associate publisher for Doubleday, Simon & Schuster and Random House for her 20 years in NY Publishing. Content exec for web startups Excite and WebMD.

Represents nonfiction books, novels. **Considers these nonfiction areas:** business, cooking, health, humor, memoirs, nature, popular culture, psychology, self help, womens narrative, parenting, aging, reference, lifestyle, cultural technology. **Considers these fiction areas:** literary, mainstream, suspense, women's quirky. Along with our love of books and publishing, we have the desire and commitment to work with fun, interesting and creative people, to do so with respect and professionalism, but also with a sense of humor. Actively seeking high-quality, nonfiction works created for the general consumer market, as well as projects with the potential to become book series. Does not want to receive fiction. Do not send packages that require signature for delivery.

How to Contact Query via e-mail only. Obtains most new clients through recommendations from others, solicitations.

Terms Offers written contract. Charges for copying and delivery charges, if any, as specified in author/agency agreement.

☑ HELEN REES LITERARY AGENCY

376 North St., Boston MA 02113-2013. (617)227-9014. Fax: (617)227-8762. E-mail: reesagency@reesagency.com. **Contact:** Joan Mazmanian, Ann Collette, Helen Rees, Lorin Rees. Member of AAR. Other memberships include PEN. Represents more than 100 clients. 50% of clients are new/unpublished writers. Currently handles nonfiction books (60%), novels (40%).

Member Agents Ann Collette (literary fiction, women's studies, health, biography, history)

Represents nonfiction books, novels. **Considers these nonfiction areas:** biography, business, current affairs, government, health, history, money, womens. **Considers these fiction areas:** historical, literary, mainstream, mystery, thriller.

How to Contact Query with SASE, outline, 2 sample chapters. No unsolicited e-mail submissions. No multiple submissions. Responds in 3-4 weeks to queries. Obtains most new clients through recommendations from others, conferences, submissions.

Terms Agent receives 15% commission on domestic sales. Agent receives 20% commission on foreign sales.

☑ JODY REIN BOOKS, INC.

7741 S. Ash Ct., Centennial CO 80122. (303)694-4430. Fax: (303)694-0687. Website: www.jodyreinbooks.com. **Contact:** Winnefred Dollar. false Other memberships include Authors' Guild. Currently handles nonfiction books (70%), novels (30%).

• Prior to opening her agency, Ms. Rein worked for 13 years as an acquisitions editor for Contemporary Books and as executive editor for Bantam/Doubleday/Dell and Morrow/Avon.

Represents nonfiction books, novels. **Considers these nonfiction areas:** business, child, current affairs, ethnic, government, history, humor, music, nature, popular culture, psychology, science, sociology, film, womens. **Considers these fiction areas:** literary, mainstream. This agency is no longer actively seeking clients.

Terms Agent receives 15% commission on domestic sales. Agent receives 25% commission on foreign sales. Agent receives 20% commission on film sales. Offers written contract. Charges clients for express mail, overseas expenses, photocopying mss.

Tips "Do your homework before submitting. Make sure you have a marketable topic and the credentials to write about it. We want well-written books on fresh and original nonfiction topics that have broad appeal, as well as novels written by authors who have spent years developing their craft. Authors must be well established in their fields and have strong media experience."

☑ JODIE RHODES LITERARY AGENCY

8840 Villa La Jolla Drive, Suite 315, La Jolla CA 92037-1957. **Contact:** Jodie Rhodes, president. Member of AAR. Represents 74 clients. 60% of clients are new/unpublished writers. Currently handles nonfiction books (45%), novels (35%), juvenile books (20%).

• Prior to opening her agency, Ms. Rhodes was a university-level creative writing teacher, workshop director, published novelist, and vice president/media director at the N.W. Ayer Advertising Agency.

Member Agents Jodie Rhodes; Clark McCutcheon (fiction); Bob McCarter (nonfiction).

Represents nonfiction books, novels. **Considers these nonfiction areas:** biography, child, ethnic, government, health, history, memoirs, military, science, womens. **Considers these fiction areas:** ethnic, family, historical, literary, mainstream, mystery, thriller, young, womens. "Actively seeking witty, sophisticated women's books about career ambitions and relationships; edgy/trendy YA and teen books; narrative nonfiction on groundbreaking scientific discoveries, politics, economics, military and important current affairs by prominent scientists and academic professors." Does not want to receive erotica, horror, fantasy, romance, science fiction, religious/inspirational, or children's books (does accept young adult/teen).

How to Contact Query with brief synopsis, first 30-50 pages, SASE. Do not call. Do not send complete ms unless requested. This agency does not return unrequested material weighing a pound or more that requires special postage. Include e-mail address with query. Accepts simultaneous submissions.

Responds in 3 weeks to queries. Obtains most new clients through recommendations from others, agent sourcebooks.

Terms Agent receives 15% commission on domestic sales. Agent receives 20% commission on foreign sales. Offers written contract; 1-month notice must be given to terminate contract. Charges clients for fax, photocopying, phone calls, postage. Charges are itemized and approved by writers upfront.

Tips "Think your book out before you write it. Do your research, know your subject matter intimately, and write vivid specifics, not bland generalities. Care deeply about your book. Don't imitate other writers. Find your own voice. We never take on a book we don't believe in, and we go the extra mile for our writers. We welcome talented, new writers."

☑ ANN RITTENBERG LITERARY AGENCY, INC.

30 Bond St., New York NY 10012. (212)684-6936. Fax: (212)684-6929. Website: www.rittlit.com. **Contact:** Ann Rittenberg, president and Penn Whaling. Member of AAR. Currently handles nonfiction books (50%), novels (50%).

Represents nonfiction books, novels. **Considers these nonfiction areas:** biography, history, social/cultural, memoirs, womens. **Considers these fiction areas:** literary. This agent specializes in literary fiction and literary nonfiction. Does not want to receive Screenplays, genre fiction, Poetry, Self-help.

How to Contact Query with SASE. Submit outline, 3 sample chapters, SASE. Query via snail mail *only*. Accepts simultaneous submissions. Responds in 6 weeks to queries. Responds in 2 months to mss. Obtains most new clients through referrals from established writers and editors.

Terms Agent receives 15% commission on domestic sales. Agent receives 20% commission on foreign sales. Offers written contract. This agency charges clients for photocopying only.

☑ RLR ASSOCIATES, LTD.

Literary Department, 7 W. 51st St., New York NY 10019. (212)541-8641. Fax: (212)262-7084. E-mail: sgould@rlrassociates.net. Website: www.rlrliterary.net. **Contact:** Scott Gould. Member of AAR. Represents 50 clients. 25% of clients are new/unpublished writers. Currently handles nonfiction books (70%), novels (25%), story collections (5%).

Represents nonfiction books, novels, short story collections, scholarly. **Considers these nonfiction areas:** interior, animals, anthropology, art, biography, business, child, cooking, current affairs, education, ethnic, gay, government, health, history, humor, language, memoirs, money, multicultural, music, nature, photography, popular culture, psychology, religion, science, self help, sociology, sports, translation, travel, true crime, womens. **Considers these fiction areas:** adventure, comic, detective, ethnic, experimental, family, feminist, gay, historical, horror, humor, literary, mainstream, multicultural, mystery, sports, thriller. "We provide a lot of editorial assistance to our clients and have connections." Actively seeking fiction, current affairs, history, art, popular culture, health and business. Does not want to receive screenplays.

How to Contact Query by either e-mail or mail. Accepts simultaneous submissions. Responds in 4-8 weeks to queries. Obtains most new clients through recommendations from others.

Terms Agent receives 15% commission on domestic sales. Agent receives 20% commission on foreign sales. Offers written contract.

Tips "Please check out our Web site for more details on our agency."

☑ B.J. ROBBINS LITERARY AGENCY

5130 Bellaire Ave., North Hollywood CA 91607-2908. (818)760-6602. E-mail: robbinsliterary@aol.com. **Contact:** (Ms.) B.J. Robbins. Member of AAR. Represents 40 clients. 50% of clients are new/unpublished writers. Currently handles nonfiction books (50%), novels (50%).

Represents nonfiction books, novels. **Considers these nonfiction areas:** biography, current affairs, ethnic, health, how-to, humor, memoirs, music, popular culture, psychology, self help, sociology, sports, film, travel, true crime, womens. **Considers these fiction areas:** detective, ethnic, literary, mainstream, mystery, sports, thriller.

How to Contact Query with SASE. Submit outline/proposal, 3 sample chapters, SASE. Accepts e-mail queries (no attachments). Accepts simultaneous submissions. Responds in 2-6 weeks to queries. Responds in 6-8 weeks to mss. Obtains most new clients through conferences, referrals.

Terms Agent receives 15% commission on domestic sales. Agent receives 20% commission on foreign sales. Offers written contract; 3-month notice must be given to terminate contract. This agency charges clients for postage and photocopying (only after sale of ms).

Writers Conferences Squaw Valley Writers Workshop; San Diego State University Writers' Conference.

☑ THE ROSENBERG GROUP

23 Lincoln Ave., Marblehead MA 01945. (781)990-1341. Fax: (781)990-1344. Website: www. rosenberggroup.com. **Contact:** Barbara Collins Rosenberg. Member of AAR. Other memberships include recognized agent of the RWA. Represents 25 clients. 15% of clients are new/unpublished writers. Currently handles nonfiction books (30%), novels (30%), scholarly books (10%), other(30% college textbooks).

• Prior to becoming an agent, Ms. Rosenberg was a senior editor for Harcourt.

Represents nonfiction books, novels, textbooks, college textbooks only. **Considers these nonfiction areas:** current affairs, popular culture, psychology, sports, womens women's health; food/wine/beverages. **Considers these fiction areas:** romance, womens. Ms. Rosenberg is well-versed in the romance market (both category and single title). She is a frequent speaker at romance conferences. Actively seeking romance category or single title in contemporary romantic suspense, and the historical subgenres. Does not want to receive inspirational or spiritual romances.

How to Contact Query with SASE. No e-mail or fax queries; will not respond. Responds in 2 weeks to queries. Responds in 4-6 weeks to mss. Obtains most new clients through recommendations from others, solicitations, conferences.

Terms Agent receives 15% commission on domestic sales. Agent receives 15% commission on foreign sales. Offers written contract; 1-month notice must be given to terminate contract. Charges maximum of $350/year for postage and photocopying.

Writers Conferences RWA National Conference; BookExpo America.

☑ JANE ROTROSEN AGENCY LLC

318 E. 51st St., New York NY 10022. (212)593-4330. Fax: (212)935-6985. E-mail: lcohen@janerotrosen. com. Website: www.janerotrosen.com. Member of AAR. Other memberships include Authors Guild. Represents over 100 clients. Currently handles nonfiction books (30%), novels (70%).

Member Agents Jane R. Berkey; Andrea Cirillo; Annelise Robey; Margaret Ruley; Christina Hogrebe; Peggy Gordijn, director of rights.

Represents nonfiction books, novels. **Considers these nonfiction areas:** biography, business, child, cooking, current affairs, health, how to, humor, money, nature, popular culture, psychology, self help, sports, true crime, womens. **Considers these fiction areas:** historical, mystery, romance, thriller, womens.

How to Contact Query with SASE. Responds in 2 weeks to writers who have been referred by a client or colleague. Responds in 2 months to mss. Obtains most new clients through recommendations from others.

Terms Agent receives 15% commission on domestic sales. Agent receives 20% commission on foreign sales. Offers written contract, binding for 3 years; 2-month notice must be given to terminate contract. Charges clients for photocopying, express mail, overseas postage, book purchase.

☑ MARLY RUSOFF & ASSOCIATES, INC.

P.O. Box 524, Bronxville NY 10708. (914)961-7939. E-mail: mra_queries@rusoffagency.com. Website: www.rusoffagency.com. **Contact:** Marly Rusoff.

• Prior to her current position, Ms. Rusoff held positions at Houghton Mifflin, Doubleday and William Morrow.

Member Agents Marly Rusoff.

Represents nonfiction books, novels. **Considers these nonfiction areas:** biography, business, health, history, memoirs, popular culture, psychology. **Considers these fiction areas:** historical, literary commercial. "While we take delight in discovering new talent, we are particularly interested in helping established writers expand readership and develop their careers."

How to Contact Query with SASE. Submit synopsis, publishing history, author bio, contact information. For e-queries, include no attachments or pdf files. "We cannot read DOCXs." This agency only responds if interested. Responds to queries. Obtains most new clients through recommendations from others.

☑ RUSSELL & VOLKENING

50 W. 29th St., #7E, New York NY 10001. (212)684-6050. Fax: (212)889-3026. **Contact:** Timothy Seldes (adult books), Jesseca Salky (adult, general fiction & nonfiction, memoirs), Carrie Hannigan (children's), Rosanna Bruno (adult, mysteries). Member of AAR. Represents 140 clients. 20% of clients are new/unpublished writers. Currently handles nonfiction books (45%), novels (50%), story collections (3%), novella(2%).

Represents nonfiction books, novels, short story collections. **Considers these nonfiction areas:** anthropology, art, biography, business, cooking, current affairs, education, ethnic, gay, government, health, history, language, military, money, music, nature, photography, popular culture, psychology, science, sociology, sports, film, true crime, womens creative nonfiction. **Considers these fiction areas:** adventure, detective, ethnic, literary, mainstream, mystery, picture books, sports, thriller. This agency specializes in literary fiction and narrative nonfiction. novels

How to Contact Query only with SASE to appropriate person. Responds in 4 weeks to queries.

Terms Agent receives 15% commission on domestic sales. Agent receives 20% commission on foreign sales. Charges clients for standard office expenses relating to the submission of materials.

Tips If the query is cogent, well written, well presented, and is the type of book we'd represent, we'll ask to see the manuscript. From there, it depends purely on the quality of the work.

☑ VICTORIA SANDERS & ASSOCIATES

241 Avenue of the Americas, Suite 11 H, New York NY 10014. (212)633-8811. Fax: (212)633-0525. E-mail: queriesvsa@hotmail.com. Website: www.victoriasanders.com. **Contact:** Victoria Sanders, Diane Dickensheid. Member of AAR. Signatory of WGA. Represents 135 clients. 25% of clients are new/unpublished writers. Currently handles nonfiction books (30%), novels (70%).

Represents nonfiction books, novels. **Considers these nonfiction areas:** biography, current affairs, ethnic, gay, government, history, humor, language, music, popular culture, psychology, film, translation, womens. **Considers these fiction areas:** contemporary, adventure, ethnic, family, feminist, gay, literary, thriller.

How to Contact Query by e-mail only.

Terms Agent receives 15% commission on domestic sales. Agent receives 20% commission on foreign sales. Offers written contract. Charges for photocopying, messenger, express mail. If in excess of $100, client approval is required.

Tips "Limit query to letter (no calls) and give it your best shot. A good query is going to get a good response."

☑ SCHIAVONE LITERARY AGENCY, INC.

236 Trails End, West Palm Beach FL 33413-2135. (561)966-9294. Fax: (561)966-9294. E-mail: profschia@ aol.com. **Contact:** Dr. James Schiavone. CEO, corporate offices in Florida; Jennifer DuVall, president, New York office. New York office: 3671 Hudson Manor Terrace, No. 11H, Bronx, NY, 10463-1139, phone: (718)548-5332; fax: (718)548-5332; e-mail: jendu77@aol.com Other memberships include National Education Association. Represents 60 + clients. 2%% of clients are new/unpublished writers. Currently handles nonfiction books (50%), novels (49%), textbooks (1%).

- Prior to opening his agency, Dr. Schiavone was a full professor of developmental skills at the City University of New York and author of 5 trade books and 3 textbooks. Jennifer DuVall has many years of combined experience in office management and agenting.

Represents nonfiction books, novels, juvenile, scholarly, textbooks. **Considers these nonfiction areas:** juvenile, animals, anthropology, biography, child, current affairs, education, ethnic, gay, government, health, history, how to, humor, language, military, nature, popular culture, psychology, science, self help, sociology, spirituality, mind and body, true crime. **Considers these fiction areas:** ethnic, family, historical, horror, humor, juvenile, literary, mainstream, science, young. This agency specializes in celebrity biography and autobiography and memoirs. Does not want to receive poetry.

How to Contact Query with SASE. Do not send unsolicited materials or parcels requiring a signature. Send no e-attachments. Accepts simultaneous submissions. Responds in 2 weeks to queries. Responds in 6 weeks to mss. Obtains most new clients through recommendations from others, solicitations, conferences.

Terms Agent receives 15% commission on domestic sales. Agent receives 20% commission on foreign sales. Offers written contract. Charges clients for postage only.

Writers Conferences Key West Literary Seminar; South Florida Writers' Conference; Tallahassee Writers' Conference, Million Dollar Writers' Conference; Alaska Writers Conference.

Tips "We prefer to work with established authors published by major houses in New York. We will consider marketable proposals from new/previously unpublished writers."

☑ SUSAN SCHULMAN LITERARY AGENCY

454 West 44th St., New York NY 10036. (212)713-1633. Fax: (212)581-8830. E-mail: queries@schulmanagency.com. Website: www.schulmanagency.com. **Contact:** Susan Schulman. Member of AAR. Signatory of WGA. Other memberships include Dramatists Guild. 10% of clients are new/unpublished writers. Currently handles nonfiction books (50%), novels (25%), juvenile books (15%), stage plays (10%).

Member Agents Linda Kiss, director of foreign rights; Katherine Stones, theater; Emily Uhry, submissions editor.

Represents Considers these nonfiction areas: anthropology, biography, business, child, cooking, current affairs, education, ethnic, gay, government, health, history, how to, language, memoirs, money, music, nature, popular culture, psychology, religion, self help, sociology, sports, true crime, womens. **Considers these fiction areas:** adventure, detective, feminist, historical, humor, juvenile, literary, mainstream, mystery, picture books, religious, young, womens. "We specialize in books for, by and about women and women's issues including nonfiction self-help books, fiction and theater projects. We also handle the film, television and allied rights for several agencies as well as foreign rights for several publishing houses." Actively seeking new nonfiction. Considers plays. Does not want to receive poetry, television scripts or concepts for television.

How to Contact Query with SASE. Submit outline, synopsis, author bio, 3 sample chapters, SASE. Accepts simultaneous submissions. Responds in 6 weeks to queries. Responds in 6 weeks to mss. Obtains most new clients through recommendations from others, solicitations, conferences.

Terms Agent receives 15% commission on domestic sales. Agent receives 20% commission on foreign sales. Offers written contract; 30-day notice must be given to terminate contract.

Writers Conferences Geneva Writers' Conference (Switzerland); Columbus Writers' Conference; Skidmore Conference of the Independent Women's Writers Group.

Tips "Keep writing!"

☑ SCRIBBLERS HOUSE, LLC LITERARY AGENCY

P.O. Box 1007, Cooper Station, New York NY 10276-1007. (212)714-7744. E-mail: query@scribblershouse.net. Website: www.scribblershouse.net. **Contact:** Stedman Mays, Garrett Gambino. 25% of clients are new/unpublished writers.

Represents nonfiction books, novels, occasionally. **Considers these nonfiction areas:** business, health, history, how to, language, memoirs, popular culture, psychology, self help, sex, spirituality diet/nutrition; the brain; personal finance; biography; politics; writing books; relationships; gender issues; parenting. **Considers these fiction areas:** historical, literary, womens suspense; crime; thrillers.

How to Contact Query via e-mail. Put "nonfiction query" or "fiction query" in the subject line followed by the title of your project (send to our submissions email on our website). Do not send attachments or downloadable materials of any kind with query. We will request more materials if we are interested. Usually respond in 2 weeks to 2 months to email queries if we are interested (if we are not interested, we will not respond due to the overwhelming amount of queries we receive). We are only accepting email queries at the present time. Accepts simultaneous submissions.

Terms Agent receives 15% commission on domestic sales. Charges clients for postage, shipping and copying.

Tips "If you must send by snail mail, we will return material or respond to a U.S. Postal Service-accepted SASE. (No international coupons or outdated mail strips, please.) Presentation means a lot. A well-written query letter with a brief author bio and your credentials is important. For query letter models, go to the bookstore or online and look at the cover copy and flap copy on other books in your general area of interest. Emulate what's best. Have an idea of other notable books that will be perceived as being in the same vein as yours. Know what's fresh about your project and articulate it in as few words as possible. Consult our Web site for the most up-to-date information on submitting."

☐ SCRIBE AGENCY, LLC

5508 Joylynne Dr., Madison WI 53716. E-mail: queries@scribeagency.com. Website: www.scribeagency.com. **Contact:** Kristopher O'Higgins. Represents 11 clients. 18% of clients are new/unpublished writers. Currently handles novels (98%), story collections (2%).

> • "We have 17 years of experience in publishing and have worked on both agency and editorial sides in the past, with marketing expertise to boot. We love books as much or more than anyone you know. Check our website to see what we're about and to make sure you jive with the Scribe vibe."

Member Agents Kristopher O'Higgins; Jesse Vogel.

Represents nonfiction books, novels, short story collections, novellas anthologies. **Considers these nonfiction areas:** ethnic, gay, memoirs, popular culture, womens. **Considers these fiction areas:** detective, erotica, experimental, fantasy, feminist, gay, horror, humor, lesbian, literary, mainstream, mystery, psychic, thriller science fiction,. Actively seeking excellent writers with ideas and stories to tell.

How to Contact E queries only. See the Web site for submission info, as it may change. Responds in 3-4 weeks to queries. Responds in 5 months to mss.

Terms Agent receives 15% commission on domestic sales. Agent receives 20% commission on foreign sales. Offers written contract. Charges for postage and photocopying.

Writers Conferences BookExpo America; The Writer's Institute; Spring Writer's Festival; WisCon; Wisconsin Book Festival; World Fantasy Convention.

SECRET AGENT MAN

P.O. Box 1078, Lake Forest CA 92609-1078. (949)698-6987. E-mail: scott@secretagentman.net. Website: www.secretagentman.net. **Contact:** Scott Mortenson.

Represents novels. **Considers these fiction areas:** detective, mystery, religious, thriller. Actively seeking selective mystery, thriller, suspense and detective fiction. Does not want to receive scripts or screenplays.

How to Contact Query with SASE. Query via e-mail or snail mail; include sample chapter(s), synopsis and/or outline. Prefers to read the real thing rather than a description of it. Obtains most new clients through recommendations from others, solicitations.

LYNN SELIGMAN, LITERARY AGENT

400 Highland Ave., Upper Montclair NJ 07043. (973)783-3631. **Contact:** Lynn Seligman. Other memberships include Women's Media Group. Represents 32 clients. 15% of clients are new/unpublished writers. Currently handles nonfiction books (60%), novels (40%).

> • Prior to opening her agency, Ms. Seligman worked in the subsidiary rights department of Doubleday and Simon & Schuster, and served as an agent with Julian Bach Literary Agency (which became IMG Literary Agency). Foreign rights are represented by Books Crossing Borders, Inc.

Represents nonfiction books, novels. **Considers these nonfiction areas:** interior, anthropology, art, biography, business, child, cooking, current affairs, education, ethnic, government, health, history, how to, humor, language, money, music, nature, photography, popular culture, psychology, science, self help, sociology, film, true crime, womens. **Considers these fiction areas:** detective, ethnic, fantasy, feminist, historical, horror, humor, literary, mainstream, mystery, romance, contemporary, gothic, historical, regency, science. "This agency specializes in general nonfiction and fiction. I also do illustrated and photography books and have represented several photographers for books."

How to Contact Query with SASE. Prefers to read materials exclusively. Accepts simultaneous submissions. Responds in 2 weeks to queries. Responds in 2 months to mss. Obtains most new clients through referrals from other writers and editors.

Terms Agent receives 15% commission on domestic sales. Agent receives 25% commission on foreign sales. Charges clients for photocopying, unusual postage, express mail, telephone expenses (checks with author first).

☑ THE SEYMOUR AGENCY

475 Miner St., Canton NY 13617. (315)386-1831. E-mail: marysue@twcny.rr.com. Website: www.theseymouragency.com. **Contact:** Mary Sue Seymour. Member of AAR. Signatory of WGA. Other memberships include RWA, Authors Guild. Represents 50 clients. 5% of clients are new/unpublished writers. Currently handles nonfiction books (50%), other(50% fiction).

• Ms. Seymour is a retired New York State certified teacher.

Represents nonfiction books, novels. **Considers these nonfiction areas:** business, health, how-to, self help Christian books; cookbooks; any well-written nonfiction that includes a proposal in standard format and 1 sample chapter. **Considers these fiction areas:** religious, Christian books, romance, any type.

How to Contact Query with SASE, synopsis, first 50 pages for romance. Accepts e-mail queries. Accepts simultaneous submissions. Responds in 1 month to queries. Responds in 3 months to mss.

Terms Agent receives 12-15% commission on domestic sales.

☑ WENDY SHERMAN ASSOCIATES, INC.

450 Seventh Ave., Suite 2307, New York NY 10123. (212)279-9027. Fax: (212)279-8863. Website: www. wsherman.com. **Contact:** Wendy Sherman. Member of AAR. Represents 50 clients. 30% of clients are new/unpublished writers. Currently handles nonfiction books (50%), novels (50%).

• Prior to opening the agency, Ms. Sherman worked for The Aaron Priest agency and served as vice president, executive director, associate publisher, subsidary rights director, and sales and marketing director in the publishing industry.

Member Agents Wendy Sherman; Michelle Brower.

Represents nonfiction books, novels. **Considers these nonfiction areas:** psychology narrative; practical. **Considers these fiction areas:** literary, womens, suspense. "We specialize in developing new writers, as well as working with more established writers. My experience as a publisher has proven to be a great asset to my clients."

How to Contact Query with SASE or send outline/proposal, 1 sample chapter. E-mail queries accepted by Ms. Brower only. Considers Accepts simultaneous submissions. Responds in 1 month to queries. Obtains most new clients through recommendations from others.

Terms Agent receives 15% commission on domestic sales. Agent receives 20% commission on foreign sales. Offers written contract.

Tips "The bottom line is: Do your homework. Be as well prepared as possible. Read the books that will help you present yourself and your work with polish. You want your submission to stand out."

▦ ☑ JEFFREY SIMMONS LITERARY AGENCY

15 Penn House, Mallory St., London NW8 8SX England. (44)(207)224-8917. E-mail: jasimmons@ unicombox.co.uk. **Contact:** Jeffrey Simmons. Represents 43 clients. 40% of clients are new/unpublished writers. Currently handles nonfiction books (65%), novels (35%).

• Prior to becoming an agent, Mr. Simmons was a publisher. He is also an author.

Represents nonfiction books, novels. **Considers these nonfiction areas:** biography, current affairs, government, history, language, memoirs, music, popular culture, sociology, sports, film, translation, true crime. **Considers these fiction areas:** adventure, confession, detective, family, literary, mainstream, mystery, thriller. "This agency seeks to handle good books and promising young writers. My long experience in publishing and as an author and ghostwriter means I can offer an excellent service all around, especially in terms of editorial experience where appropriate." Actively seeking quality fiction, biography, autobiography, showbiz, personality books, law, crime, politics, and world affairs. Does not want to receive science fiction, horror, fantasy, juvenile, academic books, or specialist subjects (e.g., cooking, gardening, religious).

How to Contact Submit sample chapter, outline/proposal, SASE (IRCs if necessary). Prefers to read materials exclusively. Responds in 1 week to queries. Responds in 1 month to mss. Obtains most new clients through recommendations from others, solicitations.

Terms Agent receives 10-15% commission on domestic sales. Agent receives 15% commission on foreign sales. Offers written contract, binding for lifetime of book in question or until it becomes out of print.

Tips "When contacting us with an outline/proposal, include a brief biographical note (listing any previous publications, with publishers and dates). Preferably tell us if the book has already been offered elsewhere."

☑ BEVERLEY SLOPEN LITERARY AGENCY

131 Bloor St. W., Suite 711, Toronto ON M5S 1S3 Canada. (416)964-9598. Fax: (416)921-7726. E-mail: beverly@slopenagency.ca. Website: www.slopenagency.ca. **Contact:** Beverley Slopen. Represents 70 clients. 20% of clients are new/unpublished writers. Currently handles nonfiction books (60%), novels (40%).

• Prior to opening her agency, Ms. Slopen worked in publishing and as a journalist.

Represents nonfiction books, novels, scholarly, textbooks, college. **Considers these nonfiction areas:** anthropology, biography, business, current affairs, psychology, sociology, true crime, womens. **Considers these fiction areas:** literary, mystery. "This agency has a strong bent toward Canadian writers." Actively seeking serious nonfiction that is accessible and appealing to the general reader. Does not want to receive fantasy, science fiction, or children's books.

How to Contact Query with SAE and IRCs. Returns materials only with SASE (Canadian postage only). Accepts simultaneous submissions. Responds in 2 months to queries.

Terms Agent receives 15% commission on domestic sales. Agent receives 10% commission on foreign sales. Offers written contract, binding for 2 years; 3-month notice must be given to terminate contract.

Tips "Please, no unsolicited manuscripts."

VALERIE SMITH, LITERARY AGENT

1746 Route 44/55, Modena NY 12548. **Contact:** Valerie Smith. Represents 17 clients. Currently handles nonfiction books (2%), novels (75%), story collections (1%), juvenile books (20%), scholarly books (1%), textbooks (1%).

Represents nonfiction books, novels, juvenile, textbooks. **Considers these nonfiction areas:** agriculture horticulture, cooking, how to, self help. **Considers these fiction areas:** fantasy, historical, juvenile, literary, mainstream, mystery, science, young women's/chick lit. "This is a small, personalized agency with a strong long-term commitment to clients interested in building careers. I have strong ties to science fiction, fantasy and young adult projects. I look for serious, productive writers whose work I can be passionate about." Does not want to receive unsolicited mss.

How to Contact Query with synopsis, bio, 3 sample chapters, SASE. Contact by snail mail only. Obtains most new clients through recommendations from others.

Terms Agent receives 15% commission on domestic sales. Agent receives 20% commission on foreign sales. Offers written contract; 6-week notice must be given to terminate contract.

☑ SPECTRUM LITERARY AGENCY

320 Central Park W., Suite 1-D, New York NY 10025. Fax: (212)362-4562. Website: www. spectrumliteraryagency.com. **Contact:** Eleanor Wood, president. SFWA Represents 90 clients. Currently handles nonfiction books (10%), novels (90%).

Member Agents Eleanor Wood, Justin Bell

Represents nonfiction books, novels. **Considers these fiction areas:** fantasy, historical, mainstream, mystery, romance, science fiction.

How to Contact Query with SASE. Submit author bio, publishing credits. No unsolicited mss will be read. Snail mail queries **only**. Eleanor and Lucienne have different addresses — see the Web site for full info. Responds in 1-3 months to queries. Obtains most new clients through recommendations from authors.

Terms Agent receives 15% commission on domestic sales. Deducts for photocopying and book orders.

Tips "Spectrum's policy is to read only book-length manuscripts that we have specifically asked to see. Unsolicited manuscripts are not accepted. The letter should describe your book briefly and include publishing credits and background information or qualifications relating to your work, if any."

☑ SPENCERHILL ASSOCIATES

P.O. Box 374, Chatham NY 12037. (518)392-9293. Fax: (518)392-9554. E-mail: ksolem@klsbooks.com; jennifer@klsbooks.com. **Contact:** Karen Solem or Jennifer Schober. Member of AAR. Represents 73 clients. 5% of clients are new/unpublished writers.

• Prior to becoming an agent, Ms. Solem was editor-in-chief at HarperCollins and an associate publisher.

Member Agents Karen Solem; Jennifer Schober.

Represents novels. **Considers these fiction areas:** detective, historical, literary, mainstream, religious, romance, thriller, young. "We handle mostly commercial women's fiction, historical novels, romance (historical, contemporary, paranormal, urban fantasy), thrillers, and mysteries. We also represent Christian fiction." No nonfiction, poetry, science fiction, children's picture books, or scripts.

How to Contact Query jennifer@klsbooks.com with synopsis and first three chapters. E-queries preferred. Responds in 6-8 weeks to queries.

Terms Agent receives 15% commission on domestic sales. Agent receives 20% commission on foreign sales. Offers written contract; 3-month notice must be given to terminate contract.

☑ THE SPIELER AGENCY

154 W. 57th St., Suite 135, New York NY 10019. E-mail: eric@spieleragency.com. **Contact:** Katya Balter. Represents 160 clients. 2% of clients are new/unpublished writers.

• Prior to opening his agency, Mr. Spieler was a magazine editor.

Member Agents Joe Spieler

Represents nonfiction books, novels children's books. **Considers these nonfiction areas:** biography, business, current affairs, film, gay, government, history, memoirs, money, music, nature, sociology, spirituality, travel. **Considers these fiction areas:** detective, feminist, gay, literary, mystery children's books, Middle Grade and Young Adult novels.

How to Contact Accepts electronic submissions (spieleragency@spieleragency.com), or send query letter and sample chapters. Prefers to read materials exclusively. Returns materials only with SASE; otherwise materials are discarded when rejected. Accepts simultaneous submissions. Responds in 2 weeks to queries. Responds in 2 months to mss. Obtains most new clients through recommendations, listing in *Guide to Literary Agents*.

Terms Agent receives 15% commission on domestic sales. Charges clients for messenger bills, photocopying, postage.

Writers Conferences London Book Fair.

Tips "Check http://www.publishersmarketplace.com/members/spielerlit/."

☑ NANCY STAUFFER ASSOCIATES

P.O. Box 1203, 1540 Boston Post Road, Darien CT 06820. (203)202-2500. Fax: (203)655-3704. E-mail: StaufferAssoc@optonline.net. **Contact:** Nancy Stauffer Cahoon. Other memberships include Authors Guild. 5% of clients are new/unpublished writers. Currently handles nonfiction books (15%), novels (85%).

Represents Considers these nonfiction areas: current affairs, ethnic creative nonfiction (narrative). **Considers these fiction areas:** contemporary, literary, regional.

How to Contact Obtains most new clients through referrals from existing clients.

Terms Agent receives 15% commission on domestic sales. Agent receives 20% commission on foreign sales. Agent receives 15% commission on film sales.

☑ STEELE-PERKINS LITERARY AGENCY

26 Island Ln., Canandaigua NY 14424. (585)396-9290. Fax: (585)396-3579. E-mail: pattiesp@aol.com. **Contact:** Pattie Steele-Perkins. Member of AAR. Other memberships include RWA. Currently handles novels (100%).

Represents novels. **Considers these fiction areas:** romance, women's All genres: category romance, romantic suspense, historical, contemporary, multi-cultural, and inspirational.

How to Contact Submit synopsis and one chapter via e-mail (no attachments) or snail mail. Snail mail submissions require SASE. Accepts simultaneous submissions. Responds in 6 weeks to queries. Obtains most new clients through recommendations from others, queries/solicitations.

Terms Agent receives 15% commission on domestic sales. Offers written contract, binding for 1 year; 1-month notice must be given to terminate contract.

Writers Conferences RWA National Conference; BookExpo America; CBA Convention; Romance Slam Jam.

Tips Be patient. E-mail rather than call. Make sure what you are sending is the best it can be.

☑ STERNIG & BYRNE LITERARY AGENCY

2370 S. 107th St., Apt. #4, Milwaukee WI 53227-2036. (414)328-8034. Fax: (414)328-8034. E-mail: jackbyrne@hotmail.com. Website: www.sff.net/people/jackbyrne. **Contact:** Jack Byrne. Other memberships include SFWA, MWA. Represents 30 clients. 10% of clients are new/unpublished writers. Currently handles nonfiction books (5%), novels (90%), juvenile books (5%).

Represents nonfiction books, novels, juvenile. **Considers these fiction areas:** fantasy, horror, mystery, science. Our client list is comfortably full and our current needs are therefore quite limited. Actively seeking science fiction/fantasy and mystery by established writers. Does not want to receive romance, poetry, textbooks, or highly specialized nonfiction.

How to Contact Query with SASE. Prefers e-mail queries (no attachments); hard copy queries also acceptable. Responds in 3 weeks to queries. Responds in 3 months to mss.

Terms Agent receives 15% commission on domestic sales. Agent receives 20% commission on foreign sales. Offers written contract; 2-month notice must be given to terminate contract.

Tips "Don't send first drafts, have a professional presentation (including cover letter), and know your field. Read what's been done - good and bad."

☑ STRACHAN LITERARY AGENCY

P.O. Box 2091, Annapolis MD 21404. E-mail: query@strachanlit.com. Website: www.strachanlit.com. **Contact:** Laura Strachan.

- Prior to becoming an agent, Ms. Strachan was (and still is) an attorney.

Represents nonfiction books, novels. **Considers these nonfiction areas:** interior, cooking, gardening, memoirs, photography, psychology, self help, travel narrative, parenting, arts. **Considers these fiction areas:** literary, mystery legal and pyschological thrillers, children's. "This agency specializes in literary fiction and narrative nonfiction." Actively seeking new, fresh voices.

How to Contact Query with cover letter outlining your professional experience and a brief synopsis. Prefers e-mail queries; send no e-mail attachments. No sample pages unless requested.

☑ THE STROTHMAN AGENCY, LLC

narrative nonfiction and literary fiction, Six Beacon St., Suite 810, Boston MA 02108. (617)742-2011. Fax: (617)742-2014. Website: www.strothmanagency.com. **Contact:** Wendy Strothman, Dan O'Connell. Member of AAR. Other memberships include Authors' Guild. Represents 50 clients. Currently handles nonfiction books (70%), novels (10%), scholarly books (20%).

- Prior to becoming an agent, Ms. Strothman was head of Beacon Press (1983-1995) and executive vice president of Houghton Mifflin's Trade & Reference Division (1996-2002).

Member Agents Wendy Strothman; Dan O'Connell.

Represents nonfiction books, novels, scholarly. **Considers these nonfiction areas:** current affairs, government, history, language, nature. **Considers these fiction areas:** literary. "Because we are highly selective in the clients we represent, we increase the value publishers place on our properties. We specialize in narrative nonfiction, memoir, history, science and nature, arts and culture, literary travel, current affairs, and some business. We have a highly selective practice in literary fiction and smart self-help. We are now opening our doors to more commercial fiction but ONLY from authors who have a platform. If you have a platform, please mention it in your query letter." "The Strothman Agency seeks out scholars, journalists, and other acknowledged and emerging experts in their fields. We are now actively looking for authors of well written young-adult fiction and nonfiction. Browse the Latest News to get an idea of the types of books that we represent. For more about what we're looking for, read Pitching an Agent: The Strothman Agency on the publishing website mediabistro.com." Does not want to receive commercial fiction, romance, science fiction or self-help.

How to Contact Open to email (strothmanagency@gmail.com) and postal submissions. See submission guidelines. Accepts simultaneous submissions. Responds in 4 weeks to queries. Responds in 6 weeks to mss. Obtains most new clients through recommendations from others.

Terms Agent receives 15% commission on domestic sales. Agent receives 20% commission on foreign sales. Offers written contract; 30-day notice must be given to terminate contract.

☑ EMMA SWEENEY AGENCY, LLC

245 East 80th St., Suite 7E, New York NY 10075. E-mail: queries@emmasweeneyagency.com; info@emmasweeneyagency.com. Website: www.emmasweeneyagency.com. **Contact:** Eva Talmadge. Member of AAR. Other memberships include Women's Media Group. Represents 50 clients. 5% of clients are new/unpublished writers. Currently handles nonfiction books (30%), novels (70%).

- Prior to becoming an agent, Ms. Sweeney was a subsidiary rights assistant at William Morrow. Since 1990, she has been a literary agent, and was most recently an agent with Harold Ober Associates.

Member Agents Emma Sweeney, president; Eva Talmadge, rights manager; Justine Wenger, junior agent/assistant (justine@emmasweeneyagency.com).

Represents nonfiction books, novels. **Considers these nonfiction areas:** agriculture horticulture, animals, biography, cooking, memoirs. **Considers these fiction areas:** literary, mystery, thriller, womens. "We specialize in quality fiction and non-fiction. Our primary areas of interest include literary and women's fiction, mysteries and thrillers; science, history, biography, memoir, religious studies and the natural sciences." Does not want to receive romance and westerns or screenplays.

How to Contact Send query letter and first ten pages in body of e-mail (no attachments) to queries@ emmasweeneyagency.com. No snail mail queries.

Terms Agent receives 15% commission on domestic sales. Agent receives 10% commission on foreign sales.

Writers Conferences Nebraska Writers' Conference; Words and Music Festival in New Orleans.

☑ TALCOTT NOTCH LITERARY

276 Forest Road, Milford CT 06460. (203)877-1146. Fax: (203)876-9517. E-mail: editorial@talcottnotch. net. Website: www.talcottnotch.net. **Contact:** Gina Panettieri, president. Represents 35 clients. 25% of clients are new/unpublished writers. Currently handles nonfiction books (25%), novels (55%), story collections (5%), juvenile books (10%), scholarly books (5%).

- Prior to becoming an agent, Ms. Panettieri was a freelance writer and editor.

Member Agents Gina Panettieri (nonfiction, mystery); Rachel Dowen (children's fiction, mystery).

Represents nonfiction books, novels, juvenile, scholarly, textbooks. **Considers these nonfiction areas:** agriculture horticulture, animals, anthropology, art, biography, business, child, computers, cooking, current affairs, education, ethnic, gay, government, health, history, how to, memoirs, military, money, music, nature, popular culture, psychology, science, self help, sociology, sports, true crime, womens New Age/metaphysics, interior design/decorating, juvenile nonfiction. **Considers these fiction areas:** adventure, detective, juvenile, mystery, thriller, young.

How to Contact Query via e-mail (preferred) or with SASE. Accepts simultaneous submissions. Responds in 1 week to queries. Responds in 4-6 weeks to mss.

Terms Agent receives 15% commission on domestic sales. Agent receives 20% commission on foreign sales. Offers written contract, binding for 1 year.

Tips "Present your book or project effectively in your query. Don't include links to a Web page rather than a traditional query, and take the time to prepare a thorough but brief synopsis of the material. Make the effort to prepare a thoughtful analysis of comparison titles. How is your work different, yet would appeal to those same readers?"

☑ PATRICIA TEAL LITERARY AGENCY

2036 Vista Del Rosa, Fullerton CA 92831-1336. Phone/Fax: (714)738-8333. **Contact:** Patricia Teal. Member of AAR. Other memberships include RWA, Authors Guild. Represents 20 clients. Currently handles nonfiction books (10%), other(90% fiction).

Represents nonfiction books, novels. **Considers these nonfiction areas:** animals, biography, child, health, how to, psychology, self help, true crime, womens. **Considers these fiction areas:** glitz, mainstream, mystery, romance (contemporary, historical). This agency specializes in women's fiction, commercial how-to, and self-help nonfiction. Does not want to receive poetry, short stories, articles, science fiction, fantasy, or regency romance.

How to Contact Published authors only may query with SASE. Accepts simultaneous submissions. Responds in 10 days to queries. Responds in 6 weeks to mss. Obtains most new clients through conferences, recommendations from authors and editors.

Terms Agent receives 10-15% commission on domestic sales. Agent receives 20% commission on foreign sales. Offers written contract, binding for 1 year. Charges clients for ms copies.

Writers Conferences RWA Conferences; Asilomar; BookExpo America; Bouchercon; Maui Writers Conference.

Tips "Include SASE with all correspondence. I am taking on published authors only."

ANN TOBIAS: A LITERARY AGENCY FOR CHILDREN'S BOOKS

520 E. 84th St., Apt. 4L, New York NY 10028. E-mail: AnnTobias84@hotmail.com. **Contact:** Ann Tobias. Represents 25 clients. 10% of clients are new/unpublished writers. Currently handles juvenile books (100%).

- Prior to opening her agency, Ms. Tobias worked as a children's book editor at Harper, William Morrow and Scholastic.

Represents juvenile. **Considers these nonfiction areas:** juvenile. **Considers these fiction areas:** picture books, poetry, for children, young illustrated mss; mid-level novels. This agency specializes in books for children.

How to Contact For all age groups and genres: Send a one-page letter of inquiry accompanied by a one-page writing sample, double-spaced. No attachments will be opened. Other Responds in 2 months to mss. Obtains most new clients through recommendations from editors.

Terms Agent receives 15% commission on domestic sales. Agent receives 20% commission on foreign sales. No written contract. This agency charges clients for photocopying, overnight mail, foreign postage, foreign telephone.

Tips "Read at least 200 children's books in the age group and genre in which you hope to be published. Follow this by reading another 100 children's books in other age groups and genres so you will have a feel for the field as a whole."

⬛ ⬛ TRANSATLANTIC LITERARY AGENCY

72 Glengowan Road, Toronto Ontario M4N 1G4 Canada. E-mail: info@tla1.com. Website: www.tla1.com. **Contact:** Lynn Bennett. Represents 250 clients. 10% of clients are new/unpublished writers. Currently handles nonfiction books (30%), novels (15%), juvenile books (50%), textbooks (5%).

Member Agents Lynn Bennett, Lynn@tla1.com, (juvenile and young adult fiction); Shaun Bradley, Shaun@tla1.com (literary fiction and narrative nonfiction); Marie Campbell, Marie@tla1.com (literary juvenile and young adult fiction); Andrea Cascardi, Andrea@tla1.com (literary juvenile and young adult fiction); Samantha Haywood, Sam@tla1.com (literary fiction, narrative nonfiction and graphic novels); Don Sedgwick, Don@tla1.com (literary fiction and narrative nonfiction).

Represents nonfiction books, novels, juvenile. **Considers these nonfiction areas:** biography, business, current affairs, nature. **Considers these fiction areas:** juvenile, literary, mainstream. In both children's and adult literature, we market directly into the United States, the United Kingdom and Canada. Actively seeking literary children's and adult fiction, nonfiction. Does not want to receive picture books, poetry, screenplays or stage plays.

How to Contact Submit E-query query with synopsis, 2 sample chapters, bio. Always refer to the Web site as guidelines will change. Responds in 2 weeks to queries. Obtains most new clients through recommendations from others.

Terms Agent receives 15% commission on domestic sales. Agent receives 20% commission on foreign sales. Offers written contract; 45-day notice must be given to terminate contract. This agency charges for photocopying and postage when it exceeds $100.

⬛ TRIADA U.S. LITERARY AGENCY, INC.

P.O. Box 561, Sewickley PA 15143. (412)401-3376. E-mail: uwe@triadaus.com. Website: www.triadaus.com. **Contact:** Dr. Uwe Stender. true Represents 65 clients. 25% of clients are new/unpublished writers.

Member Agents Rebecca Post.

Represents fiction, nonfiction. **Considers these nonfiction areas:** biography, business, education, memoirs, popular culture, science, sports advice, relationships, health, cooking, lifestyle. **Considers these fiction areas:** adventure, detective, ethnic, historical, horror, juvenile, literary, mainstream, mystery, occult, romance, women's, young adult. "We are looking for great writing and story platforms. Our response time is fairly unique. We recognize that neither we nor the authors have time to waste, so we guarantee a 5-day response time. We usually respond within 24 hours. " Actively looking for both fiction and nonfiction in all areas. De-emphasizing fiction, although great writing will always be considered.

How to Contact E-mail queries preferred; otherwise query with SASE. Accepts simultaneous submissions. Responds in 1-5 weeks to queries. Responds in 2-6 weeks to mss. Obtains most new clients through recommendations from others, conferences.

Terms Agent receives 15% commission on domestic sales. Agent receives 20% commission on foreign sales. Offers written contract; 30-day notice must be given to terminate contract.

Tips "I comment on all requested manuscripts that I reject."

⬛ VANGUARD LITERARY AGENCY

81 E. Jefryn Blvd., Suite E,, Deer Park NY 11729. (718)710-3662. Fax: (917)591-7088. E-mail: sandylu@vanguardliterary.com; sandy@lperkinsagency.com. Website: www.vanguardliterary.com. **Contact:** Sandy

Lu. Represents 15 clients. 60% of clients are new/unpublished writers. Currently handles nonfiction books (20%), novels (80%).

- Prior to becoming an agent, Ms. Lu held managerial positions in commercial theater. "Ms. Lu is also an associate agent at the L. Perkins Agency. Please only send queries to one of her e-mail addresses."

Represents nonfiction books, novels, short story collections, novellas. **Considers these nonfiction areas:** anthropology, biography, cooking, ethnic, gay, history, memoirs, music, popular culture, psychology, science, sociology, translation, true crime, womens. **Considers these fiction areas:** adventure, confession, detective, ethnic, historical, horror, humor, literary, mainstream, mystery, regional, thriller, womens, (no chick lit). "Very few agents in the business still edit their clients' manuscripts, especially when it comes to fiction. Vanguard Literary Agency is different. I care about the quality of my clients' works and will not send anything out to publishers without personally going through each page first to ensure that when the manuscript is sent out, it is in the best possible shape." Actively seeking literary and commercial fiction with a unique voice. Does not want to receive movie or TV scripts, stage plays or poetry; unwanted fiction genres include science fiction/fantasy, Western, YA, children's; unwanted nonfiction genres include self-help, how-to, parenting, sports, dating/relationship, military/war, religion/spirituality, New Age, gift books.

How to Contact Only accepts e-mail queries. No fax queries. Accepts simultaneous submissions. Responds in 2 weeks to queries. Responds in 6-8 weeks to mss. Obtains most new clients through recommendations from others, solicitations, conferences.

Terms Agent receives 15% commission on domestic sales. Agent receives 20% commission on foreign sales. Offers written contract, binding for 1 year; 30-day notice must be given to terminate contract. This agency charges for photocopying and postage, and discusses larger costs (in excess of $100) with authors prior to charging.

Tips "Do your research. Do not query an agent for a genre he or she does not represent. Personalize your query letter. Start with an interesting hook. Learn how to write a succinct yet interesting synopsis or proposal."

☑ VENTURE LITERARY

8895 Towne Centre Drive, Suite 105, #141, San Diego CA 92122. (619)807-1887. Fax: (772)365-8321. E-mail: submissions@ventureliterary.com. Website: www.ventureliterary.com. **Contact:** Frank R. Scatoni. Represents 50 clients. 40% of clients are new/unpublished writers. Currently handles nonfiction books (80%), novels (20%).

- Prior to becoming an agent, Mr. Scatoni worked as an editor at Simon & Schuster.

Member Agents Frank R. Scatoni (general nonfiction, biography, memoir, narrative nonfiction, sports, serious nonfiction, graphic novels, narratives).

Represents nonfiction books, novels graphic novels, narratives. **Considers these nonfiction areas:** anthropology, biography, business, current affairs, ethnic, government, history, memoirs, military, money, multicultural, music, nature, popular culture, psychology, science, sports, true crime. **Considers these fiction areas:** adventure, detective, literary, mainstream, mystery, sports, thriller, womens. Specializes in nonfiction, sports, biography, gambling and nonfiction narratives. Actively seeking nonfiction, graphic novels and narratives.

How to Contact Considers e-mail queries only. *No unsolicited mss* and no snail mail whatsoever. See Web site for complete submission guidelines. Obtains most new clients through recommendations from others.

Terms Agent receives 15% commission on domestic sales. Agent receives 20% commission on foreign sales. Offers written contract.

☑ BETH VESEL LITERARY AGENCY

80 Fifth Ave., Suite 1101, New York NY 10011. (212)924-4252. E-mail: mlindley@bvlit.com. **Contact:** Julia Masnik, assistant. Represents 65 clients. 10% of clients are new/unpublished writers. Currently handles nonfiction books (75%), novels (10%), story collections (5%), scholarly books (10%).

- Prior to becoming an agent, Ms. Vesel was a poet and a journalist.

Represents nonfiction books, novels. **Considers these nonfiction areas:** biography, business, ethnic, health, how to, memoirs, psychology, self help, true crime, womens cultural criticism. **Considers these fiction areas:** detective, literary Francophone novels. "My specialties include serious nonfiction, psychology, cultural criticism, memoir, and women's issues." Actively seeking cultural criticism, literary psychological thrillers, and sophisticated memoirs. No uninspired psychology or run-of-the-mill first novels.

How to Contact Query with SASE. Accepts simultaneous submissions. Responds in 2 weeks to queries. Responds in 1 month to mss. Obtains most new clients through referrals, reading good magazines, contacting professionals with ideas.

Terms Agent receives 15% commission on domestic sales. Agent receives 20% commission on foreign sales. Offers written contract.

Writers Conferences Squaw Valley Writers Workshop, Iowa Summer Writing Festival.

Tips "Try to find out if you fit on a particular agent's list by looking at his/her books and comparing yours. You can almost always find who represents a book by looking at the acknowledgements."

CHRISTINA WARD LITERARY AGENCY

PO Box 7144, Lowell MA 01852. (978)656-8389. E-mail: christinawardlit@mac.com.
Represents nonfiction books, novels. **Considers these nonfiction areas:** biography, health, history, medicine, memoirs, nature, psychology, science literary nonfiction, including narrative nonfiction. **Considers these fiction areas:** literary, mystery, suspense, thriller.

JOHN A. WARE LITERARY AGENCY

392 Central Park W., New York NY 10025-5801. (212)866-4733. Fax: (212)866-4734. **Contact:** John Ware. Represents 60 clients. 40%% of clients are new/unpublished writers. Currently handles nonfiction books (75%), novels (25%).

- Prior to opening his agency, Mr. Ware served as a literary agent with James Brown Associates/Curtis Brown, Ltd., and as an editor for Doubleday & Co.

Represents nonfiction books, novels. **Considers these nonfiction areas:** anthropology, biography, current affairs, health, academic credentials required, history, oral history, Americana, folklore, language, music, nature, popular culture, psychology, academic credentials required, science, sports, true crime, womens social commentary. **Considers these fiction areas:** detective, mystery, thriller accessible literary noncategory fiction. Does not want personal memoirs.

How to Contact Query with SASE. Send a letter only. Other Responds in 2 weeks to queries.

Terms Agent receives 15% commission on domestic sales. Agent receives 20% commission on foreign sales. Agent receives 15% commission on film sales. Charges clients for messenger service and photocopying.

Tips "Writers must have appropriate credentials for authorship of proposal (nonfiction) or manuscript (fiction); no publishing track record required. I am open to good writing and interesting ideas by new or veteran writers."

IRENE WEBB LITERARY

822 Bishop's Lodge Road, Santa Fe NM 87501. E-mail: webblit@gmail.com. Website: www.irenewebb. com. **Contact:** Irene Webb.
Represents nonfiction books, novels. **Considers these nonfiction areas:** memoirs, popular culture, sports true stories. **Considers these fiction areas:** mystery, thriller, young adult middle grade, literary and commercial fiction. Irene Webb Literary is known as one of the top boutique agencies selling books to film and TV. We have close relationships with top film producers and talent in Hollywood. Does not want to receive unsolicited manuscripts or screenplays.

How to Contact Query via e-mail only. Obtains most new clients through recommendations from others, solicitations.

CHERRY WEINER LITERARY AGENCY

28 Kipling Way, Manalapan NJ 07726-3711. (732)446-2096. Fax: (732)792-0506. E-mail: cherry8486@ aol.com. **Contact:** Cherry Weiner. Represents 40 clients. 10% of clients are new/unpublished writers. Currently handles nonfiction books (10-20%), novels (80-90%).

Represents nonfiction books, novels. **Considers these nonfiction areas:** self help. **Considers these fiction areas:** contemporary, psychic, adventure, detective, family, fantasy, historical, mainstream, mystery, romance, science, thriller, western. This agency is currently not accepting new clients except by referral or by personal contact at writers' conferences. Specializes in fantasy, science fiction, Western's, mysteries (both contemporary and historical), historical novels, Native-American works, mainstream and all genre romances.

How to Contact Query with SASE. Prefers to read materials exclusively. Responds in 1 week to queries. Responds in 2 months to mss.

Terms Agent receives 15% commission on domestic sales. Agent receives 15% commission on foreign sales. Offers written contract. Charges clients for extra copies of mss, first-class postage for author's copies of books, express mail for important documents/mss.

Tips "Meet agents and publishers at conferences. Establish a relationship, then get in touch with them and remind them of the meeting and conference."

☑ THE WEINGEL-FIDEL AGENCY

310 E. 46th St., 21E, New York NY 10017. (212)599-2959. **Contact:** Loretta Weingel-Fidel. Currently handles nonfiction books (75%), novels (25%).

• Prior to opening her agency, Ms. Weingel-Fidel was a psychoeducational diagnostician.

Represents nonfiction books, novels. **Considers these nonfiction areas:** art, biography, memoirs, music, psychology, science, sociology, womens investigative journalism. **Considers these fiction areas:** literary, mainstream. This agency specializes in commercial and literary fiction and nonfiction. Actively seeking investigative journalism. Does not want to receive genre fiction, self-help, science fiction, or fantasy.

How to Contact Accepts writers by referral only. *No unsolicited mss.*

Terms Agent receives 15% commission on domestic sales. Agent receives 20% commission on foreign sales. Offers written contract, binding for 1 year with automatic renewal. Bills sent back to clients are all reasonable expenses, such as UPS, express mail, photocopying, etc.

Tips "A very small, selective list enables me to work very closely with my clients to develop and nurture talent. I only take on projects and writers about which I am extremely enthusiastic."

☑ LARRY WEISSMAN LITERARY, LLC

526 8th St., #2R, Brooklyn NY **Contact:** Larry Weissman. Represents 35 clients. Currently handles nonfiction books (80%), novels (10%), story collections (10%).

Represents nonfiction books, novels, short story collections. **Considers these fiction areas:** literary. "Very interested in established journalists with bold voices. He's interested in anything to do with food. Fiction has to feel "vital" and short stories are accepted, but only if you can sell him on an idea for a novel as well." Nonfiction, including food & lifestyle, politics, pop culture, narrative, cultural/social issues, journalism. No genre fiction, poetry or children's.

How to Contact Send e-queries only.

Terms Agent receives 15% commission on domestic sales. Agent receives 20% commission on foreign sales.

☐ WHIMSY LITERARY AGENCY, LLC

New York/Los Angeles E-mail: whimsynyc@aol.com. **Contact:** Jackie Meyer. Other memberships include Center for Independent Publishing Advisory Board. Represents 30 clients. 20% of clients are new/unpublished writers. Currently handles nonfiction books (100%).

• Prior to becoming an agent, Ms. Meyer was with Warner Books for 19 years; Ms. Vezeris and Ms. Legette have 30 years experience at various book publishers.

Member Agents Jackie Meyer; Olga Vezeris (fiction and nonfiction); Nansci LeGette, senior associate in LA.

Represents nonfiction books. **Considers these nonfiction areas:** agriculture, art, biography, business, child guidance, cooking, education, health, history, horticulture, how-to, humor, interior design, memoirs, money, New Age, popular culture, psychology, religious, self-help, true crime, women's issues, women's studies. **Considers these fiction areas:** mainstream, religious, thriller, womens. "Whimsy looks for projects that are concept and platform driven. We seek books that educate, inspire and entertain." Actively seeking experts in their field with good platforms.

How to Contact Send a query letter via e-mail. Send a synopsis, bio, platform and proposal. No snail mail submissions. Responds "quickly, but only if interested" to queries. Obtains most new clients through recommendations from others, solicitations.

Terms Agent receives 15% commission on domestic sales. Agent receives 20% commission on foreign sales. Offers written contract. Charges for posting and photocopying.

☐ WOLFSON LITERARY AGENCY

P.O. Box 266, New York NY 10276. E-mail: query@wolfsonliterary.com. Website: www.wolfsonliterary.com/. **Contact:** Michelle Wolfson. Other memberships include Adheres to AAR canon of ethics. Currently handles nonfiction books (70%), novels (30%).

- Prior to forming her own agency, Michelle spent two years with Artists & Artisans, Inc. and two years with Ralph Vicinanza, Ltd.

Represents nonfiction books, novels. **Considers these nonfiction areas:** business, health, humor, memoirs, popular culture. **Considers these fiction areas:** mainstream, mystery, romance, thriller. Actively seeking commercial fiction, mainstream, mysteries, thrillers, suspense, women's fiction, romance, YA, practical nonfiction (particularly of interest to women), advice, medical, pop culture, humor, business.
How to Contact Query with SASE. E-queries only! Accepts simultaneous submissions. Responds in 4 weeks to queries. Responds in 3 months to mss. Obtains most new clients through recommendations from others, solicitations.
Terms Agent receives 15% commission on domestic sales. Agent receives 25% commission on foreign sales. Offers written contract; 30-day notice must be given to terminate contract.
Writers Conferences SDSU Writers' Conference; New Jersey Romance Writers of America Writers' Conference; American Independent Writers Conference in Washington DC.
Tips Be persistent.

☑ WRITERS' REPRESENTATIVES, LLC

116 W. 14th St., 11th Floor, New York NY 10011-7305. Fax: (212)620-0023. E-mail: transom@writersreps.com. Website: www.writersreps.com. Represents 130 clients. 10% of clients are new/unpublished writers. Currently handles nonfiction books (90%), novels (10%).

- Prior to becoming an agent, Ms. Chu was a lawyer; Mr. Hartley worked at Simon & Schuster, Harper & Row, and Cornell University Press.

Member Agents Lynn Chu; Glen Hartley; Christine Hsu.
Represents nonfiction books, novels. **Considers these fiction areas:** literary. Serious nonfiction and quality fiction. No motion picture or television screenplays.
How to Contact Query with SASE. Prefers to read materials exclusively. Considers simultaneous queries, but must be informed at time of submission.
Terms Agent receives 15% commission on domestic sales. Agent receives 20% commission on foreign sales.
Tips "Always include a SASE; it will ensure a response from the agent and the return of your submitted material."

☑ YATES & YATES

1100 Town & Country Road, Suite 1300, Orange CA 92868. Website: www.yates2.com. Represents 60 clients.
Represents nonfiction books, novels. **Considers these nonfiction areas:** business, current affairs, government, memoirs, religion. **Considers these fiction areas:** literary, regional, religious, thriller, womens.

☑ SUSAN ZECKENDORF ASSOC., INC.

171 W. 57th St., New York NY 10019. (212)245-2928. **Contact:** Susan Zeckendorf. Member of AAR. Represents 15 clients. 25% of clients are new/unpublished writers. Currently handles nonfiction books (50%), novels (50%).

- Prior to opening her agency, Ms. Zeckendorf was a counseling psychologist.

Represents nonfiction books, novels. **Considers these nonfiction areas:** biography, health, history, music, psychology, sociology, womens. **Considers these fiction areas:** detective, ethnic, historical, literary, mainstream, mystery, thriller. Actively seeking mysteries, literary fiction, mainstream fiction, thrillers, social history, classical music, and biography. Does not want to receive science fiction, romance, or children's books.
How to Contact Query with SASE. Accepts simultaneous submissions. Responds in 10 days to queries. Responds in 3 weeks to mss.
Terms Agent receives 15% commission on domestic sales. Agent receives 20% commission on foreign sales. Charges for photocopying and messenger services.

Writers Conferences Frontiers in Writing Conference; Oklahoma Festival of Books.

Tips "We are a small agency giving lots of individual attention. We respond quickly to submissions."

☑ HELEN ZIMMERMANN LITERARY AGENCY

3 Emmy Lane, New Paltz NY 12561. (845)256-0977. Fax: (845)256-0979. E-mail: helen@zimmagency. com. Website: www.zimmermannliterary.com. **Contact:** Helen Zimmermann. Represents 25 clients. 50% of clients are new/unpublished writers. Currently handles nonfiction books (80%), other(20% fiction).

• Prior to opening her agency, Ms. Zimmermann was the director of advertising and promotion at Random House and the events coordinator at an independent bookstore.

Represents nonfiction books, novels. **Considers these nonfiction areas:** animals, child, how to, humor, memoirs, nature, popular culture, sports. **Considers these fiction areas:** family, historical, literary, mystery. "As an agent who has experience at both a publishing house and a bookstore, I have a keen insight for viable projects. This experience also helps me ensure every client gets published well, through the whole process." Actively seeking memoirs, pop culture, women's issues and accessible literary fiction. Does not want to receive science fiction, poetry or romance.

How to Contact Accepts e-mail queries only. E-mail should include a short description of project and bio, whether it be fiction or nonfiction. Accepts simultaneous submissions. Responds in 2 weeks to queries. Responds in 1 month to mss. Obtains most new clients through recommendations from others, solicitations.

Terms Agent receives 15% commission on domestic sales. Offers written contract; 30-day notice must be given to terminate contract. Charges for photocopying and postage (reimbursed if project is sold).

Writers Conferences BEA/Writer's Digest Books Writers' Conference, Portland, ME Writers Conference, Berkshire Writers and Readers Conference.

Literary Magazines

This section contains markets for your literary short fiction. Although definitions of what constitutes "literary" writing vary, editors of literary journals agree they want to publish the best fiction they can acquire. Qualities they look for in fiction include fully developed characters, strong and unique narrative voice, flawless mechanics, and careful attention to detail in content and manuscript preparation. Most of the authors writing such fiction are well read and well educated, and many are students and graduates of university creative writing programs.

Please also review our Online Markets section, page 322, for electronic literary magazines. At a time when paper and publishing costs rise while funding to small and university presses continues to be cut or eliminated, electronic literary magazines are helping generate a publishing renaissance for experimental as well as more traditional literary fiction. These electronic outlets for literary fiction also benefit writers by eliminating copying and postage costs and providing the opportunity for much quicker responses to submissions. Also notice that some magazines with Web sites give specific information about what they offer online, including updated writer's guidelines and sample fiction from their publications.

STEPPING STONES TO RECOGNITION

Some well-established literary journals pay several hundred or even several thousand dollars for a short story. Most, though, can only pay with contributor's copies or a subscription to their publication. However, being published in literary journals offers the important benefits of experience, exposure and prestige. Agents and major book publishers regularly read literary magazines in search of new writers. Work from these journals is also selected for inclusion in annual prize anthologies. (See next page for a list of anthologies.)

You'll find most of the well-known prestigious literary journals listed here. Many, including *The Southern Review* and *Ploughshares*, are associated with universities, while others like *The Paris Review* are independently published.

SELECTING THE RIGHT LITERARY JOURNAL

Once you have browsed through this section and have a list of journals you might like to submit to, read those listings again carefully. Remember this is information editors provide to help you submit work that fits their needs. You've Got a Story, starting on page 2, will guide you through the process of finding markets for your fiction.

Note that you will find some magazines that do not read submissions all year long. Whether limited reading periods are tied to a university schedule or meant to accommodate the capabilities of a very small staff, those periods are noted within listings (when the editors notify us). The staffs of university journals are usually made up of student editors and a managing editor who is also a faculty member. These staffs often change every year.

Whenever possible, we indicate this in listings and give the name of the current editor and the length of that editor's term. Also be aware that the schedule of a university journal usually coincides with that university's academic year, meaning that the editors of most university publications are difficult or impossible to reach during the summer.

FURTHERING YOUR SEARCH

It cannot be stressed enough that reading the listings for literary journals is only the first part of developing your marketing plan. The second part, equally important, is to obtain fiction guidelines and to read with great care the actual journal you'd like to submit to. Reading copies of these journals helps you determine the fine points of each magazine's publishing style and sensibility. There is no substitute for this type of hands-on research.

Unlike commercial periodicals available at most newsstands and bookstores, it requires a little more effort to obtain some of the magazines listed here. The super-chain bookstores are doing a better job these days of stocking literaries, and you can find some in independent and college bookstores, especially those published in your area. The Internet is an invaluable resource for submission guidelines, as more and more journals establish an online presence. You may, however, need to send for a sample copy. We include sample copy prices in the listings whenever possible. In addition to reading your sample copies, pay close attention to the **Tips** section of each listing. There you'll often find a very specific description of the style of fiction the editors at that publication prefer.

Another way to find out more about literary magazines is to check out the various prize anthologies and take note of journals whose fiction is being selected for publication in them. Studying prize anthologies not only lets you know which magazines are publishing award-winning work, but it also provides a valuable overview of what is considered to be the best fiction published today. Those anthologies include:

- *Best American Short Stories*, published by Houghton Mifflin.
- *New Stories from the South: The Year's Best*, published by Algonquin Books of Chapel Hill.
- *The O. Henry Prize Stories*, published by Doubleday/Anchor.
- *Pushcart Prize: Best of the Small Presses*, published by Pushcart Press.

At the beginnings of listings, we include symbols to help you narrow your search. Keys to those symbols can be found on the inside covers of this book.

Literary Magazines

☑ ACM (ANOTHER CHICAGO MAGAZINE)

Left Field Press, 3709 N. Kenmore, Chicago IL 60613. E-mail: anotherchicagomagazine@yahoo.com. Website: www.anotherchicagomag.org. **Contact:** Jacob S. Knabb, Managing/Fiction editor. Magazine: 5½ × 8½; 200-220 pages; "art folio each issue." Biannual. Estab. 1977. Circ. 2,000.

Needs Ethnic/multicultural, experimental, feminist, gay, lesbian, literary, translations, contemporary, prose poem. No religious, strictly genre or editorial. Receives 300 unsolicited mss/month. Reads mss from February 1-August 31. Publishes ms 6-12 months after acceptance. **Publishes 10 new writers/year.** Recently published work by Stuart Dybek and Steve Almond.

How to Contact Responds in 3 months to queries; 6 months to mss. Accepts simultaneous, multiple submissions. Sample copy for $8 ppd. Writer's guidelines online.

Payment/Terms Pays small honorarium when possible, contributor's copies and 1 year subscription. Acquires first North American serial rights.

Tips "Support literary publishing by subscribing to at least one literary journal—if not ours, another. Get used to rejection slips, and don't get discouraged. Keep introductory letters short. Make sure manuscript has name and address on every page, and that it is clean, neat and proofread. We are looking for stories with freshness and originality in subject angle and style, and work that encounters the world and is not stuck in its own navel."

☑ $ AFRICAN AMERICAN REVIEW

Saint Louis University, Humanities 317, 3800 Lindell Boulevard, St. Louis MO 63108-3414. (314) 977-3688. Fax: (314) 977-1514. E-mail: keenanam@slu.edu. Website: aar.slu.edu. **Contact:** Nathan Grant, editor; Aileen Keenan, managing editor. Magazine: 7X10; 200 pages; 55 lb., acid-free paper; 100 lb. skid stock cover; illustrations; photos. "Essays on African-American literature, theater, film, art and culture generally; interviews; poetry and fiction; book reviews." Quarterly. Estab. 1967. Circ. 2,000.

- *African American Review* is the official publication of the Division of Black American Literature and Culture of the Modern Language Association. The magazine received American Literary Magazine Awards in 1994 and 1995.

Needs Ethnic/multicultural, experimental, feminist, literary, mainstream. "No children's/juvenile/young adult/teen." Receives 35 unsolicited mss/month. Accepts 10 mss/year. Publishes ms 1 year after acceptance. Agented fiction 0%. Recently published work by Solon Timothy Woodward, Eugenia Collier, Jeffery Renard Allen, Patrick Lohier, Raki Jones, Olympia Vernon. Length: 2,500-5,000 words; average length: 3,000 words. Also publishes literary essays, literary criticism, poetry. Sometimes comments on rejected mss.

How to Contact Responds in 1 week to queries; 3 months to mss. Sample copy for $12. Writer's guidelines online. Reviews fiction.

Payment/Terms Pays $25-75, 1 contributor's copy and 5 offprints. Pays on publication for first North American serial rights. Sends galleys to author.

☑ $ ☑ AGNI

Boston University, 236 Bay State Rd., Boston MA 02215. (617) 353-7135. Fax: (617) 353-7134. E-mail: agni@bu.edu. Website: www.agnimagazine.org. **Contact:** Sven Birkerts, editor. Magazine: 5⅜ × 8½; 240 pages; 55 lb. booktext paper; art portfolios. "Eclectic literary magazine publishing first-rate poems, essays, translations and stories." Biannual. Estab. 1972. Circ. 4,000.

- Founding editor Askold Melnyczuk won the 2001 Nora Magid Award for Magazine Editing. Work from *AGNI* has been included and cited regularly in the *Pushcart Prize* and *Best American* anthologies.

Needs Translations, stories, prose poems. "No science fiction or romance." Receives 500 unsolicited mss/month. Accepts 3-5 mss/issue; 6-10 mss/year. Reading period September 1 through May 31 only. Publishes ms 6 months after acceptance. **Publishes 30 new writers/year.** Recently published work by Rikki Ducornet, Phong Nguyen, Jack Pulaski, David Foster Wallace, Lise Haines, Gania Barlow and Nicholas Montemarano.

How to Contact Responds in 2 weeks to queries; 4 months to mss. Accepts simultaneous submissions. Sample copy for $10 or online. Writer's guidelines for #10 SASE or online.

Payment/Terms Pays $10/page up to $150, 2 contributor's copies, 1-year subscription, and 4 gift copies. Pays on publication for first North American serial rights, rights to reprint in *AGNI* anthology (with author's consent). Sends galleys to author.

Tips "Read *AGNI* and other literary magazines carefully to understand the kinds of stories we do and do not publish. It's also important for artists to support the arts."

☑ THE AGUILAR EXPRESSION

1329 Gilmore Ave., Donora PA 15033-2228. (724) 379-8019. E-mail: xyz0@access995.com. Website: www.wordrunner.com/xfaguilar. **Contact:** Xavier F. Aguilar, editor. Magazine: 8½ × 11; 4-20 pages; 20 lb. bond paper; illustrations. "We are open to all writers of a general theme—something that may appeal to everyone." Publishes in October. Estab. 1986. Circ. 300.

Needs Adventure, ethnic/multicultural, experimental, horror, mainstream, mystery/suspense (romantic suspense), romance (contemporary). "No religious or erotic stories. Want more current social issues." Receives 15 unsolicited mss/month. Accepts 1-2 mss/year. Reading period: January, February, March. Publishes ms 1 month to 1 year after acceptance. **Publishes 2-4 new writers/year.** Recently published work by Ken Bennet. Length: 250-1,000 words; average length: 1,000 words. Also publishes poetry.

How to Contact Send a disposable copy of ms with SASE for reply. "We do not return any manuscripts and discard rejected works. If we decide to publish, we contact within 30 days." Responds in 1 month to mss. No simultaneous submissions. Sample copy for $8. Guidelines for first-class stamp.

Payment/Terms Pays 2 contributor's copies for lead story; additional copies at a reduced rate of $3. Acquires one-time rights. Not copyrighted.

Tips "We would like to see more social issues worked into fiction."

☑ $ ALASKA QUARTERLY REVIEW

ESB 208, University of Alaska-Anchorage, 3211 Providence Dr., Anchorage AK 99508. (907) 786-6916. E-mail: ayaqr@uaa.alaska.edu. Website: www.uaa.alaska.edu/aqr. **Contact:** Ronald Spatz, fiction editor. Magazine: 6 × 9; 232-300 pages; 60 lb. Glatfelter paper; 12 pt. C15 black ink or 4-color; varnish cover stock; photos on cover and photo essays. AQR "publishes fiction, poetry, literary nonfiction and short plays in traditional and experimental styles." Semiannual. Estab. 1982. Circ. 2,700.

• Two stories selected for inclusion in the 2004 edition of *The O'Henry Prize Stories*.

Needs Experimental, literary, translations, contemporary, prose poem. "If the works in *Alaska Quarterly Review* have certain characteristics, they are these: freshness, honesty and a compelling subject. What makes a piece stand out from the multitude of other submissions? The voice of the piece must be strong—idiosyncratic enough to create a unique persona. We look for the demonstration of craft, making the situation palpable and putting it in a form where it becomes emotionally and intellectually complex. One could look through our pages over time and see that many of the pieces published in the *Alaska Quarterly Review* concern everyday life. We're not asking our writers to go outside themselves and their experiences to the absolute exotic to catch our interest. We look for the experiential and revelatory qualities of the work. We will, without hesitation, champion a piece that may be less polished or stylistically sophisticated, if it engages me, surprises me, and resonates for me. The joy in reading such a work is in discovering something true. Moreover, in keeping with our mission to publish new writers, we are looking for voices our readers do not know, voices that may not always be reflected in the dominant culture and that, in all instances, have something important to convey." Receives 200 unsolicited mss/ month. Accepts 7-18 mss/issue; 15-30 mss/year. Does not read mss May 10-August 25. Publishes ms 6 months after acceptance. **Publishes 6 new writers/year.** Recently published work by Howard Norman, Douglas Light, Courtney Angela Brkic, Alison Baker, Lindsay Fitz-Gerald, John Fulton, Ann Stapleton, Edith Pearlman. Publishes short shorts.

How to Contact Responds in 4 months to queries; 4 months to mss. Simultaneous submissions "undesirable, but will accept if indicated." Sample copy for $6. Writer's guidelines online.

Payment/Terms Pays $50-200 subject to funding; pays in contributor's copies and subscriptions when funding is limited. Honorariums on publication when funding permits. Acquires first North American serial rights. Upon request, rights will be transferred back to author after publication.

Tips "Professionalism, patience and persistence are essential. One needs to do one's homework and know the market. The competition is very intense, and funding for the front-line journals is generally inadequate, so staffing is low. It takes time to get a response, and rejections are a fact of life. It is important not to take the rejections personally, and also to know that editors make decisions for better or worse, and they make mistakes too. Fortunately there are many gatekeepers. *Alaska Quarterly Review* has published many pieces that had been turned down by other journals—including pieces that then went on to win national awards. We also know of instances in which pieces *Alaska Quarterly Review* rejected later appeared in other magazines. We haven't regretted that we didn't take those pieces. Rather, we're happy that the authors have made a good match. Disappointment should *never* stop anyone. Will counts as much as talent, and new writers need to have confidence in themselves and stick to it."

☑ ◎ ALIMENTUM, The Literature of Food

P.O. Box 210028, Nashville TN 37221. E-mail: submissions@alimentumjournal.com. Website: www.alimentumjournal.com. **Contact:** Submissions editor. Literary magazine/journal: 6 × 7½, 128 pages, matte cover. Contains illustrations. "All of our stories, poems and essays have food or drink as a theme." Semiannual. Estab. 2005.

Needs Literary. Special interests: food related. Receives 100 mss/month. Accepts 20-24 mss/issue. Manuscript published one to two years after acceptance. **Publishes average of 2 new writers/year.** Published Mark Kurlansky, Oliver Sacks, Dick Allen, Ann Hood, Carly Sachs. Length: 3,000 words (max). Average length: 1,000-2,000 words. Publishes short shorts. Also publishes literary essays, poetry, spot illustrations. Rarely comments on/critiques rejected mss.

How to Contact Send complete ms with cover letter. Snail mail only. No previously published work. 5-poem limit per submission. Simultaneous submissions okay." Responds to queries and mss in 1-3 months. Send either SASE (or IRC) for return of ms or disposable copy of ms and #10 SASE for reply only. Sample copy available for $10. Guidelines available on Web site. Check for submission reading periods as they vary from year to year.

Payment/Terms Writers receive 1 contributor's copy. Additional contributor's copies $8. Pays on publication. Acquires first North American serial rights. Publication is copyrighted.

Tips "Write a good story, no clichés, attention to style, strong voice, memorable characters and scenes."

☑ ALLIGATOR JUNIPER

Prescott College, 220 Grove Ave., Prescott AZ 86301. (928) 350-2012. Fax: (928) 776-5137. E-mail: aj@prescott.edu. Website: www.prescott.edu/highlights/alligator_juniper/index.html. **Contact:** Jeff Fearnside, managing editor. Literary magazine/journal: 7.5 × 10.5; 182 pages; photographs. "Alligator Juniper was founded with the intention of furthering the environmental and experimental mission of Prescott College, its sponsoring institution, by featuring environmentally-aware and socially-conscious writing and art. Since its premiere issue in 1995, AJ has provided regional, national, and international artists, both established and emerging, a forum in which to publish writing with timely, emotional themes. AJ is proud to showcase a perennially diverse range of artisits." Annual. Estab. 1995. Circ. 1500. Member CLMP.

  • AJhas received the AWP Director's Award for Content (2001 & 2004), annual funding from the Arizona Commission on the Arts, and a Gregory Kolovakos Seed Grant from the Council of Literary Magazines and Presses (1997).

Needs Experimental, literary. Does not want genre fiction or children's literature. "Includes an open submissions section on a special theme in each issue. The theme for the 2010 special section is "International Writing," complete information available on Web site." Accepts 5-6 mss/year. Does not read November-April. Mss published 4 months after acceptance.

How to Contact Primarily accepts submissions via annual *Alligator Juniper* National Writing Contest. See separate listing under Contests and Awards.

☑ $ AMERICAN SHORT FICTION

Badgerdog Literary Publishing, P.O. Box 301209, Austin TX 78703. (512) 538-1305. Fax: (512) 538-1306. E-mail: editors@americanshortfiction.org. Website: www.americanshortfiction.org. **Contact:** Stacy Swann, Editor; Jill Meyers, Managing Editor. Literary magazine/journal. 6X9.5, 140 pages. Contains illustrations. Includes photographs. "American Short Fiction (ASF) strives to discover and publish new fiction in which transformations of language, narrative, and character occur swiftly, deftly, and unexpectedly. We are drawn to evocative language, unique subject matter, and an overall sense of immediacy. We target readers who love literary fiction, are drawn to independent publishing, and enjoy short fiction. ASF is one of the few journals that focuses solely on fiction." Quarterly. Estab. 1991. Circ. 2,500. Member CLMP.

• ASF has had a selection included in *Best Nonrequired Reading*, 2007 and *New Stories from the Southwest*, 2008. Awards from the previous incarnation of ASF (when published by The University of Texas, 1991-1998) include selections in *Best American Short Stories*, *The O. Henry Prize Stories*, the *Graywolf Annual*, the *Pushcart Prize* anthology, and two time finalist for the National Magazine Award.

Needs Experimental, literary, translations. Does not want young adult fiction or genre fiction. "However, we are open to publishing mystery or speculative fiction if we feel it has literary value." Receives 300-400 mss/month. Accepts 5-6 mss/issue; 20-25 mss/year. Manuscript published 3 months after acceptance. Agented fiction 20%. **Publishes 2-3 new writers/year.** Published Joice Carol Oates, Maud Casey, Chris Bachelder, Vendela Vida, Benjamin Percy, Jack Pendarvis, Paul Yoon, and Dagoberto Gilb. Length: 2,000 words (min)-15,000 words (max). Average length: 6,000 words. Publishes short shorts. Average length of short shorts: 500 words. Also publishes literary essays, literary criticism. Sometimes comments on/critiques rejected mss.

How to Contact Submit complete ms electronically on Web site. Include estimated word count, brief bio. Responds to queries in 2 weeks. Responds to mss in 4-5 months. Guidelines available for SASE, via e-mail, on Web site.

Payment/Terms Writers receive $250-500, 2 contributor's copies, free subscription to the magazine. Additional copies $5. Pays on publication. Acquires first North American serial rights, electronic rights. Sends galleys to author. Publication is copyrighted. Sponsors Short Story Contest. See separate listing or Web site.

Tips "We publish fiction that speaks to us emotionally, uses evocative and precise language, and takes risks in subject matter and/or form. Try to read an issue or two of *American Short Fiction* to get a sense of what we like. Also, to be concise is a great virtue."

☑ AMOSKEAG, THE JOURNAL OF SOUTHERN NEW HAMPSHIRE UNIVERSITY

2500 N. River Road, Manchester NH 03106. (603) 668-2211 x2376. E-mail: a.cummings@snhu.edu. Website: www.amoskeagjournal.com. **Contact:** Allison Cummings, Editor. Magazine has revolving editor and occasional themes (see Web site). Editorial term: 3 yrs; 2007-2009. Literary magazine/journal. 6 × 9, 105-140 pages. Contains photographs. "We select workt that appeals to general readers, writers, and academics alike. We accept work from writers nationwide, but also try to include New England writers. We tend not to accept much experimental work, but the language of poetry or prose must nevertheless be dense, careful and surprising." Annual. Journal estab. 1983; literary journal since 2005. Circ.1,500.

Needs Ethnic/multicultural (general), experimental, feminist, gay, humor/satire, literary. Does not want genre fiction. Receives 200 mss/month. Accepts 10 prose mss and 15-20 poems/issue. Does not read December-August. Reading period is Sept-Dec. Ms published in late April. Published Jessica Bacal, Merle Drown, Pat Parnell, Octavio Quintanilla, Darryl Halbrooks, Simon Perchik and Baron Wormser. Length: 2,500 words (max). Average length: 1,250 words. Publishes short shorts. Average length of short shorts: 120 words. Also publishes poetry, creative non-fiction. Sometimes comments on/critiques rejected mss.

How to Contact Send complete ms with cover letter. Include brief bio, list of publications. Responds to queries in 1 month. Responds to mss in 4-7 months. Send either SASE (or IRC) for return of ms or disposable copy of ms and #10 SASE for reply only. Considers simultaneous submissions, multiple submissions. Sample copy available for $2. Guidelines available for SASE.

Payment/Terms Writers aren't paid, but receive 3 contributor's copies. Additional copies $5. Pays on publication. Acquires one-time rights. Publication is copyrighted.

Tips "Stories need good pacing, believable characters and dialogue, as well as unusual subjects to stand out. Most stories we get are 'domestic fiction;' middle-class family dramas. We're drawn to stories about qypsies, the supernatural, travel, work, non-American perspectives, poverty or legends. Read the news, especially from other places and times, for inspiration. Try to entertain an editor who reads clever knock-offs ad nauseum."

☑ ◎ $ ANCIENT PATHS

P.O. Box 7505, Fairfax Station VA 22039. Website: www. editorskylar.com. Contact: Skylar H. Burris, editor. Magazine: digest size; 80+ pages; 20 lb. plain white paper; cardstock cover; perfect bound; illustrations. "Ancient Paths publishes quality fiction and creative nonfiction for a literate Christian audience. Religious themes are usually subtle, and the magazine has non-Christian readers as well as some content by non-Christian authors. However, writers should be comfortable appearing in a Christian magazine." Annual. Estab. 1998. Circ. 175-200.

Needs Historical, humor/satire, literary, mainstream, novel excerpts, religious/inspirational (general religious/literary), science fiction (Christian), slice-of-life vignettes. No retelling of Bible stories. Literary fiction favored over genre fiction. Receives 10+ unsolicited mss/month. Accepts 7-10 mss/issue. Publishes ms 2-4 months after acceptance. Recently published work by Diane Rosier, Mary Chandler, Larry Marshall Sams, Erin Tocknell, and Chris Williams. Length: 250-2,500 words; average length: 1,500 words. Publishes short shorts. Often comments on rejected mss.

How to Contact Send complete ms. Accepts submissions by e-mail (ssburris@msn.com [only international submissions]). Include estimated word count. Send SASE for return of ms or send a disposable copy of ms and #10 SASE for reply only. Responds in 1 week to queries; 4-5 weeks to mss. Accepts simultaneous, multiple submissions and reprints. Sample copy for $5; make checks payable to Skylar Burris *not* to *Ancient Paths*. Writer's guidelines online. Reviews fiction.

Payment/Terms Pays $6, 1 copy, and discount on additional copies. Pays on publication for one-time rights. Not copyrighted.

Tips "We look for fluid prose, intriguing characters and substantial themes in fiction manuscripts."

⬧ ✏ $ THE ANTIGONISH REVIEW

St. Francis Xavier University, P.O. Box 5000, Antigonish NS B2G 2W5 Canada. (902)867-3962. Fax: (902)867-5563. Website: www.antigonishreview.com. **Contact:** Bonnie McIsaac, office manager. Literary magazine for educated and creative readers. Quarterly. Estab. 1970. Circ. 1,000.

Needs Literary, translations, contemporary, prose poem. No erotica. Receives 50 unsolicited mss/month. Accepts 6 mss/issue. Publishes ms 4 months after acceptance. **Publishes some new writers/year.** Recently published work by Arnold Bloch, Richard Butts and Helen Barolini. Sometimes comments on rejected mss.

How to Contact Send complete ms. Accepts submissions by fax. Accepts electronic (disk compatible with WordPerfect/IBM and Windows) submissions. Prefers hard copy with disk submission. Responds in 1 month to queries; 6 months to mss. No simultaneous submissions. Sample copy for $7 or online. Writer's guidelines for #10 SASE or online.

Payment/Terms Pays $100 per accepted story. Pays on publication. Rights retained by author.

Tips "Learn the fundamentals and do not deluge an editor."

✏ $ ANTIOCH REVIEW

P.O. Box 148, Yellow Springs OH 45387-0148. E-mail: review@antioch.edu. Website: www.review. antioch.edu. **Contact:** Fiction editor. Magazine: 6 × 9; 200 pages; 50 lb. book offset paper; coated cover stock; illustrations "seldom." "Literary and cultural review of contemporary issues, and literature for general readership." Quarterly. Estab. 1941. Circ. 4,000.

Needs Literary, experimental, contemporary, translations. No science fiction, fantasy or confessions. Receives 275 unsolicited mss/month. Accepts 5-6 mss/issue; 20-24 mss/year. No mss accepted June 1-September 1. Publishes ms 10 months after acceptance. Agented fiction 1-2%. **Publishes 1-2 new writers/year.** Recently published work by Edith Pearlman, Peter LaSalle, Rosellen Brown, Nathan Oates, Benjamin Percy, and Gordon Lish.

How to Contact Send complete ms with SASE, preferably mailed flat. Responds in 4-6 months to mss. Sample copy for $7. Writer's guidelines online.

Payment/Terms Pays $15/printed page. Pays on publication.

Tips "Our best advice always is to read the *Antioch Review* to see what type of material we publish. Quality fiction requires an engagement of the reader's intellectual interest supported by mature emotional relevance, written in a style that is rich and rewarding without being freaky. The great number of stories submitted to us indicates that fiction still has great appeal. We assume that if so many are writing fiction, many must be reading it."

✏ APALACHEE REVIEW

Apalachee Press, P.O. Box 10469, Tallahassee FL 32302. (850) 644-9114. Website: http://apalacheereview. org/index.html. **Contact:** Michael Trammell, editor; Mary Jane Ryals, fiction editor. Literary magazine/ journal: trade paperback size, 100-140 pages. Includes photographs. "At Apalachee Review, we are interested in outstanding literary fiction, but we especially like poetry, fiction, and nonfiction that addresses intercultural issues in a domestic or international setting/context." Annual. Estab. 1976. Circ. 500. Member CLMP.

Needs Ethnic/multicultural, experimental, fantasy/sci-fi (with a literary bent), feminist, historical, humor/satire, literary, mainstream, mystery/suspense, new age, translations. Does not want cliché-filled genre-oriented fiction. Receives 60-100 mss/month. Accepts 5-10 mss/issue. Manuscript published 1 yr after acceptance. Agented fiction 0.5%. **Publishes 1-2 new writers/year**. Recently published Lu Vickers, Joe Clark, Joe Taylor, Jane Arrowsmith Edwards, Vivian Lawry, Linda Frysh, Charles Harper Webb, Reno Raymond Gwaltney. Length: 600 words (min)-5,500 words (max). Average length: 3,500 words. Publishes short shorts. Average length of short shorts: 250 words. Also publishes literary essays, book reviews, poetry. Send review copies to Michael Trammell, editor. Sometimes comments on/critiques rejected mss.

How to Contact Send complete ms with cover letter. Include brief bio, list of publications. Responds to queries in 4-6 weeks. Responds to mss in 3-14 months. Send either SASE (or IRC) for return of ms or disposable copy of ms and #10 SASE for reply only. Considers simultaneous submissions. Sample copy available for $8 (current issue), $5 (back issue). Guidelines available for SASE, or check the Web site.

Payment/Terms Writers receive 2 contributors copies. Additional copies $5/each. Pays on publication. Acquires one-time rights, electronic rights. Publication is copyrighted.

☑ ◎ APPALACHIAN HERITAGE

CPO 2166, Berea KY 40404. (859)985-3699. Fax: (859)985-3903. E-mail: george-brosi@berea.edu. Website: http://community.berea.edu/appalachianheritage/. **Contact:** George Brosi. Magazine: 6 × 9; 104 pages; 60 lb. stock; 10 pt. Warrenflo cover; drawings; b&w photos. "Appalachian Heritage is a Southern Appalachian literary magazine. We try to keep a balance of fiction, poetry, essays, scholarly works, etc., for a general audience and/or those interested in the Appalachian mountains." Quarterly. Estab. 1973. Circ. 750.

Needs Historical, literary, regional. "We do not want to see fiction that has no ties to Southern Appalachia." Receives 60-80 unsolicited mss/month. Accepts 2-3 mss/issue; 12-15 mss/year. Publishes ms 3-6 months after acceptance. **Publishes 8 new writers/year.** Recently published work by Wendell Berry, Charles Wright, Jayne Anne Phillips, Silas House, Ron Rash, and Lee Smith. Publishes short shorts. Occasionally comments on rejected mss.

How to Contact Send complete ms. Send SASE for reply, return of ms or send a disposable copy of ms. Responds in 1 month to queries; 6 weeks to mss. Sample copy for $6. Writer's guidelines free.

Payment/Terms Pays 3 contributor's copies; $6 charge for extras. Acquires first North American serial rights.

Tips "Get acquainted with *Appalachian Heritage*, as you should with any publication before submitting your work."

ℕ ☑ ARGESTES LITERARY REVIEW

Collen Tree Press, 2941 170th St., South Amana IA 52334. (319) 899-0994. E-mail: ctp_argestes@yahoo. com. **Contact:** Robert Bruce Kelsey, Fiction Editor. Literary magazine/journal. 100-150 pages. Contains illustrations. Includes photographs. "Argestes is a literary review of poetry and short story. We are a print-only journal. We are open to most forms of poetry and short story. We publish work of both established and new writers. We are an independent journal with no university affiliations." Semiannual. Estab. 1998. Circ. 200.

Needs Ethnic/multicultural (general), experimental, fantasy, feminist, gay, lesbian, literary, science fiction (soft/sociological), translations. Does not want gratuitous violence. Receives 30-60 mss/month. Accepts 3-6 mss/issue; 6-12 mss/year. Ms published 3-6 months after acceptance. **Publishes 3-6 new writers/year.** Published Joseph Hart, J. Cochran, Martin Galvin, Robert Parham, Tim Hurley and Joanne Lowery. Length: 2500 words (max). Average length: 1,700 words. Publishes short shorts. Average length of short shorts: 1,000 words. Also publishes literary essays, literary criticism, book reviews, poetry. Send review copies to Robert Bruce Kelsey-short story collections only. Sometimes comments on/critiques rejected mss.

How to Contact Send complete ms with cover letter. Include estimated word count, brief bio. Responds to queries in 4-8 weeks. Responds to mss in 4-8 weeks. Send disposable copy of ms and #10 SASE for reply only. Considers simultaneous submissions, multiple submissions. Sample copy available for $7. Guidelines available for SASE.

Payment/Terms Writers receive 2 contributor's copies. Additional copies $7. Pays on publication. Acquires first North American serial rights. Publication is copyrighted.

Tips "We look for a unique voice; an ear for language, dialogue; an obviously unique perception or emotional engagement with the subject matter. Read broadly and deeply, but craft your own stories in your own voice."

☑ ◎ ARKANSAS REVIEW

Department of English and Philosophy, P.O. Box 1890, Arkansas State University, State University AR 72467-1890. (870) 972-3043. Fax: (501) 972-3045. E-mail: jcollins@astate.edu. Website: www.clt.astate.edu/arkreview. **Contact:** fiction editor. Magazine: 8¼ × 11; 64-100 pages; coated, matte paper; matte, 4-color cover stock; illustrations; photos. Publishes articles, fiction, poetry, essays, interviews, reviews, visual art evocative of or responsive to the Mississippi River Delta. Triannual. Estab. 1996. Circ. 700.

Needs Literary (essays and criticism), regional (short stories). "No genre fiction. Must have a Delta focus." Receives 30-50 unsolicited mss/month. Accepts 2-3 mss/issue; 5-7 mss/year. Publishes ms 6-12 months after acceptance. Agented fiction 1%. **Publishes 3-4 new writers/year.** Recently published work by Susan Henderson, George Singleton, Scott Ely and Pia Erhart. Also publishes literary essays, poetry. Sometimes comments on rejected mss.

How to Contact Accepts submissions by e-mail, fax. Send SASE for reply, return of ms or send a disposable copy of ms. Responds in 1 week to queries; 4 months to mss. Sample copy for $7.50. Writer's guidelines for #10 SASE.

Payment/Terms Pays 3 contributor's copies; additional copies for $5. Acquires first North American serial rights.

Tips "We see a lot of stories set in New Orleans but prefer fiction that takes place in other parts of the Delta. We'd love more innovative and experimental fiction too but primarily seek stories that involve and engage the reader and evoke or respond to the Delta natural and/or cultural experience."

☑ THE ARMCHAIR AESTHETE

Pickle Gas Press, 19 Abbotswood Crescent, Penfield NY 14526. (585)381-1003. E-mail: bypaul@frontiernet.net or thearmchairaesthete@yahoo.com. **Contact:** Paul Agosto, editor. Magazine: 5½ × 8½; 145-175 pages; 20 lb. paper; 110 lb. card stock color cover and plastic spiral bound. "The Armchair Aesthete seeks quality writing that enlightens and entertains a thoughtful audience (ages 9-90) with a 'good read.'" 2-3 issues per year. Estab. 1996. Circ. 100.

Needs Adventure, fantasy (science fantasy, sword and sorcery), historical (general), horror, humor/satire (satire), mainstream (contemporary), mystery/suspense (amateur sleuth, cozy, police procedural, private eye/hard-boiled, romantic suspense), science fiction (soft/sociological), western (frontier, traditional). "No racist, pornographic, overt gore; no religious or material intended for or written by children. Receives 60 unsolicited mss/month. Accepts 16-24 mss/issue; 60-80 mss/year. Publishes ms 1-12 months after acceptance. Agented fiction 5%. **Publishes 15-25 new writers/year.** Recently published work by Chris Brown, Laverne and Carol Frith, Lydia Williams, Andrew Bynom, and Douglas Empringham. Average length: 4,500 words. Publishes short shorts. Also publishes poetry. Sometimes comments on rejected mss.

How to Contact Accepts submissions by e-mail. Send SASE for reply, return of ms or send a disposable copy of ms. Responds in 2-3 weeks to queries; 3-6 months to mss. Accepts simultaneous, multiple submissions and reprints. Sample copy for $6.95 (paid to P. Agosto, Ed.) and 5 first-class stamps. Writer's guidelines for #10 SASE. No longer reviews fiction or poetry chapbooks.

Payment/Terms Pays 1 contributor's copy; additional copies for $6.95 (pay to P. Agosto, editor). Pays on publication for one-time rights.

Tips "Clever, compelling storytelling has a good chance here. We look for a clever plot, thought-out characters, something that surprises or catches us off guard. Write on innovative subjects and situations. Submissions should be professionally presented and technically sound."

☑ ◧ AXE FACTORY REVIEW

Cynic Press, P.O. Box 40691, Philadelphia PA 19107. **Contact:** Joseph Farley, editor. Magazine: 11 × 17 folded to 8½ × 11; 30-60 pages; 20 lb. stock paper; 70 lb. stock cover; illustrations; photos on occasion. "We firmly believe that literature is a form of (and/or expression/manifestations of) madness. We seek to spread the disease called literature. We will look at any genre, but we search for the quirky, the off-center, the offensive, the annoying, but always the well-written story, poem, essay." Biannual. Estab. 1986. Circ. 200.

Needs Adventure, comics/graphic novels, erotica, ethnic/multicultural (Asian), experimental, fantasy (space fantasy, sword and sorcery), feminist, gay, historical, horror (dark fantasy, futuristic, psychological, supernatural), humor/satire, lesbian, literary, mainstream, military/war, mystery/suspense, New Age, psychic/supernatural/occult, regional (Philadelphia area), religious/inspirational (general religious, inspirational, religious mystery/suspense), romance, science fiction (hard science/technological, soft/sociological, cross genre), thriller/espionage, translations, western (frontier saga, traditional). "We would like to see more hybrid genres, literary/science fiction, Beat writing. No genteel professional gibberish." Receives 20 unsolicited mss/month. Accepts 1-2 mss/issue; 3 mss/year. Publishes ms 6-12 months after acceptance. Recently published work by Tim Gavin and Michael Hafer. Length: 500-5,000 words; average length: 3,000 words. Publishes short shorts. Also publishes literary essays, literary criticism, poetry. Often comments on rejected mss.

How to Contact Send SASE (or IRC) for return of ms. Responds in 6 weeks to mss. Accepts simultaneous, multiple submissions and reprints. Sample copy for $8. Current issue $9. Reviews fiction.

Payment/Terms Pays 1-2 contributor's copies; additional copies $8. Pays on publication for one-time rights, anthology rights.

Tips "In fiction we look for a strong beginning, strong middle, strong end; memorable characters; and most importantly language, language, language."

☑ THE BALTIMORE REVIEW

P.O. Box 36418, Towson MD 21286. Website: www.baltimorereview.org. **Contact:** Susan Muaddi Darraj, managing editor. Magazine: 6 × 9; 150 pages; 60 lb. paper; 10 pt. CS1 gloss film cover. Showcase for the best short stories, creative nonfiction and poetry by writers in the Baltimore area and beyond. Semiannual. Estab. 1996.

Needs Ethnic/multicultural, literary, mainstream. "No science fiction, westerns, children's, romance, etc." Accepts 20 mss/issue; approx. 40 mss/year. Publishes ms 1-9 months after acceptance. **Publishes "at least a few" new writers/year.** Average length: 3,000 words. Publishes short shorts. Also publishes poetry.

How to Contact Accepts submissions via online system only. Please visit Web site. Responds in 4-6 months to mss. Accepts simultaneous submissions. Sample copy: $10, which included postage/handling.

Payment/Terms Pays 2 contributor's copies. Acquires first North American serial rights.

Tips "We look for compelling stories and a masterful use of the English language. We want to feel that we have never heard this story, or this voice, before. Read the kinds of publications you want your work to appear in. Make your reader believe and care."

☑ BARBARIC YAWP

Bone World Publishing, 3700 County Rt. 24, Russell NY 13684-3198. (315)347-2609. **Contact:** Nancy Berbrich, fiction editor. Magazine: digest-size; 60 pages; 24 lb. paper; matte cover stock. "We publish what we like. Fiction should include some bounce and surprise. Our publication is intended for the intelligent, open-minded reader." Quarterly. Estab. 1997. Circ. 120.

Needs Adventure, experimental, fantasy (science, sword and sorcery), historical, horror, literary, mainstream, psychic/supernatural/occult, regional, religious/inspirational, science fiction (hard, soft/sociological). "We don't want any pornography, gratuitous violence or whining." Wants more suspense and philosophical work. Receives 30-40 unsolicited mss/month. Accepts 10-12 mss/issue; 40-48 mss/year. Publishes ms up to 6 months after acceptance. **Publishes 4-6 new writers/year.** Recently published work by Francine Witte, Jeff Grimshaw, Thaddeus Rutkowski and Holly Interlandi. Length: 1,500 words; average length: 600 words. Publishes short shorts. Also publishes literary essays, literary criticism, poetry. Often comments on rejected mss.

How to Contact Send SASE for reply, return of ms or send a disposable copy of ms. Responds in 2 weeks to queries; 4 months to mss. Accepts simultaneous, multiple submissions and reprints. Sample copy for $4. Writer's guidelines for #10 SASE.

Payment/Terms Pays 1 contributor's copy; additional copies $3. Acquires one-time rights.

Tips "Don't give up. Read much, write much, submit much. Observe closely the world around you. Don't borrow ideas from TV or films. Revision is often necessary—grit your teeth and do it. Never fear rejection."

☐ BATHTUB GIN

Pathwise Press, 2311 Broadway St, New Orleans, LA 70125. (812) 327-2855. E-mail: pathwisepress@hotmail.com. Website: www. pathwisepress.com. **Contact:**Fiction Editor. Magazine: 8½ × 5½; 60 pages; reycled 20-lb. paper; 80-lb. card cover; illustrations; photos. "Bathtub Gin is looking for work that has some kick to it. We are very eclectic and publish a wide range of styles. Audience is anyone interested in new writing and art that is not being presented in larger magazines." Semiannual. Estab. 1997. Circ. 250.

Needs Condensed novels, experimental, humor/satire, literary. "No horror, science fiction, historical unless they go beyond the usual formula." "We want more experimental fiction." Receives 20 unsolicited mss/month. Accepts 2-3 mss/issue. Reads mss for two issues June 1st-September 15th. "We publish in mid-October and mid-April." **Publishes 10 new writers/year.** Recently published work by J.T. Whitehead and G.D. McFetridge. Publishes short shorts. Also publishes literary essays, literary criticism, poetry. Often comments on rejected mss.

How to Contact Accepts submissions by e-mail. Send cover letter with a 3-5 line bio. Send SASE for reply, return of ms or send a disposable copy of ms. Responds in 1-2 months to queries. Accepts simultaneous, multiple submissions and reprints. Sample copy for $5. Writer's guidelines for #10 SASE. Reviews fiction.

Payment/Terms Pays 2 contributor's copies; discount on additional copies. Rights revert to author upon publication.

Tips "Please be advised that magazine is currently on hiatus and not accepting work until at least 2009."

☐ BELLEVUE LITERARY REVIEW

Dept. of Medicine, NYU School of Medicine, 550 First Avenue, OBV-A612, New York NY 10016. (212) 263-3973. Fax: (212) 263-3206. E-mail: info@blreview.org. Website: http://blreview.org. **Contact:** Ronna Wineberg, senior fiction editor. Magazine: 6 × 9; 160 pages. "The BLR is a literary journal that examines human existence through the prism of health and healing, illness and disease. We encourage creative interpretations of these themes." Semiannual. Estab. 2001. Member CLMP.

Needs Literary. No genre fiction. Receives 100 unsolicited mss/month. Accepts 12 mss/issue; 24 mss/year. Publishes mss 3-6 months after acceptance. Agented fiction 1%. **Publishes 3-6 new writers/year.** Recently published work by Amy Hempel, Sheila Kohler, Martha Cooley. Length: 5,000 words; average length: 2,500 words. Publishes short shorts. Also publishes literary essays, poetry. Sometimes comments on rejected mss.

How to Contact Submit online at www.blreview.org (preferred). Also accepts mss via regular mail. Send complete ms. Send SASE (or IRC) for return of ms or disposable copy of the ms and #10 SASE for reply only. Responds in 3-6 months to mss. Accepts simultaneous submissions. Sample copy for $7. Writer's guidelines for SASE, e-mail or on Website.

Payment/Terms Pays 2 contributor's copies, 1-year subscription and 1 year gift subscription; additional copies $6. Pays on publication for first North American serial rights. Sends galleys to author.

☑ BELLINGHAM REVIEW

Mail Stop 9053, Western Washington University, Bellingham WA 98225. (360) 650-4863. E-mail: bhreview@cc.wwu.edu. Website: www.wwu.edu/~bhreview. **Contact:** Fiction Editor. Magazine: 6 × 8¼; 150 pages; 60 lb. white paper; four-color cover." Bellingham Review seeks literature of palpable quality; stories, essays and poems that nudge the limits of form or execute traditional forms exquisitely. Semiannual. Estab. 1977. Circ. 1,600.

• The editors are actively seeking submissions of creative nonfiction, as well as stories that push the boundaries of the form. The Tobias Wolff Award in Fiction Contest runs December 1-March 15; see Web site for guidelines or send SASE.

Needs Experimental, humor/satire, literary, regional (Northwest). Does not want anything nonliterary.

Accepts 3-4 mss/issue. Does not read ms February 2-September 14. Publishes ms 6 months after acceptance. Agented fiction 10%. **Publishes 10 new writers/year.** Recently published work by Patricia Vigderman, Joshua Rolnick, and A.G. Harmon. Publishes short shorts. Also publishes poetry.

How to Contact Send complete ms. Responds in 3 months to mss. Accepts simultaneous submissions. Sample copy for $7. Writer's guidelines online.

Payment/Terms Pays on publication when funding allows. Acquires first North American serial rights.

Tips "We look for work that is ambitious, vital and challenging both to the spirit and the intellect."

BELLOWING ARK

P.O. Box 55564, Shoreline WA 98155. E-mail: bellowingark@bellowingark.org. **Contact:** Fiction Editor. Tabloid: 11½ × 17½; 32 pages; electro-brite paper and cover stock; illustrations; photos. "We publish material we feel addresses the human situation in an affirmative way. We do not publish academic fiction." Bimonthly. Estab. 1984. Circ. 650.

• Work from *Bellowing Ark* appeared in the *Pushcart Prize* anthology.

Needs Literary, mainstream, serialized novels. "No science fiction or fantasy." Receives 30-70 unsolicited mss/month. Accepts 2-5 mss/issue; 700-1,000 mss/year. Publishes ms 6 months after acceptance. **Publishes 6-10 new writers/year.** Recently published work by Tom Cook, Tanyo Ravicz, Mindy Aber Barad, Shelley Uva, and E.R. Romaine. Also publishes literary essays, literary criticism, poetry. Sometimes comments on rejected mss.

How to Contact Send complete ms and SASE. Responds in 6 weeks to mss. No simultaneous submissions. Sample copy for $4, 9½ × 12½ SAE and $1.43 postage.

Payment/Terms Pays in contributor's copies. Acquires one-time rights.

Tips "*Bellowing Ark* began as (and remains) an alternative to the despair and negativity of the workshop/ academic literary scene; we believe that life has meaning and is worth living—the work we publish reflects that belief. Learn how to tell a story before submitting. Avoid 'trick' endings; they have all been done before and better. *Bellowing Ark* is interested in publishing writers who will develop with the magazine, as in an extended community. We find good writers and stick with them. This is why the magazine has grown from 12 to 32 pages."

BELOIT FICTION JOURNAL

Box 11, 700 College St., Beloit College WI 53511. (608)363-2577. E-mail: bfj@beloit.edu. Website: www.beloit.edu/ ~ english/bfjournal.htm. **Contact:** Chris Fink, editor-in-chief. Literary magazine: 6 × 9; 250 pages; 60 lb. paper; 10 pt. C1S cover stock; illustrations; photos on cover; ad-free. "We are interested in publishing the best contemporary fiction and are open to all themes except those involving pornographic, religiously dogmatic or politically propagandistic representations. Our magazine is for general readership, though most of our readers will probably have a specific interest in literary magazines." Annual. Estab. 1985.

• Work first appearing in Beloit Fiction Journal has been reprinted in award-winning collections, including the Flannery O'Connor and the Milkweed Fiction Prize collections, and has won the Iowa Short Fiction award.

Needs Literary, mainstream, contemporary. Wants more experimental and short shorts. Would like to see more "stories with a focus on both language and plot, unusual metaphors and vivid characters. No pornography, religious dogma, science fiction, horror, political propaganda or genre fiction." Receives 200 unsolicited mss/month. Accepts 20 mss/year. Publishes ms 9 months after acceptance. **Publishes 3 new writers/year.** Recently published work by Dennis Lehane, Silas House and David Harris Ebenbach. Length: 250-10,000 words; average length: 5,000 words. Sometimes comments on rejected mss.

How to Contact "Our reading period is from August 1st to December 1st only. " No fax, e-mail or disk submissions. Responds in 2 weeks to queries; 2 months to mss. Accepts simultaneous submissions if identified as such. Please send one story at a time. Always include SASE. Sample copy for $ 10 (new issue), $8 (back issue, double issue), $ 6 (back issue, single issue). Writer's guidelines for #10 SASE or on Web site.

Payment/Terms Buys first North American serial rights only. Payment in copies.

Tips "Many of our contributors are writers whose work we had previously rejected. Don't let one rejection slip turn you away from our—or any—magazine."

☑ BERKELEY FICTION REVIEW

10B Eshleman Hall, University of California, Berkeley CA 94720. (510) 642-2892. E-mail: bfictionreview@ yahoo.com. Website: www.OCF.Berkeley.EDU/~bfr/. **Contact:** Rhoda Piland, editor. Magazine: 5½ × 8½; 180 pages; perfect-bound; glossy cover; some b&w art; photographs. "The mission of Berkeley Fiction Review is to provide a forum for new and emerging writers as well as writers already established. We publish a wide variety of contemporary short fiction for a literary audience." Annual. Estab. 1981. Circ. 1,000.

Needs Experimental, literary, mainstream. "Quality, inventive short fiction. No poetry or formula fiction." Receives 70 unsolicited mss/month. Accepts 10-15 mss/issue. **Publishes 12-15 new writers/year.** Publishes short shorts. Occacionally comments on rejected mss.

How to Contact Responds in 3-9 months to mss. Accepts simultaneous, multiple submissions. Sample copy for $9.50. Writer's guidelines for SASE. Accepts e-mail submissions in.pdf or word attachments.

Payment/Terms Pays one contributor's copy. Acquires first rights. Sponsors awards/contests.

Tips "Our criteria is fiction that resonates. Voices that are strong and move a reader. Clear, powerful prose (either voice or rendering of subject) with a point. Unique ways of telling stories-these capture the editors. Work hard, don't give up. Don't let your friends or family critique your work. Get someone honest to point out your writing weaknesses, and then work on them. Don't submit thinly veiled autobiographical stories; it's been done before-and better. With the proliferation of computers, everyone thinks they're a writer. Not true, unfortunately. The plus side though is ease of transmission and layout and diversity and range of new work."

$ BIBLIOPHILOS

The Bibliophile Publishing Co., Inc., 200 Security Building, Fairmont WV 26554. (304)366-8107. **Contact:**Gerald J. Bobango, editor. Literary magazine: 5½ × 8; 68-72 pages; white glossy paper; illustrations; photos. "We see ourself as a forum for new and unpublished writers, historians, philosophers, literary critics and reviewers, and those who love animals. Audience is academic-oriented, college graduate, who believes in traditional Aristotelian-Thomistic thought and education and has a fair streak of the Luddite in him/her. Our ideal reader owns no television, has never sent or received e-mail, and avoids shopping malls at any cost. He loves books." Quarterly. Estab. 1981. Circ. 400.

Needs Adventure, ethnic/multicultural, family saga, historical (general, US, Eastern Europe), horror (psychological, supernatural), humor/satire, literary, mainstream, military/war, mystery/suspense (police procedural, private eye/hard -boiled, courtroom), novel excerpts, regional (New England, Middle Atlantic), romance (gothic, historical, regency period), slice-of-life vignettes, suspense, thriller/ espionage, translations, western (frontier saga, traditional), utopian, Orwellian. "No 'I found Jesus and it turned my life around'; no 'I remember Mama, who was a saint and I miss her terribly'; no gay or lesbian topics; no drug culture material; nothing harping on political correctness; nothing to do with healthy living, HMOs, medical programs, or the welfare state, unless it is against statism in these areas." *No unsolicited submissions.*Accepts 5-6 mss/issue; 25-30 mss/year. Publishes ms 12-18 months after acceptance. **Publishes 2-6 new writers/year.** Recently published work by Mardelle Fortier, Clevenger Kehmeier, Gwen Williams, Manuel Sanchez-Lopez, Janet Tyson, Andrea C. Poe, Norman Nathan. Also publishes literary essays, literary criticism, poetry. Often comments on rejected mss.

How to Contact Query with clips of published work. Include bio, SASE and $5.25 for sample issue. Responds in 2 weeks to queries; 1 month to mss. Sample copy for $5.25. Writer's guidelines for 9½ × 4 SAE and 2 first-class stamps.

Payment/Terms Pays $15-40. Pays on publication for first North American serial rights.

Tips "Write for specifications, send for a sample issue, then *read* the thing, study the formatting, and follow the instructions, which say query first before sending anything. We shall not respond to unsolicited material. We don't want touchy-feely maudlin stuff where hugging kids solves all of life's problems, and we want no references anywhere in the story to e-mail, the Internet, or computers, unless it's to berate them."

☑ ☒ BIG MUDDY: A JOURNAL OF THE MISSISSIPPI RIVER VALLEY

Southeast Missouri State University Press, MS2650 English Dept., Southeast MO State University, Cape Girardeau MO 63701. E-mail: sswartwout@semo.edu. Website: www6.semo.edu/universitypress/ hearne.htm. **Contact:** Susan Swartwout, publisher/editor. Magazine: 8½ × 5½ perfect-bound; 150

pages; acid-free paper; color cover stock; layflat lamination; illustrations; photos. "Big Muddy explores multidisciplinary, multicultural issues, people, and events mainly concerning the 10-state area that borders the Mississippi River, by people who have lived here, who have an interest in the area, or who know the River Basin. We publish fiction, poetry, historical essays, creative nonfiction, environmental essays, biography, regional events, photography, art, etc." Semiannual. Estab. 2001. Circ. 500.

Needs Adventure, ethnic/multicultural, experimental, family saga, feminist, historical, humor/satire, literary, mainstream, military/war, mystery/suspense, regional (Mississippi River Valley; Midwest), translations. "No romance, fantasy or children's." Receives 50 unsolicited mss/month. Accepts 7-10 mss/issue. Publishes ms 6 months after acceptance.

How to Contact Send SASE for return of ms or send a disposable copy of ms and #10 SASE for reply only. Responds in 12 weeks to mss. Accepts multiple submissions. Sample copy for $6. Writer's guidelines for SASE, e-mail, fax or on Web site. Reviews fiction, poetry, nonfiction.

Payment/Terms Pays 2 contributor's copies; additional copies $5. Acquires first North American serial rights.

Tips "We look for clear language, avoidance of clichés except in necessary dialogue, a fresh vision of the theme or issue. Find some excellent and honest readers to comment on your work-in-progress and final draft. Consider their viewpoints carefully. Revise."

☑ THE BITTER OLEANDER

4983 Tall Oaks Dr., Fayettville NY 13066-9776. (315) 637-3047. Fax: (315) 637-5056. E-mail: info@ bitteroleander.com. Website: www.bitteroleander.com. **Contact:** Paul B. Roth. Zine specializing in poetry and short fiction: 6 × 9; 128 pages; 55 lb. paper; 12 pt. CIS cover stock; photos. "We're interested in the surreal; deep image particularization of natural experiences." Bi-annual. Estab. 1974. Circ. 1,500.

Needs Experimental, translations. "No pornography; no confessional; no romance." Receives 200 unsolicited mss/month. Accepts 4-5 mss/issue; 8-10 mss/year. Does not read in July. Publishes ms 4-6 months after acceptance. Recently published work by Daniel J. Doehr, V. Ulea, Emily Soto and Jeannette Ane Encinias. Max length: 2,500 words. Publishes short shorts. Also publishes literary essays, poetry. Always comments on rejected mss.

How to Contact Send SASE for reply, return of ms. Responds in 1 week to queries; 1 month to mss. Accepts multiple submissions. Sample copy for $10. Writer's guidelines for #10 SASE.

Payment/Terms Pays 1 contributor's copy; additional copies $10. Acquires first rights.

Tips "If within the first 100 words my mind drifts, the rest rarely makes it. Be yourself and listen to no one but yourself."

☑ $ ☑ BLACK WARRIOR REVIEW

P.O. Box 862936, Tuscaloosa AL 35486-0027. (205)348-4518. E-mail: bwr@ua.edu. Website: www.bwr. ua.edu. **Contact:** Christopher Hellwig, fiction editor. Magazine: 6 × 9; 160 pages; color artwork. "We publish contemporary fiction, poetry, reviews, essays and art for a literary audience. We publish the freshest work we can find." Semiannual. Estab. 1974. Circ. 2,000.

• Work that appeared in the *Black Warrior Review* has been included in the *Pushcart Prize* anthology, *Harper's Magazine*, *Best American Short Stories*, *Best American Poetry* and *New Stories from the South*.

Needs Literary, contemporary, short and short-short fiction. Wants "work that is conscious of form and well crafted. We are open to good experimental writing and short-short fiction. No genre fiction, please." Receives 300 unsolicited mss/month. Accepts 5 mss/issue; 10 mss/year. Unsolicited novel excerpts are not considered unless the novel is already contracted for publication. Publishes ms 6 months after acceptance. **Publishes 5 new writers/year.** Recently published work by Eric Maxon, Gary Parks, Gary Fincke, Anthony Varallo, Wayne Johnson, Jim Ruland, Elizabeth Wetmore, Bret Anthony Johnston, Rick Bass, Sherri Flick. Length: 7,500 words; average length: 2,000-5,000 words. Occasionally comments on rejected mss.

How to Contact Send complete ms with SASE (1 story per submission). Responds in 4 months to mss. Accepts simultaneous submissions if noted. Sample copy for $10. Writer's guidelines online.

Payment/Terms Pays up to $100, copies, and a 1-year subscription. Pays on publication for first rights.

Tips "We look for attention to language, freshness, honesty, a convincing and sharp voice. Send us a clean, well-printed, proofread manuscript. Become familiar with the magazine prior to submission."

☑ ◎ BLUELINE

125 Morey Hall, Department of English and Communication, SUNY Potsdam, Postdam NY 13676. (315) 267-2043. E-mail: blueline@potsdam.edu. Website: http://www2.potsdam.edu/blueline/blue.html. **Contact:**fiction editor. Magazine: 6 × 9; 200 pages; 70 lb. white stock paper; 65 lb. smooth cover stock; illustrations; photos. "Blueline is interested in quality writing about the Adirondacks or other places similar in geography and spirit. We publish fiction, poetry, personal essays, book reviews and oral history for those interested in Adirondacks, nature in general, and well-crafted writing." Annual. Estab. 1979. Circ. 400.

Needs Adventure, humor/satire, literary, regional, contemporary, prose poem, reminiscences, oral history, nature/outdoors. No urban stories or erotica. Receives 8-10 unsolicited mss/month. Accepts 6-8 mss/issue. Does not read January-August. Publishes ms 3-6 months after acceptance. **Publishes 2 new writers/year.** Recently published work by Joan Connor, Laura Rodley and Ann Mohin. Length: 500-3,000 words; average length: 2,500 words. Also publishes literary essays, poetry. Occasionally comments on rejected mss.

How to Contact Accepts simultaneous submissions. Sample copy for $6.

Payment/Terms Pays 1 contributor's copy; charges $7 each for 3 or more copies. Acquires first rights.

Tips "We look for concise, clear, concrete prose that tells a story and touches upon a universal theme or situation. We prefer realism to romanticism but will consider nostalgia if well done. Pay attention to grammar and syntax. Avoid murky language, sentimentality, cuteness or folkiness. We would like to see more good fiction related to the Adirondacks and more literary fiction and prose poems. If manuscript has potential, we work with author to improve and reconsider for publication. Our readers prefer fiction to poetry (in general) or reviews. Write from your own experience, be specific and factual (within the bounds of your story) and if you write about universal features such as love, death, change, etc., write about them in a fresh way. Triteness and mediocrity are the hallmarks of the majority of stories seen today."

☐ ◎ BLUE MESA REVIEW

University of New Mexico, MSC03 2170, 1 University of New Mexico, Albuquerque NM 87131-0001. Fax: (505)277-5573. E-mail: bmrinfo@unm.edu. Website: www.unm.edu/~bluemesa. **Contact:** Skye Pratt. Magazine: 6 × 9; 300 pages; 55 lb. paper; 10 pt CS1 photos. Blue Mesa Review publishes the best/most current creative writing on the market. Annual. Estab. 1989. Circ. 1,000.

Needs Literary fiction, including but not limited to ethnic/multicultural, experimental, feminist, gay, historical, humor/satire, lesbian, literary, mainstream, regional, western themes. Accepts 25 mss/year. Accepts mss year round; all submissions must be post marked by October 1; reads mss September-March; responds in 3-6 months. Publishes ms 5-6 months after acceptance. Also publishes literary essays, poetry, author interviews, and book reviews.

How to Contact Send SASE for reply. Sample copy for $12. Writer's guidelines online.

Payment/Terms Pays 2 contributor's copies. Acquires first North American serial rights.

☑ BOGG

A Journal of Contemporary Writing Bogg Publications, 422 N. Cleveland St., Arlington VA 22201-1424. E-mail: boggmag@aol.com. Contact: John Elsberg, US editor. Magazine: 6 × 9; 72 pages; 70 lb. white paper; 70 lb. cover stock; line illustrations. "Poetry (to include prose poems, haiku/tanka and experimental forms), experimental short fiction, reviews." Published 2 times a year. Estab. 1968. Circ. 800.

Needs Very short experimental fiction and prose poems. Receives 25 unsolicited prose mss/month. Accepts 4-6 mss/issue. Publishes ms 3-18 months after acceptance. **Publishes 40-80 new writers/year.** Recently published work by Linda Bosson, Brian Johnson, Katrina Holden Bronson, Karen Rosenberg, Carla Mayfield, and Elizabeth Bernays. Also occasionally publishes interviews and essays on small press history. Rarely comments on rejected mss.

How to Contact Responds in 1 week to queries; 2 weeks to mss. Sample copy for $4 or $6 (current issue). Reviews fiction. Does not consider e-mail or simultaneous submissions.

Payment/Terms Pays 2 contributor's copies; reduced charge for extras. Acquires one-time rights.

Tips "We look for voice and originality. Read magazine first. Bogg is mainly a poetry journal, and we look for prose poems and short experimental or wry fiction that works well with the poetry."

▦ ◻ BOOK WORLD MAGAZINE

Christ Church Publishers Ltd., 2 Caversham Street, London England SW3 4AH United Kingdom. 0207 351 4995. Fax: 0207 3514995. E-mail: leonard.holdsworth@btopenworld.com. **Contact:** James Hughes. Magazine: 64 pages; illustrations; photos. "Subscription magazine for serious book lovers, book collectors, librarians and academics." Monthly. Estab. 1971. Circ. 6,000.

Needs Also publishes literary essays, literary criticism.

How to Contact Query. Send IRC (International Reply Coupon) for return of ms. Responds in 3 months to queries; 3 months to mss. Accepts simultaneous submissions. Sample copy for $7.50. Writer's guidelines for IRC.

Payment/Terms Pays on publication for one-time rights.

Tips "Always write to us before sending any mss."

☑ THE BRIAR CLIFF REVIEW

Briar Cliff University, 3303 Rebecca St., Sioux City IA 51104-0100. (712) 279-5477. E-mail: curranst@briarcliff.edu. Website: www.briarcliff.edu/bcreview. **Contact:** Phil Hey or Tricia Currans-Sheehan, fiction editors. Magazine: 8½ × 11; 120 pages; 70 lb. 100# Altima Satin Text; illustrations; photos. "The Briar Cliff Review is an eclectic literary and cultural magazine focusing on (but not limited to) Siouxland writers and subjects. We are happy to proclaim ourselves a regional publication. It doesn't diminish us; it enhances us." Annual. Estab. 1989. Circ. 750.

Needs Ethnic/multicultural, feminist, historical, humor/satire, literary, mainstream, regional. "No romance, horror or alien stories." Accepts 5 mss/year. Reads mss only between August 1 and November 1. Publishes ms 3-4 months after acceptance. **Publishes 10-14 new writers/year.** Recently published work by Jenna Blum, Brian Bedard, Christian Michener, Rebecca Tuch, Scott H. Andrews, and Josip Novakovich. Length: 2,500-5,000 words; average length: 3,000 words. Also publishes literary essays, literary criticism, poetry. Sometimes comments on rejected mss.

How to Contact Send SASE for return of ms. Does not accept electronic submissions (unless from overseas). Responds in 4-5 months to mss. Accepts simultaneous submissions. Sample copy for $15 and 9 × 12 SAE. Writer's guidelines for #10 SASE. Reviews fiction.

Payment/Terms Pays 2 contributor's copies; additional copies available for $12. Acquires first rights.

Tips "So many stories are just telling. We want some action. It has to move. We prefer stories in which there is no gimmick, no mechanical turn of events, no moral except the one we would draw privately."

☑ ◎ BRILLANT CORNERS

Lycoming College, Williamsport PA 17701. (570) 321-4279. Fax: (570) 321-4090. E-mail: feinstein@lycoming.edu. **Contact**: Sascha Feinstein, editor. Journal: 6 × 9; 90 pages; 70 lb. Cougar opaque, vellum, natural paper; photographs. "We publish jazz-related literature—fiction, poetry and nonfiction." Semiannual. Estab. 1996. Circ. 1,200.

Needs Condensed novels, ethnic/multicultural, experimental, literary, mainstream, romance (contemporary). Receives 10-15 unsolicited mss/month. Accepts 1-2 mss/issue; 2-3 mss/year. Does not read mss May 15-September 1. Publishes ms 4-12 months after acceptance. Publishes short shorts. Also publishes literary essays, literary criticism, poetry. Rarely comments on rejected mss.

How to Contact SASE for return of ms or send a disposable copy of ms. Accepts unpublished work only. Responds in 2 weeks to queries; 1-2 months to mss. Sample copy for $7. Reviews fiction.

Payment/Terms Acquires first North American serial rights. Sends galleys to author when possible.

Tips "We look for clear, moving prose that demostrates a love of both writing and jazz. We primarily publish established writers, but we read all submissions carefully and welcome work by outstanding young writers."

◻ THE BROADKILL REVIEW, A JOURNAL OF LITERATURE

John Milton and Company Quality Used Books, 104 Federal Street, Milton DE 19968. (302) 684-0174. E-mail: the_broadkill_review@earthlink.net. **Contact:** Jamie Brown, Publisher/Editor. PDF Literary magazine/journal. Contains illustrations, photographs. "Quality is the most important factor. This isn't to suggest that we are snobs, for I'm not talking about subject matter, but about the bell-like resonance of the work (evoked within the reader) and clarity. We want the reader left with the feeling that it matters to the reader personally that they read the story. Writing is the first interactive medium, after all, and although 100% communication cannot ever be achieved, owing to all sorts of internal and unconscious filters and the differences between two peoples' perceptions of the same thing, the stories we like are those that understand that and which encourage a kind of divestiture of the self and an investment in the story with whatever they, the reader, can bring to it of an emotional commitment. We are fans of John Gardner's On Becoming a Novelist, and firmly believe in establishing 'the waking dream' as the responsibility of the author." Bimonthly. Estab. 2007. Circ. 12,000. Member CLMP, Delaware Press Assn.

Needs Literary. Does not want anything gratuitous. Receives 8-20 mss/month. Accepts 1-4 mss/issue; 16-20 mss/year. Manuscript published 1-3 months after acceptance. **Publishes 30 new writers/year.** Published Thom Wade Myers, Chad Clifton, Tina Hession, Joshua D. Isard, Maryanne Khan, Richard Myers Peabody, H. A. Maxson, Bob Yearick, Gaylene Carbis, Louise D'Arcy, and Andee Jones. Length: 6,000 words (max). Average length: 3,300 words. Publishes short shorts. Also publishes literary essays, literary criticism, book reviews, poetry. Send two review copies to Editor, The Broadkill Review, 104 Federal Street, Milton, DE 19968. Sometimes comments on/critiques rejected mss, if requested by the author.

How to Contact Send complete ms with cover letter—preferably by e-mail. Include estimated word count, brief bio, list of publications. Responds to queries in 1 week. Responds to mss in 4-26 weeks. Send either SASE (or IRC) for return of ms or disposable copy of ms and #10 SASE for reply only. Considers simultaneous submissions, multiple submissions. Sample copy delivered electronically free upon request. Guidelines available via e-mail.

Payment/Terms Writers receive contributor's copy. Pays on publication. Acquires first rights. Publication is copyrighted.

Tips "Finish the work. Getting to the end of your first draft may be emotionally satisfying and physically enervating, but that is the point where the WORK of writing begins. Don't stint on the effort it may take you to revise your work. We are interested in publishing in our pages that which rises above the ordinary. We are not, on the other hand, interested in stories about your three-headed cat, zombies, flesh-eating bacteria, BEMs from outer-space, or psychopathic axe murderers. In short, your stories and poems should not rely on the unusual circumstance in place of actually having work which is finely crafted, insightful of the human condition, or which manages to make the reader continue to think about it after they have finished reading it. We are open to almost everything that does what Literature should do, which is to exact a price greater than the effort required to read it. The selection process is entirely subjective. We are not representative of the whole world. We publish what moves US. "

☑ BROKEN BRIDGE REVIEW, For Emerging Writers

Pomfret School, 398 Pomfret St., Pomfret CT 06258-0128. (860)963-5220. E-mail: bdavis@pomfretschool.org. Website: www.brokenbridge.us. **Contact:** Brad Davis, editor. Literary magazine/journal: 5½ × 11, 8-16 pages, b&w debossed cover, sewn binding. "Neither for beginners nor A-list writers; think 'on the cusp'. A journal of interest for new writers, college and MFA writers, established writers—with an eye for the best new work by emerging writers." Triannual. Estab. 2006.

Needs Experimental, literary, mainstream, regional. Reads fiction in November only. Manuscript published 2 months after acceptance. Length: 2,500 words (min)-5,000 words (max). Publishes short shorts. Also publishes poetry and creative nonfiction. Never comments on/critiques rejected manuscripts.

How to Contact Send complete ms with cover letter by online submission manager. Include estimated word count, brief bio, list of publications, e-mail address and (if any) private school connection. Responds to mss in 1-3 months. Replies by e-mail. Sample copy available for $8. Guidelines available on Web site.

Payment/Terms Writers receive 50 contributors copies. Additional copies $8. Pays on publication. Acquires one-time rights. Sends galleys to author.

☑ BUFFALO CARP

Quad City Arts, 1715 2nd Avenue, Rock Island IL 61201.(309)793-1213. Website: www.quadcityarts.com. **Contact:** Ryan Collins, managing editor. Literary magazine/journal: 6 × 9, 100 pages, 60 lb. paper, glossy, four-color with original artwork cover. "Buffalo Carp is a hybrid, an amalgam, unique, surprising and yet somehow inevitable. The works range from the factual to the fanciful, from fascinating to frightening, and everything in between." Annual. Estab. 2002. Circ. 350.

Needs High quality fiction of any style, genre, etc. "We are more concerned with the quality of the work than the classification of the work." Receives 15 mss/month. Accepts 8-10 mss/issue. Does not read May-August. Manuscript published 6-12 months after acceptance. Agented fiction 5%. Publishes 1-2 new writers/year. Length: 3,000 words (max). Average length: 1,500-3,000 words. Publishes short shorts. Also publishes poetry. Rarely comments on/critiques rejected mss. Flash Fiction Contest opens for submissions September 1 of each year; contest guidelines available on Web site.

How to Contact Send complete ms with cover letter. Accepts submissions by e-mail. Include estimated word count, brief bio. Responds to queries in 2 weeks. Responds to mss in 6-12 weeks. Send disposable copy of ms and #10 SASE for reply only. Considers simultaneous submissions, multiple submissions. Sample copy available for $7. Guidelines available on Web site.

Payment/Terms Writers receive 2 contributors copies. Pays on publication. Publication is copyrighted.

Tips "Send us your best, most interesting work. Worry less about how you would classify the work and more about it being high-quality and stand-out. We are looking to go in new directions with upcoming issues, so send us what you think best represents you and not who your influences are. *Buffalo Carp* is not interested in blending in, and has no interest in homogenized work. Blow us away!"

BUTTON

Box 77, Westminster, MA 014 73. Website: www.moonsigns.net. **Contact**: W.M. Davies, fiction editor. Magazine: 4 × 5; 34 pages; bond paper; color cardstock cover; illustrations; photos. "Button is New England's tiniest magazine of poetry, fiction and gracious living, published once a year. As 'gracious living' is on the cover, we like wit, brevity, cleverly conceived essay/recipe, poetry that isn't sentimental or song lyrics. I started Button so that a century from now, when people read it in landfils or, preferably, libraries, they'll say, 'Gee, what a great time to have lived. I wish I lived back then.'" Annual. Estab. 1993. Circ. 1,500.

Needs Literary. "No genre fiction, science fiction, techno-thriller." Wants more of "anything Herman Melville, Henry James or Betty MacDonald would like to read." Receives 20-40 unsolicited mss/month. Accepts 1-2 mss/issue; 3-5 mss/year. Publishes ms 3-9 months after acceptance. Recently published work by Ralph Lombreglia, John Hanson Mitchell, They Might Be Giants and Lawrence Millman. Also publishes literary essays, poetry. Sometimes comments on rejected mss. "Only reads between April 1 and September 30. We will send samples but will discard mss not sent during those periods."

How to Contact Send complete ms with bio, list of publications and explain how you found magazine. Include SASE. Responds in 1 month to queries; 2 months to mss. Sample copy for $2.50 and 1 first class stamp. Writer's guidelines for #10 SASE. Reviews fiction.

Payment/Terms Honorium, subscription and copies. Pays on publication for first North American serial rights.

Tips "What makes a manuscript stand out? Flannery O'Connor once said, 'Don't get subtle till the fourth page,' and I agree. We look for interesting, sympathetic, believable characters and careful setting. I'm really tired of stories that start strong then devolve into dialogue uninterrupted by further exposition. Also, no stories from a mad person's POV unless it's really tricky and skillful. Advice to prospective writers: Continue to read at least 10 times as much as you write. Read the best, and read intelligent criticism if you can find it. *No beginners please*. Please don't submit more than once a year; it's more important that you work on your craft rather than machine-gunning publications with samples, and don't submit more than 3 poems in a batch (this advice goes for other places, you'll find)."

CAIRN

The New St. Andrews Review St. Andrews College Press, 1700 Dogwood Mile, Laurinburg NC 28352. (910)277-5310. Fax: (910)277-5020. E-mail: pressemail@sapc.edu. Website: www.sapc.edu/sapress.html. **Contact:** Fiction Editor. Magazine: 50-60 lb. paper. "Cairn is a nonprofit, national/international literary magazine which publishes established as well as emerging writers." Estab. 1969. Member CLMP and AWP.

Needs Literary, short stories and short-short fiction. "We're looking for original, imaginative short fiction with style and insight." **Publishes 10-15 new writers/year.**

How to Contact Accepts no submissions by e-mail. Send only snail-mail disposable copy of ms with SASE for reply only. Responds in 3-4 months to mss. Accepts simultaneous submissions with notice.

Payment/Terms Pays 1 contributor copy.

☑ ◎ ☒ CALLALOO

Dept. of English, TAMU 4212, Texas A&M University, College Station TX 77843-4227. (979) 458-3108. Fax: (979) 458-3275. E-mail: callaloo@tamu.edu. Website: http://callaloo.tamu.edu. **Contact:** Charles H. Rowell, editor. Magazine: 7X10; 250 pages. "Devoted to publishing fiction, poetry, drama of the African diaspora, including North, Central and South America, the Caribbean, Europe and Africa. Visually beautiful and well-edited, the journal publishes 3-5 short stories in all forms and styles in each issue." Quarterly. Estab. 1976. Circ. 2,000.

- One of the leading voices in African-American literature, Callaloo has recieved NEA literature grants. Several pieces every year are chosen for collections of the year's best stories, such as Beacon's Best John Wideman's "Weight" from Callaloo won the 2000 O. Henry Award.

Needs Ethnic/multicultural (black culture), feminist, historical, humor/satire, literary, regional, science fiction, serialized novels, translations, contemporary, prose poem. "No romance, confessional. Would like to see more experimental fiction, science fiction and well-crafted literary fiction particularly dealing with the black middle class, immigrant communities and/or the black South." Accepts 3-5 mss/issue; 10-20 mss/year. **Publishes 5-10 new writers/year.** Recently published work by Charles Johnson, Edwidge Danticat, Thomas Glave, Nallo Hopkinson, John Edgar Wideman, Jamaica Kincaid, Percival Everett and Patricia Powell. Also publishes poetry.

How to Contact Generally accepts unpublished work, rarely accepts reprints. Responds in 2 weeks to queries; 6 months to mss. Accepts multiple submissions. Sample copy for $12. Writer's guidelines online.

Payment/Terms Pays in contributor's copies. Aquires some rights. Sends galleys to author.

Tips "We look for freshness of both writing and plot, strength of characterization, plausibilty of plot. Read what's being written and published, especially in journals such as *Callaloo*."

☑ ◎ CALYX

Calyx, Inc., P.O. Box B, Corvallis OR 97339. (541) 753-9384. Fax: (541) 753-0515. E-mail: calyx@proaxis. com. Website: www. calyxpress.org. **Contact:** Editor. Magazine: 6 × 8; 128 pages per single issue; 60 lb. coated matte stock paper; 10 pt. chrome coat cover; original art. Publishes prose, poetry, art, essays, interviews and critical and review articles. "Calyx exists to publish fine literature and art by women and is committed to publishing the work of all women, including women of color, older women, working class women and other voices that need to be heard. We are committed to discovering and nurturing beginning writers." Biannual. Estab. 1976. Circ. 6,000.

Needs Receives approximately 1,000 unsolicited prose and poetry mss when open. Accepts 4-8 prose mss/issue; 9-15 mss/year. Reads mss October 1-December 31; submit only during this period. Mss received when not reading will be returned. Publishes ms 4-12 months after acceptance. **Publishes 10-20 new writers/year.** Recently published work by M. Evelina Galang, Chitrita Banerji, Diana Ma, Catherine Brady. Also publishes literary essays, literary criticism, poetry.

How to Contact Responds in 4-12 months to mss. Accepts simultaneous submissions. Sample copy for $ 10 plus $4 postage. Include SASE.

Payment/Terms "Combination of free issues and 1 volume subscription.

Tips Most mss are rejected because "The writers are not familiar with *Calyx*. Writers should read *Calyx* and be familar with the publication. We look for good writing, imagination and important/interesting subject matter."

☒ ☑ $ THE CAPILANO REVIEW

2055 Purcell Way, North Vancouver BC V7J 3H5 Canada. Website: www.capcollege.bc.ca/thecapilanoreview. Magazine: 7 × 9; 90-120 pages; book paper; glossy cover; perfect-bound; visual art. "Triannual visual and literary arts magazine that publishes experimental art and writing." Estab. 1972. Circ. 800.

Needs "No traditional, conventional fiction. Want to see innovative, genre-blurring work." Receives 100 unsolicited mss/month. Accepts 1 mss/issue; 3 mss/year. Publishes ms 4-6 months after acceptance. **Publishes some new writers/year.** Recently published work by Michael Turner, Lewis Buzbee, George Bowering. Also publishes literary essays, poetry.

How to Contact Include 2- to 3-sentence bio and brief list of publications. Send Canadian SASE or IRCs for reply. Responds in 1 month to queries; 4 months to mss. No simultaneous submissions. Sample copy for $14.70. Writer's guidelines online.

Payment/Terms Pays $50-200. Pays on publication for first North American serial rights.
Tips "Read the magazine before submitting."

☐ CC&D, CHILDREN, CHURCHES & DADDIES MAGAZINE: THE UNRELIGIOUS, NONFAMILY-ORIENTED LITERARY AND ART MAGAZINE

Scars Publications and Design, 829 Brian Court, Gurnee IL 60031-3155. (847) 281-9070. E-mail: ccandd96@scars.tv. Website: http://scars.tv. **Contact:** Janet Kuypers, editor in chief. Literary magazine/journal: 5x7, 60 lb paper. Contains illustrations & photographs. Monthly. Estab. 1993.

Needs "Our biases are works that relate to issues such as politics, sexism, society, and the like, but are definitely not limited to such. We publish good work that makes you think, that makes you feel like you've lived through a scene instead of merely reading it. If it relates to how the world fits into a person's life (political story, a day in the life, coping with issues people face), it will probably win us over faster. We have received comments from readers and other editors saying that they thought some of our stories really happened. They didn't, but it was nice to know they were so concrete, so believable people thought they were nonfiction. Do that to our readers." Interested in many topics including adventure, ethnic/multicultural, experimental, feminist, gay, historical, lesbian, literary, mystery/suspense, new age, psychic/supernatural/occult, science fiction. Does not want religious or rhyming or family-oriented material. Manuscript published 1 yr after acceptance. Published Mel Waldman, Kenneth DiMaggio, Pat Dixon, Robert William Meyers, Troy Davis, G.A. Scheinoha, Ken Dean. Average length: 1,000 words. Publishes short shorts, essays and stories. Also publishes poetry. Always comments on/critiques rejected mss if asked.

How to Contact Send complete ms with cover letter or query with clips of published work. Prefers submissions by e-mail. "If you have e-mail and send us a snail-mail submission, we will accept writing only if you e-mail it to us." Responds to queries in 2 weeks; mss in 2 weeks. "Responds much faster to e-mail submissions and queries." Send either SASE (or IRC) for return of ms or disposable copy of ms and #10 SASE for reply only, but if you have e-mail PLEASE send us an electronic submission instead. ("If we accept your writing, we'll only ask for you to e-mail it to us anyway.") Considers simultaneous submissions, previously published submissions, multiple submissions. Sample copy available for $6. Guidelines available for SASE, via e-mail, on Web site. Reviews fiction, essays, journals, editorials, short fiction.

☑ CENTER

University of Missouri, 202 Tate Hall, Columbia MO 65211 -1500. (573) 882-4971. E-mail: cla@missouri.edu. Website: http://center.missouri.edu. **Contact:** Fiction editor. Magazine: 6 × 9; 150-250 pages; perfect bound, with 4-color card cover. "Center aims to publish the best in literary fiction, poetry, and creative nonfiction by previously unpublished and emerging writers, as well as work by more established writers. Annual. Estab. 2000. Circ. 500.

Needs Ethnic/multicultural, experimental, humor/satire, literary. Receives 40-60 unsolicited mss/month. Accepts 2-4 mss/year. Reads mss from July 1-December 1 only. Publishes ms 6 months after acceptance. **Publishes 35% new writers/year.** Recently published work by Kim Chinquee, William Eisner, and April Ayers Lawson. Publishes short shorts. Also publishes literary essays, poetry. Sometimes comments on rejected mss.

How to Contact Send SASE (or IRC) for return of ms or send a disposable copy of ms and #10 SASE for reply only. Responds in 1 month to queries; 3-4 months to mss. Accepts simultaneous, multiple submissions. Sample copy for $3.50, current copy $7. Writer's guidelines online.

Payment/Terms Pays 2 contributor's copies; additional copies $3.50. Pays on publication for one-time rights.

☑ CHAFFIN JOURNAL

English Department, Eastern Kentucky University, Case Annex 467, Richmond KY 40475-3102. (859) 622-3080. E-mail: robert.witt@eku.edu. Website: www.english.eku.edu/chaffin_journal. **Contact:** Robert Witt, editor. Magazine: 8 × 5½; 120-130 pages; 70 lb. paper; 80 lb. cover. "We publish fiction on any subject; our only consideration is the quality." Annual. Estab. 1998. Circ. 150.

Needs Ethnic/multicultural, historical, humor/satire, literary, mainstream, regional (Appalachia). "No erotica, fantasy." Receives 20 unsolicited mss/month. Accepts 6-8 mss/year. Does not read mss October

1 through May 31. Publishes ms 6 months after acceptance. **Publishes 2-3 new writers/year.** Recently published work by Meridith Sue Willis, Marie Manilla, Raymond Abbott, Marjorie Bixler, Chris Helvey. Length: 10,000 words per submission period; average length: 5,000 words.

How to Contact Send SASE for return of ms. Responds in 1 week to queries; 3 months to mss. Accepts simultaneous, multiple submissions. Sample copy for $6.

Payment/Terms Pays 1 contributor's copy; additional copies $6. Pays on publication for one-time rights.

Tips "All manuscripts submitted are considered."

🖩 $ CHAPMAN

Chapman Publishing, 4 Broughton Place, Edinburgh Scotland EH1 3RX United Kingdom. (+44)131 557 2207. E-mail: chapman-pub@blueyonder.co.uk. Website: www.chapman-pub.co.uk. **Contact:** Joy Hendry, editor. "Chapman, Scotland's quality literary magazine, is a dynamic force in Scotland—publishing poetry; fiction; criticism; reviews; articles on theatre, politics, language and the arts. Our philosophy is to publish new work, from known and unknown writers, mainly Scottish, but also worldwide." Published three times a year. Estab. 1970. Circ. 2,000.

Needs Experimental, historical, humor/satire, literary, Scottish/international. "No horror, science fiction." Accepts 10-14 mss/issue. Publishes ms 6 months after acceptance. **Publishes 50 new writers/ year.**

How to Contact No simultaneous submissions. Writer's guidelines by e-mail or send SASE/IRC.

Payment/Terms Pays by negotiation. Pays on publication for first rights.

Tips "Keep your stories for six months and edit carefully. We seek challenging work which attempts to explore difficult/new territory in content and form, but lighter work, if original enough, is welcome."

✓ CHICAGO QUARTERLY REVIEW

517 Sherman Ave., Evanston IL 60202-2815. **Contact:** Syed Afzal Haider and Elizabeth McKenzie, editors. Magazine: 6 × 9; 125 pages; illustrations; photos. Annual. Estab. 1994. Circ. 300.

Needs Literary. Receives 60-80 unsolicited mss/month. Accepts 8-10 mss/issue; 16-20 mss/year. Publishes ms 6 months-1 year after acceptance. Agented fiction 5%. **Publishes 8-10 new writers/year.** Length: 5,000 words; average length: 2,500 words. Publishes short shorts. Also publishes literary essays, poetry. Sometimes comments on rejected mss.

How to Contact Send a disposable copy of ms and #10 SASE for reply only. Responds in 2 months to queries; 6 months to mss. Accepts simultaneous submissions. Up to 5 poems in a single submission; does not accept multiple short story submissions. Sample copy for $9.

Payment/Terms Pays 2 contributor's copies; additional copies $9. Pays on publication for one-time rights.

Tips "The writer's voice ought to be clear and unique and should explain something of what it means to be human. We want well-written stories that reflect an appreciation for the rhythm and music of language, work that shows passion and commitment to the art of writing."

✓ CHICAGO REVIEW

5801 S. Kenwood Ave., Chicago IL 60637. (773)702-0887. E-mail: chicago-review@uchicago.edu. Website: http://humanities.uchicago.edu/review. **Contact:** Joshua Adams, editor. Magazine for a highly literate general audience: 6 × 9; 128 pages; offset white 60 lb. paper; illustrations; photos. Quarterly. Estab. 1946. Circ. 3,500.

Needs Experimental, literary, contemporary. Receives 200 unsolicited mss/month. Accepts 2 mss/issue; 8 mss/year. Recently published work by Harry Mathews, Tom House, Viet Dinh and Doris Doörrie. Also publishes literary essays, literary criticism, poetry.

How to Contact SASE. Responds in 3-6 months to mss. No simultaneous submissions. Sample copy for $10. Guidelines via Web site or SASE.

Payment/Terms Pays 3 contributor's copies and subscription.

Tips "We look for innovative fiction that avoids cliché."

🖩 ✓ ◎ $ ⊞ CHROMA, AN INTERNATIONAL QUEER LITERARY JOURNAL

P.O. Box 44655, London, England N16 0WQ. +44-20-7193-7642. E-mail: editor@chromajournal.co.uk.

Website: www.chromajournal.co.uk. **Contact:** Shaun Levin, editor. Literary magazine/journal. 52 pages. Contains illustrations. Includes photographs. "Chroma is the only international queer literary and arts journal based in Europe. We publish poetry, short prose and artwork by lesbian, gay, bisexual and transgendered writers and artists. We are always looking for new work and encourage work in translation. Each issue is themed, so please check the website for details. Past themes have included: Foreigners, Beauty, Islands, and Tormented." Semiannual. Estab. 2004. Circ. 1,000.

Needs Comics/graphic novels, erotica, ethnic/multicultural, experimental, feminist, gay, lesbian, literary. Receives 100 mss/month. Accepts 12 mss/issue; 24 mss/year. Ms published 3 months after acceptance. **Publishes 20 new writers/year.** Length: 2,000 words (min)-5,000 words (max). Average length: 3,000 words. Publishes short shorts. Average length of short shorts: 1,000 words. Also publishes book reviews, poetry. Send review copies to Eric Anderson, books editor. Sometimes comments on/critiques rejected mss.

How to Contact Send complete ms with cover letter. Include brief bio. Responds to queries in 1 month via e-mail. Considers simultaneous submissions, multiple submissions. Guidelines available on Web site.

Payment/Terms Writers receive up to $150. Additional copies $7. Pays on publication. Acquires first rights. Publication is copyrighted. "The *Chroma* International Queer Writing Competition runs every two years. The first was in 2006. Check guidelines on our Web site."

Tips "We look for a good story well told. We look for writers doing interesting things with language, writers who are not afraid to take risks in the stories they tell and the way they tell them. Read back issues. If you like what we do, send us your work."

☑ ◎ $ CHRYSALIS READER

1745 Gravel Hill Road, Dillwyn VA 23936. (434) 983-3021. E-mail: chrysalis@hovac.com. Website: www. swedenborg.com /chrysalis. **Contact:** Robert Tucker, fiction editor. Book series: 7½ × 10; 192 pages; coated cover stock; illustrations; photos. "The Chrysalis Reader audience includes people from numerous faiths and backgrounds. Many of them work in psychology, education, religion, the arts, sciences, or one of the helping professions. The style of writing may be humorous, serious, or some combination of these approaches. Essays, poetry, and fiction that are not evangelical in tone but that are unique in addressing the Chrysalis Reader theme are more likely to be accepted. Our readers are interested in expanding, enriching, or challenging their intellects, hearts, and philosophies, and many also just want to enjoy a good read. For these reasons the editors attempt to publish a mix of writings. Articles and poetry must be related to the theme; however, you may have your own approach to the theme not written in our description." Estab. 1985. Circ. 3,000.

- This journal explores contemporary questions of spirituality from a Swedenborgian multifaith perspective.; This journal explores contemporary questions of spirituality from the perspective of Swedenborg theology.

Needs Adventure, experimental, historical, literary, mainstream, mystery/suspense, science fiction, fiction (leading to insight), contemporary, spiritual, sports. No religious works. Upcoming theme: "Lenses" (Fall 2009). Receives 50 unsolicited mss/month. Accepts 20-40 mss/year. Publishes ms 9 months after acceptance. **Publishes 10 new writers/year.** Recently published work by Robert Bly, William Kloefkorn, Raymond Moody, Virgil Suárez, Carol Lem, Alan Magee, John Hitchcock. Also publishes literary essays, literary criticism, poetry. Sometimes comments on rejected mss.

How to Contact Query with SASE. Accepts submissions by e-mail and USPS. Responds in 1 month to queries; 4-6 months to mss. No previously published work. Sample copy for $10 and 8½ × 11 SAE. Writer's guidelines and themes for issues for SASE or on Web site.

Payment/Terms Pays $25-100. Pays at page-proof stage. Acquires first rights, makes work-for-hire assignments. Sends galleys to author.

Tips Looking for "1: Quality; 2. appeal for our audience; 3. relevance to/illumination of an issue's theme."

☑ CIMARRON REVIEW

Oklahoma State University, 205 Morrill Hall, Stillwater OK 74078-0135. (405)744-9476. Website: http:// cimarronreview.okstate.edu. **Contact:** Toni Graham, fiction editor. Magazine: 6 × 9; 110 pages. "Poetry and fiction on contemporary themes; personal essays on contemporary issues that cope with life in the

21st century. We are eager to receive manuscripts from both established and less experienced writers who intrigue us with their unusual perspective, language, imagery and character." Quarterly. Estab. 1967. Circ. 600.

Needs Literary-quality short stories and novel excerpts. No juvenile or genre fiction. Accepts 3-5 mss/issue; 12-15 mss/year. Publishes ms 2-6 months after acceptance. **Publishes 2-4 new writers/year.** Recently published work by Molly Giles, Gary Fincke, David Galef, Nona Caspers, Robin Beeman, Edward J. Delaney. Also publishes literary essays, literary criticism, poetry.

How to Contact Send complete ms with SASE. Responds in 2-6 months to mss. Accepts simultaneous submissions. Sample copy for $7. Reviews fiction.

Payment/Terms Pays 2 contributor's copies. Acquires first North American serial rights.

Tips "In order to get a feel for the kind of work we publish, please read an issue or two before submitting."

☑ $ THE CINCINNATI REVIEW

P.O. Box 210069, Cincinnati OH 45221-0069. (513) 556-3954. E-mail: editors@cincinnatireview.com. Website: www.cincinnatireview.com. **Contact:** Brock Clarke, fiction editor. Magazine: 6 × 9; 180-200 pages; 60 lb. white offset paper. "A journal devoted to publishing the best new literary fiction and poetry as well as book reviews, essays and interviews." Semiannual. Estab. 2003.

Needs Literary. Does not want genre fiction. Accepts 10-15 mss/year. Reads submissions September 1-May 31. Manuscripts arriving during June, July and August will be returned unread.

How to Contact Send complete ms with SASE. Does not consider e-mail submissions. Responds in 2 weeks to queries; 6 weeks to mss. Accepts simultaneous submissions with notice. Sample copy for $9, subscription $15. Writer's guidelines online or send SASE.

Payment/Terms Pays $25/page. Pays on publication for first North American serial, electronic rights. All rights revert to author upon publication.

☒ ☐ ◎ THE CLAREMONT REVIEW

The Claremont Review Publishers, 4980 Wesley Rd., Victoria BC V8Y 1Y9 Canada. (250) 658-5221. Fax: (250) 658-5387. E-mail: editor@theClaremontReview.ca. Website: www.theClaremontReview.ca. **Contact:** Lucy Bashford (managing editor), Susan Stenson, Janice McCachen, Terence Young, editors. Magazine: 6 × 9; 110-120 pages; book paper; soft gloss cover; b&w illustrations. "We are dedicated to publishing emerging young writers aged 13-19 from anywhere in the English-speaking world, but primarily Canada and the U.S." Biannual. Estab. 1992. Circ. 700.

Needs Young adult/teen ("their writing, not writing for them "). No science fiction, fantasy. Receives 20-30 unsolicited mss/month. Accepts 10-12 mss/issue; 20-24 mss/year. Publishes ms 3 months after acceptance. **Publishes 100 new writers/year.** Recently published work by Selina Boan, Blaise Lucey, Gillian Harper, Julianne Yip. Length: 5,000 words; average length: 1,500-3,000 words. Publishes short shorts. Also publishes poetry. Always comments on rejected mss.

How to Contact Responds in 3 months to mss. Accepts multiple submissions. Sample copy for $10.

Payment/Terms Pays 1 contributor's copy. Additional copies for $8. Acquires first North American serial, one-time rights. Sponsors awards/contests.

Tips Looking for "good concrete narratives with credible dialogue and solid use of original detail. It must be unique, honest and have a glimpse of some truth. Send an error-free final draft with a short cover letter and bio. Read us first to see what we publish."

☐ COAL CITY REVIEW

Coal City Press, University of Kansas, Lawrence KS 66045. E-mail: coalcity@sunflower.com. **Contact:** Mary Wharff, fiction editor. Literary magazine/journal: 812 X 512, 124 pages, heavy cover. Includes photographs. Annual. Estab. 1990. Circ. 200.

Needs Experimental, literary. Does not want erotica, horror, romance, mystery. Receives 20-30 mss/month. Accepts 6-8 mss/issue. Reads year round. Manuscript published up to 1 year after acceptance. Agented fiction 0%. **Publishes new writers every year.** Published Judy Bauer, Olivia V. Ambroglio, Susan B. Cokal, Daniel A. Hoyt, Tasha Haas, Paul Levine. Length: 50 words (min)—4,000 words (max). Average length: 2,000 words. Also publishes literary criticism, poetry. Sometimes comments on/critiques rejected manuscripts.

How to Contact Submit via e-mail to coalcity@sunflower.com. Attach Word file. Include estimated word count, brief bio, list of publications. Responds to mss in 4 months. Send disposable copy of ms and #10 SASE for reply only. Considers simultaneous submissions. Guidelines available via e-mail.

Payment/Terms Writers receive 2 contributor's copies. Additional copies $5. Pays on publication. Acquires one-time rights. Publication is copyrighted.

Tips "We are looking for artful stories—with great language and great heart. Please do not send work that has not been thoughtfully and carefully revised or edited."

☑ $ COLORADO REVIEW

Center for Literary Publishing, Department of English, 9105 Campus Delivery, Colorado State University, Fort Collins CO 80523. (970) 491-5449. E-mail: creview@colostate.edu. Website: http://coloradoreview. colostate.edu. **Contact:** Stephanie G'Schwind, editor. Literary journal: 224 pages; 60 lb. book weight paper. Estab. 1956. Circ. 1,100.

Needs Ethnic/multicultural, experimental, literary, mainstream, contemporary. "No genre fiction." Receives 1,000 unsolicited mss/month. Accepts 4-5 mss/issue. Does not read mss May-August. Publishes ms within 1 year after acceptance. Recently published work by Paul Mandelbaum, Ann Hood, Kent Haruf, Charles Baxter, and Bret Lott. Also publishes poetry.

How to Contact Send complete ms. Responds in 2 months to mss. Sample copy for $10. Writer's guidelines online. Reviews fiction, poetry, and nonfiction.

Payment/Terms Pays $5/page plus two contributor's copies. Pays on publication for first North American serial rights. Rights revert to author upon publication. Sends galleys to author.

Tips "We are interested in manuscripts that show craft, imagination and a convincing voice. If a story has reached a level of technical competence, we are receptive to the fiction working on its own terms. The oldest advice is still the best: persistence. Approach every aspect of the writing process with pride, conscientiousness—from word choice to manuscript appearance. Be familiar with the *Colorado Review*; read a couple of issues before submitting your manuscript."

CONCHO RIVER REVIEW

Angelo State University, English Dept., Box 10894 ASU Station, San Angelo TX 76904. (325) 942-2269, ext. 230. Fax: (325) 942-2208. E-mail: me.hartje@angelo.edu. Website: www.angelo.edu/dept/english/concho_river_review.htm. **Contact:** Terry Dalrymple, fiction editor. Magazine: 6½ × 9; 100-125 pages; 60 lb. Ardor offset paper; Classic Laid Color cover stock; b&w drawings. "We publish any fiction of high quality—no thematic specialties." Semiannual. Estab. 1987. Circ. 300.

Needs Ethnic/multicultural, historical, humor/satire, literary, regional, western. Also publishes poetry, nonfiction, book reviews. "No erotica; no science fiction." Receives 10-15 unsolicited mss/month. Accepts 3-6 mss/issue; 8-10 mss/year. Publishes ms 4-6 months after acceptance. **Publishes 4 new writers/year.** Recently published work by Gordon Alexander, Riley Froh, Gretchen Geralds, Kimberly Willis Holt. Length: 1,500-5,000 words; average length: 3,500 words.

How to Contact Send electric copy upon acceptance. Responds in 3 weeks to queries. Accepts simultaneous submissions (if noted). Sample copy for $4. Writer's guidelines for #10 SASE. Reviews fiction.

Payment/Terms Pays in contributor's copies; $5 charge for extras. Acquires first rights.

Tips "We prefer a clear sense of conflict, strong characterization and effective dialogue."

☐ $ ☑ CONFRONTATION

Long Island University, Brookville NY 11548. (516)299-2720. Fax: (516)299-2735. **Contact:** Jonna Semeiks. Magazine: 6 × 9; 250-350 pages; 70 lb. paper; 80 lb. cover; illustrations; photos. "We are eclectic in our taste. Excellence of style is our dominant concern." Semiannual. Estab. 1968. Circ. 2,000.

- *Confrontation* has garnered a long list of awards and honors, including the Editor's Award for Distinguished Achievement from CCLP and NEA grants. Work from the magazine has appeared in numerous anthologies including the *Pushcart Prize, Best Short Stories* and *The O. Henry Prize Stories*.

Needs Experimental, literary, mainstream, novel excerpts (if they are self-contained stories), regional, slice-of-life vignettes, contemporary, prose poem s. "No 'proselytizing' literature or genre fiction." Receives 250-300 unsolicited mss/month. Accepts 30 mss/issue; 60 mss/year. Does not read June-September. Publishes ms 6 months to 1 year after acceptance. Agented fiction approximately 10-15%. **Publishes 20-**

30 new writers/year. Recently published work by Susan Vreeland, Lanford Wilson, Tom Stacey, Elizabeth Swados and Sallie Bingham. Publishes short shorts. Also publishes literary essays, poetry.

How to Contact Send complete ms to Confrontation, English Dept., C.W. Post campus of Long Island University, 720 Northern Blvd., Brookville NY 11548. Accepts e-mail for international submissions only (martin.tucker@liu.edu). "Cover letters acceptable, not necessary. We accept simultaneous submissions but do not prefer them." Responds in 3 weeks to queries; 6-8 weeks to mss. Sample copy for $3. Writer's guidelines not available. Reviews fiction, poetry, nonfiction.

Payment/Terms Pays $25-250. Pays on publication for first North American serial, first, one-time rights.

Tips "We look for literary merit. Keep trying."

☑ COTTONWOOD

Box J, 400 Kansas Union, University of Kansas, Lawrence KS 66045-2115. (785) 864-2516. Fax: (785) 864-4298. E-mail: tlorenz@ku.edu. **Contact:** Tom Lorenz, fiction editor. Magazine: 6 × 9; 100 pages; illustrations; photos. "Cottonwood publishes high quality prose, poetry and artwork and is aimed at an audience that appreciates the same. We have a national scope and reputation while maintaining a strong regional flavor." Semiannual. Estab. 1965. Circ. 500.

Needs "We publish literary prose and poetry." Receives 25-50 unsolicited mss/month. Accepts 5-6 mss/issue; 10-12 mss/year. Publishes ms 6-18 months after acceptance. Agented fiction 10%. **Publishes 1-3 new writers/year.** Recently published work by Connie May Fowler, Oakley Hall, Cris Mazza. Length: 1,000-8,000 words; average length: 2,000-5,000 words. Publishes short shorts. Also publishes literary essays, literary criticism, poetry.

How to Contact SASE for return of ms. Responds in 6 months to mss. Accepts simultaneous submissions. Sample copy for $8.50, 9 × 12 SAE and $1.90. Reviews fiction.

Payment/Terms Acquires one-time rights.

Tips "We're looking for depth and/or originality of subject matter, engaging voice and style, emotional honesty, command of the material and the structure. *Cottonwood* publishes high quality literary fiction, but we are very open to the work of talented new writers. Write something honest and that you care about and write it as well as you can. Don't hesitate to keep trying us. We sometimes take a piece from a writer we've rejected a number of times. We generally don't like clever, gimmicky writing. The style should be engaging but not claim all the the attention itself."

☑ $ ☑ CRAB ORCHARD REVIEW

Dept. of English, Faner Hall, 2380-Mail Code 4503, Southern Illinois University Carbondale, 1000 Faner Dr., Carbondale IL 62901-4503. (618)453-6833. Fax: (618)453-8224. E-mail: jtribble@siu.edu. Website: www.siu.edu/~crborchd. **Contact:** Jon Tribble, managing editor. Magazine: 5½ × 8½; 275 pages; 55 lb. recycled paper, card cover; photo on cover. "We are a general interest literary journal published twice/year. We strive to be a journal that writers admire and readers enjoy. We publish fiction, poetry, creative nonfiction, fiction translations, interviews and reviews." Estab. 1995. Circ. 2,500.

• *Crab Orchard Review* has won Illinois Arts Council Literary Awards and a 2008 Program Grant from the Illinois Arts Council.

Needs Ethnic/multicultural, literary, excerpted novel. No science fiction, romance, western, horror, gothic or children's. Wants more novel excerpts that also stand alone as pieces. List of upcoming themes available on Web site. Receives 900 unsolicited mss/month. Accepts 15-20 mss/issue; 20-40 mss/year. Reads February-April and August-October. Publishes ms 9-12 months after acceptance. Agented fiction 1%. **Publishes 4 new writers/year.** Recently published work by Francisco Aragón, Kerry Neville Bakken, Timothy Crandle, Amina Gautier, Jodee Stanley, Alia Yunis. Length: 1,000-6,500 words; average length: 2,500 words. Also publishes literary essays, poetry. Rarely comments on rejected mss.

How to Contact Send SASE for reply, return of ms. Responds in 3 weeks to queries; 9 months to mss. Accepts simultaneous submissions. Sample copy for $10. Writer's guidelines for #10 SASE.

Payment/Terms Pays $100 minimum; $20/page maximum, 2 contributor's copies and a year subscription. Acquires first North American serial rights.

Tips "We look for well-written, provocative, fully realized fiction that seeks to engage both the reader's senses and intellect. Don't submit too often to the same market, and don't send manuscripts that you haven't read over carefully. Writers can't rely on spell checkers to catch all errors. Always include a SASE. Read and support the journals you admire so they can continue to survive."

$ CRAZYHORSE

College of Charleston, Dept. of English, 66 George St., Charleston SC 29424. (843)953-7740. E-mail: crazyhorse@cofc.edu. Website: http://crazyhorse.cofc.edu. **Contact:** Anthony Varallo, fiction editor. Literary magazine: 8¾ × 8¼; 150 pages; illustrations; photos. "Crazyhorse publishes writing of fine quality regardless of style, predilection, subject. Editors are especially interested in original writing that engages in the work of honest communication." Raymond Carver called Crazyhorse "an indispensable literary magazine of the first order." Semiannual. Estab. 1961. Circ. 2,000.

• Karen Brown's "Galatea" won a 2008 *Best American Short Stories* inclusion for *Crazyhorse*.

Needs All fiction of fine quality. Receives 200 unsolicited mss/month. Accepts 8-10 mss/issue; 16-20 mss/year. Publishes ms 6-12 months after acceptance. Recently published work by Luke Blanchard, Karen Brown, E. V. Slate, Melanie Rae Thon, Lia Purpura, Carolyn Walker. Length: 25 pages; average length: 15 pages. Publishes short shorts. Also publishes literary essays, poetry.

How to Contact Send SASE for return of ms or disposable copy of ms and #10 SASE for reply only. Responds in 1 week to queries; 3 months to mss. Accepts simultaneous submissions. Sample copy for $5; year subscription for $16. Writer's guidelines for SASE or by e-mail.

Payment/Terms Pays $20 per page and 2 contributor's copies; additional copies $5. Acquires first North American serial rights. Sends galleys to author.

Tips "Write to explore subjects you care about. Clarity of language; subject is one in which something is at stake."

⬚ CUTTHROAT, A JOURNAL OF THE ARTS

P.O. Box 2414, Durango CO 81302. (970) 903-7914. E-mail: cutthroatmag@gmail.com. Website: www.cutthroatmag.com. **Contact:** Beth Alvardo, fiction editor. Literary magazine/journal and "one separate online edition of poetry, translations, short fiction, and book reviews yearly. 6 × 9, 180 + pages, fine cream paper, slick cover. Includes photographs. "We publish only high quality fiction and poetry. We are looking for the cutting edge, the endangered word, fiction with wit, heart, soul and meaning." Annual. Estab. 2005. Member CCLMP.

Needs Ethnic/multicultural, experimental, feminist, humor/satire, literary, mainstream. Does not want romance, horror, historical, fantasy, religious, teen, juvenile. List of upcoming themes available on Web site. Receives 100 + mss/month. Accepts 6 mss/issue; 10-12 mss/year. Does not read from October 1st-March 1st and from June 1st-July 15th. **Publishes 5-8 new writers/year.** Published Michael Schiavone, Rusty Harris, Timothy Rien, Summer Wood, Peter Christopher, Jamey Genna, Doug Frelke, Sally Bellerose, Marc Levy. Length: 500 words (min)-5,000 words (max). Publishes short shorts. Also publishes book reviews. Send review copies to Pamela Uschuk. Sometimes comments on/critiques rejected mss.

How to Contact Send complete ms with cover letter. Accepts submissions by e-mail for online edition and from authors living overseas only. Include estimated word count, brief bio. Responds to queries in 1-2 weeks. Responds to mss in 16-24 weeks. Send either SASE (or IRC) for return of ms or disposable copy of ms and #10 SASE for reply only. Considers simultaneous submissions, multiple submissions. Sample copy available for $10. Guidelines available for SASE, on Web site.

Payment/Terms Writers receive contributor's copies. Additional copies $10. Pays on publication. Acquires first North American serial rights. Sends galleys to author. Publication is copyrighted. "Sponsors the Rick DeMarinis Short Fiction Prize ($1250 first prize). See separate listing and Web site for more information."

Tips "Read our magazine and see what types of stories we've published. The piece must have heart and soul, excellence in craft."

⬚ DISLOCATE

English Department, University of Minnesota, 222 Lind Hall, 207 Church St. SE, Minneapolis MN 55455. E-mail: dislocate.magazine@gmail.com. Website: http://dislocate.org. **Contact:** Shantha Susman. Magazine has revolving editor. Editorial term: 2006-2007. Literary magazine/journal: 5½ × 8½, 128 pages. Annual. Estab. 2005. Circ. 2,000.

Needs Literary fiction. Receives 25-50 mss/month. Accepts 2-3 mss/year. Publishes short shorts. Also publishes literary essays, poetry.

How to Contact Send complete ms with cover letter. Send SASE for reply or return of ms. Considers simultaneous submissions, multiple submissions. Guidelines available on Web site.

Payment/Terms Pays on publication.

Tips "Looking for excellent writing that rearranges the world."

⊠ ◎ $ ⊠ DOWNSTATE STORY

1825 Maple Ridge, Peoria IL 61614. (309)688-1409. Website: www.wiu.edu/users/mfgeh/dss. **Contact:** Elaine Hopkins, editor. Magazine: includes illustrations. "Short fiction—some connection with Illinois or the Midwest." Annual. Estab. 1992. Circ. 250.

 • Fiction received the Best of Illinois Stories Award.

Needs Adventure, ethnic/multicultural, experimental, historical, horror, humor/satire, literary, mainstream, mystery/suspense, psychic/supernatural/occult, regional, romance, science fiction, suspense, western. No porn. Accepts 10 mss/issue. Publishes ms 1 year after acceptance. Publishes short shorts. Also publishes literary essays.

How to Contact Send complete ms with a cover letter. SASE for return of ms. Responds "ASAP" to mss. Accepts simultaneous submissions. Sample copy for $8. Writer's guidelines online.

Payment/Terms Pays $50. Pays on acceptance for first rights.

⊠ ECLIPSE

Glendale College, 1500 N. Verdugo Rd., Glendale CA 91208. (818)240-1000. Fax: (818)549-9436. E-mail: eclipse@glendale.edu. **Contact:** Bart Edelman, editor. Magazine: 8½ × 5½; 150-200 pages; 60 lb. paper. "Eclipse is committed to publishing outstanding fiction and poetry. We look for compelling characters and stories executed in ways that provoke our readers and allow them to understand the world in new ways." Annual. Circ. 1,800. CLMP.

Needs Ethnic/multicultural, experimental, literary. "Does not want horror, religious, science fiction or thriller mss." Receives 50-100 unsolicited mss/month. Accepts 10 mss/year. Publishes ms 6-12 months after acceptance. **Publishes 8 new writers/year.** Recently published work by Amy Sage Webb, Ira Sukrungruang, Richard Schmitt, George Rabasa. Length: 6,000 words; average length: 4,000 words. Publishes short shorts. Also publishes poetry. Sometimes comments on rejected mss.

How to Contact Send complete ms. Responds in 2 weeks to queries; 4-6 weeks to mss. Accepts simultaneous submissions. Sample copy for $8. Writer's guidelines for #10 SASE or by e-mail.

Payment/Terms Pays 2 contributor's copies; additional copies $ 7. Pays on publication for first North American serial rights.

Tips "We look for well crafted fiction, experimental or traditional, with a clear unity of elements. A good story is important, but the writing must transcend the simple act of conveying the story."

⊠ ECOTONE, REIMAGINING PLACE

UNCW Dept. of Creative Writing, 601 South College Road, Wilmington NC 28403-3297. E-mail: info@ ecotonejournal.com. Website: www.ecotonejournal.com. Literary magazine/journal: 6 × 9. "Ecotone is a literary journal of place seeking to publish creative work that illuminates the edges between science and literature, the urban and rural, and the personal and biological." Semiannual. Estab. 2005. Circ. 1,500.

Needs Ethnic/multicultural, experimental, historical, literary, mainstream. Does not want genre (fantasy, horror, sci-fi, etc.) or young adult fiction. Receives 90-100 mss/month. Accepts 5-7 mss/issue; 10-12 mss/year. Does not read mss April 15-August 15. Manuscript published 6-8 months after acceptance. Publishes 5-7 new writers/year. Published Kevin Brockmeier, Michael Branch, Brock Clarke, Daniel Orozco, and Steve Almond and Pattiann Rogers. Length: 2,000 words (min)-6,000 words (max). Average length: 4,500 words. Also publishes literary essays, poetry.

How to Contact Send complete ms with cover letter. Include brief bio, list of publications. Send either SASE (or IRC) for return of ms or disposable copy of ms and #10 SASE for reply only. Considers simultaneous submissions. Sample copy available for $9. Guidelines available for SASE, via e-mail, on Web site.

Payment/Terms Writers receive 2 contributor's copies, and payment subject to available funding. Pays on publication. Acquires first North American serial rights. Sends galleys to author. Publication is copyrighted.

◻ $ ELLIPSIS MAGAZINE

Westminster College of Salt Lake City, 1840 S. 1300 E., Salt Lake City UT 84105. (801)832-2321. Website: www.westminstercollege.edu/ellipsis. **Contact:** Stephanie Peterson (revolving editor; changes every year). Magazine: 6 × 9; 110-120 pages; 60 lb. paper; 15 pt. cover stock; illustrations; photos. Ellipsis Magazine needs good literary poetry, fiction, essays, plays and visual art. Annual. Estab. 1967. Circ. 2,000.

Needs Receives 110 unsolicited mss/month. Accepts 4 mss/issue. Does not read mss November 1-July 31. Publishes ms 3 months after acceptance. **Publishes 2 new writers/year.** Length: 6,000 words; average length: 4,000 words. Also publishes poetry. Rarely comments on rejected mss.

How to Contact Send complete ms. Send SASE (or IRC) for return of ms or send disposable copy of the ms and #10 SASE for reply only. Responds in 6 months to mss. Accepts simultaneous submissions. Sample copy for $7.50. Writer's guidelines online.

Payment/Terms Pays $50 per story and one contributor's copy; additional copies $3.50. Pays on publication for first North American serial rights. Not copyrighted.

Tips "Have friends or mentors read your story first and make suggestions to improve it."

☑ EMRYS JOURNAL

The Emrys Foundation, P.O. Box 8813, Greenville SC 29604. E-mail: lydia.dishman@gmail.com. Website: www.emrys.org. Contact: L.B. Dishman. Catalog: 9 × 9¾; 120 pages; 80 lb. paper. "We publish short fiction, poetry and creative nonfiction. We are particularly interested in hearing from women and other minorities." Annual. Estab. 1984. Circ. 400.

Needs Literary, contemporary. No religious, sexually explicit or science fiction mss. Accepts approx 18 mss/issue. Reading period: August 1-November 1, no ms will be read outside the reading period. Publishes mss in April. **Publishes several new writers/year.** Recently published work by Jessica Goodfellow and Ron Rash. Length: 5,000 words; average length: 3,500 words. Publishes short shorts.

How to Contact Send complete ms with SASE. Responds after end of reading period. Does not accept simultaneous submissions. Accepts multiple submissions. Sample copy for $15 and 7 × 10 SAE with 4 first-class stamps. Writer's guidelines for #10 SASE.

Payment/Terms Pays in contributor's copies. Acquires first rights.

Tips Looks for previously unpublished literary fiction.

☑ $ ☑ EPOCH

Cornell University, 251 Goldwin Smith Hall, Cornell University, Ithaca NY 14853. (607)255-3385. Fax: (607)255-6661. Contact: Joseph Martin, senior editor. Magazine: 6 × 9; 128 pages; good quality paper; good cover stock. "Well-written literary fiction, poetry, personal essays. Newcomers always welcome. Open to mainstream and avant-garde writing." Estab. 1947. Circ. 1,000.

- Work originally appearing in this quality literary journal has appeared in numerous anthologies including *Best American Short Stories, Best American Poetry, Pushcart Prize, The O. Henry Prize Stories, Best of the West* and *New Stories from the South.*

Needs Ethnic/multicultural, experimental, literary, mainstream, novel excerpts, literary short stories. "No genre fiction. Would like to see more Southern fiction (Southern US)." Receives 500 unsolicited mss/month. Accepts 15-20 mss/issue. Does not read in summer (April 15-September 15). Publishes ms an average of 6 months after acceptance. **Publishes 3-4 new writers/year.** Recently published work by Antonya Nelson, Doris Betts, Heidi Jon Schmidt. Also publishes poetry. Sometimes comments on rejected mss.

How to Contact Send complete ms. Responds in 2 weeks to queries; 6 weeks to mss. No simultaneous submissions. Sample copy for $5. Writer's guidelines for #10 SASE.

Payment/Terms Pays $5 and up/printed page. Pays on publication for first North American serial rights.

Tips "Read the journals you're sending work to."

☑ EUREKA LITERARY MAGAZINE

300 E. College Ave., Eureka College, Eureka IL 61530-1500. (309)467-6591. E-mail: elm@eureka.edu. **Contact:** Zeke Jarvis, editor. Magazine: 6 × 9; 120 pages; 70 lb. white offset paper; 80 lb. gloss cover; photographs (occasionally). "We seek to be open to the best stories that are submitted to us. Our

audience is a combination of professors/writers, students of writing and literature, and general readers."
Semiannual. Estab. 1992. Circ. 500.

Needs ethnic/multicultural, experimental, fantasy (science), feminist, historical, humor/satire, literary, mainstream, mystery/suspense (private eye/hard-boiled, romantic), science fiction (soft/sociological), translations. Would like to see more "good literary fiction stories, good magical realism, historical fiction. We try to achieve a balance between the traditional and the experimental. We look for the well-crafted story, but essentially any type of story that has depth and substance to it is welcome." Receives 100 unsolicited mss/month. Accepts 10-12 mss/issue; 20-30 mss/year. Does not accept mss in summer (May-August). **Publishes 5-6 new writers/year.** Recently published work by Jane Guill, Sarah Strickley, Ray Bradbury, Patrick Madden, Virgil Suarez, Cynthia Gallaher, Wendell Mayo, Tom Noyes, and Brian Doyle. Length: 4,000-6,000 words; average length: 5,000 words. Also publishes short shorts, flash fiction and poetry.

How to Contact Accepts submissions by e-mail. Send SASE for reply, return of ms or send disposable copy of ms. Responds in 2 weeks to electronic queries; 4 months to mss. Accepts simultaneous submissions. Sample copy for $7.50.

Tips "Do something that hasn't been done a thousand times already. Give us unusual but believable characters in unusual but believable conflicts—clear resolution isn't always necessary, but it's nice. We don't hold to hard and fast rules about length, but most stories could do with some cutting. Make sure your title is relevant and eye-catching. Please do not send personal gifts or hate mail. We're a college-operated magazine, so we do not actually exist in summer. If we don't take a submission, that doesn't automatically mean we don't like it—we try to encourage authors who show promise to revise and resubmit. Order a copy if you can."

☑ EVANSVILLE REVIEW

University of Evansville, 1800 Lincoln Ave., Evansville IN 47722. (812)488-1042. **Contact:** Fiction editor. Magazine: 6 × 9; 180 pages; 70 lb. white paper; glossy full-color cover; perfect bound. Annual. Estab. 1989. Circ. 1,000.

Needs Does not want erotica, fantasy, experimental or children's fiction. "We're open to all creativity. No discrimination. All fiction, screenplays, nonfiction, poetry, interviews and anything in between." Receives 70 unsolicited mss/month. Does not read mss January-August. Agented fiction 2%. **Publishes 20 new writers/year.** Recently published work by John Updike, Arthur Miller, X.J. Kennedy, Jim Barnes, Rita Dove. Also publishes literary essays, poetry.

How to Contact Send SASE for reply, or send a disposable copy of ms. Responds in 1 month to queries; 3 months to mss. Accepts simultaneous, multiple submissions and reprints. Sample copy for $5. Writer's guidelines free.

Payment/Terms Pays 2 contributor's copies. Pays on publication for one-time rights. Not copyrighted.

Tips "Because editorial staff rolls over every 1-2 years, the journal always has a new flavor."

☑ ◎ FEMINIST STUDIES

0103 Taliaferro, University of Maryland, College Park MD 20742-7726. (301) 405-7415. Fax: (301) 405-8395. E-mail: creative@feministstudies.org. Website: www.feministstudies.org. **Contact:** Minnie Bruce Pratt, creative writing editor. Magazine: journal-sized; about 200 pages; photographs. "We are interested in work that addresses questions of interest to the feminist studies audience, particularly work that pushes past the boundaries of what has been done before. We look for creative work that is intellectually challenging and aesthetically adventurous, that is complicated in dialogue with feminist ideas and concepts, and that shifts our readers into new perspectives on women/gender." Triannual. Estab. 1974. Circ. 7,500.

Needs Ethnic/multicultural, feminist, LGBT, contemporary. Receives 20 unsolicited mss/month. Accepts 2-3 mss/issue. "We review fiction and poetry twice a year. Deadline dates are May 1 and December 1. Authors will recieve notice of the board's decision by July 15 and February 15, respectively." Recently published work by Grace M. Cho, Dawn McDuffie, Susanne Davis, Liz Robbins, Maria Mazziotti Gillan, Cathleen Calbert, and Mary Ann Wehler. Sometimes comments on rejected mss.

How to Contact No simultaneous submissions. Sample copy for $15. Writer's guidelines at Web site.

Payment/Terms Pays 2 contributor's copies and 10 tearsheets.

☑ $ ☑ FICTION

Department of English, The City College of New York, 138th St. & Convent Ave., New York NY 10031. (212) 650-6319. E-mail: fictionmagazine@yahoo.com. Website: www.fictioninc.com. **Contact:** Mark J. Mirsky, editor. Magazine: 6 × 9; 150-250 pages; illustrations; occasionally photos. "As the name implies, we publish only fiction; we are looking for the best new writing available, leaning toward the unconventional. Fiction has traditionally attempted to make accessible the unaccessible, to bring the experimental to a broader audience." Semiannual. Estab. 1972. Circ. 4,000.

• Stories first published in *Fiction* have been selected for inclusion in the *Pushcart Prize*, *Best of the Small Presses* anthologies and more recently *Best American Short Stories*.

Needs Experimental, humor/satire (satire), literary, translations, contemporary. No romance, science fiction, etc. Receives 200 unsolicited mss/month. Accepts 12-20 mss/issue; 24-40 mss/year. Reads mss September 15-April 15. Publishes ms 1 year after acceptance. Agented fiction 10-20%. Recently published work by Joyce Carol Oates, John Barth, Robert Musil, Romulus Linney. Publishes short shorts. Sometimes comments on rejected mss.

How to Contact Send complete ms with cover letter and SASE. No e-mail submissions. Responds in 3 months to mss. Accepts simultaneous submissions. Sample copy for $5. Writer's guidelines online.

Payment/Terms Pays $75 plus subscription. Acquires first rights.

Tips "The guiding principle of *Fiction* has always been to go to terra incognita in the writing of the imagination and to ask that modern fiction set itself serious questions, if often in absurd and comical voices, interrogating the nature of the real and the fantastic. It represents no particular school of fiction, except the innovative. Its pages have often been a harbor for writers at odds with each other. As a result of its willingness to publish the difficult, experimental, unusual, while not excluding the well known, *Fiction* has a unique reputation in the U.S. and abroad as a journal of future directions."

☒ ☑ $ THE FIDDLEHEAD

University of New Brunswick, Campus House, 11 Garland Court, Box 4400, Fredericton NB E3B 5A3 Canada. (506)453-3501. Website: www.lib.und.ca/texts/fiddlehead. **Contact**: Mark A. Jarman, fiction editor. Magazine: 6 × 9; 128-180 pages; ink illustrations; photos. "No criteria for publication except quality. For a general audience, including many poets and writers." Quarterly. Estab. 1945. Circ. 1,200.

Needs Literary. Receives 100-150 unsolicited mss/month. Accepts 4-5 mss/issue; 20-40 mss/year. Publishes ms 1 year after acceptance. Agented fiction: small percentage. **Publishes high percentage of new writers/year.** Recently published work by Maureen Bilerman, Randy DeVita, Julie Paul, and Russell Wangersky. Average length: 3,000 words. Publishes short shorts. Occasionally comments on rejected mss.

How to Contact Send SASE and *Canadian* stamps or IRCs for return of mss. Responds in 6 months to mss. No simultaneous submissions. Sample copy for $15 (US).

Payment/Terms Pays up to $30 (Canadian)/published page and 1 contributor's copy. Pays on publication for first or one-time rights.

Tips "Less than 2% of the material received is published."

☑ FIRST CLASS

P.O. Box 86, Friendship IN 47021. E-mail: christopherm@four-sep.com. Website: www.four-sep.com. **Contact:** Christopher M, editor. Magazine: 4¼ × 11; 48-60 + pages; 24 lb./60 lb. offset paper; craft cover; illustrations; photos. "First Class features short fiction and poetics fr om the cream of the small press and killer unknowns—mingling before your very hungry eyes. I publish plays, too." Biannual. Estab. 1995. Circ. 200-400.

Needs Erotica, literary, science fiction (soft/socialogical), satire, drama. "No religious or traditional poetry, or 'boomer angst'—therapy-driven self loathing." Receives 50-70 unsolicited mss/month. Accepts 4-6 mss/issue; 10-12 mss/year. Publishes ms 1 month after acceptance. **Publishes 10-15 new writers/ year.** Recently published work by Gerald Locklin, John Bennnet, B.Z. Niditch. Length: 5,000-8,000; average length: 2,000-3,000 words. Publishes short shorts. Also publishes poetry. Sometimes comments on rejected mss.

How to Contact Send SASE or send a disposable copy of ms and #10 SASE for reply only. Responds in 3-5 week to queries. Accepts simultaneous submissions and reprints. Sample copy for $6. Writer's guidelines for #10 SASE. Reviews fiction.

Literary Magazines

Payment/Terms Pays 1 contributor's copy; additional copies $5. Acquires one-time rights.

Tips "Don't bore me with puppy dogs and the morose/sappy feeling you have about death. Belt out a good, short, thought-provoking, graphic, uncommon piece."

☑ ◎ FLINT HILLS REVIEW

Dept. of English, Box 4019, Emporia State University, Emporia KS 66801-5087. (620)341-6916. Fax: (620)341-5547. E-mail: krabas@emporia.edu. Website: www.emporia.edu/fhr/. **Contact:** Kevin Rabas, co-editor. Magazine: 9 × 6; 115 pages; 60 lb. paper; glossy cover; illustrations; photos. "FHR seeks work informed by a strong sense of place or region, especially Kansas and the Great Plains region. We seek to provide a publishing venue for writers of the Great Plains and Kansas while also publishing authors whose work evidences a strong sense of place, writing of literary quality, and accomplished use of language and depth of character development." Annual. Estab. 1996. Circ. 300. CLMP.

Needs Ethnic/multicultural, gay, historical, regional (Plains), translations. "No religious, inspirational, children's." Want to see more "writing of literary quality with a strong sense of place." List of upcoming themes online. Receives 5-15 unsolicited mss/month. Accepts 2-5 mss/issue; 2-5 mss/year. Does not read mss April-December. Publishes ms 4 months after acceptance. **Publishes 4 new writers/year.** Recently published work by Kim Stafford, Elizabeth Dodd, Bart Edelman, and Jennifer Henderson. Length: 1 page-5,000; average length: 3,000 words. Publishes short shorts. Also publishes literary essays, literary criticism, poetry.

How to Contact Send a disposable copy of ms and #10 SASE for reply only. Responds in 5 weeks to queries; 6 months to mss. Accepts simultaneous, multiple submissions. Sample copy for $5.50. Writer's guidelines for SASE, by e-mail, fax or on Web site. Reviews fiction.

Payment/Terms Pays 2 contributor's copies; additional copies $5.50. Acquires one-time rights.

Tips "Strong imagery and voice, writing that is informed by place or region, writing of literary quality with depth of character development. Hone the language down to the most literary depiction that is possible in the shortest space that still provides depth of development without excess length."

☑ FLORIDA REVIEW

Dept. of English, University of Central Florida, P.O. Box 161346, Orlando FL 32816-1346. (407) 823-2038. E-mail: flreview@mail.ucf.edu. Website: www.english.ucf.edu/~flreview. **Contact:** Jocelyn Bartkevicius, editor. Magazine: 6 × 9; 185 pages; semi-gloss full color cover, perfect bound. "We publish fiction of high 'literary' quality—stories that delight, instruct and take risks. Our audience consists of avid readers of fiction, poetry and creative nonfiction." Semiannual. Estab. 1972. Circ. 1,500. Needs Experimental, literary. "We aren't particularly interested in genre fiction (sci-fi, romance, adventure, etc.) but a good story can transcend any genre." Receives 500 unsolicited mss/month. Accepts 5-7 mss/issue; 10-14 mss/year. Publishes ms 4 months after acceptance. **Publishes 3-5 new writers/year.** Recently published work by Billy Collins, Kelly Clancy, Denise Duhamel, Tony Hoagland, Baron Wormser, and Farnoosh Moshiri. Length: 2,000-7,000 words; average length: 5,000 words. Publishes short shorts. Also publishes creative nonfiction, poetry. Rarely comments on rejected mss.

How to Contact Send complete ms. Send SASE (or IRC) for return of the ms or send disposable copy of the ms and #10 SASE for reply only. Responds in 2 weeks to queries; 3 months to mss. Accepts simultaneous submissions. Sample copy for $8. Writer's guidelines for #10 SASE or online.

Payment/Terms Rights held by UCF, revert to author after publication.

Tips "We're looking for writers with fresh voices and original stories. We like risk."

☑ FLYWAY

Iowa State University, 206 Ross Hall, Ames IA 50011. (515)294-8273. Fax: (515)294-6814. E-mail: flyway@iastate.edu. Website: www.flyway.org. **Contact:** Stephen Pett, editor. Literary magazine: 6 × 9; 120 pages; quality paper; cover stock; some illustrations; photos. "We publish quality fiction with a particular interest in place as a component of 'story,' or with an 'enviromental' sensibility. Our stories are accompanied by brief commentaries by their authors, the sort of thing a writer might say introducing a piece at a reading." Biannual. Estab. 1995. Circ. 500.

Needs Literary. Receives 50 unsolicited mss/month. Accepts 2-5 mss/issue; 10-12 mss/year. Reads mss September 1-May. Publishes ms 5 months after acceptance. **Publishes 7-10 new writers/year.** Recently published work by Naomi Shihab Nye, Gina Ochsner, Ted Kooser, Michael Martone. Length: 5,000;

average length: 3,500 words. Publishes short shorts. Often comments on rejected mss.

How to Contact Send SASE. Sample copy for $8. Writer's guidelines for SASE.

Payment/Terms Pays 2 contributor's copies; additional copies $6. Acquires one-time rights.

Tips "Quality, originality, voice, drama, tension. Make it as strong as you can."

☐ FOLIATE OAK LITERARY MAGAZINE

University of Arkansas-Monticello, MCB 113, Monticello AR 71656. (870) 460-1247. E-mail: foliateoak@ uamont.edu. Website: www.foliateoak.uamont.edu. **Contact**: Diane Payne, faculty advisor. Magazine: 6 × 9; 80 pages. Monthly. Estab. 1980. Circ. 500.Needs Adventure, comics/graphic novels, ethnic/ multicultural, experimental, family saga, feminist, gay, historical, humor/satire, lesbian, literary, mainstream, science fiction (soft/sociological). No religious, sexist or homophobic work. Receives 80 unsolicited mss/month. Accepts 20 mss/issue; 160 mss/year. Does not read mss May-August. Publishes ms 1 month after acceptance. **Publishes 130 new writers/year.** Recently published work by David Barringer, Thom Didato, Joe Taylor, Molly Giles, Patricia Shevlin, Tony Hoagland. Length: 50-2,500 words; average length: 1,500 words. Publishes short shorts. Also publishes literary essays, literary criticism, poetry. Rarely comments on rejected mss.

How to Contact Send complete ms as an e-mail attachment (Word or RTF). Postal submissions will not be read. Please include author's name and title of story/poem/essay in e-mail header. In the e-mail, please send contact information and a short bio. Responds in 4 weeks. Only accepts submissions August through April. Accepts simultaneous submissions and multiple submissions. Please contact ASAP if work is accepted elsewhere. Sample copy for SASE and 6 × 8 envelope. Writer's guidelines online. Reviews fiction.

Payment/Terms Pays contributor's copy. Acquires electronic rights. Sends galleys to author. Not copyrighted.

Tips "We're open to honest, experimental, offbeat, realistic and surprising writing, if it has been edited. Limit poems to five per submission, and one short story or creative nonfiction (less than 2,500 words. You may send up to three flash fictions. PLease put your flash fiction in one attachment. Please don't send more writing until you hear from us regarding your first submission. We are also looking for art-work sent as.jpg or.gif files."

☑ FOLIO

Doyle, Department of Literature, American University, Washington DC 20016. (202)885-2971. E-mail: folio.editors@gmail.com. Website: www.foliojournal.org. **Contact:** Amina Hafiz. Magazine: about 70 pages; illustrations; photos. "Folio is a journal of poetry, fiction and creative nonfiction. We look for work that ignites and endures, is artful and natural, daring and elegant." Semiannual. Estab. 1984. Circ. 300.

Needs Literary. Does not want anything that is sexually offensive. Receives 50-60 unsolicited mss/ month. Accepts 2-3 mss/issue; 5-8 mss/year. Does not read mss May-August. **Publishes 2-3 new writers/ year.** Length: 3,500 words; average length: 2,500 words. Publishes short shorts. Also publishes poetry. Sometimes comments on rejected mss.

How to Contact Send complete ms. Send a SASE (or IRC) for return of the ms or send a disposable copy of the ms and #10 SASE for reply only. Responds in 3-4 months to mss. Accepts simultaneous, multiple submissions. Sample copy for $6. Writer's guidelines for #10 SASE or online.

Payment/Terms Pays 2 contributor's copies. Pays on publication for first North American serial rights.

Tips "Visit our Web site and/or read the journal to get a sense of *Folio* style."

☑ ☑ FREEFALL MAGAZINE

The Alexandra Writers' Centre Society, 922 Ninth Ave. SE, Calgary AB T2G 0S4 Canada. (403) 264-4730. E-mail: freefallmagazine@yahoo.com. Website: www.freefallmagazine.ca. **Contact:** Micheline Maylor, editor-in-chief; Lynn Fraser, managing editor. Magazine: 8½ × 5¾; 100 pages; bond paper; bond stock; b&w illustrations; photos. "FreeFall features the best of new, emerging writers and gives them the chance to get into print along with established writers. Now in its 18th year, FreeFall seeks to attract readers looking for well-crafted stories, poetry and artwork." Semiannual. Estab. 1990. Circ. 650. Alberta Magazine Publishers Association (AMPA). Canadian Magazines.

Needs Literary fiction, poetry, non-fiction, artwork, photography, and reviews. Accepts 3-5 mss/issue; 6-10 mss/year. Reads July and January. Publishes ms 4-6 months after acceptance. **Publishes 40% new**

writers/year. Length: 500-3,000 words.

How to Contact Send SASE (or IRC) for return of ms, or send a disposable copy of ms with e-mail address or #10 SASE for reply only. Responds in 3 months to mss. Sample copy for $10 (US). Writer's guidelines for SASE, e-mail or on Web site.

Payment/Terms Pays 1 contributor's copy; additional copies $10 (US). Acquires first North American serial, one-time rights.

Tips "We look for thoughtful word usage, craftmanship, strong voice and unique expression coupled with clarity and narrative structure. Professional, clean presentation of work is essential. Carefully read *FreeFall* guidelines before submitting. Do not fold manuscript, and submit 9 × 11 envelope. Include SASE/IRC for reply and/or return of manuscript. You may contact us by e-mail after initial hardcopy submission. For accepted pieces a request is made for disk or e-mail copy. Strong Web presence attracts submissions from writers all over the world."

▣ ☑ FRONT & CENTRE

Black Bile Press, 573 Gainsborough Ave., Ottawa ON K2A 2Y6 Canada. (613) 729-8973. E-mail: firth@istar.ca. Website: www.ardentdreams.com/bbp. **Contact:** Matthew Firth, editor. Magazine: half letter-size; 40-50 pages; illustrations; photos. "We look for new fiction from Canadian and international writers—bold, aggressive work that does not compromise quality." Three issues per year. Estab. 1998. Circ. 500.

Needs Literary ("contemporary realism/gritty urban"). "No science fiction, horror, mainstream, romance or religious." Receives 20 unsolicited mss/month. Accepts 6-7 mss/issue; 10-20 mss/year. Publishes ms 6 months after acceptance. Agented fiction 10%. **Publishes 8-9 new writers/year.** Recently published work by Len Gasparini, Katharine Coldiron, Salvatore Difalco, Gerald Locklin, Amanda Earl, Tom Johns. Length: 50-4,000 words; average length: 2,500 words. Publishes short shorts. Always comments on rejected mss.

How to Contact Send SASE (from Canada) (or IRCs from USA) for return of ms or send a disposable copy of ms with #10 SASE for reply only. Responds in 2 weeks to queries; 4 months to mss. Accepts multiple submissions. Sample copy for $5. Writer's guidelines for SASE or by e-mail. Reviews fiction.

Payment/Terms Acquires first rights. Not copyrighted.

Tips "We look for attention to detail, unique voice, not overtly derivative, bold writing, not pretentious. We should like to see more realism. Read the magazine first—simple as that!"

☑ $ FUGUE

200 Brink Hall, University of Idaho, P.O. Box 441102, Moscow ID 83844-1102. (208)885-6156. Fax: (208)885-5944. E-mail: fugue@uidaho.edu. Website: www.uidaho.edu/fugue. **Contact:** Fiction editor. Magazine: 6 × 9; 175 pages; 70 lb. stock paper. By allowing the voices of established writers to lend their authority to new and emerging writers, Fugue strives to provide its readers with the most compelling stories, poems, essays, interviews and literary criticism possible. Semiannual. Estab. 1990. Circ. 1,400.

• Work published in *Fugue* has won the Pushcart Prize and has been cited in *Best American Essays*.

Needs Ethnic/multicultural, experimental, humor/satire, literary. Receives 80 unsolicited mss/month. Accepts 6-8 mss/issue; 12-15 mss/year. Does not read mss May 1-August 31. Publishes ms 6 months after acceptance. **Publishes 4-6 new writers/year.** Recently published work by Kent Nelson, Marilyn Krysl, Cary Holladay, Padgett Powell, Dean Young, W.S. Merwin, Matthew Vollmer. Publishes short shorts. Also publishes literary essays, literary criticism, poetry. Sometimes comments on rejected mss.

How to Contact Send complete ms. Send SASE (or IRC) for return of the ms or disposable copy of the ms and #10 SASE for reply only. Responds in 3-4 months to mss. Accepts simultaneous submissions. Sample copy for $8. Writer's guidelines for SASE or on Web site.

Payment/Terms Pays $10 minimum and 1 contributor copy as well as a one-year subscription to the magazine; additional copies $5. Pays on publication for first North American serial, electronic rights.

Tips "The best way, of course, to determine what we're looking for is to read the journal. As the name *Fugue* indicates, our goal is to present a wide range of literary perspectives. We like stories that satisfy us both intellectually and emotionally, with fresh language and characters so captivating that they stick with us and invite a second reading. We are also seeking creative literary criticism which illuminates a piece of literature or a specific writer by examining that writer's personal experience."

☑ GARGOYLE

3819 N. 13th St., Arlington VA 22201. (703)525-9296. E-mail: gargoyle@gargoylemagazine.com. Website: www.gargoylemagazine.com. **Contact:** Richard Peabody and Lucinda Ebersole, editors. Literary magazine: 5½ × 8½; 200 pages; illustrations; photos. "Gargoyle Magazine has always been a scallywag magazine, a maverick magazine, a bit too academic for the underground and way too underground for the academics. We are a writer's magazine in that we are read by other writers and have never worried about reaching the masses." Annual. Estab. 1976. Circ. 2,000.

Needs Erotica, ethnic/multicultural, experimental, gay, lesbian, literary, mainstream, translations. "No romance, horror, science fiction." Wants "edgy realism or experimental works. We run both." Wants to see more Canadian, British, Australian and Third World fiction. Receives 50-200 unsolicited mss/month. Accepts 10-15 mss/issue. Accepts submissions during June, July, and Aug. Publishes ms 6-12 months after acceptance. Agented fiction 5%. **Publishes 2-3 new writers/year.** Recently published work by Nin Andrews, Toby Barlow, Nicole Blackman, Myronn Hardy, Nik Houser, Elise Levine, Dora Malech, Mark Maxwell, Holly Prado, Kit Reed, Eleanor Ross Taylor. Length: 30 pages maximum; average length: 5-10 pages. Publishes short shorts. Also publishes literary essays, literary criticism, poetry. Sometimes comments on rejected mss.

How to Contact "We prefer electronic submissions. Please use submission engine online." For snail mail, send SASE for reply, return of ms or send a disposable copy of ms. Responds in 2 weeks to queries; 3 months to mss. Accepts simultaneous submissions. Sample copy for $12.95.

Payment/Terms Pays 1 contributor's copy; additional copies for 12 price. Acquires first North American serial, and first British rights. Sends galleys to author.

Tips "We have to fall in love with a particular fiction."

☐ GEORGETOWN REVIEW

G and R Publishing, Box 227, 400 East College St., Georgetown KY 40324. (502)863-8308. Fax: (502)868-8888. E-mail: gtownreview@georgetowncollege.edu. Website: http://georgetownreview.georgetowncollege.edu. **Contact:** Steven Carter, editor. Literary magazine/journal: 6 × 9, 192 pages, 20 lb. paper, four-color 60 lb. glossy cover. "We publish the best fiction we receive, regardless of theme or genre." Annual. Estab. 1993. Circ. 1,000. Member CLMP.

Needs Ethnic/multicultural (general), experimental, literary. Does not want adventure, children's, fantasy, romance. Receives 100-125 mss/month. Accepts 8-10 mss/issue; 15-20 mss/year. Does not read March 16-August 31. Manuscript published 1 month-2 years after acceptance. Agented fiction 0%. **Publishes 3-4 new writers/year.** Published Andrew Plattner, Sallie Bingham, Alison Stine. Average length: 4,000 words. Publishes short shorts. Average length of short shorts: 500-1,500 words. Also publishes literary essays, poetry. Sometimes comments on/critiques rejected manuscripts.

How to Contact Send complete ms with cover letter. Include brief bio, list of publications. Responds to queries in 1 month. Responds to mss in 1-3 months. Send either SASE (or IRC) for return of ms or disposable copy of ms and #10 SASE for reply only. Considers simultaneous submissions. Sample copy available for $7. Guidelines available on Web site.

Payment/Terms Writers receive 2 contributor's copies, free subscription to the magazine. Additional copies $5. Pays on publication. Acquires first North American serial rights. Publication is copyrighted. "Sponsors annual contest with $1,000 prize. Check Web site for guidelines."

Tips "We look for fiction that is well written and that has a story line that keeps our interest. Don't send a first draft, and even if we don't take your first, second, or third submission, keep trying."

☑ $ ☑ THE GEORGIA REVIEW

The University of Georgia, 012 Gilbert Hall, University of Georgia, Athens GA 30602-9009. (706)542-3481. Fax: (706)542-0047. Website: www.thegeorgiareview.com. **Contact:** Stephen Corey, editor. Journal: 7 × 10; 208 pages (average); 50 lb. woven old-style paper; 80 lb. cover stock; illustrations; photos. "Our readers are educated, inquisitive people who read a lot of work in the areas we feature, so they expect only the best in our pages. All work submitted should show evidence that the writer is at least as well educated and well-read as our readers. Essays should be authoritative but accessible to a range of readers." Quarterly. Estab. 1947. Circ. 4,000.

• Stories first published in *The Georgia Review* have been anthologized in *Best American Short Stories*, *Best American Mystery Stories*, *New Stories from The South* and the *Pushcart Prize Collection*. *The*

Georgia Review won the National Magazine Award in essays in 2007.

Needs "Ordinarily we do not publish novel excerpts or works translated into English, and we strongly discourage authors from submitting these." Receives 300 unsolicited mss/month. Accepts 3-4 mss/issue; 12-15 mss/year. Does not read unsolicited mss May 5-August 15. Publishes ms 6 months after acceptance. **Publishes some new writers/year.** Recently published work by Lee K. Abbot, Kevin Brockmeier, Mary Hood, Joyce Carol Oates, George Singleton. Also publishes literary essays, literary criticism, poetry. Occasionally comments on rejected mss.

How to Contact Send complete ms. Responds in 2 weeks to queries; 2-4 months to mss. No simultaneous submissions. Sample copy for $7. Writer's guidelines online.

Payment/Terms Pays $50/published page. Pays on publication for first North American serial rights. Sends galleys to author.

☑ GERTRUDE

PO Box 83948, Portland OR 97283. **Contact:** Eric Delehoy, editor. Magazine: 5 × 8½; 64-72 pages; perfect bound; 60 lb. paper; glossy card cover; illustrations; photos. Gertrude is a "annual publication featuring the voices and visions of the gay, lesbian, bisexual, transgender and supportive community." Estab. 1999. Circ. 400.

Needs Ethnic/multicultural, feminist, gay, humor/satire, lesbian, literary, mainstream. "No romance, pornography or mystery." Wants more multicultural fiction. "We'd like to publish more humor and positive portrayals of gays—steer away from victim roles, pity." Receives 15-20 unsolicited mss/month. Accepts 4-8 mss/issue; 4-8 mss/year. Publishes ms 1-2 months after acceptance. **Publishes 4-5 new writers/year.** Recently published work by Carol Guess, Demrie Alonzo, Henry Alley and Scott Pomfret. Length: 200-3,000 words; average length: 1,800 words. Publishes short shorts. Also publishes poetry.

How to Contact Send SASE for reply to query and a disposable copy of ms. Responds in 6-9 months to mss. Accepts multiple submissions Simultaneous submissions okay. Sample copy for $5, 6 × 9 SAE and 4 1st class stamps. Writer's guidelines for #10 SASE.

Payment/Terms Pays 1-2 contributor's copies; additional copies $4. Pays on publication. Author retains rights upon publication. Not copyrighted.

Tips "We look for strong characterization, imagery and new, unique ways of writing about universal experiences. Follow the construction of your work until the ending. Many stories start out with zest, then flipper and die. Show us, don't tell us."

☑ $ ☑ THE GETTYSBURG REVIEW

Gettysburg College, Gettysburg PA 17325. (717)337-6770. Fax: (717)337-6775. Website: www.gettysburgreview.com. **Contact:** Peter Stitt, editor. Magazine: 6¼ × 10; 170 pages; acid free paper; full color illustrations. "Our concern is quality. Manuscripts submitted here should be extremely well written." Reading period September-May. Quarterly. Estab. 1988. Circ. 4,000.

- Work appearing in *The Gettysburg Review* has also been included in *Prize Stories: The O. Henry Awards, Pushcart Prize* anthology, *Best American Fiction, New Stories from The South, Harper's,* and elsewhere. It is also the recipient of a Lila Wallace-Reader's Digest grant and NEA grants.

Needs Experimental, historical, humor/satire, literary, mainstream, novel excerpts, regional, serialized novels, contemporary. "We require that fiction be intelligent and esthetically written." Receives 350 unsolicited mss/month. Accepts 15-20 mss/issue; 60-80 mss/year. Publishes ms within 1 year after acceptance. **Publishes 1-5 new writers/year.** Recently published work by Nicholas Montemarano, Victoria Lancelotta, Leslie Pietrzyk, Kyle Minor, Kerry Neville-Bakken, Margot Singer. Length: 2,000-7,000 words; average length: 3,000 words. Publishes short shorts. Also publishes literary essays, literary criticism, poetry. Sometimes comments on rejected mss.

How to Contact Send complete ms with SASE. Responds in 1 month to queries; 3-6 months to mss. Accepts simultaneous submissions. Sample copy for $10. Writer's guidelines online.

Payment/Terms Pays $30/page. Pays on publication for first North American serial rights.

Tips "Reporting time can take more than three months. It is helpful to look at a sample copy of *The Gettysburg Review* to see what kinds of fiction we publish before submitting."

☑ GINOSKO

P.O. Box 246, Fairfax CA 94978. Website: www.GinoskoLiteraryJournal.com. Ghin-oce-koe: to perceive, understand, come to know; knowledge that has an inception, an attainment; the recognition of truth by personal experience. Published semiannually. Selects material from ezine for printed anthology. Estab. 2003. Circ. 4,000 + . Web site traffic has 750-1,000 hits/month.

Needs Short fiction, poetry, creative non-fiction interviews, and excerpts. Receives 80-100 unsolicited mss/month. **Publishes 4 new writers/year.** Selects work from ezine for printed anthology.

How to Contact Send complete ms. Accepts submissions by e-mail (ginoskoeditor@aol.com) and snail mail. Responds in 1-3 months to mss. Accepts simultaneous and reprints submissions.

Payment/Terms Copyright reverts to author.

Tips "Check downloadable issues on Web site for style and tone: use latest version of Adobe Reader."

☑ $ ☑ GLIMMER TRAIN STORIES

Glimmer Train Press, Inc., 1211 NW Glisan St. #207, Portland OR 97209. (503) 221-0836. Fax: (503) 221-0837. E-mail: eds@glimmertrain.org. Website: www.glimmertrain.org. **Contact:** Susan Burmeister-Brown and Linda B. Swanson-Davies. Magazine: 225 pages; recycled; acid-free paper; 12 photographs. "We are interested in literary short stories published by new and established writers." Quarterly. Estab. 1991. Circ. 16,000.

• The magazine also sponsors a short story contest for new writers, a very short fiction (under 3,000 words) contest and a family-themed contest.

Needs Literary. Receives 4,000 unsolicited mss/month. Accepts 10 mss/issue; 40 mss/year. Publishes ms up to 18 months after acceptance. Agented fiction 5%. **Publishes 20 new writers/year.** Recently published work by Charles Baxter, Thisbe Nissen, Herman Carrillo, Andre Dubus III, William Trevor, Patricia Henley, Alberto Rios, Ann Beattie. Sometimes comments on rejected mss.

How to Contact Submit work online at www.glimmertrain.org. Different submission categories are open each month of the year. Accepted work published in *Glimmer Train Stories.* Responds in 2 months to mss. Accepts simultaneous submissions. Sample copy for $12 on Web site. Writer's guidelines online.

Payment/Terms Pays $700 for standard submissions, up to $2,000 for contest winning stories. Pays on acceptance for first rights.

Tips "We are very open to the work of new writers. Of the 100 Distinguished Short Stories listed in the current edition of Best American Short Stories, 10 first appeared in Glimmer Train Stories, more than in any other publication, including the New Yorker. Three of those 10 were the author's first publication."

☑ GRASSLIMB

Grasslimb, P.O. Box 420816, San Diego CA 92142. E-mail: editor@grasslimb.com. Website: www. grasslimb.com. **Contact:** Valerie Polichar, editor. Magazine: 14 × 20; 8 pages; 60 lb. white paper; illustrations. "Grasslimb publishes literary prose, poetry and art. Fiction is best when it is short and avant-garde or otherwise experimental." Semiannual. Estab. 2002. Circ. 200.

Needs Ethnic/multicultural, experimental, gay, literary, mystery/suspense (crime), regional, thriller/espionage, translations. Does not want romance or religious writings. Accepts 2-4 mss/issue; 4-8 mss/year. Publishes ms 3-6 months after acceptance. **Publishes 4 new writers/year.** Recently published work by Kuzhali Manickvel, David Yost, Sandra Maddux-Creech. Length: 500-2,000 words; average length: 1,500 words. Publishes short shorts. Also publishes poetry. Rarely comments on rejected mss.

How to Contact Send complete ms. Send SASE for return of ms or disposable copy of ms and #10 SASE for reply only. Responds in 4 months to mss. Accepts simultaneous and reprints, multiple submissions. Sample copy for $2.50. Writer's guidelines for SASE, e-mail or on Web site. Reviews fiction.

Payment/Terms Writers receive $5 minimum; $50 maximum, and 2 contributor's copies; additional copies $3. Pays on acceptance for first print publication serial rights.

Tips "We publish brief fiction work that can be read in a single sitting over a cup of coffee. Work can be serious or light, but is generally 'literary' in nature, rather than mainstream. Experimental work welcome. Remember to have your work proofread and to send short work. We cannot read over 2,500 and prefer under 2,000 words. Include word count."

☑ ☑ GREEN MOUNTAINS REVIEW

Johnson State College, Johnson VT 05656. (802) 635-1350. E-mail: gmr@jsc.vsc.edu. Website: http://greenmountainsreview.jsc.vsc.edu. **Contact:** Leslie Daniels, fiction editor. Magazine: digest-sized; 160-200 pages. Semiannual. Estab. 1975. Circ. 1,700.

• *Green Mountains Review* has received a Pushcart Prize and Editor's Choice Award.

Needs Adventure, experimental, humor/satire, literary, mainstream, serialized novels, translations. Receives 100 unsolicited mss/month. Accepts 6 mss/issue; 12 mss/year. "Manuscripts received between March 1 and September 1 will not be read and will be returned." Publishes ms 6-12 months after acceptance. **Publishes 0-4 new writers/year.** Recently published work by Tracy Daugherty, Terese Svoboda, Walter Wetherell, T.M. McNally, J. Robert Lennon, Louis B. Jones, and Tom Whalen. Publishes short shorts. Also publishes literary criticism, poetry. Sometimes comments on rejected mss.

How to Contact Send complete ms and SASE. Responds in 1 month to queries; 6 months to mss. Accepts simultaneous submissions if advised. Sample copy for $7.

Payment/Terms Pays contributor's copies, 1-year subscription and small honorarium, depending on grants. Acquires first North American serial rights. Rights revert to author upon request.

☑ ☑ THE GREENSBORO REVIEW

3302 Moore Humanities and Research Administration, UNC Greensboro, P.O. Box 26170, Greensboro NC 27402-6170. (336) 334-5459. E-mail: anseay@uncg.edu. Website: www.greensbororeview.org. **Contact:** Jim Clark, editor. Magazine: 6 × 9; approximately 128 pages; 60 lb. paper; 80 lb. cover. Literary magazine featuring fiction and poetry for readers interested in contemporary literature. Semiannual. Circ. 800.

• Stories for *The Greensboro Review* have been included in *Best American Short Stories, The O. Henry Awards Prize Stories, New Stories from The South,* and *Pushcart Prize.*

Needs Accepts 6-8 mss/issue; 12-16 mss/year. Unsolicited manuscripts must arrive by September 15 to be considered for the spring issue and by February 15 to be considered for the fall issue. Manuscripts arriving after those dates may be held for the next consideration. **Publishes 10% new writers/year.** Recently published work by Robert Morgan, George Singleton, Robert Olmstead, Natasha Trethewey, Claudia Emerson, Dale Ray Phillips, Linda Gregg.

How to Contact Responds in 4 months to mss. Accepts multiple submissions. No simultaneous submissions. Sample copy for $5.

Payment/Terms Pays in contributor's copies. Acquires first North American serial rights.

Tips "We want to see the best being written regardless of theme, subject or style."

THE GRIFFIN

Gwynedd-Mercy College, P.O. Box 901, 1325 Sumneytown Pike, Gwynedd Valley PA 19437-0901. (215)646-7300, ext. 256. Fax: (215)641-5517. E-mail: allego.d@gmc.edu. **Contact:** Donna Allego, editor. Literary magazine: 8½ × 5½; 112 pages. "The Griffin is a literary journal sponsored by Gwynedd-Mercy College. Its mission is to enrich society by nurturing and promoting creative writing that demonstrates a unique and intelligent voice. We seek writing which accurately reflects the human condition with all its intellectual, emotional and ethical challenges." Annual. Estab. 1999. Circ. 500.

Needs Short stories, essays and poetry. Open to genre work. "No slasher, graphic violence or sex." Accepts mss depending on the quality of work submitted. Receives 20-30 unsolicited mss/month. Publishes ms 6-9 months after acceptance. **Publishes 10-15 new writers/year.** Length: 2,500 words; average length: 2,000 words. Publishes short shorts. Also publishes literary essays, poetry.

How to Contact Send complete ms. All submissions must be on disk and include a hard copy. Send disposable copy of ms, disk and #10 SASE for reply only. Responds in 2-3 months to queries; 6 months to mss. Accepts simultaneous submissions "if notified." Sample copy for $8.

Payment/Terms Pays 2 contributor's copies; additional copies for $8.

Tips "Looking for well-constructed works that explore universal qualities, respect for the individual and community, justice and integrity. Check our description and criteria. Rewrite until you're sure every word counts. We publish the best work we find regardless of industry needs."

GUD MAGAZINE

Greatest Uncommon Denominator Publishing, P.O. Box 1537, Laconia CA 03247. (603)397-3843. E-mail: editor@gudmagazine.com. Website: www.gudmagazine.com. **Contact:** Kaolin Fire, founding editor. Literary magazine/journal. "GUD Magazine transcends and encompasses the audiences of both genre and literary fiction. Published twice a year in an attractive 5" × 8" perfect bound, 200 + page format, GUD features fiction (from flash to 15,000 word stories), art, poetry, essays, comics, reports and short drama. See Web site for more." Estab. 2006.

Needs Adventure, erotica, ethnic/multicultural, experimental, fantasy, horror, humor/satire, literary, science fiction, alternate history, mystery, why. Accepts 40 mss/year. Manuscript published 6 months after acceptance. Length: 15,000 words (max).

How to Contact Submit via online form only. Responds to mss in up to 6 months. Considers simultaneous submissions, previously published submissions, and multiple submissions (art and poetry only). Guidelines available on Web site.

Tips "Be warned: We read a lot. We've seen it all before. We are not easy to impress. Is your work original? Does it have something to say? Read it again. If you genuinely believe it to be so, send it. But first read the guidelines."

☑ $ ☑ GULF COAST

Dept. of English, University of Houston, Houston TX 77204-3013. (713)743-3223. Fax: (713)743-3229. Website: www.gulfcoast mag.org. **Contact:** Casey Fleming, David MacLean, Oindrila Murherdee, fiction editors. Magazine: 7 × 9; approx. 300 pages; stock paper, gloss cover; illustrations; photos. "Innovative fiction for the literary-minded." Estab. 1987. Circ. 2,300.

• Work published in Gulf Coast has been selected for inclusion in the *Pushcart Prize* anthology, *The O'Henry Prize Stories* anthology and *Best American Short Stories*.

Needs Ethnic/multicultural, experimental, literary, regional, translations, contemporary. "No children's, genre, religious/inspirational." Wants more "cutting-edge, experimental" fiction. Receives 300 unsolicited mss/month. Accepts 4-8 mss/issue; 12-16 mss/year. Publishes ms 6 months-1 year after acceptance. Agented fiction 5%. **Publishes 2-8 new writers/year.** Recently published work by Justin Cronin, Cary Holladay, Holiday Reinhorn, Michael Martone, Joe Meno, Karen An-hwei Lee. Publishes short shorts. Sometimes comments on rejected mss.

How to Contact Responds in 6 months to mss. Accepts simultaneous submissions. Back issue for $7, 7 × 10 SASE with 4 first-class stamps. Writer's guidelines for #10 SASE or on Web site.

Payment/Terms Pays $50-100. Acquires one-time rights.

Tips "Rotating editorship, so please be patient with replies. As always, please send one story at a time."

☑ GULF STREAM MAGAZINE

Florida International University, English Dept., Biscayne Bay Campus, 3000 N.E. 151st St., N. Miami FL 33181-3000. (305)919-5599. E-mail: gulfstreamfiu@yahoo.com. **Contact:** Corey Ginsberg, editor. Magazine: 5½ × 8½; 124 pages; recycled paper; 80 lb. glossy cover; cover illustrations. "We publish good quality —fiction, nonfiction and poetry for a predominately literary market." Semiannual. Estab. 1989. Circ. 300.

Needs Literary, mainstream, contemporary. Does not want romance, historical, juvenile or religious work. Receives 250 unsolicited mss/month. Accepts 5 mss/issue; 10 mss/year. Does not read mss during the summer. Publishes ms 3-6 months after acceptance. **Publishes 2-5 new writers/year.** Recently published work by Leonard Nash, Jesse Millner, Lyn Millner, Peter Meinke, Susan Neville. Length: 7,500 words; average length: 5,000 words. Publishes short shorts. Also publishes poetry.

How to Contact Responds in 6 months to mss. Accepts simultaneous submissions "if noted." Sample copy for $5. Writer's guidelines for #10 SASE.

Payment/Terms Pays in gift subscriptions and contributor's copies. Acquires first North American serial rights.

Tips "Looks for fresh, original writing—well plotted stories with unforgettable characters, fresh poetry and experimental writing. Usually longer stories do not get accepted. There are exceptions, however."

☒ ☑ HAPA NUI: READER-DRIVEN CONTENT

967 Garden Street, East Palo Alto CA 94303. E-mail: editors@hapanui.com. Website: www.hapanui.com. **Contact:** Julianne Bonnet, editor. Print and online literary magazine/journal. Size: 4.25 × 5.5, 200 pages. Contains illustrations. Includes photographs. "In Hawaiian, 'hapa nui' means majority or large part. The concept of the reader-driven lit mag is at the heart of what we see as a new movement in literature. One part on-line venue and one part print journal, Hapa Nui is a placce where readers determine through a democratic voting process what they like and, ultimately, which work makes it into print. Submit your work or just come back and vote to participate in this new literary revolution." Annual. Estab. 2008.

Circ. 250. Member CLMP.

Needs Ethnic/multicultural (general), experimental, family saga, feminist, gay, historical (general), humor/satire, lesbian, literary, mainstream, mystery. Does not want space fantasy, sword and sorcery, religious, overly spiritual or children's/juvenile. Receives 100 mss/month. Accepts up to 52 mss/year. Ms published 1-12 months after acceptance. **Publishes 37% new writers/year.** Published Joyce Nower, Changming Yuan and Rob Carney. Length: 2,500 words (max). Average length: 1,500 words. Publishes short shorts. Average length of short shorts: 250 words. Also publishes literary essays, poetry. Sometimes comments on/critiques rejected mss.

How to Contact Send complete ms with cover letter by e-mail. Include estimated word count, brief bio. Responds to mss in 12 weeks. Considers previously published submissions, multiple submissions. Sample copy available for $5. Guidelines available on Web site.

Payment/Terms Writers receive 2 contributer's copies. Additional copies $5. Pays on publication. Acquires first North American serial rights, anthology rights. Sends galleys to author. Publication is copyrighted.

Tips "The first paragraph really needs to pull the reader in. The ending has to support a conclusion to everything leading up to that point. We tend to look for work that really speaks to the human struggle-no matter what the circumstances or surroundings. Read the publication or visit the Web site often to get a idea for editorial preferences."

☑ $ HAPPY

46 St. Paul's Avenue, Jersey City, NJ 07306. E-mail: bayardx@gmail.com. Contact: Bayard, fiction editor. Magazine: 6X8 inches; 150-200 pages; 60 lb. text paper; 150 lb.cover; perfect-bound; illustrations; photos. "Frequency depends on quality and quantity of submissions. Erratic at the moment." Estab. 1995. Circ. 500.

Needs Erotica, ethnic/multicultural, experimental, fantasy, feminist, gay, horror, humor/satire, lesbian, literary, novel excerpts, psychic/supernatural/occult, science fiction, short stories. No "television rehash or religious nonsense." Wants more work that is "strong, angry, empowering, intelligent, God-like, expressive." Receives 300-500 unsolicited mss/month. Accepts 30-40 mss/issue; 100-150 mss/year. Publishes ms 6-12 months after acceptance. **Publishes 25-30 new writers/year.** Length: 6,000 words maximum; average length: 1,000-3,500 words. Publishes short shorts. Often comments on rejected mss.

How to Contact Send complete ms. Include estimated word count. Send SASE for reply, return of ms or send a disposable copy of ms. Responds in 1 month to queries. Accepts simultaneous submissions. Sample copy for $20. Writer's guidelines for #10 SASE.

Payment/Terms Pays minimum $25 per story, more funds permitting. Pays on publication for one time rights.

Tips "Original, evocative, well-written, and new!"

☑ HARPUR PALATE

English Department, P.O. Box 6000, Binghamton University, Binghamton NY 13902-6000. E-mail: harpur. palate@gmail.com. Website: http://harpurpalate.binghamton.edu. **Contact:** Kim Vose, Barrett Bowlin, editor. Magazine: 6 × 9; 180-200 pages; coated or uncoated paper; 100 lb. coated cover; 4-color art portfolio insert. "We have no restrictions on subject matter or form. Quite simply, send us your highest-quality prose or poetry." Semiannual. Estab. 2000. Circ. 800.

Needs Adventure, ethnic/multicultural, experimental, historical, humor/satire, mainstream, mystery/suspense, novel excerpts, literary, fabulism, magical realism, metafiction, slipstream. Receives 400 unsolicited mss/month. Accepts 5-10 mss/issue; 12-20 mss/year. Publishes ms 1-2 months after acceptance. **Publishes 5 new writers/year.** Recently published work by Lee K. Abbott, Jaimee Wriston Colbert, Joan Connor, Stephen Corey, Viet Dinh, Andrew Farkas, Timothy Liu, Mary Ann Mohanraj, Maura Stanton, Michael Steinberg, Martha Witt. Length: 250-8,000 words; average length: 2,000-4,000 words. Publishes short shorts. Also publishes poetry. Sometimes comments on rejected mss.

How to Contact Send complete ms with a cover letter. Include e-mail address on cover. Include estimated word count, brief bio, list of publications. Send a disposable copy of ms and #10 SASE for reply only. Responds in 1-3 week to queries; 4- 8 months to mss. Accepts simultaneous submissions if stated in the cover letter. Sample copy for $10. Writer's guidelines online.

Payment/Terms Pays 2 copies. Pays on publication for first North American serial, electronic rights. Sponsors awards/contests.

Tips "*Harpur Palate* accepts submissions between July 15 and November 15 for the winter issue, between December 15 and April 15 for the summer issue. *Harpur Palate* sponsors a fiction contest for the summer issue and a poetry contest for the winter issue. We do not accept submissions via e-mail. Almost every literary magazine already says this, but it bears repeating: Look at a recent copy of our publication to get an idea of the kind of writing published."

⚉ HARVARD REVIEW

Harvard University, Lamont Library, Cambridge MA 02138. (617)495-9775. E-mail: harvrev@fas.harvard. edu. Website: http://hcl.harvard.edu/harvardreview. **Contact:** Christina Thompson, editor. Magazine: 6 × 9; 256-272 pages; b&w illustrations; photographs. Semiannual. Estab. 1992. Circ. 2,000.

Needs Literary. Receives 200 unsolicited mss/month. Accepts 4 mss/issue; 8 mss/year. Publishes ms 3-6 months after acceptance. **Publishes 3-4 new writers/year.** Recently published work by Joyce Carol Oates, Alice Hoffman, William Lychack, Jim Crace, and Karen Bender. Length: 1,000-7,000 words; average length: 3,000-5,000 words. Publishes short shorts. Also publishes literary essays, literary criticism, poetry, and plays. Sometimes comments on rejected mss.

How to Contact Send SASE for return of ms or disposable copy of ms and SASE for reply only. Responds within 6 months to queries. Accepts simultaneous submissions. Writer's guidelines online.

Payment/Terms Pays 2 contributor's copies; additional copies $7. Pays on publication for first North American serial rights. Sends galleys to author.

⚉ HAWAI'I PACIFIC REVIEW

Hawai'i Pacific University, 1060 Bishop St., Honolulu HI 96813. (808) 544-1108. Fax: (808) 544-0862. E-mail: pwilson@hpu.edu. Website: www.hpu.edu. **Contact:** Patrice M. Wilson, editor. Magazine: 6 × 9; 100 pages; glossy coated cover. "Hawai'i Pacific Review is looking for poetry, short fiction and personal essays that speak with a powerful and unique voice. We encourage experimental narrative techniques and poetic styles, and we welcome works in translation." Annual.

Needs Ethnic/multicultural (general), experimental, fantasy, feminist, historical (general), humor/satire, literary, mainstream, regional (Pacific), translations. "Open to all types as long as they're well done. Our audience is adults, so nothing for children/teens." Receives 30-50 unsolicited mss/month. Accepts 5-10 mss/year. Reads mss September- December each year. Publishes ms 10 months after acceptance. **Publishes 2-4 new writers/year.** Recently published work by Wendell Mayo, Elizabeth Crowell, Janet Flora, Mary Ann Cain, and Jean Giovanetti. Publishes short shorts. Also publishes literary essays, poetry. Sometimes comments on rejected mss.

How to Contact Send SASE for return of ms or send a disposable copy of ms and SASE for reply only. Responds in 2 weeks to queries; 15 weeks to mss. Accepts simultaneous submissions but must be cited in the cover letter. Sample copy for $5.

Payment/Terms Pays 2 contributor's copies; additional copies $5. Pays on publication for first North American serial rights.

Tips "We look for the unusual or original plot; prose with the texture and nuance of poetry. Character development or portrayal must be unusual/original; humanity shown in an original insightful way (or characters); sense of humor where applicable. Be sure it's a draft that has gone through substantial changes, with supervision from a more experienced writer, if you're a beginner. Write about intense emotion and feeling, not just about someone's divorce or shaky relationship. No soap-opera-like fiction."

⚉ ⚉ HAYDEN'S FERRY REVIEW

The Virginia G. Piper Center for Creative Writing at Arizona State University, Box 875002, Arizona State University, Tempe AZ 85287-5002. (480) 965-1337. E-mail: hfr@asu.edu. Website: www. haydensferryreview.org. **Contact:** Beth Staples. Editors change every 1-2 years. Magazine: 6¾ × 9¾; 150 pages; fine paper; illustrations; photos. "Hayden's Ferry Review publishes best quality fiction, poetry, translations, and creative nonfiction from new, emerging and established writers." Semiannual. Estab. 1986. Circ. 1,300.

- Work from *Hayden's Ferry Review* has been selected for inclusion in *Pushcart Prize* anthologies and *Best Creative Nonfiction.*

Needs Ethnic/multicultural, experimental, humor/satire, literary, regional, slice-of-life vignettes, contemporary, prose poem. Possible special issue. Receives 250 unsolicited mss/month. Accepts 5 mss/issue; 10 mss/year. Publishes ms 6 months after acceptance. Recently published work by Joseph Heller, Ron Carlson, Norman Dubie, John Updike, Richard Ford, Yusef Komunyakaa, Joel-Peter Witkin, Ai, David St. John, Gloria Naylor, Tess Gallagher, Ken Kesey, Naomi Shihab Nye, Allen Ginsberg, T.C. Boyle, Raymond Carver, Rita Dove, Chuck Rosenthal, Rick Bass, Charles Baxter, Pam Houston, and Denise Duhamel. Publishes short shorts. Also publishes literary criticism.
How to Contact Send complete ms. SASE. Responds in 2 weeks to queries; 5 months to mss. Accepts simultaneous submissions. Sample copy for $7.50. Writer's guidelines online.
Payment/Terms Pays $25-100. Pays on publication for first North American serial rights. Sends galleys to author.

☑ ☑ HOME PLANET NEWS

Home Planet Publications, P.O. Box 455, High Falls NY 12440. (845)687-4084. **Contact:** Donald Lev, editor. Tabloid: 11½ × 16; 24 pages; newsprint; illustrations; photos. "Home Planet News publishes mainly poetry along with some fiction, as well as reviews (books, theater and art) and articles of literary interest. We see HPN as a quality literary journal in an eminently readable format and with content that is urban, urbane and politically aware." Triannual. Estab. 1979. Circ. 1,000.

• *HPN* has received a small grant from the Puffin Foundation for its focus on AIDS issues.
Needs Ethnic/multicultural, experimental, feminist, gay, historical, lesbian, literary, mainstream, science fiction (soft/sociological). No "children's or genre stories (except rarely some science fiction)." Publishes special fiction issue or anthology. Receives 12 unsolicited mss/month. Accepts 1 mss/issue; 3 mss/year. Publishes ms 1 year after acceptance. Recently published work by Hugh Fox, Walter Jackman, Jim Story. Length: 500-2,500 words; average length: 2,000 words. Publishes short shorts. Also publishes literary criticism.
How to Contact Send complete ms. Send SASE for reply, return of ms or send a disposable copy of the ms. Responds in 6 months to mss. Sample copy for $4. Writer's guidelines for SASE.
Payment/Terms Pays 3 contributor's copies; additional copies $1. Acquires one-time rights.
Tips "We use very little fiction, and a story we accept just has to grab us. We need short pieces of some complexity, stories about complex people facing situations which resist simple resolutions."

☑ $ ICONOCLAST

1675 Amazon Rd., Mohegan Lake NY 10547-1804. **Contact:** Phil Wagner, editor. Magazine: 8 × 10½; 80-96 pages; 20 lb. white paper; 50 lb. cover stock; illustrations. "Aimed for a literate general audience with interests in fine (but accessible) fiction and poetry." Bimonthly. Estab. 1992. Circ. 700.
Needs Adventure, ethnic/multicultural, experimental, humor/satire, literary, mainstream, novel excerpts, science fiction, literary. No character studies, slice-of-life, pieces strong on attitude/weak on plot. Receives 150 unsolicited mss/month. Accepts 3-6 mss/issue; 25-30 mss/year. Publishes ms 9-12 months after acceptance. **Publishes 8-10 new writers/year.** Publishes short shorts. Also publishes literary essays, poetry. Sometimes comments on rejected mss.
How to Contact Send complete ms. Send SASE for reply, return of ms or send a disposable copy of the ms labeled as such. Responds in 2 weeks to queries; 5 weeks to mss. No simultaneous submissions. Sample copy for $5. Writer's guidelines for #10 SASE. Reviews fiction.
Payment/Terms Pays 1¢/word. Pays on publication for first North American serial rights.
Tips "We like fiction that has something to say (and not about its author). We hope for work that is observant, intense and multi-leveled. Follow Pound's advice—'make it new.' Write what you want in whatever style you want without being gross, sensational or needlessly explicit—then pray there's someone who can appreciate your sensibility. Read good fiction. It's as fundamental as learning how to hit, throw and catch is to baseball. With the increasing American disinclination towards literature, stories must insist on being heard. Read what is being published—then write something better—and different. Do all rewrites before sending a story out. Few editors have time to work with writers on promising stories; only polished ones."

☑ $ ☑ THE IDAHO REVIEW

Boise State University, English Dept., 1910 University Dr., Boise ID 83725. (208)426-1002. Fax: (208)426-

4373. E-mail: mwieland@boisestate.edu. **Contact:** Mitch Wieland, editor. Magazine: 6 × 9; 180-200 pages; acid-free accent opaque paper; coated cover stock; photos. "A literary journal for anyone who enjoys good fiction." Annual. Estab. 1998. Circ. 1,000. Member CLMP.

   • Recent stories reprinted in *The Best American Short Stories, The O. Henry Prize Stories, The Pushcart Prize*, and *New Stories from The South*.

Needs Experimental, literary. "No genre fiction of any type." Receives 150 unsolicited mss/month. Accepts 5-7 mss/issue; 5-7 mss/year. "We do not read from May 1-August 31." Publishes ms 1 year after acceptance. Agented fiction 5%. **Publishes 1 new writers/year.** Recently published work by Rick Bass, Melanie Rae Thon, Ron Carlson, Joy Williams, Madison Smartt Bell, Carolyn Cooke. Length: open; average length: 7,000 words. Publishes short shorts. Also publishes literary essays, poetry. Sometimes comments on rejected mss.

How to Contact Send SASE for return of ms or send a disposable copy of ms and #10 SASE for reply only. Responds in 3-5 months to mss. Accepts simultaneous, multiple submissions. Sample copy for $8.95. Writer's guidelines for SASE. Reviews fiction.

Payment/Terms Pays $100 when funds are available plus 2 contributor's copies; additional copies $5. Pays on publication for first North American serial rights. Sends galleys to author.

Tips "We look for strongly crafted work that tells a story that needs to be told. We demand vision and intlligence and mystery in the fiction we publish."

☑ ILLUMINATIONS

Dept. of English, College of Charleston, 66 George St., Charleston SC 29424-0001. (843)953-1920. Fax: (843)953-1924. E-mail: lewiss@cofc.edu. Website: www.cofc.edu/illuminations. **Contact:** Simon Lewis, editor. Magazine: 5 × 8; 80 pages; illustrations. "Illuminations is one of the most challengingly eclectic little literary magazines around, having featured writers from the United States, Britain and Romania, as well as Southern Africa." Annual. Estab. 1982. Circ. 500.

Needs Literary. Receives 5 unsolicited mss/month. Accepts 1 mss/year. **Publishes 1 new writer/year.** Recently published work by John Michael Cummings. Also publishes poetry. Sometimes comments on rejected mss.

How to Contact Send SASE for reply, return of ms or send a disposable copy of ms. Responds in 2 weeks to queries; 2 months to mss. No simultaneous submissions. Sample copy for $10 and 6 × 9 envelope. Writer's guidelines free.

Payment/Terms Pays 2 contributor's copies of current issue; 1 of subsequent issue. Acquires one-time rights.

☑ ◎ $ IMAGE

3307 Third Ave. W, Seattle WA 98119. (206) 281-2988. E-mail: gwolfe@imagejournal.org. Website: www.imagejournal.org. **Contact:** Gregory Wolfe. Magazine: 7 × 10; 136 pages; glossy cover stock; illustrations; photos. "Image is a showcase for the encounter between religious faith and world-class contemporary art. Each issue features fiction, poetry, essays, memoirs, an in-depth interview and articles about visual artists, film, music, etc. and glossy 4-color plates of contemporary visual art." Quarterly. Estab. 1989. Circ. 4,500. Member CLMP.

Needs Literary, translations. Receives 100 unsolicited mss/month. Accepts 2 mss/issue; 8 mss/year. Publishes ms 1 year after acceptance. Agented fiction 5%. Recently published work by Annie Dillard, David James Duncan, Robert Olen Butler, Bret Lott, Melanie Rae Thon. Length: 4,000-6,000 words; average length: 5,000 words. Also publishes literary essays, poetry.

How to Contact Send SASE for reply, return of ms or send disposable copy of ms. Responds in 1 month to queries; 3 months to mss. Sample copy for $16. Reviews fiction.

Payment/Terms Pays $10/page and 4 contributor's copies; additional copies for $6. Pays on acceptance. Sends galleys to author.

Tips "Fiction must grapple with religious faith, though the settings and subjects need not be overtly religious."

☑ $ ☑ INDIANA REVIEW

Indiana University, Ballantine Hall 465, 1020 E. Kirkwood, Bloomington IN 47405-7103. (812)855-3439. Website: www.indianareview.org. **Contact**: Fiction editor. Magazine: 6 × 9; 160 pages; 50 lb. paper;

Glatfelter cover stock. "Indiana Review, a nonprofit organization run by IU graduate students, is a journal of previously unpublished poetry and fiction. Literary interviews and essays also considered. We publish innovative fiction and poetry. We're interested in energy, originality and careful attention to craft. While we publish many well-known writers, we also welcome new and emerging poets and fiction writers." Semiannual. Estab. 1976. Circ. 2,000.

- Work published in *Indiana Review* received a Pushcart Prize (2001) and was included in *Best New American Voices* (2001). *IR* also received an Indiana Arts Council Grant and a NEA grant.

Needs Ethnic/multicultural, experimental, literary, mainstream, novel excerpts, regional, translations. No genre fiction. Receives 300 unsolicited mss/month. Accepts 7-9 mss/issue. Reads year round, but refer to web site for closed submission periods. Publishes ms an average of 3-6 months after acceptance. **Publishes 6-8 new writers/year.** Recently published work by Kim Addonizio, Stuart Dybek, Marilyn Chin, Ray Gonzalez, Abby Frucht. Also publishes literary essays, poetry.

How to Contact Send complete ms. Accepts online submissions. Cover letters should be *brief* and demonstrate specific familiarity with the content of a recent issue of *Indiana Review*. Include SASE. Responds in 4 months to mss. Accepts simultaneous submissions if notified *immediately* of other publication. Sample copy for $9. Writer's guidelines online.

Payment/Terms Pays $5/page, plus 2 contributor's copies. Pays on publication for first North American serial rights. Sponsors awards/contests.

Tips "Because our editors change each year, so do our literary preferences. It's important that potential contributors are familiar with our most recent issue of *Indiana Review* via library, sample copy or subscription. Beyond that, we look for prose that is well crafted and socially relevant. Dig deep. Don't accept your first choice descriptions when you are revising. Cliché and easy images sink 90% of the stories we reject. Understand the magazines you send to—investigate!"

☑ INKWELL MAGAZINE

Manhattanville College, 2900 Purchase St., Purchase NY 10577. (914) 323-7239. E-mail: inkwell@mville. edu. Website: www.inkwelljournal.org. **Contact:** Fiction editor. Literary Journal: 5½ × 7½; 120-170 pages; 60 lb. paper; 10 pt C1S, 4/c cover; illustrations; photos. "Inkwell Magazine is committed to presenting top quality poetry, prose and artwork in a high quality publication. Inkwell is dedicated to discovering new talent and to encouraging and bringing talents of working writers and artists to a wider audience. We encourage diverse voices and have an open submission policy for both art and literature." Annual. Estab. 1995. Circ. 1,000. Member CLMP.

Needs Experimental, humor/satire, literary. "No erotica, children's literature, romance, religious." Receives 120 unsolicited mss/month. Accepts 45 mss/issue. Does not read mss December-July. Publishes ms 2 months after acceptance. **Publishes 3-5 new writers/year.** Recently published work by Alice Quinn, Margaret Gibson, Benjamin Cheever, Paul Muldoon, Pablo Medina, Carol Muske-Dukes. Length: 5,000 words; average length: 3,000 words. Publishes short shorts. Also publishes poetry.

How to Contact Send a disposable copy of ms and #10 SASE for reply only. Responds in 1 month to queries; 4-6 months to mss. Sample copy for $6. Writer's guidelines for SASE.

Payment/Terms Pays contributor's copies and sends complimentary copies; additional copies $8. Acquires first North American serial, first rights. Sponsors awards/contests.

Tips "We look for well-crafted original stories with a strong voice."

☑ $ THE IOWA REVIEW

308 EPB, The University of Iowa, Iowa City IA 52242. (319)335-0462. Fax: (319)335-2535. Website: www. iowareview.org. **Contact:** Fiction Editor. Magazine: 5½ × 8½; 200 pages; first-grade offset paper; Carolina CS1 10-pt. cover stock. "Stories, essays, poems for a general readership interested in contemporary literature." Triannual magazine. Estab. 1970. Circ. 2,500.

Needs "We are open to a range of styles and voices and always hope to be surprised by work we then feel we need." Receives 600 unsolicited mss/month. Accepts 4-6 mss/issue; 12-18 mss/year. Does not read mss January-August. Publishes ms an average of 12-18 months after acceptance. Agented fiction less than 2%. **Publishes some new writers/year.** Recently published work by Benjamin Chambers, Pierre Hauser, Stellar Kim. Also publishes literary essays, literary criticism, poetry.

How to Contact Send complete ms with cover letter. "Don't bother with queries." SASE for return of ms. Responds in 3 months to queries; 3 months to mss. "We discourage simultaneous submissions." Sample copy for $9 and online. Writer's guidelines online. Reviews fiction.

Payment/Terms Pays $25 for the first page and $15 for each additional page, plus 2 contributor's copies; additional copies 30% off cover price. Pays on publication for first North American serial, nonexclusive anthology, classroom, online serial rights.

Tips "We have no set guidelines as to content or length; we look for what we consider to be the best writing available to us and are pleased when writers we believe we have discovered catch on with a wider range of readers. It is never a bad idea to look through an issue or two of the magazine prior to a submission."

☑ ◎ $ ISOTOPE

A Journal of Literary Nature and Science Writing, 3200 Old Main Hill, Logan UT 84322-3200. (435)797-3697. Fax: (435)797-3797. E-mail: leslie.brown@usu.edu. Website: isotope.usu.edu. **Contact:** Charles Waugh, fiction editor. Literary magazine/journal: 8½ × 11, 56 pages. Contains illustrations. Includes photographs. "Focus on nature and science writing that meditates on and engages in the varied and complex relations among the human and non-human worlds." Semiannual. Estab. 2003. Circ.1,200. Member CLMP.

Needs Experimental, humor/satire, literary, translations. Special interests: nature and science. Receives 10 mss/month. Accepts 1-2 mss/issue; 2-4 mss/year. Does not read October 16 through June 30. Manuscript published 6-18 months after acceptance. **Publishes 2 new writers/year.** Published Jill Stegman, Emily Doak, Janette Fecteau. Length: 250-7,500. Average length: 5,000. Publishes short shorts. Average length of short shorts: 500. Also publishes literary essays, poetry. Rarely comments on/critiques rejected mss.

How to Contact Send complete ms with cover letter. Include brief bio, list of publications. Send either SASE (or IRC) for return of ms or disposable copy of ms and #10 SASE for reply only. Considers simultaneous submissions, multiple short submissions. Sample copy available for $5. Guidelines available on Web site.

Payment/Terms Writers receive $100 per story, 4 contributor's copies, free subscription to the magazine. Additional copies $4. Pays on publication. Acquires first North American serial rights. Sends galleys to author. Publication is copyrighted.

☑ JABBERWOCK REVIEW

New Writing on Justice Dept. of English, John Jay College of Criminal Justice, 619 West 54th Street, 7th Floor, New York NY 10019. E-mail: journal@jjay.cuny.edu. **Contact:** Adam Berlin and Jeffrey Heiman, editors. Literary magazine/journal: 6x9; 120 pages; 60 lb paper; 80 lb cover. "J Journal publishes literary fiction, creative nonfiction and poetry on the subjects of crime, criminal justice, law and law enforcement. While the themes are specific, they need not dominate the work. We're interested in questions of justice from all perspectives." Semiannual. Estab. 2008. Mississippi State University, Drawer E, Dept. of English, Mississippi State MS 39762. (662)325-3644. E-mail: jabberwockreview@english. msstate.edu. Website: www.msstate.edu/org/jabberwock. **Contact:** fiction editor (revolving editorship). Magazine: 8½ × 5½; 120 pages; glossy cover; illustrations; photos. "We are located in the South—love the South—but we publish good writing from anywhere and everywhere. And from anyone. We respect writers of reputation—and print their work—but we take great delight in publishing new and emerging writers as well." Semiannual. Estab. 1979. Circ. 500.

Needs Ethnic/multicultural, experimental, feminist, gay, literary, mainstream, regional, translations. "No science fiction, romance." Receives 150 unsolicited mss/month. Accepts 7-8 mss/issue; 15 mss/year. "We do not read March 15 to September 1." Publishes ms 4-6 months after acceptance. **Publishes 1-5 new writers/year.** Recently published work by Robert Morgan, Charles Harper Webb, Ted Kooser, Alison Baker, Alyce Miller, Lorraine Lopez, J.D. Chapman. Length: 250-5,000 words; average length: 4,000 words. Publishes short shorts. Also publishes literary essays, poetry. Sometimes comments on rejected mss.

How to Contact Send SASE (or IRC) for return of ms. Responds in 5 months to mss. Accepts simultaneous submissions "with notification of such." Sample copy for $6. Writer's guidelines for SASE.

Payment/Terms Pays 2 contributor's copies. Sponsors awards/contests.

Tips "It might take a few months to get a response from us, but your manuscript will be read with care. Our editors enjoy reading submissions (really!) and will remember writers who are persistent and committed to getting a story 'right' through revision."

☑ ◎ J JOURNAL

New Writing on Justice Dept. of English, John Jay College of Criminal Justice, 619 West 54th Street, 7th Floor, New York NY 10019. E-mail: journal@jjay.cuny.edu. **Contact:** Adam Berlin and Jeffrey Heiman, editors. Literary magazine/journal: 6x9; 120 pages; 60 lb paper; 80 lb cover. "J Journal publishes literary fiction, creative nonfiction and poetry on the subjects of crime, criminal justice, law and law enforcement. While the themes are specific, they need not dominate the work. We're interested in questions of justice from all perspectives." Semiannual. Estab. 2008.

Needs Experimental, gay, historical (general), literary, military/war, mystery, regional. Receives 100 mss/month. Accepts 5 mss/issue; 10 mss/year. Ms. published 6 months after acceptance. Length: 750-6,000 words (max). Average length: 4,000 words. Also publishes poetry. Sometimes comments on/critiques rejected mss.

How to Contact Send complete ms with cover letter. Include estimated word count, brief bio, list of publications. Responds to queries in 4 weeks; mss in 12 weeks. Send recyclable copy of ms and #10 SASE for reply only. Considers simultaneous submissions. Sample copy available for $10.

Payment/Terms Writers receive 2 contributor's copies. Additional copies $10. Pays on publication. Acquires first rights. Publication is copyrighted.

Tips "We're looking for literary fiction/memoir with a connection, direct or tangential, to the theme of justice."

☑ ▣ KARAMU

English Dept., Eastern Illinois University, 600 Lincoln Ave., Charleston IL 61920. (217) 581-6297. E-mail: oabella@eiu.edu. **Contact:** Fiction Editor. Literary magazine: 5 × 8; 132-150 pages; illustrations. "Karamu is a literary magazine of ideas and artistic expression independently produced by the faculty members and associates of Eastern Illinois University. We publish writing that captures something essential about life, which goes beyond superficial, and which develops voice genuinely. Contributions of creative non-fiction, fiction, poetry and artwork of interest to a broadly educated audience are welcome." Annual. Estab. 1966. Circ. 500.

   • *Karamu* has received three Illinois Arts Council Awards.

Needs Adventure, ethnic/multicultural, experimental, feminist, gay, historical, humor/satire, lesbian, literary, mainstream, regional. "No pornographic, science fiction, religious, political or didactic stories—no dogma or proselytizing." List of upcoming editorial themes available for SASE. Receives 80-90 unsolicited mss/month. Accepts 10-15 mss/issue. Does not read February 16-September 1. Publishes ms 1 year after acceptance. **Publishes 3-6 new writers/year.** Recently published work by Geer Austin, Patricia Brieschke, Pappi Tomas, Kathleen Spivack, Richard Thieme, and Mary Lynn Reed. Publishes short shorts. Also publishes poetry. Sometimes comments on rejected mss.

How to Contact Send SASE for reply. Responds in 1 week to queries. Does not accept simultaneous submissions. Sample copy for $8 or 2 for $6 for back issues. Writer's guidelines for SASE.

Payment/Terms Pays 1 contributor's copy; additional copies at discount. Acquires one-time rights.

Tips Looks for "convincing, well-developed characters and plots expressing aspects of human nature or relationships in a perceptive, believable and carefully considered and written way."

☑ $ ▣ THE KENYON REVIEW

Walton House, 102 W. Wiggin St., Finn House, Gambier OH 43022. (740)427-5208. Fax: (740)427-5417. E-mail: kenyonreview@kenyon.edu. Website: www.kenyonreview.org. **Contact:** Marlene Landefeld. An international journal of literature, culture and the arts dedicated to an inclusive representation of the best in new writing (fiction, poetry, essays, interviews, criticism) from established and emerging writers. Estab. 1939. Circ. 6,000.

   • Work published in the *Kenyon Review* has been selected for inclusion in *The O. Henry Prize Stories, Pushcart Prize* anthologies, *Best American Short Stories,* and *Best American Poetry.*

Needs Excerpts from novels, condensed novels, ethnic/multicultural, experimental, feminist, gay, historical, humor/satire, lesbian, literary, mainstream, translations, contemporary. Receives 900 unsolicited mss/month. Unsolicited mss read only from September 15-January 15. Publishes ms 1 year after acceptance. Recently published work by Alice Hoffman, Beth Ann Fennelly, Romulus Linney, John Koethe, Albert Goldbarth, Erin McGraw.

How to Contact Only accepting mss via online submissions program. Please visit Web site for instructions.

Do not submit via e-mail or snail mail. No simultaneous submissions. Sample copy $12 single issue, includes postage and handling. Please call or e-mail to order. Writer's guidelines online.

Payment/Terms Pays $15-40/page. Pays on publication for first rights.

Tips "We look for strong voice, unusual perspective, and power in the writing."

☐ ◎ KEREM

Jewish Study Center Press, Inc., 3035 Porter St. NW, Washington DC 20008. (202) 364-3006. E-mail: langner@erols.com. Website: www.kerem.org. **Contact:** Sara R. Horowitz and Gilah Langner, editors. Magazine: 6 × 9; 128 pages; 60 lb. offset paper; glossy cover; illustrations; photos. "Kerem publishes Jewish religious, creative, literary material—short stories, poetry, personal reflections, text study, prayers, rituals, etc." Estab. 1992. Circ. 2,000.

Needs Jewish: feminist, humor/satire, literary, religious/inspirational. Receives 10-12 unsolicited mss/month. Accepts 1-2 mss/issue. Publishes ms 2-10 months after acceptance. **Publishes 2 new writers/year.** Also publishes literary essays, poetry.

How to Contact Prefers submissions by e-mail. Send SASE for reply, return of ms or send disposable copy of ms. Responds in 2 months to queries; 5 months to mss. Accepts simultaneous, multiple submissions. Sample copy for $8.50. Writer's guidelines online.

Payment/Terms Pays free subscription and 2-10 contributor's copies. Acquires one-time rights.

Tips "Should have a strong Jewish content. We want to be moved by reading the manuscript!"

☐ $ THE KIT-CAT REVIEW

244 Halstead Ave., Harrison NY 10528. (914)835-4833. E-mail: kitcatreview@gmail.com. **Contact:** Claudia Fletcher, editor. Magazine: 8½ × 5½; 75 pages; laser paper; colored card cover stock; illustrations. "The Kit-Cat Review is named after the 18th Century Kit-Cat Club, whose members included Addison, Steele, Congreve, Vanbrugh and Garth. Its purpose is to promote/discover excellence and originality." The Kit-Cat Review is part of the collections of the University of Wisconsin (Madison) and State University of New York (Buffalo). Quarterly. Estab. 1998. Circ. 500.

Needs Ethnic/multicultural, experimental, literary, novel excerpts, slice-of-life vignettes. No stories with "O. Henry-type formula endings. Shorter pieces stand a better chance of publication." No science fiction, fantasy, romance, horror or new age. Receives 40 unsolicited mss/month. Accepts 6 mss/issue; 24 mss/year. Time between acceptance and publication is 6 months. **Publishes 14 new writers/year.** Recently published work by Chayym Zeldis, Michael Fedo, Louis Phillips, Elisha Porat. Length: 5,000 words maximum; average length: 2,000 words. Publishes short shorts. Also publishes literary essays, literary criticism, poetry.

How to Contact Send complete ms. Accepts submissions by disk. Send SASE (or IRC) for return of ms, or send disposable copy of ms and #10 SASE for reply only. Responds in 1 week to queries; 2 months to mss. Accepts simultaneous, multiple submissions. Sample copy for $7 (payable to Claudia Fletcher). Writer's guidelines not available.

Payment/Terms Pays $25-200 and 2 contributor's copies; additional copies $5. Pays on publication for first rights.

▦ ◎ LA KANCERKLINIKO

c/o Laurent Septier, 162 rue Paradis, P.O. Box 174, 13444 Marseille Cantini Cedex France. (33) 2-48-61-81-98. Fax: (33) 2-48-61-81-98. E-mail: lseptier@hotmail.com. **Contact:** Laurent Septier. "An Esperanto magazine which appears 4 times annually. Each issue contains 32 pages. La Kancerkliniko is a political and cultural magazine." Quarterly. Circ. 300.

Needs Science fiction, short stories or very short novels. "The short story (or the very short novel) must be written only in Esperanto, either original or translation from any other language." Wants more science fiction. **Publishes 2-3 new writers/year.** Recently published work by Mao Zifu, Manuel de Sabrea, Peter Brown and Aldo de'Giorgi.

How to Contact Accepts submissions by e-mail, fax. Accepts disk submissions. Accepts multiple submissions. Sample copy for 3 IRCs from Universal Postal Union.

Payment/Terms Pays in contributor's copies.

☑ LAKE EFFECT, A Journal of the Literary Arts

Penn State Erie, Humanities and Social Sciences, 4951 College Dr., Erie PA 16563-1501. (814) 898-6281. Fax: (814) 898-6032. E-mail: goL1@psu.edu. **Contact:** George Looney, editor-in-chief. Magazine: 5½ × 8½; 180-200 pages; 55 lb. natural paper; 12 pt. C1S cover. "In addition to seeking strong, traditional stories, Lake Effect is open to more experimental, language-centered fiction as well." Annual. Estab. as Lake Effect, 2001; as Tempest, 1978. Circ. 500. Member CLMP.

Needs Experimental, literary, mainstream. "No children's/juvenile, fantasy, science fiction, romance or young adult/teen." Receives 120 unsolicited mss/month. Accepts 5-9 mss/issue. Publishes ms 1 year after acceptance. **Publishes 6 new writers/year.** Recently published work by Edith Pearlman, Francois Camoin, Cris Mazza, Joan Connor, Aimee Parkison, Joanna Howard. Length: 4,500-5,000 words; average length: 2,600-3,900 words. Publishes short shorts. Also publishes literary essays, poetry.

How to Contact Send SASE for return of ms or send a disposable copy of ms and #10 SASE for reply only. Responds in 3 weeks to queries; 4-6 months to mss. Accepts simultaneous submissions. Sample copy for $6. Writer's guidelines for SASE.

Payment/Terms Pays 2 contributor's copies; additional copies $2. Acquires first, one-time rights. Not copyrighted.

Tips "We're looking for strong, well-crafted stories that emerge from character and language more than plot. The language is what makes a story stand out (and a strong sense of voice). Be sure to let us know immediately should a submitted story be accepted elsewhere."

▦ LANDFALL/OTAGO UNIVERSITY PRESS

Otago University Press, P.O. Box 56, Dunedin New Zealand. Fax: (643)479-8385. E-mail: landfall@otago.ac.nz. **Contact:** Landfall Editor.

Needs Publishes fiction, poetry, commentary and reviews of New Zealand books.

How to Contact Send copy of ms with SASE. Sample copy not available.

Tips "We concentrate on publishing work by New Zealand writers, but occasionally accept work from elsewhere."

◐ THE LAUREL REVIEW

Northwest Missouri State University, Dept. of English, Maryville MO 64468. (660)562-1739. E-mail: tlr@nwmissouri.edu. Website: http://catpages.nwmissouri.edu/m/tlr. **Contact:** John Gallaher, Richard Black, or Brenda Lewis. Magazine: 6 × 9; 124-128 pages; good quality paper. "We publish poetry and fiction of high quality, from the traditional to the avant-garde. We are eclectic, open and flexible. Good writing is all we seek." Biannual. Estab. 1960. Circ. 900.

Needs Literary, contemporary. "No genre or politically polemical fiction." Receives 120 unsolicited mss/month. Accepts 3-5 mss/issue; 6-10 mss/year. Reading period: September 1-May 1. Publishes ms 1-12 months after acceptance. **Publishes 1-2 new writers/year.** Recently published work by Albert Goldbarth, Zachary Schomburg, Craig Morgan Teicher, and Ethan Paquin. Also publishes literary essays, poetry.

How to Contact Responds in 4 months to mss. No simultaneous submissions. Sample copy for $5.

Payment/Terms Pays 2 contributor's copies and 1 year subscription. Acquires first rights. Copyright reverts to author upon request.

Tips "Nothing really matters to us except our perception that the story presents something powerfully felt by the writer and communicated intensely to a serious reader. (We believe, incidentally, that comedy is just as serious a matter as tragedy, and we don't mind a bit if something makes us laugh out loud; we get too little that makes us laugh, in fact.) We try to reply promptly, though we don't always manage that. In short, we want good poems and good stories. We hope to be able to recognize them, and we print what we believe to the best work submitted."

☑ THE LEDGE MAGAZINE

40 Maple Ave., Bellport NY 11713-2011.(631)219-5969. E-mail: tkmonaghan@aol.com. Website: www.theledgemagazine.com. **Contact:** Tim Monaghan, publisher. Literary magazine/journal: 6 × 9, 192 pages, offset paper, glossy stock cover. "The Ledge Magazine publishes cutting-edge contemporary fiction by emerging and established writers." Annual. Estab. 1988. Circ. 1,000.

Needs Erotica, ethnic/multicultural (general), literary. Receives 90 mss/month. Accepts 6-8 mss/issue. Manuscript published 6 months after acceptance. Published Pia Chatterjee, Xujun Eberlein, Franny

French, Clifford Garstang, Richard Jespers, Al Sims. Length: 2,500 words (min)-7,500 words (max). Average length: 6,000 words. Also publishes poetry. Rarely comments on/critiques rejected mss.

How to Contact Send complete ms with cover letter. Include estimated word count, brief bio. Responds to queries in 6 weeks. Responds to mss in 8 months. Send SASE (or IRC) for return of ms. Considers simultaneous submissions. Sample copy available for $10. Subscription: $20 (2 issues), $36 (4 issues). Guidelines available for SASE.

Payment/Terms Writers receive 1 contributor's copy. Additional copies $6. Pays on publication. Acquires first North American serial rights. Sends galleys to author. Publication is copyrighted.

Tips "We seek compelling stories that employ innovative language and complex characterization. We especially enjoy poignant stories with a sense of purpose. We dislike careless or hackneyed writing."

☑ ◎ LE FORUM, Supplement Littéraire

Franco-American Research Opportunity Group, University of Maine, Franco American Center, Orono ME 04469-5719. (207) 581-3764. Fax: (207) 581-1455. E-mail: lisa_michaud@umit.maine.edu. Website: www. francomaine.org. **Contact:** Lisa Michaud, managing editor. Magazine: 56 pages; illustrations; photos. Publication was founded to stimulate and recognize creative expression among Franco-Americans, all types of readers, including literary and working class. This publication is used in classrooms. Circulated internationally. Quarterly. Estab. 19 72. Circ. 5,000.

Needs "We will consider any type of short fiction, poetry and critical essays having to with Franco-American experience. They must be of good quality in French or English. We are also looking for Canadian writers with French-North American experiences." Receives 10 unsolicited mss/month. Accepts 2-4 mss/issue. **Publishes some new writers/year.** Length: 750-2,500 words; average length: 1,000 words. Occasionally comments on rejected mss.

How to Contact Include SASE. Responds in 3 weeks to queries; 1 month to mss. Accepts simultaneous submissions and reprints. Sample copy not available.

Payment/Terms Pays 3 copies. Acquires one-time rights.

Tips "Write honestly. Start with a strongly felt personal Franco-American experience. If you make us feel what you have felt, we will publish it. We stress that this publication deals specifically with the Franco-American experience."

☑ THE LISTENING EYE

Kent State University Geauga Campus, 14111 Claridon-Troy Rd., Burton OH 44021. (440)286-3840. E-mail: grace_butcher@msn.com. **Contact:** Grace Butcher, editor. Magazine: 5½ × 8½; 60 pages; photographs. "We publish the occasional very short stories (750 words/3 pages double spaced) in any subject and any style, but the language must be strong, unusual, free from cliché and vagueness. We are a shoestring operation from a small campus but we publish high-quality work." Annual. Estab. 1970. Circ. 250.

Needs Literary. "Pretty much anything will be considered except porn." Reads mss January 1-April 15 only. Publishes ms 3-4 months after acceptance. Recently published work by Elizabeth Scott, Sam Ruddick, H.E. Wright. Publishes short shorts. Also publishes poetry. Sometimes comments on rejected mss.

How to Contact Send SASE for return of ms or disposable copy of ms with SASE for reply only. Responds in 4 weeks to queries; 4 months to mss. Accepts reprint submissions. Sample copy for $3 and $1 postage. Writer's guidelines for SASE.

Payment/Terms Pays 2 contributor's copies; additional copies $3 with $1 postage. Pays on publication for one-time rights.

Tips "We look for powerful, unusual imagery, content and plot. Short, short."

☐ LITERAL LATTE

Word Sci, Inc., 200 East 10th Street Suite 240, New York NY 10003. (212)260-5532. E-mail: litlatte@aol. com. Website: www.literal-latte.com. **Contact:** Jeff Bockman, editor. Magazine: illustrations; photos. "Publishes great writing in many flavors and styles. Literal Latte expanded the readership for literary magazines by offering free copies in New York coffeehouses and bookstores. Now online only and free to the world." Bimonthly. Estab. 1994. CLMP.

Needs Experimental, fantasy, literary, science fiction. Receives 4,000 unsolicited mss/month. Accepts 5-8 mss/issue; 40 mss/year. Agented fiction 5%. **Publishes 6 new writers/year.** Length: 500-6,000 words;

average length: 4,000 words. Publishes short shorts. Often comments on rejected mss.

How to Contact Send SASE for return of mss or send a disposable copy of ms and #10 SASE for reply only or e-mail for reply only. Responds in 6 months to mss. Accepts simultaneous, multiple submissions. Sample copy for $3. Writer's guidelines for SASE, e-mail or check Web site. Reviews fiction.

Payment/Terms Pays 10 contributor's copies, a free subscription to the magazine and 2 gift certificates; additional copies $1. First rights. May request additional rights to put piece in annual anthology. Pays on publication for first, one-time rights. Sponsors awards/contests.

Tips "Keeping free thought free and challenging entertainment are not mutually exclusive. Words make a manuscript stand out, words beautifully woven together in striking and memorable patterns."

☐ 🖪 THE LITERARY REVIEW

Fairleigh Dickinson University, 285 Madison Ave., Madison NJ 07940. (973) 443-8564. Fax: (973) 443-8364. E-mail: tlr@fdu.edu. Website: www.theliteraryreview.org. **Contact:** Minna Proctor, editor-in-chief. Magazine: 6 × 9; 160 pages; professionally printed on textpaper; semigloss card cover; perfect-bound. "Literary magazine specializing in fiction, poetry and essays with an international focus. Our audience is general with a leaning toward scholars, libraries and schools." Quarterly. Estab. 1957. Circ. 2,000.

• Work published in *The Literary Review* has been included in *Editor's Choice, Best American Short Stories* and *Pushcart Prize* anthologies.

Needs Works of high literary quality only. Does not want to see "overused subject matter or pat resolutions to conflicts." Receives 90-100 unsolicited mss/month. Accepts 20-25 mss/year. Does not read submissions June 1-September 1. Publishes ms 112-2 years after acceptance. Agented fiction 1-2%. **Publishes 80% new writers/year.** Recently published work by Irvin Faust, Todd James Pierce, Joshua Shapiro, Susan Schwartz Senstadt. Also publishes literary essays, literary criticism, poetry. Occasionally comments on rejected mss.

How to Contact Responds in 3-4 months to mss. Submit online at www.theliteraryreview.org/submit.html only. Accepts multiple submissions. Sample copy for $7. Writer's guidelines for SASE. Reviews fiction.

Payment/Terms Pays 2 contributor's copies; $3 discount for extras. Acquires first rights.

Tips "We want original dramatic situations with complex moral and intellectual resonance and vivid prose. We don't want versions of familiar plots and relationships. Too much of what we are seeing today is openly derivative in subject, plot and prose style. We pride ourselves on spotting new writers with fresh insight and approach."

☐ THE LONG STORY

18 Eaton St., Lawrence MA 01843. (978)686-7638. E-mail: rpburnham@mac.com. Website: http://web. mac.com/rpburnham/iWeb/Site/LongStory.html. **Contact:** R. P. Burnham. Magazine: 5½ × 8½; 150-200 pages; 60 lb. cover stock; illustrations (b&w graphics). For serious, educated, literary people. Annual. Estab. 1983. Circ. 1,200.

Needs Ethnic/multicultural, feminist, literary, contemporary. "No science fiction, adventure, romance, etc. We publish high literary quality of any kind but especially look for stories that have difficulty getting published elsewhere—committed fiction, working class settings, left-wing themes, etc." Receives 30-40 unsolicited mss/month. Accepts 6-7 mss/issue. Publishes ms 3 months to 1 year after acceptance. **Publishes 90% new writers/year.** Length: 8,000-20,000 words; average length: 8,000-12,000 words.

How to Contact Include SASE. Responds in 2 months to mss. Accepts simultaneous submissions "but not wild about it." Sample copy for $7.

Payment/Terms Pays 2 contributor's copies; $5 charge for extras. Acquires first rights.

Tips "Read us first and make sure submitted material is the kind we're interested in. Send clear, legible manuscripts. We're not interested in commercial success; rather we want to provide a place for long stories, the most difficult literary form to publish in our country."

☑ ◎ LOUISIANA LITERATURE

Southeastern Louisiana University, SLU 792, Hammond LA 70402. (985) 549-5022. Fax: (985) 549-5021. E-mail: lalit@selu.edu. Website: www.louisianaliterature.org. **Contact:** Norman German, fiction editor. Magazine: 6 × 9; 150 pages; 70 lb. paper; card cover; illustrations. "Essays should be about Louisiana material; preference is given to fiction and poetry with Louisiana and Southern themes, but creative work can be set anywhere." Semiannual. Estab. 1984. Circ. 600 paid; 750-1,000 printed.

Needs Literary, mainstream, regional. "No sloppy, ungrammatical manuscripts." Receives 100 unsolicited mss/month. May not read mss June-July. Publishes ms 6-12 after acceptance. **Publishes 4 new writers/year.** Recently published work by Anthony Bukowski, Aaron Gwyn, Robert Phillips, R.T. Smith. Length: 1,000-6,000 words; average length: 3,500 words. Sometimes comments on rejected mss.

How to Contact Include SASE. Responds in 3 months to mss. Sample copy for $8. Reviews fiction.

Payment/Terms Pays usually in contributor's copies. Acquires one-time rights.

Tips "Cut out everything that is not a functioning part of the story. Make sure your manuscript is professionally presented. Use relevant specific detail in every scene. We love detail, local color, voice and craft. Any professional manuscript stands out."

◎ THE LOUISIANA REVIEW

Division of Liberal Arts, Louisiana State University at Eunice, P.O. Box 1129, Eunice LA 70535. (337) 550-1315. E-mail: bfonteno@lsue.edu. **Contact:** Dr. Billy Fontenot, editor. Magazine: 812X512 bound; 100-200 pages; b&w illustrations. "We are looking for excellent work by Louisiana writers as well as those outside the state who tell us their connection to it. Non-Louisiana material is considered, but Louisiana/Gulf Coast themed work gets priority." Annual. Estab. 1999. Circ. 300-600.

Needs Ethnic/multicultural (Cajun or Louisiana culture), historical (Louisiana-related or setting), regional (Louisiana, Gulf Coast). Receives 25 unsolicited mss/month. Accepts 5-7 mss/issue. Reads year-round. Publishes ms 6-12 months after acceptance. Recently published work by Ronald Frame, Tom Bonner, Laura Cario, Sheryl St. Germaine. Length: up to 9,000 words; average length: 2,000 words. Publishes short shorts. Also publishes poetry and b&w artwork. Sometimes comments on rejected mss.

How to Contact Send SASE for return of ms. Responds in 5 weeks to queries; 10 weeks to mss. Accepts multiple submissions. Sample copy for $5.

Payment/Terms Pays 1 contributor's copy. Pays on publication for one-time rights. Not copyrighted but has an ISSN number.

Tips "We do like to have fiction play out visually as a film would rather than static and undramatized. Louisiana or Gulf Coast settings and themes preferred."

◪ THE LOUISVILLE REVIEW

Spalding University, 851 S. Fourth St., Louisville KY 40203. (502) 585-9911, ext. 2777. E-mail: louisvillereview@spalding.edu. Website: www.louisvillereview.org. **Contact:** Sena Jeter Naslund, editor. Literary magazine. "We are a literary journal seeking original stories with fresh imagery and vivid language." Semiannual. Estab. 1976.

Needs Literary. Receives 200 + unsolicited mss/month. Accepts 4-6 fiction mss/issue; 8-12 fiction mss/year. Publishes ms 6 months after acceptance. **Publishes 8-10 new writers/year.** Recently published work by Scott Russell Sanders, Lawrence Millman, Aleda Shirley, Bill Roorbach, and Piotr Florczyk. Publishes essays, fiction, nonfiction and poetry.

How to Contact Send a disposable copy of ms and #10 SASE for reply only. Responds in 6 months to queries; 6 months to mss. Accepts multiple submissions.

Payment/Terms Pays 2 contributor's copies.

◪ THE MACGUFFIN

Schoolcraft College, Department of English, 18600 Haggerty Rd., Livonia MI 48152-2696. (734) 462-4400, ext. 5327. Fax: (734) 462-4679. E-mail: macguffin@schoolcraft.edu. Website: www.schoolcraft.edu/macguffin/. **Contact:** Steven A. Dolgin, editor; Nicholle Cormier, managing editor; Elizabeth Kircos, fiction editor; Carol Was, poetry editor. Magazine: 6 × 9; 164 + pages; 60 lb. paper; 110 lb. cover; b&w illustrations; photos. "The MacGuffin is a literary magazine which publishes a range of material including poetry, creative nonfiction and fiction. Material ranges from traditional to experimental. We hope our periodical attracts a variety of people with many different interests." Triannual. Estab. 1984. Circ. 600.

Needs Adventure, ethnic/multicultural, experimental, historical (general), humor/satire, literary, mainstream, translations, contemporary, prose poem. "No religious, inspirational, juvenile, romance, horror, pornography." Receives 35-55 unsolicited mss/month. Accepts 10-15 mss/issue; 30-50 mss/year. Does not read mss between July 1-August 15. Publishes ms 6 months to 2 years after acceptance. Agented fiction 10-15%. **Publishes 30 new writers/year.** Recently published work by Gerry LaFemina, Gail Waldstein, Margaret Karmazin, Linda Nemec Foster, Laurence Lieberman, Conrad Hilberry, Thomas

Lux and Vivian Shipley. Length: 100-5,000 words; average length: 2,000-2,500 words. Publishes short shorts. Also publishes literary essays. Occasionally comments on rejected mss.

How to Contact Send SASE or e-mail. Responds in 4-6 months to mss. Sample copy for $6; current issue for $9. Writer's guidelines free.

Payment/Terms Pays 2 contributor's copies. Acquires one-time rights.

Tips "We want to give promising new fiction writers the opportunity to publish alongside recognized writers. Be persistent. If a story is rejected, try to send it somewhere else. When we reject a story, we may accept the next one you send us. When we make suggestions for a rewrite, we may accept the revision. There seems to be a great number of good authors of fiction, but there are far too few places for publication. However, this is changing. Make your characters come to life. Even the most ordinary people become fascinating if they live for your readers."

THE MADISON REVIEW

Department of English, Helen C. White Hall, 600 N. Park St., University of Wisconsin, Madison WI 53706. (608) 263-0566. E-mail: madisonreview@yahoo.com. Website: http://themadisonreview.blogspot.com and www.madisonreview.org. **Contact:** Miles Johnson and Elzbieta Beck, fiction editors. Magazine: 6 × 9; 180 pages. "We are an independent literary journal featuring quality fiction, poetry, artwork and interviews. Both established and emerging writers are encouraged to submit." Semiannual. Estab. 1978. Circ. 1,000.

Needs "Well-crafted, compelling fiction featuring a wide range of styles and subjects." Receives 300 unsolicited mss/period. Accepts 6 mss/issue. Does not read May-September. Publishes ms 4 months after acceptance. **Publishes 4 new writers/year.** Recently published work by Lori Rader Day and Ian Williams. Average length: 4,000 words. Also publishes poetry.

How to Contact Accepts multiple submissions. Sample copy for $4 via postal service or e-mail.

Payment/Terms Pays 2 contributor's copies; $5 charge for extras. Acquires first North American serial rights.

$ THE MALAHAT REVIEW

The University of Victoria P.O. Box 1700, STN CSC, Victoria BC V8W 2Y2 Canada. (250)721-8524. E-mail: malahat@uvic.ca. Website: www.malahatreview.ca. **Contact:** John Barton, editor. "We try to achieve a balance of views and styles in each issue. We strive for a mix of the best writing by both established and new writers." Quarterly. Estab. 1967. Circ. 1,700.

• *The Malahat Review* has received Canada's National Magazine Award for poetry and fiction.

Needs "General fiction, poetry, and creative nonfiction." Accepts 3-4 fiction mss/issue and 1 creative nonfiction ms/issue. Publishes ms within 6 months after acceptance. **Publishes 4-5 new writers/year.** Recently published work by Ian Bullock, Harold Rhenish, Anne Fleming, Vaia Barkas, and Scott Randall.

How to Contact Send complete ms. "Enclose proper postage on the SASE (or send IRC)." Responds in 2 weeks to queries; 3 months to mss. No simultaneous submissions. Sample copy for $16.45 (US). Writer's guidelines online.

Payment/Terms Pays $40 CAD/magazine page. Pays on acceptance for second serial (reprint), first world rights.

Tips "We do encourage new writers to submit. Read the magazines you want to be published in, ask for their guidelines and follow them. Check Web site for information on *Malahat's* novella competition, *Far Horizons for Short Fiction* award, and creative nonfiction award."

$ MANOA

English Dept., University of Hawaii, Honolulu HI 96822. (808) 956-3070. Fax: (808) 956-3083. E-mail: mjournal-l@hawaii.edu. Website: http://manoajournal.hawaii.edu. **Contact**: Frank Stewart, editor. Magazine: 7 × 10; 240 pages. "High quality literary fiction, poetry, essays, personal narrative, reviews. Most of each issue devoted to new work from Pacific and Asian nations. Please see Web site for current projects and needs. Semiannual. Estab. 1989. Circ. 2,000 print; 10,000 digital.

• *Manoa* has received numerous awards, and work published in the magazine has been selected for prize anthologies.

Needs Literary, mainstream, translations (from U.S. and nations in or bordering on the Pacific), contemporary, excerpted novel. Accepts 1-2 mss/issue. Agented fiction 10%. **Publishes 1-2 new writers/**

year. Recently published fiction by Wang Ping, Larissa Behrendt, Tony Birch, Roger McDonald, Alexis Wright, Prafulla Roy. Also publishes poetry.

How to Contact Please query first before sending in mss. Include SASE. Does not accept submissions by e-mail. Responds in 3 weeks to queries; 1 month to poetry mss; 6 months to fiction to mss. Accepts simultaneous submissions. Sample copy for $20 (U.S.). Writer's guidelines online. Reviews fiction.

Payment/Terms Pays $100-500 normally ($25/printed page). Pays on publication for first North American serial, non-exclusive, one-time print rights. Sends galleys to author.

☑ $ ⚇ THE MASSACHUSETTS REVIEW

South College, University of Massachusetts, Amherst MA 01003-9934. (413) 545-2689. Fax: (413) 577-0740. E-mail: massrev@external.umass.edu. Website: www.massreview.org. **Contact:** Fiction Editor. Magazine: 6 × 9; 172 pages; 52 lb. paper; 65 lb. vellum cover; illustrations; photos. Quarterly. Estab. 1959. Circ. 1,200.

- Stories from *The Massachusetts Review* have been anthologized in the *100 Best American Short Stories of the Century* and the *Pushcart Prize* anthology.

Needs Short stories. Wants more prose less than 30 pages. Does not read fiction mss June 1-September 30. Publishes ms 18 months after acceptance. Agented fiction Approximately 5%. **Publishes 3-5 new writers/year.** Recently published work by Ahdaf Soueif, Elizabeth Denton, Nicholas Montemarano. Also publishes poetry. Sometimes comments on rejected mss.

How to Contact Send complete ms. No returned ms without SASE. Responds in 3 months to mss. Accepts simultaneous, multiple submissions. Sample copy for $8. Writer's guidelines online.

Payment/Terms Pays $50. Pays on publication for first North American serial rights.

Tips "Shorter rather than longer stories preferred (up to 28-30 pages)." Looks for works that "stop us in our tracks." Manuscripts that stand out use "unexpected language, idiosyncrasy of outlook and are the opposite of ordinary."

⚇ METAL SCRATCHES

P.O. Box 685, Forest Lake MN 55025. E-mail: metalscratches@aol.com. **Contact:** Kim Mark, editor. Magazine: 5½ × 8½; 35 pages; heavy cover-stock. "Metal Scratches focuses on literary fiction that examines the dark side of humanity. We are not looking for anything that is 'cute' or 'sweet'." Semiannual. Estab. 2000.

Needs Experimental, horror (psychological), literary. "No poetry, science fiction, rape, murder or horror as in gore." Receives 20 unsolicited mss/month. Accepts 5-6 mss/issue; 20 mss/year. Publishes ms 6 months after acceptance. **Publishes 3 new writers/year.** Length: 3,500 words; average length: 3,000 words. Publishes short shorts. Sometimes comments on rejected mss.

How to Contact Send complete ms. Accepts submissions by e-mail. (No attachments.) Send disposable copy of ms and #10 SASE for reply only. Responds in 1 month to mss. Accepts simultaneous, multiple submissions. Sample copy for $3. Writer's guidelines for SASE or by e-mail.

Payment/Terms Pays 2 contributor's copies and one year subscription; additional copies for $2.50. Pays on publication for one-time rights. Not copyrighted.

Tips "Clean manuscripts prepared according to guidelines are a must. Send us something new and inventive. Don't let rejections from any editor scare you. Keep writing and keep submitting."

$ ⚇ MICHIGAN QUARTERLY REVIEW

3574 Rackham Bldg., 915 E. Washington, University of Michigan, Ann Arbor MI 48109-1070. (734) 764-9265. E-mail: mqr@umich.edu. Website: www.umich.edu/~mqr. **Contact:** Fiction Editor. "An interdisciplinary journal which publishes mainly essays and reviews, with some high-quality fiction and poetry, for an intellectual, widely read audience." Quarterly. Estab. 1962. Circ. 1,500.

- Stories from *Michigan Quarterly Review* have been selected for inclusion in *The Best American Short Stories*, *The O. Henry Prize Stories* and *Pushcart Prize* volumes.

Needs Literary. "No genre fiction written for a market. Would like to see more fiction about social, political, cultural matters, not just centered on a love relationship or dysfunctional family." Receives 200 unsolicited mss/month. Accepts 2 mss/issue; 8 mss/year. Publishes ms 1 year after acceptance. **Publishes 1-2 new writers/year.** Recently published work by Robert Boyers, Herbert Gold, Alice Mattison, Joyce Carol Oates, Vu Tran. Length: 1,500-7,000 words; average length: 5,000 words. Also publishes literary essays, poetry.

How to Contact Send complete ms. "I like to know if a writer is at the beginning, or further along, in his or her career. Don't offer plot summaries of the story, though a background comment is welcome." Include SASE. Responds in 2 months to queries; 6 weeks to mss. No simultaneous submissions. Sample copy for $4. Writer's guidelines online.

Payment/Terms Pays $10/published page. Pays on publication. Buys first serial rights. Sponsors awards/contests.

Tips "There's no beating a good plot, interesting characters and a fresh use of the English language. (Most stories fail because they're written in such a bland manner, or in TV-speak.) Be ambitious, try to involve the social world in the personal one, be aware of what the best writing of today is doing, don't be satisfied with a small slice-of-life narrative but think how to go beyond the ordinary."

☑ ☑ MID-AMERICAN REVIEW

Department of English Box W, Bowling Green State University, Bowling Green OH 43403. (419)372-2725. Fax: (419)372-6805. Website: www.bgsu.edu/midamericanreview. **Contact:** Ashley Kaine, fiction editor. Magazine: 6 × 9; 232 pages; 60 lb. bond paper; coated cover stock. "We try to put the best possible work in front of the biggest possible audience. We publish serious fiction and poetry, as well as critical studies in contemporary literature, translations and book reviews." Semiannual. Estab. 1981.

Needs Experimental, literary, translations, memoir, prose poem, traditional. "No genre fiction. Would like to see more short shorts." Receives 700 unsolicited mss/month. Accepts 4-8 mss/issue. Publishes ms 6 months after acceptance. Agented fiction 5%. **Publishes 4-8 new writers/year.** Recently published work by Matthew Eck, Becky Hagentson, and Kevin Wilson. Occasionally comments on rejected mss.

How to Contact Send complete ms with SASE. Responds in 4 months to mss. Sample copy for $9 (current issue), $5 (back issue); rare back issues $10. Writer's guidelines online. Reviews fiction.

Payment/Terms Pays $10/page up to $50, pending funding. Pays on publication when funding is available. Acquires first North American serial, one-time rights. Sponsors awards/contests.

Tips "We look for well-written stories that make the reader want to read on past the first line and page. Cliché themes and sloppy writing turn us off immediately. Read literary journals to see what's being published in today's market. We tend to publish work that is more non-traditional in style and subject, but are open to all literary non-genre submissions."

☑ THE MINNESOTA REVIEW

Dept. of English, Carnegie Mellon University, Pittsburgh PA 15213. (412) 268- 9825. E-mail: editors@theminnesotareview.org. Website: http://theminnesotareview.org. **Contact:** Jeffrey Williams, editor. Magazine: 5¼ × 7½; approximately 200 pages; some illustrations; occasional photos. "We emphasize socially and politically engaged work." Semiannual. Estab. 1960. Circ. 1,500.

Needs Experimental, feminist, gay, historical, lesbian, literary. Receives 50-75 unsolicited mss/month. Accepts 3-4 mss/issue; 6-8 mss/year. Publishes ms 6-12 months after acceptance. **Publishes 3-5 new writers/year.** Recently published work by E. Shaskan Bumas, Carlos Fuentes, Maggie Jaffe, James Hughes. Publishes short shorts. Also publishes literary essays, literary criticism, poetry. Occasionally comments on rejected mss.

How to Contact Include SASE. Responds in 3 weeks to queries; 3 months to mss. Accepts simultaneous, multiple submissions. Sample copy for $15. Reviews fiction.

Payment/Terms Pays in contributor's copies. Charge for additional copies. Acquires first rights.

Tips "We look for socially and politically engaged work, particularly short, striking work that stretches boundaries."

☑ MINNETONKA REVIEW

Minnetonka Review Press, LLC, P.O. Box 386, Spring Park MN 55384. E-mail: query@minnetonkareview.com. Website: www.minnetonkareview.com. **Contact:** Troy Ehlers, Editor-in-Chief. Literary magazine/journal. 6x9, 200 pages, recycled natural paper, glossy cover. Contains illustrations. Includes photographs. "We publish work of literary excellence. We are particularly attracted to fiction with careful prose, engaging and tension filled stories, and new perspectives, forms and styles." Semiannual. Estab. 2007. Circ. 1,000.

Needs Literary, mainstream. Receives 100 mss/month. Accepts 7 mss/issue; 15 mss/year. Does not read during the summer between May 15th and October 15th. Ms published 6-8 months after acceptance.

Publishes 6 new writers/year. Published Bev Jafek, Daniel DiStasio, Nathan Leslie, Robin Lippincott, Megan Cass, Arthur Saltzman, Gary Amdahl, and Arthur Winfield Knight. Length: 1,200 words (min)-6,000 words (max). Average length: 4,000 words. Publishes short shorts. Average length of short shorts: 1,200 words. Also publishes literary essays, poetry. Rarely comments on/critiques rejected mss.

How to Contact Send complete ms with cover letter. Accepts submissions by e-mail. Include brief bio. Responds to queries in 2 weeks. Responds to mss in 4 months. Send either SASE (or IRC) for return of ms or disposable copy of ms and #10 SASE for reply only. Considers simultaneous submissions. Sample copy available for $9. Guidelines available for SASE, via e-mail, on Web site.

Payment/Terms Writers receive 3 contributor's copies. Additional copies $7. Pays on publication. Acquires first North American serial rights. Publication is copyrighted. "Two authors from each issue receive a $150 Editor's Prize. Other contests with $1,000 prize are held from time to time. Details are available on our Web site"

Tips "The trick seems to be holding our attention, whether via novelty, language, style, story, good descriptions or tension. Always be honing your craft, reading and writing. And when you read, it helps to be familiar with what we publish, but in general, you should be reading a number of literary journals and anthologies. Think of your work as a contribution to a greater literary dialogue."

◙ MISSISSIPPI REVIEW

University of Southern Mississippi, 118 College Dr. #5144, Hattiesburg MS 39406-0001. (601) 266-4321. Fax: (601) 266-5757. E-mail: rief@mississippireview.com. Website: www.mississippireview.com. **Contact:** Rie Fortenberry, managing editor. Semiannual. Estab. 1972. Circ. 1,500.

Needs Annual fiction and poetry competition. $1,000 awarded in each category plus publication of all winners and finalists. Fiction entries 5,000 words or less. Poetry entry equals 1-3 poems, page limit is 10. $15 entry fee includes copy of prize issue. No limit on number of entries. Deadline October 1. No mss returned. **Publishes 25-30 new writers/year.**

How to Contact Sample copy for $8. Writer's guidelines online.

Payment/Terms Acquires first North American serial rights.

◙ $ ◙ THE MISSOURI REVIEW

1507 Hillcrest Hall, University of Missouri, Columbia MO 65211. (573)882-4474. Fax: (573)884-4671. E-mail: question@missourireview.com. Website: www.missourireview.com. **Contact:** Speer Morgan, editor; Evelyn Somers, associate editor. Magazine: 6¾ × 10; 200 pages. "We publish contemporary fiction, poetry, interviews, personal essays, cartoons, special features for the literary and the general reader interested in a wide range of subjects." Estab. 1978. Circ. 5,500.

• This magazine had stories anthologized in the *Pushcart Prize, Best American Short Stories, The O. Henry Prize Stories, Best American Essays, Best American Mystery Stories, Best American Nature and Science Writing, Best American Erotica*, and *New Stories from The South*.

Needs Literary fiction on all subjects, novel excerpts. No genre fiction. Receives 500 unsolicited mss/month. Accepts 5-7 mss/issue; 16-20 mss/year. **Publishes 6-10 new writers/year.** Recently published work by Nat Akin, Jennifer Bryan, Bruce Ducker, William Lychack, Cynthia Morrison Phoel. Also publishes literary essays, poetry. Often comments on rejected mss.

How to Contact Send complete ms. May include brief bio and list of publications. Send SASE for reply, return of ms or send disposable copy of ms. Online submissions via Web site. Responds in 2 weeks to queries; 12 weeks to mss. Sample copy for $8 or online. Writer's guidelines online.

Payment/Terms Pays $30/printed page up to $750. Offers signed contract. Sponsors awards/contests.

◙ MOBIUS

505 Christianson, Madison WI 53714. (608) 242-1009. E-mail: fmschep@charter.net. Website: www.mobiusmagazine.com. **Contact:** Fred Schepartz, editor. Magazine: 8½ × 11; 16-24 pages; 60 lb. paper; 60 lb. cover. "Looking for fiction which uses social change as either a primary or secondary theme. This is broader than most people think. Need social relevance in one way or another. For an artistically and politically aware and curious audience." Quarterly. Estab. 1989. Circ. 1,500.

Needs Ethnic/multicultural, experimental, fantasy, feminist, gay, historical, horror, humor/satire, lesbian, literary, mainstream, science fiction, contemporary, prose poem. "No porn, no racist, sexist or any other kind of -ist. No Christian or spirituality proselytizing fiction." Wants to see more science fiction, erotica "assuming it relates to social change." Receives 15 unsolicited mss/month. Accepts 3-5 mss/issue, "however we are now doubling as a webzine, which means a dramatic change in how we operate. Any work considered suitable will first be published in the web version and will be held for further consideration for the print version." Publishes ms 3-9 months after acceptance. **Publishes 10 new writers/year.** Recently published work by Margaret Karmazin, Benjamin Reed, John Tuschen, Ken Byrnes. Length: 500-5,000 words; average length: 3,500 words. Publishes short shorts. Always comments on rejected mss.

How to Contact Include SASE. Responds in 4 months to mss. Accepts simultaneous, multiple submissions and reprints. Sample copy for $2, 9 × 12 SAE and 3 first class stamps. Writer's guidelines for SASE.

Payment/Terms Pays contributor's copies. Acquires one-time rights, electronic rights for www version.

Tips "Note that fiction and poetry may be simultaneously published in e-version of Mobius. Due to space constraints of print version, some works may be accepted in e-version, but not print version. We like high impact, we like plot and character-driven stories that function like theater of the mind. Looks for first and foremost, good writing. Prose must be crisp and polished; the story must pique my interest and make me care due to a certain intellectual, emotional aspect. Second, *Mobius* is about social change. We want stories that make some statement about the society we live in, either on a macro or micro level. Not that your story neeeds to preach from a soapbox (actually, we prefer that it doesn't), but your story needs to have *something* to say."

☑ THE MOCHILA REVIEW

Hignell Book Printing. Website: www.missouriwestern.edu/EFLJ /mochila. **Contact:** Bill Church, editor. Magazine: 9 × 6; 120-160 pages; photos. "Good readership, no theme." Annual. Estab. 2000.

Needs Literary. Does not accept genre work, erotica. Receives 25 unsolicited mss/month. Accepts 5-10 mss/issue. Does not read mss December-July. Publishes ms 6 months after acceptance. **Publishes 2-3 new writers/year.** Length: 5,000 words (max); average length: 3,000 words. Publishes short shorts; average 500 words. Also publishes literary essays, poetry. Rarely comments on rejected mss.

How to Contact Send complete disposable copy of ms with cover letter and #10 SASE for reply only. Include estimated word count, brief bio and list of publications. Responds in 3-5 months to mss. Accepts simultaneous submissions. Sample copy for $7. Writer's guidelines for SASE or on Web site.

Payment/Terms Pays 2 contributor's copies; additional copies $5. Acquires first rights. Publication not copyrighted.

Tips "Manuscripts with fresh language, energy, passion and intelligence stand out. Study the craft and be entertaining and engaging."

☑ NASSAU REVIEW

Nassau Community College, State University of New York, 1 Education Dr., Garden City NY 11530-6793. (516)572-7792. **Contact:** Editorial Board. Magazine: 6½ × 9½; 200 pages; heavy stock paper and cover; illustrations; photos. "Looking for high-level, professionally talented fiction on any subject matter except science fiction. Intended for a college and university faculty-level audience. Not geared to college students or others of that age who have not yet reached professional competency." Annual. Estab. 1964. Circ. 1,200. Member Council of Literary Magazines & Presses.

Needs Historical (general), humor/satire, literary, mainstream, mystery/suspense (amateur sleuth, cozy). "No science fiction." Receives 200-400 unsolicited mss/month. Accepts 5-6 mss/year. Does not read mss April-October. Publishes ms 6 months after acceptance. **Publishes 3-4 new writers/year.** Recently published work by Louis Phillips, Dick Wimmer, Norbert Petsch, Mike Lipstock. Length: 2,000-6,000 words; average length: 3,000-4,000 words. Publishes short shorts. Also publishes literary essays, literary criticism, poetry.

How to Contact Send 3 disposable copies of ms and #10 SASE for reply only. Responds in 2 weeks to queries; 6 months to mss. No simultaneous submissions. Sample copy free.

Payment/Terms Pays contributor's copies. Acquires one-time rights. Sponsors awards/contests.

Tips "We look for narrative drive, perceptive characterization and professional competence. Write concretely. Does not want over-elaborate details, and avoid digressions."

☑ NERVE COWBOY

Liquid Paper Press, P.O. Box 4973, Austin TX 78765. Website: www.jwhagins.com/nervecowboy.html.

Contact: Joseph Shields or Jerry Hagins, editors. Magazine: 7 × 8½; 64 pages; 20 lb. paper; card stock cover; illustrations. "Nerve Cowboy publishes adventurous, comical, disturbing, thought-provoking, accessible poetry and fiction. We like to see work sensitive enough to make the hardest hard-ass cry, funny enough to make the most helpless brooder laugh and disturbing enough to make us all glad we're not the author of the piece." Semiannual. Estab. 1996. Circ. 400.

Needs Literary. No "racist, sexist or overly offensive work. Wants more unusual stories with rich description and enough twists and turns that leave the reader thinking." Receives 40 unsolicited mss/month. Accepts 2-3 mss/issue; 4-6 mss/year. Publishes ms 6-12 months after acceptance. **Publishes 5-10 new writers/year.** Recently published work by Lori Jakiela, Michele Anne Jaquays, Tom Schmidt, David Elsey, Michael A. Flanagan. Length: 1,500 words; average length: 750-1,000 words. Publishes short shorts. Also publishes poetry.

How to Contact Send SASE for reply, return of ms or send a disposable copy of ms. Responds in 6 weeks to queries; 3 months to mss. Accepts reprint submissions. No simultaneous submissions. Sample copy for $6. Writer's guidelines for #10 SASE or online.

Payment/Terms Pays 1 contributor's copy. Acquires one-time rights.

Tips "We look for writing which is very direct and elicits a visceral reaction in the reader. Read magazines you submit to in order to get a feel for what the editors are looking for. Write simply and from the gut."

☑ ☑ NEW DELTA REVIEW

Louisiana State University, Dept. of English, 214 Allen Hall, Baton Rouge LA 70803-5001. (225) 578-4079. E-mail: new-delta@lsu.edu. Website: http://www.lsu.edu/newdeltareview/. **Contact:** Editors change every year. Check Web site. Magazine: 6 × 9; 75-125 pages; high quality paper; glossy card cover; color artwork. "We seek vivid and exciting work from new and established writers. We have published fiction from writers such as Stacy Richter, Mark Poirier and George Singleton." Semiannual. Estab. 1984. Circ. 500.

- *New Delta Review* also sponsors the Matt Clark Prizes for fiction and poetry. Work from the magazine has been included in the *Pushcart Prize* anthology.

Needs Humor/satire, literary, mainstream, translations, contemporary, prose poem. "No Elvis stories, overwrought 'Southern' fiction, or cancer stories." Receives 150 unsolicited mss/month. Accepts 3-4 mss/issue; 6-8 mss/year. Reads from August 15-April 15. **Publishes 1-3 new writers/year.** Average length: 15 ms pages. Publishes short shorts. Also publishes poetry. Rarely comments on rejected mss.

How to Contact SASE (or IRC). Responds in 3 weeks to queries; 3 months to mss. Accepts simultaneous submissions only when stated in the cover letter. Sample copy for $7.

Payment/Terms Pays in contributor's copies. Charge for extras. Acquires first North American serial, electronic rights. Sponsors awards/contests.

Tips "Our staff is open-minded and youthful. We base decisions on merit, not reputation. The manuscript that's most enjoyable to read gets the nod. Be bold, take risks, surprise us."

☑ $ ☑ NEW LETTERS

University of Missouri-Kansas City, University House, 5101 Rockhill Road, Kansas City MO 64110-2499. (816) 235-1168. Fax: (816) 235-2611. E-mail: newletters@umkc.edu. Website: www.newletters. org. **Contact:** Robert Stewart, editor. Magazine: 6X9, 14 lb. cream paper; illustrations. "New Letters is intended for the general literary reader. We publish literary fiction, nonfiction, essays, poetry. We also publish art." Quarterly. Estab. 1934. Circ. 2,500.

Needs Ethnic/multicultural, experimental, humor/satire, literary, mainstream, translations, contemporary. No genre fiction. Does not read mss May 1-October 1. Publishes ms 5 months after acceptance. Recently published work by Thomas E. Kennedy, Sheila Kohler, Charlotte Holmes, Rosellen Brown, Janet Burroway. Publishes short shorts.

How to Contact Send complete ms. Do not submit by e-mail. Responds in 1 month to queries; 3 months to mss. No simultaneous submissions. Sample copy for $10 or sample articles on Web site. Writer's guidelines online.

Payment/Terms Pays $30-75 for fiction and $15 for single poem. Pays on publication for first North American serial rights. Sends galleys to author. $4,500 awarded annually in writing contest for short fiction, essay, and poetry. Visit www.newletters.org for contest guidelines.

Tips "Seek publication of representative chapters in high-quality magazines as a way to the book contract. Try literary magazines first."

⌾ ☑ NEW MADRID

Murray State University, 7C Faculty Hall, Murray KY 42071. (270) 809-4730. E-mail: newmadrid@ murraystate.edu. Website: www.newmadridjournal.org. **Contact:** Ann Neelon, editor. Literary magazine/ journal: 160 pages. "New Madrid is the national journal of the low-residency MFA program at Murray State University. It takes its name from the New Madrid seismic zone, which falls within the central Mississippi Valley and extends through western Kentucky." Semiannual. Estab. 2007. Circ.1,000.

Needs Literary. See Web site for guidelines and upcoming themes. "We have two reading periods, one from August 15-November 1, and one from January 15-April 1." Also publishes poetry and creative nonfiction. Rarely comments on/critiques rejected mss.

How to Contact Accepts submissions by Online Submissions Manager only. Include brief bio, list of publications. Considers multiple submissions. Guidelines available on Web site.

Payment/Terms Pays 2 contributor's copies on publication. Acquires first North American serial rights. Publication is copyrighted.

Tips "Quality is the determining factor for breaking in *New Madrid*. We are looking for well-crafted, compelling writing in a range of genres, forms and styles."

⌾ $ NEW MILLENNIUM WRITINGS

New Messenger Writing and Publishing, P.O. Box 2463, Knoxville TN 37901. Phone/fax: (865) 428-0389. E-mail: donwilliams7@charter.net. Website: http://newmillenniumwritings.com. **Contact:** Don Williams, editor. Annual anthology. 6 × 9, 204 pages, 50 lb. white paper, glossy 4-color cover. Contains illustrations. Includes photographs. "Superior writing is the sole criterion." Annual. Estab. 1996. Circ. 3,000. Received Golden Presscard Award from Sigma Delta Chi (1997)

Needs "While we no longer accept unsolicited submissions, except for profiles or interviews of famous authors, we hold four contests twice each year for all types of fiction, nonfiction, short-short fiction and poetry." Receives average of 200 mss/month. Accepts 60 mss/year. Manuscript published 6 months to one year after acceptance. Agented fiction 0%. Publishes 10 new writers/year. Published Charles Wright, Ted Kooser, Allen Wier, Lucille Clifton, and Don Williams. Length: 200 words (min)-6,000 words (max). Average length: 4,000 words for fiction. Publishes short shorts. Also publishes literary essays, poetry. Rarely comments on/critiques rejected manuscripts.

How to Contact Accepts ms through biannual *New Millennium Writing* Awards only. Visit Web site for more information.

Payment/Terms See listing for *New Millennium Writing* Awards in Contests & Awards section.

Tips "Looks for originality, accessibility, musicality, psychological insight, moral sensibility. E-mail for list of writing tips or send SASE. No charge."

☑ ☑ NEW ORLEANS REVIEW

Box 195, Loyola University, New Orleans LA 70118. (504)865-2295. Fax: (504)865-2294. E-mail: noreview@loyno.edu. Website: www.loyno.edu/~noreview/. **Contact:** Christopher Chambers, editor. Journal: 6 × 9; perfect bound; 200 pages; photos. "Publishes poetry, fiction, translations, photographs, nonfiction on literature, art and film. Readership: those interested in contemporary literature and culture." Biannual. Estab. 1968. Circ. 1,500.

- Work from the *New Orleans Review* has been anthologized in *New Stores from theSouth* and the *Pushcart Prize Anthology. Best American Non required reading, Best American Poetry, O. Henry Prize Anthology.*

Needs "Quality fiction from conventional to experimental." **Publishes 12 new writers/year.** Recently published work by Gordon Lish, Michael Martone, Dylan Landis, Stephen Graham Jones, Carolyn Sanchez and Josh Russell.

How to Contact Responds in 4 months to mss. Accepts simultaneous submissions "if we are notified immediately upon acceptance elsewhere." Sample copy for $6. Reviews fiction.

Payment/Terms Pays $25-50 and 2 copies. Pays on publication for first North American serial rights.

Tips "We're looking for dynamic writing that demostrates attention to the language, and a sense of the medium, writing that engages, surprises, moves us. We're not looking for genre fiction, or academic articles. We subscribe to the belief that in order to truly write well, one must first master the rudiments: grammar and syntax, punctuation, the sentence, the paragraph, the line, the stanza. We recieve about 3,000 manuscripts a year, and publish about 3% of them. Check out a recent issue, send us your best, proofread your work, be patient, be persistent."

☼ ☑ ☑ THE NEW ORPHIC REVIEW

New Orphic Publishers, 706 Mill St., Nelson BC V1L 4S5 Canada. (250)354-0494. Website: www3.telus. net/neworphicpublishers-hekkanen. **Contact:** Ernest Hekkanen, editor-in-chief. Magazine; 5½ × 8½; 120 pages; common paper; 100 lb. color cover. "In the traditional Orphic fashion, our magazine accepts a wide range of styles and approaches—from naturalism to the surreal, but, please, get to the essence of the narrative, emotion, conflict, state of being, whatever." Semiannual. Estab. 1998. Circ. 300.

• Margrith Schraner's story, "Dream Dig" was included in *The Journey Prize Anthology*, 2001.

Needs Ethnic/multicultural, experimental, fantasy, historical (general), literary, mainstream. "No detective or sword and sorcery stories." List of upcoming themes available for SASE. Receives 20 unsolicited mss/month. Accepts 10 mss/issue; 22 mss/year. Publishes ms 1 year after acceptance. **Publishes 6-8 new writers/year.** Recently published work by Eveline Hasler (Swiss), Leena Krohn (Finnish), Pekka Salmi. Length: 2,000-10,000 words; average length: 3,500 words. Publishes short shorts. Also publishes literary essays, literary criticism, poetry. Sometimes comments on rejected mss.

How to Contact Send SASE (or IRC) for return of ms or send a disposable copy of ms and #10 SASE for reply only. Responds in 1 month to queries; 4 months to mss. Accepts simultaneous, multiple submissions. Sample copy for $17.50. Writer's guidelines for SASE. Reviews fiction.

Payment/Terms Pays 1 contributor's copy; additional copies $14. Pays on publication for first North American serial rights.

Tips "I like fiction that deals with issues, accounts for every motive, has conflict, is well written and tackles something that is substantive. Don't be mundane; try for more, not less."

☑ NEW SOUTH

Georgia State University, Campus P.O. Box 1894, MSC 8R0322 Unit 8, Atlanta GA 30303-3083. (404) 413-5874. Fax: (404) 413-5830. Website: www.review.gsu.edu. **Contact:** Prose Editor. Literary journal. "New South is a biannual literary magazine publishing poetry, fiction, creative nonfiction, and visual art. We're looking for original voices and well-written manuscripts. No subject or form biases." Biannual.

Needs Literary fiction and creative nonfiction. Receives 200 unsolicited mss/month. Publishes and welcomes short shorts.

How to Contact Include SASE for notification. Responds in 3-5 months. Sample copy for $5. Writer's guidelines for SASE or on Web site.

Payment/Terms Pays in contributor's copy. Acquires one-time rights.

▦ ☑ THE NEW WRITER

P.O. Box 60, Cranbrook TN17 2ZR United Kingdom. 01580 212626. E-mail: editor@the newwriter. com. Website: www.thenewwriter.com. **Contact:** Suzanne Ruthven, editor. Magazine: A4; 56 pages; illustrations; photos. Contemporary writing magazine which publishes "the best in fact, fiction and poetry." Publishes 6 issues per annum. Estab. 1996. Circ. 1,500.

Needs "We will consider most categories apart from stories written for children. No horror, erotic or cosy fiction." Accepts 4 mss/issue; 24 mss/year. Publishes ms 1 year after acceptance. Agented fiction 5%. **Publishes 12 new writers/year.** Recently published work by Sally Zigmond, Lorna Dowell, Wes Lee, Amy Licence, Cathy Whitfield, Katy Darby, Clio Gray. Length: 2,000-5,000 words; average length: 3,500 words. Publishes short shorts. Also publishes literary essays, literary criticism, poetry. Often comments on rejected mss.

How to Contact Query with published clips. Accepts submissions by e-mail, fax. Send SASE (or IRC) for return of ms or send a disposable copy of ms and #10 SASE for reply only. "We consider short stories from subscribers only but we may also commission guest writers." Responds in 2 months to queries; 4 months to mss. Accepts simultaneous submissions. Sample copy for SASE and A4 SAE with IRCs only. Writer's guidelines for SASE. Reviews fiction.

Payment/Terms Pays £10 per story by credit voucher; additional copies for £1.50. Pays on publication for one-time rights. Sponsors awards/contests.

Tips "Hone it—always be prepared to improve the story. It's a competitive market."

☑ NIMROD

University of Tulsa, 800 S. Tucker Dr., Tulsa OK 74104-3189. (918)631-3080. Fax: (918)631-3033. E-mail: nimrod@utulsa.edu. Website: www.utulsa.edu/nimrod/. **Contact:** Gerry McLoud, fiction editor. Magazine: 6 × 9; 192 pages; 60 lb. white paper; illustrations; photos. "We publish one thematic issue and one awards issue each year. A recent theme was 'Crossing Borders,' a compilation of poetry and prose from all over the world. We seek vigorous, imaginative, quality writing. Our mission is to discover new writers and publish experimental writers who have not yet found a 'home' for their work." Semiannual. Estab. 1956. Circ. 3,000.

Needs "We accept contemporary poetry and/or prose. May submit adventure, ethnic, experimental, prose poem or translations. No science fiction or romance." Receives 120 unsolicited mss/month. **Publishes 5-10 new writers/year.** Recently published work by Felicia Ward, Ellen Bass, Jeanette Turner Hospital, Kate Small. Also publishes poetry.

How to Contact SASE for return of ms. Accepts queries by e-mail. Does not accept submissions by e-mail unless the writer is living outside the U.S. Responds in 5 months to mss. Accepts simultaneous, multiple submissions.

Payment/Terms Pays 2 contributor's copies.

Tips "We have not changed our fiction needs: quality, vigor, distinctive voice. We have, however, increased the number of stories we print. See current issues. We look for fiction that is fresh, vigorous, distinctive, serious and humorous, unflinchingly serious, ironic—whatever. Just so it is quality. Strongly encourage writers to send #10 SASE for brochure for annual literary contest with prizes of $1,000 and $2,000."

◎ $ ☑ THE NORTH AMERICAN REVIEW

University of Northern Iowa, Cedar Falls IA 50614-0516. (319)273-6455. Fax: (319)273-4326. Website: www.webdelsol.com/NorthAmReview/NAR/. **Contact:** Grant Tracey, fiction editor. "The NAR is the oldest literary magazine in America and one of the most respected. Though we have no prejudices about the subject matter of material sent to us, our first concern is quality." Bimonthly. Estab. 1815. Circ. under 5,000.

• Works published in *The North American Review* have won the Pushcart Prize.

Needs Open (literary). "No flat narrative stories where the inferiority of the character is the paramount concern." Wants to see more "well-crafted literary stories that emphasize family concerns. We'd also like to see more stories engaged with environmental concerns." Reads fiction mss all year. Publishes ms an average of 1 year after acceptance. **Publishes 2 new writers/year.** Recently published work by Lee Ann Roripaugh, Dick Allen, Rita Welty Bourke.

How to Contact Accepts submissions by USPS mail only. Send complete ms with SASE. Responds in 3 months to queries; 4 months to mss. No simultaneous submissions. Sample copy for $5. Writer's guidelines online.

Payment/Terms Pays $5/350 words; $20 minimum, $100 maximum. Pays on publication for first North American serial, first rights.

Tips "Stories that do not condescend to the reader or their character are always appealing to us. We also like stories that have characters doing things (acting upon the world instead of being acted upon). We also like a strong narrative arc. Stories that are mainly about language need not apply. Your first should be your second best line. Your last sentence should be your best. Everything in the middle should approach the two."

◎ NORTH CAROLINA LITERARY REVIEW, A Magazine of North Carolina Literature, Literary History and Culture

English Dept., East Carolina University, Greenville NC 27858-4353. (252) 328-1537. Fax: (252) 328-4889. E-mail: bauerm@ecu.edu. Website: www.ecu.edu/nclr. "Articles should have a North Carolina literature slant. First consideration is always for quality of work. Although we treat academic and scholarly subjects, we do not wish to see jargon-laden prose; our readers, we hope, are found as often in bookstores and libraries as in academia. We seek to combine the best elements of a magazine for serious readers with the best of a scholarly journal." Annual. Estab. 1992. Circ. 750.

Needs Regional (North Carolina). Must be North Carolina related—either a North Carolina-connected writer or set in North Carolina. Publishes ms 1 year after acceptance.

How to Contact Query. Accepts queries by e-mail. Responds in 1 month to queries; within 6 months to mss. Sample copy for $10-25. Writer's guidelines online.

Payment/Terms Pays on publication for first North American serial rights. Rights returned to writer on request.

☐ ◉ NORTH CENTRAL REVIEW, YOUR UNDERGRADUATE LITERARY JOURNAL

North Central College, 30 N. Brainard St., CM #235, Naperville IL 60540. (630)637-5280. Fax: (630) 637-5221. E-mail: nccreview@noctrl.edu. Website: http://orgs.northcentralcollege.edu/review. **Contact:** Dr. Richard Guzman, advisor. Magazine has revolving editor. Editorial term: Editor changes each year in the Fall. Literary magazine/journal: 5½ × 8½, 120 pages, perfect binding, color card-stock cover. Includes black and white art. "The North Central Review is an undergraduate literary journal soliciting fiction, poetry, nonfiction and drama from around the country and the globe—but only from college students. This offers undergraduates a venue for sharing their work with their peers." Semiannual. Estab. 1936, undergraduate focus as of 2005. Circ. 500-750, depending on funding.

Needs Considers all categories. Deadlines: February 15 and October 15. Does not read February 15-August 15. Accepts 4-8 mss/issue; 8-16 mss/year. Manuscript published 2-3 months after acceptance. Agented fiction 0%. **Publishes "at least half, probably more" new writers/year.**Length: 5,000 words (max). Average length: 2,000 words. Publishes short shorts. Average length of short shorts: 100-700 words. Also publishes literary essays, poetry. Rarely comments on/critiques rejected manuscripts.

How to Contact Send complete ms with cover letter. Accepts submissions by e-mail. Include student (.edu) e-mail address or copy of student ID with ID number marked. Responds to queries in 2 weeks. Responds to mss in 4 months. Send disposable copy of ms and #10 SASE for reply only. Considers multiple submissions. Sample copy free upon request (older issue) or available for $5 (most recent issue). Guidelines available at Web site, for SASE, via e-mail.

Payment/Terms Writers receive 2 contributors copies. Additional copies $5. Pays on publication. Acquires one-time rights.

Tips "The reading staff changes year to year (and sometimes from one academic term to the next) so tastes change. That said, at least three readers evaluate each submission, and there's usually a widespread agreement on the best ones. While all elements need to work together, readers take notice when one element—maybe setting or character—captivates and even teaches the reader something new. Don't send something you just drafted and printed. Give your work some time, revise it, and polish what you plan to send us. That said, don't hesitate to submit and submit again to the *North Central Review*. Undergraduates are beginners, and we welcome new voices."

☑ ☒ NORTH DAKOTA QUARTERLY

University of North Dakota, Merrifield Hall Room 110, 276 Centennial Drive Stop 7209 Grand Forks ND 58202-7209. (701) 777-3322. Fax: (701) 777-2373. E-mail: ndq@und.edu. Website: www.und.nodak.edu/org/ndq. **Contact:** Robert W. Lewis, editor. Magazine: 6 × 9; 200 pages; bond paper; illustrations; photos. "North Dakota Quarterly is a literary journal publishing essays in the humanities; some short stories, some poetry. Occasional special topic issues." General audience. Quarterly. Estab. 1911. Circ. 600.

• Work published in *North Dakota Quarterly* was selected for inclusion in *The O. Henry Prize Stories, The Pushcart Prize Series,* and *Best American Essays*.

Needs Ethnic/multicultural, experimental, feminist, historical, literary, Native American. Receives 125-150 unsolicited mss/month. Accepts 4 mss/issue; 16 mss/year. Publishes ms 2 years after acceptance. **Publishes 4-5 new writers/year.** Recently published work by Louise Erdrich, Robert Day, Maxine Kumin and Fred Arroyo. Average length: 3,000-4,000 words. Also publishes literary essays and criticism. Sometimes comments on rejected mss.

How to Contact SASE. Responds in 3 months to mss. Sample copy for $10. Reviews fiction.

Payment/Terms Pays 2-4 contributor's copies; 30% discount for extras. Acquires one-time rights. Sends galleys to author.

☑ $ ☒ NOTRE DAME REVIEW

University of Notre Dame, 840 Flanner Hall, Notre Dame IN 46556. (574)631-6952. Fax: (574)631-8209. Website: www.nd.edu/~ndr/review.htm. **Contact:** William O'Rourke, fiction editor. Literary magazine: 6 × 9; 200 pages; 50 lb. smooth paper; illustrations; photos. "The Notre Dame Review is an indepenent, noncommercial magazine of contemporary American and international fiction, poetry, criticism and art. We are especially interested in work that takes on big issues by making the invisible seen, that gives voice to the voiceless. In addition to showcasing celebrated authors like Seamus Heaney and Czelaw Milosz, the Notre Dame Review introduces readers to authors they may have never encountered before, but who are doing innovative and important work. In conjunction with the Notre Dame Review, the online companion to the printed magazine engages readers as a community centered in literary rather than commercial concerns, a community we reach out to through critique and commentary as well as aesthetic experience." Semiannual. Estab. 1995. Circ. 1,500.

• Pushcart prizes in fiction and poetry. Best American Short stories; Best American Poetry.

Needs No genre fiction. Upcoming theme issues planned. Receives 75 unsolicited mss/month. Accepts 4-5 mss/issue; 10 mss/year. Does not read mss November-January or April-August. Publishes ms 6 months after acceptance. **Publishes 1 new writer/year.** Recently published work by Ed Falco, Jarda Cerverka, David Green. Publishes short shorts. Also publishes literary criticism, poetry.

How to Contact Send complete ms with cover letter. Include 4-sentence bio. Send SASE for response, return of ms, or send a disposable copy of ms. Responds in 6 months to mss. Accepts simultaneous submissions. Sample copy for $6. Writer's guidelines online. Mss sent during summer months will be returned unread.

Payment/Terms Pays $5-25. Pays on publication for first North American serial rights.

Tips "We're looking for high quality work that takes on big issues in a literary way. Please read our back issues before submitting."

◎ OBSIDIAN III

Dept. of English, North Carolina State University, Raleigh NC 27695-8105. (919)515-4153. Fax: (919)515-1836. E-mail: obsidian@social.chass.ncsu.edu. Website: www.ncsu.edu/chass/obsidian/. **Contact:** Sheila Smith McKoy, editor. Magazine: 130 pages. "Creative works in English by black writers, scholarly critical studies by all writers on black literature in English." Published 2 times/year (spring/summer, fall/winter). Estab. 1975. Circ. 500.

Needs Ethnic/multicultural (Pan-African), feminist, literary. Accepts 7-9 mss/year. Publishes ms 4-6 months after acceptance. **Publishes 20 new writers/year.** Recently published work by R. Flowers Rivera, Terrance Hayes, Eugene Kraft, Arlene McKanic, Pearl Bothe Williams, Kwane Dawes, Jay Wright, and Octavia E. Butler.

How to Contact Accepts submissions by e-mail. Responds in 4 months to mss. Sample copy for $10.

Payment/Terms Pays in contributor's copies. Acquires one-time rights. Sponsors awards/contests.

Tips "Following proper format is essential. Your title must be intriguing and text clean. Never give up. Some of the writers we publish were rejected many times before we published them."

☑ ◎ OHIO TEACHERS WRITE

Ohio Council of Teachers of English Language Arts, 644 Overlook Dr., Columbus OH 43214. E-mail: rmcclain@bright.net. **Contact:** Scott Parsons, editor. Editors change every 3 years. Magazine: 8½ × 11; 50 pages; 60 lb. white offset paper; 65 lb. blue cover stock; illustrations; photos. "The purpose of the magazine is three fold: (1) to provide a collection of fine literature for the reading pleasure of teachers and other adult readers; (2) to encourage teachers to compose literary works along with their students; (3) to provide the literate citizens of Ohio a window into the world of educators not often seen by those outside the teaching profession." Annual. Estab. 1995. Circ. 1,000. Submissions are limited to Ohio Educators.

Needs Adventure, ethnic/multicultural, experimental, fantasy (science fantasy), feminist, gay, historical, humor/satire, lesbian, literary, mainstream, regional, religious/inspirational, romance (contemporary), science fiction (hard science, soft/sociological), western (frontier, traditional), senior citizen/retirement, sports, teaching. Receives 2 unsolicited mss/month. Accepts 7 mss/issue. "We read only in May when editorial board meets." Recently published work by Lois Spencer, Harry R. Noden, Linda J. Rice, June Langford Berkley. Publishes short shorts. Also publishes poetry. Often comments on rejected mss.

How to Contact Send SASE with postage clipped for return of ms or send a disposable copy of ms. Accepts multiple submissions. Sample copy for $6.

Payment/Terms Pays 2 contributor's copies; additional copies $6. Acquires first rights.

▣ ▢ OPEN WIDE MAGAZINE

40 Wingfield Road, Lakenheath, Brandon, Suffolk IP27 9HR United Kingdom. E-mail: contact@ openwidemagazine.co.uk. Website: www.openwidemagazine.co.uk. **Contact:** Liz Roberts. Online literary magazine/journal: Quarterly. Estab. 2001.

Needs Christian-based journal enjoyes adventure, ethnic/multicultural, experimental, feminist, humor/ satire, mainstream, mystery/suspense, principle beat. Receives 100 mss/month. Accepts 25 mss/issue. Manuscript published 3 months after acceptance. **Publishes 30 new writers/year.** Length: 500-4,000. Average length: 2,500. Publishes short shorts. Also publishes poetry, reviews (music, film, art) and interviews. Rarely comments on/critiques rejected mss.

How to Contact Accepts submissions by e-mail. Include estimated word count, brief bio. Send either SASE (or IRC) for return of ms or disposable copy of ms and #10 SASE for reply only.

Payment/Terms Acquires one-time rights. Publication is copyrighted.

▢ OYEZ REVIEW

Roosevelt University, Dept. of Literature and languages, 430 S. Michigan Ave., Chicago IL 60605.(312)341-3770. E-mail: oyezreview@roosevelt.edu. Website: www.roosevelt.edu/oyezreview. **Contact:** Dr. Janet Wondra, editor. Literary magazine/journal. "Oyez Review publishes fiction, creative nonfiction, poetry and art. There are no restrictions on style, theme, or subject matter." Annual. Estab. 1965. Circ. 800.

Needs Publishes short stories and flash fiction from established authors and newcomers. Literary excellence is our goal and our primary criterion. Send us your best work, and you will receive a thoughtful, thorough reading. Recently published J. Weintraub, Lori Rader Day, Joyce Goldenstern, Norman Lock, Peter Obourn, Jotham Burrello.

How to Contact Accepts art and international submissions by e-mail. Sample copy available for $5. Guidelines available on Web site.

Payment/Terms Writers receive 2 contributors copies. Acquires first North American serial rights.

Tips "Writers should familiarize themselves with a variety of literary magazines in addition to ours in order to understand what contemporary literary magazines do and do not publish. Note that e-mail submissions, simultaneous submissions, work received without an SASE, and mss received before or after our August 1-October 1 reading period will not be read. We read complete manuscripts rather than queries."

OYSTER BOY REVIEW

P.O. Box 299, Pacifica CA 94044. E-mail: fiction@oysterboyreview.com. Website: www.oysterboyreview. com. **Contact**: Craig Nelson, fiction editor. Damon Suave, editor/publisher. Electronic and print magazine. "We publish kick-ass, teeth-cracking stories." Published 2-3 times a year.

Needs No genre fiction. "Fiction that revolves around characters in conflict with themselves or each other; a plot that has a beginning, a middle, and an end; a narrative with a strong moral center (not necessarily 'moralistic'); a story with a satisfying resolution to the conflict; and an ethereal something that contributes to the mystery of a question, but does not necessarily seek or contrive to answer it." Submissions closed for 2009. **Publishes 4 new writers/year.** Recently published work by Todd Goldberg, Ken Wainio, Elisha Porat, Kevin McGowan.

How to Contact Accepts multiple submissions. Sample copy not available.

Tips "Keep writing, keep submitting, keep revising."

▢ PACIFIC COAST JOURNAL

French Bread Publications, P.O. Box 56, Carlsbad CA 92018. E mail: paccoastj@frenchbreadpublications. com. Website: www.frenchbreadpublications.com/pcj. **Contact:**Stephanie Kylkis, fiction editor. Magazine: 5½ × 8½; 40 pages; 20 lb. paper; 67 lb. cover; illustrations; b&w photos. "Slight focus toward Western North America/Pacific Rim." Quarterly. Estab. 1992. Circ. 200.

Needs Ethnic/multicultural, experimental, feminist, historical, humor/satire, literary, science fiction (soft/sociological, magical realism). "No children's, religious, or hard sci-fi." Receives 150unsolicited mss/month. Accepts 3-4 mss/issue; 10-12 mss/year. Publishes ms 6-18 months after acceptance. Length: 4,000 words; average length: 2,500 words. Publishes short shorts. Also publishes literary essays, poetry. Sometimes comments on rejected mss.

How to Contact Send SASE for reply, return of ms or send a disposable copy of ms. Also accepts e-mail address for response instead of SASE. Responds in 6-9 months to mss. Accepts simultaneous submissions and reprints. Sample copy for $3, 6 × 9 SASE and 3oz. postage. Reviews fiction.

Payment/Terms Pays 1 contributor's copy. Acquires one-time rights.

Tips *"PCJ* is an independent magazine and we have a limited amount of space and funding. We are looking for experiments in what can be done with the short fiction form. The best stories will entertain as well as confuse."

PACIFIC REVIEW

Dept. of English and Comparative Lit., San Diego State University, 5500 Campanile Dr. MC8140, San Diego CA 92182-6020. E-mail: pacificreview_sdsu@yahoo.com. Website: http://pacificreview.sdsu.edu. **Contact:** Lester O'Connor, fiction editor. Magazine: 6 × 9; 200 pages; book stock paper; paper back, extra heavy cover stock; b&w illustrations, b&w photos. "pacific REVIEW publishes the work of emergent literati, pairing their efforts with those of established artists. It is available at West Coast independent booksellers and university and college libraries and is taught as text in numerous university literature and creative writing classes." Circ. 2,000.

Needs "We welcome submissions of previously published poems, short stories, translations, and creative nonfiction, including essays and reviews." For information on theme issues see Web site. **Publishes 15 new writers/year.** Recently published work by Ai, Alurista, Susan Daitch, Lawrence Ferlinghetti, William T. Vollmann.

How to Contact Responds in 3 months to mss. Sample copy for $10.

Payment/Terms Pays 2 contributor's copies. Aquires first serial rights. All other rights revert to author.

Tips "We welcome all submissions, especially those created in or in the context of the West Coast/California and the space of our borders."

PACKINGTOWN REVIEW

University of Illinois, Chicago. E-mail: editors@packingtownreview.com. Website: www. packingtownreview.com. **Contact:** Tasha Fouts and Snezana Zabic, Editors-in-Chief. Magazine has revolving editor. Editorial term: 3 years. Next term: 2011. Literary magazine/journal. 812X11, 250 pages. "Packingtown Review publishes imaginative and critical prose by emerging and established writers. We welcome submissions of poetry, scholarly articles, drama, creative nonfiction, fiction, and literary translation, as well as genre-bending pieces." Annual. Estab. 2008.

Needs Comics/graphic novels, ethnic/multicultural (general), experimental, feminist, gay, glitz, historical (general), literary, mainstream, military/war, translations. Does not want to see uninspired or unrevised work. "We also would like to avoid fantasy, science fiction, overtly religious, or romantic pieces." Ms published max of nine months after acceptance. Length: 3,000 words (min)-8,000 words (max). Publishes short shorts. Also publishes literary essays, literary criticism, book reviews, poetry. Send review copies to Tasha Fouts or Snezana Zabic (Editors-in-Chief). Sometimes comments on/critiques rejected mss.

How to Contact Send complete ms with cover letter. Include estimated word count, brief bio. Responds to queries in 3 weeks. Responds to mss in 3 months. Considers simultaneous submissions. See Web site for price guidelines. Guidelines available for SASE, via e-mail.

Payment/Terms Writers receive 2 contributor's copies. Pays on publication. Acquires first North American serial rights. Sends galleys to author. Publication is copyrighted.

Tips "We are looking for well crafted prose. We are open to most styles and forms. We are also looking for prose that takes risks and does so successfully. We will consider articles about prose."

PADDLEFISH

1105 W. 8th Street, Yankton SD 5708. (605) 688-1362. E-mail: james.reese@mtmc.edu. Website: www. mmcpaddlefish.com. **Contact:** Dr. Jim Reese, editor. Literary magazine/journal. 6 × 9, 150 pages. Includes photographs. "We publish unique and creative pieces." Annual. Estab. 2007.

Needs Adventure, comics/graphic novels, erotica, ethnic/multicultural, experimental, family saga, fantasy, feminist, gay, glitz, historical, horror, humor/satire, lesbian, literary, mainstream, military/war, mystery, new age, psychic/supernatural/occult, religious, romance, science fiction, thriller/espionage, translations, western, young adult/teen. Does not want excessive or gratuitous language, sex or violence. Receives 300 mss/month. Accepts 30 mss/year. Submission period is Nov 1-Feb 28. Ms published 3-9 months after acceptance. **Publishes 5-10 new writers/year.** Published David Lee, William Kloefkorn,

David Allen Evans, Jack Anderson and Maria Mazziotti Gillan. Length: 2,500 words (max). Publishes short shorts. Also publishes literary essays, poetry. Rarely comments on/critiques rejected mss.

How to Contact Send complete ms with cover letter. Include estimated word count, brief bio, list of publications. Send disposable copy of ms and #10 SASE for reply only. Guidelines available for SASE.

Payment/Terms Writers receive 1 contributor's copy. Additional copies $8. Pays on publication. Acquires one-time rights. Sends galleys to author. Publication is copyrighted. "Cash prizes are award to Mount Marty students."

☑ PAINTED BRIDE QUARTERLY

Drexel University, Dept. of English, 3141 Chestnut Street, Philadelphia PA 19104. E-mail: pbq@drexel. edu. Website: http://pbq.drexel.edu. **Contact:** Kathleen Volk-Miller, managing editor. "PBQ seeks literary fiction, experimental and traditional." Publishes online each quarter and a print annual each spring. Estab. 1973.

Needs Ethnic/multicultural, experimental, feminist, gay, lesbian, literary, translations. "No genre fiction." "Publishes theme-related work, check Web site; holds annual fiction contests. **Publishes 24 new writers/ year.** Length: 5,000 words; average length: 3,000 words. Publishes short shorts. Also publishes literary essays, literary criticism, poetry. Occasionally comments on rejected mss.

How to Contact Send complete ms. No electronic submissions. Responds in 6 months to mss. Sample copy online. Writer's guidelines online. Reviews fiction.

Payment/Terms Acquires first North American serial rights.

Tips We look for "freshness of idea incorporated with high-quality writing. We receive an awful lot of nicely written work with worn-out plots. We want quality in whatever—we hold experimental work to as strict standards as anything else. Many of our readers write fiction; most of them enjoy a good reading. We hope to be an outlet for quality. A good story gives, first, enjoyment to the reader. We've seen a good many of them lately, and we've published the best of them."

☑ ☒ $ PALO ALTO REVIEW

Palo Alto College, 1400 W. Villaret, San Antonio TX 78224. (210)486-3249. Fax: (210)486-3231. E-mail: eshull@mail.accd.edu. **Contact**: Ellen Shull, editor. Magazine: 8½ × 11; 64 pages; 60 lb. gloss white paper; illustrations; photos. More than half of each issue is devoted to articles and essays. "We select stories that we would want to read again. Not too experimental nor excessively avant-garde, just good fiction." Semiannual. Estab. 1992. Circ. 500.

• *Palo Alto Review* was awarded the Pushcart Prize for 2001.

Needs Adventure, ethnic/multicultural, experimental, fantasy, feminist, historical, humor/satire, literary, mainstream, mystery/suspense, regional, romance, science fiction, translations, western. Upcoming themes available for SASE. Receives 100-150 unsolicited mss/month. Accepts 2-3 mss/issue; 4-6 mss/ year. Does not read mss April -May and October-December when putting out each issue. Publishes ms 2-15 months after acceptance. **Publishes 20 new writers/year.** Recently published work by Char Miller, Naveed Noori, E.M. Schorb, Louis Phillips, Tom Filer, Jo Lecoeur, H. Palmer Hall. Publishes short shorts. Also publishes poetry, essays, articles, memoirs, book reviews. Always comments on rejected mss.

How to Contact Send SASE for reply, return of ms or send a disposable copy of ms. "Request sample copy and guidelines." Accepts submissions by e-mail only if outside the US. Responds in 4 months to mss. Accepts simultaneous submissions. Sample copy for $5. Writer's guidelines for #10 SASE or e-mail to eshull@accd.edu.

Payment/Terms Pays 2 contributor's copies; additional copies for $5. Acquires first North American serial rights.

Tips "Good short stories have interesting characters confronted by a dilemma working toward a solution. So often what we get is 'a moment in time,' not a story. Generally, characters are interesting because readers can identify with them. Edit judiciously. Cut out extraneous verbiage. Set up a choice that has to be made. Then create tension—who wants what and why they can't have it."

☐ ◉ $ ☒ PARADOX, THE MAGAZINE OF HISTORICAL AND SPECULATIVE FICTION

Paradox Publications, P.O. Box 22897, Brooklyn NY 11202-2897. E-mail: editor@paradoxmag.com. Website: www.paradoxmag.com. **Contact:** Christopher M. Cevasco, editor/publisher. Literary magazine/ journal: 8½ × 11, 57 pages, standard white paper with b&w interior art, glossy color cover. Contains illustrations. Includes photographs. "Paradox is the only English-language print magazine exclusively devoted to historical fiction in either its mainstream or genre forms." Semiannual. Estab. 2003. Circ. 600. Member Speculative Literature Foundation Small Press Co-operative. Awards: 2008 WSFA Small Press Award (Best Story); two stories were finalists for the 2006 Sidewise Award for Alternate History; numerous Honorable Mentions 2003-2007 in both Year's Best Fantasy & Horror, edited by Ellen Datlow, Kelly Link, and Gavin Grant and Year's Best Science Fiction, edited by Gardner Dozois.

Needs Fantasy (historical), horror (historical), military/war, historical mystery/suspense, science fiction (historical, e.g. time travel and alternate history), western (historical). Does not want children's stories, gratuitous erotica, vampires, werewolves. Receives 75 mss/month. Accepts 6-8 mss/issue; 12-16 mss/year. Manuscript published 6 months after acceptance. Agented fiction 5%. **Publishes 1-2 new writers/year.** Published Jack Whyte, Sarah Monette, Darrell Schweitzer, Paul Finch, Eugie Foster, Matthew Kirby (debut). Length: 500 words (min)-15,000 words (max). Average length: 6,000 words. Publishes short shorts. Average length of short shorts: 1,200 words. Also publishes literary essays, book reviews, poetry. Send review copies to Christopher M. Cevasco. Frequently comments on/critiques rejected manuscripts.

How to Contact Send complete ms with cover letter. Include estimated word count. Responds to mss in 4 months. Send SASE (or IRC) for return of ms or disposable copy of ms and #10 SASE for reply only; will reply to international submissions by e-mail. Sample copy available for $7.50 (includes postage), or for $8 to Canada, or for $11 elsewhere. Guidelines available on Web site.

Payment/Terms Writers receive 3¢-5¢/word, 4 contributor's copies. Additional copies 1/3 off cover price. Pays on publication. Acquires first world English-language rights. Sends galleys to author. Publication is copyrighted. "Offers periodic fiction writing contests; details posted in magazine and on Web site."

☑ PASSAGES NORTH

Northern Michigan University, Department of English, Gries Hall, Rm 229, Marquette MI 49855. (906) 227-1203. Fax: (906) 227-1096. E-mail: passages@nmu.edu. Website: http://myweb.nmu.edu/ ~ passages. **Contact:** Kate Myers Hanson, Editor-in-Chief. Magazine: 7 × 10; 200-300 pgs; 60 lb. paper. "Passages North publishes quality fiction, poetry and creative nonfiction by emerging and established writers." Annual. Estab. 1979. Circ. 1,500.

Needs Ethnic/multicultural, literary, short-short fiction. No genre fiction, science fiction, "typical commercial press work." Receives 200 unsolicited mss/month. Accepts 12-15 mss/year. Reads mss September 1-April 15. **Publishes 10% new writers/year.** Recently published work by John McNally, Steve Almond, Tracy Winn and Midege Raymond. Length: 5,000 words (max). Average lenth 3,000 words. Publishes short shorts. Average length: 1,000 words. Also publishes literary essays, poetry. Comments on rejected mss when there is time.

How to Contact Send complete ms with cover letter. Responds in 2-4 months to mss. Accepts simultaneous submissions. Sample copy for $3-7. Guidelines for SASE, e-mail, on Web site.

Payment/Terms Pays 2 contributor's copies. Rights revert to author upon publication. Publication is copyrighted. Occasionally sponsors contests; check Web site for details.

Tips "We look for voice, energetic prose, writers who take risks. We look for an engaging story in which the author evokes an emotional response from the reader through carefully rendered scenes, complex characters, and a smart, narrative design. Revise, revise. Read what we publish."

☑ ☒ THE PATERSON LITERARY REVIEW

Passaic County Community College, One College Blvd., Paterson NJ 07505. (973) 684-6555. Fax: (973) 523-6085. E-mail: mgillan@pccc.edu. Website: www.pccc.edu/poetry. **Contact:** Maria Mazziotti Gillan, editor. Magazine: 6 × 9; 400 pages; 60 lb. paper; 70 lb. cover; illustrations; photos. Annual.

• Work for *PLR* has been included in the *Pushcart Prize* anthology and *Best American Poetry*.

Needs Ethnic/multicultural, literary, contemporary. "We are interested in quality short stories, with no taboos on subject matter." Receives 60 unsolicited mss/month. Publishes ms 6-12 months after acceptance. **Publishes 5% new writers/year.** Recently published work by Robert Mooney and Abigail Stone. Also publishes literary essays, literary criticism, poetry.

How to Contact Send SASE for reply or return of ms. "Indicate whether you want story returned." Accepts simultaneous submissions. Sample copy for $13 plus $1.50 postage. Reviews fiction.

Payment/Terms Pays in contributor's copies. Acquires first North American serial rights.

Tips Looks for "clear, moving and specific work."

☑ ◎ PEARL

3030 E. Second St., Long Beach CA 90803-5163. (562) 434-4523. E-mail: pearlmag@aol.com. Website: www.pearlmag.com. **Contact:** Marilyn Johnson, editor. Magazine: 5½ × 8½; 96 pages; 60 lb. recycled, acid-free paper; perfect bound; coated cover; b &w drawings and graphics. "We are primarily a poetry magazine, but we do publish some very short fiction. We are interested in lively, readable prose that speaks to real people in direct, living language; for a general literary audience." Biannual. Estab. 1974. Circ. 600.

Needs Humor/satire, literary, mainstream, contemporary, prose poem. "We will consider short-short stories up to 1,200 words. Longer stories (up to 4,000 words) may only be submitted to our short story contest. All contest entries are considered for publication. Although we have no taboos stylistically or subject-wise, obscure, predictable, sentimental, or cliché-ridden stories are a turn-off." Publishes an all-fiction issue each year. Receives 30-40 unsolicited mss/month. Accepts 15-20 mss/issue; 12-15 mss/year. Submissions accepted January-June only. Publishes ms 6-12 months after acceptance. **Publishes 1-5 new writers/year.** Recently published work by James D. McCallister, Heidi Rosenberg, W. Joshua Heffernan, Suzanne Greenberg, Fred McGavran, Gerald Locklin, Robert Perchan, Lisa Glatt. Length: 500-1,200 words; average length: 1,000 words. Also publishes poetry.

How to Contact Include SASE. Responds in 2 months to mss. Accepts simultaneous, multiple submissions. Sample copy for $8 (postpaid). Writer's guidelines for #10 SASE.

Payment/Terms Pays 1 contributor's copy. Acquires first North American serial rights. Sends galleys to author. Sponsors awards/contests.

Tips "We look for vivid, *dramatized* situations and characters, stories written in an original 'voice,' that make sense and follow a clear narrative line. What makes a manuscript stand out is more elusive, though—more to do with feeling and imagination than anything else."

☑ $ PEEKS & VALLEYS

E-mail: editor@peeksandvalleys.com. Website: http://peeksandvalleys.com/. **Contact**: Mary Anne DeYoung, editor. "Peeks & Valleys is a fiction journal that seeks traditional, character driven fiction. Our goal is to encourage and offer an outlet for both accomplished and new writers and to cause contemplation on the part of the reader." Quarterly. Estab. 1999, under new ownership as of 2007.

Needs "Please no sci-fi, formulaic, interview/profile or erotica." Receives 50 unsolicited mss/month. Accepts 7-8 mss/issue; 28-32 mss/year. Publishing time after acceptance varies. **Publishes 70% new writers/year.** Length: 5,000 words max; average length: 2,400 words. Also publishes poetry.

How to Contact Send complete ms. or poems electronically only. Check Web site for guidelines. Responds in 3 months. Accepts simultaneous submissions if advised with submissions. some reprints considered but prefers new, never-before published stories.

Payment/Terms Pays $10.00 plus 2 contributor's copies. Pays on publication for one-time or second serial (reprint) rights.

Tips "Please follow Writer's guidelines carefully. Submissions not following guidelines may not be read. Study the journal to become familiar with the type of material we are seeking."

☐ PENNSYLVANIA ENGLISH

Penn State DuBois, College Place, DuBois PA 15801. (814) 375-4814. Fax: (814) 375-4784. E-mail: ajv2@psu.edu. "Mention Pennsylvania English in the subject line." **Contact:** Antonio Vallone, editor. Magazine: 5¼ × 8¼; up to 200 pages; perfect bound; full color cover featuring the artwork of a Pennsylvania artist. "Our philosophy is quality. We publish literary fiction (and poetry and nonfiction). Our intended audience is literate, college-educated people." Annual. Estab. 1985. Circ. 300.

Needs Literary, mainstream, contemporary. "No genre fiction or romance." Reads mss during the summer. Publishes ms up tp 12 months after acceptance. **Publishes 4-6 new writers/year.** Recently published work by Dave Kress, Dan Leone and Paul West. Publishes short shorts. Also publishes literary essays, literary criticism, poetry. Sometimes comments on rejected mss.

How to Contact SASE. Does not normally accept electronic submissions. "We are creating Pennsylvania English Online —www.pennsylvaniaenglish.com— for electronic submissions and expanded publishing oppurtunities." Responds in up to 12 months to mss. Accepts simultaneous submissions. Does not accept previously published work. Sample copy for $10.

Payment/Terms Pays in 2 contributor's copies. Acquires first North American serial rights.

Tips "Quality of the writing is our only measure. We're not impressed by long-winded cover letters detailing awards and publications we've never heard of. Beginners and professionals have the same chance with us. We receive stacks of competently written but boring fiction. For a story to rise out of the rejection pile, it takes more than the basic competence."

☑ PEREGRINE

Amherst Writers & Artists Press, P.O. Box 60111, Florence MA 01062. (413) 253-3307. E-mail: peregrine@amherstwriters.com. Website: www.amherstwriters.com. **Contact:** Nancy Rose, editor. Magazine: 6 × 9; 100 pages; 60 lb. white offset paper; glossy cover. "Peregrine has provided a forum for national and international writers since 1983, and is committed to finding excellent work by emerging as well as established writers. We welcome work reflecting diversity of voice. We like to be surprised. We look for writing that is honest, unpretentious, and memorable. We like to be surprised. All decisions are made by the editors." Annual. Member CLMP.

Needs Poetry and prose. "No previously published work. No children's stories." Short pieces have a better chance of publication. No electronic submissions. Accepts 6-12 mss/issue. Reads January-April. Publishes ms 4 months after acceptance. **Publishes 8-10 new writers/year.** Recently published work by Douglas Andrew, Brad Buchanan, Krikor N. Der Hohannesian, Myron Ernst, Laura Hogan, Lucy Honig, Dana Kroos, M.K. Meder, Pat Schneider, John Surowiecki, Edwina Trentham, Sacha Webley, Fred Yannantuono. Publishes short shorts.

How to Contact Enclose sufficiently stamped SASE for return of ms; if disposable copy, enclose #10 SASE for response. Deadline for submission: April 15. Accepts simultaneous submissions. Sample copy for $12. Writer's guidelines for #10 SASE or Web site.

Payment/Terms Pays contributor's copies. All rights return to writer upon publication.

Tips "Check guidelines before submitting your work. Familiarize yourself with Peregrine. We look for heart and soul as well as technical expertise. Trust your own voice."

☑ ◎ PHILADELPHIA STORIES

Fiction/Art/Poetry of the Delaware Valley, 2021 S. 11th Street, Philadelphia PA 19148. (215) 551-5889. Fax: (215) 635-0195. E-mail: info@philadelphiastories.org. Website: www.philadelphiastories.org. **Contact:** Carla Spataro, Fiction Editor/Co-Publisher. Literary magazine/journal. 8½ × 11; 24 pages; 70# Matte Text, all four-color paper; 70# Matte Text cover. Contains illustrations, photographs. "Philadelphia Stories Magazine publishes fiction, poetry, essays and art written by authors living in, or originally from, Pennsylvania, Delaware, or New Jersey." Quarterly. Estab. 2004. Circ. 10,000. Member CLMP.

Needs Experimental, literary, mainstream. "We will consider anything that is well written but are most inclined to publish literary or mainstream fiction. We are NOT particularly interested in most genres (sci fi/fantasy, romance, etc.)." List of upcoming themes available for SASE, on Web site. Receives 45-80 mss/month. Accepts 3-4 mss/issue for print, additional 1-2 online; 12-16 mss/year for print, 4-8 online. Ms published 1-2 months after acceptance. **Publishes 50% new writers/year.** Published Justin St. Germain, Christine, Tim Zatzariny Jr., Lee W. Doty, Shantee' Cherese, Victoria Sprow. Length: 5,000 words (max). Average length: 4,000 words. Publishes short shorts. Average length of short shorts: 800 words. Also publishes literary essays, book reviews, poetry. Send review queries to: info@philadelphiastories.org. Rarely comments on/critiques rejected mss.

How to Contact Send complete ms with cover letter via online submission form only. Include estimated word count, list of publications, affiliation to the Philadelphia area. Responds to mss in 12 weeks. Considers simultaneous submissions. Sample copy available for $5, on Web site. Guidelines available on Web site.

Payment/Terms Writers receive 2 + contributor's copies. Pays on publication. Acquires one-time rights. Publication is copyrighted. "Occasionally sponsores contests; visit our Web site for opportunities"

Tips "All work is screened by three editorial board members, who rank the work. These scores are processed at the end of the quarterly submission period, and then the board meets to decide which pieces will be published in print and online. We look for exceptional, polished prose, a controlled voice, strong characters and place, and interesting subjects. Follow guidelines. We cannot stress this enough. Read every guideline carefully and thoroughly before sending anything out. Send out only polished material. We reject many quality pieces for various reasons; try not to take rejection personally. Just because your piece isn't right for one publication doesn't mean it's bad. Selection is an extremely subjective process."

◫ ☑ THE PINCH

(formerly *River City*) Dept. of English, The University of Memphis, Memphis TN 38152. (901) 678-4591. E-mail: editor@thepinchjournal.com. Website: www.thepinchjournal.com. **Contact**: Kristen Iversen, Editor-in-Chief. Magazine: 7 × 10; 168 pages. Semiannual. Estab. 1980. Circ. 1,500.

Needs Short stories, poetry, creative nonfiction, essays, memoir, travel, nature writing, photography, art. **Publishes some new writers every year.** Recently published work by Chris Fink, George Singleton, Stephen Dunn, Denise Duhamel, Floyd Skloot, and Beth Ann Fennelly.

How to Contact Send complete ms. Responds in 2 months to mss. Sample copy for $12.

Payment/Terms Pays 2 contributor's copies. Acquires first North American serial rights.

Tips "We have a new look and a new edge. We're soliciting work from writers with a national or international reputation as well as strong, interesting work from emerging writers. The Pinch Literary Award (previously River City Writing Award) in Fiction offers a $1,500 prize and publication. Check our Web site for details."

PINDELDYBOZ

Pindeldyboz, 23-55 38th St., Astoria NY 11105. E-mail: editor@pindeldyboz.com. @pindeldyboz.com. Website: www.pindeldyboz.com. **Contact:** Whitney Pastorek, executive editor. "Pindeldyboz is dedicated to publishing work that challenges what a short story can be. We don't ask for anything specific—we only ask that people take chances. We like heightened language, events, relationships—stories that paint the world a little differently, while still showing us the places we already know." Bimonthly. Estab. 2000.

Needs Comics/graphic novels, experimental, literary. Reads mss September 1-February 1 only. Publishes ms 3 months after acceptance. Has published work by Tai Dong Huai, Vanessa Wieland, Kyle Minor, Brandi Wells, Alex Burford, Daniel Pinkerton. Length: 250 + ; average length: 2,000 words. Publishes short shorts. Also publishes literary essays, poetry. Always comments on rejected mss.

How to Contact Send complete copy of ms with cover letter. Accepts mss by e-mail and disk. Include brief bio and phone number with submission. Send SASE (or IRC) for return of the ms and disposable copy of ms and #10 SASE for reply only. Responds in 2 weeks to queries; 3 months to mss. Accepts simultaneous, multiple submissions. Sample copy for $12. Writer's guidelines online.

Payment/Terms Pays 2 contributor's copies; additional copies $10. Pays on publication for one-time rights.

Tips "Good grammar, spelling, and sentence structure help, but what's more important is a willingness to take risks. Surprise us. And we will love it."

☐ PISGAH REVIEW

Department of Humanities, Brevard College, Brevard NC 28712. (828) 884-8349. E-mail: tinerjj@brevard. edu. Website: www.pisgahreview.com **Contact:** Jubal Tiner, editor, or contact Lonnie Busch, fiction editor; or Ken Chamlee, poetry editor. Literary magazine/journal: 5½ × 8½, 120 pages. Includes cover photograph. "Pisgah Review publishes primarily literary short fiction, creative nonfiction and poetry. Our only criteria is quality of work; we look for the best. The magazine does give a small preference to work that is based evocatively on place, but we will look at any work of quality." Semiannual. Estab. 2005. Circ. 200.

Needs Ethnic/multicultural, experimental, literary, mainstream. Special interests: stories rooted in the theme of place—physical, psychological, or spiritual. Does not want genre fiction or inspirational stories. Receives 30 mss/month. Accepts 6-8 mss/issue; 12-15 mss/year. Manuscript published 6 months after acceptance. **Publishes 5 new writers/year.** Published Ron Rash, Thomas Rain Crowe, Joan Conner, Gary Dincke, Aaron Gwyn. Length: 2,000 words (min)-7,500 words (max). Average length: 4,000 words. Publishes short shorts. Average length of short shorts: 1,000 words. Also publishes poetry and creative nonfiction. Sometimes comments on/critiques rejected mss.

How to Contact Send complete ms with cover letter. Accepts submissions by e-mail. Responds to mss in 4-6 months. Send either SASE (or IRC) for return of ms or disposable copy of ms and #10 SASE for reply only. Considers simultaneous submissions. Sample copy available for $7. Guidelines available for SASE, via e-mail.

Payment/Terms Writers receive 2 contributor's copies. Additional copies $7. Pays on publication. Acquires first North American serial rights. Sends galleys to author. Publication is copyrighted.

Tips "We select work only of the highest quality. Grab us from the beginning and follow through. Engage us with your language and characters. A clean manuscript goes a long way toward acceptance. Stay true to the vision of your work, revise tirelessly, and submit persistently."

▦ $ PLANET-THE WELSH INTERNATIONALIST

P.O. Box 44, Aberystwyth Ceredigion Cymru/Wales SY23 3ZZ United Kingdom. 01970-611255. Fax: 01970-611197. Website: www.planetmagazine.org.uk. **Contact:** John Barnie, fiction editor. "A literary/cultural/political journal centered on Welsh affairs but also covering international issues, with a strong interest in minority cultures in Europe and elsewhere." Quarterly. Circ. 1,100.

Needs No horror or science fiction. Recently published work by Emyr Humphreys, Anne Stevenson, and Robert Minhinnick.

How to Contact No submissions returned unless accompanied by an SAE. Writers submitting from abroad should send at least 3 IRCs for return of typescript; 1 IRC for reply only. E-mail queries accepted. Sample copy for £5.75. Writer's guidelines online.

Payment/Terms Pays £50/1,000 words.

Tips "We do not look for fiction which necessarily has a 'Welsh' connection, which some writers assume from our title. We try to publish a broad range of fiction and our main criterion is quality. Try to read copies of any magazine you submit to. Don't write out of the blue to a magazine which might be completely inappropriate for your work. Recognize that you are likely to have a high rejection rate, as magazines tend to favor writers from their own countries."

☑ $ ☒ PLEIADES

Pleiades Press, Department of English & Philosophy, University of Central Missouri, Martin 336, Warrensburg MO 64093. (660)543-4425. Fax: (660)543-8544. E-mail: kdp8106@yahoo.com. Website: www.ucmo.edu/englphil/pleiades. **Contact:** G.B. Crump, Matthew Eck, Phong Nguyen, Prose editors. Magazine: 5½ × 8½; 250 pages; 60 lb. paper; perfect-bound; 8 pt. color cover. "We publish contemporary fiction, poetry, interviews, literary essays, special-interest personal essays, reviews for a general and literary audience." Semiannual. Estab. 1991. Circ. 3,000.

• Work from *Pleiades* appears in recent volumes of *The Best American Poetry, Pushcart Prize* and *Best American Fantasy and Horror.*

Needs Ethnic/multicultural, experimental, feminist, gay, humor/satire, literary, mainstream, novel excerpts, regional, translations, magical realism. No science fiction, fantasy, confession, erotica. Receives 100 unsolicited mss/month. Accepts 8 mss/issue; 16 mss/year. "We're slower at reading manuscripts in the summer." Publishes ms 9 months after acceptance. **Publishes 4-5 new writers/year.** Recently published work by Sherman Alexie, Edith Pearlman, Joyce Carol Oates, James Tate. Length: 2,000-6,000 words; average length: 3,000-6,000 words. Also publishes literary essays, literary criticism, poetry. Sometimes comments on rejected mss.

How to Contact Send complete ms. Include 75-100 word bio and list of publications. Send SASE for reply, return of ms or send a disposable copy of ms. Responds in 2 months to queries; 2 months to mss. Accepts simultaneous submissions. Sample copy for $5 (back issue), $6 (current issue). Writer's guidelines for #10 SASE.

Payment/Terms Pays $10. Pays on publication for first North American serial, second serial (reprint) rights. Occasionally requests rights for TV, radio reading, Web site.

Tips Looks for "a blend of language and subject matter that entices from beginning to end. Send us your best work. Don't send us formula stories. While we appreciate and publish well-crafted traditional pieces, we constantly seek the story that risks, that breaks form and expectations and wins us over anyhow."

☑ $ ☒ PLOUGHSHARES

Emerson College, Department M, 120 Boylston St., Boston MA 02116. Website: www.pshares.org. **Contact:** Fiction Editor. "Our mission is to present dynamic, contrasting views on what is valid and important in contemporary literature and to discover and advance significant literary talent. Each issue is guest-edited by a different writer. We no longer structure issues around preconceived themes." Estab. 1971. Circ. 6,000.

• Work published in *Ploughshares* has been selected regularly for inclusion in the *Best American Short Stories* and *O. Henry Prize* anthologies. In fact, the magazine has the honor of having the most stories selected from a single issue (three) to be included in *Best American Short Stories*. Guest editors have included Richard Ford, Tim O'Brien and Ann Beattie.

Needs Literary, mainstream. "No genre (science fiction, detective, gothic, adventure, etc.), popular formula or commerical fiction whose purpose is to entertain rather than to illuminate." Receives 1,000 unsolicited mss/month. Accepts 30 mss/year. Reading period: postmarked August 1 to March 31. Publishes ms 6 months after acceptance. **Publishes some new writers/year.** Recently published work by ZZ Packer, Antonya Nelson, Stuart Dybek.

How to Contact Cover letter should includ "previous pubs." Send SASE. Responds in 5 months to mss. Accepts simultaneous submissions. Sample copy for $9 (back issue). Writer's guidelines online.

Payment/Terms Pays $25/printed page, $50-250. Pays on publication for first North American serial rights.

Tips "Be familiar with our fiction issues, fiction by our writers and by our various editors (e.g., Sue Miller, Tobias Wolff, Rosellen Brown, Richard Ford, Jayne Anne Phillips, James Alan McPherson), and more generally acquaint yourself with the best short fiction currently appearing in the literary quarterlies and the annual prize anthologies (*Pushcart Prize*, *O. Henry Awards*, *Best American Short Stories*). Also realistically consider whether the work you are submitting is as good as or better than—in your own opinion—the work appearing in the magazine you're sending to. What is the level of competition? And what is its volume? Never send 'blindly' to a magazine, or without carefully weighing your prospect there against those elsewhere. Always keep a log and a copy of the work you submit."

☑ ◎ ☐ PMS, POEMMEMOIRSTORY

University of Alabama at Birmingham, HB 217, 1530 3rd Avenue South, Birmingham AL 35294-4450. (205) 934-8583. Fax: (205) 975-8125. E-mail: lfrost@uab.edu. Website: http://www.pms-journal.org. **Contact:** Tina Harris, editor-in-chief. Literary magazine/journal: 6X9; 120 pages; recycled white; matte paper; cover photos. "We print one issue a year, our cover price is $7, and our journal publishes fine creative work by women writers from across the nation (and beyond) in the three genres listed in the title. One of our distinctive features is a memoir that we feature in each issue written by a woman who has experienced something of historic, national import but who would not necessarily call herself a writer. Our first issue, for instance, featured a piece by Emily Lyons, the nurse who was critically injured in the 1998 bombing of the Birmingham New Woman All Women clinic. We've published a wide range of these featured pieces including a memoir by a woman who was in the World Trade Center on 9-11, another by a woman who was serving in Iraq, another by a student who lived through Katrina in New Orleans, and another by a woman who married her lesbian partner in a wedding in Boston during that initial window of opportunity. PMS 8 was our first special issue, guest edited by Honorée Fanonne Jeffers and featuring all African-American women writers. We are currently distributed by Ingram Periodicals, Inc." Annual. Estab. 2001. Circ. 1,500. Member Council of Literary Magazines and Presses and the Council of Editors of Learned Journals.

• Work from PMS has been reprinted in a number of award anthologies: *New Stories from the South 2005*, *The Best Creative Nonfiction 2007* and *2008*, *Best American Poetry 2003* and *2004*, and *Best American Essays 2005* and*2007*.

Needs Comics/graphic novels, ethnic/multicultural (general), experimental, feminist, literary, translations. "We don't do erotic, mystery work, and most popular forms, per se. We publish short stories and essays including memoirs and other brands of creative nonfiction." Receives 30 mss/month. Accepts 4-6 mss/issue. As of 2009, reading period is January 1 through March 30. Ms published within 6 months after acceptance. **Publishes 5 new writers/year.** Published Vicki Covington, Kim Aubrey, Patricia Brieschke, Gaines Marsh. Length: 4,500 words (max). Average length: 3,500-4,000 words. Publishes short shorts. Average length of short shorts: 300-350 words. Also publishes literary essays, poetry. Rarely comments on/critiques rejected mss.

How to Contact Send complete ms with cover letter. Include list of publications. Responds to queries in 1 month. Responds to mss in 1-4 months. Send disposable copy of ms and #10 SASE for reply only. Considers simultaneous submissions, multiple submissions. Sample copy available for $7. Guidelines available for SASE, on Web site.

Payment/Terms Writers receive 2 contributor's copies. Additional copies $7. Pays on publication. Acquires one-time rights. Publication is copyrighted.

Tips "Send your best work; excellent work with a strong eye for detail and a sense of a fresh use of the language. Read a lot, write a lot, and get into the habit of sending your work out a lot."

☑ POINTED CIRCLE

Portland Community College-Cascade, 705 N. Killingsworth St., Portland OR 97217. (503) 978-5251. E-mail: lutgarda.cowan@pcc.edu. **Contact:** Lutgarda Cowan, English instructor, faculty advisor. Magazine: 80 pages; b&w illustrations; photos. "Anything of interest to educationally/culturally mixed audience." Annual. Estab. 1980.

Needs Ethnic/multicultural, literary, regional, contemporary, prose poem. "We will read whatever is sent, but encourage writers to remember we are a quality literary/arts magazine intended to promote the arts in the community. No pornography, nothing trite. Be mindful of deadlines and length limits." Accepts submissions only October 1-March 1, for July 1 issue.

How to Contact Accepts submissions by e-mail, mail. Prose up to 3,000 words; poetry up to 6 pages; artwork in high-resolution digital form. Submitted materials will not be returned; SASE for notification only. Accepts multiple submissions.

Payment/Terms Pays 2 copies. Acquires one-time rights.

☐ ◎ POLYPHONY H.S., A STUDENT-RUN NATIONAL LITERARY MAGAZINE FOR HIGH SCHOOL WRITERS

Polyphony H.S., c/o Educational Endeavors, 1535 N. Dayton, Chicago IL 60622. (312) 266-0123. Fax: (312) 643-1036. E-mail: polyphonyhs@gmail.com. Website: www.polyphonyhs.com. **Contact:** Billy Lombardo, managing editor. Literary magazine/journal: 9 × 6, 70-120 pages, silk finish 80 lb. white paper, silk finish 100 lb. cover. " We are a 501(c)3 organization. Our goal is to seek out the finest high school writers in the country, to work with them to grow as writers, and to exhibit their fiction before a national audience. Every submission is edited, commented upon, by at least three high school editors from around the country. Polyphony H.S. invites high school students to serve as National First readers, and hosts summer workshops National Editors. Just partnered with the Claudia Ann Seaman Awards for Young Writers; 4500 awards for the best poem, best story, best work of creative nonfiction. See Web site for details." Annual. Estab. 2005. Circ. 2,000.

Needs Poetry, fiction, and creative nonfiction. Receives 500-1,000 mss/year. Accepts 50-75 mss/issue. Publishes new writers/year. Length: 3,000 words (max). Average length: 2,000 words.

How to Contact See Web site. Online submission process. Deadline: day after Valentine's Day (February 15). Responds in 4-6 weeks. Considers simultaneous submissions. Sample copy available for $7.50 + $2.50 shipping/handling.

Payment/Terms Writers receive 2 contributor's copies. Additional copies $3.50. Pays on publication. Acquires first rights.

Advice: "We think this is the most important literary magazine in the world. Inherent in it is the collective value of every other magazine in circulation. If you're a high school teacher, you should have us in your classroom. If you teach in a university you should be paying attention to our writers."

☑ PORTLAND REVIEW

Portland State University, Box 347, Portland OR 97207-0347. (503)725-4533. E-mail: theportlandreview@gmail.com. Website: www.portlandreview.org. **Contact:** Chris Cottrell, editor. Magazine: 9 × 6; 100-150 pages; b&w art and photos. Triannual. Estab. 1956. Circ. 500.

Needs Unpublished poetry and prose. Fiction/Nonfiction prose of up to 5,000 words or 5 poems per submission. Receives 200 unsolicited mss/week. Accepts up to 24 mss/issue.

How to Contact Ms and SASE for submissions. Review queries via e-mail. Submission guidelines online. All ms submissions not following guidelines are immediately rejected.

Payment/Terms Pays contributor's copies. Acquires first North American serial rights.

☑ POST ROAD

P.O. Box 600725, Newtown MA 02460. E-mail: mary@postroadmag.com. Website: www.postroadmag.com. **Contact:** Mary Cotton. Literary magazine/journal. 8½ × 11½, 240 pages, 60 lb. opaque paper, gloss cover. "Post Road is a nationally distributed literayy magazine based out of New York and Boston that publishes work in the following genres: art, criticism, fiction, nonfiction, and poetry. Post Road also features two innovations: the Recommendations section, where established writers write 500-1,000 words on a favorite book(s) or author(s); and the Etcetera section, where we publish interviews, profiles, translations, letters, classic reprints, documents, topical essays, travelogues, etc." Estab. 2000. Circ. 2,000.

- Work from *Post Road* has received the following honors: honorable mention in the 2001 O. Henry Prize Issue guest-edited by Michael Chabon, Mary Gordon, and Mona Simpson; the Pushcart Prize; honorable mention in *The Best American Nonfiction* series; and inclusion in the *Best American Short Stories* 2005.

Needs Literary. Receives 100 mss/month. Accepts 4-6 mss/issue; 8-12 mss/year. See Web site for reading periods. Manuscript published 6 months after acceptance. Published Brian Booker, Louis E. Bourgeois, Becky Bradway, Adam Braver, Ashley Capps, Susan Choi, Lisa Selin Davis, Rebecca Dickson, Rick Moody. Average length: 5,000 words. Average length of short shorts: 1,500 words. Also publishes literary essays, literary criticism, poetry. Sometimes comments on/critiques rejected manuscripts.

How to Contact Accepts submissions by e-mail. Electronic submissions only. Include brief bio. Responds to mss in 1 months. Send SASE (or IRC) for return of ms. Considers simultaneous submissions. Guidelines available on Web site.

Payment/Terms Writers receive 2 contributor's copies. Pays on publication. Acquires first North American serial rights. Sends galleys to author. Publication is not copyrighted.

Tips "Looking for interesting narrative, sharp dialogue, deft use of imagery and metaphor. Be persistent and be open to criticism."

☑ POTOMAC REVIEW

Montgomery College, Paul Peck Humanities Institute, 51 Mannakee St., Rockville MD 20850. (301) 251-7417. Fax: (301) 738-1745. E-mail: potomacrevieweditor@montgomerycollege.edu. Website: www. montgomerycollege.edu/potomacreview. **Contact:** Julie Wakeman-Linn, editor. Magazine: 5½ × 8½; 175 pages; 50 lb. paper; 65 lb. color cover. Potomac Review "reflects a view of our region looking out to the world, and in turn, seeks how the world views the region." Bi-annual. Estab. 1994. Circ. 750.

Needs "Stories and poems with a vivid, individual quality that get at 'the concealed side' of life." Essays and creative non-fiction pieces welcome. No themes. Recieves 300+ unsolicited mss/month. Accepts 40-50 mss/issue. Publishes ms within 1 year after acceptance. Recently published work by Jim Tomilson, Tim Wendel, Rose Solari, Moira Egan, Martin Galvin, Elizabeth Murawski, Richard Peabody, Jeff Hardin, and Nancy Naomi Carlson. Length: 5,000 words; average length: 2,000 words.

How to Contact Send SASE with adequate postage for reply and/or return of ms. Responds in 3 -6 months to mss. Accepts simultaneous submissions. Sample copy for $10. Writer's guidelines on Web site.

Payment/Terms Pays 2 or more contributor's copies; additional copies for a 40% discount.

Tips " Send us interesting, well crafted stories. Have something to say in an original, prov ocative voice. Read recent issue to get a sense of the journal's new direction."

☒ ☑ $ THE PRAIRIE JOURNAL

Prairie Journal Trust, P.O. Box 61203, Brentwood P.O., Calgary AB T2L 2K6 Canada. Website: www. geocities.com/prairiejournal. **Contact:** A.E. Burke, editor. Journal: 7 × 8½; 50-60 pages; white bond paper; Cadillac cover stock; cover illustrations. "The audience is literary, university, library, scholarly and creative readers/writers." Semiannual. Estab. 1983. Circ. 600.

Needs Literary, regional. No genre (romance, horror, western—sagebrush or cowboys—erotic, science fiction, or mystery). Receives 100 unsolicited mss/month. Accepts 10-15 mss/issue; 20-30 mss/year. Suggested deadlines: April 1 for spring/summer issue; October 1 for fall/winter. Publishes ms 4-6 months after acceptance. **Publishes 60 new writers/year.** Recently published work by Robert Clark, Sandy Campbell, Darcie Hasack, Christopher Blais. Length: 100-3,000 words; average length: 2,500 words. Also publishes literary essays, literary criticism, poetry. Sometimes comments on rejected mss.

How to Contact Send complete ms with SASE (IRC). Include cover letter of past credits, if any. Reply to queries for SAE with 55¢ for postage or IRC. No American stamps. Responds in 2 weeks to queries; 6 months to mss. No simultaneous submissions. No e-mail submissions. Sample copy for $6. Writer's guidelines online. Reviews fiction.

Payment/Terms Pays $10-75. Pays on publication for first North American serial rights. In Canada, author retains copyright with acknowledgement appreciated.

Tips "We like character-driven rather than plot-centered fiction." Interested in "innovational work of quality. Beginning writers welcome! There is no point in simply republishing known authors or conventional, predictable plots. Of the genres we receive, fiction is most often of the highest calibre. It is a very competitive field. Be proud of what you send. You're worth it."

⊘ ⚏ PRAIRIE SCHOONER

University of Nebraska, English Department, 201 Andrews Hall, P.O. Box 880334, Lincoln NE 68588-0334. (402) 472-0911. Fax: (402) 472-9771. E-mail: jengelhardt2@unl.edu. Website: http://prairieschooner.unl. edu. Contact: Hilda Raz, editor. Magazine: 6 × 9; 200 pages; good stock paper; heavy cover stock. "A fine literary quarterly of stories, poems, essays and reviews for a general audience that reads for pleasure." Estab. 1926. Circ. 3,000.
   • *Prairie Schooner*, one of the oldest publications in this book, has garnered several awards and honors over the years. Work appearing in the magazine has been selected for anthologies including the *Pushcart Prize* anthology and *Best American Short Stories*.
Needs Good fiction (literary). Receives 500 unsolicited mss/month. Accepts 4-5 mss/issue. Mss are read September through May only. **Publishes 5-10 new writers/year.** Recently published work by Robert Olen Butler, Janet Burroway, Aimee Phan, Valerie Sayers, Daniel Stern. Also publishes poetry.
How to Contact Send complete ms with SASE and cover letter listing previous publications—where, when. Responds in 4 months to mss. Sample copy for $6. Writer's guidelines and excerpts online. Reviews fiction.
Payment/Terms Pays in contributor's copies and prize money awarded. Will reassign rights upon request after publication. Sponsors awards/contests.
Tips "*Prairie Schooner* is eager to see fiction from beginning and established writers. Be tenacious. Accept rejection as a temporary setback and send out rejected stories to other magazines. *Prairie Schooner* is not a magazine with a program. We look for good fiction in traditional narrative modes as well as experimental, meta-fiction or any other form or fashion a writer might try. Create striking detail, well-developed characters, fresh dialogue; let the images and the situations evoke the stories' themes. Too much explication kills a lot of otherwise good stories. Be persistent. Keep writing and sending out new work. Be familiar with the tastes of the magazines where you're sending. We are receiving record numbers of submissions. Prospective contributors must sometimes wait longer to receive our reply."

⚏ ⊘ $ ⚏ PRISM INTERNATIONAL

Department of Creative Writing, Buch E462-1866 Main Mall, University of British Columbia, Vancouver BC V6T 1Z1 Canada. (604) 822-2514. Fax: (604) 822-3616. E-mail: prism@interchange.ubc.ca. Website: http://prismmagazine.ca. **Contact:** Editor. Magazine: 6 × 9; 80 pages; Zephyr book paper; Cornwall, coated one-side cover; artwork on cover. "An international journal of contemporary writing—fiction, poetry, drama, creative nonfiction and translation." Readership: "public and university libraries, individual subscriptions, bookstores—a worldwide audience concerned with the contemporary in literature." Quarterly. Estab. 1959. Circ. 1,200.
   • *Prism International* has won numerous magazine awards, and stories first published in Prism International have been included in the *Journey Prize Anthology* every year since 1991.
Needs Experimental, traditional. New writing that is contemporary and literary. Short stories and self-contained novel excerpts (up to 25 double-spaced pages). Works of translation are eagerly sought and should be accompanied by a copy of the original. Would like to see more translations. "No gothic, confession, religious, romance, pornography, or sci-fi." Also looking for creative nonfiction that is literary, not journalistic, in scope and tone. Receives over 100 unsolicited mss/month. Accepts 70 mss/year. "PRISM publishes both new and established writers; our contributors have included Franz Kafka, Gabriel Garciía Márquez, Michael Ondaatje, Margaret Laurence, Mark Anthony Jarman, Gail Anderson-Dargatz and Eden Robinson." Publishes ms 4 months after acceptance. **Publishes 7 new writers/year.** Recently published work by Ibi Kaslik, Melanie Little, Mark Anthony Jarman. Publishes short shorts. Also publishes poetry.
How to Contact Send complete ms by mail. "Keep it simple. U.S. contributors take note: Do not send SASEs with U.S. stamps, they are not valid in Canada. Send International Reply Coupons instead." Responds in 4 months to queries; 3-6 months to mss. Sample copy for $11 or on Web site. Writer's guidelines online.

Payment/Terms Pays $20/printed page of prose, $40/printed page of poetry, and 1-year subscription. Pays on publication for first North American serial rights. Selected authors are paid an additional $10/page for digital rights. Cover art pays $300 and 4 copies of issue. Sponsors awards/contests, including annual short fiction and nonfiction contests.

Tips "Read several issues of our magazine before submitting. We are committed to publishing outstanding literary work. We look for strong, believeable characters; real voices; attention to language; interesting ideas and plots. Send us fresh, innovative work which also shows a mastery of the basics of good prose writing."

☐ PUERTO DEL SOL

New Mexico State University, MSC 3E, Las Cruces NM 88003. (575)646-3931. Fax: (575)646-7755. E-mail: contact@puertodelsol.org. Website: www.puertodelsol.org. **Contact:** Carmen Gimenez Smith, editor-in-chief and poetry editor; Evan Lavendar-Smith, prose editor. Magazine: 7 × 9; 200 pages; 60 lb. paper; 70 lb. cover stock. "We publish innovative work from emerging and established writers and artists. Poetry, fiction, nonfiction, drama, theory, artwork, interviews, reviews, and interesting combinations thereof." Semiannual. Estab. 1960. Circ. 1,500.

Needs Literary, experimental, theory, drama, work in translation. Accepts 8-12 mss/issue; 16-24 mss/year. Does not accept mss April 1-September 14. **Publishes 8-10 new writers/year.** Recently accepted and published work by Kim Chinquee, Joanna Scott, Peter Markus, Shya Scanlon.

How to Contact Responds in 3-6 months to mss. Accepts simultaneous submissions. Sample copy for $8.

Payment/Terms Pays 2 contributor's copies. Acquires one-time print and electronic rights and anthology rights. Rights revert to author after publication.

Tips "We are especially pleased to publish emerging writers who work to push their art form or field of study in new directions."

▦ ☑ QUALITY FICTION

(formerly Quarterly Women's Fiction), c/o AllWriters' Workplace & Workshop, 234 Brook St., Unit 2, Waukesha WI 53188. E-mail: qwfsubmissionsusa@yahoo.com. Website: www.allwriters.org (click on QWF) **Contact:** Kathie Giorgio, Editor. Magazine: A5; 100 pages; glossy paper. "Whether a story is about a woman's highest point in her life, or her lowest, the stories must resonate with an emotional chord. All QWF stories must have impact." Published twice a year. Estab. 1994. Circ. 1,000.

Needs Accepts all genres, as long as the main characters are women and the stories are written by women. Receives 300 unsolicited mss/reading period. Accepts 20 mss/issue; 40 mss/year. Only reads during reading periods. Publishes ms in next issue after acceptance. Publishes new writers. Length: up to 5,000 words; average length: 2,500 words. Publishes short shorts. Always comments on rejected mss.

How to Contact Send complete ms. Accepts submissions by e-mail only. Send complete ms as Word document. Responds in 2 months to queries; 2 months to mss. Simultaneous submissions okay, but not preferred. Back issues available for sale on Web site.

Payment/Terms Pays in copies. Acquires first rights.

Tips "Evoking emotion is the most important characteristic of a QWF story. There is no room for a dry reporting of the facts here. Rather, the stories should present the expanse that is every woman's emotional lifetime and experience."

☑ $ ▨ QUARTERLY WEST

University of Utah, 255 S. Central Campus Dr., Dept. of English, LNCO 3500, Salt Lake City UT 84112-9109. (801) 581-3938. E-mail: quarterlywest@yahoo.com. Website: www.utah.edu/quarterlywest. **Contact:** Rachel Marston and Pam Balluck. Magazine: 7 × 10; 50 lb. paper; 4 color cover stock. "We publish fiction, poetry, and nonfiction in long and short formats, and will consider experimental as well as traditional works." Semiannual. Estab. 1976. Circ. 1,900.

 • *Quarterly West* was awarded First Place for Editorial Content from the American Literary Magazine Awards. Work published in the magazine has been selected for inclusion in the *Pushcart Prize* anthology and *The Best American Short Stories* anthology.

Needs Ethnic/multicultural, experimental, humor/satire, literary, mainstream, novel excerpts, slice-of-life vignettes, translations, short shorts, translations. No detective, science fiction or romance. Receives

300 unsolicited mss/month. Accepts 6-10 mss/issue; 12-20 mss/year. Reads mss between September 1 and May 1 only. "Submissions received between May 2 and August 31 will be returned unread." Publishes ms 6 months after acceptance. **Publishes 3 new writers/year.** Recently published work by Steve Almond, Linh Dinh.

How to Contact Send complete ms. Brief cover letters welcome. Send SASE for reply or return of ms. Responds in 6 months to mss. Accepts simultaneous submissions if notified. Sample copy for $7.50. Writer's guidelines online.

Payment/Terms Pays $15-50, and 2 contributor's copies. Pays on publication for first North American serial rights.

Tips "We publish a special section of short shorts every issue, and we also sponsor a biennial novella contest. We are open to experimental work—potential contributors should read the magazine! We solicit occasionally, but tend more toward the surprises—unsolicited. Don't send more than one story per submission, and wait until you've heard about the first before submitting another."

☑ $ THE RAMBLER

Rambler Publications, LLC, P.O. Box 5070, Chapel Hill NC 27514-5001. (919) 545-9789. Fax: (919) 545-0921. E-mail: editor@ramblermagazine.com. Website: www.ramblermagazine.com. **Contact:** Elizabeth Oliver, Managing Editor. Magazine: 8⅛ × 10⅞, 64 pages, full color. Includes photographs. "The Rambler, a magazine of personal expression, features in-depth interviews with artists, writers and performers as well as selections of fiction, poetry and essays." Bimonthly. Estab. Jan/Feb 2004. Circ. 4,000.

Needs Literary. Does not want any kind of genre fiction. Receives 150 mss/month. Accepts 1-2 mss/issue; 6-12 mss/year. Manuscript published 6-18 months after acceptance. Agented fiction 5%. **Publishes 15 new writers/year.** Published Marjorie Kemper, Lawrence Naumoff, Christopher Locke, Catherine McCall, Kathryn Hughes, and Marianne Gingher. Length: 8,000 words max. Average length: 4,000 words. Publishes short shorts. Average length of short shorts: 300 1,000 words. Also publishes nonfiction, poetry. Sometimes comments on/critiques rejected manuscripts.

How to Contact Send complete ms with cover letter. Include estimated word count, brief bio, list of publications. Prose submissions may also be sent by e-mail to fiction@ramblermagazine.com or nonfiction@ramblermagazine.com. Responds to queries in 2 months. Responds to mss in 4-6 months. Send either SASE (or IRC) for return of ms or disposable copy of ms and #10 SASE for reply only. Considers multiple submissions. Sample copy available for $7. Guidelines available for SASE, on Web site.

Payment/Terms Writers receive $25-$50 flat-rate payment, 1 contributors copy, complimentary one-year subscription to the magazine. Additional copies $6. Pays on publication. Acquires first North American serial rights. Sends galleys to author. Publication is copyrighted.

Tips "We're looking for stories that are well written with well-developed characters, believable dialogue and satisfying plots. A story that moves us in some way, connects us to something larger. Something that stays with us long after the story is finished. Send us your best work."

☑ RATTAPALLAX

Rattapallax Press, 532 La Guardia Place, Suite 353, New York NJ 10012. E-mail: info@rattapallax.com. Website: www.rattapallax.com. **Contact:** Alan Cheuse, fiction editor. Literary magazine: 9 × 12; 128 pages; bound; some illustrations; photos. "General readership. Our stories must be character driven with strong conflict. All accepted stories are edited by our staff and the writer before publication to ensure a well-crafted and written work." Semiannual. Estab. 1999. Circ. 2,000.

Needs Literary. Receives 15 unsolicited mss/month. Accepts 3 mss/issue; 6 mss/year. Publishes ms 3-6 months after acceptance. Agented fiction 15%. **Publishes 3 new writers/year.** Recently published work by Stuart Dybek, Howard Norman, Molly Giles, Rick Moody. Length: 1,000-10,000 words; average length: 5,000 words. Publishes short shorts. Also publishes poetry. Often comments on rejected mss.

How to Contact Send SASE for return of ms. Responds in 3 months to queries; 3 months to mss. Sample copy for $7.95. Writer's guidelines for SASE or on Web site.

Payment/Terms Pays 2 contributor's copies; additional copies for $7.95. Pays on publication for first North American serial rights. Sends galleys to author.

Tips "Character driven, well crafted, strong conflict."

☑ $ THE RAVEN CHRONICLES

The Raven Chronicles, Warren Building, 909 NE 43rd Street., Seattle WA 98105- 6020. (206)364-2045. E-mail: editors@ravenchronicles.org. Website: www.ravenchronicles.org. **Contact:** Fiction editor. Magazine: 8½ × 11; 88-100 pages; 50 lb. book; glossy cover; b&w illustrations; photos. "The Raven Chronicles is designed to promote transcultural art, literature and the spoken word." Bi -annual. Estab. 1991. Circ. 2,500-5,000.

Needs Ethnic/multicultural, literary, regional, political, cultural essays. "No romance, fantasy, mystery or detective." Receives 300-400 unsolicited mss/month. Accepts 35-60 mss/issue; 105-150 mss/year. Publishes ms 12 months after acceptance. **Publishes 50-100 new writers/year.** Recently published work by David Romtvedt, Sherman Alexie, D.L. Birchfield, Nancy Redwine, Diane Glancy, Greg Hischak, Sharon Hashimoto. Length: 2,500 words (but negotiable); average length: 2,000 words. Publishes short shorts. Also publishes literary essays, literary criticism, poetry. Sometimes comments on rejected mss.

How to Contact Send SASE for return of ms. Does not accept unsolicited submissions by e-mail (except foreign submissions). Responds in 3 months to mss. Does not accept simultaneous submissions. Sample copy for $5.19-10.19. Writer's guidelines for #10 SASE.

Payment/Terms Pays $10-40 and 2 contributor's copies; additional copies at half cover cost. Pays on publication for first North American serial rights. Sends galleys to author.

Tips Looks for "clean, direct language, written from the heart, and experimental writing. Read sample copy, or look at *Before Columbus* anthologies and *Greywolf Annual* anthologies."

⊕ ☑ THE READER

19 Abercromby Square, Liverpool, Merseyside LG9 7ZG.01517942830. E-mail: readers@liv.ac.uk. Website: www.thereader.co.uk. **Contact:** Jane Davis. Literary magazine/journal: 216 × 138 mm, 130 pages, 80 gsm (Silver Offset) paper. Includes photographs. "The Reader is a quarterly literary magazine aimed at the intelligent 'common reader'—from those just beginning to explore serious literary reading to professional teachers, academics and writers. As well as publishing short fiction and poetry by new writers and established names, the magazine features articles on all aspects of literature, language, and reading; regular features, including a literary quiz and 'Our Spy in NY', a bird's-eye view of literary goings-on in New York; reviews; and readers'recommendations of books that have made a difference to them. The Reader is unique among literary magazines in its focus on reading as a creative, important and pleasurable activity, and in its combination of high-quality material and presentation with a genuine commitment to ordinary but dedicated readers." Quarterly. Estab. 1997. Circ. 700.

Needs Literary. Receives 10 mss/month. Accepts 1-2 mss/issue; 8 mss/year. Manuscript published 16 months after acceptance. Publishes 4 new writers/year. Published Karen King Arbisala, Ray Tallis, Sasha Dugdale, Vicki Seal, David Constantine, Jonathan Meades, Ramesh Avadhani. Length: 1,000 words (min)-3,000 words (max). Average length: 2,300 words. Publishes short shorts. Average length of short shorts: 1,500 words. Also publishes literary essays, literary criticism, poetry. Sometimes comments on/ critiques rejected mss.

How to Contact Send complete ms with cover letter. Include estimated word count, brief bio, list of publications. Responds to queries in 2 months; mss in 2 months. Send SASE (or IRC) for return of ms. Considers simultaneous submissions, multiple submissions. Guidelines available for SASE.

Payment/Terms Additional copies $14. Pays on publication. Sends galleys to author.

Tips "The style or polish of the writing is less important than the deep structure of the story (though of course, it matters that it's well written). The main persuasive element is whether the story moves us— and that's quite hard to quantify—it's something to do with the force of the idea and the genuine nature of enquiry within the story. When fiction is the writer's natural means of thinking things through, that'll get us. "

☑ THE RED CLAY REVIEW

M. A. in Professional Writing Program, Dept of English, Bldg. #27, Kennesaw State University, Kennesaw GA 30144-5591. E-mail: redclayreview@gmail.com. Website: http://rcr.kaitopia.com. **Contact:** Dr. Jim Elledge, Director M.A. in Professional Writing Program or student Editor-in-Chief. Magazine has revolving editor. Editorial term: 1 year. Literary magazine/journal. 8½ × 5½, 80-120 pages, 60# white paper, 10 pt matte lam. cover. "The Red Clay Review is dedicated to publishing only the most outstanding graduate literary pieces. It has been established by members of the Graduate Writers Association at Kennesaw

State University. It is unique because it only includes the work of graduate writing students. We publish poems (must be limited to 300 words, double spaced, 12 pt. font, 3-5 poems per submission), fiction/non-fiction pieces (must not exceed 10 pages, double spaced, 12 pt. font), and 10 minute plays/scenes (should be limited to 11 total pages since the first page will usually be mostly taken up by character listing/setting description.)" Annual. Estab. 2008.

Needs "We do not have any specific themes or topics, but keep in mind that we are a literary publication. We will read whatever is sent in. We will publish whatever we deem to be great literary writing. So in essence, every topic is open to submission, and we are all interested in a wide variety of subjects. We do not prohibit any topic or subject matter from being submitted. As long as submissions adhere to our guidelines, we are open to reading them. However, subject matter in any area that is too extreme may be less likely to be published because we want to include a broad collection of literary graduate work, but on the other hand, we cannot morally reject great writing." Receives 12 mss/month. Does not read November 1- June 1. Ms published 6 months after acceptance. Length: 2,500 words (min)- 8,000 words (max). Publishes short shorts. Also publishes literary essays, poetry. Never comments on/critiques rejected mss.

How to Contact Send complete ms with cover letter. Include brief bio, list of publications, and an e-mail address must be supplied for the student, as well as the student's advisor's contact information (to verify student status). Responds to mss in 12-16 weeks. Considers simultaneous submissions, multiple submissions. Guidelines available on Web site.

Payment/Terms Writers receive 2 contributor's copies. Pays on publication. Acquires first rights. Publication is copyrighted.

Tips "Because the editors of *RCR* are graduate student writers, we are mindful of grammatical proficiency, vocabulary, and the organizational flow of the submissions we receive. We appreciate a heightened level of writing from fellow graduate writing students; but we also hold it to a standard to which we have learned in our graduate writing experience. Have your submission(s) proofread by a fellow student or professor."

☑ REDIVIDER

120 Boylston St., Emerson College, Boston MA 02116. E-mail: redivider@emerson.edu. Website: www.redividerjournal.org. **Contact:** Prose Editor. Editors change each year. Magazine: 5½ × 8½; 160 pages; 60 lb. paper. Redivider, a journal of literature and art, is published twice a year by students in the graduate writing, literature and publishing department of Emerson College. Biannual. Estab. 1986. Circ. 1000.

Needs Literary. Receives 100 unsolicited mss/month. Accepts 6-8 mss/issue; 10-12 mss/year. Publishes ms 3-6 months after acceptance. Publishes short shorts. Also publishes poetry. Sometimes comments on rejected mss.

How to Contact Send disposable copy of ms. Accepts simultaneous submissions with notification. Sample copy for $6 with a #10 SASE. Writer's guidelines for SASE.

Payment/Terms Pays 2 contributor's copies; additional copies $6. Pays on publication for one-time rights. Sponsors awards/contests.

☑ RED ROCK REVIEW

College of Southern Nevada, 3200 E. Cheyenne Ave. N., Las Vegas NV 89030. (702) 651-5634. Fax: (702) 651-4639. E-mail: richard.logsdon@ccsn.nevada.edu. Website: http://sites.csn.edu/english/redrockreview/. **Contact:** Dr. Richard Logsdon, senior editor. Magazine: 5 × 8; 125 pages. "We're looking for the very best literature. Stories need to be tightly crafted, strong in character development, built around conflict. Poems need to be tightly crafted, characterised by expert use of language." Semiannual. Estab. 1995. Circ. 250.

Needs Experimental, literary, mainstream. Receives 350 unsolicited mss/month. Accepts 40-60 mss/issue; 80-120 mss/year. Does not read mss during summer. Publishes ms 3-5 after acceptance. **Publishes 5-10 new writers/year.** Recently published work by Charles Harper Webb, Mary Sojourner, Mark Irwin. Length: 1,500-5,000 words; average length: 3,500 words. Publishes short shorts. Also publishes literary essays, literary criticism, poetry. Sometimes comments on rejected mss.

How to Contact Send SASE (or IRC) for return of ms. Responds in 2 weeks to queries; 3 months to mss. Accepts simultaneous, multiple submissions. Sample copy for $5.50. Writer's guidelines for SASE, by e-mail or on Web site.

Payment/Terms Pays 2 contributor's copies. Pays on acceptance for first rights.

☑ RED WHEELBARROW

De Anza College, 21250 Stevens Creek Blvd., Cupertino CA 95014-5702. (408) 864-8600. E-mail: splitterrandolph@fhda.edu. Website: www.deanza.edu/redwheelbarrow. **Contact:** Randy Splitter or Ken Weisner. Magazine: 200-275 pages; photos. "Contemporary poetry, fiction, creative nonfiction, b&w graphics, comics and photos." Annual. Estab. 1976 as Bottomfish; 2000 as Red Wheelbarrow. Circ. 250-500.

Needs "Thoughtful, meaningful writing. We welcome submissions of all kinds, and we seek to publish a diverse range of styles and voices from around the country and the world." Receives 75 unsolicited mss/month. Accepts 30-50 mss/issue. Reads mss September through February. Submission deadline: January 31; publication date: Spring or Summer. Publishes ms 2-4 months after acceptance. Agented fiction 1%. **Publishes 0-2 new writers/year.** Recently published work by Joan Connor, Brian Friesen, Caroline Marwitz, Garry Craig Powell, Chad Simpson, and Bill Teitelbaum. Length: 4,000 words; average length: 2,500 words. Publishes short shorts. Also publishes poetry.

How to Contact Accepts submissions by e-mail. Responds in 2-4 months to mss. Accepts simultaneous submissions. Sample copy for $10; back issues $2.50. Writer's guidelines online.

Payment/Terms Pays 1 contributor's copy. Acquires first North American serial rights.

Tips "Write freely, rewrite carefully. Resist clichés and stereotypes. We are not affiliated with Red Wheelbarrow Press or any similarly named publication."

☑ REED MAGAZINE

San Jose State University, Dept. of English, One Washington Square, San Jose CA 95192-0090. (408) 927-4458. E-mail: reed@email.sjsu.edu. Website: http://www.reedmag.org/drupal/. **Contact:** Nick Taylor, editor. Literary magazine/journal. 9 × 5.75, 200 pages, semi-gloss paper, card cover. Contains illustrations. Includes photographs. "Reed Magazine is one of the oldest student-run literary journals west of the Mississippi. We publish outstanding fiction, poetry, nonfiction and art as a service to the South Bay literary community." Annual. Estab. 1944. Circ. 3500. Member CLMP.

Needs Ethnic/multicultural (general), experimental, feminist, gay, historical (general), humor/satire, lesbian, literary, mainstream, regional (northern California). Does not want children's, young adult, fantasy, or erotic. Receives 30 mss/month. Accepts 5-7 mss/issue. Does not read Nov 2-May 31. Ms published 6 months after acceptance. Publishes 3-4 new writers/year. Published Tommy Mouton, Alan Soldofsky, Gwen Goodkin and Al Young. Length: 2,000 words (min)-6,000 words (max). Average length: 3,500 words. Also publishes literary essays, book reviews, poetry. Send review copies to Nick Taylor, Editor. Never comments on/critiques rejected mss.

How to Contact Submit online. Include estimated word count, brief bio. Responds to mss in 6 months. Considers simultaneous submissions, multiple submissions. Sample copy available for $8. Guidelines available on Web site.

Payment/Terms Writers receive free subscription to the magazine. Additional copies $5. Pays on publication. Acquires first North American serial rights. Sends galleys to author. Publication is copyrighted. "Sponsors the Steinbeck Award, given annually for the best short story. The prize is $1,000 and there's a $15 entry fee."

Tips "Well-writen, original, clean grammatical prose is essential. Keep submitting! The readers are students and change every year."

☑ REFLECTIONS LITERARY JOURNAL

Piedmont Community College, P.O. Box 1197, Roxboro NC 27573. (336) 599-1181. E-mail: reflect@piedmontcc.edu. **Contact**: Dawn Langley, editor. Magazine: 100-150 pages. Annual. Estab. 1999. Circ. 250.

Needs Literary. "Accepts mss from Person and Caswell county, NC authors only (residents or natives). If time and space permit, we'll consider submissions from other North Carolina authors." Publishes mss 6-10 months after acceptance. **Publishes 3-5 new writers/year.** Recently published work by Maureen Sherbondy, Dainiel Green, Betty Moffett, Lian Gouw, Sejal Badani Ravani, Donna Conrad. Max Length: 4,000 words; average length: 2,500 words. Publishes short shorts. Also publishes poetry and essays, photographs, videos, digital animation, and artwork.

How to Contact Send SASE for return of ms or #10 SASE for reply only. Sample copy for $5. Writer's guidelines for SASE or by e-mail.

Payment/Terms Publication is online. Acquires first North American serial rights. Sponsors awards/contests.

Tips "We look for good writing with a flair, which captivates an educated lay audience. Don't take rejection letters personally. We turn away many submissions simply because we don't have room for everything we like or because the author is not from our region. For that reason, we're more likely to accept shorter well-written stories than longer stories of the same quality. Also, stories containing profanity that doesn't contribute to the plot, structure or intended tone are rejected immediately."

☑ $ THE REJECTED QUARTERLY

P.O. Box 1351, Cobb CA 95426. E-mail: bplankton@juno.com. Contact: Daniel Weiss, Jeff Ludecke, fiction editors. Magazine: 8½ × 11; 36-44 pages; 60 lb. paper; 10 pt. coated cover stock; illustrations. "We want the best literature possible, regardless of genre. We do, however, have a bias toward the unusual and toward speculative fiction. We aim for a literate, educated audience. The Rejected Quarterly believes in publishing the highest quality rejected fiction and other writing that doesn't fit anywhere else. We strive to be different, but will go for quality every time, whether conventional or not." Semiannual. Estab. 1998.

Needs Experimental, fantasy, historical, humor/satire, literary, mainstream, mystery/suspense, romance (futuristic/time travel only), science fiction (soft/sociological), sports. Accepts poetry about being rejected. Receives 30 unsolicited mss/month. Accepts 3-6 mss/issue; 8-12 mss/year. Publishes ms 1-12 months after acceptance. **Publishes 2- 4 new writers/year.** Recently published work by Sharon Ellis, Hannah Gersen and John C. Carter. Length: 8,000 words. Publishes short shorts (literature related), literary criticism, rejection-related poetry. Often comments on rejected mss.

How to Contact Send SASE for reply, return of ms or send a disposable copy of ms. No longer accepting e-mail submissions. Responds in 2-4 weeks to queries; 1-9 months to mss. Accepts reprint submissions. Sample copy for $6 (IRCs for foreign requests). Reviews fiction.

Payment/Terms Pays $15 and 1 contributor's copy; additional copies $5. Pays on acceptance for first rights.

Tips "We are looking for high-quality writing that tells a story or expresses a coherent idea. We want unique stories, original viewpoints and unusual slants. We are getting far too many inappropriate submissions. Please be familiar with the magazine. Be sure to include your rejection slips! Send out quality rather than quantity."

☑ RIVER OAK REVIEW

Elmhurst College, 190 Prospect Ave, Elmhurst IL 60126-3296. (630) 617-3137. Fax: (630) 617-3609. E-mail: riveroak@elmhurst.edu. Website: www.riveroakreview.org. **Contact:** Ron Wiginton, editor. Literary magazine/journal: 6 × 9, 195 pages; perfect bound paper; glossy, 4 color cover. "We try with each issue to showcase many voices of America, loud and soft, radical and sublime. Each piece we publish, prose or poetry, is an attempt to capture a part of 'us', with the notion that it is through our art that we are defined as a culture." Estab. 1993. Circ. 500.

Needs Ethnic/multicultural (general), experimental, literary, mainstream, translations. Does not want genre fiction or "lessons of morality; 'idea' driven stories usually do not work." Receives 50-75 mss/month. Accepts 7-8 mss/issue; 14-16 mss/year. Ms published 3 months after acceptance. Agented fiction 1%. **Publishes 2-3 new writers/year.** Published Adam Lichtenstein, Robert Moulthrop, J. Malcom Garcia and Laura Hope-Gill. Length: 250 words (min)-7,000 words (max). Average length: 3,000 words. Publishes short shorts. Average length of short shorts: 750 words. Also publishes literary essays, book reviews, poetry. Send review copies to Ron Wiginton, Editor. Sometimes comments on/critiques rejected mss.

How to Contact Send complete ms with cover letter. Accepts submissions by e-mail. Include list of publications. Responds to mss in 6 months. Send disposable copy of ms and #10 SASE for reply only. Considers simultaneous submissions. Sample copy available for $5. Guidelines available for SASE, via e-mail, on Web site, via fax.

Payment/Terms Writers receive 2 contributor's copies. Additional copies $10. Pays on publication. Acquires first North American serial rights. Publication is copyrighted.

Tips "The voice is what we notice first. Is the writer in command of the language? Secondly, does the story have anything to say? It's not that 'fluff' cannot be good, but we note our favorites stories tend to have meaning beyond the surface of the plot. Thirdly, the story must by populated by 'real' peoples who are also interesting, characters, in other words, who have lives underneath the storyline. Finally, look before you leap."

☑ ⚐ RIVER STYX

Big River Association, 3547 Olive Street, Suite 107, St. Louis MO 63103. (314)533-4541. Fax: (314)289-4019. Website: www.riverstyx.org. **Contact:** Richard Newman, editor. Magazine: 6 × 9; 100 pages; color card cover; perfect-bound; b&w visual art. "River Styx publishes the highest quality fiction, poetry, interviews, essays, and visual art. We are an internationally distributed multicultural literary magazine." Mss read May-November. Estab. 1975.

- *River Styx* has had stories appear in *New Stories from the South* and has been included in *Pushcart* anthologies.

Needs Ethnic/multicultural, experimental, feminist, gay, lesbian, literary, mainstream, novel excerpts, translations, short stories, literary. "No genre fiction, less thinly veiled autobiography." Receives 350 unsolicited mss/month. Accepts 2-6 mss/issue; 6-12 mss/year. Reads only May through November. Publishes ms 1 year after acceptance. **Publishes 20 new writers/year.** Recently published work by George Singleton, Philip Graham, Katherine Min, Richard Burgin, Nancy Zafris, Jacob Appel, and Eric Shade. Publishes short shorts. Also publishes poetry. Sometimes comments on rejected mss.

How to Contact Send complete ms. SASE required. Responds in 4 months to mss. Accepts simultaneous submissions "if a note is enclosed with your work and if we are notified immediately upon acceptance elsewhere." Sample copy for $8. Writer's guidelines online.

Payment/Terms Pays 2 contributor copies, plus 1-year subscription; $8/page if funds are available. Pays on publication for first North American serial, one-time rights.

Tips "We want high-powered stories with well-developed characters. We like strong plots, usually with at least three memorable scenes, and a subplot often helps. No thin, flimsy fiction with merely service-able language. Short stories shouldn't be any different than poetry—every single word should count. One could argue every word counts more since we're being asked to read 10 to 30 pages."

☑ RIVERWIND

Hocking College, 3301 Hocking Parkway, Nelsonville OH 45764. (740)753-3591. E-mail: williams_k@hocking.edu. **Contact:** Kristine Williams, co-editor. Magazine: 7 × 7; 125-150 pages; 60 lb. offset paper; illustrations; photos. Riverwind is an established magazine that prints fiction, poetry, black and white photos and prints, drawings, creative nonfiction, book reviews and plays. Special consideration is given to writers from the Appalachian region. Annual. Estab. 1976. Circ. 200-400.

Needs Adventure, ethnic/multicultural (Appalachian), humor/satire, literary, mainstream, regional. DOES NOT WANT erotica, fantasy, horror, experimental, religious, children's/juvenile. Receives 25 unsolicited mss/month. Does not read mss June-September. Publishes ms 6-9 months after acceptance. **Publishes many new writers/year.** Recently published work by Gerald Wheeler, Wendy McVicker, Roy Bentley, Perry A. White, Tom Montag, Beau Beadreaux. Length: 500-2,500 words; average length: 1,750 words. Publishes short shorts. Also publishes literary essays, literary criticism, poetry. Rarely comments on rejected mss.

How to Contact Send complete ms. Accepts submissions by e-mail, disk. Send disposable copy of ms and #10 SASE for reply only. Responds in 4 weeks to queries; 8-16 weeks to mss. Accepts simultaneous, multiple submissions. Sample copy for $5. Writer's guidelines for #10 SASE or by e-mail.

Payment/Terms Pays 2 contributor's copies. Pays on publication for first North American serial rights.

Tips "Avoid stereotypical plots and characters. We tend to favor realism but not sentimentality."

☑ $ ROANOKE REVIEW

Roanoke College, 221 College Lane, Salem VA 24153-3794. (540)375-2380. E-mail: review@roanoke.edu. **Contact:** Paul Hanstedt, editor. Magazine: 6 × 9; 200 pages; 60 lb. paper; 70 lb. cover. "We're looking for fresh, thoughtful material that will appeal to a broader as well as literary audience. Humor encouraged." Annual. Estab. 1967. Circ. 500.

Needs Feminist, gay, humor/satire, lesbian, literary, mainstream, regional. Receives 150 unsolicited mss/month. Accepts 5-10 mss/year. Does not read mss February 1-September 1. Publishes ms 6 months after acceptance. **Publishes 1-5 new writers/year.** Recently published work by Siobhan Fallon, Jacob M. Appel, and JoeAnn Hart. Length: 1,000-5,000 words; average length: 3,000 words. Publishes short shorts. Also publishes poetry. Sometimes comments on rejected mss.

How to Contact Send SASE for return of ms or send a disposable copy of ms and #10 SASE for reply only. Responds in 1 month to queries; 6 months to mss. Sample copy for 8 × 11 SAE with $2 postage. Writer's guidelines for SASE.

Payment/Terms Pays $10-50/story (when budget allows) and 2 contributor's copies; additional copies $5. Pays on publication for one-time rights.

Tips "Pay attention to sentence-level writing—verbs, metaphors, concrete images. Don't forget, though, that plot and character keep us reading. We're looking for stuff that breaks the MFA story style."

☑ THE ROCKFORD REVIEW

The Rockford Writers Guild, P.O. Box 858, Rockford IL 61105. E-mail: daveconnieross@aol.com. Website: http://writersguild1.tripod.com. **Contact:** David Ross, editor. Magazine: 100 pages; perfect bound; color illustrations; b&w photos. "We look for prose and poetry with a fresh approach to old themes or new insights into the human condition." Semiannual. Estab. 1971. Circ. 600.

Needs Ethnic/multicultural, experimental, fantasy, humor/satire, literary, regional, science fiction (hard science, soft/sociological). "No graphic sex, translations or overly academic work." Recently published work by James Bellarosa, Sean Michael Rice, John P. Kristofco, L.S. Sedishiro. Also publishes literary essays.

How to Contact Include SASE. Responds in 2 months to mss. Accepts simultaneous, multiple submissions. Sample copy for $9. Writer's guidelines for SASE or online.

Payment/Terms Pays contributor's copies. "Two $25 editor's choice cash prizes per issue." Acquires first North American serial rights.

Tips "We're wide open to new and established writers alike—particularly short satire."

☷ ☑ ◎ $ ROOM

Magazine: A Canadian Quarterly of Women's Literature and Criticism West Coast Feminist Literary Magazine Society, P.O. Box 46160, Station D, Vancouver BC V6J 5G5 Canada. Website: www.roommagazine.com. **Contact:** Growing Room Collective. Magazine: 112 pages; illustrations; photos. "Room of One's Own is Canada's oldest feminist literary journal. Since 1975, Room has been a forum in which women can share their unique perspectives on the world, each other and themselves." Quarterly. Estab. 1975. Circ. 1,000.

Needs Feminist literature—short stories, creative nonfiction, essays—by, for and about women. "No humor, science fiction, romance." Receives 60-100 unsolicited mss/month. Accepts 18-20 mss/issue; 75-80 mss/year. Publishes ms 1 year after acceptance. **Publishes 15-20 new writers/year.** Publishes poetry by Canadian authors only.

How to Contact Send complete ms with a cover letter. Include estimated word count and brief bio. Send a disposable copy of ms and #10 SASE or IRC for reply only. Responds in 6 months to mss. Sample copy for $13 or online. Writer's guidelines online. Reviews fiction.

Payment/Terms Pays $50 (Canadian) and a 1-year subscription. Pays on publication for first North American serial rights.

☑ ☷ SALMAGUNDI

Skidmore College, 815 North Broadway, Saratoga Springs NY 12866. Fax: (518)580-5188. E-mail: pboyes@skidmore.edu. **Contact:** Peg Boyers. Magazine: 8 × 5; 200-300 pages; illustrations; photos. "Salmagundi publishes an eclectic variety of materials, ranging from short-short fiction to novellas from the surreal to the realistic. Authors include Nadine Gordimer, Russell Banks, Steven Millhauser, Gordon Lish, Clark Blaise, Mary Gordon, Joyce Carol Oates and Cynthia Ozick. Our audience is a generally literate population of people who read for pleasure." Quarterly. Estab. 1965. Circ. 4,800. Member CLMP.

• *Salmagundi* authors are regularly represented in *Pushcart* collections and *Best American Short Story* collections.

Needs Ethnic/multicultural (multicultural), experimental, family saga, gay, historical (general), literary, poetry. Receives 300-500 unsolicited mss/month. Accepts 2 mss/year. Read unsolicited mss October 1-May 1 "but from time to time close the doors even during this period because the backlog tends to grow out of control." Publishes ms up to 2 years after acceptance. Agented fiction 10%. Also publishes literary essays, literary criticism, poetry.

How to Contact Send complete ms by e-mail (pboyes@skidmore.edu). Responds in 6 months to mss. Sample copy for $5. Writer's guidelines for #10 SASE.

Payment/Terms Pays 6-10 contributor's copies and subscription to magazine. Acquires first, electronic rights.

Tips "I look for excellence and a very unpredictable ability to appeal to the interests and tastes of the editors. Be brave. Don't be discouraged by rejection. Keep stories in circulation. Of course, it goes without saying: Work hard on the writing. Revise tirelessly. Study magazines and send only to those whose sensibility matches yours."

☑ SANTA MONICA REVIEW

Santa Monica College, 1900 Pico Blvd., Santa Monica CA 90405. (310)434-4242. **Contact:** Andrew Tonkovich, editor. Magazine: 250 pages. "The editors are committed to fostering new talent as well as presenting new work by established writers. There is also a special emphasis on presenting and promoting writers who make their home in Southern California." Estab. 1989. Circ. 4,000.

Needs Experimental, literary, memoirs. "No crime and detective, mysogyny, footnotes, TV, dog stories. We want more self-conscious, smart, political, humorous, digressive, meta-fiction." Receives 250 unsolicited mss/month. Accepts 10 mss/issue; 20 mss/year. Agented fiction 10%. **Publishes 5 new writers/year.** Recently published work by Ed Skoog, Trini Dalton, Judith Grossman, John Peterson. Also publishes literary essays.

How to Contact Send complete ms. Send disposable copy of ms. Responds in 3 months to mss. Accepts simultaneous, multiple submissions. Sample copy for $7.

Payment/Terms Pays 5 contributor's copies. Acquires first North American serial rights. Sends galleys to author.

☑ THE SARANAC REVIEW

Suny Plattsburgh, Dept. of English, Champlain Valley Hall, Plattsburgh NY 12901. (518) 564-5151. Fax: (518) 564-2140. E-mail: saranacreview@plattsburgh.edu. Website: http://research.plattsburgh.edu/saranacreview/. **Contact**: fiction editor. Magazine: 5½ × 8½; 180-200 pages; 80 lb. cover/70 lb. paper; glossy cover stock; illustrations; photos. "The Saranac Review is committed to dissolving boundaries of all kinds, seeking to publish a diverse array of emerging and established writers from Canada and the U.S. The Saranac Review aims to be a textual clearing in which a space is opened for cross-pollination between American and Canadian writers. In this way the magazine reflects the expansive bright spirit of the etymology of it's name, Saranac, meaning 'cluster of stars.'" Annual. Estab. 2004.

Needs Ethnic/multicultural, historical, literary. Publishes ms 8 months after acceptance. Publishes flash fiction. Also publishes poetry and literary/creative nonfiction. Sometimes comments on rejected mss.

How to Contact Send complete ms. Send SASE (or IRC) for return of ms or send disposable copy of the ms and #10 SASE for reply only. Responds in 4 months to mss. Accepts simultaneous submissions. Sample copy for $6. Writer's guidelines online, or by e-mail. "Please send one story at a time." Maximum length: 7,000 words.

Payment/Terms Pays 2 contributor's copies; discount on extras. Pays on publication for first North American serial, first rights.

Tips "We publish serious, generous fiction."

☑ THE SEATTLE REVIEW

Box 354330, University of Washington, Seattle WA 98195. (206)543-2302. E-mail: seaview@u.washington.edu. Website: www.seattlereview.org. **Contact:** Andrew Feld, editor-in-chief. Magazine: 6 × 9; 150 pages; illustrations; photos. "Includes fiction, nonfiction, poetry and one interview per issue with an established writer." Semiannual. Estab. 1978. Circ. 1,000. Needs Literary. Nothing in "bad taste (porn, racist, etc.)." Receives 200 unsolicited mss/month. Accepts 2-4 mss/issue; 4-8 mss/year. Does not read mss May 31-October 1. Publishes ms 1-212 years after acceptance. **Publishes 3-4 new writers/ year.** Recently published work by Rick Bass, Lauren Whitehurst, Martha Hurwitz. Length: 4,000 words; average length: 3,000 words.

How to Contact Send complete ms. Send SASE (or IRC) for return of ms or send disposable copy of ms and #10 SASE for reply only. Responds in 4-6 months to mss. No simultaneous submissions, accepts multiple submissions. Sample copy for $8. Writer's guidelines for #10 SASE, online or by e-mail.

Payment/Terms Pays 2 contributor's copies. Acquires first North American serial rights.

Tips "Know what we publish: no genre fiction; look at our magazine and decide if your work might be appreciated."

$ THE SEWANEE REVIEW

University of the South, 735 University Ave., Sewanee TN 37383-1000. (931)598-1246. Website: www. sewanee.edu/sewanee_review. **Contact:** George Core. "A literary quarterly, publishing original fiction, poetry, essays on literary and related subjects, and book reviews for well-educated readers who appreciate good American and English literature." Quarterly. Estab. 1892. Circ. 2,000.

Needs Literary, contemporary. No erotica, science fiction, fantasy or excessively violent or profane material.

How to Contact Responds in 8-10 weeks to mss. Sample copy for $8.50. Writer's guidelines online, or e-mail Leigh Anne Couch at lcouch@sewanee.edu.

Payment/Terms Pays $10-12/printed pages of prose; $2.50/line of poetry. 2 contributor copies. Pays on publication for first North American serial, second serial (reprint) rights.

$ SHENANDOAH

Washington and Lee University, Mattingly House, 2 Lee Avenue, Washington and Lee University, Lexington VA 24450-2116. (540) 458-8765. E-mail: shenandoah@wlu.edu. Website: http://shenandoah. wlu.edu. Triannual. Estab. 1950. Circ. 2,000.

Needs Mainstream, novel excerpts. No sloppy, hasty, slight fiction. Publishes ms 10 months after acceptance.

How to Contact Send complete ms. Responds in 2 months to mss. Sample copy for $10. Writer's guidelines online.

Payment/Terms Pays $25/page (cap $250). Pays on publication for first North American serial, one-time rights.

☑ SLEEPINGFISH

Calamari Press. E-mail: white@sleepingfish.net. Website: www.sleepingfish.net. **Contact:** Derek White, editor. Literary magazine/journal: 6 × 8, 160 pages, 60 lb. vellum paper, card stock cover. More recently publishing a Web version. Contains illustrations. Includes photographs. "Sleepingfish publishes an eclectic mix of flash fiction, prose and visual poetry, experimental texts, text/image and art." Published every 9 months. Estab. 2003. Circ. 500.

Needs Adventure, comics/graphic novels, ethnic/multicultural, experimental, literary. Does not want to see any fiction or writing that fits into a genre or that is written for any other reason except for the sake of art. Receives 250 mss/month. Accepts 25 mss/issue; 25 mss/year. Manuscript published less than 3 months after acceptance. **Publishes 2-3 new writers/year.** Published Rick Moody, Dawn Raffel, Terese Svoboda, Laird Hunt, Normon Lock, Peter Markus, Kevin Sampsell, Brian Evenson, Thurston Moore, and Kim Chinquee. Length: 1 word (min)-8,000 words (max). Average length: 2,000 words. Publishes short shorts. Average length of short shorts: 1,000 words. Rarely comments on/critiques rejected mss.

How to Contact Send complete ms with cover letter. Only accepts submissions by e-mail. Include brief bio. Responds to queries in 4 weeks. Responds to mss in 3 months. Send SASE (or IRC) for return of ms. Considers simultaneous submissions, multiple submissions. Guidelines available on Web site.

Payment/Terms Writers receive 1 contributor copy. Additional copies half price. Pays on publication. Acquires first rights. Sends galleys to author. Publication is copyrighted.

Tips "Write or create what's true to yourself and find a publication where you think your work honestly fits in."

☑ $ SNOWY EGRET

The Fair Press, P.O. Box 9265, Terre Haute IN 47808. **Contact:**Editors. Magazine: 8½ × 11; 60 pages; text paper; heavier cover; illustrations. "We publish works which celebrate the abundance and beauty of nature and examine the variety of ways in which human beings interact with landscapes and living things. Nature writing from literary, artistic, psychological, philosophical and historical perspectives." Semiannual. Estab. 1922. Circ. 400.

Needs "No genre fiction, e.g., horror, western, romance, etc." Receives 25 unsolicited mss/month.

Accepts up to 6 mss/issue; up to 12 mss/year. Publishes ms 6 months after acceptance. **Publishes 20 new writers/year.** Recently published work by James Hinton, Ron Gielgun, Tom Noyes, Alice Cross, Maeve Mullin Ellis. Length: 500-10,000 words; average length: 1,000-3,000 words. Publishes short shorts. Sometimes comments on rejected mss.

How to Contact Send complete ms with SASE. Cover letter optional: do not query. Responds in 2 months to mss. Accepts simultaneous submissions if noted. Sample copy for 9 × 12 SASE and $8. Writer's guidelines for #10 SASE.

Payment/Terms Pays $2/page plus 2 contributor's copies. Pays on publication for first North American serial, one-time anthology rights, or reprint rights. Sends galleys to author.

Tips Looks for "honest, freshly detailed pieces with plenty of description and/or dialogue which will allow the reader to identify with the characters and step into the setting; fiction in which nature affects character development and the outcome of the story."

☑ SONORA REVIEW

University of Arizona's Creative Writing MFA Program, University of Arizona, Dept. of English, Tucson AZ 85721. E-mail: sonora@email.arizona.edu. Website: www.coh.arizona.edu/sonora. **Contact:** Jake Levine, Jon Walter, editors. Magazine: 6 × 9; approx. 150 pages; photos. "We look for the highest quality poetry, fiction, and nonfiction, with an emphasis on emerging writers. Our magazine has a long-standing tradition of publishing the best new literature and writers. Check out our Web site for a sample of what we publish and our submission guidelines, or write us for a sample back issue." Semiannual. Estab. 1980. Circ. 500.

Needs Ethnic/multicultural, experimental, literary, mainstream, novel excerpts. Receives 200 unsolicited mss/month. Accepts 2-3 mss/issue; 6-8 mss/year. Does not read in the summer (June-August). Publishes ms 3-4 months after acceptance. **Publishes 1-3 new writers/year.** Recently published work by Michael Martone, Sawako Nakayasu. Also publishes literary essays, literary criticism, poetry. Sometimes comments on rejected mss.

How to Contact Send complete ms. Send disposable copy of the ms and #10 SASE for reply only. Responds in 2-5 weeks to queries; 3 months to mss. Accepts simultaneous, multiple submissions. Sample copy for $6. Writer's guidelines online. Reviews fiction.

Payment/Terms Pays 2 contributor's copies; additional copies for $4. Pays on publication for first North American serial, one-time, electronic rights.

Tips "Send us your best stuff."

☑ ◎ SO TO SPEAK

George Mason University, 4400 University Dr., MS 2 C5, Fairfax VA 22030. (703)993-3625. E-mail: sts@gmu.edu. Website: www.gmu.edu/org/sts. **Contact:** Norah Vawter, fiction editor. Magazine: 5½ × 8½; approximately 100 pages. "We are a feminist journal of language and art." Semiannual. Estab. 1993. Circ. 1,000.

Needs Ethnic/multicultural, experimental, feminist, lesbian, literary, mainstream, regional, translations. "No science fiction, mystery, genre romance." Receives 100 unsolicited mss/month. Accepts 3-5 mss/issue; 6-10 mss/year. Publishes ms 6 months after acceptance. **Publishes 7 new writers/year.** Length: For fiction, up to 5,000 words; for poetry, 3-5 pages per submission; average length: for fiction, up to 5,000 words; for poetry, 3-5 pages per submission. Publishes flash and short fiction, creative nonfiction, poetry, and visual art.

How to Contact Send complete ms. Include bio (50 words maximum) and SASE for return of ms or send a disposable copy of ms. Responds in 6 months to mss. Accepts simultaneous submissions. Sample copy for $7. Reviews fiction.

Payment/Terms Pays contributor copies. Acquires first North American serial rights. Sponsors awards/contests.

Tips "We do not read between March 15 and August 15. Every writer has something they do exceptionally well; do that and it will shine through in the work. We look for quality prose with a definite appeal to a feminist audience. We are trying to move away from strict genre lines. We want high quality fiction, nonfiction, poetry, art, innovative and risk-taking work."

☑ SOUTH CAROLINA REVIEW

611 Strode Tower Box 340522, Clemson University, Clemson SC 29634-0522. (864) 656-5399. Fax: (864) 656-1345. E-mail: cwayne@clemson.edu. Website: www.clemson.edu/caah/cedp. **Contact:** Wayne Chapman, editor. Magazine: 6 × 9; 200 pages; 60 lb. cream white vellum paper; 65 lb. color cover stock. Semiannual. Estab. 1967. Circ. 500.

Needs Literary, mainstream, poetry, essays, reviews. Does not read mss June-August or December. Receives 50-60 unsolicited mss/month. Recently published work by Ronald Frame, Dennis McFadden, Dulane Upshaw Ponder, and Stephen Jones. Rarely comments on rejected mss.

How to Contact Send complete ms. Requires text on disk upon acceptance in WordPerfect or Microsoft Word in PC format. Responds in 2 months to mss. Sample copy for $16 includes postage inside the U.S. Reviews fiction.

Payment/Terms Pays in contributor's copies.

☑ SOUTHERN CALIFORNIA REVIEW

(Formally Southern California Anthology) Master of Professional Writing, 3501 Trousdale Parkway, Mark Taper Hall, THH 355J University of Southern California, Los Angeles CA 90089-4034. (213)740-3253. Fax: (213)740-5775. E-mail: scr@college.usc.edu. Website: www.usc.edu/dept/LAS/mpw/students/sca. php. **Contact**: Fiction Editor. Magazine: 150 pages; semiglosss cover stock. "Formerly known as the Southern California Anthology, Southern California Review (SCR) is the literary journal of the Master of Professional Writing program at the University of Southern California. It has been publishing fiction and poetry since 1982 and now also accepts submissions of creative nonfiction, plays, and screenplays. Printed every October and April with original cover artwork, every issue contains new, emerging, and established authors." Semiannual. Estab. 1983. Circ. 1,000.

Needs "We accept short shorts but rarely use stories more than 8,000 words. Novel excerpts are acceptable if they can stand alone. We do consider genre work (horror, mystery, romance, sci-fi) if it transcends the boundaries of the genre." Receives 120 unsolicited mss/month. Accepts 10-15 mss/issue. Publishes ms 4 months after acceptance. **Publishes 20-30 new writers/year**. Recently published work by James Ragan, James Tate, Alice Fulton, John Updike, Joyce Carol Oates, Hubert Selby Jr., Marge Piercy, Stephen Dunn, Ruth Stone, Gay Talese. Publishes short shorts.

How to Contact Send complete, typed, double-spaced ms. Cover letter should include list of previous publications. Address to the proper editor (Fiction, Poetry, etc.). Please include a cover letter. Be sure your full name and contact information (address, phone, and e-mail) appear on the first page of the manuscript. Response time for submissions is 3 to 6 months. No electronic or e-mail submissions are accepted. Every submission must include a self-addressed stamped envelope (SASE). Sample copy for $10. Writer's guidelines for SASE and on Web site.

Payment/Terms Pays in 2 contributor copies. Acquires first rights.

Tips "The Anthology pays particular attention to craft and style in its selection of narrative writing."

☑ ◎ SOUTHERN HUMANITIES REVIEW

Auburn University, 9088 Haley Center, Auburn University AL 36849. Website: www.auburn.edu. **Contact:** Fiction Editor. Magazine: 6 × 9; 100 pages; 60 lb neutral pH, natural paper; 65 lb. neutral pH medium coated cover stock; occasional illustration; photos. "We publish essays, poetry, fiction and reviews. Our fiction has ranged from very traditional in form and content to very experimental. Literate, college-educated audience. We hope they read our journal for both enlightenment and pleasure." Quarterly. Estab. 1967. Circ. 800.

Needs Feminist, humor/satire, regional. Slower reading time in summer. Receives 25 unsolicited mss/month. Accepts 1-2 mss/issue; 4-6 mss/year. Recently published work by Chris Arthur, Andrea Deagon, Sheryl St. Germain, Patricia Foster, Janette Turner Hospital, Paula Koöhlmeier, David Wagner, Yves Bonnefoy, Neil Grimmett, and Wayne Flynt. Also publishes literary essays, literary criticism, poetry. Sometimes comments on rejected mss.

How to Contact Send complete ms, cover letter with an explanation of the topic chosen—"special, certain book, etc., a little about the author if he/she has never submitted." No e-mail submissions. No simultaneous submissions. Responds in 3 months to mss.

Payment/Terms Pays in contributor copies. Rights revert to author on publication.

Tips "Send us the ms with SASE. If we like it, we'll take it or we'll recommend changes. If we don't like it, we'll send it back as promptly as possible. Read the journal. Send typewritten, clean copy, carefully proofread. We also award the annual Hoepfner Prize of $100 for the best published essay or short story of the year. Let someone whose opinion you respect read your story and give you an honest appraisal. Rewrite, if necessary, to get the most from your story."

☑ $ ▣ THE SOUTHERN REVIEW

Old President's House, Louisiana State University, Baton Rouge LA 70803. (225) 578-5108. Fax: (225) 578-5098. E-mail: southernreview@lsu.edu. Website: www.lsu.edu/thesouthernreview. **Contact:** Jeanne Leiby, editor. Magazine: 6¼ × 10; 240 pages; 50 lb. Glatfelter paper; 65 lb. #1 grade cover stock. Quarterly. Estab. 1935. Circ. 3,000.

• Several stories published in *The Southern Review* were *Pushcart Prize* selections.

Needs Literary. "We select fiction that conveys a unique and compelling voice and vision." Receives approximately 300 unsolicited mss/month. Accepts 4-6 mss/issue. Reading period: September-May. Publishes ms 6 months after acceptance. Agented fiction 1%. **Publishes 10-12 new writers/year.**Recently published work by David Bottoms, Robert Cording, Rita Dove, Ivonne Lamazeres, Nadine Sabra Meyer, and more. Also publishes literary essays, literary criticism, poetry and book reviews.

How to Contact Mail hard copy of ms with cover letter and SASE. No queries. "Prefer brief letters giving author's prefessional information, including recent or notable publcations. Biographical info not necessary." Responds within 10 weeks to mss. Sample copy for $8. Writer's guidelines online. Reviews fiction, poetry.

Payment/Terms Pays $30/page. Pays on publication for first North American serial rights. Sends page proof to author via e-mail. Sponsors awards/contests.

Tips "Careful attention to craftsmanship and technique combined with a developed sense of the creation of story will always make us pay attention."

☑ ◎ SOUTHWESTERN AMERICAN LITERATURE

Center for the Study of the Southwest, Texas State University-San Marcos, 601 University Drive, San Marcos TX 78666. (512)245-2224. Fax: (512)245-7462. E-mail: mb13@txstate.edu. Website: http://swrhc.txstate.edu/cssw/. **Contact:** Twister Marquiss, assistant editor; Mark Busby, co-editor; Dick Maurice Heaberlin, co-editor. Magazine: 6 × 9; 125 pages; 80 lb. cover stock. "We publish fiction, nonfiction, poetry, literary criticism and book reviews. Generally speaking, we want material covering the Greater Southwest or material written by Southwest writers." Biannual. Estab. 1971. Circ. 300.

Needs Ethnic/multicultural, literary, mainstream, regional. "No science fiction or romance." Receives 10-15 unsolicited mss/month. Accepts 1-2 mss/issue; 4-5 mss/year. Publishes ms 6 months after acceptance. **Publishes 1-2 new writers/year.** Recently published work by Keith Ekiss, Michelle Brooks, Donald Lucio Hurd, Walt McDonald, Carol Hamilton, Larry D. Thomas. Length: 6,250 words; average length: 4,000 words. Also publishes literary essays, literary criticism, poetry. Sometimes comments on rejected mss.

How to Contact Send complete ms. Include cover letter, estimated word count, 2-5 line bio and list of publications. Does not accept e-mail submissions. Responds in 3-6 months to mss. Sample copy for $8. Writer's guidelines free.

Payment/Terms Pays 2 contributor copies. Acquires first rights.

Tips "We look for crisp language, an interesting approach to material; a regional approach is desired but not required. Read widely, write often, revise carefully. We are looking for stories that probe the relationship between the tradition of Southwestern American literature and the writer's own imagination in creative ways. We seek stories that move beyond stereotype and approach the larger defining elements and also ones that, as William Faulkner noted in his Nobel Prize acceptance speech, treat subjects central to good literature—the old verities of the human heart, such as honor and courage and pity and suffering, fear and humor, love and sorrow."

☑ SOUTHWEST REVIEW

P.O. Box 750374, Dallas TX 75275-0374. (214)768-1037. Fax: (214)768-1408. E-mail: swr@smu.edu. Website: www.smu.edu/southwestreview. **Contact:** Jennifer Cranfill, Senior Editor. Magazine: 6 × 9; 150 pages. "The majority of our readers are well read adults who wish to stay abreast of the latest and best in contemporary fiction, poetry, and essays in all but the most specialized disciplines." Quarterly. Estab. 1915. Circ. 1,600.

Needs "High literary quality; no specific requirements as to subject matter, but cannot use sentimental, religious, western, poor science fiction, pornographic, true confession, mystery, juvenile or serialized or condensed novels." Receives 200 unsolicited mss/month. Publishes ms 6-12 months after acceptance. Recently published work by Alice Hoffman, Sabina Murray, Alix Ohlin. Also publishes literary essays, poetry. Occasionally comments on rejected mss.

How to Contact Mail complete ms or submit on line. Responds in 1-4 months to mss. Accepts multiple submissions. Sample copy for $6. Writer's guidelines for #10 SASE or on Web site.

Payment/Terms Pays negotiable rate and 3 contributor copies. Acquires first North American serial rights. Sends galleys to author.

Tips "Despite the title, we are not a regional magazine. Before you submit your work, it's a good idea to take a look at recent issues to familiarize yourself with the magazine. We strongly advise all writers to include a cover letter. Keep your cover letter professional and concise and don't include extraneous personal information, a story synopsis, or a resume. When authors ask what we look for in a strong story submission the answer is simple regarless of graduate degrees in creative writing, workshops, or whom you know. We look for good writing, period."

▢ ☒ SPOUT

Spout Press, P.O. Box 581067, Minneapolis MN 55458-1067. E-mail: editors@spoutpress.org. Website: www.spoutpress.org. **Contact:** Carrie Eidem, fiction editor. Literary magazine/journal: 5¾ × 8½, 60 pages. Contains illustrations. Includes photographs. "With Spout we strive to publish experimental writing. We don't focus on any certain style, tone or approach for the stories we publish. Spout also has an annual fiction story of the year contest. Please see Web site for details." Semiannual. Estab. 1989. Member CLMP.

Needs Adventure, comics/graphic novels, ethnic/multicultural (general), experimental, feminist, gay, science fiction. Does not want children's fiction. Receives 15-20 mss/month. Accepts 3-5 mss/issue; 6-10 mss/year. Ms published 1-2 months after acceptance. **Publishes 6-10 new writers/year.** Published Jeri Blazek, Ryan Van Cleave and Mike Tuohy. Length: 500 words (min)-7,000 words (max). Average length: 5,000 words. Publishes short shorts. Average length of short shorts: 500 words. Also publishes poetry. Rarely comments on/critiques rejected mss.

How to Contact Send complete ms with cover letter. Include estimated word count, brief bio. Responds to queries within one month. Responds to mss in 6-8 weeks. Send either SASE (or IRC) for return of ms or disposable copy of ms and #10 SASE for reply only. Considers simultaneous submissions, multiple submissions. Sample copy available for $5. Guidelines available for SASE, via e-mail, on Web site.

Payment/Terms Writers receive 1 contributor copy. Additional copies $5. Pays on publication. Acquires one-time rights. Publication is not copyrighted. "We take submissions from the fall to spring for our Story of the Year contest. See Web site for details."

Tips "Please look at our *Spout Magazine* to see if your submissions will fit our journal."

STAND MAGAZINE

North American Office: Department of English, VCU, Richmond VA 23284-2005. (804) 828-1331. E-mail: dlatane@vcu.edu. Website: www.standmagazine.org. "Stand Magazine is concerned with what happens when cultures and literatures meet, with translation in its many guises, with the mechanics of language, with the processes by which the policy receives or disables its cultural makers. Stand promotes debate of issues that are of radical concern to the intellectual community worldwide." Quarterly. Estab. 1952 in Leeds UK. Circ. 3,000 worldwide.

Needs "No genre fiction." Publishes ms 12 months after acceptance.

How to Contact Send complete ms. Responds in 6 weeks to queries; 3 months to mss. Sample copy for $12. Writer's guidelines for #10 SASE with sufficient number of IRCs or online.

Payment/Terms Payment varies. Pays on publication. Aquires first world rights.

▢ ◎ $ ☒ STONE SOUP

Children's Art Foundation, P.O. Box 83, Santa Cruz CA 95063-0083. (831)426-5557. Fax: (831)426-1161. Website: www.stonesoup.com. **Contact:** Ms. Gerry Mandel, editor. Magazine: 7 × 10; 48 pages; high quality paper; photos. Audience is children, teachers, parents, writers, artists. "We have a preference for writing and art based on real-life experiences; no formula stories or poems. We only publish writing by children ages 8 to 13. We do not publish writing by adults." Bimonthly. Estab. 1973. Circ. 20,000.

- This is known as "the literary journal for children." *Stone Soup* has previously won the Ed Press Golden Lamp Honor Award and the Parent's Choice Award.

Needs Adventure, ethnic/multicultural, experimental, fantasy, historical, humor/satire, mystery/suspense, science fiction, slice-of-life vignettes, suspense. "We do not like assignments or formula stories of any kind." Receives 1,000 unsolicited mss/month. Accepts 10 mss/issue. Publishes ms 4 months after acceptance. **Publishes some new writers/year.** Also publishes literary essays, poetry.

How to Contact Send complete ms. "We like to learn a little about our young writers, why they like to write, and how they came to write the story they are submitting." Please do not include SASE. Do not send originals. Responds only to those submissions being considered for possible publication. "If you do not hear from us in 4 to 6 weeks it means we were not able to use your work. Don't be discouraged! Try again!" No simultaneous submissions. Sample copy for $5 or online. Writer's guidelines online.

Payment/Terms Pays $40 for stories. Authors also receive 2 copies, a certificate, and discounts on additional copies and on subscriptions. Pays on publication.

Tips Mss are rejected because they are "derivatives of movies, TV, comic books, or classroom assignments or other formulas. Go to our Web site, where you can see many examples of the kind of work we publish."

▦ ☑ $ STORIE

Leconte Press, Via Suor Celestina Donati 13/E, Rome 00167 Italy. (+39) 06 614 8777. Fax: (+39) 06 614 8777. E-mail: storie@tiscali.it. Website: www.storie.it. **Contact**: Gianluca Bassi, editor; Barbara Pezzopane, assistant editor; George Lerner, foreign editor. Magazine: 186 pages; illustrations; photographs. "Storie is one of Italy's leading literary magazines. Committed to a truly crossover vision of writing, the bilingual (Italian/English) review publishes high quality fiction and poetry, interspersed with the work of alternative wordsmiths such as filmmakers and musicians. Through writings bordering on narratives and interviews with important contemporary writers, it explores the culture and craft of writing." Bimonthly. Estab. 1989. Circ. 20,000.

Needs Literary. Receives 150 unsolicited mss/month. Accepts 6-10 mss/issue; 30-50 mss/year. Does not read mss in August. Publishes ms 2 months after acceptance. Publishes 20 new writers/year. Recently published work by Joyce Carol Oates, Haruki Murakami, Paul Auster, Robert Coover, Raymond Carver, T.C. Boyle, Ariel Dorfman, Tess Gallagher. Length: 2,000-6,000 words; average length: 1,500 words. Publishes short shorts. Also publishes literary essays, literary criticism, poetry. Sometimes comments on rejected mss.

How to Contact Accepts submissions by e-mail or on disk. Include brief bio. Send complete ms with cover letter. "Manuscripts may be submitted directly by regular post without querying first; however, we do not accept unsolicited m anus cripts via e-mail. Please query via e-mail first. We only contact writers if their work has been accepted. We also arrange for and oversee a high-quality, professional translation of the piece." Responds in 1 month to queries; 6 months to mss. Accepts multiple submissions. Sample copy for $ 10. Writer's guidelines online.

Payment/Terms Pays $30-600 and 2 contributor's copies. Pays on publication for first (in English and Italian) rights.

Tips "More than erudite references or a virtuoso performance, we're interested in the recording of human experience in a genuine, original voice. *Storie* reserves the right to include a brief review of interesting submissions not selected for publication in a special column of the magazine."

▢ STRAYLIGHT

UW-Parkside, English Dept., 900 Wood Rd., P.O. Box 2000, Kenosha WI 53141. (262)595-2139. Fax: (262)595-2271. E-mail: straylight@litspot.net. Website: www.litspot.net/straylight. **Contact:** fiction editor. Magazine has revolving editor. Editorial term: 1 years. Literary magazine/journal: 6¼ × 9½, 75 pages, quality paper, uncoated index stock cover. Contains illustrations. Includes photographs. "Straylight publishes high quality, character-based fiction of any style. We tend not to publish strict genre pieces, though we may query them for future special issues. We do not publish erotica." Biannual with special issues. Estab. 2005.

Needs Ethnic/multicultural (general), experimental, gay, lesbian, literary, mainstream, regional. Special interests: genre fiction in special theme issues. Accepts 5-7 mss/issue; 10-14 mss/year. Does not read

May-August. Manuscript published 6 months after acceptance. Agented fiction 10%. Length: 1,000 words (min)-5,000 words (max). Average length: 2,500 words. Publishes short shorts. Also publishes poetry. Rarely comments on/critiques rejected mss.

How to Contact Send complete ms with cover letter. Accepts submissions by e-mail. Include brief bio, list of publications. Responds to queries in 2 weeks. Responds to mss in 2 months. Send either SASE (or IRC) for return of ms or disposable copy of ms and #10 SASE for reply only. Sample copy available for $6. Guidelines available for SASE, on Web site.

Payment/Terms Writers receive 2 contributor's copies. Additional copies $3. Pays on publication. Acquires first North American serial rights. Publication is copyrighted.

Tips "We tend to publish character-based and inventive fiction with cutting-edge prose. We are unimpressed with works based on strict plot twists or novelties. Read a sample copy to get a feel for what we publish."

☑ STRUGGLE

Detroit MI 48213-0261. (213) 273-9039. E-mail: timhall11@yahoo.com. Contact: Tim Hall, editor. Magazine: 5½ × 8½; 36-72 pages; 20 lb. white bond paper; colored cover; illustrations; occasional photos. Publishes material related to "the struggle of the working class and all progressive people against the rule of the rich—including their war policies, repression, racism, exploitation of the workers, oppression of women and general culture, etc." Quarterly. Estab. 1985.

Needs Ethnic/multicultural, experimental, feminist, historical, humor/satire, literary, regional, science fiction, translations, young adult/teen (10-18), prose poem, senior citizen/retirement. "The theme can be approached in many ways, including plenty of categories not listed here. Readers would like fiction about anti-globalization, the fight against racism, prison conditions, neo-conservatism and the Iraq War. Would also like to see more fiction that depicts life, work and struggle of the working class of every background; also the struggles of the 1930s and '60s illustrated and brought to life. No romance, psychic, mystery, western, erotica, religious." Receives 10-12 unsolicited mss/month. Recently published work by Gregory Alan Norton, Paris Smith, Keith Laufenberg. Length: 4,000 words; average length: 1,000-3,000 words. Publishes short shorts. Normally comments on rejected mss.

How to Contact Send complete ms. Accepts submissions by e-mail. "Tries to" report in 3-4 months to queries. Accepts simultaneous, multiple submissions and reprints. Sample copies for $3; $5 for double-size issues; subscriptions $10 for 4 issues; make checks payable to Tim Hall, Special Account, not to *Struggle*.

Payment/Terms Pays 1 contributor's copy. No rights acquired. Not copyrighted.

Tips "Write about the oppression of the working people, the poor, the minorities, women and, if possible, their rebellion against it—we are not interested in anything which accepts the status quo. We are not too worried about plot and advanced technique (fine if we get them!)—we would probably accept things others would call sketches, provided they have life and struggle. For new writers: just describe for us a situation in which some real people confront some problem of oppression, however seemingly minor. Observe and put down the real facts. Experienced writers: try your 'committed'/experimental fiction on us. We get poetry all the time. We have increased our fiction portion of our content in the last few years. The quality of fiction that we have published has continued to improve. If your work raises an interesting issue of literature and politics, it may get discussed in letters and in my editorial. I suggest ordering a sample."

▣ ☑ $ SUBTERRAIN

P.O. Box 3008, MPO, Vancouver BC V6B 3X5 Canada. (604) 876-8710. Fax: (604) 879-2667. E-mail: subter@portal.ca. Website: www.subterrain.ca. **Contact:** Fiction editor. Magazine: 8¼ × 10⅞; 56 pages; gloss stock paper; color gloss cover stock; illustrations; photos. "Looking for unique work and perspectives from Canada and beyond." Triannual. Estab. 1988. Circ. 3,000.

Needs Literary. Does not want genre fiction or children's fiction. Receives 100 unsolicited mss/month. Accepts 4 mss/issue; 10-15 mss/year. Publishes ms 4 months after acceptance. Recently published work by John Moore. Also publishes literary essays, literary criticism. Rarely comments on rejected mss.

How to Contact Send complete ms. Include disposable copy of the ms and #10 SASE for reply only. Responds in 2-4 months to mss. Accepts multiple submissions. Sample copy for $5. Writer's guidelines online.

Payment/Terms Pays $25 per page for prose. Pays on publication for first North American serial rights. **Tips** "Read the magazine first. Get to know what kind of work we publish."

☑ ◎ $ SUBTROPICS

P.O. Box 112075, Turlington Hall, Univ. of FL, Gainesville FL 32611-2075. (352)392-6650 x234. Fax: (352)392-0860. E-mail: subtropics@english.ufl.edu. Website: http://www.english.ufl.edu/subtropics. **Contact:** David Leavitt, fiction editor. Literary magazine/journal: 9 × 6, 160 pages. Includes photographs. "Subtropics—headed by fiction editor David Leavitt, poetry editor Sidney Wade, and managing editor Mark Mitchell—is committed to publishing the best new fiction, poetry, literary nonfiction, and translation by emerging and established writers. In addition to new work, Subtropics also, from time to time, republishes important and compelling stories, essays, and poems that have lapsed out of print." Triannual. Estab. 2006. Circ. 3,500. Member CLMP.

• Stories included in *Best American Short Stories 2007* and *The O. Henry Prize Stories 2007*. Poems included in *Best American Poetry 2007 and 2008*.

Needs Literary. Does not want genre fiction. Receives 1,000 mss/month. Accepts 5-6 mss/issue; 15-18 mss/year. Does not read between May 1 and August 31. Ms published 3-6 months after acceptance. Agented fiction 33%. **Publishes 1-2 new writers/year.** Published John Barth, Ariel Dorfman, Tony D'Souza, Allan Gurganus, Frances Hwang, Kuzhali Manickavel, Eileen Pollack, Padgett Powell, Nancy Reisman, Jarret Rosenblatt, Joanna Scott, and Olga Slavnikova. Average length: 5,000 words. Publishes short shorts. Average length of short shorts: 400 words. Also publishes literary essays, poetry. Rarely comments on/critiques rejected mss.

How to Contact Send complete ms with cover letter. Responds to mss in 2-6 weeks. Send disposable copy of ms. Replies via e-mail only. Do not include SASE. Considers simultaneous submissions. Sample copy available for $12.95. Guidelines available on Web site.

Payment/Terms Writers receive $500-1,000, 2 contributor's copies. Additional copies $12.95. Pays on acceptance. Acquires first North American serial rights. Publication is copyrighted.

Tips "Please read the guidelines and at least one issue of the magazine before submitting."

☑ $ THE SUN

The Sun Publishing Co., 107 N. Roberson St., Chapel Hill NC 27516. (919)942-5282. Fax: (919)932-3101. Website: www.thesunmagazine.org. **Contact:** Sy Safransky, editor. Magazine: 8½ × 11; 48 pages; offset paper; glossy cover stock; photos. "We are open to all kinds of writing, though we favor work of a personal nature." Monthly. Estab. 1974. Circ. 72,000.

Needs Literary. Open to all fiction. Receives 800 unsolicited mss/month. Accepts 20 short stories/year. Publishes ms 12-24 months after acceptance. Recently published work by Alex Mindt, John Tait, Mark Wisniewski, April Wilder, Theresa Williams. Also publishes poetry and nonfiction. No science fiction, horror, fantasy, or other genre fiction.

How to Contact Send complete ms. Accepts reprint submissions. Sample copy for $5. Writer's guidelines online.

Payment/Terms Pays $300-2,000. Pays on publication for first, one-time rights.

Tips "We favor honest, personal writing with an intimate point of view. No science fiction, fantasy, or historical fiction."

☑ SYCAMORE REVIEW

Purdue University, Department of English, 500 Oval Drive, West Lafayette IN 47907. (765) 494-3783. Fax: (765) 494-3780. E-mail: sycamore@purdue.edu. Website: www.sycamorereview.com **Contact:** Editor-in-Chief. Magazine: 8 × 8; 100-150 pages; heavy, textured, uncoated paper; heavy laminated cover. "Journal devoted to contemporary literature. We publish both traditional and experimental fiction, personal essay, poetry, interviews, drama and graphic art. Novel excerpts welcome if they stand alone as a story." Semiannual. Estab. 1989. Circ. 1,000.

Needs Experimental, humor/satire, literary, mainstream, regional, translations. "We generally avoid genre literature but maintain no formal restrictions on style or subject matter. No romance, children's." Would like to see more experimental fiction. Publishes ms 11 months after acceptance. Recently published work by Lucia Perillo, June Armstrong, W. P. Osborn, William Giraldi. Also publishes poetry. Sometimes comments on rejected mss.

How to Contact Send complete ms with SASE, cover letter with previous publications and address. Responds in 4 months to mss. Accepts simultaneous submissions. Sample copy for $5. Writer's guidelines for #10 SASE or online.

Payment/Terms Acquires one-time rights.

Tips "We publish both new and experienced authors but we're always looking for stories with strong emotional appeal, vivid characterization and a distinctive narrative voice; fiction that breaks new ground while still telling an interesting and significant story. Avoid gimmicks and trite, predictable outcomes. Write stories that have a ring of truth, the impact of felt emotion. Don't be afraid to submit, send your best."

▦ $ TAKAHE

P.O. Box 13-335, Christchurch 8001 New Zealand. (03)359-8133. Website: http://takahe.org.nz. "Takahe is a hardcopy literary magazine which appears three times a year and publishes short stories, poetry, and artwork by both established and emerging writers. The publisher is Takahe Collective Trust, a non-profit organization formed by established writers to help new writers get into print."

Needs "We are particularly losing interest in stories offer a new perspective; something a little different."

Publishes 20 new writers/year. Recently published work by Raewyn Alexander, Simon Minto, Claire Baylis, Hayden Williams, Sarah Penwarden, Michael Botur, Doc Drumheller, Andrew McIntyre.

How to Contact Send complete ms. by e-mail (poetry in hardcopy). Include e-mail address, mailing address, 40 word bio and SASE (IRC for overseas submissions). See website for formatting. No simultaneous submissions. Copyright reverts to author on publication.

Payment/Terms NZ residents receive $30 (amount subject to change) and all contributors receive two hard copies of the issue in which their work appears. Overseas contributors receive a one year subscription to *Takahe* in lieu of payment.

Tips "We pay a flat rate to each writer/poet appearing in a particular issue regardless of the number/ length of items. Editorials and literary commentaries are by invitation only."

☑ TALKING RIVER REVIEW

Lewis-Clark State College, Division of Literature and Languages, 500 8th Ave., Lewiston ID 83501. (208)792-2189. Fax: (208)792-2324. **Contact:** Kevin Goodan, editorial advisor. Magazine: 6 × 9; 150-200 pages; 60 lb. paper; coated, color cover; illustrations; photos. "We look for new voices with something to say to a discerning general audience." Semiannual. Estab. 1994. Circ. 250.

Needs Condensed novels, ethnic/multicultural, feminist, humor/satire, literary, regional. "Wants more well-written, character-driven stories that surprise and delight the reader with fresh, arresting yet unself-conscious language, imagery, metaphor, revelation." No stories that are sexist, racist, homophobic, erotic for shock value; no genre fiction. Receives 400 unsolicited mss/month. Accepts 5-8 mss/issue; 10-15 mss/year. Reads mss September 1-May 1 only. Publishes ms 1-2 year s after acceptance. **Publishes 10-15 new writers/year.** Recently published work by X.J. Kennedy and Gary Fincke. Length: 4,000 words; average length: 3,000 words. Also publishes literary essays, poetry. Sometimes comments on rejected mss.

How to Contact Send complete manuscript with cover letter. Include estimated word count, 2-sentence bio and list of publications. Send SASE for reply, return of ms or send disposable copy of ms. Responds in 3 months to mss. Does not accept simultaneous submissions. Sample copy for $6. Writer's guidelines for #10 SASE.

Payment/Terms Pays contributor's copies; additional copies $4. Acquires one-time rights.

Tips "We look for the strong, the unique; we reject clichéd images and predictable climaxes."

☑ $ TAMPA REVIEW

University of Tampa Press, 401 W. Kennedy Blvd., Tampa FL 33606. (813)253-6266. Fax: (813)258-7593. Website: tampareview.ut.edu. **Contact:** Lisa Birnbaum and Kathleen Ochshorn, fiction editors. Magazine: 7½ × 10½; hardback; approximately 100 pages; acid-free paper; visual art; photos. An international literary journal publishing art and literature from Florida and Tampa Bay as well as new work and translations from throughout the world. Semiannual. Estab. 1988. Circ. 800.

Needs Ethnic/multicultural, experimental, fantasy, historical, literary, mainstream, translations. "We are far more interested in quality than in genre. Nothing sentimental as opposed to genuinely moving, nor

Literary Magazines

self-conscious style at the expense of human truth." Accepts 4-5 mss/issue. Reads September-December; reports January-May. Publishes ms 10 months after acceptance. Agented fiction 20%. Recently published work by Elizabeth Spencer, Lee K. Abbott, Lorrie Moore, Gordon Weaver, Tim O'Brien. Publishes short shorts. Also publishes literary essays, poetry.

How to Contact Send complete ms. Include brief bio. Responds in 5 months to mss. Accepts multiple submissions. Sample copy for $7. Writer's guidelines online.

Payment/Terms Pays $10/printed page. Pays on publication for first North American serial rights. Sends digital proofs to author.

Tips "There are more good writers publishing in magazines today than there have been in many decades. Unfortunately, there are even more bad ones. In T. Gertler's Elbowing the Seducer, an editor advises a young writer that he wants to hear her voice completely, to tell (he means 'show') him in a story the truest thing she knows. We concur. Rather than a trendy workshop story or a minimalism that actually stems from not having much to say, we would like to see stories that make us believe they mattered to the writer and, more importantly, will matter to a reader. Trim until only the essential is left, and don't give up belief in yourself. And it might help to attend a good writers' conference."

☑ TAPROOT LITERARY REVIEW

Taproot Writer's Workshop, Inc., Box 204, Ambridge PA 15003. (724) 266-8476. E-mail: taproot10@aol.com. **Contact**: Tikvah Feinstein, editor. Magazine: 5½ × 8½; 93 pages; 20 lb. paper; hardcover; attractively printed; saddle-stitched. "We select on quality, not topic. Variety and quality are our appealing features." Annual. Estab. 1987. Circ. 500.

Needs Literary. "No pornography, religious, popular, romance fiction. Wants more stories with multicultural themes, showing intensity, reality and human emotions that readers can relate to, learn from, and most importantly—be interesting." The majority of ms published are received through annual contest. Receives 20 unsolicited mss/month. Accepts 6 mss/issue. **Publishes 2-4 new writers/year.** Recently published work by Jim Meirose, Ginny Cunningham, Alicia Stankay, Lorraine Loiselle, Alena Horowitz, Lonnie Goldman, Shirley Barasch. Publishes short shorts. Also publishes poetry. Sometimes comments on rejected mss.

How to Contact Accepts submissions by e-mail. Send for guidelines first. Send complete ms with a cover letter. Include estimated word count and bio. Responds in 6 months to mss. No simultaneous submissions. Sample copy for $5, 6 × 12 SAE with 5 first-class stamps. Writer's guidelines for #10 SASE.

Payment/Terms Awards $25 in prize money for first place fiction and poetry winners each issue; certificate for 2nd and 3rd place; 1 contributor's copy. Additionally, *Taproot* offers a coveted literary prize, promotion, and $15 for the winner. Acquires first rights. Sponsors awards/contests.

Tips "*Taproot* is getting more fiction submissions, and every one is read entirely. This takes time, so response can be delayed at busy times of year. Our contest is a good way to start publishing. Send for a sample copy and read it through. Ask for a critique and follow suggestions. Don't be offended by any suggestions—just take them or leave them and keep writing. Looks for a story that speaks in its unique voice, told in a well-crafted and complete, memorable style, a style of signature to the author. Follow writer's guidelines. Research markets. Send cover letter. Don't give up."

☑ THE TEXAS REVIEW

Texas Review Press at Sam Houston State University, P.O. Box 2146, Huntsville TX 77341-2146. (936) 294-1992. Fax: (936) 294-3070 (inquiries only). E-mail: eng_pdr@shsu.edu. Website: www.shsu.edu/~www_trp/. **Contact:** Paul Ruffin, editor. Magazine: 6 × 9; 148-190 pages; best quality paper; 70 lb. cover stock; illustrations; photos. "We publish top quality poetry, fiction, articles, interviews and reviews for a general audience." Semiannual. Estab. 1976. Circ. 1,200. A member of the Texas A&M University Press consortium.

Needs Humor/satire, literary, mainstream, contemporary fiction. "We are eager enough to consider fiction of quality, no matter what its theme or subject matter. No juvenile fiction." Receives 40-60 unsolicited mss/month. Accepts 4 mss/issue; 6 mss/year. Does not read mss May-September. Publishes ms 6-12 months after acceptance. **Publishes some new writers/year.** Recently published work by George Garrett, Ellen Gilchrist, Fred Chappell. Also publishes literary essays, literary criticism, poetry. Sometimes comments on rejected mss.

How to Contact Send complete ms. No mss accepted via fax. Send disposable copy of ms and #10 SASE for reply only. Responds in 2 weeks to queries; 3-6 months to mss. Accepts multiple submissions. Sample copy for $5. Writer's guidelines for SASE and on Web site.

Payment/Terms Pays contributor's copies and one year subscription. Pays on publication for first North American serial, one-time rights. Sends galleys to author.

Tips "Submit often; be aware that we reject 90% of submissions due to overwhelming number of mss sent."

☑ $ THEMA

Box 8747, Metairie LA 70011-8747. (504)940-7156. **Contact:** Virginia Howard, editor. Magazine: 5½ × 8½; 150 pages; Grandee Strathmore cover stock; b&w illustrations. "Thema is designed to stimulate creative thinking by challenging writers with unusual themes, such as 'rage over a lost penny.' Appeals to writers, teachers of creative writing, and general reading audience." Estab. 1988. Circ. 350.

Needs Adventure, ethnic/multicultural, experimental, fantasy, historical, humor/satire, literary, mainstream, mystery/suspense, novel excerpts, psychic/supernatural/occult, regional, religious/inspirational, science fiction, slice-of-life vignettes, western, contemporary, sports, prose poem. "No erotica." Themes with deadlines for submission in 2009 (publication in 2010): "Put It in Your Pocket, Lillian" (March 1); "The Dean's Cat" (July 1); "About Two Miles Down the Road" (July 1); and "One Thing Done Superbly" (November 1). For more information, visit *THEMA*'s Web site. Publishes ms within 6 months after acceptance. **Publishes 9 new writers/year.** Recently published work by Toby Tucker Hecht, Cheryl Mathis, Jeffrey Melton, and Teresa Burns Murphy. Publishes short shorts. Also publishes poetry. Sometimes comments on rejected mss.

How to Contact Send complete ms with SASE, cover letter, include "name and address, brief introduction, specifying the intended target issue for the mss." SASE. Responds in 1 week to queries; 5 months to mss. Accepts simultaneous, multiple submissions and reprints. Does not accept e-mailed submissions. Sample copy for $10. Writer's guidelines for #10 SASE.

Payment/Terms Pays $10-25. Pays on acceptance for one-time rights.

Tips "Do not submit a manuscript unless you have written it for a specified theme. If you don't know the upcoming themes, send for guidelines first before sending a story. We need more stories told in the Mark Twain/O. Henry tradition in magazine fiction."

☑ ⚑ THIRD COAST

Dept. of English, Western Michigan University, Kalamazoo MI 49008-5331. (269)387-2675. Fax: (269)387-2562. E-Mail: editors@thirdcoastmagazine.com Website: www.thirdcoastmagazine.com. Rachel Swearingen, editor. **Contact:** Jessi Phillips and James Miranda, fiction editors. Magazine: 6 × 9; 176 pages. "We will consider many different types of fiction and favor those exhibiting a freshness of vision and approach." Twice-yearly. Estab. 1995. Circ. 2,875.

• *Third Coast* has received *Pushcart Prize* nominations. The section editors of this publication change with the university year.

Needs Literary. "While we don't want to see formulaic genre fiction, we will consider material that plays with or challenges generic forms." Receives 200 unsolicited mss/month. Accepts 6-8 mss/issue; 15 mss/year. Recently published work by Keith Banner, Peter Ho Davies, Moira Crone, Lee Martin, John McNally, and Peter Orner. Also publishes literary essays, poetry, one-act plays. Sometimes comments on rejected mss.

How to Contact Visit our Web site at http://www.thirdcoastmagazine.com for guidelines. *Third Coast* only accepts submissions submitted to its online submission manager. All hard copy submissions will be returned unread. Reads mss from August through May of each year.

Payment/Terms Pays 2 contributor's copies as well as a 1 year subscription to the publication; additional copies for $4. Acquires first North American serial rights.

Tips "We seek superior fiction from short-shorts to 30-page stories."

☑ $ THIRD WEDNESDAY: A LITERARY ARTS MAGAZINE

174 Greenside Up, Ypsilanti, MI 48197. (734) 434-2409. E-mail: submissions@thirdwednesday.org. Website: http://thirdwednesday.org. **Contact:** Laurence Thomas, editor. Literary magazine/journal. 60-65 pages. Contains illustrations. Includes photographs. "Third Wednesday publishes quality (a subjective term at best) poetry, short fiction and artwork by experienced writers and artists. We welcome work by

established writers/artists, as well as those who are not yet well known, but headed for prominence." Quarterly. Estab. 2007.

Needs Experimental, fantasy, humor/satire, literary, mainstream, romance, translations. Does not want "purely anecdotal accounts of incidents, sentimentality, pointless conclusions, or stories without some characterization or plot development." Receives 5-10 mss/month. Accepts 3-5 mss/issue. Ms published 3 months after acceptance. Length: 1,500 words (max). Average length: 1,000 words. Publishes short shorts. Also publishes poetry. Sometimes comments on/critiques rejected mss.

How to Contact Send complete ms with cover letter. Accepts submissions by e-mail. Include estimated word count, brief bio. Responds to mss in 6-8 weeks. Considers simultaneous submissions. Sample copy available for $8. Guidelines available for SASE, via e-mail.

Payment/Terms Writers receive $3, 1 contributor's copy. Additional copies $8. Pays on acceptance. Acquires first rights.

Tips "Of course, originality is important along with skill in writing, deft handling of language and meaning which goes hand in hand with beauty, whatever that is. Short fiction is specialized and difficult, so the writer should read extensively in the field."

☑ ◖ TICKLED BY THUNDER

Tickled By Thunder Publishing Co., 14076 86A Ave., Surrey BC V3W 0V9 Canada. (604) 591-6095. E-mail: info@tickledbythunder.com. Website: www.tickledbythunder.com. **Contact:** Larry Lindner, publisher. Magazine: digest-sized; 24 pages; bond paper; bond cover stock; illustrations; photos. "Tickled By Thunder is designed to encourage beginning writers of fiction, poetry and nonfiction." Quarterly. Estab. 1990. Circ. 1,000.

Needs Fantasy, humor/satire, literary, mainstream, mystery/suspense, science fiction, western. "No overly indulgent horror, sex, profanity or religious material." Receives 25 unsolicited mss/month. Accepts 3 mss/issue; 12 mss/year. Publishes ms 3-9 months after acceptance. **Publishes 5 new writers/ year.** Recently published work by John Connors and J-Ann Godfrey. Length: 2,000 words; average length: 1,500 words. Also publishes literary essays, literary criticism, poetry.

How to Contact Send complete ms. Include estimated word count and brief bio. Send SASE or IRC for return of ms; or send disposable copy of ms and #10 SASE for reply only. No e-mail submissions. Responds in 3 months to queries; 6 months to mss. Accepts simultaneous, multiple submissions and reprints. Writer's guidelines online.

Payment/Terms Pays on publication for first, second serial (reprint) rights.

Tips "Allow your characters to breathe on their own. Use description with action."

☑ ◎ ☑ TRANSITION

104 Mount Auburn St., 3R, Cambridge MA 02138. (617) 496-2845. Fax: (617) 496-2877. E-mail: transition@ fas.harvard.edu. Website: www.transitionmagazine.com. **Contact:** Laurie Calhoun, executive editor. Magazine: 9½ × 6½; 150-175 pages; 70 lb. Finch Opaque paper; 100 lb. White Warren Lustro dull cover; illustrations; photos. "Transition magazine is a trimestrial international review known for compelling and controversial writing from and about Africa and the diaspora. This prestigious magazine is edited at Harvard University, and editorial board members include such heavy-hitters as Toni Morrison, Jamaica Kincaid and bell hooks. The magazine also attracts famous contributors such as Spike Lee, Philip Gourevitch and Carolos Fuentes." Quarterly. Estab. 1961. Circ. 3,000.

- Essays first published in a recent issue of *Transition* were selected for inclusion in *Best American Essays 2008*, *Best American Nonrequired Reading 2008*, and *Best African American Writing 2009*. Four-time winner of the Alternative Press Award for international reporting (2001, 2000, 1999, 1995); finalist in the 2001 National Magazine Award in General Excellence category.

Needs Ethnic/multicultural, historical, humor/satire, literary, regional (African diaspora, Third World, etc.). Receives 40 unsolicited mss/month. Accepts 2-4 mss/year. Publishes ms 6-8 months after acceptance. Agented fiction 30-40%. **Publishes 5 new writers/year.** Recently published work by Wole Soyinka, Nuruddin Farah, Chimamanda Adichie, John Wideman, and Emily Raboteau. Length: 4,000-8,000 words; average length: 7,000 words. Also publishes literary essays, literary criticism. Sometimes comments on rejected mss.

How to Contact Query with published clips or send complete ms. Include brief bio and list of publications. Send disposable copy of ms and #10 SASE for reply only. Responds in 2 months to queries; 6 months to

mss. Accepts simultaneous submissions. Sample copy not available. Writer's guidelines for #10 SASE.
Payment/Terms 2 contributor's copies. Sends galleys to author.
Tips "We look for a non-white, alternative perspective, dealing with issues of race, ethnicity and identity in an upredictable, provocative way."

⬚ ☑ UNDER HWY 99, Showcasing the Untold Story

Seattle WA. E-mail: info@underhwy99.com. Website: http://underhwy99.com. **Contact:** Erica Goodkind, editor. Literary magazine/journal: 8.5X11; 25-35 pages; 60# paper; 80# glossy cover. Contains illustrations, photographs. "The 'untold story' is the story that is most important to you—the one you feel most compelled to tell. This is a publication for people who like a good read, and for those who have an undying devotion to and special knack for writing." Biannual. Estab. 2008. Circ. 300.
Needs Adventure, ethnic/multicultural (general), historical (general), humor/satire, literary, mainstream. Special interests: slice-of-life, music inspired prose. Does not want horror, romance, science fiction, evangelic. Receives 20-30 mss/month. Accepts 5-15 mss/issue; 15-30 mss/year. Manuscript published 2-4 months after acceptance. **Publishes 75% new writers/year.** Length: 3,500 words (max). Average length: 2,500 words. Publishes short shorts. Average length of short shorts: 500 words. Sometimes comments on/critiques rejected mss.
How to Contact Send complete ms with cover letter. Accepts submissions by e-mail only. Include estimated word count, brief bio. Responds to queries in 4 weeks; mss in 2 months. Considers simultaneous submissions, multiple submissions. Sample copy available for $4.95. Guidelines available on Web site.
Payment/Terms Writers receive 1 contributor's copy. Additional copies $4.95. Pays on publication. Acquires first rights, electronic rights. Publication is not copyrighted.
Tips "We have weakness for smart, imaginative pieces that bring out the uniqueness in any given situation. We tend to find stories that cast ordinary things in an unusal light and unusual things in an ordinary light particularly irresistible. Pieces should balance all othe usual elements of any good piece of literature: character, setting, theme, voice, pacing, etc."

⬚ ▢ UNDERSTANDING

Dionysia Press, 127 Milton Rd. West, 7 Duddingston House Courtyard, Edinburgh Scotland EH15 1JG United Kingdom. Magazine: A5; 200 pages. Annual. Estab. 1989. Circ. 500. Member: Scottish Publishing Association.
Needs Translations. Publishes ms 10 months after acceptance. **Publishes 100 new writers/year.** Publishes short shorts. Also publishes literary essays, poetry. Sometimes comments on rejected mss.
How to Contact Responds in 1 year to queries. Sample copy for $4.50 + postage. Writer's guidelines for SASE.
Payment/Terms Pays in contributor's copies.

⬚ ☑ UPSTREET

Ledgetop Publishing, P.O. Box 105, Richmond MA 01254-0105. (413) 441-9702. E-mail: editor@upstreet-mag.org. Website: http://www.upstreet-mag.org. **Contact:** editor. Literary magazine/journal. 7 × 8.5, 224 pages, 60# white offset paper. "A literary annual containing the best new fiction, poetry, and creative nonfiction available. First four issues feature interviews with Jim Shepard, Lydia Davis, Wally Lamb, and Michael Martone. Independently owned and published, nationally distributed. Founded by Vivian Dorsel, former managing editor of The Berkshire Review for eight years, who selected the members of the editorial staff for their love of the written word, their high standards of literary judgment, and their desire to offer a voice to prose writers and poets who might not find publication opportunities in more mainstream journals." Annual. Estab. 2005. Circ. 4,000. Member CLMP.
Needs Ethnic/multicultural (general), experimental, humor/satire, literary, mainstream. Does not want juvenile/YA, religious, or "any genre fiction that is not 'literary' (i.e., imaginative, sophisticated, innovative)." Does not read March-September. Ms published 2-4 months after acceptance. Length: 5,000 words (max). Publishes short shorts. Also publishes literary essays, poetry. Rarely comments on/critiques rejected mss.
How to Contact Send complete ms with cover letter. Accepts submissions by e-mail. Include estimated word count, brief bio, contact information. Considers simultaneous submissions, multiple submissions. Sample copy available for $10 plus postage. Guidelines available via e-mail.

Payment/Terms Writers receive 1 contributor's copy. Additional copies $10. Pays on publication. Acquires first North American serial rights. Publication is copyrighted.

▦ ☑ VERSAL

Wordsinhere, Amsterdam, The Netherlands. E-mail: versal@wordsinhere.com. Website: http://versal. wordsinhere.com. **Contact:** Robert Glick, fiction editor. Literary magazine/journal: 20 cm × 20 cm, 100 pages, offset, perfect-bound, acid-free color cover. Includes artwork. "Versal is the only English-language literary magazine in the Netherlands and publishes new poetry, prose and art from around the world. We publish writers with an instinct for language and line break, content and form that is urgent, involved and unexpected." Annual. Estab. 2002. Circ. 750.

Needs Experimental, literary. Receives 85 mss/month. Accepts 10 mss/year. Does not read mss January 16-September 14. Manuscript published 4-7 months after acceptance. **Publishes 2 new writers/year.** Published Jenny Arnold, Tom Bass, Selfa Chew, Russell Edson, Alissa Nutting. Length: 3,000 words (max). Publishes short shorts. Average length of short shorts: 1,500 words. Also publishes poetry. Sometimes comments on/critiques rejected mss.

How to Contact Send complete ms with cover letter. Accepts submissions electronically only. Include brief bio. Responds to queries in 1 week. Responds to mss in 2 months. Considers simultaneous submissions. Guidelines available on Web site.

Payment/Terms Writers receive 1 contributor copy. Additional copies $15. Pays on publication. Acquires one-time rights. Sends galleys to author. Publication is copyrighted.

Advice "We are drawn to good pacing, varied tone and something out of the ordinary. Above all, we look for surprise and richness of detail in representing this surprise. We especially love something written in an unusual voice that also contains depth of content. For more traditional voices, we look for surprise within the story, either by giving us an unusual situation or by having characters surprise us with their actions. Nasty sex and drug adventures don't really shock us, so unless there's a fantastic twist to the tale, they don't provide a jump out of the slush pile. In flash fiction, we are less inclined to the purely anecdotal than to work that somehow manages to convey depth and/or tension."

☑ $ VIRGINIA QUARTERLY REVIEW

University of Virginia, One West Range, P.O. Box 400223, Charlottesville VA 22904-4223. (434)924-3124. Fax: (434)924-1397. Website: www.vqronline.org. **Contact:** Ted Genoways, editor. "A national journal of literature and discussion, featuring nonfiction, fiction, and poetry for educated general readers." Quarterly. Estab. 1925. Circ. 6,000.

Needs Ethnic/multicultural, feminist, historical, humor/satire, literary, mainstream, mystery/suspense, novel excerpts, translations. Accepts 3 mss/issue; 20 mss/year. Publishes ms 3-6 months after acceptance.

How to Contact Submit complete ms. online. No queries. Responds in 3-4 months to mss. Sample copy for $14. Writer's guidelines online.

Payment/Terms Pays $100/page maximum. $5 per line for poetry. Pays on publication for first North American rights and nonexclusive online rights. Submissions only accepted online.

☑ WHR/WESTERN HUMANITIES REVIEW

Western Humanities Review, University of Utah, English Department, 255 S. Central Campus Dr., Room 3500, Salt Lake City UT 84112-0494. (801)581-6070. E-mail: whr@mail.hum.utah.edu. Website: www. hum.utah.edu/whr. **Contact:** Dawn Lonsinger, managing editor or Lance Olsen, fiction editor. Biannual. Estab. 1947. Circ. 1,300.

Needs "Looking for work that continues to resonate after reading is over. Especially interested in experimental and innovative fiction." Does not want genre (romance, sci-fi, etc.). Receives 100 mss/ month. Accepts 5-6 mss/issue; 6-8 mss/year. Does not read April September. Publishes ms up to 1 year after acceptance. **Publishes 3-5 new writers/year.** Recently published work by Michael Martone, Steve Almond, Craig Dworkin, Benjamin Percy, Francois Camoin, Kate Bernheimer, Lidia Yuknavitch. Publishes short shorts. Also innovative literary criticism and poetry. Rarely comments on rejected mss.

How to Contact Send one story per reading period. No e-mail submissions or queries. Sample copy for $10. Writer's guidelines online.

Payment/Terms Pays in contributor's copies on publication.Additional Information Runs Utah Writers' Contest every fall.

☑ WHISKEY ISLAND MAGAZINE

Dept. of English, Cleveland State University, Cleveland OH 44115-2440. (216) 687-2056. Fax: (216) 687-6943. E-mail: whiskeyisland@csuohio.edu. Website: www.csuohio.edu/whiskey_island. Editors change each year. Magazine of fiction, creative nonfiction, theater writing, poetry and art. "We provide a forum for new writers, for themes and points of view that are both traditional and experimental." Semiannual. Estab. 1977. Press run: 1,000.

Needs "From flash fiction to 5,000 words." Receives 100 unsolicited mss/month. Accepts 46 mss/issue. Recently published work by Carolyn Furnish, Carl Peterson, and Shannon Robinson. "Most recent issue features three writers' first publications. We nominate for *Pushcart Prize.*"

How to Contact Send complete ms. Accepts submissions by mail and e-mail. Accepts simultaneous submissions. Responds in 6 months. Sample copy for $6. Subscription $12.

Payment/Terms Pays 2 contributor copies and 1-year subscription. Acquires one-time rights. Sponsors annual fiction contest with $500 prize and publication. $10 per entry.

Tips "We read manuscripts year round. We seek engaging writing of any style."

▩ ☑ ⊞ WHITE FUNGUS: AN EXPERIMENTAL ARTS MAGAZINE

P.O. Box 6173, Wellington, Aotearoa, New Zealand. (64) 4 382 9113. E-mail: whitefungusmail@yahoo.com. Website: www.whitefungus.com. **Contact:** Ron Hanson, Editor. Literary magazine/journal. Oversize A5, 104 pages, matte paper, matte card cover. Contains illustrations, photographs. "White Fungus covers a range of experimental arts including literature, poetry, visual arts, comics and music. We are interested in material that is bold, innovative and well-researched. Independence of thought and meaningful surprises are a high priority." Semiannual. Estab. 2004. Circ. 2,000.

Needs Comics/graphic novels, ethnic/multicultural, experimental, feminist, gay, historical (general), humor/satire, lesbian, literary, science fiction. "*White Fungus* considers submissions on the basis of quality rather than genre." Receives 20 mss/month. Accepts 3 mss/issue; 6 mss/year. Ms published 1-12 months after acceptance. **Publishes 2 new writers/year.** Published Hamish Low, Cyril Wong, Aaron Coyes, Hamish Wyn, Tim Bollinger, Kate Montgomery, Tessa Laird and Tobias Fischer. Average length: 1,200 words. Publishes short shorts. Average length of short shorts: 1,000 words. Also publishes literary criticism, poetry. Sometimes comments on/critiques rejected mss.

How to Contact Query with clips of published work. Accepts submissions by e-mail, on disk. Include brief bio, list of publications. Responds to queries in 1 week. Responds to mss in 1 week. Send either SASE (or IRC) for return of ms or disposable copy of ms and #10 SASE for reply only. Considers simultaneous submissions, multiple submissions. Sample copy available for $10. Guidelines available via e-mail.

Payment/Terms Writers receive 10 contributor's copies, free subscription to the magazine. Additional copies $6. Pays on publication. Acquires first rights. Publication is copyrighted.

Tips "We like writing that explores the world around it rather than being self-obsessed. We're not interested in personal fantasies or self-projections, just an active critical responce to one's enviroment. Be direct, flexible and consider how your work might be considered in an international context. What can you contribute or shed light on?"

☑ WILLARD & MAPLE

163 South Willard Street, Freeman 302, Box 34, Burlington VT 05401. (802)860-2700 ext. 2462. E-mail: willardandmaple@champlain.edu. **Contact:** fiction editor. Magazine: perfect bound; 125 pages; illustrations; photos. "Willard & Maple is a student-run literary magazine from Champlain College that publishes a wide array of poems, short stories, creative essays, short plays, pen and ink drawings, black and white photos, and computer graphics. We now accept color." Annual. Estab. 1996.

Needs We accept all types of mss. Receives 20 unsolicited mss/month. Accepts 1 mss/year. Does not read mss March 31-September 1. Publishes ms within 1 year after acceptance. **Publishes 10 new writers/year.** Recently published work by Ian Frisch, Mark Belair, Rachel Chalmers, Robin Gaines, W.J. Everts, and Shirley O. Length: 5,000 words; average length: 2,500 words. Publishes short shorts. Also publishes literary essays, poetry. Sometimes comments on rejected mss.

How to Contact Send complete mss. Send SASE for return of ms or send disposable copy of mss and #10 SASE for reply only. Responds in 6 months to queries; 6 months to mss. Accepts simultaneous, multiple submissions. Sample copy for $10. Writer's guidelines for SASE or send e-mail. Reviews fiction.

Payment/Terms Pays 2 contributor's copies; additional copies $12. Pays on publication for one-time rights.

Tips "The power of imagination makes us infinite."

☑ WILLOW REVIEW

College of Lake County, 19351 W. Washington, Grayslake IL 60030.(847) 543-2956. E-mail: com426@ clcillinois.edu. Website: www.clcillinois.edu/community/willowreview.asp. **Contact:** Michael Latza, editor. Literary magazine/journal. 6 × 9, 110 pages. Annual. Estab. 1969. Circ. 800.

Needs Literary. Receives 10 mss/month. Accepts 3-5 mss/issue. Does not read mss May 1-September 1. Publishes 2-3 new writers/year. Published Patricia Smith, Tim Joyce. Length: 7,500 words (max). Publishes short shorts. Average length of short shorts: 500 words. Also publishes literary criticism. Rarely comments on/critiques rejected manuscripts.

How to Contact Send complete ms with cover letter. Include estimated word count, brief bio, list of publications. Responds to mss in 3-4 months. Send either SASE (or IRC) for return of ms or disposable copy of ms and #10 SASE for reply only. Considers simultaneous submissions, multiple submissions. Sample copy available for $5. Guidelines available for SASE, via e-mail.

Payment/Terms Writers receive 2 contributors copies. Additional copies $7. Pays on publication. All rights revert to author upon publication.

☑ ☑ WILLOW SPRINGS

501 N. Riverpoint Blvd., Ste. 425, Spokane WA 99202. (509)623-4349. Website: http://willowsprings. ewu.edu. Contact: Fiction Editor. Magazine: 9 × 6; 120 pages; 80 lb. matte cover. "We publish quality contemporary fiction, poetry, nonfiction, interviews with notable authors, and works in translation." Semiannual. Estab. 1977. Circ. 1,500. Member CLMP, AWP.

• *Willow Springs* has received grants from the NEA and a CLMP excellence award.

Needs Literary short shorts, nonfiction, translations, short stories, prose poems, poems. "No genre fiction, please." Receives 200 unsolicited mss/month. Accepts 2-4 mss/issue; 4-8 mss/year. Reads mss year round, but expect slower response between July and October. Publishes ms 4 months after acceptance. **Publishes some new writers/year.** Recently published work by Imad Rahman, Deb Olin Unferth, Jim Daniels, Kirsten Sundberg Lunstrum, Robert Lopez, Stacey Richter. Also publishes literary essays, literary criticism, poetry. Rarely comments on rejected mss.

How to Contact Send complete ms. Prose submissions now accepted online. Responds in 2 months to queries; 2 months to mss. Simultaneous submissions encouraged. Sample copy for $10. Writer's guidelines for #10 SASE.

Payment/Terms Pays 2 contributor's copies. Acquires first North American serial, first rights.

Tips "We hope to attract good fiction writers to our magazine, and we've made a commitment to publish 3-4 stories per issue. We like fiction that exhibits a fresh approach to language. Our most recent issues, we feel, indicate the quality and level of our commitment."

☐ WINDHOVER

University of Mary Hardin-Baylor, P.O. Box 8008, 900 College St., Belton TX 76513. (254)295-4561. E-mail: windhover@umhb.edu. **Contact:** D. Audell Shelburne, editor. Magazine: 6 × 9; white bond paper. "We accept poetry, short fiction, nonfiction, creative nonfiction. Windhover is devoted to promoting writers and literature with a Christian perspective and with a broad definition of that perspective." Annual. Estab. 1997. Circ. 500.

Needs Ethnic/multicultural, experimental, fantasy, historical, humor/satire, literary. No erotica. Receives 30 unsolicited mss/month. Accepts 5 mss/issue; 5 mss/year. Publishes ms 1 year after acceptance. **Publishes 5 new writers/year.** Recently published work by Walt McDonald, Cleatus Rattan, Greg Garrett, Barbara Crooker. Length: 1,500-4,000 words; average length: 3,000 words. Publishes short shorts. Also publishes literary essays, poetry. Sometimes comments on rejected mss.

How to Contact Send complete ms. Estimated word count, brief bio and list of publications. Include SASE postcard for acknowledgement. No submissions by e-mail. "Deadlines for submissions in June 1st for next issue. Editors read during summer months and notify writers in early September." Accepts simultaneous submissions. Sample copy for $10. Writer's guidelines by e-mail.

Payment/Terms Pays 2 contributor copies. Pays on publication for first rights.

Tips "Be patient. We have an editorial board and it sometimes take s longer than I like. We particularly look for convincing plot and character development."

☑ ☑ WISCONSIN REVIEW

University of Wisconsin-Oshkosh, 800 Algoma Blvd., Oshkosh WI 54902. (920)424-2267. E-mail:

wisconsin.review@uwosh.edu. Website: http://www.english.uwosh.edu/review.html. "The publication is for an adult contemporary audience. We seek art/photography, prose, poetry, and essays." Publishes twice a year in fall and spring. Estab. 1966. Circ. 2,000.

• *Wisconsin Review* won the Pippistrelle Best of the Small Press Award #13.

Needs Experimental, literary. Receives 30-50 unsolicited mss/month. Publishes ms 4-6 months after acceptance.

How to Contact Send complete ms with cover letter and SASE. Sample copy $5; yearly subscription $10/year.

Payment/Terms 2 contributor copies. Acquires first rights. Simultaneous submissions are not accepted.

☒ ☑ ◎ $ ☒ WITHERSIN MAGAZINE, DARK, DIFFERENT; PLEASANTLY SINISTER

30318 Deer Meadow Rd, Temecula CA 92591. (951) 795-5498. Fax: (951) 699-0486. E-mail: withersin@hotmail.com. Website: http://www.withersin.com. **Contact:** Misty L. Gersley, Editor-in-Chief. Literary magazine/journal. 6 × 9, 100 pages. Contains illustrations. Includes photographs. "A literary chimera, Withersin explores the bittersweet stain of the human condition. Comprised of an impressive array of original razor wire fiction, oddments and incongruities, obscure historical footnotes, unconventional research articles, delectable interviews, highlights, reviews and releases in film, music and print; all sewn together with threads of deviant art." Triannual. Estab. 2007. Circ. 600.

Needs Comics/graphic novels, experimental, historical (general), horror, literary, psychic/supernatural/occult, regional (specific and unique places; legends and lore). Does not want romance, erotica (read: pornography), or politically charged pieces. List of upcoming themes available for SASE, on Web site. Receives 100-300 mss/month. Accepts 3-5 mss/issue; 9-15 mss/year. Does not read July-March. Ms published 9-18 months after acceptance. **Publishes 5 new writers/year.** Published David Bain, Robert Heinze, Edward Morris, Michael Pignatella, M.W. Anderson, Sunil Sadanand, David Sackmyster, Mark Allan Gunnells and Chet Gottfried. Length: 500 words (min)-3,000 words (max). Average length: 2,000 words. Publishes short shorts. Average length of short shorts: 500 words. Also publishes literary essays, literary criticism, book reviews, poetry. Send review copies to *Withersin* Reviews, P.O. Box 892665 Temucula, CA 92589-2665 or *Withersin* Reviews 30318 Deer Meadow Rd, Temecula CA 92591. Often comments on/critiques rejected mss.

How to Contact Send complete ms with cover letter. Accepts submissions by e-mail, on disk. Include estimated word count, brief bio. Responds to queries in 2-3 weeks. Responds to mss in 4-6 weeks. Send either SASE (or IRC) for return of ms or disposable copy of ms and #10 SASE for reply only. Considers previously published submissions (reprints have different pay scale), multiple submissions. Sample copy available for $7.25, on Web site. Guidelines available for SASE, via e-mail, on Web site.

Payment/Terms Writers receive 1-5¢ per word, 3000 word payment cap, 1 contributor's copy. Additional copies $7.25. Pays on publication. Acquires first North American serial rights, one-time rights. Publication is copyrighted. Occasionally sponsors contests, check Web site for details. "We also sponsor videography contests on www.youtube.com/withersin."

Tips "Beyond an interesting plot structure and ideology, we definitely look for 'complete' pieces i.e. short works that have a distinct beginning, middle and end—Emphasis on END. It is actually difficult to complete a work of short fiction with all of these elements present, and it is important to continue to work and rework your piece until this comes to fruition. Your work should be free of errors, and each sentence should flow well into the next. Stand out works feature looking at the world from an odd, oblique angle. Make us think. Look outside the box, and tell us what you see—Elements of horror can always be presented in a non-traditional, yet still somehow gut-wrenching and unsettling way. Stay away from cliché. Before turning in your manuscript, read it aloud. Then have someone else unfamiliar with the piece read it aloud to you. This will highlight any unintentional snafus in grammar, spelling, sentence structure and flow. It will also allow you some great feedback. Look for open endings and correct them. Remember, you must articulate your writing so the reader can understand your message."

☑ THE WORCESTER REVIEW

Worcester County Poetry Association, Inc., 1 Ekman St., Worcester MA 01607. (508)797-4770. Website: www.geocities.com/Paris/LeftBank/6433. **Contact:** Fiction Editor. Magazine: 6 × 9; 100 pages; 60 lb. white offset paper; 10 pt. CS1 cover stock; illustrations; photos. "We like high quality, creative poetry, artwork and fiction. Critical articles should be connected to New England." Annual. Estab. 1972. Circ. 1,000.

Needs Literary, prose poem. "We encourage New England writers in the hopes we will publish at least 30% New England but want the other 70% to show the best of writing from across the U.S." Receives 20-30 unsolicited mss/month. Accepts 2-4 mss/issue. Publishes ms 11 months after acceptance. Agented fiction less than 10%. Recently published work by Robert Pinsky, Marge Piercy, Wes McNair, Ed Hirsch. Length: 1,000-4,000 words; average length: 2,000 words. Publishes short shorts. Also publishes literary essays, literary criticism, poetry. Sometimes comments on rejected mss.

How to Contact Send complete ms. Responds in 1 year to mss. Accepts simultaneous submissions only if other markets are clearly identified. Sample copy for $8. Writer's guidelines free.

Payment/Terms Pays 2 contributor copies and honorarium if possible. Acquires one-time rights.

Tips "Send only one short story—reading editors do not like to read two by the same author at the same time. We will use only one. We generally look for creative work with a blend of craftsmanship, insight and empathy. This does not exclude humor. We won't print work that is shoddy in any of these areas."

☐ $ WORKERS WRITE!

Blue Cubicle Press, LLC, P.O. Box 250382, Plano TX 75025-0382. (972)824-0646. E-mail: info@workerswritejournal.com. Website: www.workerswritejournal.com. **Contact:** David LaBounty, editor. Literary magazine/journal: 100-164 pages, 20 lb. bond paper paper, 80 lb. cover stock cover. "We publish stories that center on a particular workplace." Annual.

Needs Ethnic/multicultural (general), humor/satire, literary, mainstream, regional. Receives 100 mss/month. Accepts 12-15 mss/year. Manuscript published 3-4 months after acceptance. **Publishes 1 new writer/year**. Length: 500 words (min)-5,000 words (max). Average length: 3,000 words. Publishes short shorts. Also publishes poetry. Often comments on rejected mss.

How to Contact Send complete ms with cover letter. Accepts submissions by e-mail. Responds to queries in 1 weeks. Responds to mss in 2-3 months. Send either SASE (or IRC) for return of ms or disposable copy of ms and #10 SASE for reply only. Considers simultaneous submissions, previously published submissions, multiple submissions. Sample copy available for $8. Guidelines available for SASE, via e-mail, on Web site.

Payment/Terms Pays $50 maximum and contributor's copies. Additional copies $4. Pays on publication.

Tips "We publish stories from the worker's point of view."

◪ XAVIER REVIEW

Xavier University, 1 Drexel Dr., New Orleans LA 70125-1098. (504)520-7549. Fax: (504)485-7197. E-mail: ngreene@xula.edu (correspondence only—no mss). **Contact:** Nicole Pepinster Greene, editor. Robert Skinner, managing editor. Magazine: 6 × 9; 75 pages; 50 lb. paper; 12 pt. CS1 cover; photographs. Magazine of "poetry/fiction/nonfiction/reviews (contemporary literature) for professional writers, libraries, colleges and universities." Semiannual. Estab. 1980. Circ. 500.

Needs Ethnic/multicultural, experimental, historical, literary, mainstream, regional (Southern, Latin American), religious/inspirational, serialized novels, translations. Receives 40 unsolicited mss/month. Accepts 2 mss/issue; 4 mss/year. **Publishes 2-3 new writers/year.** Recently published work by Andrei Codrescu, Terrance Hayes, Naton Leslie, Patricia Smith. Also publishes literary essays, literary criticism. Occasionally comments on rejected mss.

How to Contact Send complete ms. Include 2-3 sentence bio. Sample copy for $5.

Payment/Terms Pays 2 contributor copies.

◎ $ ZYZZYVA

P.O. Box 590069, San Francisco CA 94159-0069. (415) 752-4393. Fax: (415) 752-4391. E-mail: editor@zyzzyva.org. Website: www.zyzzyva.org. **Contact:** Howard Junker, editor. "We feature work by writers currently living on the West Coast or in Alaska and Hawaii only. We are essentially a literary magazine, but of wide-ranging interests and a strong commitment to nonfiction." Estab. 1985. Circ. 3,500.

Needs Ethnic/multicultural, experimental, humor/satire, mainstream. Receives 300 unsolicited mss/month. Accepts 10 mss/issue; 30 mss/year. Publishes ms 3 months after acceptance. Agented fiction 1%. **Publishes 15 new writers/year.** Recently published work by Amanda Field, Katherine Karlin, Margaret Weatherford. Publishes short shorts. Also publishes literary essays, poetry.

How to Contact Send complete ms. Responds in 1 week to queries; 1 month to mss. Sample copy for $7 or online. Writer's guidelines online.

Payment/Terms Pays $50. Pays on acceptance for first North American serial and one-time anthology rights.

Small Circulation Magazines

This section of *Novel & Short Story Writer's Market* contains general interest, special interest, regional and genre magazines with circulations under 10,000. Although these magazines vary greatly in size, theme, format and management, the editors are all looking for short stories. Their specific fiction needs present writers of all degrees of expertise and interests with an abundance of publishing opportunities. Among the diverse publications in this section are magazines devoted to almost every topic, every level of writing, and every type of writer. Some of the markets listed here publish fiction about a particular geographic area or by authors who live in that locale.

Although not as high-paying as the large-circulation consumer magazines, you'll find some of the publications listed here do pay writers 1-5¢/word or more. Also, unlike the big consumer magazines, these markets are very open to new writers and relatively easy to break into. Their only criterion is that your story be well written, well presented and suitable for their particular readership.

In this section you will also find listings for zines. Zines vary greatly in appearance as well as content. Some paper zines are photocopies published whenever the editor has material and money, while others feature offset printing and regular distribution schedules. A few have evolved into very slick four-color, commercial-looking publications.

SELECTING THE RIGHT MARKET

First, zero in on those markets most likely to be interested in your work. Begin by looking at the Category Index starting on page 599. If your work is more general—or conversely, very specialized—you may wish to browse through the listings, perhaps looking up those magazines published in your state or region. Also check the Online Markets section for other specialized and genre publications.

In addition to browsing through the listings and using the Category Index, check the openness icons at the beginning of listings to find those most likely to be receptive to your work. This is especially true for beginning writers, who should look for magazines that say they are especially open to new writers (❏) and for those giving equal weight to both new and established writers (◪). For more explanation about these icons, see the inside covers of this book.

Once you have a list of magazines you might like to try, read their listings carefully. Much of the material within each listing carries clues that tell you more about the magazine. You've Got a Story, starting on page 2, describes in detail the listing information common to all the markets in our book.

The physical description appearing near the beginning of the listings can give you clues about the size and financial commitment to the publication. This is not always an indication of quality, but chances are a publication with expensive paper and four-color artwork on the cover has more prestige than a photocopied publication featuring a clip-art cover. For more information on some of the paper, binding and printing terms used in these descriptions, see Printing and Production Terms Defined on page 554.

FURTHERING YOUR SEARCH

It cannot be stressed enough that reading the listing is only the first part of developing your marketing plan. The second part, equally important, is to obtain fiction guidelines and read the actual magazine. Reading copies of a magazine helps you determine the fine points of the magazine's publishing style and philosophy. There is no substitute for this type of hands-on research.

Unlike commercial magazines available at most newsstands and bookstores, it requires a little more effort to obtain some of the magazines listed here. You may need to send for a sample copy. We include sample copy prices in the listings whenever possible. See The Business of Fiction Writing on page 77 for the specific mechanics of manuscript submission. Above all, editors appreciate a professional presentation. Include a brief cover letter and send a self-addressed, stamped envelope for a reply. Be sure the envelope is large enough to accommodate your manuscript, if you would like it returned, and include enough stamps or International Reply Coupons (for replies from countries other than your own) to cover your manuscript's return. Many publishers today appreciate receiving a disposable manuscript, eliminating the cost to writers of return postage and saving editors the effort of repackaging manuscripts for return.

Most of the magazines listed here are published in the U.S. You will also find some English-speaking markets from around the world. These foreign publications are denoted with a (▩) symbol at the beginning of listings. To make it easier to find Canadian markets, we include a (▣) symbol at the start of those listings.

▣ ☑ ◎ THE ABIKO ANNUAL WITH JAMES JOYCE

ALP Ltd., c/o T. Hamada, Hananoi 1787-28, Kashiwa-shi 277-0812, Japan. (011) 81-471-69-8036. E-mail: hamada-tatsuo@jcom.home.ne.jp.   Website: http://members.jcom.home.ne.jp/hamada-tatsuo/. **Contact**: Tatsuo Hamada. Magazine: A5; 350 pages; illustrations; photos. "We primarily publish James Joyce Finnegans Wake essays from writers here in Japan and abroad." Annual. Estab. 1989. Circ. 300.

Needs Experimental (in the vein of James Joyce), literary, inspirational. Also essays on James Joyce's *Finnegans Wake* from around the world. Receives very few unsolicited mss/month. Also publishes literary essays, literary criticism, poetry. Always comments on rejected mss.

How to Contact Send a disposable copy of ms or e-mail attachment. Responds in 1 week to queries; 3 months to mss. Accepts multiple submissions. Sample copy for $20. Guidelines for SASE. Reviews fiction.

Payment/Terms Pays 1 contributor's copy; additional copies $25. Copyright reverts to author upon publication.

Tips "We require camera-ready copy. The writer is welcome to accompany it with appropriate artwork."

▣ ☑ ◎ $ ALBEDO ONE

Albedo One, 2 Post Rd., Lusk, Co Dublin Ireland. (+353)1-8730177. E-mail: bobn@yellowbrickroad.ie. Website: www.albedo1.com. **Contact:** editor, Albedo One. Magazine: A4; 64 pages. "We hope to publish interesting and unusual fiction by new and established writers. We will consider anything, as long as it is well written and entertaining, though our definitions of both may not be exactly mainstream. We like stories with plot and characters that live on the page. Most of our audience are probably committed genre fans, but we try to appeal to a broad spectrum of readers." Triannual. Estab. 1993. Circ. 900.

Needs Experimental, fantasy, horror, literary, science fiction. Receives more than 80 unsolicited mss/ month. Accepts 15-18 mss/year. Publishes ms 1 year after acceptance. **Publishes 6-8 new writers/year.** Length: 2,000-9,000 words; average length: 4,000 words. Also publishes literary criticism. Sometimes comments on rejected mss.

How to Contact Responds in 3 months to mss. PDF—electronic—sample copies are available for download at a reduced price. Guidelines available by e-mail or on Web site. Reviews fiction.

Payment/Terms Pays €3 per 1,000 words, and 1 contributor's copy; additional copies $5 plus p&p. Pays on publication for first rights.

Tips "We look for good writing, good plot, good characters. Read the magazine, and don't give up."

☑ ANY DREAM WILL DO REVIEW

Any Dream Will Do, Inc., 1830 Kirman Ave., C1, Reno NV 89502-3381. (775)786-0345. E-mail: cassjmb@ intercomm.com. Website: www.willigocrazy.org/Ch08.htm. **Contact**: Dr. Jean M. Bradt, editor and publisher. Magazine: 5½ × 8½; 52 pages; 20 lb. bond paper; 12pt. Carolina cover stock. "The Any Dream Will Do Review showcases a new literary genre, Fiction In The Raw, which attempts to fight the prejudice against consumers of mental-health services by touching hearts, that is, by exposing the consumers' deepest thoughts and emotions. In the Review's stories, accomplished authors honestly reveal their most intimate secrets. See www.willigocrazy.org/Ch09a.htm for detailed instructions on how to write Fiction In The Raw." Published every 1 or 2 years. Estab. 2001. Circ. 200.

Needs Adapted ethnic/multicultural, mainstream, psychic/supernatural/occult, romance (contemporary), science fiction (soft/sociological), all of which must follow the guidelines at Web site. No pornography, true-life stories, black humor, political material, testimonials, experimental fiction, or depressing accounts of hopeless or perverted people. Accepts 10 mss/issue; 20 mss/year. Publishes ms 12 months after acceptance. **Publishes 10 new writers/year.** Publishes short shorts. Often comments on rejected mss.

How to Contact Send complete ms. Accepts submissions by e-mail (cassjmb@intercomm.com). Please submit by e-mail. If you must submit by hardcopy, please send disposable copies. No queries, please. Responds in 8 weeks to mss. Sample copy for $4 plus postage. Writer's guidelines online.

Payment/Terms Pays in contributor's copies; additional copies $4 plus postage. Acquires first North American serial rights.

Tips "Read several stories on www.willigocrazy.org before starting to write. Proof your story many times before submitting. Make the readers think. Above all, present people (preferably diagnosed with mental illness) realistically rather than with prejudice." Now publishing booklets; check Web site for more info.

Small Circulation

☑ $ APEX SCIENCE FICTION AND HORROR DIGEST

Apex Publications, P.O. Box 24323, Lexington KY 40524. (859) 312-3974. E-mail: jason@apexdigest.com. Website: www.apexdigest.com. **Contact:** Jason Sizemore, editor-in-chief. Magazine: 5½ × 8½, 128 pages, 70 lb. white offset paper, glossy #120 cover. Contains illustrations. "We publish dark sci-fi with horror elements. Our readers are those that enjoy speculative fiction with dark themes." Monthly. Estab. 2005. Circ. 3,000.

Needs Dark science fiction. "We're not fans of 'monster' fiction." Receives 200-250 mss/month. Accepts 2 mss/issue; 24 mss/year. Manuscript published 3 months after acceptance. **Publishes 10 new writers/year**. Published Brian Keene, Cherie Priest, Ben Bova, William F. Nolan, Tom Piccirilli, M.M. Buckner, JA Rourath, and James P. Hogan. Length: 200 words (min)-7,500 words (max). Average length: 4,000 words. Publishes short shorts. Average length of short shorts: 500 words. Often comments on/critiques rejected manuscripts.

How to Contact Send complete ms with cover letter. Include estimated word count, brief bio. Responds to queries in 3-4 weeks. Responds to mss in 3-4 weeks. E-mail submissions only. Guidelines available via e-mail, on Web site.

Payment/Terms Writers receive 5¢/word. Pays on publication. Acquires first North American web rights. Non-exclusive print anthology rights. Publication is copyrighted.

Tips "Be professional. Be confident. Remember that any criticisms offered are given for your benefit."

☐ ◎ $ ☒ THE APUTAMKON REVIEW: VOICES FROM DOWNEAST MAINE AND THE CANADIAN MARITIMES (OR THEREABOUTS)

the WordShed, LLC, P.O. Box 190, Jonesboro MA 04648. (207) 434-5661. Fax: (207) 434-5661. E-mail: thewordshed@tds.net. **Contact:** Les Simon, Publisher. Magazine. Approx. 160 pages. Contains illustrations. Includes photographs. "All age groups living in downeast Maine and the Canadian Maritimes, or thereabouts, are invited to participate. The Aputamkon Review will present a mismash of truths, half truths and outright lies, including but not limited to short fiction, tall tales, creative non-fiction, essays, (some) poetry, haiku, b&w visual arts, interviews, lyrics and music, quips, quirks, quotes that should be famous, witticisms, follies, comic strips, cartoons, jokes, riddles, recipes, puzzles, games. Stretch your imagination. Practically anything goes." Annual. Estab. 2006. Circ. 500. Member Maine Writers and Publishers Alliance.

Needs Adventure, children's/juvenile, comics/graphic novels, ethnic/multicultural, experimental, family saga, fantasy, glitz, historical, horror, humor/satire, literary, mainstream, military/war, mystery, psychic/supernatural/occult, religious, romance, science fiction, thriller/espionage, translations, western, young adult/teen. Does not want mss which are heavy with sex or religion. Receives 1-20 mss/month. Accepts 10-20 mss/year. Ms published max of 12 months after acceptance. Length: 250 words (min)-4,000 words (max). Average length: 500 words. Publishes short shorts. Also publishes literary essays, literary criticism, poetry. Rarely comments on/critiques rejected mss.

How to Contact Send complete ms with cover letter. Accepts submissions by e-mail, on disk. Submission period is September 1 through December 31. Include age if under 18, and a bio will be requested upon acceptance of work. Responds to queries in 2-4 weeks. Responds to mss in 1-6 months. Send SASE (or IRC) for return of ms or a disposable copy of ms and #10 SASE for reply only. Considers simultaneous submissions, multiple submissions. Sample copy available for $12 plus s/h. Guidelines available for SASE, via e-mail, via fax.

Payment/Terms Writers receive $10-35 depending on medium. Pays on acceptance. Acquires first North American serial rights. Publication is copyrighted.

Tips "Be colorful, heartfelt and honest, not mainstream. Write what you want and then submit."

THE BINNACLE

University of Maine at Machias, 9 O'Brien Ave., Machias ME 04654. E-mail: ummbinnacle@maine.edu. Website: www.umm.maine.edu/binnacle. "We are looking for the fresh voices of people who know what dirt under their fingernails, a belly laugh, and hard luck feel like, and of writers who are not afraid to take a chance." Semiannual, plus annual Ultra-Short Competition editon. Estab. 1957. Circ. 300.

Needs Ethnic/multicultural, experimental, humor/satire, mainstream, slice-of-life vignettes. No extreme erotica, fantasy, horror, or religious, but any genre attuned to a general audience can work. Publishes ms 3 months after acceptance.

How to Contact Submissions by e-mail preferred. Responds in 1 month to queries; 3 months to mss. Accepts simultaneous submissions. Sample copy for $7. Writer's guidelines online at Web site or by e-mail.
Payment/Terms $300 in prizes for Ultra-Short. $50 per issue for one work of editor's choice. Acquires one-time rights.

☐ ◎ $ BLACK LACE

BLK Publishing CO., P.O. Box 83912, Los Angeles CA 90083-0912. (310)410-0808. Fax: (310)410-9250. E-mail: newsroom@blk.com. Website: www.blacklace.org. **Contact:** Fiction Editor. Magazine: 8⅛ × 10⅝; 48 pages; book stock; color glossy cover; illustrations; photos. "Black Lace is a lifestyle magazine for African-American lesbians. Its content ranges from erotic imagery to political commentary." Quarterly. Estab. 1991.
Needs Ethnic/multicultural, lesbian. "Avoid interracial stories of idealized pornography." Accepts 4 mss/year. Recently published work by Nicole King, Wanda Thompson, Lynn K. Pannell, Sheree Ann Slaughter, Lyn Lifshin, JoJo and Drew Alise Timmens. Publishes short shorts. Also publishes literary essays, literary criticism, poetry.
How to Contact Query with published clips or send complete ms. Send a disposable copy of ms. No simultaneous submissions. Accepts electronic submissions. Sample copy for $7. Writer's guidelines free.
Payment/Terms Pays $50 and 2 contributor's copies. Acquires first North American serial rights. Right to anthologize.
Tips "*Black Lace* seeks erotic material of the highest quality. The most important thing is that the work be erotic and that it feature black lesbians or themes. Study the magazine to see what we do and how we do it. Some fiction is very romantic, other is highly sexual. Most articles in *Black Lace* cater to black lesbians between two extremes."

Ⓝ ☒ BROKEN PENCIL

P.O. Box 203 STN P, Toronto ON M5S 2S7 Canada.(416)204-1700. E-mail: editor@brokenpencil.com. Website: www.brokenpencil.com. **Contact:** Hal Niedzviecki, fiction editor. Magazine. "Founded in 1995 and based in Toronto, Canada, Broken Pencil is a Web site and print magazine published four times a year. It is one of the few magazines in the world devoted to underground culture and the independent arts. We are a great resource and a lively read. A cross between the Utne Reader, an underground Reader's Digest, and the now defunct Factsheet15, Broken Pencil reviews the best zines, books, Web sites, videos, and artworks from the underground and reprints the best articles from the alternative press. Also, ground-breaking interviews, original fiction, and commentary on all aspects of the independent arts. From the hilarious to the perverse, Broken Pencil challenges conformity and demands attention." Quarterly. Estab. 1995. Circ. 5,000.
Needs Adventure, erotica, ethnic/multicultural, experimental, fantasy, historical, horror, humor/satire, amateur sleuth, romance, science fiction. Accepts 8 mss/year. Manuscript published 2-3 months after acceptance. Length: 500-3,000 words.
How to Contact Accepts submissions by e-mail.
Payment/Terms Acquires first rights.
Tips "Write to receive a list of upcoming themes and then pitch us stories based around these themes. If you keep your ear to the ground in alternative and underground arts communities, you will be able to find content appropriate for *Broken Pencil*."

☑ $ CONCEIT MAGAZINE

P.O. Box 884223, San Francisco CA 94188-4333 or P.O. Box 8544, Emeryville CA 94662. (415) 401-8370. Fax: (415) 401-8370. E-mail: conceitmagazine2007@yahoo.com. Website: www.myspace.com/conceitmagazine. **Contact:** Perry Terrell, Editor. Magazine. 8½ × 5½, 44 pages, copy paper paper. Contains illustrations, photographs. "If it's on your mind, write it down and send it to Perry Terrell at Conceit Magazine. Writing is good therapy." Monthly. Estab. 2007. Circ. 300 + .
Needs Adventure, children's/juvenile, ethnic/multicultural, experimental, family saga, fantasy, feminist, gay, historical, horror (futuristic, psychological, supernatural), humor/satire, lesbian, literary, mainstream, military/war, mystery, new age, psychic/supernatural/occult, religious, romance

(contemporary, futuristic/time travel, historical, regency, suspense), science fiction (soft/sociological), thriller/espionage, translations, western, young adult/teen (adventure, easy-to-read, fantasy/science fiction, historical, mystery/suspense, problem novels, romance, series, sports, western). Does not want profanity, porn, gruesomeness. List of upcoming themes available for SASE and on Web site. Receives 40-50 mss/month. Accepts 20-22 mss/issue; up to 264 mss/year. Ms published 3-10 months after acceptance. **Publishes 150 new writers/year.** Published Dr. C. David Hay, D. Neil Simmers, Tamara Fey Turner, Zachary Nahrstadt, Eve J. Blohm, Barbara Hantman, Wayne Sheer. Length: 100 words (min)-3,000 words (max). Average length: 1,500-2,000 words. Publishes short shorts. Average length of short shorts: 50-500 words. Also publishes literary essays, literary criticism, book reviews, poetry. Send review copies to Perry Terrell. Sometimes comments on/critiques rejected mss.

How to Contact Query first or send complete ms with cover letter. Accepts submissions by e-mail, by fax, mail and on disk. Include estimated word count, brief bio, list of publications. Responds to queries in 1-2 weeks. Responds to mss in 1-4 weeks. Send either SASE (or IRC) for return of ms or disposable copy of ms and #10 SASE for reply only. Considers simultaneous submissions, previously published submissions, multiple submissions. Sample copy free with SASE. Guidelines available for SASE, via e-mail, on Web site, via fax.

Payment/Terms Writers receive 1 contributor copy and subscribers vote on who receives a $100 monthly stipend. Additional copies $4.50. Pays on publication. Acquires one-time rights. Publication is copyrighted. "Occassionly sponsors contests. Send SASE or check blog on Web site for details."

Tips "Uniqueness and creativity make a manuscript stand out. Be brave and confident. Let me see what you created."

⚡ ◎ $ THE COUNTRY CONNECTION

Pinecone Publishing, P.O. Box 100, Boulter ON K0L 1G0 Canada. (613) 332-3651. E-mail: editor@pinecone. on.ca. Website: www.pinecone.on.ca. "The Country Connection is a magazine for true nature lovers and the rural adventurer. Building on our commitment to heritage, cultural, artistic, and environmental themes, we continually add new topics to illuminate the country experience of people living within nature. Our goal is to chronicle rural life in its many aspects, giving 'voice' to the countryside." Estab. 1989. Circ. 5,000.

Needs Ontario history and heritage, humor/satire, nature, environment, the arts, country living. "Canadian material by Canadian authors only." Publishes ms 4 months after acceptance.

How to Contact Send complete ms. Accepts submissions by e-mail, disk. Sample copy for $ 6.68. Writer's guidelines online.

Payment/Terms Pays 10¢/word. Pays on publication for first rights.

☐ CREATIVE WITH WORDS PUBLICATIONS

Creative With Words Publications, P.O. Box 223226, Carmel CA 93922. Fax: (831)655-8627. E-mail: geltrich@mbay.net. Website: members.tripod.com/CreativeWithWords. **Contact:** Brigitta Geltrich, general editor.

Needs Ethnic/multicultural, humor/satire, mystery/suspense (amateur sleuth, private eye), regional (folklore), young adult/teen (adventure, historical). "Do not submit essays." No violence or erotica, overly religious fiction or sensationalism. "Twice a year we publish *the* Eclectics written by adults only (20 and older); throughout the year we publish thematic anthologies written by all ages." List of upcoming themes available for SASE. Limit poetry to 20 lines or less, 46 characters per line or less. Receives 50-200 unsolicited mss/month. Accepts 50-80 mss/anthology. Publishes ms 1-2 months after acceptance. Recently published work by Najwa Salam Brax, Sirock Brighton, Roger D. Coleman, Antoinette Garrick and Maria Dickerhof. Sometimes comments on rejected mss.

How to Contact Send complete ms with a cover letter with SASE. Include estimated word count. Responds in 2 weeks to queries; 1-2 months after a specific theme's due date to mss. Please request a list of themes with SASE before sending manuscript. Sample copy for $7. Writer's guidelines for #10 SASE.

Payment/Terms 20% reduction cost on 1-9 copies ordered, 30% reduction on 10 to 19 copies, 40% reduction on each copy on order of 20 or more. Acquires one-time rights.

Tips "We offer a great variety of themes. We look for clean family-type fiction/poetry. Also, we ask the writer to look at the world from a different perspective, research topic thoroughly, be creative, apply brevity, tell the story from a character's viewpoint, tighten dialogue, be less descriptive, proofread before submitting and be patient. We will not publish every manuscript we receive. It has to be in standard English, well written, proofread. We do not appreciate receiving manuscripts where we have to do the proofreading and the correcting of grammar."

✔ ◎ $ DARK DISCOVERIES

Dark Discoveries Publications, 142 Woodside Drive, Longview WA 98632. (360) 425-5796. E-mail: info@ darkdiscoveries.com. Website: www.darkdiscoveries.com. **Contact:** James R. Beach, Editor-in-Chief/ Publisher. Magazine. 8½ × 11, 64 pages. Contains illustrations. Includes photographs. "We publish dark fiction in the horror/fantasy realm with a lean towards the psychological side. We do publish mystery and supernatural as well. We also feature interviews, articles and reviews." Quarterly. Estab. 2004. Circ. 3,000.

• Four stories published in Dark Discoveries have been Honorable Mentions in the Year's Best Fantasy & Horror and three stories have been nominated for the Bram Stoker Awards. Magazine was runner-up for Best Horror Magazine in the first Black Quill Awards.

Needs Horror (dark fantasy). Does not want straight science fiction or mystery, "but will look at hybrid horror stories with elements of each. No straight sword and socery or fantasy either." Receives 50-70 mss/month. Accepts 25 mss/year. Ms published within 12 months after acceptance. **Publishes 2-4 new writers/year.** Published William F. Nolan, Elizabeth Engstrom, Kealan Partick Burke, Jay Lake, Tony Richards, John Everson, Tim Waggoner, Cindy Foster, Stephen Mark Rainey, Kurt Newton, and Brian Knight. Length: 1,000-5,000 words. Average length: 4,000 words. Publishes short shorts. Average length of short shorts: 1,000 words. Also publishes literary essays, literary criticism, book reviews. Send review copies to James R. Beach. Often comments on/critiques rejected mss.

How to Contact Send complete ms with cover letter. Accepts submissions by e-mail. Include estimated word count, brief bio, list of publications. Responds to queries in 1-2 weeks. Responds to mss in 6-7 months. Send either SASE (or IRC) for return of ms or disposable copy of ms and #10 SASE for reply only. Considers simultaneous submissions, previously published submissions if you query first. Sample copy available for $6.99. Guidelines available for SASE, via e-mail, on Web site.

Payment/Terms Writers receive ¢1-2 per word, 2 contributor's copies. Additional copies at 40% of cover price. Pays on publication. Acquires one-time rights. Publication is copyrighted. "Occasionally sponsors contests. Check the Web site for details."

Tips "I look for well-written and thought provoking tales. I don't like to see the same well-tread themes. Be it a new or established writer, I like to see the writer's voice show through. Take our suggestions to heart, and if you don't succeed at catching our eye at first keep trying."

◎ ✔ ◎ $ DARK TALES

Dark Tales, 7 Offley Street, Worcester, UK WR3 8BH. E-mail: sean@darktales.co.uk. Website: www. darktales.co.uk. **Contact:** Sean Jeffery, editor. Magazine: Contains illustrations. "We publish horror and speculative short fiction from anybody, anywhere, and the publication is professionally illustrated throughout." Estab. 2003. Circ. 350+.

Needs Horror (dark fantasy, futuristic, psychological, supernatural), science fiction (soft/sociological). Receives 25+ mss/month. Accepts 10-15 mss/issue; 25-40 mss/year. Ms published 6 months after acceptance. **Publishes 20 new writers/year.** Published Davin Ireland, Niall McMahon, David Robertson, Valerie Robson, K.S. Dearsley and Mark Cowley. Length: 500-3,500 words. Average length: 2,500 words. Publishes short shorts. Average length of short shorts: 500 words. Sometimes comments on/critiques rejected mss. Has occasional contests; see Web site for details.

How to Contact Send complete ms with cover letter. Include estimated word count, list of publications. Responds to queries in 1 week. Responds to mss in 12 weeks. Send disposable copy of ms and #10 SASE for reply only. Sample copy available for $3. Guidelines available on Web site.

Payment/Terms Writers receive $5 per thousand words. Additional copies $7.10. Pays on publication. Acquires first British serial rights. Sends galleys to author. Publication is copyrighted.

Tips "Have a believable but inspiring plot, sympathetic characters, an original premise, and a human heart no matter how technical or disturbing a story. Read a copy of the magazine! Make sure you get your writing basics spot-on. Don't rehash old ideas—if you must go down the werewolf/vampire route, put a spin on it."

❏ **DOWN IN THE DIRT**

Scars Publications and Design, 829 Brian Court, Gurnee IL 60031-3155. (847) 281-9070. E-mail: alexrand@scars.tv. Website: scars.tv. **Contact**: Alexandria Rand, editor. Magazine: 5½ × 8½; 60 lb. paper; illustrations; photos. Monthly. Estab. 2000.

Needs Adventure, ethnic/multicultural, experimental, fantasy, feminist, gay, historical, horror, lesbian, literary, mystery/suspense, New Age, psychic/supernatural/occult, science fiction. No religious or rhyming or family-oriented material. Publishes ms within 1 year after acceptance. Recently published work by Pat Dixon, Mel Waldman, Ken Dean Aeon Logan, Helena Wolfe. Average length: 1,000 words. Publishes short shorts. Also publishes poetry. Always, if asked, comments on rejected mss.

How to Contact Query with e-mail submission. "99.5% of all submissions are via e-mail only, so if you do not have electronic access, there is a strong chance you will not be considered. Responds in 1 month to queries; 1 month to mss. Accepts simultaneous, multiple submissions and reprints. Sample copy for $6. Writer's guidelines for SASE, e-mail or on the Web site.

▣ ◎ **$ DREAMS & VISIONS**

Skysong Press, 35 Peter St. S., Orillia ON L3V 5A8 Canada. (705) 329-1770. E-mail: skysong@bconnex.net. Website: www.bconnex.net/~skysong. **Contact:** Steve Stanton, editor. Magazine: 5½ × 8½; 60 pages; 20 lb. bond paper; glossy cover. "Innovative literary fiction for adult Christian readers." Semiannual. Estab. 1988. Circ. 300.

Needs Experimental, fantasy, humor/satire, literary, mainstream, mystery/suspense, novel excerpts, religious/inspirational, science fiction, slice-of-life vignettes. "We do not publish stories that glorify violence or perversity. All stories should portray a Christian worldview or expand upon Biblical themes or ethics in an entertaining or enlightening manner." Receives 20 unsolicited mss/month. Accepts 5 mss/issue; 10 mss/year. Publishes ms 4-8 months after acceptance. **Publishes 3 new writers/year.** Recently published work by Fred McGavran, Steven Mills, Donna Farley, and Michael Vance. Length: 2,000-6,000 words; average length: 2,500 words.

How to Contact Send complete ms. Responds in 3 weeks to queries; 3 months to mss. Accepts simultaneous submissions and reprints. Sample copy for $ 5.95. Writer's guidelines online.

Payment/Terms Pays 1¢/word (Canadian). Pays on publication for one-time rights.

Tips "In general we look for work that has some literary value, that is in some way unique and relevant to Christian readers today. Our first priority is technical adequacy, though we will occasionally work with a beginning writer to polish a manuscript. Ultimately, we look for stories that glorify the Lord Jesus Christ, stories that build up rather than tear down, that exalt the sanctity of life, the holiness of God, and the value of the family."

▣ **$ THE FIRST LINE**

Blue Cubicle Press, LLC, P.O. Box 250382, Plano TX 75025-0382. (972) 824-0646. E-mail: submission@ thefirstline.com. Website: www.thefirstline.com. **Contact:** Robin LaBounty, manuscript coordinator. Magazine: 8 × 5; 64-72 pages; 20 lb. bond paper; 80 lb. cover stock. "We only publish stories that start with the first line provided. We are a collection of tales—of different directions writers can take when they start from the same place. Quarterly. Estab. 1999. Circ. 1,000.

Needs Adventure, ethnic/multicultural, fantasy, gay, humor/satire, lesbian, literary, mainstream, mystery/suspense, regional, romance, science fiction, western. Receives 200 unsolicited mss/month. Accepts 12 mss/issue; 48 mss/year. Publishes ms 1 month after acceptance. **Publishes 6 new writers/year.** Length: 300-3,000 words; average length: 1,500 words. Publishes short shorts. Also publishes literary essays, literary criticism. Often comments on rejected mss.

How to Contact Send complete ms. Accepts submissions by e-mail. Send SASE for return of ms or disposable copy of the ms and #10 SASE for reply only. Responds in 1 week to queries; 3 months to mss. Accepts multiple submissions. No simultaneous submissions. Sample copy for $3.50. Writer's guidelines for SASE, e-mail or on Web site. Reviews fiction.

Payment/Terms Pays $20 maximum and contributor's copy; additional copy $2. Pays on publication.

Tips "Don't just write the first story that comes to mind after you read the sentence. If it is obvious, chances are other people are writing about the same thing. Don't try so hard. Be willing to accept criticism."

Small Circulation

☑ ◎ $ HARDBOILED

Gryphon Publications, P.O. Box 209, Brooklyn NY 11228. Website: www.gryphonbooks.com. **Contact:** Gary Lovisi, editor. Magazine: Digest-sized; 100 pages; offset paper; color cover; illustrations. "Hard-hitting crime fiction and private-eye stories—the newest and most cutting-edge work and classic reprints." Semiannual. Estab. 1988. Circ. 1,000.

Needs Mystery/suspense (private eye, police procedural, noir), hard-boiled crime, and private-eye stories, all on the cutting edge. No "pastiches, violence for the sake of violence." Wants to see more non-private-eye hard-boiled. Receives 40-60 unsolicited mss/month. Accepts 10-20 mss/issue. Publishes ms 18 months after acceptance. **Publishes 5-10 new writers/year.** Recently published work by Andrew Vachss, Stephen Solomita, Joe Hensley, Mike Black. Sometimes comments on rejected mss.

How to Contact Query with or without published clips or send complete ms. Accepts submissions by fax. Query with SASE only on anything over 3,000 words. All stories must be submitted in hard copy. If accepted, e-mail as an attachment in a Word document. Responds in 2 weeks to queries; 1 month to mss. Accepts simultaneous submissions and reprints. Sample copy for $10 or double issue for $20 (add $1.50 book postage). Writer's guidelines for #10 SASE.

Payment/Terms Pays $5-50. Pays on publication for first North American serial, one-time rights.

Tips By "hardboiled" the editor does not mean rehashing of pulp detective fiction from the 1940s and 1950s but rather realistic, gritty material. We look for good writing, memorable characters, intense situations. Lovisi could be called a pulp fiction "afficionado," however he also publishes *Paperback Parade* and holds an annual vintage paperback fiction convention each year. "It is advisable new writers try a subscription to the magazine to better see the type of stories and writing I am looking for. $35 gets you the next 4 hard-hitting issues."

☑ ◎ IRREANTUM

The Association for Mormon Letters, P.O. Box 970874, Orem UT 84097-0874. (801) 582- 2090. Website: www.mormonletters.org/irreantum/. **Contact:** Managing Editor. Magazine or Zine: 8½ × 7½; 100-120 pages; 20 lb. paper; 20 lb. color cover; illustrations; photos. "While focused on Mormonism, Irreantum is a cultural, humanities-oriented magazine, not a religious magazine. Our guiding principle is that Mormonism is grounded in a sufficiently unusual, cohesive, and extended historical and cultural experience that it has become like a nation, an ethnic culture. We can speak of Mormon literature at least as surely as we can of a Jewish or Southern literature. Irreantum publishes stories, one-act dramas, stand-alone novel and drama excerpts, and poetry by, for, or about Mormons (as well as author interviews, essays, and reviews). The magazine's audience includes readers of any or no religious faith who are interested in literary exploration of the Mormon culture, mindset, and worldview through Mormon themes and characters. Irreantum is currently the only magazine devoted to Mormon literature." Bi-annual. Estab. 1999. Circ. 300.

Needs Adventure, ethnic/multicultural (Mormon), experimental, family saga, fantasy, feminist, historical, horror, humor/satire, literary, mainstream, mystery/suspense, New Age, psychic/supernatural/occult, regional (Western USA/Mormon), religious/inspirational, romance, science fiction, thriller/espionage, translations, young adult/teen. Receives 5 unsolicited mss/month. Accepts 3 mss/issue; 6 mss/year. Publishes ms 3-12 months after acceptance. **Publishes 3 or more new writers/year.** Recently published work by Anne Perry, Brady Udall, Brian Evenson and Robert Kirby. Length: 1,000-5,000 words; average length: 5,000 words. Publishes short shorts. Also publishes literary essays, literary criticism, poetry. Sometimes comments on rejected mss. Annual fiction contest and annual personal essay contest with cash prizes.

How to Contact Accepts submissions by e-mail only to irreantum@mormonletters.org, in Microsoft Word or WordPerfect file format. Short pieces (such as Poetry or Readers Write) may be included in the body of the email message. Please include the category of work you are submitting in the subject line (e.g., Poetry submission, Critical Essay submission). Writers will receive a copy of the Irreantum issue in which their work appears (Readers Write contributors excepted). Send complete ms with cover letter. Include brief bio and list of publications. Responds in 2 weeks to queries; 2 months to mss. Accepts simultaneous and reprints, multiple submissions. Sample copy for $8. Writer's guidelines at http://www.mormonletters.org/irreantum/submit.html. Reviews fiction.

Payment/Terms Pays $0-100. Pays on publication for one-time rights.

Tips "*Irreantum* is not interested in didactic or polemical fiction that primarily attempts to prove or disprove Mormon doctrine, history or corporate policy. We encourage beginning writers to focus on human elements first, with Mormon elements introduced only as natural and organic to the story. Readers can tell if you are honestly trying to explore the human experience or if you are writing with a propagandistic agenda either for or against Mormonism. For conservative, orthodox Mormon writers, beware of sentimentalism, simplistic resolutions, and foregone conclusions."

☑ ◎ ITALIAN AMERICANA

URI/CCE, 80 Washington Street, Providence RI 02903-1803. (401)277-5306. Fax: (401)277-5100. E-mail: bonomoal@etal.uri.edu. Website: www.italianamericana.com. **Contact:** C.B. Albright, editor. Magazine: 6 × 9; 240 pages; varnished cover; perfect bound; photos. "Italian Americana contains historical articles, fiction, poetry and memoirs, all concerning the Italian experience in the Americas." Semiannual. Estab. 1974. Circ. 1,200.

Needs Literary, Italian American. No nostalgia. Wants to see more fiction featuring "individualized characters." Receives 10 unsolicited mss/month. Accepts 3 mss/issue; 6-7 mss/year. Publishes ms up to 1 year after acceptance. Agented fiction 5%. **Publishes 2-4 new writers/year.** Publishing 2 issues a year of historical articles, fiction, memoir, poetry and reviews. Award winning authors in all categories, such as Mary Caponegro, Sal La Puma, Dana Gioia (past poetry editor).

How to Contact Send complete ms (in duplicate) with a cover letter. Include 3-5 line bio, list of publications. Responds in 1 month to queries; 2 months to mss. No simultaneous submissions. Subscription: $20/year; $35/2 years. Sample copy for $7. Writer's guidelines for #10 SASE. Reviews fiction.

Payment/Terms 1 contributor's copy; additional copies $7. Acquires first North American serial rights.

Tips "Check out our new Web site supplement to the journal at www.italianamericana.com. Read *Wild Dreams: The Best of Italian Americana* (Fordham University Press), the best stories, poems and memoirs in the journal's 35- year history."

☑ KELSEY REVIEW

Mercer County College, P.O. Box B, Trenton NJ 08690. (609) 586-4800. Fax: (609) 586-2318. E-mail: kelsey.review@mccc.edu. Website: www.mccc.edu. **Contact**: Ed Carmien, Holly-Katherine Mathews, editors. Magazine: 7 × 14; 98 pages; glossy paper; soft cover. "Must live or work in Mercer County, NJ." Annual. Estab. 1988. Circ. 2,000.

Needs Regional (Mercer County, NJ only), open. Receives 10 unsolicited mss/month. Accepts 24 mss/issue. Reads mss only in May. **Publishes 10 new writers/year.** Recently published work by Thom Beachamps, Janet Kirk, Bruce Petronio. Publishes short shorts. Also publishes literary essays, poetry.

How to Contact SASE for return of ms. Responds no later than September 1 to mss. Accepts multiple submissions. Sample copy free.

Payment/Terms 3 contributor's copies. Rights revert to author on publication.

Tips Look for "quality, intellect, grace and guts. Avoid sentimentality, overwriting and self-indulgence. Work on clarity, depth and originality."

▦ ◎ KRAX MAGAZINE

63 Dixon Lane, Leeds Yorkshire LS12 4RR United Kingdom. **Contact:** A. Robson, co-editor. "Krax publishes lighthearted, humorous and whimsical writing. It is for anyone seeking light relief at a gentle pace. Our audience has grown middle-aged along with us, especially now that we're annual and not able to provide the instant fix demanded by teens and twenties."

Needs "No war stories, horror, space bandits, boy-girl soap opera. We publish mostly poetry of a lighthearted nature but use comic or spoof fiction, witty and humorous essays. Would like to see more whimsical items, trivia ramblings or anything daft." Accepts 1 mss/issue. **Publishes 1 new writer/year.** Recently published work by Aaron Dabrowski, Rovert L. Voss.

How to Contact No specific guidelines but cover letter appreciated. Sample copy for $2.

Tips "Look at what you enjoy in all forms of fiction—from strip cartoons to novels, movies to music lyrics—then try to put some of this into your own writing. Go for the idea first, then find the scenery to set it in. There are plenty of unreal worlds out there."

⊠ $ ⊟ LADY CHURCHILL'S ROSEBUD WRISTLET

Small Beer Press, 150 Pleasant St., #306, Easthampton MA 01017. E-mail: info@lcrw.net. Website: www. lcrw.net/lcrw. **Contact:** Gavin Grant, editor. Zine: half legal size; 60 pages; 60 lb. paper; glossy cover; illustrations; photos. Semiannual. Estab. 1996. Circ. 1,000.

Needs Comics/graphic novels, experimental, fantasy, feminist, literary, science fiction, translations, short story collections. Receives 25 unsolicited mss/month. Accepts 4-6 mss/issue; 8-12 mss/year. Publishes ms 6-12 months after acceptance. **Publishes 2-4 new writers/year.** Recently published work by Amy Beth Forbes, Jeffrey Ford, Carol Emshwiller and Theodora Goss. Length: 200-7,000 words; average length: 3,500 words. Also publishes literary essays, poetry. Sometimes comments on rejected mss.

How to Contact Send complete ms with a cover letter. Include estimated word count. Send SASE (or IRC) for return of ms, or send a disposable copy of ms and #10 SASE for reply only. Responds in 4 weeks to queries; 3-6 months to mss. Sample copy for $5. Writer's guidelines online. Reviews fiction.

Payment/Terms Pays 1¢/word, $20 minimum and 2 contributor's copies; additional copies contributor's discount 40%. Pays on publication for first, one-time and electronic rights.

Tips "I like fiction that tends toward the speculative."

◎ LEADING EDGE

4087 JKB, Provo, UT 84602. E-mail: fiction@leadingedgemagazine.com. Website: www. leadingedgemagazine.com. **Contact:** Fiction Director. Magazine specializing in science fiction and fantasy. Leading Edge is dedicated to helping new writers make their way into publishing. "We send back critiques with every story. We don't print anything with explicit language, graphic violence or sex." Semiannual. Estab. 1981.

Needs Fantasy and science fiction short stories, poetry, and artwork. Receives 50 unsolicited mss/month. Accepts 6 mss/issue; 12 mss/year. Publishes ms 1-6 months after acceptance. **Publishes 9-10 new writers/year.** Have published work by Orson Scott Card, Brandon Sanderson, and Dave Wolverton. Max length: 15,000; average length: 10,000 words.

How to Contact Send complete ms with cover letter and SASE. Include estimated word count. Send #10 SASE for reply only if disposable ms. Responds in 3 months to mss. Sample copy for $5.95. Writer's guidelines on Web site or send a SASE.

Payment/Terms 1¢/word for fiction; $10 for first 4 pages of poetry, $1.50 for each subsequent page; 2 contributor's copies; additional copies $4.95. Pays for publication for first North American serial rights. Sends galleys to author.

Tips "Buy a sample issue to know what is currently selling in our magazine. Also, make sure to follow the writer's guidelines when submitting."

◎ LEFT CURVE

P.O. Box 472, Oakland CA 94604-0472. (510)763-7193. E-mail: editor@leftcurve.org. Website: www. leftcurve.org. Contact: Csaba Polony, editor. Magazine: 8½ × 11; 144 pages; 60 lb. paper; 100 pt. C1S gloss layflat lamination cover; illustrations; photos. "Left Curve is an artist-produced journal addressing the problem(s) of cultural forms emerging from the crises of modernity that strive to be independent from the control of dominant institutions, based on the recognition of the destructiveness of commodity (capitalist) systems to all life." Published irregularly. Estab. 1974. Circ. 2,000.

Needs Ethnic/multicultural, experimental, historical, literary, regional, science fiction, translations, contemporary, prose poem, political. "No topical satire, religion-based pieces, melodrama. We publish critical, open, social/political-conscious writing." Receives 50 unsolicited mss/month. Accepts 3-4 mss/issue. Publishes ms 6-12 months after acceptance. Recently published work by Mike Standaert, Ilan Pappe, Terrence Cannon, John Gist. Length: 500-5,000 words; average length: 1,200 words. Publishes short shorts. Sometimes comments on rejected mss.

How to Contact Send complete ms. Accepts submissions by e-mail (editor@leftcurve.org). Send complete ms with cover letter. Include "statement of writer's intent, brief bio and reason for submitting to *Left Curve*." Accepts electronic submissions and hard copy, though for accepted work we request e-mail copy, either in body of text or as attachments." Responds in 6 months to mss. Sample copy for $12. Writer's guidelines available with SASE.

Payment/Terms Contributor's copies. Rights revert to author.

Tips "We look for continuity, adequate descriptive passages, endings that are not simply abandoned (in both meanings). Dig deep; no superficial personalisms, no corny satire. Be honest, realistic and gouge out the truth you wish to say. Understand yourself and the world. Have writing be a means to achieve or realize what is real."

▦ $ THE LONDON MAGAZINE

The London Magazine, 32 Addison Grove, London England W4 1ER United Kingdom. (00)44 0208 400 5882. Fax: (00)44 0208 994 1713. E-mail: admin@thelondonmagazine.net. Website: www. thelondonmagazine.ukf.net. Bimonthly. Estab.1732. Circ. 1,000.

Needs Adventure, literature, critique, confessions, erotica, ethnic/multicultural, experimental, fantasy, historical, humor/satire, mainstream, mystery/suspense, novel excerpts, religious/inspirational, romance, slice-of-life vignettes, suspense. Publishes ms 4 months after acceptance.

How to Contact Send complete ms by post or e-mail. If by post, include SASE. Responds in 1 month to queries; 4 months to mss. Accepts simultaneous submissions. Writer's guidelines free.

Payment/Terms Currently unpaid publications.

▨ ◎ $ ▣ MOM WRITER'S LITERARY MAGAZINE: MOM WRITERS WHO HAVE SOMETHING TO SAY

Mom Writer's Productions, LLC., P.O. Box 447, St. Johnsbury, VT 05719. (877) 382-6771. E-mail: publisher@momwriterslitmag.com. Website: www.momwriterslitmag.com. **Contact:** Samantha Gianulis, Editor-in-Chief. Online and print literary magazine. Print: 8x10, 84 pages. Contains illustrations. Includes photographs. "Mom Writer's Literary Magazine is a publication written by moms for moms across the globe who come together to share their stories. We publish creative nonfiction essays, fiction, columns, book reviews, profiles about mom writers and visual art. Mom Writer's Literary Magazine seeks writing that is vivid, complex and practical. We are not looking for 'sugar-coated' material. We believe the art of Motherhood is deserving of literary attention. We are a literary magazine for mothers with something to say. We're proud to have published essays that are emotionally moving, smart, raw and, sometimes, humorous. Mom Writer's Literary Magazine honors the fulfilling and tedious work that women do by making their stoires visible through print." Semiannual. Estab. 2005-Online, 2007- Print. Circ. 6,000. Member Mom Writers Publishing Cooperative.

> • *Mom Writer's Literary Magazine* was picked by *Writer's Digest* magazine as one of the Best Web Sites for Writers in 2006, 2007, and 2008.

Needs Adventure, ethnic/multicultural, family saga, feminist, literary, mainstream, romance (contemporary, suspense). Special interests: motherhood. Does not want children/juvenile, religious, horror, or western. Receives 20-30 mss/month. Accepts 2 mss/issue; 4 mss/year. Ms published 1-4 months after acceptance. **Publishes 2 new writers/year.**Length: 800-1,500 words. Average length: 1,400 words. Publishes short shorts. Average length of short shorts: 1,200 words. Also publishes literary essays, book reviews, poetry. Send review copies to Kathy Schlaeger, Reviews Editor. Rarely comments on/critiques rejected mss.

How to Contact Send complete ms with cover letter. Accepts submissions by e-mail. Include estimated word count, brief bio. Responds to mss in 1-3 months. Considers simultaneous submissions. Guidelines available on Web site.

Payment/Terms Writers receive $100 max., 1 contributor's copy. Additional copies $10. Pays on publication. Acquires one-time rights. Publication is copyrighted.

Tips "May be any genre. Story must flow smoothly and really get our attention (all editors). Must be within the word limits and submitted correctly. Also, please have a title for your story."

❏ ◎ THE NOCTURNAL LYRIC

The Nocturnal Lyric, P.O. Box 542, Astoria OR 97103. E-mail: nocturnallyric@melodymail.com. Website: www.angelfire.com/ca/nocturnallyric. **Contact:** Susan Moon, editor. Magazine: 8½ × 11; 40 pages; illustrations. "Fiction and poetry submitted should have a bizarre horror theme. Our audience encompasses people who stand proudly outside of the mainstream society." Annual. Estab. 1987. Circ. 400.

Needs Horror (dark fantasy, futuristic, psychological, supernatural, satirical). "No sexually graphic material—it's too overdone in the horror genre lately." Receives 25-30 unsolicited mss/month. Accepts

10-11 mss/issue; 10-11 mss/year. Publishes ms 1 year after acceptance. **Publishes 20 new writers/year.** Recently published work by Robert Essig, Mike Bayles, Prologue, Wanda Morrow-Clevenger, and Will Finnegan. Length: 2,000 words maximum; average length: 1,500 words. Publishes short shorts. Also publishes literary essays, poetry. Rarely comments on rejected mss.

How to Contact Send complete ms with cover letter. Include estimated word count. Responds in 3 month to queries; 8 months to mss. Accepts simultaneous, multiple submissions and reprints. Sample copy for $2 (back issue); $3 (current issue). Writer's guidelines online.

Payment/Terms Pays with discounts on subscriptions and discounts on copies of issue. Pays on acceptance Not copyrighted.

Tips "A manuscript stands out when the story has a very original theme and the ending is not predictable. Don't be afraid to be adventurous with your story. Mainstream horror can be boring. Surreal, satirical horror is what true nightmares are all about."

☑ ◎ $ NOVA SCIENCE FICTION MAGAZINE

Nova Publishing Company, 17983 Paseo Del Sol, Chino Hills CA 91709-3947. (909)393-0806. **Contact:** Wesley Kawato, editor. Zine specializing in evangelical Christian science fiction: 8½ × 5½; 64 pages; cardstock cover. "We publish religious science fiction short stories, no fantasy or horror. One story slot per issue will be reserved for a story written from an evangelical Christian viewpoint." Biannual. Estab. 1999. Circ. 25.

Needs Science fiction (hard science/technological, soft/sociological, religious). "No stories where the villain is a religious fanatic and stories that assume the truth of evolution." Accepts 6 mss/issue; 12 mss/year. Publishes ms 3 months after acceptance. **Publishes 7 new writers/year.** Recently published work by Jonathan Cooper, Lawrence Dagstine, Don Kerr, Gary Carter, Wesley Lambert, Susan Taylor, Erik Leinhart, David Baumann, Francis Alexander, Mark Galbert, Howard Bowman. Length: 250-7,000 words; average length: 4,000 words. Publishes short shorts. Sometimes comments on rejected mss.

How to Contact Query first. Include estimated word count and list of publications. Responds in 3 months to queries and mss. Send SASE (or IRC) for return of ms. Accepts reprints, multiple submissions. Sample copy for $6. Guidelines free for SASE.

Payment/Terms Pays $1.25-35. Pays on publication for first North American serial rights. Not copyrighted.

Tips "Make sure your plot is believable and describe your characters well enough so I can visualize them. If I like it, I buy it. I like happy endings and heroes with a strong sense of faith."

☑ NUTHOUSE

Twin Rivers Press, P.O. Box 119, Ellenton FL 34222. **Contact:** Dr. Ludwig "Needles" Von Quirk, chief of staff. Zine: digest-sized; 12-16 pages; bond paper; illustrations; photos. "Humor of all genres for an adult readership that is not easily offended." Published every 2-3 months. Estab. 1993. Circ. 100.

Needs Humor/satire (erotica, experimental, fantasy, feminist, historical [general], horror, literary, mainstream/contemporary, mystery/suspense, psychic/supernatural/occult, romance, science fiction and westerns). Receives 30-50 unsolicited mss/month. Accepts 5-10 mss/issue; 50-60 mss/year. Publishes ms 6-12 months after acceptance. **Publishes 10-15 new writers/year.** Recently published work by Michael Fowler, Dale Andrew White, and Jim Sullivan. Length: 100-1,000 words; average length: 500 words. Publishes short shorts. Also publishes literary essays, literary criticism, poetry. Often comments on rejected mss.

How to Contact Send complete ms with a cover letter. Include estimated word count, bio (paragraph) and list of publications. SASE for return of ms or send disposable copy of ms. Sample copy for $1. 50 (payable to Twin Rivers Press). Writer's guidelines for #10 SASE.

Payment/Terms Pays 1 contributor's copy. Acquires one-time rights. Not copyrighted.

Tips Looks for "laugh-out-loud prose. Strive for original ideas; read the great humorists—Saki, Woody Allen, Robert Benchley, Garrison Keillor, John Irving—and learn from them. We are turned off by sophomoric attempts at humor built on a single, tired, overworked gag or pun; give us a story with a beginning, middle and end."

☑ THE OAK

1530 Seventh Street, Rock Island IL 61201. (309)788-3980. **Contact:** Betty Mowery, editor. Magazine: 8½ × 11; 8-10 pages. "To provide a showcase for new authors while showing the work of established authors as well; to publish wholesome work, something with a message." Bimonthly. Estab. 1991. Circ. 300.

Needs Mainstream, contemporary, poems. Fiction up to 500 words. No erotica or love poetry. "No killing of humans or animals." "Gray Squirrel" appears as a section in Oak, accepts poetry and fiction from seniors age 50 and up. Length: 500 words. Receives 25 unsolicited mss/month. Accepts 12 mss/issue. Publishes ms 3 months after acceptance. **Publishes 25 new writers/year.**

How to Contact Send complete ms. Responds in 1 week to mss. Accepts simultaneous, multiple submissions. Sample copy for $4; subscription $12. Writer's guidelines for #10 SASE.

Payment/Terms None, but not necessary to buy a copy in order to be published. Acquires first rights.

Tips "I do not want erotica, extreme violence or killing of humans or animals for the sake of killing. Just be yourself when you write. Also, write tight. Please include SASE or manuscripts will be destroyed. Be sure name and address are on the manuscript. Study the markets for length of manuscript and what type of material is wanted. *The Shepherd* needs inspirational fiction up to 500 words, poetry, and Biblical character profiles. Same address as *The Oak*. Sample $3; subscription $12."

▨ ☑ $ ON SPEC

P.O. Box 4727, Station South, Edmonton AB T6E 5G6 Canada. (780) 413-0215. Fax: (780) 413-1538. E-mail: onspec@onspec.ca. Website: www.onspec.ca/. **Contact**: Diane L. Walton, editor. Magazine: 5¼ × 8; 112-120 pages; illustrations. "We publish speculative fiction by new and established writers, with a strong preference for Canadian authored works." Quarterly. Estab. 1989. Circ. 2,000.

Needs Fantasy, horror, science fiction, magic realism. No media tie-in or shaggy-alien stories. No condensed or excerpted novels, Religious/inspirational stories, fairy tales. "We would like to see more horror, fantasy, science fiction—well-developed stories with complex characters and strong plots." Receives 100 unsolicited mss/month. Accepts 10 mss/issue; 40 mss/year. "We read manuscripts during the month after each deadline: February 28/May 31/August 31/November 30." Publishes ms 6-18 months after acceptance. **Publishes 10-15 new writers/year.** Recently published work by Mark Shainblum, Hugh Spencer and Leah Bobet. Length: 1,000-6,000 words; average length: 4,000 words. Also publishes poetry. Often comments on rejected mss.

How to Contact Send complete ms. Accepts submissions by disk. SASE for return of ms or send a disposable copy of ms plus #10 SASE for response. Include Canadian postage or IRCs. No e-mail or fax submissions. Responds in 2 weeks to queries; 4 months after deadline to mss. Accepts simultaneous submissions. Sample copy for $8. Writer's guidelines for #10 SASE or on Web site.

Payment/Terms Pays $50-180 for fiction. Short stories (under 1,000 words): $50 plus 1 contributor's copy. Pays on acceptance for first North American serial rights.

Tips "We're looking for original ideas with a strong SF element, excellent dialogue, and characters who are so believable, our readers will really care about them."

▢ OPIUM MAGAZINE

Literary Humor for the Deliriously Captivated, 166 Albion St., San Francisco, CA 94110. (347)229-2443. E-mail: todd@opiummagazine.com. Website: www.opiumden.org. **Contact:** Todd Zuniga, editor-in-chief. Biannual magazine. Contains black and white cartoons, illustrations, and photographs. "Opium Magazine displays an eclectic mix of stories, poetry, reviews, cartoons, interviews and much more. It features 'estimated reading times' that precede each piece. While the focus is often humorous literature, we love to publish heartbreaking, serious work. Our rule is that all work must be well written and engaging from the very first sentence. While we publish traditional pieces, we're primarily engaged by writers who take risks." Updated daily. Estab. 2001. Circ. 25,000 hits/month. Member CLMP.

Needs Comics/graphic novels, experimental, humor/satire, literary, mainstream. "Vignettes and first-person 'look at what a whacky time I had going to Spain' stories aren't going to get past first base with us." Receives 200 mss/month. Accepts 60 mss/year. Manuscript published 4 months after acceptance. Agented fiction 10%. **Publishes 10-12 new writers/year.** Published Etgar Keret, Art Spiegelman, Jack Handey, Terese Svoboda. Length: 50-1,200 words. Average length: 700 words. Publishes short shorts. Average length of short shorts: 400 words. Also publishes literary essays, literary criticism, poetry.

Sometimes comments on/critiques rejected mss.

How to Contact Send complete ms with cover letter by e-mail only. Ms received via snail mail will not be read. Include estimated word count, brief bio, list of publications, and your favorite book. Responds to queries in 2 weeks. Responds to mss in 15 weeks. Considers simultaneous submissions. Guidelines available via e-mail or on Website.

Payment/Terms Acquires first North American serial rights. Publication is copyrighted.

Tips "If you don't strike out in that first paragraph to expose something definitive or new, then you better by the second. We get scores of stories, and like the readers we want to attract, we demand to be engaged immediately. Tell us it's your first time, we'll be gentle, and our editors usually give thoughts and encouragement if a piece has promise, even if we reject it."

☑ ☒ ORACLE STORY & LETTERS

Rising Star Publishers, 7510 Lake Glen Drive, Glen Dale MD 20769. (301)352-2533. Fax: (301)352-2529. E-mail: hekwonna@aol.com. **Contact:** Obi H. Ekwonna, publisher. Magazine: 5½ × 8½; 60 lb. white bound paper. Quarterly. Estab. 1989. Circ. 1,000.

Needs Adventure, children's/juvenile (adventure, fantasy, historical, mystery, series), comics/graphic novels, ethnic/multicultural, family saga, fantasy (sword and sorcery), historical, literary, mainstream, military/war, romance (contemporary, historical, suspense), thriller/espionage, western (frontier saga), young adult/teen (adventure, historical). Does not want gay/lesbian or erotica works. Receives 10 unsolicited mss/month. Accepts 7 mss/issue. Publishes ms 4 months after acceptance. **Publishes 5 new writers/year.** Recently published work by Joseph Manco, I.B.S. Sesay. Publishes short shorts. Also publishes literary essays, literary criticism, poetry. Rarely comments on rejected mss.

How to Contact Send complete ms. Accepts submissions by disk. Send SASE (or IRC) for return of the ms, or send a disposable copy of the ms and #10 SASE for reply only. Responds in 1 month to mss. Accepts multiple submissions. Sample copy for $10. Writer's guidelines for #10 SASE, or by e-mail.

Payment/Terms Pays 1 contributor's copy. Pays on publication for first North American serial rights.

Tips "Read anything you can lay your hands on."

☑ ◎ ☒ OUTER DARKNESS

Outer Darkness Press, 1312 N. Delaware Place, Tulsa OK 74110. Website: http://members.cox.net/outerdarkness. **Contact**: Dennis Kirk, editor. Zine: 8½ × 5½; 50-60 pages; 20 lb. paper; perfect-bound, 90 lb. glossy cover; illustrations. Specializes in imaginative literature. "Variety is something I strive for in Outer Darkness. In each issue we present readers with great tales of science fiction and horror along with poetry, cartoons and interviews/essays. I seek to provide readers with a magazine which, overall, is fun to read. My readers range in age from 16 to 70." Quarterly. Estab. 1994. Circ. 500.

• Fiction published in *Outer Darkness* has received honorable mention in *The Year's Best Fantasy and Horror.*

Needs Fantasy (science), horror, mystery/suspense (with horror slant), psychic/supernatural/occult, romance (gothic), science fiction (hard science, soft/sociological). No straight mystery, pure fantasy— works which do not incorporate elements of science fiction and/or horror. Also, no slasher horror with violence, gore, sex instead of plot. Wants more "character driven tales—especially in the genre of science fiction and well-developed psychological horror. I do not publish works with children in sexual situations, and graphic language should be kept to a minimum." Receives 75-100 unsolicited mss/month. Accepts 5-7 mss/issue; 2 0-25 mss/year. **Publishes 2-5 new writers/year.** Recently published work by John Sunseri, Christopher Fulbright, Melinda Arnett, and James M. Steimle. Length: 1,500-5,000 words; average length: 3,000 words. Also publishes poetry. Comments on rejected mss when possible.

How to Contact Send complete ms with a cover letter. Include estimated word count, 50- to 75-word bio, list of publications and "any awards, honors you have received." Send SASE for reply, return of ms, or send a disposable copy of ms. Responds in 2 weeks to queries; 4 months to mss. Accepts simultaneous, multiple submissions. Sample copy for $4.95. Writer's guidelines for #10 SASE.

Payment/Terms Pays 2 contributor's copies for fiction; 1 for poetry and 2 for art. Pays on publication for one-time rights.

Tips "I look for strong characters and well -developed plot. And I definitely look for suspense. I want stories which move—and carry the reader along with them. Be patient and persistent. Often it's simply a matter of linking the right story with the right editor. I've received many stories which were good, but not what I wanted at the time. However, these stories worked well in another horror-sci-fi zine."

☑ ◎ PANGAIA

BBI Media, Inc., P.O. Box 687, Forest Grove OR 97116. (503)430-8817. Website: www.pangaia.com. **Contact**: Anne Niven, chief editor. Magazine: 8½ × 11; 80 pages; 50 lb. recycled book paper; 80 lb. book cover stock. "We are the only publication of this type. PanGaia explores Pagan and Gaian earth-based spirituality at home and around the world. We envision a world in which living in spirit and living on earth support and enrich each other; a spirituality that honors what is sacred in all life; a future in which ancient ritual and modern science both have a place. Intended audience: thinking adult Pagans of every sort. Women and men of all earth-affirming spiritual paths." Quarterly. Estab. 1997. Circ. 8,000.

• Nominated for the *Utne Reader's* Alternative Press Award for best spirituality coverage.

Needs Pagan/Gaian. Receives 2-4 unsolicited mss/month. Accepts 1-4 mss/year. Publishes ms 6 months after acceptance. **Publishes some new writers/year.** Length: 500-5,000 words; average length: 3,500 words. Publishes short shorts. Also publishes poetry. Sometimes comments on rejected mss.

How to Contact Send complete ms. Accepts submissions by e-mail, fax, disk. Include SASE (or IRC) for return of ms, or send disposable copy of the ms and #10 SASE for reply only. Responds in 3-6 weeks to mss. Accepts reprints submissions. Sample copy free. Writer's guidelines for #10 SASE, online, or by e-mail.

Payment/Terms Pays.025¢-4¢/word. Pays on publication for first North American serial, electronic rights.

Tips "Read the magazine! Must know who we are and what we like."

◎ PARADOXISM

University of New Mexico, 200 College Rd., Gallup NM 87301. Fax: (503) 863-7532. E-mail: smarand@ unm.edu. Website: www.gallup.unm.edu/ ~ smarandache/a/paradoxism.htm. **Contact:** Dr. Florentin Smarandache. Magazine: 8½ × 11; 100 pages; illustrations. "Paradoxism is an avant-garde movement based on excessive use of antinomies, antitheses, contraditions, paradoxes in the literary creations set up by the editor in the 1980s as an anti-totalitarian protest." Annual. Estab. 1993. Circ. 500.

Needs Experimental, literary. "Contradictory, uncommon, experimental, avant garde." Plans specific themes in the next year. Publishes annual special fiction issue or anthology. Receives 5 unsolicited mss/ month. Accepts 10 mss/issue. Recently published work by Mircea Monu, Doru Motoc and Patrick Pinard. Publishes short shorts. Also publishes literary essays, literary criticism, poetry. Sometimes comments on rejected mss.

How to Contact Send a disposable copy of ms. Responds in 2 months to mss. Accepts simultaneous submissions. Sample copy for $19.95 and 8½ × 11 SASE. Writer's guidelines online.

Payment/Terms Pays subscription. Pays on publication. Not copyrighted.

Tips "We look for work that refers to the paradoxism or is written in the paradoxist style. The Basic Thesis of the paradoxism: everything has a meaning and a non-meaning in a harmony with each other. The Essence of the paradoxism: a) the sense has a non-sense, and reciprocally B) the non-sense has a sense. The Motto of the paradoxism: 'All is possible, the impossible too!' The Symbol of the paradoxism: a spiral—optic illusion, or vicious circle."

☐ ◎ PRAYERWORKS

The Master's Work, P.O. Box 301363, Portland OR 97294-9363. (503) 761-2072. E-mail: vannm1@aol. com. Website: www.prayerworksnw.org. **Contact**: V. Ann Mandeville, editor. Newsletter: 5½ × 8; 4 pages; bond paper. "Our intended audience is 70% retired Christians and 30% families. We publish 350-500 word devotional material—fiction, nonfiction, biographical, poetry, clean quips and quotes. Our philosophy is evangelical Christian serving the body of Chirst in the area of prayer." Estab. 1988. Circ. 1,100.

Needs Religious/inspirational. "No nonevangelical Christian. Subject matter may include anything which will build relationship with the Lord—prayer, ways to pray, stories of answered prayer, teaching on a Scripture portion, articles that will build faith, or poems will all work." We even use a series occasionally. Publishes ms 2-6 months after acceptance. **Publishes 30 new writers/year.** Recently published work by

Allen Audrey and Petey Prater. Length: 350-500 words; average length: 350-500 words. Publishes short shorts. Also publishes poetry. Often comments on rejected mss.

How to Contact Send complete ms with cover letter. Include estimated word count and a very short bio. Responds in 1 month to mss. Accepts simultaneous, multiple submissions and reprints. Writer's guidelines for #10 SASE.

Payment/Terms Pays free subscription to the magazine and contributor's copies. Pays on publication. Not copyrighted.

Tips Stories "must have a great take-away—no preaching; teach through action. Be thrifty with words— make them count."

☐ $ PURPOSE

616 Walnut Ave., Scottdale PA 15683-1999. (724) 887-8500. Fax: (724) 887-3111. E-mail: horsch@mph.org. Website: www.mph.net. **Contact:** James E. Horsch, editor. Magazine: 5⅜ × 8⅜; 8 pages; illustrations; photos. Monthly. Estab. 1968. Circ. 8,500.

Needs Historical (related to discipleship theme), humor/satire, religious/inspirational. No militaristic, narrow patriotism, or racist themes. Receives 150 unsolicited mss/month. Accepts 12 mss/issue; 140 mss/year. Publishes ms 1 year after acceptance. **Publishes 15-25 new writers/year.** Length: 600 words; average length: 400 words. Occasionally comments on rejected mss.

How to Contact Send complete ms. Send all submissions by Word attachment via e-mail. Responds in 3 months to queries. Accepts simultaneous submissions, reprints, multiple submissions. Sample copy and writer's guidelines for $2, 6 × 9 SAE and 2 first-class stamps. Writer's guidelines online.

Payment/Terms Pays up to 7¢/word for stories, and 2 contributor's copies. Pays on acceptance for one-time rights.

Tips "Many stories are situational, how to respond to dilemmas. Looking for first-person storylines. Write crisp, action moving, personal style, focused upon an individual, a group of people, or an organization. The story form is an excellent literary device to help readers explore discipleship issues. The first two paragraphs are crucial in establishing the mood/issue to be resolved in the story. Work hard on the development of these."

☒ ☐ ◎ $ QUEEN'S QUARTERLY

Queen's Quarterly, 144 Barrie St. Kingston ON K7L 3N6 Canada. (613)533-2667. Fax: (613)533-6822. E-mail: q ueens.quarter ly@queensu.ca. Website: www.queensu.ca/quarterly. **Contact**: Boris Castel, editor. Magazine: 6 × 9; 800 pages/year; illustrations. "A general interest intellectual review, featuring articles on science, politics, humanities, arts and letters. Book reviews, poetry and fiction." Quarterly. Estab. 1893. Circ. 3,000.

Needs Historical, literary, mainstream, novel excerpts, short stories, women's. "Special emphasis on work by Canadian writers." Accepts 2 mss/issue; 8 mss/year. Publishes ms 6-12 months after acceptance. **Publishes 5 new writers/year.** Recently published work by Gail Anderson-Dargatz, Tim Bowling, Emma Donohue, Viktor Carr, Mark Jarman, Rick Bowers and Dennis Bock. Also publishes literary essays, literary criticism, poetry.

How to Contact "Send complete ms with SASE and/or IRC. No reply with insufficient postage." Responds in 2-3 months to queries. Sample copy online. Writer's guidelines online. Reviews fiction.

Payment/Terms Pays $100-300 for fiction, 2 contributor's copies and 1-year subscription; additional copies $5. Pays on publication for first North American serial rights. Sends galleys to author.

☐ SILENT VOICES

Ex Machina Press, LLC, P.O. Box 11180, Glendale CA 91226.(818)244-7209. E-mail: exmachinapag@aol. com. Website: www.exmachinapress.com. **Contact:** Peter Balaskas, editor. Literary magazine/journal. "Silent Voices is an annual literary anthology whose purpose is to publish fiction of a variety of styles and genres. By taking stories of a diverse nature and placing them in a specific order, we produce a creative mosaic that tells a larger story." Annual. Estab. 2004. Circ. 1,000.

Needs Adventure, erotica, ethnic/multicultural, experimental, fantasy, historical, horror, humor/satire, mainstream, mystery, religious, romance, science fiction, western. Manuscript published 4-5 months after acceptance. Length: 10,000 words. *We are not accepting new fiction submissions at this time.* Please check Web site for updates.

How to Contact Send complete ms with cover letter via e-mail only. Considers simultaneous submissions. Guidelines available on Web site. Please read Web site guidelines before submitting.

Payment/Terms Pays 2 contributor's copies. Acquires first North American serial rights.

☐ ◉ SLATE & STYLE

NFB Writer's Division, 2704 Beach Drive, Merrick NY 11566. (516)868-8718. E-mail: loristay@aol.com. **Contact**: Lori Stayer, editor. Quarterly magazine: 28-32 print/40 Braille pages; e-mail, cassette and large print. "Articles of interest to writers, and resources for blind writers." Estab. 1982. Circ. 200.

Needs Adventure, fantasy, humor/satire, contemporary, blindness. No erotica. "Avoid theme of death." Does not read mss in June or July. **Publishes 2 new writers/year.** Recently published work by Bruce Adkins, Patricia Hubschman, Kristen Diaz, and Amy Krout-horn. Accepts short stories up to 2,000 words. Publishes short shorts. Also publishes literary criticism, poetry. Sometimes comments on rejected mss.

How to Contact Accepts submissions by e-mail. Responds in 3-6 weeks to queries; 3-6 weeks to mss. Sample copy for $3.

Payment/Terms Pays in contributor's copies. Acquires one-time rights. Sponsors awards/contests.

Tips "The best advice I can give is to send your work out; manuscripts left in a drawer have no chance at all."

◉ SOLEADO

IPFW, CM 267 2101 E. Coliseum Blvd., Fort Wayne IN 46805.(260)481-6630. Fax: (260)481-6985. E-mail: summersj@ipfw.edu. Website: www.soleado.org. **Contact:** Jason Summers, editor. Magazine. "We are looking for good literary writing in Spanish, from Magical Realism á la García Márquez, to McOndo-esque writing similiar to that of Edmundo Paz-Soldá and Alberto Fuguet, to Spanish pulp realism like that of Arturo Pérez-Reverte. Testimonials, experimental works like those of Diamela Eltit, and women's voices like Marcela Serrano and Zoé Valdés are also encouraged. We are not against any particular genre writing, but such stories do have to maintain their hold on the literary, as well as the genre, which is often a difficult task. Please do not send anything in English. We publish a very limited selection of work in Spanglish—Do not send us anything without having read what we have already published." Annual. Estab. 2004.

Needs Children's/juvenile, ethnic/multicultural, experimental, fantasy, historical, humor/satire, mainstream, mystery, science fiction. Accepts 2-6 mss/year. Length: 8,000 words (max).

How to Contact Send complete ms with cover letter. Accepts submissions by e-mail. Responds to queries in 2 weeks. Responds to mss in 3 months. Guidelines available on Web site.

Payment/Terms Acquires first rights, first North American serial rights, one-time rights, electronic rights.

☑ ◉ $ SPACE AND TIME MAGAZINE: THE MAGAZINE OF FANTASY, HORROR, AND SCIENCE

HDi Consulting, Inc. 1308 Centennial Ave, Ste 101, Piscataway, NJ 08854. (732) 512-8789. E-mail: fictioneditor@spaceandtimemagazine.com. Website: http://spaceandtimemagazine.com. **Fiction Contact:** Gerard Houarner, fiction editor. Magazine. 8½ × 11, 48 pages, matte paper, glossy cover. Contains illustrations. "We love stories that blend elements—horror and science fiction, fantasy with SF elements, etc. We challenge writers to try something new and send us their unclassifiable works—what other publications reject because the work doesn't fit in their 'pigeonholes.'" Quarterly. Estab. 1966. Circ. 2,000.

Needs Fantasy (high, sword and sorcery, modern), horror (dark fantasy, futuristic, psychological, supernatural), romance (futuristic/time travel), science fiction (hard science/technological, soft/sociological). Does not want anything without some sort of speculative element. Receives 250 mss/month. Accepts 8 mss/issue; 32 mss/year. Closes periodically due to backlog. Check Web site to see if submissions are open. Ms published 3-6 months after acceptance. **Publishes 2-4 new writers/year.** Published PD Cacek, AR Morlan, Jeffrey Ford, Charles De Lint and Jack Ketchum. Length: 1,000-10,000 words. Average length: 6,500 words. Publishes short shorts. Average length of short shorts: 1,000 words. Also publishes poetry, occasional book reviews. Send review copies to Publisher Hildy Silverman, hildy@spaceandtimemagazine.com. Sometimes comments on/critiques rejected mss.

How to Contact Send complete ms with cover letter. Accepts submissions by e-mail. Include estimated word count, brief bio, list of publications. Responds to queries in 4-6 weeks. Responds to mss in 4-6 weeks. Send disposable query letter and #10 SASE for reply only if unable to email submission. Sample copy available for $5. Guidelines available via e-mail, on Web site.

Payment/Terms Writers receive 1¢ per word, 2 contributor's copies. Additional copies $ 5. Pays on publication. Acquires first North American serial rights, one-time rights. Publication is copyrighted.

Tips "Be well written—that means proper grammar, punctuation and spelling. Proofread! The greatness of your story will not supersede sloppy construct. Strong internal logic no matter how 'far out' the story. New twists on familiat plots or truly unique offerings will make your manuscript stand out. Blend genre elements in a new and interesting way, and you'll get our attention."

STEAMPUNK MAGAZINE, PUTTING THE PUNK BACK INTO STEAMPUNK

Strangers In A Tangled Wilderness. E-mail: strangers@riseup.net. Website: http://www. steampunkmagazine.com. **Contact:** Magpie Killjoy, editor. Magazine/Online magazine. 8.5 × 7, 80 pages, recycled paper. Contains illustrations. "SteamPunk Magazine is involved in supporting the SteamPunk subculture, a subculture that offers a competing vision of humanity's interaction with technology, a subculture that wears too many goggles." Quarterly. Estab. 2007. Circ. 1,000 print; 60,000 online.

Needs Adventure, comics/graphic novels, ethnic/multicultural, experimental, fantasy (space fantasy), feminist, horror (dark fantasy, supernatural), humor/satire, literary, military/war, mystery, romance (gothic, historical), science fiction, western. Special interests: steampunk. "We are not interested in promoting misogynist, nationalistic, pro-colonial, monarchical, homophobic, or otherwise useless text." List of upcoming themes available on Web site. Receives 5-12 mss/month. Accepts 1-2 mss/issue; 3-6 mss/year. Manuscript published 2 months after acceptance. **Publishes 6-10 new writers/year.** Published John Reppion, Margaret Killjoy, GD Falksen, Will Strop, Catastraphone Orchestra and Olga Izakson. Length: 500-6,000 words. Average length: 3,500 words. Publishes short shorts. Average length of short shorts: 800 words. Also publishes literary essays, literary criticism, book reviews. Send review copies to Magpie Killjoy. Sometimes comments on/critiques rejected mss.

How to Contact Send complete ms with cover letter. Accepts submissions by e-mail only. Include brief bio, list of publications. Responds to queries in 2 weeks. Responds to mss in 2 months. Considers simultaneous submissions, previously published submissions, multiple submissions. Sample copy available for $3, on Web site. Guidelines available on Web site.

Payment/Terms Pays $30 per story. Pays on publication.

Tips "We want work that does not simply repeat the stereotypical steampunk genre ideas; work that offers something tangible other than shiny brass thing-a-mabobs. Don't write about a steam-powered robot, unless you really have to."

$ THE STORYTELLER

2441 Washington Road, Maynard AR 72444. (870) 647-2137. E-mail: storyteller1@hightowercom.com. Website: www.thestorytellermagazine.com. **Contact:** Regina Williams, editor. Tabloid: 8½ × 11; 72 pages; typing paper; glossy cover; illustrations. "This magazine is open to all new writers regardless of age. I will accept short stories in most genres and poetry in any type. Please keep in mind, this is a family publication." Quarterly. Estab. 1996.

• Offers *People's Choice Awards* and nominates for a *Pushcart Prize.*

Needs Adventure, historical, humor/satire, literary, mainstream, mystery/suspense, religious/inspirational, romance, western, senior citizen/retirement, sports. "I will not accept pornography, erotica, science fiction, new age, foul language, graphic horror or graphic violence." No children's stories or young adult. Wants more well-plotted mysteries. Publishes ms 3-9 months after acceptance. **Publishes 30-50 new writers/year.** Recently published work by Jodi Thomas, Jory Sherman, David Marion Wilkinson, Dusty Richards and Tony Hillerman. Publishes short shorts. Also publishes literary essays, poetry. Sometimes comments on rejected mss. Word length 2,500.

How to Contact Send complete ms with cover letter. Include estimated word count and 5-line bio. Submission by mail only. Responds in 1-2 weeks to mss. No queries. Accepts simultaneous submissions and reprints. Sample copy for $6. Writer's guidelines for #10 SASE.

Payment/Terms Pays 14 ¢ per word. Sponsors awards/contests.

Tips "Follow the guidelines. No matter how many times this has been said, writers still ignore this basic and most important rule." Looks for "professionalism, good plots and unique characters. Purchase a sample copy so you know the kind of material we look for." Would like more "well-plotted mysteries and suspense and a few traditional westerns. Avoid sending anything that children or young adults would not (or could not) read, such as really bad language. Polish, polish, polish before sending anything out."

🌐 ☑ STUDIO

727 Peel Street, Albury 2640. Australia. (+61) 26021-1135. E-mail: studio00@bigpond.net.au. **Contact:** Paul Grover, managing editor. Quarterly. Circ. 300.

Needs "*Studio* publishes prose and poetry of literary merit, offers a venue for new and aspiring writers, and seeks to create a sense of community among Christians writing." Accepts 30-40 mss/year. **Publishes 40 new writers/year.** Recently published work by Andrew Lansdown and Benjamin Gilmour.

How to Contact Accepts submissions by e-mail. Send SASE. "Overseas contributors must use International postal coupons in place of stamped envelope." Responds in 1 month to mss. Sample copy for $10 (Aus).

Payment/Terms Pays in copies; additional copies are discounted. Subscription $60 (Australian) for 4 issues (1 year). International draft in Australian dollars and IRC required, or Visa and Mastercard facilities available. "Copyright of individual published pieces remains with the author, while each collection is copyright to *Studio*."

☑ TALEBONES

Fairwood Press, 21528 104th Street Court East, Bonney Lake WA 98391. (253) 269-2640. E-mail: info@talebones.com. **Contact:** Patrick Swenson, editor. Magazine: digest size; 100 pages; standard paper; glossy cover stock; illustrations; photos. "We like stories that have punch, but still entertain. We like science fiction and dark fantasy, humor, psychological and experimental works." Published 2-3 times a year. Estab. 1995. Circ. 1,000.

Needs Fantasy (dark), humor/satire, science fiction (hard science, soft/sociological, dark). "No straight slash and hack horror. No cat stories or stories told by young adults." "Would like to see more science fiction." Receives 200 unsolicited mss/month. Accepts 8-10 mss/issue; 16-30 mss/year. Publishes ms 3-4 months after acceptance. **Publishes 2-3 new writers/year.** Recently published work by William F. Nolan, Nina Kiriki Hoffman, Paul Melko, Ken Scholes, and James Van Pelt. Length: 1,000-6,000 words; average length: 3,000-4,000 words. No short shorts or flash. Also publishes poetry.

How to Contact Send complete ms with cover letter. Include estimated word count and 1-paragraph bio. Responds in 1 week to queries; 1-2 months to mss. Sample copy for $7. Writer's guidelines for #10 SASE. Reviews fiction.

☑ ◎ $ ☑ TALES OF THE TALISMAN

Hadrosaur Productions, P.O. Box 2194, Mesilla Park NM 88047-2194. E-mail: hadrosaur@zianet.com. Website: www.talesofthetalisman.com. **Contact:** David L. Summers, editor. Zine specializing in science fiction: 8½ × 10½; 90 pages; 60 lb. white stock; 80 lb. cover. "Tales of the Talisman is a literary science fiction and fantasy magazine published 4 times a year. We publish short stories, poetry, and articles with themes related to science fiction and fantasy. Above all, we are looking for thought-provoking ideas and good writing. Speculative fiction set in the past, present, and future is welcome. Likewise, contemporary or historical fiction is welcome as long as it has a mythic or science fictional element. Our target audience includes adult fans of the science fiction and fantasy genres along with anyone else who enjoys thought-provoking and entertaining writing." Quarterly. Estab. 1995. Circ. 200.

• Received an honorable mention in *The Year's Best Science Fiction 2004* edited by Gardner Dozois.

Needs Fantasy (space fantasy, sword and sorcery), horror, science fiction (hard science/technological, soft/sociological). "We do not want to see stories with graphic violence. Do not send 'mainstream' fiction with no science fictional or fantastic elements. Do not send stories with copyrighted characters, unless you're the copyright holder." Receives 60 unsolicited mss/month. Accepts 7-10 mss/issue; 21-30 mss/year. Publishes ms 9 months after acceptance. **Publishes 8 new writers/year.** Recently published work by Tyree Campbell, Carol Hightshoe Ed Cox, Richard Harland, Janni Lee Simner and Jill Knowles. Length: 1,000-6,000 words; average length: 4,000 words. Also publishes poetry. Often comments on rejected mss.

How to Contact Send complete ms. Accepts submissions by e-mail (hadrosaur@zianet.com). Accepts submissions from January 1-February 15 and July 1-August 15. Include estimated word count, brief bio and list of publications. Send SASE (or IRC) for return of ms or send a disposable copy of ms and #10 SASE for reply only. Responds in 1 week to queries; 1 month to mss. Sometimes comments on rejected works. Accepts reprint submissions. No simultaneous submissions. Sample copy for $8. Writer's guidelines online.

Payment/Terms Pays $6-10. Pays on acceptance for one-time rights.

Tips "First and foremost, I look for engaging drama and believable characters. With those characters and situations, I want you to take me someplace I've never been before. The story I'll buy is the one set in a new world or where the unexpected happens, but yet I cannot help but believe in the situation because it feels real. Read absolutely everything you can get your hands on, especially stories and articles outside your genre of choice. This is a great source for original ideas."

☐ ◎ TEA, A MAGAZINE

Olde English Tea Company, Inc., 3 Devotion Road P.O. Box 348, Scotland CT 06264. (860) 456-1145. Fax: (860) 456-1023. E-mail: teamag@teamag.com. Website: www.teamag.com. **Contact:** Jobina Miller, assistant to the editor. Magazine. "An exciting quarterly magazine all about tea, both as a drink and for its cultural significance in art, music, literature, history and society." Quarterly. Estab. 1994. Circ. 9,500.

Needs Needs fiction that is tea related.

How to Contact Send complete ms with cover letter. Responds to mss in 6 months. Guidelines available for SASE.

Payment/Terms Pays on publication. Acquires all rights.

◙ $ TIMBER CREEK REVIEW

P.O. Box 16542, Greensboro NC 27416. E-mail: timber_creek_review@hoopsmail.com. **Contact:** John M. Freiermuth, editor; Willa Schmidt, associate editor. Newsletter: 5½ × 8½; 76-80 pages; computer generated on copy paper; saddle-stapled with colored paper cover; some illustrations. "Fiction, humor/satire, poetry and travel for a general audience." Quarterly. Estab. 1992. Circ. 130-150.

Needs Adventure, ethnic/multicultural, feminist, historical, humor/satire, literary, mainstream, mystery/suspense, regional, western, literary nonfiction, and one-act plays. "No religious, children's, gay, modern romance, and no reprints please!" Receives 50 unsolicited mss/month. Accepts 30-36 stories and 75-85 poems a year. Publishes ms 2-6 months after acceptance. Length: 3,500-6,000 words. **Publishes 0-3 new writers/year.** Recently published work by Roslyn Willett, Alex Girtti, Joseph Love, Michael Fessler, John L. Campbell, Eugene R. Baker, Dennis Vannatta, Marylyn Dorf, and Ramon A. Klitzke.

How to Contact Cover letter expected. Accepts simultaneous submissions. Sample copy for $5.00, subscription $18. Overseas mail add $8 for postage.

Payment/Terms Pays $10-40, plus subscription. Acquires first North American serial rights. Not copyrighted.

Tips "Stop watching TV and read that literary magazine where your last manuscript appeared. There are no automatons here, so don't treat us like machines. We may not recognize your name at the top of the manuscript. Include a statement that the mss have previously not been published on paper nor on the internet, nor have they been accepted by others. A few lines about yourself breaks the ice, the names of three or four magazines that have published you in the last year or two would show your reality, and a bio blurb of 27 words including the names of 2 or 3 of the magazines you send the occasional subscription check (where you aspire to be?) could help. If you are not sending a check to some little magazine that is supported by subscriptions and the blood, sweat and tears of the editors, why would you send your manuscript to any of them and expect to receive a warm welcome? No requirement to subscribe or buy a sample, but they're available and are encouraged. There are no phony contests and never a reading fee. We read all year long, but may take 3-8 months to respond."

☐ ◎ TRAIL OF INDISCRETION

Fortress Publishing, Inc., 3704 Hartzdale Dr., Camp Hill PA 17011. (717) 350-8760. E-mail:

fortresspublishinginc@yahoo.com. Website: www.fortresspublishinginc.com. **Contact:** Brian Koscienski, editor in chief. Zine specializing in genre fiction: digest (5½ × 8½), 48 pages, 24 lb. paper, glossy cover. "We publish genre fiction—sci-fi, fantasy, horror, etc. We'd rather have a solid story containing great characters than a weak story with a surprise 'trick' ending." Quarterly. Estab. 2006. Circ. 100.

Needs Adventure, fantasy (space fantasy, sword and sorcery), horror (dark fantasy, futuristic, psychological, supernatural), humor/satire, psychic/supernatural/occult, science fiction (hard science/ technological, soft/sociological). Does not want "touchy-feely 'coming of age' stories or stories where the protagonist mopes about contemplating his/her own mortality." Accepts 5-7 mss/issue. Manuscript published 3-9 months after acceptance. **Publishes 2-10 new writers/year.** Published Cliff Ackman (debut), Roger Arnold, Susan Kerr (debut), Kristine Ong Muslim, Tala Bar, CJ Henderson, Danielle Ackley-McPhail. Length: 5,000 words (max). Average length: 3,000 words. Publishes short shorts. Sometimes comments on/critiques rejected mss.

How to Contact Send complete ms with cover letter. Accepts submissions by e-mail. Include estimated word count, brief bio, list of publications. Responds to queries in 1-2 weeks. Responds to mss in 1-10 weeks. Send either SASE (or IRC) for return of ms or disposable copy of ms and #10 SASE for reply only. Considers simultaneous submissions, previously published submissions. Sample copy available for $4 or on Web site. Guidelines available for SASE, via e-mail, on Web site.

Payment/Terms Writers receive 1 contributor copy. Additional copies $2.50. Pays on publication. Acquires one-time rights. Publication is copyrighted.

Tips "If your story is about a 13-year-old girl coping with the change to womanhood while poignantly reflecting the recent passing of her favorite aunt, then we *don't* want it. However, if your story is about the 13-year-old daughter of a vampire cowboy who stumbles upon a government conspiracy involving unicorns and aliens while investigating the grizzly murder of her favorite aunt, then we'll look at it. Please read the magazine to see what we want. Love your story, but listen to advice."

◪ ◎ TRANSCENDENT VISIONS

Toxic Evolution Press, 251 S. Olds Blvd., 84-E, Fairless Hills PA 19030-3426. (215)547-7159. **Contact:** David Kime, editor. Zine: letter size; 50-60 pages; Xerox paper; illustrations. "*Transcendent Visions* is a literary zine by and for people who have been labeled mentally ill. Our purpose is to illustrate that we are creative and articulate people." Annual. Estab. 1992. Circ. 250.

• *Transcendent Visions* has received excellent reviews in many underground publications.

Needs Experimental, feminist, gay, humor/satire, lesbian. Especially interested in material dealing with mental illness. "I do not like stuff one would find in a mainstream publication. No porn." Would like to see more "quirky, non-mainstream fiction." Receives 5 unsolicited mss/month. Accepts 7 mss/year. Publishes ms 3-8 months after acceptance. Recently published work by White Elephant, Gabe Kaufman, Jamey Damert, Marc Pernaino, Teacup Mary, K.J. Kabza, and Arthur Longworth. Publishes short shorts. Also publishes poetry.

How to Contact Send complete ms with cover letter. Include half-page bio. Send disposable copy of ms. Responds in 3-4 months to mss. Accepts simultaneous submissions and reprints. Sample copy for $3.

Payment/Terms Pays 1 contributor's copy. Pays on publication for one-time rights.

Tips "We like unusual stories that are quirky. We like shorter pieces. Please do not go on and on about what zines you have been published in or awards you have won, etc. We just want to read your material, not know your life story. Please don't swamp me with tons of submissions. Send up to five stories. Please print or type your name and address."

◪ ◎ $ WATERMEN

Fine & Finer Graphic, 2428 Gramercy Ave, Torrance CA 90501. (310) 850-6431. E-mail: tomlockie@ sbcglobal.net. Website: http://freedivingfilms.com/watermen.htm. **Contact:** Tom Lockie, Editor. Magazine. 8.5 × 11, 32 pages. Contains illustrations. Includes photographs. "Watermen is a term referring to the lifeguarding, bodysurfing, surfing, spearfishing, SCUBA diving lifestyle. The magazine is dedicated to the ocean lifestyle, arts, fashion and sports: diving, surfing, kayaking, paddleboating, underwater photography. We publish stories and articles dealing with adventure travel and above all ecological issues—protecting oceans and water health. Also publishes medical articles, travel articles, poems and short stories." Semiannual. Estab. 2006. Circ. 5,000.

Needs Adventure, humor/satire, literary, mainstream. Special interests: watersport stories. Receives 10-

12 mss/month. Accepts 2-3 mss/issue; 4-6 mss/year. Ms published 1-5 months after acceptance. Agented fiction 10%. **Publishes 1-2 new writers/year.** Published Brian Donahue and Matteo Verna. Length: 500-1,500 words. Average length: 1,200 words. Publishes short shorts. Average length of short shorts: 400-500 words. Also publishes book reviews, poetry. Send review copies to Tom Lockie; has to be watersport based. Sometimes comments on/critiques rejected mss.

How to Contact Accepts submissions by e-mail only. Please query first. Include brief bio. Responds to queries in 3 weeks. Responds to mss in 1 months. Sample copy free with 812X11 SASE and $2.60 postage. Guidelines available via e-mail.

Payment/Terms Writers receive $20 per page. Additional copies $5 & $1.90 postage. Pays on publication. Acquires electronic rights, archive rights. Publication is not copyrighted.

Tips "Writer must be seriously involved in watersports to stand out. Pay some heavy dues in the water."

☑ $ WEIRD TALES

Business Office: 9710 Traville Gateway Drive #234, Rockville MD 20850. Editorial address (all fiction submissions): P.O. Box 38190, Tallahassee FL 32315. E-mail: weirdtales@gmail.com. Website: www. weirdtales.net. **Contact:** Ann VanderMeer, fiction editor. Magazine: 8½ × 11; 80-96 pages; white, newsprint paper; glossy 4-color cover; illustrations and comics. "We publish fantastic fiction, supernatural horror for an adult audience." Published 6 times a year. Estab. 1923. Circ. 5,000.

Needs Fantasy (sword and sorcery), horror, psychic/supernatural/occult, translations. No hard science fiction or non-fantasy. "Looking for darkly fantastical fiction, work that is unique and unusual. Stories that are recognized as Weird Tales for the 21st Century." Receives 1,200 unsolicited mss/month. Accepts 8 mss/issue; 48 mss/year. Publishes ms 6-18 months after acceptance. Agented fiction 10%. **Publishes 8 new writers/year.** Recently published work by Michael Moorcock, Tanith Lee, Thomas Ligotti, Darrell Schweitzer, Sarah Monette and Michael Boatman. Length: up to 10,000 words, but very few longer than 8,000; average length: 4,000 words. Publishes short shorts.

How to Contact Send complete ms. You must include SASE for reply and return of ms or send a disposable copy of ms with SASE. Responds in 6-8 weeks to mss. Accepts simultaneous submissions. No multiple submissions. Also accepts email submissions to weirdtales@gmail.com. If sending via e-mail please note: have the first 3-4 paragraphs pasted into the body of the email and the entire document attached, either as a PC Word document or an RTF file. Sample copy for $6. Writer's guidelines for #10 SASE or by e-mail. Reviews books of fantasy fiction.

Payment/Terms Pays 3-4¢/word and 2 contributor's copies on acceptance. Acquires first North American serial, plus anthology option rights.

Tips "Traditional fantasy tropes are fine as long as it's a new and different take on the genre. Do not send any familiar story lines and do not send any pastiches of Lovecraft."

☑ ◎ $ THE WILLOWS

E-mail: editor@thewillowsmagazine.com. Website: www.thewillowsmagazine.com. **Contact:** Ben Thomas, lead editor. Literary magazine/journal. 8½ × 11, 70-90 pages, matte paper, glossy cover. Contains illustrations. "Founded to give voice to a unique but neglected corner of horror literature, The Willows strives to publish only the best in true classic-style weird fiction. We pride ourselves on our gentlemanly aesthetic, as well as our love of mad science, strange monstrosities, and ethereal wonder. Our readers share our passion for this bygone age, and the scientific romances of its greatest literary minds." Bimonthly. Estab. 2007. Circ. 50.

Needs Horror (dark fantasy, supernatural). Special interests: classic-style weird fiction. Does not want gory horror, slashers, splatterpunk, or "anything not fitting to be told over brandy in a gentleman's lounge in 1920s London." Receives 50-60 mss/month. Accepts 10 mss/issue; 60 mss/year. Manuscript published 2-4 months after acceptance. **Publishes 5 new writers/year.** Published Paul Melniczek, Charles Muir, Paul Marlowe, Nike Bourke, Nickolas Cook, G.W. Thomas, Lawrence Dagstine, Kristine Ong Muslim, Sarah Monette, and Steven Shrewsbury. Length: 1,000-5,500 words. Average length: 3,500 words. Publishes short shorts. Average length of short shorts: 500 words. Also publishes literary essays, literary criticism, poetry. Often comments on/critiques rejected mss.

How to Contact Send complete ms with cover letter. Accepts submissions by e-mail. Include estimated word count, brief bio, list of publications, expression of interest in the classic weird tale genre. Responds to queries in 2 weeks. Responds to mss in 1 month. Considers previously published submissions.

Guidelines available on Web site.

Payment/Terms Writers receive $25. Additional copies $5 each. Pays on publication. Acquires first North American serial rights. Sends galleys to author. Publication is copyrighted.

Tips "We love work set in Victorian times, in the European countryside, in a twisted fairyland, in the underbelly of an enchanted city, or in the ruins of an undiscovered civilization. We want tales of cosmic fright; eerie fireside memories of nature's deadly mystery; adventures among the aether, the hemera, the spirit realm; tragedies of mad academics who take science too far; warnings of monstrosities that lurk in the sea, in the air, beneath the ground; stories of strange mechanical devices with unholy purposes; or anything else fitting the classic weird motifs. We do not accept stories set in postmodern times. This means nothing after the 1940s. In fact, we prefer stories that are timeless, or at least set in Victorian or Edwardian times. Weird fiction does not merely mean 'stories that are weird.' Weird Fiction refers to a specific genre, and if this genre is one with which you are unfamiliar, we ask that you not submit here until you have become sufficiently familiar."

☑ $ ZAHIR,

Zahir Publishing, 315 South Coast Hwy. 101, Suite U8, Encinitas CA 92024. E-mail: stempchin@zahirtales. com. Website: www.zahirtales.com. **Contact:** Sheryl Tempchin, editor. Magazine: Digest-size; 80 pages; heavy stock paper; glossy, full color cover stock. "We publish literary speculative fiction." Triannual. Estab. 2003.

Needs Fantasy, literary, psychic/supernatural/occult, science fiction, surrealism, magical realism. No children's stories, excessive violence or pornography. Accepts 6-8 mss/issue; 18-24 mss/year. Publishes ms 2-12 months after acceptance. **Publishes 6 new writers/year.** Sometimes comments on rejected mss.

How to Contact Send complete ms. Send SASE (or IRC) for return of ms, or send disposable copy of the ms and #10 SASE for reply only. E-mail queries okay. No e-mail mss except from writers living outside the U.S. Responds in 1-2 weeks to queries; 1-3 months to mss. Accepts reprints submissions. No simultaneous submissions. Sample copy for $8 (US), $8.50 (Canada) or $10.50 (International). Writer's guidelines for #10 SASE, by e-mail, or online.

Payment/Terms Pays $10 and 2 contributor's copies. Pays on publication for first, second serial (reprint) rights.

Tips "The stories we are most likely to buy are well written, have interesting, well-developed characters and/or ideas that fascinate, chill, thrill, or amuse us. They must have some element of the fantastic or surreal."

Online Markets

As production and distribution costs go up and the number of subscribers falls, more and more magazines are giving up print publication and moving online. Relatively inexpensive to maintain and quicker to accept and post submissions, online fiction sites are growing fast in numbers and legitimacy. The benefit for writers is that your stories can get more attention in online journals than in small literary journals. Small journals have small print runs—500-1,000 copies—so there's a limit on how many people will read your work. There is no limit when your work appears online.

There is also no limit to the types on online journals being published, offering outlets for a rich and diverse community of voices. These include genre sites, particular those for science fiction/fantasy and horror, and mainstream short fiction markets. Online literary journals range from the traditional to those with a decidedly more quirky bent. Writers will also find online outlets for more highly experimental and multimedia work.

While the medium of online publication is different, the traditional rules of publishing apply to submissions. Writers should research the site and archives carefully, looking for a match in sensibility for their work. Follow submission guidelines exactly and submit courteously. True, these sites aren't bound by traditional print schedules, so your work theoretically may be published more quickly. But that doesn't mean online journals have larger staffs, so exercise patience with editors considering your manuscript.

Also, while reviewing the listings in this market section, notice they are grouped differently from other market listings. In our Literary Magazines section, for example, you'll find primarily publications searching for only literary short fiction. But Online Markets are grouped by medium, so you'll find publishers of mystery short stories listed next to those looking for horror next to those specializing in flash fiction, so review with care. In addition, online markets with print counterparts can be found listed in the print markets sections.

A final note about online publication: Like literary journals, the majority of these markets are either nonpaying or very low paying. In addition, writers will not receive print copies of the publications because of the medium. So in most cases, do not expect to be paid for your exposure.

5-TROPE

E-mail: editor.5trope@gmail.com. Website: www.5trope.com. **Contact:** Gunnar Benediktsson, editor. Online literary journal. "We aim to publish the new and original in fiction, poetry and new media. We are seeking writers with a playful seriousness about language and form." Quarterly. Estab. 1999. Circ. 5,000.

Needs Avant-garde prose, experimental, literary. "No religious, horror, fantasy, espionage." Receives 75 unsolicited mss/month. Accepts 6 mss/issue; 18 mss/year. Publishes ms 6-12 months after acceptance. **Publishes 5 new writers/year.** Recently published work by Cole Swensen, Carol Novack, Christopher Kennedy, Mike Topp, Norman Lock, Jeff Johnson, Peter Markus, Mandee Wright, and Jane Unrue. Length: 25-5,000 words; average length: 1,000 words. Publishes short shorts. Also publishes poetry. Sometimes comments on rejected mss.

How to Contact Accepts submissions by e-mail. Send complete mss electronically. Sample copy online.

Payment/Terms Acquires first rights. Sends galleys to author.

Tips "Before submitting, please visit our site, read an issue, and consult our guidelines for submission. Include your story within the body of an e-mail, not as an attachment. Include a descriptive subject line to get around spam filters. Experimental work should have a clarity about it, and should never be sentimental. Our stories are about the moment of rupture, not the moment of closure."

☑ THE 13TH WARRIOR REVIEW

Asterius Press, P.O. Box 5122, Seabrook NJ 08302-3511. E-mail: theeditor@asteriusonline.com. Website: www.13thwr.org. **Contact:** John C. Erianne, publisher/editor. Online magazine. Estab. 2000.

Needs Literary/mainstream, erotica, experimental, magical realism, meta-fiction. Receives 500 unsolicited mss/month. Accepts 4-8 mss/issue; 10-15 mss/year. Publishes ms 6 months after acceptance. **Publishes 1-2 new writers/year.** Recently published work by Cindy Rosmus, Jeff Blechle, Elizabeth Farren, and Andrew Hellem. Length: 500-6,000 words; average length: 1,800 words. Publishes short shorts. Also publishes literary essays, literary criticism, poetry, and book reviews. Sometimes comments on rejected mss.

How to Contact Send complete ms. Include estimated word count, brief bio and address/e-mail. Send SASE or IRC for return of ms or send a disposable copy of ms and #10 SASE for reply only. Accepts submissions by e-mail (will accept file attachments, but prefers text in message body). Responds in 1 week to queries; 1-2 months to mss. Accepts simultaneous submissions. Sample copy online at www.13thwr.org. Reviews fiction.

Payment/Terms Acquires first rights, Internet archival rights.

☑ THE ADIRONDACK REVIEW

Black Lawrence Press, 8405 Bay Parkway #C8, c/o Diane Goettel, Brooklyn NY 11214. E-mail: tar@blacklawrencepress.com. Website: http://adirondackreview.homestead.com. **Contact:** Diane Goettel, editor. Online literary magazine/journal. Contains illustrations & photographs. Estab. 2000.

Needs Adventure, experimental, family saga, gay, historical (general), psychological, translations. Does not want SciFi, fantasy. Receives over 200 mss/month. Accepts 5-10 mss/issue; 20-30 mss/year. Manuscript published 1-5 months after acceptance. Agented fiction 5%. **Publishes 15% new writers/year.** Published Frank Haberle, Steve Gillis, Melinda Misrala, Kate Swoboda. Length: 700-8,000 words. Average length: 2,000 words. Publishes short shorts. Average length of short shorts: 800 words. Also publishes literary essays, literary criticism, book reviews, poetry. Send review copies to Diane Goettel. Rarely comments on/critiques rejected mss.

How to Contact Send complete ms with cover letter. Accepts submissions by e-mail. Include estimated word count, brief bio, list of publications, and "how they learned about the magazine." Responds to queries in 1-2 months. Responds to mss in 2-4 months. Send either SASE (or IRC) for return of ms or disposable copy of ms and #10 SASE for reply only. Considers simultaneous submissions, multiple submissions.

Payment/Terms Acquires first rights. Sponsors contests. See Web site for details.

☑ $ ALIENSKIN MAGAZINE

Froggy Bottom Press, 465 Market St., Beaver PA 15009. E-mail: alienskin@alienskinmag.com. Website: www.alienskinmag.com. **Contact:** Feature fiction: Kay Patterson; Flash fiction: Phil Adams. Online magazine. "Our magazine was created for, and strives to help, aspiring writers of SFFH. We endeavor to promote genre writers." Bimonthly. Estab. 2002. Circ. 2,800 + internet.

Needs Fantasy (dark fantasy, sword and sorcery), horror (dark fantasy, futuristic, psychological, psychic/supernatural/occult), science fiction (hard science/technological, soft/sociological). "No excessive blood, gore, erotica, vulgarity or child abuse. No experimental or speculative fiction that does not use basic story elements of character, conflict, action and resolution. No esoteric ruminations." Receives 250-400 unsolicited mss/month. Accepts 30-37 mss/issue; 180-222 mss/year. Publishes ms 30-60 days after acceptance. **Publishes 24-48 new writers/year.** Recently published work by Jason Brannon, Todd Austin Hunt, Mark Lee Pearson, Ginger Burton. Length: 500-1,000 words; average length: 995 words. Publishes micro fiction of exactly 150 words and Fibonacci sequence poetry (6 lines, 20 syllables). Always comments on rejected mss.

How to Contact Send complete ms. Accepts submissions by e-mail only. Include estimated word count, brief bio, name, address, and e-mail address. Responds in 1-2 weeks to queries; 2 months to mss. Accepts multiple submissions; no simultaneous submissions or previously published material. Sample copy and writer's guidelines online.

Payment/Terms $10 flat fee for 500-1,000 words. Exposure only for for 150 word micro fiction and Fibonacci poetry. Pays on publication for first, electronic rights. Sponsors a pro-payment contest each year.

Tips "We look for interesting stories, offer ing something unique; stories that use basic story elements of character, conflict, action and resolution. We like the dark, twisted side of SFFH genres. Read our guidelines and follow the rules. Treat the submission process as a serious business transaction. Only send stories that have been spell-checked, and proofread at least twice. Try to remember: editors who offer a critique on manuscripts do so to help you as a writer, not to hamper or dissuade you as a writer."

▢ ◉ $ ⚑ ALLEGORY

(formerly Peridot Books) 1225 Liberty Bell Dr., Cherry Hill NJ 08003. E-mail: submissions@allegoryezine.com. Website: www.allegoryezine.com. **Contact:** Ty Drago, editor. Online magazine specializing in science fiction, fantasy and horror. "We are an e-zine by writers for writers. Our articles focus on the art, craft and business of writing. Our links and editorial policy all focus on the needs of fiction authors." Triannual. Estab. 1998.

• Peridot Books won the Page One Award for Literary Contribution.

Needs Fantasy (space fantasy, sword and sorcery, sociological), horror (dark fantasy, futuristic, supernatural), science fiction (hard science/technological, soft/sociological). "No media tie-ins (Star Trek, Star Wars, etc., or space opera, vampires)." Receives 150 unsolicited mss/month. Accepts 8 mss/issue; 24 mss/year. Publishes ms 1-2 months after acceptance. Agented fiction 5%. **Publishes 10 new writers/year.** Length: 1,500-7,500 words; average length: 4,500 words. Also publishes literary essays, literary criticism. Often comments on rejected mss.

How to Contact Send complete ms with a cover letter, electronic only. Include estimated word count, brief bio, list of publications and name and e-mail address in the body of the story. Responds in 8 weeks to mss. Accepts simultaneous submissions and reprints. Writer's guidelines online.

Payment/Terms $15/story-article. Pays on publication for one-time, electronic rights.

Tips "Give us something original, preferably with a twist. Avoid gratuitous sex or violence. Funny always scores points. Be clever, imaginative, but be able to tell a story with proper mood and characterization. Put your name and e-mail address in the body of the story. Read the site and get a feel for it before submitting."

▣ ⚑ ANDERBO.COM

Anderbo Publishing, 270 Lafayette St. Suite 1412, New York NY 10012-3364. (917) 705-4081. Fax: (212) 777-3400. E-mail: editors@anderbo.com. Website: www.anderbo.com. **Contact:** Rick Rofihe, editor-in-chief. Online literary magazine/journal. "Quality fiction, poetry, 'fact' and photography on a Web site with 'print-feel' design." Estab. 2005. Member CLMP.

• Received the Best New Online Magazine or Journal, *storySouth* Million Writers Award in 2005.

Needs Literary. Does not want any genre literature. "We're interested only in literary fiction, poetry, and literary 'fact.'" Receives 120 mss/month. Accepts 14 mss/year. Ms published one month after acceptance. **Publishes 6 new writers/year.** Published Lisa Margonelli, Lucille Lang Day, Martha Wilson and Susan Breen. Length: 3,500 words (max). Average length: 2,600 words. Publishes short shorts. Average length of short shorts: 1,400 words. Also publishes literary essays, poetry. Rarely comments on/ critiques rejected mss.

How to Contact Send complete ms with cover letter. Accepts submissions by e-mail. Include brief bio, list of publications. Responds to queries in 2 weeks. Responds to mss in 2 weeks. Considers simultaneous submissions. Guidelines available on Web site.

Payment/Terms Acquires first rights, first North American serial rights, one-time rights, electronic rights. Publication is copyrighted.

Tips "We are looking for fiction that is unique, urgent, accessible and involving. Look at our site and read what we've already published."

APPLE VALLEY REVIEW, A JOURNAL OF CONTEMPORARY LITERATURE

Queen's Postal Outlet, Box 12, Kingston ON K7L 3R9 Canada. E-mail: editor@leahbrowning.net. Website: www.applevalleyreview.com. **Contact:** Leah Browning, editor. Online literary magazine. Includes photographs/artwork on cover. "Each issue features a selection of beautifully crafted poetry, short fiction and essays. We prefer work that has both mainstream and literary appeal. As such, we avoid erotica, work containing explicit language and anything violent or extremely depressing. Our audience includes teens and adults of all ages." Semiannual. Estab. 2005. Member CLMP.

Needs Ethnic/multicultural (general), experimental, humor/satire, literary, mainstream, regional (American South, Southwest), translations, literary women's fiction (e.g. Barbara Kingsolver, Anne Tyler, Lee Smith, Elinor Lipman, Perri Klass). Does not want strict genre fiction, erotica, work containing explicit language, or anything violent or extremely depressing. Receives 50+ mss/month. Accepts 1-3 mss/issue; 2-12 mss/year. Manuscript published 3-6 months after acceptance. Published Miriam Sagan, Barry Jay Kaplan, Jenny Steele, Kerri Quinn, Patricia Gosling. Length: 100-3,000 words. Average length: 2,000 words. Publishes short shorts. Average length of short shorts: 1,200 words. Also publishes literary essays, poetry. Sometimes comments on/critiques rejected mss.

How to Contact Send complete ms with cover letter. Accepts submissions only via e-mail. Include estimated word count, brief bio. Responds to mss in 1 week-3 months. Considers multiple submissions. Guidelines available on Web site. Sample copy on Web site.

Payment/Terms Acquires first rights, right to archive online. Publication is copyrighted.

Tips "Excellent writing always makes a manuscript stand out. Beyond that, I look for stories and poems that I want to read again, and that I want to give to someone else to read—work so interesting for one reason or another that I feel compelled to share it. Please read at least some of the previously published work to get a feel for our style, and follow the submission guidelines as closely as possible. We accept submissions only via e-mail."

ASCENT ASPIRATIONS

Ascent Aspirations Magazine, 1560 Arbutus Dr., Nanoose Bay BC C9P 9C8 Canada. E-mail: ascentaspirations@shaw.com. Website: www.ascentaspirations.ca. **Contact:** David Fraser, editor. E-zine specializing in short fiction (all genres) and poetry, essays, visual art: 40 electronic pages; illustrations; photos. Ascent publishes two additional issues in print each year. "Ascent Aspirations Magazine publishes quarterly online and semi-annually in print. The print issues are operated as contests. Please refer to current guidelines before submitting. Ascent Aspirations is a quality electronic publication dedicated to the promotion and encouragement of aspiring writers of any genre. The focus however is toward interesting experimental writing in dark mainstream, literary, science fiction, fantasy and horror. Poetry can be on any theme. Essays need to be unique, current and have social, philosophical commentary." Quarterly online. Estab. 1997.

Needs Erotica, experimental, fantasy (space fantasy), feminist, horror (dark fantasy, futuristic, psychological, supernatural), literary, mainstream, mystery/suspense, New Age, psychic/supernatural/ occult, science fiction (hard science/technological, soft/sociological). Receives 100-200 unsolicited mss/ month. Accepts 40 mss/issue; 240 mss/year. Publishes ms 3 months after acceptance. **Publishes 10-50 new writers/year.** Recently published work by Taylor Graham, Janet Buck, Jim Manton, Steve Cartwright, Don Stockard, Penn Kemp, Sam Vargo, Vernon Waring, Margaret Karmazin, Bill Hughes. Length: 1,000 words or less. Publishes short shorts. Also publishes literary essays, literary criticism, poetry. Sometimes comments on rejected mss.

How to Contact "Query by e-mail with Word attachment." Include estimated word count, brief bio and list of publications. If you have to submit by mail because it is your only avenue, provide a SASE with either International Coupons or Canadian stamps only. Responds in 1 week to queries; 3 months to mss. Accepts simultaneous, multiple submissions, and reprints. Guidelines by e-mail or on Web site. Reviews fiction and poetry collections.

Payment/Terms "No payment at this time. Rights remain with author."

Tips "Short fiction should, first of all tell, a good story, take the reader to new and interesting imaginary or real places. Short fiction should use language lyrically and effectively, be experimental in either form or content and take the reader into realms where they can analyze and think about the human condition. Write with passion for your material, be concise and economical and let the reader work to unravel your story. In terms of editing, always proofread to the point where what you submit is the best it possibly can be. Never be discouraged if your work is not accepted; it may just not be the right fit for a current publication."

☐ ◎ $ ⊞ ATOMJACK

Susurrus Press, 409 Alabama Street, Huntington WV 25704. (304) 634-9867. E-mail: atomjackmagazine@yahoo.com. Website: http://atomjackmagazine.com. **Contact:** Adicus Ryan Garton, editor. Online magazine. Contains illustrations. Includes photographs. "There are many online science fiction magazines, but they rarely combine a visual aesthetic with powerful stories. Atomjack, being a Susurrus publication, strives to achieve the prominence and quality of big print magazines in a free online publication. Atomjack is aimed at adults, as some stories have excessive violence or language unsuited for most children." Quarterly. Estab. 2006. Circ. 300-600 viewers per month.

Needs Comics/graphic novels, fantasy (space fantasy, science fantasy), horror (futuristic), science fiction (hard science/technological, soft/sociological). Does not want any stories that do NOT contain an element of science fiction."Atomjack very rarely considers romance or erotic stories, though we do not entirely discount them." List of upcoming themes available for SASE, on Web site. Receives 200 mss/month. Accepts 8-12 mss/issue; 40 mss/year. Ms published 2 months after acceptance. **Publishes 10 new writers/year.** Published Lawrence Dagstine, Kristine Ong Muslim, Anthony Bernstein, Amanda Underwood, and Cameron Pierce. Length: 100 words-5,000 words. Average length: 3,500 words. Publishes short shorts. Average length of short shorts: 500 words. Also publishes literary criticism. Always comments on/critiques rejected mss.

How to Contact Send complete ms with cover letter. Accepts submissions by e-mail only. Include estimated word count, brief bio. Responds to queries in 2 weeks. Responds to mss in 3 months. Considers simultaneous submissions, previously published submissions, multiple submissions. Sample copy, guidelines available on Web site.

Payment/Terms Writers receive $20. Pays on publication. Acquires electronic rights. Sends galleys to author. Publication is not copyrighted.

Tips "Character development and plot are the most important aspect of an *Atomjack* story. We routinely publish stories that have great characters in unique situations in what may not be an original SF environment. We also reject many stories with an amazing concept but no story to reinforce it. Atomjack occasionally gives a curt response for some stories. Queries about rejections welcome. Re-submit. Atomjack has published stories that were rewritten with the critique in mind and re-submitted."

BABEL, the Multilingual, Multicultural Online Journal and Community of Arts and Ideas

E-mail: submissions@towerofbabel.com. Website: www.towerofbabel.com. **Contact**: Malcolm Lawrence, Editor-in-Chief. Electronic zine. "Recognized by the United Nations as one of the most important social and human sciences online periodicals." Publishes "regional reports from international stringers all over the planet, as well as features, round table discussions, fiction, columns, poetry, erotica, travelogues, and reviews of all of the arts and editorials. We are an online community involving an extensive group of artists, writers, programmers and translators representing 250 of the world's languages."

Needs "There are no specifc categories of fiction we are not interested in. Possible exceptions: lawyers/vampires, different genders hailing from different planets, cold war military scenarios and things that go bump in the suburban night." Recently published work by Nicholas P. Snoek, Yves Jaques, Doug Williamson, A.L. Fern, Laura Feister, Denzel J. Hankinson, and Pete Hanson.

How to Contact Send queries/mss by email. "Please send submissions with a resumé/cover letter or biography attached to the email." Reviews novels and short story collections.

Tips "We would like to see more fiction with first-person male characters written by female authors, as well as more fiction first-person female characters written by male authors. We would also like to see that dynamic in action when it comes to other languages, cultures, races, classes, sexual orientations and ages. The best advice we could give to writers wanting to be published in our publication is simply to know what you are writing about and write passionately about it."

▦ ☑ ☑ THE BARCELONA REVIEW

Correu Vell 12-2, Barcelona 08002 Spain. (00) 34 93 319 15 96. E-mail: editor@barcelonareview.com. Website: www.barcelonareview.com. **Contact:** Jill Adams, editor. "TBR is an international review of contemporary, cutting-edge fiction published in English, Spanish and Catalan. Our aim is to bring both new and established writers to the attention of a larger audience. Well-known writers such as Alicia Erian in the U.S., Michel Faber in the U.K., Carlos Gardini in Argentina, and Nuria Amat in Spain, for example, were not known outside their countries until appearing in TBR. Our multilingual format increases the audience all the more. Internationally known writers, such as Irvine Welsh and Douglas Coupland, have contributed stories that ran in small press anthologies available only in one country. We try to keep abreast of what's happening internationally and to present the best finds every two months. Our intended audience is anyone interested in high-quality contemporary fiction that often (but not always) veers from the mainstream; we assume that our readers are well read and familiar with contemporary fiction in general."

Needs Short fiction. "Our bias is towards potent and powerful cutting-edge material; given that general criteria, we are open to all styles and techniques and all genres. No slice-of-life stories, vignettes or reworked fables, and nothing that does not measure up, in your opinion, to the quality of work in our review, which we expect submitters to be familiar with." **Publishes 20 new writers/year.** Recently published work by Niall Griffiths, Adam Haslett, G.K. Wuori, Adam Johnson, Mary Wornov, Emily Carter, Jesse Shepard and Julie Orringer.

How to Contact Send submissions by e-mail as an attached file. Hard copies accepted but cannot be returned. No simultaneous submissions.

Payment/Terms "In lieu of pay we offer a highly professional Spanish translation to English language writers and vice versa to Spanish writers."

Tips "Send top drawer material that has been drafted two, three, four times—whatever it takes. Then sit on it for a while and look at it afresh. Keep the text tight. Grab the reader in the first paragraph and don't let go. Keep in mind that a perfectly crafted story that lacks a punch of some sort won't cut it. Make it new, make it different. Surprise the reader in some way. Read the best of the short fiction available in your area of writing to see how yours measures up. Don't send anything off until you feel it's ready and then familiarize yourself with the content of the review/magazine to which you are submitting."

☑ BLACKBIRD

Virginia Commonwealth University Department of English, P.O. Box 843082, Richmond VA 23284. (804)225-4729. E-mail: blackbird@vcu.edu. Website: www.blackbird.vcu.edu. **Contact:** Mary Flinn, Gregory Donovan, editors. Online journal: 80+ pages if printed; illustrations; photos. "We strive to maintain the highest quality of writing and design, bringing the best things about a print magazine to the outside world. We publish fiction that is carefully crafted, thoughtful and suprising." Semiannual. Estab. 2001. Circ. 30,000 readers per month.

Needs Literary, novel excerpts. Does not want science fiction, religious/inspirational, condensed novels, horror, romance, children's. Receives 400-600 unsolicited mss/month. Accepts 4-5 mss/issue; 8-10 mss/year. Does not read from April 15- September 15. Publishes ms 3-6 months after acceptance. **Publishes 1-2 new writers/year.** Length: 5,000-10,000 words; average length: 5,000-6,500 words. Also publishes literary essays, literary criticism, poetry. Sometimes comments on rejected mss.

How to Contact Send complete ms. In clude cover letter, name, address, telephone number, brief biographical comment. Responds in 6 months to mss. Accepts simultaneous submissions. Sample copy online. Writer's guidelines online.

Payment/Terms Pays $200 for fiction, $40 for poetry. Pays on publication for first North American serial rights.

Tips "We like a story that invites us into its world, that engages our senses, soul and mind."

Online Markets

$ BURST

Terra Media, LLC. E-mail: burst@terra-media.us. Website: www.terra-media.us/burst. **Contact:** Kevin Struck, editor. E-zine. "Burst is a literary e-zine specifically designed for mobile devices, such as cell phones. Content must be short, entertaining, and get to the point. Material that is ambiguous and meaningful only to the writer is not for us. Specialize in flash fiction." Estab. 2006.

Needs Adventure, experimental, fantasy, humor/satire, mainstream, mystery, romance, science fiction. Accepts 35 mss/year. Ms published 3 months after acceptance. Length: 50-700 words.

How to Contact Accepts submissions only by e-mail. Responds to queries in 3 weeks. Considers simultaneous submissions, previously published submissions. Guidelines available on Web site.

Payment/Terms Acquires one-time rights. Pays flat rate of $10.

$ THE CAFE IRREAL

E-mail: editors@cafeirreal.com. Website: www.cafeirreal.com. **Contact:** Alice Whittenburg, G.S. Evans, editors. E-zine: illustrations. "The Cafe Irreal is a webzine focusing on short stories and short shorts of an irreal nature." Quarterly. Estab. 1998.

Needs Experimental, fantasy (literary), science fiction (literary), translations. "No horror or 'slice-of-life' stories; no genre or mainstream science fiction or fantasy." Accepts 8-10 mss/issue; 30-40 mss/year. Recently published work by Ignacio Padilla, Charles Simic, Michal Ajvaz, Stephanie Hammer, and Norman Lock. Length: 2,000 words (max). Publishes short shorts. Also publishes literary essays, literary criticism. Sometimes comments on rejected mss.

How to Contact Accepts submissions by e-mail. "No attachments, include submission in body of e-mail. Include estimated word count." Responds in 2-4 months to mss. No simultaneous submissions. Sample copy online. Writer's guidelines online.

Payment/Terms Pays 1¢/word, $2 minimum. Pays on publication for first-time electronic rights. Sends galleys to author.

Tips "Forget formulas. Write about what you don't know, take me places I couldn't possibly go, don't try to make me care about the characters. Read short fiction by writers such as Franz Kafka, Kobo Abe, Donald Barthelme, Mangnus Mills, Ana Maria Shua and Stanislaw Lem. Also read our Web site and guidelines."

CEZANNE'S CARROT, A LITERARY JOURNAL OF FRESH OBSERVATIONS

Spiritual, Transformational & Visionary Art, Inc., P.O. Box 6037, Santa Fe NM 87502-6037. E-mail: query@cezannescarrot.org. Website: www.cezannescarrot.org. **Contact:** Barbara Jacksha and Joan Kremer, editors. Online magazine. "Cezanne's Carrot publishes fiction, creative nonfiction, and art that explores spiritual, transformational, visionary, metaphysical or contemplative themes. We publish work that explores the higher, more expansive aspects of human nature, the integration of inner and outer worlds, and the exciting thresholds where the familiar meets the unknown." Quarterly. Estab. 2005.

Needs Experimental, fantasy (speculative), literary, new age, psychic/supernatural/occult, science fiction (soft/sociological), magical realism, irrealism, visionary, surrealism, metaphysical, spiritual. "Does not want horror, gore, murder, serial-killers, abuse stories, drug stories, vampires or other monsters, political stories, war stories, stories written for children, stories that primarily promote an agenda or a particular religion. We're not interested in dogma in any form." Receives 100 mss/month. Accepts 10-15 mss/issue; 40-60 mss/year. Manuscript published 4-12 weeks after acceptance. **Publishes 1-5 new writers/year.** Published Bruce Holland Rogers, Tamara Kaye Sellman, Utahna Faith, Margaret Frey, Corey Mesler, Christine Boyka kluge, and Charles P. Ries. Length: 100 words (min)-3,000 words (max). Average length: 1,800 words. Publishes short shorts.

How to Contact Send complete ms with cover letter. Accepts submissions by e-mail only. Include estimated word count, brief bio, list of publications. Responds to mss in 1-4 months. Considers simultaneous submissions, previously published submissions. Guidelines available on Web site.

Payment/Terms Acquires one-time rights, reprint rights.

Tips "We only accept work with a strong tie to our journal's mission and theme. Read our guidelines and mission statement carefully. Read previous issues to understand the kind of work we're looking for. Only submissions sent to the correct e-mail address will be considered."

⬕ ☑ ◎ $ ⬔ CHIZINE: TREATMENT OF LIGHT AND SHADE IN WORDS

E-mail: savory@rogers.com. Website: www.chizine.com. **Contact:** Brett Alexander Savory, editor-in-chief. E-zine. "Subtle, sophisticated dark fiction with a literary bent." Quarterly. Estab. 1997.

• Received Bram Stoker Award for Other Media in 2000

Needs Experimental, fantasy, horror (dark fantasy, futuristic, psychological, supernatural), literary, mystery, science fiction (soft/sociological), Does not want "tropes of vampires, werewolves, mummies, monsters, or anything that's been done to death." Receives 100 mss/month. Accepts 3-4 mss/issue; 12-16 mss/year. Does not read June, July and August due to Chizine/Leisure Short Story Contest. Length: 4,000 words (max). Publishes short shorts. Average length of short shorts: 500 words. Also publishes poetry. Send to savory@rogers.com to query. Always comments on/critiques rejected mss.

How to Contact Send complete ms with cover letter. Accepts only submissions by e-mail. Include estimated word count, brief bio. Responds to queries in 1 week. Responds to mss within 3 months. Considers simultaneous submissions so long as we're told it is simultaneous. Guidelines available on Web site.

Payment/Terms Writers receive 7¢/word, with a $280 max. Pays on publication. Acquires all rights for 90 days, then archival rights for one year. Sends any edits to author. Publication is copyrighted. Sponsors the Chizine/Leisure Short Story contest. Guidelines posted on Web site around May. See entry in Contests & Awards section.

▦ ☑ CONTE ONLINE, A JOURNAL OF NARRATIVE WRITING

E-mail: prose@conteonline.net. Website: www.conteonline.net. **Contact:** Robert Lieberman, editor. Online magazine. "We aim to publish narrative writing of all kinds. Relating a sequence of events is a primary method of human communication; we are interested in the narrative form as a means of relating ideas, experiences, and emotions, and we love how the act of telling a story unites the perspectives of listeners and speakers. We are dedicated to the concept of disseminating fresh, stellar writing to as many people as possible, as quickly and as often as possible, hence our online basis. We are enthusiastic about publishing the latest works of writers from all backgrounds and of varying experience. We hope Conte will be a mechanism not only for publication, but communication among writers as well as between readers and authors, and above all that we continue the ancient and perhaps sacred tradition of telling a good yarn." Semiannual. Estab. 2005.

Needs "We'll consider fiction on essentially any topic; our primary focus is the effective use of narrative. We discourage fiction which does not present a clear (sequential or non-sequential) narrative progression; work without a distinctive and engaging plot of some form isn't what we are looking for. We tend to be frustrated by stories that merely raise questions but don't attempt to address them, or that end early without seeming complete." Receives 20-30 mss/month. Accepts 5-7 mss/issue; 10-14 mss/year. Manuscript published 2-3 months or less after acceptance. Agented fiction <5%. **Publishes 4 new writers/year.** Published Joanna Catherine Scott, Louis E. Bourgeois, Adam Sirois, Lyn Lifshin, Steve MacKinnon, James J. Cho, Jessica Murakami, Charles Rafferty, Kristin Berger, R.T. Castleberry and Bertha Rogers. Length: 8,000 words (max). Average length: 5,000 words. Publishes short shorts. Average length of short shorts: 1,000 words. Also publishes poetry. Sometimes comments on/critiques rejected mss.

How to Contact Send complete ms with cover letter. Accepts submissions by e-mail only. Include estimated word count, brief bio. Responds to queries in 3-4 weeks. Responds to mss in 8-10 weeks. Considers simultaneous submissions. Guidelines available via e-mail, on Web site.

Payment/Terms Acquires electronic rights. Sends galleys to author. Publication is not copyrighted.

Tips "We love to see stories that let us take something away—a fact, a perspective, a great bit of dialogue, some piece of the world you create we can keep with us after it's over. Writing that leads us somewhere unexpected is always a delight; immersive worlds and characters are the hallmarks of our favorite fiction. Stories that investigate the overlooked and show us the significance of something often missed are likely to grab our attention. In all, the clarity of the senses you lend us, the adroitness of your storytelling, and the joy we take in reading your tale are the primary barometers of our selection process. Tell your story completely; if you start us on a journey, we want to be taken all the way to the end. Details and imagery are what make a narrative come alive, but try not to lose momentum in them. Have the confidence to tell your story the way it needs to be told; we love reading, so we're already on your side to begin with."

☑ $ CONTRARY

3114 S. Wallace Street, Suite 2, Chicago IL 60616-3299. E-mail: chicago@contrarymagazine.com. Website: www.contrarymagazine.com. **Contact:** Jeff McMahon, editor. Online literary magazine/journal. Contains illustrations. "Contrary publishes fiction, poetry, literary commentary, and prefers work that combines the virtues of all those categories. Founded at the University of Chicago, it now operates independently and not-for-profit on the South Side of Chicago. We like work that is not only contrary in content, but contrary in its evasion of the expectations established by its genre. Our fiction defies traditional story form. For example, a story may bring us to closure without ever delivering an ending. We don't insist on the ending, but we do insiste on the closure. And we value fiction as poetic as any poem." Quarterly. Estab. 2003. Circ. 38,000 unique readers. Member CLMP.

Needs Literary. Receives 650 mss/month. Accepts 3 mss/issue; 12 mss/year. Ms published no more than 21 days after acceptance. **Publishes 1 new writer/year.** Published Andrew Coburn, Thomas King, Clare Kirwan, Liz Prato, Laurence Davies, Edward Mc Whinney, and Amy Reed. Length: 2,000 words (max). Average length: 750 words. Publishes short shorts. Average length of short shorts: 750 words. Also publishes literary essays, poetry. Rarely comments on/critiques rejected mss.

How to Contact Accepts submissions through Web site only. www.contrarymagazine.com/Contrary/Submissions.html. Include estimated word count, brief bio, list of publications. Responds to queries in 2 weeks. Responds to mss in 3 months. Considers simultaneous submissions. Guidelines available on Web site.

Payment/Terms Pays $20-60. Pays on publication. Acquires first rights and perpetual archive and anthology rights. Publication is copyrighted.

Tips "Beautiful writing catches our eye first. If we realize we're in the presence of unanticipated meaning, that's what clinches the deal. Also, we're not fond of expository fiction. We prefer to be seduced by beauty, profundity and mystery than to be presented with the obvious. We look for fiction that entrances, that stays the reader's finger above the mouse button. That is, in part, why we favor microfiction, flash fiction and short-shorts. Also, we hope writers will remember that most editors are looking for very particular species of work. We try to describe our particular species in our mission statement and our submission guidelines, but those descriptions don't always convey nuance. That's why many editors urge writers to read the publication itself; in the hope that they will intuit an understanding of its particularities. If you happen to write that particular species of work we favor, your submission may find a happy home with us. If you don't, it does not necessarily reflect on your quality or your ability. It usually just means that your work has a happier home somewhere else."

☑ CONVERGENCE

E-mail: clinville@csus.edu. Website: www.convergence-journal.com. **Contact:** Cynthia Linville, editor. Convergence seeks to unify the literary and visual arts and draw new interpretations of the written word by pairing poems and flash fiction with complementary art. Quarterly. Estab. 2003. Circ. 400.

Needs Ethnic/multicultural, experimental, feminist, gay, lesbian, literary, regional, translations. Accepts 10 mss/issue. Publishes ms 3 weeks after acceptance. Recently published work by Andrena Zawinski, Grace Cavalieri, Lola Haskins, Molly Fisk, Renato Rosaldo. Publishes short shorts. Also publishes poetry. Sometimes comments on rejected mss.

How to Contact Send complete ms. E-mail submissions only with "Convergence" in subject line. No simultaneous submissions. Responds in 2 weeks to queries; 4 months to mss. Writer's guidelines online.

Payment/Terms Acquires electronic rights.

Tips "We look for freshness and originality and a mastery of the craft of flash fiction."

☑ ◎ THE COPPERFIELD REVIEW

E-mail: info@copperfieldreview.com. Website: www.copperfieldreview.com. **Contact:** Meredith Allard, executive editor. "We are an online literary journal that publishes historical fiction and articles, reviews and interviews related to historical fiction. We believe that by understanding the lessons of the past through historical fiction we can gain better insight into the nature of our society today, as well as a better understanding of ourselves." Quarterly. Estab. 2000.

Needs Historical (general), romance (historical), western (frontier saga, traditional). "We will consider submissions in most fiction categories, but the setting must be historical in nature. We don't want to see anything not related to historical fiction." Receives 30 unsolicited mss/month. Accepts 7-10 mss/issue; 28-40 mss/year. Responds to mss during the months of January, April, July and October. **Publishes "between 30 and 40 percent" new writers/year.** Publishes short shorts. Also publishes literary essays, literary criticism, poetry. Seldom comments on rejected mss.

How to Contact Send complete ms. Accepts submissions by e-mail. Responds in 6 weeks to queries. Accepts simultaneous, multiple submissions and reprints. Sample copy online. Writer's guidelines online. Reviews fiction.

Payment/Terms Acquires one-time rights.

Tips "We wish to showcase the very best in literary historical fiction. Stories that use historical periods and details to illuminate universal truths will immediately stand out. We are thrilled to receive thoughtful work that is polished, poised and written from the heart. Be professional, and only submit your very best work. Be certain to adhere to a publication's submission guidelines, and always treat your e-mail submissions with the same care you would use with a traditional publisher. Above all, be strong and true to your calling as a writer. It is a difficult, frustrating but wonderful journey. It is important for writers to review our online submission guidelines prior to submitting."

◎ THE DEAD MULE

P.O. Box 835, Winterville NC 28590. E-mail: submit.mule@gmail.com. Website: www.deadmule.com. **Contact:** Valerie MacEwan, editor; Rebecca Cowell, fiction editor; or Helen Losse, poetry editor. "The Dead Mule School Alumni Association recruits year 'round. Want to join the freshman class of 2014? Submit today. The Mule proudly claims a long heritage of Southern literary excellence." Estab. 1996.

Needs Fiction, creative nonfiction, interviews with Southerners, essays, poetry. "Always, always, stories about mules."

How to Contact Send complete ms. Accepts submissions by e-mail only at submit.mule@gmail.com. "Read and follow the guidelines online—you need a Southern Legitimacy Statement."

Tips "You are a writer—obviously, or you would not be reading this book. So: remember to follow submission guidelines; match your work to the publication; spellcheck and edit your work before submitting; and don't track mud all over your mother's clean floor. Don't send a personally published blog entry to an online journal—you're wasting good bandwidth when you do that. It's 2010, if sending a .doc is beyond your level of expertise, spend some quality time playing technological catch-up. And remember to be patient, we're Southern, so haste is not a word in our vocabulary. No good Southern fiction is complete without a dead mule."

☑ DIAGRAM

New Michigan Press, 648 Crescent NE, Grand Rapids MI 49503. E-mail: editor@thediagram.com. Website: http://thediagram.com. **Contact:** Ander Monson, editor. "We specialize in work that pushes the boundaries of traditional genre or work that is in some way schematic. We do publish traditional fiction and poetry, too, but hybrid forms (short stories, prose poems, indexes, tables of contents, etc.) are particularly welcome! We also publish diagrams and schematics (original and found). Bimonthly. Estab. 2001. Circ. 200,000 + hits/month. Member CLMP.

Needs Experimental, literary. "We don't publish genre fiction, unless it's exceptional and transcends the genre boundaries." Receives 100 unsolicited mss/month. Accepts 2-3 mss/issue; 15 mss/year. **Publishes 6 new writers/year.** Average length: 250-2,000 words. Publishes short shorts. Also publishes literary essays, poetry. Often comments on rejected mss.

How to Contact Send complete ms. Accepts submissions by Web submissions manager; no e-mail please. Send SASE for return of the ms, or send disposable copy of the ms and #10 SASE for reply only. Responds in 2 weeks to queries; 1-2 months to mss. Accepts simultaneous submissions. Sample copy for $12 for print version. Writer's guidelines online.

Payment/Terms Acquires first, serial, electronic rights.

Tips "We value invention, energy, experimentation and voice. When done very well, we like traditional fiction, too. Nearly all the work we select is propulsive and exciting, but first the sentences have to be beautiful."

☑ DUCTS

P.O. Box 3203, Grand Central Station, New York NY 10163. (718) 383-6728. E-mail: editor@ducts.org.

Website: http://ducts.org. **Contact:** Jonathan Kravetz. DUCTS is a Webzine of personal stories, fiction, essays, memoirs, poetry, humor, profiles, reviews and art. "DUCTS was founded in 1999 with the intent of giving emerging writers a venue to regularly publish their compelling, personal stories. The site has been expanded to include art and creative works of all genres. We believe that these genres must and do overlap. DUCTS publishes the best, most compelling stories and we hope to attract readers who are drawn to work that rises above." Semiannual. Estab. 1999. Circ. 12,000. CLMP.

Needs Ethnic/multicultural, humor/satire, literary, mainstream. "Please do not send us genre work, unless it is extraordinarily unique." Receives 50 unsolicited mss/month. Accepts 40 mss/issue; 80 mss/year. Publishes ms 1-6 months after acceptance. **Publishes 10-12 new writers/year.** Recently published work by Charles Salzberg, Mark Goldblatt, Richard Kostelanz, and Helen Zelon. Publishes short shorts. Also publishes literary essays, literary criticism, poetry. Sometimes comments on rejected mss.

How to Contact Reading period is January 1 through August 31. Send complete ms. Accepts submissions by e-mail to appropriate departments. Responds in 1-4 weeks to queries; 1-6 months to mss. Accepts simultaneous and reprints submissions. Writer's guidelines on ducts.org.

Payment/Terms $15. Acquires one-time rights.

Tips "We prefer writing that tells a compelling story with a strong narrative drive."

◪ THE EXTERNALIST: A JOURNAL OF PERSPECTIVES

c/o Larina Warnock, Corvallis OR 97339-2052. E-mail: editor@theexternalist.com. Website: www.theexternalist.com. **Contact:** Larina Warnock, editor. Online magazine, PDF format, 45-60 pgs. "The Externalist embraces the balance between craft, entertainment and substance with a focus on subjects that are meaningful in human context. The externalist writer is the writer who is driven by a desire to write well while also writing in such a way that others can understand their perspective (even if they disagree or can't relate), and in this way, keeps an eye on the world outside of self. Externalism values craft and content equally. It recognizes there are still important lessons to be learned, there is still a need to understand and relate to the world around us, and differences are as important as similiarites, and vice versa. The externalist believes there are significant human concerns across the globe and here in the United States, and that good litereature has the power to create discussion around these concerns. The externalist also believes the multiplicity of perspectives found in today's quickly changing world can (and should) be valued as a means to comprehension—a way to change the things that do not work and give force to the things that do." Bimonthly. Estab. 2007. Circ. approx.1,000 unique visitors a month.

• *The Externalist* has been nominated for "Best of the Web" and "Best of the Net." Nominates for the *Pushcart Prize.*

Needs Adventure, ethnic/multicultural, family saga, fantasy, feminist, gay, historical, horror, humor/satire, lesbian, literary, mainstream, military/war, mystery, new age, psychic/supernatural/occult, religious, science fiction, thriller/espionage, and western, but "all fiction must have an externalist focus regardless of genre." Does not want children's or young adult literature, erotica or pornography, or standard romance. "We do not publish any work that is designed to inspire hate or violence against any population. Highly experimental work is strongly discouraged. Slice-of-life fiction that does not deal with a significant social issue will not be accepted." List of upcoming themes available on Web site. Receives 20-25 mss/month. Accepts 2-3 mss/issue; 12-18 mss/year. Ms published 4 months after acceptance. **Publishes 10-15 new writers/year.** Published Bill Tietelbaum, Lois Shapley Bassen, and Shaul Hendel. Length: 500-5,000 words. Average length: 3,500 words. Publishes short shorts. Average length of short shorts: 750 words. Also publishes literary essays, literary criticism, poetry. Often comments on/critiques rejected mss.

How to Contact E-mail submissions only. Include estimated word count, brief bio. Responds to queries in 2-3 weeks. Responds to mss in 6-8 weeks. Considers simultaneous submissions, previously published submissions. Guidelines available on Web site.

Payment/Terms Contributor's link on Web page (see Web site for details). Acquires first North American serial rights. Sends galleys to author. Publication is copyrighted. "All work published in *The Externalist* is eligible for Editor's Choice (each issue) and our annual Best of *The Externalist* anthology."

Tips "The fiction that appears in *The Externalist* is well-crafted and speaks subtly about significant social issues in our world today. The more thought-provoking the story, the more likely we will accept it for publication. The editor has a soft spot for well written satire. However, read the work we publish before submitting. Familiarize yourslef with externalism. This information is on our Web site free of charge, and even a brief look at the material we publish will improve your chances. Follow the guidelines! We do not open unsolicated attachments, and manuscripts that do not follow our e-mail formatting guidelines stand a good chance of hitting our junk mail folder and not being seen."

☑ ⚑ FAILBETTER.COM

Failbetter, 2022 Grove Avenue, Richmond, VA 23221. E-mail: submissions@failbetter.com. Website: www. failbetter.com. **Contact:** Thom Didato, publisher. Andrew Day, managing editor. "We are a quarterly online magazine published in the spirit of a traditional literary journal—dedicated to publishing quality fiction, poetry, and artwork. While the Web plays host to hundreds, if not thousands, of genre-related sites (many of which have merit), we are not one of them." Quarterly. Estab. 2000. Circ. 50,000. Member CLMP.

Needs Literary, short stories, novel excerpts. "No genre fiction—romance, fantasy or science fiction." Always would like to see more "character-driven literary fiction where something happens!" Receives 175-200 unsolicited mss/month. Accepts 3-5 mss/issue; 12-20 mss/year. Publishes ms 4-8 months after acceptance. **Publishes 4-6 new writers/year.** Recently published work by Michael Martone, Daniel Alarcon, Pascal Mercier, Jeffrey Lent, and Elizabeth Crane. Publishes short shorts. Often comments on rejected mss.

How to Contact Accepts submissions by e-mail. Include the word "submission" in the subject line. Responds in 3-4 months to email submissions; 4-6 month s to snail mail mss. Accepts simultaneous submissions. All issues are available online.

Payment/Terms Acquires one-time rights.

Tips "Read an issue. Read our guidelines! We place a high degree of importance on originality, believing that even in this age of trends it is still possible. We are not looking for what is current or momentary. We are not concerned with length: One good sentence may find a home here, as the bulk of mediocrity will not. Most importantly, know that what you are saying could only come from you. When you are sure of this, please feel free to submit."

☑ ◎ FICKLE MUSES, An Online Journal of Myth and Legend

E-mail: fiction@ficklemuses.com. Website: www.ficklemuses.com. **Contact:** Leslie Fox, fiction editor. Online magazine. Contains illustrations. Includes photographs. "We feature poetry and short stories that re-imagine old myths or reexamine mythic themes contemporarily." Weekly. Estab. 2007.

Needs Literary. "Stories may cross over into any genre as long as the story is based in a myth or legend. Does not want stories that treat myth as a false belief or stereotype (e.g. the myth of beauty). No pure genre (romance, horror, mystery, etc.)." Receives 13-15 mss/month. Accepts 12-24 mss/year. Ms published up to 3 months after acceptance. **Publishes approx 10% new writers/year.** Published Neil de la Flor, Maureen Seaton, Virginia Mohlere and M.M. De Voe. Length: 1,000-5,000 words. Average length: 2,000 words. Publishes short shorts. Average length of short shorts: 500 words. Also publishes literary essays, literary criticism, book reviews, poetry. Send review query to fiction@ficklemuses.com. Rarely comments on/critiques rejected mss.

How to Contact Send complete ms with cover letter. Accepts submissions by e-mail only. Include estimated word count and "a brief description of the myth or legend your story is based on if it is not standard knowledge." Responds to queries in 3 weeks. Responds to mss in 3 weeks. Considers simultaneous submissions, previously published submissions. Guidelines available on Web site.

Payment/Terms Acquires one-time rights. Publication is not copyrighted.

Tips "Originality. An innovative look at an old story. I'm looking to be swept away. Get a feel for our Web site."

☐ $ FLASH ME MAGAZINE: THE ONLINE MAGAZINE EXCLUSIVELY FOR FLASH FICTION STORIES

Winged Halo Productions, P.O. Box 803, O'Fallon, IL 62269-0803. E-mail: info@wingedhalo.com. Website: www.wingedhalo.com. **Contact:** Jennifer Dawson, Editor-in-Chief. Online magazine. "Flash Me Magazine is a quartly magazine, accepting all genres of fiction, as long as the story is under 1000 words. There are no restrictions on content, though we will not publish stories with excess gore, violence, profanity or sex." Quarterly. Estab. 2003. Circ. 1,000 visitors per month. Member Small Press Co-op.

Needs Fantasy (space fantasy, sword and sorcery), historical, horror (dark fantasy, futuristic, psychological, supernatural), humor/satire, literary, mainstream, military/war, mystery, romance (contemporary, futuristic/time travel, gothic, historical, regency, suspense), science fiction (soft/sociological). Receives 100 mss/month. Accepts 6-12 mss/issue; 24-48 mss/year. Ms published 3 months or less after acceptance. **Publishes 20 new writers/year.** Published Debbie Mumford, Bruce Holland Rogers, Angie Smibert and Amy Herlihy. Publishes short shorts only. Average length of short shorts: 750, max 1,000 words. Also publishes book reviews. Send review queries to reviews@wingedhalo.com. Always comments on/critiques rejected mss.

How to Contact Send complete ms with cover letter. Accepts submissions by e-mail. Include brief bio. Responds to queries in 1 week. Responds to mss in 3 months. Considers previously published submissions, multiple submissions. Guidelines available on Web site.

Payment/Terms Writers receive $5-20. Pays on publication. Acquires electronic rights. Sends galleys to author. Publication is copyrighted.

Tips "Anything well-written stands a chance, and anything with a good plot, as well. To really catch our eye though, a story has be unique and memorable. Read our guidelines carefully before submitting work."

☑ FLUENT ASCENSION

Fierce Concepts, P.O. Box 14581, Phoenix AZ 85063. E-mail: submissions@fluentascension.com. Website: www.fluentascension.com. **Contact:** Warren Norgaard, editor. Online magazine. Quarterly. Estab. 2003.

Needs Comics/graphic novels, erotica, ethnic/multicultural, experimental, gay, humor/satire, lesbian, literary, translations. Receives 6-10 unsolicited mss/month. Accepts 1-3 mss/issue. Publishes short shorts. Also publishes literary essays, literary criticism, poetry. Sometimes comments on rejected mss.

How to Contact Send complete ms. Accepts submissions by e-mail. Include estimated word count, brief bio and list of publications. Send SASE (or IRC) for return of ms or send disposable copy of ms and #10 SASE for reply only. Responds in 8-12 weeks to queries; 8-12 weeks to mss. Accepts simultaneous, multiple submissions. Sample copy online. Writer's guidelines online.

Payment/Terms Acquires electronic rights. Sponsors awards/contests.

☑ FRINGE MAGAZINE: THE NOUN THAT VERBS YOUR WORLD

8 Willow Ave, #2, Somerville MA 02144. (617) 413-8674. E-mail: fringeeditors@gmail.com. Website: www.fringemagazine.org. **Contact:** Katie Spencer, editor. Online magazine/E-zine specializing in literature. Contains illustrations and photographs. "Fringe Magazine is dedicated to political and experimental literature, and was founded to fight the homogenization of culture and the loss of revolutionary writing at the high literary and popular levels. Our audience is diverse, garnering more than 16,000 page views each month from more than 40 countries. Fringe is a 501(c)3 public charity organized under the laws of Delaware whose nonprofit purpose is to diversify the existing literary aesthetic, publish genres that other magazines do not print, and to give crucial early publication credits to young writers, particularly to writers of color and women writers. In each issue, Fringe features one artist per genre." Quarterly. Estab. 2006. Circ. over 16,000 page views per month. Member CLMP.

Needs Ethnic/multicultural (general), experimental, feminist, gay, humor/satire, lesbian, literary, mainstream. Special interest in experimental literature, cross-genre work, hypertext and flash-based literature. Does not want to see erotica or pornography, unless it has a higher literary purpose. "We enjoy stories that span cultures, but have recently received a lot of work in the genre of 'I went on vacation and got an exotic lover.' In general, we do not like work that is sentimental." The third anniversary issue, February 2009, will be themed "environment." Submissions for this issue will open August 1, 2008 and close December 15, 2008. List of upcoming themes available on Web site. Receives 30-60 mss/month. Accepts 1-4 mss/issue; 9-12 mss/year. Ms published 6-8 weeks after acceptance. **Publishes 5 new writers/year.** Published Sarah Sweeney, Amy Clark, Chris Siteman, Jasmin Saigal, TJ Dietderich, Kirstin Chen, and Chip Cheek. Length: 100-15,000 words. Average length: 3,000 words. Publishes short shorts. Average length of short shorts: 450 words. Also publishes literary essays, literary criticism, book reviews, poetry. Send review copies to Sarah Miles c/o the magazine address. "Reviews will not appear in the journal itself, but do appear on our blog." Often comments on/critiques rejected mss.

How to Contact Send complete ms with cover letter. Accepts submissions by e-mail. Include estimated word count, brief bio. Responds to queries in 3 weeks. Responds to mss in 3 months. Considers simultaneous submissions, multiple submissions. Guidelines available on Web site.

Payment/Terms Acquires first rights, electronic rights, archive rights.

Tips "We really enjoy fiction that takes risks, that dares to be off-beat, that experiments with form or content. Often, when we are torn between two pieces, we end up taking the one that seems 'more fringey,' or the one that engages with core political issues in the most complex and nuanced way. We are suckers for fiction that explores feminist themes in new, non-cliché, non-preachy manners. We love the postmodern. We drool over work that successfully engages with myth. Be careful with politics—they can add a lot to a work, but can also make it come across as preachy and flat. Do not summarize your story in your cover letter—it deprives us of whatever wonderful surprises your story has in store."

✍ FULLOSIA PRESS

Rockaway Park Philosophical Society, P.O. Box 280, Ronkonkoma NY 11779. E-mail: deanofrpps@aol. com. Website: rpps_fullosia_press.tripod.com. **Contact:** J.D. Collins, editor; Geoff Jackson, assoc. editor. E-zine. "Part-time publisher of fiction and non-fiction. Our publication is right wing and conservative, leaning to views of Patrick Buchanan but amenable to the opposition's point of view. We promote an independent America. We are anti-global, anti-UN. Collects unusual news from former British or American provinces. Fiction interests include military, police, private detective, courthouse stories." Monthly. Estab. 1999. Circ. 175.

Needs Historical (American), military/war, mystery/suspense, thriller/espionage. Christmas, St. Patrick's Day, Fourth of July. Publishes ms 1 week after acceptance. **Publishes 10 new writers/year.** Recently published work by Geoff Jasckson, 'Awesome' Dave Lawrence, Robert E.L. Nesbitt, MD, John Grey, Dr. Kelly White, James Davies, Andy Martin, Michael Levy, and Peter Vetrano's class. Length: 500-2,000 words; average length: 750 words. Publishes short shorts. Also publishes literary essays. Always comments on rejected mss.

How to Contact Query with or without published clips. Accepts submissions by e-mail. Include brief bio and list of publications. Mail submissions must be on 314 floppy disk. Responds in 1 month to mss. Please avoid mass mailings. Sample copy online. Reviews fiction.

Payment/Terms Acquires electronic rights.

Tips "Make your point quickly. If you haven't done so, after five pages, everybody hates you and your characters."

▢ THE FURNACE REVIEW

E-mail: editor@thefurnacereview.com. Website: www.thefurnacereview.com. Contact: Ciara LaVelle, editor. "We reach out to a young, well-educated audience, bringing them new, unique, fresh work they won't find elsewhere." Quarterly. Estab. 2004.

Needs Erotica, experimental, feminist, gay, historical, humor/satire, lesbian, literary, mainstream, military/war. Does not want children's, science fiction, or religious submissions. Receives 50-60 unsolicited mss/month. Accepts 1-3 mss/issue; 5-8 mss/year. **Publishes 5-8 new writers/year.** Recently published work by Amy Greene, Dominic Preziosi, and Sandra Soson. Length: 7,000 words; average length: 4,000 words. Publishes short shorts. Also publishes poetry.

How to Contact Send complete ms. Accepts submissions by e-mail only. Responds in 4 month to queries. Accepts simultaneous submissions.

Payment/Terms Acquires first North American serial rights.

✍ THE GREEN HILLS LITERARY LANTERN

Published by Truman State University, Division of Language & Literature, Kirksville MO 63501. (660) 785-4487. E-mail: adavis@truman.edu. Website: http://ll.truman.edu/ghllweb. **Contact:** Fiction editor. "The mission of GHLL is to provide a literary market for quality fiction writers, both established and beginners, and to provide quality literature for readers from diverse backgrounds. We also see ourselves as a cultural resource for North Missouri. Our publication works to publish the highest quality fiction—dense, layered, subtle—and, at the same time, fiction which grabs the ordinary reader. We tend to publish traditional short stories, but we are open to experimental forms." Annual. Estab. 1990. The GHLL is now an online, open-access journal.

Needs Ethnic/multicultural, experimental, feminist, humor/satire, literary, mainstream, regional. "Our main requirement is literary merit. Wants more quality fiction about rural culture. No adventure, crime, erotica, horror, inspirational, mystery/suspense, romance." Receives 40 unsolicited mss/month. Accepts

15-17 mss/issue. Publishes ms 6-12 months after acceptance. **Publishes 0-3 new writers/year.** Recently published work by Karl Harshbarger, Mark Jacobs, J. Morris, Gary Fincke, Dennis Vannatta. Length: 7,000 words; average length: 3,000 words. Publishes short shorts. Also publishes poetry. Sometimes comments on rejected mss.

How to Contact SASE for return of ms. Responds in 4 months to mss. Accepts simultaneous, multiple submissions. Electronic submissions in.doc or.txt format also acceptable from writers livingoutside North America, but our manuscript readers still prefer hardcopy. E-mail attachment to adavis@truman.edu.

Payment/Terms No payment. Acquires one-time rights.

Tips "We look for strong character development, substantive plot and theme, visual and forceful language within a multilayered story. Make sure your work has the flavor of life, a sense of reality. A good story, well crafted, will eventually get published. Find the right market for it, and above all, don't give up."

☑ $ IDEOMANCER

Website: www.ideomancer.com. **Contact:** Leah Bobet, Publisher. Online magazine. Contains illustrations. "Ideomancer publishes science fiction, fantasy, horror, slipstream and poetry. We look for stories that explore the edges of ideas, stories that subvert, refute and push the limits. We want unique pieces from authors willing to explore non-traditional narratives, take chances with tone, structure and execution, and take risks. Our aim is to showcase speculative stories in all categores which provoke, reflect and marry ideas to resonance and character." Quarterly. Estab. 2001.

Needs Fantasy (mythic, urban, historical, low), horror (dark fantasy, futuristic, psychological, supernatural), science fiction (hard science/technological, soft/sociological). Special interests: slipstream and poetry. Does not want fiction without a speculative element. Receives 200 mss/month. Accepts 3-4 mss/issue; 9-12 mss/year. Does not read February, May, August and November. Ms published within 12 months of acceptance. **Publishes 1-2 new writers/year.** Published Sarah Monette, Ruth Nestvold, Astrid Atkinson, Becca de la Rosa, January Mortimer, Yoon Ha Lee and David Kopaska-Merkel. Length: 7,000 words (max). Average length: 4,000 words. Publishes short shorts. Average length of short shorts: 1,000 words. Also publishes book reviews, poetry. *Requests only* to have a novel or collection reviewed should be sent to the publisher. Often comments on/critiques rejected mss.

How to Contact Send complete ms with cover letter. Accepts submissions by e-mail only. Include estimated word count. Responds to queries in 3 weeks. Responds to mss in 6 weeks. Guidelines available on Web site.

Payment/Terms Writers receive 3¢ per word, max of $40. Pays on acceptance. Acquires electronic rights. Publication is copyrighted.

Tips "Beyond the basics of formatting the fiction as per our guidelines, good writing and intriguing characters and plot, where the writer brings depth to the tale, make a manuscript stand out. We receive a number of submissions which showcase good writing, but lack the details that make them spring to life for us. Visit our Web site and read some of our fiction to see if we're a good fit. Read our submission guidelines carefully and use rtf formatting as requested. We're far more interested in your story than your cover letter, so spend your time polishing that."

☑ ◎ KENNESAW REVIEW

Kennesaw State University, Dept. of English, Building 27, 1000 Chastain Rd., Kennesaw GA 30144-5591. (770) 375-0706. E-mail: kenrev@gmail.com. Website: www.kennesawreview.org. **Contact:** Robert W. Hill and Robert Barrier, editors. Online literary journal. "Just good literary fiction, all themes, for an eclectic audience." Ongoing updates to Web site. Estab. 1987.

Needs Short stories and flash fiction. "No formulaic genre fiction." Receives 25 unsolicited mss/month. Accepts 2-4 mss/issue. Publishes ms 4-6 months after acceptance. Recently published work by Ellen Lundquist, Michael Cadnum, and Robert Philips.

How to Contact Accepts.doc attachments via e-mail only. Guidelines on Web site. Responds in 2 months to mss. Accepts simultaneous, multiple submissions. Writer's guidelines online.

Payment/Terms Acquires first rights.

Tips "Use the language well and tell an interesting story."

☑ $ THE KING'S ENGLISH

(503) 709-1917. E-mail: thekingsenglish@comcast.net. Website: www.thekingsenglish.org. **Contact:** Benjamin Chambers, editor. "We're an online publication only. Our focus is long literary fiction, especially if it's stuffed with strong imagery and gorgeous prose. Novellas 11,000-48,000 words (150 double-spaced pages). In very rare instances, we'll include detective fiction or sci-fi/fantasy, as long as there's a strong element of suspense, the setting is unusual, and the writing first-rate." Estab. 2003.

• Three-time winner of the Million Writers Award for Best Publisher of Novella-Length Fiction.

Needs Experimental, historical, literary, mainstream, mystery/suspense (private eye/hardboiled), thriller/espionage, translations. No horror, religious or heartwarming tales of redemption. Accepts 3 mss/issue; 12 mss/year. Also publishes literary essays, poetry.

How to Contact Send complete ms. Electronic submissions only. Responds in 2 weeks to queries; 1-2 months to mss. Accepts simultaneous, multiple submissions. Writer's guidelines by e-mail or on the Web site.

Payment/Terms Pays $20/story or essay, $10/poem. Acquires one-time, non-exclusive rights to anthologize and archive on the Web site.

Tips "Surprise us. With language, mostly, though concept and execution can do just as well or better. If your first page makes us long for a rainy day and a cozy armchair in which to curl up with your manuscript, you'll get our attention. Make sure your story deserves to be a long one. Write what you'd like to read. Save yourself some heartbreak and read our guidelines before submitting."

▦ ☑ $ LONE STAR STORIES, SPECULATIVE FICTION AND POETRY

E-mail: submissions@erictmarin.com. Website: www.lonestarstories.com. **Contact:** Eric T. Marin, editor. Online magazine. Contains illustrations and photographs. "Lone Star Stories publishes quality speculative fiction and poetry." Bimonthly. Estab. 2004.

Needs Speculative fiction (fantasy, dark fantasy, science fiction, and interstitial). Receives 100+ mss/month. Accepts 3 mss/issue; 18 mss/year. Manuscript published 2 months after acceptance. Average length: 5,000 words. Publishes short shorts. Average length of short shorts: 500 words. Also publishes poetry.

How to Contact Send complete ms with cover letter. Accepts submissions by e-mail. Include estimated word count. Responds to queries in 1 weeks. Responds to mss in 1 week. Considers simultaneous submissions, previously published submissions. Guidelines available on Web site.

Payment/Terms Writers receive $20 per story; $10 per poem. **Pays on acceptance.** Publication is copyrighted.

Tips "The standard advice applies: Read the current issue of *Lone Star Stories* to get a feel for what is likely to be published."

☑ ▣ ▨ MAD HATTERS' REVIEW: EDGY AND ENLIGHTENED ART, LITERATURE AND MUSIC IN THE AGE OF DEMENTIA

E-mail: madhattersreview@gmail.com. Website: www.madhattersreview.com. **Contact:** Carol Novack, Publisher/Editor-in-Chief. Online magazine. "Mad Hatters' Review is a socially aware/progressive, multi-media/literary journal, featuring original works of fiction, flash fiction, poetry, creative/literary nonfiction, whatnots, drama, collages, audios, book reviews, columns, contests and more. We also feature cartoons and comic strips, including the 'The Perils of Patriotic Polly' and 'Coconuts.' All of our contributing authors' writings are accompanied by original art created specifically for the material, as well as original, custom made music or recitations by authors. We are proud of our spectacular featured artists' galleries, as well as our mini-movies, parodies, and featured foreign sections. Our staff musicians and visual artists are wonderful. Webdelsol took us on board (the first and only multimedia) in 2006 and hosts our site." Semiannual. Estab. 2005. Member CLMP.

• Mad Hatters' Review has received an Artistry Award from Sixty Plus Design, 2006-7 Web Design Award from Invision Graphics, and a Gold Medal Award of Excellence for 2006-7 from ArtSpace2000. com.

Needs Inventive works, mixed media, translations, humor, literary prose and poetry that demonstrate a unique, unconventional, intellectual, sophisticated and emotional perspective on the world and a delight in craft. Does not want mainstream prose/story that doesn't exhibit a love of language and a sophisticated mentality. No religious or inspirational writings, confessionals, boys sowing oats, sentimental and coming of age stories. Accepts 3-6 mss/issue. Submissions are open briefly for each issue: check guidelines periodically for dates or subscribe free to newsletter. Ms published 5-6 months after acceptance. **Publishes 1 new writer/year.** Published Alastair Gray, Kass Fleisher, Vanessa Place, Harold Jaffe, Andrei Codrescu, Sheila Murphy, Simon Perchik, Terese Svoboda, Niels Hav, Martin, Nakell, and Juan Jose Millas (translated from the Spanish). Length: 3,000 words (max). Average length of fictions: 1,500-2,500 words. Publishes short shorts. Average length of short shorts: 500-800 words. Also publishes literary essays, literary criticism, book reviews, and interviews. Send review queries to madhattersreview@gmail.com. Sometimes comments on/critiques rejected mss.

How to Contact Accepts submissions by e-mail only. Include estimated word count, brief bio. Now has a submission form for most issues. Responds to queries in 1 week. Responds to mss in 1-6 weeks. Considers simultaneous submissions. Guidelines available on Web site.

Payment/Terms Acquires first rights. Sends galleys to author. "We offer contests in most issues."

Tips "Imagination, skill with and appreciation of language, inventiveness, rhythm, sense of humor/irony/satire and compelling style make a manuscript stand out. Read the magazine. Don't necessarily follow the rules you've been taught in the usual MFA program or workshop."

TIMOTHY MCSWEENEY'S INTERNET TENDENCY

826 Valencia Street, San Francisco CA 94110. E-mail: websubmissions@mcsweeneys.net. Website: www.mcsweeneys.net. **Contact:** Dave Eggers, John Warner, Christopher Monks, editors. Online literary journal. "Timothy McSweeney's Internet Tendency is an offshoot of Timothy McSweeney's Quarterly Concern, a journal created by nervous people in relative obscurity, and published four times a year." Daily.

Needs Literate humor. Sometimes comments on rejected mss.

How to Contact Accepts submissions by e-mail. "For submissions to the Web site, paste the entire piece into the body of an e-mail. Absolute length limit of 1,500 words, with a preference for pieces significantly shorter (700-1,000 words)." Sample copy online. Writer's guidelines online.

Tips "Do not submit your work to both the print submissions address and the Web submissions address, as seemingly hundreds of writers have been doing lately. If you submit a piece of writing intended for the magazine to the Web submissions address, you will confuse us, and if you confuse us, we will accidentally delete your work without reading it, and then we will laugh and never give it another moment's thought, and sleep the carefree sleep of young children. This is very, very serious."

☑ ◎ MICROHORROR: SHORT STORIES. ENDLESS NIGHTMARES

5300 Merceron Ave, Baltimore, MD 21207. (443) 670-6133. E-mail: microhorror@gmail.com. Website: www.microhorror.com. **Contact:** Nathan Rosen, editor. Online magazine. "MicroHorror is not a magazine in the traditional sense. Instead, it is a free online archive for short-short horror fiction. With a strict limit of 666 words, MicroHorror showcases the power of the short-short horror to convey great emotional impact in only a few brief paragraphs." Estab. 2006.

• Golden Horror Award from Horrorfind.com in 2007.

Needs Horror (dark fantasy, futuristic, psychological, supernatural), young adult/teen (horror). Receives 25 mss/month. Accepts 300 mss/year. Ms published 1-3 days after acceptance. **Publishes 50 new writers/year.** Published D.W. Green, Michael A. Kechula, Oonah V. Joslin, Kevin Sweeney, James Lacey, Jeff Ryan, Sean Ryan, R. K. Gemienhardt, K. A. Patterson, Andrew JM Stone, Rod Drake, Yuichi Mendez, and Santiago Eximeno. Length: 666 words (max). Publishes short shorts. Average length of short shorts: 500 words. Often comments on/critiques rejected mss.

How to Contact Send complete ms with cover letter. Accepts submissions by e-mail. Include estimated word count, brief bio. Responds to queries in 1 week. Responds to mss in 1 week. Send either SASE (or IRC) for return of ms or disposable copy of ms and #10 SASE for reply only. Considers simultaneous submissions, previously published submissions, multiple submissions. Guidelines available on Web site.

Payment/Terms Acquires one-time rights. Publication is copyrighted.

Tips "This is horror. Scare me. Make shivers run down my spine. Make me afraid to look behind the shower curtain. Pack the biggest punch you can into a few well chosen sentences. Read all the horror you can, and figure out what makes it scary. Trim away all the excess trappngs until you get right to the core, and use what you find."

☐ MIDNIGHT TIMES

E-mail: editor@midnighttimes.com. Website: www.midnighttimes.com. **Contact:** Jay Manning, editor. Midnight Times is an online literary magazine dedicated to publishing quality poetry and fiction by both previously unpublished as well as published writers. The primary theme is darkness, but this doesn't necessarily mean evil. There can be a light at the end of the tunnel. Quarterly. Estab. 2003.

Needs Fantasy (sword and sorcery), horror (dark fantasy, futuristic, psychological, supernatural), literary, mainstream, psychic/supernatural/occult, science fiction, vampires. No pornography. Accepts 5-9 mss/issue; 20-36 mss/year. Publishes ms 3-9 months after acceptance. **Publishes many new writers/year.** Length: 500-10,000 words; average length: 4,000 words. Publishes short shorts. Also publishes poetry. Sometimes comments on rejected mss.

How to Contact Send complete ms. Submissions accepted by e-mail only. Responds in 2 months to mss. Accepts simultaneous, multiple submissions and reprints. Writer's guidelines on Website.

Payment/Terms No payment. Acquires one-time, electronic rights.

Tips "Please read the submission guidelines on MidnightTimes.com before submitting your work! Thanks."

☑ MIDWAY JOURNAL

P.O. Box 14499, St. Paul MN 55114. (612) 825-4811. E-mail: editors@midwayjournal.com. Website: www.midwayjournal.com. **Contact:** Raph Pennel, fiction editor. Online magazine. "Midway Journal accepts submissions of aesthetically ambitious work that occupies the realms between the experimental and trasitional. Midway, or its position is midway, is a place of boundary crossing, where work complicates and even questions the boundaries between forms, binaries and genres." Bimonthly. Estab. 2006. Member CLMP.

Needs Comics/graphic novels, ethnic/multicultural (general), experimental, feminist, gay, historical (general), humor/satire, lesbian, literary, science fiction (soft/sociological), translations. Does not want new age, young adult/teen, children/juvenile or erotica. "Writers should visit current and back issues to see what we have or have not published in the past." Receives 30 mss/month. Accepts 3-4 mss/issue; 18-24 mss/year. Does not read June 1-Nov 30. Ms published 4-12 months after acceptance. Agented fiction 1%. **Publishes 2-5 new writers/year.** Published Harrison Bas Wein, Frank Miller, Richard Hollinger and Noelle Sickels. Length: 250-25,000 words. Average length: 3,000 words. Publishes short shorts. Average length of short shorts: 600 words. Also publishes literary essays, poetry. Sometimes comments on/critiques rejected mss.

How to Contact Send complete ms with cover letter. Accepts international submissions by e-mail. Include estimated word count, brief bio, list of publications. Responds to queries in 1-2 weeks. Please see Web site for submission guidelines. Send either SASE (or IRC) for return of ms or disposable copy of ms and #10 SASE for reply only. Considers simultaneous submissions, previously published submissions. Guidelines available on Web site.

Payment/Terms Acquires one-time rights. Publication is copyrighted.

Tips "An interesting story with engaging writing, both in terms of style and voice, make a manuscript stand out. Round characters are a must. Writers who take chances either with content or with form grab an editor's immediate attention. Spend time with the words on the page. Spend time with the language. The language and voice are not vehicles, they, too, are tools."

☐ ◎ $ MINDFLIGHTS

Double-Edged Publishing, 9618 Misty Brook Cove, Cordova TX 38016. (901) 213-3768. E-mail: editor@mindflights.com. Website: http://www.Mindflights.com. **Contact:** Selena Thomason, Managing Editor. Magazine/E-zine. "Publishes science fiction, fantasy, and all genres of speculative fiction and poetry. We want work that is grounded in a Christian or Christian friendly worldview, without being preachy. Please see our vision and guidelines page for details. MindFlights is the merging of two established magazines: The Sword Review andDragons, Knights, & Angels." Monthly ezine, quarterly print edition. Estab. 2008.

Needs Fantasy (space fantasy, sword and sorcery), science fiction (hard science/technological, soft/sociological), special interests: speculative fiction and poetry with Christian themes. Does not want to see work "that would be offensive to a Christian audience. Also, we are a family-friendly market and thus do not want to see explicit sex, illicit drug use, gratuitous violence or excessive gore." Receives 30 mss/month. Accepts 6 mss/issue; 72 mss/year. Ms published 2 months after acceptance. **Publishes 6-12 new writers/year.** Length: 500-5,000 words. Average length: 3,000 words. Publishes short shorts. Average length of short shorts: 700 words. Also publishes poetry. Always comments on/critiques rejected mss.

How to Contact Send complete ms via online form. Include estimated word count. Responds to queries in 2 weeks. Responds to mss in 4 weeks. Considers previously published submissions, multiple submissions. Guidelines available on Web site.

Payment/Terms Writers receive 1/2¢ per word, $5 min and $25 max, 1 contributor's copy if selected for print edition. Additional copies $7.50. Pays on acceptance. Acquires first rights, first North American serial rights, one-time rights, electronic rights. Sends galleys to author. Publication is copyrighted. Occasional contests. "Details and entry process would be on our website when contest is announced."

Tips "We look for speculative fiction that entertains, enlightens, and uplifts. We also prefer work that is family-friendly and grounded in a Christian world-view. We especially seek work that successfully melds the speculative with Christian themes. Please read our guidelines and proof your work carefully. (It is helpful to also have someone else proof your work as writers often miss typos in their own work.) Please do not submit work that is clearly inappropriate for our magazine and/or is full of typos, misspellings, and grammar errors."

☑ NEW WORKS REVIEW

520 10TH Street, Tell, City IN 47586. (812) 547-6787. E-mail: brettalansanders@gmail.com. Website: www. new-works.org. **Contact:** Brett Alan Sanders, managing editor. Online magazine. Contains illustrations and photographs. "Our philosphy is to publish outstanding work suitable for all readers. All genres are published." Quarterly. Estab. 1998.

Needs Adventure, family saga, humor/satire, literary, mainstream, military/war, peace studies, mystery/suspense (amateur sleuth, cozy, police procedural, private eye/hard-boiled), thriller/espionage, translations, western. Does not want porn, anti-religious, erotica, or use of obscenities. Receives 30 mss/month. Accepts 10 mss/issue; 40 mss/year. Manuscript published 3 months after acceptance. **Publishes 5-10 new writers/year.** Published Irving Greenfield, Lynn Strongin, Tom Sheehan, Michael Corrigan, Brett Alan Sanders and Diane Sawyer. Average length: 3,000 words. Also publishes literary essays, literary criticism, poetry, and book reviews. Often comments on/critiques rejected manuscripts.

How to Contact *Not accepting new submissions at this time*. Watch Web site for updates. Guidelines available on Web site.

Payment/Terms All rights retained by author. Sends galleys to author. Publication is copyrighted.

Tips "Read established writers, edit and re-edit your stories, follow the guidelines."

☑ NUVEIN ONLINE

(626) 401-3466. Fax: (626) 401-3460. E-mail: editor@nuvein.com. Website: www.nuvein.com. **Contact:** Enrique Diaz, editor. Online magazine published by the Nuvein Foundation for Literature and the Arts. "We are open to short fiction, poetry and essays that explore topics divergent from the mainstream. Our vision is to provide a forum for new and experienced voices rarely heard in our global community."

• *Nuvein Online* has received the Visionary Media Award.

Needs Fiction, poetry, plays, movie/theatre reviews/articles and art. Wants more "experimental fiction, ethnic works, and pieces dealing with the exploration of gender and sexuality, as well as works dealing with the clash of cultures." **Publishes 20 new writers/year.** Recently published work by J. Knight, Paul A. Toth, Rick Austin, Robert Levin and Scott Essman, as well as interviews with film directors Guillermo Del Toro, Alejandro Gonzalez Inñarritu and Frank Darabont.

How to Contact Query. Accepts submissions by e-mail. Send work as attachment. Sample copy online.

Tips "Read over each submission before sending it, and if you, as the writer, find the piece irresistable, e-mail it to us immediately!"

☐ $ ON THE PREMISES: A GOOD PLACE TO START

On The Premises, LLC, 4323 Gingham Court, Alexandria, VA 22310. (202)262-2168. E-mail: questions@ onthepremises.com. Website: www.OnThePremises.com. **Contact:** Tarl Roger Kudrick or Bethany Granger, Co-Publishers. E-zine. "Stories published in On the Premises are winning entries in contests that are held every four months. Each contest challenges writers to produce a great story based on a broad premise that our editors supply as part of the contest. On the Premises aims to promote newer and/or relatively unknown writers who can write what we feel are creative, compelling stories told in effective, uncluttered and evocative prose. Entrants pay no fees, and winners recieve cash prizes in addition to publication." Triannual. Estab. 2007. Member Small Press Promotions.

Needs Adventure, ethnic/multicultural (general), experimental, family saga, fantasy, feminist, historical (general), horror, humor/satire, literary, mainstream, military/war, mystery, new age, psychic/supernatural/occult, romance, science fiction, thriller/espionage, western. Does not want young adult fiction, children's fiction, x-rated fiction. "In general, we don't like stories that were written solely to make a social or political point, especialy if the story seems to assume that no intelligent person could possibly disagree with the author. Save the idealogy for editorial and opinion pieces, please. But above all, we NEVER EVER want to see stories that do not use the contest premise! Use the premise, and make it 'clear' and 'obvious' that you are using the premise." Themes are announced the day each contest is launched. List of past and current premises available on Web site. Receives 10-40 mss/month. Accepts 3-6 mss/issue; 9-18 mss/year. Does not read February, June and October. Ms published a month or less after acceptance. **Publishes 3-6 new writers/year.** Published A'llyn Ettien, Cory Cramer, Mark Tullius, Michael Van Ornum, Ken Liu and K. Stodard Hayes. Length: 1000 words (min)-5000 words (max). Average length: 3500 words. Sometimes comments on/critiques rejected mss.

How to Contact Send complete ms with cover letter. "We are a contest-based magazine and we strive to judge all entries 'blindly.' We request that an author's name and contact information be in the body of the email." Accepts submissions by e-mail only. Responds to mss in 2 weeks after contest deadline. Guidelines available on Web site.

Payment/Terms Writers receive $25-140. Pays on acceptance. Acquires electronic rights. Sends galleys to author. Publication is copyrighted.

Tips "Make sure you use the premise, not just interpret it. If the premise is 'must contain a real live dog,' then think of a creative, compelling way to use a real dog. Revise you draft, then revise again and again. Remember, we judge blindly, so craftmanship and creativety matter, not how well known you are."

⊡ ◖ THE ORACULAR TREE

The Oracular Tree, 29 Hillyard St., Chatham ON N7L 3E1 Canada. E-mail: editor@oraculartree.com. Website: www.oraculartree.com. **Contact:** Jeff Beardwood, editor. E-zine specializing in practical ideas for transforming our lives. "The stories we tell ourselves and each other predict the outcome of our lives. We can affect gradual social change by transforming our deeply rooted cultural stories. The genre is not as important as the message and the high quality of the writing. We accept stories, poems, articles and essays which will reach well-educated, open-minded readers around the world. We offer a forum for those who see a need for change, who want to add their voices to a growing search for positive alternatives." Monthly. Estab. 1997. Circ. 250,000 hits/month.

Needs Serial fiction, poetry, essays, novels and novel excerpts, visual art, short fiction, news. "We'll look at any genre that is well written and can examine a new cultural paradigm. No tired dogma, no greeting card poetry, please." Receives 20-30 unsolicited mss/month. Accepts 80-100 mss/year. Publishes ms 3 months after acceptance. **Publishes 20-30 new writers/year.** Recently published work by Elisha Porat, Lyn Lyfshin, Rattan Mann, and Dr. Elaine Hatfield. Publishes short shorts. Also publishes literary essays, poetry. Often comments on rejected mss.

How to Contact Send complete ms. Accepts submissions by e-mail. Responds in 2 weeks to queries; 2 months to mss. Accepts simultaneous, multiple submissions and reprints. Sample copy online. Writer's guidelines online.

Payment/Terms Author retains copyright; one-time archive posting.

Tips "The underlying idea must be clearly expressed. The language should be appropriate to the tale, using creative license and an awareness of rhythm. We look for a juxtaposition of ideas that creates resonance in the mind and heart of the reader. Write from your honest voice. Trust your writing to unfold."

☑ ◎ $ ORSON SCOTT CARD'S INTERGALACTIC MEDICINE SHOW

Hatrack River Publications, P.O. Box 18184, Greensboro, NC 27419. Website: http://InterGalacticMedicineShow.com or www.oscIGMS.com. **Contact:** Edmund R. Schubert, Editor. E-zine specializing in science fiction and fantasy. Contains illustrations. "We like to see well-developed milieus and believeable, engaging characters. We also look for clear, unaffected writing. Asimov, Niven, Tolkien, Yolen and Hobb are more likely to be our literary exemplars than James Joyce." Quarterly. Estab. 2005.

Needs fantasy (space fantasy, sword and sorcery), horror (dark fantasy, futuristic), science fiction (hard science/technological, soft/sociological), young adult/teen (fantasy/science fiction). Receives 300-400 mss/month. Accepts 7 mss/issue; 28 mss/year. Ms published 4-9 months after acceptance. Agented fiction 5%. **Publishes 4-6 new writers/year.** Published Peter S. Beagle, Tim Pratt, Eugie Fodter, James Maxey, Eric James Stone, Alethea Kontis, Steven Savile and Cat Rambo. Length: 1000 words (min)-10000 words (max). Average length: 4000-7000 words. Publishes short shorts. Average length of short shorts: 750 words. Also publishes book reviews. Sometimes comments on/critiques rejected mss.

How to Contact Submit ms via submission form on website. Include estimated word count, email address. Responds to queries in 2 weeks. Responds to mss in 3-6 months. Considers simultaneous submissions, previously published submissions (if obscure publication). Guidelines available on Web site.

Payment/Terms Writers receive ¢6 per word for first 7500 words, ¢5 per word beyond 7500, contributor's copy. Pays on publication. Acquires first North American serial rights, electronic rights. Publication is copyrighted.

Tips "Plain and simple, we want to see plots that go somewhere, filled with people we care about. Stories that show the author has a real undersanding of the subtleties of human nature. Proper manuscript formatting and up-to-date contact information are overlooked by more writers than you could imagine. Also, please bear in mind that all stories must be PG-13 suitable. Gratuitous sex, violence or language will get you rejected right away."

◎ OUTER ART

The University of New Mexico, 200 College Road, Gallup NM 87301. (505) 863-7647. Fax: (505) 863-7532. E-mail: smarand@unm.edu. Website: www.gallup.unm.edu/~smarandache/a/outer-art.htm. **Contact:** Florentin Smarandache, editor. E-zine. Annual. Estab. 2000.

Needs Experimental, literary, outer-art. Publishes ms 1 month after acceptance. Publishes short shorts. Also publishes literary essays, literary criticism.

How to Contact Accepts submissions by e-mail. Send SASE (or IRC) for return of the ms. Responds in 1 month to mss. Accepts simultaneous submissions and reprints. Writer's guidelines online.

▣ ☑ PAPERPLATES

Perkolator Kommunikation, 19 Kenwood Ave., Toronto ON M6C 2R8 Canada. (416) 651-2551. E-mail: magazine@paperplates.org. Website: www.paperplates.org. **Contact:** Bethany Gibson, fiction editor. Electronic magazine. Quarterly. Estab. 1990.

Needs Condensed novels, ethnic/multicultural, feminist, gay, lesbian, literary, mainstream, translations. "No science fiction, fantasy or horror." Receives 12 unsolicited mss/month. Accepts 2-3 mss/issue; 6-9 mss/year. Publishes ms 6-8 months after acceptance. Recently published work by Lyn Fox, David Bezmozgis, Fraser Sutherland and Tim Conley. Length: 1,500-3,500 words; average length: 3,000 words. Publishes short shorts. Also publishes literary essays, literary criticism, poetry.

How to Contact Accepts submissions by e-mail and land mail. Responds in 6 weeks to queries; 6 months to mss. Accepts simultaneous submissions. Sample copy online. Writer's guidelines online.

Payment/Terms No payment. Acquires first North American serial rights.

☑ THE PAUMANOK REVIEW

E-mail: submissions@paumanokreview.com. Website: www.paumanokreview.com. **Contact:** Katherine Arline, editor. Online literary magazine. "TPR is dedicated to publishing and promoting the best in world art and literature." Quarterly. Estab. 2000.

• J.P. Maney's *Western Exposures* was selected for inclusion in the *E2INK Best of the Web Anthology.*

Needs Mainstream, narrative, experimental, historical, mystery, horror, western, science fiction, slice-of-life vignette, serial, novel excerpt. Receives 100 unsolicited mss/month. Accepts 6-8 mss/issue; 24-32 mss/year. Publishes ms 6 weeks after acceptance. **Publishes 4 new writers/year.** Recently published work by Patty Friedman, Elisha Porat, Barry Spacks and Walt McDonald. Length: 1,000-6,000 words; average length: 3,000 words. Publishes short shorts. Also publishes literary essays, poetry. Usually comments on rejected mss.

How to Contact Send complete ms as attatchment (Word, RTF, HTML, TXT) or pasted in body of e-mail. Include estimated word count, brief bio, two ways to contact you, list of publications, and how you discovered *TPR*. Responds in 1 week to queries; 1 month to mss. Accepts simultaneous submissions and reprints. No multiple submissions. Sample copy online. Writer's guidelines online.

Payment/Terms Acquires one-time, anthology rights. Galleys offered in HTML or PDF format.

Tips "Though this is an English-language publication, it is not US-or UK-centric. Please submit accordingly. *TPR* is a publication of Wind River Press, which also publishes *Critique* magazine and select print and electronic books."

☑ PBW

513 N. Central Ave., Fairborn OH 45324. (937) 878-5184. E-mail: rianca@aol.com. Electronic disk zine; 700 pages, specializing in avant-garde fiction and poetry. "PBW is an experimental floppy disk (CD-Rom) that prints strange and 'unpublishable' in an above-ground-sense writing." Twice per year. Estab. 1988.

How to Contact "Manuscripts are only taken if they are submitted on disk or by e-mail." Send SASE for reply, return of ms. Sample copy not available.

Payment/Terms All rights revert back to author. Not copyrighted.

Ⓝ ☑ $ THE PEDESTAL MAGAZINE

Pedestal Enterprises, Inc., 6815 Honors Court, Charlotte NC 28210. (704) 643-0244. E-mail: pedmagazine@ carolina.rr.com. Web site www.thepedestalmagazine.com **Contact:** Nathan Leslie, editor; John Amen, editor-in-chief. Online literary magazine/journal. "We publish poetry, fiction, reviews and interviews. We are committed to the individual voice and publish an eclectic mix of high-quality work." Bimonthly. Estab. 2000. Member CLMP.

Needs Adventure, ethnic/multicultural, experimental, family saga, fantasy, feminist, gay, glitz, historical, horror, humor/satire, lesbian, literary, mainstream, military/war, mystery, new age, psychic/ supernatural/occult, romance, science fiction, thriller/espionage. Receives 100-150 mss/month. Accepts 3-5 mss/issue; 18-24 mss/year. Closed to submissions at the following times: January, March, May, July, September, November: from the 12th-19th; February, April, June, August, October, December: from the 14th-28th. Ms published 1-3 weeks after acceptance. **Publishes 1-2 new writers/year.** Published Grant Tracy, Mary Grabar, Karen Heuler, James Scott Iredell, Don Shea, Mary Carroll-Hackett, R.T. Smith and Richard Peabody. Publishes short shorts. Also publishes book reviews, poetry. Send review query to pedmagazine@carolina.rr.com. Rarely comments on/critiques rejected mss.

How to Contact Submit via the online form provided on the Web site. Include brief bio, list of publications. Responds to queries in 2-3 days. Responds to mss in 4-6 weeks. Considers simultaneous submissions, multiple submissions. Guidelines available on Web site.

Payment/Terms Writers receive 5¢/word. Pays on publication. Acquires first rights. Sends galleys to author. Publication is copyrighted.

Tips "Strong characterization, imagery and a distinct voice are always important. Also, we always look for startling or unusual themes and content. Writers we publish should be willing to push their readers and themselves into unfamiliar terrain. We read too many generic stories that read like bad television. Read the magazine to get a sense of what we publish. Polish your work as much as possible before submitting. Be professional."

THE PINK CHAMELEON

E-mail: dpfreda@juno.com. Website: http://www.geocities.com/thepinkchameleon/index.html. **Contact:** Mrs. Dorothy Paula Freda, editor/publisher. Family-oriented electronic magazine. Annual. Estab. 2000. Reading period from January-April 30 and September-October 31.

Needs Short stories, adventure, family saga, fantasy, humor/satire, literary, mainstream, mystery/ suspense, religious/inspirational, romance, science fiction, thriller/espionage, western, young adult/ teen, psychic/supernatural. "No violence for the sake of violence." Receives 20 unsolicited mss/month. Publishes ms within 1 year after acceptance. **Publishes 50% new writers/year.** Recently published work by Deanne F. Purcell, Martin Green, Albert J. Manachino, James W. Collins, Lanette Kissel, Mel Grillo/ Carmella Prochnau, and Denise Noe. Length: 500-2,500 words; average length: 2,000 words. Publishes short shorts. No novels or novel excerpts. Also publishes literary essays, poetry. Sometimes comments on rejected mss.

How to Contact Send complete ms in the body of the e-mail. No attachments. Responds in 1 month to mss. Accepts reprints. No simultaneous submissions. Sample copy online. Writer's guidelines online.

Payment/Terms "Non-profit. Acquires one-time rights for one year but will return rights earlier on request."

Tips "Simple, honest, evocative emotion, upbeat submissions that give hope for the future; well-paced plots; stories, poetry, articles, essays that speak from the heart. Read guidelines carefully. Use a good, but not ostentatious, opening hook. Stories should have a beginning, middle and end that make the reader feel the story was worth his or her time. This also applies to articles and essays. In the latter two, wrap your comments and conclusions in a neatly packaged final paragraph. Turnoffs include violence, bad language. Simple, genuine and sensitive work does not need to shock with vulgarity to be interesting and enjoyable."

☑ ◎ $ PSEUDOPOD, THE SOUND OF HORROR

Escape Artists, Inc., P.O. Box 1538, Stone Mountain GA 30086. (678) 389-6700. Fax: (206) 666-3763. E-mail: editor@pseudopod.org. Website: http://pseudopod.org. **Contact:** Ben Phillips, Editor. Online magazine. 25-40 min weekly episode, 5-10 min for sporadic specials like flash fiction or movie/book reviews. "Pseudopod is a genre magazine in audio form. We're looking for horror: dark, weird fiction. We run the spectrum from grim realism or magic-realism to blatantly supernatural dark fantasy. We publish highly literary stories reminiscent of Poe or Lovecraft, as well as vulgar, innovative, and/or shock-value-focused pulp fiction. We don't split hairs about genre definitions, and we don't have any hard and fast taboos about what kind of content can appear in our stories. Originality demands that you're better off avoiding vampires, zombies, and other recognizable horror tropes unless you have put a very original spin on them. (Ghosts are currently somewhat more smiled upon, mainly because they haven't settled into such predictably canonical treatment; you don't know what a ghost can do until the author establishes it, so fear of the unknown is intact - which is the real lesson here.) What matters most is just that the stories are dark and entertaining." Weekly. Estab. 2006. Circ. 5,500.

- Episode 27 was a finalist nominee for the 2007 Parsec (podcasting) award for Best SF Story (short form).

Needs Horror (dark fantasy, futuristic, psychological, supernatural, sentimental, literary, erotic, splatterpunk, romantic, humorours). Does not want archetypical vampire, zombie, or werewolf fiction. Receives 100 mss/month. Accepts 1 mss/issue; 70 mss/year. Manuscript published 1 month after acceptance. **Publishes 20 new writers/year.** Published Joel Arnold, Kevin J. Anderson, Richard Dansky, Scott Sigler, Paul Jessup, Nicholas Ozment, and Stephen Gaskell. Length: 2,000-6,000 words. Average length: 3,000 words. Publishes short shorts. Average length of short shorts: 800 words. Often comments on/critiques rejected manuscripts.

How to Contact Send complete ms with cover letter. Accepts submissions by e-mail. Include estimated word count, brief bio, brief list of publications. Responds to queries in 2 weeks. Responds to mss in 2 months. Considers simultaneous submissions, previously published submissions. Sample copy, guidelines available on Web site.

Payment/Terms Writers receive $20 under 2,000 words, $50 over 2,000 words. Pays on acceptance. "*Pseudopod* is released under a Creative Commons Attribution-Noncommercial-No Derivative Works 3.0 License - see http://creativecommons.org for more info."

Tips "Fast pacing is very important for audio listeners, but we forgive a lot in the name of literary value for outstanding stories. Be original, disturbing, and preferably character-focused. Have it critiqued first by a local writer's group (horror-oriented or not, it shouldn't matter—you want to tell a good story by conventional standards as well as have appeal for horror fans), or barring that, by an online critique group such as critters.org."

◎ $ RAVING DOVE

E-mail: ravingdove@gmail.com. Website: www.ravingdove.org. **Contact:** Jo-Ann Moss, Editor. Online literary magazine. "Raving Dove publishes writing, poetry, and art with universal, anti-violence, anti-hate, human rights, and social justice themes. We share sentiments that oppose physical and psychological violence in all its forms, including war, discrimination against sexual orientation, and every shade of bigotry." Quarterly. Estab. 2004.

Needs Literary, mainstream. "*Raving Dove* is not a political publication. Material for or against one specific person or entity will not be considered, fictitious or otherwise." Ms published up to 3 months after acceptance. Length: 2,000 words (max). Also publishes poetry.

How to Contact Accepts submissions by e-mail only. Include brief bio, submission genre, i.e., fiction, nonfiction, poetry, etc., in the e-mail subject line. Responds to mss in 3 months. Considers simultaneous submissions. Guidelines available on Web site.

Payment/Terms Payment is based on available funding. (Check Web site for current information.) Acquires one-time North American and Internet serial rights, exclusive for the duration of the edition in which the work appears (3 months).

☑ ◎ RESIDENTIAL ALIENS, Speculative Fiction from the Seven Stars

ResAliens, 7412 E Brookview Cir., Wichita KS 67226. (316) 871-1200. E-mail: resaliens@gmail.com. Website: http://residentialaliens.blogspot.com. **Contact:** Lyn Perry, Founding Editor. Online magazine/E-zine. "Because reading and writing speculative fiction is a strong interest of mine, I thought I'd contribute to the genre of faith-informed spec fic by offering other writers and readers of science fiction, fantasy, spiritual and supernatural thrillers a quality venue in which to share their passion. You could say ResAliens is speculative fiction with a spiritual thread." Monthly. Estab. 2007.

Needs Fantasy (space fantasy, sword and sorcery), horror (supernatural), science fiction (soft/sociological). Does not want horror, gore, erotica. Will publish another Sci-Fi/Fantasy anthology. List of upcoming themes available for SASE, on Web site. Receives 20 mss/month. Accepts 5-6 mss/issue; 65-75 mss/year. Ms published 1-2 months after acceptance. **Publishes 25 new writers/year.** Published George L. Duncan (author of novel *A Cold and Distant Memory*), Patrick G. Cox (author of novel *Out of Time*), Merrie Destefano (editor of *Victorian Homes Magazine*), Brandon Barr (co-author of upcoming novel *When the Sky Fell*), Ilaria Dal Brun (short story "Foul Breath"), Alex Moisi (short story "Up or Down"), Curtis Schweitzer (short story "Colossus"), and Glyn Shull (short story "Demonic Intent"). Length: 500-5,000 words. Average length: 3,500 words. Publishes short shorts. Average length of short shorts: 900 words. Will take serial novellas of 2-5 installments (up to 20,000 words). Also publishes book reviews. Send review copies to lyngperry@yahoo.com. Often comments on/critiques rejected mss.

How to Contact Send complete ms with cover letter. Accepts submissions by e-mail. Include estimated word count, brief bio. Responds to queries in 2-5 days; to mss in 1-2 weeks. Considers simultaneous submissions, previously published submissions, multiple submissions. Sample copy and guidelines available on Web site.

Payment/Terms Writers receive PDF file as their contributor's copy. Acquires one-time rights, electronic rights, 6 month archive rights. Sends galleys to author. Publication is copyrighted. "Occasionally sponsors contests."

Tips "We want stories that read well and move quickly. We enjoy all sorts of speculative fiction, and 'tried and true' forms and themes are fine as long as the author has a slightly different take or a fresh perspective on a topic. For example, time machine stories are great—how is yours unique or interesting?"

☑ R-KV-R-Y, A QUARTERLY LITERARY JOURNAL

90 Meetings in 90 Days Press, 499 North Canon Dr., Suite 400, Beverly Hills CA 90210. (323)217-5162. Fax: (323)852-1535. E-mail: victoriapynchon@gmail.com. Website: www.ninetymeetingsinninetydays. com. **Contact:** Victoria Pynchon, editor-in-chief. Online magazine. 100 Web pages. Contains illustrations. Includes photographs. "R-KV-R-Y publishes half a dozen short stories of high literary quality every quarter. We publish fiction that varies widely in style. We prefer stories of character development, psychological penetration, and lyricism, without sentimentality or purple prose. We ask that all submissions address issues related to recovery from any type of physical, psychological, or cultural loss, dislocation or oppression. We include but do not limit ourselves to issues of substance abuse. We do not publish the standard 'what it was like, what happened and what it is like now' recovery narrative. Works published by R-KV-R-Y embrace almost every area of adult interest related to recovery: literary affairs, history, folklore, fiction, poetry, literary criticism, art, music, and the theatre. Material should be presented in a fashion suited to a quarterly that is neither journalistic nor academic. We welcome academic articles from varying fields. We encourage our academic contributors to free themselves from the contraints imposed by academic journals, letting their knowledge, wisdom, and experience rock and roll on these pages. Our intended audience is people of discriminating taste, original ideas, heart, and love of narrative and language." Quarterly. Estab. 2004. Circ. 15,000 quarterly readers.

Needs Literary. List of upcoming themes available on Web site. Receives 10 mss/month. Accepts 5 mss/issue; 20 mss/year. Manuscript published 2-3 months after acceptance. Agented fiction 10%. **Publishes**

5-6 new writers/year. Published Rita Coleman (debut fiction), Anne LaBorde (debut literary nonfiction), Richard Wirick, Joseph Mockus, Birute Serota, Zoe Kiethley, Lee Patton, Nathan Leslie, Kathleen Wakefield, Sherry Lynne Maze (debut). Length: 5,000 words (max). Average length: 2,000 words. Publishes short shorts. Average length of short shorts: 1,000 words. Also publishes literary essays, book reviews, poetry. Sometimes comments on/critiques rejected manuscripts.

How to Contact Send complete ms with cover letter. Accepts submissions by e-mail. Include brief bio, list of publications. Responds to queries in 2 weeks. Responds to mss in 1-3 months. Considers simultaneous submissions, previously published submissions. Guidelines available on Web site.

Payment/Terms Acquires electronic rights. Posts proof pages on site. Publication is copyrighted.

Tips "Wants strong focus on character development and lively writing style with strong voice. Read our present and former issues (archived online) as well as fiction found in such journals and magazines as *Granta*, *The New Yorker*, *Tri-Quarterly*, *The Atlantic*, *Harper's*, *Story* and similar sources of the highest quality fiction."

☑ $ ☒ THE ROSE & THORN LITERARY E-ZINE

E-mail: BAQuinn@aol.com. Website: www.theroseandthornezine.com. **Contact:** Barbara Quinn, fiction editor, publisher, managing editor. E-zine specializing in literary works of fiction, nonfiction, poetry and essays. "We created this publication for readers and writers alike. We provide a forum for emerging and established voices. We blend contemporary writing with traditional prose and poetry in an effort to promote the literary arts." Quarterly. Circ. 120,000.

Needs Adventure, ethnic/multicultural, experimental, fantasy, historical, horror (dark fantasy, futuristic, psychological, supernatural), humor/satire, literary, mainstream, mystery/suspense, New Age, regional, religious/inspirational, romance (contemporary, futuristic/time travel, gothic, historical, regency, romantic suspense), science fiction, thriller/espionage, western. Receives "several hundred" unsolicited mss/month. Accepts 8-10 mss/issue; 40-50 mss/year. **Publishes many new writers/year.** Publishes short shorts. Also publishes literary essays, poetry. Sometimes comments on rejected mss.

How to Contact Query with or without published clips or send complete ms. Accepts submissions by e-mail. Include estimated word count, 150-word bio, list of publications and author's byline. Responds in 1 week to queries; 1 month to mss. Accepts simultaneous submissions and reprints. Sample copy free. Writer's guidelines online. Length: 2,000 word limit.

Payment/Terms Writer retains all rights. Sends galleys to author. Pays $5 for each piece published.

Tips "Clarity, control of the language, evocative stories that tug at the heart and make their mark on the reader long after it's been read. We look for uniqueness in voice, style and characterization. New twists on old themes are always welcome. Use all aspects of good writing in your stories, including dynamic characters, strong narrative voice and a riveting original plot. We have eclectic tastes, so go ahead and give us a shot. Read the publication and other quality literary journals so you'll see what we look for. Always check your spelling and grammar before submitting. Reread your submission with a critical eye and ask yourself, 'Does it evoke an emotional response? Have I completely captured my reader?' Check your submission for 'it' and 'was' and see if you can come up with a better way to express yourself. Be unique."

☑ SLOW TRAINS LITERARY JOURNAL

P.O. 4741, Denver CO 80155. E-mail: editor@slowtrains.com. Website: www.slowtrains.com. **Contact**: Susannah Indigo. Quarterly. Estab. 2000.

Needs Literary. No romance, sci-fi, or other specific genre-writing. Receives 100+ unsolicited mss/month. Accepts 10-15 mss/issue; 40-50 mss/year. Publishes ms 3 months after acceptance. **Publishes 20- 40 new writers/year.** Length: 1,000-5,000 words; average length: 3,500 words. Publishes short shorts. Also publishes literary essays, poetry. Rarely comments on rejected mss.

How to Contact Accepts submissions by e-mail. Responds in 4-8 weeks to mss. Accepts simultaneous and reprints submissions. Sample copy online. Writer's guidelines online.

Payment/Terms Pays 2 contributor's copies. Acquires one-time, electronic rights.

Tips "The first page must be able to pull the reader in immediately. Use your own fresh, poetic, compelling voice. Center your story around some emotional truth, and be sure of what you're trying to say."

☐ SNREVIEW

197 Fairchild Ave., Fairfield CT 06825-4856. (203) 366-5991. E-mail: editor@snreview.org. Website: www.snreview.org. **Contact:** Joseph Conlin, editor. E-zine and print edition specializing in literary short stories, essays and poetry. "We search for material that not only has strong characters and plot but also a devotion to imagery." Now available in a print edition. Quarterly. Estab. 1999.

Needs Literary, mainstream. Receives 200 unsolicited mss/month. Accepts 40 + mss/issue; 150 mss/year. Publishes ms 6 months after acceptance. **Publishes 50 new writers/year.** Recently published work by Frank X. Walker, Adrian Louis, Barbara Burkhardt, E. Lindsey Balkan, Marie Griffin and Jonathan Lerner. Length: 1,000-7,000 words; average length: 4,000 words. Also publishes literary essays, literary criticism, poetry.

How to Contact Accepts submissions by e-mail only. Include 100 word bio and list of publications. Responds in 3 months to mss. Accepts simultaneous and reprints submissions. Sample copy online. Writer's guidelines online. A printe edition of SNReview is now available from an on-demand printer.

Payment/Terms Acquires first electronic and print rights.

☑ $ SPACESUITS AND SIXGUNS

Silvern Studios, 3704 E. Main, #204, Gatesville TX 76528. E-mail: submissions@spacesuitsandsixguns.com. Website: http://www.spacesuitsandsixguns.com. **Contact:** Dave Duggins (editor@spacesuitandsixguns.com). Online magazine. "Spacesuits and Sixguns is a magazine of contemporary pulp fiction—simple, straightforward storytelling with an emphasis on humor and action. We're not looking for Lovecraft or Howard pastiches, or stories set in the 1930's. Read a dozen pulp fiction stories, soak it all up, then ask yourself: what if this happened in my hometown today? Write close to home, write about what you love, and follow Elmore Leonard's maxim: leave out the parts people skip. All genres accepted—detective, horror, mystery, adventure, SF, sword and sorcery. We love them all. Give us about 4,000 words. Shorter is fine. We're flexible. If it's longer and it's good, no problem. Rule number one—be fun!" Quarterly. Estab. 2007. Circ. 2,500. Member SLF Small Press co-op.

Needs Fantasy (space fantasy), horror (dark fantasy, futuristic, psychological, supernatural), humor/satire, mystery (amateur sleuth, police procedural, private eye/hard-boiled), science fiction (space opera). Does not want erotica. List of upcoming themes available for SASE, on Web site. Receives 500 mss/month. Accepts 4-6 mss/issue; 16-24 mss/year. Ms published 1-3 months after acceptance. **Publishes few new writers/year.** Published Mike Wiecek, Lucy Snyder, Andrew Nicolle. Length: 4,000 words (max). Average length: 3,000 words. Publishes short shorts. Average length of short shorts: 1,000 words. Sometimes comments on/critiques rejected mss.

How to Contact Send complete ms with cover letter. Accepts submissions by e-mail. Include estimated word count, brief bio. Sample copy and guidelines available on Web site.

Payment/Terms Writers receive 3¢-$100. Pays on publication. Acquires first North American serial rights. Sends galleys to author. Publication is copyrighted.

Tips "Originality and authenticity stand out. The easiest way to accomplish this is to follow James Magnuson's dictum: find the most powerful experience in your life and write about it. Read well and exhaustively. If you decide to write a story about robots rebelling against their human masters, be aware of the enormous body of work already concerned with that subject. Read it all, then evaluate your own idea."

☐ ◎ $ ⧉ SPACEWESTERNS: THE E-ZINE OF THE SPACE WESTERN SUB-GENRE

P.O. Box 93, Parker Ford, PA 19457. (610) 410-7400. E-mail: submissions2018@spacewesterns.com. Website: www.spacewesterns.com. **Contact:** N.E. Lilly, Editor-in-chief. E-zine. "Aside from strictly short stories we also like to see stage plays, screen plays, comics, audio files of stories, short form videos and animation." Weekly. Estab. 2007.

Needs Adventure, comics/graphic novels, ethnic/multicultural, fantasy (space fantasy), horror (dark fantasy, futuristic, psychological, supernatural), humor/satire, mystery, science fiction (hard science/technological, soft/sociological), western (frontier saga, traditional), but it *must be space western*, science fiction western. List of upcoming themes available on Web site. Receives 12 mss/month. Accepts 52 mss/year. Ms published within 6 months after acceptance. **Publishes 12 new writers/year.** Published Camille Alexa, Vonnie Winslow Crist, Jens Rushing, Amanda Spikol, Donald Jacob Uitvlugt, John M. Whalen, A.R. Yngve, Filamena Young. Length: 2,500-7,500 words. Average length: 4,000-5,000 words. Also publishes literary essays, literary criticism, book reviews, poetry. Send review copies to N. E. Lilly. Often comments on/critiques rejected mss.

How to Contact Send complete ms with cover letter. Accepts submissions by e-mail only. Include estimated word count. Responds to queries immediately. Responds to mss in 6 weeks. Considers previously published submissions, multiple submissions. Guidelines available on Web site.

Payment/Terms Writers receive 1¢ per word, $50 max. Pays on publication. Publication is copyrighted.

Tips "First of all, have a well-crafted manuscript (no spelling or grammar errors). Secondly, a good idea—many errors will be forgiven for a solid concept and fresh idea. Be yourself. Write what you love. Familiarize yourself with the scope of the Universe and astronomical concepts."

☑ ◎ STILL CRAZY: AN ONLINE LITERARY MAGAZINE

(614) 746-0859. E-mail: editor@crazylitmag.com. Website: www.crazylitmag.com. **Contact:** Barbara Kussow, editor. "Still Crazy publishes writing by people over age 50 and writing by people of any age if the topic is about people over 50. The editor is particularly interested in material that challenges the stereotypes of older people and that portrays older people's inner lives as rich and rewarding." Semiannual. Estab. 2007.

Needs Feminist. Special interests: seniors (over 50). "Does not want material that is too sentimental or inspirational." Accepts 6-8 mss/issue; 12-16 mss/year. Manuscript published 6-12 months after acceptance. Length: 5,000 words (max) under 3,000 words more likely to be published. Publishes short shorts. Also publishes poetry and short non-fiction. Sometimes comments on/critiques rejected mss.

How to Contact Submit via e-mail form on Web site. Attach MS Word doc or cut and paste into text of email. Include estimated word count, brief bio, age of writer. Responds to mss in 6 months. Considers simultaneous submissions, previously published submissions (please indicate when and where), multiple submissions. Guidelines available on Web site.

Payment/Terms Acquires one-time rights. Publication is not copyrighted.

Tips Looking for "interesting characters and interesting situations. Humor and Lightness welcome."

☑ STORY BYTES

E-mail: editor@storybytes.com. Website: www.storybytes.com. **Contact:** M. Stanley Bubien, editor. Electronic zine. "We are strictly an electronic publication, appearing on the Internet in three forms. First, the stories are sent to an electronic mailing list of readers. They also get placed on our Web site, both in PDF and HTML format."

Needs "Stories must be very short—having a length that is the power of 2, specifically: 2, 4, 8, 16, 32, etc." No sexually explicit material. "Would like to see more material dealing with religion—not necessarily 'inspirational' stories, but those that show the struggles of living a life of faith in a realistic manner." **Publishes 33% new writers/year.** Recently published work by Richard K. Weems, Joseph Lerner, Lisa Cote and Thomas Sennet.

How to Contact Please query first. Query with or without published clips or send complete ms. Accepts submissions by e-mail. "I prefer plain text with story title, authorship and word count. Only accepts electronic submissions. See Web site for complete guidelines." Sample copy online. Writer's guidelines online.

Tips "In Story Bytes the very short stories themselves range in topic. Many explore a brief event—a vignette of something unusual, unique and at times something even commonplace. Some stories can be bizarre, while others quite lucid. Some are based on actual events, while others are entirely fictional. Try to develop conflict early on (in the first sentence if possible!), and illustrate or resolve this conflict through action rather than description. I believe we'll find an audience for electronic published works primarily in the short story realm."

☑ STORYSOUTH

5603B W. Friendly Ave., Suite 282, Greensboro NC 27410. E-mail: editors@storysouth.com. Website: www.storysouth.com. **Contact:** Terry Kennedy, editor. "storySouth is interested in fiction, creative nonfiction, and poetry by writers from the New South. The exact definition New South varies from person to person and we leave it up to the writer to define their own connection to the southern United States." Quarterly. Estab. 2001.

Needs Experimental, literary, regional (south), translations. Receives 70 unsolicited mss/month. Accepts 5 mss/issue; 20 mss/year. Publishes ms 1 month after acceptance. **Publishes 5-10 new writers/year.** Average length: 4,000 words. Publishes short shorts. Also publishes literary essays, literary criticism, poetry. Often comments on rejected mss.

How to Contact Send complete ms. Accepts online submissions only. Responds in 4 months to mss. No simultaneous submissions. Writer's guidelines online.

Payment/Terms Acquires one-time rights.

Tips "What really makes a story stand out is a strong voice and a sense of urgency—a need for the reader to keep reading the story and not put it down until it is finished."

☑ $ THE SUMMERSET REVIEW

25 Summerset Dr., Smithtown NY 11787. E-mail: editor@summersetreview.org. Website: www. summersetreview.org. **Contact:** Joseph Levens, editor. Magazine: illustrations and photographs. "Our goal is simply to publish the highest quality literary fiction and essays intended for a general audience. This is a simple online literary journal of high quality material, so simple you can call it unique." Periodically releaseses print issues. Quarterly. Estab. 2002.

• Several editors-in-chief of very prominent literary publications have done interviews for *The Summerset Review*: M.M.M. Hayes of *StoryQuarterly*, Gina Frangello of *Other Voices*, Jennifer Spiegel of *Hayden's Ferry Review*.

Needs Literary. No sci-fi, horror, or graphic erotica. Receives 100 unsolicited mss/month. Accepts 4 mss/issue; 18 mss/year. Publishes ms 2-3 months after acceptance. **Publishes 5-10 new writers/year.** Length: 8,000 words; average length: 3,000 words. Publishes short shorts. Also publishes literary essays. Usually critiques on mss that were almost accepted.

How to Contact Send complete ms. Accepts submissions by e-mail. Responds in 1-2 weeks to queries; 4-12 weeks to mss. Accepts simultaneous and reprints submissions. Writer's guidelines online.

Payment/Terms $25 per story/essay. Acquires no rights other than one-time publishing, although we request credit if first published in *The Summerset Review*. Sends galleys to author.

Tips "Style counts. We prefer innovative or at least very smooth, convincing voices. Even the dullest of premises or the complete lack of conflict make for an interesting story if it is told in the right voice and style. We like to find little, interesting facts and/or connections subtly sprinkled throughout the piece. Harsh language should be used only if/when necessary. If we are choosing between light and dark subjects, the light will usually win."

☑ ◎ $ SUSURRUS: THE LITERATURE OF MADNESS

Susurrus Press, 535 4th Ave Suite 3, Huntington WV 25701-1248. (304) 622-9434. E-mail: editor@ susurrusmagazine.com. Website: www.susurrusmagazine.com. **Contact:** Brian Worley, James Maddox, Fiction Editors. Online magazine. "Susurrus is a highly experimental venue for fiction that deals with the human condition in speculative situations. We publish fiction that shows that to be human is to be at least a little bit crazy. (Keeping this in mind, we publish very few insane asylum/psychiatric ward stories. We know crazy people are crazy. We want stories that show the rest of us are, too.)" Quarterly. Estab. 2005. Circ. 1,000 unique hits a month.

Needs Adventure, experimental, humor/satire, literary, science fiction (soft/sociological). Special interests: cross-genre, slipstream, magical realism, surreal. Does not want serial killers, goth vampires, stories that turn out to be delusions by a person in an asylum, or stories that only detail a murder/suicide. Receives 50-100 mss/month. Accepts 6-8 mss/issue; 24-32 mss/year. Ms published 1-3 months after acceptance. **Publishes 5-10 new writers/year.** Published Cameron Pierce, Ashley Kaufman, James Swingle, Chris Pritchard, Tamara Kaye Sellman and Laura Sanger Kelly. Length: 25-5,000 words. Average length: 2,000 words. Publishes short shorts. Average length of short shorts: 500 words. Also publishes literary essays, literary criticism, book reviews, poetry. Send review copies to Brian Worley or James Maddox. Often comments on/critiques rejected mss.

How to Contact Send complete ms with cover letter. Accepts submissions by e-mail. Include estimated word count, brief bio. Responds to queries in 1-2 weeks. Responds to mss in 1-3 months. Considers simultaneous submissions, previously published submissions, multiple submissions. Guidelines and sample available on Web site.

Payment/Terms Pays on publication. Acquires electronic rights. Publication is copyrighted.

Tips "As an online publisher, we have to remember that our readers are only three clicks away from seeing their house from outer space. Therefore, we like fiction that is paced for short attention spans. Beautiful, detailed description is great, but don't let it weigh down your story. Know both the genre you're writing in, and the magazine to which you're submitting. In other words, read the magazine, read from the section of the bookstore that's like what you write, then read some more."

☑ TERRAIN.ORG: A JOURNAL OF THE BUILT & NATURAL ENVIROMENTS

Terrain.org, P.O. Box 19161, Tucson, AZ 19161. (520) 241-7390. E-mail: contact2@terrain.org. Website: www.terrain.org. **Contact:** Simmons Buntin, Editor/Publisher. E-zine. "Terrain.org is searching for that interface-the integration-among the built and natural enviroments, that might be called the soul of place. The works contained within Terrain.org ultimately examine the physical realm around us, and how those enviroments influence us and each other physically, mentally, emotionally and spiritually." Semiannual. Estab. 1998.
* PLANetizen Top 50 Website 2002 & 2003.

Needs Adventure, ethnic/multicultural, experimental, family saga, fantasy, feminist, gay, glitz, historical, horror, humor/satire, lesbian, literary, mainstream, military/war, mystery, new age, psychic/supernatural/ occult, science fiction, thriller/espionage, translations, western. Special interests: enviromental. Does not want erotica. All issues are theme-based. List of upcoming themes available on Web site. Receives 10 mss/month. Accepts 3-5 mss/issue; 6-10 mss/year. Does not read June 1-August 1 and December 1-February 1. Manuscript published five weeks to 18 months after acceptance. Agented fiction 5%. **Publishes 1-3 new writers/year.** Published Al Sim, Jacob MacAurthur Mooney, T.R. Healy, Deborah Fries, Andrew Wingfield, Martin Ott, Scott Spires and Tiel Aisha Ansari. Length: 1,000-8,000 words. Average length: 5,000 words. Publishes short shorts. Average length of short shorts: 750 words. Also publishes literary essays, literary criticism, book reviews, poetry. Send review copies to Simmon Buntin. Sometimes comments on/critiques rejected mss.

How to Contact Send complete ms with cover letter. Accepts submissions online@ http://sub.terrain.org. Include brief bio. Responds to queries in 2 weeks. Responds to mss in 4 weeks. Considers simultaneous submissions, previously published submissions. Guidelines available on Web site.

Payment/Terms Acquires one-time rights. Sends galleys to author. Publication is copyrighted.

Tips "We have three primary criteria in reviewing fiction: 1) The story is compelling and well-crafted. 2) The story provides some element of surprise; i.e., whether in content, form or delivery we are unexpectedly delighted in what we've read. 3) The story meets an upcoming theme, even if only peripherally. Read fiction in the current issue and perhaps some archived work, and if you like what you read—and our overall enviromental slant—then send us your best work. Make sure you follow our submission guidelines (including cover note with bio), and that your manuscript is as error-free as possible."

☐ TOASTED CHEESE

E-mail: editors@toasted-cheese.com. Website: www.toasted-cheese.com. **Contact:** submit@toasted-cheese.com. E-zine specializing in fiction, creative nonfiction, poetry and flash fiction. "Toasted Cheese accepts submissions of previously unpublished fiction, flash fiction, creative nonfiction and poetry. Our focus is on quality of work, not quantity. Some issues will therefore contain fewer/more pieces than previous issues. We don't restrict publication based on subject matter. We encourage submissions from innovative writers in all genres." Quarterly. Estab. 2001.

Needs Adventure, children's/juvenile, ethnic/multicultural, fantasy, feminist, gay, historical, horror, humor/satire, lesbian, literary, mainstream, mystery/suspense, New Age, psychic/supernatural/occult, romance, science fiction, thriller/espionage, western. "No fan fiction. No chapters or excerpts unless they read as a stand-alone story. No first drafts." Receives 70 unsolicited mss/month. Accepts 1-10 mss/ issue; 5-30 mss/year. **Publishes 15 new writers/year.** Publishes short shorts. Also publishes poetry.

How to Contact Send complete ms in body of e-mail; no attachments. Accepts submissions by e-mail. Responds in 4 months to mss. No simultaneous submissions. Sample copy online. Writer's guidelines online.

Payment/Terms Acquires electronic rights. Sponsors awards/contests.

Tips "We are looking for clean, professional writing from writers of any level. Accepted stories will be concise and compelling. We are looking for writers who are serious about the craft: tomorrow's literary stars before they're famous. Take your submission seriously, yet remember that levity is appreciated. You are submitting not to traditional 'editors' but to fellow writers who appreciate the efforts of those in the trenches."

◪ ◎ $ TOWER OF LIGHT FANTASY FREE ONLINE

9701 Harford Road, Carney MD 21234. (410) 661-3362. E-mail: tol@tolfantasy.com. Website: www.tolfantasy.com **Contact:** Michael Southard, editor. Online magazine. "To publish great fantasy stories, especially the genre-blending kind such as dark fantasy, urban, science, and superhero fantasy. Romantic fantasy (not erotic, however) is also acceptable. And Tower of Light would very much like to showcase new work by beginning writers." Biannual. Estab. 2007.

Needs Fantasy (space fantasy, sword and sorcery), horror (dark fantasy, futuristic, supernatural), psychic/supernatural/occult, religious (fantasy), romance (fantasy). Does not want erotic fantasy, or anything that does not have a mystical or supernatural element. List of upcoming themes available on Web site. Receives 15-30 mss/month. Accepts 6 mss/issue; 12 mss/year. Reading period: Jan 1-Mar 31; July 1-Aug 31. Ms published 6-12 months after acceptance. Published Ian Whates, Christopher Heath, Tom Williams, Daniel Henderson, Alice M. Roelke, Matthew Baron, Eric S. Brown, Ryder Patzuk-Russell and Mischell Lyne. Length: 500-4,000 words. Average length: 3,500 words. Publishes short shorts. Also publishes book reviews. Send review copies to Michael Southard. Sometimes comments on/critiques rejected mss.

How to Contact Send ms in the body of e-mail. Unfortunately, artwork must be sent as an attachment. Responds to mss in 6-12 weeks. Considers previously published submissions, multiple submissions. Guidelines, sample copy available on Web site.

Payment/Terms Writers and artists receive $5. Pays on publication. Acquires one-time rights, electronic rights. Occasionally sends galleys to author. Publication is not copyrighted.

Tips "Strong, well-developed characters that really elicit an emotional response, good writing, original plots and world-building catch my attention. Send me a good story, and make sure to check your spelling and grammar. I don't mind a couple of errors, but when there's more than half a dozen, it gets really irritating. Make sure to study the guidelines thoroughly; I'm looking for character-driven stories, preferably in third person limited point-of-view."

Ⓝ ◻ ◲ UGLY ACCENT, A Literary Adversaria Brought to You by the Midwest

2310 40th Pl NW, #302, Washington DC 20007. E-mail: editor@uglyaccent.com. Website: www.uglyaccent.com. **Contact:** Juli Obudzinski, Fiction Editor. Online and print literary magazine: 8.5 × 11; 40 pages; newsprint paper; contains illustrations, photographs. "Ugly Accent is an emerging literary journal out of Madison, Wisconsin. The focus of our journal is not only to publish exceptional writing, but also to glorify the cesspool of talent this region breeds. We put forth a challenge to our submitters to find that inherent degree of separation from the good ole heartland." Semiannual. Estab. 2006. Circ. 2,000.

Needs Experimental, feminist, gay, humor/satire, lesbian, literary, regional (midwest). Does not want pieces containing unnessesary violence or those that are sexist, racist or homophobic in nature. Receives 10 mss/month. Accepts 2-7 mss/issue; 15-20 mss/year. Ms published 6 months after acceptance. **Publishes 5-10 new writers/year**. Published Susan Yount, Brian Nealon, C.J. Krueger, Joseph Fronczak, Ryan Chapman, Shanley Erin Kane, Bayard Godsave, Erica Goodkind, Louis Bourgeois, Erin Pringle,and Nicolette Kittinger. Length: 1,000-6,000 words. Average length: 3,000 words. Publishes short shorts. Average length of short shorts: 1,000 words. Also publishes literary essays, literary criticism, book reviews, poetry. Send review copies to Juli Obudzinski. Often comments on/critiques rejected mss.

How to Contact Send complete ms with cover letter. Include estimated word count, brief bio, list of publications. Responds to queries in 2-4 weeks; mss in 4-6 months. Send disposable copy of ms and #10 SASE for reply only. Considers simultaneous submissions, previously published submissions. Sample copy available on Web site. Guidelines available on Web site.

Payment/Terms Writers receive contributor's copies. Pays on publication. Acquires one-time rights, electronic rights. Publication is not copyrighted.

Tips "We are looking for writers with subtlety and a predilection for experimentation with language and form. We believe that prose should test the elasticity of language and utilize the form for all its worth. We seek literary pieces that challenge everything else that ends up filling the shelves of chain stores littered across the country. Those looking for fame need not apply. Instead, those whose writing challenges the mold, works against the metaphorical grain. We like good writing, who doesn't, but it also has to catch our attention somehow. Satires, absurdity, form stretching free style prose are all goodies for us. We like when you bend the rules a little and things become messy and a little strange."

VERBSAP.COM, CONCISE PROSE. ENOUGH SAID.

VERBSAP.COM, Concise Prose. Enough Said. E-mail: editor@verbsap.com. Website: www.verbsap.com. **Contact:** Laurie Seider, editor. Online magazine. "Verbsap showcases an eclectic selection of the finest in concise prose by established and emerging writers." Published quarterly. Estab. 2005. Needs Literary, mainstream. Does not want violent, racist or pornographic content. Accepts 200 mss/year. Ms published 2-4 weeks after acceptance. Length: 3,000 words (max). Average length: 2,000 words. Publishes short shorts. Average length of short shorts: 900 words. Also publishes literary essays, author and artist interviews, and book reviews. Always comments on/critiques rejected mss.

How to Contact Follow online guidelines. Accepts submissions by e-mail. Responds to mss in 1-3 weeks. Considers simultaneous submissions. Guidelines available on Web site.

Payment/Terms Sends galleys to author. Publication is copyrighted.

Tips "We're looking for stark, elegant prose. Make us weep or make us laugh, but move us. You might find our 'Editor's Notebook' essays helpful."

WILD VIOLET

Wild Violet, P.O. Box 39706, Philadelphia PA 19106-9706. E-mail: wildvioletmagazine@yahoo.com. Website: www.wildviolet.net. **Contact:** Alyce Wilson, editor. Online magazine: illustrations, photos. "Our goal is to make a place for the arts: to make the arts more accessible and to serve as a creative forum for writers and artists. Our audience includes English-speaking readers from all over the world, who are interested in both 'high art' and pop culture." Quarterly. Estab. 2001.

Needs Comics/graphic novels, ethnic/multicultural, experimental, fantasy (space fantasy, sword and sorcery), feminist, gay, horror (dark fantasy, futuristic, psychological, supernatural), humor/satire, lesbian, literary, New Age, psychic/supernatural/occult, science fiction. "No stories where sexual or violent content is just used to shock the reader. No racist writings." Receives 30 unsolicited mss/month. Accepts 5 mss/issue; 20 mss/year. **Publishes 30 new writers/year.** Recently published work by Deen Borok, Wayne Scheer, Jane McDonald, Mark Joseph Kiewlak, Susan Snowden, and Kent Robinson. Length: 500-6,000 words; average length: 3,000 words. Also publishes literary essays, literary criticism, poetry. Sometimes comments on rejected mss.

How to Contact Send complete ms. Accepts submissions by e-mail. Include estimated word count and brief bio. Send SASE for return of ms or send a disposable copy of ms and #10 SASE for reply only. Responds in 1 week to queries; 3-6 months to mss. Accepts simultaneous, multiple submissions. Sample copy online. Writer's guidelines by e-mail.

Payment/Terms Writers receive bio and links on contributor's page. Request limited electronic rights, for online publication and archival only. Sponsors awards/contests.

Tips "We look for stories that are well paced and show character and plot development. Even short shorts should do more than simply paint a picture. Manuscripts stand out when the author's voice is fresh and engaging. Avoid muddying your story with too many characters and don't attempt to shock the reader with an ending you have not earned. Experiment with styles and structures, but don't resort to experimentation for its own sake."

WORD RIOT

Word Riot Press, P.O. Box 414, Middletown NJ 07748-3143. (732)706-1272. Fax: (732)706-5856. E-mail: wr.submissions@gmail.com. Website: www.wordriot.org. **Contact:** Jacki Corley, publisher; Timmy Waldron and Kevin O'cuinn, fiction editors; Charles P. Ries, poetry editor. Online magazine. Monthly. Estab. 2002. Member, CLMP.

Needs Humor/satire, literary, mainstream. "No fantasy, science fiction, romance." Accepts 20-25 mss/issue; 240-300 mss/year. Publishes ms 1-2 months after acceptance. Agented fiction 5%. Publishes 8-10 new writers/year. Length: 300-6,000 words; average length: 2,700 words. Publishes flash fiction, short stories, creative non-fiction and poetry. Also publishes literary essays, poetry. Often comments on rejected mss.

How to Contact Accepts submissions by e-mail. Include estimated word count and brief bio. Responds in 4-6 weeks to mss. Accepts multiple submissions. Sample copy online. Writer's guidelines online.

Payment/Terms Acquires electronic rights. Not copyrighted. Sponsors awards/contests.

Tips "We're always looking for something edgy or quirky. We like writers who take risks."

Consumer Magazines

I n this section of *Novel & Short Story Writer's Market* are consumer magazines with circulations of more than 10,000. Many have circulations in the hundreds of thousands or millions. And among the oldest magazines listed here are ones not only familiar to us, but also to our parents, grandparents and even great-grandparents: *The Atlantic Monthly* (1857); *Esquire* (1933); and *Ellery Queen's Mystery Magazine* (1941).

Consumer periodicals make excellent markets for fiction in terms of exposure, prestige and payment. Because these magazines are well known, however, competition is great. Even the largest consumer publications buy only one or two stories an issue, yet thousands of writers submit to these popular magazines.

Despite the odds, it is possible for talented new writers to break into print in the magazines listed here. Your keys to breaking into these markets are careful research, professional presentation and, of course, top-quality fiction.

TYPES OF CONSUMER MAGAZINES

In this section you will find a number of popular publications, some for a broad-based, general-interest readership and others for large but select groups of readers—children, teenagers, women, men and seniors. There are also religious and church-affiliated magazines, publications devoted to the interests of particular cultures and outlooks, and top markets for genre fiction.

SELECTING THE RIGHT MARKET

Unlike smaller journals and publications, most of the magazines listed here are available at newsstands and bookstores. Many can also be found in the library, and guidelines and sample copies are almost always available by mail or online. Start your search by reviewing the listings, then familiarize yourself with the fiction included in the magazines that interest you.

Don't make the mistake of thinking that just because you are familiar with a magazine, their fiction is the same today as when you first saw it. Nothing could be further from the truth. Consumer magazines, no matter how well established, are constantly revising their fiction needs as they strive to expand their audience base.

In a magazine that uses only one or two stories an issue, take a look at the nonfiction articles and features as well. These can give you a better idea of the audience for the publication and clues to the type of fiction that might appeal to them.

If you write genre fiction, look in the Category Index beginning on page 599. There you will find a list of markets that say they are looking for a particular subject.

FURTHERING YOUR SEARCH

See You've Got a Story (page 2) for information about the material common to all listings in this book. In this section in particular, pay close attention to the number of submissions a magazine receives in a given period and how many they publish in the same period. This will give you a clear picture of how stiff your competition can be.

While many of the magazines listed here publish one or two pieces of fiction in each issue, some also publish special fiction issues once or twice a year. When possible, we have indicated this in the listing information. We also note if the magazine is open to novel excerpts as well as short fiction, and we advise novelists to query first before submitting long work.

The Business of Fiction Writing, beginning on page 77, covers the basics of submitting your work. Professional presentation is a must for all markets listed. Editors at consumer magazines are especially busy, and anything you can do to make your manuscript easy to read and accessible will help your chances of being published. Most magazines want to see complete manuscripts, but watch for publications in this section that require a query first.

As in the previous section, we've included our own comments in many of the listings, set off by a bullet (•). Whenever possible, we list the publication's recent awards and honors. We've also included any special information we feel will help you in determining whether a particular publication interests you.

The maple leaf symbol (🍁) identifies our Canadian listings. You will also find some English-speaking markets from around the world. These foreign magazines are denoted with (🌐) at the beginning of the listings. Remember to use International Reply Coupons rather than stamps when you want a reply from a country other than your own.

☑ ADVOCATE, PKA'S PUBLICATION

PKA Publications, 1881 Little Westkill Rd. CO2, Prattsville NY 12468. (518)299-3103. Tabloid: $9\frac{3}{8} \times 12\frac{1}{4}$; 20-24 pages; newsprint paper; line drawings; color and b&w photographs. "Eclectic for a general audience." Bimonthly. Estab. 1987. Circ. 10,000.

Needs Adventure, children's/juvenile (5-9 years), ethnic/multicultural, experimental, fantasy, feminist, historical, humor/satire, literary, mainstream, mystery/suspense, regional, romance, science fiction, western, young adult/teen (10-18 years), contemporary, prose poem, senior citizen/retirement, sports. "Nothing religious, pornographic, violent, erotic, pro-drug or anti-enviroment. Currently looking for equine (horses) stories, poetry, art, photos and cartoons. *The Gaited Horse Newsletter* is currently published within the pages of PKA's *Advocate*." Receives 60 unsolicited mss/month. Accepts 6-8 mss/issue; 34-48 mss/year. Publishes ms 4 months to 1 year after acceptance. Also publishes poetry. Sometimes comments on rejected mss.

How to Contact Send a complete ms with cover letter. Responds in 2 months to mss. No simultaneous submissions. "No work that has appeared on the Internet." Sample copy for $5 (US currency for inside US; $6.50 US currency for Canada). Writer's Guidelines with purchase of sample copy.

Payment/Terms Pays contributor copies. Acquires first rights.

Tips "The highest criterion in selecting a work is its entertainment value. It must first be enjoyable reading. It must, of course, be orginal. To stand out, it must be thought provoking or strongly emotive, or very cleverly plotted. Will consider only previously unpublished works by writers who do not earn their living principally through writing. We are currently very backed up on short stories. We are mostly looking for art, photos and poetry."

☑ AFRICAN VOICES

African Voices Communications, Inc., 270 W. 96th St., New York NY 10025. (212)865-2982. Fax: (212)316-3335. Website: www.africanvoices.com. **Contact:** Kim Horne, fiction editor. Magazine: 52 pages; illustrations; photos. "African Voices is dedicated to highlighting the art, literature, and history of people of color." Quarterly. Estab. 1992. Circ. 20,000.

Needs Adventure, children's/juvenile, condensed novels, erotica, ethnic/multicultural, experimental, fantasy, gay, historical (general), horror, humor/satire, literary, mainstream, mystery/suspense, novel excerpts, psychic/supernatural/occult, religious/inspirational, romance, science fiction, serialized novels, slice-of-life vignettes, suspense, young adult/teen (adventure, romance), African-American. List of upcoming themes available for SASE. Publishes special fiction issue. Receives 20-50 unsolicited mss/ month. Accepts 20 mss/issue. Publishes ms 3-6 months after acceptance. Agented fiction 5%. **Publishes 30 new writers/year.** Recently published work by Anton Nimblett, Latoya Wolfe, and novelist Ngugiwa Thiong'o. Length: 500-2,500 words; average length: 2,000 words. Publishes short shorts. Also publishes literary essays, poetry.

How to Contact Send complete ms. Include short bio. Send SASE for return of ms. Responds in 3 months to queries. Accepts simultaneous and reprints submissions. Sample copy for $5 or online. Writer's guidelines online. Reviews fiction.

Payment/Terms Pays $25-50. Pays on publication for first North American serial rights.

Tips "A manuscript stands out if it is neatly typed with a well-written and interesting story line or plot. Originality encouraged. We are interested in more horror, erotic and drama pieces. *AV* wants to highlight the diversity in our culture. Stories must touch the humanity in us all."

☑ $ AIM MAGAZINE

Aim Publishing Co., P.O. Box 390, Milton WA 98354-0390. (253) 815-9030. Fax: (206) 543-2746. Website: aimmagazine.org. **Contact:** Ruth Apilado, associate editor. Magazine: $8\frac{1}{2} \times 11$; 48 pages; slick paper; photos and illustrations. Publishes material "to purge racism from the human bloodstream through the written word—that is the purpose of Aim Magazine." Quarterly. Estab. 1975. Circ. 10,000.

Needs Ethnic/multicultural, historical, mainstream, suspense. Open. No "religious" mss. Published special fiction issue last year; plans another. Receives 25 unsolicited mss/month. Accepts 15 mss/issue; 60 mss/year. Publishes ms 3 months after acceptance. **Publishes 40 new writers/year.** Recently published work by Christina Touregny, Thomas Lee Harris, Michael Williams and Jake Halpern. Publishes short shorts. Sometimes comments on rejected mss.

How to Contact Send complete ms. Accepts submissions by e-mail. Include SASE with cover letter and author's photograph. Responds in 2 months to queries; 1 month to mss. Accepts simultaneous submissions. Sample copy and writer's guidelines for $4 and 9 × 12 SAE with $1.70 postage or online.

Payment/Terms Pays $25-35. Pays on publication for first, one-time rights.

Tips "Search for those who are making unselfish contributions to their community and write about them. Write about your own experiences. Be familar with the background of your characters. Known for stories with social significance, proving that people from different ethnic, racial backgrounds are more alike than they are different."

☑ $ ☒ ANALOG SCIENCE FICTION & FACT

Dell Magazine Fiction Group, 475 Park Ave. S., 11th Floor, New York NY 10016. (212) 686-7188. Fax: (212) 686-7414. E-mail: analog@dellmagazines.com. Website: www.analogsf.com. **Contact:** Stanley Schmidt, editor. Magazine: 144 pages; illustrations; photos. Monthly. Estab. 1930. Circ. 50,000.

• Fiction published in *Analog* has won numerous Nebula and Hugo Awards.

Needs Science fiction (hard science/technological, soft/sociological). "No fantasy or stories in which the scientific background is implausible or plays no essential role." Receives 500 unsolicited mss/month. Accepts 6 mss/issue; 70 mss/year. Publishes ms 10 months after acceptance. Agented fiction 5%. **Publishes 3-4 new writers/year.** Recently published work by Ben Bova, Stephen Baxter, Larry Niven, Michael F. Flynn, Timothy Zahn, Robert J. Sawyer, and Joe Haldeman. Length: 2,000-80,000 words; average length: 10,000 words. Publishes short shorts. Sometimes comments on rejected mss.

How to Contact Send complete ms with a cover letter. Accepts queries for serials and fact articles only; query by mail. Include estimated word count. Send SASE for return of ms or send a disposable copy of ms and #10 SASE for reply only. Responds in 1 month to queries. Accepts multiple submissions. No simultaneous submissions. Sample copy for $5. Writer's guidelines online. Reviews fiction.

Payment/Terms Pays 4¢/word for novels; 5-6¢/word for novelettes; 6-8¢/word for shorts under 7,500 words; $450-600 for intermediate lengths. Pays on acceptance for first North American serial, nonexclusive foreign serial rights. Sends galleys to author. Not copyrighted.

Tips "I'm looking for irresistibly entertaining stories that make me think about things in ways I've never done before. Read several issues to get a broad feel for our tastes, but don't try to imitate what you read."

☒ ☑ ◎ $ THE ANNALS OF SAINT ANNE DE BEAUPRE

9795 St. Anne Blvd., St. Anne de Beaupre QC G0A 3C0 Canada. (418)827-4538. Fax: (418)827-4530. E-mail: mag@revuesaintanne.ca (for subscriptions only). **Contact:** Fr. Guy Desrochers, C.Ss.R., editor. Magazine: 32 pages; glossy paper; photos. "Promotes Catholic family values and devotion to St. Anne." Bimonthly. Estab. 1885. Circ. 25,000.

Needs Religious/inspirational. "No senseless mockery." Receives 50-60 unsolicited mss/month. Recently published work by Beverly Sheresh. Always comments on rejected mss.

How to Contact Send complete ms. Include estimated word count. Send SASE for reply or return of ms. Responds in 4-6 weeks to queries; send SASE for reply or return of ms. No disc or e-mail submission. Rights must be clearly stated. Typed manuscripts only. Included estimated word count.

Payment/Terms Pays $40 for Adult/Religious fiction (one page only, 700 words). Pays on acceptance for first North American serial rights. Please state "rights" for sale.

Tips "Writing must be uplifting and inspirational, clearly written, not filled with long quotations. We tend to stay away from extreme controversy and focus on the family, good family values, devotion, and Christianity. Most open to Christian education, Christian living, Christian growth, Church life and testimonies. Write a well-researched, current story with 'across the board' appeal."

☑ $ ART TIMES

P.O. Box 730, Mount Marion NY 12456-0730. (914)246-6944. Fax: (914)246-6944. Website: www.arttimesjournal.com. **Contact:** Raymond J. Steiner, fiction editor. Magazine: 12 × 15; 24 pages; Jet paper and cover; illustrations; photos. "Art Times covers the art fields and is distributed in locations most frequented by those enjoying the arts. Our copies are distributed throughout the Northeast region as well as in most of the galleries of Soho, 57th Street and Madison Avenue in the metropolitan area; locations include theaters, galleries, museums, cultural centers and the like. Our readers are mostly over 40, affluent, art-conscious and sophisticated. Subscribers are located across U.S. and abroad (Italy, France, Germany, Greece, Russia, etc.)." Monthly. Estab. 1984. Circ. 28,000.

Needs Adventure, ethnic/multicultural, fantasy, feminist, gay, historical, humor/satire, lesbian, literary, mainstream, science fiction, contemporary. "We seek quality literary pieces. Nothing violent, sexist, erotic, juvenile, racist, romantic, political, etc." Receives 30-50 unsolicited mss/month. Accepts 1 mss/issue; 10 mss/year. Publishes ms 3 years after acceptance. **Publishes 6 new writers/year.** Publishes short shorts.

How to Contact Send complete ms with SASE. Responds in 6 months to mss. Accepts simultaneous, multiple submissions. Sample copy for 9 × 12 SAE and 6 first-class stamps. Writer's guidelines for #10 SASE or on Web site.

Payment/Terms Pays $25 maximum (honorarium) and 1 year's free subscription. Pays on publication for first North American serial, first rights.

Tips "Competition is greater (more submissions received), but keep trying. We print new as well as published writers."

☑ ◎ $ ☑ ASIMOV'S SCIENCE FICTION

Dell Magazine Fiction Group, 475 Park Ave. S., 11th Floor, New York NY 10016. (212) 686-7188. Fax: (212) 686-7414. E-mail: asimovs@dellmagazines.com. Website: www.asimovs.com. **Contact:** Sheila Williams, editor. Magazine: 5⅞ × 8⅝ (trim size); 112 pages; 30 lb. newspaper; 70 lb. to 8 pt. C1S cover stock; illustrations; rarely photos. Magazine consists of science fiction and fantasy stories for adults and young adults. Publishes "the best short science fiction available." Estab. 1977. Circ. 50,000.

• Named for a science fiction "legend," *Asimov's* regularly receives Hugo and Nebula Awards. Editor Gardner Dozois has received several awards for editing including Hugos and those from *Locus* magazine.

Needs Fantasy, science fiction (hard science, soft sociological). No horror or psychic/supernatural. Would like to see more hard science fiction. Receives approximately 800 unsolicited mss/month. Accepts 10 mss/issue. Publishes ms 6-12 months after acceptance. Agented fiction 10%. **Publishes 10 new writers/year.** Recently published work by Robert Silverberg and Larry Niven. Publishes short shorts. Sometimes comments on rejected mss.

How to Contact Send complete ms with SASE. Responds in 2 months to queries; 3 months to mss. No simultaneous or reprint submissions. Sample copy for $5. Writer's guidelines for #10 SASE or online. Reviews fiction.

Payment/Terms Pays 5-8¢/word. Pays on acceptance. Buys first North American serial, nonexclusive foreign serial rights; reprint rights occasionally. Sends galleys to author.

Tips "We are looking for character stories rather than those emphasizing technology or science. New writers will do best with a story under 10,000 words. Every new science fiction or fantasy film seems to 'inspire' writers—and this is not a desirable trend. Be sure to be familiar with our magazine and the type of story we like; workshops and lots of practice help. Try to stay away from trite, clichéd themes. Start in the middle of the action, starting as close to the end of the story as you possibly can. We like stories that extrapolate from up-to-date scientific research, but don't forget that we've been publishing clone stories for decades. Ideas must be fresh."

$ THE ATLANTIC MONTHLY

The Watergate, 600 New Hampshire Ave. NW, Washington DC 20037. (202)266-7083. Fax: (202)266-6388. Website: www.theatlantic.com. **Contact:** C. Michael Curtis, fiction editor. General magazine for an educated readership with broad cultural interests. Monthly. Estab. 1857. Circ. 500,000.

Needs Literary and contemporary fiction. "Seeks fiction that is clear, tightly written with strong sense of 'story' and well-defined characters." Receives 1,000 unsolicited mss/month. Accepts 7-8 mss/year. **Publishes 3-4 new writers/year.** Recently published work by Mary Gordon, Tobias Wolff.

How to Contact Send complete ms. Responds in 2 months to mss. Accepts multiple submissions. Writer's guidelines online.

Payment/Terms Pays $3,000. Pays on acceptance for first North American serial rights.

Tips When making first contract, "cover letters are sometimes helpful, particularly if they cite prior publications or involvement in writing programs. Common mistakes: melodrama, inconclusiveness, lack of development, unpersuasive characters and/or dialogue."

$ BABYBUG

Carus Publishing Co., 70 E. Lake, Suite 300, Chicago IL 60601. (312)701-1720. Website: www.cricketmag. com. "*Babybug* is 'the listening and looking magazine for infants and toddlers,' intended to be read aloud by a loving adult to foster a love of books and reading in young children ages 6 months-2 years." Estab. 1994. Circ. 45,000.

Needs Very simple stories for infants and toddlers.

How to Contact Send complete ms. Accepts simultaneous submissions. Sample copy for $5. Writer's guidelines online.

Payment/Terms Pays $25 and up. Pays on publication for variable rights.

Tips *"Babybug* is a board-book magazine. Study back issues before submitting."

$ BACKROADS, Motorcycles, Travel & Adventure

Backroads, Inc., P.O. Box 317, Branchville NJ 07826. (973)948-4176. Fax: (973)948-0823. E-mail: editor@ backroadsusa.com. Website: www.backroadsusa.com. *"Backroads* is a motorcycle tour magazine geared toward getting motorcyclists on the road and traveling. We provide interesting destinations, unique roadside attractions and eateries, plus Rip & Ride Route Sheets. We cater to all brands. If you really ride, you need Backroads." Monthly. Estab. 1995. Circ. 50,000.

Needs Travel, motorcycle-related stories. Publishes ms 3 months after acceptance. Articles must be motorcycle-related and include images of motorcycles to accompany story. It helps if you actually ride a motorcycle.

How to Contact Query. Accepts submissions by e-mail. Sample copy for $5. Writer's guidelines on Web site.

Payment/Terms Pays 5¢/word. Pays on publication for one-time rights.

☑ $ THE BEAR DELUXE MAGAZINE

Orlo, P.O. Box 10342, Portland OR 97296. (503)242-1047. E-mail: bear@orlo.org. Website: www.orlo. org. **Contact:** Tom Webb, editor. Magazine: 9 × 12; 48 pages; newsprint paper; Kraft paper cover illustrations; photos. *"The Bear Deluxe Magazine* provides a fresh voice amid often strident and polarized environmental discourse. Street level, solution-oriented, and nondogmatic, The Bear Deluxe presents lively creative discussion to a diverse readership." Semiannual. Estab. 1993. Circ. 20,000.

  • *The Bear Deluxe* has received publishing grants from the Oregon Cultural Trust, Regional Arts and Culture Council, Oregon Council for the Humanities, Literary Arts, Regional Arts and Culture Council, Tides Foundation.

Needs Adventure, condensed novels, historical, horror, humor/satire, mystery/suspense, novel excerpts, western. "No detective, children's or horror." Enviromentally focused: humor/satire, literary, science fiction. "We would like to see more nontraditional forms." List of upcoming themes available for SASE. Receives 20-30 unsolicited mss/month. Accepts 2-3 mss/issue; 8-12 mss/year. Publishes ms 3 months after acceptance. **Publishes 5-6 new writers/year.** Recently published work by Peter Houlahan, John Reed and Karen Hueler. Length: 750-4,500 words; average length: 2,500 words. Publishes short shorts. Also publishes literary essays, literary criticism, poetry. Sometimes comments on rejected mss.

How to Contact Query with or without published clips or send complete ms. Send disposable copy of mss. Responds in 3 months to queries; 6 months to mss. Accepts simultaneous submissions and reprints. Sample copy for $5. Writer's guidelines for #10 SASE or on Web site. Reviews fiction. Also send SASE for guides to new Doug Fir Fiction Award ($1,000 top prize).

Payment/Terms Pays free subscription to the magazine, contributor's copies and 5¢/word; additional copies for postage. Pays on publication for first, one-time rights.

Tips "Keep sending work. Write actively and focus on the connections of man, nature, etc., not just flowery descriptions. Urban and suburban enviroments are grist for the mill as well. Have not seen enough quality humorous and ironic writing. Interview and artist profile ideas needed. Juxtaposition of place welcome. Action and hands-on great. Not all that interested in enviromental ranting and simple 'walks through the park.' Make it powerful, yet accessible to a wide audience."

☑ $ BOMB MAGAZINE

A Journal of Contemporary Writing Bogg Publications, 422 N. Cleveland St., Arlington VA 22201-1424. E-mail: boggmag@aol.com. Contact: John Elsberg, US editor. Magazine: 6 × 9; 72 pages; 70 lb. white paper; 70 lb. cover stock; line illustrations. "Poetry (to include prose poems, haiku/tanka and experimental forms), experimental short fiction, reviews." Published 2 times a year. Estab. 1968. Circ. 800.80 Hanson Place, Suite 703, Brooklyn NY 11217. (718) 636-9100. Fax: (718) 636-9200. E-mail: generalinquiries@bombsite.com. Website: www.bombsite.com. Magazine: 11 × 14; 104 pages; 70 lb.

glossy cover; illustrations; photos. Written, edited and produced by industry professionals and funded by those interested in the arts. Publishes writing which is unconventional and contains an edge, whether it be in style or subject matter. Quarterly. Estab. 1981. Circ. 36,000.

Needs Experimental, novel excerpts, contemporary. No genre: romance, science fiction, horror, western. Receives 200 unsolicited mss/month. Accepts 6 mss/issue; 24 mss/year. Publishes ms 3-6 months after acceptance. Agented fiction 70%. **Publishes 2-3 new writers/year.** Recently published work by Lynne Tillman, Dennis Cooper, Susan Wheeler, and Laurie Sheck.

How to Contact SASE. Responds in 3-5 months to mss. Accepts multiple submissions. Sample copy for $10, plus $2.13 postage and handling. Writer's guidelines in FAQ on Web site. Accepts submissions from January 1 to August 31; mss sent "outside those dates will be returned unread."

Payment/Terms Pays $100, and contributor's copies. Pays on publication for first, one-time rights. Sends galleys to author.

Tips "We are committed to publishing new work that commercial publishers often deem too dangerous or difficult. The problem is, a lot of young writers confuse difficult with dreadful. Read the magazine before you even think of submitting something."

☑ $ ⧫ BOSTON REVIEW

35 Medford St., Suite 302, Sommerville, MA 02143. E-mail: review@bostonreview.net. Website: www. bostonreview.net. **Contact:** Junot Diaz, fiction editor. Magazine: 10¾ × 14¾; 60 pages; newsprint. "The editors are committed to a society and culture that foster human diversity and a democracy in which we seek common grounds of principle amidst our many differences. In the hope of advancing these ideals, the Review acts as a forum that seeks to enrich the language of public debate." Bimonthly. Estab. 1975. Circ. 20,000.

- *Boston Review* is the recipient of a Pushcart Prize in poetry.

Needs Ethnic/multicultural, experimental, literary, regional, translations, contemporary, prose poem. Receives 150 unsolicited mss/month. Accepts 4-6 mss/year. Publishes ms 4 months after acceptance. Recently published work by Dagberto Gilb, Charles Johnson, Deb Olin Unferth, T.E. Holt, and Yvonne Woon. Length: 1,200-5,000 words; average length: 2,000 words. Occasionally comments on rejected mss.

How to Contact Send complete ms. Responds in 4 months to queries. Accepts simultaneous submissions if noted. Sample copy for $5 or online. Writer's guidelines online. Reviews fiction. "The editors are looking for fiction in which a heart struggles against itself, in which the messy unmanageable complexity of the world is revealed. Sentences that are so sharp they cut the eye."

Payment/Terms Pays $300, and 3 contributor's copies. Acquires first North American serial, first rights.

◎ BOWHUNTER

Primedia Consumer Media & Magazine Group, 6405 Flank Dr., Harrisburg PA 17112. (717)657-9555. Fax: (717)657-9552. E-mail: bowhunter_magazine@primediamags.com. Website: www.bowhunter.com. **Contact:** Dwight Schuh, editor. Magazine: 7¾ × 10½: 150 pages; 75 lb. glossy paper; 150 lb. glossy cover stock; illustrations; photos. "We are a special-interest publication, produced by bowhunters for bowhunters, covering all aspects of the sport. Material included in each issue is designed to entertain and inform readers, making them better bowhunters." Bimonthly. Estab. 1971. Circ. 154,446.

Needs Bowhunting, outdoor adventure. "Writers must expect a very limited market. We buy only one or two fiction pieces a year. Writers must know the market—bowhunting—and let that be the theme of their work. No 'me and my dog' types of stories; no stories by people who have obviously never held a bow in their hands." Receives 25 unsolicited mss/month. Accepts 30 mss/year. Publishes ms 3 months to 2 years after acceptance. **Publishes 3-4 new writers/year.** Length: 500-2,000 words; average length: 1,500 words. Publishes short shorts. Sometimes comments on rejected mss.

How to Contact Send complete ms. Accepts submissions by e-mail, fax. Responds in 2 weeks to queries; 1 month to mss. Sample copy for $2 and 8½ × 11 SAE with appropriate postage. Writer's guidelines for #10 SASE or on Web site.

Payment/Terms Pays $100-350. Pays on acceptance. Buys exclusive first, worldwide publication rights.

Tips "We have a resident humorist who supplies us with most of the 'fiction' we need. But if a story comes through the door which captures the essence of bowhunting and we feel it will reach out to our readers, we will buy it. Despite our macho outdoor magazine status, we are a bunch of English majors who love to read. You can't bull your way around real outdoor people—they can spot a phony at 20 paces. If you've never camped out under the stars and listened to an elk bugle and try to relate that experience without really experiencing it, someone's going to know. We are very specialized; we don't want stories about shooting apples off people's heads or of Cupid's arrow finding its mark. James Dickey's *Deliverance* used bowhunting metaphorically, very effectively... while we don't expect that type of writing from everyone, that's the kind of feeling that characterizes a good piece of outdoor fiction."

☑ ▣ BRAIN, CHILD, The Magazine for Thinking Mothers

March Press, P.O. Box 5566, Charlottesville VA 22905. (434) 977-4151. E-mail: editor@brainchildmag. com. Website: www.brainchildmag.com. **Contact:** Jennifer Niesslein and Stephanie Wilkinson, co-editors. Magazine: 7¼ × 10; 60-100 pages; 80lb. matte cover; illustrations; photos. "Brain, Child reflects modern motherhood—the way it really is. We like to think of Brain, Child as a community, for and by mothers who like to think about what raising kids does for (and to) the mind and soul. Brain, Child isn't your typical parenting magazine. We couldn't cupcake-decorate our way out of a paper bag. We are more 'literary' than 'how-to,' more New Yorker than Parents. We shy away from expert advice on childrearing in favor of first-hand reflections by great writers (Jane Smiley, Barbara Ehrenreich, Anne Tyler) on life as a mother. Each quarterly issue is full of essays, features, humor, reviews, fiction, art, cartoons, and our readers' own stories. Our philosophy is pretty simple: Motherhood is worthy of literature. And there are a lot of ways to mother, all of them interesting. We're proud to be publishing articles and essays that are smart, down to earth, sometimes funny, and sometimes poignant." Quarterly. Estab. 2000. Circ. 30,000. Member, IPA, ASME.

- *Brain, Child* has either won or been nominated for the *Utne* Independent Prss Award each year it has been in existence.

Needs Literary, mainstream, literary. No genre fiction. Receives 200 unsolicited mss/month. Accepts 1 mss/issue; 4 mss/year. Publishes ms 6 months after acceptance. Recently published work by Anne Tyler, Barbara Kingsolver and Jane Smiley. Length: 800-5,000 words; average length: 2,500 words. Also publishes literary essays. Sometimes comments on rejected mss.

How to Contact Send complete ms. Accepts submissions by e-mail (be sure to copy and paste the ms into the body of the e-mail). Include estimated word count, brief bio and list of publications. Send SASE (or IRC) for return of ms or send a disposable copy of ms and #10 SASE for reply only. Responds in 1 month to queries; 1-3 months to mss. Accepts simultaneous and reprints, multiple submissions. Sample copy online. Writer's guidelines online. Reviews fiction.

Payment/Terms Payment varies. Pays on publication for first North American serial, electronic rights. *Brain, Child* anthology rights Sends galleys to author.

Tips "We only publish fiction with a strong motherhood theme. But, like every other publisher of literary fiction, we look for well-developed characters, a compelling story, and an ending that is as strong as the rest of the piece."

☑ ◙ $ CADET QUEST MAGAZINE

P.O. Box 7259, Grand Rapids MI 49510-7259. (616) 241-5616. Fax: (616) 241-5558. E-mail: submissions@ calvinistcadets.org. Website: www.calvinistcadets.org. **Contact:** G. Richard Broene, editor. Magazine: 8½ × 11; 24 pages; illustrations; photos. "Cadet Quest Magazine shows boys 9-14 how God is at work in their lives and in the world around them." Estab. 1958. Circ. 8,000.

Needs Adventure, children's/juvenile, religious/inspirational (Christian), spiritual, sports, comics. "Need material based on Christian perspective and articles on Christian role models. Avoid long dialogue and little action." No fantasy, science fiction, fashion, horror or erotica. List of upcoming themes available for SASE or on Web site in February. Receives 60 unsolicited mss/month. Accepts 3 mss/issue; 18 mss/year. Publishes ms 4-11 months after acceptance. **Publishes 0-3 new writers/year.** Length: 900-1,500 words; average length: 1,200 words. Publishes short shorts.

How to Contact Send complete ms by mail or send submissions in the body of the e-mail. Not as an attachment. Responds in 2 months. No queries. Accepts simultaneous, multiple submissions and reprints. Sample copy for 9 × 12 SASE. Writer's guidelines for #10 SASE.

Payment/Terms Pays 4-6¢/word, and 1 contributor's copy. Pays on acceptance for first North American serial, one-time, second serial (reprint), simultaneous rights. Rights purchased vary with author and material.

Tips "On a cover sheet, list the point your story is trying to make. Our magazine has a theme for each issue, and we try to fit the fiction to the theme. All fiction should be about a young boy's interests—sports, outdoor activities, problems—with an emphasis on a Christian perspective. No simple moralisms. Best time to submit material is February-April."

❑ CANADIAN WRITER'S JOURNAL

P.O. Box 1178, New Liskeard ON P0J 1P0 Canada. (705)647-5424. Fax: (705)647-8366. Website: www. cwj.ca. Accepts well-written articles by all writers. Annual. Estab. 1984. Circ. 350.

Needs Requirements being met by annual contest. Send SASE for rules, or see guidelines on Web site. "Does not want gratuitous violence, sex subject matter." Publishes ms 9 months after acceptance. **Publishes 40 new writers/year.** Also publishes poetry. Rarely comments on rejected mss.

How to Contact Accepts submissions by e-mail. Responds in 2 months to queries. Writer's guidelines online.

Payment/Terms Pays on publication for one-time rights.

❑ ◎ $ CLUBHOUSE JR.

Focus on the Family, 8605 Explorer Drive, Colorado Springs CO 80920. (719)531-3400. Website: www. clubhousejr.com. **Contact**: Jamie Dangers, editorial assistant. Magazine: 8½ × 11; 24 pages; illustrations; photos. *Clubhouse Jr.* is designed to inspire, entertain, and teach Christian values to children 4-8. Estab. 1988. Circ. 57,000.

Needs Children's/juvenile (adventure, animal, preschool, sports), ethnic/multicultural, religious/inspirational. Receives 160 unsolicited mss/month. Accepts 1 mss/issue; 12 mss/year. Publishes ms 1 year after acceptance. **Publishes 2-3 new writers/year.** Recently published work by Laura Sassi, Nancy Sanders, Manfred Koehler, and Mary Manz Simon. Length: 250-1,000 words; average length: 250-700 words. Publishes short shorts. Also publishes poetry. Sometimes comments on rejected mss.

How to Contact Send complete ms. Send SASE (or IRC) for return of the ms or send disposable copy of the ms and #10 SASE for reply only. Responds in 6-8 weeks to mss. Does not accept simultaneous submissions. Sample copy for $1.25. Writer's guidelines for #10 SASE.

Payment/Terms Pays $125-200. Pays on acceptance for all rights.

Tips "Fresh, inviting, creative; stories that explore a worthy theme without an obvious *moral*. Characters are well-developed, story line fast-moving and interesting; built on Christian beliefs and values."

❑ ◎ $ CLUBHOUSE MAGAZINE

Focus on the Family, 8605 Explorer Dr., Colorado Springs CO 80920. (719)531-3400. Website: www. clubhousemagazine.com. **Contact:** Jamie Dangers, editorial assistant. Magazine: 8 × 11; 24 pages; illustrations; photos. "*Clubhouse* readers are 8-12 year old boys and girls who desire to know more about God and the Bible. Their parents (who typically pay for the membership) want wholesome, educational material with Scriptural or moral insight. The kids want excitement, adventure, action, humor, or mystery. Your job as a writer is to please both the parent and child with each article." Monthly. Estab. 1987. Circ. 90,000.

Needs Adventure, children's/juvenile (8-12 years), humor/satire, mystery/suspense, religious/inspirational, holiday. Avoid contemporary, middle-class family settings (existing authors meet this need), stories dealing with boy-girl relationships. "No science fiction." Receives 150 unsolicited mss/month. Accepts 1 mss/issue. Publishes ms 6-12 months after acceptance. Agented fiction 15%. **Publishes 8 new writers/year.** Recently published work by Jonathan Friesen and Nancy Rue.

How to Contact Send complete ms. Send SASE for reply, return of ms or send a disposable copy of ms. Responds in 2 months to mss. Sample copy for $1.50 with 9 × 12 SASE. Writer's guidelines for #10 SASE.

Payment/Terms Pays $200 and up for first time contributor and 5 contributor's copies; additional copies available. Pays on acceptance for non-exclusive license.

Tips Looks for "humor with a point, historical fiction featuring great Christians or Christians who lived during great times; contemporary, exotic settings; holiday material (Christmas, Thanksgiving, Easter, President's Day); parables; avoid graphic descriptions of evil creatures and sorcery; mystery stories; choose-your-own adventure stories. No contemporary, middle-class family settings (we already have authors who can meet these needs) or stories dealing with boy-girl relationships."

❑ ◎ $ ❑ CRICKET

Carus Publishing Co., 70 E. Lake Suite 300, Chicago IL 60601. (312)701-1720. Website: www.cricketmag.

com. Marianne Carus, editor-in-chief. **Contact:** Submissions Editor. Magazine: 8 × 10; 64 pages; illustrations; photos. Magazine for children, ages 9-14. Monthly. Estab. 1973. Circ. 73,000.

 • *Cricket* has received a Parents' Choice Award, and awards from EdPress. Carus Corporation also publishes *Spider, the Magazine for Children*; *Ladybug, the Magazine for Young Children; Babybug*; and *Cicada*.

Needs Adventure, children's/juvenile, ethnic/multicultural, fantasy, historical, humor/satire, mystery/ suspense, novel excerpts, science fiction, suspense, thriller/espionage, western, folk and fairy tales. No didactic, sex, religious, or horror stories. All issues have different "mini-themes." Receives 1,100 unsolicited mss/month. Accepts 150 mss/year. Publishes ms 6-24 months after acceptance. Agented fiction 1-2%. **Publishes some new writers/year.** Recently published work by Aaron Shepard, Arnold Adoff, and Nancy Springer.

How to Contact Send complete ms. Responds in 3 months to mss. Accepts reprints submissions. Sample copy for $5 and 9 × 12 SAE. Writer's guidelines for SASE and on Web site.

Payment/Terms Pays 25¢/word maximum, and 6 contributor's copies; $2.50 charge for extras. Pays on publication. Rights vary. Sponsors awards/contests.

Tips "Do not write *down* to children. Write about well-researched subjects you are familiar with and interested in, or about something that concerns you deeply. Children *need* fiction and fantasy. Carefully study several issues of *Cricket* before you submit your manuscript."

☑ $ ☑ ESQUIRE

Hearst, 300 West 57th Street, 21st Floor, New York NY 10019. (212)649-4050. Website: www.esquire.com. **Contact:** Adrienne Miller, literary editor. Magazine. Monthly magazine for smart, well-off men. General readership is college educated and sophisticated, between ages 30 and 45. Written mostly by contributing editors on contract. Rarely accepts unsolicited manuscripts. Monthly. Estab. 1933. Circ. 750,000.

 • *Esquire* is well respected for its fiction and has received several National Magazine Awards. Work published in *Esquire* has been selected for inclusion in the *Best American Short Stories* and *O. Henry* anthologies.

Needs Novel excerpts, short stories, some poetry, memoirs, and plays. No "pornography, science fiction or 'true romance' stories." Publishes special fiction issue in July. Receives 800 unsolicited mss/month. Rarely accepts unsolicited fiction. Publishes ms 2-6 months after acceptance. Recently published work by Russell Banks, Tim O'Brien, Richard Russo and David Means.

How to Contact Send complete ms. Accepts simultaneous submissions. Writer's guidelines for SASE.

Payment/Terms Pays in cash on acceptance, amount undisclosed. Retains first worldwide periodical publication rights for 90 days from cover date.

Tips "Submit one story at a time. We receive over 10,000 stories a year, so worry a little less about publication, a little more about the work itself."

☑ ◎ $ EVANGEL

Free Methodist Publishing House, P.O. Box 535002, Indianapolis IN 46253-5002. (317)244-3660. Magazine: 5½ × 8½; 8 pages; 2 and 4-color illustrations; color and b&w photos. Sunday school take-home paper for distribution to adults who attend church. Fiction involves people coping with everday crises, making decisions that show spiritual growth. Weekly distribution. Printed quarterly. Estab. 1897. Circ. 10,000.

Needs Religious/inspirational. "No fiction without any semblance of Christian message or where the message clobbers the reader. Looking for more short pieces of devotional nature of 500 words or less." Receives 300 unsolicited mss/month. Accepts 3-4 mss/issue; 156-200 mss/year. Publishes ms 18-36 months after acceptance. **Publishes 7 new writers/year.** Recently published work by Kelli Wise and Hope Byler.

How to Contact Send complete ms. Responds in 4-6 weeks to queries. Accepts multiple submissions. Sample copy and writer's guidelines for #10 SASE.

Payment/Terms Pays 4¢/word and 2 contributor's copies. Pays on publication. Buys second serial (reprint) or one-time rights.

Tips "Desire, concise, tight writing that supports a solid thesis and fits the mission expressed in the quidelines."

☑ $ FUNNY TIMES

Funny Times, Inc., P.O. Box 18530, Cleveland Heights OH 44118. (216)371-8600. Fax: (216)371-8696.

Website: www.funnytimes.com. **Contact:** Ray Lesser and Susan Wolpert, editors. Zine specializing in humor: tabloid; 24 pages; newsprint; illustrations. "Funny Times is a monthly review of America's funniest cartoonists and writers. We are the Reader's Digest of modern American humor with a progressive/peace-oriented/environmental/politically activist slant." Monthly. Estab. 1985. Circ. 70,000.

Needs Humor/satire. "Anything funny." Receives hundreds unsolicited mss/month. Accepts 5 mss/issue; 60 mss/year. Publishes ms 3 months after acceptance. Agented fiction 10%. **Publishes 10 new writers/year.** Publishes short shorts.

How to Contact Query with published clips. Include list of publications. Send SASE for return of ms or disposable copy of ms. Responds in 3 months to mss. Accepts simultaneous and reprints submissions. Sample copy for $3 or 9 × 12 SAE with 4 first-class stamps ($1.17 postage). Writer's guidelines online.

Payment/Terms Pays $50-150. Pays on publication for one-time, second serial (reprint) rights.

Tips "It must be funny."

☑ ◎ $ ☑ HIGHLIGHTS FOR CHILDREN

Manuscript Submissions, 803 Church St., Honesdale PA 18431-1824. (570)253-1080. Fax: (570)251-7847. Website: www.highlights.com. **Contact:** Manuscript Coordinator. Magazine: 42 pages; uncoated paper; coated cover stock; illustrations; photos. "This magazine of wholesome fun is dedicated to helping children grow in basic skills and knowledge, in creativeness, in ability to think and reason, in sensitivity to others, in high ideals and worthy ways of living—for children are the world's most important people. Publishes stories for children up to age 12; up to 500 words for beginners (ages 3-7), up to 800 words for advanced (ages 8-12)." Monthly. Estab. 1946.

- *Highlights* has won the Parent's Guide to Children's Media Award, Parent's Choice Award, and Editorial Excellence Awards from the Association of Educational Publishers.

Needs Adventure, fantasy, mystery, historical, humor, mystery, animal, contemporary, retellings of folktales, multicultural, sports. Prefers stories appealing to both girls and boys and stories with good characterization, strong emotional appeal, action, strong plot, believable setting. Receives 600-800 unsolicited mss/month. **Publishes 30 new writers/year.**

How to Contact Send complete ms. Responds in 4 to 6 weeks. Accepts multiple submissions. Sample copy free. Writer's guidelines in "About Us" section of Web site.

Payment/Terms Pays $150 minimum, plus 2 contributor's copies. **Pays on acceptance.** Sends galleys to author.

Tips "We accept a story on its merit whether written by an unpublished or an experienced writer. Mss are rejected because of poor writing, lack of plot, trite or worn-out plot, or poor characterization. Children *like* stories and learn about life from stories. Children learn to become lifelong fiction readers by enjoying stories. Feel passion for your subject. Create vivid images. Write a child-centered story; leave adults in the background."

☑ ◎ ☑ ALFRED HITCHCOCK'S MYSTERY MAGAZINE

Dell Magazines, 475 Park Ave. S., 11th Floor, New York NY 10016. Website: www.themysteryplace. com. **Contact:** Linda Landrigan, editor. Mystery fiction magazine: 5½ × 8⅜; 112 pages; 28 lb. newsprint paper; 70 lb. machine-coated cover stock; illustrations; photos. 10 issues/year (2 double). Estab. 1956. Readership: 100,000.

- Stories published in *Alfred Hitchcock's Mystery Magazine* have won Edgar Awards for "Best Mystery Story of the Year," Shamus Awards for "Best Private Eye Story of the Year" and Robert L. Fish Awards for "Best First Mystery Short Story of the Year."

Needs Mystery/suspense (amateur sleuth, private eye, police procedural, suspense, etc.). No sensationalism. Number of mss/issue varies with length of mss. Recently published work by Rhys Bowen, Doug Allyn, I.J. Parker, and Martin Limón.

How to Contact Send complete ms. Responds in 4 months to mss. Sample copy for $5. Writer's guidelines for SASE or on Web site.

Payment/Terms Payment varies. Pays on publication for first serial, foreign rights.

◎ JEWISH CURRENTS MAGAZINE

45 E. 33rd Street, New York NY 10016-1919. (845) 626-2427. E-mail: lawrencebush@earthlink.net. **Contact:** Lawrence Bush. Magazine: 8½ × 11; 48 pages. A secular, progressive, independent Jewish bimonthly, printing fiction, poetry articles and reviews on Jewish politics and history. Holocaust/

Resistance; Mideast peace process, Black-Jewish relations; labor struggles, women's issues. Audience is secular, left/progressive, Jewish, mostly urban. Bimonthly. Estab.1946. Circ.16,000.

Needs Ethnic/multicultural, feminist, historical, humor/satire, translations, contemporary. "No no porn or hard sex, no escapist stuff. Go easy on experimentation, but we're interested." Must be well written! We are interested in *authentic* experience and readable prose; humanistic orientation. Jewish themes." Receives 6-10 unsolicited mss/month. Accepts 1-2 mss/issue; 6-12 mss/year. Publishes ms 2-24 months after acceptance. Recently published work by Elizabeth Swados, Esther Cohen, Lawrence Bush, David Rothenberg, Paul Buhle, Mikhail Horowitz. Length: 1,000-3,000 words; average length: 2,000 words. Publishes short shorts. Also publishes literary essays, literary criticism, poetry.

How to Contact Send complete ms with cover letter. "Writers should include brief biographical information, especially their publishing histories." SASE. Responds in 2 months to mss. Sample copy for $3 with SAE and 3 first class stamps. Reviews fiction.

Payment/Terms Pays complimentary one-year subscription and 6 contributor's copies. "We readily give reprint permission at no charge." Sends galleys to author.

☑ ◎ ☒ KALEIDOSCOPE

Kaleidoscope Press, 701 S. Main St., Akron OH 44311-1019. (330)762-9755. Fax: (330)762-0912. E-mail: mshiplett@udsakron.org. Website: www.udsakron.org. **Contact:** Gail Willmott, editor-in-chief. Magazine: 8½ × 11; 64 pages; non-coated paper; coated cover stock; illustrations (all media); photos. Subscribers include individuals, agencies, and organizations that assist people with disabilities and many university and public libraries. Open to new writers but appreciates work by established writers as well. Especially interested in work by writers with a disability, but features writers both with and without disabilities. "Writers without a disability must limit themselves to our focus, while those with a disability may explore any topic (although we prefer original perspectives about experiences with disability)." Semiannual. Estab. 1979. Circ. 1,000.

* *Kaleidoscope* has received awards from the American Heart Association, the Great Lakes Awards Competition and Ohio Public Images.

Needs "We look for well-developed plots, engaging characters and realistic dialogue. We lean toward fiction that emphasizes character and emotions rather than action-oriented narratives. No fiction that is stereotypical, patronizing, sentimental, erotic, or maudlin. No romance, religious or dogmatic fiction; no children's literature." Receives 35-40 unsolicited mss/month. Accepts 20 mss/year. Agented fiction 1%. **Publishes 2 new writer/year.** Recently published work by Carole hall, Deshae E. Lott, and Natalie E. Illum. Also publishes poetry.

How to Contact Accepts submissions by fax and e-mail, double-spaced with full address. Query first or send complete ms and cover letter. Include author's education and writing background and, if author has a disability, how it influenced the writing. SASE. Responds in 3 weeks to queries; 6 months to mss. Accepts simultaneous, multiple submissions and reprints. Sample copy for $6 prepaid. Writer's guidelines online.

Payment/Terms Pays $10-125, and 2 contributor's copies; additional copies $6. Pays on publication for first rights, reprints permitted with credit given to original publication. Rights revert to author upon publication.

Tips "Read the magazine and get submission guidelines. We prefer that writers with a disability offer original perspectives about their experiences; writers without disabilities should limit themselves to our focus in order to solidify a connection to our magazine's purpose. Do not use stereotypical, patronizing and sentimental attitudes about disability."

☑ ◎ $ ☒ LADYBUG

Carus Publishing Co., 70 E. Lake St., Suite 300, Chicago IL 60601. (312)701-1720. Website: www.ladybugmagkids.com. **Contact:** Alice Letvin, editor; Jenny Gillespie, assistant editor. Magazine: 8 × 10; 36 pages plus 4-page pullout section; illustrations. "We look for quality writing—quality literature, no matter the subject. For young children, ages 3-6." Monthly. Estab. 1990. Circ. 134,000.

* *Ladybug* has received the Parents Choice Award; the Golden Lamp Honor Award and the Golden Lamp Award from Ed Press, and Magazine Merit awards from the Society of Children's Book Writers and Illustrators.

Needs "Looking for age-appropriate read-aloud stories for preschoolers."

How to Contact Send complete ms. SASE. Responds in 6-8 months to mss. Accepts reprints submissions.

Sample copy for $5 and 9 × 12 SAE. Writer's guidelines online.

Payment/Terms Pays 25¢/word (less for reprints). Pays on publication. Rights purchased vary. For recurring features, pays flat fee and copyright becomes property of Cricket Magazine Group.

Tips Looks for "well-written stories for preschoolers: age-appropriate, not condescending. We look for rich, evocative language and sense of joy or wonder."

☑ ◎ $ LISTEN MAGAZINE

The Health Connection, 55 W. Oak Ridge Dr., Hagerstown MD 21740. (301)393-4082. Fax: (301)393-4055. E-mail: editor@listenmagazine.org. Website: www.listenmagazine.org. **Contact:** Celeste Perrino-Walker, editor. Magazine: 16 pages; glossy paper; illustrations; photos. "Listen is used in many high school classes and by professionals: medical personnel, counselors, law enforcement officers, educators, youth workers, etc. Listen publishes true lifestories about giving teens choices about real-life situations and moral issues in a secular way." Monthly. Circ. 12,000.

Needs Young adult/teen (easy-to-read, sports), anti-drug, alcohol, tobacco, positive role models. Publishes ms 6 months after acceptance. Length: 350-700; average length: 500 words.

How to Contact Query with published clips or send complete ms. Accepts submissions by e-mail. Prefers submissions by e-mail. Considers manuscripts once a year-around October. Accepts simultaneous and multiple submissions, and reprints. Sample copy for $2 and 9 × 12 SASE. Writer's guidelines for SASE, by e-mail, fax or on Web site.

Payment/Terms Pays $50-200, and 3 contributor's copies; additional copies $2. Pays on acceptance for first rights.

☑ ◎ $ LIVE

Gospel Publishing House, 1445 N. Boonville Ave., Springfield MO 65802-1894. (417)862-2781. Fax: (417)862-6059. E-mail: rl-live@gph.org. Website: www.radiantlife.org. **Contact:** Richard Bennett, editor. "*LIVE* is a take-home paper distributed weekly in young adult and adult Sunday school classes. We seek to encourage Christians to live for God through fiction and true stories which apply Biblical principles to everyday problems." Weekly. Estab. 1928. Circ. 60,000.

Needs Religious/inspirational, inspirational, prose poem. No preachy fiction, fiction about Bible characters, or stories that refer to religious myths (e.g., Santa Claus, Easter Bunny, etc.). No science fiction or Biblical fiction. No controversial stories about such subjects as feminism, war or capital punishment, 'city, ethnic, racial settings.' Accepts 2 mss/issue. Publishes ms 18 months after acceptance. **Publishes 50-70 new writers/year.** Recently published work by Rick Barry, Amy Steiner, Marie Latta, and Sarah Gitlin.

How to Contact Send complete ms. Accepts submissions by e-mail or regular mail. Responds in 6 weeks to mss. Accepts simultaneous submissions. Sample copy for #10 SASE. Writer's guidelines for #10 SASE or by e-mail request.

Payment/Terms Pays 7-10¢/word. Pays on acceptance for first, second serial (reprint) rights.

Tips "Write good, inspirational stories that will encourage people to become all they can be as Christians. Stories should go somewhere! Action, not just thought life; interaction, not just insights. Heroes and heroines, suspense and conflict. Avoid simplistic, pietistic, preachy, or critical conclusions or moralizing. We don't accept science fiction or Biblical fiction. Stories should be encouraging, challenging, humorous. Even problem-centered stories should be upbeat. Reserves the right to change the titles, abbreviate length and clarify flashbacks for publication."

◎ $ THE LUTHERAN JOURNAL

Apostolic Publishing Co., Inc., P.O. Box 28158, Oakdale MN 55128. (651)702-0086. Fax: (651)702-0074. E-mail: lutheran2@msn.com. **Contact:** Vance E. Lichty. "A family magazine providing wholesome and inspirational reading material for the enjoyment and enrichment of Lutherans." Annual. Estab. 1938. Circ. 200,000.

Needs Literary, religious/inspirational, romance (historical), young adult/teen, senior citizen/retirement. Must be appropriate for distribution in the churches. Accepts 3-6 mss/issue.

How to Contact Send complete ms. Responds in 4 months to queries. Accepts simultaneous submissions. Sample copy for 9 × 12 SASE with 60¢ postage.

Payment/Terms Pays $50-300 and one contributor's copy. Pays on publication for first rights.

☑ ◎ $ ▣ **THE MAGAZINE OF FANTASY & SCIENCE FICTION**

Spilogale, Inc., P.O. Box 3447, Hoboken NJ 07030. (201) 876-2551. E-mail: fandsf@aol.com. Website: www.fsfmag.com. **Contact**: Gordon Van Gelder, editor. Magazine: 5 × 8; 160 pages; groundwood paper; card stock cover; illustrations on cover only. "For almost sixty years, we have been one of the leading publishers of fantastic fiction (which includes fantasy stories, science fiction, and some horror fiction). Our vision has changed little over six decades—we remain committed to publishing great stories without regard for whether they're classified as sf or fantasy. The Magazine of Fantasy and Science Fiction publishes various types of science fiction and fantasy short stories and novellas, making up about 80% of each issue. The balance of each issue is devoted to articles about science fiction, a science column, book and film reviews, cartoons, and competitions." Monthly. Estab. 1949. Circ. 30,000.

- The *Magazine of Fantasy & Science Fiction* won a Nebula Award for Best Novelet for "The Merchant and the Alchemist's Gate" by Ted Chiang in in 2008. Also won the 2007 World Fantasy Award for Best Short Story for "Journey into the Kingdom" by M. Rickert. Editor Van Gelder won the Hugo Award for Best Editor (short form), 2007 and 2008.

Needs Adventure, fantasy (space fantasy, sword and sorcery), horror (dark fantasy, futuristic, psychological, supernatural), psychic/supernatural/occult, science fiction (hard science/technological, soft/sociological), young adult/teen (fantasy/science fiction, horror). "We're always looking for more science fiction." Receives 600-900 unsolicited mss/month. Accepts 5-10 mss/issue; 60-100 mss/year. Publishes ms 6-9 months after acceptance. **Publishes 3-6 new writers/year.** Agented fiction 5%. Recently published work by Peter S. Beagle, Ursula K. Le Guin, Alex Irvine, Pat Murphy, Joyce Carol Oates, Gene Wolfe, Ted Chiang, S.L. Gilbow and Robert Silverberg. Length: Up to 25,000 words; average length: 7,500 words. Publishes short shorts. Send book review copies to Gordon Van Gelder. Sometimes comments on rejected mss.

How to Contact Send complete ms with SASE (or IRC). Include list of publications, estimated word count. No electronic submissions. Responds in 2 months to queries, 6-8 weeks to mss. Accepts reprint submissions. Sample copy for $5. Writer's guidelines for SASE or on Web site.

Payment/Terms Pays 6-9¢/word, 2 contributor's copies; additional copies $2.70. Pays on acceptance for first North American serial rights. Sends galleys to author. Publication is copyrighted.

Tips "Good storytelling makes a submission stand out. Regarding manuscripts, a well-prepared manuscript (i.e., one that follows the trafitional format, like that describted here: http://www.sfwa.org/writing/vonda/vonda.htm) stands out more than any gimmicks. Read an issue of the magazine before submitting. New writers should keep their submissions under 15,000 words—we rarely publish novellas by new writers."

☑ ◎ **MATURE LIVING**

Lifeway Christian Resources, One Lifeway Plaza, Nashville TN 37234-0175. (615)251-5677. E-mail: matureliving@lifeway.com. **Contact:** Rene Holt, content editor. Magazine: 8½ × 11; 52 pages; slick cover stock; full-color illustrations; photos. "Our magazine is Christian in content, and the material required is what would appeal to 55 and over age group: inspirational, informational, nostalgic, humorous. Our magazine is distributed mainly through churches (especially Southern Baptist churches) that buy the magazine in bulk and distribute it to members in this age group." Monthly. Estab. 1977. Circ. 315,000.

Needs Humor/satire, religious/inspirational, senior citizen/retirement. No reference to liquor, dancing, drugs, gambling; no pornography, profanity or occult. Accepts 8-10 mss/issue. Publishes ms 7-8 months after acceptance. Length: 600-1,200 words preferred; average length: 1,000 words.

How to Contact Send complete ms. "No queries please." Responds in 2 months to mss. Sample copy for 9 × 12 SAE with 4 first-class stamps. Writer's guidelines for #10 SASE.

Payment/Terms Pays $75-105 for feature articles; 3 contributor's copies. Pays on publication.

Tips Mss are rejected because they are too long or subject matter unsuitable. "Our readers seem to enjoy an occasional short piece of fiction. It must be believable, however, and present senior adults in a favorable light."

☑ ◎ $ **MATURE YEARS**

The United Methodist Publishing House, 201 Eighth Ave. S., Nashville TN 37202-0801. (615) 749-6292. Fax: (615) 749-6512. E-mail: matureyears@umpublishing.org. **Contact:** Marvin Cropsey, editor. Magazine: 8½ × 11; 112 pages; illustrations; photos. Magazine "helps persons in and nearing retirement to appropriate the resources of the Christian faith as they seek to face the problems and opportunities related to aging." Quarterly. Estab. 1954. Circ. 55,000.

Needs Humor/satire, religious/inspirational, slice-of-life vignettes, retirement years issues, intergenerational relationships. "We don't want anything poking fun at old age, saccharine stories or anything not for older adults. Must show older adults (age 55 plus) in a positive manner." Accepts 1 mss/issue; 4 mss/year. Publishes ms 1 year after acceptance. **Publishes some new writers/year.** Recently published work by Harriet May Savitz, Donita K. Paul and Ann Gray.

How to Contact Send complete ms. Responds in 2 weeks to queries; 2 months to mss. No simultaneous submissions. Sample copy for $6 and 9 × 12 SAE. Writer's guidelines for #10 SASE or by e-mail.

Payment/Terms Pays $60-125. Pays on acceptance for first North American serial rights.

Tips "Practice writing dialogue! Listen to people talk; take notes; master dialogue writing! Not easy, but well worth it! Most inquiry letters are far too long. If you can't sell me an idea in a brief paragraph, you're not going to sell the reader on reading your finished article or story."

🖼 ◎ $ MSLEXIA

Mslexia Publications Ltd., P.O. Box 656, Newcastle Upon Tyne NE99 1PZ United Kingdom. (00) 44-191-2616656. Fax: (00) 44-191-2616636. E-mail: postbag@mslexia.co.uk. Website: www.mslexia.co.uk. **Contact**: Daneet Steffens, editor. Magazine: A4; 6 8 pages; some illustrations; photos. "*Mslexia* is for women who write, who want to write, who have a specialist interest in women's writing or who teach creative writing. *Mslexia* is a blend of features, articles, advice, listings, and original prose and poetry. Many parts of the magazine are open to submission from any women. Please request contributors' guidelines prior to sending in work." Quarterly. Estab. 1999. Circ. 20,000.

Needs No work from men accepted, except on letters' page. Prose and poetry in each issue is to a specific theme (e.g. sins, travel, rain). Send SASE for themes. Publishes ms 1-2 months after acceptance. **Publishes 40-50 new writers/year.** Length: 2,500 words; average length: 2,000 words. Publishes short shorts to a specific theme and autobiography (800 words). Recent themes have been: The Four Elements, Bugs, Zoo, and Gloves. Also publishes poetry.

How to Contact Accepts submissions by post, and by e-mail from overseas only (postbag@mslexia.co.uk). See www.mslexia.co.uk to read contributors' guidelines before submitting. Responds in 3 months to mss. Guidelines for SAE, e-mail, fax or on Web site.

Payment/Terms Pays £25 per poem; £15 per 1,000 words prose; features by negotiation. Plus contributors' copies.

Tips "Well structured, short pieces preferred. We look for intelligence and a strong sense of voice and place. Consider the obvious interpretations of the theme—then try to think of a new slant. Dare to be different. Make sure the piece is strong on craft as well as content. Extracts from novels are unlikely to be suitable."

◎ $ NA'AMAT WOMAN

NA'AMAT USA, 350 Fifth Ave., Suite 4700, New York NY 10118. (212)563-5222. Fax: (212)563-5710. **Contact:** Judith A. Sokoloff, editor. "Magazine covering a wide variety of subjects of interest to the Jewish community—including political and social issues, arts, profiles; many articles about Israel and women's issues. Fiction must have a Jewish theme. Readers are the American Jewish community." Estab. 1926. Circ. 15,000.

Needs Ethnic/multicultural, historical, humor/satire, literary, novel excerpts, women-oriented. Receives 10 unsolicited mss/month. Accepts 3-5 mss/year.

How to Contact Query with published clips or send complete mss. Responds in 6 months to queries; 6 months to mss. Sample copy for 9 × 11½ SAE and $1.20 postage. Writer's guidelines for #10 SASE.

Payment/Terms Pays 10¢/word and 2 contributor's copies. Pays on publication for first North American serial, first, one-time, second serial (reprint) rights, makes work-for-hire assignments.

Tips "No maudlin nostalgia or romance; no hackneyed Jewish humor."

$ NEWWITCH

BBI, Inc., P.O. Box 687, Forest Grove, OR 97116. (503)430-8817. E-mail: meditor@newwitch.com. Website: www.newwitch.com. **Contact:** Kenaz Filan, managing editor. Magazine. "*newWitch* is dedicated to Witches, Wiccans, Neo-Pagans, and various other earth-based, ethnic, pre/post-christian, shamanic and magical practitioners. We hope to reach not only those already involved in what we cover, but also the curious and completely new as well." Quarterly. Estab. 2002. Circ. 15,000.

Needs Needs contemporary Pagan-themed fiction only. Does not accept fictionalized retellings of real events. Avoid gratuitous sex and violence: in movie rating terms think PG-13. Also avoid gratuitous sentimentality and Pagan moralizing: don't beat our readers with the Rede or the Threefold Law. Accepts 3-4 mss/year. Length: 1,000 words (min)-5,000 words (max).

How to Contact Send complete ms with cover letter. Accepts submissions by e-mail. Responds to queries in 1-2 weeks. Responds to mss in 1 month. Sample copy available for. Guidelines available on Web site.

Tips "Read the magazine, do your research, write the piece, send it in. That's really the only way to get started as a writer: Everything else is window dressing."

☑ ◎ $ PAKN TREGER

National Yiddish Book Center, 1021 West Street, Amherst MA 01002. (413) 256-4900. Fax: (413) 256-4700. E-mail: aatherley@bikher.org. Website: www.yiddishbookcenter.org. **Contact:** Anne Atherley, editor's assistant. Literary magazine/journal. "*Pakn Treger* is looking for high-quality writing for a secular audience interested in Yiddish and Jewish history, literature, and culture." Triannual. Estab. 1980. Circ. 30,000.

Needs Historical, humor/satire, mystery. Accepts 2 mss/year. Manuscript published 4 months after acceptance. Length: 1,200-5,000 words.

How to Contact Query first. Accepts submissions by e-mail. Responds to queries in 2 weeks; mss in 2 months. Sample copy available via e-mail request or viewed on Web site. Guidelines available via e-mail.

Payment/Terms Acquires one-time rights.

Tips "Read the magazine and visit Web site."

☑ ☺ ☑ PLAYBOY MAGAZINE

730 5th Avenue, New York NY 10019. (212)261-5000. Website: www.playboy.com. **Contact:** Fiction Department. "As the world's largest general interest lifestyle magazine for men, *Playboy* spans the spectrum of contemporary men's passions. From hard-hitting investigative journalism to light-hearted humor, the latest in fashion and personal technology to the cutting edge of the popular culture, *Playboy* is and always has been guidebook and dream book for generations of American men, the definitive source of information and ideas for over 10 million readers each month. In addition, *Playboy*'s 'Interview' and '20 Questions' present profiles of politicians, athletes and today's hottest personalities." Monthly. Estab. 1953. Circ. 3,283,000.

Needs Humor/satire, mainstream/literary, mystery/suspense. Does not consider poetry, plays, story outlines or novel-length mss. Writers should remember that the magazine's appeal is chiefly to a well-informed, young male audience. Fairy tales, extremely experimental fiction and out-right pornography all have their place, but it is not in *Playboy*. Handwritten submissions will be returned unread. Writers who submit mss without including a SASE will receive neither the ms nor a printed rejection. "We will not consider stories submitted electronically or by fax."

How to Contact Agented submissions only. Responds in 1 month to queries. No simultaneous submissions. Writer's guidelines for #10 SASE or online at Web site.

Payment/Terms Acquires first North American serial rights.

Tips "*Playboy* does not consider poetry, plays, story outlines or novel-length manuscripts."

◎ $ POCKETS

The Upper Room, 1908 Grand Ave., P.O. Box 340004, Nashville TN 37203-0004. (615) 340-7333. Fax: (615) 340-7267. E-mail: pockets@upperroom.org. Website: www.pockets.org. **Contact:** Lynn W. Gilliam, editor. Magazine: 7 × 11; 48 pages; some photos. "*Pockets* is a Christian, inter-denominational publication for children 6-11 years of age. Each issue reflects a specific theme." Estab. 1981. Circ. 96,000.

• *Pockets* has received honors from the Educational Press Association of America.

Needs Adventure, ethnic/multicultural, historical (general), religious/inspirational, slice-of-life vignettes. No fantasy, science fiction, talking animals. "All submissions should address the broad theme of the magazine. Each issue is built around one theme with material which can be used by children in a variety of ways. Scripture stories, fiction, poetry, prayers, art, graphics, puzzles and activities are included. Submissions do not need to be overtly religious. They should help children experience a Christian lifestyle that is not always a neatly-wrapped moral package, but is open to the continuing revelation of God's will. Seasonal material, both secular and liturgical, is desired. No violence, horror, sexual, racial stereotyping or fiction containing heavy moralizing." Receives 200 unsolicited mss/month. Accepts 3-4 mss/issue; 33-44 mss/year. Publishes ms 1 year to 18 months after acceptance. **Publishes 15 new writers/ year.** Length: 600-1,400 words; average length: 1,200 words.

How to Contact Send complete ms. Cover letter not required. Responds in 6 weeks to mss. Accepts one-time reprints, multiple submissions. For a sample copy, themes and/or guidelines send 9 × 12 SASE with 4 first-class stamps. Writer's guidelines, themes, and due dates available online.

Payment/Terms Pays 14¢/word, plus 2-5 contributor's copies. Pays on acceptance for first North American serial rights. Sponsors an annual fiction-writing contest.

Tips "We receive many inappropriate maunscripts. Study guidelines and themes before submitting. Many manuscripts we receive are simply inappropriate. New themes published in December of each year. We strongly advise sending for themes or reading them on the Web site before submitting." Include SASE with all submissions.

☑ ◎ $ PORTLAND MONTHLY

722 Congress St., Portland ME 04102. (207)775-4339. Fax: (207)775-2334. E-mail: editor@portlandmonthly. com. Website: www.portlandmagazine.com. **Contact:** Colin Sargent, editor. Magazine: 200 pages; 60 lb. paper; 100 lb. cover stock; illustrations; photos. "City lifestyle magazine—fiction, style, business, real estate, controversy, fashion, cuisine, interviews and art relating to the Maine area." Monthly. Estab. 1986. Circ. 100,000.

Needs Contemporary, literary (Maine connection). Query first. Receives 20 unsolicited mss/month. Accepts 1 ms/issue; 10 mss/year. **Publishes 50 new writers/year.** Recently published work by Rick Mood y, Ann Hood, C.D.B Bryan, Joan Connor, Mameve Medwed, Jason Brown, Sarah Graves, Tess Gerritsor and Sebastian Junger.

How to Contact Send complete ms. SASE.

Payment/Terms Pays on publication for first North American serial rights.

Tips "We publish ambitious short fiction featuring everyone from Rick Moody to newly discovered fiction by Edna St. Vincent Millay."

◎ $ ☑ ELLERY QUEEN'S MYSTERY MAGAZINE

Dell Magazines Fiction Group, 475 Park Ave. S., 11th Floor, New York NY 10016. (212)686-7188. Fax: (212)686-7414. E-mail: elleryqueen@dellmagazines.com. Website: www.themysteryplace.com. **Contact**: Janet Hutchings, editor. Magazine: 5¼ × 8⅓, 144 pages with special 240-page combined March/April and September/October issues. *"Ellery Queen's Mystery Magazine* welcomes submissions from both new and established writers. We publish every kind of mystery short story: the psychological suspense tale, the deductive puzzle, the private eye case, the gamut of crime and detection from the realistic (including the policeman's lot and stories of police procedure) to the more imaginative (including "locked rooms" and "impossible crimes"). *EQMM* has been in continuous publication since 1941. From the beginning, three general criteria have been employed in evaluating submissions: We look for strong writing, an original and exciting plot, and professional craftsmanship. We encourage writers whose work meets these general criteria to read an issue of *EQMM* before making a submission." Magazine for lovers of mystery fiction. Estab. 1941. Circ. 180,780 readers.

• *EQMM* has won numerous awards and sponsors its own award yearly for the best EQMM stories nominated by its readership.

Needs Mystery/suspense. No explicit sex or violence, no gore or horror. Seldom publishes parodies or pastiches. "We accept only mystery, crime, suspense and detective fiction." 2,500-8,000 words is the preferred range. Also publishes minute mysteries of 250 words; novellas up to 20,000 words from established authors. Publishes ms 6-12 months after acceptance. Agented fiction 50%. **Publishes 10 new writers/year.** Recently published work by Jeffery Deaver, Joyce Carol Oates and Margaret Maron. Sometimes comments on rejected mss.

How to Contact Send complete ms with SASE for reply. No e-mail submissions. Responds in 3 months to mss. Accepts simultaneous, multiple submissions. Sample copy for $5.50. Writer's guidelines for SASE or online.

Payment/Terms Pays 5-8¢/ a word, occasionally higher for established authors. Pays on acceptance for first North American serial rights.

Tips "We have a Department of First Stories and usually publish at least one first story an issue, i.e., the author's first published fiction. We select stories that are fresh and of the kind our readers have expressed a liking for. In writing a detective story, you must play fair with the reader, providing clues and necessary information. Otherwise you have a better chance of publishing if you avoid writing to formula."

☑ ◎ $ SEEK

Standard Publishing, 8805 Governor's Hill Drive, Suite 400, Cincinnati OH 45239. (513) 728-6822. Fax: (513) 931-0950. E-mail: seek@standardpub.com. Website: www.standardpub.com. Magazine: 5½ × 8½; 8 pages; newsprint paper; art and photo in each issue. "Inspirational stories of faith-in-action for Christian adults; a Sunday School take-home paper." Quarterly. Estab. 1970. Circ. 27,000.

Needs Religious/inspirational, Religious fiction and religiously slanted historical and humorous fiction. No poetry. List of upcoming themes available online. Accepts 150 mss/year. Publishes ms 1 year after acceptance.

How to Contact Send complete ms. Accepts submissions by e-mail. Prefers submissions by e-mail. Writer's guidelines online.

Payment/Terms Pays 7¢/word. Pays on acceptance for first North American serial, pays 5¢ for second serial (reprint) rights.

Tips "Write a credible story with a Christian slant—no preachments; avoid overworked themes such as joy in suffering, generation gaps, etc. Most manuscripts are rejected by us because of irrelevant topic or message, unrealistic story, or poor charater and/or plot development. We use fiction stories that are believable."

☑ ◎ $ ☑ SHINE BRIGHTLY

GEMS Girls' Clubs, P.O. Box 7259, Grand Rapids MI 49510. (616)241-5616. Fax: (616)241-5558. E-mail: sara@gemsgc.org. Website: www.gemsgc.org. **Contact:** Jan Boone, editor; Sara Hilton, Senior Editor. Monthly with combined summer issue. Circ. 17,000. "*SHINE brightly* is designed to help girls ages 9-14 see how God is at work in their lives and in the world around them."

Needs adventure, animal, contemporary, health, history, humorous, multicultural, nature/environment, problem-solving, religious, sports. Does not want "unrealistic stories and those with trite, easy endings. We are interested in manuscripts that show how girls can change the world." Buys 30 mss/year. Length: 400-1,000 words; average length: 800 words.

How to Contact Send complete ms. Responds to mss in 1 month. Will consider simultaneous submissions. Guidelines are on Web site.

Payment/Terms Pays 3¢/word. Pays on publication for first North American serial, second serial (reprint), simultaneous rights. Original artwork not returned at job's completion. Pays $35 for stories, assigned articles, and unsolicited articles and contributor's copies.

Tips "Please check our Website before submitting. We have a specific style and theme that deals with how girls can impact the world. The stories should be current, deal with pre-adolescent problems and joys, and help girls see God at work in their lives through humor as well as problem-solving."

☑ ◎ $ STANDARD

Nazarene Publishing House, 2923 Troost, Kansas City MO 64109. (816) 931-1900. Fax: (816)412-8306. E-mail: clyourdon@wordaction.com. Website: www.wordaction.com. **Contact:** Charlie L. Yourdon, editor; Everett Leadingham, senior editor. Magazine: 8½ × 11; 8 pages; illustrations; photos. Inspirational reading for adults. "In Standard we want to show Christianity in action, and we prefer to do that through stories that hold the reader's attention." Weekly. Estab. 1936. Circ. 100,000.

Needs "Looking for stories that show Christianity in action." Accepts 200 mss/year. Publishes ms 14-18 months after acceptance. **Publishes some new writers/year.**

How to Contact Accepts submissions by e-mail. Postal submissions: send complete ms. SASE. Accepts simultaneous submissions but pays at reprint rates. Writer's guidelines and sample copy for SAE with 2 first-class stamps or available by e-mail request.

Payment/Terms Pays 3½¢/word for first rights; 2¢/word for reprint rights, and contributor's copies. Pays on acceptance for one-time rights, whether first or reprint rights.

Tips "Be conscientious in your use of Scripture; don't overload your story with quotations. When you quote the Bible, quote it exactly and cite chapter, verse, and version used. (We prefer NIV.) *Standard* will handle copyright matters for Scripture. Except for quotations from the Bible, written permission for the use of any other copyrighted material (especially song lyrics) is the responsibility of the writer. Keep in mind the international audience of *Standard* with regard to geographic ref erences and holidays. We cannot use stories about cultural, national, or secular holidays. Do not mention specific church affiliations. *Standard* is read in a variety of denominations. Do not submit any man uscrip ts which has been submitted to or published in any of the following: *Vista, Wesleyan Advocate, Holiness Today, Preacher's Magazine, World Mission, Women Alive*, or various teen and children's publications produced by WordAction Publishing Company. These are overlapping markets."

✅ ◎ $ ✅ ST. ANTHONY MESSENGER

28 W. Liberty St., Cincinnati OH 45202-6498. (513) 241-5615. Fax: (513) 241-0399. E-mail: patm@ americancatholic.org. Website: www.americancatholic.org. **Contact:** Father Pat McCloskey, O.F.M., editor. Magazine: 8 × 10¾; 60 pages; illustrations; photos. "St. Anthony Messenger is a Catholic family magazine which aims to help its readers lead more fully human and Christian lives. We publish articles which report on a changing church and world, opinion pieces written from the perspective of Christian faith and values, personality profiles, and fiction which entertains and informs." Estab. 1893. Circ. 308,884.

> • This is a leading Catholic magazine, but has won awards for both religious and secular journalism and writing from the Catholic Press Association, the International Association of Business Communicators, and the Society of Professional Journalists.

Needs Mainstream, religious/inspirational, senior citizen/retirement. "We do not want mawkishly sentimental or preachy fiction. Stories are most often rejected for poor plotting and characterization; bad dialogue—listen to how people talk; inadequate motivation. Many stories say nothing, are 'happenings' rather than stories." No fetal journals, no rewritten Bible stories. Receives 60-70 unsolicited mss/month. Accepts 1 mss/issue; 12 mss/year. Publishes ms 1 year after acceptance. **Publishes 3 new writers/ year.** Recently published work by Geraldine Marshall Gutfreund, John Salustri, Beth Dotson, Miriam Pollikatsikis and Joseph Pici. Sometimes requests revisions before acceptance.

How to Contact Send complete ms. Accepts submissions by e-mail, fax. "For quickest response send self-addressed stamped postcard with choices: "Yes, we're interested in publishing; Maybe, we'd like to hold for future consideration; No, we've decided to pass on the publication." Responds in 3 weeks to queries; 2 months to mss. No simultaneous submissions. Sample copy for 9 × 12 SASE with 4 first-class stamps. Writer's guidelines online. Reviews fiction.

Payment/Terms Pays 16¢/word maximum and 2 contributor's copies; $1 charge for extras. Pays on acceptance for first North American serial, electronic rights.

Tips "We publish one story a month and we get up to 1,000 a year. Too many offer simplistic 'solutions' or answers. Pay attention to endings. Easy, simplistic, deus ex machina endings don't work. People have to feel characters in the stories are real and have a reason to care about them and what happens to them. Fiction entertains but can also convey a point and sound values."

$ WASHINGTON RUNNING REPORT

13710 Ashby Rd, Rockville MD 20853. (301) 871-0006. Fax: (301) 871-0005. E-mail: kathy@runwashington. com. Website: www.runwashington.com. **Contact:** Kathy Freedman, editor. Magazine. "Written by runners for runners, Washington Running Report covers the running and racing scene in metropolitan Washington DC. Features include runner rankings, training tips and advice, feature articles on races, race results, race calendar, humor, product reviews and other articles of interest to runners." Bimonthly. Estab. 1984. Circ. 35,000.

Needs Adventure, fantasy, historical, humor/satire, mainstream, mystery. Accepts 1-2 mss/year. Manuscript published 2-4 months after acceptance. Length: 750-1,500 words. Stories must be about running.

How to Contact Send complete ms with cover letter. Accepts submissions by e-mail. Responds to queries in 2-3 weeks. Responds to mss in 1-2 months. Considers simultaneous submissions, previously published submissions. Sample copy free upon request.

Payment/Terms Acquires first rights, one-time rights, electronic rights.

▦ □ $ WRITERS' FORUM

Select Publisher Services, P.O. Box 6337, Bournemouth BH1 9EH United Kingdom. (44)1202 586848. E-mail: carl@selectps.com. Website: www.writers-forum.com. **Contact:** Carl Styants, editor. Monthly: A4; 68 pages; illustrations; photos. "In each issue *Writers' Forum* covers the who, why, what, where, when and how of writing. You will find the latest on markets, how-to articles, courses/holidays for writers and much more. There is also a short story competition in every issuea poetry competition, and a young writer's competition in every issue with cash prizes and all winning entries and runners-up printed in the magazine. Prizes range from £300 to £100. Monthly. Estab. 1995.

Needs Historical, horror (psychological), literary, mainstream, mystery/suspense (cozy, private eye/hardboiled), romance (contemporary, futuristic/time travel, historical, romantic suspense), science fiction (soft/sociological), thriller/espionage, western (frontier saga, traditional), young adult/teen (adventure, easy-to-read, historical, problem novels, romance). Receives hundreds unsolicited mss/month. Accepts 3-4 mss/issue; 33 mss/year. Publishes ms 2-3 months after acceptance. Length: 1,000-3,000 words; average length: 1,800 words. Also publishes literary essays, literary criticism, and poetry. Full critique on all rejected competition mss.

How to Contact Query. Accepts submissions by e-mail, post; $15 fee per competition entry. Send SASE (or IRC) for return of ms or send disposable copy of the ms and #10 SASE for reply only. Responds in 2-3 weeks to queries; 3-4 weeks to mss. Accepts simultaneous submissions. Sample copy online. Writer's guidelines online. Reviews fiction.

Payment/Terms Pays £300 maximum and 1 contributor's copy; additional copies $6. Pays 1 month following publication. Acquires first rights. Sponsors awards/contests.

Tips "A good introduction and a original slant on a common theme. Always read the competition rules and our guidelines."

$ WRITERS' JOURNAL

Val-Tech Media, P.O. Box 394, Perham MN 56573-0394. (218) 346-7921. Fax: (218) 346-7924. E-mail: editor@writersjournal.com. Website: www.writersjournal.com. "*WRITERS' Journal* is read by thousands of aspiring writers whose love of writing has taken them to the next step: Writing for money. We are an instructional manual giving writers the tools and information necessary to get their work published. We also print works by authors who have won our writing contests." Bimonthly. Estab. 1980. Circ. 20,000.

Needs "We publish fiction stories from winners of our contests—16 contests/year." Receives 200 contest entries mss/month. Publishes article submissions 5-7 mss/issue; 30-40 mss/year. **Publishes 100 new writers/year.** Also publishes poetry.

How to Contact Accepts contest submissions by postal mail only. Responds in 6 weeks to queries; 6 months to article mss. Accepts unpublished simultaneous submissions. Sample copy for $ 6.

Payment/Terms Pays prize money on publication for one-time rights.

Book Publishers

In this section, you will find many of the "big name" book publishers. Many of these publishers remain tough markets for new writers or for those whose work might be considered literary or experimental. Indeed, some only accept work from established authors, and then often only through an author's agent. Although having your novel published by one of the big commercial publishers listed in this section is difficult, it is not impossible. The trade magazine *Publishers Weekly* regularly features interviews with writers whose first novels are being released by top publishers. Many editors at large publishing houses find great satisfaction in publishing a writer's first novel.

On page 548, you'll find the publishing industry's "family tree," which maps out each of the large book publishing conglomerates' divisions, subsidiaries and imprints. Remember, most manuscripts are acquired by imprints, not their parent company, so avoid submitting to the conglomerates themselves. (For example, submit to Dutton or Berkley Books, not their parent Penguin.)

Also listed here are "small presses" publishing four or more titles annually. Included among them are independent presses, university presses and other nonprofit publishers. Introducing new writers to the reading public has become an increasingly important role of these smaller presses at a time when the large conglomerates are taking fewer chances on unknown writers. Many of the successful small presses listed in this section have built their reputations and their businesses in this way and have become known for publishing prize-winning fiction.

These smaller presses also tend to keep books in print longer than larger houses. And, since small presses publish a smaller number of books, each title is equally important to the publisher, and each is promoted in much the same way and with the same commitment. Editors also stay at small presses longer because they have more of a stake in the business—often they own the business. Many smaller book publishers are writers themselves and know firsthand the importance of a close editor-author or publisher-author relationship.

TYPES OF BOOK PUBLISHERS

Large or small, the publishers in this section publish books "for the trade." That is, unlike textbook, technical or scholarly publishers, trade publishers publish books to be sold to the general consumer through bookstores, chain stores or other retail outlets. Within the trade book field, however, there are a number of different types of books.

The easiest way to categorize books is by their physical appearance and the way they are marketed. Hardcover books are the more expensive editions of a book, sold through bookstores and carrying a price tag of around $20 and up. Trade paperbacks are soft-bound books, also sold mostly in bookstores, but they carry a more modest price tag of usually around $10 to $20. Today a lot of fiction is published in this form because it means a lower financial risk than hardcover.

Mass market paperbacks are another animal altogether. These are the smaller "pocket-size" books available at bookstores, grocery stores, drug stores, chain retail outlets, etc. Much genre or category fiction is published in this format. This area of the publishing industry is very open to the work of talented new writers who write in specific genres such as science fiction, romance and mystery.

At one time publishers could be easily identified and grouped by the type of books they produce. Today, however, the lines between hardcover and paperback books are blurred. Many publishers known for publishing hardcover books also publish trade paperbacks and have paperback imprints. This enables them to offer established authors (and a very few lucky newcomers) hard-soft deals in which their book comes out in both versions. Thanks to the mergers of the past decade, too, the same company may own several hardcover and paperback subsidiaries and imprints, even though their editorial focuses may remain separate.

CHOOSING A BOOK PUBLISHER

In addition to checking the bookstores and libraries for books by publishers that interest you, you may want to refer to the Category Index at the back of this book to find publishers divided by specific subject categories. The subjects listed in the Index are general. Read individual listings to find which subcategories interest a publisher. For example, you will find several romance publishers listed, but read the listings to find which type of romance is considered—gothic, contemporary, regency or futuristic. See You've Got a Story on page 2 for more on how to refine your list of potential markets.

The icons appearing before the names of the publishers will also help you in selecting a publisher. These codes are especially important in this section, because many of the publishing houses listed here require writers to submit through an agent. The ⓐ symbol indicates that a publisher accepts agented submissions only. A ⓜ icon identifies those that mostly publish established and agented authors, while a ☐ points to publishers most open to new writers. See the inside front cover of this book for a complete list and explanations of symbols used in this book.

IN THE LISTINGS

As with other sections in this book, we identify new listings with a ⓝ symbol. In this section, most with this symbol are not new publishers, but instead are established publishers who were unable or decided not to list last year and are therefore new to this edition.

In addition to the ⓝ symbol indicating new listings, we include other symbols to help you in narrowing your search. English-speaking foreign markets are denoted by a ⓖ. The maple leaf symbol ⁌ identifies Canadian presses. If you are not a Canadian writer but are interested in a Canadian press, check the listing carefully. Many small presses in Canada receive grants and other funds from their provincial or national government and are, therefore, restricted to publishing Canadian authors.

We also include editorial comments set off by a bullet (•) within listings. This is where we include information about any special requirements or circumstances that will help you know even more about the publisher's needs and policies. The star ⁌ signals that this market is an imprint or division of a larger publisher. The ⓥ symbol identifies publishers who have recently received honors or awards for their books. The ⓖ denotes publishers who produce comics and graphic novels.

Each listing includes a summary of the editorial mission of the house, an overarching principle that ties together what they publish. Under the heading **Contact** we list one or more editors, often with their specific area of expertise.

Book editors asked us again this year to emphasize the importance of paying close attention to the **Needs** and **How to Contact** subheads of listings for book publishers. Unlike magazine editors who want to see complete manuscripts of short stories, most of the book publishers listed here ask that writers send a query letter with an outline and/or synopsis and several chapters of their novel. The Business of Fiction Writing, beginning on page 77 of this book, outlines how to prepare work to submit directly to a publisher.

There are no subsidy book publishers listed in *Novel & Short Story Writer's Market*. By subsidy, we mean any arrangement in which the writer is expected to pay all or part of the cost of producing, distributing and marketing his book. We feel a writer should not be asked to share in any cost of turning his manuscript into a book. All the book publishers listed here told us that they *do not charge writers* for publishing their work. **If any of the publishers listed here ask you to pay any part of publishing or marketing your manuscript, please let us know.** See our Complaint Procedure on the copyright page of this book.

A NOTE ABOUT AGENTS

Some publishers are willing to look at unsolicited submissions, but most feel having an agent is in the writer's best interest. In this section more than any other, you'll find a number of publishers who prefer submissions from agents. That's why we've included a section of agents open to submissions from fiction writers (page 125). For even more agents along with a great deal of helpful articles about approaching and working with them, refer to *Guide to Literary Agents* (Writer's Digest Books).

If you use the Internet or another resource to find an agent not listed in this book, be wary of any agents who charge large sums of money for reading a manuscript. Reading fees do not guarantee representation. Think of an agent as a potential business partner and feel free to ask tough questions about his or her credentials, experience and business practices.

□ ABERDEEN BAY

5676 Ridge View Drive, Alexandria VA 22310. Website: www.aberdeenbay.com. **Contact:** Andy Zhang, principal editor. Estab. 2007. "We're a small independent publisher who publishes trade paperback originals with outstanding quality." Publishes paperback originals, paperback reprints, e-books. Format: POD printing. **Published 5 new writers last year.** Plans 20 debut novels this year. Averages 20 total titles/year; 15 fiction titles/year. Distributes/promotes titles through various retailers.

Needs Ethnic/multicultural (Asian), family saga, feminist, gay, glitz, historical, lesbian, literary, mainstream, young adult/teen (adventure, easy-to-read, historical, mystery/suspense, problem novels, romance, series, sports, western). Published *Memories of an Eastern Sky, When Summer was in the Meadow, Uncle Si's Secret.*

How to Contact Query with outline/synopsis and 3 sample chapters. Accepts queries by snail mail. Include brief bio, list of publishing credits. Send disposable copy of ms and SASE for reply only. Responds to queries in 8 weeks. Accepts unsolicited mss. Considers simultaneous submissions. Sometimes critiques/comments on rejected mss. Responds to mss in 12 weeks.

Terms Ms published 6 months after acceptance. Writer's guidelines on Web site. Pays royalties 10%, 1 author's free copy. Book catalogs on Web site.

HARRY N. ABRAMS, INC.

La Martiniere Groupe, Attn: Managing Editor, 115 West 18th St., New York NY 10011. (212)206-7715. Fax: (212)645-8437. Website: www.abramsbooks.com. **Contact:** Managing editor. Estab. 1949. Publishes hardcover and "a few" paperback originals. Averages 150 total titles/year.

Imprints Abrams Books; Stewart, Tabori & Chang; Abrams Books for Young Readers (including Amulet Books for Middle Grade and Young Adult); Abrams Gifts and Stationery.

How to Contact Responds in 6 months to queries. No simultaneous submissions, electronic submissions.

Terms Pays royalty. Average advance: variable. Publishes ms 2 years after acceptance. Book catalog for $5.

☑ ABSEY & CO.

23011 Northcrest Drive, Spring TX 77389. (281)257-2340. E-mail: abseyandco@aol.com. Website: www.absey.com. **Contact:** Edward E. Wilson, publisher. "We are interested in book-length fiction of literary merit with a firm intended audience." Publishes hardcover, trade paperback and mass market paperback originals. **Published 3-5 debut authors within the last year.** Averages 6-10 total titles, 6-10 fiction titles/year.

Needs Juvenile, mainstream/contemporary, short story collections. Published *Where I'm From*, by George Ella Lyon; *Blast Man Standing*, by Robert V. Spelleri.

How to Contact Accepts unsolicited mss. Query with SASE. Responds in 3 months to queries; 9 months to mss. No simultaneous submissions, electronic submissions.

Terms Royalty and advance vary. Publishes ms 1 year after acceptance. Ms guidelines online.

☑ ACADEMY CHICAGO PUBLISHERS

363 W. Erie St., Suite 7E., Chicago IL 60610-3125. (312)751-7300. Fax: (312)751-7306. E-mail: info@academychicago.com. Website: www.academychicago.com. **Contact:** Anita Miller, senior editor. Estab. 1975. Midsize independent publisher. Publishes hardcover originals and trade paperback reprints. Averages 15 total titles/year.

Needs Historical, mainstream/contemporary, military/war, mystery. "We look for quality work, but we do not publish experimental, avant-garde novels." Biography, history, academic and anthologies. Only the most unusual mysteries, no private-eyes or thrillers. No explicit sex or violence. Serious fiction, no romance/adventure. "We will consider historical fiction that is well researched. No science fiction/fantasy, no religious/inspirational, no how-to, no cookbooks. In general, we are very conscious of women's roles. We publish very few children's books." Published *Clean Start*, by Patricia Margaret Page (first fiction); *Cutter's Island: Caesar in Captivity*, by Vincent Panella (first fiction, historical); *Murder at the Paniomic Games*, by Michael B. Edward.

How to Contact Accepts unsolicited mss. Do not submit by e-mail. Submit 3 sample chapter(s), synopsis. Accepts queries by mail. Include cover letter briefly describing the content of your work. Send SASE or IRC. "Manuscripts without envelopes will be discarded. *Mailers* are a *must* even from agents." Responds in 3 months to queries. No electronic submissions.

Terms Pays 7-10% royalty on wholesale price. Average advance: modest. Publishes ms 18 months after acceptance. Ms guidelines online.

☑ ◎ ACE SCIENCE FICTION AND FANTASY

The Berkley Publishing Group, Penguin Group (USA), Inc., 375 Hudson St., New York NY 10014. (212)366-2000. Website: www.penguin.com. **Contact:** Susan Allison, editor-in-chief; Anne Sowards, editor. Estab. 1953. Publishes hardcover, paperback and trade paperback originals and reprints. Averages 75 total titles, 75 fiction titles/year.

Needs Fantasy, science fiction. No other genre accepted. No short stories. Published *Iron Sunrise*, by Charles Stross; *Neuromancer*, by William Gibson; *King Kelson's Bride*, by Katherine Kurtz.

How to Contact Does not accept unsolicited mss. Submit 1-2 sample chapter(s), synopsis. Send SASE or IRC. Responds in 2-3 months to queries. Accepts simultaneous submissions.

Terms Pays royalty. Offers advance. Publishes ms 1-2 years after acceptance. Ms guidelines for #10 SASE.

◎ ACME PRESS

P.O. Box 1702, Westminster MD 21158-1702. (410)848-7577. **Contact:** (Ms.) E.G. Johnston, managing editor. Estab. 1991. "We operate on a part-time basis." Publishes hardcover and trade paperback originals. **Published some debut authors within the last year.** Averages 1-2 total titles/year.

Needs Humor. "We accept submissions on any subject as long as the material is humorous; prefer full-length novels. No cartoons or art (text only). No pornography, poetry, short stories or children's material." Published *She-Crab Soup*, by Dawn Langley Simmons (fictional memoir); *Biting the Wall*, by J.M. Johnston (mystery); *SuperFan*, by Lyn A. Sherwood (football); and *Hearts of Gold*, by James Magorian (caper).

How to Contact Accepts unsolicited mss. Agented fiction 25%. Responds in 2 weeks to queries; 2 months to mss. Accepts simultaneous submissions. Always comments on rejected mss.

Terms Pays 25 author's copies and 50% of profits. Average advance: small. Publishes ms 1 year after acceptance. Book catalog and ms guidelines for #10 SASE.

☑ ◎ AGELESS PRESS

3759 Collins St., Sarasota FL 34232. E-mail: irishope@comcast.net. Website: http://irisforrest.com. **Contact:** Iris Forrest, editor. Estab. 1992. Independent publisher. Publishes paperback originals. Books: acid-free paper; notched perfect binding; no illustrations. Averages 1 total title/year.

Needs Experimental, fantasy, humor, literary, mainstream/contemporary, mystery, new age/mystic, science fiction, short story collections, thriller/espionage. Looking for material "based on personal computer experiences." Stories selected by editor. Published *Computer Legends, Lies & Lore*, by various (anthology); and *Computer Tales of Fact and Fantasy*, by various (anthology).

How to Contact Does not accept unsolicited mss. Query with SASE. Accepts queries by e-mail, fax, mail. Responds in 1 week to queries; 1 week to mss. Accepts simultaneous submissions, electronic submissions, submissions on disk. Sometimes comments on rejected mss.

Terms Average advance: negotiable. Publishes ms 6-12 months after acceptance.

ALGONQUIN BOOKS OF CHAPEL HILL

Workman Publishing, P.O. Box 2225, Chapel Hill NC 27515-2225. (919)967-0108. Website: www.algonquin.com. **Contact:** Editorial Department. Publishes hardcover originals. Averages 24 total titles/year.

Needs Literary fiction and nonfiction, cookbooks and lifestyle books (about family, animals, food, flowers, adventure, and other topics of interest). No poetry, genre fiction (romance, science fiction, etc.) or children's books. Recently published *Saving the World*, by Julia Alvarez; *Which Brings Me to You*, by Steve Almond and Julianna Baggott; *Hope and Other Dangerous Pursuits*, by Laila Lalami.

How to Contact Send a 20-page sample of your work, along with a cover letter, SASE, and a check for return postage (if you wish to have your mss returned). No phone, e-mail or fax queries or submissions.

Terms Ms guidelines online.

◎ AMERICAN ATHEIST PRESS

P.O. Box 5733, Parsippany NJ 07054-6733. (908)276-7300. Fax: (908)276-7402. E-mail: info@atheists.org.

Website: www.atheists.org. Contact: Frank Zindler, editor. Estab. 1963. Publishes trade paperback originals and reprints. Publishes monthly journal, American Atheist, for which are needed articles of interest to atheists. Published 40-50% debut authors within the last year. Averages 12 total titles/year.

Imprints Gustav Broukal Press.

Needs Humor (satire of religion or of current religious leaders), anything of particular interest to atheists. "We rarely publish any fiction. But we have occasionally released a humorous book. No mainstream. For our press to consider fiction, it would have to tie in with the general focus of our press, which is the promotion of atheism and free thought."

How to Contact Submit outline, sample chapter(s). Responds in 4 months to queries. Accepts simultaneous submissions.

Terms Pays 5-10% royalty on retail price. Publishes ms within 2 years after acceptance. Ms to be submitted as MS Word attachments with e-mail. Hard copy may be requested.

AMIRA PRESS

(443) 421-6831. E-mail: yvette@amirapress.com. Website: www.amirapress.com. **Contact:** Yvette A. Lynn, CEO (sensual and erotic only); Deborah Herald, managing editor—erotica (erotica, westerns, nonfiction). Estab. 2007. "We are a small press which likes to publish works from all backgrounds and groups. Our authors and stories are diverse. Our slogan is 'Fiction that is Coloring the World,' which means we are bringing all types of people together with our books." Publishes paperback originals, e-books. POD printing. **Published 30 new writers last year.** Averages 50 fiction titles/year. Member EPIC. Distributes/promotes titles through Amazon, Mobipocket, Fictionwise, BarnesandNoble.com, Target.com, Amirapress.com, All Romance Ebooks, and Ingrams.

Needs Adventure romance, erotica, ethnic/multicultural, fantasy, historical, mystery/suspense, science fiction, psychic/supernatural, contemporary, futuristic/time travel, historical, regency period. Special interests: interracial, paranormal, fantasy. Published *Tempting a Wolf*, by Tressie Lockwood (interracial romance), *Accidental Mates*, by Brenda Steele(erotic fantasy romance); *Shifter: Stefan's Mark*, by Jaden Sinclair (paranormal erotic romance).

How to Contact Submit complete ms with cover letter. Accepts queries by e-mail. Include estimated word count, brief bio, list of publishing credits. Accepts unsolicited mss. Considers simultaneous submissions, submissions on CD or disk. Sometimes critiques/comments on rejected mss. Responds to mss in 3 months.

Terms Ms published 1-4 months after acceptance. Writer's guidelines on Web site. Pays royalties, 15% net (print)-50% net (Ebooks). Book catalogs on Web site.

ANNICK PRESS, LTD.

15 Patricia Ave., Toronto ON M2M 1H9 Canada. (416)221-4802. Fax: (416)221-8400. E-mail: annickpress@annickpress.com. Website: www.annickpress.com. Publisher of children's books. Publishes hardcover and trade paperback originals. Average print order; 9,000. First novel print order: 7,000. Plans 18 first novels this year. Averages 25 total titles/year. Distributes titles through Firefly Books Ltd.

Needs Juvenile, young adult. fiction, and non-fiction.

How to Contact Query with SASE. Responds in 1 month queries; 3 months to mss. No simultaneous submissions, electronic submissions. Sometimes comments on rejected mss. Does not accept unsolicted mss.

Terms Publishes ms 2 years after acceptance. Ms guidelines online.

ANTARCTIC PRESS

7272 Wurzbach, Suite 204, San Antonio TX 78240. (210)614-0396. Website: www.antarctic-press.com. "Antarctic Press is a Texas-based company that was started in 1984. Since then, we have grown to become one of the largest publishers of comics in the United States. Over the years we have produced over 850 titles with a total circulation of over 5 million. Among our titles are some of the most respected and longest-running independent series in comics today. Since our inception, our main goal has been to establish a series of titles that are unique, entertaining, and high in both quality and profitability. The titles we currently publish exhibit all these traits, and appeal to a wide audience." Publishes comic books, graphic novels.

Terms Pays royalty on net receipts. Ms guidelines online.

⬡ ☑ ◎ ANVIL PRESS

278 East First Avenue, Vancouver BC V5T 1A6 Canada. (604)876-8710. Fax: (604)879-2667. E-mail: info@anvilpress.com. Website: www.anvilpress.com. **Contact:** Brian Kaufman, publisher. Estab. 1988. "Three-person operation with volunteer editorial board." Publishes trade paperback originals. Canadian authors only. Books: offset or web printing; perfect bound. **Published some debut authors within the last year.** Averages 8-10 total titles/year.

Needs Experimental, literary, short story collections. Contemporary, modern literature—no formulaic or genre. Published *Stolen*, by Annette Lapointe (novel); *Suburban Pornography*, by Matthew Firth (stories); *Elysium and Other Stories*, by Pamela Stewart; *Dirtbags*, by Teresa McWhirter (novel); *Black Rabbit and Other Stories* by Salvatore DiFalco.

How to Contact Accepts unsolicited mss, or query with SASE. Include estimated word count, brief bio. Send SASE for return of ms or send a disposable ms and SASE for reply only. Responds in 2 months to queries; 6 months to mss. Accepts simultaneous submissions.

Terms Pays 15% royalty on net receipts. Average advance: $500. Publishes ms 8 months after acceptance. Book catalog for 9 × 12 SAE with 2 first-class stamps. Ms guidelines online.

⬡ ☑ ARCADE PUBLISHING

116 John St., Suite 2810, New York NY 10038. (212)475-2633. **Contact:** Richard Seaver, Jeannette Seaver, Cal Barksdale, Casey Ebro, James Jayo, and Tessa Ayel. Estab. 1988. Independent publisher. Publishes hardcover originals, trade paperback reprints. Books: 50-55 lb. paper; notch, perfect bound; illustrations. **Published some debut authors within the last year.** Averages 35 total titles, 10 fiction titles/year. Distributes titles through Hachette Book Group USA.

Needs Literary, mainstream/contemporary, short story collections. Published *Trying to Save Piggy Sneed*, by John Irving; *It Might Have Been What He Said*, by Eden Collinsworth; *Music of a Life*, by Andrei Makine; *The Last Song of Dusk*, by Siddharth Dhanvant Shanghvi; *Bibliophilia,* by Michael Griffith.

How to Contact Does not accept unsolicited mss. *Agented submissions only*. Agented fiction 100%. Responds in 1 month to queries; 4 months to mss.

Terms Pays royalty on retail price, 10 author's copies. Offers advance. Publishes ms within 18 months after acceptance. Ms guidelines for #10 SASE.

⬡ ⬡ ARCHAIA

586 Devon St., 3rd Floor, Kearny NJ 07032-2804. E-mail: editorial@aspcomics.com. Website: www. archaiasp.com. "Archaia was founded as a home originally for Mark S. Smylie's comic Artesia. Now Mark and publishing partner Aki Liao have expanded ASP to include a line of idiosyncratic and creator-driven comic books and graphic novels in the fantasy, science fiction, and horror genres, as well as translations of several of Europe's best titles."

Needs "Archaia Studios Press (ASP) is interested in publishing creator-owned comic books in the fantasy, horror, pulp noir, and science fiction genres that contain idiosyncratic and atypical writing and art. ASP does not hire freelancers or arrange for freelance work, so submissions should only be for book and series proposals. ASP is primarily interested in full-color projects, but proposals for black & white projects will also be considered."

How to Contact Query with outline/synopsis and photocopies of completed pages. Accepts queries by snail mail. Include estimated page count and other technical details."

Terms Writer's guidelines on Web site.

⬡ ⬡ ARCHIE COMIC PUBLICATIONS, INC

325 Fayette Ave., Mamaroneck NY 10543.(914)381-5155. Fax: (914)381-2335. Website: http://www. archiecomics.com/index.html.

☑ ARIEL STARR PRODUCTIONS, LTD.

P.O. Box 17, Demarest NJ 07627. E-mail: darkbird@aol.com. **Contact:** Acquisitions department. Estab. 1991. Publishes paperback originals. **Published 2 debut authors within the last year.**

How to Contact Submit outline, 1 sample chapter. Accepts queries by e-mail. Include brief bio. Send SASE or IRC. Responds in 6 weeks to queries; 4 months to mss. Sometimes comments on rejected mss.

Terms Publishes ms one year after acceptance.

⚏ ☑ ◎ ARSENAL PULP PRESS

341 Water Street, Suite 200, Vancouver BC V6B 1B8 Canada. (604)687-4233. Fax: (604)687-4283. Website: www.arsenalpulp.com. **Contact:** Bethanne Grabham, Editorial Asst. Estab. 1980. Literary press. Publishes hardcover and trade paperback originals, and trade paperback reprints. **Published some debut authors within the last year.** Plans 1,500 first novels this year. Plans 2 first novels this year. Averages 20 total titles/year. Distributes titles through Whitecap Books (Canada) and Consortium (U.S.). Promotes titles through reviews, excerpts and print advertising.

Needs Gay/lesbian, literary fiction and nonfiction, multicultural, regional (British Columbia), cultural studies, pop culture, political/sociological issues, cookbooks. No poetry.

How to Contact Accepts unsolicited mss. Submit outline, 2-3 sample chapter(s), synopsis. Include list of publishing credits. Send copy of ms and SASE (or with International Reply Coupons if sent from outside Canada) OR include e-mail address if manuscript does not need to be returned. Agented fiction 10%. Responds in 2 months to queries; 4 months to mss. Accepts simultaneous submissions. Sometimes comments on rejected mss.

Terms Publishes ms 1 year after acceptance. Book catalog and submission guidelines on Web site.

◻ ◎ ARTEMIS PRESS

SRS Internet Publishing, 236 W. Portal Avenue #525, San Francisco CA 94127. (866)216-7333. E-mail: submissions@artemispress.com. Website: www.artemispress.com. **Contact:** Susan R. Skolnick, publisher and editor-in-chief; Chloe Greenberg, editor. Estab. 2000. "Publisher of short fiction of interest to the worldwide women's community. We specialize in lesbian-related titles but are interested in all women-centered titles. We are open to working with new authors." Publishes electronic editions of original, previously published material. **Published no debut authors within the last year.** Titles distributed and promoted online to target market.

Needs Mystery, suspense, romance, erotica, psychic/supernatural, and science fiction. Published *Zoo Gang Girls*, by Joan Arndt (science fiction); *Against a White Sky: A Memoir of Closets and Classrooms*, by Laurie Stapleton (lesbian studies/gender studies); *Clicking Stones*, by Nancy Tyler Glenn (new age/mystic); *Moon Madness and Other Stories*, by Liann Snow (short story collection); *Faith in Love*, by Liann Snow (humor/satire); *Luna Ascending: Stories of Love and Magic*, by Renee Brown (short story collection); *Windrow Garden*, by Janet McClellan (romance); *Never Letting Go*, by Suzanne Hollo (humor/satire); *Minding Therapy*, by Ros Johnson (humor/satire).

How to Contact Does not accept unsolicited mss. Agented fiction 5%. Responds in 3 months to queries. Does not accept simultaneous submissions.

Terms Buys all rights. Publishes ms 6 months after acceptance. Ms guidelines online.

☑ ◎ ARTE PUBLICO PRESS

University of Houston, 452 Cullen Performance Hall, Houston TX 77204-2004. Fax: (713)743-3080. Website: www.artepublicopress.com. E-mail: appinfo@uh.edu. **Contact**: Dr. Nicolas Kanellos, editor. Estab. 1979. "Small press devoted to the publication of contemporary U.S.-Hispanic literature." Publishes hardcover originals, trade paperback originals and reprints. Averages 36 total titles/year.

  • Arte Publico Press is the oldest and largest publisher of Hispanic literature for children and adults in the United States.

Imprints Pinata Books featuring children's and young adult literature by U.S.-Hispanic writers.

Needs Ethnic, literary, mainstream/contemporary, written by U.S.-Hispanic authors. Published *Project Death*, by Richard Bertematti (novel, mystery); *A Perfect Silence*, by Alba Ambert; *Song of the Hummingbird*, by Graciela Limón; *Little Havana Blues: A Cuban-American Literature Anthology*.

How to Contact Accepts unsolicited mss. Query with SASE or submit 2 sample chapter(s), synopsis or submit complete ms. Agented fiction 1%. Responds in 2-4 months to queries; 3-6 months to mss. Accepts simultaneous submissions. Sometimes comments on rejected mss.

Terms Pays 10% royalty on wholesale price. Provides 20 author's copies; 40% discount on subsequent copies. Average advance: $1,000-3,000. Publishes ms 2 years after acceptance. Ms guidelines online.

⋈ ☑ ASPEN MOUNTAIN PRESS

P.O. Box 473543, Aurora CO 80047-3543. E-mail: submissions@aspenmountainpress.com. Website: www.AspenMountainPress.com. **Contact:** Sandra Hicks, editor-in-chief (gay, mystery, erotica, science fiction, fantasy); Nikita Gordyn (paranormal romance, science fiction romance). Estab. 2006. "We are a small electronic press that specializes in e-books. A few outstanding stories are considered for print. We currently encourage newer, outstanding writers to take their craft to the next level. The bulk of our stories are romantic with varying degrees of sensuality/sexuality. We encourage romances between consenting adults. We encourage discussion among our authors; we frequently discuss marketing, we take author input into covers seriously, we pay every month royalties are earned." Publishes paperback originals, e-books. Format: POD printing; perfect bound. Average print order: 250-500. Debut novel print order: 250. **Published 30 debut writers last year**. Plans 25-30 debut novels this year. Averages 65 fiction titles/year. Member CIPA. Distributes/promotes titles through Fictionwise, AllRomance Ebooks, Mobipocket, Amazon, Ingrams, and Baker and Taylor.

Needs Adventure, erotica, fantasy (space fantasy, sword and sorcery), gay, historical (erotic regencey), horror (dark fantasy, futuristic, psychological, supernatural), lesbian, military/war, mystery/suspense (amateur sleuth, cozy, police procedural, private eye/hardboiled), psychic/supernatural, romance (contemporary, futuristic/time travel, gothic, historical, regency, romantic suspense), science fiction (hard science/technological, soft/sociological), short story collections, thriller/espionage, western (frontier saga, traditional, gay). Special interests: "military/paramilitary with heroes the reader can identify with and science fiction romance—No first person!" Published *Cold Warriors*, by Clare Dargin (science fiction romance); *Del Fantasma: Texas Tea*, by Maura Anderson (erotic paranormal romance); and *Soul Sacrifice*, by Elisabeth Jason (erotic paranormal romance).

How to Contact Query with outline/synopsis and 2-4 sample chapters. Accepts queries by e-mail only. Include estimated word count, brief bio, list of publishing credits, and indicate whether the ms is finished. Responds to queries in 1 month. Accepts unsolicited mss. Often critiques/comments on rejected mss. Responds to mss in 2-3 months.

Terms Sends pre-production galleys to author. Ms published 3-12 months after acceptance. Writer's guidelines on Web site. Pays royalties of 8% min for print, 35-40% max for e-books.

ATHENEUM BOOKS FOR YOUNG READERS

Simon & Schuster, 1230 Avenue of the Americas, New York NY 10020. (212) 698-7000. Fax: (212) 698-2796. Website: www.simonsayskids.com. **Contact:** Emma D. Dryden, VP/Publisher, Caitlyn Dlouhy, editorial director; Namrata Tripathi, executive editor. **Art Acquisitions:** Ann Bobco, executive art director. Estab. 1960. Atheneum Books for Young Readers is a hardcover imprint with a focus on literary fiction and fine picture books for preschoolers through young adults. Publishes special interest, first novels and new talent. Publishes 20 + picture books/year; 20 + middle readers/year; 20 + young adult titles/year.

> • In recent years, Atheneum has received the Newberry Medal for *Kira-Kira* by Cynthia Kadohata and *The Higher Power of Lucky* by Susan Patron; the Caldecott Honor for international bestseller *Olivia* written and illustrated by Ian Falconer; the Siebert Honor for *Lightship* written and illustrated by Brian Floca; and National Book Award finalists *Skin Hunger* by Kathleen Duey and *The Underneath* by Kathi Appelt.

Needs Middle grade and YA adventure, fantasy, humor, mainstream/contemporary, mystery, suspense, and picture books. "We do not need how-to pamphlets, ABC books, coloring books, or board books."

How to Contact "We do not accept unsolicited queries, partial, or full manuscript submissions, unless from an agent."

Terms Average print order is 10,000 -15,000 for a first middle grade or young adult book; 7,500-20,000 for a first picture book. Pays royalty on hardcover retail price: 10% fiction; 5% author, 5% illustrator (picture book). Offers $5,000-$8,000 advance for new authors. Publishes ms up to 3 years after acceptance.

AUNT LUTE BOOKS

P.O. Box 410687, San Francisco CA 94141. (415) 826-1300. Fax: (415) 826-8300. E-mail: submissions@ auntlute.com. Website: www.auntlute.com. **Contact:** Noella de la Paz, first reader. Small feminist and women-of-color press. Publishes hardcover and paperback originals. Does not publish single-author collections of poetry. Averages 4 total titles/year.

Needs Ethnic, feminist, lesbian.

How to Contact Accepts unsolicited ms queries. Please include SASE. Alternately, submit cover letter, two sample chapters (approx 50 pages), brief synopsis, and SASE. Responds in 4 months.

Terms Pays royalty.

▨ ◖◗ AURORA PUBLISHING

Ohzora Publishing Co., 3655 Torrance Blvd., Suite 430, Torrance CA 90503. (310)540-2800. Fax: (310)540-2877. E-mail: info@aurora-publishing.com. Website: www.aurora-publishing.com. Estab. 2006.

◪ AUTUMN HOUSE PRESS

87 12 Westwood Street, Pittsburgh PA 15211. (412) 381-4261. E-mail: info@autumnhouse.org. Website: http://autumnhouse.org. **Contact:** Michael Simms, editor-in-chief. Estab. 1998. "We are a non-profit literary press specializing in high-quality poetry and fiction. Our editions are beautifully designed and printed, and they are distributed nationally. Approximately one-third of our sales are to college literature and creative writing classes." Publishes hardcover originals, paperback originals. Format: acid-free paper; offset printing; perfect and casebound (cloth) bound; sometimes contains illustrations. Average print order: 1,500. Debut novel print order: 1,500. **Published 2 new writers last year.** Plans 2 debut novels this year. Averages 6 total titles/year; 2 fiction titles/year. Member CLMP, AWP, Academy of American Poets. "We distribute our own titles. We do extensive national promotion through ads, web-marketing, reading tours, bookfairs and conferences."

Needs "We are open to all genres. The quality of writing concerns us, not the genre. We are looking for well-crafted prose fiction." Published *New World Order*, by Derek Green (collection of stories) and *Drift and Swerve*, by Samuel Ligon (collection of stories).

How to Contact All submissions come through our annual contests, deadline June 30 each year. See Web site for official guidelines. Responds to queries in 2 days. Accepts mss only through contest. Never critiques/comments on rejected mss. Responds to mss by August.

Terms Sends pre-production galleys to author. Ms published 9-12 months after acceptance. Submission guidelines on Web site. Pays royalties 7%, advance average of $2,500. Book catalogs free upon request, on Web site.

AVALON BOOKS

Thomas Bouregy & Co., Inc., 160 Madison Ave., 5th Floor, New York NY 10016. (212)598-0222. Fax: (212)979-1862. E-mail: editorial@avalonbooks.com. Website: www.avalonbooks.com. **Contact:** Faith Black, associate editor. Estab. 1950. Publishes hardcover originals. **Published some debut authors within the last year.** Averages 60 total titles/year. Distributes titles through Baker & Taylor, libraries, Barnes&Noble.com and Amazon.com. Promotes titles through Library Journal, Booklist, Publishers Weekly and local papers.

Needs Historical (romance), mystery, contemporary romance, western. "We publish wholesome contemporary romances, mysteries, historical romances and westerns. Our books are read by adults as well as teenagers, and the main characters are all adults. All mysteries are contemporary. We publish contemporary romances (four every two months), historical romances (two every two months), mysteries (two every two months) and westerns (two every two months). Submit first 3 sample chapters, a 2-3 page synopsis and SASE. The manuscripts should be between 40,000 to 70,000 words. Manuscripts that are too long will not be considered. Time period and setting are the author's preference. The historical romances will maintain the high level of reading expected by our readers. The books shall be wholesome fiction, without graphic sex, violence or strong language." Published *Death in the French Quarter*, by Kent Conwell (mystery); *Judgment at Gold Butte,*, by Terrell L. Bowers (western); *Adieu, My Love,* by Lynn Turner (historical romance); *Everything But a Groom*, by Holly Jacobs (romantic comedy).

How to Contact Does not accept unsolicited mss. Query with SASE or IRC. Responds in 1 month to queries; 6-10 months to mss.

Terms Average advance: $1,000. Publishes ms 8-12 months after acceptance. Ms guidelines online.

◙ ◖◗ AVATAR PRESS

515 N. Century Blvd, Rantoul IL 61866.Fax: (217)893-9671. E-mail: submissions@avatarpress.net; william@avatarpress.net. Website: http://www.avatarpress.com/.

Needs Comic books both freelance artists working within company-owned storylines, or creator-owned comics. Published Warren Ellis' Anna Mercury, George A. Romero's Night of the Living Dead, Frank Miller's Robocop, and Alan Moore's The Courtyard and more. Doktor Sleepless, Gravel.

How to Contact "Send us an 8-12 page story with panel to panel descriptions and in full script format. The story should feature an adventure by any Avatar Press company-owned character. Do not send us stories featuring characters owned by other comic companies or any creator-owned characters (even if

the creator who owns the character is you - if you want to submit a creator-owned project see our listed guidelines for that ... these are the guidelines for freelance writing submissions). E-mail submissions are OK. If you have been previously published you may send copies of those comics. Don't forget to include your name, address, e-mail address and/or a phone number at which you can be contacted."
Terms Writer's guidelines on Web site.

AVON BOOKS

Harper Collins Publishers, 10 E. 53 Street, New York NY 10022. (212)207-7000. Website: www.harpercollins. com. **Contact:** Michael Morrison, publisher. Estab. 1941. "Avon has been publishing award-winning books since 1941. It is recognized for having pioneered the historical romance category and continues to bring the best of commercial literature to the broadest possible audience." Publishes hardcover and paperback originals and reprints. Averages 400 total titles/year.
Imprints Avon, EOS.
Needs Historical, literary, mystery, romance, science fiction, young adult, health, pop culture.
How to Contact Does not accept unsolicited mss. Query with SASE. Send SASE or IRC.
Terms Varies.

☑ ◎ B & H PUBLISHING

LifeWay Christian Resources, 127 Ninth Ave. N., Nashville TN 37234. (615)251-2438. Fax: (615)251-3752. Website: www.bhpublishinggroup.com/Fiction. **Contact:** David Webb, executive editor. Estab. 1934. Publishes hardcover and paperback originals. B & H is the book division of LifeWay, the world's largest publisher of Christian materials. Averages 90 total titles, 20 fiction titles/year. Member: ECPA.
Needs Religious/inspirational (contemporary women's fiction, suspense, romance, thriller, historical romance). Engaging stories told from a Christian worldview. Published*Elvis Takes a Back Seat*, by Leanna Ellis (contemporary); *Snow Angel*, by Jamie Carie (romance); *The Moon in the Mango Tree*, by Pamela Binnings Ewin (historical); *Shade*, by John B. Olson (thriller); and *Forsaken*, by James David Jordan (suspense).
How to Contact Does not accept unsolicited mss. Query with SASE. Accepts queries by e-mail. Include synopsis, estimated word count, brief bio, list of publishing credits. Agented fiction 75%. Responds in 3 months to queries. Accepts simultaneous submissions.
Terms Pays negotiable royalty. Publishes ms 10-12 months after acceptance. Ms guidelines for #10 SASE.

☑ ◎ BAEN PUBLISHING ENTERPRISES

P.O. Box 1403, Riverdale NY 10471-0671. (718) 548-3100. E-mail: info@baen.com. Website: www.baen. com. **Contact:** Toni Weisskopf, publisher. Estab. 1983. "We publish books at the heart of science fiction and fantasy." Publishes hardcover, trade paperback and mass market paperback originals and reprints. **Published some debut authors within the last year.** Plans 2-3 first novels this year. Averages 120 total titles, 120 fiction titles/year. Distributes titles through Simon & Schuster.
Imprints Baen Science Fiction and Baen Fantasy.
Needs Fantasy, science fiction. Interested in science fiction novels (based on real science) and fantasy novels "that at least strive for originality." Length: 110,00-150,000 words. Published *In Fury Born*, by David Weber; *Music to My Sorrow*, by Mercedes Lackey and Rosemary Edghill; *Ghost*, by John Ringo.
How to Contact Submit synopsis and complete ms. "Electronic submissions are strongly preferred. Attach manuscript as a Rich Text Format (.rtf) file. Any other format will not be considered." Additional submission guidelines online. Include estimated word count, brief bio. Send SASE or IRC. Responds in 9-12 months. No simultaneous submissions. Sometimes comments on rejected mss.
Terms Pays royalty on retail price. Offers advance. Ms guidelines online.

☑ ◎ BAKER BOOKS

Baker Book House Company, P.O. Box 6287, Grand Rapids MI 49516-6287. (616)676-9185. Fax: (616)676-2315. Website: www.bakerbooks.com. **Contact:** Jeanette Thomason, special projects editor (mystery, literary, women's fiction); Lonnie Hull DuPont, editoral director (all genres); Vicki Crumpton, aquisitions editor (all genres). Estab. 1939. "Midsize publisher of work that interests Christians." Publishes hardcover and trade paperback originals and trade paperback reprints. Books: web offset print. Plans 5 first novels this year. Averages 200 total titles/year. Distributes titles through Ingram and Spring Arbor into both CBA and ABA markets worldwide.

Needs Literary, mainstream/contemporary, mystery, picture books, religious. "We are mainly seeking fiction of two genres: contemporary women's fiction and mystery." Published *Praise Jerusalem!* and *Resting in the Bosom of the Lamb*, by Augusta Trobaugh (contemporary women's fiction); *Touches the Sky*, by James Schaap (western, literary); and *Face to Face*, by Linda Dorrell (mystery); *Flabbergasted*, by Ray Blackston; *The Fisherman*, by Larry Huntsberger.

How to Contact Does not accept unsolicited mss.

Terms Pays 14% royalty on net receipts. Offers advance. Publishes ms within 1 year after acceptance. Ms guidelines for #10 SASE.

ⓐ BALLANTINE BOOKS

Random House, Inc., 1745 Broadway, New York NY 10019. (212)782-9000. E-mail: bfi@randomhouse. com. Website: www.randomhouse.com/BB. **Contact:** Julia Cheiffetz, editor. Estab. 1952. "Ballantine's list encompasses a large, diverse offering in a variety of formats." Publishes hardcover, trade paperback, mass market paperback originals

Imprints Ballantine Books; Del Ray; Fawcett (mystery line); Ivy (romance); The Modern Library; One World; Strivers Row; Presidio Press; Random House Trade Paperbacks; Villard Books.

Needs Confession, ethnic, fantasy, feminist, gay/lesbian, historical, humor, literary, mainstream/ contemporary (women's), military/war, multicultural, mystery, romance, short story collections, spiritual, suspense, general fiction.

How to Contact *Agented submissions only.*

Terms Pays 8-15% royalty. Average advance: variable. Ms guidelines online.

ⓐ ⓩ ⓥ BANCROFT PRESS

P.O. Box 65360, Baltimore MD 21209-9945. (410)358-0658. Fax: (410)764-1967. Website: www. bancroftpress.com. **Contact:** Bruce Bortz, publisher (health, investments, politics, history, humor); Fiction Editor (literary novels, mystery/thrillers, young adult). "Small independent press publishing literary and commercial fiction, often by journalists." Publishes hardcover and trade paperback originals. Also packages books for other publishers (no fee to authors). **Published 5 debut authors within the last two years.** Averages 4-6 fiction titles/year.

• *The Re-Appearance of Sam Webber*, by Jonathon Scott Fugua is an ALEX Award winner; *Uncovering Sadie's Secrets*, by Libby Sternberg, is an Edgar Award finalist.

Needs Ethnic (general), family saga, feminist, gay/lesbian, glitz, historical, humor, lesbian, literary, mainstream/contemporary, military/war, mystery (amateur sleuth, cozy, police procedural, private eye/ hard-boiled), new age/mystic, regional, science fiction (hard science/technological, soft/sociological), thriller/espionage, young adult (historical, problem novels, series. "Our current focuses are young adult fiction, women's fiction, and literary fiction." Published *The Re-Appearance of Sam Webber*, by Scott Fugua (literary); *Hume's Fork*, by Ron Cooper (literary); *The Case Against My Brother*, by Libby Sternberg (historical/young adult), *Finn* by Matthew Olshan (young adult); and *The Sinful Life of Lucy Burns*, by Elizabeth Leikness (fantasy/women's).

How to Contact Accepts unsolicited mss. Query with SASE or submit outline, 2 sample chapter(s), synopsis, by mail or e-mail or submit complete ms. Accepts queries by e-mail, fax. Include brief bio, list of publishing credits. Send SASE for return of ms or send a disposable ms and SASE for reply only. Agented fiction 100%. Responds in 6-12 months to mss. Accepts simultaneous submissions. Sometimes comments on rejected mss.

Terms Pays various royalties on retail price. Average advance: $1500. Publishes ms up to 3 years after acceptance. Ms guidelines online.

ⓐ BANTAM DELL PUBLISHING GROUP

Random House, Inc., 1745 Broadway, New York NY 10019. (212)782-9000. Fax: (212)782-8890. Website: www.bantamdell.com. Estab. 1945. "In addition to being the nation's largest mass market paperback publisher, Bantam publishes a select yet diverse hardcover list." Publishes hardcover, trade paperback and mass market paperback originals; mass market paperback reprints. Averages 350 total titles/year.

Imprints Bantam Hardcover; Bantam Trade Paperback; Bantam Mass Market; Crimeline; Dell; Delta; Domain; DTP; Delacorte Press; The Dial Press; Fanfare; Island; Spectra.

Needs Adventure, fantasy, horror.

How to Contact Agented submissions only.

Terms Offers advance. Publishes ms 1 year after acceptance.

Ⓐ Ⓦ BANTAM DOUBLEDAY DELL BOOKS FOR YOUNG READERS

Random House Children's Publishing, Random House, Inc., 1745 Broadway, New York NY 10019. (212)782-9000. Fax: (212)782-8234. Website: www.randomhouse.com/kids. **Contact:** Michelle Poplof, editorial director. Publishes hardcover, trade paperback and mass market paperback series originals, trade paperback reprints. Averages 300 total titles/year.

• *Bud, Not Buddy*, by Christopher Paul Curtis won the Newbery Medal and the Coretta Scott King Award.

Imprints Delecorte Books for Young Readers; Doubleday Books for Young Readers; Laurel Leaf; Skylark; Starfire; Yearling Books.

Needs Adventure, fantasy, historical, humor, juvenile, mainstream/contemporary, mystery, picture books, suspense, chapter books, middle-grade. Published *Bud, Not Buddy*, by Christopher Paul Curtis; *The Sisterhood of the Traveling Pants*, by Ann Brashares.

How to Contact Does not accept unsolicited mss. *Agented submissions only.*

Terms Pays royalty. Average advance: varied. Publishes ms 2 years after acceptance. Book catalog for 9 × 12 SASE.

Ⓞ BARBOUR PUBLISHING, INC.

P.O. Box 719, Uhrichsville OH 44683. (740)922-6045. Fax: (740)922-5948. E-mail: fictionsubmit@ barbourbooks.com. Website: www.barbourpublishing.com. **Contact:** Rebecca Germany, senior editor (fiction). Estab. 1981. Publishes hardcover, trade paperback and mass market paperback originals and reprints. **Published 40% debut authors within the last year.** Averages 250 total titles/year.

Imprints Heartsong Presents; Barbour Books.

Needs Historical, contemporary, religious, romance, western, mystery. All submissions must be Christian mss. "Heartsong romance is 'sweet'—no sex, no bad language. All stories must have Christian faith as an underlying basis. Common writer's mistakes are a sketchy proposal, an unbelieveable story, and a story that doesn't fit our guidelines for inspirational romances." Published *A Sister's Secret*, by Wanda E. Brunstetter (fiction).

How to Contact Submit 3 sample chapter(s), synopsis by e-mail only. Responds in 6 months to mss. Accepts simultaneous submissions.

Terms Pays 8-16% royalty on net price. Average advance: $1,000-8,000. Publishes ms 1-2 years after acceptance. Book catalog online or for 9 × 12 SAE with 2 first-class stamps; ms guidelines for #10 SASE or online.

Ⓞ BAREFOOT BOOKS

2067 Massachusetts Avenue, Cambridge MA 02140. Website: www.barefootbooks.com. **Contact:** Submissions editor. Publishes hardcover and trade paperback originals. **Published 35% debut authors within the last year.** Averages 30 total titles/year.

Needs Juvenile. Barefoot Books only publishes children's picture books and anthologies of folktales. We just started publishing young adult fiction, so new ideas are welcome. *Little Leap Forward*, by Guo Yue and Clare Farrow (young fiction); *The Prince's Bedtime*, by Joanne Oppenheim (picture book); *The Barefoot Book of Fairy Tales*, by Malachy Doyle (illustrated anthology).

How to Contact "We do accept query letters but prefer to receive full manuscripts." Include SASE. Responds in 4 months to mss. Accepts simultaneous submissions. No phone calls, or e-mails, please.

Terms Pays 2½-5% royalty on retail price. Offers advance. Publishes ms 2 years after acceptance. Ms guidelines online.

Ⓞ BARRON'S EDUCATIONAL SERIES, INC.

250 Wireless Blvd., Hauppauge NY 11788. (631) 434-3311. Fax: (631) 434-3394. E-mail: waynebarr@ barronseduc.com. Website: barronseduc.com. **Contact:** Wayne Barr, director of acquisitions. Estab. 1941. Publishes hardcover, paperback and mass market originals and software. **Published 10% debut authors within the last year.** Averages 400 total titles/year.

Needs Middle grade, YA.

How to Contact Accepts simultaneous submissions. E-mail queries only, no attachments.

Terms Pays 12-13% royalty on net receipts. Average advance: $3-4,000. Publishes ms 18 months after acceptance. Ms queries online.

☑ **FREDERIC C. BEIL, PUBLISHER, INC.**

609 Whitaker St., Savannah GA 31401. (912)233-2446. Fax: (912)233-6456. E-mail: beilbook@beil.com. Website: www.beil.com. **Contact:** Frederic C. Beil III, president; Mary Ann Bowman, editor. Estab. 1982. "Our objectives are (1) to offer to the reading public carefully selected texts of lasting value; (2) to adhere to high standards in the choice of materials and bookmaking craftsmanship; (3) to produce books that exemplify good taste in format and design; and (4) to maintain the lowest cost consistent with quality." Publishes hardcover originals and reprints. Books: acid-free paper; offset printing; Smyth-sewn, hardcover binding; illustrations. Plans 3 first novels this year. Averages 10 total titles, 4 fiction titles/year.

Imprints The Sandstone Press, Hypermedia.

Needs History, biography, fiction. Published *Dancing by The River*, by Marlin Barton; *Joseph Jefferson*, by Arthur Bloom (biography); *The Invisible Country*, by H.E. Francis (fiction).

How to Contact Does not accept unsolicited mss. Query with SASE. Responds in 3 days to queries. Accepts simultaneous submissions.

Terms Pays 712% royalty on retail price. Publishes ms 20 months after acceptance.

☑ ◎ **BELLEVUE LITERARY PRESS**

Dept. of Medicine, NYU School of Medicine, 550 First Avenue, OBV A-640, New York NY 10016. (212) 263-7802. Fax: (212) 263-7803. E-mail: egoldman@blreview.org. Website: http://blpress.org. **Contact:** Erika Goldman, editorial director (literary fiction); Leslie Hodgkins, editor (literary fiction). Estab. 2005. "We're a small literary press that publishes nonfiction and fiction that ranges the intersection of the sciences (or medicine) and the arts." Publishes hardcover originals, paperback originals. Debut novel print order: 3000. Plans 2 debut novels this year. Averages 8 total titles/year; 2 fiction titles/year. Member CLMP. Distributes/promotes titles through Consortium.

Needs Literary. Published *The Cure*, by Varley O'Connor; *The Leper Compound*, by Paula Nangle (literary); *A Proper Knowledge*, by Michelle Latiolais; and *Tinkers*, by Paul Harding.

How to Contact Send query letter or query with outline/synopsis and 3 sample chapters. Accepts queries by snail mail, e-mail. Include estimated word count, brief bio, list of publishing credits. Send disposable copy of ms and SASE for reply only. Agented fiction: 75%. Responds to queries in 2 weeks. Accepts unsolicited mss. Considers simultaneous submissions. Rarely critiques/comments on rejected mss. Responds to mss in 6 weeks.

Terms Sends pre-production galleys to author. Manuscript published 8-12 months after acceptance. Writer's guidelines not available. Pays royalties 6-15%, advance $1,000. Book catalogs on Web site.

⚏ **THE BERKLEY PUBLISHING GROUP**

Penguin Putnam, Inc., 375 Hudson St., New York NY 10014. (212)366-2000. Website: www.penguinputnam. com. Estab. 1954. "Berkley is proud to publish in paperback some of the country's most significant best-selling authors." Publishes paperback and mass market originals and reprints. Averages approximately 800 total titles/year.

Imprints Ace Books, Berkley Books, HP Books, Perigee, Riverhead Books.

Needs Adventure, historical, literary, mystery, romance, spiritual, suspense, western, young adult.

How to Contact Does not accept unsolicited mss.

Terms Pays 4-15% royalty on retail price. Offers advance. Publishes ms 2 years after acceptance.

☑ ◎ **BILINGUAL REVIEW PRESS**

Hispanic Research Center, Arizona State University, P.O. Box 875303, Tempe AZ 85287-5303. (480)965-3867. Fax: (480)965-0315. E-mail: brp@asu.edu. Website: www.asu.edu/brp. **Contact:** Gary Keller, publisher. Estab. 1973. "University affiliated." Publishes hardcover and paperback originals and reprints. Books: 60 lb. acid-free paper; single sheet or web press printing; perfect-bound.

Needs Ethnic, literary, short story collections. Always seeking Chicano, Puerto Rican, Cuban-American or other U.S. Hispanic themes with strong and serious literary qualities and distinctive and intellectually important themes. Does *not* publish children's literature or trade genres such as travelogues and adventure fiction. Novels set in a pre-Columbian past are not likely to be published. Published *Moving Target: A Memoir of Pursuit*, by Ron Arias; *Contemporary Chicano and Chicana Art: Artists, Works, Culture, and Education*, Gary Keller, et al; *Triumph of Our Communities: Four Decades of Mexican American Art*, Gary Keller et al; *Assumption and Other Stories*, by Daniel A. Olivas; *Renaming Ecstasy: Latino Writings on the Sacred*, edited by Orlando Ricardo Menes.

How to Contact Accepts unsolicited mss. Query with SASE or submit 2-3 sample chapter(s). Accepts queries by email, mail. Include brief bio, list of publishing credits. Send SASE or IRC. Responds in 6 weeks to queries; 2-6 months to mss.

Terms Pays 10% royalty. Average advance: $500. Publishes ms 2 years after acceptance. Ms guidelines by email.

BIRCH BROOK PRESS

P.O. Box 81, Delhi NY 13753. Fax: (607)746-7453. Website: www.birchbrookpress.info. Contact: Tom Tolnay, publisher. Estab. 1982. Small publisher of popular culture and literary titles in mostly handcrafted letterpress editions. Specializes in fiction anthologies with specific theme, and an occasional novella. "Not a good market for full-length novels." Occasionally publishes hardcover and trade paperback originals. Books: 80 lb. vellum paper; letterpress printing; wood engraving illustrations. Averages 6 total titles, 2 fiction titles/year. Member, Small Press Center, Publishers Marketing Association, Academy of American Poets. Distributes titles through Baker and Taylor, Barnes&Noble.com, Amazon.com, Gazelle Book Services in Europe, Multicultural Books in Canada. Promotes titles through Web site, catalogs, direct mail and group ads.

Imprints Birch Brook Press, Persephone Press and Birch Brook Impressions.

Needs Literary, regional (Adirondacks), popular culture, special interest (flyfishing, baseball, books about books, outdoors). "Mostly we do anthologies around a particular theme generated inhouse. We make specific calls for fiction when we are doing an anthology." Published *Magic and Madness in the Library* (fiction collection); *Life & Death of a Book*, by William MacAdams; *Kilimanjaro Burning*, by John B. Robinson; *A Punk in Gallows America*, by P.W. Fox; *White Buffalo*, by Peter Skinner; *The Suspense of Loneliness* (anthology); *Tales for the Trail* (anthology); *Sexy Sixties*, by Harry Smith; *Human/Nature*, by Lance Lee; *Jack's Beans*, by Tom Smith; *The Alchemy of Words*, by Edward Francisco; *Where Things Are When You Lose Them*, by Martin Golan; *The Sea-Crossing of St. Brendan*, by Matthew Brennan; *Woodstoves & Ravens*, by Robert Farmer.

How to Contact Query with SASE or submit sample chapter(s), synopsis. Responds in 2 months to queries. Accepts simultaneous submissions. Sometimes comments on rejected mss.

Terms Modest flat fee on anthologies. Usually publishes ms 10-18 months after acceptance. Ms guidelines for #10 SASE.

BKMK PRESS

University of Missouri-Kansas City, 5101 Rockhill Rd., Kansas City MO 64110-2499. (816)235-2558. Fax: (816)235-2611. E-mail: bkmk@umkc.edu. Website: www.umkc.edu/bkmk. Estab. 1971. Publishes trade paperback originals. Averages 4 total titles/year.

Needs Literary, short story collections. Not currently acquiring novels.

How to Contact Query with SASE or submit 2-3 sample stories between January 1 and June 30. Responds in 8 months to mss. Accepts simultaneous submissions.

Terms Pays 10% royalty on wholesale price. Publishes ms 1 year after acceptance. Ms guidelines online.

BLACK HERON PRESS

P.O. Box 13396, Mill Creek WA 98082. Website: www.blackheronpress.com. **Contact:** Jerry Gold, publisher. Estab. 1984. Two-person operation; no immediate plans to expand. "We're known for literary fiction. We've done several Vietnam titles and several surrealistic fictions." Publishes hardcover and trade paperback originals. **Published 1-2 debut authors within the last year.** Averages 4 total titles, 4 fiction titles/year.

• Ten books published by Black Heron Press have won regional or national awards.

Needs Experimental, humor, literary, mainstream/contemporary, science fiction (surrealism), war novels (literary). Published *Infinite Kindness*, by Laurie Blauner (historical fiction); and *Moses in Sinai*, by Simone Zelitch (historical fiction).

How to Contact Query letter with first 30 pages of completed manuscript, and SASE with SASE. Responds in 3 months to queries; 6 months to mss. Accepts simultaneous submissions.

Terms Pays 8% royalty on retail price.

JOHN F. BLAIR, PUBLISHER

1406 Plaza Dr., Winston-Salem NC 27103-1470. (336)768-1374. Fax: (336)768-9194. Website: www.

blairpub.com. **Contact:** Carolyn Sakowski, president. Estab. 1954. Small, independent publisher. Publishes hardcover originals and trade paperbacks. Books: Acid-free paper; offset printing; illustrations. Averages 20 total titles/year.

Needs Prefers regional material dealing with southeastern U.S. "We publish one work of fiction per season relating to the Southeastern U.S. Our editorial focus concentrates mostly on nonfiction." Published *The Minotaur Takes a Cigarette Break*, by Steven Sherrill; *Rocks That Float*, by Kathy Steele.

How to Contact Accepts unsolicited mss. Query with SASE or submit complete ms with SASE or IRC. Responds in 3 months to queries. Accepts simultaneous submissions.

Terms Royalty negotiable. Offers advance. Publishes ms 18 months after acceptance. Book catalog for 9 × 12 SAE with 5 first-class stamps. Ms guidelines online.

◙ BLEAK HOUSE BOOKS

923 Williamson St., Madison WI 53703. (608)467-0133. Website: www.bleakhousebooks.com. Benjamin LeRoy, publisher; Alison Janssen, editor. Estab. 1995. Publisher hardcover and paperback originals. Averages 15-20 titles annually.

Needs Mysteries and literary fiction. " We aren't looking for big budget special effects and car chases. The best part of the story isn't in the distractions, it's in the heart. Characters need to be well drawn. We don't want formula fiction. We don't want rehashes of CSI. We don't want unqualified 'experts' writing books with plot holes. We don't want authors who are so married to their words that they can't see when something doesn't work." Published *Toros and Torsos*, by Craig Mcdonald; *Empty Ever After*, by Reed Farrel Coleman; *Easy Innocence*, by Libby Fischer Hellmann; *In the Light of You*, by Nathan Singer; *Yellow Medicine*, by Anthony Neil Smith.

How to Contact Does not accept unsolicited mss. Any unsolicited mss we receive will be recycled without ever being read. Query with SASE. Include estimated word count, brief bio, list of publishing credits. Agented fiction 85%. "Responds as fast as we can to queries. Depending on when we receive them, it may take awhile. Same holds true for submitted manuscripts, but we'll keep you abreast of what's going on when we know it." Responds in 3 weeks to queries; 2 months to mss. Accepts simultaneous submissions. No electronic submissions. Check Web site for up-to-date guidelines.

Terms All contracts negotiable depending on author, market viability, etc. Our average royalty rate is somewhere between 7.5-15% depending on hardcover/paperback, print run, and many other factors. Advances range from $1,000-$10,000. Publishes ms 12-18 months after acceptance.

ⓝ ◎ BLIND EYE BOOKS

1141 Grant Street, Bellingham WA 98225. E-mail: editor@blindeyebooks.com. Website: www. blindeyebooks.com. **Contact:** Nicole Kimberling, editor. Estab. 2007. "Blind Eye Books publishes science fiction, fantasy and paranormal romance novels featuring gay or lesbian protagonists. We do not publish short story collections, poetry, erotica, horror or non-fiction. We would hesitate to publish any manuscript that is less than 70,000 or over 150,000 words."

Needs Science fiction, fantasy, and paranormal romance novels featuring gay or lesbian protagonists. Published *The Archer's Heart* by Astrid Amara, *Tangle* (anthology), and *Wicked Gentlemen* by Ginn Hale.

How to Contact Submit complete ms with cover letter. Accepts queries by snail mail. Send disposable copy of ms and SASE for reply only. Does not return rejected mss.

Terms Writer's guidelines on Web site.

◩ BLOODFIRE STUDIOS

P.O Box 710451, San Diego CA 92171. E-mail: likewecare@bloodfire.com. Website: http://www.bloodfire. com. **Contact:** Dennis Greenhill, VP of Publishing; Lee Kohse, Creative Director. Estab. 1997. "Midsize Independent Publisher working mostly in Sci/Fi, Horror, and Manga. We pride ourselves on maintaining a high level of quality comparable to the big publishers. Art, Story, paper, etc meet or exceed Marvel and DC standards." Publishes paperback originals, paperpack reprints. Format: 60-80 lb gloss paper; saddle stitch, perfect bound binding; illustrations. **Publishes 4 debut writers/year.** Publishes 6-10 titles/year. Various distributors including Diamond Comics, direct sales, conventions, etc. Advertising and self-promotion through various channels;

How to Contact Prefers submissions from writers, artists, writer-artists, creative teams. Email to warn of pending submission and then a hard copy of submission should be sent to PO Box listed above. Follow guidelines posted on website closely or submissions will be trashed. "We attend major industry shows such as San Diego Comic Con, Wizard World LA and Wizard World Chicago." Responds to mss/art packets in a few weeks. Considers simultaneous submissions. Often comments on rejected mss.

Terms Payment and rights varies on contract terms for each book. Ms published about a year after acceptance. Writer's and artist's guidelines, book catalog on Web site.

▦ Ⓐ ☑ BL PUBLISHING

Games Workshop Ltd., Willow Road, Lenton, Nottingham NG7 2WS. (+44)(115)900-4100. Fax: (+44)(115)900-4111. E-mail: publishing@games-workshop.co.uk. Website: www.blacklibrary.com. **Contact:** Christian Dunn. Estab. 1997. Publishes paperback originals. Published 3 new writers last year. Averages 65 total titles/year; 65 fiction titles/year.

Imprints Black Library, Solaris.

Needs Fantasy (space fantasy, sword and sorcery), horror (dark fantasy, futuristic), science fiction (hard science/technological, soft/sociological), short story collection, young adult/teen (fantasy/science fiction, horror). Published *The Summoner*, by Gail Z. Martin (fantasy); *Horus Rising*, by Dan Abnett (science fiction); *The Vampire Genevieve*, by Jack Yeovil (fantasy).

How to Contact Submit through agent only. Accepts queries by snail mail, e-mail. Include brief bio, list of publishing credits. Send SASE or IRC for return of ms or disposable copy of ms and SASE/IRC for reply only. Agented fiction: 5%. Responds to mss in 3 months. No unsolicited mss. Considers simultaneous submissions, e-mail submissions. Rarely critiques/comments on rejected mss.

Terms Sends pre-production galleys to author. Writer's guidelines on Web site.

☒ ◎ BOOKS FOR ALL TIMES, INC.

P.O. Box 202, Warrenton VA 20188. Website: www.bfat.com. **Contact:** Joe David, publisher/editor. Estab. 1981. One-man operation. Publishes paperback originals.

Needs Literary, mainstream/contemporary, short story collections. "No novels at the moment; hopeful, though, of publishing a collection of quality short stories. No popular fiction or material easily published by the major or minor houses specializing in mindless entertainment. Only interested in stories of the Victor Hugo or Sinclair Lewis quality."

How to Contact Query with SASE. Responds in 1 month to queries. Sometimes comments on rejected mss.

Terms Pays negotiable advance. "Publishing/payment arrangement will depend on plans for the book."

☒ BRANDEN PUBLISHING CO., INC.

P.O. Box 812094, Wellesley MA 02482. Phone-Fax; (781)235-3634. Website: www.brandenbooks.com. **Contact:** Adolph Caso, editor. Estab. 1909. Publishes hardcover and trade paperback originals, reprints and software. Books: 55-60 lb. acid-free paper; case—or perfect-bound; illustrations. Averages 15 total titles, 5 fiction titles/year.

Imprints I.P.L; Dante University Press; Four Seas; Branden Publishing Co., Branden Books.

Needs Ethnic (histories, integration), historical, literary, military/war, religious (historical-reconstructive), short story collections. Looking for "contemporary, fast pace, modern society." Published *I, Morgain*, by Harry Robin; *The Bell Keeper*, by Marilyn Seguin; and *The Straw Obelisk*, by Adolph Caso; *Priest to Mafia Don* by Father Bascio.

How to Contact Does not accept unsolicited mss. Query with SASE. Responds in 1 month to queries.

Terms Pays 5-10% royalty on net receipts. 10 author's copies. Average advance: $1,000 maximum. Publishes ms 10 months after acceptance.

☒ BRIDGE WORKS PUBLISHING CO.

Box 1798, 221 Bridge Lane, Bridgehampton NY 11932. (631)537-3418. Fax: (631)537-5092. **Contact:** Barbara Phillips, editorial director. Estab. 1992. "Bridge Works is very small, doing only 1-6 titles a year." **Published some debut authors within the last year.** Distributes titles through National Book Network. "Our books are routinely reviewed in major publications, and we work closely with authors in both the editorial and marketing processes."

Needs Publishes mainstream quality fiction and nonfiction, also thrillers. "Query with SASE before submitting ms. First-time authors should have manuscripts vetted by freelance editors before submitting. We do not accept or read multiple submissions." Recent publications include *Mineral Spirits*, by Heather

Sharfeddin and *The Polish Woman*, by Eva Mekler.

How to Contact Write to address above, including synopsis and estimated word count. Responds in one month to query and 50 pages, two months to entire ms. Sometimes comments on rejected mss. Query with SASE before submitting ms or query by email. First-time authors should have manuscripts vetted by freelance editors before submitting. Does not accept or read simultaneous submissions.

Terms Pays 8% of net received from wholesalers and bookstores. Average advance: $1,000. Publishes ms 1 year after acceptance. Book catalog and ms guidelines for #10 SASE.

▣ BROADWAY BOOKS

Doubleday Broadway Publishing Group, Random House, Inc., 1745 Broadway, New York NY 10019. (212)782-9000. Fax: (212)782-9411. Website: www.broadwaybooks.com. **Contact:** William Thomas, editor-in-chief. Estab. 1995. Broadway publishes general interest nonfiction and fiction for adults. Publishes hardcover and trade paperback originals and reprints.

Needs Publishes a limited list of commercial literary fiction. Published *Freedomland*, by Richard Price.

How to Contact *Agented submissions only.*

▤ ◎ BROWN SKIN BOOKS

Pentimento, Ltd., P.O. Box 57421, London England E5 0ZD United Kingdom. E-mail: info@brownskinbooks. co.uk. Website: www.brownskinbooks.co.uk. Estab. 2002. Publishes trade paperback originals. Averages 4 total titles/year.

Needs Erotica. "We are looking for erotic short stories or novels written by women of color, or sensual crime thrillers."

How to Contact Submit proposal package including 2 sample chapter(s), synopsis. Responds in 2 months to queries; 3 months to mss. Accepts simultaneous submissions.

Terms Pays 5-50% royalty or makes outright purchase. Publishes ms 18 months after acceptance. Ms guidelines online.

◪ CALAMARI PRESS

E-mail: derek@calamaripress.com. Website: www.calamaripress.com. **Contact:** Derek White, editor. Estab. 2003. "Calamari Press publishes book objects of literary text and art and experimental fiction." Publishes paperback originals. Format: 60 lb. natural finch opaque paper; digital printing; perfect or saddle-stitched bound. Average print order: 500. Debut novel print order: 300. Averages 5 total titles/year; 4 fiction titles/year.

Needs Adventure, comics/graphic novels, ethnic/multicultural, experimental, literary, short story collections. Published *Land of the Snow Men*, by George Belden (Norman Lock) (fictional literary canard with illustrations); *The Singing Fish*, by Peter Markus (prose poem/short fiction collection); *The Night I Dropped Shakespeare On The Cat*, by John Olson; *The Revisionist*, by Miranda Mellis; *Part of the World*, by Robert Lopez.

How to Contact Query with outline/synopsis and 3 sample chapters. Accepts queries by e-mail only. Include brief bio. Send SASE or IRC for return of ms. Responds to queries in 2 weeks. Accepts unsolicited mss. Considers e-mail submissions only. Sometimes critiques/comments on rejected mss. Responds to mss in 2 weeks.

Terms Sends pre-production galleys to author. Manuscript published 2-6 months after acceptance. Writer's guidelines on Web site. Pays in author's copies.

◎ ◎ CALYX BOOKS

P.O. Box B, Corvallis OR 97339-0539. (541)753-9384. Fax: (541)753-0515. **Contact:** M. Donnelly, director. Estab. 1986 for Calyx Books; 1976 for Calyx, Inc. "Calyx exists to publish women's literary and artistic work and is committed to publishing the works of all women, including women of color, older women, lesbians, working-class women, and other voices that need to be heard." Publishes fine literature by women, fiction, nonfiction and poetry. Publishes hardcover and paperback originals. Books: offset printing; paper and cloth binding. **Published 1 debut author within the last year.** Averages 1-2 total titles/year. Distributes titles through Consortium Book Sale and Distribution. Promotes titles through author reading tours, print advertising (trade and individuals), galley and review copy mailings, presence at trade shows, etc.

Needs Ethnic, experimental, feminist, gay/lesbian, lesbian, literary, mainstream/contemporary, short story collections. Published *Forbidden Stitch: An Asian American Women's Anthology; Women and Aging: Present Tense; Writing and Art by Young Women*; and *A Line of Cutting Women*.

How to Contact Closed to submissions until further notice.

Terms Pays 10-15% royalty on net receipts. Average advance: depends on grant support. Publishes ms 2 years after acceptance. Ms guidelines for #10 SASE.

◎ ☑ CANDLEWICK PRESS

2067 Massachusetts Ave., Cambridge MA 02140. (617) 661-3330. Fax: (617) 661-0565. E-mail: bigbear@candlewick.com. Website: www.candlewick.com. **Contact:** Joan Powers, editor-at-large; Deb Wayshak Noyes, senior editor; Liz Bicknell, editorial director/associate publisher (poetry, picture books, fiction); Mary Lee Donovan, executive editor (picture books, fiction); Sarah Ketchersid, senior editor (board, toddler); Hilary Breed Van Dusen, editor. Estab. 1991. "We are a truly child-centered publisher." Publishes hardcover originals, trade paperback originals and reprints. Averages 200 total titles/year.

- *The Tale of Despereaux*, by Kate DiCamillo won the 2004 Newbery Medal. *The Astonishing Life of Octavian Nothing, Traitor to the Nation, Volume One: The Pox Party*, by M.T. Anderson won the 2007 National Book Award.

Needs Juvenile, picture books, young adult. Published *The Tale of Despereaux*, by Kate DiCamillo; the Judy Moody series, by Megan McDonald, illustrated by Peter Reynolds; *Feed*, by M.T. Anderson; *Fairieality*, by David Ellwand.

How to Contact Does not accept unsolicited mss.

☐ CAROLINA WREN PRESS

120 Morris St., Durham NC 27701. (919) 560-2738. E-mail: carolinawrenpress@earthlink.net. Website: www.carolinawrenpress.org. **Contact:** Andrea Selch, president. Estab. 1976. "We publish poetry, fiction, nonfiction, biography, autobiography, literary nonfiction work by and/or about people of color, women, gay/lesbian issues, health and mental health topics in children's literature." Books: 6 × 9 paper; typeset; various bindings; illustrations. **Published 2 debut authors within the last year.** Distributes titles through Amazon.com, Barnes & Noble, Borders, Ingram and Baker & Taylor and on their Web site.

Needs "Though we accept unsolicited manuscripts of fiction and nonfiction September-December, we very rarely accept any. We suggest you submit to our Doris Bakwin Award for Writing by a Woman; contests is held in fall of odd-numbered years" Does not publish genre fiction or religious texts or self-help books. Published *Downriver* by Jeanne Leiby in 2007.

How to Contact Reads unsolicited mss in September only. Accepts queries by e-mail, mail. Include brief bio. Send SASE or IRC. Responds in 3 months to queries; 6 months to mss. "Please query before you send or else plan to enter one of our contests. The Doris Bakwin Award for Writing by a Woman accepts entries in odd-numbered years, with a deadline of December 1, 2009, 2011, etc; entry fee is required. Guidelines on our Web site in summer."

Terms Publishes ms 2 year after acceptance. Ms guidelines online.

◎ CAVE BOOKS

277 Clamer Rd., Trenton NJ 08628-3204. (609)530-9743. E-mail: pddb@juno.com. Website: www.cavebooks.com. **Contact:** Paul Steward, managing editor. Estab. 1980. Small press devoted to books on caves, karst and speleology. Fiction: novels about cave exploration only. Publishes hardcover and trade paperback originals and reprints. Books: acid-free paper; offset printing. Averages 2 total titles, 1 fiction title/year.

Needs Adventure, historical, literary, caves, karst, speleology. Recently published *Cave Geology*, by Arthur N. Palmer.

How to Contact Accepts unsolicited mss. Query with SASE or submit complete ms. Accepts queries by e-mail. Send SASE for return of ms or send a disposable ms and SASE for reply only. Responds in 2 weeks to queries; 3 months to mss. Accepts simultaneous submissions, electronic submissions. Sometimes comments on rejected mss.

Terms Pays 10% royalty on retail price. Publishes ms 18 months after acceptance.

ℕ ☑ CHAMPAGNE ROSE PRESS

The Wild Rose Press, P.O. Box 708, Adam's Basin NY 14410.E-mail: queryus@thewildrosepress.com. Website: www.thewildrosepress.com. **Contact:** Roseann Armstrong, editor. Estab. 2006. "The Champagne

Rose line is the contemporary romance line of the Wild Rose Press. Our contemporary stories are filled with sexual tension and passionate chemistry. The setting can take place anywhere in the world today. Champagne Rose couples explore their relationship both emotionally and physically. In each full-length novel, there must be one fully consummated love scene. In the case of short stories, if this isn't realistic for the plot of the story, then the physical encounters must be ripe with tension. The characters should leave us remembering them long after we turn the last page. We should feel their feelings, share their joys and their heartaches. And, as with all romances, we should close the book completely satisfied by the happy-ever-after ending." Publishes paperback originals, reprints, and e-books in a POD format. **Published 25 debut authors last year**. Publishes approximately 60 fiction titles/year. Member: EPIC, Romance Writers of America. Distributes/promotes titles through major distribution chains, including Ingrams, Baker & Taylor, Sony, Amazon.com, as well as smaller and online distributors.

- Has received two Eppie Awards (2007) for First Place, and the New Jersey Golden Leaf Award for 2006 and 2007.

Needs Religious romance, contemporary, futuristic/time travel, gothic, historical, regency, romantic suspense, YA, erotic, and paranormal romances. Plans several anthologies "in several lines of the company in the next year, including Cactus Rose, Yellow Rose, American Rose, Black Rose, and Scarlet Rose." Has published *Holly and the Millionaire*, by Margaret Tanner; *Jake's Return*, by Liana Laverentz; and *Beauty and the Geek,* by Roni Adams.

How to Contact *Does not accept unsolicited mss*. Send query letter with outline and synopsis of up to 5 pages. Prefers queries by e-mail; accepts by mail. Include estimated word count, brief bio, and list of publishing credits. Send SASE or IRC for return of ms. Agented fiction less than 1%. Responds to queries in 4 weeks; to mss in 12 weeks. Does not consider simultaneous submissions. Always comments on rejected mss.

Terms Pays royalty of 7% minimum; 35% maximum. Sends prepublication galleys to author. Time between acceptance and publication is approximately 1 year. Writer's guidelines available on Web site.

ⓝ ⓞ CHANGELING PRESS LLC

P.O. Box 1046, Martinsburg WV 25402. (304)885-4993. E-mail: Submissions@changelingpress.com. Website: www.changelingpress.com. **Contact:** Sheri Ross Fogarty, editor-in-chief. Publishes print and e-books.

Needs Special interests: "We publish Sci-Fi, Futuristic, Paranormal, Fantasy, Suspense, Horror, and Humor, BDSM, and Fetish Love Stories. We publish Interludes and Novellas only, from 8,000 to 25,000 words total length — NO 100,000 word sagas, please! (Series and Serials welcome)."

How to Contact Submit complete ms with cover letter via e-mail only. Responds to queries in 2 months. Accepts unsolicited mss. Considers e-mail submissions.

Terms Pays royalties of 35% gross paid monthly.

CHARLESBRIDGE PUBLISHING

85 Main St., Watertown MA 02472. Website: www.charlesbridge.com/school. Estab. 1980. Publishes hardcover and paperback nonfiction and fiction children's picture books, early readers, and middle-grade chapter books. Averages 36 total titles/year.

Needs Multicultural, nature, science, social studies, bedtime, math, etc. Recently published *The Searcher and Old Tree*, by David McPhail; *Wiggle and Waggle*, by Caroline Arnold.

How to Contact Submit complete ms as exclusive submission for three months. Responds only to ms of interest. Please do not include SASE.

Terms Royalty and advance vary. Publishes ms 2 years after acceptance. Ms guidelines online.

CHRONICLE BOOKS

Adult Trade Division, 680 Second St., San Francisco CA 94107. (415)537-4200. Fax: (415)537-4460. E-mail: frontdesk@chroniclebooks.com. Website: www.chroniclebooks.com. **Contact:** Editorial Dept., Adult Trade Division. Estab. 1966. Publishes hardcover and trade paperback originals. Averages 175 total titles/year.

Needs Novels and story collections. No genre fiction.

How to Contact Submit complete ms and SASE. Responds in 3 months to mss. Accepts simultaneous submissions.

Terms Publishes ms 18 months after acceptance. Ms guidelines online.

◎ CHRONICLE BOOKS FOR CHILDREN

680 Second St., San Francisco CA 94107. (415) 537-4400. Fax: (415) 537-4415. E-mail: kided@ chroniclebooks.com. Website: www.chroniclekids.com. **Contact:** Victoria Rock, founding publisher and editor-at-large; Andrea Menotti, editor; Julie Romeis, editor; Melissa Manlove, assistant editor; Naomi Kirsten, assistant editor, Mary Colgan, editorial assistant. Publishes hardcover and trade paperback originals. **Published 5% debut authors within the last year.** Averages 90 total titles/year.

Needs Mainstream/contemporary, multicultural, young adult, picture books, middle grade fiction, young adult projects. Published *Wave*, by Suzy Lee (all ages, picture book); Ivy and Bean series, by Annie Barrows, illustrated by Sophie Blackwell (ages 6-11, chapter book); *Delicious: The Art and Life of Wayne Theibaud*, by Susan Goldman Rubin (ages 9-14, chapter book).

How to Contact Submit complete ms (picture books); submit outline synopsis and 3 sample chapters (for older readers). Responds to queries in 1 month; will not respond to submissions unless interested. Do not send SASE; send SASP to confirm receipt. No electronic submissions, submissions on disk or fax.

Terms Royalty varies. Average advance: variable. Publishes ms 18-24 months after acceptance. Ms guidelines online.

CITY LIGHTS BOOKS

261 Columbus Ave., San Francisco CA 94133. (415)362-1901. Fax: (415)362-4921. E-mail: staff@citylights. com. Website: www.citylights.com. **Contact:** Editorial staff. Estab. 1955. Publishes paperback originals. Plans 1-2 first novels this year. Averages 12 total titles, 4-5 fiction titles/year.

Needs Fiction, essays, memoirs, translations, poetry and books on social and political issues.

How to Contact Submit one-page description of the book and a sample chapter or two with SASE. Does not accept unsolicited mss. Does not accept queries by e-mail. See Web site for guidelines.

◎ ⚄ CLARION BOOKS

Houghton Mifflin Co., 215 Park Ave. S., New York NY 10003. Website: www.clarionbooks.com. **Contact:** Dinah Stevenson, vice-president and publisher (YA, middle-grade, chapter book); Jennifer B. Greene, senior editor (YA, middle-grade, chapter book); Jennifer Wingertzahn, editor (YA, middle-grade, chapter book); Marcia Leonard, editor (middle-grade, chapter book), Lynne Polvino, editor (YA, middle-grade, chapter book). Estab. 1965. "Clarion is a strong presence in the fiction market for young readers. We are highly selective in the areas of historical and contemporary fiction. We publish chapter books for children ages 7-10 and middle-grade novels for ages 9-12, as well as picture books and nonfiction." Publishes hardcover originals for children. Averages 50 total titles/year.

Needs Adventure, historical, humor, mystery, suspense, strong character studies. Clarion is highly selective in the areas of historical fiction, fantasy and science fiction. A novel must be superlatively written in order to find a place on the list. Mss are not responded to unless there is an interest in publishing. Accepts fiction translations. Published *A Taste for Red*, by Lewis Harris (contemporary, middle-grade); *The Wednesday Wars*, by Gary D. Schmidt (historical fiction); *Keeping Score*, by Linda Sue Park (middle-grade historical fiction).

How to Contact Submit complete ms. Responds in 2 months to queries. Prefers no multiple submissions of mss.

Terms Pays 5-10% royalty on retail price. Average advance: start at $6,000. Publishes ms 2 years after acceptance. Ms guidelines available at Web site.

⚄ CLEIS PRESS

P.O. Box 14697, San Francisco CA 94114. (415)575-4700. Fax: (415)575-4705. Website: www.cleispress. com. **Contact:** Frederique Delacoste, editor. Estab. 1980. "Cleis Press publishes provocative works by women and men in the areas of gay and lesbian studies sexual politics, fiction, feminism, self-help, erotica, gender studies, and human rights." Publishes trade paperback originals and reprints. **Published some debut authors within the last year.** Averages 20 total titles, 5 fiction titles/year.

Needs Feminist, gay/lesbian, literary. "We are looking for high quality fiction by women and men." *Black Like Us* (fiction); *Arts and Letters*, by Edmund White (essays); and *A Fragile Union*, by Joan Nestle (essays), which won a Lambda Literary Award.

How to Contact Accepts unsolicited mss. Submit complete ms. Accepts queries by email. Include brief bio, list of publishing credits. Send SASE for return of ms or send a disposable ms and SASE for reply only. Agented fiction 10%. Responds in 1 month to queries.

Terms Pays variable royalty on retail price. Publishes ms 2 years after acceptance.

⬛ ⬛ COFFEE HOUSE PRESS

79 Thirteenth Ave. NE, Ste. 110, Minneapolis, MN 55413. Fax: (612)338-4004. **Contact:** Chris Fischbach, senior editor. Estab. 1984. "Nonprofit publisher with a small staff. We publish literary titles: fiction and poetry." Publishes trade paperback originals. Books: acid-free paper; cover illustrations. **Published some debut authors within the last year.** Averages 12 total titles, 6 fiction titles/year.

• This successful nonprofit small press has received numerous grants from various organizations including the NEA, the McKnight Foundation and Target.

Needs Ethnic, experimental, literary, mainstream/contemporary, short story collections, novels. Publishes anthologies, but they are closed to unsolicited submissions. Published *Miniatures*, by Norah Labiner (novel); *Circle K Cycles*, by Karen Yamashita (stories); *Little Casino*, by Gilbert Sorrentino (novel).

How to Contact Accepts unsolicited mss. Query with SASE. Agented fiction 10%. Responds in 1 month to queries; up to 4 months to mss. No electronic submissions.

Terms Pays 8% royalty on retail price. Provides 15 author's copies. Publishes ms 18 months after acceptance. Book catalog and ms guidelines for #10 SASE with 2 first-class stamps. Ms guidelines for #10 SAE with 55¢ first-class stamps.

⬛ ⬛ CONSTABLE & ROBINSON, LTD.

(formerly Constable Publishers), Constable & Robinson, 3 The Lanchesters, 162 Fulham Palace Rd., London England W6 9ER United Kingdom. 0208-741-3663. Fax: 0208-748-7562. Contact: Krystyna Green, editorial director (crime fiction). Publishes hardcover and trade paperback originals. Averages 160 total titles/year.

Needs Publishes "crime fiction (mysteries) and historical crime fiction." Length 80,000 words minimum; 130,000 words maximum. Recently published *Roma* and *The Judgement of Caesar*, by Steven Saylor; *The Yeane's Midnight*, by Ed O'Connor; *The More Deceived*, by David Roberts.

How to Contact *Agented submissions only.* No e-mail submissions. Submit by post 3 sample chapter(s), synopsis and cover letter. Responds in 1 month to queries; 3 months to mss. Accepts simultaneous submissions.

Terms Pays royalty. Offers advance. Publishes ms 1 year after acceptance.

⬛ ⬛ COTEAU BOOKS

AKA Thunder Creek Publishing Co-operative Ltd., 2517 Victoria Ave., Regina SK S4P 0T2 Canada. (306) 777-0170. Fax: (306) 522-5152. E-mail: coteau@cotcaubooks.com. Website: www.coteaubooks.com. **Contact:** Nik L. Burton, managing editor. Estab. 1975. "Coteau Books publishes the finest Canadian fiction, poetry, drama and children's literature, with an emphasis on western writers." Publishes trade paperback originals and reprints. Books: 20 lb. offset or 60 lb. hi-bulk paper; offset printing; perfect bound; 4-color illustrations. Averages 16 total titles, 4-6 fiction titles/year. Distributes titles through Fitzhenry & Whiteside.

Needs Ethnic, fantasy, feminist, gay/lesbian, historical, humor, juvenile, literary, mainstream/contemporary, multicultural, multimedia, mystery, regional, short story collections, spiritual, sports, young adult. Canadian authors *only*. Published *God of the Plains*, by Gail Robinson (fiction); *Morningstar: A Warrior's Spirit*, by Morningstar Mercedi (memoir); *Peacekeepcrs*, by Dianne Linden (young adult).

How to Contact Accepts unsolicited mss. Submit complete manuscript, or 3-4 sample chapter(s), author bio. Responds in 2-3 months to queries; 6 months to mss. No simultaneous submissions. Sometimes comments on rejected mss.

Terms Pays 10% royalty on retail price. "We're a co-operative and receive subsidies from the Canadian, provincial and local governments. We do not accept payments from authors to publish their works." Publishes ms 1-2 years after acceptance. Ms guidelines online.

⬛ COVENANT COMMUNICATIONS, INC.

920 E. State Rd., American Fork UT 84003-0416. (801)756-9966. E-mail: info@covenant-lds.com. Website: www.covenant-lds.com. Averages 80+ total titles/year.

Needs Historical fiction, suspense, mystery, romance, children's; all submissions must have strong LDS (Church of Jesus Christ of Latter-day Saints, or "Mormons") content.

How to Contact Follow submission guidelines on web site at www.covenant-lds.com. Requires electronic submission. Responds in 4 months to mss.

Terms Pays 6½-15% royalty on retail price. Generally publishes ms 6-12 months after acceptance. Ms guidelines online.

CROSSQUARTER PUBLISHING GROUP

P.O. Box 23749, Santa Fe NM 87502. (505)438-2666. Website: www.crossquarter.com. **Contact:** Anthony Ravenscroft. Publishes trade paperback originals and reprints. **Published 90% debut authors within the last year.** Averages 1-2 total titles/year. We are no longer accepting ficiton manuscripts. We do continue to have the annual science fiction short story contest.

How to Contact Currently closed to submissions unless for Crosstime Science Fiction contest (see Crosstime listing).

Terms Pays 8-10% royalty on wholesale or retail price. Publishes ms 1 year after acceptance. Book catalog for $1.75. Ms guidelines online.

☑ CROSSTIME

Crossquarter Publishing Group, P.O. Box 23749, Santa Fe, NM 87502. (505)690-3923. Fax: (214)975-9715. E-mail: info@crossquarter.com. Website: www.crossquarter.com. **Contact:** Anthony Ravenscroft. Estab. 1985. Small Publisher. Publishes paperback originals. Books: recycled paper; docutech or offset printing; perfect bound. **Published 2 debut authors within the last year.** Plans 2 first novels this year. Member SPAN, PMA.

Needs Mystery (occult), new age/mystic, psychic/supernatural, romance (occult), science fiction, young adult (fantasy/science fiction). Plans an anthology of Paul B. Duquette Memorial Short Science Fiction contest winners. Guidelines on Web site. Recently published *Many Voices, One Song,* by Barbara Percival; *When Dharma Fails Its King,* by Spencer Johnson; *Swamp Poet,* by Ben Goodridge; *CrossTIME Science Fiction Anthology Vol VI.*

Terms Pays 6-10% royalty. Publishes ms 6-9 months after acceptance. Ms guidelines online.

☑ ☑ CROSSWAY BOOKS

Division of Good News Publishers, 1300 Crescent St., Wheaton IL 60187-5800. (630)682-4300. Fax: (630)682-4785. Website: www.crossway.com. **Contact:** Jill Carter. Estab. 1938. "'Making a difference in people's lives for Christ' as its maxim, Crossway Books lists titles written from an evangelical Christian perspective." Midsize evangelical Christian publisher. Publishes hardcover and trade paperback originals. Averages 85 total titles, 1 fiction titles/year. Member ECPA. Distributes titles through Christian bookstores and catalogs. Promotes titles through magazine ads, catalogs.

Needs *Currently not accepting fiction manuscripts.*

How to Contact Does not accept unsolicited mss. Agented fiction 5%.

Terms Pays negotiable royalty. Average advance: negotiable. Publishes ms 18 months after acceptance. Ms guidelines online.

☑ CROWN BOOKS FOR YOUNG READERS

Bantam, Doubleday, Dell/Delacorte, Knopf and Crown Books for Young Readers, Random House Children's Books, A Division of Random House, Inc., 1540 Broadway, New York NY 10171. (212)572-2600 or (800)200-3552. Website: www.randomhouse.com/kids. See listing for Bantam, Doubleday, Dell/Delacorte, Knopf and Crown Books for Young Readers.

CROWN PUBLISHING GROUP

Random House, Inc., 1745 Broadway, New York NY 10019. (212)572-2600. Fax: (212)940-7408. E-mail: crownbiz@randomhouse.com. Website: www.randomhouse.com/crown. Estab. 1933. "The group publishes a selection of popular fiction and nonfiction by both established and rising authors."

Imprints Crown, Harmony Books; Shaye Areheart Books; Three Rivers Press; The Princeton Review; Watson-Guptill.

☑ JOHN DANIEL AND CO.

Daniel & Daniel, Publishers, Inc., P.O. Box 2790, McKinleyville CA 95519. (707)839-3495. Fax: (707)839-3242. E-mail: dandd@danielpublishing.com. Website: www.danielpublishing.com. **Contact:** John Daniel, publisher. Estab. 1980. "We publish small books, usually in small editions, but we do so with pride." Publishes hardcover originals and trade paperback originals. Publishes poetry, fiction and nonfiction. Averages 4 total titles/year. Distributes through SCB Distributors. Promotes through direct mail, reviews.

Needs Literary, short story collections. Publishes poetry, fiction and nonfiction; specializes in belles lettres, literary memoir. Published *Murder in Los Lobos*, by Sue McGinty (mystery novel); *Wolf Tones*, by Irving Weinman (novel).

How to Contact Currently closed to fiction submissions.

Terms Pays 10% royalty on wholesale price. Average advance: $0-500. Publishes ms 1 year after acceptance. Ms guidelines online.

☐ DAN RIVER PRESS

Conservatory of American Letters, P.O. Box 298, Thomaston ME 04861-0298. (207)226-7528. E-mail: cal@americanletters.org. Website: www.americanletters.org. **Contact:** Richard S. Danbury, III, fiction editor. Estab. 1977. "Small press publisher of fiction and biographies owned by a non-profit foundation." Publishes hardcover and paperback originals. Books: paperback; offset or digital printing; perfect and cloth binding; illustrations. Averages 3-4 fiction titles/year, plus the annual (since 1984) Dan River Anthology. Promotes titles through the author's sphere of influence. Distributes titles by mail order to libraries and bookstores, as well as by Amazon, Barnesandnoble.com, Baker & Taylor, Ingram, 10 UK distributors, and author's influence.

Needs Adventure, family saga, fantasy (space fantasy, sword and sorcery), historical (general), horror (dark fantasy, futuristic, psychological, supernatural), humor, literary, mainstream/contemporary, military/war, mystery (amateur sleuth, police procedural, private eye/hard-boiled), new age/mystic, psychic/supernatural, religious (general religious, inspirational, religious mystery/suspense, religious thriller, religious romance), romance (contemporary, futuristic/time travel, gothic, historical, romantic suspense), science fiction (hard science/technological, soft/sociological), short story collections, thriller/espionage, western (frontier saga, traditional), young adult, outdoors/fishing/hunting/camping/trapping. Accepts anything but porn, sedition, evangelical, and children's literature. Publishes poetry and fiction anthology (submission guidelines to Dan River Anthology on the Web, or send #10 SASE).

How to Contact Accepts queries by mail. Do not send ms until requested. Include estimated word count, brief bio, list of publishing credits. Send SASE for return of ms or send a disposable ms and SASE for reply only. Responds in 2-3 days to queries; 1-2 weeks to mss. Accepts simultaneous submissions. No electronic submissions. Do not submit until you've read our guidlines.Terms Pays 10-15% royalty and 5 author's copies. Average advance: occasional. Publishes ms 3-4 months after acceptance. Book catalog for 6 × 9 SASE with 68¢ postage affixed. Ms guidelines online or by #10 SASE.

☑ DARK HORSE COMICS, INC.

10956 SE Main St., Milwaukie OR 97222. (503)652-8815. Website: www.darkhorse.com. "In addition to publishing comics from top talent like Frank Miller, Mike Mignola, Stan Sakai and internationally-renowned humorist Sergio Aragonés, Dark Horse is recognized as the world's leading publisher of licensed comics."

Needs Comic books, graphic novels. Published *Astro Boy Volume 10 TPB*, by Osamu Tezuka and Reid Fleming; *Flaming Carrot Crossover #1* by Bob Burden and David Boswell.

How to Contact Submit synopsis.

☑ ◎ MAY DAVENPORT, PUBLISHERS

26313 Purissima Rd., Los Altos Hills CA 94022. (650) 947-1275. Fax: (650) 947-1373. E-mail: mdbooks@ earthlink.net. Website: www.maydavenportpublishers.com. **Contact:** May Davenport, editor/publisher. Estab. 1976. "We prefer books which can be used in high schools as supplementary readings in English or creative writing courses. Reading skills have to be taught, and novels by humourous authors can be more pleasant to read than Hawthorne's or Melville's novels, war novels, or novels about past generations. Humor has a place in literature." Publishes hardcover and paperback originals. Averages 4 total titles/year. Distributes titles through direct mail order.

Imprints md Books (nonfiction and fiction).

Needs Humor, literary. "We want to focus on novels junior and senior high school teachers can share with the reluctant readers in their classrooms." Published *Charlie and Champ*, by Allyson Wagoner; *Senioritis,* by Tate Thompson; *A Life on The Line*, by Michael Horton; *Matthew Livingston & The Prison of Souls,* by Marco Conelli; *Summer of Suspense*, by Frances Drummond Waines.

How to Contact Query with SASE. Responds in 1 month to queries.

Terms Pays 15% royalty on retail price. Publishes ms 1 year after acceptance. Ms guidelines for #10 SASE.

◻ ◎ DAW BOOKS, INC.

Penguin Group, Inc., 375 Hudson St., 3rd Floor, New York NY 10014-3658. (212) 366-2096. Fax: (212) 366-2090. E-mail: daw@us.penguingroup.com. Website: www.dawbooks.com. **Contact:** Peter Stampfel, submissions editor. Estab. 1971. Publishes hardcover and paperback originals and reprints. Averages 60 total titles/year.

Needs Fantasy, science fiction. "We are interested in science fiction and fantasy novels. We are also interested in paranormal romantic fantasy. We like character-driven books. We accept both agented and unagented manuscripts. Long books are not a problem. We are not seeking short stories or ideas for anthologies. We do not want any nonfiction manuscripts."

How to Contact Submit complete ms with SASE. Do not submit your only copy of anything. Responds within 3 months to mss.

Terms Pays in royalties with an advance negotiable on a book-by-book basis. Ms guidelines online.

ℕ ⊘ ⊟ DC UNIVERSE

1700 Broadway, New York NY 10019-5905. Website: http://www.dccomics.com/dcu/. Imprints: Vertigo, Wildstorm, CMX Manga, DC Direct, Mad, DC Kids, Zuda.

How to Contact No unsolicited submissions. Recycles unsolicited manuscripts. Artists should contact through Comic Con conventions. See submission guidelines on Web site for more information. International Comic-Cons.

Terms Writer's and artist's guidelines on Web site.

◐ DELACORTE BOOKS FOR YOUNG READERS

Random House Children's Books, 1540 Broadway, New York NY 10036. (212)782-900. Website: www. randomhouse.com/kids. Distinguished literary fiction and commercial fiction for the middle grade and young adult categories.

Terms Ms guidelines online.

Ⓐ ◎ DEL REY BOOKS

The Random House Publishing Group, Random House, Inc., 1745 Broadway, 18th Floor, New York NY 10019. (212)782-9000. Website: www.delreybooks.com. **Contact:** Betsy Mitchell, editor-in-chief; Chris Schluep, senior editor, Liz Scheier, senior editor. Estab. 1977. "We are a long-established imprint with an eclectic frontlist. We're seeking interesting new voices to add to our best-selling backlist. Publishes hardcover, trade paperback, and mass market originals and mass market paperback reprints. Averages 120 total titles, 80 fiction titles/year.

Imprints Imprints: Del Rey Manga, managed by Dallas Middaugh, publishes translations of Japanese comics as well as original graphic novels.

Needs Fantasy (should have the practice of magic as an essential element of the plot), science fiction (well-plotted novels with good characterizations and interesting extrapolations), alternate history. Published *Gentlemen of the Road*, by Michael Chabon; *Un Lun Dun*, by China Mieville; *His Majesty's Dragon*, by Naomi Novik; *The Man With the Iron Heart,* by Harry Turtledove; and *Star Wars: Order 66,* by Karen Traviss.

How to Contact Does not accept unsolicited mss. *Agented submissions only.*

Terms Pays royalty on retail price. Average advance: competitive. Publishes ms 1 year after acceptance. Ms guidelines online.

◎ DIAL BOOKS FOR YOUNG READERS

Penguin Group USA, 345 Hudson St., 14th Floor, New York NY 10014. (212)366-2000. Website: www. us.penguingroup.com. **Contact:** Submissions Editor. Estab. 1961. Trade children's book publisher. Publishes hardcover originals. Averages 50 total titles/year.

Needs Adventure, fantasy, juvenile, picture books, young adult. Especially looking for "lively and well-written novels for middle grade and young adult children involving a convincing plot and believable characters. The subject matter or theme should not already be overworked in previously published books. The approach must not be demeaning to any minority group, nor should the roles of female characters (or others) be stereotyped, though we don't think books should be didactic, or in any way message-y. No topics inappropriate for the juvenile, young adult and middle grade audiences. No plays." Published *A Year Down Yonder*, by Richard Peck; *The Missing Mitten Mystery,* by Steven Kellog.

How to Contact Accepts unsolicited mss. "Submit entire picture book manuscript or the first three chapters of longer works. Please include a cover letter with brief bio and publication credits. Please note that, unless interested in publishing your book, Dial will not respond to unsolicited submissions. Please do NOT include a SASE. If Dial is interested, expect a reply from us within four months."

Terms Pays royalty. Average advance: varies.

☒ DIAL PRESS

Bantam Dell Publishing Group, Random House, Inc., 1745 Broadway, New York NY 10019. (212)782-9000. Fax: (212)782-9523. Website: www.randomhouse.com/bantamdell/. **Contact:** Susan Kamil, vice president, editorial director. Estab. 1924. Averages 6-12 total titles/year.

Needs Literary (general). Published *Mary and O'Neil* (short story collection); *Niagara Falls Over Again*, by Elizabeth Mccracken (fiction).

How to Contact *Agented submissions only.* Accepts simultaneous submissions.

Terms Pays royalty on retail price. Offers advance. Publishes ms 18 months after acceptance.

☒ ☒ DIGITAL MANGA PUBLISHING

1487 West 178th St., Suite 300, Gardenia CA 90248. (310)817-8010. Fax: (310)817-8018. E-mail: dmp@emanga.com. Website: www.dmpbooks.com.

☒ DOUBLEDAY

Knopf Doubleday Broadway Publishing Group, Random House, Inc., 1745 Broadway, New York NY 10019. (212)782-9000. Fax: (212)782-9700. Website: www.randomhouse.com. Estab. 1897. Publishes hardcover originals. Averages 70 total titles/year.

Imprints Nan A. Talese, Doubleday Religion, Currency, Black Ink/Harlem Moon, Doubleday Graphic Novels.

Needs Adventure, confession, ethnic, experimental, feminist, gay/lesbian, historical, humor, literary, mainstream/contemporary, religious, short story collections.

How to Contact *Agented submissions only.* No simultaneous submissions.

Terms Pays royalty on retail price. Offers advance. Publishes ms 1 year after acceptance.

☒ DOUBLEDAY BOOKS FOR YOUNG READERS

Random House Children's Books, 1540 Broadway, New York NY 10036. (212)782-9000. Website: www.randomhouse.com/kids.

☒ ☒ DOUBLEDAY CANADA

Random House of Canada, 1 Toronto Street, Suite 300, Toronto ON M5C 2V6 Canada. (416)364-4449. Website: www.randomhouse.ca. Publishes hardcover and paperback originals. Averages 50 total titles/year.

Imprints Doubleday Canada (hardcover and paperback publisher); Bond Street Books Canada (hardcover publisher of international titles); Seal Books (mass market publisher); Anchor Canada (trade paperback publisher).

How to Contact Does not accept unsolicited mss. *Agented submissions only.*

☒ ☒ DOUBLEDAY RELIGIOUS PUBLISHING

Doubleday Broadway Publishing Group, Random House, Inc., 1745 Broadway, New York NY 10019. (212)782-9000. Website: www.randomhouse.com. **Contact:** Eric Major, vice president, religious division; Trace Murphy, executive editor; Andrew Corbin, editor. Estab. 1897. Publishes hardcover and trade paperback originals and reprints. Averages 45-50 total titles/year.

Imprints Image Books, Anchor Bible Commentary, Anchor Bible Reference, Galilee, New Jerusalem Bible.

Needs Religious.

How to Contact *Agented submissions only.* Accepts simultaneous submissions.

Terms Pays 712-15% royalty. Offers advance. Publishes ms 1 year after acceptance. Book catalog for SAE with 3 first-class stamps.

☑ ◎ DOWN EAST BOOKS

Down East Enterprise, Inc., P.O. Box 679, Camden ME 04843-0679. Fax: (207)594-7215. E-mail: msteere@downeast.com. Website: www.downeast.com. **Contact**: Michael Steere, managing editor. Estab. 1967. "We are primarily a regional publisher concentrating on Maine or New England." Publishes hardcover and trade paperback originals, trade paperback reprints. First print order: 3,000. Averages 20-24 total titles/year.

Needs Juvenile, mainstream/contemporary, regional. "We publish 1-2 juvenile titles/year (fiction and nonfiction), and 1-2 adult fiction titles/year." See bookshelf on our Web site.

How to Contact Query with SASE. Responds in 3 months to queries. Accepts simultaneous submissions.

Terms Pays 10-15% royalty on net receipts. Average advance: $500 average. Publishes ms 18 months- 2 years after acceptance. Ms guidelines for 9 × 12 SAE with 2 first-class stamps.

⚒ ◌ ◎ DRAGON MOON PRESS

3521 43A Ave, Red Deer AB T4N 3W9 Canada. E-mail: publisher@dragonmoonpress.com. Website: www.dragonmoonpress.com. **Contact:** Gwen Gades, publisher. Estab. 1994. "Dragon Moon Press is dedicated to new and exciting voices in science fiction and fantasy." Publishes trade paperback and electronic originals. Books: 60 lb. offset paper; short run printing and offset printing. Average print order: 250-3,000. **Published several debut authors within the last year.** Plans 5 first novels this year. Averages 4-6 total titles, 4-5 fiction titles/year. Distributed through Baker & Taylor. Promoted locally through authors and online at leading retail bookstores like Amazon, Barnes & Noble, Chapters, etc.

Imprints Dragon Moon Press, Gwen Gades publisher (fantasy and science fiction).

Needs Fantasy, science fiction (soft/sociological). No horror or children's fiction, short stories or poetry. "We seek out quality manuscripts and authors who are eager to participate in the marketing of their book.

How to Contact Please visit our Web site at www.dragonmoonpress.com for submission guidelines. Accepts simultaneous submissions. No submissions on disk. "All submissions are requested electronically—do not mail submissions, as we will not respond. All mailed submissions are shredded and recycled."

Terms Pays 8-15% royalty on retail price. Publishes ms 2 years after acceptance.

⚒ ☑ ◎ DREAMCATCHER BOOKS & PUBLISHING

55 Canterbury St., #8 &9 Saint John NB E2L 2C6. (506)632-4008, Fax:(506)632-4009 E-mail: info@dreamcatcherpublishing.ca. Website: www.dreamcatcherpublishing.nb.ca. Established in 1998. **Contact:** Elizabeth Margaris, Publisher. Publishes mainstream fiction, with first consideration to Atalantic Canadian writers. "Especially interested in green themes, hope & inspiration (including autobiographies) with a humourous twist." **Imprints:** Magi Press (vanity press).;

⚐ ☑ DUTTON (ADULT TRADE)

Penguin Putnam, Inc., 375 Hudson St., New York NY 10014. (212)366-2000. Website: www.penguinputnam.com. **Contact:** Editor-in-Chief: Brian Tart. Estab. 1852. Publishers hardcover originals. Averages 40 total titles/year.

Needs Adventure, historical, literary, mainstream/contemporary, mystery, short story collections, suspense. Published *The Darwin Awards II*, by Wendy Northcutt (humor); *Falling Angels*, by Tracy Chevalier (fiction); *The Oath*, by John Lescroart (fiction).

How to Contact *Agented submissions only.* Responds in 6 months to queries. Accepts simultaneous submissions.

Terms Pays royalty. Average advance: negotiable. Publishes ms 12-18 months after acceptance.

☑ ◎ DUTTON CHILDREN'S BOOKS

Imprint of Penguin Group (USA), inc. 345 Hudson St., New York NY 10014. (212)4143700. Fax:(212)414-3397. Website: www.penquin.com/youngreaders. **Contact**: Lauri Hornik, president and publisher (picture books and fiction); Maureen Sullivan, executive editor (books for all ages with distinct narrative style); Lucia Monfried, senior editor (picture books and middle grade fiction); Julie Strauss-Gabel, associate publisher (literary contemporary young adult fiction); Sarah Shumway, editor (commercial young adult fiction). Estab.1852. Dutton Children's Books publishes fiction and nonfiction for readers ranging from preschoolers to young adults on a variety of subjects. Publishes hardcover originals as well as novelty formats Averages 50 titles/year. 10% of books form first-time authors.

Needs Dutton Children's Books has a diverse, general-interest list that includes picture books, and fiction for all ages, from "middle grade"books to young adult readers. Published *Big Chickens Fly the Coop*, by Leslie Helakoski, illustrated by Henry Cole (picture book); *Antsy Does Time*, by Neal Shusterman (middle-grade novel); *Paper Towns*, by John Green (young adult novel).

How to Contact Query letter only; include SASE

Terms Pays royalty on retail price. Offers advance

☑ DZANC BOOKS, INC.

Dzanc Books, Inc., 2702 Lillian, Ann Arbor MI 48104. E-mail: info@dzancbooks.org. Website: http://www.dzancbooks.org. **Contact:** Steve Gillis, editor (literary fiction); Dan Wickett, editor (literary fiction); Keith Taylor, editor (literary fiction). "We're an independent non-profit publishing literary fiction. We also set up writer-in-residence programs and help literary journals develop their subscription bases." Publishes paperback originals. **Published some debut authors within the last year.** Averages 6 fiction titles/year, 20 titles/year when imprints are included.

Imprints OV Books, Gina Frangello/Stacy Bierlein, editors (literary fiction); Black Lawrence Press, Colleen Ryor/Diane Goettel, editors (literary fiction/nonfiction/poetry).

Needs Literary. Plans anthology *The Best of the Web*, in which online journal editors nominate stories and poems - series and press editors select from that list and selected reading. Published Roy Kesey, Yannick Murphy, Peter Markus, Hesh Kestin, Kyle Minor.

How to Contact Query with outline/synopsis and 35 sample pages. Accepts queries by e-mail. Include brief bio. Agented fiction: 3%. Accepts unsolicited mss. Considers simultaneous submissions, submissions on CD or disk. Rarely critiques/comments on rejected mss. Responds to mss in 5 months.

Terms Sends pre-production galleys to author. Manuscript published 12-36 months after acceptance. Writer's guidelines on Web site.

▣ ☑ THE ECCO PRESS

HarperCollins, 10 E. 53rd St., New York NY 10022. (212)207-7000. Fax: (212)702-2460. Website: www.harpercollins.com. **Contact:** Daniel Halpern, editor-in-chief. Estab. 1970. Publishes hardcover and trade paperback originals and reprints. Books: acid-free paper; offset printing; Smythe-sewn binding; occasional illustrations. First novel print order: 3,000 copies Averages 60 total titles, 20 fiction titles/year.

Needs Literary, short story collections. "We can publish possibly one or two original novels a year." Published *Blonde*, by Joyce Carrol Oates; *Pitching Around Fidel*, by S.L. Price.

How to Contact Does not accept unsolicited mss. Query with SASE.

Terms Pays royalty. Average advance: negotiable. Publishes ms 1 year after acceptance.

⚑ ECW PRESS

2120 Queen St. E., Suite 200, Toronto ON M4E 1E2 Canada. (416) 694-3348. Fax: (416) 698-9906. E-mail: info@ecwpress.com. Website: www.ecwpress.com. **Contact:** Jack David, publisher. Estab. 1979. Publishes hardcover and trade paperback originals. Averages 40 total titles/year.

Needs Only Canadian authored fiction, specializes in mystery.

How to Contact Accepts simultaneous submissions.

Terms Pays 8-12% royalty on net receipts. Average advance: $300-5,000. Publishes ms 18 months after acceptance. Book catalog and ms guidelines free. Ms guidelines online.

⚑ ◎ EDGE SCIENCE FICTION AND FANTASY PUBLISHING

Box 1714, Calgary AB T2P 2L7 Canada. (403)254-0160. Fax: (403)254-0456. E-mail: publisher@hadespublications.com. Website: www.edgewebsite.com. **Contact:** Anita Hades, acquistions manager (science fiction/fantasy). Estab. 1996. "We are an independent publisher of science fiction and fantasy novels in hard cover or trade paperback format. We produce high-quality books with lots of attention to detail and lots of marketing effort. We want to encourage, produce and promote thought-provoking and fun-to-read science fiction and fantasy literature by 'bringing the magic alive: one world at a time' (as our motto says) with each new book released." Publishes hardcover and trade paperback originals. Books: natural offset paper; offset/web printing; HC/perfect binding; b&w illustration only. Average print order: 2,000-3,000. Plans 20 first novels this year. Averages 16-20 total titles/year. Member of Book Publishers Association of Alberta (BPAA), Independent Publishers Association of Canada (IPAC),

Publisher's Marketing Association (PMA), Small Press Center.

Imprints Tesseract Books, Dragon Moon Press, Alien Vistas, Riverbend.

Needs Fantasy (space fantasy, sword and sorcery), science fiction (hard science/technological, soft/sociological). "We are looking for all types of fantasy and science fiction, horror except juvenile/young adlut, erotica, religious fiction, short stories, dark/gruesome fantasy, or poetry." Published *Stealing Magic*, by Tanya Huff; *Forbidden Cargo*, by Rebecca K. Rowe, *The Hounds of Ash and other tales of Fool Wolf* by Greg Keyes.

How to Contact Accepts unsolicited mss. Submit first 3 chapters and synopsis, Check Web site for guidelines or send SAE & IRCs for same. Include estimated word count. Responds in 4-5 months to mss. No simultaneous submissions, electronic submissions. Rarely comments on rejected mss.

Terms Pays 10% royalty on wholesale price. Average advance: negotiable. Publishes ms 18-20 months after acceptance. Ms guidelines online.

☑ EMPYREAL PRESS

P.O. Box 1708, Champlain, NY 12919-9998. E-mail: empyrealpress@hotmail.com. Website: www.skarwood.com. **Contact:** Colleen B. McCool. "Our mission is the publishing of literature which doesn't fit into any standard 'mold'—writing which is experimental yet grounded in discipline, imagination." Publishes trade paperback originals. **Published no debut authors within the last year.** Averages 0-1 total titles/year.

Needs "Empyreal Press is not currently accepting unsolicited manuscripts due to extremely limited resources."

ℕ ◎ ⚹ ENGLISH TEA ROSE PRESS

The Wild Rose Press, P.O. Box 708, Adams Basin NY 14410-0708.(585)752-8770. E-mail: queryus@thewildrosepress.com. Website: www.thewildrosepress.com. **Contact:** Nicole D'Arienzo, editor. Estab. 2006. "In the English Tea Rose line we have conquering heroes, high seas adventure, and scandalous gossip. The love stories that will take you back in time. From the windswept moors of Scotland, to the Emerald Isle, to the elegant ballrooms of Regency England, the men and women of this time are larger than life and willing to risk it all for the love of a lifetime. English Tea Rose stories encompass historical romances set before 1900 which are not set on American soil. Send us your medieval knights, Vikings, Scottish highlanders, marauding pirates, and ladies and gentlemen of the Ton. English Tea Rose romances should have strong conflict and be emotionally driven; and, whether the story is medieval, Regency, set during the renaissance, or any other pre-1900 time, they must stay true to their period in historical accuracy and flavor. English Tea Roses can range from sweet to spicy, but should not contain overly explicit language."Publishes paperback originals, reprints, and e-books in a POD format. Published 5 debut authors last year. Publishes approximately 10 fiction titles/year. Member: EPIC, Romance Writers of America. Distributes/promotes titles through major distribution chains, including Ingrams, Baker & Taylor, Sony, Amazon.com, as well as smaller and online distributors.

- Has received two Eppie Awards (2007) for First Place, and the New Jersey Golden Leaf Award for 2006 and 2007.

Imprints American Rose (American historical romance), Nicole D'Arienzo, editor;

Needs Religious romance, contemporary, futuristic/time travel, gothic, historical, regency, romantic suspense, YA, erotic, and paranormal romances. Plans several anthologies "in several lines of the company in the next year, including Cactus Rose, Yellow Rose, American Rose, Black Rose, and Scarlet Rose." Has published *The Raven's Revenge*, by Gina Black; *By King's Command*, by Linda Lea Castle; and *Patience,* by C.H. Admirand.

How to Contact *Does not accept unsolicited mss.* Send query letter with outline and synopsis of up to 5 pages. Prefers queries by e-mail; accepts by mail. Include estimated word count, brief bio, and list of publishing credits. Send SASE or IRC for return of ms. Agented fiction less than 1%. Responds to queries in 4 weeks; to mss in 12 weeks. Does not consider simultaneous submissions. Always comments on rejected mss.

Terms Pays royalty of 7% minimum; 35% maximum. Sends prepublication galleys to author. Time between acceptance and publication is approximately 1 year. Writer's guidelines available on Web site.

Advice "Polish your manuscript, make it as error free as possible, and follow our submission guidelines."

☑ ◎ EROS BOOKS

463 Barlow Ave., Staten Island NY 10308. (718) 317-7484. E-mail: marynicholaou@aol.com. Website: www.eros.thecraze.com. **Contact:** Mary Nicholaou, fiction editor. Estab. 2000. "Small independent publisher of postmodern romance, short fiction and translations." Publishes paperback originals, e-books. Format: 20 lb. paper; offset printing. Average print order: 500. Debut novel print order: 500. **Published 5 new writers last year.** Plans 10 debut novels this year. Averages 5 total titles/year; 4 fiction titles/year.

Needs Postmodern, short, romance fiction, translations. Published *Cracks*, by Mary Nicholaou (postmodern romance); *Chimera*, by Clara Smith (postmodern romance).

How to Contact Query with outline/synopsis. Reads submissions June-September. Accepts queries by snail mail, e-mail. Include social security number. Send SASE or IRC for return of ms or disposable copy of ms and SASE/IRC for reply only. Agented fiction: 10%. Responds to queries in 2 weeks. Considers simultaneous submissions, submissions on CD or disk. Always critiques/comments on rejected mss. Responds to mss in 2 months.

Terms Pays in author's copies. Manuscript published 12 months after acceptance. Writer's guidelines available for SASE. Book catalogs available for SASE.

Ⓝ ☷ ☑ ETERNAL PRESS

E-mail: ceo@eternalpress.ca. Website: www.eternalpress.ca. **Contact:** Ally Robertson. Estab. 2007. Publishes e-books.

Needs Mystery, sci-fi, paranormal, historical, suspense, horror, women's fiction, fantasy, thrillers, erotica, gay, and all sub genres of romance. Accepts short stories, novellas, and full-length manuscripts, from 5,000 to 110,000 words.

How to Contact Query with outline/synopsis and Accepts queries by e-mail.

Terms Writer's guidelines on Web site. Pays royalties of 35% on ebooks, 10% on print. "We hold all rights for 2 years from date of publication."

Ⓝ ◎ ☑ FAERY ROSE

The Wild Rose Press, P.O. Box 708, Adams Basin NY 14410-0708.(585)752-8770. E-mail: queryus@ thewildrosepress.com. Website: www.thewildrosepress.com. **Contact:** Amanda Barnett, editor (paranormal romance). Estab. 2006. " Fairy Tales are not just for children. The Faery Rose line is a place where you can allow your imagination a free rein to create romance with mystical and mythical characters. Picture if you will, a faery hero who is a strong sensual male who knows what he wants and goes after his leading lady. Dragons don't just frolic in the mist but turn into mortal men and women with love and lust on their minds. Elves have minds and hearts, looking for love with a bit of mischief thrown in. Ghosts who come back to life for the love of their life and wizards, warlocks, and witches who crank up the romance like they spit out a spell. Futuristic worlds, filled with science fiction warriors who can wield a sword as well as a laser and not afraid, be they woman or man, to go after what their heart desires. Time travels moving through centuries with the hero and heroine seeking not the secrets of the ages but love." Publishes paperback originals, reprints, and e-books in a POD format. Published 25 debut authors last year. Publishes approximately 60 fiction titles/year. Member: EPIC, Romance Writers of America. Distributes/promotes titles through major distribution chains, including Ingrams, Baker & Taylor, Sony, Amazon.com, as well as smaller and online distributors.

- Has received two Eppie Awards (2007) for First Place, and the New Jersey Golden Leaf Award for 2006 and 2007.

Needs Religious romance, contemporary, futuristic/time travel, gothic, historical, regency, romantic suspense, YA, erotic, and paranormal romances. Plans several anthologies "in several lines of the company in the next year, including Cactus Rose, Yellow Rose, American Rose, Black Rose, and Scarlet Rose." Has published *Anam Cara*, by Keena Kincaid; *A Forever Kind of Thing*, by Sharon Cullen; and *Rogue's Challenge*, by Jo Barrett.

How to Contact *Does not accept unsolicited mss.* Send query letter with outline and synopsis of up to 5 pages. Prefers queries by e-mail; accepts by mail. Include estimated word count, brief bio, and list of publishing credits. Send SASE or IRC for return of ms. Agented fiction less than 1%. Responds to queries in 4 weeks; to mss in 12 weeks. Does not consider simultaneous submissions. Always comments on rejected mss.

Terms Pays royalty of 7% minimum; 35% maximum. Sends prepublication galleys to author. Time between acceptance and publication is approximately 1 year. Writer's guidelines available on Web site.

☑ ☐ ☑ FANTAGRAPHICS BOOKS

7563 Lake City Way NE, Seattle WA 98115. Fax: (206)524-2104. E-mail: fbicomix@fantagraphics.com. Website: www.fantagraphics.com. **Contact:** Michael Dowers (all genres). Estab. 1976. "Fantagraphics Books has been a leading proponent of comics as a legitimate form of art and literature since it began publishing the critical trade magazine The Comics Journal in 1976. By the early 1980s, Fantagraphics found itself at the forefront of the burgeoning movement to establish comics as a medium as eloquent and expressive as the more established popular arts of film, literature, poetry, et al. Fantagraphics quickly established a reputation as an advocacy publisher that specialized in seeking out and publishing the kind of innovative work that traditional comics corporations who dealt almost exclusively in superheroes and fantasy either didn't know existed or wouldn't touch: serious, dramatic, historical, journalistic, political and satirical work by a new generation of alternative cartoonists, as well as many artists who gained prominence as part of the seminal underground comix movement of the '60s. Fantagraphics has since gained an international reputation for its literate and audacious editorial standards and its exacting production values." Publishes hardcover originals, paperback originals, hardcover reprints, paperpack reprints. Average print run: 3,000 (debut writer). **Publishes 3-4 debut writers/year.** Publishes 60 titles/ year. Titles promoted/distributed by W.W. Norton & Co. Awards: Harvey Awards, Eisner Awards, Ignatz Awards, Quills nomination.

Needs All categories. Does not want superheros. Anthologies: MOME, Comic Books, Hotwire, Blab. Editors select stories.

How to Contact Prefers submissions from writer-artists. Detailed submission guidelines at www. fantagraphics.com/submissions.html. Agented submissions: less than 5%. Responds to queries and ms/ art packages in 4 months. Often comments on rejected manuscripts.

Terms Creators paid royalty. Sends pre-publication galleys to author. Writer's and artist's guidelines on Web site. Book catalog free upon request.

☑ FARRAR, STRAUS & GIROUX

19 Union Square West, New York NY 10003. (212)741-6900. E-mail: fsg.editorial@fsgbooks.com. Website: www.fsgbooks.com. Eric Chinski, editor-in-chief. Publishes hardcover and trade paperback books. Averages 180 total titles/year.

Needs Literary.

How to Contact Does not accept unsolicited mss.

☐ ☑ ☑ FARRAR, STRAUS & GIROUX BOOKS FOR YOUNG READERS

Farrar Straus Giroux, Inc., 18 West 18th Street., New York NY 10011. (212)741-6900. **Contact:** Margaret Ferguson, editorial director (children's); Wesley Adams, executive editor (children's); Jill Davis, executive editor (children's); Janine O'Malley, senior editor (children's). Estab. 1946. "We publish original and well-written materials for all ages." Publishes hardcover originals and trade paperback reprints. **Published some debut authors within the last year.** Averages 75 total titles/year.

Imprints Frances Foster Books, edited by Frances Foster (children's); Melanie Kroupa Books, edited by Melanie Kroupa (children's).

Needs Children's/juvenile, picture books, middle grade, young adult, narrative nonfiction. "Do not query picture books; just send manuscript. Do not fax queries or manuscripts." Published *Adele and Simon*, by Barbara McClintock; *The Cabinet of Wonders*, by Marie Rutkoski.

How to Contact For novels and other longer mss, query with SASE and three sample chapters. Do not query picture books, just send ms with cover letter. Include brief bio, list of publishing credits. Agented fiction 50%. Responds in 2 months to queries; 4 months to mss. Accepts simultaneous submissions. No electronic submissions or submissions on disk.

Terms Pays 2-6% royalty on retail price for paperbacks, 3-10% for hardcovers. Average advance: $3,000-25,000. Publishes ms 18 months after acceptance. Book catalog for 9 × 12 SAE with $2.00 postage. Ms guidelines for #10 SASE.

☑ FARRAR, STRAUS & GIROUX PAPERBACKS

19 Union Square W., New York NY 10003. (212)741-6900. FSG Paperbacks emphasizes literary nonfiction and fiction, as well as poetry. Publishes hardcover and trade paperback originals and reprints. Averages 180 total titles/year.

Needs Literary. Published The Corrections, by Jonathan Franzen; The Haunting of L., by Howard Norman.

How to Contact Does not accept unsolicited mss. Agented submissions only.

FC2

Center for Publications, School of Arts and Sciences-UHV, 3007 N. Ben Wilson, Victoria TX 77901. E-mail: fc2@uhv.edu. Website: http://fc2.org. **Contact:** Carmen Edington, assistant editor. Estab. 1974. Publisher of innovative fiction. Publishes hardcover and paperback originals. Books: perfect/Smyth binding; illustrations. Average print order: 2,200. **Published some debut authors within the last year.** Plans 2 first novels this year. Averages 6 total titles, 6 fiction titles/year. Titles distributed through University of Alabama Press. No open submissions except through Ronald Sukenick Innovative Fiction Prize.

Needs Experimental, feminist, gay/lesbian, innovative; modernist/postmodern; avant-garde; anarchist; minority; cyberpunk. Published *Book of Lazarus,* by Richard Grossman; *Is It Sexual Harassment Yet?,* by Cris Mazza; *Liberty's Excess,* by Lidia Yuknavitch; *The Wavering Knife,* by Brian Evenson.

How to Contact Does not accept unsolicited mss. See Web site for contest info. Agented fiction 5%. Responds in 3 weeks to queries; 2-6 months to mss. Accepts simultaneous submissions.

Terms Pays 10% royalty. Publishes ms 1-3 years after acceptance. Ms guidelines online.

⊘ ⊚ THE FEMINIST PRESS AT THE CITY UNIVERSITY OF NEW YORK

365 Fifth Ave., Suite 5406, New York NY 10016. (212)817-7917. Fax: (212)817-1593. E-mail: jpannasch@gc.cuny.edu. Website: www.feministpress.org. **Contact:** Jeanann Pannasch, managing editor. Estab. 1970. Small, nonprofit literary and educational publisher. The Feminist Press publishes mainly fiction reprints by classic American women authors and translations of distinguished international women writers. Publishes hardcover and trade paperback originals and reprints. Publishes original fiction occasionally; exceptions are anthologies and international works. We use acid-free paper and cloth for library sales; we prouduce four-color covers, perfect bind our books, and shoot from the original text when possible. We always include a scholarly and literary afterword, since we are introducing a text to a new audience. Average print run: 2,500. Averages 15-20 total titles, 4-8 fiction titles/year. Member: CLMP, Small Press Association, AAP. Distributes titles through Consortium Book Sales and Distribution. Promotes titles through author tours, advertising, exhibits and conferences. Charges permission fees (reimbursement).

Needs Ethnic, feminist, gay/lesbian, literary, short story collections, women's. The Feminist Press publishes mainly fiction reprints by classic women authors and imports and translations of distinguished international women writers. Very little original fiction is considered. Needs fiction by U.S. women of color writers from 1920-1970 who have fallen out of print. Published *Apples From the Desert,* by Savyon Liebrecht (short stories, translation); *The Parish and the Hill,* by Mary Doyle Curran (fiction reprint); *Allegra Maud Goldman,* by Edith Konecky (fiction, reprint); and *Still Alive,* by Ruth Kluger (memoir).

How to Contact Does not accept unsolicited mss. Email Jeanann Pannasch with the word "submission"in the subject heading. Describe in no more than 200 words the type of book you are proposing and who you are. If we wish to see a portion of the manuscript or other materials, we will reply to your email requesting that you send those. Before writing, please consult our website to research if your book project fits the Feminist Press's publishing line. Usually responds within 6 weeks to queries. Accepts simultaneous submissions, electronic submissions.

Terms Pays 10% royalty on net receipts. Pays 5-10 author's copies. Average advance: $1,000. Publishes ms 18-24 months after acceptance. Ms guidelines online.

FIRST SECOND BOOKS

Roaring Book Press (a division of Holtzbrinck Publishers), 175 Fifth Ave, New York NY 10010.(908)955-4060. E-mail: mail@firstsecondbooks.com. Website: www.firstsecondbooks.com. **Contact:** MarK Siegel, editorial director. "First Second aims for high quality, literate graphic novels for a wide age-range, from Middlegrade to Young Adult to Adult readers." Publishes hardcover originals, paperback originals, paperback reprints.

How to Contact *Does not accept unsolicited submissions.*

FLORIDA ACADEMIC PRESS

P.O. Box 540, Gainesville FL 32602. (352) 332-5104. Fax: (352) 331-6003. E-mail: fapress@gmail.com. Contact: Florence Dusek, assistant editor (fiction). Publishes hardcover and trade paperback originals. **Published 90% debut authors within the last year.** Averages 10 total titles/year.

Needs Serious fiction and scholarly social science manuscripts. Does not want "children's books, poetry, science fiction, religious tracts, anthologies, or booklets."

How to Contact Submit complete ms. Responds in 4-12 weeks to mss.

Terms Pays 5-8% royalty on retail price, depending if paperback or hardcover. Publishes ms 3-5 months after acceptance.

☑ ⚏ FORGE AND TOR BOOKS

Tom Doherty Associates, LLC, 175 Fifth Ave. 14th Floor, New York NY 10010. (212)388-0100. Fax: (212)388-0191. Website: www.tor.com. **Contact:** Melissa Ann Singer, senior editor (general fiction, mysteries, thriller); Patrick Nielsen Hayden, senior editor (science fiction, fantasy). Estab. 1980. "Tor Books are science fiction, fantasy and horror, and occasionally, related nonfiction. Forge books are everything else—general fiction, historical fiction, mysteries and suspense, women's fiction and nonfiction. Orb titles are trade paperback reprint editions of science fiction, fantasy and horror books." Publishes hardcover, trade paperback and mass market paperback originals, trade and mass market paperback reprints. **Published some debut authors within the last year.**

• Tor was named Best Publisher at the Locus Awards for the sixteenth consecutive year.

Imprints Forge, Tor, Orb.

Needs Historical, horror, mainstream/contemporary, mystery (amateur sleuth, police procedural, private eye/hard-boiled), science fiction, suspense, thriller/espionage, western (frontier saga, traditional), thriller; general fiction and fantasy.

How to Contact Accepts unsolicited mss. Do not query; "submit only the first three chapters of your book and a synopsis of the entire book. Your cover letter should state the genre of the submission and previous sales or publications if relevant." Include estimated word count, brief bio, list of publishing credits. Agented fiction 95%. Sometimes comments on rejected mss. Responds in 4-6 months. No simultaneous submissions. Additional guidelines on Web site.

Terms Paperback: Pays 6-8% royalty for first-time authors, 8-10% royalty for established authors. Hardcover: Pays 10% first 5,000; 1212% second 5,000; 15% thereafter. Offers advance. Publishes ms 12-18 months after acceptance.

◎ FORT ROSS INC. RUSSIAN-AMERICAN PUBLISHING PROJECTS

26 Arthur Place, Yonkers NY 10701. (914) 375-6448. E-mail: fortross@optonline.net. Website: www.fortrossinc.com. **Contact:** Dr. Vladimir P. Kartsev. Estab. 1992. "We welcome Russia-related manuscripts as well as books from well-established fantasy and romance novel writers who would like to have their novels translated in Russia by our publishing house in cooperation with the local publishers." Publishes hard cover and paperback originals. **Published 2 debut authors within the last year.** Averages 20 total titles/year.

Needs Adventure, fantasy (space fantasy, sword and sorcery), horror, mainstream/contemporary, mystery (amateur sleuth, police procedural, private eye/hard-boiled), romance (contemporary, regency), science fiction (hard science/technological, soft/sociological), suspense, thriller

How to Contact Does not accept unsolicited mss. Query with SASE. Include estimated word count, brief bio, list of publishing credits. Send SASE for return of ms or send a disposable ms and SASE for reply only. Responds in 1 month to queries; 3 months to mss. Accepts simultaneous submissions.

Terms Pays 5-10% royalty on wholesale price or makes outright purchase of $500-1,500. Average advance: $500-$1,000; negotiable.

☑ FREYA'S BOWER

Wild Child Publishing, P.O. Box 4897, Culver City CA 90231. E-mail: mbaun@freyasbower.com. Website: http://www.freyasbower.com. **Contact:** Marci Baun, editor-in-chief; Faith Bicknell-Brown, managing editor. Estab. 2006. "Freya's Bower is a small, independent press that started out in March 2006. We are known for working with newer/unpublished authors and editing to the standards of NYC publishers. We respond promptly to submissions." Publishes paperback originals, e-books. Average print order: 50-200. Debut novel print order: 50. **Published over 30 new writers last year.** Plans 10-15 debut novels this year. Averages 75 total titles/year; 75 fiction titles/year. Member EPIC. Distributes/promotes titles through Ingram, All Romance eBooks, Fictionwise, Mobipocket and Web site.

Needs Adventure, erotica, ethnic/multicultural, experimental, fantasy, feminist, gay, historical, horror, humor/satire, lesbian, literary, mainstream, military/war, mystery/suspense, new age/mystic, psychic/supernatural, romance, science fiction, short story collections, thriller/espionage, western, young adult (fantasy/science fiction). Anthologies planned include Faeries, Dreams & Desires, vol. 2, M/M. Published

Dreams & Desires: A Collection of Romance & Erotic Tales (romance/erotica); *Conspiracy of Angels*, by Zinnia Hope (contemporary romance/erotica); *Dragon Queen: Book 1 & Book 2*, by Emily Ryan-Davis (paranormal/contemporary erotica).

How to Contact Query with outline/synopsis and 1 sample chapter. Accepts queries by e-mail. Include estimated word count, brief bio. Writers submit material per submissions guidelines. See Web site for details. Responds to queries in 2-4 weeks. Accepts unsolicited mss. Often critiques/comments on rejected mss. Responds to mss in 2-4 weeks.

Terms Sends pre-production galleys to author. Ms published 2-5 months after acceptance. Writer's guidelines on Web site. Pays royalties 10-40%. Book catalogs on Web site.

☑ ◎ ☒ FRONT STREET

An imprint of Boyds Mills Press, Inc., 815 Church St., Honesdale PA 18431. Website: www.frontstreetbooks. com. **Contact:** Manuscript Submissions. Estab. 1994. "High-quality fiction for children and young adults." Publishes hardcover originals and trade paperback reprints. Books: coated paper; offset printing; case binding; 4-color illustrations. Averages 15 fiction titles/year. Distributes titles through independent sales reps, wholesalers, and via order line directly from Front Street. Promotes titles through sales and professional conferences, sales reps, reviews, catalogs, web site, and direct marketing.

Needs Adventure, ethnic, historical, humor, juvenile, literary, picture books, young adult (adventure, fantasy/science fiction, historical, mystery/suspense, problem novels, sports). "We look for fresh voices for children and young adults. Titles on our list entertain, challenge, or enlighten, always employing novel characters whose considered voices resonate." Published *The Bear Makers* by Andrea Cheng; *Drive* by Nathan Clement; *The Adventurous Deeds of Deadwood Jones* by Helen Hemphill.

How to Contact Accepts unsolicited and international mss. Query with outline/synopsis, 3 sample chapters, and SASE and label the package "Manuscript Submission." Agented fiction 30%. Responds in 3 months to mss. Accepts simultaneous submissions.

Terms Pays royalty on retail price. Offers advance.

◎ GASLIGHT PUBLICATIONS

Empire Publishing Services, P.O. Box 1344, Studio City CA 91614. (818)784-8918. **Contact**: Simon Waters, fiction editor (Sherlock Holmes only). Estab. 1960. Publishes hardcover and paperback originals and reprints. Books: paper varies; offset printing; binding varies; illustrations. Average print order: 5,000. **Published 1 debut author within the last year.** Averages 4-12 total titles, 2-4 fiction titles/year. Promotes titles through sales reps, trade, library, etc.

Needs Sherlock Holmes only. Recently published *Schlock Homes, The Complete Bagel Street Saga*, by Robert L. Fish; *Subcutaneously: My Dear Watson*, by Jack Tracy (all Sherlock Holmes).

How to Contact Accepts unsolicited mss. Query with SASE. Include estimated word count, brief bio, list of publishing credits. Send SASE for return of ms or send a disposable ms and SASE for reply only. Agented fiction 10%. Responds in 2 weeks to queries; 1 year to mss.

Terms Pays 8-10% royalty. Royalty and advance dependent on the material. Publishes ms 1-6 months after acceptance.

Ⓝ ◎ ☐ GEMSTONE PUBLISHING

Diamond Comic Distributors, 3679 Concord Road, York PA 17402. (888) 375-9800 ext. 1617. Fax: 717-434-1690. E-mail: hjenna@gemstonepub.com. Website: www.gemstonepub.com. "Best known as the home of The Overstreet Comic Book Price Guide, Gemstone Publishing, a division of Geppi's Entertainment Publishing & Auctions, was formed by Diamond Comic Distributors President and Chief Executive Officer Stephen A. Geppi as a conduit for his efforts in preserving and promoting the history of the comics medium."

Imprints Walt Disney's Comics.

GENESIS PRESS, INC.

200 6th Street N., Suite 601/P.O. Box 101, Columbus MS 39703. (662)329-9927. Fax: (662) 329-9399. E-mail: customerservice@genesis-press.com. Website: www.genesis-press.com. Publishes hardcover and trade paperback originals and reprints. **Published 50% debut authors within the last year**. Averages 30 total titles/year.

- *Tomorrow's Promise*, by Leslie Esdale won a Gold Pen Award.

Needs Erotica, ethnic, literary, multicultural, romance, women's. Published *Cherish the Flame,* by Beverly Clark; *No Apologies,* by Seressia Glass.

How to Contact Query with SASE or submit 3 sample chapter(s), synopsis. Responds in 2 months to queries; 4 months to mss.Terms Pays 6-12% royalty on invoice price. Average advance: $750-5,000. Publishes ms 1 year after acceptance. Ms guidelines online.

☑ GERTRUDE PRESS

P.O. Box 83948, Portland OR 97283. Website: www.gertrudepress.org. **Contact:** Justus Ballard (all fiction). Estab. 2005. "Gertrude Press is a nonprofit organization developing and showcasing the creative talents of lesbian, gay, bisexual, trans, queer-identified and allied individuals. We publish limited-edition fiction and poetry chapbooks plus the biannual literary journal, Gertrude." Format: 60 lb. paper; high-quality digital printing; perfect (lit mag) or saddle-stitch (chapbook) bound. Average print order: 350. Published 5-10 new writers last year. Averages 4 total titles/year; 1 fiction title/year.

Needs Ethnic/multicultural, experimental, feminist, gay, humor/satire, lesbian, literary, mainstream, short story collections.

How to Contact Submit complete ms with cover letter. Submissions accepted year-round. Accepts queries by snail mail, e-mail. Include estimated word count, brief bio, list of publishing credits. Send disposable copy of ms and SASE for reply only. Responds to queries in 3-4 weeks; mss in 3-6 months. Accepts unsolicited mss. Considers simultaneous submissions, e-mail submissions. Sometimes critiques/comments on rejected mss.

Terms Manuscript published 3 months after acceptance. Writer's guidelines on Web site. Pays in author's copies (1 for lit mag, 50 for chapbook). Book catalogs not available.

GHOST ROAD PRESS

820 S. Monaco Pkwy #288, Denver CO 80224. (303)758-7623. E-mail: matt@ghostroadpress.com; evan@ghostroadpress.com. Website: http://ghostroadpress.com.

Needs "Genre-based mss in literary, science fiction, young adult, fantasy, mystery, and crime fiction."

How to Contact Query via e-mail. "Send an attachment (word or.rtf only) that includes a complete synopsis, a description of your marketing plan and platform, and the first three chapters. To view a complete list of our titles and changing submission guidelines, please visit Website." Responds in 2-3 months. Accepts simultaneous submissions.

☐ GIVAL PRESS

P.O. Box 3812, Arlington VA 22203. (703)351-0079. E-mail: givalpress@yahoo.com. Website: www.givalpress.com. **Contact:** Robert L. Giron, publisher. Estab. 1998. A small, award-winning independent publisher that publishes quality works by a variety of authors from an array of walks of life. Works are in English, Spanish and French and have a philosophical or social message. Publishes paperback originals and reprints and e-books. Books: perfect-bound. Average print order: 500. **Publishes established and debut authors.** Plans 2 first novels this year. Member AAP, PMA, Literary Council of Small Presses and Magazines. Distributes books through Ingram and BookMasters, Inc.

Needs Literary, ethnic, gay/lesbian. "Looking for French books with English translation." The Annual Gival Press Novel Award contest deadline is May 30th. The Annual Gival Press Short Story Award contest deadline is August 8th. Guidelines on Web site. *Recently published 'Twelve Rivers of the Body,*, by Elizabeth Oness, and *A Tomb of the Periphery*, by John Domini.

How to Contact Does not accept unsolicited mss. Query by e-mail first. Include description of project, estimated word count, brief bio, list of publishing credits. Agented fiction 5%. Responds by e-mail within 2 weeks. Rarely comments on rejected mss.

Terms Pays 20 contributor's copies. Offers advance. Publishes ms 1 year after acceptance. For book catalog send SASE and on Web site. Ms guidelines by SASE or on Web site.

☐ ◎ THE GLENCANNON PRESS

P.O. Box 1428, El Cerrito CA 94530. (510) 528-4216. Fax: (510) 528-3194. E-mail: merships@yahoo.com. Website: www.glencannon.com. **Contact:** Bill Harris (maritime, maritime children's). Estab. 1993. "We publish quality books about ships and the sea." Publishes hardcover and paperback originals and hardcover reprints. Books: Smyth: perfect binding; illustrations. Average print order: 1,000. First novel print order: 750. Averages 4-5 total titles, 1 fiction titles/year. Member PMA, BAIPA. Distributes titles through Quality Books, Baker & Taylor. Promotes titles through direct mail, magazine advertising and word of mouth.

Imprints Palo Alto Books (any except maritime); Glencannon Press (merchant marine and Navy).

Needs Adventure, children's/juvenile (adventure, fantasy, historical, mystery, preschool/picture book), ethnic (general), historical (maritime), humor, mainstream/contemporary, military/war, mystery, thriller/espionage, western (frontier saga, traditional maritime), young adult (adventure, historical, mystery/suspense, western). Currently emphasizing children's maritime, any age. Recently published *Good Shipmates*, by Ernest F. Imhoff (anthology, merchant marine); *Fort Ross*, by Mark West (Palo Alto Books, western).

How to Contact Accepts unsolicited mss. Submit complete ms. Include brief bio, list of publishing credits. Send SASE for return of ms or send a disposable ms and SASE for reply only. Responds in 1 month to queries; 2 months to mss. Accepts simultaneous submissions. Often comments on rejected mss.

Terms Pays 10-20% royalty. Publishes ms 6-24 months after acceptance.

Ⓝ Ⓜ Ⓞ Ⓗ GO! COMI

Go! Media Entertainment, LLC, 5737 Kanan Rd. #591, Agoura Hills CA 91301. E-mail: info@gomedia-ent. com. Website: http://www.gocomi.com/index.php.

Needs *Go! Comi is closed to unsolicited submissions for original material.* See the jobs section on Web site for information about possible freelance opportunities on existing manga.

⬥ Ⓞ Ⓞ GOOSE LANE EDITIONS

500 Beaverbrook Court, Suite 330, Fredericton NB E3B 5X4 Canada. (506)450-4251. Fax: (506)459-4991. Website: www.gooselane.com. **Contact:** Susanne Alexander, publisher. Estab. 1954. Publishes hardcover and paperback originals and occasional reprints. Books: some illustrations. Average print order: 3,000. First novel print order: 1,500. Averages 16-18 total titles, 6-8 fiction titles/year. Distributes titles through University of Toronto Press (UTP).

Needs Literary (novels), mainstream/contemporary, short story collections. "Our needs in fiction never change: substantial, character-centered literary fiction." Published *Reading by Lightning*, by Joan Thomas.

How to Contact Accepts unsolicited mss. Query with SASE. Responds in 6 months to mss. No simultaneous submissions.

Terms Pays 8-10% royalty on retail price. Average advance: $200-1,000, negotiable. Ms guidelines online.

Ⓞ GOTHIC CHAPBOOK SERIES

Gothic Press, 2272 Quail Oak, Baton Rouge LA 70808-9023. E-mail: gothicpt12@aol.com. Website: www. gothicpress.com. **Contact:** Gary W. Crawford, editor (horror, fiction, poetry and scholarship). Estab. 1979. "One person operation on a part-time basis." Publishes paperback originals. Books: printing or photocopying. Average print order: 150-200. Distributes titles through direct mail and book dealers.

Needs Horror (dark fantasy, psychological, supernatural). Need novellas and short stories.

How to Contact Accepts unsolicited mss. Query with SASE. Accepts queries by e-mail, phone. Include estimated word count, brief bio, list of publishing credits. Send SASE for return of ms or send a disposable ms and SASE for reply only. Responds in 2 weeks to queries; 2 months to mss. Sometimes comments on rejected mss.

Terms Pays 10% royalty. Ms guidelines for #10 SASE.

Ⓤ GRAYWOLF PRESS

2402 University Ave., Suite 203, St. Paul MN 55114. E-mail: wolves@graywolfpress.org. Website: www. graywolfpress.org. **Contact:** Polly Carden, editorial assistant. Estab. 1974. Growing independent literary press, nonprofit corporation. Publishes trade cloth and paperback originals. Books: acid-free quality paper; offset printing; hardcover and soft binding. Average print order: 3,000-10,000. First novel print order: 3,000-7,500. Averages 27 total titles, 8-10 fiction titles/year. Distributes titles nationally through Farrar, Straus and Giroux.

Needs Literary novels, short story collections. "Familiarize yourself with our list before submitting your work." Published *Out Stealing Horses*, by Per Petterson; *The Water Cure*, by Percival Everett; *Holding Pattern*, by Jeffery Renard Allen; *Black Glasses Like Clark Kent*, by Terese Svoboda.

How to Contact Send query letter including SASE/IRC, estimated word count, brief bio, list of publishing credits. Agented fiction 90%. Responds in 3 months to queries. Accepts simultaneous submissions.
Terms Pays royalty on retail price, author's copies. Average advance: $2,500-15,000. Publishes ms 18-24 months after acceptance. Ms guidelines online.

✪ ◉ GREENE BARK PRESS

P.O. Box 1108, Bridgeport CT 06601. (610)434-2802. Fax: (610)434-2803. E-mail: service@greenebarkpress. com. Website: www.greenebarkpress.com. **Contact:** Tara Maroney, associate publisher. Estab. 1991. "We only publish children's fiction—all subjects, but usually reading picture book format appealing to ages 3-9 or all ages." Publishes hardcover originals. **Published some debut authors within the last year.** Averages 1-6 total titles/year. Distributes titles through Baker & Taylor and Quality Books. Promotes titles through ads, trade shows (national and regional), direct mail campaigns.
Needs Juvenile. Published *Edith Ellen Eddy*, by Julee Granger.
How to Contact Submit complete ms. Responds in 3 months to queries; 6 months to mss. Accepts simultaneous submissions. No electronic submissions.
Terms Pays 10-15% royalty on wholesale price. Publishes ms 1 year after acceptance. Ms guidelines for SASE or e-mail request.

✪ GREENWILLOW BOOKS

HarperCollins Publishers, 1350 Avenue of the Americas, New York NY 10019. (212)261-6500. Website: www.harpercollinschildrens.com. Estab. 1974. Publishes hardcover originals and reprints. Averages 40-50 total titles/year.
Needs Childrens books: fantasy, humor, literary, mystery. *Criss Cross* by Lynne Rae Perkins, 2006 Newbery Medal Winner; *Deadline*, by Chris Crutcher; *Ida B*, by Katherine Hannigan.
How to Contact Does not accept unsolicited mss. "Unsolicited mail will not be opened and will not be returned."
Terms Pays 10% royalty on wholesale price for first-time authors. Average advance: variable. Publishes ms 2 years after acceptance.

✪ GROVE/ATLANTIC, INC.

841 Broadway 4th Floor, New York NY 10003. (212)614-7850. Fax: (212)614-7886. Website: www. groveatlantic.com. Estab. 1952. Publishes hardcover originals, trade paperback originals and reprints. Averages 60-70 total titles/year.
Imprints Grove Press (estab. 1952), Atlantic Monthly Press (estab. 1917), Black Cat (estab. 1961, revived 2004).
Needs Literary. Published *Halfway House*, by Katharine Noel; *A Killing in This Town*, by Olympia Vernon; *I Love You More Than You Know*, by Jonathan Ames.
How to Contact Does not accept unsolicited mss. *Agented submissions only*. Accepts simultaneous submissions.
Terms Pays 712-15% royalty on retail price. Average advance: varies. Publishes ms 1 year after acceptance.

✪ ✪ ✪ GUERNICA EDITIONS

11 Mount Royal, Toronto ON M6H 2S2 Canada. (416)658-9888. Fax: (416)657-8885. E-mail: guernicaeditions@cs.com. Website: www.guernicaeditions.com. **Contact:** Antonio D'Alfonso, fiction editor (novel and short story). Estab. 1978. "Guernica Editions is a small press that produces works of fiction and nonfiction on the viability of pluriculturalism." Publishes trade paperback originals, reprints and software. Books: various paper; offset printing; perfect binding. Average print order: 1,000. **Published 4 debut authors within the last year.** Averages 25 total titles, 18-20 fiction titles/year. Distributes titles through professional distributors.
• Three titles by Guernica Editions have won American Book Awards.
Imprints Prose Series (original); Picas Series (reprints).
Needs literary, multicultural. "We wish to open up into the fiction world and focus less on poetry. We specialize in European, especially Italian, translations." Publishes anthology of Arab women/Italian women writers. Published *At the Copa*, by Marisa Labozzetta; *In the Claws of the Cat*, by Claude Forand; *Unholy Stories*, by Carole David; *girls Closed In,* by France Theoret.

How to Contact Accepts unsolicited mss. Query with SASE. Include estimated word count, brief bio, list of publishing credits. Responds in 1 month to queries; 1 year to mss. No simultaneous submissions.
Terms Pays 8-10% royalty on retail price. Or makes outright purchase of $200-5,000. Average advance: $200-2,000. Publishes ms 15 months after acceptance.

HACHETTE BOOK GROUP USA

Hachette Livre, New York NY. (800)759-0190. Fax: (800)331-1664. Website: www.hachettebookgroupusa.com. "Hachette Book Group (HBG) was created when Hachette Livre, a global publishing company based in France, acquired Time Warner Book Group from Time Warner in 2006. Hachette Livre is a wholly-owned subsidiary of Lagardère, a company that is active worldwide in the areas of communications and media (books, press, audiovisual and distribution/retailing of cultural products)." Publishes hardcover originals, paperback originals, hardcover reprints, paperback reprints.
Imprint(s) Grand Central Publishing; Little, Brown and Company; Yen Press; Faith Words; Orbit; Center Street.
How to Contact Submit through agent only.

HADLEY RILLE BOOKS

P.O. Box 25466, Overland Park KS 66225. E-mail: contact@hadleyrillebooks.com. Website: http://www.hadleyrillebooks.com. **Contact:** Eric T. Reynolds, Editor (science fiction, fantasy). Estab. 2005. "Small publisher, one to two person operation. The first 9 titles are anthologies, mostly science fiction, with a little fantasy (in two titles). We've published new works by well-know authors (for example, new works by Sir Arthur C. Clarke, Mike Resnick, Stephen Baxter, Jay Lake, G. David Nordley, Robert Sheckley, Terry Bisson) as well as up-and-coming and new authors. At present time, about half of our anthologies are by invitation only, the other half are open to unsolicited submissions. We publish the kind of innovative anthologies that are generally not considered by larger publishers (somewhat common in the SF genre). Some of our anthologies are experimental, for example, the first title (Golden Age SF) had well-known authors write 'Golden Age' SF stories as if they were living during that time. The second title, Visual Journeys, asked each contributing author to choose a work of space art and write a story based on it. We included color plates of the art with each story. We're currently in the middle of a Ruins anthology series with stories that are set in or are about ruins. An anthology in 2009 will feature stories that deal with the consequences of global warming. Well-known futurists and SF writers are writing for this." Publishes hardcover originals, paperback originals. Format: Offset and POD printing. Published 50 new writers last year. Averages 6 fiction titles/year. Distributes/promotes titles via distrubtors, promotes at conventions, online advertising and by reviews.

- One story from *Golden Age SF: Tales of a Bygone Future* (2006) selected for David Hartwell and Kathryn Cramer's *Year's Best SF* #12, another selected for Rich Horton's *Space Opera 2007*. Two stories reprinted in Gardner Dozois' *The Year's Best Science Fiction #2* and ten stories received honorable mentions.

Needs Science fiction, fantasy, short story collections. Check Web site for current needs. Some anthologies are and will be open to unsolicited submissions, and will be announced on Web site. Published *Golden Age SF: Tales of a Bygone Future* (science fiction), *Visual Journeys: A Tribute to Space* (science fiction), *Ruins Terra* (SF/fantasy/horror).
How to Contact Send query letter. Accepts queries by e-mail. Include estimated word count, brief bio. Agented fiction: less than 5%. Accepts unsolicited mss. Often critiques/comments on rejected mss.
Terms Sends pre-production galleys to author. Ms published generally 6 months after acceptance. Writer's guidelines on Web site. Pays royalties of 12 of the ratio of 1 to the number of stories in the book, advance of $30 for unsolicated work. Book catalogs on Web site.

HARCOURT CHILDREN'S BOOKS

Imprint of Houghton Mifflin Harcourt Children's Book Group, 215 Park Ave South, New York, NY 10003. Website: www.harcourtbooks.com. **Senior Vice President and Publisher:** Betsy Groban. **Associate Publisher:** Jennifer Haller. 20% of books by first-time authors; 50% of books from agented writers. "Harcourt Children's Books publishes hardcover picture books and fiction only."

- Harcourt Children's Books no longer accepts unsolicited manuscripts, queries, or illustrations. Recent Harcourt titles:*Tails*, by Matthew Van Fleet; *Leaf Man*, by Lois Ehlert; *The Great Fuzz Frenzy*, by Janet Stevens and Susan Steven Crummel; *How I Became a Pirate* and *Pirates Don't Change Diapers*, by Melinda Long, illustrated by David Shannon; and *Frankenstein Makes a Sandwich*, by Adam Rex, are all New York Times bestsellers. Other Harcourt titles include *Evil Genius*, by Catherine Jinks; and *Each Little Bird That Sings*, by Deborah Wiles, a 2005 finalist for the National Book Award

How to Contact Only interested in agented material. Illustration Only interested in agented material.

Terms Pays authors royalty based on retail price. Sends preproduction galleys to authors.

HARLEQUIN AMERICAN ROMANCE

a Harlequin book line, 233 Broadway, Suite 1001, New York NY 10279. (212)553-4200. Website: www. eharlequin.com. **Contact:** Melissa Jeglinski, associate senior editor. "Upbeat and lively, fast paced and well plotted, American Romance celebrates the pursuit of love in the backyards, big cities and wide-open spaces of America." Publishes paperback originals and reprints. Books: newspaper print paper; web printing; perfect bound.

Needs Romance (contemporary, American). Needs "all-American stories with a range of emotional and sensual content that are supported by a sense of community within the plot's framework. In the confident and caring heroine, the tough but tender hero, and their dynamic relationship that is at the center of this series, real-life love is showcased as the best fantasy of all!"

How to Contact Query with SASE. No simultaneous submissions, electronic submissions, or submissions on disk.

Terms Pays royalty. Offers advance. Ms guidelines online.

HARLEQUIN BLAZE

a Harlequin book line, 225 Duncan Mill Road, Don Mills ON M3B 3K9 Canada. (416)445-5860. Website: www.eharlequin.com. **Contact:** Brenda Chin, associate senior editor. "Harlequin Blaze is a red-hot series. It is a vehicle to build and promote new authors who have a strong sexual edge to their stories. It is also the place to be for seasoned authors who want to create a sexy, sizzling, longer contemporary story." Publishes paperback originals. Books: newspaper print; web printing; perfect bound. **Published some debut authors within the last year.**

Needs Romance (contemporary). "Sensuous, highly romantic, innovative plots that are sexy in premise and execution. The tone of the books can run from fun and flirtatious to dark and sensual. Submissions should have a very contemporary feel—what it's like to be young and single today. We are looking for heroes and heroines in their early 20s and up. There should be a a strong emphasis on the physical relationship between the couples. Fully described love scenes along with a high level of fantasy and playfulness."

How to Contact No simultaneous submissions, electronic submissions, submissions on disk.

Terms Pays royalty. Offers advance. Ms guidelines online.

HARLEQUIN HISTORICALS

a Harlequin book line, Eton House, 18-24 Paradise Road, Richmond Surrey TW9 1SR United Kingdom. (212)553-4200. Website: www.eharlequin.com. **Contact:** Linda Fildew, senior editor. "The primary element of a Harlequin Historical novel is romance. The story should focus on the heroine and how her love for one man changes her life forever. For this reason, it is very important that you have an appealing hero and heroine, and that their relationship is a compelling one. The conflicts they must overcome—and the situations they face—can be as varied as the setting you have chosen, but there must be romantic tension, some spark between your hero and heroine that keeps your reader interested." Publishes paperback originals and reprints. Books: newsprint paper; perfect bound. **Published some debut authors within the last year.**

Needs Romance (historical). "We will not accept books set after 1900. We're looking primarily for books set in North America, England or France between 1100 and 1900 A.D. We do not buy many novels set during the American Civil War. We are, however, flexible and will consider most periods and settings. We are not looking for gothics or family sagas, nor are we interested in the kind of comedy of manners typified by straight Regencies. Historical romances set during the Regency period, however, will definitely be considered."

How to Contact Submit the first three chapters along with a 1-2 page synopsis of your novel.

Terms Pays royalty. Offers advance. Ms guidelines online.

▦ **HARLEQUIN MILLS & BOON, LTD.**

Harlequin Enterprises, Ltd., Eton House, 18-24 Paradise Rd., Richmond Surrey TW9 1SR United Kingdom. (+44)0208-288-2800. Website: www.millsandboon.co.uk. **Contact:** K. Stoecker, editorial director; Tessa Shapcott, senior editor (Mills & Boon Modern Romance); Bryony Green, senior editor (Mills & Boon Tender Romance); Linda Fildew, senior editor (Mills & Boon Historicals); Sheila Hodgson, senior editor (Mills & Boon Medicals). Estab. 1908-1909. Publishes mass market paperback originals. **Published some debut authors within the last year.** Plans 3-4 first novels this year.

Imprints Mills & Boon Modern Romance (Harlequin Presents); Mills & Boon Tender Romance (Harlequin Romance); Mills & Boon Historicals; Mills & Boon Medicals.

Needs Romance (contemporary, historical, regency period, medical).

How to Contact Send query letter. No simultaneous submissions.

Terms Pays advance against royalty. Publishes ms 2 years after acceptance. Ms guidelines online.

▣ ▯ **HARLEQUIN SUPERROMANCE**

a Harlequin book line, 225 Duncan Mill Road, Don Mills ON M3B 3K9 Canada. (416)445-5860. Website: www.eharlequin.com. **Contact:** Laura Shin, senior editor. "The aim of Superromance novels is to produce a contemporary, involving read with a mainstream tone in its situations and characters, using romance as the major theme. To achieve this, emphasis should be placed on individual writing styles and unique and topical ideas." Publishes paperback originals. Books: newspaper print; perfect bound. **Published 5 debut authors in 2006.**

Needs Romance (contemporary). "The criteria for Superromance books are flexible. Aside from length, the determining factor for publication will always be quality. Authors should strive to break free of stereotypes, clichés and worn-out plot devices to create strong, believable stories with depth and emotional intensity. Superromance novels are intended to appeal to a wide range of romance readers."

How to Contact Accepts unsolicited submissions. Submit 3 sample chapter(s) and synopsis. Send SASE for return of ms or send a disposable ms and SASE for reply only. No simultaneous submissions, electronic submissions, submissions on disk.

Terms Pays royalty. Offers advance. Ms guidelines online.

▣ ▣ ▢ ▣ **HARPERCOLLINS CANADA LTD.**

2 Bloor St. East, 20th Floor, Toronto ON M4W 1A8 Canada. (416)975-9334. Fax: (416)975-5223. Website: www.harpercanada.com. Harpercollins is not accepting unsolicited material at this time.

▣ **HARPERCOLLINS CHILDREN'S BOOKS**

1350 Avenue of the Americas, New York NY 10019. (212)261-6500. Website: www.harperchildrens.com. Imprints: HarperTrophy, HarperTeen, EOS, HarperFestival, Greenwillow Books, Joanna Cotler Books, Laura Geringer Books, Katherine Tegen Books.

How to Contact Writers Only interested in agented material

Illustration Art samples may be sent to Martha Rago or Stephanie Bart-Horvath. **Please do not send original art.** Works with over 100 illustrators/year. Responds only if interested. Samples returned with SASE; samples filed only if interested.

  • HarperCollins Children's Books is not accepting unsolicited and/or unagented manuscripts or queries. "Unfortunately, the volume of these submissions is so large that we cannot give them the attention they deserve. Such submissions will not be reviewed or returned."

Terms Art guidelines available for SASE.

HARPERCOLLINS GENERAL BOOKS GROUP

Division of HarperCollins Publishers, 10 East 53 Street, New York NY 10022. (212)207-7000. Fax: (212)207-7633. Website: www.harpercollins.com. "HarperCollins, one of the largest English language publishers in the world, is a broad-based publisher with strengths in academic, business and professional, children's, educational, general interest, and religious and spiritual books, as well as multimedia titles." Publishes hardcover and paperback originals and paperback reprints.

Imprints Amistad Press, Avon, Caedmon, Ecco, Eos, Haper Perennial, HarperAudio, HarperCollins, HarperEntertainment, HarperLargePrint, HarperSanFranciso, HarperTorch PerfectBound, Rayo, ReganBooks, William Morrow.

How to Contact See imprint for specific guidelines.

ⒶⓂ HARVEST HOUSE PUBLISHERS

990 Owen Loop N., Eugene OR 97402. (541)343-0123. Fax: (541)302-0731. Website: www. harvesthousepublishers.com. **Contact:** Acquisitions. Estab. 1974. "Our mission is to glorify God by providing high-quality books and products that affirm biblical values, help people grow spiritually strong, and proclaim Jesus Christ as the answer to every human need." Publishes hardcover originals and reprints, trade paperback originals and reprints, and mass market paperback originals and reprints. Books: 40 lb. ground wood paper; offset printing; perfect binding. Average print order: 10,000. First novel print order: 10,000-15,000. **Published 20 debut authors within the last year.** Averages 175 total titles, 15-20 fiction titles/year.

Needs Harvest House no longer accepts unsolicited manuscripts, proposals, or artwork.

How to Contact Does not accept unsolicited mss.

⒪ HELICON NINE EDITIONS

Subsidiary of Midwest Center for the Literary Arts, Inc., P.O. Box 22412, Kansas City MO 64113. (816) 753-1016. E-mail: helicon9@aol.com. Website: www.heliconnine.com. **Contact:** Gloria Vando Hickok. Estab. 1990. Small not-for-profit press publishing poetry, fiction, creative nonfiction and anthologies. Publishes paperback originals. Also publishes one-story chapbooks called feuillets, which come with envelope, 250 print run. Books: 60 lb. paper; offset printing; perfect bound; 4-color cover. Average print order: 1,000-5,000. **Published 1 debut author within the last year.** Distributes titles through Baker & Taylor, Brodart, Ingrams, Follet (library acquisitions), and booksellers. Promotes titles through reviews, readings, radio and television interviews.

How to Contact Does not accept unsolicited mss.

Terms Pays royalty. Author's copies. Offers advance. Publishes ms 12-18 months after acceptance.

Ⓜ HENDRICK-LONG PUBLISHING CO., INC.

10635 Tower Oaks Dr., Suite D, Houston TX 77070. (832)912-7323. Fax: (832)912-7353. E-mail: hendricklong@worldnet.att.net. Website: hendricklongpublishing.com. **Contact:** Michael Long. Estab. 1969. Only considers manuscripts with Texas theme. Publishes hardcover and trade paperback originals and hardcover reprints. Averages 4 total titles/year.

Needs Juvenile, young adult.

How to Contact Submit outline, 2 sample chapter(s), synopsis. Responds in 3 months to queries. No simultaneous submissions. Please, no e-mail submissions.

Terms Pays royalty on selling price. Offers advance. Publishes ms 18 months after acceptance. Book catalog for 8½ × 11 or 9 × 12 SASE with 4 first-class stamps. Ms guidelines online.

▦Ⓐ HESPERUS PRESS

4 Rickett Street, London England SW6 1RU United Kingdom. 44 20 7610 3331. Fax: 44 20 7610 3337. E-mail: info@hesperuspress.com. Website: www.hesperus press.com. Estab. 2001. Hesperus is a small independent publisher mainly of classic literary fiction translated fiction, and biographies of literary figures. Publishes paperback originals. Books: munken paper; traditional printing; sewn binding. Average print order: 5,000. Distributes titles through Trafalgar Square in the US, Grantham Book Services in the UK.

Needs Literary. Published *Carlyle's House*, by Virginia Woolf (rediscovered modern classic); *No Man's Land*, by Graham Greene (rediscovered modern classic); *The Princess of Mantua*, by Marie Ferranti (award-winning fiction in translation); *The Maytrees*, by Annie Dillard (new fiction).

How to Contact Does not accept unsolicited mss. *Agented submissions only.* Query with SASE. Accepts queries by mail. Include estimated word count, brief bio, list of publishing credits. Agented fiction 100%. Responds in 8-10 weeks to queries; 8-10 weeks to mss. Accepts simultaneous submissions. No submissions on disk.

⒪Ⓥ HIGHLAND PRESS PUBLISHING

P.O. Box 2292, High Springs FL 32655. (386) 454-3927. Fax: (386) 454-3927. E-mail: The.Highland. Press@gmail.com. Website: http://www.highlandpress.org. **Contact:** Leanne Burroughs, CEO (fiction); she will forward all mss to appropriate editor. Estab. 2005. "With our focus on historical romances, Highland Press Publishing is known as your 'Passport to Romance.' We focus on historical romances and our award-winning anthologies. Many people have told us they can once again delight in reading with the anthologies, since they do not have to feel guilty about reading and then putting a book down before it is finished. With the short stories/novellas, they can read a heart warming story, yet still get back to the demands of today's busy lives. As for our historicals, we publish historical novels like many of us grew up with and loved. History is a big part of the story and is tactfully woven throughout the romance." Publishes paperback originals, paperback reprints. Format: off set printing; perfect bound. Average print order: 1000. Debut novel print order: 1,000. **Published 15 new writers last year.** Plans 25 debut authors this year. Averages 30 total titles/year; 30 fiction titles/year. Distributes/promotes titles through Ingrams, Baker & Taylor, Nielsen, Powells.

- *Highland Wishes* was a Finalist, 2005 Readers and Booksellers Best and 2006 Winner, Reviewers International Award of Excellence. *Faery Special Romances* was a nominee for 2007 Night Owl Romances. *Blue Moon Enchantment* won the 2007 P.E.A.R.L. Award (two separate stories). *Christmas Wishes* had several stories nominated for the 2007 P.E.A.R.L. Award and received the 2007 Linda Howard Award of Excellence. *Her Highland Rogue* recieved the 2006 Reviewer's International Award, the 2006 National Readers Choice Award, and was a 2007 finalist for Readers and Booksellers Best. *Cat O'Nine Tales* had several stories as finalists or win the 2007 P.E.A.R.L. Award, 2007 Linda Howard Award of Excellence, and the 2007 Reviewers International Organization Award of Excellence.

Imprints A Wee Dram (short stories/novellas), The Wee Ones (children's illustrated), Regency Royale (Regency/romance), Thistle (Scottish historicals), Grace (inspirationals), Eire (Irish historicals), Pandora (young adult), Western (western/romance), Paranormal.

Needs Children's/juvenile (adventure, animal, easy-to-read, fantasy, historical, mystery, preschool/picture book, series), family saga, fantasy (space fantasy), historical, horror (dark fantasy, futuristic, supernatural), mainstream, military/war, mystery/suspense (amateur/sleuth, cozy, police procedural, private eye/hardboiled), religious (children's, general, family, inspirational, fantasy, mystery/suspense, thriller, romance), romance (contemporary, futuristic/time travel, gothic, historical, regency period, suspense), short story collections, thriller/espionage, western (frontier saga, traditional), young adult/teen (adventure, paranormal, fantasy/science fiction, historical, horror, mystery/suspense, romance, series, western). Special interests: Children's ms must come with illustrator. "We will always be looking for good historical manuscripts. In addition, we are actively seeking inspirational romances and Regency period romances." Numerous romance anthologies are planned. Topics and word count are posted on the Web site. Writers should query with their proposal. After the submission deadline has passed, editors select the stories. Published *Saving Tampa*, by Jo Webnar; *The Zero Day Event*, by Eric Fullilove; *Dark Well of Decision*, by Anne Kimberly; *The Bride of Blackbeard*, by Brynn Chapman; *The Barefoot Queen*, by Jean Harrington, and more.

How to Contact Send query letter. Query with outline/synopsis and sample chapters. Accepts queries by snail mail, e-mail. Include estimated word count, target market. Send disposable copy of ms and SASE for reply only. Agented fiction: 10%. Responds to queries in 8 weeks. Accepts unsolicited mss. Considers simultaneous submissions, e-mail submissions. Sometimes critiques/comments on rejected mss. Responds to mss in 3-9 months.

Terms Sends pre-production galleys to author. Ms published within 12 months after acceptance. Writer's guidelines on Web site. Pays royalties 7.5-8%. Book catalogs on Web site.

◎ HOLIDAY HOUSE, INC.

425 Madison Ave., New York NY 10017. (212)688-0085. Fax: (212)421-6134. Website: www.holidayhouse. com. Estab. 1935. Book publisher. **Vice President/Editor-in-Chief:** Mary Cash. **Acquisitions:** Acquisitions Editor. Publishes 35 picture books/year; 3 young readers/year; 15 middle readers/year; 8 young adult titles/year. 20% of books by first-time authors; 10% from agented writers. Mission Statement: "To publish high-quality books for children."

Needs All levels of young readers: adventure, contemporary, fantasy, folktales, ghost, historical, humor, literary, multicultural, school, suspense/mystery, sports. Recently published *Anansi's Party Time*, by Eric Kimmel, illustrated by Janet Stevens; *The Blossom Family* series, by Betsy Byars; *Washington at Valley Forge*, by Russell Freedman.

How to Contact Send queries only to editor. Responds to queries in 3 months; mss in 4 months. "If we find your book idea suits our present needs, we will notify you by mail." Once a ms has been requested, the writers should send in the exclusive submission, with a SASE, otherwise the ms will not be returned.

Terms Pays authors and illustrators an advance against royalties. Originals returned at job's completion. Book catalog, ms guidelines available for a SASE.

◎ HENRY HOLT & CO. BOOKS FOR YOUNG READERS

Henry Holt & Co., LLC, 175 Fifth Avenue, New York NY 10010. (646)307-5087. Website: www.henryholtchildrensbooks.com. **Contact:** Submissions editor, Books for Young Readers. Henry Holt Books for Young Readers publishes excellent books of all kinds (fiction, nonfiction, illustrated) for all ages, from the very young to the young adult. Publishes hardcover originals of picture books, chapter books, middle grade and young adult novels. Averages 70-80 total titles/year.

Needs Adventure, fantasy, historical, mainstream/contemporary, multicultural, picture books, young adult. Juvenile: adventure, animal, contemporary, fantasy, history, multicultural. Picture books: animal, concept, history, mulitcultural, sports. Young adult: contemporary, fantasy, history, multicultural, nature/environment, problem novels, sports. Published *When Zachary Beaver Came to Town*, by Kimberly Willis Holt (middle grade fiction); *The Gospel According to Larry*, by Janet Tashjian (YA fiction); *Visiting Langston*, by Willie Perdomo, illustrated by Bryan Collier (picture book); *Keeper of the Night*, by Kimberly Willis Holt; *Alphabet Under Construction*, by Denise Fleming (picture book).

How to Contact Accepts unsolicited mss. Include estimated word count, brief bio, list of publishing credits. Do not send SASE; publisher will not respond unless making an offer for publication.

Terms See Web site for complete guidelines, www.henryholtchildrensbooks.com/submissions.htm.

◪ HENRY HOLT

Henry Holt and Company, 175 Fifth Avenue, New York NY 10011. (646)307-5095. Website: www.henryholt.com. Publishes hardcover and paperback originals and reprints.

Imprints Metropolitan Books; Times Books; Henry Holt; Holt Paperbacks.

How to Contact Closed to submissions. *Agented submissions only.*

◩ ◎ HOUGHTON MIFFLIN BOOKS FOR CHILDREN

Houghton Mifflin Company, 222 Berkeley St., Boston MA 02116. (617)351-5959. Fax: (617)351-1111. E-mail: children's_books@hmco.com. Website: www.houghtonmifflinbooks.com. **Contact:** Submissions coordinator; Kate O'Sullivan senior editor; Ann Rider, senior editor; Margaret Raymo, editorial director. "Houghton Mifflin gives shape to ideas that educate, inform and, above all, delight." Publishes hardcover originals and trade paperback originals and reprints. **Published 12 debut authors within the last year.** Averages 100 total titles/year. Promotes titles through author visits, advertising, reviews.

Imprints Clarion Books, New York City, Graphia Boston; Sand Pipers, Boston.

Needs Adventure, ethnic, historical, humor, juvenile (early readers), literary, mystery, picture books, suspense, young adult, board books. Published *Trainstop*, by Barbara Lehman; *The Willowbys*, by Lois Lowry; *Just Grace Walker the Dog*, by Cherise Mericle Harper.

How to Contact Accepts unsolicited mss. Responds only if interested. Do not send SASE. Accepts simultaneous submissions. No electronic submissions.

Terms Pays 5-10% royalty on retail price. Average advance: variable. Publishes ms 18-24 months after acceptance. Book catalog for 9 × 12 SASE with 3 first-class stamps. Ms guidelines online.

◪ HOUGHTON MIFFLIN CO.

222 Berkeley St., Boston MA 02116. (617)351-5000. Website: www.hmco.com. **Contact:** Submissions Editor. Estab. 1832. Publishes hardcover originals and trade paperback originals and reprints. **Published 5 debut authors within the last year.** Averages 250 total titles/year.

Needs Literary. "We are not a mass market publisher. Study the current list." Published *Extremely Loud and Incredibly Close*, by Jonathan Safran Foer; *The Plot Against America*, by Philip Roth; *Heir to the Glimmering World*, by Cynthia Ozick.

How to Contact Does not accept unsolicited mss. *Agented submissions only.* Accepts simultaneous submissions.

Terms Hardcover: pays 10-15% royalty on retail price, sliding scale or flat rate based on sales; paperback: 712% flat rate, but negotiable. Average advance: variable. Publishes ms 3 years after acceptance.

Ⓝ ◎ ◪ IMAGE COMICS

2134 Allston Way, 2nd Floor, Berkeley CA 94704. E-mail: submissions@imagecomics.com. Website: www.imagecomics.com. Estab. 1992. "Image is a comics and graphic novels publisher formed by seven of Marvel Comics' best-selling artists: Erik Larsen, Jim Lee, Rob Liefeld, Todd McFarlane, Whilce Portacio, Marc Silvestri, and Jim Valentino. Since that time, Image has gone on to become the third largest comics publisher in the United States."

Needs "We are not looking for any specific genre or type of comic book. We are looking for comics that are well written and well drawn, by people who are dedicated and can meet deadlines."

How to Contact Query with 1 page synopsis and 5 pages or more of samples. "We do not accept writing (that is plots, scripts, whatever) samples! If you're an established pro, we might be able to find somebody willing to work with you but it would be nearly impossible for us to read through every script that might find its way our direction. Do not send your script or your plot unaccompanied by art — it will be discarded, unread." Accepts queries by snail mail, e-mail. Sometimes critiques/comments on rejected mss.

Terms Writer's guidelines on Web site.

⊘ IMAGES SI, INC

.Imprint of Images Publishing, 109 Woods of Arden Rd., Staten Island NY 10312. (718)966-3964. Fax: (718)966-3695. Website: www.imagesco.com/publishing/index.html. **Contact:** Acquisitions Editor. Estab. 1990. Publishes 2 audio books a year.

Needs Hard science fiction for audiocassettes and CDs. Published *Centauri III*, by George L. Griggs (science fiction print book); *Nova-Audio, Issues 1-3*, by Hoyt, Franklin, Schoen, Wild, Silverberg and Catelli (science fiction audio).

How to Contact Closed to submissions through Fall, 2009.

Terms Pays 10-20% royalty on wholesale price. Publishes stories 6 months-2 years after acceptence.

⊘ IMAJINN BOOKS

P.O. Box 545, Canon City CO 81212-0545. (719)275-0060. Fax: (719)276-0746. E-mail: editors@ imajinnbooks.com. Website: www.imajinnbooks.com. **Contact:** Linda J. Kichline, editor. Estab. 1998. "ImaJinn Books is a small independent print-on-demand publishing house that specializes in Regency Romance,Urban Fantasy, and paranormal romances with story lines involving psychics or psychic phenomena, witches, vampires, werewolves, space travel, the future." Publishes trade paperback originals. Books: print-on-demand; perfect binding; no illustrations. **Published 3-4 debut authors per year.** Member: SPAN. Distributes titles through Ingram Books and imajinnbooks.com. Promotes titles through advertising and review magazines.

Needs Fantasy (romance), horror (romance), psychic/supernatural (romance), all Urban Fantasy story lines,and all Regency romance story lines. "We look for specific story lines based on what the readers are asking for and what story lines in which we're short. We post our current needs on our Web site." Published *Dancing with The Devil*, by Keri Arthur (horror romance); *Half Past Hell*, by Jay Roycraft (Urban Fantasy); and *Marry Me, Millie*, by J.A. Ferguson (Regency romance).

How to Contact Query by e-mail only. Include estimated word count, brief bio, list of publishing credits. Agented fiction 20%. Responds in 3 months to queries; 9-12 months to mss. Often comments on rejected mss.

Terms Pays 6-10% royalty on retail price. Average advance: 100-200. Publishes ms 1-3 years after acceptance. Book catalog and ms guidelines for #10 SASE or online. Ms guidelines online.

⊘ INGALLS PUBLISHING GROUP, INC

197 New Market Center, #135, Boone NC 28607. (828) 297-7127. Fax: (828) 297-1057. E-mail: sales@ ingallspublishinggroup.com. Website: www.ingallspublishinggroup.com. **Contact:** Wendy Dingwall, Operations and Sales Manager. Estab. 2001. "We are a small regional house focusing on popular fiction and memoir. At present, we are most interested in regional fiction, historical fiction and mystery fiction." Publishes hardcover originals, paperback originals and paperback reprints. Books: 60# paper; offset printing; b&w illustrations. Average print order: 1,500-5,000. First novel print order: 1,500-3,000. **Published 1 debut author within the last year.** Plans 3 first novels this year. Member IBPA, MWA, SIBA. Distributes titles through Atlas Books Distribution, a division of Bookmasters, Inc.

Needs regional (southeast US), mystery (amateur sleuth, cozy, police procedural, private eye/hard-boiled), regional (southern Appalachian), romance (contemporary, historical, romantic suspense adventure), young adult (historical, mystery/suspense). Published *Perfect for Framing*, by Maggie Bishop (regional mystery); *In the Shadows of Chimney Rock*, by Rose Senehi (romance suspense); *Blood of Caesar*, by Albert A. Bell, Jr. (historical mystery); *Getorix; The Eagle and the Bull*, by Judith Geary (young adult historical).

How to Contact Accepts unsolicited mss. Query first. Will specifically request if interested in reading

synopsis and 3 sample chapters. Reading period open from July to October. Accepts queries by e-mail, mail. Include estimated word count, brief bio, list of publishing credits. Send copy of ms and SASE. Agented fiction 10%. Responds in 6 months to queries; 6 months to mss. Accepts simultaneous submissions, electronic submissions. No submissions on disk. Often comments on rejected mss.
Terms Pays 10% royalty. Publishes ms 6 months-2 years after acceptance. Ms guidelines online.

⬚ INSOMNIAC PRESS

520 Princess Ave., London ON N6B 2B8 Canada. (416)504-6270. E-mail: mike@insomniacpress.com. Website: www.insomniacpress.com. Estab. 1992. "Midsize independent publisher with a mandate to produce edgy experimental fiction." Publishes trade paperback originals and reprints, mass market paperback originals, and electronic originals and reprints. First novel print order: 3,000. **Published 15 debut authors within the last year.** Plans 4 first novels this year. Averages 20 total titles, 5 fiction titles/year.
Needs Comic books, ethnic, experimental, gay/lesbian, humor, literary, mainstream/contemporary, multicultural, mystery, suspense. We publish a mix of commercial (mysteries) and literary fiction. Published *Pray For Us Sinners*, by Patrick Taylor (novel).
How to Contact Accepts unsolicited mss. Accepts queries by email. Include estimated word count, brief bio, list of publishing credits. Send SASE for return of ms or send a disposable ms and SASE for reply only. Agented fiction 5%. Responds in 1 week to queries; 2 months to mss. Accepts simultaneous submissions. Sometimes comments on rejected mss.
Terms Pays 10-15% royalty on retail price. Average advance: $500-1,000. Publishes ms 6 months after acceptance. Ms guidelines online.

INTERLINK PUBLISHING GROUP, INC.

46 Crosby St., Northampton MA 01060. (413)582-7054. Fax: (413)582-7057. E-mail: editor@interlinkbooks. com. Website: www.interlinkbooks.com. **Contact:** Michel Moushabeck, publisher; Pam Thompson, editor. Estab. 1987. "Midsize independent publisher specializing in world travel, world literature, world history and politics." Publishes hardcover and trade paperback originals. Books: 55 lb. Warren Sebago Cream white paper; web offset printing; perfect binding. Average print order: 5,000. **Published new writers within the last year.** Averages 50 total titles, 2-4 fiction titles/year. Distributes titles through Baker & Taylor. Promotes titles through book mailings to extensive, specialized lists of editors and reviews; authors read at bookstores and special events across the country.
Imprints Interlink Books and Olive Branch Press.
Needs Ethnic, international. "Adult—We are looking for translated works relating to the Middle East, Africa or Latin America." Recently published *Everything Good Will Come*, by Sefi Atta (first novel); *The Gardens of Light*, by Amin Maalouf (novel translated from French); *War in the Land of Egypt*, by Yusef Al-Qaid (novel translated from Arabic).
How to Contact Does not accept unsolicited mss. Query with SASE and a brief sample. Responds in 3 months to queries. Accepts simultaneous submissions. No electronic submissions.
Terms Pays 6-8% royalty on retail price. Average advance: small. Publishes ms 18 months after acceptance. Ms guidelines online.

▣ INVERTED-A

P.O. Box 267, Licking MO 65542. E-mail: amnfn@well.com. **Contact:** Aya Katz, chief editor (poetry, novels, political); Nets Katz, science editor (scientific, academic). Estab. 1985. Publishes paperback originals. Books: offset printing. Average print order: 1,000. Average first novel print order: 500. Distributes through Baker & Taylor, Amazon, Bowker.
Needs Utopian, political. Needs poetry submission for our newsletter, *Inverted-A Horn*.
How to Contact Does not accept unsolicited mss. Query with SASE. Reading period open from January 2 to March 15. Accepts queries by e-mail. Include estimated word count. Responds in 1 month to queries; 3 months to mss. Accepts simultaneous submissions. Sometimes comments on rejected mss.
Terms Pays in 10 author's copies. Publishes ms 1 year after acceptance. Ms guidelines for SASE.

▣ ◎ ITALICA PRESS

595 Main St., Suite 605, New York NY 10044-0047. (212)935-4230. Fax: (212)838-7812. E-mail: inquiries@italicapress.com. Website: www.italicapress.com. **Contact:** Ronald G. Musto and Eileen

Gardiner, publishers. Estab. 1985. Small independent publisher of Italian fiction in translation. "First-time translators published. We would like to see translations of Italian writers who are well-known in Italy who are not yet translated for an American audience." Publishes trade paperback originals. Books: 50-60 lb. natural paper; offset printing; illustrations. Average print order: 1,500. Averages 6 total titles, 2 fiction titles/year. Distributes titles through Web site. Promotes titles through Web site.

Needs Translations of 20th century Italian fiction. Published *Game Plan for a Novel*, by Gianna Manzini; *The Great Bear*, by Ginevra Bompianai; *Sparrow*, by Giovanni Verga.

How to Contact Accepts unsolicited mss. Query with SASE. Accepts queries by e-mail, fax. Responds in 1 month to queries; 2 months to mss. Accepts simultaneous submissions, electronic submissions, submissions on disk.

Terms Pays 7-15% royalty on wholesale price. Pays author's copies. Publishes ms 1 year after acceptance. Ms guidelines online.

☑ ◎ JOURNEYFORTH

BJU Press, 1700 Wade Hampton Blvd., Greenville SC 29614-0001. (864)242-5100, ext. 4350. E-mail: jb@bjupress.com. Website: www.bjupress.com. **Contact:** Nancy Lohr, acquisitions editor (juvenile fiction). Estab. 1974. "Small independent publisher of excellent, trustworthy novels for readers pre-school through high school. We desire to develop in our children a love for and understanding of the written word, ultimately helping them love and understand God's word." Publishes paperback originals and reprints. Average print order varies. **Published some debut authors within the last year.** Averages 20-24 total titles. Distributes titles through Genesis Marketing, Spring Arbor and Appalachian.

Needs Adventure (children's/juvenile, young adult), historical (children's/juvenile, young adult), juvenile (animal, easy-to-read, series), mystery (children's/juvenile, young adult), sports (children's/juvenile, young adult), suspense (young adult), western (young adult), young adult (series). "Our fiction is all based on a moral and Christian wolrdview." Published *Susannah and the Secret Coins*, by Elaine Schulte (historical children's fiction); *Arby Jenkins Meets His Match*, by Sharon Hambrick (contemporary children's fiction); *Over the Divide*, by Catherine Farnes (young adult fiction).

How to Contact Accepts unsolicited mss. Query with SASE or submit outline, 5 sample chapters or submit complete ms. Include estimated word count, brief bio, list of publishing credits. Send SASE for return of ms or send a disposable ms and SASE for reply only. Responds in 1 month to queries; 3 months to mss.

Terms Pays royalty. Publishes ms 12-18 months after acceptance. Ms guidelines online.

☑ ◎ JUNO BOOKS

Wildside Press. (301) 762-1305. Fax: (301) 762-1306. E-mail: editor@juno-books.com. Website: www.juno-books.com. **Contact:** Paula Guran, Editor (fantasy). Estab. 2006; Wildside 1989. "Juno Books is a small independent, but professional, publisher of a wide range of fantasy featuring strong female protagonists." Publishes hardcover originals, paperback originals, paperback reprints, e-books. Format: offset printing; mass market paperback or trade paperback bound. Average print order: mmp first printing 10,000-25,000, trade 2,000-5,000. Debut novel print order: mmp 10,000, trade 2,000. **Published 6 new writers last year.** Plans 3 debut novels this year. Averages 14-18 fiction titles/year. Distributes/promotes titles nationally through Diamond Book Distribution. Promotion includes Web contests, conventions, print samplers, print ads, etc.

Needs "We welcome a cross-genre mix of contemporary and traditional FANTASY with mystery, thriller, paranormal romance, sf, adventure, historical fiction, detective, sensual, etc. Right now we're looking for contemporary and urban fantasy featuring strong female protagonists with 'kickassitude.'" Published *Dancing With Werewolves*, by Carole Nelson Douglas; *Personal Demons*, by Stacia Kane; *Matters of the Blood* by Maria Lima.

How to Contact *Currently closed to submissions.* See Web site for when submissions will open again. Query with outline/synopsis and 3 sample chapters. Accepts queries by e-mail only. Include estimated word count, brief bio, list of best publishing credits. Agented fiction: 30%. Responds to queries in 3 months. Accepts unsolicited mss. Considers simultaneous submissions. Sometimes critiques/comments on rejected mss.

Terms Sends pre-production galleys to author. Ms published 6-24 months after acceptance. Writer's guidelines on Web site. Pays 6-10% royalties, average $1000 advance, author's copies. Advance is negotiable. Book catalog on Web site.

◙ JUST US BOOKS, INC.

356 Glenwood Ave 3rd FL, East Orange NJ 07017. (973) 672-7701. Fax: (973) 677-7570. E-mail: info@ justusbooks.com. Website: www.justusbooks.com. Estab. 1988. Small independent publisher of children's books that focus on Black history, culture, and experiences (fiction and nonfiction). Publishes hardcover originals, paperback originals, hardcover reprints and paperback reprints (under its Sankofa Books imprint for previously published titles). Averages 4-8 total titles, 2-4 fiction titles/year. Member, Small Press Association; Children Book Council.

Needs Ethnic (African American), young adult (adventure, easy-to-read, historical, mystery/suspense, problem novels, series, sports). Published *Path to my African Eyes*, by Ermila Moodley; *12 Brown Boys*, by Omar Tyree.

How to Contact Does not accept unsolicited mss. Query with SASE, ms synopsis and pitch letter by mail only. Include brief bio, list of publishing credits. Send SASE for reply. Responds to queries in 10-12 weeks. Accepts simultaneous submissions.

Terms Pays royalty. Ms guidelines for SASE or on Web site.

◎ KEARNEY STREET BOOKS

P.O. Box 2021, Bellingham WA 98227. (360)738-1355. E-mail: garyrmc@mac.com. Website: http://kearneystreetbooks.com.

Needs Only publishes books about music or musicians. Published *Such a Killing Crime*, Robert Lopresti (mystery); *Tribute to Orpheus* (short story collection).

How to Contact Send query letter. Accepts queries by e-mail. Send disposable copy of ms and SASE for reply only. Responds to queries in 1 week. Accepts unsolicited mss. Responds to mss in 6-10 months. Considers simultaneous submissions, submissions on CD or disk. Never critiques/comments on rejected mss. Does not return rejected mss.

Terms Sends pre-production galleys to author. Manuscript published 18 months after acceptance. Pays "after expenses, profits split 50/50."

◪ KENSINGTON PUBLISHING CORP.

850 Third Ave., 16th Floor, New York NY 10022. (212)407-1500. Fax: (212)935-0699. Website: www.kensingtonbooks.com. **Contact:** John Scognamiglio, editor in chief (Kensington); Kate Duffy, editorial director (romance); Selena James, executive editor (African American fiction, Dafina Books); Audrey LaFehr, editorial director (wormen's fiction). Michaela Hamilton, executive editor. Estab. 1975. Full service trade commercial publisher, all formats. Publishes hardcover and trade paperback originals, mass market paperback originals and reprints. Averages over 500 total titles/year.

Needs Book-length fiction and nonfiction for popular audiences. Adult and YA.

How to Contact Accepts unsolicited and unagented mss. Responds in 1 month to queries; 4 months to mss. Accepts simultaneous submissions.

Terms Advance against royalties based on net sales. Publishes ms 12-24 months after acceptance.

◪ ALFRED A. KNOPF

Knopf Publishing Group, Random House, Inc., 1745 Broadway, 21st Floor, New York NY 10019. Website: www.randomhouse.com/knopf. **Contact:** Senior Editor. Estab. 1915. Publishes hardcover and paperback originals. **Published some debut authors within the last year.** Averages 200 total titles/year.

Needs Publishes book-length fiction of literary merit by known or unknown writers. Length: 40,000-150,000 words. Published *Gertrude and Claudius*, by John Updike; *The Emperor of Ocean Park*, by Stephen Carter; *Balzac and the Little Chinese Seamstress*, by Dai Sijie.

How to Contact *Agented submissions only.* Query with SASE or submit sample chapter(s). Responds in 2-6 months to queries. Accepts simultaneous submissions.

Terms Pays 10-15% royalty. Royalty and advance vary. Offers advance. Must return advance if book is not completed or is unacceptable. Publishes ms 1 year after acceptance. Book catalog for 7½ × 10½ SAE with 5 first-class stamps.

KNOPF PUBLISHING GROUP

Division of Random House, Inc., 1745 Broadway, New York NY 10019. (212)751-2600. Website: www.randomhouse.com/knopf. Estab. 1915. "Throughout history, Knopf has been dedicated to publishing distinguished fiction and nonfiction." Publishes hardcover and paperback originals.

Imprints Everyman's Library; Alfred A. Knopf; Pantheon Books; Shocken Books; Vintage Anchor Publishing, Doubleday, and Nan A. Talese.

☑ L&L DREAMSPELL

P.O. Box 1984, Friendswood TX 77546. E-mail: Administrator@lldreamspell.com. Website: http://www.lldreamspell.com. **Contact:** Lisa Rene'Smith, editor (fiction). "L&L Dreamspell is a micro publishing company based in the Houston, Texas area, publishing both fiction and nonfiction. Run by two gusty women, Linda Houle and Lisa Rene'Smith, we believe in making new author's dreams come true! We are a standard royalty paying publisher, and accept submissions for consideration through our website. We want to read outstanding mysteries, romance novels, and anything paranormal. New genres include thriller, horror, and young adult. Check our Web site for more information. We're still a young company—our nonfiction line was added in 2008. Linda and Lisa encourage all authors to follow their dreams..." Publishes paperback originals, e-books. Debut novel print order: 150. **Published 12 new writers last year.** Plans 36 or more books this year. Averages at least 24- to 36 books per year. Member PMA, SPAN. Distributes/promotes titles via Lightningsource, in addition to using a local printer (we also distribute our titles).

Needs adventure, erotica, fantasy, horror, mainstream, mystery/suspense, new age/mystic, romance. "We still have anthologies open for submission. Writers may submit stories per our Web site's guidelines." Published *The Key*, by Pauline Baird Jones (mainstream romance/sci fi); *Cold Tears*, by John Foxjohn (mystery), voted best mystery in 2007 by preditors and editors readers poll; *Dance on His Grave*, by Sylvia Dickey Smith (mystery); *Murder New York* style mystery anthology featuring an Agatha Award winning story by Elizabeth Zelvin.

How to Contact Query with outline/synopsis and 1 sample chapter. Accepts queries, submissions by e-mail only. Include estimated word count, list of publishing credits. Responds to queries in 2 weeks. Accepts unsolicited mss. Considers simultaneous submissions. Often critiques/comments on rejected mss. Responds to mss in 3 months.

Terms Sends pre-production galleys to author. Ms published 1 year after acceptance. Writer's guidelines on Web site. Pays royalties min 15%. Book catalogs not available.

☒ ☐ LACHESIS PUBLISHING

1787 Cartier Court, RR 1, Kingston, Nova Scotia B0P 1R0. Fax: (902) 242-2178. E-mail: louise@louisebohmer.com. Website: www.lachesispublishing.com. **Contact:** Louise Bohmer, editor-in-chief (horror /speculative). Estab. 2005. "Midsize independent publisher. Will assess all fiction but no poetry, collections of short stories or children's stories." Publishes paperback originals, paperback reprints, e-books. Format: POD printing;some illustrations. Debut novel print order: 150. **Published 12 new writers last year.** Plans 8 debut novels this year. Averages 12 fiction titles/year.

Imprint(s) LBF Books; Sinful Moments Press.

Needs Adventure, juvenile (fantasy, mystery, series), erotica, family saga, fantasy, gay, historical, horror, mainstream, military/war, mystery/suspense, regional, romance, science fiction, thriller/espionage, western, young adult/teen. Need erotica, gay and lesbian, and all types of romance

How to Contact Query with outline/synopsis and 3 sample chapters. Accepts queries by e-mail. Include estimated word count, brief bio, list of publishing credits, any connection with a writer's association. Responds to queries in 2 weeks. Accepts unsolicited mss. Considers simultaneous submissions. Always critiques/comments on rejected mss. Responds to mss in 3-5 months.

Terms Ms published 18 months after acceptance. Writer's guidelines on Web site. Pays royalties 10% min for print, 20% max for e-book.

☑ LEAPFROG PRESS

Box 2110, Teaticket, MA 02536. E-mail acquisitions@leapfrogpress.com. Website: www.leapfrogpress.com. **Contact**: Tasha Enseki, acquisitions editor. Estab. 1996. "We search for beautifully written literary titles and market them aggressively to national trade and library accounts. We also sell film, translation, foreign, and book club rights." Publishes paperback originals. Books: acid-free paper; sewn binding. Average print order: 3,000. First novel print order: 2,000-5,000 (average). Member, Publishers Marketing Association, PEN. Distributes titles through Consortium Book Sales and Distribution, St. Paul, MN. Promotes titles through all national review media, bookstore readings, author tours, Web site, radio shows, chain store promotions, advertisements, book fairs.

• *The Devil and Daniel Silverman* by Theodore Rosak was nominated for the American Library Association Stonewall Award and was a San Francisco Chronicle best seller. *The German Money* by Lev Raphael was a Booksense 76 pick.

Needs "Genres often blur; look for good writing. We are most interested in works that are quirky, that fall outside of any known genre, and of course are well written and finely crafted. We are most interested in literary fiction." Published *The War at Home*, by Nora Eisenberg; *Junebug*, by Maureen McCoy; *Paradise Dance*, by Michael Lee; *Waiting for Elvis*, by Toni Graham; and *Losing Kei*, by Suzanne Kamata. See web site for more recent titles.

How to Contact Query letter and first 5 to 10 ms pages within e-mail message. No attachments. Responds in 2-3 weeks to queries by e-mail; 6 months to mss. may consider simultaneous submissions.

Terms Pays 4-8% royalty on net receipts. Average advance: negotiable. Publishes ms 1-2 years after acceptance.

LEAPING DOG PRESS

P.O. Box 90473, Raleigh NC 27675-0473. (877) 570-6873. Fax: (877) 570-6873. E-mail: editor@ leapingdogpress.com. Website: www.leapingdogpress.com. **Contact:** Jordan Jones, editor and publisher. Member: CLMP, SPAN, and PMA. "Leaping Dog Press and Asylum Arts Press publish accessible, edgy, witty, and challenging contemporary poetry, fiction, and works in translation, with Asylum Arts Press having an additional focus on surrealism and the avant garde."

Needs "Please bear in mind that we are a small press that publishes only 4-6 titles a year. Additionally, we are currently under contract for titles through calendar year 2008, so the soonest newly accepted titles could appear is 2009." Does not want "genre fiction, self help, dog books, etc."

How to Contact Query by mail with a cover letter "containing your reasons for considering LPD or AA and your ideas for marketing your title; a proposed table of contents; a bio or CV and a list of publications; two chapters or 20 pages of fiction." Does not accept e-mail or electronic submissions or queries. Include SASE.

☑ ◎ LEE & LOW BOOKS INC.

95 Madison Ave., New York NY 10016-7801. (212)779-4400. Fax: (212) 683-1894. E-mail: info@leeandlow. com. Website: www.leeandlow.com. **Acquisitions:** Louise May, editor-in-chief; Jennifer Fox, senior editor. Publishes 12-14 children's books/year. 25% of books by first-time authors. Lee & Low Books publishes books with diverse themes. "One of our goals is to discover new talent and produce books that reflect the diverse society in which we live.

• Lee & Low Books is dedicated to publishing culturally authentic literature. The company makes a special effort to work with writers and artists of color and encourages new voices.

Needs Picture books, young readers: anthology, contemporary, history, multicultural, poetry. "We are not considering folktales or animal stories." Picture book, middle reader: contemporary, history, multicultural, nature/environment, poetry, sports. Average word length: picture books—1,000-1,500 words. Recently published Jazz Baby by Carol Boston Weatherford, illustrated by Laura Freeman; Home at Last by Susan Middleton Elya, illustrated by Felipe Davalos.

How to Contact Fiction/nonfiction: Submit complete ms. No e-mail submissions. Publishes a book 1-2 years after acceptance. Will consider simultaneous submissions. Guidelines on Web site. No SASE; Writer will be notified within 6 monthsif we have interest in the work. Manuscripts will not be returned.

Terms Pays authors advances against royalty. Pays illustrators advance against royalty. Photographers paid advance against royalty. Book catalog available for 9 × 12 SAE and $1.65 postage; ms and art guidelines available via Web site or with SASE.

☑ LEISURE BOOKS

Dorchester Publishing Co., 200 Madison Ave., Suite 2000, New York NY 10016. (212)725-8811. Fax: (212)532-1054. Website: www.dorchesterpub.com. **Contact:** Alissa Davis, editorial assistant. Estab. 1970. Publishes mass market paperback originals and reprints. Publishes romances, westerns, horrors, chick lit and thrillers only. Books: newsprint paper; offset printing; perfect bound. Average print order: variable. First novel print order: variable. Plans 25 first novels this year. Averages 255 total titles/year. Promotes titles through national reviews, ads, author readings, promotional items and on the Web site.

Imprints Leisure Books.

Needs Horror, romance, western, and thrillers. "We strongly back first time writers. All historical romance should be set pre-1900. Horrors and westerns are growing as well. No sweet romance, science fiction, cozy mysteries." Published *The Price of Pleasure*, by Connie Mason (historical romance); *The Last Twilight*, by Marjorie M. Liu (paranormal romance); *Cuts*, by Richard Laymon (horror).

How to Contact Accepts unsolicited mss. Query with SASE or submit outline, first 3 sample chapters, synopsis. Agented fiction 70%. Responds in 6-8 months to queries. No simultaneous submissions, electronic submissions.

Terms Pays royalty on retail price. Average advance: negotiable. Publishes ms 12 months after acceptance. Book catalog for free (800)481-9191. Ms guidelines online.

☑ LERNER PUBLISHING GROUP

241 First Ave. N., Minneapolis MN 55401. (612)332-3344. Fax: (612)332-7615. E-mail: info@lernerbooks. com. Website: www.lernerbooks.com. **Manuscript Acquisitions:** Jennifer Zimian, nonfiction submissions editor; Zelda Wagner, fiction submissions editor. Primarily publishes books for children ages 7-18. List includes titles in geography, natural and physical science, current events, ancient and modern history, high interest, sports, world cultures, and numerous biography series.

- Starting in 2007, Lerner Publishing Group no longer accepts submission in any of their imprints except for Kar-Ben Publishing.

How to Contact "We will continue to seek targeted solicitations at specific reading levels and in specific subject areas. The company will list these targeted solicitations on our Web site and in national newsletters, such as the SCBWI *Bulletin*."

Ⓝ ☑ ◎ LETHE PRESS

NJ. (609)410-7391. E-mail: editor@lethepressbooks.com. Website: www.lethepressbooks.com. **Contact:** Steve Berman, publisher. Estab. 2001. "Named after the Greek river of memory and forgetfulness (and pronounced Lee-Thee), Lethe Press is a small press devoted to ideas that are often neglected or forgotten by mainstream, profit-oriented publishers." Distributes/promotes titles Lethe Books are distributed by Ingram Publications and Bookazine, and are available at all major bookstores, as well as the major online retailers.

Needs Primarily interested in gay fiction, poetry and non-fiction titles. Has imprint for gay spirituality titles. Also releases work of occult and supernatural, sci-fi, and east asian interests.

How to Contact Send query letter. Accepts queries by e-mail.

☑ ARTHUR A. LEVINE BOOKS

Scholastic Inc., 557 Broadway, New York NY 10012. (212)343-4436. Website: www.scholastic.com. **Contact:** Arthur Levine, VP, publisher. "Arthur A. Levine is looking for distinctive literature, for children and young adults, for whatever's extraordinary." Averages 18-20 total titles/year.

Needs Juvenile, picture books, young adult, middle grade novels. Published *Her Mother's Face*, by Roddy Doyle, illustrated by Freya Blackwood; *Carlos Is Gonna Get It*, by Kevin Emerson; *A Curse Dark as Gold*, by Elizabeth C Bunce, *At the Crossing-Places*, by Kevin Crossley-Holland.

How to Contact Query with SASE.

Terms Pays variable royalty on retail price. Average advance: variable. Book catalog for 9 × 12 SASE.

Ⓝ ▢ ◎ ☑ LINDEN BAY ROMANCE, LLC

3529 Greenglen Circle, Palm Harbor FL 34684. E-mail: service@lindenbayromance.com. Website: www. lindenbayromance.com. **Contact:** Barbabra Perfetti, managing editor (romance); Stephanie Wardall-Gaw, editor (romance). Estab. 2005. "Linden Bay Romance is an independent small press that publishes romance in electronic format and trade paperback. Our catalogue contains short stories, novellas and novels ranging in length from 10,000-80,000 words in all the usual romance sub-genres. We publish strictly romance, and do not publish drama or comedies whose main focus is not on the relationship of the main characters. Linden Bay is a royalty paying publisher, with no fees paid by authors." Publishes paperback originals, e-books. Format: POD printing. **Published 7 new writers last year.** Plans 9 debut novels this year. Averages 65 total titles/year; 65 fiction titles/year. Plans for 2009 were to release 80 novels. Member AIPD, NYCIP; RWA non-subsidy, non-vanity press. Distributes/promotes print titles with Ingram, Baker & Taylor, then distriubtes through Amazon.com (US, Canada, UK and Europe), Borders.com, Waldenbooks.com, and Target.com as well as from Web site. E-books are distributed through Allromancebooks.com, Mobipocket.com, Fictionwise.com, and Lightnightsource.com as well as through their affiliates. Promotional efforts are handled by Julie Cummings, Manager of Marketing and Promotions.

Needs Romance (all sub-genres). Unsolicited mss are being accepted electronically, no agent required. See Web site for submission guidelines. Wants 40,000-65,000 word single stories or 3 short story collections with interrelated theme. Currently seeking non-traditional relationships (multiple partner, older female/younger male, etc.), gay romance in all sub-genres, contemporaries, sensual, edgy (light bondage, etc.) with heroes involved in action/adventure careers (police, firemen, spies, cowboys, race car drivers, etc.), sci-fi/urban fantasy (particularly shapeshifters), and cross-genre historicals; highly sensual, particularly if unusual time periods or locales, and crossed with mystery, sci-fi/urban fantasy, or adventure. Published *Articles of Way series)Random, Winds of Change, Eye of the Storm)*, by Lee Rowan (GLBT historical romance); *Forbidden series (The Calm, The Awakening)*, by Samantha Sommersby (paranormal romance/urban fantasy); *Task Force Zeta series*, by Cat Johnson (contemporary action/adventure military romance), and more.

How to Contact Query with outline/synopsis and 3 sample chapters. Accepts queries by e-mail only. Include estimated word count, brief bio, list of publishing credits. Agented fiction: less than 5 %. Responds to queries in 2-6 weeks. Accepts unsolicited mss. Considers simultaneous submissions, e-mail submissions. Always critiques/comments on rejected mss. Responds to mss in 2-4 weeks.

Terms Sends pre-production galleys to author. Ms published 3-6 months after acceptance. Writer's guidelines on Web site. Pays royalties. Book catalog on Web site.

Ⓝ ◎ LIQUID SILVER BOOKS

E-mail: support@liquidsilverbooks.com. Website: www.liquidsilverbooks.com. **Contact:** Tracey West, aqcuisitions editor. "Romance is the key to our stories. The stories must hold on their own if the sex scenes are omitted. Stories must have well developed characters, with depth and explosive chemistry that entice the reader to like and/or identify with them. Mix in an imaginative and fully realized plot, vivid settings, and clear dialog and you've got the ingredients for a story we'd be interested in publishing." Publishes paperback originals and e-books.

Needs Contemporary, gay and lesbian, paranormal, supernatural, sci-fi, fantasy, historical, suspense, and western romances.

How to Contact Query with outline/synopsis and three sample chapters in.rtf form, ariel 12 pt font only. Accepts queries by e-mail. Include estimated word count, author bio, thoughts on e-Publishing, and a snapshot synopsis of book including title and series title, if applicable, in body of e-mail. Mss must include pen name, real name, snail mail, and e-mail contact information on first page top left corner. No headers, footers, or page numbers. Responds to queries in 4-6 weeks.

Terms Manuscript published 4 months after acceptance. Writer's guidelines on Web site. Pays royalties 40%.

Ⓐ LITTLE, BROWN AND CO. ADULT TRADE BOOKS

Hachette Book Group USA (formerly Time Warner Book Group), 237 Park Avenue, New York NY 10017. (212)364-1100. Website: www.hachettebookgroup.com. **Contact:** Editorial dept. Estab. 1837. "The general editorial philosophy for all divisions continues to be broad and flexible, with high quality and the promise of commercial success as always the first considerations." Publishes hardcover originals and paperback originals and reprints. Averages 100 total titles/year.

Imprints Little, Brown; Arcade Books; Back Bay Books; Bulfinch Press.

Needs Literary, mainstream/contemporary. Published *Cross Country*, by James Patterson; *Outliers*, by Malcolm Gladwell; *The Historian*, by Elizabeth Kostova; *When You Are Engulfed in Flames*, by David Sedaris.

How to Contact *Agented submissions only*.

Terms Pays royalty. Offers advance. Ms guidelines online.

Ⓐ ◎ LITTLE, BROWN AND CO. BOOKS FOR YOUNG READERS

Division of Hachette Book Group, Inc., 237 Park Avenue, New York NY 10017. (212)522-8700. Website: www.lb-kids.com. **Contact:** Submissions editor. Estab. 1837. "We are looking for strong writing and presentation but no predetermined topics." Publishes hardcover originals, trade paperback reprints. Averages 100-150 total titles/year.

Imprints Poppy; LB Kids; Megan Tingley Books (Megan Tingley, VP publisher).

Needs Adventure, ethnic, fantasy, historical, humor, juvenile, mystery, novelty, picture books, science fiction, suspense, young adult. "We are looking for strong fiction for children of all ages in any area, including multicultural. We always prefer full manuscripts for fiction."

How to Contact *Agented submissions only.*

Terms Pays royalty on retail price. Average advance: negotiable. Publishes ms 2 years after acceptance. Ms guidelines online.

LIVINGSTON PRESS

University of West Alabama, Station 22, Livingston AL 35470. E-mail: jwt@uwa.edu. Website: www. livingstonpress.uwa.edu. **Contact:** Joe Taylor, literary editor. Estab. 1984. "Small university press specializing in offbeat and/or Southern literature." Publishes hardcover and trade paperback originals. Books: acid free; offset; some illustrations. Average print order: 2,500. First novel print order: 2,500. Plans 5 first novels this year. Averages 10 fiction titles/year.

Imprints Swallow's Tale Press.

Needs Experimental, literary, short story collections, off-beat or southern. "We are interested in form and, of course style." Published *The Gin Girl*, by River Jordan (novel); *Pulpwood*, by Scott Ely (stories); *Live Cargo*, by Paul Toutonghi (stories).

How to Contact Query with SASE. Include estimated word count, brief bio, list of publishing credits. Send SASE for return of ms or send a disposable ms and SASE for reply only. Responds in 1 month to queries; 1 year to mss. Accepts simultaneous submissions. Send only in June and July.

Terms Pays 10% of 1,500 print run, 150 copies; thereafter pays a mix of royalties and books. Publishes ms 18 months after acceptance. Book catalog for SASE. Ms guidelines online.

ⓝ ◎ LOOSE ID

1802 N. Carson St., Suite 212-2924, Carson City NE 89701.E-mail: submissions@loose-id.com. Website: www.loose-id.com. **Contact:** Treva Harte, editor-in-chief. Estab. 2004. "Loose Id is love unleashed. We're taking romance to the edge." Publishes e-books. Distributes/promotes titles "The company promotes itself through web and print advertising wherever readers of erotic romance may be found, creating a recognizable brand identity as the place to let your id run free and the people who unleash your fantasies. It is currently pursuing licensing agreements for foreign translations, and developing a print program of 2 to 5 titles per month."

Needs Wants non-traditional erotic romance stories, including gay, lesbian, non-traditional heroes and heroines, multi-culturalism, cross-genre, fantasy, and science fiction. No straight contemporary or historical romances.

How to Contact Query with outline/synopsis and three sample chapters. Accepts queries by e-mail. Include estimated word count, list of publishing credits, and why your submission is "Love Unleashed™". Responds to queries in 1 months. Considers e-mail submissions.

Terms Manuscript published within 1 year after acceptance. Writer's guidelines on Web site. Pays royalties 35%.

☑ ◎ LOST HORSE PRESS

105 Lost Horse Lane, Sandpoint ID 83864. (208) 255-4410. E-mail: losthorsepress@mindspring.com. Website: www.losthorsepress.org. **Contact:** Christine Holbert, publisher. Estab. 1998. Publishes hardcover and paperback originals. Books: 60-70 lb. natural paper; offset printing; b&w illustration. Average print order: 500-2,500. First novel print order: 500. **Published 2 debut authors within the last year.** Averages 4 total titles/year. Distributed by Eastern Washington University Press.

- *Woman on the Cross*, by Pierre Delattre, won the *ForeWord Magazine's* 2001 Book of the Year Award for literary fiction.

Needs Literary, regional (Pacific NW), short story collections, poetry. Published *Tales of a Dalai Lama*, by Pierre Delattre (literary fiction); *Love*, by Valerie Martin (short stories); *The Baseball Field At Night Poems*, by Patricia Goedicke; *Thistle*, by Melissa Kwasny; *Willing To Choose* and *Composing Voices*, by Robert Pack.

Terms Publishes ms 6 months-1 year after acceptance. Please check submission guidelines on Web site before submitting ms.

☑ ◎ LOVE SPELL

Dorchester Publishing Co., Inc., 200 Madison Ave., 20th Floor, New York NY 10016. (212)725-8811. Fax: (212)532-1054. Website: www.dorchesterpub.com. **Contact:** Alissa Davis, Editorial Assistant. Love Spell publishes the quirky sub-genres of romance: time-travel, paranormal, futuristic. "Despite the exotic settings, we are still interested in character-driven plots." Publishes mass market paperback originals. Books: newsprint paper; offset printing; perfect bound. Average print order: varies. First novel print order: varies. Averages 48 total titles/year.

Needs Romance (futuristic, time travel, paranormal, historical), whimsical contemporaries. "Books industry-wide are getting shorter; we're interested in 90,000 words." Published *Deep Magic*, by Joy Nash (historical romance); *Immortals: The Calling*, by Jennifer Ashley (paranormal romance).

How to Contact Accepts unsolicited mss. Query with SASE or submit 3 sample chapter(s), synopsis. Send SASE or IRC. Agented fiction 70%. Responds in 6-8 months to mss. No simultaneous submissions.

Terms Pays royalty on retail price. Average advance: varies. Publishes ms 1 year after acceptance. Book catalog for free (800)481-9191. Ms guidelines online.

◎ MARINE TECHNIQUES PUBLISHING, INC.

126 Western Ave., Suite 266, Augusta ME 04330-7249. (207)622-7984. Fax: (207)621-0821. E-mail: marinetechniques@midmaine.com. Website: www.MarineTechPublishing.com **Contact:** James L. Pelletier, president/owner (commercial marine or maritime international and national and international maritime-related properties). **Published 15% debut authors within the last year.** Averages 3-5 total titles/year.

Needs Must be commercial maritime/marine related.

How to Contact Submit complete ms. Responds in 2 months to queries; 6 months to mss. Accepts simultaneous submissions.

Terms Pays 25-43% royalty on wholesale or retail price. Publishes ms 6-12 months after acceptance.

☐ ◙ MARVEL COMICS

417 5th Ave., New York NY 10016. (212)576-4000. Fax: (212)576-8547. Website: www.marvel.com. Publishes hardcover originals and reprints, trade paperback reprints, mass market comic book originals, electronic reprints. Averages 650 total titles/year.

Needs Adventure, comic books, fantasy, horror, humor, science fiction, young adult. "Our shared universe needs new heroes and villains; books for younger readers and teens needed."

How to Contact "Please send us an inquiry letter, detailing your writing experience and why you would like to write for Marvel. Based on your inquiry letter, we may request to read a sample of your work. Please note: Unsolicited writing samples will not be read. Any unsolicited or solicited writing sample received without a signed Marvel Idea Submission Form will be destroyed unread." (Download Marvel Idea Submission Form from Web site). Responds only if interested in 3-5 weeks.

Terms Pays on a per page work-for-hire basis which is contracted. Ms guidelines online.

◙ ◎ MCBOOKS PRESS

ID Booth Building, 520 N. Meadow St., Ithaca NY 14850. (607) 272-2114. Fax: (607) 273-6068. E-mail: jackie@mcbooks.com. Website: www.mcbooks.com. **Contact:** Jackie Swift. Estab. 1979. Small independent publisher. Publishes Julian Stockwin, John Biggins, Colin Sargent, and Douglas W. Jacobson. Publishes trade paperback and hardcover originals and reprints. Averages t otal titles, fiction titles/year. Distributes titles through Independent Publishers Group.

Needs "We are looking for a few good novels and are open to almost any genre or style, except romance, inspirational, science fiction, fantasy, and children's. Our main criteria is an exceptionally strong story combined with an author who can show he/she has a good grasp on self-promotion through networking, personal appearances, and tireless internet presence."

How to Contact Does not accept unsolicited mss. Submission guidelines available on Web site. Query with SASE or via e-mail. Include list of publishing credits and a well thought-out marketing plan. Responds in 3 months to queries. Accepts simultaneous submissions.

Terms Pays 5-10% royalty on retail price. Average advance: $1,000-5,000.

◎ ◙ MARGARET K. MCELDERRY BOOKS

Simon & Schuster Children's Publishing Division, Simon & Schuster, 1230 Sixth Ave., New York NY 10020.

(212)698-7605. Fax: (212)698-2797. Website: www.simonsayskids.com. **Contact:** Emma D. Dryden, vice president/publisher. Estab. 1971. Publishes quality material for preschoolers to 18-year-olds. Publishes hardcover and paperback originals. Books: high quality paper; offset printing; three piece and POB bindings; illustrations. Average print order: 15,000. First novel print order: 10,000. **Published some debut authors within the last year.** Averages 35 total titles/year.

• Books published by Margaret K. McElderry Books have received numerous awards, including the Newbery and Caldecott Medals.

Needs Adventure, fantasy, historical, mainstream/contemporary, mystery, picture books, young adult (or middle grade). All categories (fiction and nonfiction) for juvenile and young adult. "We will consider any category. Results depend on the quality of the imagination, the artwork and the writing." Published *Dr. Ted,* by Andrea Beaty; illustrated by by Pascal LeMaitre and *Bear Feels Sick* by Karma Wilson; Illustrated by Jane Cahpeman (picture books); *Sight,* by Adrienne Maria Vrettos (middle-grade fiction); *City of Bones and City of Ashes* by Cassandra Clare (teen fiction), by *OOPS!* by AlanKaatz; illustrated by Edward Koren (poetry).

Terms *"We do not accept unsolicited queries or submissions. Submissions must be sent through an agent."* Average print order is 10,000-15,000 for a first middle grade or young adult book; 7,500-20,000 for a first picture book. Pays royalty on hardcover retail price: 10% fiction; 5% author, 5% illustrator (picture book). Offers $5,000-8,000 advance for new authors. Publishes ms up to 3 years after acceptance. Ms guidelines for #10 SASE.

☑ MEDALLION PRESS, INC.

8988 South Sheridan Road, Suite L, Box 216, Tulsa OK 74133. Website: www.medallionpress.com. **Contact**: Christy Phillippe, acquisitions editor. Estab. 2003. "We are an independent publisher looking for books that are outside of the box. Please do not submit to us if you are looking for a large advance. We reserve our funds for marketing the books." Publishes paperback originals. Average print order: 5,000. **Published 20+ debut authors within the last year.**

Imprints Platinum/Hardcover; Gold/Mass Market; Silver/Trade Paper; Bronze/Young Adult; Jewel/Romance; Amethyst/Fantasy, Sci-Fi, Paranormal; Emerald/Suspense; Ruby/Contemporary; Sapphire/Historical.

Needs Adventure, ethnic, fantasy (space fantasy, sword and sorcery), glitz, historical, horror (dark fantasy, futuristic, psychological, supernatural), humor, literary, mainstream/contemporary, military/war, mystery (amateur slueth, police procedural, private eye/hard-boiled), romance, science fiction (hard science/technological, soft/sociological), thriller/espionage, western (frontier saga), young adult. Published *Siren's Call*, by Mary Ann Mitchell (horror); *Grand Traverse*, by Michael Beres (mainstream fiction); *Memories of Empire*, by Django Wexler (epic fantasy).

How to Contact Does not accept unsolicited mss. "Minimum word count 80K for adult fiction, 55K for YA, no exceptions." No poetry, anthologies, erotica or inspirational. Submit first 3 consecutive chapters and a chapter-by-chapter synopsis. "Without the synopsis, the submission will be rejected." Accepts queries only by mail. No e-mail queries. Include estimated word count, brief bio, list of publishing credits. Send SASE or IRC. Responds in 4-8 months to mss. Accepts simultaneous submissions. Sometimes comments on rejected mss.

Terms Offers advance. Publishes ms 1-2 years after acceptance. Ms guidelines online.

◎ MERIWETHER PUBLISHING, LTD.

885 Elkton Dr., Colorado Springs CO 80907-3557. (719)594-4422. Fax: (719)594-9916. E-mail: editor@meriwether.com. Website: www.meriwetherpublishing.com; www.contemporarydrama.com. **Contact:** Rhonda Wray, associate editor (church plays); Ted Zapel, editor (school plays, comedies, books). Estab. 1969. "Mid-size, independent publisher of plays. We publish plays for teens, mostly one-act comedies, holiday plays for churches and musical comedies. Our books are on the theatrical arts." Publishes paperback originals and reprints. Books: quality paper; printing house specialist; paperback binding. Average print order: 5,000-10,000. **Published 25-35 debut authors within the last year.**

Needs Mainstream/contemporary, comedy, religious (children's plays and religious Christmas and Easter plays), suspense—all in playscript format. Published *Pirates and Petticoats*, by Pat Cook (a two-act pirate comedy); *Let Him Sleep Until it's Time for His Funeral*, by Peg Kehret (two-act play).

How to Contact Accepts unsolicited mss. Query with SASE. Accepts queries by e-mail. Include list of publishing credits. Send SASE for return of ms or send a disposable ms and SASE for reply only. Responds in 3 weeks to queries; 2 months to mss. Accepts simultaneous submissions. Sometimes comments on rejected mss.

Terms Pays 10% royalty on retail price or makes outright purchase. Publishes ms 6-12 months after acceptance. Book catalog and ms guidelines for $2 postage.

☐ MID-LIST PRESS

4324 12th Ave S., Minneapolis MN 55407-3218. (612)432-8062. Fax: (612)823-8387. E-mail: guide@ midlist.org. Website: www.midlist.org. **Contact:** Marianne Nora, executive director. Estab. 1989. "We are a nonprofit literary press dedicated to the survival of the mid-list, those quality titles that are being neglected by the larger commercial houses. Our focus is on new and emerging writers." Publishes hardcover and trade paperback originals. Books: acid-free paper; offset printing; perfect or Smyth-sewn binding. Average print order: 2,000. Averages 4 total titles, 1 fiction titles/year. Distributes titles through Baker & Taylor, Midwest Library Service, Brodart, Follett and Emery Pratt. Promotes titles through publicity, direct mail, catalogs, author's events and review and awards.

Needs General fiction. Published *The Woman Who Never Cooked*, by Mary L. Tabor; *The Echo of Sand*, by Gail Chehab (first novel).

How to Contact Accepts unsolicited mss. Agented fiction less than10%. Do not include SASE. Responds only if interested by telephone or e-mail. Accepts simultaneous submissions. Ms guidelines online.

Terms Pays 40-50% royalty on net receipts. Average advance: $1,000. Publishes ms 12-18 months after acceptance.

☑ MILKWEED EDITIONS

1011 Washington Ave. S., Suite 300, Minneapolis MN 55415. (612) 332-3192. Fax: (612) 215-2550. E-mail: editor@milkweed.org. Website: www.milkweed.org. **Contact:** Daniel Slager, Publisher; The Editors, first reader. Estab. 1984. Nonprofit publisher. Publishes hardcover originals and paperback originals and reprints. Books: book text quality—acid-free paper; offset printing; perfect or hardcover binding. Average print order: 4,000. First novel print order depends on book. **Published some debut authors within the last year.** Averages 15 total titles/year. Distributes through Publisher's Group West. Each book has its own marketing plan involving print ads, tours, conferences, etc.

Needs Literary. Novels for adults and for readers 8-13. High literary quality. For adult readers: literary fiction, nonfiction, poetry, essays; for children (ages 8-13): literary novels. Translations welcome for both audiences. Published *The Blue Sky*, by Galsan Tschinag (translation); *Visigoth*, by Gary Amdahl (first fiction, short stories); *The Farther Shore*, by Matthew Eck.

How to Contact Submit complete ms. Responds in 2 months to queries; 6 months to mss. Accepts simultaneous submissions.

Terms Variable royalty on retail price. Average advance: varied. Publishes ms 1-2 years after acceptance. Book catalog for $1.50 postage. Ms guidelines online.

◎ MILKWEED FOR YOUNG READERS

Milkweed Editions, 1011 Washington Ave. South, Open Book, Suite 300, Minneapolis MN 55415. (612)332-3192. Fax: (612)215-2550. Website: www.milkweed.org. **Contact**: Daniel Slager, Publisher; Children's reader. Estab. 1984. "Milkweed for Young Readers are works that embody humane values and contribute to cultural understanding." Publishes hardcover and trade paperback originals. Averages 1-2 total titles/year. Distributes titles through Publishers Group West. Promotes titles individually through print advertising, Web site and author tours.

• *Perfect*, by Natasha Friend, was chosen as a Book Sense 76 Children's Book selection.

Needs Adventure, historical, humor, mainstream/contemporary, animal, environmental. For ages 8-13. Published *The Cat*, By Jutta Richter, and *The Linden Tree* by Ellie Mathews.

How to Contact Query with SASE. Agented fiction 30%. Responds in 2 months to queries. Accepts simultaneous submissions.

Terms Pays 6% royalty on retail price. Average advance: variable. Publishes ms 1 year after acceptance. Book catalog for $1.50. Ms guidelines for #10 SASE or on the Web site.

Advice "Familiarize yourself with our books before submitting. You need not have a long list of credentials—excellent work speaks for itself."

⊠ ⬚ $ MONDIAL

203 W. 107th St., Suite 6C, New York NY 10025.(212)851-3252. E-mail: contact@mondialbooks.com. Website: www.mondialbooks.com.

Needs adventure, erotica, ethnic, gay, historical, literary, mainstream, multicultural, mystery, poetry, romance, short, translation. Published *Two People*, by David Windham; *Bitterness*, by Malama Katulwende; *Winter Ridge: A Love Story*, by Bruce Kellner.

How to Contact Query through online submission form. Responds to queries in 3 months. Terms Pays 10% royalty of the selling price of each book copy sold.

⬡ ⬚ MONSOON BOOKS

52 Telok Blangah Road, #03-05 Telok Blangah House, 098829 Singapore. (+65)63776272. Fax: (+65)62761743. E-mail: sales@monsoonbooks.com.sg. Website: www.monsoonbooks.com.sg. **Contact:** Philip Tatham (all fiction). Estab. 2002. "Monsoon Books is an independent publisher of fiction and nonfiction with Asian themes, based in Singapore with worldwide distribution." Publishes paperback originals, paperback reprints. Books: Mungken 80 gram paper; offset printing; threadsewn binding. Average print order: 3,000. First novel print order: 3,000. **Published 7 new writers last year**. Plans 10 first novels this year. Averages 20 total titles/year; 12 fiction titles/year. Distributes titles through Worldwide Distribution and promotes through Freelance Publicists for USA and Asia.

Needs erotica, ethnic/multicultural, family saga, gay, historical, horror (supernatural), humor satire, literary, mainstream, military/war, mystery/suspense (police procedural, private eye/hard-boiled), regional (Asia), thriller/espionage, translations, young adult (romance). Special interests: Southeast Asia. Published *Rouge Raider*, by Nigel Barley (historical fiction); *Straights and Narrow*, by Grace McClurg (thriller); *Private Dancer*, by Stephen Leather (general fiction/international relationships).

How to Contact Query with outline/synopsis and submit complete ms with cover letter. Accepts queries by snail mail, fax and e-mail. Please include estimated word count, brief bio, list of publishing credits, and list of three comparative titles. Send SASE or IRC for return of ms. Agented fiction 20%. Responds in 1 week to queries; 12 weeks to manuscripts. Accepts simultaneous submissions, submissions on CD or disk. Rarely comments on rejected manuscripts.

Terms Pays 7-10% royalty. Advance is negotiable. Publishes ms 6-12 months after acceptance. Guidelines online.

⬚ ◉ MOODY PUBLISHERS

Moody Bible Institute, 820 N. LaSalle Blvd., Chicago IL 60610. E-mail: acquisitions@moody.edu. **Contact:** Acquistions Coordinator (fiction only). Estab. 1894. Small, evangelical Christian publisher. "We publish fiction that reflects and supports our evangelical worldview and mission." Publishes hardcover, trade and mass market paperback originals. Averages 70 total titles, 10-12 fiction titles/year. Member, CBA. Distributes and promotes titles through sales reps, print advertising, promotional events, Internet, etc.

Needs Contemporary, historical, literary, mystery, suspense, science fiction. Recently published *My Hands Came Away Red*, by Lisa McKay (suspense novel); *Feeling for Bones*, by Bethany Pierce (contemporary/literary).

How to Contact Accepts unsolicited fiction mss. proposal with SASE and two chapters. Accepts queries by mail only (no electronic submissions). Include estimated word count, brief bio, list of publishing credits. Send SASE for return of ms or send a disposable ms and SASE for reply only. Agented fiction 75%. Responds in 4-5 months to queries. Accepts electronic submissions.

Terms Royalty varies. Average advance: $1,000-10,000. Publishes ms 9-12 months after acceptance. Ms guidelines for SASE and on Web site.

⊠ MOUNTAINLAND PUBLISHING, INC

P.O. Box 150891, Ogden UT 84415. (801)475-4387. E-mail: editor@mountainlandpublishing.com. Website: http://www.mountainlandpublishing.com. **Contact:** Michael Combs, Managing Editor. Estab. 2001. Publishes paperback originals, e-books. Published 50% new writers last year. Averages 6-10 total titles/year.

Needs adventure, fantasy, historical, horror, humor, juvenile, literary, mainstream, military/war, multicultural, mystery, regional, religious, romance, science fiction, short story collections, suspense, western, young adult.

How to Contact Query with outline/synopsis and 1 sample chapter. Include SASE. Considers simultaneous submissions.

Terms Manuscript published 3 months after acceptance. Pays royalties.

NBM PUBLISHING

40 Exchange Pl., Ste. 1308, New York NY 10005. Website: www.nbmpub.com. **Contact:** Terry Nantier, editor/art director. Estab. 1976. "One of the best regarded quality graphic novel publishers. Our catalog is determined by what will appeal to a wide audience of readers." Publishes hardcover originals, paperback originals. Format: offset printing; perfect binding. Average print order: 3,000-4,000; average debut writer's print order: 2,000. Publishes 1-2 debut writers/year. Publishes 30 titles/year. Member: PMA, CBC. Distributed/promoted "ourselves." Imprints: ComicsLit (literary comics), Eurotica (erotic comics).

Needs Literary fiction mostly, children's/juvenile (especially fairy tales, classics), creative nonfiction (especially true crime), erotica, ethnic/multicultural, humor (satire), manga, mystery/suspense, translations, young adult/teen. Does not want superhero or overly violent comics.

How to Contact Prefers submissions from writer-artists, creative teams. Send a one-page synopsis of story along with a few pages of comics (copies NOT originals) and a SASE. Attends San Diego Comicon. Agented submissions: 2%. Responds to queries in 1 week; to ms/art packages in 3-4 weeks. Sometimes comments on rejected manuscripts.

Terms Royalties and advance negotiable. Publishes ms 6 months to 1 year after acceptance. Writer's guidelines on Web site. Artist's guidelines on Web site. Book catalog free upon request.

THOMAS NELSON, INC.

Box 141000, Nashville TN 37214-1000. (615)889-9000. Website: www.thomasnelson.com. **Contact:** Acquisitions Editor. "Largest Christian book publishers." Publishes hardcover and paperback orginals. Averages 75 total titles/year.

Needs Publishes commercial fiction authors who write for adults and teens 12 and up from a Christian worldview. Published The Yada Yada Prayer Group Series by Neta Jackson, *Hood* by Stephen Lawhead, *Sinner* by Ted Dekker, *The Convenient Groom* by Denise Hunter, *Plain Perfect* by Beth Wiseman, *and The Inheritance* by Tamara Alexander.

How to Contact Does not accept unsolicited mss or queries.

Terms Pays royalty on net receipts. Rates negotiated for each project. Offers advance. Publishes ms 1-2 years after acceptance. Ms guidelines online.

NEWEST PUBLISHERS LTD.

201, 8540 109 St., Edmonton AB T6G 1E6 Canada. (780) 432-9427. Fax: (780) 433-3179. E-mail: info@ newestpress.com. Website: www.newestpress.com. **Contact:** Lou Morin, General Manager. Estab. 1977. Publishes trade paperback originals. **Published some debut authors within the last year.** Averages 11-14 total titles/year. Promotes titles through Facebook, audio files, online networking, newsletters, book launches, media interviews, review copy mailings.

Imprints Prairie Play Series (drama); Writer as Critic (literary criticisim); Nunatak First Fiction.

Needs Literary. "Our press is interested in Canadian fiction, mysteries, poetry and drama, and non-fiction with a Western Canadian focus." Published *Icefields,* by Thomas Wharton (novel); *Blood Relations and Other Plays,* by Sharon Pollock (drama); *A Hummingbird Dance,* by Garry Ryan (mystery).

How to Contact Accepts unsolicited mss. Submit complete ms. Send SASE or IRC. Responds in 9-12 months to queries. Accepts simultaneous submissions.

Terms Pays 10% royalty. Publishes ms 24-30 months after acceptance. Book catalog for 9 × 12 SASE. Ms guidelines online.

NEW ISSUES POETRY & PROSE

Western Michigan University, 1903 W. Michigan Ave., Kalamazoo MI 49008-5463. (269)387-8185. Fax: (269)387-2562. E-mail: new-issues@wmich.edu. Website: wmich.edu/newissues. Estab. 1996. Publishes hardcover originals and trade paperback originals. Averages 8 titles/year. Has recently published The Truth, by Geoff Rips; One Tribe, by M. Evelina Galang.

Needs literary, poetry, translations.

How to Contact Query first. All unsolicited mss returned unopened. 50% of books published are by first time authors. Agented submissions: less than 5%. Responds to mss in 6 months.

Terms Pays 10-12% royalty on wholesale price. Manuscript published 18 months after acceptance. Accepts simultaneous submissions. Writer's guidelines by SASE, e-mail, or online.

☑ ◎ ☑ NEW VICTORIA PUBLISHERS

P.O. Box 13173, Chicago IL 60613-0173. (800)326-5297. E-mail: queries@NewVictoria.com. Website: www.newvictoria.com. **Contact:** Patricia Feuerhaken, president. Estab. 1976. "Publishes mostly lesbian fiction—strong female protagonists. Most well known for Stoner McTavish mystery series." Publishes trade paperback originals. Averages 2-3 total titles/year. Distributes titles through Amazon Books, Bella books, Bulldog Books (Sydney, Australia), and Women and Children First Books (Chicago). Promotes titles "mostly through lesbian feminist media."

• *Mommy Deadest*, by Jean Marcy, won the Lambda Literary Award for Mystery.

Needs Lesbian, feminist fiction including adventure, erotica, fantasy, historical, humor, mystery (amateur sleuth), or science fiction. "Looking for strong feminist, well drawn characters, with a strong plot and action. We will consider any original, well written piece that appeals to the lesbian/feminist audience." Publishes anthologies or special editions. Published *Sparkling rain*, by Barbara Summerhawk and Kimberly Hughes (2008); *Killing at the Cat*, by Carlene Miller (mystery); *Queer Japan*, by Barbara Summerhawk (anthology); *Skin to Skin*, by Martha Miller (erotic short fiction); *Talk Show*, by Melissa Hartman (novel); *Flight from Chador*, by Sigrid Brunel (adventure); *Owl of the Desert*, by Ida Swearingen (novel).

How to Contact Accepts unsolicited mss, but prefers query first. Submit outline, synopsis, and sample chapters (50 pages). No queries by e-mail or fax; please send SASE or IRC. No simultaneous submissions.

Terms Pays 10% royalty. Publishes ms 1 year after acceptance. Ms guidelines for SASE.

☑ W.W. NORTON CO., INC.

500 Fifth Ave., New York NY 10110. (212)354-5500. Fax: (212)869-0856. E-mail: manuscripts@wwnorton. com. Website: www.wwnorton.com. **Contact:** Acquisitions editor. Midsize independent publisher of trade books and college textbooks. Publishes literary fiction. Estab. 1923. Publishes hardcover and paperback originals and reprints. Averages 300 total titles/year.

Needs Literary, poetry, poetry in translation, religious. High-qulity literary fiction. Published *Ship Fever*, by Andrea Barrett; *Oyster,* by Jannette Turner Hospital; *Power,* by Linda Hogan.

How to Contact Does not accept unagented submissions. If you would like to submit your proposal (6 pages or less) by e-mail, paste the text of your query letter and/or sample chapter into the body of the e-mail message. Do not send attachments. Responds in 2 months to queries. No simultaneous submissions.

Terms Pays royalty. Offers advance. Ms guidelines online.

☐ ☑ OAK TREE PRESS

140 E. Palmer St., Taylorville IL 62568. (217)824-6500. Fax: (217)824-2040. E-mail: oaktreepub@aol. com. Website: www.oaktreebooks.com. **Contact:** Billie Johnson, publisher (mysteries, romance, nonfiction); Sarah Wasson, acquisitions editor (all); Barbara Hoffman, senior editor (children's, young adult, educational). Estab. 1998. "Small independent publisher with a philosophy of author advocacy. Welcomes first-time authors, and sponsors annual contests in which the winning entries are published." Publishes hardcover, trade paperback and mass market paperback originals and reprints. Books: acid-free paper; perfect binding. First novel print order: 1,000. **Published 5 debut authors within the last year.** Plans 8 first novels this year. Averages 12 total titles, 8 fiction titles/year. Member: SPAN, SPAWN. Distributes through Ingram, Baker & Taylor and Amazon.com. Promotes through Web site, conferences, PR, author tours.

• *Affinity for Murder*, by Anne White, was an Agatha Award finalist.*Timeless Love*, by Mary Montague Sikes, received a Prism Award.

Imprints Oak Tree Press, Dark Oak Mysteries, Timeless Love, Coptales, Acorn Books for Children (children's, YA).

Needs Adventure, confession, ethnic, fantasy (romance), feminist, humor, mainstream/contemporary, mystery (amateur sleuth, cozy, police procedural, private eye/hard-boiled), new age/mystic, picture books, romance (contemporary, futuristic/time travel, romantic suspense), suspense, thriller/espionage, young adult (adventure, mystery/suspense, romance). Emphasis on mystery and romance novels. Recently published *The Poetry of Murder*, by Bernadette Steele (mystery); *Media Blitz*, by Joe Nowlan(mystery); *Lake Meade*, by Heather Mosko (romance); *Secrets by the Sea*, by Mary Montague Sikes (paranormal romance); *Easy Money,* by Norm Maher (memoir-police officer), and *The Last Stop: Lincoln and the Mud Circuit*, by Alan Bower (history).

How to Contact Does not accept or return unsolicited mss. Query with SASE. Accepts queries by e-mail. Include estimated word count, brief bio, list of publishing credits, brief description of ms. Send SASE for return of ms or send a disposable ms and SASE for reply only. Agented fiction 5%. Responds in 4-6 weeks to queries; 2 months to proposals; 3-6 months to mss. Accepts simultaneous submissions, electronic submissions. No submissions on disk. Rarely comments on rejected mss.

Terms Pays 10-20% royalty on wholesale price. Average advance: negotiable. Publishes ms 9-18 months after acceptance. Book catalog for SASE or on Web site www.oaktreebooks.com. Ms guidelines for SASE or on Web site.

☒ ☑ ☒ OBRAKE BOOKS

Obrake Canada, Inc., 3401 Dufferin Street, P.O. Box 27538, Toronto, ON M6Λ3B8. Fax: (416) 907-5734. E-mail: editors@obrake.com. Website: www.obrake.com. **Contact:** Echez Godoy, acquisitions editor (fiction-suspense, thriller, multicultural, science fiction, literary, romance, short story collection, mystery, ethnic, African based novels, African American characters and interest). Estab. 2006. "We're a small independent publisher of hardcover and trade-paper fiction and nonfiction books. We publish mainly thriller, suspense, romance, mystery, multicutural, and ethnic novels and short story collections." Publishes hardcover originals, paperback originals, paperback reprints. Average print order: 1,500. Debut novel print order: 1,500. **Published 1 new writer last year.** Plans 3 debut novels this year. Averages 10 total titles/year; 7 fiction titles/year. Member Independent Publishers Association PMA (USA), Canadian Booksellers Association (CBA), Book Promoters Association of Canada (BPAC). Distributes/promotes titles through national distributors in USA and Canada, Library Suppliers/Buyers, Chain bookstores (e.g. Barnes and Nobles [USA], Chapters/Indigo Bookstore [Canada]), Indigo Books & Music, Online (Amazon), worldwide distribution.

Needs Adventure, children's/juvenile (adventure, fantasy, historical, mystery), comics/graphic novels, erotica, ethnic/multicultural, feminist, gay, historical (general), horror (psychological, supernatural), lesbian, literary, mainstream, mystery/suspense, psychic/supernatural, regional, religious (mystery/suspense, thriller, romance), romance (contemporary, historical, romantic suspense), short story collections, thriller/espionage, young adult/teen (adventure, fantasy/science fiction, historical, horror, romance). Published *Corrupted Ambition*, by Obi Orakwue (thriller/suspense); *The Terrorist Creed*, by Obi Orakwue (suspense); *Overqualified Labourer*, by Obi Orakwue (mystery).

How to Contact Send query letter. Query with outline/synopsis and 3 sample chapters, 50 pages max. Accepts queries by snail mail, e-mail. Include estimated word count, brief bio. Send SASE or IRC for return of ms or disposable copy of ms and SASE/IRC for reply only. Agented fiction: 5%. Responds to queries in 3-6 weeks. Accepts unsolicited mss. Considers simultaneous submissions, submissions on CD or disk. Rarely critiques/comments on rejected mss. Responds to mss in 3-6 months.

Terms Sends pre-production galleys to author. Ms published 10 months after acceptance. Writer's guidelines available for SASE, on Web site. Pays royalties 8-15%, advance $350 average. Book catalogs free upon request.

☒ ☐ ☒ ORCA BOOK PUBLISHERS

P.O. Box 5626, Victoria BC V8R 6S4 Canada. (250)380-1229. Fax: (250)380-1892. E-mail: orca@orcabook.com. Website: www.orcabook.com. **Contact:** Christi Howes, editor (picture books); Sarah Harvey, editor (young readers); Andrew Wooldridge, editor (juvenile fiction, teen fiction); Bob Tyrrell, publisher (YA, teen). Estab. 1984. Only publishes Canadian authors. Publishes hardcover and trade paperback originals, and mass market paperback originals and reprints. Books: quality 60 lb. book stock paper; illustrations. Average print order: 3,000-5,000. First novel print order: 3,000-5,000. Averages 30 total titles/year.

Needs Hi-lo, juvenile (5-9 years), literary, mainstream/contemporary, young adult (10-18 years). "Ask for guidelines, find out what we publish." Looking for "children's fiction."

How to Contact Query with SASE, or submit proposal package including outline, 2-5 sample chapter(s), synopsis, SASE. Agented fiction 20%. Responds in 1 month to queries; 1-2 months to mss. No simultaneous submissions. Sometimes comments on rejected mss.

Terms Pays 10% royalty. Publishes ms 12-18 months after acceptance. Book catalog for 8½ × 11 SASE. Ms guidelines online.

☒ OUTRIDER PRESS, INC.

2036 North Winds Drive, Dyer IN 46311. (219)322-7270. Fax: (219)322-7085. E-mail: outriderpress@

sbcglobal.net. Website: www.outriderpress.com. **Contact:** Whitney Scott, editor. Estab. 1988. Small literary press and hand bindery; publishes many first-time authors. Publishes paperback originals. Books: 70 lb. paper; offset printing; perfect bound. Average print order: 2,000. **Published 25-30 debut authors within the last year.** Distributes titles through Baker & Taylor.

• Was a *Small Press Review* "Pick" for 2000.

Needs Ethnic, experimental, family saga, fantasy (space fantasy, sword and sorcery), feminist, gay/ lesbian, historical, horror (psychological, supernatural), humor, lesbian, literary, mainstream/ contemporary, mystery (amateur slueth, cozy, police procedural, private eye/hard-boiled), new age/ mystic, psychic/supernatural, romance (contemporary, futuristic/time travel, gothic, historical, regency period, romantic suspense), science *fiction (soft/sociological), short story collections, thriller/espionage, western (frontier saga, traditional). Published Telling Time*, by Cherie Caswell Dost; *If Ever I Cease to Love*, by Robert Klein Engler; *62000 Reasons*, by Paul Miller; *Aquarium Octopus*, by Claudia Van Gerven; and *Heat*, by Deborah Thompson.

How to Contact Accepts unsolicited mss. Query with SASE. Accepts queries by mail. Include estimated word count, brief bio, list of publishing credits. Agented fiction 10%. Responds in 6 weeks to queries; 4 months to mss. Accepts simultaneous submissions, electronic submissions, submissions on disk. Sometimes comments on rejected mss. In affiliation with Tallgrass Writers Guild, publishes an annual anthonlogy with cash prizes. 2010 anthology theme is: "'The Changing Seasons.' As always, broadly interpreted with a variety of historic/geographic settings welcomed." Deadline is February 27, 2010. For details and complete guidelines, e-mail outriderpress@sbcglobal.net.

Terms Pays honorarium. Publishes ms 6 months after acceptance. Ms guidelines for SASE.

PANTHEON BOOKS

Knopf Publishing Group, Random House, Inc., 1745 Broadway, 3rd Floor, New York NY 10019. (212)751-2600. Fax: (212)572-6030. Website: www.pantheonbooks.com. **Contact:** Adult Editorial Department. Estab. 1942. "Small but well-established imprint of well-known larger house." Publishes hardcover and trade paperback originals and trade paperback reprints.

Needs Quality fiction and nonfiction. Published *Crooked Little Heart*, Anne Lamott.

How to Contact Does not accept unsolicited mss. Send SASE or IRC. No simultaneous submissions.

Terms Pays royalty. Offers advance.

☑ PATHWISE PRESS

2311 Broadway St., New Orleans, LA 70125. E-mail: pathwisepress@hotmail.com. Website: www. pathwisepress.com. **Contact:** Christopher Harter. Estab. 1997. Small independent publisher interested in work that is neither academic or Bukowski. "We publish chapbooks only." Publishes paperback originals. Books: 20 lb. white linen paper; laser printing; saddle-stitch bound; illustrations. Average print order: 200-300.

Needs Experimental, literary, short story collections.

How to Contact "Pathwise Press currently on hiatus. Interested parties should e-mail or check Web site for updates."

Terms Pays 10-20% royalty. Publishes ms 6 months after acceptance. Ms guidelines online.

☑ PAYCOCK PRESS

3819 No. 13th St., Arlington VA 22201. (703)525-9296. E-mail: hedgehog2@erols.com. Website: www. gargoylemagazine.com. **Contact:** Lucinda Ebersole and Richard Peabody. Estab. 1976. "Too academic for underground, too outlaw for the academic world. We tend to be edgy and look for ultra-literary work." Publishes paperback originals. Books: POD printing. Average print order: 500. Averages 1 total title/year. Member CLMP. Distributes through Amazon and Web site.

Needs Experimental, literary, short story collections.

How to Contact Accepts unsolicited mss. Accepts queries by e-mail. Include brief bio. Send SASE for return of ms or send a disposable ms and SASE for reply only. Agented fiction 5%. Responds in 1 month to queries; 4 months to mss. Accepts simultaneous submissions, electronic submissions. Rarely comments on rejected mss.

Terms Publishes ms 12 months after acceptance.

☑ ◎ PEACHTREE CHILDREN'S BOOKS

Peachtree Publishers, Ltd., 1700 Chattahoochee Avenue, Atlanta GA 30318-2112. (404) 876-8761. Fax: (404) 875-2578. E-mail: hello@peachtree-online.com. Website: www.peachtree-online.com. **Contact:** Helen Harriss, acquisitions editor. "We publish a broad range of subjects and perspectives, with emphasis on innovative plots and strong writing." Publishes hardcover and trade paperback originals. Averages 30 total titles, 20-25 fiction titles/year.

Needs Juvenile, picture books, young adult. Looking for very well written middle grade and young adult novels. No adult fiction. No short stories. Published *Martina the Beautiful Cockroach, Night of the Spadefoot Toads, The Boy Who Was Raised by Librarians*.

How to Contact Submit 3 sample chapter(s) or submit complete ms. Responds in 6 months to queries; 6 months to mss. Accepts simultaneous submissions.

Terms Pays royalty on retail price; advance varies. Publishes ms 1 year or more after acceptance. Book catalog for 6 first-class stamps. Ms guidelines online.

◎ PEACHTREE PUBLISHERS, LTD.

1700 Chattahoochee Ave., Atlanta GA 30318-2112. (404)876-8761. Fax: (404)875-2578. E-mail: hello@peachtree-online.com. Website: www.peachtree-online.com. **Acquisitions:** Helen Harriss. Publishes 30-35 titles/year.

Needs Picture books, young readers: adventure, animal, concept, history, nature/environment. Middle readers: adventure, animal, history, nature/environment, sports. Young adults: fiction, mystery, adventure. Does not want to see science fiction, romance.

How to Contact Submit complete ms (picture books) or 3 sample chapters (chapter books) by postal mail only. Responds to queries/mss in 6-7 months. Publishes a book 1-2 years after acceptance. Will consider simultaneous submissions.

Terms "Manuscript guidelines for SASE, visit Web site or call for a recorded message. No fax or e-mail submittals or queries please."

☒ ⊘ ◎ PEDLAR PRESS

P.O. Box 26, Station P, Toronto ON M5S 2S6 Canada. (416) 534-2011. E-mail: feralgrl@interlog.com. **Contact:** Beth Follett, owner/editor. Publishes hardcover and trade paperback originals. **Published 50% debut authors within the last year.** Averages 7 total titles/year. Distributes in Canada through LitDistCo.; in the US distributes directly through publisher.

Needs Experimental, feminist, gay/lesbian, literary, picture books, short story collections. Canadian writers only. Published Black Stars in a White Night Sky, by Jonarno Lawson, illustrated by Sherwin Tjia.

How to Contact Query with SASE, sample chapter(s), synopsis.

Terms Pays 10% royalty on retail price. Average advance: $200-400. Publishes ms 1 year after acceptance. Ms guidelines for #10 SASE.

☑ ◎ ☒ PELICAN PUBLISHING CO.

1000 Burmaster St., Gretna LA 70053. (504)368-1175. Website: www.pelicanpub.com. **Contact:** Nina Kooij, editor-in-chief. Estab. 1926. "We seek writers on the cutting edge of ideas. We believe ideas have consequences. One of the consequences is that they lead to a best-selling book." Publishes hardcover, trade paperback and mass market paperback originals and reprints. Books: hardcover and paperback binding; illustrations sometimes. Buys juvenile mss with illustrations. Averages 65 total titles/year. Distributes titles internationally through distributors, bookstores, libraries. Promotes titles at reading and book conventions, in trade magazines, in radio interviews, print reviews and TV interviews.

• *The Warlord's Puzzle*, by Virginia Walton Pilegard, was #2 on *Independent Bookseller's Book Sense 76* list.

Needs Considers picture books for young readers or Louisiana historical middle-grade novels.

How to Contact Does not accept unsolicited mss except for picture books (1,100 words). For Louisiana historical middle-grade novels, submit outline, 2 sample chapters. Responds in 1 month to queries; 3 months to mss. No simultaneous or multiple submissions. Rarely comments on rejected mss.

Terms Pays royalty on actual receipts. Average advance: considered. Publishes ms 9-18 months after acceptance. Book catalog for SASE or on Web site. Writer's guidelines for SASE or on Web site.

⬍ ☑ ◎ PEMMICAN PUBLICATIONS

150 Henry Ave., Main Floor RM 12, Winnipeg MB R3B 0J7 Canada. (204) 589-6346. Fax: (204) 589-2063. E-mail: rmcilroy@pemmican.mbc.ca. Website: www.pemmican.mb.ca. **Contact:** Randal McIlroy, managing editor. Estab. 1980. Metis adult and children's books. Publishes paperback originals. Books: stapled-bound smaller books and perfect-bound larger ones; 4-color illustrations, where applicable. Average print order: 1,500. First novel print order: 1,000. **Published some debut authors within the last year.** Averages 6 total titles/year. Distributes titles through press releases, Web site, fax, catalogues, and book displays.

Needs Stories by and about the Canadian Metis experience, especially from a modern adult or young-adult perspective. Recently published *Cries from a Metis Heart,* by Lorraine Mayer (adult non-fiction); *Goose Girl,* by Joe and Matrine McClellan(children's fiction); and *The Bannock Book,* by Linda Ducharme (children's fiction).

How to Contact Accepts unsolicited mss by conventional mail only. Submit samples and synopsis. Send SASE for return of ms or send a disposable ms and SASE for reply only. Return postage for outside of Canada must be provided in IRC's. Accepts simultaneous submissions.

Terms Pays 10% royalty. Provides 10 author's copies. Average advance: $350.

☑ PENGUIN GROUP USA

375 Hudson St., New York NY 10014. (212)366-2000. Website: www.penguin.com. "The company possesses perhaps the world's most prestigious list of best-selling authors and a backlist of unparalleled breadth, depth and quality." General interest publisher of both fiction and nonfiction.

Imprints Viking (hardcover); Dutton (hardcover); The Penguin Press (hardcover); Daw (hardcover and paperback); G P Putnam's Sons (hardcover and children's); Riverhead Books (hardcover and paperback); Tarcher (hardcover and paperback); Grosset/Putnam (hardcover); Putnam (hardcover); Avery; Viking Compass (hardcover); Penguin (paperback); Penguin Classics (paperback); Plume (paperback); Signet (paperback); Signet classics (paperback); Onyx (paperback); Roc (paperback); Topaz (paperback); Mentor (paperback); Meridian (paperback); Berkley Books (paperback); Jove (paperback); Ace (paperback); Prime Crime (paperback); HPBooks (paperback); Penguin Compass (paperback); Dial Books for Young Readers (children's); Dutton Children's Books (children's); Viking Children's Books (children's); Puffin (children's); Frederick Warne (children's); Philomel Books (children's); Grosset and Dunlap (children's); Wee Sing (children's); PaperStar (children's); Planet Dexter (children's); Berkely (hardcover); Gothom (hardcover and paperback); Portfolio (hard and paperback); NAL (hardcover).

How to Contact "Due to the high volume of manuscripts we receive, Penguin Group (USA) Inc. imprints do not normally accept unsolicited manuscripts. On rare occasion, however, a particular imprint may be open to reading such. The Penguin Group (USA) web site features a listing of which imprints (if any) are currently accepting unsolicited manuscripts." Continue to check Web site for updates to the list.

Terms Pays advance and royalties, depending on imprint.

☑ THE PERMANENT PRESS/SECOND CHANCE PRESS

4170 Noyac Rd., Sag Harbor NY 11963. (631)725-1101. Fax: (631)725-8215. Website: www.thepermanentpress.com. **Contact:** Judith and Martin Shepard, publishers. Estab. 1978. Mid-size, independent publisher of literary fiction. "We keep titles in print and are active in selling subsidiary rights." Publishes hardcover originals. Average print order: 1,500. Averages 12 total titles, 11 fiction titles/year. Distributes titles through Baker & Taylor and Brodart. Promotes titles through reviews.

Needs Literary, mainstream/contemporary, mystery. Especially looking for high-line literary fiction, "artful, original and arresting." Accepts any fiction category as long as it is a "well-written, original full-length novel." Published *The Last Refuge, Two Time and Head Wounds* by Chris Knopf; *The Contractor,* by Charles Holdefer; *The Night Battles* by M.F. Bloxam; *A Richer Dust* by Amy Boaz.

How to Contact Accepts unsolicited mss. Send SASE for return of ms or send a disposable ms and SASE for reply only. Responds in 12 weeks to queries; 8 months to mss. Accepts simultaneous submissions.

Terms Pays 10-15% royalty on wholesale price. Offers $1,000 advance for Permanent Press books; royalty only on Second Chance Press titles. Publishes ms 18 months after acceptance. Ms guidelines for #10 SASE.

🌐 ◎ DAVID PHILIP PUBLISHERS

P.O. Box 46962, Glosderry 7702 South Africa. Fax: (+21)6743358. Website: www.newafricabooks.co.za.

Needs "Fiction with southern African concern or focus. Progressive, often suitable for school or university prescription, literary, serious but wtih commercial potential."

How to Contact Submit 1 sample chapter(s), detailed synopsis and letter of motivation.

Terms Pays royalty. Write for guidelines.

☑ PHILOMEL BOOKS

Penguin Putnam Inc., 345 Hudson St., New York NY 10014. (212)414-3610. **Contact**: Patricia Lee Gauch, editor-at-large; Michael Green, vice president and publisher. Estab. 1980. "A high-quality oriented imprint focused on stimulating picture books, middle-grade novels and young adult novels." Publishes hardcover originals. Averages 20-25 total titles/year.

Needs Adventure, ethnic, family saga, fantasy, historical, juvenile (5-9 years), literary, picture books, regional, short story collections, western (young adult), young adult (10-18 years). Children's picture books (ages 3-8); middle-grade fiction and illustrated chapter books (ages 7-10); young adult novels (ages 10-15). Particularly interested in picture book mss with original stories and regional fiction with a distinct voice. Looking for "story-driven novels with a strong cultural voice but which speak universally." Published *The Big Field*, by Mike Lupica; *Ranger's Apprentice*, by John Flanagan; *The Book Eating Boy*, by Oliver Jeffers.

How to Contact Does not accept unsolicited mss. Query with SASE or submit outline, 3 sample chapter(s), synopsis. Send SASE or IRC. Agented fiction 40%. Responds in 3 months to queries; 4 months to mss. Accepts simultaneous submissions. Sometimes comments on rejected mss.

Terms Pays royalty. Also gives complimentary author's copies. Average advance: negotiable. Publishes ms 1-2 years after acceptance. Ms guidelines for #10 SASE.

▦ ◻ PIATKUS BOOKS

An imprint of Little, Brown Book Group, 100 Victoria Embankment, London England EC4Y 0DY United Kingdom. (+0)207 911 8000. Fax: (+02)07 911 8100. E-mail: info@piatkus.co.uk. Website: www.piatkus.co.uk. **Contact:** Emma Beswetherick, senior editor; Donna Condon, editor; Kim Mackay, editorial assistant. "Until 2007, Piatkus operated as an independent publishing house. Now it exists as a commercial imprint of Hachette-owned Little, Brown Book Group. The fiction list is highly commercial and includes women's fiction, crime, and thriller, general fiction, paranormal and historical romance, and some horror. Publishes hardcover originals, paperback originals, and paperback reprints.

Needs Quality women's fiction, family saga, historical, literary, mainstream/contemporary, mystery (amateur sleuth, police procedural, private eye/hard-boiled), regional, romance (contemporary, historical, regency period, romantic suspense, paranormal romance), thriller/espionage, horror. Bestselling authors include: Nora Roberts, JD Robb, Christina Jones, Julia Quinn, Nick Brownlee.

How to Contact Accepts unsolicited mss. Query with SASE or submit first 3 sample chapter(s), synopsis. Accepts queries by mail. Include estimated word count, brief bio, list of publishing credits. Send SASE for return of ms or send a disposable ms and SASE for reply only. Agented fiction 90%. Hopes to respond in 12 weeks to mss. Accepts simultaneous submissions. No submissions on disk or via e-mail. Rarely comments on rejected mss.

Terms Pays royalty. Average advance: negotiable. Publishes ms 1 year after acceptance. Ms guidelines for SASE.

▣ ☑ ▢ PICADOR USA

St. Martin's Press, 175 Fifth Ave., New York NY 10010. (212)674-5151. Website: www.picadorusa.com. **Contact:** Frances Coady, publisher (literary fiction); Joshua Kendall, associate editor (literary fiction); Sam Douglas, associate editor; David Rogers, assistant editor. Estab. 1994. Picador publishes high-quality literary fiction and nonfiction. "We are open to a broad range of subjects, well written by authoritative authors." Publishes hardcover and trade paperback originals and reprints. Averages 70-80 total titles/year. Titles distributed through Von Holtzbrinck Publishers. Titles promoted through national print advertising and bookstore co-op.

- *The Amazing Adventures of Kavalier & Clay*, by Michael Chabon, won the Pulitzer Prize for fiction; *In America*, by Susan Sontag, won National Book Award; Jame Crace's *Being Dead* won the National Book Critics Circle Award.

Needs Literary. Published *No One Thinks of Greenland*, by John Griesmer (first novel, literary); *Summerland*, by Malcolm Knox (first novel, literary fiction); *Half a Heart*, by Rosellen Brown (literary fiction).

How to Contact Does not accept unsolicited mss. *Agented submissions only.* Accepts queries by e-mail, fax, mail. Responds in 2 months to queries. Accepts simultaneous submissions.

Terms Pays 712-15% royalty on retail price. Average advance: varies. Publishes ms 18 months after acceptance. Book catalog for 9 × 12 SASE and $2.60 postage; ms guidelines for #10 SASE or online.

☑ PIÑATA BOOKS

Arte Publico Press, University of Houston, 452 Cullen Performance Hall, Houston TX 77204-2004. (713)743-2841. Fax: (713)743-3080. Website: www.latinoteca.com. **Contact:** Nicolas Kanellos, director. Estab. 1994. Piñata Books is dedicated to the publication of children's and young adult literature focusing on U.S. Hispanic culture by U.S. Hispanic authors. Publishes hardcover and trade paperback originals. **Published some debut authors within the last year.** Averages 10-15 total titles/year.

Needs Adventure, juvenile, picture books, young adult. Published *Trino's Choice*, by Diane Gonzales Bertrand (ages 11-up); *Delicious Hullabaloo/Pachanga Deliciosa*, by Pat Mora (picture book); and *The Year of Our Revolution*, by Judith Ortiz Cofer (young adult).

How to Contact Does not accept unsolicited mss. Query with SASE or submit 2 sample chapter(s), synopsis, SASE. Responds in 1 month to queries; 6 months to mss. Accepts simultaneous submissions.

Terms Pays 10% royalty on wholesale price. Average advance: $1,000-3,000. Publishes ms 2 years after acceptance. Book catalog and ms guidelines available via Web site or with #10 SASE.

☑ ◎ PINEAPPLE PRESS, INC.

P.O. Box 3889, Sarasota FL 34230. (941)739-2219. Fax: (941)739-2296. E-mail: info@pineapplepress.com. Website: www.pineapplepress.com. **Contact:** June Cussen, editor. Estab. 1982. Small independent trade publisher. Publishes hardcover and trade paperback originals. Books: quality paper; offset printing; Smyth-sewn or perfect bound; illustrations occasionally. Averages 25 total titles/year. Distributes titles through Pineapple, Ingram, and Baker & Taylor. Promotes titles through reviews, advertising in print media, direct mail, author signings, and the World Wide Web.

Needs Will only consider fiction set in Florida.

How to Contact Does not accept unsolicited mss. Query with sample, SASE. Responds in 2 months to queries. Accepts simultaneous submissions.

Terms Pays 6½-15% royalty on net receipts. Average advance: rare. Publishes ms 18 months after acceptance. Book catalog for 9 × 12 SAE with $1.34 postage.

▦ ◻ PIPERS' ASH, LTD.

Pipers' Ash, Church Rd., Christian Malford, Chippenham, Wiltshire SN15 4BW United Kingdom. (+44)1249 720 563. Fax: 0870 056 8917. E-mail: pipersash@supamasu.com. Website: www.supamasu.com. **Contact:** Manuscript Evaluation Desk. Estab. 1976. "Small press publisher. Considers all submitted manuscripts fairly—without bias or favor. This company is run by book lovers, not by accountants." Publishes hardcover and electronic originals. **Published 18 debut authors within the last year.** Averages 18 total titles, 18 fiction titles/year. Distributes and promotes titles through press releases, catalogues, Web site shopping basket, direct mail and the Internet.

Needs Adventure, children's/juvenile (adventure), confession, feminist, historical, literary, mainstream/contemporary, military/war, regional, religious, romance (contemporary, romantic suspense), science fiction (hard science/technological, soft/sociological), short story collections, sports, suspense, young adult (adventure,science fiction). "We publish 30,000-word novellas and short story collections. Visit our Web site for submission guidelines and tips. Authors are invited to submit collections of short stories and poetry for consideration for our ongoing programs." Published *Belly-Button Tales and Other Things*, by Sandra McTavish; *Cosmic Women*, by Margaret Karamazin; *A Sailor's Song*, by Leslie Wilkie.

How to Contact Accepts unsolicited mss. Query with SASE or IRC or submit sample chapter(s), 25-word synopsis (that sorts out the writers from the wafflers). Accepts queries by e-mail, fax, phone. Include estimated word count. Send SASE or IRC for return of ms or send a disposable ms and SASE or IRC for reply only. Responds in 1 month to queries; 3 months to mss. Accepts electronic submissions, submissions on disk. No simultaneous submissions. Always comments on rejected mss.

Terms Pays 10% royalty on wholesale price. Also gives 5 author's copies. Publishes ms 6 months after acceptance. Ms guidelines online, www.supumasu.com.

Ⓐ Ⓜ PLUME

Division of Penguin Putnam Inc., 375 Hudson St., New York NY 10014. (212)366-2000. Website: www. penguinputnam.com. **Contact:** Trena Keating, editor-in-chief/associate publisher (literary fiction). Estab. 1948. Publishes paperback originals and reprints. **Published some debut authors within the last year.**
Needs "All kinds of commercial and litearary fiction, including mainstream, historical, New Age, western, thriller, gay. Full length novels and collections." Published *Girl with a Pearl Earring*, by Tracy Chevalier; *Liar's Moon*, by Phillip Kimball; *The True History of Paradise*, by Margaret Cezain-Thompson.
How to Contact *Agented submissions only.* Accepts simultaneous submissions.
Terms Pays in royalties and author's copies. Offers advance. Publishes ms 12-18 months after acceptance. Book catalog for SASE.

Ⓒ POCOL PRESS

6023 Pocol Drive, Clifton VA 20124. (703) 830-5862. E-mail: chrisandtom@erols.com. Website: www. pocolpress.com. **Contact:** J. Thomas Hetrick, editor (baseball history and fiction). Pocol Press publishes first-time, unagented authors. Our fiction deals mainly with single author short story collections from outstanding niche writers. Publishes paperback originals. Books: 50 lb. paper; offset printing; perfect binding. Average print order: 500. **Published 2 debut authors within the last year.** Averages 4-6 total titles, 3 fiction titles/year. Member: Small Press Publishers Association. Distributes titles through Web site, authors, e-mail, word-of-mouth and readings.
Needs Horror (psychological, supernatural), literary, mainstream/contemporary, short story collections, baseball. Published *Believers*, by Nathan Leslie (short fiction); *A Collection of Friends*, by Thomas Sheehan (memoir); *Journeymen*, by Michael Rychlik (baseball fiction).
How to Contact Does not accept or return unsolicited mss. Query with SASE or submit 1 sample chapter(s). Accepts queries by mail. Include estimated word count, brief bio, list of publishing credits. Responds in 2 weeks to queries; 2 months to mss. No simultaneous submissions, submissions on disk. Sometimes comments on rejected mss.
Terms Pays 10-12% royalty. Publishes ms 1 year or less after acceptance. Book catalog for SASE or on Web site. Ms guidelines for SASE or on Web site.

Ⓒ Ⓞ Ⓥ POISONED PEN PRESS

6962 E. 1st Ave. #103, Scottsdale AZ 85251. (480) 945-3375. Fax: (480) 949-1707. E-mail: info@ poisonedpenpress.com. Website: www.poisonedpenpress.com. **Contact:** editor@poisonedpenpress.com (mystery, fiction). Estab. 1997. Publishes hardcover originals and paperback reprints. Books: 60 lb. paper; offset printing; hardcover binding. Average print order: 3,500. First novel print order: 3,000. **Published 4 debut authors within the last year.** Plans 5 first novels this year. Member Publishers Marketing Associations, Arizona Book Publishers Associations, Publishers Association of West. Distributes through Ingram, Baker & Taylor, Brodart.
 • Was nominated in 2002 for the LA Times Book Prize. Also the recipient of several Edgar and Agatha Awards.
Needs Mystery (amateur sleuth, cozy, police procedural, private eye/hard-boiled, historical). Published *Sweeping Up Glass*, by Carolyn D. Wall (mystery/fiction); *Impulse*, by Frederick Ramsay (mystery/ fiction); *Murder in the Dark*, by Kerry Greenwood(mystery/fiction); *Drive*, by James Sallis (mystery/ fiction).
How to Contact Accepts unsolicited mss. Electronic queries only. Accepts queries by e-mail to editor@ poisonedpenpress.com. Responds in 1-3 weeks to queries; 6-9 months to mss. Only accepts electronic submissions. No simultaneous submissions. Often comments on rejected mss.
Terms Pays 9-15% royalty. Average advance: $1,000. Publishes ms 12-15 months after acceptance. Ms guidelines online.

Ⓥ Ⓙ Ⓞ PRAIRIE JOURNAL PRESS

Prairie Journal Trust, P.O. Box 61203, Brentwood Postal Services, Calgary AB T2L 2K6 Canada. E-mail: prairiejournal@yahoo.com. Website: www.geocities.com/prairiejournal/. **Contact:** Anne Burke, literary editor. Estab. 1983. Small-press, noncommercial literary publisher. Publishes paperback originals. Books: bond paper; offset printing; stapled binding; b&w line drawings. **Published some debut authors within the last year.** Distributes titles by mail and in bookstores and libraries (public and university). Promotes titles through direct mail, reviews and in journals.

• Prairie Journal Press authors have been nominees for The Journey Prize in fiction and finalists and honorable mention for the National Magazine awards.

Needs Literary, short story collections. Published *Prairie Journal Fiction, Prairie Journal Fiction II* (anthologies of short stories); *Solstice* (short fiction on the theme of aging); and *Prairie Journal Prose.*

How to Contact Accepts unsolicited mss. Sometimes comments on rejected mss.

Terms Pays 1 author's copy; honorarium depends on grant/award provided by the government or private/corporate donations. SAE with IRC for individuals. No U.S. stamps please.

Ⓝ ☑ $ PS BOOKS

Philadelphia Stories, Inc., 2021 S. 11th St., Philadelphia PA 19148. (215)551-5889. Fax: (215)635-0195. E-mail: info@psbookspublishing.org. Website: www.psbookspublishing.org. **Contact:** Marc Schuster, editor. Estab. 2008. "In 2008, the publishers of Philadelphia Stories magazine launched a books division called PS Books. The needs of PS Books closely mirror those of the magazine; we are looking for novel-length fiction and narrative nonfiction manuscripts featuring polished prose, a controlled voice, strong characters, and interesting subjects. Please read our current titles to get a sense of what we publish. For information on submitting a query package, please visit our Web site." Publishes paperback originals. Format: cougar smooth paper;off-set commercial printing;perfect-bound. Average print order: 500-1,000. Debut novel print order: 500-1,000. Plans 1 debut novel this year. Averages 2 total titles/year; 1-2 fiction titles/year. Member CLMP. Distributes/promotes titles Baker & Taylor, direct marketing.

Needs Humor, Literary, Mainstream, Regional (Delaware valley, greater Philadelphia). Anthologies planned include *The Best of Philadelphia Stories, vol. 2*; *By Any Other Name.* Published *Broad Street*, by Christine Weiser (upmarket commercial fiction); *The Singular Exploits of Wonder Mom and Party Girl*, by Marc Schuster (literary fiction).

How to Contact Query with outline/synopsis and first 20 pages. Accepts queries by e-mail. Include estimated word count, brief bio, list of publishing credits.Send disposable copy of ms and SASE for reply only. Responds to queries in 2 months. No unsolicited mss. Considers simultaneous submissions, e-mail submissions. Rarely critiques/comments on rejected mss. Responds to mss in 3 months.

Terms Manuscript published within 1 year after acceptance.

☑ ◎ PUFFIN BOOKS

Penguin Group (USA), Inc., 345 Hudson St., New York NY 10014. (212)366-2000. Website: www.penguinputnam.com. **Contact:** Sharyn November, senior editor; Kristin Gilson, editorial director. Puffin Books publishes high-end trade paperbacks and paperback reprints for preschool children, beginning and middle readers, and young adults. Publishes trade paperback originals and reprints. Averages 175-200 total titles/year.

Needs Young adult, middle grade; easy-to-read grades 1-3. "We publish paperback reprints and original titles. We do not publish original picture books." Published *Three Cups of Tea, Young Readers Edition,* by Greg Mortenson and David Oliver Relin, adapted for young readers by Sarah Thomson.

How to Contact Does not accept unsolicited mss. Send SASE or IRC. Responds in 3 months to mss. No simultaneous submissions.

Terms Royalty varies. Average advance: varies. Publishes ms 1 year after acceptance. Book catalog for 9 × 12 SAE with 7 first-class stamps; send request to Marketing Department.

☐ ◎ ⊞ PUREPLAY PRESS

11353 Missouri Ave., Los Angeles CA 90025. (310)479-8773. Fax: (310)473-9384. E-mail: editor@pureplaypress.com. Website: www.pureplaypress.com. **Contact**: David Landau. "We are a small, niche publisher devoted to Cuba's history and culture. We publish high-quality books that people will want to read for years to come." Books are in English, Spanish and bilingual formats. Publishes hardcover and paperback originals. Ms guidelines online.

▣ G.P. PUTNAM'S SONS

Penguin Putnam Books For Young Readers, 345 Hudson St., New York NY 10014. (212)414-3610. Website: www.us.penguingroup.com. **Manuscript Acquisitions:** Susan Kochan, associate editorial director; John Rudolph, executive editor; Timothy Travaglini, senior editor; Stacey Barney, editor. **Art Acquisitions:** Cecilia Yung, art director, Putnam and Philomel. Publishes 25 picture books/year; 15 middle readers/year; 5 young adult titles/year. 5% of books by first-time authors; 50% of books from agented authors.

- G. Putnam's Sons 2007 titles *Slam*, by Nick Hornby and *The Three Snow Bears*, by Jan Brett were #1 on the New York Times Bestseller List.

Needs Juvenile picture books: animal, concept, contemporary, humor, multicultural. Young readers: adventure, contemporary, history, humor, multicultural, special needs, suspense/mystery. Middle readers: adventure, contemporary, history, humor, fantasy, multicultural, problem novels, sports, suspense/mystery. Young adults: contemporary, history, fantasy, problem novels, special needs. Does not want to see series. Average word length: picture books—200-1,000; middle readers—10,000-30,000; young adults—40,000-50,000. Recently published *Good Night, Goon: A Parody* by Michael Rex (ages 4-8); *Geek Magnet*, by Kieran Scott (ages 12 and up).

How to Contact Accepts unsolicited mss. No SASE required, as will only respond if interested. Picture books: send full mss. Fiction: Query with outline/synopsis and 10 manuscript pages. Do not send art unless requested. Responds to mss within 4 months if interested. Will consider simultaneous submissions.

Terms Pays authors royalty based on retail price. Sends prepublication galleys to authors.

☐ ◎ QUIXOTE PRESS

3544 Blakslee St., Wever IA 52658. (800)571-2665. Fax: (319)372-7485. **Contact:** Bruce Carlson, president. Quixote Press specializes in humorous and/or regional folklore and special-interest cookbooks. Publishes trade paperback originals and reprints. **Published many debut authors within the last year.**

Needs Humor, short story collections. Published *Eating Ohio*, by Rus Pishnery (short stories about Ohio); *Lil' Red Book of Fishing Tips*, by Tom Whitecloud (fishing tales); *How to Talk Hoosier*, by Netha Bell (humor); *Cow Whisperer*, by Skip Holmes (humor); *Flour Sack Bloomers*, by Lucy Fetterhoff (history).

How to Contact Query with SASE. Accepts simultaneous submissions.

Terms Pays 10% royalty on wholesale price. Publishes ms 1 year after acceptance.

▣ ◎ RANDOM HOUSE, INC.

Division of Bertelsmann Book Group, 1745 Broadway, New York NY 10013. (212)782-9000. Fax: (212)302-7985. E-mail: editor@randomhouse.com. Website: www.randomhouse.com. Estab. 1925. "Random House has long been committed to publishing the best literature by writers both in the United States and abroad."

Imprints Alfred A. Knopf; Anchor Books; Shaye Areheart Books; Ballantine Books; Bantam Hardcover; Bantam Mass Market; Bantam Trade Paperbacks; Bell Tower; Black Ink/Harlem Moon; Broadway; Clarkson Potter; Crown Books for Young Readers; Crown Publishers, Inc; Currency; Del Ray; Del Ray/Lucas; Delacorte; Dell; Dell Dragonfly; Dell Laurel-Leaf; Dell Yearling; Delta; The Dial Press; Domain; Doubleday; Doubleday Religion; Doubleday Graphic Novels; DTP; Everyman's Library; Fanfare; Fawcett; David Fickling Books; First Choice Chapter Books; Fodor's; Grammercy Book; Harmony Books; Island; Ivy; Knopf Books for Young Readers; Knopf Paperbacks; Library of Contemporary Thought; Main Street Books; The Modern Library; Nan A. Talese; One World; Pantheon Books; Picture Yearling; Presidio Press; Random House Children's Publishing; Random House Large Print Publishing; Shocken Books; Spectra; Strivers Row; Three Rivers Press; Times Books; Villard Books; Vintage Books; Wings Books.

Terms Pays royalty. Offers advance. Ms guidelines online.

▣ ◎ RANDOM HOUSE CHILDREN'S BOOKS

Division of Random House, Inc., 1745 Broadway, New York NY 10019. (212)782-9000. Fax: (212)782-9452. Website: www.randomhouse.com/kids. **Contact:** Kate Klimo, editorial director of Random House Golden Books Young Readers Group; Beverly Horowitz, editorial director for Knopf Delacorte Dell Young Readers Group; Heidi Kilgras, editorial director for Step Into Reading; Jennifer Dussling, senior director for Stepping Stone; Jim Thomas, senior editor (fantasy). Estab. 1925. "Producing books for preschool children through young adult readers, in all formats from board to activity books to picture books and novels, Random House Children's Books brings together world-famous franchise characters, multimillion-copy series and top-flight, award-winning authors and illustrators."

Imprints *For Knopf Delacorte Dell Young Readers Group*—Doubleday, Alfred A. Knopf, Crown, Delacorte Press, Wendy Lamb Books, David Fickling Books, Dragonfly Books, Yearling Books, Laurel-Leaf Books, Bantam, Swartz & Wade Books. *For Random House/Golden Books Young Readers Group*—Picturebacks, Beginner Books, Step Into Reading, Stepping Stone Books, Landmark Books, Disney Books for Young Readers, First Time Books, Sesame Workshop.

Needs "Random House publishes a select list of first chapter books and novels, with an emphasis on

fantasy and historical fiction." Chapter books, middle-grade readers, young adult.
How to Contact Does not accept unsolicited mss. *Agented submissions only.* Accepts simultaneous submissions.

⊠ RANDOM HOUSE TRADE PUBLISHING GROUP

Random House, Inc., 1745 Broadway, 17th Floor, New York NY 10019. (212)782-9000. Fax: (212)572-4960. Website: www.randomhouse.com. Estab. 1925. "The flagship imprint of Random House, Inc." Publishes hardcover and trade paperback books. Averages 120 total titles/year.
Imprints The Modern Library, Random House Trade Books, Random House Trade Paperbacks, Villard Books, Strivers Row, Ballantine Books, Dial Press, Spiegel and Grau, and Bantam Dell.
Needs Adventure, confession, experimental, fantasy, historical, horror, humor, mainstream/contemporary, mystery, suspense.
How to Contact *Agented submissions only.* Accepts simultaneous submissions.
Terms Pays royalty on retail price. Offers advance. Ms guidelines online.

▦ ▢ ◎ RANSOM PUBLISHING LTD.

51 Southgate Street, Winchester, SO23 9EH United Kingdom. (+44) 01962 862307. Fax: (+44) 05601 148881. E-mail: rebecca@ransom.co.uk. Website: www.ransom.co.uk. **Contact:** Jenny Ertle, editor; Rebecca Pash, Marketing Manager. Estab. 1995. Independent UK publisher with distribution in English speaking markets throughout the world. Specializes in books for reluctant and struggling readers. One of the few English language publishers to publish books with very high interest age and very low reading age. Has a developing list of children's books for home and school use. Specializes in phonics and general reading programs. Publishes paperback originals. **Published 5 debut authors within the last year.** Member BESA (UK), IPG (UK).
Needs Easy reading for young adults. Books for reluctant and struggling readers.
How to Contact Accepts unsolicited mss. Query with SASE or submit outline/proposal. Prefers queries by e-mail. Include estimated word count, brief bio, list of publishing credits. Responds in 3-4 weeks to queries. Accepts simultaneous submissions, electronic submissions, submissions on disk. Never comments on rejected mss.
Terms Pays 10% royalty on net receipts. Ms guidelines by e-mail.

▨ ☑ ◎ ⬚ RED DEER PRESS

195 Allstate Parkway, Markham, ON L3R 4TB Canada. (905)477-9700. Fax: (905)477-9179. E-mail: rdp@reddeerpress.com. Website: www.reddeerpress.com. **Contact:** Richard Dionne, publisher. Estab. 1975. Publishes young adult, adult non-fiction, science fiction, fantasy, and paperback originals "focusing on books by, about, or of interest to Canadians." Books: offset paper; offset printing; hardcover/perfect-bound. Average print order: 5,000. First novel print order: 2,500. Distributes titles in Canada and the US, the UK, Australia and New Zealand.
• Red Deer Press has received numerous honors and awards from the Book Publishers Association of Alberta, Canadian Children's Book Centre, the Governor General of Canada and the Writers Guild of Alberta.
Imprints Robert J Sawyer Books (Sci-fi), Flea Circus Books (fantasy).
Needs Young adult (juvenile and early reader), contemporary. No romance or horror. Published *A Fine Daughter*, by Catherine Simmons Niven (novel); *The Kappa Child*, by Hiromi Goto (novel); *The Dollinage*, by Martine Leavitt; and *The Game*, by Teresa Toten (nominated for the Governor General's Award); *The Drum Calls Softly*, by David Bouchard (Aboriginal Picture Book); *Egghead*, by Caroline Pignat (Novel); *Big Big Sky*, by Kristyn Dunnion (Novel).
How to Contact Accepts unsolicited mss. Query with SASE. Responds in 6 months to mss. Accepts simultaneous submissions. No submissions on disk.
Terms Pays 8-10% royalty. Advance is negotiable. Publishes ms 1 year after acceptance. Book catalog for 9 × 12 SASE.

RENAISSANCE HOUSE

465 Westview Ave, Englewood, NJ.07631. (800)547-5113. Website: www.renaissancehouse.net. **Contact:** Sam Laredo, publisher; Raquel Benatar, editor. Publishes hardcover and trade paperback originals. **Published 25-30% debut authors within the last year.** Averages 30 total titles/year.

Needs Fantasy, juvenile, multicultural, picture books, legends, fables. Recently published *Go, Milka, Go—Corre, Milka, Corre*, by Raquel Benatar.

How to Contact Query with SASE. Agented fiction 25%. Responds in 2 months to queries; 2 months to mss. Accepts simultaneous submissions.

Terms Pays 5-10% royalty on net receipts. Ms guidelines online.

☑ ☑ RIVER CITY PUBLISHING

River City Publishing, LLC, 1719 Mulberry St., Montgomery AL 36106. (334) 265-6753. Fax: (334) 265-8880. E-mail: jgilbert@rivercitypublishing.com. Website: www.rivercitypublishing.com. **Contact:** Jim Gilbert, editor. Estab. 1989. Midsize independent publisher (8-10 books per year). "We publish books of national appeal, with an emphasis on Southern writers and Southern stories." Publishes hardcover and trade paperback originals. Averages 6 total titles, 2 fiction titles/year.

- Had three nominees to *Foreword* fiction book of the year awards (2002); won Ippy for Short Fiction (2005).

Needs Literary fiction, narrative nonfiction, regional (southern), short story collections. No poetry, memoir, or children's books. Published *Murder Creek*, by Joe Formichella (true crime); *Breathing Out the Ghost*, by Kirk Curnutt (novel); *The Bear Bryant Funeral Train*, by Brad Vice (short story collection).

How to Contact Accepts unsolicited submissions and submissions from unagented authors, as well as those from established and agented writers. Submit 5 consecutive sample chapters or entire manuscript for review. "Please include a short biography that highlights any previous writing and publishing experience, sales opportunities the author could provide, ideas for marketing the book, and why you think the work would be appropriate for River City." Send appropriate-sized SASE or IRC, "otherwise, the material will be recycled." Also accepts queries by e-mail. "Please include your electronic query letter as inline text and not as an attachment; we do not open unsolicited attachments of any kind. Please do not include sample chapters or your entire manuscript as inline text. We do not field or accept queries by telephone." Agented fiction 25%. Responds in three to nine months; "please wait at least 3 months before contacting us about your submission." Accepts simultaneous submissions. No multiple submissions. Rarely comments on rejected mss.

Terms Pays 10-15% royalty on retail price. Average advance: $500-5,000. Publishes ms 1 year after acceptance.

Ⓝ ☑ ☑ RIVERHEAD BOOKS

Penguin Putnam, 375 Hudson Street, Office #4079, New York NY 10014.

Needs Literary, mainstream, contemporary. Among the award-winning writers whose careers Riverhead has launched so far are Pearl Abraham (*The Romance Reader*; *Giving Up America*), Jennifer Belle (*Going Down*; *High Maintenance)*, Adam Davies (*The Frog King*), Junot Diíaz (*Drown*), Alex Garland (*The Beach*; *The Tesseract*), Nick Hornby (*High Fidelity*; *About a Boy*; *How to Be Good*), Khaled Hosseini (*The Kite Runner*), ZZ Packer (*Drinking Coffee Elsewhere*), Iain Pears (*The Dream of Scipio*; *Instance of the Fingerpost*), Danzy Senna (*Caucasia*), Gary Shteyngart (*The Russian Debutante's Handbook*), Aryeh Lev Stollman (*The Far Euphrates*; *The Illuminated Soul*; *The Dialogues of Time and Entropy*), Sarah Waters (*Tipping the Velvet*; *Affinity*; *Fingersmith*).

How to Contact Submit through agent only. No unsolicited mss.

☑ ☑ ◎ RONSDALE PRESS

3350 W. 21st Ave., Vancouver BC V6S 1G7 Canada. (604) 738-4688. Fax: (604) 731-4548. E-mail: ronsdale@shaw.ca. Website: www.ronsdalepress.com. **Contact:** Ronald B. Hatch, president/editor; Veronica Hatch, editor (YA historical). Estab. 1988. Ronsdale Press is "dedicated to publishing books that give Canadians new insights into themselves and their country." Publishes trade paperback originals. Books: 60 lb. paper; photo offset printing; perfect binding. Average print order: 1,500. **Published some debut authors within the last year.** Averages 10 total titles, 3 fiction titles/year. Sales representation: Literary Press Group. Distribution: LitDistco. Promotes titles through ads in BC Bookworld and Globe & Mail and interviews on radio.

Needs Literary, short story collections, novels. Canadian authors *only*. Published *The City in the Egg*, by Michel Tremblay (novel); *Jackrabbit Moon*, by Sheila McLeod Arnopoulos (novel); and *What Belongs*, by F.B. André (short story collection).

How to Contact Accepts unsolicited mss. Accepts queries by e-mail. Send SASE or IRC. Responds in

2 weeks to queries; 2 months to mss. Accepts simultaneous submissions. Sometimes comments on rejected mss.

Terms Pays 10% royalty on retail price. Publishes ms 1 year after acceptance. Ms guidelines online.

☑ ☒ SAMHAIN PUBLISHING, LTD

577 Mulberry Street, Ste. 1520, Macon GA 31201. (478)314-5144. Fax: (478)314-5148. E-mail: books@ samhainpublishing.com. Website: www.samhainpublishing.com. **Contact:** Angela James, executive editor (fiction). Estab. 2005. "A small, independent publisher, Samhain's motto is 'It's all about the story.'We look for fresh, unique voices who have a story to share with the world. We encourage our authors to let their muse have its way and to create tales that don't always adhere to current trends. One never knows what the next 'hot genre' will be or when it will start, so write what's in your soul. These are the books that, whether the story is based on 'formula' or is an 'original,' when written from the heart will earn you a life-time readership." Publishes paperback originals, e-books. Format: POD/offset printing; line illustrations. **Published 20-30 new writers last year.** Plans 20 or more debut novels this year. Averages 240 fiction titles/year. Distributes/promotes titles through Ingrams Publisher Services and through a variety of media outlets both online and offline.

- Preditor and Editors Best Publisher 2006

Needs Erotica, fantasy (space fantasy, sword and sorcery), gay, glitz, historical, horror (dark fantasy, futuristic, pyschological, supernatural), lesbian, mainstream, military/war, mystery/suspense, psychic/ supernatural, religious, romance (contemporary, futuristic/time travel, gothic, historical, paranormal, regency period, romantic suspense), science fiction, thriller/espionage, western (frontier saga, traditional), young adult/teen (problem novel). "Samhain is looking to expand outside the romance genre and appreciates submissions of fantasy, science fiction, horror and mainstream/women's fiction. Within the romance genre we are actively seeking unique paranormals, futuristics and non-erotic books. However, all genres of fiction are currently accepted." Anthologies planned include a 2008 untitled Christmas anthology and a 2008 untitled annual Samhain anthology. Open call for submissions is placed on Web site. Full manuscript is required for special anthologies and the editor in charge of anthology selects final stories. Published *Steelflower*, by Lilith Saincrow (fantasy); *Annabell's Courtship*, by Lucy Monroe (historical romance); *Blackmailed*, by Annmarie McKenna (erotic romance).

How to Contact Query with outline/synopsis and 3 sample chapters. Accepts queries by e-mail. Include estimated word count, brief bio, list of publishing credits and "how an author is working to improve craft: association, critique groups, etc." Responds to queries in 10-12 weeks. Accepts unsolicited mss. Sometimes critiques/comments on rejected mss. Responds to mss in 10-12 weeks.

Terms Sends pre-production galleys to author. Ms published 6-18 months after acceptance. Writer's guidelines on Web site. Pays royalties 30-40% for e-books, average of 8% for tradepaper, an advance and author's copies (quantity varies). Book catalogs on Web site.

☑ ◎ ☒ SARABANDE BOOKS, INC.

2234 Dundee Rd., Suite 200, Louisville KY 40205. (502)458-4028. Fax: (502)458-4065. E-mail: info@ sarabandebooks.org. Website: www.sarabandebooks.org. **Contact:**Sarah Gorham, editor-in-chief; Kirby Gann, managing editor. Estab. 1994. "Small literary press publishing poetry, short fiction and literary nonfiction." Publishes trade paperback originals. **Published some debut authors within the last year.** Averages 12 total titles, 3-4 prose titles/year. Distributes titles through Consortium Book Sales & Distribution. Promotes titles through advertising in national magazines, sales reps, brochures, newsletters, postcards, catalogs, press release mailings, sales conferences, book fairs, author tours and reviews.

- Marjorie Sander's story collection *Portrait of My Mother Who Posed Nude in Wartime* won the 2004 National Jewish Book Award. *When It Burned to the Ground*, by Yolanda Barnes won the 2006 Independent Publisher Award for Best Multicultural Fiction.

Needs Literary, novellas, short novels, 250 pages maximum, 150 pages minimum. Submissions to Mary McCarthy Prize in Short Fiction accepted January through February. Published *Other Electricities*, by Ander Monson; *More Like Not Running Away*, by Paul Shepherd, and *Water: Nine Stories*, by Alyce Miller.

How to Contact See Web site for McCarthy Contest entry form. Accepts simultaneous submissions.

Terms Pays royalty of 10% on actual income received. Publishes ms 18 months after acceptance. Ms guidelines for #10 SASE.

⬛ ⬛ ⬛ ⬛ SCHOLASTIC CANADA, LTD.

604 King St. West, ON M5V 1E1 Canada. (416)915-3500. Fax: (416)849-7912. Website: www.scholastic. ca; for ms/artist guidelines: www.scholastic.ca/aboutscholastic/manuscripts.htm. **Acquisitions:** Editor, children's books. Publishes hardcover and trade paperback originals. Imprints: Scholastic Canada; North Winds Press; Les Editions Scholastic. Publishes 70 titles/year; imprint publishes 4 titles/year. 3% of books from first-time authors; 50% from unagented writers. Canadian authors, theme or setting required.

  • At presstime Scholastic Canada was not accepting unsolicited manuscripts. For up-to-date information on their current submission policy, call their publishing status line at (905)887-7323, ext. 4308 or view their submission guidelines on their Web site.

Needs Juvenile picture books, young readers, young adult. Average word length: picture books—under 1,000; young readers—7,000-10,000; middle readers—15,000-30,000; young adult—25,000-40,000.

How to Contact Query with synopsis, 3 sample chapters and SASE. Nonfiction: Query with outline, 1-2 sample chapters and SASE (IRC or Canadian stamps only). Responds in 3 months. Publishes book 1 year after acceptance.

Terms Pays authors royalty of 5-10% based on retail price. Offers advances. Book catalog for 8½ × 11 SAE with $2.55 postage stamps (IRC or Canadian stamps only).

⬛ ⬛ SCHOLASTIC PRESS

Scholastic Inc., 557 Broadway, New York NY 10012. (212)343-6100. Fax: (212)343-4713. Website: www. scholastic.com. **Contact:** David Saylor, editorial director (picture books) David Levithan, editorial director, middle grade, young adult; Dianne Hess, executive editor (picture books, early chapter books, middle grade, YA); Tracy Mack, executive editor (picture books, middle grade, young adult); Kara LaReau, executive editor; Anamika Bhatnager, senior editor (picture books, early chapter books, middle grade). Publishes hardcover originals. **Published some debut authors within the last year.** Averages 30 total titles/year. Promotes titles through trade and library channels.

Needs Juvenile, picture books, novels. Wants "fresh, exciting picture books and novels—inspiring, new talent." Published *Chasing Vermeer*, by Blue Balliet; *Here Today*, by Ann M. Martin; *Detective LaRue*, by Mark Teague.

How to Contact Does not accept unsolicited mss. *Agented submissions and submissons by published authors only.* No simultaneous submissions.

Terms Pays royalty on retail price. Average advance: variable. Publishes ms 18-24 months after acceptance.

⬛ ⬛ SEAL PRESS

Avalon Publishing Group, 1400 65th Street, Suite 250, Emeryville, CA 94608. E-mail: sealacquisitions@ avalonpub.com. Website: www.sealpress.com. **Contact:** Ingrid Emerick, editor/publisher; Leslie Miller, senior editor; Christina Henry, editor. Estab. 1976. "Midsize independent feminist book publisher interested in original, lively, radical, empowering and culturally diverse books by women." Publishes mainly trade paperback originals. Books: 55 lb. natural paper; Cameron Belt, Web or offset printing; perfect binding; illustrations occasionally. Averages 22 total titles/year. Titles distributed by Publishers Group West.

Imprints Adventura (women 's travel/outdoors), Live Girls (Third-Wave, pop culture, young feminist).

Needs Ethnic, feminist, gay/lesbian, literary, multicultural. "We are interested in alternative voices." Published *Valencia*, by Michelle Tea (fiction); *Navigating the Darwin Straits*, by Edith Forbes (fiction); and *Bruised Hibiscus*, by Elizabeth Nunez (fiction).

How to Contact Does not accept unsolicited mss. Query with SASE or submit outline, 2 sample chapter(s), synopsis. Responds in 2 months to queries. Accepts simultaneous submissions.

Terms Pays 7-10% royalty on retail price. Pays variable advance. Publishes ms 18 months after acceptance. Book catalog and ms guidelines for SASE or online. Ms guidelines online.

⬛ SILVER LEAF BOOKS, LLC

P.O. Box 6460, Holliston MA 01746. (508)740-6270. E-mail: editor@silverleafbooks.com. Website: www. silverleafbooks.com. **Contact:** Brett Fried, editor. Estab. 2003. "Silver Leaf Books is a small press featuring primarily new and upcoming talent in the fantasy, science fiction, mystery, thrillers, suspense, and horror genres. Our editors work closely with our authors to establish a lasting and mutually beneficial relationship, helping both the authors and company continue to grow and thrive." Publishes hardcover originals, trade paperback originals, paperback originals, paperback reprints. Average print order: 3,000. Debut novel print order: 3,000. **Published 1 new writer last year**. Plans 2 debut novels this year. Averages 6 total titles/year; 6 fiction titles/year. Distributes/promotes titles through Baker & Taylor Books and Ingram.

Needs Fantasy (space fantasy, sword and sorcery), horror (dark fantasy, futuristic, psychological, supernatural), mystery/suspense (amateur sleuth, cozy, police procedural, private eye/hard-boiled), science fiction (hard science/technological, soft/sociological), young adult (adventure, fantasy/science fiction, horror, mystery/suspense). Published *The Apprentice of Zoldex* and *The Darkness Within*, by Clifford B. Bowyer, and *When the Sky Fell* by Mike Lynch and Brandon Barr.

How to Contact Query with outline/synopsis and 3 sample chapters. Accepts queries by snail mail. Include estimated word count, brief bio and marketing plan. Send SASE or IRC for return of ms or disposable copy of ms and SASE/IRC for reply only. Agented fiction: 25%. Responds to queries in 6 months. Responds to mss in 4 months. Accepts unsolicited mss. Sometimes critiques/comments on rejected mss.

Terms Manuscript published 12-24 months after acceptance. Writer's guidelines on Web site. Pays royalties, and provides author's copies.

⬛ SIMON & SCHUSTER

1230 Avenue of the Americas, New York NY 10020. (212)698-7000. Website: www.simonsays.com.

Imprints Simon & Schuster Adult Publishing Group: Simon & Schuster; Scribner (Scribner, Lisa Drew, Simple Abundance Press); The Free Press; Atria Books; Kaplan; Touchstone; Scribner Paperback Fiction; S&S Libros en Espanol; Simon & Schuster Source; Wall Street Journal Books; Pocket Books (Pocket Star; Washington Square Press; MTV Books; Sonnet Books; Star Trek; The New Fogler Shakespeare; VH-1 Books; WWF Books). Simon & Schuster Children's Publishing: Aladdin Paperbacks; Atheneum Books for Young Readers (Richard Jackson Books); Beach Lane Books; Little Simon (Simon Spotlight; Rabbit Ears Books & Audio); Margaret K. McElderry Books, (Archway Paperbacks; Minstreal Books); Simon & Schuster Books for Young Readers (Paula Wiseman Books).

How to Contact Agented submissions only.

Terms Pays royalty. Offers advance. Ms guidelines online.

⬛ SIMON & SCHUSTER ADULT PUBLISHING GROUP

(formerly Simon & Schuster Trade Division, Division of Simon & Schuster), 1230 Avenue of the Americas, New York NY 10020. E-mail: ssonline@simonsays.com. Website: www.simonsays.com. Estab. 1924.

Imprints H&R Block; Lisa Drew Books; Fireside; The Free Press; Pocket Book Press; Rawson Associates; Scribner; Scribner Classics; Scribner Paperback Fiction; Scribner Poetry; S&S—Libros en Espanol; Simon & Schuster; Simon & Schuster Source; Simple Abundance Press; Touchstone; Wall Street Journal Books.

How to Contact *Agented submissions only.*

🔲 ☑ SKYSONG PRESS

35 Peter St. S, Orillia ON L3V 5A8 Canada. (705)329-1770. E-mail: skysong@bconnex.net. Website: www. bconnex.net/ ~skysong/. **Contact:** Steve Stanton. Estab. 1988. Skysong Press is a small independent Christian publisher. **Published 3 debut authors within the last year. Imprint(s)** Dreams & Visions.

Needs Short stories 2000-6000 words: Ethnic, experimental, fantasy, literary, mainstream/contemporary, religious, romance, science fiction.

How to Contact Accepts unsolicited mss. Submit complete ms and SASE. Accepts queries by e-mail. Include estimated word count, list of publishing credits. Responds in 2-6 weeks to queries; 2-6 months to mss. Accepts simultaneous submissions. Rarely comments on rejected mss.

Terms Average advance: 1 cent/word. Publishes ms 6-12 months after acceptance. Ms guidelines online.

☑ 🔲 SMALL BEER PRESS

150 Pleasant St., #306, Easthampton MA 01017. (413) 203-1636. Fax: (413) 203-1636. E-mail: info@lcrw. net. Website: www.lcrw.net. **Contact:** Gavin J. Grant. Estab. 2000. Averages 3-6 fiction titles/year.

• Small Beer Press also publishes the zine *Lady Churchill's Rosebud Wristlet*. SBP's books have been Hugo and Locus Award winners, as well as BookSense Picks and finalists for The Story Prize.

Needs Literary, experimental, speculative, story collections. Recently published *Generation Loss: A*

Novel, by Elizabeth Hand (post-punk lit thriller); *Interfictions: An Anthology of Interstitial Writing*, Delia Sherman and Theodora Goss, editors; *Skinny Dipping in the Lake of the Dead*, by Alan DeNiro (story collection); *Mothers & Other Monsters*, by Maureen F. McHugh (story collection); *Magic for Beginners*, by Kelly Link.
How to Contact "We do not accept unsolicited novel or short story collection manuscripts. Queries are welcome. Please send queries with an SASE by mail."

☑ SOHO PRESS, INC.

853 Broadway, New York NY 10003. (212) 260-1900. Fax: (212) 260-1902. E-mail: soho@sohopress. com. Website: www.sohopress.com. **Contact:** Laura Hruska, editor-in-chief (literary novels, mysteries with foreign or exotic settings); Katie Herman, editor (literary novels, mysteries with foreign or exotic settings), and Bronwen Hruska (literary novels, mysteries with foreign or exotic settings). Estab. 1986. "Independent publisher known for sophisticated fiction, mysteries set abroad, women's interest (no genre) novels and multicultural novels." Publishes hardcover and trade paperback originals and reprint editions. Books: perfect binding; halftone illustrations. First novel print order varies. **Published 7 debut authors within the last year.** Averages 70 total titles, 65 fiction titles/year. Distributes titles through Consortium Book Sales & Distribution in the US and Canada, Turnaround in England.
Imprints Soho Crime: procedural series set abroad.
Needs Adventure, ethnic, feminist, historical, literary, mainstream/contemporary, mystery (police procedural), suspense, multicultural. Published *Thirty-Three Teeth*, by Colin Cotterill; *When Red is Black*, by Qiu Xiaolong; *Murder on the Ile Saint-Louis*, by Cara Black; *The Farming of Bones*, by Edwidge Danticat; *The Darkest Child*, by Delores Phillips; *The First Wave*, by James R. Benn.
How to Contact Send first three chapters. Include estimated word count, brief bio, list of publishing credits. Send SASE for return of ms or send a disposable ms and SASE for reply only. Agented fiction 85%. Responds in 3 months to queries; 3 months to mss. Accepts simultaneous submissions. No electronic submissions. Sometimes comments on rejected mss.
Terms Pays 10-15% royalty on retail price for harcovers, 7.5% on trade paperbacks. Offers advance. Publishes ms 18-24 months after acceptance. Ms guidelines online.

☒ SOURCEBOOKS LANDMARK

Sourcebooks Inc, P.O. Box 4410, Naperville IL 60567-4410.Website: www.sourcebooks.com. "Our fiction imprint, Sourcebooks Landmark, publishes a variety of commercial fiction, including specialties in historical fiction and Austenalia. We are interested first and foremost in books that have a story to tell."
How to Contact Submit through agent only. Agented fiction: 100. Responds to queries in 6-8 weeks.

☑ SOUTHERN METHODIST UNIVERSITY PRESS

P.O. Box 750415, Dallas TX 75275-0415. (214)768-1433. Fax: (214)768-1428. Website: www.tamu.edu/ upress. **Contact**: Kathryn Lang, senior editor. Estab. 1937. "Small university press publishing in areas of film/theater, Southwest life and letters, medical ethics, sports, creative nonfiction and contemporary fiction." Publishes hardcover and trade paperback originals and reprints. Books: acid-free paper; perfect bound; some illustrations. Average print order: 2,000. **Published 2 debut authors within the last year.** Averages 10-12 total titles, 3-4 fiction titles/year. Distributes titles through Texas A&M University Press Consortium. Promotes titles through writers' publications.
Needs Literary, short story collections, novels. "We are willing to look at 'serious' or 'literary' fiction." No "mass market, science fiction, formula, thriller, romance." Published *The Trespasser*, by Edra Ziesk(a novel) and *The End of the Straight and Narrow*, by David McGlynn(a short story collection).
How to Contact Accepts unsolicited mss. Query with SASE. Responds in 2 weeks to queries; up to 1 year to mss. No simultaneous submissions. Sometimes comments on rejected mss.
Terms Pays 10% royalty on wholesale price, 10 author's copies. Average advance: $500. Publishes ms 1 year after acceptance. Ms guidelines online.

N ◻ ◎ SPEAK UP PRESS

P.O. Box 100506, Denver CO 80250. (303)715-0837. Fax: (303)715-0793. E-mail: gbryant@speakuppress. org; info@speakuppress.org. Website: www.speakuppress.org. Estab. 1999. "Speak Up Press is a small, nonprofit publisher of young adult fiction and nonfiction." Publishes paperback originals. Plans 3 debut novels this year. Averages 3 fiction titles/year.

Needs Young adult adventure, historical, mystery/suspense, problem novels, series, and nonfiction.

How to Contact Query with outline/synopsis and 3 sample chapters. Accepts queries by snail mail, e-mail. Send disposable copy of ms and SASE for reply only. Responds to queries in 6 weeks. Considers simultaneous submissions, e-mail submissions. Never critiques/comments on rejected mss.

Terms Writer's guidelines on Web site. Payment is determined "per individual author depending on book."

☑ ◎ SPIRE PRESS

532 LaGuardia Place, Suite 298, New York NY 10012. E-mail: editor@spirepress.org. Website: www. spirepress.org. **Contact:** Shelly Reed. Publishes 5-6 books/year. **Publishes 1-2 new writers/year.Needs** Literary story collections. Also publishes memoir, poetry. No novels. No horror, romance, or religious work. Length: 30,000 + words. Recently published work by Richard Weems.

How to Contact Send first 15 pages and synopsis in August only. Send disposable copy and #10 SASE for reply only. Responds in 3 months. Accepts simultaneous submissions. Rarely comments on rejected queries. Writer's guidelines online.

Terms Pays in advance copies and 15% royalty.

☑ SPOUT PRESS

P.O. Box 581067, Minneapolis MN 55458. (612) 782-9629. E-mail: editors@spoutpress.org. Website: www. spoutpress.org. **Contact:** Chris Watercott, fiction editor. Estab. 1989. "Small independent publisher with a permanent staff of five—interested in experimental fiction for our magazine and books." Publishes paperback originals. Books: perfect bound; illustrations. Average print order: 1,000. **Published 1 debut author within the last year.** Distibutes and promotes books through the Web site, events and large Web-based stores such as Amazon.com.

Needs Ethnic, experimental, literary, short story collections. Published *I'm Right Here*, by Tony Rauch. Runs annual fiction of the year story contest for Spout magazine. First prize is cash. Accepts submissions fall through spring. See Web site for specfic dates and details.

How to Contact Does not accept unsolicited mss. Query with SASE. Accepts queries by mail. Include estimated word count, brief bio, list of publishing credits. Send SASE for return of ms or send a disposable ms and SASE for reply only. Responds in 1 month to queries; 3-5 months to mss. Accepts simultaneous submissions. Rarely comments on rejected mss.

Terms Individual arrangement with author depending on the book. Publishes ms 12-15 months after acceptance. Ms guidelines for SASE or on Web site.

STARCHERONE BOOKS

P.O. Box 303, Buffalo NY 14201-0303. (716) 885-2726. E-mail: publisher@starcherone.com. Website: www.starcherone.com. **Contact:** Ted Pelton, publisher. Estab. 2000. Non-profit publisher of literary and experimental fiction. Publishes paperback originals and reprints. Books: acid-free paper; perfect bound; occasional illustrations. Average print order: 1,000. Average first novel print order: 1,000. **Published 2 debut authors within the last year.** Member CLMP. Titles distributed through Web site, Small Press Distribution, Amazon, independent bookstores.

Needs Experimental, literary. Published *Quinnehtukqut*, by Joshua Harmon (debut author, novel); *Hangings*, by Nina Shope (debut author, short stories); *My Body in Nine Parts*, by Raymond Federman (experimental).

How to Contact Accepts queries by mail or e-mail during August and September of each year. Include brief bio, list of publishing credits. Always query before sending ms. Responds in 2 months to queries; 6-10 months to mss. Accepts simultaneous submissions if noted in cover letter.

Terms Pays 10-12.5% royalty. Publishes ms 9-18 months after acceptance. Guidelines and catalog available on Web site.

☑ ST. MARTIN'S PRESS

175 Fifth Ave., New York NY 10010. (212)674-5151. Fax: (212)420-9314. Website: www.stmartins. com. Estab. 1952. General interest publisher of both fiction and nonfiction. Publishes hardcover, trade paperback and mass market originals. Averages 1,500 total titles/year.

Imprints Bedford Books; Buzz Books; Thomas Dunne Books; Forge; Minotaur; Picador USA; Stonewall Inn Editions; TOR Books; Griffin.

Needs Fantasy, historical, horror, literary, mainstream/contemporary, mystery, science fiction, suspense, western (contemporary), general fiction; thriller.

How to Contact *Agented submissions only.*

Terms Pays royalty. Offers advance. Ms guidelines online.

SYNERGEBOOKS

32700 River Bend Rd. #5 P.O. Box 685, Chiloquin OR 97624. (541)783-7512. E-mail: synergebooks@ aol.com. Website: www.synergebooks.com. **Contact:** Debra Staples, editor. Estab. 1999. Small press publisher, specializing in quality e-books from talented new writers in a myriad of genres, including print-on-demand. SynergEbooks "works together" with the author to edit and market each book. Publishes paperback originals and e-books. Books: 60 lb. paper; print-on-demand; perfect bound. Average first novel print order: 30. **Published 10-20 debut authors within the last year.** Averages 50 total titles, 30 fiction titles/year.

• Authors have received EPPIES and other awards.

Needs Adventure, business, family saga, fantasy (space fantasy, sword and sorcery), historical, horror, humor, mainstream/contemporary, mystery, new age/mystic, religious (children's religious, inspirational, religious fantasy, religious mystery/suspense, religious thriller, religious romance), romance (contemporary, futuristic/time travel, historical, regency period, romantic suspense), science fiction, short story collections, western (frontier saga, traditional), young adult (adventure, fantasy/science fiction, historical, horror, mystery/suspense, romance), native american, new age, and spirituality. Welcomes series books (1-9 in a series, with at least 1 title completed at time of submission.) Published *A Talent to Deceive: Who REALLY Killed the Lindberg Baby?*, by William Norris (nonfiction); *The Witchlock Series*, by Cyrese Covelli (fantasy/young adult), *A Banana Patch*, by Michael David (new age).

How to Contact Accepts unsolicited mss. Query via e-mail or snail mail, email preferred, 3 sample chapter(s), synopsis via attached mail in.doc format. Include estimated word count, brief bio, list of publishing credits, and e-mail address. Agented fiction 1%. Responds in 3 weeks to queries; 3 months to mss. Accepts simultaneous submissions, submissions on disk. Sometimes comments on rejected mss.

Terms Pays 15-40% royalty. Publishes ms 3-6 months after acceptance. Ms guidelines online.

NAN A. TALESE

Random House, Inc., 1745 Broadway, New York NY 10019. (212)782-8918. Fax: (212)782-8448. Website: www.nantalese.com. **Contact:** Nan A. Talese, editorial director. "Nan A. Talese publishes nonfiction with a powerful guiding narrative and relevance to larger cultural trends and interests, and literary fiction of the highest quality." Publishes hardcover originals. Averages 15 total titles/year.

Needs Literary. "We want well-written narratives with a compelling story line, good characterization and use of language. We like stories with an edge." *Agented submissions only.* Published *The Blind Assassin*, by Margaret Atwood; *Atonement,* by Ian McEwan; *Great Shame*, Thomas Keneally.

How to Contact Responds in 1 week to queries; 2 weeks to mss. Accepts simultaneous submissions.

Terms Pays variable royalty on retail price. Average advance: varying. Publishes ms 1 year after acceptance. Agented submissions only.

THIRD WORLD PRESS

P.O. Box 19730, 7822 S. Dobson Ave., Chicago IL 60619. (773) 651-0700. Fax: (773) 651-7286. E-mail: TWPress3@aol.com. Website: www.thirdworldpressinc.com. **Contact:** Gwendolyn Mitchell, editor. Estab. 1967. Black-owned and operated independent publisher of fiction and nonfiction books about the black experience throughout the Diaspora. Publishes hardcover and trade paperback originals and reprints. Averages 20 total titles/year. Distibutes titles through Independent Publisher Group. Needs Materials for literary, ethnic, contemporary, juvenile and children's books. "We publish nonfiction, primarily, but will consider fiction." Published The Covenant with Black America, with an introduction by Tavis Smiley; 1996, by Gloria Naylor.

How to Contact Accepts unsolicited mss. Submit outline, 5 sample chapter(s), synopsis. Responds in 8 weeks to queries; 5 months to mss. Accepts simultaneous submissions.

Terms Pays royalty on net revenues. Individual arrangement with author depending on the book, etc. Publishes ms 18 months after acceptance. Ms guidelines for #10 SASE.

▲ ☑ TIN HOUSE BOOKS

2601 NW Thurman St., Portland OR 97210. (503) 219-0622. Fax: (503) 222-1154. E-mail: meg@tinhouse.com. Website: www.tinhouse.com. **Contact:** Lee Montgomery, editorial director; Meg Storey, associate editor; Tony Perez, assistant editor. Estab. 2005. "We are a small independent publisher dedicated to nurturing new, promising talent as well as showcasing the work of established writers. Our Tin House New Voice series features work by authors who have not previously published a book." Publishes hardcover originals, paperback originals, paperback reprints. **Plans 3 debut novels this year.** Averages 8-10 total titles/year; 4-6 fiction titles/year. Distributes/promotes titles through Publishers Group West.

Needs Literary, novels, short story collections, poetry, translations. Publishes A New Voice series.

How to Contact Agented mss only. Accepts queries by snail mail, e-mail, phone. Include brief bio, list of publishing credits. Send SASE or IRC for return of ms or disposable copy of ms and SASE/IRC for reply only. Agented fiction 80%. Responds to queries in 2-3 weeks. Responds to mss in 2-3 months. Considers simultaneous submissions. Sometimes critiques/comments on rejected mss.

Terms Sends pre-production galleys to author. Manuscript published approximately one year after acceptance. Writer's guidelines on Web site. Advance is negotiable. Book catalogs not available.

☑ TITAN PRESS

PMB 17897, Encino CA 91416. E-mail: titan91416@yahoo.com. Website: www.calwriterssfv.com. **Contact:** Stefanya Wilson, editor. Estab. 1981. Publishes hardcover originals and paperback originals. Books: recycled paper; offset printing; perfect bound. Average print order: 2,000. Average first novel print order: 1,000. **Published 3 debut authors within the last year.** Averages 12 total titles, 6 fiction titles/year. Distributed at book fairs and through the Internet and at Barnes & Noble.

Needs Literary, mainstream/contemporary, short story collections. Published *Orange Messiahs*, by Scott Alixander Sonders (fiction).

How to Contact Does not accept unsolicited mss. Query with SASE. Include brief bio, social security number, list of publishing credits. Agented fiction 50%. Responds in 3 months to mss. Accepts simultaneous submissions. Sometimes comments on rejected mss.

Terms Pays 20-40% royalty. Publishes ms 1 year after acceptance. Ms guidelines for #10 SASE.

TOKYOPOP

5900 Wilshire Blvd., Suite 2000, Los Angeles CA 90036-5020. Website: www.tokyopop.com.

Ⓝ ☑ Ⓓ TOP COW PRODUCTIONS

10390 Santa Monica Blvd., Suite 340, Los Angeles CA 90025. E-mail: editorial@topcowent.com. Website: http://www.topcow.com/Site/.

How to Contact *No unsolicited submissions.* Prefers submissions from artists. See Web site for details and advice on how to break into the market.

☒ ◎ TRADEWIND BOOKS

202-1807 Maritime Mews, Vancouver BC V6H 3W7 Canada. (604)662-4405. Fax: (604)730-0454. E-mail: tradewindbooks@yahoo.com. Web site.www.tradewindbooks.com. **Manuscript Acquisitions:** Michael Katz, publisher. **Senior Editor:** R. David Stephens. Publishes 2 picture books; 3 young adult titles/year; 1 book of poetry. 15% of books by first-time authors.

Needs Juvenile Picture books: adventure, multicultural, folktales. Average word length: 900 words. Recently published *Broken*, by Alyxandra Harvey-Fitzhenry; *The Graveyard Hounds*, by Vi Hughes; *The Eco-Diary of Kiran Singer*, by Sue Ann Alderson.

How to Contact Picture books: submit complete ms. YA novels by Canadian authors only. Chapter books by US authors considered. Will consider simultaneous submissions. Do not send query letter. Responds to mss in 12 weeks. Unsolicited submissions accepted only if authors have read a selection of books published by Tradewind Books. Submissions must include a reference to these books.

Terms : Royalties negotiable. Offers advances against royalties. Catalog available on Web site.

☑ ☒ TRICYCLE PRESS

P.O. Box 7123, Berkeley CA 94707. (510)559-1600. Website: www.tricylepress.com. **Contact:** Nicole Geiger, publisher. Estab. 1993. "Tricycle Press is a children's book publisher that publishes picture books, board books, middle grade novels and early young adult novels. As an independent publisher, Tricycle

Press brings to life kid-friendly books that address the universal truths of childhood in an off-beat way." Publishes hardcover and trade paperback originals. **Published 3 debut authors within the last year.** Averages 25-30 total titles, 20-25 fiction titles/year.

• Received a 2007 notable children's book citation from the American Library Association for middle grade novel *Hugging the Rock* by Susan Taylor Brown.

Needs Children's/juvenile (adventure, historical, board book, preschool/picture book), preteen. "One-off middle grade novels—quality fiction, tween fiction." Published *Hugging The Rock*, by Susan Taylor Brown (middle grade); *Time Bomb*, by Nigel Hinton (middle grade); *Brand-New Emily*, by Ginger Rue (young adult); and *Shifty* by Lynn E. Hazen (young adult).

How to Contact Accepts unsolicited mss. Include three chapters and outline, brief bio, list of publishing credits, e-mail address. Send SASE for return of ms or send a disposable ms and SASE for reply only. Agented fiction 60%. Responds in 4-6 months to mss. Accepts simultaneous submissions.

Terms Pays 15-20% royalty on net receipts. Average advance: $1,000-9,000. Publishes ms 1-2 years after acceptance. Book catalog and ms guidelines for 9 × 12 SASE with 3 first-class stamps, or visit the Web site.

☑ TWILIGHT TIMES BOOKS

P.O. Box 3340, Kingsport TN 37664. (423)323-0183. Fax: (423)323-0183. E-mail: publisher@ twilighttimesbooks.com. Website: www.twilighttimesbooks.com. **Contact:** Ardy M. Scott, managing editor. Estab. 1999. "We publish compelling literary fiction by authors with a distinctive voice." Publishes hardcover and paperback originals and paperback reprints and e-books. Book: 60 lb. paper; offset and digital printing; perfect bound. Average print order: 1500. **Published 3 debut authors within the last year.** Averages 50 total titles, 12 fiction titles/year. Member: AAP, PAS, SPAN, SLF. Nationally distributed by Midpoint Trade Books.

Needs Historical, literary, mystery, nonfiction, science fiction, and young adult. Published *Hudson Lake*, by Laura Toops; *The New Bedford Samurai*, by Anca Vlaspolos; *Valley of the Raven*, By Ken Ramirez.

How to Contact Accepts unsolicited mss. Query with SASE or submit 2 sample chapter(s). Do not send complete mss. Accepts queries by e-mail, mail. Include estimated word count, brief bio, list of publishing credits, marketing plan. Send copy of ms and SASE. Agented fiction 10%. Responds in 4 weeks to queries; 2 months to mss. Accepts electronic submissions, submissions on disk. Rarely comments on rejected mss.

Terms Pays 8-15% royalty. Ms guidelines online.

☐ UNBRIDLED BOOKS

200 North 9th Street, Suite A, Columbia MO 65201. 573-256-4106. Fax: 573-256-5207. Website: www. unbridledbooks.com. **Contact**: Greg Michalson and Fred Ramey, editors. Estab. 2004. "Unbridled Books is a premier publisher of works of rich literary quality that appeal to a broad audience." Publishes both fiction and creative nonfiction. Hardcover and trade paperback originals. **Published 6 debut authors within the last year.** Averages 10-12 total titles, 8-10 fiction titles/year.

Needs Literary, nonfiction, memoir. *The Green Age of Asher Witherow*, by M. Allen Cunningham; *The Distance Between Us*, by Masha Hamilton; *Fear Itself*, by Candida Lawrence; *Lucky Strike*, by Nancy Zafris.

How to Contact Query with SASE. Accepts queries by mail. No electronic submissions.

☑ UNIVERSITY OF IOWA PRESS

119 W. Park Rd, Iowa City IA 52242-1000. (319)335-2000. Fax: (319)335-2055. E-mail: uipress@uiowa. edu. Website: www.uiowapress.org. **Contact:** Holly Carver, director; Joe Parsons, acquisitions editor. Estab. 1969. Publishes paperback originals. Average print run for a first book is 1,000-1,500. Averages 35 total titles/year.

Needs Currently publishes the Iowa Short Fiction Award selections.

How to Contact Responds in 6 months to queries. See Web site for details.

Terms Pays 7-10% royalty on net receipts. Publishes ms 1 year after acceptance. Ms guidelines online.

☑ ◎ ☑ UNIVERSITY OF NEVADA PRESS

MS 166, Reno NV 89557. (775)682-7393. Fax: (775)784-6200. Website: www.unpress.nevada.edu. **Contact**: Margaret Dalrymple (fiction). Estab. 1961. "Small university press. Publishes fiction that primarily focuses on the American West." Publishes hardcover and paperback originals. Averages 25 total titles, 2 fiction titles/year. Member: AAUP

- *Strange White Male*, by Gerald Haslam won the WESTAF Award for Fiction in 2000 and *Foreword Magazine's* second place winner for Book of the Year.

Needs "We publish in Basque Studies, Gambling Studies, Western literature, Western history, Natural science, Environmental Studies, Travel and Outdoor books, Archeology, Anthropology, and Political Studies, all focusing on the West". Has published *The Mechanics of Falling and Other Stories*, by Catherine Brady; *Little Lost River*, by Pamela Johnston; *Moon Lily*, by Susan Lang.

How to Contact Submit outline, 2-4 sample chapter(s), synopsis. Include estimated word count, brief bio, list of publishing credits. Send SASE or IRC. Responds in 2 months to queries. No simultaneous submissions.

Terms Publishes ms 18 months after acceptance. Book catalog and ms guidelines free Ms guidelines online.

◨ ◎ VEHICULE PRESS

Box 125, Place du Parc Station, Montreal QC H2X 4A3 Canada. (514)844-6073. Fax: (514)844-7543. E-mail: vp@vehiculepress.com. Website: www.vehiculepress.com. **Contact:** Andrew Steinmetz, fiction editor. Estab. 1973. Small publisher of scholarly, literary and cultural books. Publishes trade paperback originals by Canadian authors only. Books: good quality paper; offset printing; perfect and cloth binding; illustrations. Average print order: 1,000-3,000. Averages 15 total titles/year.

Imprints Signal Editions (poetry), Esplande Books (fiction).

Needs Literary, regional, short story collections. Published *Optique*, by Clayton Bailey; *Seventeen Tomatoes: Tales from Kashmir*, by Jaspreet Singh; *A Short Journey by Car*, by Liam Durcan.

How to Contact Query with SASE. Responds in 4 months to queries.

Terms Pays 10-15% royalty on retail price. Average advance: $200-500. "Depends on press run and sales. Translators of fiction can receive Canada Council funding, which publisher applies for." Publishes ms 1 year after acceptance. Book catalog for 9 × 12 SAE with IRCs.

⊠ ◎ ⊟ VERTIGO

DC Universe, Vertigo-DC Comics, 1700 Broadway, New York NY 10019.(212)636-5400. E-mail: dcovemail@aol.com. Website: www.dccomics.com.

⊡ VIKING

Penguin Putnam Inc., 375 Hudson St., New York NY 10014. (212)366-2000. **Contact:** Acquisitions Editor. Publishes a mix of literary and popular fiction and nonfiction. Publishes hardcover and originals.

Needs Literary, mainstream/contemporary, mystery, suspense. Published *Lake Wobegon Summer 1956*, by Garrison Keillor; *A Day Late and A Dollar Short*, by Terry McMillian; *A Common Life*, by Jan Karon; *In the Heart of the Sea*, by Nathaniel Philbrick.

How to Contact *Agented submissions only.* Responds in 6 months to queries. Accepts simultaneous submissions.

Terms Pays 10-15% royalty on retail price. Average advance: negotiable. Publishes ms 12-18 months after acceptance.

◪ ◎ VIKING CHILDREN'S BOOKS

A division of Penguin Young Readers Group, 345 Hudson St., New York NY 10014. (212)366-3600. Website: www.penguin.com. **Contact:** Catherine Frank, Tracy Gates, Joy Peskin, Anne Gunton, Kendra Levin. "Viking Children's books publishes high quality trade hardcover books for children through young adults. These include fiction and nonfiction." Publishes hardcover originals. **Published some debut authors within the last year.** Averages 70 total titles/year. Promotes titles through press kits, institutional ads.

Needs Juvenile, picture books, young adult. Published *Just Listen*, by Sarah Dessen (novel); *Llama, Llama Red Pajama*, by Anna Dewdney (picture book).

How to Contact Only accepts solicited mss. Submit complete ms. Send SASE. Responds in 12 months to queries.

Terms Pays 5-10% royalty on retail price. Average advance: negotiable. Publishes ms 1 year after acceptance.

ⓐ VINTAGE ANCHOR PUBLISHING

The Knopf Publishing Group, A Division of Random House, Inc., 1745 Broadway, New York NY 10019. Website: www.randomhouse.com. **Contact:** Furaha Norton, editor. Publishes trade paperback originals and reprints.

Needs Literary, mainstream/contemporary, short story collections. Published *Snow Falling on Cedars*, by Guterson (contemporary); *Martin Dressler*, by Millhauser (literary).

How to Contact *Agented submissions only.* Accepts simultaneous submissions. No electronic submissions.

Terms Pays 4-8% royalty on retail price. Average advance: $2,500 and up. Publishes ms 1 year after acceptance.

Ⓝ ⓖ VIZ MEDIA LLC

295 Bast Street, P.O. Box 77010, San Francisco CA 94133. (415)546-7073. Fax: (415)546-7086. Website: www.viz.com. "VIZ Media, LLC is one of the most comprehensive and innovative companies in the field of manga (graphic novel) publishing, animation and entertainment licensing of Japanese content. Owned by three of Japan's largest creators and licensors of manga and animation, Shueisha Inc., Shogakukan Inc., and Shogakukan-Shueisha Productions, Co., Ltd., VIZ Media is a leader in the publishing and distribution of Japanese manga for English speaking audiences in North America, the United Kingdom, Ireland, and South Africa and is a global ex-Asia licensor of Japanese manga and animation. The company offers an integrated product line including magazines such as SHONEN JUMP and SHOJO BEAT, graphic novels, and DVDs, and develops, markets, licenses, and distributes animated entertainment for audiences and consumers of all ages."

How to Contact Accepts queries by snail mail to P.O. Box 77010, San Francisco CA 94133.

WALKER AND CO.

Walker Publishing Co., 175 Fifth Ave., 8th Floor, New York NY 10010. Website: www.walkeryoungreaders.com. **Contact:** Emily Easton, publisher (picture books, middle grade & young adult novels); Stacy Cantor, Associate editor (picture books, middle grade, and young adult novels); Mary Kate Castellani, assistant editor (picture books, middle grade, and young adult novels). Estab. 1959. Midsize publisher. Publishes hardcover trade originals. Average first novel print order: 5,000-7,500. Averages 25 total titles/year.

Needs Juvenile (fiction, nonfiction), picture books (juvenile). Published *Stolen Car*, by Patrick Jones; *Skinny*, by Ibi Kaslik, *Violent Raines Almost Got Struck by Lightning*, by Danette Haworth, *Gimme Cracked Corn and I Will Share*, by Kevin O'Malley.

How to Contact Accepts unsolicited mss. Query with SASE. Include "a concise description of the story line, including its outcome, word length of story, writing experience, publishing credits, particular expertise on this subject and in this genre. Common mistake: not researching our publishing program and forgetting SASE." Agented fiction 75%. Sometimes comments on rejected mss. Send SASE for our reponse to your submission. We do not return manuscripts and proposals.

Terms Pays 5%-10% royalty. Average advance: competitive. Generally publishes ms 1 year after acceptance.

ⓐ ◎ WHITE MANE KIDS

White Mane Publishing, P.O. Box 708, Shippensburg PA 17257. (717) 532-2237. Fax: (717) 532-6110. E-mail: marketing@whitemane.com. Website: www.whitemane.com. Publishes hardcover orginals and paperback originals.

Needs Children's/juvenile (historical), young adult (historical). Published *Anybody's Hero: Battle of Old Men & Young Boys*, by Phyllis Haslip; *Crossroads at Gettysburg*, by Alan Kay.

How to Contact Accepts unsolicited mss. Query with SASE. Accepts queries by fax, mail. Include estimated word count, brief bio, summary of work and marketing ideas. Send SASE for return of ms or send a disposable ms and SASE for reply only. Responds in 1 month to queries; 3-4 months to mss. Accepts simultaneous submissions. Rarely comments on rejected mss.

Terms Pays royalty. Publishes ms 12-18 months after acceptance. Ms guidelines for #10 SASE.

ⓐ WILD CHILD PUBLISHING

P.O. Box 4897, Culver City CA 90231. E-mail: mgbaun@wildchildpublishing.com. Website: http://www.wildchildpublishing.com/. **Contact:** Marci Baun, editor-in-chief (genres not covered by other editors);

Faith Bicknell-Brown, managing editor (horror and romance); S.R. Howen, editor (science fiction and non-fiction). Estab. 2006. Wild Child Publishing is a small, independent press that started out as a magazine in September 1999. We are known for working with newer/unpublished authors and editing to the standards of NYC publishers. Publishes paperback originals, e-books. Format: POD printing; perfect bound. Average print order: 50-200. Debut novel print order: 50. **Published 12 new writers last year.** Plans 10 debut novels this year. Averages 12 fiction titles/year. Member EPIC. Distributes/promotes titles through Ingrams and own Web site, Mobipocket Kindle, Amazon, and soon with Fictionwise. Freya's Bower already distributed with through Fictionwise.

• Was named a Top 101 Writers' Web sites in 2005.

Imprints Freya's Bower.

Needs Adventure, children's/juvenile, erotica for Freya's Bower only, ethnic/multicultural, experimental, fantasy, feminist, gay, historical, horror, humor/satire, lesbian, literary, mainstream, military/war, mystery/suspense, New Age/mystic, psychic/supernatural, romance, science fiction, short story collections, thriller/espionage, western, young adult/teen (fantasy/science fiction). Multiple anthologies planned. Writers should submit material per our submissions guidelines. Published *Weirdly: A Collection of Strange Tales*, by Variety(horror/psychological thriller); *Quits: Book 2: Devils*, by M.E. Ellis (horror, psychological thriller, paranormal).

How to Contact Query with outline/synopsis and 1 sample chapter. Accepts queries by e-mail only. Include estimated word count, brief bio. Responds to queries in 2-4 weeks. Often critiques/comments on rejected mss. Responds to mss in 2-4 weeks.

Terms Sends pre-production galleys to author. Ms published 2-4 months after acceptance. Pays royalties 10-40%. Book catalogs on Web site.

☑ ◎ ☑ THE WILD ROSE PRESS

P.O. Box 708, Adams Basin NY 14410. E-mail: queryus@thewildrosepress.com. Website: http://www. thewildrosepress.com. **Contact:** Nicole D'Arienzo, editor. "The American Rose lines publishes stories about the French and Indian wars; Colonial America; the Revolutionary War; the war of 1812; the War Between the States; the Reconstruction era; the dawn of the new century. These are the struggles at the heart of the American Rose story. The central romantic relationship is the key driving force, set against historically accurate backdrop. These stories are for those who long for the courageous heroes and heroines who fought for their freedom and settled the new world; for gentle southern belles with spines of steel and the gallant gentlemen who sweep them away. This line is wide open for writers with a love of American history." Estab. 2006. Publishes paperback originals, reprints, and e-books in a POD format. Published 5 debut authors last year. Publishes approximately 10 fiction titles/year. Member: EPIC, Romance Writers of America. Distributes/promotes titles through major distribution chains, including Ingrams, Baker & Taylor, Sony, Amazon.com, as well as smaller and online distributors.

• Has received two Eppie Awards (2007) for First Place, and the New Jersey Golden Leaf Award for 2006 and 2007.

Imprints American Rose (American historical romance), Nicole D'Arienzo, editor; Climbing Roses (YA), Jill Williamson, editor; and more.

Needs Religious romance, contemporary, futuristic/time travel, gothic, historical, regency, romantic suspense, YA, erotic, and paranormal romances. Plans several anthologies "in several lines of the company in the next year, including Cactus Rose, Yellow Rose, American Rose, Black Rose, and Scarlet Rose." Has published *Where the Heart Is*, by Sheridon Smythe; *Cost of Freedom*, by Carol A. Spradling; and *My Valentine,* by Sheridon Smythe.

How to Contact *Does not accept unsolicited mss*. Send query letter with outline and synopsis of up to 5 pages. Prefers queries by e-mail; accepts by mail. Include estimated word count, brief bio, and list of publishing credits. Send SASE or IRC for return of ms. Agented fiction less than 1%. Responds to queries in 4 weeks; to mss in 12 weeks. Does not consider simultaneous submissions. Always comments on rejected mss.

Terms Pays royalty of 7% minimum; 35% maximum. Sends prepublication galleys to author. Time between acceptance and publication is approximately 1 year. Writer's guidelines available on Web site.

Ⓝ ☑ Ⓗ WILDSTORM

DC Universe, 1700 Broadway, New York NY 10019. (212)636-5400. Website: http://www.dccomics.com/ wildstorm/. Wildstorm is part of the DC Universe.

Ⓝ Ⓐ WILLIAM MORROW

HarperCollins, 10 E. 53rd St., New York NY 10022. (212)207-7000. Fax: (212)207-7606. Website: www. harpercollins.com. **Contact:** Acquisitions Editor. Estab. 1926. Approximately half of the books published are fiction. Averages 160 total titles/year.

Needs Publishes adult fiction. "Morrow accepts only the highest quality submissions" in adult fiction.

How to Contact *Agented submissions only.*

Terms Pays standard royalty on retail price. Average advance: varying. Publishes ms 2 years after acceptance.

Ⓐ Ⓞ WILSHIRE BOOK CO.

9731 Variel Ave., Chatsworth, CA 92311-4315. (818)700-1522. Fax: (818)700-1527. E-mail: mpowers@ mpowers.com. Website: www.mpowers.com. **Contact:** Melvin Powers, publisher; editorial department (adult fables). Estab. 1947. "You are not only what you are today, but also what you choose to become tomorrow." Looking for adult fables that teach principles of psychological growth. Publishes trade paperback originals and reprints. **Published 7 debut authors within the last year.** Averages 25 total titles/year. Distributes titles through wholesalers, bookstores and mail order. Promotes titles through author interviews on radio and television.

Needs Adult allegories that teach principles of psychological growth or offer guidance in living. Minimum 25,000 words. Published *The Princess Who Believed in Fairy Tales*, by Marcia Grad; *The Knight in Rusty Armor*, by Robert Fisher; *The Dragon Slayer With a Heavy Heart*, by Marcia Powers.

How to Contact Accepts unsolicited mss. Query with SASE or submit 3 sample chapter(s), synopsis or submit complete ms. Accepts queries by e-mail. Responds in 2 months to queries. Accepts simultaneous submissions.

Terms Pays standard royalty. Offers advance. Publishes ms 6 months after acceptance. Ms guidelines online.

Ⓐ WIND RIVER PRESS

E-mail: submissions@windriverpress.com. Website: www.windriverpress.com. **Contact:** Katherine Arline, editor (mainstream, travel, literary, historical, short story collections, translations). Estab. 2002. Publishes full and chapbook length paperback originals and reprints and electronic books. "Wind River Press works closely with the author to develop a cost-effective production, promotion and distribution strategy."

Needs Historical, literary, mainstream/contemporary, short story collections. Plans anthology of works selected from Wind River Press's magazines (*Critique* and *The Paumanok Review*). Recently published books by Elisha Porat, Gaither Stewart and Rochelle Mass.

How to Contact Accepts unsolicited mss. Accepts queries by e-mail. Include estimated word count, brief bio, list of publishing credits. Agented fiction 5%. Responds in 3 weeks to queries; 2 months to mss. Accepts simultaneous submissions. Always comments on rejected mss.

Terms Individual arrangement depending on book formats and target audience. Publishes ms 6 months after acceptance. Guidelines and book catalog available on Web site.

WINDRIVER PUBLISHING, INC.

72 N. Windriver Road, Silverton ID 83867-0446. (208)752-1836. Fax: (208)752-1876. E-mail: info@ windriverpublishing.com. Website: www.windriverpublishing.com. Estab. 2003. Publishes hardcover originals and reprints, trade paperback originals, mass market originals. Averages 8 total titles/year.

Needs Adventure, fantasy, historical, humor, juvenile, literary, military/war, mystery, religious, science fiction, spiritual, suspense, young adult.

How to Contact Responds in 2 months to queries; 4-6 months to mss. Accepts simultaneous submissions.

Terms Pays 8-15% royalty on wholesale price. Publishes ms 12-18 months after acceptance. Ms guidelines online.

Ⓞ WOODLEY MEMORIAL PRESS

English Dept., Washburn University, Topeka KS 66621. Website: www.washburn.edu/reference/woodley-press. **Contact:** Kevin Rabas, acquisitions editor at Dept. of English, Box 4019, Emporia State University, 1200 Commercial St., Emporia KS 66801. Estab. 1980. "Woodley Memorial Press is a small, nonprofit press which publishes novels and fiction collections by Kansas writers only; by 'Kansas writers' we mean writers who reside in Kansas or have a Kansas connection." Publishes paperback originals.

Book Publishers

Needs Literary, mainstream/contemporary, short story collections. Published KS Notable Book winner *Great Blues*, by Steve Semken; *The Trouble With Campus Security*, by G.W. Clift; and *Loading The Stone*, by Harley Elliot.
How to Contact Accepts unsolicited mss. Accepts queries by e-mail. Responds in 2 weeks to queries; 6 months to mss. Often comments on rejected mss.
Terms Publishes ms 1 year after acceptance. Ms guidelines online.

☐ YELLOW SHOE FICTION SERIES
Louisiana State University Press, P.O. Box 25053, Baton Rouge LA 70894-5053. Website: www.lsu.edu/lsupress. **Contact:** Michael Griffith, editor. Estab. 2004. Literary fiction series. Averages 2 titles/year.
Needs Literary. "Looking first and foremost for literary excellence, especially good manuscripts that have fallen through the cracks at the big commercial presses. I'll cast a wide net." Published *If the Heart is Lean*, by Margaret Luongo.
How to Contact Does not accept unsolicited mss. Accepts queries by mail; Attn: John Easterly. No electronic submissions.
Terms Pays royalty. Offers advance. Ms guidelines online.

Contests & Awards

In addition to honors and, quite often, cash prizes, contests and awards programs offer writers the opportunity to be judged on the basis of quality alone without the outside factors that sometimes influence publishing decisions. New writers who win contests may be published for the first time, while more experienced writers may gain public recognition of an entire body of work.

Listed here are contests for almost every type of fiction writing. Some focus on form, such as short stories, novels or novellas, while others feature writing on particular themes or topics. Still others are prestigious prizes or awards for work that must be nominated, such as the Pulitzer Prize in Fiction. Chances are, no matter what type of fiction you write, there is a contest or award program that may interest you.

SELECTING & SUBMITTING TO A CONTEST

Use the same care in submitting to contests as you would sending your manuscript to a publication or book publisher. Deadlines are very important, and where possible, we've included this information. At times contest deadlines were only approximate at our press deadline, so be sure to write, call or look online for complete information.

Follow the rules to the letter. If, for instance, contest rules require your name on a cover sheet only, you will be disqualified if you ignore this and put your name on every page. Find out how many copies to send. If you don't send the correct amount, by the time you are contacted to send more, it may be past the submission deadline. An increasing number of contests invite writers to query by e-mail, and many post contest information on their Web sites. Check listings for e-mail and Web site addresses.

One note of caution: Beware of contests that charge entry fees that are disproportionate to the amount of the prize. Contests offering a $10 prize, but charging $7 in entry fees, are a waste of your time and money.

If you are interested in a contest or award that requires your publisher to nominate your work, it's acceptable to make your interest known. Be sure to leave the publisher plenty of time, however, to make the nomination deadline.

◎ "BEST OF OHIO WRITER" CONTEST

(Formerly Ohio Writer) Muse Magazine, 2570 Superior, #203, Cleveland OH 44114. (216) 694-0000. Fax: (216) 694-0004. E-mail: info@the-lit.org. Website: www.the-lit.org. **Contact:** Judith Mansour-Thomas, executive director. Award "to promote and encourage the work of writers in Ohio." Prize: $500. Judged by "a selected panel of prominent Ohio writers." Entry fee: $25. **Deadline: September 30.** Entries must be unpublished. Guidelines available after June 1 for SASE or e-mail. Accepts inquiries by e-mail and phone. "No cliché plots; we're looking for fresh unpublished voices." Results announced December 1. Winners notified by mail. For contest results, send SASE or e-mail after December 1.

▦ AEON AWARD

Albedo One/Aeon Press, c/o 8 Bachelor's Walk, Dublin 1, Ireland. Fax: +353 (1) 8730177. E-mail: fraslaw@yahoo.co.uk. Website: www.albedo1.com. **Contact:** Frank Ludlow, Event Coordinator. "We aim to encourage new writers into the genre and to encourage existing writers to push at their boundaries" Annual. Competition/award for short stories. Prize: First prize €1,000, second €200, and third €100. The top three stories are guaranteed publication in Albedo One. Categories: any speculative genre, "i.e. fantasy, SF horror or anything in between or unlcassifiable (like slipstream)." A short list is drawn up by the Albedo One editorial team and the final decision is made by renowned author Ian Watson. Entry Fee: €7. Pay via Web site. Guidelines available in December. Accepts inquiries by fax, e-mail. The best stories of each submission period are shortlisted for the grand prize. **The competition is run in four quarterly periods with probable deadlines of the end of March, June, September and November.** Check the website for definite dates. Entries should be unpublished. Award open to "anyone with €7 and a burning desire to be the best." Length: under 8,000 words. Cover letter should include name, address, e-mail, word count, novel/story title. It is essential the story is marked so it can be identified with its author. Writers may submit own work. "As the contest is initially judged by the editorial staff of Albedo One, I think it is fair to say that choices will be influenced by the individual tastes of these people. You can see what they like in Albedo One on a regular basis. I wish I could say there is a certain formula, but we pick the best stories submitted to us and although there can often be little evidence of genre influence visible on the page, we always feel that the stories are informed by the author's genre sensibilities. In other words, we like stories by authors who used to like/write science fiction. Confused? Pick up an issue of the magazine and check it out." Results announced within two months of the final deadline. Winners notified by e-mail, and at event/banquet. Winners in 2007 were announced at Eurocon in Copenhagen. Results made available to entrants on Web site.

▦ ◎ AHWA FLASH & SHORT STORY COMPETITION

AHWA (Australian Horror Writers Association), P.O. Box 3023, Murrumbeena VIC 3163, Austrailia. E-mail: competitions@australianhorror.com. Website: http://www.australianhorror.com. **Contact:** David Carroll, Competitions Officer. "To showcase the diversity and talent of writers of horror fiction." Annual. Competition/award for short stories and flash fiction. The writers of the winning story in each category will receive an engraved plaque, plus the stories will be published (TBA) at paying rates. There are 2 categories: short stories (1,500 to 8,000 words) and flash fiction (less than 1,000 words). We have received more than 100 entries in the past two years. Writers may submit to one or both categorics, but entry is limited to 1 story per author per category. There will be a panel of 3 judges who will announce a shortlist of 5 stories prior to the announcement of the winners. Entry free for AHWA members; for non-members, $5 for flash, $10 for short story. Payment can be made via our secure Paypal option using ahwa@australianhorror.com. Alternatively, contact us and we can arrange other payment methods (eg, direct debit). Cheques will not be accepted due to the cost associated with banking them. Guidelines available in January. Accepts inquiries by e-mail. Entry deadline each year is May 31. Entries should be unpublished. Anyone may enter the contest by submitting a story to competitions@australianhorror.com as an attached doc or rtf. Please do not send the story in the body of the email. Alternatively, contact us to arrange postal submissions. Cover letter should include name, address, e-mail, word count, novel/ story title. Please do not include your name, address, or email on the ms as we hand the entries to the judges blind to remove any possible bias. Only include the title and word count at the start, plus title and page number on each page. "We're after horror stories, tales that frighten, yarns that unsettle us in our comfortable homes. All themes in this genre will be accepted, from the well-used (zombies, vampires, ghosts etc) to the highly original, so long as the story is professional and well written. No previously published entries will be accepted— all tales must be an original work by the author. Stories can be as violent or as bloody as the storyline dictates, but those containing gratuitous sex or violence will not be considered. Please check your entries for spelling and grammar mistakes and follow standard submission guidelines (eg, 12 point font, Ariel, Times New Roman, or Courier New, one and a half spacing between lines, with title and page number on each page." Results announced July/August. Winners notified at national convention in Australia. Results made available to entrants on Web site.

☐ AIM MAGAZINE SHORT STORY CONTEST

P.O. Box 390, Milton WA 98354-0390. (253) 815-9030. E-mail: editor@aimmagazine.org. Website: www. aimmagazine.org. **Contact**: Ruth Apilado, associate editor. $100 prize offered to contest winner for best unpublished short story (4,000 words maximum) "promoting brotherhood among people and cultures." Judged by staff members. No entry fee. Deadline: August 15. Competition receives 20 submissions per category. Guidelines available anytime. Accepts inquiries by e-mail and phone. Winners are announced in the autumn issue and notified by mail on September 1. List of winners available for SASE. Open to any writer.

◎ ALABAMA STATE COUNCIL ON THE ARTS INDIVIDUAL ARTIST FELLOWSHIP

201 Monroe St., Montgomery AL 36130-1800. (334) 242-4076, ext. 224. Fax: (334) 240-3269. E-mail: randy. shoults@arts.alabama.gov. Website: www.arts.state.al.us. **Contact:** Randy Shoults, literature program manager. "To recognize the achievements and potential of Alabama writers." Judged by independent peer panel. Guidelines available in January. For guidelines, fax, e-mail, visit Web site. Accepts inquiries by fax, e-mail and phone. "Two copies of the following should be submitted: a résumé and a list of published works with reviews, if available. A minimum of 10 pages of poetry or prose, but no more than 20 pages. Please label each page with title, artist's name and date. If published, indicate where and the date of publication." Winners announced in June and notified by mail. List of winners available for SASE, fax, e-mail or visit Web site. No entry fee. Deadline: March. Competition receives 25 submissions annually. Two-year residency required.

☑ ALLIGATOR JUNIPER'S NATIONAL WRITING CONTEST

Alligator Juniper, 220 Grove Ave, Prescott AZ 86301. (928) 350-2012. Fax: (928) 776-5137. E-mail: aj@ prescott.edu. Website: http://www.prescott.edu/highlights/alligator_juniper/index.html. **Contact:** Jeff Fearnside, managing editor. Annual. Competition/award for short stories. Prize: Winner receives $500 and publication. Finalists are published and receive copies. Categories: fiction, creative nonfiction, poetry. "All entries are read and discussed by advanced writing students at Prescott College enrolled in the Alligator Juniper practicum class. This class is overseen by two faculty members, each of whom is a working writer in the genres of poetry, fiction and creative nonfiction. All entrants receive a personal letter from one of our staff regarding the status of their submission. We usually inform in late January. The individual attention we devote to each manuscript takes time. We appreciate your patience." Entry fee: $15 (includes copy of issue). Make checks payable to Alligator Juniper. Accepts inquiries by fax, e-mail, phone. **Submission period is May 1-October 1.** Entries should be unpublished. Deadline: **October 1.** Anyone may enter contest. Length: Prose should be under 30 pages; poetry 5 poems or less. Cover letter should include name, address, phone, e-mail, word count, novel excerpt/story title. Writers may submit own work. "Send us your best work; we often don't know what we're looking for until we read it. Historically, winning work has grappled poetically and honestly with issues of race, sexuality, patriotism, politics, the environment, and language itself. We publish work that is both long and short, traditional and experimental in its approaches. Our editorial staff is composed of savvy, college-aged readers; do your best to wow us." Results announced January. Winners notified by phone, by e-mail. Winners announced December. Results made available to entrants with SASE, by fax, by e-mail, on Web site.

◎ AMERICAN ASSOCIATION OF UNIVERSITY WOMEN AWARD IN JUVENILE LITERATURE

North Carolina Literary and Historical Association, 4610 Mail Service Center, Raleigh NC 27699-4610. (919) 807-7290. Fax: (919) 733-8807. E-mail: michael.hill@ncmail.net. **Contact:** Michael Hill, awards coordinator. Award's purpose is to "select the year's best work of literature for young people by a North Carolina writer." Annual award for published books. Award: cup. Competition receives 10-15 submissions per category. Judged by three-judge panel. No entry fee. **Deadline: July 15.** Entries must be previously published. Contest open to "residents of North Carolina (three-year minimum)." Guidelines available

July 15. For guidelines, send SASE, fax, e-mail or call. Accepts inquiries by fax, e-mail, phone. Winners announced October 15. Winners notified by mail. List of winners available for SASE, fax, e-mail.

☐ AMERICAN MARKETS NEWSLETTER SHORT STORY COMPETITION

American Markets Newsletter, 1974 46th Ave., San Francisco CA 94116. E-mail: sheila.oconnor@juno. com. Award is "to give short story writers more exposure." Accepts fiction and nonfiction up to 2,000 words. Entries are eligible for cash prizes and all entries are eligible for worldwide syndication whether they win or not. Send double-spaced manuscripts with your story/article title, byline, word count and address on the first page above your article/story's first paragraph (no need for separate cover page). There is no limit to the number of entries you may send. Prize: 1st Place: $300; 2nd Place: $100; 3rd Place: $50. Judged by a panel of independent judges. Entry fee: $12 per entry; $20 for 2; $25 for 3; $30 for 4; $5 each entry thereafter. For guidelines, send SASE, fax or e-mail. **Deadline: June 30 and December 31.** Contest offered biannually. Published and unpublished stories are actively encouraged. Add a note of where and when previously published. Open to any writer. "All kinds of fiction are considered. We especially want women's pieces—romance, with a twist in the tale—but all will be considered." Results announced within 3 months of deadlines. Winners notified by mail if they include SASE.

◎ AMERICAN SCANDINAVIAN FOUNDATION TRANSLATION PRIZE

American Scandinavian Foundation, 58 Park Ave., New York NY 10016. (212) 879-9779. Fax: (212) 686-2115. E-mail: info@amscan.org. Website: www.amscan.org. **Contact:**Valerie Hymas. Award to recognize excellence in fiction, poetry and drama translations of Scandinavian writers born after 1800. Prize: $2,000 grand prize; $1,000 prize. No entry fee. Cover letter should include name, address, phone, e-mail and title. Deadline: June 1. Entries must be unpublished. Length: no more than 50 pages for drama, fiction; no more than 35 pages for poetry. Open to any writer. Guidelines available in January for SASE, by fax, phone, e-mail or on Web site. Accepts inquiries by fax, e-mail, phone. Results announced in November. Winners notified by mail. Results available for SASE or by fax, e-mail, Web site.

☐ AMERICAN SHORT FICTION SHORT STORY CONTEST

American Short Fiction, P.O. Box 301209, Austin TX 78703. (512) 5538-1305. Fax: (512) 5538-1306. E-mail: editors@americanshortfiction.org. Website: www.americanshortfiction.org. **Contact:** Stacey Swann, editor. "To reward the best short fiction being written with prize money and publication in American Short Fiction." Annual. Competition/award for short stories. Prize: $1,000 and publication for first place, $500 for second place. Receives about 400 entries per category. The first round of judging is a blind read by American Short Fiction editorial staff. Ten stories are sent to guest judge for final blind judging. The guest judge changes every year. Entry fee: $20. Make payment and submit story via electronic database manager on Web site. Guidelines available in August. Accepts inquiries by e-mail. **Contest submission period is September 15th through December 1st**. Entries should be unpublished. Anyone may enter contest. Length: 6,000 max. Writers may submit own work. "Familiarize yourself with our journal and aesthetic." Results announced mid to late March. Winners notified by e-mail. Results made available to entrants with SASE, by e-mail, on Web site.

☑ THE SHERWOOD ANDERSON FOUNDATION FICTION AWARD

The Sherwood Anderson Foundation, 216 College Rd., Richmond, VA 23229.(804)289-8324. Fax: (804) 287-6052. E-mail: mspear@richmond.edu. Web site: www.sherwoodandersonfoundation.org. Contact: Michael M. Spear, foundation co-president. Contest is to honor, preserve and celebrate the memory and literary work of Sherwood Anderson, American realist for the first half of the 20th century. Annual award to support developing writers of short stories and novels. Entrants must have published at least one book of fiction or have had several short stories published in major literary and/or commercial publications. Self-published stories do not qualify. Award:$15,000 grant. Judged by a committee established by the foundation. Entryfee: $20 application fee (payable to The Sherwood Anderson Foundation).Deadline: April 1. Send a detailed resumé that includes a bibliography of your publications. Include a cover letter that provides a history of your writing experience and your future plans for writing projects. Also, submit2 or 3 examples of what you consider to be your best work. Do not send manuscripts by e-mail. Only mss in English will be accepted. Open to any writer who meets the qualifications listed above. Accepts inquiries by e-mail. Mail your application to the above address. No mss or publications will be returned.

ANNUAL ATLANTIC WRITING COMPETITION

Writer's Federation of Nova Scotia, 1113 Marginal Road, Halifax NS B3H 4P7 Canada. (902) 423-8116. Fax: (902) 422-0881. E-mail: talk@writers.ns.ca. Website: www.writers.ns.ca. **Contact**: Jane Buss, director. Award's purpose is "to provide feedback to emerging writers and create a venue for their work to be considered against that of other beginning authors. Annual award to residents of Atlantic Canada for short stories, poetry, and novels as well as children's literature, YA novels, poetry and essay." Prize: In Canadian money: $200, $150, $100 for adult novel; $150, $75, $50 for children's literature and YA novel; $150, $75, $50 for short stories and essay/magazine article. Judged by a jury of professionals from the writing/literature field—authors, librarians, publishers, teachers. Entry fee: $25 per novel entry ($20 for WFNS members); $15 per entry in other categories ($10 members). **Deadline: first Friday in December of each year.** Entries must be unpublished. Length: story 3,000 words maximum; novel 100,000 words maximum; children's writing 20,000 words maximum, YA novel 75,000 words maximum. Writers must use pseudonym; use 8½ × 11 white paper (one side only); and format entry typed and double-spaced. To be eligible, writers must be residents of Atlantic Canada, older than 16 and not extensively published in the category they are entering. Guidelines available by SASE or on Web site. Accepts inquiries by e-mail, phone. Winners announced in August. List of winners available on Web site.

ANNUAL BOOK COMPETITION

Washington Writers' Publishing House, P.O. Box 15271, Washington D.C 20003. E-mail: wwph@gmail.com. Website: www.wwph.org. **Contact:** Elisavietta Ritchie at P.O. Box 298, Broomes Island MD 20615. "To award literary excellence in the greater Washington DC-Baltimore area." Annual. Competition/award for novels, story collections. Prize: $500, publication, and 50 copies of book. Categories: fiction (novel or collection of short stories). Receives about 40 entries per category. Judged by members of the press. Entry fee: $25. Make checks payable to WWPH. Guidelines available all year with SASE, on Web site. Accepts inquiries by e-mail. Deadline: Nov. 1. Entries should be unpublished. "Individual stories or excerpts may have been published in journals and anthologies." Open to fiction writers living within 60 miles of the Capitol (Baltimore area included). Length: no more than 350 pages, double or 112 spaced. Cover letter should include name, address, phone, e-mail, novel/collection title, acknowledgments. None of this information should appear on the actual manuscript. Results announced January of each year. Winners notified by phone, by e-mail.

ARROWHEAD REGIONAL ARTS COUNCIL INDIVIDUAL ARTIST CAREER DEVELOPMENT GRANT

Arrowhead Regional Arts Council, 1301 Rice Lake Rd., Suite 111, Duluth MN 55811. (218) 722-0952 or (800) 569-8134. Fax: (218) 722-4459. E-mail: info@aracouncil.org. Website: www.aracouncil.org. Award to "provide financial support to regional artists wishing to take advantage of impending, concrete opportunities that will advance their work or careers." Prize: up to $1,000. Categories: novels, short stories, story collections and translations. Judged by ARAC Board. No entry fee. Guidelines available by phone, e-mail or on Web site. **See Web site for 2009 deadlines.** Entries must be unpublished. Award is offered 3 times per year. Applicants must live in the seven-county region of Northeastern Minnesota. Results announced approximately 6 weeks after deadline. Winners notified by mail. List of winners available by phone and also listed on the Web site.

ART AFFAIR SHORT STORY AND WESTERN SHORT STORY CONTESTS

P.O. Box 54302, Oklahoma City OK 73154.E-mail: okpoets@aol.com. Website: www.shadetreecreations.com. **Contact:** Barbara Shepherd. The annual Art Affair Writing Contests include (General) Short Story and Western Short Story categories and offer 1st Prize: $50 and certificate; 2nd Prize: $25 and certificate; and 3rd Prize: $15 and certificate in both categories. Honorable Mention certificates will be awarded at the discretion of the judges. Open to any writer. All short stories must be unpublished. Multiple entries accepted in both categories with separate entry fees for each. Submit original stories on any subject and timeframe for general Short Story category and submit original western stories for Western Short Story - word limit for all entries is 5,000 words. (Put word count in the upper right-hand corner of first page; mark " Western" if applicable). Include cover page with writer's name, address, phone number, and ms title. Do not include SASE; mss will not be returned. Guidelines available on website. **Deadline: October 1, 2009 (postmark). Entry Fee:** $5/short story; $5/western short story. Make check payable to Art Affair. Winners' list will be published on the Art Affair website in December.

☑ ◎ ◙ ARTIST TRUST/ WASHINGTON STATE ARTS COMMISSION FELLOWSHIP AWARDS

Artist Trust, 1835 12th Ave, Seattle WA 98122. (209)467-8734 ext 9. Fax: (206) 467-9633. E-mail: info@ artisttrust.org. Website: http://artisttrust.org. **Contact:** Monica Miller, Director of Programs. "Artist Trust/ Washington State Arts Commission Fellowship awards practicing professional Washington State artists of exceptional talent and demonstrated ability." Annual. Prize: $7,500. "The Fellowship awards are multidisciplinary awards. The categories for 2009 are Literary, Music, Media and Craft. Accepted genres for Literary are: poetry, fiction, graphic novels, experimental works, creative non-fiction, screen plays, film scripts and teleplays." Receives about 175 entries per category. Entries are judged by work samples as specified in the guidelines. Winners are selected by a multidisciplinary panel of artists and arts professionals. No entry fee. Guidelines available in April. Accepts inquiries by e-mail, phone. April-June is the submission period. **Deadline is approximately the 4th Friday of June.** Web site should be consulted for the exact date. Entries can be unpublished or previously published. Washington State residents only. Length: up to 15 pages for poetry, fiction, graphic novels, experimental works and creative non-fiction, and up to 20 pages for screen plays, film scripts and teleplays. All mss must be typed with a 12-pnt font size or larger and cannot be single spaced (except for poetry). Include artist statement and resume with name, address, phone, e-mail, and novel/story title. "The Fellowship awards are highly competitive. Please follow guidelines with care." Results announced October. Winners notified by mail. Results made available to entrants on Web site.

◎ THE ART OF MUSIC ANNUAL WRITING CONTEST

The Art of Music, Inc., P.O. Box 85, Del Mar CA 92014-0085. (619) 884-1401. Fax: (858) 755-1104. E-mail: info@theartofmusicinc.org. Website: www.pianopress.com. **Contact:** Elizabeth C. Axford. Offered annually. Categories are: essay, short story, poetry, song lyrics, and illustrations for cover art. All writings must be on music-related topics. The purpose of the contest is to promote the art of music through writing. Acquires one-time rights. All entries must be accompanied by an entry form indicating category and age; parent signature is required of all writers under age 18. Poems may be of any length and in any style; essays and short stories should not exceed five double-spaced, typewritten pages. All entries shall be previously unpublished (except poems and song lyrics) and the original work of the author. Guidelines and entry form for SASE, on Web site or by e-mail. Prize: Cash, medal, certificate, publication in the anthology titled The Art of Music: A Collection of Writings, and copies of the book. Judged by a panel of published poets, authors and songwriters. Entry fee: $20 fee. Inquiries accepted by e-mail, phone. **Deadline: June 30.** Short stories should be no longer than five pages typed and double spaced. Open to any writer. "Make sure all work is fresh and original. Music-related topics only." Results announced October 31. Winners notified by mail. For contest results, send SASE or visit Web site.

♻ ◙ ◎ ASTED/GRAND PRIX DE LITTERATURE JEUNESSE DU QUEBEC-ALVINE-BELISLE

Association pour l'avancement des sciences et des techniques de la documentation, 3414 Avenue du Parc, Bureau 202, Montreal QC H2X 2H5 Canada. (514)281-5012. Fax: (514)281-8219. E-mail: info@ asted.org. Website: www.asted.org. **Contact:** Brigitte Moreau and Olivia Marleau, co-presidents. "Prize granted for the best work in youth literature edited in French in the Quebec Province. Authors and editors can participate in the contest." Offered annually for books published during the preceding year. Prize: $1,000. No entry fee. Deadline: June 1. Entries must be previously published. Open to editors and authors with books published during the preceding year.

☑ ◎ THE ATHENAEUM LITERARY AWARD

The Athenaeum of Philadelphia, 219 S. Sixth St., Philadelphia PA 19106-3794. (215) 925-2688. Fax: (215) 925-3755. E-mail: erose@PhilaAthenaeum.org. Website: www.PhilaAthenaeum.org. **Contact**: Ellen L. Rose. Annual award to recognize and encourage outstanding literary achievement in Philadelphia and its vicinity. Prize: A certificate bearing the name of the award, the seal of the Athenaeum, the title of the book, the name of the author and the year. Categories: The Athenaeum Literary Award is granted for a work of general literature, not exclusively for fiction. Judged by a committee appointed by the Board of Directors. No entry fee. Deadline: December. Entries must be previously published. Nominations shall be made in writing to the Literary Award Committee by the author, the publisher, or a member of the Athenaeum, accompanied by a copy of the book. Open to work by residents of Philadelphia and its vicinity. Guidelines available for SASE, by fax, by e-mail and on Web site. Accepts inquiries by fax, e-mail and phone. Juvenile fiction is not included. Results announced in Spring. Winners notified by mail. For contest results, see Web site.

AUTUMN HOUSE FICTION PRIZE

Autumn House Press, 87 12 Westwood Street, Pittsburgh PA 15211. (412) 381-4261. E-mail: info@autumnhouse.org. Website: http://autumnhouse.org. **Contact:** Michael Simms, executive editor. "To identify and publish the best fiction manuscripts we can find" Annual. Competition/award for short stories, novels, story collections, translations. Prize: $2,500 and book publication. Only one category: all genres of fiction (short stories, short-shorts, novellas, and novels, or any combination of genres) are eligible. Entries are judged by Sharon Dillworth, who is assisted by an able team of experienced, published writers. Entry fee: $25. Make checks payable to Autumn House Press. Accepts inquiries by e-mail, phone. **Entry deadline is June 30, 2009.** Entries should be unpublished. Open to all writers over the age of 18. Length: approx 200-300 pgs. Cover letter should include name, address, phone, e-mail, novel/story title. The mss are judged blind, so please include two cover pages, one with contact information and one without. "The competition is tough, so submit only your best work!" Results announced September. Winners notified by mail, by phone, by e-mail. Results made available to entrants with SASE, by fax, by e-mail, on Web site.

✍ AWP AWARD SERIES IN THE NOVEL, CREATIVE NONFICTION AND SHORT FICTION

The Association of Writers & Writing Programs, Mail Stop 1E3, George Mason University, Fairfax VA 22030. (703) 993-4301. Fax: (703) 993-4302. E-mail: awp@awpwriter.org. Website: www.awpwriter.org. **Contact:** Supriya Bhatnagar, director of publications. The AWP Award Series was established in cooperation with several university presses in order to publish and make fine fiction and nonfiction available to a wide audience. Offered annually to foster new literary talent. Guidelines for SASE and on Web site. Categories: novel ($2,000), Donald Hall Prize in Poetry ($4,000), Grace Paley Prize in Short Fiction ($4,000), and creative nonfiction ($2,000). Entry fee: $25 for nonmembers, $10 for members. Entries must be unpublished. **Mss must be postmarked between January 1-February 28.** Cover letter should include name, address, phone number, e-mail and title. "This information should appear in cover letter only." Open to any writer. Guidelines available on Web site in November. No phone calls, please. Manuscripts published previously in their entirety, including self-publishing, are not eligible. No mss returned. Results announced in August. Winners notified by mail or phone. For contest results send SASE, or visit Web site. No phone calls, please.

☐ ◎ AWP INTRO JOURNALS PROJECT

Dept. of English, Bluffton University, 1 University Drive, Bluffton OH 45817-2104. E-mail: awp@gmu.edu. Website: www.awpwriter.org. **Contact**: Susan Streeter Carpenter. "This is a prize for students in AWP member university creative writing programs only. Authors are nominated by the head of the creative writing department. Each school may nominate no more than one work of nonfiction, one work of short fiction and three poems. Nominations must be accompanied by a cover letter from the program director, which verifies that the enclosed nominations are by students currently enrolled in the university's creative writing program. In the letter, the program must provide a permanent address for each nominated student." Prize: $100 plus publication in participating journal. Winning works will appear in the fall or winter issues of Hayden's Ferry Review, Mid-American Review, Colorado Review, Puerto del Sol, Controlled Burn, Quarterly West, Tampa Review, and Artful Dodge. Categories: Short stories, nonfiction and poetry. Judged by AWP. No entry fee. **Deadline: first week of December** (postmark). Entries must be unpublished. Open to students in AWP Member University Creative Writing Programs only. Accepts inquiries by e-mail, fax and phone. Guidelines available for SASE or on Web site. Results announced in Spring. Winners notified by mail in Spring. For contest results, send SASE or visit Web site.

BAKELESS PRIZE

Bread Loaf Writers'Conference/Middlebury College and Houghton Mifflin Bakeless Prize, Bread Loaf Writers'Conf., Middlebury College, Middlebury VT 05753. (802) 443-2018. E-mail: bakelessprize@middlebury.edu. Website: http://www.bakelessprize.org. **Contact:** Jennifer Bates, Contest Coordinator. "To promote first books of the highest caliber." Annual. Prize: Publication by Graywolf Press and fellowship to attend Bread Loaf Writers'Conference. Categories: One award each for Fiction (average 500 entries), Poetry (average 700 entries) and Creative Nonfiction (average 100 entries). Judges and guidelines announced on web site in June. Entry fee: $10. Make checks payable to Middlebury College. Accepts inquiries by e-mail. **Submission period is September 15 to November 1.** Entries should be unpublished. Anyone writing in English may enter contest. Cover letter should include name, address, phone, e-mail, novel/story title. No identifying information on ms. Writers may submit own work. "Make sure your manuscript is ready." Results announced May. Winners notified by phone in April. Results made available to entrants with SASE, on Web site.

☑ ◎ BARD FICTION PRIZE

Bard College, P.O. Box 5000, Annandale-on-Hudson NY 12504-5000. (845)758-7087. Fax: (845)758-7043. E-mail: bfp@bard.edu. Website: www.bard.edu/bfp. **Contact:** Irene Zedlacher. The Bard Fiction Prize is intended to encourage and support young writers of fiction to pursue their creative goals and to provide an opportunity to work in a fertile and intellectual environment. Prize: $30,000 cash award and appointment as writer-in-residence at Bard College for 1 semester. Judged by committee of 5 judges (authors associated with Bard College). No entry fee. Cover letter should include name, address, phone, e-mail and name of publisher where book was previously published. Guidelines available by SASE, fax, phone, e-mail or on Web site. Deadline: July 15. Entries must be previously published. Open to US citizens aged 39 and below. Accepts inquiries by fax, e-mail and phone. Results announced by October 15. Winners notified by phone. For contest results, e-mail or visit Web site.

☑ ◎ MILDRED L. BATCHELDER AWARD

Association for Library Service to Children, 50 E. Huron St., Chicago IL 60611. (800)545-2433 ext. 2163. Fax: (312)944-7671. E-mail: alsc@ala.org. Website: www.ala.org/alsc. **Contact:** ALSC, attn: Batchelder Award. Award is to "encourage international exchange of quality children's books by recognizing US publishers of such books in translation." Prize: Citation. Judged by Batchelder Award selection committee. No entry fee. Deadline: December 31. Books should be US trade publications for which children, up to and including age 14, are the potential audience. Previously published translations only. Accepts inquiries by fax, e-mail and phone. Guidelines available in February for SASE, by fax, phone, e-mail or on Web site. Results announced at ALA Midwinter Meeting. Winners notified by phone. Contest results by phone, fax, for SASE or visit Web site.

☒ BELLEVUE LITERARY REVIEW GOLDENBERG PRIZE FOR FICTION

Bellevue Literary Review, NYU Dept of Medicine, 550 First Ave. OBV-A612, New York NY 10016. (212)263-3973. E-mail: info@blreview.org. Website: www.blreview.org. **Contact:** Stacy Bodziak, Managing Editor. "The BLR prizes award outstanding writing related to themes of health, healing, illness, the mind and the body." Annual. Competition/award for short stories. Prize: $1,000 and publication. Receives about 200-300 entries per category. BLR editors select semi-finalists to be read by an independent judge who chooses the winner. Previous judges include Ray Gonzalez (2006), Amy Hempel (2007), Rick Moody (2008) and Rosellen Brown (2009). Entry fee: $15, or $20 to include one year subscription. Send credit card information or make checks payable to Bellevue Literary Review. Guidelines available in February. Accepts inquiries by e-mail, phone, mail. Submissions open in March. **Entry deadline is August 1st**. Entries should be unpublished. Anyone may enter contest. Length: no minimum, maximum of 5,000 words. Cover letter should include name, address, phone, e-mail, story title. Title and word count should appear on ms. Writers may submit own work. Results announced December. Winners notified by mail, by e-mail. Results made available to entrants with SASE, by e-mail, on Web site.

☐ GEORGE BENNETT FELLOWSHIP

Phillips Exeter Academy, 20 Main St., Exeter NH 03833-2460. Website: www.exeter.edu. Annual award for fellow and family "to provide time and freedom from material considerations to a person seriously contemplating or pursuing a career as a writer. Applicants should have a manuscript in progress which they intend to complete during the fellowship period." Duties: To be in residency for the academic year; to make oneself available informally to students interested in writing. Guidelines for SASE or on Web site. The committee favors writers who have not yet published a book with a major publisher. Residence at the Academy during the fellowship period required. Prize: $10,000 stipend, room and board. Judged by committee of the English department. $10 application fee. Application form and guidelines for SASE and on Web site. **Deadline: December 1**. Results announced in March. Winners notified by letter or phone. List of winners available in March. All entrants will receive an announcement of the winner. "Stay within a few pages of the limit. (We won't read more anyway.) Trust us to recognize that what you are sending is a work in progress. (You have the chance to talk about that in your statement.) Hope, but don't expect anything. If you don't win, some well-known writers have been in your shoes—at least as many as have won the fellowship."

◎ BEST LESBIAN EROTICA

BLE 2010, Kathleen Warnock, 31-64 21st St., #319, Long Island City, NY 11106. E-mail: KWarnockble@gmail.com. **Contact**: Kathleen Warnock, series editor. Categories: Novel excerpts, short stories, other prose; poetry will be considered but is not encouraged. No entry fee. Include cover page with author's name, title of submission(s), address, phone, fax, e-mail. All submissions must be typed and double-spaced. Also number the pages. Length: 5,000 words. You may submit a maximum of 3 different pieces of work. Submit 2 hard copies of each submission. No e-mail submissions will be accepted; accepts inquiries by e-mail. Accepts both previously published and unpublished material. Open to any writer. All submissions must include SASE or an e-mail address for response. No mss will be returned.

◎ BINGHAMTON UNIVERSITY JOHN GARDNER FICTION BOOK AWARD

Binghamton Center for Writers, State University of New York, P.O. Box 6000, Binghamton NY 13902. (607) 777-2713. Fax: (607) 777-2408. E-mail: cwpro@binghamton.edu. Website: english.binghamton.edu/cwpro. **Contact**: Maria Mazziotti Gillan, director. Award's purpose is "to serve the literary community by calling attention to outstanding books of fiction." Prize: $1,000. Categories: novels and short story collections. Judged by "rotating outside judges." No entry fee. Entry must have been published in book form with a minimum press run of 500. Each book submitted must be accompanied by an application form, available online or send SASE to above address. Submit three copies of the book; copies will not be returned. Publishers may submit more than one book for prize consideration. **Deadline: March 1**. Entries must have appeared in print between January 1 and December 31 of the year preceding the award. Open to any writer. Results announced in Summer. Winners notified by e-mail or phone. For contest results, send SASE or visit Web site.

☑ ◎ IRMA S. AND JAMES H. BLACK AWARD

Bank Street College of Education, 610 W. 112th St., New York NY 10025-4458. (212) 875-4450. Fax: (212) 875-4558. E-mail: kfreda@bankstreet.edu. Website: http://streetcat.bankstreet.edu/children/awards.html. **Contact:** Kristen Freda, award director. Offered annually for a book for young children, for excellence of both text and illustrations. Entries must have been published during the previous calendar year. Prize: press function and scroll and seals by Maurice Sendak for attaching to award winner's book run. Judged by adult children's literature experts and children 6-10 years old. No entry fee. Guidelines for SASE, fax, e-mail or on Web site. Accepts inquiries by phone, fax, e-mail. Deadline: December 15. Entries must be previously published. "Write to address above. Usually publishers submit books they want considered, but individuals can too. No entries are returned." Winners notified by phone in April and announced in May. A list of winners will be available on Web site.

▦ ☑ JAMES TAIT BLACK MEMORIAL PRIZES

Department of English Literature, University of Edinburgh, David Hume Tower, George Square, Edinburgh Scotland EH8 9JX United Kingdom. (44-13) 1650-3619. Fax: (44-13) 1650-6898. E-mail: s.strathdee@ed.ac.uk. Website: www.englit.ed.ac.uk/jtbinf.htm. **Contact:** Sheila Strathdee, Department of English Literature. "Two prizes each of £10,000 are awarded: one for the best work of fiction, one for the best biography or work of that nature, published during the calendar year January 1 to December 31." Judged by professors of English Literature with the assistance of teams of postgraduate readers. No entry fee. Accepts inquiries by fax, e-mail, phone. **Deadline: December 1.** Entries must be previously published. "Eligible works are those written in English and first published or co-published in Britain in the year of the award. Works should be submitted by publishers." Open to any writer. Winners notified by phone, via publisher. Contact department of English Literature for list of winners or check Web site.

▦ ☑ ◎ THE BOARDMAN TASKER AWARD FOR MOUNTAIN LITERATURE

The Boardman Tasker Charitable Trust, Pound House, Llangennith, Swansea Wales SA3 1JQ United Kingdom. Phone/fax: (44-17)9238-6215. E-mail: margaretbody@lineone.net. Website: www.boardmantasker.com. **Contact:** Margaret Body. "The award is to honor Peter Boardman and Joe Tasker, who disappeared on Everest in 1982." Offered annually to reward a work of nonfiction or fiction, in English or in translation, which has made an outstanding contribution to mountain literature. Books must be published in the UK between November 1 of previous year and October 31 of year of the prize. Writers may obtain information, but entry is by publishers only. "No restriction of nationality, but work must be published or distributed in the UK." Prize: £3,000. Judged by a panel of 3 judges elected by trustees. No entry fee. "May be fiction, nonfiction, poetry or drama. Not an anthology. Subject must be concerned with a mountain environment. Previous winners have been books on expeditions, climbing experiences, a biography of a mountaineer, novels." Guidelines available in January for SASE, by fax, e-mail or on Web site. Deadline: August 1. Entries must be previously published. Publisher's entry only. Open to any writer. Results announced in November. Winners notified by phone or e-mail. For contest results, send SASE, fax, e-mail or visit Web site. "The winning book needs to be well written to reflect a knowledge of and a respect and appreciation for the mountain environment."

☐ THE BRIAR CLIFF POETRY, FICTION & CREATIVE NONFICTION COMPETITION

The Briar Cliff Review, Briar Cliff University, 3303 Rebecca St., Sioux City IA 51104-0100. (712) 279-5321. Fax: (712) 279-5410. E-mail: curranst@briarcliff.edu. Website: www.briarcliff.edu/bcreview. **Contact:** Tricia Currans-Sheehan, editor. Award "to reward good writers and showcase quality writing." Offered annually for unpublished poem, story and essay. Prize: $ 1,000, and publication in Spring issue. All entrants receive a copy of the magazine with winning entries. Judged by editors. "We guarantee a considerate reading." Entry fee: $20. Guidelines available in August for SASE. Inquiries accepted by e-mail. **Deadline: Submissions between August 1 and November 1.** No mss returned. Entries must be unpublished. Length: 6,000 words maximum. Open to any writer. Results announced in December or January. Winners notified by phone or letter around December 20. For contest results, send SASE with submission. "Send us your best. We want stories with a plot."

⊕ ☐ THE BRIDPORT PRIZE

P.O. Box 6910, Bridport, Dorset DT6 9QB United Kingdom. (01308) 428333. E-mail: frances@bridportprize. org.uk. Website: www.bridportprize.org.uk. **Contact:** Frances Everitt, administrator. Award to "promote literary excellence, discover new talent." Prize: £5,000 sterling; £1,000 sterling; £500 sterling, plus various runners-up prizes and publication of approximately 13 best stories and 13 best poems in anthology. Categories: short stories and poetry. Judged by 1 judge for fiction (in 2009, Jackie Kay) and 1 judge for poetry (in 2009, David Harsent). Entry fee: £6 sterling for each entry. **Deadline: June 30.** Entries must be unpublished. Length: 5,000 maximum for short stories; 42 lines for poetry. Open to any writer. Guidelines available in January for SASE or visit Web site. Accepts inquiries by fax, e-mail, phone. Results announced in November of year of contest. Winners notified by phone or mail in October. For contest results, send SASE.

⬛ ◎ BURNABY WRITERS' SOCIETY CONTEST

Burnaby Writers' Society, 6584 Deer Lake Ave., Burnaby BC V5G 3T7 Canada. E-mail: info@bws. bc.ca. Website: www.bws.bc.ca. Offered annually for unpublished work. Open to all residents of British Columbia. Categories vary from year to year. Send SASE for current rules. Purpose is to encourage talented writers in all genres. Prize: 1st Place: $200; 2nd Place: $100; 3rd Place: $50; and public reading. Entry fee: $5. Guidelines available by e-mail, for SASE or on Web site. Accepts inquiries by e-mail. Deadline: May 31. Results announced in September. Winners notified by mail, phone, e-mail. Results available for SASE or on Web site.

◎ BUSH ARTIST PROGRAM

Bush Foundation, 332 Minnesota St., Suite E-900, St. Paul MN 55101. Fax: (651)297-6485. E-mail: artists@ bushfoundation.org. Website: www.bushfoundation.org. **Contact:** Julie Sholing, program director. Award to "provide artists with significant financial support that enables them to further their work and their contributions to their communities. Fellows may decide to take time for solitary work or reflection, engage in collaborative or community projects, or embark on travel or research." Prize: $50,000 for 12-24 months. Categories: Literary Arts, Script Works, Performance-Based Work, Traditional and Ethnic Performing Arts, Media Arts, Visual Arts, Traditional and Functional Craft Arts. Judged by a panel of artists and arts professionals who reside outside of Minnesota, South Dakota, and North Dakota. No entry fee. Applications available in September. Accepts inquiries by fax and e-mail. Applicants must be at least 25 years old, U.S. citizens or Permanent Residents, and residents of Minnesota, South Dakota, and North Dakota. Students not eligible. Must meet certain publication requirements. Results announced in Spring. Winners notified by letter. List of winners available in May and sent to all applicants.

▦ ☑ ◎ THE CAINE PRIZE FOR AFRICAN WRITING

51a Southwark St., London England SE1 1RU United Kingdom. E-mail: info@caineprize.com. Website: www.caineprize.com. **Contact:** Nick Elam, administrator. Annual award for a short story (3,000-15,000 words) by an African writer. "An 'African writer' is normally taken to mean someone who was born in Africa, who is a national of an African country, or whose parents are African, and whose work has reflected African sensibilities." Entries must have appeared for the first time in the 5 years prior to the closing date for submissions, which is January 31 each year. Publishers should submit 6 copies of the published original with a brief cover note (no pro forma application). Prize: £10,000. Judged by a panel of judges appointed each year. No entry fee. Cover letter should include name, address, phone, e-mail, title and publication where story was previously published. Deadline: January 31. Entries must be previously published. Word length: 3,000-10,000 words. Manuscripts not accepted. Entries must be submitted by publishers not authors. Results announced in mid-July. Winners notified at event/banquet. For contest results, send fax, e-mail or visit our Web site.

◎ CALIFORNIA BOOK AWARDS

Commonwealth Club of California, 595 Market St., San Francisco CA 94105. (415) 597-6703. Fax: (415) 597-6729. E-mail: bookawards@commonwealthclub.org. Website: www.commonwealthclub.org/features/caBookAwards/. **Contact:** Gina Baleria, literary director. Award to honor excellence in literature written by California residents. Prize: $2,000, gold medal; $300, silver medal. Categories: fiction, first work of fiction, nonfiction, juvenile, young adult, poetry, Californiana, contribution to publishing. Judged by jury. No entry fee. **Deadline: Friday, December 17, 2010 by 5pm**. Entries must be previously published. California residents only. Writer or publisher may nominate work. Guidelines available in January on Web site. Results announced in Spring. Winners notified by phone. For contest results, send e-mail.

☑ JOHN W. CAMPBELL MEMORIAL AWARD FOR BEST SCIENCE FICTION NOVEL OF THE YEAR

Center for the Study of Science Fiction, English Department, University of Kansas, Lawrence KS 66045. (785) 864-3380. Fax: (785)864-1159. E-mail: jgunn@ku.edu. Website: www.ku.edu/~sfcenter. **Contact:** James Gunn, professor and director. Award to "honor the best science fiction novel of the year." Prize: Trophy. Winners receive an expense-paid trip to the university to receive their award. Their names are also engraved on a permanent trophy. Categories: novels. Judged by a jury. No entry fee. Deadline: see Web site. Entries must be previously published. Open to any writer. Accepts inquiries by e-mail and fax. "Ordinarily publishers should submit work, but authors have done so when publishers would not. Send for list of jurors." Results announced in July. For contest results, send SASE.

$ CHIZINE/LEISURE SHORT STORY CONTEST

Website: http://chizine.com. **Contact:** Brett Alexander Savpry, editor-in-chief. Held annually "to find the top three dark fiction stories." Competition/award for short stories. Prize: 7¢/word, up to 4,000 words. Judged by a revolving panel of writers and editors of dark fiction selected by the Editor-in-Chief of Chizine. No entry fee. Guidelines available in May. Accepts inquiries by e-mail. **Submissions accepted June 1st through 30th.** Entries should be unpublished. Contest open to anyone. Cover letter and ms should include name, address, e-mail, word count, short story title. Writers may submit own work. Results announced end of July. Winners and honorable mentions notified by e-mail. Results made available to entrants on Web site.

☐ CRAZYHORSE FICTION PRIZE

College of Charleston, Dept. of English, 66 George St., Charleston SC 29424. (843) 953-7740. E-mail: crazyhorse@cofc.edu. Website: http://crazyhorse.cofc.edu. **Contact:** Editors. Prize: $2,000 and publication in Crazyhorse. Judged by anonymous writer whose identity is disclosed when the winners are announced in April. Past judges: Charles Baxter (2002), Michael Martone (2003), Diana Abu-Jaber (2004), T.M. McNally (2005), Dan Chaon (2006), Antonya Nelson (2007), Ha Jin (2008). Entry fee: $16 (covers 1-yr subscription to Crazyhorse; make checks payable to Crazyhorse). To enter, please send up to 25 pages of prose. Include a detachable cover sheet with your name, address and telephone number; please do not include this information on the ms itself. Send SASE or see Web site for additional details. **Deadline: December 15th of each year**; see Web site. Open to any writer.

❒ THE CRUCIBLE POETRY AND FICTION COMPETITION

Crucible, Barton College, College Station, Wilson NC 27893. (252)399-6456. E-mail: tgrimes@barton.edu. **Contact**: Terrence L. Grimes, editor. Offered annually for unpublished short stories. Prize: $150 (1st Prize); $100 (2nd Prize) and publication in Crucible. Competition receives 300 entries. Categories: Fiction should be 8,000 words or less. Judged by in-house editorial board. No entry fee. Guidelines available in January for SASE, e-mail or in publication. **Deadline: April**. Open to any writer. "The best time to submit is December through April." Results announced in July. Winners notified by mail. For contest rules, send e-mail.

❒ DEAD OF WINTER

E-mail: editors@toasted-cheese.com. Website: www.toasted-cheese.com. **Contact:** Stephanie Lenz, editor. The contest is a winter-themed short fiction contest with a new topic each year. Topic and word limit announced Nov. 1. The topic is usually geared toward a supernatural theme. Prize: Amazon gift certificates in the amount of $20, $15 and $10; publication in Toasted Cheese. Also offers honorable mention. Categories: short stories. Judged by two Toasted Cheese editors who blind judge each contest. Each judge uses her own criteria to rate entries. No entry fee. Cover letter should include name, address, e-mail, word count and title. **Deadline: December 21.** Entries must be unpublished. Word limit varies each year. Open to any writer. Guidelines available in November on Web site. Accepts inquiries by e-mail. "Follow guidelines. Write a smart, original story. We have further guidelines on the Web site." Results announced January 31. Winners notified by e-mail. List of winners on Web site.

❒ ◉ DELAWARE DIVISION OF THE ARTS

820 N. French St., Wilmington DE 19801. (302)577-8278. Fax: (302)577-6561. Website: www.artsdel.org. **Contact**: Kristin Pleasanton, art & artist services coordinator. Award "to help further careers of emerging and established professional artists." For Delaware residents only. Prize: $10,000 for masters; $5,000 for established professionals; $2,000 for emerging professionals. Judged by out-of-state, nationally recognized professionals in each artistic discipline. No entry fee. Guidelines available after January 1 on website. Accepts inquiries by e-mail, phone. Expects to receive 25 fiction entries. Deadline: August 15. Open to any writer. Results announced in December. Winners notified by mail. Results available on Web site. "Follow all instructions and choose your best work sample."

RICK DEMARINIS SHORT FICTION PRIZE

Cuthroat, A Journal of the Arts, P.O. Box 2414, Durango CO 81302. (970) 903-7914. E-mail: cutthroatmag@gmail.com. Website: http://www.cutthroatmag.com. **Contact:** Pamela Uschuk, editor-In-chief. "To recognize a fine piece of fiction by giving the author an honorarium and a venue for publication." Annual. Competition/award for short stories. $1,250 plus publication for First Prize; $250 plus publication for Second Prize. Receives about 250 plus entries. Magazine staff chooses 20-25 finalists, and a different nationally known fiction writer is selected each year as the final judge. Entry fee: $15. Make checks payable to Raven's Word Writers Center. Guidelines available in January. **Entries postmark deadline is October 10, 2009.** Entries should be unpublished. Anyone writing anywhere in english may enter contest. Length: 5,000 word limit. Cover letter should include name, address, phone, e-mail, novel/story title. No identifying information may appear anywhere on the ms. "Our criteria is excellence" Results announced December. Winners notified by phone. Results made available to entrants with SASE.

◉ DOBIE/PAISANO FELLOWSHIPS

Dobie Paisano Fellowship Program. The University of Texas at Austin, Graduate School, 1 University Station (G0400), Austin, TX 78712-0531. ((512) 471-8528. Fax (512) 471-7620. E-mail: adameve@mail.utexas.edu. Website: www.utexas.edu/orgs/Paisano. **Contact**: Michael Adams, Director. Two fellowship awards for writers of fiction, poetry, and non-fiction: one for four months with a stipend of $5,000 a month. Requires previous publication; one for six months with a stipend of $3,000 a month (previous publication not required but permitted. Fellow lives (rent and bills free) at Paisano ranch southwest of Austin, Texas. Judged by committee from Texas Institute of Letters and the University of Texas. Entry fee: $20 Deadline: January 15. Entries must be unpublished. Open to writers with a Texas connection—native Texans, people who have lived in Texas at least three years, or writers with published significant work on Texas." Winners announced early May. List of winners available at Web site.

DZANC PRIZE

Dzanc Books, 2702 Lillian, Ann Arbor MI 48104. E-mail: prize@dzancbooks.org. Website: www.dzancbooks.org. **Contact:** Dan Wickett, executive director. "Our goal is to help authors find means of producing their work and doing community service." Annual. Prize: $5,000. Single category of a combination of work in progress and literary community service. Entries are judged by Dzanc editors (Steve Gillis, Dan Wickett and Keith Taylor). No entry fee. Accepts inquiries by e-mail. **Entry deadline is Nov. 1, 2009.** Entries should be unpublished. Any author with a work of literary fiction in progress, and community service that is based in the United States, may enter contest. Writers may submit own work. "Have a good idea of what we're looking for in terms of literary community service (see Web site)" Results announced in December. Winners notified by e-mail. Results made available to entrants via email, and on Web site.

☐ EATON LITERARY AGENCY'S ANNUAL AWARDS PROGRAM

Eaton Literary Agency, P.O. Box 49795, Sarasota FL 34230. (941) 366-6589. Fax: (941) 365-4679. E-mail: eatonlit@aol.com. Website: www.eatonliterary.com. **Contact:** Richard Lawrence, vice president. Offered biannually for unpublished mss. Prize: $2,500 (over 10,000 words); $500 (under 10,000 words). Judged by an independent agency in conjunction with some members of Eaton's staff. No entry fee. Guidelines available for SASE, by fax, e-mail, or on Web site. Accepts inquiries by fax, phone and e-mail. **Deadline: March 31 (mss under 10,000 words); August 31 (mss over 10,000 words).** Entries must be unpublished. Open to any writer. Results announced in April and September. Winners notified by mail. For contest results, send SASE, fax, e-mail or visit Web site.

☑ EMERGING VOICES ROSENTHAL FELLOWSHIP

PEN USA, c/o Antioch University, 400 Corporate Pointe, Culver City CA 90230. (310) 862-1555. Fax: (310) 862-1556. E-mail: ev@penusa.org. Website: www.penusa.org. **Contact:** Adam Somers, Executive Director. "Annual program offering $1,000 stipend and 8-month fellowship to writers in the early stages of their literary careers. Program includes one-on-one sessions with mentors, seminars on topics such as editing or working with agents, courses in the Writers' Program at UCLA Extension, and literary readings. Participants selected according to potential and lack of access to traditional publishing and/or educational opportunities.No age restrictions; selection is not based solely on economic need. Participants need not be published, but the 'program is directed toward poets and writers of fiction and creative nonfiction with clear ideas of what they hope to accomplish through their writing. Mentors are chosen from PEN's comprehensive membership of professional writers and beyond. Participants are paired with established writers sharing similar writing interests and often with those of the same ethnic and cultural backgrounds.' Program gets underway in January. See Web site for brochure and complete guidelines." **Deadline: September 5, 2009** (for 2010 cycle). Materials must arrive in the PEN offices by the submission deadline— no exceptions.

◎ THE EMILY CONTEST

West Houston Chapter Romance Writers of America, 18207 Heaton Drive, Houston TX 77084. E-mail: emily@whrwa.com. Website: www.whrwa.com. **Contact:** Pamela Stephens, Emily Contest chair. " The mission of The Emily is to professionally support writers and guide them toward a path to publication. Prize: first place entry in each category receives an Emily brooch and are entered into the Best of the Best Contest; all finalists receive certificates. First round judging is by two judges, at least one is a published author. All judges are experienced critiquers or trained. Each entry has two final round judges and include both editors at major romance publishing houses and agents from major literary agencies." Categories include: Comtemporary Single Title, Contemporary Series, Paranormal, and Historical. Entry fee: $20 for WHRWA members; $30 for non-members. Deadline: October 6, 2009. Entries submitted via e-mail, length: first 35 pages of an unpublished novel. Open to all "unpublished romance writers not contracted by the contest deadline and published authors entering a category they're not published in." Guidelines available on the Web site. Inquiries can be made by e-mail. "We look for dynamic, interesting romance stories with a hero and heroine readers can relate to and love. Hook us from the beginning and keep the level of excitement high." Results announced the second Saturday in February. Winners notified by e-mail or phone. For contest results, visit Web site.

☑ ◎ THE VIRGINIA FAULKNER AWARD FOR EXCELLENCE IN WRITING

Prairie Schooner, 201 Andrews Hall, P.O. Box 880334, Lincoln NE 68588-0334. (402) 472-0911. Fax: (402) 472-9771. E-mail: jengelhardt2@unl.edu. Website: www.unl.edu/schooner/psmain.htm. **Contact:** Hilda Raz, editor. Offered annually for work published in Prairie Schooner in the previous year. Prize: $1,000. Categories: short stories, essays, novel excerpts and translations. Judged by Editorial Board. No entry fee. Guidelines for SASE or on Web site. Accepts inquiries by fax and e-mail. "We only read mss from September 1 through May 1." Winning entry must have been published in Prairie Schooner in the year preceeding the award. Results announced in the Spring issue. Winners notified by mail in February or March.

▦ ◻ FISH ONE PAGE PRIZE

Fish Publishing, Durrus, Bantry, County Cork Ireland. E-mail: info@fishpublishing.com. Website: www.fishpublishing.com. **Contact:** Clem Cairns, editor. Prize: 1st prize: 1,000 Euro (approx. $1,300). Nine runners up get 50 Euro (approx. $80). The authors of the 10 best works of short short fiction will be published in the Fish Short Story Prize Anthology. Entry fee: $15 per story. Enter online. **Deadline: March 19**. Entries must be unpublished. Stories must fit on one A4 page. Entries can be in any style or format and can be on any subject. The competition is open to writers from all countries, but entries must be written in English. Guidelines on Web site or by e-mail.

▦ ◻ FISH SHORT STORY PRIZE

Fish Publishing, E-mail: info@fishpublishing.com. Website: www.fishpublishing.com. **Contact:** Clem Cairns, editor. Prize: 1st Prize: 3,000 Euros (approx. $4,000) plus prizes for nine runners up, including week's residence in Anam Cara Writers Retreat in the West of Ireland. **Deadline: November 30**. Length: 5,000 words maximum. Best stories are published in annual Fish anthology. Winners announced March 17, anthology distributed in summer. No restriction on theme or style. Online entry. Honorary Patrons Frank McCourt, Roddy Doyle.

◻ FLORIDA FIRST COAST WRITERS' FESTIVAL NOVEL, SHORT FICTION, PLAYWRITING & POETRY AWARDS

Writers' Festival & Florida Community College at Jacksonville, FCCJ North Campus, 4501 Capper Road, Jacksonville FL 32218-4499. (904) 766-6760. E-mail: dathomas@fccj.edu. Website: www.fccj.edu/wf. **Contact:** Dr. Dana Thomas, festival contest director. Conference and contest "to create a healthy writing environment, honor writers of merit and find a novel manuscript to recommend to New York publishers for 'serious consideration.'" Judged by university faculty and freelance and professional writers. Entry fee: $7 for poetry or $18 for 3 poems. **Deadline: December 1 for poetry**. Entries must be unpublished. Word length: 30 lines for poetry. Open to any writer. Guidelines available on the Web site or in the fall for SASE. Accepts inquiries by fax and e-mail. "For stories and novels, make the opening pages sparkle. For plays, make them at least two acts and captivating. For poems, blow us over with imagery and insight and avoid clichés and wordiness." Results announced on the Web site and at FCCJ's Florida First Coast Writers' Festival held in the spring.

◻ H.E. FRANCIS SHORT STORY AWARD

The Ruth Hindman Foundation, University of Alabama English Dept., Department of English, Huntsville AL 35899. E-mail: MaryH71997@aol.com. Website: http://www.uah.edu/colleges/liberal/english/hefranciscontest/. **Contact:** Patricia Sammon. Offered annually for unpublished work not to exceed 5,000 words. Acquires first time publication rights. Prize: $1,000. Judged by a panel of nationally recognized, award-winning authors, directors of creative writing programs, and editors of literary journals. Entry fee: $15 reading fee (make check payable to the Ruth Hindman Foundation). **Deadline:** December 31.

JOHN GARDNER FICTION BOOK AWARD

Binghamton Center for Writers, State University of New York, P.O. Box 6000, Binghamton NY 13902. (607) 777-2713. E-mail: cwpro@binghamton.edu. Website: http://english.binghamton.edu/cwpro. **Contact:** Maria Mazziotti Gillan, director. "To recognize the strongest novel or collection of short stories published the preceding year." Annual. Competition/award for novels, story collections. Prize: $1,000. Entries are judged by a rotating guest judge. Entry fee: send 3 copies of the book. Guidelines available in June. Accepts inquiries by e-mail, phone. **Entry deadline is March 1st.** Entries should be previously published, with a min press run of 500. Author or publishers may submit. Publishers may submit as many as their authors published that year as they would like. Winners notified by e-mail. Winners announced by mid-summer. Results made available to entrants with SASE, on Web site.

☑ GEORGETOWN REVIEW PRIZE

Georgetown Review, 400 East College St, Box 227, Georgetown KY 40324. E-mail: gtownreview@ georgetowncollege.edu. Website: http://georgetownreview.georgetowncollege.edu. **Contact:** Steven Carter, editor. "Contest for short stories, poetry and creative nonfiction." Annual. Competition/award for short stories. Prize: $1,000 and publication; runners-up receive publication. Receives about 400 entries for each category. Entries are judged by the editors. Entry fee: $10 for first entry, $5 for each one thereafter. Make checks payable to Georgetown Review. Guidelines available in July. Accepts inquiries by e-mail. **Entry deadline is Nov. 15th, 2009.** Entries should be unpublished. Contest open to anyone except family, friends of the editors. Cover letter, ms should include name, address, phone, e-mail, novel/story title. Writers may submit own work. "We're just looking to publish quality work. Sometimes our contests are themed, so check the Web site for details." Results announced Feb or March. Winners notified by e-mail. Results made available to entrants with SASE.

☐ GIVAL PRESS NOVEL AWARD

Gival Press LLC, P.O. Box 3812, Arlington VA 22203. (703) 351-0079. E-mail: givalpress@yahoo.com. Website: www.givalpress.com. **Contact:** Robert L. Giron, publisher. "To award the best literary novel." Annual. Prize: $3,000 (USD), publication and author's copies. Categories: literary novel. Receives about 60-80 entries per category. Final judge for 2008 was John Domini. Entries read anonymously. Entry fee: $50 (USD). Make checks payable to Gival Press, LLC. Guidelines with SASE, by phone, by e-mail, on Web site, in journals. Accepts inquiries by e-mail. **Deadline: May 30 of each year.** Entries should be unpublished. Open to any author who writes original work in English. Length: 30,000-100,000 words. Cover letter should include name, address, phone, e-mail, word count, novel title. Only the title and word count should appear on the actual ms. Writers may submit own work. "Review the types of mss Gival Press has published. We stress literary works." Results announced late fall of same year. Winners notified by phone. Results made available to entrants with SASE, by e-mail, on Web site.

☐ GIVAL PRESS SHORT STORY AWARD

Gival Press, P.O. Box 3812, Arlington VA 22203. (703) 351-0079. E-mail: givalpress@yahoo.com. Website: www.givalpress.com. **Contact:** Robert L. Giron, publisher. "To award the best literary short story." Annual. Prize: $1,000 and publication on Web site. Category: literary short story. Receives about 60-80 entries per category. Entries are judged anonymously. Entry fee: $25. Make checks payable to Gival Press, LLC. Guidelines available online, via e-mail, or by mail. Deadline: Aug. 8th of every year. Entries must be unpublished. Open to anyone who writes original short stories in English. Length: 5,000-15,000 words. Include name, address, phone, e-mail, word count, title on cover letter. Only the title and word count should be found on ms. Writers may submit their own ficiton. "We publish literary works." Results announced in the fall of the same year. Winners notified by phone. Results available with SASE, by e-mail, on Web site.

GLIMMER TRAIN'S FAMILY MATTERS

Glimmer Train Press, Inc., 1211 NW Glisan St. Suite 207, Portland OR 97209. (503) 221-0836. Fax: (503) 221-0837. Website: www.glimmertrain.org. **Contact:** Susan Burmeister-Brown, co-editor. Offered quarterly for unpublished stories about family. Length: 1,200-12,000 words. Prize: 1st place: $1,200, publication in Glimmer Train Stories, and 20 copies of that issue; 1st/2nd runners up receive $500/$300, respectively, and possible publication in Glimmer Train Stories. Entry fee: $15. **Contest open the months of January, April, July, and October.** Open to all writers. Entries should be unpublished. Make your submissions online at www.glimmertrain.org. Winners will be notified and results will be posted three months after the close of each competition.

☐ GLIMMER TRAIN'S FICTION OPEN

Glimmer Train Press, Inc., 1211 NW Glisan St., Suite 207, Portland OR 97209. (503) 221-0836. Fax: (503) 221-0837. Website: www.glimmertrain.org. **Contact:** Susan Burmeister-Brown, co-editor. Offered quarterly for unpublished stories on any theme. Word count: 2,000-20,000. Prize: 1st place: $2,000, publication in Glimmer Train Stories, and 20 copies of that issue; 1st/2nd runners-up: $1,000/$600 respectively, and possible publication in Glimmer Train Stories. Entry fee: $20/story. **Contest open the months of March, June, September and December.** Make your submissions online (www. glimmertrain.org). Winners will be called and results announced three months after the close of each contest.

☐ GLIMMER TRAIN'S SHORT STORY AWARD FOR NEW WRITERS

Glimmer Train Press, Inc., 1211 NW Glisan St., Suite 207, Portland OR 97209. (503) 221-0836. Fax: (503) 221-0837. Website: www.glimmertrain.org. **Contact:** Susan Burmeister-Brown, co-editor. Offered for any writer whose fiction hasn't appeared in a nationally-distributed publication with a circulation over 5,000. Word limit: 500-12,000 words. Stories must be previously unpublished. **Entry fee:** $15/story. Contest open in the months of May and November. Make your submissions online at www.glimmertrain.org. Prize: First place: receives $1,200, publication in Glimmer Train Stories, and 20 copies of that issue. First/ second runners-up receive $500/$300, respectively, and possible publication in Glimmer Train Stories. Winners will be called and results announced three months after the close of each contest.

☐ GLIMMER TRAIN'S VERY SHORT FICTION AWARD

Glimmer Train Press, Inc., 1211 NW Glisan St., Suite 207, Portland OR 97209. (503) 221-0836. Fax: (503) 221-0837. Website: www.glimmertrain. org. **Contact:** Susan Burmeister-Brown, co-editor. Award to encourage the art of the very short story. "We want to read your original, unpublished, very short story— word count not to exceed 3,000 words." Prize: $1,200 and publication in Glimmer Train Stories and 20 author's copies (1st place); First/Second runners-up: $500/$300 respectively and possible publication. Entry fee: $15/story. **Contest open in the months of February and August**. Open to all writers. Make your submissions online at www.glimmertrain.org. Winners will be called and results announced three months after the close of each contest.

THE GOODHEART PRIZE FOR FICTION

Shenandoah: The Washington and Lee University Review, Mattingly House, 2 Lee Ave., Lexington VA 24450-2116. (540) 458-8765. Fax: (540) 458-8461. E-mail: shenandoah@wlu.edu. Website: shenandoah. wlu.edu. **Contact:** Lynn Leech, managing editor. Awarded to best story published in Shenandoah during a volume year. Prize: $1,000. Judged by writer whose identity is revealed after the prize winner has been selected. No entry fee. All stories published in the review are automatically considered for the prize. Winners are notified by mail or e-mail each Spring. Results are available on Web site. "Read Shenandoah to familiarize yourself with the work we publish."

☑ ☒ GRANTS FOR ARTIST'S PROJECTS

Artist Trust, 1835 12th Ave, Seattle, WA 98122. (206) 467-8734 x9. Fax: (206) 467-9633. E-mail: info@ artisttrust.org. Website: www.artisttrust.org. **Contact:** Monica Miller, Director of Programs. "The GAP Program provides support for artist-generated projects, which can include (but are not limited to) the development, completion or presentation of new work." Annual. Prize: maximum of $1,500 for projects. Accepted are poetry, fiction, graphic novels, experimental works, creative non-fiction, screen plays, film scripts and teleplays. Entries are judged by work sample as specified in the guidelines. Winners are selected by a multidisciplinary panel of artists and artist professionals. No entry fee. Guidelines available in December. Accepts inquiries by mail, phone. Submission period is Dec-Feb.**Deadline is approximately the 4th Friday of Feb.** Web site should be consulted for exact date. Entries can be unpublished or previously published. Washington state residents only. Length: 8 pages max for poetry, fiction, graphic novels, experimental work and creative nonfiction; up to 12 pages for screen plays, film scripts and teleplays. All mss must be typed with a 12-point font size or larger and cannot be single-spaced (except for poetry). Include application with project proposal and budget, as well as resume with name, address, phone, e-mail, and novel/story title. "GAP awards are highly competitive. Please follow guidelines with care." Results announced June. Winners notified by mail. Results made available to entrants by mail and on Web site.

☑ GREAT LAKES COLLEGES ASSOCIATION NEW WRITERS AWARD

Great Lakes Colleges Association Inc., 535 W. William, Suite 301, Ann Arbor MI 48103. (734) 661-2350. Fax: (734) 661-2349. E-mail: shackelford@glca.org. **Contact:** Greg Wegner. Award for first publication, one in each category of fiction, creative non-fiction and poetry. Writer must be nominated by publisher or can submit work if self-published. Prize: Winners are invited to tour the GLCA colleges. An honorarium of $500 will be guaranteed the author by each GLCA member college they visit. Judged by professors from member colleges. No entry fee. **Deadline: July 25, 2009 for 2010 competition**. Open to any writer. Submit 4 copies of the book to Greg Wegner. Guidelines available early 2009. Accepts inquiries by e-mail. Results announced in winter.

THE GRUB STREET BOOK PRIZE IN FICTION

Grub Street, 160 Boylston Street, Boston MA 02116. Phone/fax: (617) 695-0075. E-mail: info@grubstreet. org. Website: http://www.grubstreet.org. **Contact:** Christopher Castellani, artistic director. "Supports writers who are publishing beyond their first or second, third, fourth (or beyond...) book, and who live outside of New England." Annual. Competition/award for short story collections, novels. Prize: Each winner receives a $1,000 honorarium and a Friday night reading/book party at Grub Street's event space in downtown Boston. The reading and party are co-sponsored by a local independent bookstore, which will sell books at the event. Winners will lead a two-hour informal craft class on a topic of their choice for a small group of aspiring Grub Street writers. Winners also invited as guest authors to " Muse and the Marketplace" literary conference. Grub Street provides accommodations for all time in Boston and covers all travel and meal expenses. Categories: Fiction, Poetry, and Non-fiction. Different deadlines apply for each category. Entries are judged by a guest judge and committee of readers drawn from the Grub Street staff. Committee members negotiate their top picks at a meeting facilitated by the guest judge. Entry fee: $10. Send credit card information or make checks payable to Grub Street. Guidelines available in June. Accepts inquiries by fax, e-mail, phone. Entry deadline is October 15th. Entries should be previously published or under contract. Publication date must be in 2010 or 2009, and the hardcover or paperback original must be available to booksellers by the time of the winner's visit to Boston. Galleys may be submitted for the contest as long as the first edition is published by May 1, 2010. All applicants must have at least one previously published novel or short story collection (self-publication not eligible), and must not primarily reside in the following states: Massachusetts, Vermont, Maine, Connecticut, New Hampshire or Rhode Island. Cover letter should include name, address, phone, e-mail, novel/ story title. Also include a curriculum vitae and a 500-word synopsis of the proposed craft class. Writers may submit own work. Grub Street's top criterion is the overall literary merit of the work submitted, the award committee especially encourages writers publishing with small presses, writers of short story collections, and writers of color to apply. Grub Street also wants the award to benefit writers for whom a trip to Boston will likely expand their readership in a meaningful way. Please give careful thought to your proposal for the craft class, and please plan it as a 2-hour gathering for a group of 15 adult writers of mixed experience." Results announced 2-3 months after submission deadline. Previous winners: Sheri Joseph's Stray (MacAdam/Cage) and Joshua Furst's The Sabotage Café (Knopf).

◎ HAMMETT PRIZE

Internatonal Association of Crime Writers/North American Branch, P.O. Box 8674, New York NY 10116-8674. Fax: (815) 361-1477. E-mail: mfrisque@igc.org. Website: www.crimewritersna.org. **Contact:** Mary A. Frisque, executive director, North American Branch. Award established "to honor a work of literary excellence in the field of crime writing by a U.S. or Canadian author." Award for novels, story collections, nonfiction by one author. Prize: trophy. Judged by committee. "Our reading committee seeks suggestions from publishers and they also ask the membership for recommendations. Eligible books are read by a committee of members of the organization. The committee chooses five nominated books, which are then sent to three outside judges for a final selection. Judges are outside the crime writing field." No entry fee. For guidelines, send SASE or e-mail. Accepts inquiries by e-mail. **Deadline: December 1.** Entries must be previously published. To be eligible "the book must have been published in the U.S. or Canada during the calendar year." The author must be a U.S. or Canadian citizen or permanent resident. Nominations announced in January, winners announced in fall. Winners notified by mail, phone and recognized at awards ceremony. For contest results, send SASE or e-mail.

WILDA HEARNE FLASH FICTION CONTEST

Big Muddy: A Journal of the Mississippi River Valley, WHFF Contest, Southeast Missouri State Univ., MS 2650, One University Plaza, Cape Girardeau MO 63701. (573) 651-2044. Fax: (573) 651-5188. E-mail: upress@semo.edu. Website: http://www6.semo.edu/universitypress/hearne.htm. **Contact:** Dr. Susan

Swartwout, Publisher/Editor. "We're searching for the best short-short story of any theme." Annual. Prize: $200 and publication in Big Muddy. Semi-finalists will be chosen by a regional team of published writers. The final ms will be chosen by Susan Swartwout, publisher of Southeast Missouri State University Press. Entry fee: $15 (includes a copy of Big Muddy in which the winning story appears). Make checks payable to SEMO UP - WHFF. Guidelines available in January. Accepts inquiries by e-mail, phone. **Submission period is Jan 1-Sept 1.** Entries should be unpublished. Anyone may enter contest. Length: 500 words max. Cover letter should include name, address, phone, e-mail, story title. The title and page numbers should appear on each page of the ms. Writers may submit own work. Results announced fall. Winners notified by mail, by phone, by e-mail. Results made available to entrants with SASE.

◎ DRUE HEINZ LITERATURE PRIZE

University of Pittsburgh Press, 3400 Forbes Ave., 5th Floor, Eureka Building, Pittsburgh PA 15260. (412)383-2492. Fax: (412)383-2466. E-mail: press@pitt.edu. Website: www.upress.pitt.edu/upressIndex. aspx. Award to "support the writer of short fiction at a time when the economics of commercial publishing make it more and more difficult for the serious literary artist working in the short story and novella to find publication." Prize: $15,000 and publication by the University of Pittsburgh Press. No entry fee. "It is imperative that entrants review complete rules of the competition before submitting a manuscript." Deadline: Submissions received only during the months of May and June. Competition for story collections. No previously published collections. Manuscripts must be unpublished in book form. Length: 150-300 typed pages. The award is open to writers who have published a book-length collection of fiction or three short stories or novellas in commercial magazines or literary journals of national distribution. On-line publication does not count toward this requirement. Cover letter should include name, address, phone, e-mail, title, name of publications where work was originally published. This information should not appear on the ms. Results announced in December or January. Winners notified by phone. For contest results, send SASE with manuscript.

❐ LORIAN HEMINGWAY SHORT STORY COMPETITION

P.O. Box 993, Key West FL 33041-0993. (305) 294-0320. E-mail: shortstorykw@aol.com. Website: www.shortstorycompetition.com. **Contact:** Carol Shaughnessy, co-director or Joanne Denning, contest development director. Award to "encourage literary excellence and the efforts of writers who have not yet had major-market success." Competition for short stories. Prize: $1,000 (first prize), $500 (second prize), $500 (third prize), honorable mentions. Judged by a panel of writers, editors and literary scholars selected by author Lorian Hemingway. Guidelines available in January for SASE, by e-mail or on Web site. Accepts inquiries by SASE, e-mail or visit Web site. **Deadline: May 15**. Entries must be unpublished. Length: 3,000 words maximum. "Open to all writers whose work has not appeared in a nationally distributed publication with a circulation of 5,000 or more." Entry fee is $12 for each story postmarked by May 1, and $15 for stories postmarked between May 1 and May 15. "We look for excellence, pure and simple—no genre restrictions, no theme restrictions. We seek a writer's voice that cannot be ignored." Results announced at the end of July during Hemingway Days festival. Winners notified by phone prior to announcement. For contest results, send e-mail or visit Web site. "All entrants will receive a letter from Lorian Hemingway and a list of winners, via mail or e-mail, by October 1."

❐ ◎ HIGHLIGHTS FOR CHILDREN FICTION CONTEST

Highlights for Children, 803 Church St., Honesdale PA 18431-1824. (570) 253-1080. Fax: (570) 251-7847. E-mail: eds@highlights-corp.com. Website: www.highlights.com. **Contact:** Joëlle Dujardin, Associate Editor. Award "to honor quality stories (previously unpublished) for young readers and to encourage children's writers." Offered for stories for children up to age 12; category varies each year. No crime or violence, please. Specify that ms is a contest entry. Prize: $1,000 to 3 winners, plus publication in Highlights. Categories: Short stories. Judged by Highlights editors, with input given by outside readers. No entry fee. "There is a different contest theme each year. We generally receive about 1,400 entries." Cover letter should include name, address, phone, e-mail, word count and title. "We prefer that these things appear on the first page of the manuscript as well." **Deadline: January 1-31 (postmarked).** Entries must be unpublished. Length: 500 words maximum for stories for beginning readers (to age 8) and 800 words for more advanced readers (ages 9-12). No minimum word count. Open to anyone 16 years of age or older. Results announced on Web site in June. Winners notified by mail or phone. Entries not accompanied by a SASE will not be returned. See www.highlights.com for current theme and guidelines or send a SASE to Highlights for Children.

THE HILLERMAN PRIZE

Wordharvest & St. Martin's Press, 304 Calle Oso, Santa Fe NM 87501. (505) 471-1565. E-mail: wordharvest@ wordharvest.com. Website: www.wordharvest.com. **Contact:** Anne Hillerman, Co-organizer; Jean Schaumberg, Co-organizer. "To honor the contributions made by Tony Hillerman to the art and craft of the mystery." Annual competition/award for novels. Prize: $10,000 advance and publication by Thomas Dunne Books/St. Martin's Minotaur imprint. Categories: unpublished mystery novels set in the southwest, written by a first-time author in the mystery genre. One entry per author. Nominees will be selected by judges chosen by the editorial staff of St. Martin's Press, with the assistance of independent judges selected by organizers of the Tony Hillerman Writers Conference (Wordharvest), and the winner will be chosen by St. Martin's editors. No entry fee. Accepts inquiries by e-mail, phone. **Entry deadline is June 1.** Entries should be unpublished; self-published work is generally accepted. All first-time writers of an unpublished mystery set in the American southwest may enter contest. Length: no less than 220 typewritten pages or approx. 60,000 words. Cover letter should include name, address, phone, e-mail, list of publishing credits. Please include SASE for response. Writers may submit their own work. "Make sure murder or another serioius crime or crimes is at the heart of the story, and emphasis is on the solution rather than the details of the crime. The story's primary setting should be the southwest US, which includes CA, AZ, CO, NV, NM, OK, TX, and UT." Results announced at the Tony Hillerman Writers Conference. St. Martin's Press notifies the winner by phone or by e-mail 2-3 weeks prior to the conference. Results made available to entrants on Web site.

☐ TOM HOWARD/JOHN H. REID SHORT STORY CONTEST

Tom Howard Books, Mail to: Winning Writers, 351 Pleasant St., PMB 222, Northampton MA 01060-3961. (866) 946-9748. Fax: (413) 280-0539. E-mail: johnreid@mail.qango.com. Website: www.winningwriters. com/tomstory. **Contact:** John H. Reid, award director. "Established in 1993, this award honors the best short stories, essays and other works of prose being written today." Annual. Prize: $2,000 (first prize), $1,000 (second prize), $500 (third prize), $250 (fourth prize). There will also be five High Distinction Awards of $200 each and six Most Highly Commended Awards of $100 each. The top fifteen entries will be published on the Winning Writers Web site and announced in Tom Howard Contest News and the Winning Writers Newsletter. Categories: All entries are judged in one category. "We received 1,847 entries for the 2008 contest." Judged by a former journalist and magazine editor, John H. Reid. Mr. Reid has judged literary contests for over 15 years. He has published several novels, a collection of poetry, a guide to winning literary contests, and 15 books of film criticism and movie history. He is assisted by Dee C. Konrad, a leading educator and published author, who served as Associate Professor of English at Barat College of DePaul University and dean of Liberal Arts and Sciences for the year 2000-2001. Entry fee: $15 per entry. Make checks payable to Winning Writers (U.S. funds only, please). Guidelines available in August on Web site. Prefers inquiries by e-mail. **Deadline: March 31, 2009.** "Both published and unpublished works are accepted. In the case of published work, the contestant must own the online publication rights." Open to all writers. Length: 5,000 words max per entry. Cover letter should include name, address, phone, e-mail, story title, place(s) where story was previously published (if any). Only the title should be on the actual ms. Writers may submit own work. "Read past winning entries at www. winningwriters.com/contests/tomstory/ts_pastwinners.php." Results announced May 15. Winners notified by e-mail. Results made available to entrants on Web site.

THE JULIA WARD HOWE/BOSTON AUTHORS AWARD

The Boston Authors Club, 79 Moore Rd., Wayland MA 01778. (617)783-1357. E-mail: bostonauthors@ aol.com. Website: www.bostonauthorsclub.org. **Contact:** Alan Lawson. This annual award honors Julia Ward Howe and her literary friends who founded the Boston Authors Club in 1900. It also honors the membership over 108 years, consisting of novelists, biographers, historians, governors, senators, philosophers, poets, playwrights, and other luminaries. There are 2 categories: trade books and books for young readers (beginning with chapter books through young adult books). Works of fiction, nonfiction, memoir, poetry, and biography published in current year (2009 for 2010 prize) are eligible. Authors must live or have lived (college counts) within a 100-mile radius of Boston. Subsidized books, cook books and picture books are not eligible. No fee. **Deadline: January 15.** Prize: $1,000 in each category.

☐ ◎ L. RON HUBBARD'S WRITERS OF THE FUTURE CONTEST

Author Services Inc., P.O. Box 1630, Los Angeles CA 90078. (323) 466-3310. Fax: (323) 466-6474. E-mail:

contests@authorservicesinc.com. Website: www.writersofthefuture.com. **Contact:** Joni, contest director. Established in 1983. Foremost competition for new and amateur writers of unpublished science fiction or fantasy short stories or novelettes. Offered "to find, reward and publicize new speculative fiction writers so they may more easily attain professional writing careers." Open to new and amateur writers who have not professionally published a novel or short novel, more than 1 novelette, or more than 3 short stories. Eligible entries are previously unpublished short stories or novelettes (under 17,000 words) of science fiction or fantasy. Guidelines for SASE or on Web site. Accepts inquiries by fax, e-mail, phone. Prize: awards quarterly: 1st place: $1,000; 2nd place: $750; and 3rd place: $500. Annual grand prize: $5,000. "Contest has four quarters. There shall be 3 cash prizes in each quarter. In addition, at the end of the year, the 4 first-place, quarterly winners will have their entries rejudged, and a grand prize winner shall be determined." Judged by K.D. Wentworth (initial judge), then by a panel of 4 professional authors. **Deadline: December 31, March 31, June 30, September 30.** Entries must be unpublished. Limit one entry per quarter. No entry fee; entrants retain all rights to their stories. Open to any writer. Manuscripts: white paper, black ink; double-spaced; typed; each page appropriately numbered with title, no author name. Include cover page with author's name, address, phone number, e-mail address (if available), as well as estimated word count and the title of the work. Results announced quarterly in e-newsletter. Winners notified by phone.

◎ INDIANA REVIEW ½ K (SHORT-SHORT/PROSE-POEM) CONTEST

Indiana Review, Ballantine Hall 465/Indiana University, 1020 E. Kirkwood Ave., Bloomington IN 47405-7103. (812) 855-3439. Fax: (812) 855-4253. E-mail: inreview@indiana.edu. Website: www.indiana. edu/~inreview. **Contact:** Abdel Shakur, editor. Competition for fiction and prose poems no longer than 500 words. Prize: $1,000 plus publication, contributor's copies and a year's subscription. All entries considered for publication. Judged by Indiana Review staff and outside judges. Entry fee: $15 fee for no more than 3 pieces (includes a year's subscription, two issues). Make checks payable to Indiana Review. **Deadline: June 9.** Entries must be unpublished. Guidelines available in March for SASE, by phone, e-mail, on Web site, or in publication. Length: 500 words, 3 mss per entry. Open to any writer. Cover letter should include name, address, phone, e-mail, word count and title. No identifying information on ms. "We look for command of language and form." Results announced in August. Winners notified by mail. For contest results, send SASE or visit Web site.

◻ INDIANA REVIEW FICTION CONTEST

Indiana Review, BH 465/Indiana University, 1020 E. Kirkwood Ave., Bloomington IN 47405-7103. (812) 855-3439. Fax: (812) 855-4253. E-mail: inreview@indiana.edu. Website: www.indiana.edu/~inreview. **Contact:** Abdel Shakur, editor. Contest for fiction in any style and on any subject. Prize: $1,000, publication in the Indiana Review and contributor's copies. Judged by Indiana Review staff and outside judges. Entry fee: $15 fee (includes a year's subscription). Deadline: Mid-October. Entries must be unpublished. Mss will not be returned. No previously published work, or works forthcoming elsewhere, are eligible. Simultaneous submissions accepted, but in the event of entrant withdrawal, contest fee will not be refunded. Length: 15,000 words (about 40 pages) maximum, double spaced. Open to any writer. Cover letter must include name, address, phone number and title of story. Entrant's name should appear only in the cover letter, as all entries will be considered anonymously. Results announced January. Winners notified by mail. For contest results, send SASE. "We look for a command of language and structure, as well as a facility with compelling and unusual subject matter. It's a good idea to obtain copies of issues featuring past winners to get a more concrete idea of what we are looking for."

◎ INDIVIDUAL EXCELLENCE AWARDS

Ohio Arts Council, 727 E. Main St., Columbus OH 43205-1796. (614)466-2613. Fax: (614)466-4479. E-mail: ken.emerick@oac.state.oh.us. Website: www.oac.state.oh.us. **Contact:** Ken Emerick, director, Individual Creativity. "An award of excellence for completed work for Ohio residents who are not students." Annual. Competition/award for short stories, novels, story collections. Prize: $5,000 or $10,000, determined by review panel. Categories: fiction/nonfiction, poetry, criticism, playwriting/screenplays. Receives about 125 poetry, 125 fiction/nonfiction, 10-15 criticism, 25-30 playwriting entries per year. Judged by three-person panel of out-of-state panelists, anonymous review. No entry fee. Guidelines available in June on Web site. Accepts inquiries by e-mail, phone. Deadline: September 1. Open to Ohio residents living and working in the state for at least one year prior to the deadline who are also not students. Length: 20-30 pages fiction/nonfiction, 10-15 pages poetry, 30-50 pages criticism, 1 play or 2 short 1-act plays. Cover letter should include name, address, title of work. None of this information should appear on the actual manuscript. Writers may submit own work. "Submit concise bodies of work or sections, not a sampling of styles." Results announced Jan. Winners notified by mail. Results made available to entrants on Web site.

INKWELL SHORT FICTION CONTEST

Inkwell Literary Magazine, Manhattanville College, 2900 Purchase Street, Purchase NY 10577. (914) 323-7239. Fax: (914) 323-3122. E-mail: inkwell@mville.edu. Website: http://www.inkwelljournal.org. **Contact:** Competition fiction editor. Annual. Competition/award for short stories. Prize: $1,500. Entries are judged by by editorial staff. Finalists are picked by a celebrity judge. Brian Morton judging 2008 contest. Entry fee: $15. Make checks payable to Inkwell-Manhattanville College. Guidelines available in June. Accepts inquiries by fax, e-mail, phone.**Entry deadline is October 30.** Entries must be unpublished. Anyone may enter contest. Length: 5,000 words max. Cover letter should include name, address, phone, e-mail, word count, novel/story title. Only title on ms. Writers may submit own work. "Follow the guidelines. Proofread your work. Don't write for editors, teachers, or critics; write for you, and for your readers." Winners notified by phone, by e-mail. Results made available to entrants with SASE, by e-mail.

INTERNATIONAL READING ASSOCIATION CHILDREN'S BOOK AWARDS

International Reading Association, P.O. Box 8139, 800 Barksdale Rd., Newark DE 19714-8139. (302) 731-1600, ext. 221. E-mail: exec@reading.com. "This award is for newly published authors of children's books who show unusual promise in the children's book field." Offered annually for an author's first or second published book in fiction and nonfiction in 3 categories: primary (preschool-age 8), intermediate (ages 9-13), and young adult (ages 14-17). Guidelines and deadlines for SASE. Prize: 6 awards of $1,000 each, and a medal for each category. Categories: fiction and nonfiction. No entry fee. The book will be considered one time during the year of first copyright in English. **Deadline: November 1**. For guidelines with specific information write to Executive Office, International Reading Association.

◎ THE IOWA SHORT FICTION AWARD

Iowa Writers' Workshop, 102 Dey House, 507 N. Clinton St., Iowa City IA 52242-1000. (319)335-2000. Fax: (319)335-2055. Website: www.uiowapress.org. **Contact:** Holly Carver, director. Award "to give exposure to promising writers who have not yet published a book of prose." Prize: publication by University of Iowa Press. Judged by Senior Iowa Writers' Workshop members who screen manuscripts; published fiction author of note makes final selections. No entry fee. Submission period: Aug. 1-Sept. 30. Entries must be unpublished, but stories previously published in periodicals are eligible for inclusion. "The manuscript must be a collection of short stories of at least 150 word-processed, double-spaced pages." Open to any writer. No application forms are necessary. Do not send original ms. Include SASE for return of ms. Announcement of winners made early in year following competition. Winners notified by phone.

◼ JUST DESERTS SHORT-SHORT FICTION PRIZE

Passages North, NMU 1401 Presque Isle Ave, Marquette MI 49855. (906) 227-1203. E-mail: passages@nmu.edu. Website: http://myweb.num.edu/~passages. Offered every other year—check Web site for details. Prize: $1,000 First Prize and 2 honorable mentions. Entry fee: $10 for up to 2 stories; includes contest issue. Make checks payable to Northern Michigan University. **Submission period is Oct 15th-Feb 15th.** Entries should be unpublished. Anyone may enter contest. Length: max of 1,000 words. Cover letter should include name, address, phone, e-mail. Writers may submit own work. Winners notified by e-mail. Results made available to entrants with SASE.

◻ E.M. KOEPPEL SHORT FICTION AWARD

Writecorner Press, P.O. Box 140310, Gainesville FL 32614-0310. Website: www.writecorner.com. **Contact:** Mary Sue Koeppel, editor. Award for short stories. Prize: $1,100 first prize, and $100 for Editors' Choices. Judged by award-winning writers. Entry fee: $15 first story, $10 each additional story. Make checks payable to Writecorner Press. Send 2 title pages: One with title only and one with title, name, address, phone, e-mail, short bio. Place no other identification of the author on the ms that will be used in the judging. Guidelines available for SASE or on Web site. Accepts inquiries by e-mail and phone. Expects 300+ entries. **Deadline: October 1-April 30.** Entries must be unpublished. Open to any writer. Results announced in Summer. Winners notified by mail, phone in July (or earlier). For results, send SASE or check Web site.

☑ ◎ THE LAWRENCE FOUNDATION AWARD

Prairie Schooner, 201 Andrews Hall, P.O. Box 880334, Lincoln NE 68588-0334. (402)472-0911. Fax: (402)472-9771. E-mail: jengelhardt2@unl.edu. Website: http://prairieschooner.unl.edu. **Contact:** Hilda Raz, editor-in-chief. Offered annually for the best short story published in Prairie Schooner in the previous year. Prize: $1,000. Judged by editorial staff of Praire Schooner. No entry fee. Only work published in Prairie Schooner in the previous year is considered. Work is nominated by editorial staff. Results announced in the Spring issue. Winners notified by mail in February or March.

◎ LAWRENCE FOUNDATION PRIZE

Michigan Quarterly Review, 0576 Rackham Building, Ann Arbor MI 48109-1070. (734) 764-9265. E-mail: mqr@umich.edu. Website: www.umich.edu/~mqr. **Contact:** Vicki Lawrence, managing editor. Competition for short stories. Prize: $1,000. Judged by editorial board. No entry fee. No deadline. "An annual cash prize awarded to the author of the best short story published in Michigan Quarterly Review each year. Stories must be already published in Michigan Quarterly Review. This is not a competition in which manuscripts are read outside of the normal submission process." Guidelines available for SASE or on Web site. Accepts inquires by e-mail and phone. Results announced in December. Winners notified by phone or mail.

Ⓝ ◎ LESBIAN WRITERS FUND

Astraea Lesbian Foundation for Justice, 116 E. 16th St., 7th flr, New York NY 10003. (212) 529-8021. E-mail: info@astraeafoundation.org. Website: www.astraeafoundation.org. "This award is to support the work of emerging lesbian writers, and to acknowledge the contributions of established writers to our movement and culture." Annual. Competition/award for short stories, novels, story collections and poetry. Prize: First place awardees and two runners-up in the poetry and fiction categories will receive cash awards ($10,000 for awardee; $1,500 for runners-up). Each year a new set of judges reviews applications. An independent team of two judges in each genre selects the winners unanimously. The names of applicants will not be known to the judges until the decisions are made and all applicants have been notified by mail. All applications will be reviewed by a panel of lesbian writers who will remain anonymous until after the process has been completed. Entry fee: $5. Make checks payable to Astraea Lesbian Foundation for Justice. Accepts inquiries by e-mail, phone. **Entry deadline is June 30, 2009.** Entries may be pubilshed or unpublished. "To be eligible for an award from the Lesbian Writers Fund, you must satisfy all of the following: You are a lesbian-identified writer of poetry and/or fiction. Your submission is a poetry or fiction sample in English (non-fiction, screenplays, or playsare ineligible). You reside in the United States. Your submitted work includes some lesbian content (e.g. lesbian desire, identity, and/or perspective). You have published at least one piece of your writing (in any genre) in a newspaper, magazine, journal, anthology, or professional web publication (excluding personal or selfproducedhomepages). You have not published more than one book, including a chapbook, in any subject or genre with a publisher. If a second book has been accepted by a publisher, but has not been published yet, you are not eligible to apply. Published books or anthologies you have edited do not count towards the maximum. If awarded, you agree to be acknowledged publicly as a lesbian writer and agree to have your work publicized as Astraea sees fit. This may include an announcement or profile in our website and newsletter. All previous finalists, except for first place winners are eligible to apply. Past judges are excluded. Current staff and Board members of the Astraea Foundation are ineligible to apply." Write to grants@astraeafoundation.org for complete guidelines and application instructions. Submit up to 20 pages from a novel or a collection of short stories. Mss must be double spaced. "While there is no minimum page limit for fiction submissions, we recommend that you submit at least 10 pages, so that the judges gain a deeper understanding of your work." Name should not appear on ms; all pages must have identification number provided with application. Writers must submit own work. Results announced January 2010. Winners notified by mail.

Contests & Awards

LITERAL LATTÉ FICTION AWARD

Literal Latté, 200 East 10th Street, Suite 240, New York NY 10003. (212) 260-5532. E-mail: litlatte@aol. com. Website: www.literal-latte.com. **Contact:** Edward Estlin, contributing editor. Award "to provide talented writers with three essential tools for continued success: money, publication and recognition." Offered annually for unpublished fiction. Guidelines for SASE or on Web site. Open to any writer. Prize: $1,000 and publication in Literal Latté (first prize), $300 (second prize), $200 (third prize), up to 7 honorable mentions. Judged by the editors. Entry fee: $10/story. Guidelines available for SASE, by e-mail or on Web site. Accepts inquiries by e-mail. Deadline: January 15. Entries must be unpublished. Length: 8,000 words maximum. Guidelines available for SASE, by e-mail or on Web site. Accepts inquiries by e-mail or on Web site. "Celebrating fifteen years of supporting great, new writers." Winners notified by phone. List of winners available in late April for SASE or by e-mail.

▣ ☐ LONG STORY CONTEST, INTERNATIONAL

White Eagle Coffee Store Press, P.O. Box 383, Fox River Grove IL 60021. (847) 639-9200. E-mail: wecspress@ aol.com. Website: whiteeaglecoffeestorepress.com. **Contact:** Frank E. Smith, publisher. Offered annually since 1993 for unpublished work to recognize and promote long short stories of 8,000-14,000 words (about 30-50 pages). Sample of previous winner: $6.95, including postage. Open to any writer, no restrictions on materials. Prize: (A.E. Coppard Prize) $1,000 and publication, plus 25 copies of chapbook and 10 press kits. Categories: No limits on style or subject matter. Entry fee: $15 fee, $10 for second story in same envelope. Guidelines available in April by SASE, e-mail or on Web site. Accepts inquiries by e-mail. Length: 8,000-14,000 words (30-50 pages double-spaced) single story; may have multiparts or be a self-contained novel segment. **Deadline: December 15.** Accepts previously unpublished submissions, but previous publication of small parts with acknowledgment is okay. Simultaneous submissions okay. Send cover with name, address, phone; second title page with title only. Submissions are not returned; they are recycled. "SASE for most current information." Results announced in late spring. Winners notified by phone. For contest results, send SASE or visit Web site in late spring. "Write with richness and depth. This has become the premiere competition in the world for long stories, giving many winners and finalists the opportunity to move to the next level of publishing success."

◎ THE HUGH J. LUKE AWARD

Prairie Schooner, 201 Andrews Hall, P.O. Box 880334, Lincoln NE 68588-0334. (402) 472-0911. Fax: (402) 472-9771. E-mail: jengelhardt2@unl.edu. Website: prairieschooner.unl.edu/. Contact: Hilda Raz, editor-in-chief. Offered annually for work published in Prairie Schooner in the previous year. Prize: $250. Judged by editorial staff of Prairie Schooner. No entry fee. Work is nominated by the editorial staff. Guidelines for SASE or on Web site. Results announced in the Spring issue. Winners notified by mail in February or March.

LUMINA

Sarah Lawrence College's graduate literary journal of poetry, fiction, and nonfiction, is accepting submissions for its 2009 issue and poetry contest, judged by Ilya Kaminsky. **Deadline**: November 15, 2008. For more information, visit www.slc.edu/lumina.

▣ ◎ MARSH AWARD FOR CHILDREN'S LITERATURE IN TRANSLATION

Marsh Christian Trust, The English-Speaking Union, Dartmouth House, 37 Charles Street, London, W1J 5ED United Kingdom. E-mail: education@esu.org. **Contact:** Elizabeth Stokes. Award "to promote the publication of translated children's books in the UK." Biennial award for children's book translations. Judged by Patricia Crampton, Caroline Horn, Wendy Cooling, Elizabeth Hammill. No entry fee. Entries must be previously published. Entries should be translations into English first published in the UK. Entries must be nominated by publishers. Open to any writer. Guidelines available for SASE. Cover letter should include name, address, phone, E-mail: and title. Accepts inquiries by e-mail: Results announced in January. Winners notified by mail and at presentation event.

◎ WALTER RUMSEY MARVIN GRANT

Ohioana Library Association, 274 E. First Ave., Suite 300, Columbus OH 43201. (614)466-3831. Fax: (614)728-6974. E-mail: ohioana@ohioana.org. Website: www.ohioana.org. **Contact:** Linda Hengst. Award "to encourage young, unpublished writers 30 years of age or younger." Competition for short stories. Prize: $1,000. No entry fee. Up to 6 pieces of prose may be submitted; maximum 60 pages, minimum 10 pages double-spaced, 12-point type. Deadline: January 31. Entries must be unpublished. Open to unpublished authors born in Ohio or who have lived in Ohio for a minimum of five years. Must be 30 years of age or younger. Guidelines for SASE or on Web site. Winner notified in May or June. Award given in October.

◎ MEMPHIS MAGAZINE FICTION AWARDS

Memphis Magazine, P.O. Box 1738, Memphis TN 38101. (901) 521-9000. E-mail: sadler@memphismagazine. com. Website: www.memphismagazine.com. **Contact:** Marilyn Sadler, senior editor/contest coordinator. Annual. Competition/award for short stories. Prize: $1,000 grand prize and publication in Memphis; two $500 honorable mention awards. Judged by a panel of five, all with fiction writing experience and publications. Entry fee: $10/story. Guidelines available in April by phone, on Web site, in publication. Accepts inquiries by fax, e-mail, phone. Deadline: Aug. 1. Entries should be unpublished. "Manuscripts may be previously published as long as previous publication was not in a national magazine with over 20,000 circulation or in a regional publication within Shelby County." Open to all authors who live within 150 miles of Memphis. Length: 3,000-4,500 words. Cover letter should include name, address, phone, story title. Do not put your name anywhere on the ms itself. Writers may submit own work. "Each story should be typed, double-spaced, with unstapled, numbered pages. Stories are not required to have a Memphis or Southern theme, but we do want a compelling story and first-rate writing." Winners contacted in late September.

DAVID NATHAN MEYERSON PRIZE FOR FICTION

Southwest Review, P.O. Box 750374, Dallas TX 75275-0374. (214) 768-1037. Fax: (214) 768-1408. E-mail: swr@smu.edu; tlewers@smu.edu. Website: www.smu.edu/southwestreview. **Contact:** Jennifer Cranfill, senior editor. Prize will consist of $1,000 and publication in the Southwest Review. Open to writers who have not yet published a book. Submissions must be no longer than 8,000 words. $25 reading fee must accompany each submission. Work should be printed without the author's name. Name and address should appear only on the cover letter. Submissions will not be returned. For notification of the winning submission, include a S.A.S.E. Postmarked deadline for receipt is May 1, 2009. Winner announced in August.

◎ A MIDSUMMER TALE

E-mail: editors@toasted-cheese.com. Website: www.toasted-cheese.com. **Contact:** Theryn Fleming, editor. A Midsummer Tale is a summer-themed creative nonfiction contest. Topic changes each year. Check Web site for current focus and word limit. "We usually receive around 20 entries." Prize: First prize: $20 Amazon gift certificate, publication; Second prize: $15 Amazon gift certificate, publication; Third prize: $10 Amazon gift certificate, publication. Some feedback is often given to entrants. Categories: creative nonfiction. Judged by two Toasted Cheese editors who blind-judge each contest. Each judge has her own criteria for selecting winners. No entry fee. Guidelines, including the e-mail address to which you should send your entry and instructions for what to include and how to format, are available May 1 on Web site. Accepts inquiries by e-mail. **Deadline: June 21.** Entries must be unpublished. Open to any writer. Results announced July 31 on Web site. Winners notified by e-mail.

MIGHTY RIVER SHORT STORY CONTEST

Big Muddy: A Journal of the Mississippi River Valley, MRSS Contest, Southeast Missouri State Univ., MS 2650, One University Plaza, Cape Girardeau MO 63701. (573) 651-2044. Fax: (573) 651-5188. E-mail: upress@semo.edu. Website: http://www6.semo.edu/universitypress/mrss.htm. **Contact:** Dr. Susan Swartwout, publisher/editor. "We're searching for the best short story relating in some way to the Mississippi River or a sister River: its landscape, people, culture, history, current events, or future." Annual. Competition/award for short stories. Prize: $500 and publication in Big Muddy. Semi-finalists will be chosen by a regional team of published writers. The final ms will be chosen by Susan Swartwout, publisher of Southeast Missouri State University Press. Entry fee: $15 (includes a copy of Big Muddy in which the winning story appears). Make checks payable to SEMO UP - MRSS. Guidelines available in January. Accepts inquiries by phone andy by e-mail. **Submission period is Jan 1- Aug 1.** Entries should be unpublished. Anyone may enter contest. Length: up to 30 pages, double-spaced. Cover letter should include name, address, phone, e-mail, story title. The title and page numbers should appear on each page of the ms. Writers may submit own work. Results announced Fall. Winners notified by mail, by phone, by e-mail. Results made available to entrants with SASE.

◪ MILKWEED EDITIONS NATIONAL FICTION PRIZE

Milkweed Editions, 1011 Washington Ave. S., Suite 300, Minneapolis MN 55415. (612) 332-3192. Fax: (612) 215-2550. E-mail: editor@milkweed.org. Website: www.milkweed.org. **Contact:** The Editors. Annual award for unpublished works. "Looking for a novel, novella, or a collection of short stories. Manuscripts should be of high literary quality and must be double-spaced and between 150-400 pages in length. Writers who need their work returned must include a SAS book mailer. Manuscripts not accompanied by a SAS book mailer will be recycled." Winner will be chosen from the mss Milkweed accepts for publication each year. All mss submitted to Milkweed will automatically be considered for the prize. Submission directly to the contest is no longer necessary. Must be written in English. Writers should have previously published fiction in magazines/journals with national distribution." Catalog available on request for $1.50. Guidelines for SASE or online. Prize: Publication by Milkweed Editions, and a cash advance of $5,000 against royalties agreed upon in the contractual arrangement negotiated at the time of acceptance. Judged by Milkweed Editions. No entry fee. Deadline: rolling. Entries must be unpublished. Previous winners: The Father Shore, by Matthew Eck; Visigoth, by Gary Amdahl; Crossing Bully Creek, by Margaret Erhart; Ordinary Wolves, by Seth Kantner; Roofwalker, by Susan Power—this is the caliber of fiction we are searching for." Winners are notified by phone.

◎ MILLION WRITERS AWARD

StorySouth, 898 Chelsea Ave., Columbus OH 43209. (614)545-0754. E-mail: storysouth@yahoo.com. Website: www.storysouth.com. **Contact:** Jason Sanford, editor. Contest "to honor and promote the best fiction published annually in online journals and magazines. The reason for the Million Writers Award is that most of the major literary prizes for short fiction (such as the O. Henry Awards) ignore Web-published fiction. This award aims to show that world-class fiction is being published online and to promote this fiction to the larger reading and literary community." Prize: Cash prize and publicity for the author and story. Categories: short stories. Judged by StorySouth judges. No entry fee. Cover letter should include e-mail address, word count, title and publication where story was previously published. Guidelines available in December on Web site. Deadline: January. Entries must be previously published. All stories must be 1,000 words or longer. Open to any writer. Results announced in March on Web site. Winners notified by e-mail.

◎ THE MILTON CENTER POSTGRADUATE FELLOWSHIP

The Milton Center at Image, 3307 Third Ave. West, Seattle WA 98119. (206)281-2988. E-mail: miltoncenter@imagejournal.org. Website: http://imagejournal.org/page/fellowships/the-milton-center. **Contact:** Gregory Wolfe, director. Award "to bring emerging writers of Christian commitment to the Center, where their primary goal is to complete their first book-length manuscript in fiction, poetry or creative nonfiction." A $16,000 stipend is offered. $25 application fee. Guidelines on Web site. **Deadline: March 15**. Open to any writer.

MISSISSIPPI REVIEW PRIZE

Mississippi Review, 118 College Dr., #5144, Hattiesburg MS 39406. (601) 266-4321. Fax: (601) 266-5757. E-mail: rief@mississippireview.com. Website: www.mississippireview.com. **Contact:** Rie Fortenberry, managing editor. Award "to reward excellence in new fiction and poetry and to find new writers who are just beginning their careers." Offered annually for unpublished fiction and poetry. Guidelines available online. Accepts inquiries by e-mail or phone. Prize: $1,000 plus publication for fiction and poetry winners; publication for all runners up. Entry fee: $15. Deadline: October 1. Entries must be unpublished. Length: 50,000 words or less. Cover letter should include author's name, address, phone, e-mail, word count and title of story. No mss returned. Winners notified in January. For contest results, visit Web site.

MONTANA PRIZE IN FICTION

Cutbank Literary Magazine, English Dept., LA 133, UMT, Missoula MT 59812. Fax: (406) 243-6156. E-mail: cutbank@umontana.edu. Website: www.cutbankonline.org. **Contact:** fiction editor. "Since CutBank was founded in 1973, we have watched as the landscape for literary and 'little' magazines has broadened considerably, resulting in more quality short stories, essays, and poems finding their way to an audience each year. Occasionally, we come across a submission that seems to stand above the already impressive work being published in its genre, the sort of piece that serves to credit the wide field of literary publications generally. The goal of CutBank 's annual contests it to provoke, identify, and reward work of that caliber." Annual. Competition/award for short stories. Prize: $500 and publication in the summer issue of CutBank. Entries are narrowed down to a pool of five to ten submissions which are then submitted to a guest judge for selection of the winner. The judge of the 2007-2008 Montana Prize in Fiction was Aimee Bender. Entry fee: $13 (includes a one-year, two-issue subscription to CutBank). Limit of one work of fiction per submitter (though writers may also submit work to our contests in other genres). Make checks payable to Cutbank Literary Magazine. Guidelines available in November. Accepts inquiries by e-mail. **Submission period is December 1, 2008 - February 28, 2009.** Entries should be unpublished. Anyone may enter contest. Please submit no more than 40 double-spaced pages. Cover letter should include name, address, phone, e-mail, novel/story title. Only name and title on ms. Writers may submit own work. "Read the magazine and get a sense of our style. We are seeking work that showcases an authentic voice, a boldness of form, and a rejection of functional fixedness." Results announced June. Winners notified by e-mail. Results made available to entrants on Web site.

▦ ◎ BRIAN MOORE SHORT STORY AWARDS

Creative Writers Network, 109-113 Royal Ave., Belfast BT1 1FF Northern Ireland, UK. E-mail: info@creativewritersnetwork.org. Website: www.creativewritersnetwork.org. **Contact:** Administrator. Award to promote the short story form. Prize: £750, £300, £200 and publication in Verbal and Ulla's Nib. Judged by renowned American short story writer and novelist Richard Bausch. Entry fee: £5. **Deadline: March 1, 2009.** Entries must be unpublished. Open to writers of Irish descent. Guidelines available on Web site. Results announced in May 2009. List of winners available on Web site.

◎ NATIONAL READERS' CHOICE AWARDS

E-mail: NRCAcontest@hotmail.com. Website: www.okrwa.com. **Contact:** Donnell Epperson, coordinator. Contest "to provide writers of romance fiction with a competition where their published novels are judged by readers." Prize: "There is no monetary award; just an awards banquet hosted at the Annual National Romance Writers Convention." Categories: The 12 categories include traditional series; short contemporary series; long contemporary series; single title contemporary; historical; Novella (25,000+ words); romantic suspense; inspirational; young adult; paranormal; erotic romance; mainstream with romantic elements. Entry fee: $25; make checks payable to NRCA. See Web site for entry address and contact information. All entries must have an original copyright date the current contest year. (See Web site for details.) Entries will be accepted from authors, editors, publishers, agents, readers, whoever wants to fill out the entry form, pay the fee and supply the books. **Deadline**: Fee deadline: 1 December; book deadline: 15 January. (See Web site for exact dates.) No limit to the number of entries, but each title may be entered only in one category. Open to any writer. For guidelines, send e-mail or visit Web site. Entry form required— available on Web site. Deadline for entry forms is 1 December. Five copies of each entry must be mailed to the category coordinator; contact information for coordinator will be provided by December 1. Results announced in July. Winners notified by phone, if not at the awards ceremony, in July. List of winners will be mailed; also available by e-mail.

❏ NATIONAL WRITERS ASSOCIATION NOVEL WRITING CONTEST

The National Writers Association, 10940 S. Parker Rd #508, Parker CO 80134. (303) 841-0246. Fax: (303) 841-2607. E-mail: natlwritersassn@hotmail.com. Website: www.nationalwriters.com. **Contact:** Sandy Whelchel, director. Annual contest "to help develop creative skills, to recognize and reward outstanding ability, and to increase the opportunity for the marketing and subsequent publication of novel manuscripts." Prize: 1st place: $500; 2nd place: $300; 3rd place: $200. Judges' evaluation sheets sent to each entry with SASE. Categories: Open to any genre or category. Judged by editors and agents. Entry fee: $35. Opens December 1. **Deadline: April 1.** Entries must be unpublished. Length: 20,000-100,000 words. Open to any writer. Entry form and information available on Benefits section of Web site.

❏ NATIONAL WRITERS ASSOCIATION SHORT STORY CONTEST

The National Writers Association, 10940 S. Parker Rd. #508, Parker CO 80134. (303) 841-0246. Fax: (303) 841-2607. E-mail: natlwritersassn@hotmail.com. Website: www.nationalwriters.com. **Contact:** Sandy

Whelchel, director. Annual contest "to encourage writers in this creative form and to recognize those who excel in fiction writing." Prize: 1st place: $200; 2nd place: $100; 3rd place: $50. Entry fee: $15. **Deadline: postmarked by July 1.** Entries must be unpublished. Length: 5,000 words maximum. Entry form and information available in January on contest section of Web site. Accepts inquiries by fax, phone and e-mail. Evaluation sheets sent to each entrant if SASE is provided. Results announced at the NWAF Summer Conference in June. Winners notified by phone or e-mail. List of winners available in Authorship or on Web site.

NELLIGAN PRIZE FOR SHORT FICTION

Colorado Review and the Center for Literary Publishing, 9105 Campus Delivery, Colorado State University, Fort Collins CO 80523. (970) 491-5449. E-mail: creview@colostate.edu. Website: http://nelliganprize. colostate.edu.**Contact:** Stephanie G'Schwind, Editor/Director. "The Nelligan Prize for Short Fiction was established in memory of Liza Nelligan, a writer, editor, and friend of many in Colorado State University's English Department, where she received her master's degree in literature in 1992. By giving an award to the author of an outstanding short story each year, we hope to honor Liza Nelligan's life, her passion for writing, and her love of fiction." Annual. Competition/award for short stories. Prize: $1,000 plus publication in Colorado Review. Receives approximately 900 stories. All entries are read blind by Colorado Review's editorial staff. Fifteen entries are selected to be sent on to a final judge. Entry fee: $10. Send credit card information or make checks payable to Colorado Review. Guidelines available in August 2009. Accepts inquiries by e-mail, phone. **Entry deadline March 12, 2010.** Entries should be unpublished. Anyone may enter contest. Cover letter should include name, address, phone, e-mail, and novel/story title. "Authors should provide two cover sheets: one with name, address, phone, e-mail, and title of story, and a second with only the title of the story. Manuscripts are read 'blind,' so authors'names should not appear anywhere else in the manuscript." Writers may submit own work. "Successful short story writers are those who are reading contemporary short fiction (short story collections, literary magazines, annual prize anthologies), reading about the craft, and actively engaging in the practice of writing." Results announced in July of each year. Winners notified by phone. Results made available to entrants with SASE.

☐ NEW LETTERS LITERARY AWARDS

New Letters, 5101 Rockhill Rd., Kansas City MO 64110-2499. (816) 235-1168. Fax: (816) 235-2611. E-mail: newletters@umkc.edu. Website: www.newletters.org. Award to "find and reward good writing from writers who need the recognition and support." Award has 3 categories (fiction, poetry and creative nonfiction) with 1 winner in each. Offered annually for previously unpublished work. Prize: 1st place: $1,500, plus publication; all entries are considered for publication. Judged by 2 rounds of regional writers (preliminary judging). Winners picked by an anonymous judge of national repute. Entry fee: $15/entry (includes year's subscription). Make checks payable to New Letters or send credit card information. **Deadline**: May 18. Entries must be unpublished. Open to any writer. Guidelines available in January for SASE, e-mail, on Web site and in publication. Cover letter should include name, address, phone, e-mail and title. Results announced in September. Winners notified by phone. For contest results, send SASE, e-mail or visit Web site.

☐ NEW MILLENNIUM WRITING AWARDS

New Millennium Writings, Room M2, P.O. Box 2463, Knoxville TN 37901. (423)428-0389. Fax: (865) 428-2302. E-mail: DonWilliams7@charter.net. Website: www.newmillenniumwritings.com/awards.html. **Contact:** Don Williams, editor. Award "to promote literary excellence in contemporary fiction." Offered twice annually for unpublished fiction, poetry, essays or nonfiction prose to encourage new fiction writers, poets and essayists and bring them to attention of publishing industry. Entrants receive an issue of NMW in which winners appear. Prize: $1,000 (fiction, poetry, nonfiction and short-short fiction, 1,000 words or less); winners published in NMW and on Web site. Judged by novelists and short story writers. Entry fee: $17 for each submission. **Deadline**: November 17 and June 17. Entries must be unpublished. Biannual competition. Length: 1,000-6,000 words. Guidelines available year round for SASE and on Web site at www.writingawards.com. "Provide a bold, yet organic opening line, sustain the voice and mood throughout, tell an entertaining and vital story with a strong ending. New Millennium Writings is a forward-looking periodical for writers and lovers of good reading. It is filled with outstanding poetry, fiction, essays and other speculations on subjects both topical and timeless about life in our astonishing times. Our pages brim with prize-winning essays, humor, illustration, writing advice and poetry from writers at all stages of their careers. First-timers find their work displayed alongside such well-known writers as Shel Silverstein, Khaled Hosseini, Ted Kooser, Lucille Clifton, John Updike, Sharyn McCrumb, Lee Smith, Norman Mailer, Madison Smartt Bell and Cormac McCarthy." Results announced October and April. Winners notified by mail and phone. All entrants will receive a list of winners, plus a copy of the annual anthology. Send letter-sized SASE with entry for list.

☐ NEW SOUTH WRITING CONTEST

New South, Georgia State University, Campus Box 1894, MSC 8R0322, Unit 8, Atlanta GA 30303-3083. E-mail: new_south@langate.gsu.edu. Website: www.review.gsu.edu. **Contact:** Editor. To promote quality work of emerging writers. Prize: $1,000 first prize; $250 second prize; publication for winners. Categories: fiction, poetry; receives more than 250 entries each. Judged by staff at New South (finalists); 2007 winners were chosen by Keith Lee Morris (fiction) and Jake Adam York (poetry). Entry fee: $15, includes copy of Spring /Summer issue with contest results. Make checks payable to GSU.**Deadline: March 4.** Entries must be unpublished. Length: should not exceed 7,500 words. Address fiction submissions to Prose Editor; and poetry submissions Poetry Editor. Mss must be typed or letter-quality printed. On the first page of the ms include name, address, phone, e-mail, word count. Limit each submission to one short story/three poems. Guidelines available by SASE or on Web site. Contest open to all except faculty, staff, students of Georgia State University. US residents only. Winners notified by e-mail. "We look for engagement with language and characters we care about."

▦ ☑ ◎ THE NOMA AWARD FOR PUBLISHING IN AFRICA

P.O. Box 128, Witney, Oxon 0X8 5XU. United Kingdom. E-mail: maryljay@aol.com. Website: www.nomaaward.org. **Contact:** Mary Jay. Sponsored by Kodansha Ltd. Award "to encourage publication of works by African writers and scholars in Africa, instead of abroad as is still too often the case at present." Categories: scholarly or academic; books for children; literature and creative writing, including fiction, drama and poetry. Judged by a committee of African scholars and book experts and representatives of the international book community. Chairman: Walter Bgoya. No entry fee. **Deadline: February 28.** Entries must be previously published. Guidelines and entry forms available in December by fax, e-mail or on Web site. Submissions are through publishers only. "Publisher must complete entry form and supply six copies of the published work." Maximum number of entries per publisher is three. Results announced in October. Winners notified through publisher. List of winners available from Secretariat or on Web site. "The award is for an outstanding book. Content is the overriding criterion, but standards of publication are also taken into account."

▦ SEAN O'FAOLAIN SHORT STORY PRIZE

The Munster Literature Centre, Frank O'Connor House, 84 Douglas Street, Cork, Ireland. + +353-214319255. E-mail: munsterlit@eircom.net. Website: www.munsterlit.ie. **Contact:** Patrick Cotter, artistic director. "To reward writers of outstanding short stories" Annual. Prize: 1st prize €1500 (approx US $2,200); 2nd prize €500 (approx $730). Four runners-up prizes of €100 (approx $146). All six stories to be published in Southword Literary Journal. Receives about 700 entries. Guest judge reads each and every story anonymously. Judge in 20098 was Philip O Ceallaigh. Entry fee: $20. Make checks payable to Munster Literature Centre. Guidelines available in November. Accepts inquiries by e-mail, phone. **Entry deadline is July 31.** Entries should be unpublished. Anyone may enter contest. Length: 3,000 words max. Cover letter should include name, address, phone, e-mail, word count, novel/story title. No identifying information on ms. "Read previous winners in Southword Journal. " Results announced last day of Frank O'Connor International Short Story Festival in third weekend of September. Winners notified by mail or by e-mail. Results made available to entrants on Web site.

◎ (ALICE WOOD MEMORIAL) OHIOANA AWARD FOR CHILDREN'S LITERATURE

Ohioana Library Association, 274 E. First Ave., Suite 300, Columbus OH 43201. (614)466-3831. Fax: (614)728-6974. E-mail: ohioana@ohioana.org. Website: www.ohioana.org. **Contact**: Linda Hengst, executive director. Offered to an author whose body of work has made, and continues to make, a significant contribution to literature for children or young adults and through their work as a writer, teacher, or administrator and through their community service, interest in children's literature has been encouraged and children have become involved with reading. Nomination forms for SASE. Recipient must have been born in Ohio or lived in Ohio at least 5 years. Prize: $1,000. No entry fee. Deadline: December 31. Guidelines for SASE. Accepts inquiries by phone and e-mail. Results announced in August or September. Winners notified by letter in May. For contest results, call or e-mail.

☑ ◎ OHIOANA BOOK AWARDS

Ohioana Library Association, 274 E. 1st Ave., Suite 300, Columbus OH 43201-3673. (614)466-3831. Fax: (614)728-6974. E-mail: ohioana@sloma.state.oh.us. Website: www.ohioana.org. **Contact**: Linda Hengst, executive director. Offered annually to bring national attention to Ohio authors and their books, published in the last 2 years. (Books can only be considered once.) Categories: Fiction, nonfiction, juvenile, poetry, and books about Ohio or an Ohioan. Writers must have been born in Ohio or lived in Ohio for at least 5 years, but books about Ohio or an Ohioan need not be written by an Ohioan. Prize: certificate and glass sculpture. Judged by a jury selected by librarians, book reviewers, writers and other knowledgeable people. Each winter the jury considers all books received since the previous jury. No entry fee. **Deadline: December 31**. A copy of the book must be received by the Ohioana Library by December 31 prior to the year the award is given; literary quality of the book must be outstanding. No entry forms are needed, but they are available July 1 of each year. Specific questions should be sent to Ohioana. Results announced in August or September. Winners notified by mail in May.

☑ $ ON THE PREMISES CONTEST

On The Premises, LLC, 4323 Gingham Court, Alexandria VA 22310. (202) 262-2168. E-mail: questions@ onthepremises.com. Website: www.onthepremises.com. **Contact:** Tarl Roger Kudrick or Bethany Granger, Co-publishers. "On the Premises aims to promote newer and/or relatively unknown writers who can write what we feel are creative, compelling stories told in effective, uncluttered and evocative prose. Each contest challenges writers to produce a great story based on a broad premise that our editors supply as part of the contest." Competition/award for short stories. Prize: First prize is $140, Second prize $100, Third prize $70, and Honorable Mentions recieve $25. All prize winners are published in On the Premises magazine in HTML and PDF format. Entries are judged blindly by a panel of judges with professional editing and writing experience. No entry fee. Submissions are accepted by e-mail only. Contests held every four months. Check Web site for exact dates. Entries should be unpublished. Open to everyone. Length: min 1,000 words, max 5,000. Email should include name, address, e-mail, novel/story title, with ms attached. No name or contact info should be in ms. Writers may submit own work. "Write something compelling, creative and well-crafted. Above all, clearly use the contest premise. Results announced within 2 weeks of contest deadline. Winners notified via newsletter and with publication of On the Premises. Results made available to entrants on Web site, in publication.

◎ OREGON BOOK AWARDS

Literary Arts, 224 NW 13th Ave., Ste. 306, Portland OR 97209. (503)227-2583. E-mail: susan@literary-arts.org. Website: www.literary-arts.org. **Contact:** Susan Denning. The annual Oregon Book Awards celebrate Oregon authors in the areas of poetry, fiction, nonfiction, drama and young readers' literature published between April 1and March 31. Prize: Finalists are invited on a statewide reading tour and are promoted in bookstores and libraries across the state. Judged by writers who are selected from outside Oregon for their expertise in a genre. Past judges include Mark Doty, Colson Whitehead and Kim Barnes. Entry fee determined by initial print run; see Web site for details. Deadline: last Friday in May. Entries must be previously published. Oregon residents only. Accepts inquiries by phone and e-mail. Finalists announced in October. Winners announced at an awards ceremony in November. List of winners available in November.

◎ OREGON LITERARY FELLOWSHIPS

Literary Arts, Inc., 224 NW 13th Ave., Suite 306, Portland OR 97209. (503) 227-2583. Fax: (503) 243-1167. E-mail: susan@literary-arts.org. Website: www.literary-arts.org. **Contact:** Susan Denning, Director of Programs and events. Annual fellowships for writers of fiction, poetry, literary nonfiction, young readers and drama. Prize: $2500 minimum award, for approximately 12 writers. Judged by out-of-state writers. No entry fee. Guidelines available in February for SASE. Accepts inquiries by e-mail, phone. **Deadline: last Friday in June.** Oregon residents only. Recipients announced in December.

☐ PEARL SHORT STORY PRIZE

Pearl Magazine, 3030 E. Second St., Long Beach CA 90803-5163. (562) 434-4523. E-mail: Pearlmag@aol.com. Website: www.pearlmag.com. **Contact:** Marilyn Johnson, fiction editor. Award to "provide a larger forum and help widen publishing opportunities for fiction writers in the small press and to help support the continuing publication of Pearl." Prize: $250, publication in Pearl and 10 copies of the journal. Judged by the editors of Pearl: Marilyn Johnson, Joan Jobe Smith, Barbara Hauk. Entry fee: $10/story. Include a brief bio and SASE for reply or return of mss. Accepts simultaneous submissions, but asks to be notified if story is accepted elsewhere. **Submission period: April 1-May 31(postmark).** Entries must be unpublished. "Although we are open to all types of fiction, we look most favorably on coherent, well-crafted narratives containing interesting, believable characters in meaningful situations." Length: 4,000 words maximum. Open to any writer. Guidelines for SASE or on Web site. Accepts queries by e-mail or fax. Results announced in September. Winners notified by mail. For contest results, send SASE, e-mail or visit Web site.

◎ PEN CENTER USA ANNUAL LITERARY AWARDS

PEN Center USA, Antioch University Los Angeles, 400 Corporate Pointe, Culver City CA 90230. (310) 862-1555. Fax: (310) 862-1556. E-mail: awards@penusa.org. Website: www.penusa.org. Offered annually for fiction, creative nonfiction, research nonfiction, poetry, children's/young adult literature, or translation published January 1-December 31 of 2008. Winners receive $1000 and are honored at the gala in Los Angeles. Judged by a panel of established writers, editors and critics. Entry fee: $35. Guidelines available in July on website. Accepts inquiries by phone and e-mail. All entries must include 4 non-returnable copies of each submission and a completed entry form. **Deadline: December 31.** Entries must be professionally published or produced. Open to authors west of the Mississippi River, including all of Minnesota and Louisiana. Results announced in summer. Winners notified by phone and mail. For contest results, visit website.

☑ ◎ PEN/FAULKNER AWARDS FOR FICTION

PEN/Faulkner Foundation, 201 E. Capitol St., Washington DC 20003. (202) 898-9063. Fax: (202) 675-0363. E-mail: jneely@penfaulkner.org. Website: www.penfaulkner.org. **Contact:** Jessica Neely, PEN/Faulkner Foundation Executive Director. Offered annually for best book-length work of fiction by an American citizen published in a calendar year (short story collections are eligible). Prize: $15,000 (one winner); $5,000 (4 finalists). Judged by three writers chosen by the directors of the Pen/Faulkner Foundation. No entry fee. **Deadline: October 31.** Open to US citizens only, but they need not be US residents. Writers and publishers submit four copies of eligible titles published during the current year. No juvenile or self-published books.

☐ ◎ POCKETS FICTION-WRITING CONTEST

Upper Room Publications, P.O. Box 340004, Nashville TN 37203-0004. (615) 340-7333. Fax: (615) 340-7267. E-mail: pockets@upperroom.org. Website: www.pockets.org. Pockets is a devotional magazine for children between the ages of 6 and 11. Contest offered annually for unpublished work to discover new children's writers. Prize: $1,000 and publication in Pockets. Categories: short stories. Judged by Pockets staff and staff of other Upper Room Publications. No entry fee. Guidelines available on Web site or send #10 SASE. **Deadline: Must be postmarked between March 1-August 15.** Entries must be unpublished. Because the purpose of the contest is to discover new writers, previous winners are not eligible. No violence, science fiction, romance, fantasy or talking animal stories. Word length 1,000-1,600 words. Open to any writer. Winner announced November 1 and notified by U.S. mail. Contest submissions accompanied by SASE will be returned Nov. 1. "Send SASE with 4 first-class stamps to request guidelines and a past issue, or go to www.pockets.org."

☐ KATHERINE ANNE PORTER PRIZE IN SHORT FICTION

c/o Laura Kopchick, general editor; English Dept., University of Texas at Arlington, 203 Carlisle Hall, Box 19035; Arlington TX 76019. E-mail: kdevinney@unt.edu. Website: www.unt.edu/untpress. **Contact:** Laura Kopchick, general editor; Karen DeVinney, managing editor. Annual. Competition/award for story collections. Prize: $1,000 and publication by UNT Press. Categories: short fiction, which may be a combination of short-shorts, short stories and novellas (single novellas and novels alone will not be accepted). Judged by anonymous judge (2006 was Dan Chaon). Entry fee: $20. Make checks payable to UNT Press. Guidelines available in Jan. with SASE, by fax, by phone, by e-mail, on Web site, in publication. Accepts inquiries by fax, e-mail, phone. **Submission period: July & August.** Entries should be unpublished in book format, but may include both unpublished and previously published stories. Open to all. Length: 27,500-50,000 words. Cover letter should include name, address, phone, e-mail, word count, ms title, place(s) where story or stories were previously published. Names should appear on the actual ms. Writers may submit their own work. "Simply follow the rules and do your best." Results announced in January. Winners notified by mail, by phone, by e-mail. Results made available to entrants with SASE, by fax, by e-mail, on Web site.

PRAIRIE SCHOONER BOOK PRIZE SERIES

Prairie Schooner, 201 Andrews Hall, PO Box 880334, Lincoln NE 68588-0334.Website: http://prairieschooner.unl.edu. **Contact:** Attn: Fiction. Annual. Competition/award for story collections. Prize: $3,000 and publication through the University of Nebraska Press for one book of short fiction and one book of poetry; one runner-up in each category will receive a $1,000 prize. Entry fee: $25. Make checks payable to Prairie Schooner. Deadline: Submissions were accepted between January 15 and March 16 for 2009 contest; check Web site for updates. Entries should be unpublished. Send full manuscript (the author's name should not appear anywhere on the ms). Send two cover pages: one listing only the title of the ms, and the other listing the title, author's name, address, telephone number, and e-mail address. Send SASE for notification of results. All mss will be recycled. You may also send an optional SAS postcard for confirmation of receipt of ms. Winners notified by phone, by e-mail. Results made available to entrants on Web site, in publication.

◎ PRAIRIE SCHOONER GLENNA LUSCHEI AWARDS

Prairie Schooner, 201 Andrews Hall, P.O. Box 880334, Lincoln NE 68588-0334. (402) 472-0911. Fax: (402) 472-9771. E-mail: jengelhardt2@unl.edu. Website: http://prairieschooner.unl.edu. Contact: Hilda Raz, editor-in-chief. Awards to honor work published the previous year in Prairie Schooner, including poetry, essays and fiction. Prize: $250 in each category. Judged by editorial staff of Prairie Schooner. No entry fee. For guidelines, send SASE or visit Web site. "Only work published in Prairie Schooner in the previous year is considered." Work nominated by the editorial staff. Results announced in the Spring issue. Winners notified by mail in February or March.

◎ PUSHCART PRIZE

Pushcart Press, P.O. Box 380, Wainscott NY 11975. (516)324-9300. Website: www.pushcartprize.com. **Contact:** Bill Henderson, president. Award to "publish and recognize the best of small press literary work." Prize: Publication in Pushcart Prize: Best of the Small Presses anthology. Categories: short stories, poetry, essays on any subject. No entry fee. Deadline: December 1. Entries must be previously published. Must have been published during the current calendar year. Open to any writer. Nomination by small press publishers/editors only.

◪ ◎ QUEBEC WRITERS' FEDERATION BOOK AWARDS

Quebec Writers' Federation, 1200 Atwater, Westmount, QC H3Z 1X4 Canada. (514) 933-0878. E-mail: admin@qwf.org. Website: www.qwf.org. **Contact:** Lori Schubert, executive director. Award "to honor excellence in writing in English in Quebec." Prize: $2,000 (Canadian) in each category. Categories: fiction, poetry, nonfiction, first book, translation, and children's and young adult. Each prize judged by panel of 3 jurors, different each year. $20 entry fee. Guidelines for submissions sent to Canadian publishers and posted on Web site in March. Accepts inquiries by e-mail. Deadline: May 31, August 15. Entries must be previously published. Length: must be more than 48 pages. "Writer must have resided in Quebec for 3 of the previous 5 years." Books may be published anywhere. Winners announced in November at Annual Awards Gala and posted on Web site.

◎ RANDOM HOUSE, INC. CREATIVE WRITING COMPETITION

Random House Inc., 1745 Broadway, New York NY 10019. (212) 782-8319. Fax: (212) 940-7590. E-mail: creativewriting@randomhouse.com. Website: www.randomhouse.com/creativewriting/. **Contact:** Melanie Fallon Hauska, director. Offered annually for unpublished work to NYC public high school seniors. Three categories: poetry, fiction/drama and personal essay. Prize: 72 awards given in literary (3) and nonliterary (2) categories. Awards range from $500-10,000. Categories: short stories and poems.

Judged by various city officials, executives, authors, editors. No entry fee. Guidelines available in October on Web site and in publication. **Deadline: February 15 for 2009.** Entries must be unpublished. Word length: 2,500 words or less. Applicants must be seniors (under age 21) at a New York high school. No college essays or class assignments will be accepted. Results announced mid-May. Winners notified by mail and phone. For contest results, send SASE, fax, e-mail or visit Web site.

▦ ◎ THE RED HOUSE CHILDREN'S BOOK AWARD

(formerly The Children's Book Award), Owned and co-ordinated by the Federation of Children's Book Groups (Reg. Charity No. 268289), 2 Bridge Wood View, Horsforth, Leeds, West Yorkshire LS18 5PE, UK. Email: info@fcbg.co.uk. Website: www.redhousechildrensbookaward.co.uk. **Contact:** Andrea Goodall, national co-ordinator. Purpose of the award is to enable children choose the best works of fiction published in the UK. Prize: silver bowl, portfolio of children's letters and pictures. Categories: Books for Younger Children, Books for Younger Readers, Books for Older Readers. No entry fee. **Closing Date is December 31.** Either author or publisher may nominate title. Guidelines available on Web site. Accepts enquiries by email and phone. Shortlist announced in February and winners announced in June. Winners notified at award ceremony and dinner at the Hay Literary Festival and via the publisher. For contest results, visit the Web site.

☐ THE SCARS EDITOR'S CHOICE AWARDS

Scars Publications and Design, 829 Brian Court, Gurnee IL 60031-3155. E-mail: editor@scars.tv. Website: http://scars.tv. **Contact:** Janet Kuypers, editor/publisher. Award "to showcase good writing in an annual book." Prize: publication of story/essay and 1 copy of the book. Categories: short stories. Entry fee: $18/ short story. Deadline: revolves for appearing in different upcoming books as winners. Entries may be unpublished or previously published. Open to any writer. For guidelines, visit Web site. Accepts inquiries by e-mail. Length: "We appreciate shorter works. Shorter stories, more vivid and more real storylines in writing have a good chance." Results announced at book publication, online. Winners notified by mail when book is printed. For contest results, send SASE or e-mail or look at the contest page at Web site.

◎ SCRIPTAPALOOZA TELEVISION WRITING COMPETITION

7775 Sunset Blvd., PMB #200, Hollywood CA 90046. (323) 654-5809. E-mail: info@scriptapalooza. com. Website: www.scriptapaloozatv.com. "Seeking talented writers who have an interest in American television writing." Prize: $500, $200, and $100 in each category (total $3,200), production company consideration. Categories: sitcoms, pilots, one-hour dramas and reality shows. Entry fee: $40; accepts Paypal credit card or make checks payable to Scriptapalooza. **Deadline: April 30 and October 1 of each year.** Length: standard television format whether one hour, one-half hour or pilot. Open to any writer 18 or older. Guidelines available now for SASE or on Web Site. Accepts inquiries by e-mail, phone. "Pilots should be fresh and new and easy to visualize. Spec scripts should stay current with the shows, up-to-date story lines, characters, etc." Winners announced February 15 and August 15. For contest results, visit Web Site.

◎ MICHAEL SHAARA AWARD FOR EXCELLENCE IN CIVIL WAR FICTION

Civil War Institute at Gettysburg College, 300 North Washington Street, Campus Box 435, Gettysburg, PA 17325. (717) 337-6590. Fax: (717) 337-6596. E-mail: civilwar@gettysburg.edu. Website: http://www. gettysburg.edu/civilwar. **Contact:** Tina Grim. Offered annually for fiction published January 1-December 31. Contest "to encourage examination of the Civil War from unique perspectives or by taking an unusual approach." All Civil War novels are eligible. Publishers should make nominations, but authors and critics can nominate as well. Prize: $5,000, which includes travel stipend. No entry fee. **Deadline: December 31.** Entries must be previously published. Judged for presentation of unique perspective, use of unusual approach, effective writing, contribution to existing body of Civil War literature. Competition open to authors of Civil War novels published for the first time in the year designated by the award (i.e. for 2008 award, only novels published in 2008 are eligible). Guidelines available on Web site. Accepts inquiries by fax, e-mail, and phone. Cover letter should include name, address, phone, e-mail, and title. Need 10 copies of novel. "Enter well before deadline. Results announced in July. Winners notified by phone. For contest results, visit Web site.

Contests & Awards

🔁 ◎ SHORT GRAIN WRITING CONTEST

Grain Magazine, Box 67, Saskatoon SK S7K 3K1 Canada. (306)244-2828. Fax: (306)244-0255. E-mail: grainmag@sasktel.net. Website: www.grainmagazine.ca. **Contact:** Mike Thompson, Business Administrator. "Two categories with 4 prizes each: poetry in any form including prose poem; short fiction of any style including postcard story. Prizes: 2 First Prizes of $1,250, 2 Secong Prizes of $750, 4 Runner-up prizes of $500, plus publication. Entry fee: $30 fee for for a maximum of 2 entries in one category; US and international entries $36; ($6 postage) in US funds (non-Canadian). Entrants receive a one-year subscription. Guidelines available by fax, e-mail, or Web site. **Deadline: April 1.**

◎ 🔣 SKIPPING STONES HONOR AWARDS

P.O. Box 3939, Eugene OR 97403-0939. Phone/fax: (541) 342-4956. E-mail: editor@skippingstones.org. Website: www.skippingstones.org. **Contact:** Arun N. Toké, executive editor. nnual awards since 1994 to "promote multicultural and/or nature awareness through creative writings for children and teens and their educators." Prize: honor certificates; seals; reviews; press release/publicity. Categories: short stories, novels, story collections, poetry and nonfiction. Judged by "a multicultural committee of teachers, librarians, parents, students and editors." Entry fee: $50 ($25 for nonprofit, low-income publishers/self-publishers). **Deadline: February 1**. Entries must be previously published. Open to published books and resources that appeared in print during a two year period prior to the deadline date. Guidelines for SASE or e-mail and on Web site. Accepts inquiries by e-mail, fax, phone. "We seek authentic, exceptional, child/youth friendly books that promote intercultural, international, intergenerational harmony and understanding through creative ways. Writings that come out of your own experiences and cultural understanding seem to have an edge." Results announced in May each year. Winners notified through personal notifications, press release and by publishing reviews of winning titles in the summer issue. Attractive gold honor seals available for winners. For contest results, send SASE, e-mail or visit Web site.

Skipping Stones received the 2007 N.A.M.E. Award for outstanding contribution to multicultural education. Now in its 21st year!

◎ 🔣 SKIPPING STONES YOUTH AWARDS

Skipping Stones Magazine, P.O. Box 3939, Eugene OR 97403-09 39. Phone/fax: (541) 342-4956. E-mail: editor@skippingstones.org. Website: www.skippingstones.org. **Contact:** Arun N. Toké, executive editor. nnual awards to "promote creativity and multicultural and nature awareness in youth." Prize: publication in Autumn issue, honor certificate, subscription to magazine, plus 5 multicultural or nature books. Categories: short stories. Entry fee: $3/entry, make checks payable to Skipping Stones. Cover letter should include name, address, phone and e-mail. Deadline: June 20. Entries must be unpublished. Length: 1,000 words maximum. Open to any writer between 7 and 17. Guidelines available by SASE, e-mail or on Web site. Accepts inquiries by e-mail or phone. "Be creative. Do not use stereotypes or excessive violent language or plots. Be sensitive to cultural diversity." Results announced in the September-October issue. Winners notified by mail. For contest results, visit Web site. Everyone who enters receives the issue which features the award winners.

Skipping Stones is a winner of the 2007 NAME award now in 2st year.

◎ THE BERNICE SLOTE AWARD

Prairie Schooner, 201 Andrews Hall, P.O. Box 880334, Lincoln NE 68588-0334. (402)472-0911. Fax: (402)472-9771. E-mail: jengelhardt2@unlnotes.unl.edu. Website: http://prairieschooner.unl.edu. **Contact**: Hilda Raz, editor-in-chief. Offered annually for the best work by a beginning writer published in Prairie Schooner in the previous year. Prize: $500. Categories: short stories, essays and poetry. Judged by editorial staff of Prairie Schooner. No entry fee. **Submissions should be postmarked between January 15 and March 15**. For guidelines, send SASE or visit Web site. "Only work published in the journal during the previous year will be considered." Work is nominated by the editorial staff. Results announced in the Spring issue. Winners notified by mail in February or March.

▢ ◎ KAY SNOW WRITING AWARDS

Willamette Writers, 9045 SW Barbur Blvd., Suite 5A, Portland OR 97219. (503) 452-1592. Fax: (503) 452-0372. E-mail: wilwrite@teleport.com. Website: www.willamettewriters.com. **Contact:** Pat MacAodha.

Contest offered annually to "offer encouragement and recognition to writers with unpublished submissions." Acquires right to publish excerpts from winning pieces 1 time in their newsletter. Prize: 1st place: $300; 2nd place: $150; 3rd place: $50; excerpts published in Willamette Writers newsletter, and winners acknowledged at banquet during writing conference. Student writers win $50 in categories for grades 1-5, 6-8, and 9-12. $500 Liam Callen Memorial Award goes to best overall entry. Entry fee: $15 fee; no fee for student writers. **Deadline: April 23.** Guidelines for #10 SASE, fax, by e-mail or on Web site. Accepts inquires by fax, phone and e-mail. Winners notified by mail and phone. For contest results, send SASE. Prize winners will be honored at the two-day August Willamette Writers' Conference. Press releases will be sent to local and national media announcing the winners, and excerpts from winning entries may appear in our newsletter.

◎ SOUTH CAROLINA ARTS COMMISSION AND THE POST AND COURIER SOUTH CAROLINA FICTION CONTEST

1800 Gervais St., Columbia SC 29201. (803)734-8696. Website: www.southcarolinaarts.com. **Contact:** Sara June Goldstein, program director for the literary arts. "This annual writing competition calls for previously unpublished short stories of 2,500 words or less. The stories do not need to be Southern, nor do they need to be set in South Carolina, although such stories are acceptable for consideration. Up to 12 short stories will be selected for publication; each writer whose work is selected will receive $500 from The Post and Courier, which purchases first publication rights. Stories will also be published electronically by posting them on The Post and Courier's Web site, which links to the Art Commission's Web site. No entry fee. Deadline: January 15. Applicant must be a legal resident of South Carolina and be 18 years of age or older at the time of application. Guidelines and application available on the Arts Commission's Web site.

◎ SOUTH DAKOTA ARTS COUNCIL

711 E. Wells Avenue, Pierre SD 57501-3369. (605)773-3301. E-mail: sdac@state.sd.us. Website: www. artscouncil.sd.gov. **Contact:** Dennis Holub, executive director. "Individual Artist Grants (up to $3,000) and Artist Collaboration Grants (up to $6,000) are planned for fiscal 2010." No entry fee. Deadline: March 1. Open to South Dakota residents only. Students pursuing an undergraduate or graduate degree are ineligible. Guidelines and application available on Web site or by mail. Applicants must submit application form with an original signature; current résumé no longer than 5 pages; appropriate samples of artistic work (see guidelines); up to 5 pages additional documentation; SASE with adequate postage for return of ms (if desired).

◻ SOUTHWEST WRITERS (SWW) CONTESTS

SouthWest Writers (SWW), 3721 Morris St. NE, Suite A, Albuquerque NM 87111-3611. (505)265-9485. E-mail: SW Writers@juno.com. Website: www.southwestwriters.org. **Contact**: Contest Chair. The SouthWest Writers (SWW) Contest encourages and honors excellence in writing. There are 16 categories, including Christian Novel. (Please see rules on Web site for more details.) Prizes: Finalists in all categories are notified by mail and are listed on the SWW Web site with the title of their entry. First, second and third place winners in each category also receive cash prizes of $150, $100, and $50 (respectively), as well as a certificate of achievement. First place winners also compete for the $1,000 Storyteller Award. Winners will be honored at a contest awards banquet (date and time TBA). Categories: Nine categories-broken down by genre-are for short story and novel writers. For novels: Mainstream and Literary; Mystery, Suspense, Thriller, or Adventure; Romance; Science Fiction, Fantasy, or Horror; Historical or American Frontier/Western; Middle Grade (4th-6th grade) or Young Adult (7th grade and up). For short stories: Middle Grade or Young Adult; Mainstream and Literary. Other Genres: Christian, Memoir, Screenplay, Poetry, etc; Middle Grade (4th-6th grade) or Young Adult (7th grade and up). Judged by editors and agents (most from New York publishing houses) who are chosen by the contest chairs. Screening panel sends top 10 entries in each category to judges. Judges rank and critique the top three entries in each category. All entries may receive an optional written critique by a qualified consultant. Entry fee: Early deadline with no critique, $20 for members; $30 for nonmembers; late deadline, an additional $5. Early deadline with critique, $45 for members; $55 for nonmembers; late deadline, an additional $5. Cash, check (made out to SouthWest Writers), money order or credit card. No cover letter is required; send copy of the SWW Contest Entry Form. Personal information should not appear anywhere on ms. Novels: The first 20 pages, beginning with the prologue and/or first chapter, plus a 2-page maximum synopsis. Short Stories: 5,000 words or less. Please follow detailed instructions for submission in Category Specific Guidelines on Web site. Deadline: May 1; late deadline: May 15. Entries must be unpublished. Open to all writers from around the world. All entries should be submitted in English and follow standard ms format. "Entrants should read the SWW Contest Rules for complete information on the SWW Web site." Guidelines available in January by SASE, e-mail, on Web site or in SouthWest Sage SWW newsletter. Accepts inquiries by e-mail, phone. Mail SASE to receive rules, entry form in hard copy. Do not use certified mail to send submissions as they will be returned unopened; enclose an SASP to verify receipt.

◎ SPUR AWARDS

Western Writers of America, Inc., 1080 Mesa Vista Hall, MSC06 3770, 1 University of New Mexico Alberquerque NM 87131. (505) 277-5234. E-mail: wwa@unm.edu. Website: www.westernwriters.org. **Contact:** Awards Coordinator. Purpose of award is "to reward quality in the fields of western fiction and nonfiction." Prize: Trophy. Categories: short stories, novels, poetry, songs, scripts and nonfiction. No entry fee. **Deadline: January 10.** Entries must be published during the contest year. Open to any writer. Guidelines available in Sept./Oct. for SASE, on Web site or by phone. Inquiries accepted by e-mail or phone. Results announced annually in Summer. Winners notified by mail. For contest results, send SASE.

JOHN STEINBECK SHORT STORY AWARD

Reed Magazine. San Jose State University, Dept. of English, One Washington Square, San Jose CA 95192. (408) 924-4458. E-mail: reed@email.sjsu.edu. Website: http://www.reedmag.org/drupal/. **Contact:** Nick Taylor, editor. "Award for an unpublished short story of up to 6,000 words." Annual. Competition/award for short stories. Prize: $1,000 prize and publication in Reed Magazine. Receives several hundred entries per category. Entries are judged by a prominent fiction writer; 2007 judge was Tobias Wolff. Entry fee: $15 (includes issue of Reed). Make checks payable to Reed Magazine. Guidelines available in April 2008. **Submission period is June 1 - November 1, 2008.** Entries should be unpublished. Anyone may enter contest. Length: less than 6,000 words. Fill out submission form online: http://reedmag.org/drupal/?q=node/19. Writers may submit own work. "Do not submit any pornographic material, science fiction, fantasy, or children's literature. The work must be your own, (no translations)." Results announced in April. Winners notified by mail. Results made available to entrants on Web site, in publication.

◎ STONY BROOK SHORT FICTION PRIZE

Department of English, State University of New York, Stony Brook NY 11794-5350. (631)632-7400. Website: www.stonybrook.edu/fictionprize. **Contact:** John Westermann. Award "to recognize excellent undergraduate fiction." Prize: $1,000 and publication on Web site. Categories: Short stories. Judged by faculty of the Department of English & Creative Writing Program. No entry fee. Guidelines available on Web site. Inquiries accepted by e-mail. Expects 300 entries. Deadline: March 2 for 2009. Word length: 7,500 words or less. "Only undergraduates enrolled full time in American or Canadian colleges and universities for the 2006-2007 academic year are eligible. Proof required. Students of all races and backgrounds are encouraged to enter. Guidelines for SASE or on website. Ms should include name, permanent address, phone, e-mail, word count and title. Winners notified by phone; results posted on Web site by June.

☑ ◎ THEODORE STURGEON MEMORIAL AWARD FOR BEST SHORT SF OF THE YEAR

Center for the Study of Science Fiction, English Department, University of Kansas, Lawrence KS 66045. (785) 864-3380. Fax: (785) 864-1159. E-mail: jgunn@ku.edu. Website: www.ku.edu/~sfcenter. **Contact:** James Gunn, professor and director. Award to "honor the best science fiction short story of the year." Prize: Trophy. Winners receive expense-paid trip to the University and have their names engraved on permanent trophy. Categories: short stories. Judged by jury. No entry fee. Entries must be previously published. Guidelines available in December by phone, e-mail or on Web site. Accepts inquiries by e-mail and fax. Entrants for the Sturgeon Award are by nomination only. Results announced in July. For contest results, send SASE.

☒ ☐ SUBTERRAIN ANNUAL LITERARY AWARDS COMPETITION: THE LUSH TRIUMPHANT

subTERRAIN Magazine, P.O. Box 3008 MPO, Vancouver BC V6B 3X5 Canada. (604) 876-8710. Fax: (604) 879-2667. E-mail: subter@portal.ca. Website: www.subterrain.ca. **Contact:** Pat Mackenzie, managing editor. Offered annually to foster new and upcoming writers. Prize: $ 1000 (Canadian) cash prizes in each category, publication, and 1-year subscription to subTERRAIN. Categories: short stories, poetry, nonfiction. Judged by an editorial collective. Entry fee: $2 5. Entrants may submit as many entries in as many categories as they like. Guidelines on Web Site. **Deadline: May 15.** Entries must be unpublished. Length: Fiction: 3,000 words maximum; Poetry: a suite of 5 related poems (max 15 pages); creative nonfiction: max 4,000 words. Results announced on Web Site. "All entries must be previously unpublished material. Submissions will not be returned, so do not send originals."

☒ RONALD SUKENICK AMERICAN BOOK REVIEW INNOVATIVE FICTION PRIZE

FC2, American Book Review University of Houston-Victoria School of Arts and Sciences, 3007 N. Ben Wilson, Victoria TX 77901.(850) 644-2260. Fax: (850) 644-6808. E-mail: FC2@uhv.edu. Website: http://fc2.org/Sukenick%20prize.htm. **Contact:** Carmen Edington, managing editor. "To discover new writers of experimental fiction, and to publish work by writers who have not previously published with FC2." Annual. Competition/award for novels, story collections. Prize: $1000 and publication. Entries are judged by Board of Directors. For the 2007 contest, the final judge was Michael Martone. Each year it will be a different member of the Board. Entry fee: $25. Make checks payable to American Book Review. Guidelines available in June. Accepts inquiries by e-mail. **Submission period is August 15-November 1.** Entries should be unpublished. Anyone who has not previously published with FC2 may enter contest. Cover letter should include name, address, phone, e-mail, novel/story title. Only the title should appear on the ms, since all mss are read blind by the judges. Writers may submit their own work. "Be familiar with our list." Results announced May. Winners notified by phone, by e-mail. Winners announced May.

☺ SYDNEY TAYLOR MANUSCRIPT COMPETITION

Association of Jewish Libraries, 204 Park St., Montclair NJ 07042. (973)744-3836. E-mail: stmacajl@aol.com. Website: www.jewishlibraries.org. **Contact**: Aileen Grossberg, coordinator. Award "to identify and encourage writers of fiction for ages 8-11 with universal appeal of Jewish content; story should deepen the understanding of Judaism for all children, Jewish and non-Jewish, and reveal positive aspects of Jewish life. No short stories or plays. Length: 64-200 pages." Judged by 5 AJL member librarians. Prize: $1,000. No entry fee. Guidelines available by SASE, e-mail or on Web site. **Deadline: December 15.** Entries must be unpublished. Cover letter should include name, address, phone, e-mail and title. Results announced April 15. Winners notified by phone or e-mail. For contest information, send e-mail or visit Web site. Check Web site for more specific details and to download release forms which must accompany entry.

☐ THREE CHEERS AND A TIGER

E-mail: editors@toasted-cheese.com. Website: www.toasted-cheese.com. **Contact:** Stephanie Lenz, editor. Purpose of contest is to write a short story (following a specific theme) within 48 hours. Contests are held first weekend in spring (mystery) and first weekend in fall (sf/f). Prize: Amazon gift certificates and publication. Categories: short stories. Blind-judged by two Toasted Cheese editors. Each judge uses his or her own criteria to choose entries. No entry fee. Cover letter should include name, address, e-mail, word count and title. Information should be in the body of the e-mail. It will be removed before the judging begins. Entries must be unpublished. Contest offered biannually. Word limit announced at the start of the contest. Contest-specific information is announced 48 hours before the contest submission deadline. Open to any writer. Accepts inquiries by e-mail. "Follow the theme, word count and other contest rules. We have more suggestions at our Web site." Results announced in April and October. Winners notified by e-mail. List of winners on Web site.

☑ ☺ THE THURBER PRIZE FOR AMERICAN HUMOR

Thurber House, 77 Jefferson Ave., Columbus OH 43215. (614)464-1032. Fax: (614)280-3645. E-mail: mkendall@thurberhouse.org. Website: www.thurberhouse.org. **Contact:** Susanne Jaffe, Executive Director. "The Award recognizes the art of humor writing." Prize: $5,000 for the finalist, non-cash prizes awarded to two runners-up. Judged by well-known members of the national arts community. Entry fee: $65 per title. Deadline: April. Published submissions or accepted for publication in U.S. for the first time.

Primarily pictorial works such as cartoon collections are not considered. Word length: no requirement. See Web site for application form and guidelines. Results announced in October. Winners notified in person at the Algonquin Hotel in New York City. For contest results, visit Web site.

✂ ▢ TICKLED BY THUNDER ANNUAL FICTION CONTEST

Tickled By Thunder, 14076-86A Ave., Surrey BC V3W 0V9 Canada. E-mail: info@tickledbythunder.com. Website: www.tickledbythunder.com. **Contact:** Larry Lindner, editor. Award to encourage new writers. Prize: $150 Canadian, 4-issue subscription (two years) plus publication. Categories: short stories. Judged by the editor and other writers. Entry fee: $10 Canadian (free for subscribers but more than one story requires $5 per entry). Deadline: February 15. Entries must be unpublished. Word length: 2,000 words or less. Open to any writer. Guidelines available for SASE, e-mail, on Web site. Accepts inquiries by e-mail. Results announced in May. Winners notified by mail. For contest results, send SASE.

✂ ◎ TORONTO BOOK AWARDS

Toronto Protocol, City Clerk's Office, 100 Queen St. West, City Hall, 10th Floor, West Tower, Toronto ON M5H 2N2 Canada. (416)392-4674. Fax: (416)392-1247. E-mail: bkurmey@toronto.ca. Website: www. toronto.ca/book_awards. **Contact:** Bev Kurmey, protocol officer. The Toronto Book Awards honor authors of books of literary or artistic merit that are evocative of Toronto. Annual award for short stories, novels, poetry or short story collections. Prize: $15,000. Each short-listed author (usually 4-6) receives $1,000 and the winner receives the remainder. Categories: No separate categories—novels, short story collections, books of poetry, biographies, history, books about sports, children's books—all are judged together. Judged by jury of five who have demonstrated interest and/or experience in literature, literacy, books and book publishing. No entry fee. Cover letter should include name, address, phone, e-mail and title of entry. Six copies of the entry book are also required. **Deadline: last week of March.** Entries must be previously published. Guidelines available in September on Web site. Accepts inquires by fax, e-mail, phone. Finalists announced in June; winners notified in September at a gala reception. More information and results available on Web site.

WAASMODE SHORT FICTION PRIZE

Passages North, NMU 1401 Presque Ilse Ave, Marquette MI 49855. (906) 227-1203. E-mail: passages@ nmu.edu. Website: http://myweb.nmu.edu/~passages. Offered every other year—check Web site for details. Competition/award for short stories. Prize: $1000 first prize; two honorable mentions. Entry fee: $10 per story, includes contest issue. Make checks payable to Northern Michigan University. **Submission period is Oct 15-Feb 15.** Entries should be unpublished. Anyone may enter contest. Length: 7,500 word max. Writers may submit own work. Winners notified by e-mail. Results made available to entrants with SASE.

▧ WABASH PRIZE FOR FICTION

Sycamore Review, Department of English, 500 Oval Dr., West Lafayette IN 47907.(765)494-3783. E-mail: syamore@purdue.edu. Website: www.sycamorereview.com. **Contact:** Mehdi Okasi, Editor-in-Chief. Submit one short story (not to exceed 10,000 words). No identifying information should appear on the manuscript. Include cover letter with all identifying information along with a word count. Include SASE to receive notification of the winner and check made payable to Sycamore Review for entry. **Deadline:** March 19 for 2009. Winner will be announced May 1, 2009. Final judge: Tobias Wolff.

▢ THE ROBERT WATSON LITERARY PRIZE IN FICTION AND POETRY

(formerly The Greensboro Review Literary Award in Fiction and Poetry) The Greensboro Review, 3302 Moore Humanities and Research Administration Building, UNCG, P.O. Box 26170, Greensboro NC 27402-6170. (336) 334-5459. E-mail: anseay@uncg.edu. Website: www.greensthroreview.org. **Contact:** Allison Seay, associate editor. Offered annually for fiction (7,500 word limit) and poetry(3-5 poems). Sample issue for $5. Prize: $500 each for best short story and poem. Judged by editors of The Greensboro Review. No entry fee. Guidelines for SASE or on Web site. **Deadline: September 15**. Entries must be unpublished. No simultaneous submissions or submissions by e-mail. Open to any writer. Winners notified by mail, phone or e-mail. List of winners published in Spring issue. "All manuscripts meeting literary award guidelines will be considered for cash award as well as for publication in the Spring issue of The Greensboro Review."

☐ WISCONSIN INSTITUTE FOR CREATIVE WRITING FELLOWSHIP

University of Wisconsin—Madison, Creative Writing/English Dept., 6195B H.C. White Hall, 600 N. Park St., Madison WI 53706. (608) 263-3374. E-mail: rfkuka@wisc.edu. Website: www.creativewriting. wisc.edu. **Contact:** Ron Kuka, program coordinator. Fellowship provides time, space and an intellectual community for writers working on first books. Receives approximately 300 applicants a year for each genre. Prize: $17,000 for a 9-month appointment. Judged by English Department faculty and current fellows. **Entry fee**: $40, payable to the Department of English. Applicants should submit up to 10 pages of poetry or one story of up to 30 pages and a résumé or vita directly to the program during the month of February. An applicant's name must not appear on the writing sample (which must be in ms form) but rather on a separate sheet along with address, social security number, phone number, e-mail address and title(s) of submission(s). Candidates should also supply the names and phone numbers of two references. Accepts inquiries by e-mail and phone. **Deadline: February**. "Candidates must not yet have published, or had accepted for publication, a book by application deadline." Open to any writer with either an M.F.A. or Ph.D. in creative writing. Please enclose a SASE for notification of results. Results announced by May 1. "Send your best work. Stories seem to have a small advantage over novel excerpts."

☐ TOBIAS WOLFF AWARD IN FICTION

Bellingham Review, Mail Stop 9053, Western Washington University, Bellingham WA 98225. (360)650-4863. E-mail: bhreview@cc.wwu.edu. Website: www.wwu.edu/~bhreview. **Contact:** Fiction Editor. Offered annually for unpublished work. Guidelines for SASE or online. Prize: $1,000, plus publication and subscription. Categories: novel excerpts and short stories. Entry fee: $18 for 1st entry; $10 each additional entry. Guidelines available in September for SASE or on Web site. **Deadline:** Contest runs Dec. 1-March 15. Entries must be unpublished. Length: 8,000 words or less per story or chapter. Open to any writer. Winner announced in August and notified by mail. For contest results, send SASE.

◎ WORLD FANTASY AWARDS

World Fantasy Awards Association, P.O. Box 43, Mukilteo WA 98275-0043. E-mail: sfexecsec@gmail.com. Website: www.worldfantasy.org. **Contact:** Peter Dennis Pautz, president. Awards "to recognize excellence in fantasy literature worldwide." Offered annually for previously published work in several categories, including life achievement, novel, novella, short story, anthology, collection, artist, special award-pro and special award-nonpro. Works are recommended by attendees of current and previous 2 years' conventions and a panel of judges. Prize: Bust of HP Lovecraft. Judged by panel. No entry fee. Guidelines available in December for SASE or on Web site. **Deadline: June 1.** Entries must be previously published. Published submissions from previous calendar year. Word length: 10,000-40,000 for novella, 10,000 for short story. "All fantasy is eligible, from supernatural horror to Tolkien-esque to sword and sorcery to the occult, and beyond." Cover letter should include name, address, phone, e-mail, word count, title and publications where submission was previously published, submitted to the address above and the panel of judges when they appear on the Web site. Results announced November 1 at annual convention. For contest results, visit Web site.

◎ WRITER'S DIGEST ANNUAL SHORT SHORT STORY COMPETITION

Writer's Digest, 700 State Street, Iola WI 54990. (715)445-4612 ext. 13430. E-mail: short-short-competition@fwpubs.com. Website: www.writersdigest.com. **Contact:** Nicole Florence, contest administrator. Annual. Competition/award for short-shorts. Prize: 1st place receives $3,000 and option for free "Best Seller Publishing Package" from Trafford Publishing; 2nd place receives $1,500; 3rd place receives $500; 4th-10th place receive $100; 11th-25th place receive $50 gift certificate for Writer's Digest Books. The names and story titles of the 1st-10th place winners will be printed in the June issue of Writer's Digest, and winners will receive the latest edition of Novel & Short Story Writer's Market. Entry fee: $15/story. Make checks payable to Writer's Digest. Deadline: Dec. 1. Entries should be unpublished. "Writer's Digest reserves the one-time publication rights to the 1st-25th place winning entries to be published in a Writer's Digest publication." Open to all except employees of F+W Media, Inc., and their immediate families and Writer's Digest contributing editors and correspondents as listed on the masthead. Length: 1,500 words or fewer. Type the word count on the first page of your entry, along with your name, address, phone number and e-mail address. All entries must be typewritten and double-spaced on one side of 8½ × 11 or A4 white paper. Mss will not be returned. Enclose a self-addressed, stamped postcard with your entry if you wish to be notified of its receipt. Write, see publication, or visit Web site for official entry form. Writers may submit own work. Results announced June. Winners notified in Feb. Results made available to entrants on Web site, in publication.

☐ WRITER'S DIGEST ANNUAL WRITING COMPETITION

Writer's Digest, 700 State Street, Iola, WI 54591. (715)445-4612, ext. 13430. E-mail: writing-competition@ fwpubs.com. Website: www.writersdigest.com. **Contact:** Terri Boes, contest administrator. Annual. Competition/award for short stories, articles, poems, scripts. Prize: Grand prize is $3,000 cash and an all-expenses-paid trip to New York City to meet with editors and agents. Writer's Digest will fly you and a guest to The Big Apple, where you'll spend 3 days and 2 nights in the publishing capital of the world. While you're there, a Writer's Digest editor will escort you to meet and share your work with four editors or agents. You'll also receive a free Diamond Publishing Package from Outskirts Press. First place in each category receives $1,000 cash and $100 worth of Writer's Digest Books. Second place in each category receives $500 cash, plus $100 worth of Writer's Digest Books. Third place in each category receives $250 cash, plus $100 worth of Writer's Digest Books. Fourth place in each category receives $100 cash, the latest editon of Writer's Market Deluxe, and a 1-yr subscription to Writer's Digest. Fifth place in each category receives $50 cash, the latest edition of Writer's Market Deluxe, and a 1-yr subscription to Writer's Digest. Sixth-tenth place in each category receives $25 cash. First through tenth place winners also receive a copy of Writer's Market Deluxe and a one-year subscription to Writer's Digest mgazine. All other winners receive distinctive certificates honoring their accomplishment. Categories: Inspirational Writing (spiritual/religious); Article: Memoir/Personal Essay; Article: Magazine Feature; Short Story: Genre; Short Story: Mainstream/Literary; Poetry: Rhyming; Poetry: Non-rhyming; Script: Stage Play; Script: TV/Movie; Children's Fiction. Judged by the editors of Writer's Digest. **Entry fee**: $15 for first poem, $10 each additional poem; all other entries are $20 for first ms, $15 each additional ms. Make checks payable to Writer's Digest. Accepts inquiries by e-mail. **Deadline: May 15.** Entries should be unpublished. "Entries in the Magazine Feature Article category may be previously published. Writer's Digest retains one-time publication rights to the grand prize and first place winning entries in each category to be published in a Writer's Digest publication." Open to all writers except employees of F + W Media, Inc, and their immediate families, Writer's Digest contributing editors and correspondents as listed on the masthead, Writer's Online Workshops instructors, and Grand Prize winners from the previous three years. Length: 2,000 words max for Memoir/Personal Essay, Feature Article, and Children's Fiction; 2,500 words max for Insipirational Writing; 4,000 words max for Short Story categtories; 32 lines max for Poetry categories; 15 pages in standard format plus 1-pg synopsis for Script categories. Write, visit www.writersdigest.com/contests/annual, or see publication for official entry form. Your name, address, phone number, and competition category must appear in the upper left-hand corner of the first page, otherwise your entry is disqualified. See additional guidelines in publication or on Web site. Winners notified by mail. Winners notified by Oct. Results made available to entrants on Web Site after the issue has been published.

☐ WRITER'S DIGEST POPULAR FICTION AWARDS

Writer's Digest Magazine, 700 State Street, Iola, WI 54990. (715) 445-4612, ext. 13430. E-mail: popularfictionawards@fwpubs.com. **Contact:** Nicole Florence, contest administrator. Annual. Competition/award for short stories. Prizes: Grand Prize is $2,500 cash and $100 worth of Writer's Digest Books. First Prize in each of the five categories receives $500 cash and $100 worth of Writer's Digest Books. Honorable Mentions receive promotion on www.writersdigest.com and the next edition of Novel & Short Story Writer's Market. Categories: Romance, Mystery/Crime, Science Fiction/Fantasy, Thriller/ Suspense, Horror. Judged by Writer's Digest editors. Entry fee: $12.50. Make checks payable to Writer's Digest. Accepts inquiries by mail, e-mail, phone. Deadline: Nov. 1. Entries should be unpublished. Open to all "except employees of F + W Publications, Inc., and their immediate family members, Writer's Digest contributing editors and correspondents as listed on our masthead, Writer's Online Workshops instructors, and Grand Prize Winners from the previous three years in any Writer's Digest competitions." Length: 4,000 words or fewer. Entries must be accompanied by an Official Entry Form or facsimile. Your name, address, phone number and competition category must appear in the upper left-hand corner of the first page of your manuscript, otherwise it is disqualified. Writers may submit own work. Results announced in the August issue of Writer's Digest. Winners notified by mail before March 1.

☐ **WRITERS-EDITORS NETWORK 26TH ANNUAL INTERNATIONAL WRITING COMPETITION**
Florida Freelance Writers Association, PO Box A, North Stratford NH 03590-0167 (603)922-8338.
E-mail: contest@writers-editorscom. Website: wwwwriters-editorscom

☐ **WRITERS-EDITORS NETWORK 26TH ANNUAL INTERNATIONAL WRITING COMPETITION**
c/o CNW Publishing, Florida Freelance Writers Association, P.O. Box A, North Stratford NH 03590-0167.
E-mail: contest@writers-editors.com. Website: www.writers-editors.com. **Contact:** Dana K. Cassell,
executive director. Annual award "to recognize publishable talent." Divisions & Categories: Nonfiction
(previously published article/essay/column/nonfiction book chapter; unpublished or self-published
article/essay/column/nonfiction book chapter); Fiction (unpublished or self-published short story or
novel chapter); Children's Literature (unpublished or self-published short story/nonfiction article/book
chapter/poem); Poetry (unpublished or self-published free verse/traditional). Prize: 1st Place: $100, plus
certificate; 2nd Place: $75, plus certificate; 3rd Place: $50, plus certificate. Honorable Mention certificates
will be awarded in each category as warranted. Judged by editors, librarians and writers. Entry fee: $5
(active or new CNW/FFWA members) or $10 (nonmembers) for each fiction/nonfiction entry under
3,000 words; $10 (members) or $20 (nonmembers) for each entry of 3,000 words or longer; and $3
(members) or $5 (nonmembers) for each poem. Guidelines for SASE or on website. Accepts inquiries by
e-mail, phone and mail. Deadline: March 15. Open to any writer. Results announced May 31. Winners
notified by mail and posted on Web site. Results available for SASE or visit Web site.

◎ **WRITERS' FELLOWSHIP**
NC Arts Council, Department of Cultural Resources, Raleigh NC 27699-4632. (919) 807-6512. Fax:
(919) 807-6532. E-mail: debbie.mcgill@ncdcr.gov. Website: www.ncarts.org. **Contact:** Deborah McGill,
literature director. Fellowships are awarded to support the creative development of NC writers and to
stimulate the creation of new work. Prize: $10,000. Categories: short stories, novels, literary nonfiction,
literary translation, spoken word. Work for children also invited. Judged by a panel of literary professionals
appointed by the NC Arts Council, a state agency. No entry fee. **Deadline: November 1, 2008.** Mss
must not be in published form. We receive approximately 300 applications. Word length: 20 double-
spaced pages (max). The work must have been written within the past 5 years. Only writers who have
been full-time residents of NC for at least 1 year as of the application deadline and who plan to remain
in the state during the grant year may apply. Guidelines available in late August on Web site. Accepts
inquiries by fax, e-mail, phone. Results announced in late summer. All applicants notified by mail.

☐ **WRITERS' JOURNAL ANNUAL FICTION CONTEST**
Val-Tech Media, P.O. Box 394, Perham MN 56573. (218) 346-7921. Fax: (218) 346-7924. E-mail:
writersjournal@writersjournal.com. Website: www.writersjournal.com. **Contact:** Leon Ogroske, editor
(editor@writersjournal.com). Offered annually for previously unpublished fiction up to 5,000 words.
Open to any writer. Prize: 1st Place: $500; 2nd Place: $200; 3rd Place: $100, plus honorable mentions.
Prize-winning stories and selected honorable mentions published in *WRITERS' Journal.* Entry fee: $15
reading fee. Guidelines and entry forms available for SASE and on Web site. Accepts inquiries by fax,
e-mail and phone. **Deadline: January 30.** "Writer's name must not appear on submission. A separate
cover sheet must include name of contest, title, word count and writer's name, address, phone and
e-mail (if available)." Results announced in July/August. Winners notified by mail. A list of winners is
published in July/August issue and posted on Web site or available for SASE.

☐ ◎ **WRITERS' JOURNAL ANNUAL HORROR/GHOST CONTEST**
Val-Tech Media, P.O. Box 394, Perham MN 56573. (218) 346-7921. Fax: (218) 346-7924. E-mail:
writersjournal@writersjournal.com. Website: www.writersjournal.com. **Contact:** Leon Ogroske, editor.
Offered annually for previously unpublished works. Open to any writer. Prize: 1st place: $250; 2nd place:
$100; 3rd place: $50, plus honorable mentions. Prize-winning stories and selected honorable mentions
published in *WRITERS' Journal.* Entry fee: $7. Guidelines available for SASE, by fax, phone, e-mail, on
Website and in publication. Accepts inquiries by e-mail, phone, fax. **Deadline: March 30.** Entries must
be unpublished. Length: 2,000 words. Cover letter should include name, address, phone, e-mail, word
count and title; just title on ms. Results announced in September annually. Winners notified by mail. For
contest results, send SASE or visit Web site.

⬚ ◉ WRITERS' JOURNAL ANNUAL ROMANCE CONTEST

Val-Tech Media, P.O. Box 394, Perham MN 56573. (218) 346-7921. Fax: (218) 346-7924. E-mail: writersjournal@writersjournal.com. Website: www.writersjournal.com. **Contact:** Leon Ogroske, editor. Offered annually for previously unpublished works. Open to any writer. Prize: 1st place: $250; 2nd place: $100; 3rd place: $50, plus honorable mentions. Prize-winning stories and selected honorable mentions published in *WRITERS' Journal.* Entry fee: $7 fee. No limit on entries per person. Guidelines for SASE, by fax, phone, e-mail, on Web site and in publication. Accepts inquiries by fax, e-mail, phone. **Deadline: July 30.** Entries must be unpublished. Length: 2,000 words maximum. Open to any writer. Cover letter should include name, address, phone, e-mail, word count and title; just title on ms. Results announced in January/February issue. Winners notified by mail. Winners list published in *WRITERS' Journal* and on Web site. Enclose SASE for winner's list.

ⓝ ◉ WRITERS' JOURNAL ANNUAL SCIENCE FICTION/FANTASY CONTEST

Val-Tech Media, P.O. Box 394, Perham MN 56573.(218)346-7921. Fax: (218)346-7924. E-mail: writersjournal@writersjournal.com. Website: www.writersjournal.com. **Contact:** Leon Ogroske, editor. Annual contest for previously unpublished fiction up to 2,000 words. Open to any writer. Prize: 1st Place: $250; 2nd Place: $100; 3rd Place: $50, plus honorable mentions. Prize-winning stories and selected honorable mentions published in *WRITERS' Journal.* Entry fee: $7 reading fee. Guidelines available for SASE and on Web site. Accepts inquiries by fax, e-mail and phone. **Deadline: November 30**. Writer's name must not appear on submission. A separate cover sheet must include name of contest, title, word count and writer's name, address, phone and e-mail (if available)." Results announced in May/June. Winners notified by mail. A list of winners is published in May/June issue and posted on Web site or available for SASE.

⬚ ◉ WRITERS' JOURNAL ANNUAL SHORT STORY CONTEST

Val-Tech Media, P.O. Box 394, Perham MN 56573. (218) 346-7921. Fax: (218) 346-7924. E-mail: writersjournal@writersjournal.com. Website: www.writersjournal.com. **Contact:** Leon Ogroske. Offered annually for previously unpublished short stories less than 2,000 words. Open to any writer. Guidelines for SASE and online. Prize: 1st place: $350; 2nd place: $125; 3rd place: $75, plus honorable mentions. Prize-winning stories and selected honorable mentions published in *WRITERS'Journal* November/December issue. Winners notified by mail. Winners list published in *WRITERS' Journal* and on Web site. Entry fee: $10 reading fee. **Deadline: May 30.**

◉ WRITERS' LEAGUE OF TEXAS BOOK AWARDS

Writers' League of Texas, 611 S. Congress Ave., Suite 130, Austin TX 78704. (512) 499-8914. Fax: (512) 499-0441. E-mail: wlt@writersleague.org. Website: www.writersleague.org. **Contact**: Kristy Bordine, program and membership administrator. Award established to honor outstanding books by American authors. Prize: $1,000 per category. Categories: fiction, nonfiction, poetry/literary prose, children's long works, children's short works. **Entry fee**: $25. **Deadline: April 30.** Open to all authors of books published during the previous year (for 2010, books should have been published in 2009). Guidelines available in January for SASE, fax, e-mail, or visit Web site. Results announced in October and awards ceremony is held at the Texas Book Festival.

◉ WRITERS' LEAGUE OF TEXAS CHILDREN'S BOOK AWARDS

Writers' League of Texas, 611 S. Congress Ave., Suite 130, Austin TX 78704. (512) 499-8914. Fax: (512) 499-0441. E-mail: wlt@writersleague.org. Website: www.writersleague.org. **Contact:** Kristy Bordine, program and membership administrator. Award established to "honor outstanding books by children's authors." Prize: $1,000. Categories: long works and short works. Entry fee: $25. **Deadline: April 30.** Open to all authors of children's books published during the previous year (for 2010, books should have been published in 2009). Guidelines available in January for SASE, fax, e-mail, or visit Web site. Results announced in October and awards ceremony is held at the Texas Book Festival.

⬚ WRITERS' LEAGUE OF TEXAS MANUSCRIPT CONTEST

Writers' League of Texas, 611 S. Congress Ave., Suite 130, Austin TX 78704. (512) 499-8914. Fax: (512) 499-0441. E-mail: wlt@writersleague.org. Website: www.writersleague.org. **Contact:** Kristy Bordine. Prize: First-place winners meet individually with an agent at the Writers' League of Texas Agents Conference in June. Categories: mainstream fiction, mystery, thriller/action adventure, romance, science fiction/fantasy/horror, historical/western, narrative nonfiction, and children's long and short works. Judged by preliminary judges (first round), then agent or editor reads finalists' manuscripts. **Entry fee**: $50 for score sheet with comments. Open to any writer. Entries must be unpublished. Submit first 10 pages of manuscript, double-spaced. Guidelines available in November by e-mail or on Web site. **Deadline: March**. Accepts inquiries by e-mail. Results announced at the June conference and on the Web site.

WRITERS' LEAGUE OF TEXAS MANUSCRIPT CONTEST

Writers' League of Texas, 1501 W. Fifth St., #E-2, Austin TX 78703. (512)499-8914. Fax: (512)499-0441. Website: www.writersleague.org. **Contact**: Kristy Bordine. Offered annually for unpublished work. Prize: "First place winners meet individually with an agent at the Writers' League of Texas Agents Conference in June." Categories: mainstream fiction, mystery, thriller/action adventure, romance, science fiction/fantasy/horror, historical/western, narrative nonfiction, and children's long and short works. Judged by preliminary judges in the first round, then an agent or editor reads finalists' manuscripts. **Entry fee:** $50 (includes score sheet with comments.) Open to any writer. Entries must be unpublished. Submit first 10 pages of novel, double-spaced. Guidelines available in November by e-mail or on Web site. **Deadline: March**. Accept inquiries by e-mail. Results announced at the June conference and on Web site.

☑ ZOETROPE SHORT STORY CONTEST

Zoetrope: All-Story, 916 Kearny St., San Francisco CA 94133. (415) 788-7500. Fax: (415) 989-7910. E-mail: contests@all-story.com. Website: www.all-story.com. **Contact:** Krista Halverson, managing editor. Annual contest for unpublished short stories. Prize: 1st place: $1,000; 2nd place: $500, 3rd place: $250; plus 7 honorable mentions. Judged by Elizabeth McCracken in 2008. Entry fee: $15. Guidelines for SASE, by e-mail, in publication, or on Web site. **Deadline: October 1.** Entries must be unpublished. Word length: 5,000 words maximum. Open to any writer. "Please mark envelope clearly 'short fiction contest'." Winners notified by phone or e mail December 1. Results announced December 1. A list of winners will be posted on Web site and published in spring issue. The winning story will be published at the Web site as a special supplement to the spring issue.

Conferences & Workshops

Why are conferences so popular? Writers and conference directors alike tell us it's because writing can be such a lonely business—at conferences writers have the opportunity to meet (and commiserate) with fellow writers, as well as meet and network with publishers, editors and agents. Conferences and workshops provide some of the best opportunities for writers to make publishing contacts and pick up valuable information on the business, as well as the craft, of writing.

The bulk of the listings in this section are for conferences. Most conferences last from one day to one week and offer a combination of workshop-type writing sessions, panel discussions and a variety of guest speakers. Topics may include all aspects of writing from fiction to poetry to scriptwriting, or they may focus on a specific type of writing, such as those conferences sponsored by the Romance Writers of America (RWA) for writers of romance or by the Society of Children's Book Writers and Illustrators (SCBWI) for writers of children's books.

Workshops, however, tend to run longer—usually one to two weeks. Designed to operate like writing classes, most require writers to be prepared to work on and discuss their fiction while attending. An important benefit of workshops is the opportunity they provide writers for an intensive critique of their work, often by professional writing teachers and established writers.

Each of the listings here includes information on the specific focus of an event as well as planned panels, guest speakers and workshop topics. It is important to note, however, some conference directors were still in the planning stages for 2010 when we contacted them. If it was not possible to include 2010 dates, fees or topics, we have provided information from 2009 so you can get an idea of what to expect. For the most current information, it's best to check the conference Web site or send a self-addressed, stamped envelope to the director in question about three months before the date(s) listed.

LEARNING AND NETWORKING

Besides learning from workshop leaders and panelists in formal sessions, writers at conferences also benefit from conversations with other attendees. Writers on all levels enjoy sharing insights. Often, a conversation over lunch can reveal a new market for your work or let you know which editors are most receptive to the work of new writers. You can find out about recent editor changes and about specific agents. A casual chat could lead to a new contact or resource in your area.

Many editors and agents make visiting conferences a part of their regular search for new writers. A cover letter or query that starts with "I met you at the Green Mountain Writers Conference," or "I found your talk on your company's new romance line at the Moonlight and Magnolias Writer's Conference most interesting . . ." may give you a small leg up on the competition.

While a few writers have been successful in selling their manuscripts at a conference, the availability of editors and agents does not usually mean these folks will have the time there to read your novel or six best short stories (unless, of course, you've scheduled an individual meeting with them ahead of time). While editors and agents are glad to meet writers and discuss work in general terms, usually they don't have the time (or energy) to give an extensive critique during a conference. In other words, use the conference as a way to make a first, brief contact.

SELECTING A CONFERENCE

Besides the obvious considerations of time, place and cost, choose your conference based on your writing goals. If, for example, your goal is to improve the quality of your writing, it will be more helpful to you to choose a hands-on craft workshop rather than a conference offering a series of panels on marketing and promotion. If, on the other hand, you are a science fiction novelist who would like to meet your fans, try one of the many science fiction conferences or ``cons'' held throughout the country and the world.

Look for panelists and workshop instructors whose work you admire and who seem to be writing in your general area. Check for specific panels or discussions of topics relevant to what you are writing now. Think about the size—would you feel more comfortable with a small workshop of eight people or a large group of 100 or more attendees?

If your funds are limited, start by looking for conferences close to home, but you may want to explore those that offer contests with cash prizes—and a chance to recoup your expenses. A few conferences and workshops also offer scholarships, but the competition is stiff and writers interested in these should find out the requirements early. Finally, students may want to look for conferences and workshops that offer college credit. You will find these options included in the listings here. Again, send a self-addressed, stamped envelope for the most current details.

ABROAD WRITERS CONFERENCES

17363 Sutter Creek Rd., Sutter Creek CA 95685. (209)296-4050. E-mail: abroadwriters@yahoo.com. Website: http://www.abroad-crwf.com/index.html. Conferences are held throughout the year in various places worldwide. See Web site for scheduling details. Conference duration: 7-10 days. "Instead of being lost in a crowd at a large conference, Abroad Writers' Conference prides itself on holding small group meetings where participants have personal contact with everyone. Stimulating talks, interviews, readings, Q&A's, writing workshops, film screenings, private consultations and social gatherings all take place within a week to ten days. Abroad Writers' Conference promises you true networking opportunities and full detailed feedback on your writing."

Costs Prices start at $2,750. Discounts and upgrades may apply. See Web site for pricing details.

Additional Information Agents participate in conference.

ALABAMA WRITERS' CONCLAVE

137 Sterline Dr., Hueytown AL 35023. E-mail: irenelatham@charter.net. Website: www. alabamawritersconclave.org. Contact: Irene Latham, program chair; Don Johnson, treasurer. Estab. 1923. Last event held July 17-19, 2009. Average attendance: 80-100. Conference to promote all phases of writing. Also offers ms critiques and eight writing contests. Site: Four Points Sherataon at the University of Alabama campus in Tuscaloosa, Alabama.

Costs Fees for conference are $150 (member)/$175 (nonmember), includes 2 meals. Critique fee $25 (member)/$30 (nonmember). Membership $25.

Accommodations Special conference rate s.

Additional Information "We have major speakers and faculty members who conduct intensive, energetic workshops. Our annual writing contest guidelines and all other information is available at www. alabamawritersconclave.org."

ℕ ALGONKIAN FIVE DAY NOVEL CAMP

2020 Pennsylvania Ave. NW, Suite 443, Washington DC 20006.E-mail: algonkian@webdelsol.com. Website: http://algonkianconferences.com/AlgonkianParkWorkshop/. Conference duration: 5 days. Average attendance: 12 students maximum per workshop. "During 45 + hours of actual workshop time, students will engage in those rigorous narrative and complication/plot exercises necessary to produce a publishable manuscript, Genres we work with include general commercial fiction, literary fiction, serious and light women's fiction, mystery/cozy/thriller, SF/F, young adult, and memoir/narrative non-fiction. The three areas of workshop emphasis will be PREMISE, PLATFORM, and EXECUTION. Site: "The Algonkian Park is located 30 miles from Washington, D.C. A good map and directions can be found here. It is 12 miles from Dulles International Airport (the perfect place to fly into—cab fares from Dulles to Algonkian are about $25.00). The cottages are fully furnished with TV, phones, linens, dishes, central air and heat. All cottages feature fireplaces, decks with grills, equipped kitchens, cathedral ceilings, and expansive riverside views of the Potomac. Participants each have their own room in the cottage. The address of the Algonkian Park Management headquarters is 47001 Fairway Drive, Sterling, Virginia, and their phone number is 703-450-4655. If you have any questions about the cottages or facilities, ask for Heather, the manager."

Costs $865.

Accommodations Offers overnight accommodations. Price includes tuition, private cottage room for five nights, breakfast and lunch. Transportation to and from the conference and dinner are not included.

Additional Information For brochure, visit Web site.

⊟ ALTERNATIVE PRESS EXPO (APE)

Comic-Con International, P.O. Box 128458, San Diego CA 92112-8458.(619)491-2475. Fax: (619)414-1022. E-mail: cci-info@comic-con.org. Website: www.comic-con.org/ape/. **Contact:** Eddie Ibrahim, director of programming. Annual. Last conference held November 1-2, 2008, in San Francisco. Conference duration: 2 days. "Hundreds of artists and publishers converge for the largest gathering of alternative and self-published comics in the country." Includes panels on graphic novels, Web comics, how to pitch your comic to publishers, and the traditional APE 'queer cartoonists' panel. Site: Large conference or expo center in host city. Check Web site for 2008 location. 2007 special guests included Kevin Huizenga, Karl Christian Krumpholz, Hope Larson, Francoise Mouly, Art Spiegelman, Brian Lee O'Malley, Gene Yang.

Costs $7 single day; $10 both days.

Accommodations Does not offer overnight accommodations. Provides list of area hotels or lodging options on Web site.

Additional Information For brochure, visit Web site. Editors participate in conference.

AMERICAN CHRISTIAN WRITERS CONFERENCES

P.O. Box 110390, Nashville TN 37222. (800) 21-WRITE. Fax: (615) 834-7736. E-mail: ACWriters@aol. com. Website: www.ACWriters.com. **Contact:** Reg Forder, director. Estab. 1988. Annual. Conferences held throughout the year in over 2 dozen cities. Conference duration: 2 days. Average attendance: 30-80. Conference's purpose is to promote all forms of Christian writing. Site: Usually located at a major hotel chain like Holiday Inn.

Costs $119 for 1 day; $209 for 2 days. Plus meals and accommodations.

Accommodations Special rates available at host hotel.

Additional Information Conference information available for SASE, e-mail, phone or fax. Accepts inquiries by fax, e-mail, phone, SASE.

AMERICAN INDEPENDENT WRITERS (AIW) AMERICAN WRITERS CONFERENCE

1001 Connecticut Ave. NW, Ste. 701, Washington DC 20036. (202) 775-5150. Fax: (202) 775-5810. E-mail: info@aiwriters.org. Website: www.aiwriters.org. **Contact:** Donald Graul Jr., executive director. Estab. 1975. Annual conference held in June. Conference duration: Saturday. Average attendance: 350. "Gives participants a chance to hear from and talk with dozens of experts on book and magazine publishing as well as meet one-on-one with literary agents." Site: George Washington University Conference Center. Past keynote speakers included Erica Jong, Diana Rehm, Kitty Kelley, Lawrence Block, John Barth, Stephen Hunter, Francine Prose.

ANNUAL NEW YORK ROUND TABLE WRITERS' CONFERENCE

20 West 44th Street, New York NY 10036. (212) 764-7021. E-mail: smallpress@aol.com. Website: www. writersconferencenyc.com. **Contact:** Karin Taylor, director. Estab. 2004. Annual. Next conference held in April, 2009. Conference duration: 2 days. Average attendance: 200. "The purpose is to educate writers about the business of getting published." Site: The conference takes place at the New York Center for Independent Publishing, based in Midtown Manhattan. Panels in 2008 included Birth of a Book, Memoir Writing, Writing Process and Fiction Writing. Speakers for 2008 included Brigid Hughes (A Public Space), Marjorie Braman (HarperCollins) and authors Sharon Mesmer, Alice Hoffman, John Berendt, and Lincoln Child.

Costs In 2008, $250 (1 day) to $350 (2 days).

Accommodations Does not offer overnight accommodations. Provides list of area hotels or lodging options.

Additional Information Information available in January. For brochure, fax request, call, e-mail or visit Web site. Agents and editors participate in conference. "We try to provide writers with useful tools to help increase their chances of finding a literary agent or publisher."

ANTIOCH WRITERS' WORKSHOP

P.O. Box 494, Yellow Springs OH 45387. (937)475-7357. E-mail: info@antiochwritersworkshop.com. Website: www.antiochwritersworkshop.com. Estab. 1986. Annual conference held July 11-17, 2009. Conference duration: 1 week. Average attendance: 80. Workshop concentration: poetry, nonfiction, fiction, personal essay, memoir, mystery. Site: Workshop located in the idyllic Glen Helen Nature Preserve and in locations around the charming village of Yellow Springs. Past faculty have included Sue Grafton, Natalie Goldberg, Sena Jeter Naslund, Ann Hagedorn, Katrina Kittle, Silas House, and Ralph Keyes.

Costs Tuition is $735 (regular) or $675 (alumni and local participants), which includes a nonrefundable $125 registration fee.

Accommodations Accommodations are available in local homes through the village host program ($150 for the week) or at area hotels and B&Bs.

Additional Information Intensive sessions for beginning and experienced writers, small group lunches with faculty, agent pitch sessions, optional ms critiques.

ARKANSAS WRITERS' CONFERENCE

AR Penwomen Pioneer Branch of the National League of American Penwomen, 13005 Misty Creek, Little Rock AR 72211. (501)224-5823. E-mail: pvining@aristotle.net. Website: http://groups.yahoo.com/group/

arpenwomen. **Contact:** Send SASE to: Peggy Vining, at the address listed above. Estab. 1944. Annual. Conference held first weekend in June. Average attendance: 175. "We have a variety of subjects related to writing. We have some general sessions, some more specific, but we try to vary each year's subjects." **Costs** Registration: $15; luncheon: $19; banquet: $20; contest entry $10 (2006 rates). **Accommodations** "We meet at a Holiday Inn Presidential in Little Rock. Rooms available at reduced rate." Holiday Inn has a bus to bring our attendees from the airport. Rooms average $79. **Additional Information** "We have 36 contest categories. Some are open only to Arkansans, most are open to all writers. Our judges are not announced before the conference. All are qualified, many from out of state." Conference information available February 15. For brochures or inquiries send SASE with full mailing address, call or fax. "We have had 226 people attending from 12 states—over 2,000 contest entries from 40 states and New Zealand, Mexico and Canada."

Ⓝ ARTIST-IN-RESIDENCE NATIONAL PARKS

E-mail: Acadia_Information@nps.gov. Website: http://www.nps.gov/acad/supportyourpark/artistinresidence.htm. **Contact:** Artist-In-Residence Coordinator. 29 National Parks offer residency programs open to two-dimensional visual artists, photographers, sculptors, performers, writers, composers, video/filmmakers, and others.
Additional Information See Web site for individual park and contact information.

ART WORKSHOPS IN GUATEMALA

4758 Lyndale Ave. S, Minneapolis MN 55419-5304. (612) 825-0747. E-mail: info@artguat.org. Website: www.artguat.org. **Contact:** Liza Fourre, director. Estab. 1995. Annual. Workshops held year-round. Maximim class size: 10 students per class. Workshop titles include: Fiction Writing: New Directions in Travel Writing with Richard Harris; Poetry: Snapshots in Words with Rosanne Lloyd; and Creative Writing: Journey of the Soul with Sharon Doubiago.
Costs $1,745 (includes tuition, lodging in a lovely colonial style B&B, and ground transportation, and some pretty interesting field trips).
Accommodations All transportation and accommodations included in price of conference.
Additional Information Conference information available now. For brochure/guidelines visit Web site, e-mail, fax or call. Accepts inquiries by e-mail, phone.

ASPEN SUMMER WORDS WRITING RETREAT & LITERARY FESTIVAL

110 E. Hallam St., #116, Aspen CO 81611. (970)925-3122. Fax: (970)925-5700. E-mail: info@aspenwriters.org. Website: www.aspenwriters.org. **Contact:** Natalie Lacy, programs manager. Estab. 1976. Annual. 2009 conference held June 21-26. Conference duration: 5 days. Average attendance: writing retreat, 150; literary festival, 300 + , 1,800 visitors. Retreat includes intensive workshops in fiction (beginning through advanced), creative nonfiction, poetry, wirting for young readers, young wirters' workshop, magazine writing and food writing, plus a "Readers' Retreat" which in 2008 focused on Indian Literature. Literary festival features approximately 18 events (craft talks, author readings, and interviews; publishing panel discussions; agent/editor meeting; and social gatherings) for readers and writers. Festival theme for 2008 was "Passage to India". Retreat faculty for 2009: Ron Carlson (Advanced Fiction); Hallie Ephron (Mystery); Gary Ferguson (Magazine Writing and Nature Writing); William Loizeaux (Narrative Nonfiction); Christopher Merrill (Poetry); Pamela Painter (Fiction); and Nic Pizzolatto (Beginning Fiction). Festival presenters for 2009 were Salman Rushdie, Anita Rau Badami, Chitra Banerjee Divakaruni, David Davidar, Indu Sundaresan, Manil Suri, and Shashi Tharoor.
Costs As of 2008, $475/retreat; $250/2 day symposia; $175/2-day reader's retreat. Tuition includes daily continental breakfast and lunch, plus one evening reception. $200 festival pass; retreat students receive a $50 discount when they sign up for the literary festival. Festival registration includes two wine and hors d'oeuvres receptions. $35/private meetings with agents and editors.
Accommodations Discount lodging at the conference site will be available. 2010 rates to be announced. Free shuttle around town.
Additional Information Application deadline: April 6. Mss must be submitted by May 25th for review by faculty, for most workshops. 10 page limit for workshop application mss. A limited number of partial-tuition scholarships are available. Deadline for agent/editor meeting registration is May 25th. Brochures available for SASE, by e-mail and phone request, and on Web site.

Conferences

⊠ ATLANTIC CENTER FOR THE ARTS

1414 Art Center Ave, New Smyrna Beach FL 32618. (386)427-6975. Website: atlanticcenterforthearts. org. **Contact:** program department. Three week long residency offered several times a year. "Associates selected will get one-on-one experience with a Master Artist. The Master Artist selects Associate Residents from the applications."

Costs $850; $25 non-refundable application fee. Financial aid is available.

Accommodations "Van transportation is provided from ACA two days per week at regularly scheduled times to the shopping center and art supply stores. Many artists do bring their own vehicles and carpooling may be an option. ACA does provide van transportation to outreaches, when possible. Master Artists are supplied with a car. Bikes are available at ACA." Offers overnight accommodations.

AWP ANNUAL CONFERENCE AND BOOKFAIR

MS 1E3, George Mason University, Fairfax VA 22030. (703)993-4301 Fax: (703)993-4302. E-mail: conference@awpwriter.org. Website: www.awpwriter.org. **Contact:** Matt Scanlon, director of conferences. Estab. 1967. Annual. Conference held February 11-14, 2009, in Chicago. Conference duration: 4 days. Average attendance: 4,000. The annual conference is a gathering of 4,000+ students, teachers, writers, readers and publishers. All genres are represented. Site: This year the conference will be held at Hilton New York. "We will offer 175 panels on everything from writing to teaching to critical analysis." In 2007, Lee Smith, John Barth, Kaye Gibbons, C.D. Wright, Ann Beattie, and Robert Olen Butler were special speakers.

Costs Early registration fees: $40 student; $140 AWP member; $160 non-member.

Accommodations Provide airline discounts and rental-car discounts. Special rate at Hilton.

Additional Information Check Web site for more information.

⊠ BACKSPACE WRITERS CONFERENCE

PO Box 454 Washington, MI 48094. (732)267-6449. E-mail: karendionne@bksp.org. Website: www. backspacewritersconference.com. **Contact**: Christopher Graham or Karen Dionne, co-founders and owners. Annual. Estab. 2004. 2009 dates: May 28th, 29th, and 30th. Conference duration: 3 days. Average attendance: 150-200. Conference. "We focus on all genres, from nonfiction to literary fiction and everything in between, covering all popular genres from mysteries, and thrillers to young adult and romance. Formal pitch sessions are a staple at most writers'conferences. However, in planning our Backspace events, we discovered that agents hate conducting pitch sessions almost as much as authors dread doing them. In fact, many of the agents we've talked to are happy to sit on a panel or conduct a workshop, but decline to participate in formal pitch sessions. The goal of the Backspace Agent-Author Seminars is to help authors connect with agents - lots of agents - thereby giving authors the opportunity to ask questions specific to their interests and concerns. That's why we've built so much free time into the program. The full fifteen minutes between panels allows plenty of opportunity for seminar registrants to talk to agents. Many of the agents will also be available during the noon hour. Remember, agents attend conferences because they want to help authors. They're looking for new talent, and welcome the chance to hear about your work. Instead of a tense, angst-filled pitch session where it's difficult for all but the most confident authors to put their best foot forward, an interesting, relaxed, enjoyable conversation leaves a much more positive impression. And even if authors don't get the chance to mention their project, the pleasant conversation gives the author a point of reference when sending a formal query letter to the agent's office after the seminar is over." Site: The Radisson Martinique in Manhattan NY located in Mid-town Manhattan just a few blocks from Madison Square Garden/NY Penn Station. 2008 agents in attendance: Jeff Kleinman, Matthew Mahoney, Eric Meyers, Scott Hoffman, Simon Lipskar, and Richard Curtis. 2008 speakers: John Searles, deputy editor, Cosmopolitan; Mark Tavani, senior editor, Random House. Also featured editors and over 35 authors.

Costs $400; offers member, group, and student discounts along with additional workshops that are priced separately.

Accommodations "We offer a special conference rate at the Radisson Martinique for conference attendees. Average price of $279/night, must be booked 30 days in advance."

Additional Information See Web site for more information. Brochures available in January. Accepts inquiries by e-mail. Agents and editors attend conference. "

Ⓝ Ⓖ BALTIMORE COMIC-CON

Baltimore Convention Center, One West Pratt St., Baltimore MD 21201. (410)526-7410. E-mail: cardscomicscollectibles@yahoo.com. Website: http://www.comicon.com/baltimore/index.htm. **Contact:** Marc Nathan. Estab. 1999. Annual. October 10-11, 2009. Conference, "promoting the wonderful world of comics to as many people as possible." Comic-Con 2009: Special Guest George Perez.

Costs Two day pass: $25; Saturday or Sunday only: $15.

Accommodations Does not offer overnight accommodations. Provides list of area hotels or lodging options.

Additional Information For brochure, visit Web site.

BAY TO OCEAN WRITERS' CONFERENCE

Presented by the Eastern Shore Writers Association, Chesapeake College, Wye Mills, MD 21679. (410) 820-8822. E-mail: info@baytoocean.com. Website: www.baytoocean.com. **Contact:** Carolyn Jaffe. Estab. 1998. Annual. Conference held last Saturday in February. Conference duration: 1 day. Average attendance: 130. Approximately 20 speakers conduct workshops on publishing, agenting, editing, marketing, craft, writing for television and movies, poetry, fiction, nonfiction and freelance writing. Site: Chesapeake College, Rt. 213 and Rt. 50, Wye Mills, on Maryland's historic Eastern Shore. Accessible to individuals with disabilities.

Costs $80-100, students $60. Includes choice of 5-15 sessions, continental breakfast and networking lunch.

Additional Information Mail-in registration form available on Web site in October prior to the conference. Pre-registration is required, no registration at door. Conference usually sells out one month in advance. Conference is for all levels of writers.

Ⓝ Ⓖ BIG APPLE CON

704 76th St., North Bergen NJ 07049. (347)581-6166. E-mail: mikecarbo@gmail.com. Website: http://bigapplecon.com. **Contact:** Michael Carbonaro, director; Brian Schutzer, director. Annual conference held in November. Conference duration: 3 days. "The Big Apple Con is the oldest and longest-running comic, art and toy, Sci-Fi show in New York City." Site: Located directly across from Madison Square Garden and Penn Station.

☐ BIG APPLE WRITING WORKSHOPS, MEET THE AUTHORS/MEET THE AGENTS

IWWG, P.O. Box 810, Gracie Station NY 10028. (212) 737-7536. Fax: (212) 737-9469. E-mail: dirhahn@aol.com. Website: www.iwwg.org. **Contact:** Hannalore Hahn, founder & executive director. Estab. 1980. Semi-annual. October 2009, April 2010, October 2010. Conference duration: 2 days. Average attendance: 150. Workshop. "The three-fold purpose entails: 1) A full day writing workshop; 2) A panel discussion with 12 recently published IWWG members about how they became authors, found agents and publishers; 3) An open house with 8 agents for authors to meet." Site: Scandinavia House is the official building for Sweden, Norway, Finland, Iceland and Denmark. It is a modern building on Park Avenue in midtown Manhattan. It offers two comfortable lecture halls and a cafeteria (with Scandinavian food). Previous panels include "Fiction and Nonfiction: Writing and Selling on Both Sides of the Aisle" and "The Writer at Work: Writing Adrift/Writing a Draft."

Costs $130 for members of IWWG/$160 for non-members for both days. Individual sections may be selected and paid for if not attending full conference.

Accommodations Does not offer overnight accommodations. Provides list of area hotels or lodging options.

Additional Information For brochure, send SASE, fax request, call, e-mail, visit Web site. Agents and editors participate in conference. "We've had over 50 Meet the Author/Meet the Agent events. Close to 4,000 books have been published by IWWG members since our inception in 1976."

BIG BEAR WRITER'S RETREAT

P.O. Box 1441, Big Bear Lake CA 92315-1441. (909)585-0059. Fax: (909)266-0710. E-mail: mike@writers-review.com. **Contact:** Mike Foley, director. Estab. 1995. Biannual. Conferences held in May or October. Conference duration: 3 days. Average attendance: 15-25. Past themes included Finding New Creativity, Character and Setting, Avoiding Common Errors, Character Depth, Embracing Yourself as a Writer. Site: "A small, intimate lodge in Big Bear, San Bernardino mountains of Southern California." Retreat is hosted annually by Mike Foley, editor of Dream Merchant Magazine, and Tom Foley, Ph.D., artistic psychologist.

Costs $499, includes meals and lodging.

Accommodations Offers overnight accommodations. On-site facilites included in retreat fee.

Additional Information Prior to arrival, submit a fiction or nonfiction sample, 10 double-spaced pages maximum. 2010 conference information is available March 2006. For brochure send SASE, e-mail, call or fax. Accepts inquiries by SASE, e-mail, phone and fax. Editors participate in conference. "This is unlike the standard writer's conference. Participants will live as writers for a weekend. Retreat includes workshop sessions, open writing time and private counseling with retreat hosts. A weekend of focused writing, fun and friendship. This is a small group retreat, known for its individual attention to writers, intimate setting and strong bonding among participants."

BLOCKBUSTER PLOT INTENSIVE WRITING WORKSHOPS

15732 Los Gatos Blvd., #505, Los Gatos CA 95032. Fax: (408) 356-1798. E-mail: contact@blockbusterplots. com. Website: www.blockbusterplots.com. **Contact:** Martha Alderson M.A., instructor. Estab. 2000. Held four times per year. Conference duration: 2 days. Average attendance: 20. Workshop is intended to help writers create an action, character and thematic plotline for a screenplay, memoir, short story, novel or creative nonfiction. Site: Conference hall.

Costs $135 per day.

Accommodations Provides list of area hotels and lodging options.

Additional Information Brochures available by fax, e-mail or on Web site. Accepts inquiries by SASE, e-mail and fax.

◪ BLOODY WORDS MYSTERY CONFERENCE

Phone/fax: (416) 497-5293. E-mail: soles@sff.net. Website: www.bloodywords.com. **Contact:** Caro Soles, chair. Estab. 1999. Annual. Last conference held June June 5-7, 2009. Average attendance: 300. Focus: Mystery/true crime/forensics, with Canadian slant. Purpose: To bring readers and writers of the mystery genre together in a Canadian setting. Site: Ottawa: Ottawa Marriott Hotel. Conference includes two workshops and two tracks of panels, one on factual information such as forensics, agents, scene of the crime procedures, etc. and one on fiction, such as "Death in a Cold Climate," "Murder on the Menu," "Elementary, My Dear Watson," and a First Novelists Panel. Canadian Guest of Honer in 2009: Louise Penny; International Guest of Honor: Denise Mina.

Costs $175 (Canadian include the banquet and all panels, readings, dealers' room and workshop.

Accommodations Offers block of rooms in hotel; list of optional lodging available. Check Web site for details.

Additional Information Sponsors short mystery story contest—5,000 word limit; judges are experienced editors of anthologies; fee is $5 (entrants must be registered). Conference information is available now. For brochure visit Web site. Accepts inquiries by e-mail and phone. Agents and editors participate in conference. "This is a conference for both readers and writers of mysteries, the only one of its kind in Canada. We also run 'The Mystery Cafe,' a chance to get to know a dozen or so authors, hear them read and ask questions (half hour each)."

▨ BLUE RIDGE "AUTUMN IN THE MOUNTAINS" NOVEL RETREAT

(800) 588-7222. E-mail: ylehman@bellsouth.net. Website: www.lifeway.com/autumninthemountains. **Contact:** Yvonne Lehman, director. Estab. 2007. Held annually in October. Retreat held October 5-9, 2008. Limited attendance: 50 (register early). Requirements: previous attendence at a writers conference "somewhere" and have a novel in progress. Mornings: classes by established authors to take your novel to a higher level. Afternoons: Writing time. Late afternoon: Discussion/Brainstorming groups. Evening: Critique Groups in your particular novel category.

Costs : $315 tuition, deluxe accommodations in Mountain Laurel on-campus hotel. See Web site for on-campus room rates.

BLUE RIDGE MOUNTAINS CHRISTIAN WRITERS CONFERENCE

(800) 588-7222. E-mail: ylehman@bellsouth.net. Website: www.lifeway.com/christianwriters. **Contact:** Yvonne Lehman, director. Estab. 1999. Annual. Last conference held May 20-24, 2007. Average attendance: 380. All areas of Christian writing including fiction, nonfiction, devotionals, women's fiction, romance, suspense, romance, craft of writing, etc. For beginning and advanced writers. Site: LifeWay/Ridgecrest Conference Center, 20 miles east of Asheville, NC. Companies represented May 18-22, 2008 include AMG Publications, B&H, Focus on the Family, Howard Books, The Upper Room, LifeWay Christian

Resources, Christian Writers Guild, Living Ink Books, Hensley Publishing, Today's Christian Woman, Benrey Literary Agency, Les Stobbe Agency, Bethan House, Big Idea (Veggie Tales), MacGregor Literary Agency, The Nashville Group, WinePress, William K. Jensen Literary Agency, et al. Faculty includes professional authors, agents and editors.

Costs 2008: $315, which includes all sessions, breaks, and a special Wednesday evening Awards Ceremony. Additional on-campus meal package available for $98/person.

Accommodations LifeWay Ridgecrest Conference Center. See Web site for on-campus room rates.

Additional Information The Blue Ridge "Autumn in the Mountains" Novel retreat will be held annually in October at Ridgecrest/Life Way Conference Center (www.lifeway.com/novelretreat). Sponsors contests for unpublished writers. Awards include trophy and $200 scholarship toward next year's conference. See Web site for critique service and daily schedule-offering keynote sessions, continuing classes and workshops.

JAMES BONNET'S STORYMAKING: THE MASTER CLASS

6, Rue de Chateau, 25330 Nans Sous Ste. Anne, France. +33 3 81 86 56 83. USA: (818)567-0521. E-mail: bonnet@storymaking.com. Website: www.storymaking.com. **Contact:** James Bonnet. Estab. 1990. Seminars held February and October. Conference duration: 2 days. Average attendance: 25. Conferences focus on fiction, mystery and screenwriting. Site: Los Angeles, California. Workshops/Retreats held May and September. Workshop duration: 7 days. Average attendance: "limited to 4." Site: Nans Sous Ste. Anne, France. "Seminars focus on mastery of the novel and screenwriting arts through an understanding of story and guiding writers from inspiration to the final draft. Topics include The High Concept Great Idea, The Creative Unconscious, Metaphor, The Character Archetypes, The Fundamentals of Plot, Structure, Genre, Conflict, Suspense, and more. Workshops/Retreats include weekend seminar plus 5 days working one-on-one with James Bonnet. James Bonnet will be the speaker.

Costs $350 for weekend seminar. $1,500 for 7 day workshop/retreat.

Accommodations Provides a list of area hotels or lodging options.

Additional Information For brochure send SASE, e-mail, visit Web site, or call. Accepts inquiries by SASE, e-mail, phone and fax. "James Bonnet is the author of *Stealing Fire From the Gods* and *The Complete Guide to Story for Writers and Filmmakers*."

BOOKEXPO AMERICA/WRITER'S DIGEST BOOKS WRITERS CONFERENCE

4700 East Galbraith Rd., Cincinnati OH 45236. (513) 531-2690. Fax: (513) 891-7185. E-mail: publicity@ fwpubs.com. Website: www.writersdigest.com/bea or www.bookexpoamerica.com/writersconference. **Contact:** Greg Hatfield, publicity manager. Estab. 2003. Annual. Conference duration: one day, 2009's date was May 27. Average attendance: 600. "The purpose of the conference is to prepare writers hoping to get their work published. We offer instruction on the craft of writing, as well as advice for submitting their work to publications, publishing houses and agents. We provide breakout sessions on these topics, including expert advice from industry professionals, and offer workshops on fiction and nonfiction, in the various genres (literary, children's, mystery, romance, etc.). We also provide attendees the opportunity to actually pitch their work to agents." Site: The conference facility varies from year to year, as we are partnered with the BookExpo America trade show. The 2009 conference took place in New York City. Themes and panels have included Writing Genre Fiction, Children's Writing, Brutal Truths About the Book Publishing Industry, Crafting a Strong Nonfiction Book Proposal, Crafting Your Novel Pitch, and Secrets to Irresistible Magazine Queries. Past speakers included Jacquelyn Mitchard, Jodi Picoult, Jerry B. Jenkins, Jonathan Karp, Steve Almond, John Warner, Heather Sellers, Donald Maass and Michael Cader.

Costs The price in 2009 was $199.

Additional Information Information available in February. For brochure, visit Web site. Agents and editors participate in conference.

BOOMING GROUND

Buch E-462, 1866 Main Mall, Creative Writing Program, UBC, Vancouver BC V6T 121 Canada. (604) 822-2469. Fax: (604) 822-3616. E-mail: apply@boomingground.com. Website: www.boomingground.com. **Contact:** Brianna Brash-Nyberg. Estab. 1998. Average attendance: 30 per session. Writing mentorships geared toward beginner, intermediate, and advanced levels in novel, short fiction, poetry, nonfiction, and children's writing. Open to students. Online mentorship program-students work for 4-8 months with a mentor by e-mail, allowing up to 120-240 pages of material to be created. Site: Online and by e-mail.

Costs $780 (Canadian) for online mentorships; individual manuscript evaluation also available.
Additional Information Workshops are based on works-in-progress. Writers must submit ms with application. For guidelines visit Web site, or e-mail brianna@boomingground.com. Accepts inquiries by e-mail and via Web site. "Classes are offered for writers at all levels—from early career to mid-career. Our mentorships are ideal for long-form work such as novels, collections of poetry, and short fiction."

BOUCHERCON
Website: www.bouchercon.com. Conference held October 15-18, 2009, in Indianapolis. The Bouchercon is "the world mystery and detective fiction event." Site: Hyatt Regency Indianapolis. See Web site for details. Special guests include Michael Connelly.
Costs $150 (prior to July 1, 2007), $250 (after July 1) registration fee covers writing workshops, panels, reception, etc.
Additional Information Sponsors Anthony Award for published mystery novel; ballots due prior to conference. Information available on Web site.

BREAD LOAF WRITERS' CONFERENCE
Middlebury VT 05753. (802)443-5286. Fax: (802)443-2087. E-mail: ncargill@middlebury.edu. Website: www.middlebury.edu/~blwc. **Contact:** Noreen Cargill, administrative manager. Estab. 1926. Annual. Last conference held August 13-24, 2008. Conference duration: 11 days. Average attendance: 230. For fiction, nonfiction, poetry. Site: Held at the summer campus in Ripton, Vermont (belongs to Middlebury College). 2007 faculty and staff included William Kittredge, Percival Everett, Sigrid Nunez, Joanna Scott, Susan Orlean.
Costs In 2007, $2,260 (included room and board). Fellowships available.
Accommodations Accommodations are at Ripton. Onsite accommodations included in fee.
Additional Information 2008 conference information available December 2007 on Web site. Accepts inquiries by fax, e-mail and phone.

▨ BROOKLYN BOOK FESTIVAL
209 Joralemon St., Brooklyn NY 11201. (718)802-3852. E-mail: ekoch@brooklynbp.nyc.gov. Website: www.brooklynbookfestival.org. **Contact:** Liz Koch. Estab. 2005. Annual 1 day festival. "The Brooklyn Book Festival is a huge, free public event presenting an array of local, national, and international literary stars and emerging authors who represent the exciting world of literature today."
Additional Information For brochure visit Web site.

▨ CAPE COD WRITERS' CONFERENCE
P.O. Box 408, Osterville MA 02655. (508)420-0200. E-mail: writers@capecodwriterscenter.org. Website: www.capecodwriterscenter.org. **Contact:** Anne Elizabeth Tom, executive director. Annual Conference. Duration: Two-part (back to back), each part three-days, 7.5 hours; two different Master Classes; six one-day workshops; offers workshops in poetry, fiction, and creative nonfiction, and getting published, as well as manuscript evaluation/mentoring sessions with faculty." Site: Held at the Craigville Conference center in a Cape Cod village overlooking Nantucket Sound.
Costs $30 per course hour; manuscript evaluation/mentoring sessions (1.5 hours) $225; $50 registration fee for non-members.

CENTRAL OHIO FICTION WRITERS ANNUAL CONFERENCE
Central Ohio Fiction Writers (COFW), P.O. Box 912, Worthington OH 43085. E-mail: cae@carolannerhardt.com. Website: www.cofw.org. **Contact:** Carol Ann Erhardt, president. Estab. 1990. Annual. Conference held in Columbus, OH. 2009 Conference dates September 18-19. Average attendance: 120. COFW is a chapter of Romance Writers of America. The conference focuses on all romance subgenres and welcomes published writers, pre-published writers and readers. Conference theme: celebrates and fosters writers at every stage of their careers. Best-selling authors provide motivation and instruction; workshops, speakers, and materials cover a broad spectrum of topics. Two agents and two editors will speak and take short appointments. Appointments to early registrants who have completed at least one manuscript.
Costs Price will include Saturday lunch.
Accommodations See www.cofw.org for exact location. There will be a special conference rate for hotel rooms.
Additional Information Registration form and information available on Web site or by e-mail.

CENTRUM'S PORT TOWNSEND WRITERS' CONFERENCE

P.O. Box 1158, Port Townsend WA 98368-0958. (360)385-3102. Fax: (360)385-2470. E-mail: info@ centrum.org. Website: www.centrum.org. **Contact:** Jordan Hartt, program manager. Estab. 1974. Annual. Conference held mid-July. Average attendance: 180. Conference to promote poetry, fiction, creative nonfiction "featuring many of the nation's leading writers." Two different workshop options: "New Works" and "Works-in-Progress." Site: The conference is held at Fort Worden State Park on the Strait of Juan de Fuca. "The site is a Victorian-era military fort with miles of beaches, wooded trails and recreation facilities. The park is within the limits of Port Townsend, a historic seaport and arts community, approximately 80 miles northwest of Seattle, on the Olympic Peninsula." Guest speakers participate in addition to full-time faculty.

Costs Tuition $495, Room and board ranges from $200-$390, depending on the option you choose.

Accommodations "Modest room and board facilities on site." Also list of hotels/motels/inns/bed & breakfasts/private rentals available.

Additional Information Brochures/guidelines available for SASE or on Web site. "The conference focus is on the craft of writing and the writing life, not on marketing."

CHILDREN'S LITERATURE CONFERENCE

239 Montauk Hwy, Southampton NY 11968-6700.(631)632-5030. Fax: (631)632-2578. Website: www. stonybrook.edu/writers. **Contact:** Adrienne Unger, administrative coordinator. Annual conference held in early July. "The seaside campus of Stony Brook Southampton is located in the heart of the Hamptons, a renowned resort area only 70 miles from New York City. During free time, participants can draw on inspiration from the Atlantic beaches or explore the charming seaside towns." Faculty have included Richard Peck, Tor Seidler, Cindy Kane, Gahan Wilson James McMullan, and Mitchell Kriegman.

Costs Application fee: $15; tuition, room and board: $1270; tuition only $1125 (includes breakfast and lunch).

Accommodations On-campus housing, doubles and small singles with shared baths, is modest but comfortable. Housing assignment is by lottery. Supplies list of lodging alternatives.

Additional Information "Applicants must complete an application and submit a writing sample of original, unpublished work. See Web for details. Brochure available in January by phone, e-mail, and on Web site. Accepts inquiries by e-mail, phone, and fax."

CLARION SCIENCE FICTION AND FANTASY WRITERS' WORKSHOP

UC San Diego, 9500 Gilman Drive # 0410, La Jolla CA 92093-0410. (858) 534-2115. E-mail: clarion@ ucsd.edu. Website: http://clarion.ucsd.edu. **Contact:** Tania Mayer, Program Coordinator. Estab. 1968. Annual. Conference duration: Six-week residency in summer (late June-early Aug.). Average attendance: 18. Workshop. "Clarion is a short-story writing workshop focused on fundamentals particular to the writing of science fiction, fantasy and horror." Site: The workshop is held at the UC San Diego campus in the beautiful beach town of La Jolla. Participants reside in campus apartments and attend workshop sessions in a seminar room. Beaches and shopping are within easy reach by public transportation. Summer temperatures in San Diego are normally 70-80°F, dry and comfortable. The instructors for the summer 2009 workshop were Holly Black, Larissa Lai, Robert Crais, Kim Stanley Robinson, Elizabeth Hand, and Paul Park.

Costs The fees for 2009 (application, tuition, room and board) were approximately $4,500. Scholarships were available.

Accommodations Participants make their own travel arrangements to and from the campus. Campus residency is required. Participants are housed in semi-private accommodations (private bedroom, shared bathroom) in student apartments. The room and board fee includes three meals a day at a campus dining facility. In 2009 the room and board fee for the six-week residency were approximately $2,500 (included in the $4,500 workshop fee).

Additional Information "Workshop participants are selected on the basis of their potential for highly successful writing careers. Applications are judged by a review panel composed of the workshop instructors. Applicants submit an application and two complete short stories, each between 2,500 words and 6,000 words in length. The application deadline (typically, March 1) is posted on the Clarion Web site." Information available in September. For brochure, visit Web site. Agents and editors frequently participate in Clarion as instructors or guest speakers.

CLARION WEST WRITERS' WORKSHOP

340 15th Avenue E, Suite 350, Seattle WA 98112-5156. (206) 322-9083. E-mail: info@clarionwest.org. Website: www.clarionwest.org. **Contact:** Leslie Howle, executive director. Estab. 1983. Annual. Workshop usually held in late June through July. Average attendance: 18. "Conference to prepare students for professional careers in science fiction and fantasy writing." Deadline for applications: March 1. Site: Conference held in Seattle's University district, an urban site close to restaurants and cafes, but not too far from downtown. Faculty: 6 teachers (professional writers and editors established in the field). "Every week a new instructor—each a well-known writer chosen for the quality of his or her work and for professional stature—teaches the class, bringing a unique perspective on speculative fiction. During the fifth week, the workshop is taught by a professional editor."
Costs Workshop tuition, dormitory housing and most meals: $3,200. ($100 discount if application received by February 1).
Accommodations Students stay on site in workshop housing at one of the University of Washington's sorority houses.
Additional Information "Students write their own stories every week while preparing critiques of all the other students' work for classroom sessions. This gives participants a more focused, professional approach to their writing. The core of the workshop remains science fiction, and short stories (not novels) are the focus." Conference information available in Fall 2008. For brochure/guidelines send SASE, visit Web site, e-mail or call. Accepts inquiries by e-mail, phone, SASE. Limited scholarships are available, based on financial need. Students must submit 20-30 pages of ms with 4-page biography and $30 fee for applications sent by mail or e-mail to qualify for admission.

THE COMPLETE WRITER INTENSIVE WRITERS' CAMP

Jones Brehony Seminars in partnership with Island Path Seminars, P.O. Box 878, Ocracoke Island NC 27960. (877)708-7284. E-mail: islandpath@ocracokenc.net. Website: www.jonesbrehony.com. **Contact:** Ruth Fordon or Ken DeBarth. Estab. July 2001. Last conference held April 30-May 3, 2009. Conference duration: 3 days. Average attendance: under 15. Conference focuses on fiction, nonfiction, publishing. Site: Ocracoke Island, NC. Panels include Understanding the Publishing Industry and How to Make it Work for You, Letting the Muse Flow: Exploring and Manifesting Your Creativity as a Writer, Building the Container: Strategies and Discipline to Capture Your Creative Flow, Techniques of Fiction.
Costs Workshop and all breakfasts, all lunches, 1 dinner—$600.
Accommodations Lightkeepers Guest House reserved on a first come basis—go to www.lightkeepers guesthouse.com to see rooms/rates.
Additional Information Brochure available by e-mail for SASE. Accepts inquiries by SASE, e-mail and phone. Agents and editors attend conference.

DESERT DREAMS CONFERENCE: REALIZING THE DREAM

P.O. Box 27407, Tempe AZ 85285. (623)910-0524. E-mail: info@desertroserwa.org. Website: www. desertroserwa.org. **Contact:** Conference coordinator. Estab. 1986. Biennial. Last conference held April 4-6, 2008. Next conference Spring 2008. Average attendance: 250. Conference focuses on romance fiction. Site: Phoenix, AZ. Past panels included: Plotting, Dialogue, Manuscript Preparation, Web site Design, Synopsis, Help for the Sagging Middle. Keynote speakers in 2006 included Debbie Macomber, Lisa Gardner, Jennifer Cruise and Debra Dixon. Guest editors/agents from St. Martin's Press, Harlequin, Irene Goodman Literary Agency, Borders Group, Ellora's Cave, Spectrum Literary Agency and more.
Costs Vary each year; approximately $175-228 for full conference.
Accommodations Hotels may vary for each conference; it is always a resort location in the Phoenix area.
Additional Information Sponsors contest as part of conference, open to conference attendees only. For brochure, inquiries, contact by e-mail, phone, fax, mail or visit Web site. Agents and editors participate in conference.

DINGLE WRITING COURSES

Ballintlea, Ventry, Co Kerry Ireland. 353 66 9159815. E-mail: info@dinglewritingcourses.ie. Website: www. dinglewritingcourses.ie. **Contact:** Abigail Joffe and Nicholas McLachlan. Estab. 1996. Annual. Writing workshops held 3 or 4 weekends per year in September and October. Average attendance: 14. Creative writing weekends for fiction, poetry, memoir, novel, writing for children, etc. Site: " Writer's Retreat on the Dingle Peninsula." Recent tutors included Niall Williams, Paula Meehan and Kate Thompson.

Costs 400€ for a weekend (Friday evening to Sunday evening) includes all meals, accommodation, tuition.

Accommodations "We arrange taxis on request; cost not included in fee." Organizes overnight accommodations. "Large communal eating facility and workroom; spectacular views." Also provides list of area lodging.

Additional Information Some workshops require material submitted in advance. Brochures available in May by e-mail, phone, fax or on Web site. Accepts inquiries by e-mail, phone, fax.

⊠ ⊟ DRAGON CON

P.O. Box 16459, Atlanta GA 30321. Fax: (770)909-0112. E mail: dragoncon@dragoncon.org. Website: www.dragoncon.org. Annual. Labor Day Weekend, September 4-7, 2009.Conference duration: 4 days. "Dragon*Con is the largest multi-media, popular culture convention focusing on science fiction and fantasy, gaming, comics, literature, art, music, and film in the US."

EAST TEXAS CHRISTIAN WRITER'S CONFERENCE

East Texas Baptist University, School of Humanities, 1209 N. Grove, Marshall TX 75670. (903) 923-2083. E-mail: jhopkins@etbu.edu or jcornish@etbu.edu. Website: www.etbu.edu/News/cwc. **Contact:** Joy Cornish. Estab. 2002. Annual. Conference held the second weekend in April, Friday and Saturday, April 9-10, 2010. Conference duration: 2 days (Friday & Saturday). Average attendance: 190. "Primarily we are interested in promoting quality Christian writing that would be accepted in mainstream publishing." Site: We use the classrooms, cafeterias, etc. of East Texas Baptist University. Past conference themes were Back to Basics, Getting Started in Fiction, Writers & Agents, Writing Short Stories, Writing for Newspapers, The Significance of Style, Writing Fillers and Articles, Writing Devotionals, Blogging for Writers, Christian Non-Fiction, Inspirational Writing, E-Publishing, Publishing on Demand, and Editor and Author Relations. Past conference speakers/workshop leaders were David Jenkins, Bill Keith, Pete Litterski, Joe Early, Jr., Mary Lou Redding, Marie Chapian, Denny Boultinghouse, Vickie Phelps, Michael Farris, Susan Farris, Pamela Dowd, Donn Taylor, Terry Burns, Donna Walker-Nixon, Lexie Smith, Marv Knox, D.D. Turner, Jim Pence, Andrea Chevalier, Marie Bagnull, and Leonard Goss.

Costs $75 for individuals before March 19, 2010; after will be $80; $60 students before March 19, after $70. Price includes meal prior to early registration deadline. Conference workshops $30 before March 19; after $40.

Additional Information "We have expanded to include publishers, small presses, publish-on-demand opportunities, e-publishing and agents. A bookstore is provided with a variety of materials for writers."

⊠ ⊟ EMERALD CITY COMICON

800 Convention Place, Seattle, WA 98037. E-mail: info@emeraldcitycomicon.com. Website: www. emeraldcitycomicon.com. Estab. 2002. Annual. Last show: April 4-5, 2009. Conference duration: 2 days. "The premiere comic book convention of the Pacific Northwest. Includes comic creators and media guests, various creative and publishing panels, exhibitors, dealers and much more." Site: Washington State Convention & Trade Center. Guests include J. Michael Straczynski, Brian Michael Bendis, David Finch, Arthur Suydam, Tim Sale and many more, as well as Image Comics, Oni Press, Fantagraphics, Dark Horse, Top Shelf and others.

Costs $15/day or $25/weekend pre-sale, $20/Sat, $15/Sun or $30/weekend on-site.

Accommodations Offers overnight accommodations. Discounted rate at Roosevelt Hotel, Crowne Plaza and Red Lion in Seattle.

Additional Information For information, visit Web site. Editors participate in conference.

FESTIVAL OF FAITH AND WRITING

Calvin College/Department of English, 1795 Knollcrest Circle SE, Grand Rapids MI 49546. (616)526-6770. E-mail: ffw@calvin.edu. Website: www.calvin.edu/festival. **Contact:** English Dept. Estab. 1990. Biennial. Conference usually held in April of even years. Conference duration: 3 days. Average attendance: 1,800. The Festival of Faith and Writing encourages serious, imaginative writing by all writers interested in the intersections of literature and belief. Site: The festival is held at Calvin College in Grand Rapids, MI, 180 miles north of Chicago. Focus is on fiction, nonfiction, memoir, poetry, drama, children's, young adult, literary criticism, film and song lyrics. Past speakers have included Annie Dillard, John Updike, Katherine Paterson, Elie Wiesel, Joyce Carol Oates, Leif Enger, Salman Rushdie, and Marilynne Robinson.

Costs Registration: consult Web site. Registration includes all sessions during the 3-day event but does not include meals, lodging or evening concerts.

Accommodations Shuttles are available to and from select local hotels. Consult festival Web site for a list of hotels with special conference rates.

Additional Information Some agents and editors attend the festival and consult with prospective writers.

⋈ FISHERMAN'S WHARF WRITERS CONFERENCE

2020 Pennsylvania Ave., NW, Suite 443, Washington DC 20006. (800)250-8290. E-mail: algonkian@webdelsol.com. Website: http://fwwriters.algonkianconferences.com. **Contact:** Michael Neff. Annual. Conference duration: 5 days. "Beside the San Francisco Bay, aspiring authors will study and apply the most effective techniques of craft and style while also learning the necessary facts about the publishing market. This event is only open to serious writers who wish to either begin the novel or work towards perfecting their novel-in-progress (while also learning to write short fiction). Genres we work with include general commercial fiction, literary fiction, serious and light women's fiction, mystery/cozy/thriller, SF/F, young adult, and memoir/narrative non-fiction." The Fort Mason Center Complex overlooks San Francisco Bay with views of the Golden Gate Bridge. Paved foot/bike paths run along the water, east to Fisherman's Wharf and west to the Marina Green.

Costs $695

Accommodations Does not offer overnight accommodations. Provides list of area hotels or lodging options.

Additional Information Pre-conference assignments and readings will begin immediately following registration. Please note: these assignments must be completed. For brochure, visit Web site. Agents and editors participate in conference.

FLATHEAD RIVER WRITERS CONFERENCE

P.O. Box 7711, Kalispell MT 59904. E-mail: conference@authorsoftheflathead.org. **Contact:** Conference Coordinator. Estab. 1990. Annual. Next conference: Intense workshops September 30-October 2, 2009, general conference October 4-4, 2009. Attendance limited to 100. Deals with all aspects of writing, including short and long fiction and nonfiction. Site: Flathead Valley Community College, Kalilspell, MT. Past speakers includes Anne Rule, Linda Seger, Donald Maass.

Costs Cost of general weekend conference; $150 includes breakfast and lunch, not lodging. Intense pre-conferences priced separately. Visit Web site for details.

FORT BEND WRITERS GUILD WORKSHOP

12523 Folkcrest Way, Stafford TX 77477-3529. Website: www.fortbendwritersguild.com. **Contact:** Roger Paulding. Estab. 1997. Annual. Conference will be held in April. Conference duration: 1 day. Average attendance: 75. Focuses on fiction (novels) and screenwriting. Site: Held at Holiday Inn Southwest, Houston.

Costs $60 (including buffet lunch) before February 28; $65 thereafter; $75 at door on day of workshop. Check Web site for updated prices. Use PayPal if you wish for workshop or contest entries. Nonmembers add $10.

Additional Information Sponsors a contest. Submit for novel competition first 15 pages plus one-page synopsis, entry fee $20 plus $10 membership fee; for short story competition 10 pages complete, $10 each. "Judges are published novelists." First prize: $300, second place: $200, third place: $100. Deadline February 28, 2010. Not necessary to attend workshop in order to win. For brochure send SASE, e-mail or check Web site.

THE GLEN WORKSHOP

Image, 3307 Third Avenue W, Seattle WA 98119. (206) 281-2979. Fax: (206) 281-2335. E-mail: glenworkshop@imagejournal.org. Website: www.imagejournal.org. Estab. 1991. Annual. Workshop held first full week in August. Conference duration: 1 week. Average attendance: 150-200. Workshop focuses on "fiction, poetry, spiritual writing, songwriting, playwriting, painting, drawing, and mixed media. Run by Image, a literary journal with a religious focus. The Glen welcomes writers who practice or grapple with religious faith." Site: 2009 conference was held July 26-August 2 in Santa Fe, NM and features "presentations and readings by the faculty." Faculty has included Lauren F. Winner (spiritual writing), B.H. Fairchild and Marilyn Nelson (poetry), Mark St. Germain (playwriting), and Over the Rhine (songwriting).

Costs $500-1010, including room and board; $425-500 for commuters (lunch only).

Accommodations Arrange transportation by shuttle. Accommodations included in conference cost.

Additional Information Prior to arrival, participants may need to submit workshop material depending on the teacher. "Usually 10-25 pages." Conference information is available in February. For brochure e-mail, visit Web site, or call. "Like *Image*, the Glen is grounded in a Christian perspective, but its tone is informal and hospitable to all spiritual wayfarers."

GOTHAM WRITERS' WORKSHOP

WritingClasses.com (online division), 555 8th Avenue, Suite 1402, New York NY 10018. (212)974-8377. Fax: (212)307-6325. E-mail: dana@write.org. Website: www.writingclasses.com. **Contact:** Dana Miller, director of student affairs. Estab. 1993. "Classes held throughout the year. There are four terms, beginning in January, April, June/July, September/October." Conference duration: 10-week, 6-week, 1-day, and online courses offered. Average attendance: approximately 1,300 students per term, 6,000 students per year. Offers craft-oriented creative writing courses in fiction writing, screenwriting, nonfiction writing, memoir writing, novel writing, children's book writing, playwriting, poetry, songwriting, mystery writing, science fiction writing, romance writing, television writing, documentary film writing, feature article writing, travel writing, creative writing, and business writing. Also, Gotham Writers' Workshop offers a teen program, private instruction and classes on selling your work. Site: Classes are held at various schools in New York City as well as online at www.writingclasses.com. View a sample online class on the Web site.

Costs 10-week and online courses—$420 (includes $25 registration fee); 6-week courses-$320 (includes $25 registration fee); 1-day courses—$150 (includes $25 registration fee). Meals and lodging not included.

Additional Information "Participants do not need to submit workshop material prior to their first class." Sponsors a contest for a free 10-week online creative writing course (value = $420) offered each term. Students should fill out a form online at www.writingclasses.com to participate in the contest. The winner is randomly selected. For brochure send e-mail, visit Web site, call or fax. Accepts inquiries by e-mail, phone, fax. Agents and editors participate in some workshops.

GREATER LEHIGH VALLEY WRITERS GROUP 'THE WRITE STUFF' WRITERS CONFERENCE

350 Nazareth Pile, PMB #136, Bethlehem PA 18020-1115. (908)479-6581. Fax: (908)479-6744. E-mail: write@glvwg.org. Website: www.glvwg.org. **Contact:** JoAnn Dahan, chair. Estab. 1993. Annual. Last conference was March 27-28, 2009. Conference duration: 2 days. Average attendance: 140. This conference features workshops in all genres. Site: "The Four Points Sheraton is located in the beautiful Lehigh Valley. The spacious hotel has an indoor swimming pool and newly renovated conference rooms. Our keynote speaker Juilene McKnight will address the conference over a wonderful, three-course meal."

Costs Members, $100 (includes all workshops, 2 meals, and a chance to pitch to an editor or agent); non-members, $120. Late registration, $135.

Additional Information "The Writer's Flash contest is judged by conference participants. Write 100 words or less in fiction, creative nonfiction, or poetry. Brochures available in March for SASE, or by phone, e-mail, or on Web site. Accepts inquiries by SASE, e-mail, phone, fax. Agents and editors attend conference. Be sure to refer to the Web site, as often with conferences, things may change. Greater Lehigh Valley Writer's Group has remained one of the most friendly conferences and we give the most for your money. Breakout rooms offer craft topics, editor and agent panels. Book fair with book signing by published authors and presenters."

GREAT LAKES WRITERS FESTIVAL

Lakeland College, P.O. Box 359, Sheboygan WI 53082-0359. (920) 565-1276. Fax: (920) 565-1260. E-mail: elderk@lakeland.edu. Website: www.greatlakeswritersfestival.org. **Contact:** Karl Elder, coordinator. Estab. 1991. Annual. Last conference held Nov. 6-7, 2008. Conference duration: 2 days. "Festival celebrates the writing of poetry, fiction and creative nonfiction." Site: Lakeland College is a small, 4-yr. liberal arts college of 235 acres, a beautiful campus in a rural setting, founded in 1862. No themes or panels, just readings and workshops. 2008 faculty included Linda Aschbrenner and Tom Franklin.

Costs Free and open to the public. Participants may purchase meals and must arrange for their own lodging.

Accommodations Does not offer overnight accommodations. Provides list of area hotels or lodging options.

Additional Information All participants who would like to have their writing considered as an object for discussion during the festival workshops must submit it to Karl Elder electronically by Oct. 15. Participants may submit material for workshops in one genre only (poetry, fiction or creative nonfiction). Sponsors contest. Contest entries must contain the writer's name and address on a separate title page, be in type, and be submitted as clear, hard copy on Friday at the festival registration table. Entries may be in each of three genres per participant, yet only one poem, one story, and/or one nonfiction piece may be entered. There are two categories—high school students on one hand, all others on the other—of cash awards for first place in each of the three genres. The judges reserve the right to decline to award a prize in one or more of the genres. Judges will be the editorial staff of *Seems* (a.k.a. *Word of Mouth*), excluding the festival coordinator, Karl Elder. Information available in September. For brochure, visit Web site. Editors

GREAT RIVER ARTS

33 Bridge Street, P.O. Box 48, Bellows Falls VT 05101. (802)463-3330. E-mail: info@greatriverarts. org. Website: www.greatriverarts.org. **Contact:** Tonia Fleming, administrator. Estab. 1999. Year-round workshops. Conference duration: 2-5 days. Average attendance: 6-8 per class. Master class and workshops in the visual and literary arts. Site: Classes are held in the Bellows Falls, Vermont/Walpole, New Hampshire region located on the shores of the Connecticut River. Classes are given in poetry, memoir, fiction and children's book arts.

Costs 2008 rates were $500-750. Does not include lodging or meals.

Accommodations Provides list of area hotels.

Additional Information Participants may need to submit material prior to arrival depending on course. Workshops for 2009 were available on Web site. Accepts inquiries by e-mail, phone, fax.

GREEN LAKE CHRISTIAN WRITERS CONFERENCE

Green Lake Conference Center, W2511 State Road 23, Green Lake WI 54941. (920) 294-3323. E-mail: janwhite@glcc.org. Website: www.glcc.org. **Contact:** Jan White. "Come learn, write and celebrate with us!" Sunday afternoon-Friday morning, August 22-27, 2009, our 61st annual conference. "Affordable, inspirational conference for new or well-published writers. May write for the secular or Christian market or both. Workshop leaders are well-published and are experienced teachers. Spend 12 hours of classroom time in any of these areas: fiction, nonfiction, poetry, inspiratiional, curriculum, publishing for pastors. Special features: writers' contest, manuscript review, one-on-one with leaders, vespers, devotions, music, bookstore, writers' own area for display and sales, Writers' Showcase celebration. A dozen or more optional afternoon seminars and evening panels which cover marketing, internet use, specialized writing, and more." Site: South Central WI on the state's deepest lake, with 212 miles of shoreline and 1,000 acres of land, including outstanding golf course.

Accommodations Hotels, lodges and all meeting rooms are a/c. Affordable rates, excellent meals.

Additional Information Party & writers'showcase. Brochure and scholarship info from website or contact Jan White (920)294-3323.

GREEN MOUNTAIN WRITERS CONFERENCE

47 Hazel St., Rutland VT 05701. (802)236-6133. E-mail: ydaley@sbcglobal.net. Website: www. vermontwriters.com. **Contact:** Yvonne Daley, director. Estab. 1999. Annual. Check website for 2010 dates. Conference duration: 5 days. Average attendance: 40. "The conference is an opportunity for writers at all stages of their development to hone their skills in a beautiful, lakeside environment where published writers across genres share tips and give feedback." Site: Conference held at an old dance pavillion on a 5-acre site on a remote pond in Tinmouth, VT. Past features include Place in story: The Importance of Environment; Creating Character through Description, Dialogue, Action, Reaction, and Thought; The Collision of Real Events and Imagination. Previous staff has included Yvonne Daley, Ruth Stone, Verandah Porche, Grace Paley, David Huddle, Sydney Lea, Joan Connor, Tom Smith and Howard Frank Mosher.

Costs $500 before June 15, $525 after. Fee includes lunch, snacks, beverages, readings.

Accommodations Offers list of area hotels and lodging.

Additional Information Participants' mss can be read and commented on at a cost. Sponsors contests. Conference publishes a literary magazine featuring work of participants. Brochures available in January on Web site or for SASE, e-mail. Accepts inquiries by SASE, e-mail, phone. "We offer the opportunity to learn from some of the nation's best writers at a small, supportive conference in a lakeside setting that allows one-to-one feedback. Participants often continue to correspond and share work after conferences." Further information available on Web site, by e-mail or by phone.

HEART TALK

Women's Center for Ministry, Western Seminary, 5511 SE Hawthorne Blvd., Portland OR 97215-3367. (503) 517-1931 or (877) 517-1800, ext. 1931. Fax: (503) 517-1889. E-mail: wcm@westernseminary.edu. Website: www.westernseminary.edu/women/. **Contact:** Kenine Stein, administrative associate. Estab. 1998. Every other year (alternates with speaker's conferences). March 14, 2009 will be our writer's conference. Robin Jones Gunn will be main keynote speaker; Cindy Hannan will speak in the afternoon. Four workshop sessions with authors and editors including: Patricia Rushford, Bette Nordberg, Deborah Hedstrom-Page, Sally Stuart, Linda Clare, Sue Miholer, Kimberly Schumate, Angela Diehl, and Chip MacGregor. Topics for new and advanced writers include: publishing, editing, fiction, market trends, dialogue, screenwriting, Web site, blogging, book proposals, critique groups, nonfiction, and more more. Editors available for 1:1 consultation. Conference duration: writing, 1 day. Average attendance: 100 +. "Heart Talk provides inspirational training for men and women desiring to write for publication and/ or speak publicly." Site: "Western Seminary has a chapel plus classrooms to accommodate various size groups. The campus has a peaceful park-like atmosphere with beautiful lawns, trees and flowers, plus an inviting fountain and pond. Heart Talk 2009 will be the next conference, scheduled for March 14th, 2009. Please check Web site for further details as they become available. March 9-12, 2010 will be a speakers conference with Carol Kent and team from Speak Up With Confidence. Original and mini-advanced seminars with a writing workshop included in mini-advanced. Last speaking conference was March 11-14, 2008."

Costs $100 in 2008 for original; $125 for mini-advanced. Optional video critiquing on March 15th.

Additional Information Conference information available in January by e-mail, phone, fax and on Web site. For inquiries, contact by mail, e-mail, phone. Conference "is open to Christian women who desire to write for publication. Please view our Web site for Heart Talk 2009 Writer's Conference details. They will be posted as they become available. E-mail us to be added to our Heart Talk mailing list."

HIGHLAND SUMMER CONFERENCE

Box 7014, Radford University, Radford VA 24142-7014. (540) 831-5366. Fax: (540) 831-5951. E-mail: dcichran@radford.edu. Website: www.radford.edu/~arsc. **Contact:** Dana Cochran, assistant to director. Estab. 1978. Annual. Conference held first 2 weeks of June. Conference duration: 2 weeks. Average attendance: 25. Three hours graduate or undergraduate credits. Site: The Highland Summer Conference is held at Radford University, a school of about 9,000 students. Radford is in the Blue Ridge Mountains of southwest Virginia, about 45 miles south of Roanoke, VA. "The HSC features one (two weeks) or two (one week each) guest leaders each year. As a rule, our leaders are well-known writers who have connections, either thematic or personal or both, to the Appalachian region. The genre emphasis depends upon the workshop leader(s). In the past we have had as guest lecturers Nikki Giovanni, Sharyn McCrumb, Gurney Norman, Denise Giardinia, George Ella Lyon, Jim Wayne Miller, Wilma Dykeman and Robert Morgan."

Costs "The cost is based on current Radford tuition for 3 credit hours plus an additional conference fee. On-campus meals and housing are available at additional cost. 2008 conference tuition was $771 for in-state undergraduates, $837 for graduate students."

Accommodations "We do not have special rate arrangements with local hotels. We do offer accommodations on the Radford University Campus in a recently refurbished residence hall. (In 2007 cost was $26.09-36.08 per night.)"

Additional Information "Conference leaders typically critique work done during the two-week conference, but do not ask to have any writing submitted prior to the conference beginning." Conference information available after February for SASE. Accepts inquiries by e-mail, fax.

HIGHLIGHTS FOUNDATION FOUNDERS WORKSHOPS

814 Court St., Honesdale PA 18431. (570)253-1192. Fax: (570)253-0179. E-mail: contact@ highlightsfoundation.org. Website: www.highlightsfoundation.org. **Contact:** Kent L. Brown Jr., executive director. Estab. 2000. "Workshops geared toward those interested in writing and illustrating for children, intermediate and advanced levels." Classes offered include: Writing Novels for Young Adults, Biography, Nonfiction Writing, Writing Historical Fiction, Wordplay: Writing Poetry for Children, Heart of the Novel, Nature Writing for Kids, Visual Art of the Picture Book, The Whole Novel Workshop, and more (see Web site for updated list).

Costs Range from $695 and up, including tuition, meals, conference supplies, and private housing. **Additional Information** "Call for application and more information."

HIGHLIGHTS FOUNDATION WRITERS WORKSHOP AT CHATAUQUA

814 Court St., Honesdale PA 18431. (570) 253-1192. Fax: (570) 253-0179. E-mail: contact@ highlightsfoundation.org. Website: www.highlightsfoundation.org. **Contact**: Kent Brown, executive director. Workshops geared toward those interested in writing for children; beginner, intermediate and advanced levels. Dozens of Classes include: Writing Poetry, Book Promotion, Characterization, Developing a Plot, Exploring Genres, The Publishing Business, What Makes a Good Book, and many more. Annual workshop. Held July 14-21, 2007, at the Chautauqua Institution, Chautauqua, NY. Registration limited to 100.

Costs Cost includes tuition, meals, conference supplies. Call for availability and pricing. Scholarships are available for first-time attendees. Call for more information or visit the Web site.

TONY HILLERMAN WRITERS CONFERENCE

304 Calle Oso, Santa FE NM 87501. (505)471-1565. E-mail: wordharvest@wordharvest.com. Website: www.wordharvest.com. **Contact**: Jean Schaumberg, co-director. Estab. 2004. Annual. November. Conference duration: 4 days. Average attendance: 160. Site: Albuquerque Hyatt Regency. Previous faculty included Tony Hillerman, David Morrell, Michael McGarrity, and Jonathan and Faye Kellerman. There was no conference in 2009.

Costs Previous year's costs: $395 per-registration.

Accommodations Previous year $99 per night at the Hyatt Regency (plus parking).

Additional Information Sponsors on-site mini contest, $1,500 short story contest with *Cowboys & Indians Magazine* and a $10,000 first mystery novel contest with Thomas Dunne Books. Brochures available in July for SASE, by phone, e-mail, fax and on Web site. Accepts inquiries by SASE, phone, e-mail.

HOW TO BE PUBLISHED WORKSHOPS

P.O. Box 100031, Birmingham AL 35210-3006. E-mail: mike@writing2sell.com. Website: www.writing2sell. com. **Contact**: Michael Garrett. Estab. 1986. Workshops are offered continuously year-round at various locations. Conference duration: 1 session. Average attendance: 10-15. Workshops to "move writers of category fiction closer to publication." Focus is not on how to write, but how to get published. Site: Workshops held at college campuses and universities. Themes include marketing, idea development and manuscript critique.

Costs $55-89.

Additional Information "Special critique is offered, but advance submission is not required." Workshop information available on Web site. Accepts inquiries by e-mail.

◪ HUMBER SCHOOL FOR WRITERS SUMMER WORKSHOP

Humber Institute of Technology and Advanced Learning, 3199 Lake Shore Blvd. West, Toronto ON M8V 1K8 Canada. (416)675-6622 ext. 3448. Fax: (416)251-7167. E-mail: antanas.sileika@humber.ca. Website: www.humber.ca/creativeandperformingarts. **Contact:**Antanas Sileika, director. Annual. Workshop held second week in July. Conference duration: 1 week. Average attendance: 100. Focuses on fiction, poetry, creative nonfiction. Site: Humber College's Lakeshore campus in Toronto. Panels cover success stories, small presses, large presses, agents. Faculty: Changes annually. 2008 included Richard Bausch, Joe Bausch, Joe Kertes, Paul Quarrington, Alistair Macleod, Lisa Moore, Karen Connelly, M.G. Vassanji, Wayson Choy, Bruce Jay Friedman, Kim Moritsugu, Olive Senior.

Costs Workshop fee is $950 Canadian.

Accommodations Provides lodging. Residence fee is $350 Canadian.

Additional Information Participants "must submit sample writing no longer than 15 pages approximately 4 weeks before workshop begins." Brochures available mid-February for e-mail, phone, fax. Accepts inquiries by e-mail, phone, fax. Agents and editors participate in conference.

INDIANA UNIVERSITY WRITERS' CONFERENCE

464 Ballantine Hall, Bloomington IN 47405-7103. (812)855-1877. Fax: (812)855-9535. E-mail: writecon@ indiana.edu. Website: www.indiana.edu/~writecon. **Contact:** Bob Bledsoe, director. Estab. 1940. Annual. Conference/workshops held in June. Average attendance: 115. "The Indiana University Writers' Conference believes in a craft-based teaching of fiction writing. We emphasize an exploration of

creativity through a variety of approaches, offering workshop-based craft discussions, classes focusing on technique, and talks about the careers and concerns of a writing life." 2009: fiction faculty: Julia Glass, Manuel Munoz, Alyce Miller, Danit Brown.

Costs 2009 cost: 4500 for workshop (included all classes); $250 for classes only. $50 application fee. Information on accommodations available on Web site.

Additional Information Fiction workshop applicants must submit up to 25 pages of prose. Registration information available for SASE, by e-mail, or on Web site.

⊞ ⊟ INTERNATIONAL COMIC-CON

Comic-Con International, P.O. Box 128458, San Diego CA 92112-8458.(619)491-2475. Fax: (619)414-1022. E-mail: cci-info@comic-con.org. Website: www.comic-con.org/cci/. **Contact:** Gary Sassaman, director of programming. Annual. Last conference held July 23-26, 2009. Conference duration: 4 days. Average attendance: 104,000. "The comics industry's largest expo, hosting writers, artists, editors, agents, publishers, buyers and sellers of comics and graphic novels." Site: San Diego Convention Center. "Nearly 300 programming events, including panels, seminars and previews, on the world of comics, movies, television, animation, art, and much more." 2006 special guests included Ray Bradbury, Forrest J. Ackerman, Sergio Aragones, John Romita Sr., J. Michael Straczynski, Daniel Clowes, George Perez.

Costs $50 by April 19, $55 by June 7, $65 at the door. Special discounts for children and seniors.

Accommodations Does not offer overnight accommodations. Provides list of area hotels or lodging options. Special conference hotel and airfare discounts available. See Web site for details.

Additional Information For brochure, visit Web site. Agents and editors participate in conference.

IOWA SUMMER WRITING FESTIVAL

C215 Seashore Hall, University of Iowa, Iowa City IA 52242-1802. (319) 335-4160. E-mail: iswfestival@uiowa.edu. Website: www.uiowa.edu/~iswfest. **Contact:** Amy Margolis, director. Estab. 1987. Annual. Festival held in June and July. Workshops are one week or a weekend. Average attendance: limited to 12/class—over 1,500 participants throughout the summer. "We offer workshops across the genres, including novel, short story, poetry, essay, memoir, humor, travel, playwriting, screenwriting, writing for children and more. All writers 21 and over are welcome. You need only have the desire to write." Site: University of Iowa campus. Guest speakers are undetermined at this time. Readers and instructors have included Lee K. Abbott, Marvin Bell, Lan Samantha Chang, Janet Desaulniers, Hope Edelman, Bret Anthony Johnston, and many more.

Costs $500-525 for full week; $250 for weekend workshop. Discounts available for early registration. Housing and meals are separate.

Accommodations Iowa House, $90/night; Sheraton, $94/night, Heartland Inn, $6 8/night (rates subject to change).

Additional Information Conference information available in February. Accepts inquiries by fax, e-mail, phone. "Register early. Classes fill quickly."

IWWG EARLY SUMMER CONFERENCE

The International Women's Writing Guild, P.O. Box 810, Gracie Station, New York NY 10028. (212)737-7536. Fax: (212)737-9469. E-mail: iwwg@iwwg.org. Website: www.iwwg.org. Established 1978. **Contact**: Hannelore Hahn, executive director. 2009 dates: June 12-19. Location: Skidmore College in Saratoga Springs, NY. Average attendance: 500 maximum. Open to all women. Around 65 workshops offered each day. 2009 poetry staff includes Barbara Garro, Marj Hahne, D.H. Melhem, Myra Shapiro, and Susan Baugh.

Accommodations 2009 cost: $1,085 (single), $945 (double) for IWWG members; $1,330 (single), $990 (double), $1,034 (single). Includes program and room and board for 7 nights, 21 meals at Skidmore College. Shorter conference stays available, such as 5 days or weekend. Commuters welcome.

Additional Information Post-conference retreat weekend also available. Information available for SASE, by e-mail, or on web site.

IWWG MEET THE AGENTS AND EDITORS: THE BIG APPLE WORKSHOPS

c/o International Women's Writing Guild, P.O. Box 810, Gracie Station, New York NY 10028-0082. (212)737-7536. Fax: (212)737-9469. E-mail: iwwg@iwwg.com. Website: www.iwwg.com. **Contact:** Hannelore Hahn, executive director. Estab. 1976. Biannual. Workshops held the second weekend in April and the second weekend in October. Average attendance: 150. Workshops to promote creative writing and professional success. Site: Private meeting space of Scandinavia House, mid-town New York City. Saturday: 1-day writing workshop. Sunday afternoon: open house/meet the agents, independent presses and editors.

Costs $130 for members; $155 for non-members for the weekend.

Accommodations Information on transportation arrangements and overnight accommodations available.

Additional Information Accepts inquiries by fax, e-mail, phone.

JACKSON HOLE WRITERS CONFERENCE

Jackson WY (307)766-2938. Fax: (307)413-3331. E-mail: tim@jacksonholewritersconference.com. Website: http://jacksonholewritersconference.com/. **Contact:** Tim Sandlin, director. Annual. Last conference held June 2 6-2 9, 200 8. Conference duration: 4 days. Average attendance: 100. The Jackson Hole Writers Conference draws a wide range of participants, from beginners to published writers. Site: Center for the Arts. The conference is directed toward fiction, poetry, travel/adventure magazine, young adult playwriting and creative nonfiction, offering programs relevant to all 6 disciplines: story structure, character development, narrative thrust, work habits and business techniques. In addition, separate sessions deal with skills particular to each specialty. "We offer three one-on-one manuscript critiques to each participant."

Costs $325 conference pre-registration; $300 conference pre-registration for past participants; $75 spouse/guest registration; $50 ms evaluation; $75 extended ms evaluation. "You must register for conference to be eligible for manuscript evaluation."

Accommodations $135/night for single or double; $145/night triple; $155/night quadruple.

Additional Information The conference faculty's goal is to help our writers get published. Agent and editor roundtable discussions are geared specifically to teach you how your writing can be crafted, shaped and packaged for sale. Ms evaluations are also available. See Web site for details.

JAMES RIVER WRITERS CONFERENCE

James River Writers, Zero East 4th St. #24, Richmond VA 23224. (804) 230-4575. Fax: (804) 230-4576. E-mail: info@jamesriverwriters.com. Website: http://jamesriverwriters.com. **Contact:** Anne Westrick, administrative director. Estab. 2003. Annual. Fri-Sat, October 9-10, 2009. Average attendance: 250. Conference. "The James River Writers Conference offers two days of cross-genre sessions to bring aspiring writers together with professionals to share the ups and downs of the writing life. By seeking to build and inspire the community of writers, the sessions address a myriad of topics related to the craft and business of writing fiction, nonfiction, poetry, fantasy/sci-fi, children's, magazine articles, short stories, memoir, biography, and romance. The purpose is to energize the creative literary community." Site: "The Library of Virginia provides a beautiful setting including a 250-seat lecture hall and four rooms seating 45-60 each for break-out sessions, all located in one wing of the Library, off the main front lobby. The site lends itself to an intimacy unusual for writers conferences." Past years'conference guests have included Sheri Reynolds, Sharyn McCrumb, Claudia Emerson, Eric VanLustbader, Mark Bowden, Rosalind Miles, Dennis McFarland, David L. Robbins, Dean King, James Campbell and Hampton Sides.

Costs In 2008 the cost was $140 early registration and $155 after September 1, 2008. A continental breakfast and box lunch were included in the fee.

Accommodations Richmond is easily accessibly by air and train. Does not offer overnight accommodations. Provides list of area hotels or lodging options. "Each year we arrange for special conference rates at an area hotel."

Additional Information Workshop material is not required, however we have offered an option for submissions: the first pages critique session in which submissions are read before a panel of agents and editors who are seeing them for the first time and are asked to react on the spot. No additional fee. No guarantee that a particular submission will be read. Details posted on the website, http://jamesriverwriters.com. Information available in June. For brochure, visit Web site. Agents participate in conference. Editors participate in conference.

▥ JOURNEY INTO THE IMAGINATION: A WEEKEND WRITING WORKSHOP

995 Chapman Rd, Yorktown NY 10598.(914)962-4432. E-mail: emily@emilyhanlon.com. Website: www. thefictionwritersjourney.com. **Contact:** Emily Hanlon, workshop leader. Estab. 2004. Annual. Held the first weekend in May. Average attendance: 15-20. "Purpose of workshop: fiction, memoir, short story, creativity and the creative process." Site: Wisdom House Retreat Center in Licthfield, CT. "We

stay in an old farmhouse on the retreat center grounds. Excellent food and lovely surroundings and accommodations. The core of this weekend's work is welcoming the unknown into your writing. We will go on a magical mystery tour to find and embrace new characters and to deepen our relationship to characters who already may people our stories. Bring something on which you are already working or simply bring along your Inner Writer, pen and a journal, and let the magic unfold!"

Costs 2009: $450-650, dependent on choic of room.

Additional Information For brochure, visit Web site.

KENTUCKY WRITER'S WORKSHOP

Pine Mountain State Resort Park, 1050 State Park Rd., Pineville KY 40977. (606)337-3066. Fax: (606)337-7250. E mail: dean.henson@ky.gov. Website: http://parks.ky.gov. **Contact:** Dean Henson, event coordinator. Estab. 1995. Annual. Workshop held each March. Average attendance: 50-65. "Focuses on writing in various genres, including fiction, mystery, poetry, novels, short stories, essays, etc." Site: Pine Mountain State Resort Park (a Kentucky State Park).

Costs Registration fee is $30 for non-package participants.

Accommodations Special all-inclusive event packages are available. Call for information.

Additional Information Brochures available 2 months in advance by e-mail or phone. Accepts inquiries by SASE, e-mail, phone, fax. "Our conference features successful and celebrated Kentucky authors speaking and instructing on various topics of the writing endeavor. This workshop is designed to help developing authors improve their writing craft."

KENYON REVIEW WRITERS WORKSHOP

The Kenyon Review, Kenyon College, Gambier OH 43022. (740) 427-5207. Fax: (740) 427-5417. E-mail: writers@kenyon review.org. Website: www.kenyonreview.org. **Contact:** Anna Duke Reach, director. Estab.1990. Annual. Workshop held mid to late June. Conference duration: 8 days. Average attendance: 60-70. Participants apply in poetry, fiction or literary nonfiction, and then participate in intensive daily workshops which focus on the generation and revision of significant new work. Site: The conference takes place on the campus of Kenyon College in the rural village of Gambier, Ohio. Students have access to college computing and recreational facilities and are housed in campus housing. Workshop leaders have included David Baker, Ron Carlson, Rebecca McClanahan, Meghan O'Rourke, Rosanna Warren, and Nancy Zafris.

Costs $1,995 including room and board.

Accommodations The workshop operates a shuttle to and from Gambier and the airport in Columbus, Ohio. Offers overnight accommodations. Participants are housed in Kenyon College student housing. The cost is covered in the tuition.

Additional Information Application includes a writing sample. Admission decisions are made on a rolling basis. Workshop information is available November 1. For brochure send e-mail, visit Web site, call, fax. Accepts inquiries by SASE, e-mail, phone, fax.

KILLALOE HEDGE-SCHOOL OF WRITING

4 Riverview, Killaloe Co. Clare Ireland. (+ 353)61 375 217. Fax: (+ 353)61 375 487. E-mail: khs@killaloe.ie. Website: www.killaloe.ie/khs. **Contact:** K.Thorne, secretary. Estab. 1999. Held every fourth weekend between October and May. Conference duration: 10 a.m. Saturday till 4 p.m. Sunday. Average attendance: 15. Holds workshops on 6 different topics: Get Started Writing; Start Your Novel; Writing a Nonfiction Book; Write for Magazines and Papers; Write Your Memoirs; Get Started Writing-Level Two. Speakers include David Rice, Catherine Thorne and others yet to be invited.

Costs 235 EURO per workshop. Includes midday meal each day. Does not include lodging.

Accommodations Runs a shuttle from Shannon Airport.

Additional Information "Please check out our Web site."

KILLER NASHVILLE

P.O. Box 680686, Franklin TN 37068-0686. (615)599-4032. E-mail: contact@killernashville.com. Website: www.KillerNashville.com. **Contact:** Clay Stafford. Estab. 2006. Annual. Next event: August 2009. Conference duration: 4 days. Average attendance: 180 + . "Conference designed for writers and fans of mysteries and thrillers, including authors (fiction and nonfiction), playwrights, and screenwriters. Sponsors include Middle Tennessee State University, Barnes & Noble Booksellers, Mystery Writers of America, Sisters in Crime, First Tennessee Bank, Landmark Booksellers, and The Nashville Scene. Law enforcement workshop parters include the Federal Bureau of Investigation (FBI), The Tennessee Bureau of Investigations (TBI), Alcohol, Tobacco, & Firearms (ATF), Franklin Police Department, Brentwood Police Department, and Wilson County Sheriff's Department. Agents, editors and industry professionals include Carey Nelson Burch (William Morris Agency), Lucienne Diver (The Knight Literary Agency), Miriam Kress (Irene Goodman Literary Agency), and Maryglenn McCombs (Oceanview Publishing). Event includes book signings and panels." Past panelists included authors Michael Connelly, Carol Higgins Clark, Bill Bass, Gregg Hurwitz, Hallie Ephron, Chris Grabenstein, Rhonda Pollero, P.J. Parrish, Reed Farrel Coleman, Kathryn Wall, Mary Saums, Don Bruns, Bill Moody, Richard Helms, Alexandra Sokoloff, and Steven Womack.

Costs Signings events are free; current prices for events available on Web site.

Additional Information "Additional information about registration is provided at www.KillerNashville. com."

LA JOLLA WRITERS CONFERENCE

P.O. Box 178122, San Diego CA 92177. (858)467-1978. Website: www.lajollawritersconference.com. **Contact:** Jared Kuritz, director. Established 2001. Annual. 2009 Conference held November 6-8. Conference duration: 3 days. Maximum attendance limited to 200. The La Jolla Writers Conference welcomes writers of all levels of experience. This three-day event, now in its 9th year, always boasts exciting, interactive workshops, lectures, and presentations by an outstanding and freely accessible faculty comprised of best-selling authors, editors from major publishing houses, and literary agents, all of whom value meeting and working with a diverse group of creative people passionate about writing. The LJWC uniquely covers the art, craft, and business of writing for both fiction and non-fiction.

Costs $385 Early, $355 Regular, $425 after August 1. Conference registration includes access to more than 85 classes, three keynote addresses, two meals, appetizer reception, and faculty author signing.

Additional Information Private Read & Critiques for an additional fee of $50 each.

LAMB'S SPRINGFED WRITING RETREAT

(formally Walloon Writer's Retreat) P.O. Box 304, Royal Oak MI 48068-0304. (248) 589-3913. Fax: (248) 589-9981. E-mail: johndlamb@ameritech.net. Website: www.springfed.org. **Contact**: John D. Lamb, director. Estab. 1999. Annual. Last conference held October 9-12, 2008. Next conference is October 8-11, 2009. Average attendance: 75. Focus includes fiction, poetry, screenwriting and nonfiction. Site: The Birchwood Inn, Harbor Spring, MI. Attendees stay in comfortable rooms, and seminars are held in conference rooms with fieldstone fireplaces and dining area. Past faculty included Billy Collins, Michael Moore, Jonathan Rand, Jacquelyn Mitchard, Jane Hamilton, Thomas Lux, Joyce Maynard, Jack Driscoll, Dorianne Laux, and Cornelius Eady.

Costs Single occupancy is $625, $560 (3 days, 2 nights, all meals included). $360 non-lodging.

Accommodations Shuttle rides from Traverse City Airport or Pellston Airport. Offers overnight accommodations. Provides list of area lodging options.

Additional Information Optional: Attendees may submit 3 poems or 5 pages of prose for conference with a staff member. Brochures available mid-June by e-mail, on Web site or by phone. Accepts inquiries by SASE, e-mail, phone.

▣ LAS VEGAS WRITERS CONFERENCE

Henderson Writers' Group, 614 Mosswood Dr., Henderson NV 89015.(702)564-2488. E-mail: president@ hendersonwritersgroup.com. Website: www.lasvegaswritersconference.com. **Contact:** Jo Wilkins, president or Stacee Halquist, conference coordinator. Annual. April. Conference duration: 4 days. Average attendance: 150 maximum. "Join writing professionals, agents, industry experts and your colleagues for four days in Las Vegas, NV, as they share their knowledge on all aspects of the writer's craft. While there are formal pitch sessions, panels, workshops, and seminars, the faculty is also available throughout the conference for informal discussions and advice. Plus, you're bound to meet a few new friends, too. Workshops, seminars and expert panels will take you through writing in many genres including fiction, creative nonfiction, screenwriting, poetry, journalism and business and technical writing. There will be many Q&A panels for you to ask the experts all your questions." Site: Sam's Town Hotel and Gambling Hall in Las Vegas.

Costs $375 Early Bird or $400 after February 1; One day registration $250.

Additional Information Sponsors contest. Agents and editors participate in conference.

▧ LEDIG HOUSE INTERNATIONAL WRITERS RESIDENCY

55 Fifth Ave., 15th Floor, New York NY 10003.Fax: (212) 206-6114. E-mail: writers@artomi.org. Website: www.artomi.org/ledig. Residency duration: 2 weeks to 2 months. Average attendance: Up to 20 writers per session. Residency. Site: "Up to 20 writers per session—10 at a given time—live and write on the stunning 300 acre grounds and sculpture park that overlooks the Catskill Mountains."

Accommodations Residents provide their own transportation. Offers overnight accommodations.

Additional Information "Agents and editors from the New York publishing community are invited for dinner and discussion. Bicycles, a swimming pool, and nearby tennis court are available for use."

LESLEY UNIVERSITY WRITER'S CONFERENCE

29 Everett Street, Cambridge MA 02138. (617) 349 8298. Fax: (617) 349-8335. E-mail: jwadling@lesley.edu. Website: www.lesley.edu/info/luwc. **Contact:** Joyce Wadlington, director continuing education. Estab. 2007. Annual. 2009 Conference July 26-July 31. Conference duration: one week. Average attendance: 40-60 people. Workshop/residency. "We focus on fiction, nonfiction, children's book writing, and poetry." Workshop limit: 10. Site: Lesley University Campus, Cambridge, MA. 2009 faculty included Marcie Hershman (Safe in America), Michael Lowenthal (Charity Girl), Afas M. Weaver (Timber and Prayer, 1996 Pulitzer Prize finalist), and David Elliot (And Here's to You !). Guest faculty included Julia Glass (Three Junes, 2002 National Book Award), M.T. Anderson (Octavian Nothing, 2006 National Book Award for Young People), and Gail Mazur (Nightfire).

Costs 2009: tuition $770 plus $30 registration fee.

Accommodations Participants commute or stay in the residence halls; commuter and resident meal plans are available. Parking available for a fee.

Additional Information Admission is selective and based on evaluation of applicant's work. For brochure, call or e-mail.

THE MACDOWELL COLONY

100 High St., Peterborough NH 03458. (603) 924-3886. Fax: (603) 924-9142. E-mail: admissions@macdowellcolony.org. Website: www.macdowellcolony.org. **Contact:** Admissions Director. Estab. 1907. Open to writers and playwrights, composers, visual artists, film/video artists, interdisciplinary artists and architects. Site: includes main building, library, 3 residence halls and 32 individual studios on over 450 mostly wooded acres, 1 mile from center of small town in southern New Hampshire. Available up to 8 weeks year-round. Provisions for the writer include meals, private sleeping room, individual secluded studio. Accommodates variable number of writers, 10 to 20 at a time.

Costs "There are no residency fees. Grants for travel to and from the Colony are available based on need. The MacDowell Colony is pleased to offer grants up to $1,000 for artists in need of financial assistance during a residency at MacDowell. At the present time, only artists reviewed and accepted by the admissions panel are eligible for this grant." Application forms available. Application deadline: January 15 for summer (June 1-Sept. 30), April 15 for fall (Oct. 1-Jan. 31), September 15 for winter/spring (Feb. 1-May 31). Submit 6 copies of a writing sample, no more than 25 pages. Please refer to work sample guidelines. Work in progress strongly recommended. Brochure/guidelines available; SASE required for return of work sample.

▧ ✦ ♿ MANITOBA COMIC CON AND SCI-FI EXPO

Winnipeg Convention Centre, 375 York Ave, Winnipeg MB. E-mail: michael@manitobacomiccon.com. Website: http://manitobacomiccon.com. Annual conference and expo in October. Conference duration: 2 days.

Costs $12.50; $7.50 one day only.

Accommodations Does not offer overnight accommodations. Provides list of area hotels or lodging options.

MARYMOUNT MANHATTAN COLLEGE WRITERS' CONFERENCE

Marymount Manhattan College, 221 E. 71st St., New York NY 10021. (212)774-4810. Fax: 212-774-0792. E-mail: lfrumkes@mmm.edu. **Contact:** Lewis Burke Frumkes or Karen Arfi. Estab. 1993. Annual. June. Conference duration: "Actual conference is one day, and there is a three-day intensive preceeding." Average attendance: 200. "We present workshops on several different writing genres and panels on publicity, editing and literary agents." Site: College/auditorium setting. 2008 conference featured 2 fiction panels, a children's book writing panel, a mystery/thriller panel and a literary agent panel.

Keynote speaker for 2008 was Stuart Woods. The conference itself included more than 50 authors.
Costs $175, includes lunch and reception.
Accommodations Provides list of area lodging.
Additional Information 2009 conference information will be available in March by fax or phone. Also accepts inquiries by e-mail. Editors and agents sometimes attend conference.

MAUI WRITERS CONFERENCE AND RETREAT

Kihei HI 96753. (808)879-0061. Fax: (808)879-6233. E-mail: writers@mauiwriters.com. Website: www.mauiwriters.com. Contact: Shannon Tullius, director. Estab. 1992. Annual. Retreat and Conference. Average attendance: 1,200 conference; 200 retreat. Conference covers fiction, nonfiction, screenwriting, playwriting, children's books. Site: Wailea Marriot Resort, "Four Diamond Resort on beach in Maui, Hawaii. Dozens of speakers, panels and workshops cover all aspects of writing and publishing fiction."
Costs See Web site for current rates.
Accommodations Offers "heavily discounted rates at Wailea Marriot Resort and Maui area condos."
Additional Information Sponsors a contest. Submit 12 pages of fiction. Judged by NY Times bestselling authors. Over $4,000 in cash prizes available. Must be attendee to participate. Guidelines/brochure available throughout the year. Send a request by letter, e-mail, fax or visit Web site. Accepts inquiries by phone, fax, e-mail or mail. "More than 50 agents and editors attend conference."

▒ ⬚ MEGACON

5757 74th Trace, Live Oak FL 32060.(386)364-1826. Fax: (386)364-1828. E-mail: info@megaconvention.com. Website: www.megaconvention.com. Annual. March 10-11, 2010. Conference duration: 3 days. "MegaCon is the southeast's largest comic book, science fiction/fantasy, anime, gaming, toys multimedia event!"
Costs $52.19 for three days; $22.37 for one day ticket in advance.

MENDOCINO COAST WRITERS CONFERENCE

College of the Redwoods, 1211 Del Mar Drive, Fort Bragg CA 95437. (707) 962-2600 ext 2167. E-mail: info@mcwc.org. Website: www.mcwc.org. **Contact:** Barbara Lee, registrar. Estab. 1989. Annual. Last conference held August 2008. Average attendance: 100. "We hope to encourage the developing writer by inviting presenters who are both fine writers and excellent teachers." Site: College of the Redwoods is a small community college located on the gorgeous northern California coast. Focuses are fiction, poetry, creative nonfiction, memoir. Special areas have included children's (2003), mystery (2002), social awareness (2007). In 200 8 faculty included James D. Houston, Jody Gehrman, Michael Datcher, Daphne Gottlieb, Amy Stewart, Susan Wooldridge, Jenoyne Adams, Marianne Villaneuva.
Costs Before June 15, 200 8: $450.00; after June 15: $495.00
Additional Information Brochures for the conference will be available in March by SASE, phone, e-mail or on the Web site. Agents and editors participate in the conference. "The conference is small, friendly and fills up fast with many returnees."

▒ ⬚ MID-OHIO-CON

(203)724-1698. Fax: (203)724-4185. E-mail: info@midohiocon.com. Website: www.midohiocon.com. Conference held annually in October."Now in its 28th consecutive year, Mid-Ohio-Con is one of America's longest-running and most successful comic book and pop-culture conventions, carrying on a fun and family-oriented tradition of bringing fans of all ages together with leading comic book writers and artists, film and television stars and creators, and publishers and retailers from across the nation."
Costs $25 for both days; $15 for Saturday or Sunday only.
Additional Information For brochure, visit Web site.

MIDWEST WRITERS WORKSHOP

Dept. of Journalism, Ball State University, Muncie IN 47306. (765) 282-1055. Fax: (765) 285-5997. E-mail: info@midwestwriters.org. Website: www.midwestwriters.org. **Contact:** Jama Bigger. Estab. 1974. Annual. Workshops is last weekend of July. Average attendance: 150. Site: Conference held at New Alumni Center, Ball State University.
Costs $295 for 3-day workshop; $100 for 1-day Intensive Session including opening reception, hospitality room and closing banquet.
Accommodations Special hotel rates offered.

Additional Information Manuscript evaluation for extra fee. Conference brochures/guidelines are available for SASE.

⊠ MONTEVALLO LITERARY FESTIVAL

Station 6420, University of Montevallo, Montevallo AL 35115.(205) 665-6420. Fax: (205) 665-6422. E-mail: murphyj@montevallo.edu. Website: www.montevallo.edu/english. **Contact:** Dr. Jim Murphy, director. Estab. 2003. Annual. Last festival held: April 18-19, 2008. Average attendance: 60-100. "Readings, panels, and workshops on all literary genres and on literary editing/publishing. Workshops with manuscript critiques in fiction, poetry, and drama." Site: Several sites on a bucolic liberal arts university campus. 2008 fiction workshop leader was Inman Majors. Past fiction workshop faculty included Patricia Foster, Tom Franklin, Sheri Joseph, Sena Jeter Naslund, Brad Vice, Brad Watson, and John Dufresne. See Web site for 2008 dates and speakers.
Costs In 2007: $45 for festival, including meals; $95 for festival, including meals and workshop.
Accommodations Free on-campus parking. Offers overnight accommodations at Ramsay Conference Center on campus. Rooms $40/night. Call (205)665-6280 for reservations. Visit www.montevallo.edu/cont_ed/ramsay.shtm for information.
Additional Information Workshop participants submit up to 5 pages of poetry/up to 15 pages of prose; e-mail as Word doc to Jim Murphy (murphyj@montevallo.edu) at least 2 weeks prior to festival. Information for upcoming festival available in February For brochure, visit Web site. Accepts inquiries by mail (with SASE), e-mail, phone, and fax. Editors participate in conference. "This is a friendly, relaxed 2-day festival dedicated to bringing literary writers and readers together on a personal scale."

MONTROSE CHRISTIAN WRITER'S CONFERENCE

5 Locust Street, Montrose Bible Conference, Montrose PA 18801-1112. (570) 278-1001 or (800) 598-5030. Fax: (570) 278-3061. E-mail: mbc@montrosebible.org. Website: www.montrosebible.org. **Contact:** Donna Kosik, MBC Secretary/Registrar. Estab. 1990. Annual. Conference held in July. Average attendance: 85. "We try to meet a cross-section of writing needs, for beginners and advanced, covering fiction, poetry and writing for children. It is small enough to allow personal interaction between conferees and faculty. We meet in the beautiful village of Montrose, Pennsylvania, situated in the mountains. The Bible Conference provides hotel/motel-like accommodation and good food. The main sessions are held in the chapel with rooms available for other classes. Fiction writing has been taught each year."
Costs In 2008 registration (tuition) was $150.
Accommodations Will meet planes in Binghamton, NY and Scranton, PA. On-site accomodations: room and board $260-305/conference; $60-70/day including food (2008 rates). RV court available.
Additional Information "Writers can send work ahead of time and have it critiqued for a small fee." The attendees are usually church related. The writing has a Christian emphasis. Conference information available in April. For brochure send SASE, visit Web site, e-mail, call or fax. Accepts inquiries by SASE, e-mail, fax, phone.

MOONLIGHT AND MAGNOLIAS WRITER'S CONFERENCE

Georgia Romance Writers, 2173 Indian Shoals Drive, Loganville GA 30052. E-mail: info@georgiaromancewriters.org. Website: www.georgiaromancewriters.org. **Contact:** Pam Mantovani. Estab. 1982. Annual. Last conference held October 3-5, 2008, in the Westin Atlanta North Hotel in Atlanta, GA. Average attendance: 175. "Conference focuses on writing of women's fiction with emphasis on romance. Includes agents and editors from major publishing houses. Previous workshops have included: beginning writer sessions, research topics, writng basics and professional issues for the published author; plus specialty sessions on writing young adult, multi-cultural, inspirational and Regency. Speakers have included experts in law enforcement, screenwriting and research. Literary raffle and advertised speaker and GRW member autographing open to the public. Published authors make up 25-30% of attendees." Brochures available for SASE in June.
Costs $170 GRW member/$180 nonmember for conference registration. Check Web site for current conference fees, hotel rates and registration forms.
Additional Information Maggie Awards for excellence are presented to unpublished writers. The Maggie Award for published writers is limited to Region 3 members of Romance Writers of America. Deadline for published Maggie is May 2. Deadline for unpublished Maggies is June 1. Entry forms and guidelines available on Web site. Published authors judge first round, category editors judge finals. Guidelines available for SASE in Spring.

MOUNT HERMON CHRISTIAN WRITERS CONFERENCE

P.O. Box 413, Mount Hermon CA 95041-0413. (831)335-4466. Fax: (831)335-9413. E-mail: info@ mhcamps.org. Website: www.mounthermon.org/writers. **Contact:** Rachel Williams, Director. Estab. 1970. Annual. Held Palm Sunday weekend, Friday through Tuesday. "A working, how-to conference with over 10 major morning tracks and 70 options afternoon workshops about the craft of writing fiction, children's books, poetry, nonfiction, articles, and educational curriculum, with varying levels of writing proficiency addressed. Site: "The conference is sponsored by and held at the 440-acre Mount Hermon Christian Conference Center near San Jose, California, in the heart of the coastal redwoods. The faculty/ student ratio is about 1:6 or 7. Faculty is made up of editors and publisher representatives from major Christian publishing houses nationwide."

Costs Registration fees include tuition, all major morning sessions, keynote sessions, and refreshment breaks. Room and board varies depending on choice of housing options. See Web site for current costs.

Accommodations Registrants stay in hotel-style accommodations, and full board is provided as part of conference fees. Housing is not required of registrants, but about 96% of our registrants use Mount Hermon's housing facilities. Meals are buffet style, with faculty joining registrants and are required and included in fees. For those flying, shuttle service is available from the San Jose International airport. Check Web site for current cost of this service.

Additional Information Registrants may submit 2 mss for critique in advance of the conference. No advance work is required, however. Conference brochures/guidelines are available online annually in December. Accepts inquiries by e-mail, fax. "The residential nature of our conference makes this a unique setting for one-on-one interaction with faculty/staff. There is an intentional spiritual flavor to the conference, with genreal sessions by well-known speakers a highlight. Come rested, with plenty of business cards and samples of works in progress."

NATCHEZ LITERARY AND CINEMA CELEBRATION

P.O. Box 1307, Natchez MS 39121-1307. (601)446-1208. Fax: (601)446-1214. E-mail: carolyn.smith@colin. edu. Website: www.colin.edu/NLCC. **Contact:** Carolyn Vance Smith, co-chairman. Estab. 1990. Annual. Conference held February 25-28, 2010. Average attendance: 3,000. Conference focuses on "all literature, including film scripts." Site: 500-seat auditorium, various sizes of break-out rooms. Theme: "Southern Humor." Scholars will speak on humor in history, literature, film, and real life.

Costs "About $100, includes a meal, receptions, book signings, workshops. Lectures/panel discussions are free."

Accommodations "Groups can ask for special assistance. Usually they can be accommodated." Call 866-296-6522.

Additional Information "Conference information is available in Fall. For brochure send SASE, e-mail, visit Web site, call or fax. Accepts inquiries by SASE, e-mail, phone and fax. Agents and editors participate in conference.

NATIONAL WRITERS ASSOCIATION FOUNDATION CONFERENCE

10940 S. Parker Rd. #508, Parker CO 80138. (303) 841-0246. Fax: (303) 841-2607. E-mail: conference@ nationalwriters.com. Website: www.nationalwriters.com. **Contact:** Sandy Whelchel, executive director. Estab. 1926. Annual. Workshop held in June. Workshop duration: 1 day. Average attendance: 100. For general writing and marketing.

Costs $100 (approximately).

Additional Information Awards for previous contests will be presented at the workshop. Workshop information available annually in December. For brochures/guidelines send SASE, visit Web site, e-mail, fax or call.

THE NEW LETTERS WEEKEND WRITERS CONFERENCE

University of Missouri-Kansas City, College of Arts and Sciences Continuing Ed. Division, 5300 Rockhill Rd., Kansas City MO 64110-2499. (816) 235-2736. Fax: (816) 235-5279. Website: www.newletters.org. **Contact:** Robert Stewart. Estab. mid-'70s as The Longboat Key Writers Conference. Annual. Conference held in June. Conference duration: 3 days. Average attendance: 75. For "craft and the creative process in poetry, fiction, screenwriting, playwriting and journalism; but the program also deals with matters of psychology, publications and marketing. The conference is appropriate for both advanced and beginning writers." Site: "The conference meets at the beautiful Diastole conference center of The University of Missouri-Kansas City."

Costs Several options are available. Participants may choose to attend as a non-credit student or they may attend for 1-3 hours of college credit from the University of Missouri-Kansas City. Conference registration includes continental breakfasts, Saturday and Sunday lunch. For complete information, contact the university.

Accommodations Information on area accommodations is made available.

Additional Information Those registering for college credit are required to submit a ms in advance. Manuscript reading and critique are included in the credit fee. Those attending the conference for non-credit also have the option of having their ms critiqued for an additional fee. Accepts inquiries by phone, fax.

NIMROD ANNUAL WRITERS' WORKSHOP

University of Tulsa, 800 S. Tucker Dr., Tulsa OK 74104. (918)631-3080. Fax: (918)631-3033. E-mail: nimrod@utulsa.edu. Website: www.utulsa.edu/nimrod. **Contact:** Eilis O'Neal, managing editor. Estab. 1978. Annual. Conference held in October. Conference duration: 1 day. Average attendance: 150-200. Workshop in fiction and poetry. "Prize winners (Nimrod Prizes) conduct workshops as do contest judges." Past judges: Rosellen Brown, Stanley Kunitz, Toby Olson, Lucille Clifton, W.S. Merwin, Ron Carlson, Mark Doty, Anita Shreve and Francine Prose.

Costs Approximately $50. Lunch provided. Scholarships available for students.

Additional Information *Nimrod International Journal* sponsors *Nimrod* Literary Awards: The Katherine Anne Porter Prize for fiction and The Pablo Neruda Prize for poetry. Poetry and fiction prizes: $2,000 each and publication (1st prize); $1,000 each and publication (2nd prize). Deadline: must be postmarked no later than April 30.

NORTH CAROLINA WRITERS' NETWORK FALL CONFERENCE

P.O. Box 954, Carrboro NC 27510-0954. (919) 967-9540. Fax: (919) 929-0535. E-mail: ed@ncwriters.org. Website: www.ncwriters.org. **Contact:** Ed Southern, executive director. Estab. 1985. Annual. Average attendance: 350. "The NCWN Fall Conference is a weekend of workshops, discussions, readings, and community-building. The Network's Fall Conference serves writers at all levels of skill and experience, from novices to published professionals. We offer workshops in fiction, nonfiction, poetry, drama, children's writing, journalism, and the publishing business. We make available agents and editors for one-on-one sessions with prospective authors." Site: "The Fall Conference is held at a different hotel conference center each year, so that it reaches all regions of North Carolina."

Costs $200-400 depending on meals and extra sessions desired.

Accommodations "Special conference hotel rates are available, but the individual makes his/her own reservations."

Additional Information "Visit Web site for more information, including faculty roster, class listings, and secure online registration form."

THE NOVEL WRITERS WORKSHOP

P.O. Box 392, Langley WA 98260. E-mail: bob@bobmayer.org. Website: www.bobmayer.org. **Contact:** Bob Mayer. Estab. 2002. Conference duration: 4 days. Average attendance: limit of 8 attendees.

Costs $550 in 2008.

Accommodations Does not include overnight accommodations. Provides list of area hotels or lodging options.

Additional Information Participants submit cover letter, one page synopsis, and first 15 pages of ms. For brochure, visit Web site.

N ☑ NYC PITCH AND SHOP CONFERENCE

Ripley Greer studios, 520 Eighth Avenue, 16th Floor, NY. (800)250-8290. E-mail: algonkian@webdelsol. com. Website: http://nycpitchconference.com/index.htm. Conference duration: Thursday through Sunday. Average attendance: maximum 60 writers; workshops divided into 15 writers each. "The NYC Pitch and Shop promotes aspiring authors writing in the genres of commercial and literary fiction, serious and light women's fiction, historical fiction, mystery/thriller and detective, high-concept young adult, as well as memoir and narrative nonfiction. The conference provides writers with the skills and knowledge necessary to stand a realistic chance of success in today's tough novel market." Site: All NYC Pitch and Shop conferences take place at the Ripley Greer studios located near Madison Square Garden and Penn Station.

Costs "Following successful application, the registration fee for the conference is $595. This fee covers all conference pitch sessions and workshops."

Accommodations Does not offer overnight accommodations. Provides list of area hotels or lodging options.

Additional Information Upon registration, writers will receive pre-conference pitch assignments. For brochure, visit Web site. Agents and editors participate in conference.

NY STATE SUMMER WRITERS INSTITUTE

Skidmore College, 815 N. Broadway, Saratoga Springs NY 12866. (518)580-5593. Fax: (518)580-5548. E-mail: cmerrill@skidmore.edu. Website: www.skidmore.edu/summer. **Contact:** Christine Merrill, program coordinator. Estab. 1987. Annual. Conference duration: Two-week or four-week session. Average attendance: 80 per two-week session. This event features fiction, nonfiction, poetry and short story workshops. College credit is available for four-week attendees. Site: held on Skidmore campus—dorm residency and dining hall meals. "Summer in Saratoga is beautiful." Past faculty has included Amy Hempel, Nick Delbanco, Margot Livesey, Jay McInerney, Rick Moody and Lee K. Abbott. Visiting faculty has included Joyce Carol Oates, Russell Banks, Ann Beattie, Michael Cunningham and Michael Ondaatje.

Additional Information For pricing information and how to apply, visit the Web site.

ODYSSEY FANTASY WRITING WORKSHOP

P.O. Box 75, Mont Vernon NH 03057-1420. Phone/fax: (603) 673-6234. E-mail: jcavelos@sff.net. Website: www.odysseyworkshop.org. **Contact:** Jeanne Cavelos, director. Estab. 1996. Annual. Last workshop held June 8 to July 17, 2009. Conference duration: 6 weeks. Average attendance: limited to 16. "A workshop for fantasy, science fiction and horror writers that combines an intensive learning and writing experience with in-depth feedback on students' manuscripts. The only six-week workshop to combine the overall guidance of a single instructor with the varied perspectives of guest lecturers. Also, the only such workshop run by a former New York City book editor." Site: conference held at Saint Anselm College in Manchester, New Hampshire. Previous guest lecturers included: George R.R. Martin, Harlan Ellison, Ben Bova, Dan Simmons, Jane Yolen, Elizabeth Hand, Terry Brooks, Nancy Kress, Patricia McKillip and John Crowley.

Costs In 2008: $1,800 tuition, $700 housing (double room), $1,400 (single room); $25 application fee, $500-600 food (approximate), $210 processing fee to receive college credit.

Accommodations "Workshop students stay at Saint Anselm College Apartments and eat at college."

Additional Information Students must apply and include a writing sample. Application deadline April 10. Students' works are critiqued throughout the 6 weeks. Workshop information available in October. For brochure/guidelines send SASE, e-mail, visit Web site, call or fax. Accepts inquiries by SASE, e-mail, fax, phone.

OPEN WRITING WORKSHOPS

Creative Writing Program, Department of English, Bowling Green State University, Bowling Green OH 43403. (419) 372-8370. Fax: (419)372-6805. E-mail: masween@bgsu.edu. Website: www.bgsu.edu/departments/creative-writing/. "Check our Web site for next workshop dates." Conference duration: 1 day. Average attendance: 10-15. Workshop covers fiction and poetry. Site: Workshops are held in a conference room, roundtable setting, on the campus of Bowling Green State University. Provides close reading and ms critique. Spring 2009 faculty will include fiction writer Wendell Mayo and poet/editor Abbie Cloud.

Costs $50 for workshop; does not include lodging or other services; $35 for alums and students.

Accommodations Parking provided on campus.

Additional Information Participants need to submit workshop material prior to conference. Fiction or non-fiction: 1 story, 15 pages double-spaced maximum; send 2 copies. Poetry: 3 poems, a total of 100 lines for all 3; send 2 copies. "Deadlines are set about 3 weeks before the workshop. This gives us time to copy all the manuscripts and mail to all participants with detailed instructions." For brochure or inquiries, e-mail, visit Web site, call or fax. "These are no-nonsense workshops whose purpose is to 'open' doors for writers who are writing in comparative isolation. We provide guidance on preparation of manuscripts for publication as well."

OXFORD CONFERENCE FOR THE BOOK

Center for the Study of Southern Culture, The University of Mississippi, University MS 38677-1848. (662)915-5993. Fax: (662)915-5814. E-mail: aabadie@olemiss.edu. Website: www.olemiss.edu/depts/ south or www.oxfordconferenceforthebook.com. **Contact:** Ann J. Abadie, associate director. Estab. 1993. Annual. Conference held in March or April. Average attendance: 300. "The conference celebrates books, writing and reading and deals with practical concerns on which the literary arts depend, including literacy, freedom of expression and the book trade itself. Each year's program consists of readings, lectures and discussions. Areas of focus are fiction, poetry, nonfiction and—occasionally—drama. We have, on occasion, looked at science fiction and mysteries. We always pay attention to children's literature." Site: University of Mississippi campus. Annual topics include Submitting Manuscripts/Working One's Way into Print; Finding a Voice/Reaching an Audience; The Endangered Species: Readers Today and Tomorrow. The 2009 program, March 26-28, was dedicated to Mississippi Gold Coast artist, author, and naturalist Walter Inglis Anderson (1903-1965). Among the more than 50 speakers scheduled to appear were authors Jay Asher, Patti Carr Black, Hodding Carter III, Major Jackson, Haven Kimmel, David Maraniss, Christopher Maurer, Lydia Millet, Jack Pendarvis, Patricia Pinson, Peggy Whitman Prenshaw, Julia Reed, and Trenton Lee Stewart. Also on the program were editors John Freeman, Terry McDonell, and JoAnne Pritchard Morris.

Costs "The conference is open to participants without charge."

Accommodations Provides list of area hotels.

Additional Information Brochures available in February by e-mail, on Web Site, by phone, by fax. Accepts inquiries by e-mail, phone, fax. Agents and editors participate in conference.

PACIFIC NORTHWEST WRITERS CONFERENCE

PMB 2717-1420 NW Gilman Blvd., Ste 2, Issaquah, WA 98027. (425)673-2665. Fax: (206)824-4559. E-mail: pnwa@pnwa.org. Website: www.pnwa.org. Annual. 2009 conference held July 30-August 2, 2009 at Seattle Airport Hilton, Seattle, WA 98188. Average attendance: 450. "Meet agents and editors, learn craft from renowned authors, uncover new marketing secrets, and more."

Additional Information Literary Contest featuring 12 categories: Mainstream, Inspirational, Romance, Mystery/Thriller, Science Fiction/Fantasy, Young Adult Novel, Nonfiction Book/Memoir, Screen Writing, Poetry, Short Story, Children's Picture Book or Chapter Book, Adult Short Topics (article, essay, short memoir). Contest deadline: February 20, 2009. For Conference and Contest information please visit Web site.

PIKES PEAK

4164 Austin Bluffs Parkway #246, Colorado Springs CO 80918.(719)531-5723. E-mail: info@ pikespeakwriters.com. Website: http://pikespeakwriters.com. Annual. Conference duration: 3 days. Conference. "The Pikes Peak Writers Conference is a project of the Pikes Peak Writers, a nonprofit organization. This conference is underwritten by the Marriott Hotel in Colorado Springs and sponsored by the Imagination Celebration."

Accommodations Offers overnight accommodations.

Additional Information For brochure, visit Web site. Agents and editors participate in conference.

PIMA WRITERS' WORKSHOP

Pima Community College, 2202 W. Anklam Road, Tucson AZ 85709-0170. (520)206-6084. Fax: (520)206-6020. E-mail: mfiles@pima.edu. **Contact:** Meg Files, director. Estab. 1988. Annual. Conference held in May. Average attendance: 300. "For anyone interested in writing—beginning or experienced writer. The workshop offers sessions on writing short stories, novels, nonfiction articles and books, children's and juvenile stories, poetry, screenplays." Site: Sessions are held in the Center for the Arts on Pima Community College's West campus. Past speakers include Michael Blake, Ron Carlson, Gregg Levoy, Nancy Mairs, Linda McCarriston, Jerome Stern, Connie Willis, Larry McMurtry, Barbara Kingsolver and Robert Morgan.

Costs $80 (can include ms critique). Participants may attend for college credit, Meals and accommodations not included.

Accommodations Information on local accommodations is made available and special workshop rates are available at a specified motel close to the workshop site (about $70/night).

Additional Information Participants may have up to 20 pages critiqued by the author of their choice.

Manuscripts must be submitted 3 weeks before the workshop. Conference brochure/guidelines available for SASE. Accepts inquiries by e-mail. "The workshop atmosphere is casual, friendly and supportive, and guest authors are very accessible. Readings, films and panel discussions are offered as well as talks and manuscript sessions."

ℕ POINT LOMA WRITERS CONFERENCE

2020 Pennsylvania Ave. NW Suite 443, Washington DC 20006.1-800-250-8290. E-mail: algonkian@ webdelsol.com. Website: http://algonkianconferences.com/PointLomaWritersConference/. Feb. 25-Mar. 1, 2009. Conference duration: 5 days. Average attendance: 15 maximum students. Conference. "Using our unique model-and-context method, Algonkian students will study and apply techniques of craft, structure, and style culled from over 20 successful authors (and dramatists) including Ann Patchett, Ken Kesey, Annie Proulx, F. Scott Fitzgerald, Tennessee Williams, Michael Chabon, Gail Godwin, Ernest Hemingway, V. Nabokov, Flannery O'Connor, Barbara Kingsolver, and Robert Graves."

Costs $965

Accommodations Offers overnight accommodations. "Price includes tuition, shuttle transportation from the airport, private room and bath for five nights, agent pitch sessions, breakfast and lunch, dinner on Friday night, the Algonkian workshop book, 'Immersed in The Art of Fiction.'"

Additional Information For more information, visit Web site.

THE POWER OF WORDS

Goddard College, 123 Pitkin Rd., Plainfield VT 05667. (802) 454-8311, x204. E-mail: TLAconference@ goddard.edu. Website: www.tlanetwork.org/conference. **Contact:** Heather A. Mandell, TLA network coordinator. Estab. 2003. Annual. Last conference held September 3-7, 2009. Conference duration: 4 days. Average attendance: 150. "Purpose is to explore social and personal transformation through the spoken, written and sung word and to share resources for making a living using writing, storytelling, drama, narrative medicine, etc. in local communities." Site: A small college campus nestled in the Green Mountains of Vermont; campus was once historic farm, and historic buildings still in use—features woodlands (with trails), dorms, meeting halls and offices. Keynoters for 2009: Lewis Mehl-Madrona, MD; Kayhan Irani; John Fox, founder of Poetic Medicine; Dovie Thomason; Caryn Mirrian-Goldberg, founder of the Transformative Language Arts Network; Sherry Reiter; Terry Hauptman; and Callid Keefe and Kristina Perry, plus 25 other writers, storytellers, and performers TBA.

Costs $220 early bird special by March 15; $250 until July 15; /$280 thereafter.

Accommodations Offers overnight accommodations. Average is $40-60/night plus $12/meal.

Additional Information Submit workshop proposals prior to conference; deadline for proposals is January 15. Visit Web site for more information.

THE PUBLISHING GAME

Peanut Butter and Jelly Press, P.O. Box 590239, Newton MA 02459. E-mail: alyza@publishinggame.com. Website: www.publishinggame.com. **Contact:** Alyza Harris, manager. Estab. 1998. Monthly. Conference held monthly, in different locales across North America: Boston, New York City, Philadelphia, Washington DC, Boca Raton, San Francisco, Los Angeles, Toronto, Seattle, Chicago. Conference duration: 9 a.m. to 4 p.m. Maximum attendance: 18 writers. "A one-day workshop on finding a literary agent, self-publishing your book, creating a publishing house and promoting your book to bestsellerdom!" Site: "Elegant hotels across the country. Boston locations alternate between the Four Seasons Hotel in downtown Boston and The Inn at Harvard in historic Harvard Square, Cambridge." Fiction panels in 2005 included Propel Your Novel from Idea to Finished Manuscript; How to Self-Publish Your Novel; Craft the Perfect Book Package; How to Promote Your Novel; Selling Your Novel to Bookstores and Libraries. Workshop led by Fern Reiss, author and publisher of The Publishing Game series.

Costs $195.

Accommodations "All locations are easily accessible by public transportation." Offers discounted conference rates for participants who choose to arrive early. Offers list of area lodging.

Additional Information Brochures available for SASE. Accepts inquiries by SASE, e-mail, phone, fax, but e-mail preferred. Agents and editors attend conference. "If you're considering finding a literary agent, self-publishing your novel or just want to sell more copies of your book, this conference will teach you everything you need to know to successfully publish and promote your work."

▣ THE RAGDALE FOUNDATION

1260 North Green Bay Road, Lake Forest IL 60045. (847)234-1036 ext. 206. Fax: (847)234-1063. E-mail: admissions@ragdale.org. Website: www.ragdale.org. **Contact:** Director of the Artist-In-Residence Program. Estab. 1976. Conference duration: Residencies are 2-8 weeks in length, year-round. Average attendance: 12 artists, writers and composers at one time; nearly 200 residents per year. "Emerging and established artists, writers and composers from all over the world apply for residencies, in order to be awarded time and space to focus on their work and escape day-to-day distractions." Site: Ragdale is located 30 miles north of Chicago. Arts and crafts architect Howard Van Doren Shaw designed two of the main residency buildings. Twelve people are in residence at any given time. It is an historical, home-like setting adjacent to 55 acres of preserved prairie. Dinners are prepared and communal 6 nights a week.

Costs The application fee is $30. The residency fee is just $25/day even though the actual cost to Ragdale is $240/day. The fee includes food and a private room in which to work.

Additional Information "Interested people must submit materials according to application guidelines. Applications may be attained from the Web site, by e-mail or phone request. For brochure, send SASE, call, e-mail, visit Web site. "The small group atmosphere is conducive to productivity, inspiration, interaction (if desired) and creative exploration."

REMEMBER THE MAGIC IWWG ANNUAL SUMMER CONFERENCE

International Women's Writing Guild, P.O. Box 810, Gracie Station, New York NY 10028-0082. (212)737-7536. Fax: (212)737-9469. Website: www.iwwg.org. **Contact:** Hannelore Hahn. Estab. 1978. Annual. Conference held in the summer. Conference duration: 1 week. Average attendance: 450. The conference features 65 workshops held every day on every aspect of writing and the arts. Site: Saratoga Springs, 30 minutes from Albany, NY, and 4 hours from New York City. Conference is held "on the tranquil campus of Skidmore College in Saratoga Springs, where the serene Hudson Valley meets the North Country of the Adirondacks."

Costs $1,085 single, $945 double (members); $1,130 single, $990 double (non-members). Five day, weekend and commuter rates are also available. Includes meals and lodging.

Accommodations Modern, air-conditioned and non-air-conditioned dormitories—single and/or double occupancy. Equipped with spacious desks and window seats for gazing out onto nature. Meals served cafeteria-style with choice of dishes. Variety of fresh fruits, vegetables and salads have been found plentiful, even by vegetarians. Conference information is available now. For brochure send SASE, e-mail, visit Web site or fax. Accepts inquiries by SASE, e-mail, phone or fax. "The conference is for women only."

ROMANCE WRITERS OF AMERICA NATIONAL CONFERENCE

14615 Benfer Rd., Houston TX 77069. (832)717-5200, ext.121. Fax: (832)717-5201. E-mail: info@rwanational.com. Website: www.rwanational.org. **Contact:** Nicole Kennedy, PR manager. Estab. 1981. Annual. Average attendance: 2,000. Over 100 workshops on the craft of writing, researching and the business side of being a working writer. Publishing professionals attend and accept appointments. Site: Conference held in Washington DC in 2009 and Nashville in 2010. Keynote speaker for 2009 was New York Times bestselling author Linda Howard.

Costs In 2009, early registration was $425 for RWA members and $500 for nonmembers.

Additional Information Annual RITA awards are presented for romance authors. Annual Golden Heart awards are presented for unpublished writers. Conference brochures/guidelines and registration forms are available on Web site in January. Accepts inquiries by SASE, e-mail, fax, phone.

▣ SAGE HILL WRITING EXPERIENCE

Box 1731, Saskatoon SK S7K 3S1 Canada. Phone: (306) 652-7395. E-mail: sage.hill@sasktel.net. Website: www.sagehillwriting.ca. **Contact:** Paula Jane Remlinger. Annual. Workshops held in July and May. Conference duration: 10-14 days. Average attendance: Summer, 30-40; Spring, 6-8. "Sage Hill Writing Experience offers a special working and learning opportunity to writers at different stages of development. Top quality instruction, low instructor-student ratio and the beautiful Sage Hill setting offer conditions ideal for the pursuit of excellence in the arts of fiction, and poetry." Site: The Sage Hill location features "individual accommodation, in-room writing area, lounges, meeting rooms, healthy meals, walking woods and vistas in several directions." Various classes are held: Introduction to Writing Fiction & Poetry; Fiction Workshop; Fiction Colloquium, Poetry Workshop; Poetry Colloquium; Writing for Young Adults Lab.

Costs Summer program, $1,095 (Canadian) includes instruction, accommodation, meals and all facilities. Spring Colloquium: $1,395 (Canadian).

Accommodations On-site individual accommodations for Summer and Fall programs located at Lumsden, 45 kilometers outside Regina.

Additional Information Application requirements for Introduction to Creative Writing: A 5-page sample of your writing or a statement of your interest in creative writing; list of courses taken required. For workshop and colloquium programs: A résumé of your writing career and a 12-page sample of your work-in-progress, plus 5 pages of published work required. Application deadline for the Summer Program is in April. Spring program deadline in March. Guidelines are available for SASE, e-mail, fax, phone or on Web site. Scholarships and bursaries are available.

SAN FRANCISCO WRITERS CONFERENCE

1029 Jones St, San Francisco CA 94109. (415) 673-0939 or (866) 862-739. Fax: (415) 673-0367. E-mail: sfwriters@aol.com. Website: http://www.sfwriters.org. **Contact:** Elizabeth Pomada. Estab. 2004. Annual. President's Day weekend. Conference duration: 3 days. Average attendance: 350-400. "Focus is on WRITING and PUBLISHING. Attendees learn from bestselling authors, literary agents, and editors. The emphasis is on producing the best possible work and finding the most effective way to get it published from traditional (major publishers to specialty houses are always at the event) to self-publishing (iUniverse is a sponsor) and cutting edge venues (including Web sites/blogging)." The event is held at the Mark Hopkins Hotel in San Francisco. "It is an elegant and historic venue at the top of Nob Hill. General sessions, keynotes and luncheons are in the Ballroom with breakout sessions in smaller rooms at the hotel. Previous panels include A Conversation on Writing (Gail Tsukiyama and Karen Joy Fowler) and Writing for Children (Lemony Snickett). Previous topics include: Romance (Passion on the Page), How to Write a Fiction Query Letter, Workshops on Plot/Dialogue/Characterization, The Art of Literary Fiction, The Perfect Murder. The founders of SFWC are Elizabeth Pomada (fiction and nonfiction literary agent) and Michael Larsen (agent and author of many writing related books including Guerrilla Marketing for Writers). Presenters for 2009 included Sheldon Siegel (The Confession), Richard Paul Evans (The Christmas Box), Jane Smiley, dozens of literary agents and editors from top publishing houses including St. Martin's, Penguin, Random House, John Wiley & Sons, and New World Library. (Nearly 100 presenters)

Costs 2010 fee is $595 (early sign-up discounts available).

Accommodations BART trains bring attendees arriving at SFO or Oakland airports to downtown San Francisco. Then use cable car or taxi from there to hotel. Does not offer overnight accommodations. "All sessions are held at the Mark Hopkins Hotel, so make reservations there or at a nearby hotel. Mark Hopkins is offering an attendee rate of just $152 a night rate (based on availability)!"

Additional Information No application needed. Sponsors contest. This contest is judged by literary agents. For brochure, visit Web site. Agents and editors participate in conference. "San Francisco Writers Conference has over 100 editors, agents, authors and book marketing professionals as its faculty each year! Additionally we limit our attendance to 300 for the best one-on-one interaction during the event. It is truly one of the best events for advancing writing careers."

N SANIBEL ISLAND WRITERS CONFERENCE

10501 FGCU Blvd. South, Fort Myers FL 33965-6565. (239)590-7421. E-mail: tdemarch@fgcu.edu. Website: www.fgcu.edu/siwc. **Contact:** Tom DeMarchi, conference director. Estab. 2006. Held annually in November. Average attendance: 150. Conference site: Big Arts of Sanibel. Conference themes for 2009 were: Fiction, Memoir, Poetry, Creative Nonfiction, Journalism, Songwriting, Screenwriting, Children's Literature, Young Adult, Freelancing, Finding an Agent, Comic Writing. Past conference and workshop leaders were Steve Almond, Julianna Baggott, Lynne Barrett, Ishmael Beah, Dan Bern, John Brandon, Christine Buckley, Tom Chiarella, John Dufresne, William Giraldi, Sue Henshon, David Hilzenrath, Jeanne Leiby, Christopher Schelling, and more.

Accommodations $300-400 Offers overnight accommodations. West wind Inn of Sanibel or the Island Inn of Sanibel.

Additional Information Individual manuscript consultations are available on a first come, first serve basis. Conference information is available in February. Agents and editors participate in conference.

SANTA BARBARA CHRISTIAN WRITERS CONFERENCE

P.O. Box 40860, Santa Barbara CA 93140. (805)682-0316. **Contact:** Opal Dailey, director. Estab. 1997.

Conference held in October. Conference duration: 1 day. Average attendance: 60-70. Site: Westmont College, "liberal arts Christian College. Beautiful campus in the Montecito Foothills at Santa Barbara." **Costs** $99; $50 for second person if paid together. Includes continental breakfast, lunch and afternoon snack.

Additional Information Conference information available in May. For brochure, send SASE or call. Accepts inquiries by e-mail, SASE and phone. Agents and editors participate in conference.

⊠ SANTA BARBARA SUMMER WRITERS CONFERENCE

P.O. Box 6627, Santa Barbara CA 93160.(805)964-0367. E-mail: info@sbwriters.com. Website: www.sbwriters.com. Annual. June 20-25, 2009. Conference duration: 6 days. Conference. See web site for more details.

SCBWI SOUTHERN BREEZE FALL CONFERENCE

Writing and Illustrating for Kids '09, P.O. Box 26282, Birmingham AL 35260. E-mail: jskittinger@bellsouth.net. Website: www.southern-breeze.org. **Contact:** Jo Kittinger, co-regional advisor. Estab. 1992. Annual. Conference held the third Saturday in October. Average Attendance: 160. This conference is designed to educate and inspire creators of quality children's literature.

Costs: About $125 for SCBWI members, $145 for non-members.

Accommodations Nearby hotel offers a group rate to Southern Breeze conference attendees. The conference is held in a fabulous school.

Additional Information This Southern Breeze conference offers an amazing lineup of 28 workshops on craft and the business of writing and illustrating. Tracks are included for the novice or professional. Speakers generally include editors, agents, authors, art directors, writers, and illustrators - all professionals in children's books. Come prepared to be WOWED! Manuscript and portfolio critiques available for an additional fee; manuscripts must be sent by deadline. Conference information is included in the Southern Breeze News, mailed in September. Visit Web site for details. Accepts inquiries by SASE or e-mail.

SCBWI SOUTHERN BREEZE SPRINGMINGLE CONFERENCE

Springmingle '09, P.O. Box 26282, Birmingham AL 35260. E-mail: jskittinger@bellsouth.net. Website: www.southern-breeze.org. **Contact:** Jo Kittinger, co-regional advisor. Estab. 1992. Annual. Conference held the last full weekend each February (Friday PM - Sunday AM). Average Attendance: 160. This is a seminar designed to educate and inspire creators of quality children's literature.

Costs About $200; SCBWI non-members pay about $30 more. Some meals are included.

Accommodations Individuals make their own reservations. Ask for the Southern Breeze group rate in the conference site's hotel.

Additional Information Manuscript and portfolio critiques available for an additional fee. Mss must be sent ahead of time. Conference information is included in the Southern Breeze News, mailed in January. Visit Web site for details. Accepts inquiries by SASE, e-mail.

SCBWI/SUMMER ANNUAL CONFERENCE ON WRITING & ILLUSTRATING FOR CHILDREN

(formerly SCBWI/International Conference on Writing & Illustrating for Children), Society of Children's Book Writers and Illustrators, 8271 Beverly Blvd., Los Angeles CA 90048. (323)782-1010. Fax: (323)782-1892. E-mail: conference@scbwi.org. Website: www.scbwi.org. **Contact**: Lin Oliver, executive director. Estab. 1972. Annual. Conference held in August. Conference duration: 4 days. Average attendance: 800. Writer and illustrator workshops geared toward all levels. Covers all aspects of children's magazine and book publishing.

Costs Approximately $400; includes all 4 days and one banquet meal. Does not include hotel room.

Accommodations Information on overnight accommodations made available.

Additional Information Ms and illustration consultations are available. Brochure/guidelines available on Web site. SCBWI also holds an annual winter conference in New York City. See the listing in the Northeast section or visit Web site for details.

SCBWI WINTER CONFERENCE ON WRITING AND ILLUSTRATING FOR CHILDREN

(formerly SCBWI Midyear Conference), Society of Children's book Writers and Illustrators, 8271 Beverly Blvd., Los Angeles CA 90048. (323)782-1010. Fax: (323)782-1892. E-mail: conference@scbwi.org. Website: www.scbwi.org. **Contact**: Stephen Mooser. Estab. 2000. Annual. Conference held in February. Average attendance: 800. Conference is to promote writing and illustrating for children: picture books;

Conferences

fiction; nonfiction; middle grade and young adult; network with professionals; financial planning for writers; marketing your book; art exhibition; etc. Site: Manhattan.

Costs See Web site for current cost and conference information.

Additional Information SCBWI also holds an annual summer conference in August in Los Angeles. See the listing in the West section or visit Web site for details.

ℕ SCWG CONFERENCE

Holiday Inn, 1300 North Atlantic Ave., Cocoa Beach FL 32931.(321)956-7193. E-mail: scwg-jm@cfl. rr.com. Website: http://www.scwg.org/conference.asp. **Contact:** Judy Mammay. Annual. Conference duration: 2 days. Conference held the fourth weekend in January.

Costs $210 for guild members; $220 non-members. One day rates are available; see Web site for rates.

Additional Information Agents and editors participate in conference.

SEACOAST WRITERS ASSOCIATION SPRING AND FALL CONFERENCES

59 River Road, Stratham NH 03885-2358. E-mail: patparnell@comcast.net. **Contact:** Pat Parnell, conference coordinator. Annual. Conferences held in May and October. Conference duration: 1 day. Average attendance: 60. "Our conferences offer workshops covering various aspects of fiction, nonfiction and poetry." Site: Chester College of New England in Chester, New Hampshire.

Costs Approximately $50.

Additional Information "We sometimes include critiques. It is up to the workshop presenter." Spring meeting includes a contest. Categories are fiction, nonfiction (essays) and poetry. Judges vary from year to year. Conference and contest information available for SASE November 1, April 1, and September 1. Accepts inquiries by SASE, e-mail and phone. For further information, check the Web site www. seacoastwritersassociation.org.

SEWANEE WRITERS' CONFERENCE

735 University Ave., Sewanee TN 37383-1000. (931) 598-1141. E-mail: swc@sewanee.edu. Website: www. sewaneewriters.org. **Contact:** Cheri B. Peters, creative writing programs manager. Estab. 1990. Annual. Conference sessaions held each July. Average attendance: 150. "We offer genre-based workshops in fiction, poetry, and playwriting along with a full schedule of readings, craft lectures, panel discussions, talks, Q&A sessions along and the like." Site: "The Sewanee Writers' Conference uses the facilities of Sewanee: The University of the South. Physically, the University is a collection of ivy-covered Gothic-style buildings, located on the Cumberland Plateau in mid-Tennessee." Invited editors, publishers, and agents structure their own presentations, but there is always opportunity for questions from the audience." 2008 faculty included fiction writers John Casey, Tony Earley, Randall Kenan, Margot Livesey, Jill McCorkle, Erin McGraw, Tim O'Brien, and Christine Schutt; poets Daniel Anderson, Claudia Emerson, Andrew Hudgins, Mark Jarman, Mary Jo Salter, Brad Leithauser, Mark Strand, and Greg Williamson; and playwrights Romulus Linney and Arlene Hutton. The faculty changes from year to year.

Costs Full conference fee (tuition, board and basic room) is $1,700.

Accommodations Participants are housed in university dormitory rooms. Motel or B&B housing is available but not abundantly so. The cost of dormitory housing is included in the full conference fee. Complimentary chartered bus service is available—on a limited basis—on the first and last days of the conference.

Additional Information "We offer each participant (excepting auditors) the opportunity for a private manuscript conference with a member of the faculty. These manuscripts are due one month before the conference begins." Conference information available begining in January. The application season runs from January 15 to May 1, or until all spaces have been filled. Early application is encouraged. For brochure send address and phone number, e-mail, visit Web site or call. "The conference has available a limited number of fellowships and scholarships; these are awarded on a competitive basis."

SILKEN SANDS CONFERENCE

E-mail: info@cynthiaeden.com. Website: www.gccrwa.com. **Contact:** Cynthia Eden, conference chair. Estab. 1995. Annual. Conference is April 2010, in Pensacola Beach, FL. Average attendance: 100. Focuses on romance fiction including paranormal, inspirational, romantic suspense, category. 2008 panelists included Sherrilyn Kenyon (keynote speaker), Catherine Mann, Sherri Cobb South, Beth White, and Roland Haas.

Costs To be announced.

Additional Information Accepts inquiries by e-mail. Agents and editors participate in conference. "The conference is noted for its relaxed, enjoyable atmosphere where participants can immerse themselves in the total writing experience from the moment they arrive. Get up close and personal with professionals in the publishing field."

SITKA CENTER FOR ART AND ECOLOGY

P.O. Box 65, Otis OR 97368. (541)994-5485. Fax: (541)994-8024. E-mail: info@sitkacenter.org. Website: www.sitkacenter.org. **Contact:** Laura Young, program manager. Estab. 1970. workshop program is open to all levels and is held annually from late May until early October. We also have a residency program from September through May." Average attendance: 10-16/workshop. A variety of workshops in creative process, including book arts and other media. Site: The Center borders a Nature Conservatory Preserve, the Siuslaw National Experimental Forest and the Salmon River Estuary, located just north of Lincoln City, OR.

Costs "Workshops are generally $60-300; they do not include meals or lodging."

Accommodations Does not offer overnight accommodations. Provides a list of area hotels or lodging options.

Additional Information Brochure available in February of each year by SASE, phone, e-mail, fax or visit Web site. Accepts inquiries by SASE, e-mail, phone, fax.

SITKA SYMPOSIUM

P.O. Box 2420, Sitka AK 99835-2420. (907)747-3794. Fax: (907)747-6554. E-mail: island@ak.net. Website: www.islandinstitutealaska.org. **Contact:** Carolyn Servid, director. Estab. 1984. Annual. Conference held in June. Conference duration: 3-5 days. Enrollment limited to 45. Conference "to consider the relationship between writing and the ideas of selected theme focusing on social and cultural issues." Site: The Symposium is held in downtown Sitka, in the heart of southeast Alaska's striking coastal mountains and temperate rain forest. Many points of visitor interest are within walking distance. Guest speakers have included Alison Deming, Scott Russell Sanders, Barbara Ras, Bill McKibben, Pattiann Rogers, Rina Swentzell, Barry Lopez, William Kittredge, Gary Syndor, Lorna Goodison, John Keeble, Terry Tempest Williams, Robert Hass, Wendell Berry and Linda Hogan.

Costs $325.

Accommodations Accommodation info is listed on Symposium brochure and Web site.

Additional Information Conference brochures/guidelines are available for SASE or online. Accepts inquiries by e-mail and fax.

⃞ SOAPSTONE: A WRITING RETREAT FOR WOMEN

622 S.E. 29th Ave., Portland OR 97214. (503)233-3936. E-mail: retreats@soapstone.org. Website: www. soapstone.org. Duration: 1-4 weeks. Average attendance: 30 writers/year. Retreat/residency. "Soapstone provides women writers with a stretch of uninterrupted time for their work and the opportunity to live in semi-solitude close to the natural world. In addition to that rare but essential commodity for a writer-a quiet space away from jobs, children, and other responsibilities-Soapstone provides something less tangible but also invaluable: the validation and encouragement necessary to embark upon or sustain a long or difficult writing project." Site: Located in Oregon's Coast Range, nine miles from the ocean, the retreat stands on twenty-two acres of densely forested land along the banks of Soapstone Creek and is home to much wildlife. The writers in residence enjoy a unique opportunity to learn about the natural world and join us in conscious stewardship of the land.

Costs $3 per day. $20 non-refundable application fee.

Accommodations Residents must provide all of their own transportation. See Web site for more information. Offers overnight accommodations.

Additional Information Application materials required include 3 copies of the completed application, a writing sample (no more than 3 pages of poetry or 5 pages, double-spaced, of prose), and application fee. Applications must be postmarked between July 1-August 1 each year.

THE SOUTHAMPTON WRITERS CONFERENCE

Stony Brook Southampton, 239 Montauk Highway, Southampton NY 11968. (631) 632-5030. Fax: (631)632-2578. E-mail: southamptonwriters@notes.cc.sunysb.edu. Website: www.stonybrook.edu/ writers. **Contact:** Adrienne Unger, administrative coordinator. Estab. 1975. Annual. Conference held in July. Conference duration: 12 days. Average attendance: 95. The primary work of the conference is conducted in writing workshops in the novel, short story, poem, play, literary essay and memoir. Site: The seaside campus of Stony Broook Southampton is located in the heart of the Hamptons, a renowned resort area only 70 miles from New York City. During free time, participants can draw inspiration from Atlantic beaches or explore the charming seaside towns. Faculty has included Frank McCourt, Billy Collins, Bharati Mukherjee, Roger Rosenblatt, Ursula Hegi, Alan Alda, and Jules Feiffer, Melissa Bank and Matt Klam.

Costs Application fee: $25; tuition, room and board: $2,175; tuition only: $1,575 (includes breakfast and lunch).

Accommodations On-campus housing-doubles and small singles with shared baths-is modest but comfortable. Housing assignment is by lottery. Supplies list of lodging alternatives.

Additional Information Applicants must complete an application form and submit a writing sample of unpublished, original work up to 20 pages (15 pages for poetry). See Web site for details. Brochures available in January by fax, phone, e-mail and on Web site. Accepts inquiries by SASE, e-mail, phone and fax. Editors and agents attend this conference.

SOUTH CAROLINA WRITERS WORKSHOP ANNUAL CONFERENCE

P.O. Box 7104, Columbia SC 29202. (803)794-0832. E-mail: conference@myscww.org. Website: www. myscww.org. Estab. 1990. Annual writers conference held in October. Conference duration: 3 days. Average attendance: 350. Conference theme varies each year. Faculty, including agents, publishers, authors, and poets, offer talks, workshops, panels, slush pile sessions, and individual critiques and consultation. Emphasis on the craft and business of writing for all major genres and all levels of skill and experience.

Additional Information Related opportunities: literary journal and cash literary awards available to registrants. Please check Web site for more information. Accepts inquiries by e-mail.

SOUTH COAST WRITERS CONFERENCE

P.O. Box 590, 29392 Ellensburg Avenue, Gold Beach OR 97444. (541)247-2741. Fax: (541)247-6247. E-mail: scwc@socc.edu. Website: www.socc.edu/scwriters. **Contact:** Janet Pretti, coordinator. Estab. 1996. Annual. Conference held President's Day weekend. Workshops held Friday and Saturday. Average attendance: 100. "We try to cover a broad spectrum: fiction, historical, poetry, children's, nature." Site: "Friday workshops are held at The Event Center on the Beach. Saturday workshops are held at the high school." 2008 keynote speaker will be David Oliver Relin. Other presenters Linda Barnes, Robin Cody, Jayel Gibson, Robert Hill, Elizabeth Lyon, Elizabeth McKenzie, Lori Ries, Elizabeth Rusch, Floyd Skloot, Leslie What.

Costs $55 before January 31; $65 after. Friday workshops are an additional $40. No meals or lodging included.

Accommodations Provides list of area hotels.

Additional Information Sponsors contest. Bob Simons Scholarship open to anyone. Contact SCWC for details.

SOUTHEASTERN WRITERS ASSOCIATION

SWA, 161 Woodstone Dr., Athens GA 30605. E-mail: whyzz@bellsouth.net. Website: www. southeasternwriters.com. **Contact**: Sheila Hudson, registrar. Estab. 1975. Annual. Conference held third week of June every year. Average attendance: 75 (limited to 100). Conference offers classes in fiction, nonfiction, juvenile, inspirational writing, poetry, etc. Site: Epworth-by-the-Sea, St. Simons Island, GA.

Costs 2009 costs: $399, no mss submitted after April 1, 2008; $150 daily tuition. Three days' tuition required for free manuscript conferences. Conference tuition includes $35 annual membership fee.

Accommodations Offers overnight accommodations. 2007 rates were approximately $650/single to $425/double and including motel-style room and 3 meals/day per person. Off site lodging also available.

Additional Information Sponsors numerous contests in several genres and up to 3 free ms evaluation conferences with instructors. Agents and editors participate in conference panels and/or private appointments. Complete information is available on the Web site in March of each year, including registration forms. E-mail or send SASE for brochure.

SOUTHWEST LITERARY CENTER OF RECURSOS DE SANTA FE

826 Camino de Monte Rey, Santa Fe NM 87505. (505)577-1125. Fax: (505)982-7125. Website: www. santafewritersconference.com. **Contact:** Literary Center director. Estab. 1984. Annual. 2008 conference

was held July 21-25, possible extension to include Santa Fe Spanish Market. Conference duration: 6 days. Average attendance: 50. This year's conference includes lectures, afternoon talks, and private conferences on fiction, and nonfiction. Faculty included Natalie Goldberg, Lisa Dale Norton, Sallie Bingham, Julie Shigekuni and Denise Chavez and more.

Costs $550. Scholarships may be available.

Additional Information Brochure available by e-mail, fax, phone and on Web site.

SOUTHWEST WRITERS CONFERENCE

3721 Morris NE Ste A, Albuquerque NM 87111. (505) 265-9485. Fax: (505) 265-9483. E-mail: swwriters@ juno.com. Website: www.southwestwriters.org. **Contact:** Conference Chair. Estab. 1983. Annual. Conferences held throughout the year. Average attendance: 50. "Conferences concentrate on all areas of writing and include appointments and networking." Workshops and speakers include writers, editors and agents of all genres for all levels from beginners to advanced.

Costs $99 and up (members); $159 and up (nonmembers); includes conference sessions and lunch.

Accommodations Usually have official airline and discount rates. Special conference rates are available at hotel. A list of other area hotels and motels is available.

Additional Information Sponsors an annual contest judged by authors, editors and agents from New York, Los Angeles, etc., and from other major publishing houses. Many categories. Deadline, fee structure on Web site. For brochures/guidelines send SASE, visit Web site, e-mail, call. "An appointment (10 minutes, one-on-one) may be set up at the conference with the editor/agent of your choice on a first-registered/first-served basis."

⊡ SPACE (SMALL PRESS AND ALTERNATIVE COMICS EXPO)

Back Porch Comics, P.O.Box 20550, Columbus OH 43220. E-mail: bpc13@earthlink.net. Website: www.backporchcomics.com/space.htm. **Contact:** Bob Corby. Next conference/trade show to be held on April 18 and 19, 2009. Conference duration: 2 days. "The Midwest's largest exhibition of small press, alternative and creator-owned comics." Site: Held at the Aladdin Shrine Complex multipurpose room in Columbus, Ohio. Over 150 small press artists, writers, and publishers. Admission: $5 per day or $8 for weekend.

Additional Information For brochure, visit Web site. Editors participate in conference.

SQUAW VALLEY COMMUNITY OF WRITERS

P.O. Box 1416, Nevada City CA 95959-1416. (530) 470-8440. E-mail: info@squawvalleywriters.org. Website: www.squawvalleywriters.org. **Contact:** Brett Hall Jones, executive director. Estab. 1969. Annual. Conference held in August. Conference duration: 7 days. Average attendance: 124. "These writers workshops in fiction, nonfiction and memoir assist talented writers by exploring the art and craft as well as the business of writing." Offerings include daily morning workshops led by writer-teachers, editors, or agents of the staff, limited to 12-13 participants; seminars; panel discussions of editing and publishing; craft colloquies; lectures; and staff readings. Past themes and panels included Personal History in Fiction, Narrative Structure, Promise and Premise: Recognizing Subject; The Nation of Narrative Prose: Telling the Truth in Memoir and Personal Essay, and Anatomy of a Short Story. Past faculty and speakers included Ron Carlson, Sue Miller, Jason Roberts, Alice Sebold, Gregory Spatz, Amy Tan, Al Young and many more.

Costs Tuition is $750, which includes 6 dinners.

Accommodations The Community of Writers rents houses and condominiums in the Valley for participants to live in during the week of the conference. Single room (one participant): $550/week. Double room (twin beds, room shared by conference participant of the same sex): $350/week. Multiple room (bunk beds, room shared with 2 or more participants of the same sex): $200/week. All rooms subject to availability; early requests are recommended. Can arrange airport shuttle pick-ups for a fee.

Additional Information Admissions are based on submitted ms (unpublished fiction, one or two stories or novel chapters); requires $30 reading fee. Submit ms to Brett Hall Jones, Squaw Valley Community of Writers, P.O. Box 1416, Nevada City, CA 95959. Deadline: May 10. Notification: June 10. Brochure/guidelines available February by phone, e-mail or visit Web site. Accepts inquiries by SASE, e-mail, phone. Agents and editors attend/participate in conferences.

STEAMBOAT SPRINGS WRITERS GROUP

Steamboat Arts Council, P.O. Box 774284, Steamboat Springs CO 80477. (970)879-8138. E-mail: info@

steamboatwriters.com. Website: www.steamboatwriters.com. **Contact:** Susan de Wardt, director. Estab. 1982. Group meets year-round on Thursdays, 12:00 to 2:00 at Arts Depot; guests welcome. Annual conference held in July. Conference duration: 1 day. Average attendance: 35. "Our conference emphasizes instruction within the seminar format. Novices and polished professionals benefit from the individual attention and camaraderie which can be established within small groups. A pleasurable and memorable learning experience is guaranteed by the relaxed and friendly atmosphere of the old train depot. Registration is limited." Site: Restored train depot.

Costs $50 before May 25, $60 after. Fee covers all seminars and luncheon.

Accommodations Lodging available at Steamboat Resorts.

Additional Information Optional dinner and activities during evening preceding conference. Accepts inquiries by e-mail, phone, mail.

STEINBECK FESTIVAL

1 Main Street, Salinas CA 93901. (831)796-3833. Fax: (831)796-3828. Website: www.steinbeck.org. Estab. 1980. Annual. Festival held August 6-9, 2009. Average attendance: 1,000 "over 4-day period." Conference "focuses on the life and writings of John Steinbeck. This year's theme (Legends, Myth, and Magic) will focus on the Arthurian Legend that so inspired John Steinbeck. Multi-day festival includes speakers, tours, events, visual and performing arts, and museum admission. Featured speakers will include Christopher Paolini, author of The Inheritance Cycle and Jonathan Young, Director of the Center for Story Story and Symbol and founding curator of the Joseph Campbell Library." Site: National Steinbeck Center, "a $15 million, multi-sensory museum located in California's Central Coast which includes a permanent exhibit that brings to life the world of Nobel Prize-winning author, John Steinbeck, the Rabobank Agricultural Museum, which shares the stories of Salinas Valley agriculture "from field to fork," through interactive displays, film and hands on exhibits, and two changing art galleries featuring a variety of art and cultural exhibits."

Costs Fees range from $17 to $75 per person, depending on the programs offered. Daily and festival passports are also offered.

Accommodations Provides a list of area hotel and lodging options.

STELLARCON

Box F4, Elliott University Center, UNCG, Greensboro NC 27412. E-mail: info@stellarcon.org. Website: www.stellarcon.org. **Contact:** Mike Monaghan, convention manager. Estab. 1976. Annual. Last conference held March 13-15, 2009. Average attendance: 500. Conference focuses on "general science fiction and fantasy (horror also) with an emphasis on literature." Site: Hotel High Point, High Point, NC. See Web site for 2009 speakers.

Costs See Web site for 2009 rates.

Accommodations "Lodging is available at the Radisson."

Additional Information Accepts inquiries by e-mail. Agents and editors participate in conference.

SUMMER WRITING PROGRAM

Naropa University, 2130 Arapahoe Ave., Boulder CO 80302. (303)245-4600. Fax: (303)546-5287. E-mail: swpr@naropa.edu. Website: www.naropa.edu/swp. **Contact:** Julie Kazimer, registration manager. Estab. 1974. Annual. Workshops held: June 15-July 12, 2009. Workshop duration: 4 weeks. Average attendance: 250. Offers college credit. "With 13 workshops to choose from each of the four weeks of the program, students may study poetry, prose, hybrid/cross-genre writing, small press printing, or book arts." Site: All workshops, panels, lectures and readings are hosted on the Naropa University main campus. Located in downtown Boulder, the campus is within easy walking distance of restaurants, shopping and the scenic Pearl Street Mall. Prose-related panels include Ecology, Poetics of Prose, Telling Stories, The Informant "Other." 2009 faculty included Samuel R. Delany, Laura Elrick, Clayton Eshleman, Simone Forti, Gloria Frym, Renee Gladman, Joyce Johnson, Bhanu Kapil, Mark McMorris, Eileen Myles, Akilah Oliver, Willie Perdomo, Janine Pommy Vega, Ed Roberson, Selah Saterstrom, Leonard Schwartz, Steven Taylor, Anne Waldman, Zhang Er, and many others.

Costs In 2008: $450/week, $1,700 for all four weeks (non-credit students); $1072/week (BA students); $1,452/week (MFA students).

Accommodations Offers overnight accommodations. Housing is available at Snow Lion Apartments. Single room is $45/night or $315/week, single bedroom apartment is $64/night or $448/week.

Additional Information If students would like to take the Summer Writing Program for academic credit, they must submit a visiting student application, transcripts, a letter of intent, and 5-10 pages of their creative work. Information available in January. For catalog of upcoming program, fill out catalog request form at http://www.naropa.edu/swp/catalog/asp. Accepts inquiries by e-mail, phone.

TAOS SUMMER WRITERS' CONFERENCE

Department of English Language and Literature MSC03 2170, 1 University of New Mexico, Albuquerque NM 87131-0001. (505)277-5572. Fax: (505)277-2950. E-mail: taosconf@unm.edu. Website: www.unm.edu/~taosconf. **Contact**: Sharon Oard Warner, director. Estab. 1999. Annual. Held each year in July. Average attendance: 180. Workshops in novel writing, short story writing, screenwriting, poetry, creative nonfiction, publishing, and special topics such as yoga and writing. Master classes in novel, memoir and poetry. For beginning and experienced writers. "Taos itself makes our conference unique. We also offer daily visits to the D.H. Lawrence Ranch, and other local historical sites." Site: Workshops and readings are all held at the Sagebrush Inn Conference Center, part of the Sagebrush Inn, an historic hotel and Taos landmark since 1929.

Costs Weeklong workshop tuition is $600, includes a Sunday evening New Mexican buffet dinner, a Friday evening barbecue and other special events. Weekend workshop tuition is $300.

Accommodations Conference participants receive special discounted rates $59-99/night. Room rates at both hotels include a full, hot breakfast.

Additional Information "We offer three Merit Scholarships, the Taos Resident Writer Award, the Hispanic Writer Award and one D.H. Lawrence Fellowship. Scholarship awards are based on submissions of poetry, fiction and creative nonfiction." They provide tuition remission; transportation and lodging not provided. To apply for a scholarship, submit 10 pages of poetry, nonfiction or fiction along with registration and deposit. Applicants should be registered for the conference. The Fellowship is for emerging writers with one book in print, provides tuition remission and cost of lodging. Brochures available late winter. "The conference offers a balance of special events and free time. If participants take a morning workshop, they'll have the afternoons free and vice versa. We've also included several outings, including a visit to historic D.H. Lawrence Ranch outside Taos."

TEXAS CHRISTIAN WRITERS' CONFERENCE

First Baptist Church, 6038 Greenmont, Houston TX 77092. (713)686-7209. E-mail: marthalrogers@sbcglobal.net. **Contact:** Martha Rogers. Estab. 1990. Annual. Conference held in August. Conference duration: 1 day. Average attendance: 60-65. "Focus on all genres." Site: Held at the First Baptist Church fellowship center and classrooms. 2009 faculty: Cecil Murphey, keynote speaker. Workshops by Gail Gaymer Martin, Cyndy Salzman, Kathy Ide, Anita Highman, Janice Thompson, and Kathleen Y'Barbo.

Costs $65 for members of IWA, $80 nonmembers, discounts for seniors (60+) and couples, meal at noon, continental breakfast and breaks.

Accommodations Offers list of area hotels or lodging options.

Additional Information Open conference for all interested writers. Sponsors a contest for short fiction; categories include articles, devotionals, poetry, short story, book proposals, drama. Fees: $8-15. Conference information available with SASE or e-mail to Martha Rogers. Agents participate in conference.

⬛ THRILLERFEST

New York NY. (636) 938-7163. E-mail: infocentral@thrillerwriters.org. Website: www.thrillerwriters.org. Estab. 2006. Annual. July 2009. Conference duration: 4 days. Average attendance: 650. Workshop/conference/festival. "To promote thriller fiction and the thriller in general, to fans, aspiring writers, and established authors in an atmosphere that encourages casual mixing, accessibility and sharing." Previous years have focused on aspects of the thriller and writing the thriller from a creative as well as business/professionally-minded approach. The various subgenres are explores as well as the traits, advantages and disadvantages of each. In addition, the fist two days of the conference, made up of CraftFest, focus on workshoips aimed toward the professional and would-be professional. 2009 guest speakers and panelists included David Morrell, Sandra Brown, Katherine Neville, Robin Cook, Brad Meltzer, David Baldacci, Clive Cussler, Steve Berry, Steve Martini, R.L. Stine, Lee Child, M.J. Rose, Kathleen Antrim, Joe Moore, Heather Graham, Douglas Preston, Joseph Finder, Carla Neggers, David Hewson, Dakota Banks, James Rollins, Christine Kling, Gayle Lynds, Michael Palmer, Shane Gericke, Karin Slaughter, and Lisa Gardner.

Costs $300-800 depending on specific event selection and available early-bird discounting. Some meals are included in some of the packages.

Accommodations Does not offer overnight accommodations. Provides list of area hotels or lodging options. Discounted room rate available at conference location.

Additional Information Information available in September. For brochure, call or e-mail. Agents and editors participate in conference. "AgentFest is a three-hour event in which authors have the oppertunity to 'speed pitch' their story to dozens of agents in a single setting. ThrillerFest boasts a very congenial, relaxed and friendly atmosphere in which the best and the brightest in our field can mix and interact comfortably with those dreaming of becoming just that."

THUNDER ARM WRITNING RETREAT WITH NORTH CASCADES INSTITUTE

North Cascades Institute, 810 Highway 20, Sedro-Wooley WA 98284-9394. (360)856-5700 ext. 209. Fax: (360) 856-1934. E-mail: nci@ncascades.org. Website: www.ncascades.org. **Contact**: Deb Martin, registrar. Estab. 1986. Annual. 2007 conference was held July 25-29. Conference duration: 4 days. Average attendance: 32. Led by three outstanding writers, the Institute's Thunder Arm Writing Retreat engages amateur and professional writers alike with lectures, discussions, readings and writing exercises centered on the natural world. "Nature writing, at its simplest, strives to explore basic principles at work in nature and to convey these in language that introduces readers to the facility and wonder of their own place in the world." Site: North Cascades Enviromental Learning Center on Diablo Lake in North Cascades National Park. Past faculty includes: Barbara Kingsolver, Robert Michael Pyle, William Kittredge, Ann Zwinger, Gary Ferguson, Kathleen Dean Moore, and William Dietrich.

Costs 2007 costs were $325 (triple occupancy), $475 (double), $695 (single). All options include meals.

Additional Information For conference information, visit Web Site, e-mail or call.

TIN HOUSE SUMMER WRITERS WORKSHOP

P.O. Box 10500, Portland OR 97296. (503)219-0622. Fax: (503)222-1154. E-mail: cheston@tinhouse.com. Website: www.tinhouse.com. **Contact:** Cheston Knapp, Director. Estab. 2003. Annual in July. Conference duration: 1 week. Average attendance: 130. A weeklong intensive of panels, seminars, workshops and readings led by the editors of Tin House magazine and Tin House Books, and their guests—prominent contemporary writers of fiction, nonfiction, poetry and film. Site: The workshop will be held at Reed College in scenic Portland, OR, just minutes from downtown and the airport. Facilities include bookstore, library, mail service, an art gallery, print shop and athletic facilities. Each afternoon agents, editors, writers and filmmakers will discuss ideas and offer a range of discussions on topics and issues concerning the craft and business of riting. See Web site for specifics. 2008 faculty included Colson Whitehead, Denis Johnson, Andrea Barrett, David Shields, and Frank Bidart.

Costs 2009 tuition was $950; food and lodging $550. Application fee $35. Scholarships available.

Additional Information Attendees must submit writing sample and attend by invitation. Deadline: April 1, then rolling while space allows. Admission is based on the strength and promise of the writing sample—up to 15 pages of fiction. Brochures available in February for SASE, by fax, phone, e-mail and on Web site. Accepts inquiries by SASE, e-mail, phone, fax. Agents and editors attend conference.

TMCC WRITERS' CONFERENCE

TMCC Workforce Development and Continuing Education Division, 5270 Neil Road Rm 216, Reno NV 89502. (775)829-9010. Fax: (775)829-9032. E-mail: wdce@tmcc.edu. Website: wdce.tmcc.edu. Estab. 1990. Annual. 2009 conference held in March. Average attendance: 125. Conference focuses on strengthening mainstream/literary fiction and nonfiction works and how to market them to agents and publisher. Site: Truckee Meadows Community College in Reno, Nevada.

Costs $89 for lectures; $29 for one-on-one appointment with an agent.

Accommodations A wide range of affordable accommodations are available nearby.

Additional Information Brochures are available the end of November through the Web site, e-mail or mail. Accepts inquires by phone or e-mail. Multiple agents, along with successful authors, participate in this event. "This conference features a supportive, informal atmosphere where questions are encouraged."

MARK TWAIN CREATIVE WRITERS WORKSHOPS

University House, 5101 Rockhill Rd., Kansas City MO 64110-2499. (816) 235-1168. Fax: (816) 235-2611. E-mail: BeasleyM@umkc.edu. Website: www.newletters.org. **Contact:** Betsy Beasley, adminstrative associate. Estab. 1990. Annual. Held 3 weeks of June, from 9:30 to 12:30 each weekday morning. Conference duration: 3 weeks. Average attendance: 40. "Focus is on fiction, poetry and literary nonfiction."

Site: University of Missouri-Kansas City Campus. Panels planned for next conference include the full range of craft essentials. Staff includes Robert Stewart, editor-in-chief of New Letters and BkMk Press, and Michael Pritchett, creative writing professor.
Costs Fees for regular and noncredit courses.
Accommodations Offers list of area hotels or lodging options.
Additional Information Submit for workshop 6 poems/one short story prior to arrival. Conference information is available in March by SASE, e-mail or on Web site. Editors participate in conference.

▨ TY NEWYDD WRITERS' CENTRE

Llanystumdwy, Cricieth Gwynedd LL52 0LW United Kingdom. 01766-522811. Fax: 01766 523095. E-mail: post@tynewydd.org. Website: www.tynewydd.org. **Contact:** Sally Baker, director, Executive Director. Estab. 1990. Year-round. Regular courses held throughout the year. Every course held Monday-Saturday. Average attendance: 14. "To give people the opportunity to work side-by-side with professional writers, in an informal atmosphere." Site: Ty Newydd, large manor house, last home of the prime minister, David Lloyd George. Situated in North Wales, Great Britain—between mountains and sea.
Costs Single room, $834/£480, shared room, $954/£420 for Monday-Saturday (includes full board, tuition).
Accommodations Transportation from railway stations arranged. Accommodation in Ty Newydd (onsite).
Additional Information Course information available by mail, phone, e-mail, fax or visit Web site. Accepts inquiries by SASE, e-mail, fax, phone. "More and more people come to us from the U.S. often combining a writing course with a tour of Wales."

UCLA EXTENSION WRITERS' PROGRAM

10995 Le Conte Avenue, #440, Los Angeles CA 90024-2883. (310) 825-9415 or (800) 388-UCLA. Fax: (310) 206-7382. E-mail: writers@UCLAextension.edu. Website: www.uclaextension.edu/writers. **Contact:** Cindy Lieberman, program manager. Courses held year-round with one-day or intensive weekend workshops to 12-week courses. Writers Studio held in February. 9-month master classes are also offered every fall. "The diverse offerings span introductory seminars to professional novel and script completion workshops. The annual Writers Studio and a number of 1-, 2- and 4-day intensive workshops are popular with out-of-town students due to their specific focus and the chance to work with industry professionals. The most comprehensive and diverse continuing education writing program in the country, offering over 550 courses a year, including screenwriting, fiction, writing for the youth market, poetry, nonfiction, playwriting and publishing. Adult learners in the UCLA Extension Writers' Program study with professional screenwriters, fiction writers, playwrights, poets and nonfiction writers, who bring practical experience, theoretical knowledge and a wide variety of teaching styles and philosophies to their classes." Site: Courses are offered in Los Angeles on the UCLA campus, in the 1010 Westwood Center in Westwood Village, at the Figueroa Courtyard in downtown Los Angeles, as well as online.
Costs Vary from $95 for one-day workshops to about $475 for quarterly courses to $3,250 for the 9-month master class.
Accommodations Students make own arrangements. The program can provide assistance in locating local accommodations.
Additional Information Writers Studio information available October. For brochures/guidelines/guide to course offerings, visit Web site, e-mail, fax or call. Accepts inquiries by e-mail, fax, phone. "Some advanced level classes have manuscript submittal requirements; instructions are always detailed in the quarterly UCLA Extension course catalog. The UCLA Extension Screenwriting Competition is now in its fourth year, featuring prizes and industry recognition to the top three winners. An annual fiction prize, The James Kirkwood Prize in Creative Writing, has been established and is given annually to one fiction writer who has produced outstanding work in a Writers' Program course."

VERMONT STUDIO CENTER

P.O. Box 613, Johnson VT 05656. (802)635-2727. Fax: (802)635-2730. E-mail: writing@vermontstudiocenter. org. Website: www.vermontstudiocenter.org. **Contact:** Gary Clark, writing program director. Estab. 1984. Ongoing residencies. Conference duration: From 2-12 weeks. Average attendance: 55 writers and visual artists/month. "The Vermont Studio Center is an international creative community located in Johnson, Vermont, and serving more than 600 American and international artists and writers each year (50 per month). A Studio Center Residency features secluded, uninterrupted writing time, the companionship of dedicated and talented peers, and access to a roster of two distinguished Visiting Writers each month. All VSC Residents receive three meals a day, private, comfortable housing and the company of an international community of painters, sculptors, poets, printmakers and writers. Writers attending residencies at the Studio Center may work on whatever they choose—no matter what month of the year they attend." Visiting writers have included Ron Carlson, Donald Revell, Jane Hirshfield, Rosanna Warren, Chris Abani, Bob Shacochis, Tony Hoagland, and Alice Notley.

Costs The cost of a 4-week residency is $3,750. Generous fellowship and grant assistance available.

Accommodations Provided.

Additional Information "Manuscript conferences may be arranged with visiting writers whose primary genre matches that of each resident's VSC application. Full Fellowship application deadlines three times a year — February 15, June 15, and October 1. Application fee is $25. Writers encouraged to visit Web site for more information. May also e-mail, call, fax."

VIRGINIA FESTIVAL OF THE BOOK

Virginia Foundation for the Humanities, 145 Ednam Dr., Charlottesville VA 22903. (434)924-6890. Fax:(434)296-4714. E-mail: vabook@virginia.edu. Website: www.vabook.org. **Contact**: Nancy Damon, program director. Estab. 1995. Annual. Festival held in March. 2009 Dates are March 18-22, 2009. Average attendance: 22,000. Festival held to celebrate books and promote reading and literacy. Site: Held throughout the Charlottesville/Albemarle area.

Costs See Web site for 2009 rates. Most events are free and open to the public. Two luncheons, a breakfast, and a reception require tickets.

Accommodations Overnight accommodations available.

Additional Information "The festival is a five-day event featuring authors, illustrators, and publishing professionals. Authors must apply to the festival to be included on a panel. Preferred method of application is by use of online form. Information is available on the Web site and inquiries can be made via e-mail, fax, or phone."

WESLEYAN WRITERS CONFERENCE

Wesleyan University, 294 High St., room 207, Middletown CT 06459. (860)685-3604. Fax: (860)685-2441. E-mail: agreene@wesleyan.edu. Website: www.wesleyan.edu/writers. **Contact:** Anne Greene, director. Estab. 1956. Annual. Conference held the third week of June. Average attendance: 100. For novel, short story, fiction techniques, poetry, short- and long-form nonfiction, journalism, memoir, multi-media work, digital media. Site: The conference is held on the campus of Wesleyan University, in the hills overlooking the Connecticut River. Meals and lodging are provided on campus. Features daily seminars, readings, lectures, panels, workshops, mss consultations, publishing advice; faculty of award-winning writers and guest speakers.

Costs In 2008, day student 4850 (tuition, no meals), day student with meals 41,125 (includes tuition, meals), boarding student $1,298 (includes tuition, meals, and room for 5 nights).

Accommodations "Participants can fly to Hartford or take Amtrak to Meriden, CT. We are happy to help participants make travel arrangements." Overnight participants stay on campus or in hotels.

Additional Information Both experienced writers and new writers are welcome. Scholarships and teaching fellowships are available, including the Joan Jakobson Scholarships for writers of fiction, poetry and nonfiction and the Jon Davidoff Scholarships for journalists." Accepts inquiries by e-mail, phone, fax.

WESTERN RESERVE WRITERS & FREELANCE CONFERENCE

Lakeland Community College, 7700 Clocktower Dr., Kirtland OH 44094. (440) 525-7812. Website: www.deannaadams.com. E-mail: deencr@aol.com. **Contact**: Deanna Adams, director and conference coordinator. Estab. 1983. Biannual. Last conference held September 20, 2008. Conference duration: One day. Average attendance: 120. "The Western Reserve Writers Conferences are designed for all writers, aspiring and professional, and offer presentations in all genres-nonfiction, fiction, poetry, essays, creative nonfiction and the business of writing, including Web writing and successful freelance writing." Site: Located in the main building of Lakeland Community College, the conference is easy to find and just off the I-90 freeway. The Fall 2008 conference featured top notch presenters from newspapers such as the Cleveland Plain Dealer, magazines such as Northern Ohio Live, along with published authors and freelance writers. Presentations included how to draft a standout book proposal, creating credible characters, contracts/copyrights, public speaking, tips on completing your novel, and when and how to get an agent. Included throughout the day are editing consults, Q & A Panel, and book sale/author signings.

Costs Fall conference, includes lunch: $95. Spring conference, no lunch: $69.

Additional Information Brochures for the conferences are available by February (for spring conference) and July (for fall). Also accepts inquiries by e-mail and phone, or see Web site. Editors and agents often attend the conferences.

WILLAMETTE WRITERS CONFERENCE

9045 SW Barbur Blvd., Suite 5-A, Portland OR 97219-4027. (503)452-1592. Fax: (503)452-0372. E-mail: wilwrite@willamettewriters.com. Website: www.willamettewriters.com. **Contact:** Bill Johnson, office manager. Estab. 1981. Annual conference held in August. Conference duration: 3 days. Average attendance: 600. "Williamette Writers is open to all writers, and we plan our conference accordingly. We offer workshops on all aspects of fiction, nonfiction, marketing, the creative process, screenwriting, etc. Also we invite top notch inspirational speakers for keynote addresses. Recent theme was 'The Writers Way.' We always include at least one agent or editor panel and offer a variety of topics of interest to both fiction and nonfiction writers and screenwriters." Recent editors, agents and film producers in attendance have included: Andrea Brown, Marilyn Allen; Angela Rinaldi; Tony Outhwaite.

Costs Cost for 3-day conference including meals is $395 members; $430 nonmembers.

Accommodations If necessary, these can be made on an individual basis. Some years special rates are available.

Additional Information Conference brochure/guidelines are available in May for catalog-size SASE, e-mail, fax, phone or on Web site. Accepts inquiries by fax, e-mail, phone, SASE.

WILLIAM PATERSON UNIVERSITY SPRING WRITER'S CONFERENCE

English Dept., Atrium 250, 300 Pompton Rd., Wayne NJ 07470-2103. (973)720-3067. Fax: (973)720-2189. E-mail: parrasj@wpunj.edu. Website: http://euphrates.wpunj.edu/WritersConference. **Contact:** John Parras, professor of English. Annual. Conference held in April. Conference duration: 1 day. Average attendance: 100-125. The 2005 conference focused on "writing the world." Several hands-on workshops were offered in many genres of creative writing, critical writing and literature. Included reading by nationally recognized author. Site: William Paterson University campus. 2005 keynote speaker: poet Linda Gregg. Past faculty has included Yusef Komunyakaa, Joyce Carol Oates, Susan Sontag and Jimmy Santiago Braca.

Costs $40 (2005) includes 2 workshops, plenary readings, meals.

Additional Information Conference information is available November/December. For brochure send e-mail, visit Web site, call or fax. Accepts inquiries by SASE, e-mail, phone and fax. Agents and editors participate in conference.

TENNESSEE WILLIAMS/NEW ORLEANS LITERARY FESTIVAL

938 Lafayette St., Suite 514, New Orleans LA 70113. (504) 581-1144. E-mail: info@tennesseewilliams.net. Website: www.tennesseewilliams.net. **Contact:** Paul J. Willis, executive director. Estab. 1987. Annual. Conference held in late March. Average attendance: "10,000 audience seats filled." Conferences focus on "all aspects of the literary arts including editing, publishing and the artistic process. Other humanities areas are also featured, including theater and music." Site: "The festival is based at the Bourbon Oreleans hotel and at historic Le Petit Theatre du Vieux Carré and other sites throughout the French Quarter."

Costs "Ticket prices range from $10 for a single event to $60 for a special event. Master classes are $35 per class. Theatre events are sold separately and range from $10-25."

Accommodations "Host hotel is Bourbon Orleans Hotel."

Additional Information "In conjunction with the University of New Orleans, we sponsor a one-act play competition. Entries are accepted from July 15 through November 1. There is a $25 fee which must be submitted with the application form. There is a $1,000 cash prize and a staged reading at the festival, as well as a full production of the work at the following year's festival." Conference information is available in late January. For brochure send e-mail, visit Web site or call. Accepts inquiries by e-mail and phone. Agents and editors participate in conference.

▦ WINCHESTER WRITERS' CONFERENCE, FESTIVAL AND BOOKFAIR, AND WEEKLONG WORKSHOPS

University of Winchester, Winchester, Hampshire S022 4NR UK email: Barbara.Large@winchester. ac.uk. Telephone +44 (0)1962 827238. Website: www.writersconference.co.uk. The 29th Winchester Writers' Conference, Festival and Bookfair will be held on the weekend of July 3-5, 2009, followed by the Weeklong Writing Workshops at the University of Winchester, Hampshire, UK. Colin Dexter, internationally renowned for the Morse crime fiction books and television series will give the Plenary Address. Network with many other leading authors, poets, literary agents, and commissioning editors. This international conference offers all writers the opportunity to harness their creative ideas and to develop their technical skills under the guidance and instruction of 65 professional writers, literary agents, commissioning editors and book industry specialists during mini courses, workshops, seminars, lectures and 500 one-to-one appointments. Enjoy a creative writing holiday in the oldest city in England. Tours to Jane Austen's home and Study Centre, the haunts of Keats and the famous Hat Fair. Enter the fifteen writing competitions attached to this conference, even if you can't attend. Book online or print down the application and post. For further information, contact Barbara Large, MBE, Conference Director, Winchester Writers' Conference, Faculty of Research and Knowledge Transfer.

N ⚹ WINDY CITY COMICON

3656 N. Halsted, Chicago IL 60613. Website: www.windycitycomicon.com. **Contact:** Chris Neseman. Estab. 2008. Annual. Conference duration: 1 day. Conference. "The 1st Annual Windy City Comicon features dozens of guests, gaming, comic vendors and more. Don't miss out on Chicago's best comic book convention!"
Costs $5

WINTER POETRY & PROSE GETAWAY IN CAPE MAY

18 North Richards Ave., Ventnor NJ 08406. (609) 823-5076. E-mail: info@wintergetaway.com. Website: www.wintergetaway.com. Established 1994. **Contact**: Peter E. Murphy, founder/director. Next held in January 15-18, 2010. Average attendance: 200 (10 or fewer participants in each workshop). Location: The Grand Hotel on the Oceanfront in Historic Cape May, NJ. Now in its 17th year, the Winter Poetry and Prose Getaway is a three-day conference well known for its challenging and supportive workshops featuring small classes led by award-winning writers. Participants focus on one workshop during the weekend and can choose from Focusing Your Fiction, Turning Memory into Memoir, Finishing Your Novel, Writing New Stories, Revising a Short Story Toward Publication, Writing Flash Fiction, Writing for the Children's Market and Creative Nonfiction. Workshops run from 9 a.m. to 4 p.m. on Saturday and Sunday and from 9 a.m.–noon on Monday. Late afternoons allow you to choose from tutorials, panels, talks, walking on the beach, or you may continue working. Evenings include special activities, receptions, open mics, socializing, a bookstore on Sunday night and more. Previous faculty has included Renee Ashley, Julianna Baggott, Christian Bauman, Anndee Hochman, Laura McCullough, Sondra Perl, Carol Plum-Ucci, David Schwartz, Mimi Schwartz, Robbie Clipper Sethi, Terese Svoboda, Richard K. Weems and many more. The Getaway also features workshops in poetry, song writing, painting and photography.
Costs $385 for 2009; includes all workshops, 2 lunches, 2 receptions, and a tutorial for poets. Room packages from $225. A $25 Early Bard discount is available if paid in full by November 15.
Additional Information "The Getaway is a conference where you will write! You will receive feedback but the workshops emphasize creating new material or revising works in progress. It is open to all writers, beginners and experienced, over the age of 18. Teachers can earn 17 hours of professional development credit as well as graduate credit from Rutgers University. Visit www.wintergetaway.com for the latest news and to sign up for our e-newsletter."d

N ⚹ WIRED WRITING STUDIO

P.O. Box 1020, Banff AB T1L 1H5. (800) 565-9989. E-mail: arts_info@banffcentre.ca; christie.rall@banffcentre.ca. Website: www.banffcentre.ca. **Contact:** Office of the Registrar. Annual. Writing workshop. Program Dates: October 5-17, 2009 (2-week on-site residency in Banff); November 1, 2009-March 31, 2010 (20-week online residency). "By delivering most of the program online, the Wired Writing Studio broadens a writer's understanding of the Internet's potential as a tool for artistic and professional development. Each participant is assigned to one faculty mentor and will continue with that mentor throughout the program. Online, the creative community is sustained by e-mail, by participation in an online discussion forum, and by readings posted on the Web site." Site: "The Banff Centre enables both emerging and established individuals to interact within a multidisciplinary and multicultural environment, allowing them to push boundaries, to experiment, to share knowledge, to create and showcase new work, and to develop new ideas and solutions for the present and the future."
Costs Workshop fee: please see Web site for up-to-date information, www.banffcentre.ca/writing/.

Accommodations please see Web site for up-to-date information. On-site only, hotel style which also serve s as private work spaces. Computers should be brought along for private use. Public computers available on campus.

Additional Information "At time of application, writers must submit writing samples and statement of expectations. Application fee: $31 Canadian. Brochure currently available for e-mail and on Web site. For inquiries, contact by SASE, e-mail, phone, fax. Other writing programs are offered at The Banff Centre include: Banff International Translation Centre, Literary Journalism, Spoken Word, Science Communications, and Mountain Writing."

WISCONSIN REGIONAL WRITERS' ASSOCIATION CONFERENCES

9708 Idell Ave., Sparta WI 54656. (608)269-8541. E-mail: registration@wrwa.net. Website: www.wrwa. net. **Contact:** Nate Scholze, Fall Conference Coordinator; Roxanne Aehl, Spring Conference Coordinator. Estab. 1948. Annual. Conferences held in May and September "are dedicated to self-improvement through speakers, workshops and presentations. Topics and speakers vary with each event." Average attendance: 100-150. "We honor all genres of writing. Fall conference is a two-day event featuring the Jade Ring Banquet and awards for six genre categories. Spring conference is a one-day event."
Costs $40-75.

Accommodations Provides a list of area hotels or lodging options. "We negotiate special rates at each facility. A block of rooms is set aside for a specific time period."

Additional Information Award winners receive a certificate and a cash prize. First place winners of the Jade Ring contest receive a jade ring. Must be a member to enter contests. For brochure, call, e-mail or visit Web site in March/July.

Ⓝ WOMEN WRITERS WINTER RETREAT

Homestead House B&B, 38111 West Spaulding, Willoughby OH 44094.(440)946-1902. E-mail: deencr@ aol.com. Website: www.deannaadams.com. **Contact:** Deanna Adams, director. Estab. 2007. Annual. Last retreat held February 27, 2009-March 1, 2009.Conference duration: 1-3 days. Average attendance: 35-40. Retreat. "The Women Writers' Winter Retreat was designed for aspiring and professional women writers who cannot seem to find enough time to devote to honing their craft. Each retreat offers class time and workshops facilitated by successful women writers, as well as allows time to do some actual writing, alone or in a group. A Friday night dinner and Keynote kick-starts the weekend, followed by Saturday workshops, free time, meals, and an open mic to read your works. Sunday wraps up with one more workshop and fellowship. All genres welcome. Choice of overnight stay or commuting." Site: Located in the heart of downtown Willoughby, this warm and attractive bed and breakfast is easy to find, around the corner from the main street, Erie Street, and behind a popular Arabica coffee house. Door prizes and book sale/author signings throughout the weekend.

Costs Single room: $269. Shared Room: $199 (includes complete weekend package, with B&B stay and all meals and workshops); weekend commute: $135; Saturday only: $100 (prices include lunch and dinner).

Additional Information "Brochures for the writers retreat are available by December. Accepts inquiries and reservations by e-mail or phone. See Web site for additional information."

Ⓝ Ⓒ WONDERCON

Comic-Con International, P.O. Box 128458, San Diego CA 92112-8458.(619)491-2475. Fax: (619)414-1022. E-mail: cci-info@comic-con.org. Website: www.comic-con.org/wc/. **Contact:** Greg Sassaman, director of programming. Estab. 1986. Annual. Last conference held February 22-24, 2008, in San Francisco. Conference duration: 3 days. Average attendance: 14,500. "In addition to comics publisher panels, you can count on special spotlights on all of our guests. We're currently talking to many major Hollywood studios to once again present exclusive material and appearances at WonderCon. WonderCon offers a giant exhibit hall filled to the brim with the finest in old and new comics, books, original art, anime, manga, movie memorabilia, action figures and toys, DVDs, and much more. WonderCon also presents one of the best Artists' Alley sections in the country with some of the most popular artists in comics, past, present and future." Site: 2008 was held at Moscone West conference center in San Francisco. WonderCon 2008 programming featured Writing with J. Michael Straczynski, Finding Truth in Comic Books, TOKYOPOP Creator Panel, The Secret Origins of Good Readers, Secret History of Comics, and much more. Check Web site for 2009 guests and programming schedule.

Accommodations Does not offer overnight accommodations. Provides list of area hotels or lodging

options. Special hotel rates available for WonderCon attendees. Check Web site for details.
Additional Information For brochure, visit Web site. Editors participate in conference.

WRITE FROM THE HEART

9827 Irvine Avenue, Upper Lake CA 95485. (707) 275-9011. E-mail: Halbooks@HalZinaBennet.com. Website: www.HalZinaBennet.com. **Contact:** Hal. Offered 4 to 6 times a year. Conference duration: 3-5 days. Also, year-long mentorships. Average attendance: 15-30. "Open to all genres, focusing on accessing the author's most individualized sources of imagery, characterization, tensions, content, style and voice." Site: Varies; California's Mt. Shasta, Mendocino California coast, Chicago, Colorado. Panels include Creativity and Life Experiences: Sourcing Story and Character from What You Have Lived, Getting Happily Published, and more. Instructor: Hal Zina Bennett.
Costs $350 and up.
Accommodations No arrangements for transportation. Provides list of area hotels.
Additional Information Brochures available. Request by SASE, e-mail, phone, fax or on Web site. Editors participate in conference. "Hal is a personal writing coach with over 200 successfully published clients, including several bestsellers. His own 30 books include fiction, nonfiction, poetry."

WRITE IT OUT

P.O. Box 704, Sarasota FL 34230-0704. (941) 359-3824. E-mail: rmillerwio@aol.com. Website: www.writeitout.com. **Contact:** Ronni Miller, director. Estab. 1997. Workshops held 2-3 times/year in March, June, July and August. Conference duration: 5-10 days. Average attendance: 4-10. Workshops retreats on "fiction, poetry, memoirs. We also offer intimate, motivational, in-depth free private conferences with instructors." Site: Workshops in Italy in a Tuscan villa, in Sarasota at a hotel, Cape Cod and the North Carolina mountains at inns. Past speakers included Arturo Vivante, novelist.
Costs 2008 fees: Italy, $1,200; Cape Cod, $550. Price includes tution, private conferences and salons. Room, board, and airfare not included.
Additional Information "Critiques on work are given at the workshops." Conference information available year round. For brochures/guidelines e-mail, call or visit Web site. Accepts inquiries by phone, e-mail. Workshops have "small groups, option to spend time writing and not attend classes, with personal appointments with instructors."

WRITE ON THE SOUND WRITERS' CONFERENCE

Edmonds Arts Commission, 700 Main Street, Edmonds WA 98020. (425) 771-0228. Fax: (425) 771-0253. E-mail: wots@ci.edmonds.wa.us. **Contact:** Kris Gillespie, conference organizer. Estab. 1986. Annual. Last conference held October 3-5, 2008. Conference duration: 2.5 days. Average attendance: 180. "Conference is limited to 200 participants, good for networking, and focuses on the craft of writing." Site: "Edmonds is a beautiful community on the shores of Puget Sound, just north of Seattle. View brochure at www.ci.edmonds.wa.us/artscommission/wpts.stm."
Costs $109 by Sept. 17, $134 after Sept. 17 for 2 days, $69 for 1 day (2008); includes registration, morning refreshments and 1 ticket to keynote lecture.
Additional Information Brochures available August 1. Accepts inquiries by phone, e-mail, fax.

WRITERS IN PARADISE

Eckerd College, 4200 54th Ave South, St. Petersburg FL 33711. (727)864-7994. Fax: (727)864-7575. E-mail: cayacr@eckerd.edu. Website: www.writersinparadise.com. **Contact:** Christine Caya, conference coordinator. Estab. 2005. Annual. January 2009. Conference duration: 8 days. Average attendance: 84 max. Workshop. Offers college credit. "Writers in Paradise Conference offers workshop classes in fiction (novel and short story), poetry and nonfiction. Working closely with our award-winning faculty, students will have stimulating opportunities to ask questions and learn valuable skills from fellow students and authors at the top of their form. Most importantly, the intimate size and secluded location of the Writers in Paradise experience allows you the time and opportunity to share your manuscripts, critique one another's work and discuss the craft of writing with experts and peers who can help guide you to the next level." Site: Located on 188 acres of waterfont property in St. Petersburg, Florida, Eckerd College is a private, coeducational college of liberal arts and sciences. In 2008, lectures were given on the craft of writing fiction by Ann Hood and Richard Price. Fiction faculty also led discussions during two mornings of informal roundtables. 2008 Faculty and Guest Faculty included: Lexy Bloom (Vintage/Anchor), Beth Ann Fennelly (Unmentionables), Marc Fitten (The Chattahooche Review), Lisa Gallagher

(HarperCollins), Ann Hood (The Knitting Circle), Tom Franklin (Smonk), Dennis Lehane (Gone, Baby, Gone and Mystic River), Laura Lippman (What the Dead Know), Peter Meinke (Unheard Music), Roland Merullo (Breakfast with Buddha), Thisbe Nissen (The Good People of New York), Richard Price (Clockers and Freedomland), David Hale Smith (DHS Literary, Inc.), Les Standiford (Last Train to Paradise), and Sterling Watson (Sweet Dream Baby).

Costs 2008 tuition fee: $675.

Accommodations Does not offer overnight accommodations. Provides list of area hotels or lodging options.

Additional Information Application materials are required of all attendees. Acceptance is based on a writing sample and a letter detailing your writing background. Submit one short story (25 pg max) or the opening 25 pages of a novel-in-progress, plus a two-page synopsis of the book. Deadline for application materials is December 3rd. "Writers in Paradise is a conference for writers of various styles and approaches. While admission is selective, the admissions committee accepts writers with early potential as well as those with strong backgrounds in writing." Sponsors contest. "At the final Evening Reading Series Event, Co-directors Dennis Lehane and Sterling Watson will announce 'The Best of' nominees of the Writers in Paradise Conference. Winners will be published in *Sabal—A Review Featuring the Best Writing of the Writers in Paradise Conference at Eckerd College*. One winner and one honorable mention will be selected from each workshop based on the material brought into the workshop for discussion. Selection will be made by the faculty member leading the workshop. There are no additional fees or entry forms needed." Information available in October 2008. For brochure, send SASE, call, e-mail. Agents participate in conference. Editors participate in conference. "The tranquil seaside landscape sets the tone for this informal gathering of writers, teachers, editors and literary agents. After 8 days of workshopping and engagemnt with peers and professionals in your field, you will leave this unique opportunity with solid ideas about how to find an agent and get published, along with a new and better understanding of your craft."

WRITERS' INSTITUTE

610 Langdon St., Room 621, Madison WI 53703. (608)262-3447. Fax: (608)265-2475. E-mail: cdesmet@dcs.wisc.edu. Website: www.dcs.wisc.edu/lsa/writing. **Contact:** Christine DeSmet. Estab. 1989. Annual. Conference usually held in April. Site: Pyle Center. Average attendance: 200.

Costs $245 includes materials, breaks.

Accommodations Provides a list of area hotels or lodging options.

Additional Information Sponsors contest. Submit 1-page writing sample and $10 entry fee. Conference speakers are judges. For brochure send e-mail, visit Web site, call, fax. Accepts inquiries by SASE, e-mail, phone, fax. Agents and editors participate in conference.

WRITERS' LEAGUE OF TEXAS AGENTS CONFERENCE

(formerly Agents & Editors Conference), Writers' League of Texas, 611 S. Congress Ave, Suite 130, Austin TX 78704. (512) 499-8914. Fax: (512) 499-0441. E-mail: wlt@writersleague.org. Website: www.writersleague.org. **Contact:** Kristy Bordine, Progam and Membership Coordinator. Estab. 1982. Conference held in June. Conference duration: Friday-Sunday. Average attendance: 350-400. "The Writers' League of Texas Agents Conference is becoming one of the premier agents conferences in the country. The conference offers writers the opportunity to meet top literary agents and editors from New York and the West Coast and learn about the publishing industry through a full program of workshops." Open to writers of both fiction and nonfiction and children's books. Conference registration includes one private consultation with an agent. Workshop topics include: Pitching to agents and editors; finding and working with agents and publishers; writing and marketing fiction and nonfiction; dialogue; characterization; querying; book proposals; publicity and marketing; the business of writing, and the birth of a book. Agents/speakers have included Sara Nelson, Andrea Brown, Mary Evans, Kimberley Cameron, Sha-Shana Crichton, Jessica Faust, Dena Fischer, Mickey Freiberg, Jill Grosjean, Jerry Gross, Lee Gutkind, Jim Hornfischer, Milton Kahn, Abigail Koons, Rebecca Oliver, David Hale Smith, Chuck Sambuchino, Uwe Stender Abraham Verghese, and Ted Weinstein.

Costs $309-450 (discounts available for early registration).

Additional Information Conference includes social events for attendees to meet agents, including cocktail parties, a luncheon, and Pitch Round Tables.

WRITERS' LEAGUE OF TEXAS SUMMER WRITING RETREAT AND WORKSHOPS

611 S. Congress Ave., Suite 130, Austin TX 78704. (512) 499-8914. Fax: (512) 499-0441. E-mail: wlt@writersleague.org. Website: www.writersleague.org. **Contact**: Kristy Bordine, Program and Membership Coordinator. "Classes and workshops provide practical advice and guidance on various aspects of fiction, creative nonfiction and screenwriting." Retreat: Annual Summer Writing Retreat in Alpine, TX, is a weeklong writing intensive with four tracks. Special Presentations: "The Secrets of the Agents" series of workshops with visiting literary agents. Classes and Workshops: Topics: E-publishing; creative nonfiction; screenwriting; novel writing; short fiction; journaling; manuscript revision; memoir writing; poetry; essays; freelance writing; publicity; author/book web sites; and blogging. Instructors include Suzy Spencer, Karleen Koen, Scott Wiggerman, Diane Fanning, Marion Winik, Carol Dawson, Marsha Moyer, Susan Wade, Lila Guzman, Laurie Lynn Drummond, Jesse Sublett, David Wilkinson, John Pipkin, Ann McCutchan, and Dao Strom.
Costs $45-$269.
Additional Information Available at www.writersleague.org.

▣ THE WRITERS' RETREAT

15 Canusa St., Stanstead QC J0B 3E5 Canada. (819) 876-2065. E-mail: info@writersretreat.com. Website: www.writersretreat.com. **Contact:** Micheline Cote, director. Estab. 1998. Year-round. The Writers' Retreat is designed to comprehensively implement, support, and promote residential retreats and literary services to writers of all literary genres. Residential retreats are open year-round and are located in Canada, Costa Rica, Mexico and the United States, coming soon in Europe. Site: The headquarters are located in Quebec on the Vermont/Quebec border with additional retreats located in Ouray, Colorado; Santa Cruz, California; Santa Fe, New Mexico; Prince Edward Island and New Brunswick, Canada. The Writers' Retreat workshops feature instruction in fiction and nonfiction writing and screeenwriting. "Our sole purpose is to provide an ambiance conducive to creativity for career and emerging writers." Residency includes a private studio, breakfast, reference books, wireless Internet, critique, on site editor.
Costs Residency varies between $475-$1,200 per week depending on location of the retreat. To join The Writers' Retreat as a retreat operator, please submit application by e-mail.
Additional Information Accepts inquiries by e-mail.

▧ WRITERS RETREAT WORKSHOP

P.O. Box 4236, Louisville KY 40204. E-mail: wrw04@netscape.net. Website: http://writersretreatworkshop.com. **Contact:** Jason Sitzes, director. Estab. 1987. Annual. May 29-June 7, 2009 and August 28-September 6, 2009Conference duration: 10 days. Average attendance: 30 participants max. Retreat/workshop. "WRW is ten days immersed in a work of narrative story (fiction, nonfiction, memoir). Primarily focused on novelists with a work-in-progress; nonfiction writers with a creative angle will also benefit from the workshop. The Marydale Retreat Center has been for the last twelve years the site of our main 10-day workshop. Rooms are private, some showers are shared, the grounds are quiet and settled near a tranquil pond wth ample walking and 'reflection' space. Weather permitting, we feature a few bonfires through the week. Our morning courses focus on novel craft, our afternoon courses focus on craft and critique, our evening classes focus on the business aspects of writing. We have many optional classes including an Early Bird Session, Shop Talk Sessions, and a Night Owl Session all led by various core and visiting staff." 2009 included author and instructor Les Edgerton (Finding Your Voice), Edgar Award winning suspense author TJ MacGregor (Running Time), NYT best-selling author Will Lavendar, WRW grads and authors Kimberly Frost (Would-be Witch) and Jack Getze (Big Numbers), a representative from the Donald Maass Literary Agency, top agents and editors (past agents include Matt Bialer, Meredith Bernstein, Rachel Vater, Simon Lipskar, Grace Morgan, Donald Maass), and the core staff of Jason Sitzes, Lorin Oberweger, and Roman White. Other guests TBA.
Costs $1750.
Accommodations Cost includes private room, three daily meals, all classes, and one-on-one meetings with staff and agents plus wine and cheese hour daily. Early registration discounts are available. See Web site for more information.
Additional Information A synopsis and three pages are used to review appropriateness of work. "The Robin Hardy Scholarship is available for each session to a first-time participant and covers full tuition. Entry is $15 and requires a partial manuscript and application. See Web site for details and application. For brochure, send SASE, e-mail. Agents and editors participate in conference. E-mail with specific questions and to be placed on our mailing list. We limit registration to 30 participants per session."

WRITERS STUDIO AT UCLA EXTENTION

1010 Westwood Blvd., Los Angeles CA 90024. (310) 825-9415. E-mail: writers@uclaextension.edu. Website: www.uclaextension.edu/writers. **Contact:** Corey Campbell. Estab. 1997. Annual in February. Conference duration: 4 days; 10 a.m. to 6 p.m. Average attendance: 150-200. Intensive writing workshops in the areas of creative writing (fiction and nonfiction), screenwriting and television writing. Site: Conducted at UCLA Extension's 1010 Westwood Center.

Costs Fee is $775 after December 5, 2008.**Accommodations** Information on overnight accommodations is available.

Additional Information For more information, call number (310) 825-9415 or send an e-mail to writers@ uclaextension.edu.

THE WRITERS WORKSHOP

E-mail: bob@bobmayer.org. Website: www.bobmayer.org. **Contact:** Bob Mayer. Estab: 2002. Held every 3 months. Last conference: November 2008. Conference duration: 4 days. Site: varies from workshop to workshop.

Costs $550 in 2007.

Additional Information Limited to eight participants and focused on their novel and marketability.

WRITERS WORKSHOP IN SCIENCE FICTION

Lawrence KS 66045-2115. (785)864-3380. Fax: (785)864-1159. E-mail: jgunn@ku.edu. Website: www. ku.edu/~sfcenter. **Contact:** James Gunn, professor. Estab. 1984. Annual. Workshop held in late June to early July. Conference duration: 2 weeks. Average attendance: 10-14. The workshop is "small, informal and aimed at writers on the edge of publication or regular publication." For writing and marketing science fiction and fantasy. Site: "Housing is provided and classes meet in university housing on the University of Kansas campus. Workshop sessions operate informally in a lounge." Past guests included Frederik Pohl, SF writer and former editor and agent; John Ordover, writer and editor; George Zebrowski, Pamela Sargent, Kij Johnson and Christopher McKittrick, writers; Lou Anders, editor. A novel workshop in science fiction and fantasy is also available.

Costs $400 tuition. Housing and meals are additional.

Accommodations Several airport shuttle services offer reasonable transportation from the Kansas City International Airport to Lawrence. During past conferences, students were housed in a student dormitory at $14/day double, $28/day single.

Additional Information "Admission to the workshop is by submission of an acceptable story. Two additional stories should be submitted by the end of May. These three stories are distributed to other participants for critiquing and are the basis for the first week of the workshop; one story is rewritten for the second week. The workshop offers a 3-hour session manuscript critiquing each afternoon. The rest of the day is free for writing, study, consultation and recreation." Information available in December. For brochures/guidelines send SASE, visit Web site, e-mail, fax, call. The workshop concludes with The Campbell Conference, a round-table discussion of a single topic, and the presentation of the Campbell and Sturgeon Awards for the Best SF Novel and Short Story of the Year. "The Writers Workshop in Science Fiction is intended for writers who have just started to sell their work or need that extra bit of understanding or skill to become a published writer."

WRITE-TO-PUBLISH CONFERENCE

9118 W Elmwood Dr., Suite 1G, Niles IL 60714-5820. (847) 296-3964. Fax: (847)296-0754. E-mail: lin@ writetopublish.com. Website: www.writetopublish.com. **Contact:** Lin Johnson, director. Estab. 1971. Annual. Conference held June 3-6, 2009. Average attendance: 250. Conference on "writing all types of manuscripts for the Christian market." Site: Wheaton College, Wheaton, IL (Chicago).

Costs approximately $450.

Accommodations In campus residence halls or discounted hotel rates. Cost approximately $225 310.

Additional Information Optional ms evaluation available. College credit available. Conference information available in January. For details, visit Web site, or e-mail brochure@writetopublish.com. Accepts inquiries by e-mail, fax, phone.

Ⓝ ⤢ WRITING STUDIO

P.O. Box 1020, Banff AB T1L 1H5. (800) 565-9989. E-mail: arts_info@banffcentre.ca. Website: www. banffcentre.ca. **Contact:** Office of the Registrar. Annual w riting workshop. Program dates: April 27,

2008 - May 30, 2009. Application deadline: November 21, 2008. " Writing Studio is a five-week program offering poets and writers of fiction and other narrative prose the time, space, and support they need to pursue a writing project, with the benefit of editorial consultation. Designed for literary writers at an early stage in their careers, the program offers an extended period of uninterrupted writing time, one-on-one editorial assistance from experienced writers/editors, and an opportunity to engage with a community of working writers. The Writing Studio is an ideal environment for artistic inspiration and growth. Situated in the majestic Canadian Rockies, The Banff Centre offers a unique natural setting for artists of all disciplines to realize their creative potential. All participants may work with at least 2 or, in the case of poets, 3 faculty mentors during the 5 weeks of the program. As part of the Banff Summer Arts Festival, Writing Studio participants and faculty offer a weekly reading series. To help writers develop their public reading skills, we offer one-on-one sessions with a voice and relaxation instructor. Activities other than the writer's individual work (i.e., guided hikes, social gatherings, concerts and performances) are voluntary, and participants are encouraged to structure their time to suit their own needs and goals." Site: The Banff Centre enables both emerging and established individuals to interact within a multidisciplinary and multicultural environment, allowing them to push boundaries, to experiment, to share knowledge, to create and showcase new work, and to develop new ideas and solutions for the present and the future

Costs Workshop fee: please see Web site for up-to-date information, www.banffcentre.ca/writing/.

Accommodations Please see Web site for up-to-date information. On-site only, hotel style which also serve as private work spaces. Computers should be brought along for private use. Public computers available on campus.

Additional Information "At time of application, writers must submit writing samples and statement of expectations. Application fee: $5 7 Canadian. Brochure currently available for e-mail and on Web site. For inquiries, contact by SASE, e-mail, phone, fax. Other writing programs are offered at The Banff Centre include: Banff International Translation Centre, Literary Journalism, Spoken Word, Science Communications, and Mountain Writing."

⚎ WRITING WITH STYLE

The Banff Centre, P.O. Box 1020, Banff AB T1L 1H5 Canada. (800) 565-9989. E-mail: arts_info@ banffcentre.ca. Website: www.banffcentre.ca. **Contact:**Office of the Registrar. Semiannual. Writing workshop. Program dates: Spring: April 20, 2009 - April 25, 2009; Fall: September 14, 2009 - September 19, 2009. Application deadline: February 01, 2009 (spring); May 15, 2009 (fall). Conference duration: 1 week. Average attendance: 30-40 participants. "Writing With Style is a unique opportunity for writers of all levels to participate in a week-long workshop at The Banff Centre, a setting for artists that is both inspiring and productive. Whether you have attended many writing workshops or this is your first, Writing With Style will be an intense and transformative experience. Amidst a diverse community of writers, you will encounter new ideas and gain confidence in your own style and voice, while shaping and editing your work-in-progress under the guidance of an experienced writer and editor. The program offers a variety of activities designed to maximize the artistic growth of each writer. Participants will enjoy morning group sessions led by a faculty member, in which their work is read and discussed by the other writers in the program. Afternoons are left free for writing and one-on-one meetings and consultations with faculty. Participants are also invited to take part in evening readings with faculty and fellow writers." Site: "The Banff Centre enables both emerging and established individuals to interact within a multidisciplinary and multicultural environment, allowing them to push boundaries, to experiment, to share knowledge, to create and showcase new work, and to develop new ideas and solutions for the present and the future." G enres include short fiction, memoir, poetry, travel writing, creative non-fiction and mystery writing.

Costs Workshop fee: please see Web site for up-to-date information, www.banffcentre.ca/writing/.

Accommodations On-site only, hotel style which also serve as private work spaces. Computers should be brought along for private use. Public computers available on campus. Please see Web site for up-to-date information, www.banffcentre.ca/writing/.

Additional Information "At time of application, writers must submit writing samples and statement of expectations. Application fee: $31 Canadian. Brochure currently available for e-mail and on Web site. For inquiries, contact by SASE, e-mail, phone, fax. Other more advanced writing programs are also offered at The Banff Centre."

▧ THE HELENE WURLITZER FOUNDATION

P.O. Box 1891, Taos NM 87571.(575)758-2413. E-mail: hwf@taosnet.com. Website: www. wurlitzerfoundation.org. Estab. 1953. Residence duration: 3 months. "The Foundation's purpose is to provide a quiet haven where artists may pursue their creative endeavors without pressure to produce while they are in residence."

Accommodations "Provides individual housing in fully furnished studio/houses (casitas), rent and utility free. Artists are responsible for transportation to and from Taos, their meals, and the materials for their work. Bicycles are provided upon request."

YADDO

Box 395, Saratoga Springs NY 12866-0395. (518)584-0746. Fax: (518)584-1312. E-mail: yaddo@yaddo. org. Website: www.yaddo.org. **Contact:** Candace Wait, program director. Estab. 1900. Two seasons: large season is in mid-May-August; small season is late September-May (stays from 2 weeks to 2 months; average stay is 5 weeks). Average attendance: Accommodates approximately 32 artists in large season, 12-15 in the small season. "Those qualified for invitations to Yaddo are highly qualified writers, visual artists, composers, choreographers, performance artists and film and video artists who are working at the professional level in their fields. Artists who wish to work collaboratively are encouraged to apply. An abiding principle at Yaddo is that applications for residencies are judged on the quality of the artists' work and professional promise." Site: includes four small lakes, a rose garden, woodland.

Costs No fee is charged; residency includes room, board and studio space. Limited travel expenses are available to artists accepted for residencies at Yaddo.

Accommodations Provisions include room, board and studio space. No stipends are offered.

Additional Information To apply: Filing fee is $20 (checks payable to Corporation of Yaddo). Two letters of recommendation are requested. Applications are considered by the Admissions Committee and invitations are issued by March 15 (deadline: January 1) and October 1 (deadline: August 1). Information available for SASE (63¢ postage), by e-mail, fax or phone and on Web site. Accepts inquiries by e-mail, fax, SASE, phone.

ZOETROPE: ALL-STORY SHORT STORY WRITERS' WORKSHOP

916 Kearny St., San Francisco CA 94133. (415)788-7500. E-mail: info@all-story.com. Website: www. all-story.com. **Contact:** Michael Ray, editor. Estab. 1997. Annual. Last workshop held June 20-27, 2009. Conference duration: 1 week. Average attendance: 20. Workshop focuses on fiction, specifically short stories. Site: Francis Ford Coppola's gorgeous Blancaneaux Lodge in Belize, on the banks of the Privassion River. Guests stay in luxurious private cabanas and villas, all with spa baths and decks with hammocks and river views. Past instructors include Philip Gourevitch, George Saunders, Robert Olen Butler, Charles D'Ambrosio, Susan Straight, and David Bezmozgis.

Costs Ranges from $2,750 to $3,850, depending on accommodations. That fee is all-inclusive, including accommodations, food, workshop, day excursions, all transfers to and from Belize City, and a camp T-shirt.

Additional Information Please submit a completed application and an original work of short fiction less than 5,000 words by June 1. Application forms are available on the Web site. Accepts inquiries by e-mail. Editors attend the workshop.

Publishers & Their Imprints

The publishing world is in constant transition. With all the buying, selling, reorganizing, consolidating, and dissolving, it's hard to keep publishers and their imprints straight. To help make sense of these changes, here's a breakdown of major publishers (and their divisions)—who owns whom and which imprints are under each company umbrella. Keep in mind that this information changes frequently. The Web site of each publisher is provided to help you keep an eye on this ever-evolving business.

HACHETTE BOOK GROUP USA

www.hachettebookgroupusa.com

Center Street

FaithWords

Grand Central Publishing
Business Plus
5-Spot
Forever
Springboard Press
Twelve
Vision
Wellness Central

Hachette Book Group Digital Media
Hachette Audio

Little, Brown and Company
Back Bay Books
Bulfinch
Reagan Arthur Books

Little, Brown Books for Young Readers
LB Kids
Poppy

Orbit

Yen Press

HARLEQUIN ENTERPRISES

www.eharlequin.com

Harlequin
Harlequin American Romance
Harlequin Bianca
Harlequin Blaze
Harlequin Deseo
Harlequin Historical
Harlequin Intrigue
Harlequin Jazmin
Harlequin Julia
Harlequin Medical Romance
Harlequin NASCAR
Harlequin NEXT

Harlequin Presents
Harlequin Romance
Harlequin Superromance
Harlequin eBooks
Harlequin Special Releases
Harlequin Nonfiction
Harlequin Historical Undone

HQN Books
HQN eBooks

LUNA
Luna eBooks

MIRA
Mira eBooks

Kimani Press Kimani Romance
Kimani Press Kimani TRU
Kimani Press New Spirit
Kimani Press Sepia
Kimani Press Special Releases
Kimani Press eBooks

Red Dress Ink
Red Dress eBooks

Silhouette
Silhouette Desire
Silhouette Nocturne
Silhouette Romantic Suspense
Silhouette Special Edition

SPICE
SPICE Books
SPICE Briefs

Steeple Hill
Steeple Hill Café©
Steeple Hill Love Inspired
Steeple Hill Love Inspired Historical
Steeple Hill Love Inspired Suspense
Steeple Hill Women's Fiction

Worldwide Library
Rogue Angel
Worldwide Mystery

HARPERCOLLINS

www.harpercollins.com

HarperMorrow
Amistad
Avon
Avon A
Avon Inspire
Avon Red

Collins
Collins Business
Collins Design
Collins Living
Ecco
Eos
Harper
Harper Mass Market
Harper Perennial
Harper Perennial
Modern Classics
Harper Audio
HarperCollins
HarperCollins e-Books
HarperEntertainment
HarperLuxe
HarperOne
HarperStudio
William Morrow
Morrow Cookbooks
Rayo

HarperCollins Children's Books
Amistad
Eos

Greenwillow Books
HarperCollins
Children's Audio
Harper Festival
HarperTeen
HarperTrophy

HarperCollins U.K.
Harper Press
Blue Door
Fourth Estate
The Friday Project
HarperPress
HarperFiction
Voyager
Avon
HarperCollins Childrens Books
Collins
Times
Jane's
HarperCollins Canada
HarperCollinsPublishers
Collins Canada
HarperPerennial Canada
HarperTrophyCanada
Phyllis Bruce Books
HarperCollins Australia
HarperCollins India
HarperCollins New
Zealand Zondervan
Zonderkids
Vida

MACMILLAN US (HOLTZBRINCK)

http://us.macmillan.com

MacMillan
Farrar, Straus & Giroux
Faber and Faber, Inc
Farrar, Straus
Hill & Wang
North Point Press
First Second
Henry Holt
Henry Holt Books for Young Readers
Holt Paperbacks
Metropolitan
Times
MacMillan Children's
Feiwel & Friends
Farrar, Straus and Giroux Books for Young Readers
Kingfisher
Holt Books for Young Readers
Priddy Books
Roaring Brook Press
Square Fish

Picador
Palgrave MacMillan
Tor/Forge Books
Tor
Forge
Orb
Tor/Seven Seas
St. Martin's Press
Minotaur Press
Thomas Dunne Books
Griffin
St. Martin's Press Paperbacks
Let's Go
Truman Talley Books
Bedford, Freeman & Worth Publishing Group
Bedford/St. Martin's
Hayden-McNeil
W.H. Freeman
Worth Publishers
MacMillan Audio

PENGUIN GROUP (USA), INC.

www.penguingroup.com
Penguin Adult Division
Ace
Alpha
Amy Einhorn Books/Putnam
Avery
Berkley
Dutton
Gotham
HPBooks
Hudson Street Press
Jeremy P. Tarcher
Jove NAL
Penguin
Penguin Press
Perigree
Plume

Portfolio
Riverhead
Sentinel
Viking
Price Stern Sloan
Young Readers Division
Dial
Dutton
Firebird
Frederick Warne
Grosset & Dunlap
Philomel
Puffin Books
Putnam
Razorbill
Speak
Viking

RANDOM HOUSE, INC. (BERTELSMANN)

www.randomhouse.com
Crown Publishing Group
Broadway Business
Crown
Crown Business
Crown Forum
Clarkson Potter
Doubleday Business
Doubleday Religion
Harmony
Potter Craft
Potter Style
Three Rivers Press
Shaye Areheart Books
Waterbrook
Multnomah
Knopf Doubleday Publishing Group
Alfred A. Knopf
Anchor Books
Doubleday
Doubleday Religion
Flying Dolphin Press
Broadway
Everyman's Library
Nan A. Talese
Pantheon Books
Schocken Books
Vintage
Monacelli Press
Random House Publishing Group
Ballantine Books
Bantam Dell
Del Rey
Del Rey/Lucas Books
The Dial Press
The Modern Library
One World
Random House Trade Group
Random House Trade Paperbacks
Reader's Circle
Spectra
Spiegel and Grau
Strivers Row Books
Villard Books

Random House Audio Publishing Group
Listening Library
Random House Audio Random House
Children's Books
Kids@Random
Golden Books
Alfred A. Knopf Children's Books
Bantam Beginner Books
Crown Children's Books
David Fickling Books
Delacorte Press
Disney Books for Young Readers
Doubleday Children's Books
Dragonfly
First Time Books
Landmark Books
Laurel-Leaf
Picturebacks
Random House Books for Young Readers
Robin Corey Books
Schwartz and Wade Books
Sesame Workshop
Step into Reading
Stepping Stone Books
Wendy Lamb Books
Yearling Random House Information Group
Fodor's Travel
Living Language
Prima Games
Princeton Review
RH Puzzles & Games
RH Reference Publishing
Sylvan Learning
Random House International
Arete
McClelland & Stewart Ltd.
Plaza & Janes
RH Australia
RH of Canada Limited
RH Mondadori
RH South America
RH United Kingdom
Transworld UK
Verlagsgruppe RH

SIMON & SCHUSTER

www.simonsays.com

Simon & Schuster Adult Publishing
Atria Books
Washington Square Press
Beyond Words
Free Press
Howard Books
Pocket Books
Scribner
Simon & Schuster
Strebor
The Touchstone & Fireside Group
Simon & Schuster Audio
Pimsleur
Simon & Schuster Audioworks
Encore

Sound Ideas
Nightingale Conant
Simon & Schuster Children's Publishing
Aladdin Paperbacks
Atheneum Books for Young Readers
Libros
Para Nin´os
Little Simon®
Little Simon
Inspirations
Margaret K. McElderry Books
Simon & Schuster Books for Young Readers
Simon Pulse
Simon Scribbles
Simon Spotlight®

Canadian Writers Take Note

While much of the information contained in this section applies to all writers, here are some specifics of interest to Canadian writers:

Postage: When sending an SASE from Canada, you will need an International Reply Coupon ($3.50). Also be aware, a GST tax is required on postage in Canada and for mail with postage under $5 going to destinations outside the country. Since Canadian postage rates are voted on in January of each year (after we go to press), contact a Canada Post Corporation Customer Service Division (located in most cities in Canada) or visit www. canadapost.ca for the most current rates.

Copyright: For information on copyrighting your work and to obtain forms, write Canadian Intellectual Property Office, Industry Canada, Place du Portage I, 50 Victoria St., Room C-114, Gatineau, Quebec K1A 0C9 or call (866)997-1936. Web site: www.cipo.gc.ca.

The public lending right: The Public Lending Right Commission has established that eligible Canadian authors are entitled to payments when a book is available through a library. Payments are determined by a sampling of the holdings of a representative number of libraries. To find out more about the program and to learn if you are eligible, write to the Public Lending Right Commission at 350 Albert St., P.O. Box 1047, Ottawa, Ontario K1P 5V8 or call (613)566-4378 or (800)521-5721 for information. Web site: www.plr-dpp.ca. The Commission, which is part of The Canada Council, produces a helpful pamphlet, *How the PLR System Works* >, on the program.

Grants available to Canadian writers: Most province art councils or departments of culture provide grants to resident writers. Some of these, as well as contests for Canadian writers, are listed in our Contests and Awards section. For national programs, contact The Canada Council, Writing and Publishing Section, 350 Alberta St., P.O. Box 1047, Ottawa, Ontario K1P 5V8 or call (613)566-4414 or (800)263-5588 for information. Fax: (613)566-4410. Web site: www.canadacouncil.ca.

For more information: Contact The Writer's Union of Canada, 90 Richmond St. E, Suite 200, Toronto, Ontario M5C 1P1; call them at (416)703-8982 or fax them at (416)504-9090. E-mail: info@writersunion.ca. Web site: www.writersunion.ca. This organization provides a wealth of information (as well as strong support) for Canadian writers, including specialized publications on publishing contracts; contract negotiations; the author/editor relationship; author awards, competitions and grants; agents; taxes for writers, libel issues and access to archives in Canada.

Printing & Production Terms Defined

In most of the magazine listings in this book, you will find a brief physical description of each publication. This material usually includes the number of pages, type of paper, type of binding and whether or not the magazine uses photographs and/or illustrations.

Although it is important to look at a copy of the magazine to which you are submitting, these descriptions can give you a general idea of what the publication looks like. This material can provide you with a feel for the magazine's financial resources and prestige. Do not, however, rule out small, simply produced publications, as these may be the most receptive to new writers. Watch for publications that have increased their page count or improved their production from year to year. This is a sign the publication is doing well and may be accepting more fiction.

You will notice a wide variety of printing terms used within these descriptions. We explain here some of the more common terms used in our listing descriptions. We do not include explanations of terms such as Mohawk and Karma which are brand names and refer to the paper manufacturer.

PAPER

A5: An international paper standard; 148 × 210 mm or 5.8 × 8.3 in.

acid-free: Paper that has low or no acid content. This type of paper resists deterioration from exposure to the elements. More expensive than many other types of paper, publications done on acid-free paper can last a long time.

bond: Bond paper is often used for stationery and is more transparent than text paper. It can be made of either sulphite (wood) or cotton fiber. Some bonds have a mixture of both wood and cotton (such as "25 percent cotton" paper). This is the type of paper most often used in photocopying or as standard typing paper.

coated/uncoated stock: Coated and uncoated are terms usually used when referring to book or text paper. More opaque than bond, it is the paper most used for offset printing. As the name implies, uncoated paper has no coating. Coated paper is coated with a layer of clay, varnish or other chemicals. It comes in various sheens and surfaces depending on the type of coating, but the most common are dull, matte and gloss.

cover stock: Cover stock is heavier book or text paper used to cover a publication. It comes in a variety of colors and textures and can be coated on one or both sides.

CS1/CS2: Most often used when referring to cover stock, CS1 means paper that is coated only on one side; CS2 is paper coated on both sides.

newsprint: Inexpensive absorbent pulp wood paper often used in newspapers and tabloids.

text: Text paper is similar to book paper (a smooth paper used in offset printing), but it has been given some texture by using rollers or other methods to apply a pattern to the paper.

vellum: Vellum is a text paper that is fairly porous and soft.

Some notes about paper weight and thickness: Often you will see paper thickness described in terms of pounds such as 80 lb. or 60 lb. paper. The weight is determined by figuring how many pounds in a ream of a particular paper (a ream is 500 sheets). This can be confusing, however, because this figure is based on a standard sheet size and standard sheet sizes vary depending on the type of paper used. This information is most helpful when comparing papers of the same type. For example, 80 lb. book paper versus 60 lb. book paper. Since the size of the paper is the same it would follow that 80 lb. paper is the thicker, heavier paper.

Some paper, especially cover stock, is described by the actual thickness of the paper. This is expressed in a system of points. Typical paper thicknesses range from 8 points to 14 points thick.

PRINTING

There are many other printing methods but these are the ones most commonly referred to in our listings.

letterpress: Letterpress printing is printing that uses a raised surface such as type. The type is inked and then pressed against the paper. Unlike offset printing, only a limited number of impressions can be made, as the surface of the type can wear down.

offset: Offset is a printing method in which ink is transferred from an image-bearing plate to a "blanket" and from the blanket to the paper.

sheet-fed offset: Offset printing in which the paper is fed one piece at a time.

web offset: Offset printing in which a roll of paper is printed and then cut apart to make individual sheets.

BINDING

case binding: In case binding, signatures (groups of pages) are stitched together with thread rather than glued together. The stitched pages are then trimmed on three sides and glued into a hardcover or board ``case'' or cover. Most hardcover books and thicker magazines are done this way.

comb binding: A comb is a plastic spine used to hold pages together with bent tabs that are fed through punched holes in the edge of the paper.

perfect binding: Used for paperback books and heavier magazines, perfect binding involves gathering signatures (groups of pages) into a stack, trimming off the folds so the edge is flat and gluing a cover to that edge.

saddle stitched: Publications in which the pages are stitched together using metal staples. This fairly inexpensive type of binding is usually used with books or magazines that are under 80 pages.

Smythe-sewn: Binding in which the pages are sewn together with thread. Smythe is the name of the most common machine used for this purpose.

spiral binding: A wire spiral that is wound through holes punched in pages is a spiral bind. This is the binding used in spiral notebooks.

Glossary

Advance. Payment by a publisher to an author prior to the publication of a book, to be deducted from the author's future royalties.

Adventure story. A genre of fiction in which action is the key element, overshadowing characters, theme and setting. The conflict in an adventure story is often man against nature. A secondary plot that reinforces this kind of conflict is sometimes included. In Allistair MacLean's *Night Without End*, for example, the hero, while investigating a mysterious Arctic air crash, also finds himself dealing with espionage, sabotage and murder.

All rights. The rights contracted to a publisher permitting a manuscript's use anywhere and in any form, including movie and book club sales, without additional payment to the writer.

Amateur sleuth. The character in a mystery, usually the protagonist, who does the detection but is not a professional private investigator or police detective.

Anthology. A collection of selected writings by various authors.

Association of Authors' Representatives (AAR). An organization for literary agents committed to maintaining excellence in literary representation.

Auction. Publishers sometimes bid against each other for the acquisition of a manuscript that has excellent sales prospects.

Backlist. A publisher's books not published during the current season but still in print.

Biographical novel. A life story documented in history and transformed into fiction through the insight and imagination of the writer. This type of novel melds the elements of biographical research and historical truth into the framework of a novel, complete with dialogue, drama and mood. A biographical novel resembles historical fiction, save for one aspect: Characters in a historical novel may be fabricated and then placed into an authentic setting; characters in a biographical novel have actually lived.

Book producer/packager. An organization that may develop a book for a publisher based upon the publisher's idea or may plan all elements of a book, from its initial concept to writing and marketing strategies, and then sell the package to a book publisher and/or movie producer.

Cliffhanger. Fictional event in which the reader is left in suspense at the end of a chapter or episode, so that interest in the story's outcome will be sustained.

Clip. Sample, usually from a newspaper or magazine, of a writer's published work.

Cloak-and-dagger. A melodramatic, romantic type of fiction dealing with espionage and intrigue.

Commercial. Publishers whose concern is salability, profit and success with a large readership.

Contemporary. Material dealing with popular current trends, themes or topics.

Contributor's copy. Copy of an issue of a magazine or published book sent to an author whose work is included.

Copublishing. An arrangement in which the author and publisher share costs and profits.

Copyediting. Editing a manuscript for writing style, grammar, punctuation and factual accuracy.

Copyright. The legal right to exclusive publication, sale or distribution of a literary work.

Cover letter. A brief letter sent with a complete manuscript submitted to an editor.

"Cozy" (or "teacup") mystery. Mystery usually set in a small British town, in a bygone era, featuring a somewhat genteel, intellectual protagonist.

Cyberpunk. Type of science fiction, usually concerned with computer networks and human-computer combinations, involving young, sophisticated protagonists.

Electronic rights. The right to publish material electronically, either in book or short story form.

E-zine. A magazine that is published electronically.

Electronic submission. A submission of material by e-mail or on computer disk.

Ethnic fiction. Stories and novels whose central characters are black, Native American, Italian-American, Jewish, Appalachian or members of some other specific cultural group. Ethnic fiction usually deals with a protagonist caught between two conflicting ways of life: mainstream American culture and his ethnic heritage.

Experimental fiction. Fiction that is innovative in subject matter and style; avant-garde, non-formulaic, usually literary material.

Exposition. The portion of the storyline, usually the beginning, where background information about character and setting is related.

Fair use. A provision in the copyright law that says short passages from copyrighted material may be used without infringing on the owner's rights.

Fanzine. A noncommercial, small-circulation magazine usually dealing with fantasy, horror or science-fiction literature and art.

Fictional biography. The biography of a real person that goes beyond the events of a person's life by being fleshed out with imagined scenes and dialogue. The writer of fictional biographies strives to make it clear that the story is, indeed, fiction and not history.

First North American serial rights. The right to publish material in a periodical before it appears in book form, for the first time, in the United States or Canada.

Flash fiction. See short short stories.

Galleys. The first typeset version of a manuscript that has not yet been divided into pages.

Genre. A formulaic type of fiction such as romance, western or horror.

Gothic. This type of category fiction dates back to the late 18th and early 19th centuries. Contemporary gothic novels are characterized by atmospheric, historical settings and feature young, beautiful women who win the favor of handsome, brooding heroes-simultaneously dealing successfully with some life-threatening menace, either natural or supernatural. Gothics rely on mystery, peril, romantic relationships and a sense of foreboding for their strong, emotional effect on the reader. A classic early gothic novel is Emily Bronte's Wuthering Heights. The gothic writer builds a series of credible, emotional crises for his ultimately triumphant heroine. Sex between the woman and her lover is implied rather than graphically detailed; the writer's descriptive talents are used instead to paint rich, desolate, gloomy settings in stark mansions and awesome castles. He composes slow-paced, intricate sketches that create a sense of impending evil on every page.

Graphic novel. A book (original or adapted) that takes the form of a long comic strip or heavily illustrated story of 40 pages or more, produced in paperback. Though called a novel, these can also be works of nonfiction.

Hard science fiction. Science fiction with an emphasis on science and technology.

Hard-boiled detective novel. Mystery novel featuring a private eye or police detective as the protagonist; usually involves a murder. The emphasis is on the details of the crime and the tough, unsentimental protagonist usually takes a matter-of-fact attitude towards violence.

High fantasy. Fantasy with a medieval setting and a heavy emphasis on chivalry and the quest.

Historical fiction. A fictional story set in a recognizable period of history. As well as telling the stories of ordinary people's lives, historical fiction may involve political or social events of the time.

Horror. Howard Phillips (H.P.) Lovecraft, generally acknowledged to be the master of the horror tale in the 20th century and the most important American writer of this genre since Edgar Allan Poe, maintained that "The oldest and strongest emotion of mankind is fear, and the oldest and strongest kind of fear is fear of the unknown. These facts few psychologists will dispute, and their admitted truth must establish for all time the genuineness and dignity of the weirdly horrible tale as a literary form." Lovecraft distinguishes horror literature from fiction based entirely on physical fear and the merely gruesome. "The true weird tale has something more than secret murder, bloody bones or a sheeted form clanking chains according to rule. A certain atmosphere of breathless and unexplainable dread of outer, unknown forces must be present; there must be a hint, expressed with a seriousness and portentousness becoming its subject, of that most terrible concept of the human brain-a malign and particular suspension or defeat of the fixed laws of Nature which are our only safeguards against the assaults of chaos and the daemons of unplumbed space." It is that atmosphere-the creation of a particular sensation or emotional level-that, according to Lovecraft, is the most important element in the creation of horror literature. Contemporary writers enjoying considerable success in horror fiction include Stephen King, Robert Bloch, Peter Straub and Dean Koontz.

Hypertext fiction. A fictional form, read electronically, which incorporates traditional elements of storytelling with a nonlinear plot line, in which the reader determines the direction of the story by opting for one of many author-supplied links.

Imprint. Name applied to a publisher's specific line (e.g. Owl, an imprint of Henry Holt).

Interactive fiction. Fiction in book or computer-software format where the reader determines the path the story will take by choosing from several alternatives at the end of each chapter or episode.

International Reply Coupon (IRC). A form purchased at a post office and enclosed with a letter or manuscript to a international publisher, to cover return postage costs.

Juveniles, Writing for. This includes works intended for an audience usually between the ages of 2 and 18. Categories of children's books are usually divided in this way: (1) picture books and storybooks (ages 2 to 8); (2) young readers or easy-to-read books (ages 5 to 8); (3) middle readers or middle grade (ages 9 to 11); (4) young adult books (ages 12 and up).

Libel. Written or printed words that defame, malign or damagingly misrepresent a living person.

Literary fiction. The general category of fiction which employs more sophisticated technique, driven as much or more by character evolution than action in the plot.

Literary fiction vs. commercial fiction. To the writer of literary, or serious, fiction, style and technique are often as important as subject matter. Commercial fiction, however, is written with the intent of reaching as wide an audience as possible. Commercial fiction is sometimes called genre fiction because books of this type often fall into categories, such as western, gothic, romance, historical, mystery and horror.

Literary agent. A person who acts for an author in finding a publisher or arranging contract terms on a literary project.

Mainstream fiction. Fiction which appeals to a more general reading audience, versus literary or genre fiction. Mainstream is more plot-driven than literary fiction and less formulaic than genre fiction.

Malice domestic novel. A mystery featuring a murder among family members, such as the murder of a spouse or a parent.

Manuscript. The author's unpublished copy of a work, usually typewritten, used as the basis for typesetting.

Mass market paperback. Softcover book on a popular subject, usually around 4X7, directed to a general audience and sold in drugstores and groceries as well as in bookstores.

Middle reader. Also called middle grade. Juvenile fiction for readers aged 9 to 11.

Ms(s). Abbreviation for manuscript(s).

Multiple submission. Submission of more than one short story at a time to the same editor. Do not make a multiple submission unless requested.

Mystery. A form of narration in which one or more elements remain unknown or unexplained until the end of the story. The modern mystery story contains elements of the serious novel: a convincing account of a character's struggle with various physical and psychological obstacles in an effort to achieve his goal, good characterization and sound motivation.

Narration. The account of events in a story's plot as related by the speaker or the voice of the author.

Narrator. The person who tells the story, either someone involved in the action or the voice of the writer.

New Age. A term including categories such as astrology, psychic phenomena, spiritual healing, UFOs, mysticism and other aspects of the occult.

Noir. A style of mystery involving hard-boiled detectives and bleak settings.

Nom de plume. French for ``pen name''; a pseudonym.

Nonfiction novel. A work in which real events and people are written [about] in novel form, but are not camouflaged, as they are in the roman a clef. In the nonfiction novel, reality is presented imaginatively; the writer imposes a novelistic structure on the actual events, keying sections of narrative around moments that are seen (in retrospect) as symbolic. In this way, he creates a coherence that the actual story might not have had. *The Executioner's Song*, by Norman Mailer, and *In Cold Blood*, by Truman Capote, are notable examples of the nonfiction novel.

Novella (also novelette). A short novel or long story, approximately 20,000-50,000 words.

#10 envelope. 4 × 9½ envelope, used for queries and other business letters.

Offprint. Copy of a story taken from a magazine before it is bound.

One-time rights. Permission to publish a story in periodical or book form one time only.

Outline. A summary of a book's contents, often in the form of chapter headings with a few sentences outlining the action of the story under each one; sometimes part of a book proposal.

Over the transom. A phrase referring to unsolicited manuscripts, or those that come in "over the transom."

Payment on acceptance. Payment from the magazine or publishing house as soon as the decision to print a manuscript is made.

Payment on publication. Payment from the publisher after a manuscript is printed.

Pen name. A pseudonym used to conceal a writer's real name.

Periodical. A magazine or journal published at regular intervals.

Plot. The carefully devised series of events through which the characters progress in a work of fiction.

Police procedural. A mystery featuring a police detective or officer who uses standard professional police practices to solve a crime.

Popular fiction. Generally, a synonym for category or genre fiction; i.e., fiction intended to appeal to audiences for certain kinds of novels. Popular, or category, fiction is defined as such primarily for the convenience of publishers, editors, reviewers and booksellers who must identify novels of different areas of interest for potential readers.

Print on demand (POD). Novels produced digitally one at a time, as ordered. Self-publishing through print on demand technology typically involves some fees for the author. Some authors use POD to create a manuscript in book form to send to prospective traditional publishers.

Proofreading. Close reading and correction of a manuscript's typographical errors.

Proofs. A typeset version of a manuscript used for correcting errors and making changes, often a photocopy of the galleys.

Proposal. An offer to write a specific work, usually consisting of an outline of the work and one or two completed chapters.

Protagonist. The principal or leading character in a literary work.

Psychological novel. A narrative that emphasizes the mental and emotional aspects of its characters, focusing on motivations and mental activities rather than on exterior events. The psychological novelist is less concerned about relating what happened than about exploring why it happened. The term is most often used to describe 20th-century works that employ techniques such as interior monologue and stream of consciousness. Two examples of contemporary psychological novels are Judith Guest's *Ordinary People* and Mary Gordon's *The Company of Women*.

Public domain. Material that either was never copyrighted or whose copyright term has expired.

Pulp magazine. A periodical printed on inexpensive paper, usually containing lurid, sensational stories or articles.

Query. A letter written to an editor to elicit interest in a story the writer wants to submit.

Reader. A person hired by a publisher to read unsolicited manuscripts.

Reading fee. An arbitrary amount of money charged by some agents and publishers to read a submitted manuscript.

Regency romance. A subgenre of romance, usually set in England between 1811-1820.

Remainders. Leftover copies of an out-of-print book, sold by the publisher at a reduced price.

Reporting time. The number of weeks or months it takes an editor to report back on an author's query or manuscript.

Reprint rights. Permission to print an already published work whose rights have been sold to another magazine or book publisher.

Roman á clef. French "novel with a key." A novel that represents actual living or historical characters and events in fictionalized form.

Romance novel. A type of category fiction in which the love relationship between a man and a woman pervades the plot. The story is often told from the viewpoint of the heroine, who meets a man (the hero), falls in love with him, encounters a conflict that hinders their relationship, then resolves the conflict. Romance is the overriding element in this kind of story: The couple's relationship determines the plot and tone of the book. The theme of the novel is the woman's sexual awakening. Although she may not be a virgin, she has never before been so emotionally aroused. Despite all this emotion, however, characters and plot both must be well developed and realistic. Throughout a romance novel, the reader senses the sexual and emotional attraction between the heroine and hero. Lovemaking scenes, though sometimes detailed, are not generally too graphic, because more emphasis is placed on the sensual element than on physical action.

Royalties. A percentage of the retail price paid to an author for each copy of the book that is sold.

SAE. Self-addressed envelope.

SASE. Self-addressed stamped envelope.

Science fiction [vs. fantasy]. It is generally accepted that, to be science fiction, a story must have elements of science in either the conflict or setting (usually both). Fantasy, on the other hand, rarely utilizes science, relying instead on magic, mythological and neomythological beings and devices and outright invention for conflict and setting.

Second serial (reprint) rights. Permission for the reprinting of a work in another periodical after its first publication in book or magazine form.

Self-publishing. In this arrangement, the author keeps all income derived from the book, but he pays for its manufacturing, production and marketing.

Sequel. A literary work that continues the narrative of a previous, related story or novel.

Serial rights. The rights given by an author to a publisher to print a piece in one or more periodicals.

Serialized novel. A book-length work of fiction published in sequential issues of a periodical.

Setting. The environment and time period during which the action of a story takes place.

Short short story. A condensed piece of fiction, usually under 1,000 words.

Simultaneous submission. The practice of sending copies of the same manuscript to several editors or publishers at the same time. Some editors refuse to consider such submissions.

Slant. A story's particular approach or style, designed to appeal to the readers of a specific magazine.

Slice of life. A presentation of characters in a seemingly mundane situation which offers the reader a flash of illumination about the characters or their situation.

Resources

Slush pile. A stack of unsolicited manuscripts in the editorial offices of a publisher.

Social fiction. Fiction written with the purpose of bringing about positive changes in society.

Soft/sociological science fiction. Science fiction with an emphasis on society and culture versus scientific accuracy.

Space opera. Epic science fiction with an emphasis on good guys versus bad guys.

Speculation (or Spec). An editor's agreement to look at an author's manuscript with no promise to purchase.

Speculative fiction (SpecFic). The all-inclusive term for science fiction, fantasy and horror.

Splatterpunk. Type of horror fiction known for its very violent and graphic content.

Subsidiary. An incorporated branch of a company or conglomerate (e.g. Alfred Knopf, Inc., a subsidiary of Random House, Inc.).

Subsidiary rights. All rights other than book publishing rights included in a book contract, such as paperback, book club and movie rights.

Subsidy publisher. A book publisher who charges the author for the cost of typesetting, printing and promoting a book. Also called a vanity publisher.

Subterficial fiction. Innovative, challenging, nonconventional fiction in which what seems to be happening is the result of things not so easily perceived.

Suspense. A genre of fiction where the plot's primary function is to build a feeling of anticipation and fear in the reader over its possible outcome.

Synopsis. A brief summary of a story, novel or play. As part of a book proposal, it is a comprehensive summary condensed in a page or page and a half.

Tabloid. Publication printed on paper about half the size of a regular newspaper page (e.g. *The National Enquirer*).

Tearsheet. Page from a magazine containing a published story.

Techno-Thriller. This genre utilizes many of the same elements as the thriller, with one major difference. In techno-thrillers, technology becomes a major character. In Tom Clancy's *The Hunt for Red October* for example, specific functions of the submarine become crucial to plot development.

Theme. The dominant or central idea in a literary work; its message, moral or main thread.

Thriller. A novel intended to arouse feelings of excitement or suspense. Works in this genre are highly sensational, usually focusing on illegal activities, international espionage, sex and violence. A thriller is often a detective story in which the forces of good are pitted against the forces of evil in a kill-or-be-killed situation.

Trade paperback. A softbound volume, usually around 5X8, published and designed for the general public, available mainly in bookstores.

Traditional fantasy. Fantasy with an emphasis on magic, using characters with the ability to practice magic, such as wizards, witches, dragons, elves and unicorns.

Unsolicited manuscript. A story or novel manuscript that an editor did not specifically ask to see.

Urban fantasy. Fantasy that takes magical characters such as elves, fairies, vampires or wizards and places them in modern-day settings, often in the inner city.

Resources

Vanity publisher. See subsidy publisher.

Viewpoint. The position or attitude of the first- or third-person narrator or multiple narrators, which determines how a story's action is seen and evaluated.

Western. Genre with a setting in the West, usually between 1860-1890, with a formula plot about cowboys or other aspects of frontier life.

Whodunit. Genre dealing with murder, suspense and the detection of criminals.

Work-for-hire. Work that another party commissions you to do, generally for a flat fee. The creator does not own the copyright and therefore cannot sell any rights.

Young adult. The general classification of books written for readers 12 and up.

Zine. Often one- or two-person operations run from the home of the publisher/editor. Themes tend to be specialized, personal, experimental and often controversial.

Genre Glossary

Definitions of Fiction Subcategories

The following were provided courtesy of The Extended Novel Writing Workshop, created by the staff of Writers Online Workshops (www.writersonlineworkshops.com).

MYSTERY SUBCATEGORIES

The major mystery subcategories are listed below, each followed by a brief description and the names of representative authors, so you can sample each type of work. Note that we have loosely classified "suspense/thriller" as a mystery category. While these stories do not necessarily follow a traditional "whodunit" plot pattern, they share many elements with other mystery categories. In addition, many traditional mysteries are marketed as suspense/ thriller because of this category's current appeal in the marketplace. Since the lines between categories are frequently blurred, it seems practical to include them all here.

Classic Mystery (Whodunit). A crime (almost always a murder or series of murders) is solved. The detective is the viewpoint character; the reader never knows any more or less about the crime than the detective, and all the clues to solving the crime are available to the reader.

Amateur detective. As the name implies, the detective is not a professional detective (private or otherwise), but is almost always a professional something. This professional association routinely involves the protagonist in criminal cases (in a support capacity), gives him or her a special advantage in a specific case, or provides the contacts and skills necessary to solve a particular crime. (Jonathan Kellerman, Patricia Cornwell, Jan Burke)

Courtroom Drama. The action takes place primarily in the courtroom; the protagonist is generally a defense attorney out to prove the innocence of his or her client by finding the real culprit. (Scott Turow, Steve Martini, Richard North Patterson, John Grisham)

Cozy. A special class of the amateur detective category that frequently features a female protagonist. (Agatha Christie's Miss Marple stories are the classic example.) There is less on-stage violence than in other categories and the plot is often wrapped up in a final scene where the detective identifies the murderer and explains how the crime was solved. In contemporary stories, the protagonist can be anyone from a chronically curious housewife to a mystery-buff clergyman to a college professor, but he or she is usually quirky, even eccentric. (Susan Isaacs, Andrew Greeley, Lillian Jackson Braun)

Espionage. The international spy novel is less popular since the end of the cold war, but stories can still revolve around political intrigue in unstable regions. (John le CarrŽ, Ken Follett)

Heists and Capers. The crime itself is the focus. Its planning and execution are seen in detail and the participants are fully-drawn characters that may even be portrayed sympathetically. One character is the obvious leader of the group (the ``brains''); the other members are often brought together by the leader specifically for this job and may or may not have a previous association. In a heist, no matter how clever or daring the characters are, they are still portrayed as criminals and the expectation is that they will be caught and punished (but not always). A caper is more light hearted, even comedic. The participants may have a noble goal (something other than personal gain) and often get away with the crime. (Eric Ambler, Tony Kenrick, Leslie Hollander)

Historical. May be any category or subcategory of mystery, but with an emphasis on setting, the details of which must be diligently researched. But beyond the historical details (which must never overshadow the story), the plot develops along the lines of its contemporary counterpart. (Candace Robb, Caleb Carr, Anne Perry)

Juvenile/Young adult. Written for the 8-12 age group (Middle Grade) or the 12 and up age group (Young Adult), the crime in these stories may or may not be murder, but it is serious. The protagonist is a kid (or group of kids) in the same age range as the targeted reader. There is no graphic violence depicted, but the stories are scary and the villains are realistic. (Mary Downing Hahn, Wendy Corsi Staub, Cameron Dokey, Norma Fox Mazer)

Medical thriller. The plot can involve a legitimate medical threat (such as the outbreak of a virulent plague) or the illegal or immoral use of medical technology. In the former scenario, the protagonist is likely to be the doctor (or team) who identifies the virus and procures the antidote; in the latter he or she could be a patient (or the relative of a victim) who uncovers the plot and brings down the villain. (Robin Cook, Michael Palmer, Michael Crichton, Stanley Pottinger)

Police procedurals. The most realistic category, these stories require the most meticulous research. A police procedural may have more than one protagonist since cops rarely work alone. Conflict between partners, or between the detective and his or her superiors is a common theme. But cops are portrayed positively as a group, even though there may be a couple of bad or ineffective law enforcement characters for contrast and conflict. Jurisdictional disputes are still popular sources of conflict as well. (Lawrence Treat, Joseph Wambaugh, Ridley Pearson, Julie Smith)

Private detective. When described as ``hard-boiled,'' this category takes a tough stance. Violence is more prominent, characters are darker, the detectiveÆwhile almost always licensed by the stateÆoperates on the fringes of the law, and there is often open resentment between the detective and law enforcement. More ``enlightened'' male detectives and a crop of contemporary females have brought about new trends in this category. (For female P.I.sÆSue Grafton, Sara Paretsky; for male P.I.sÆJohn D. MacDonald, Lawrence Sanders, Robert Parker)

Suspense/Thriller. Where a classic mystery is always a whodunit, a suspense/thriller novel may deal more with the intricacies of the crime, what motivated it, and how the villain (whose identity may be revealed to the reader early on) is caught and brought to justice. Novels in this category frequently employ multiple points of view and have a broader scope than a more traditional murder mystery. The crime may not even involve murder—it may be a threat to global economy or regional ecology; it may be technology run amok or abused at the hands of an unscrupulous scientist; it may involve innocent citizens victimized for personal or corporate gain. Its perpetrators are kidnappers, stalkers, serial killers, rapists, pedophiles, computer hackers, or just about anyone with an evil intention and the means to carry it out. The protagonist may be a private detective or law enforcement official, but is just as likely to be a doctor, lawyer, military officer or other individual in a unique position to identify the villain and bring him or her to justice. (James Patterson, John J. Nance, Michael Connelly)

Technothriller. These are replacing the traditional espionage novel, and feature technology as an integral part of not just the setting, but the plot as well. (Tom Clancy, Stephen Coonts)

Woman in Jeopardy. A murder or other crime may be committed, but the focus is on the woman (and/or her children) currently at risk, her struggle to understand the nature of the danger, and her eventual victory over her tormentor. The protagonist makes up for her lack of physical prowess with intellect or special skills, and solves the problem on her own or with the help of her family (but she runs the show). Closely related to this category is the Romantic Suspense. But, while the heroine in a romantic suspense is certainly a "woman in jeopardy," the mystery or suspense element is subordinate to the romance. (Mary Higgins Clark, Mary Stewart, Jessica Mann)

ROMANCE SUBCATEGORIES

These categories and subcategories of romance fiction have been culled from the *Romance Writer's Sourcebook* (Writer's Digest Books) and Phyllis Taylor Pianka's *How to Write Romances* (Writer's Digest Books). We've arranged the "major" categories below with the subcategories beneath them, each followed by a brief description and the names of authors who write in each category, so you can sample representative works.

Category or Series. These are published in ``lines'' by individual publishing houses (such as Harlequin and Silhouette); each line has its own requirements as to word length, story content and amount of sex. (Debbie Macomber, Nora Roberts, Glenda Sanders)

Christian. With an inspirational, Christian message centering on the spiritual dynamic of the romantic relationship and faith in God as the foundation for that relationship; sensuality is played down. (Janelle Burnham, Ann Bell, Linda Chaikin, Catherine Palmer, Dee Henderson, Lisa Tawn Bergen)

Glitz. So called because they feature (generally wealthy) characters with high-powered positions in careers that are considered to be glamorousÆhigh finance, modeling/acting, publishing, fashionÆand are set in exciting or exotic (often metropolitan) locales such as Monte Carlo, Hollywood, London or New York. (Jackie Collins, Judith Krantz)

Historical. Can cover just about any historical (or even prehistorical) period. Setting in the historical is especially significant, and details must be thoroughly researched and accurately presented. For a sampling of a variety of historical styles try Laura Kinsell (*Flowers from the Storm*), Mary Jo Putney (*The Rake and the Reformer*) and Judy Cuevas (*Bliss*). Some currently popular periods/themes in historicals are:

- *Gothic:* historical with a strong element of suspense and a feeling of supernatural events, although these events frequently have a natural explanation. Setting plays an important role in establishing a dark, moody, suspenseful atmosphere. (Phyllis Whitney, Victoria Holt)

- *Historical fantasy:* with traditional fantasy elements of magic and magical beings, frequently set in a medieval society. (Amanda Glass, Jayne Ann Krentz, Kathleen Morgan, Jessica Bryan, Taylor Quinn Evans, Carla Simpson, Karyn Monk)

- *Early American:* usually Revolution to Civil War, set in New England or the South, but "frontier" stories set in the American West are quite popular as well. (Robin Lee Hatcher, Elizabeth Lowell, Heather Graham)

- *Native American:* where one or both of the characters are Native Americans; the conflict between cultures is a popular theme. (Carol Finch, Elizabeth Grayson, Karen Kay, Kathleen Harrington, Genell Dellin, Candace McCarthy)

- *Regency:* set in England during the Regency period from 1811-1820. (Carol Finch, Elizabeth Elliott, Georgette Heyer, Joan Johnston, Lynn Collum)

Multicultural. Most currently feature African-American or Hispanic couples, but editors are looking for other ethnic stories as well. Multiculturals can be contemporary or historical, and fall into any sub-category. (Rochelle Alers, Monica Jackson, Bette Ford, Sandra Kitt, Brenda Jackson)

Paranormal. Containing elements of the supernatural or science fiction/fantasy. There are numerous subcategories (many stories combine elements of more than one) including:

- *Time travel:* One or more of the characters travels to another timeÆusually the pastÆto find love. (Jude Devereaux, Linda Lael Miller, Diana Gabaldon, Constance O'Day Flannery)

- *Science fiction/Futuristic:* S/F elements are used for the story's setting: imaginary worlds, parallel universes, Earth in the near or distant future. (Marilyn Campbell, Jayne Ann Krentz, J.D. Robb [Nora Roberts], Anne Avery)

- *Contemporary fantasy:* From modern ghost and vampire stories to "New Age" themes such as extraterrestrials and reincarnation. (Linda Lael Miller, Anne Stuart, Antoinette Stockenberg, Christine Feehan)

Romantic Comedy. Has a fairly strong comic premise and/or a comic perspective in the author's voice or the voices of the characters (especially the heroine). (Jennifer Crusie, Susan Elizabeth Phillips)

Romantic Suspense. With a mystery or psychological thriller subplot in addition to the romance plot. (Mary Stewart, Barbara Michaels, Tami Hoag, Nora Roberts, Linda Howard, Catherine Coulter)

Single title. Longer contemporaries that do not necessarily conform to the requirements of a specific romance line and therefore feature more complex plots and nontraditional characters. (Mary Ruth Myers, Nora Roberts, Kathleen Gilles Seidel, Kathleen Korbel)

Young Adult. Focus is on first love with very little, if any, sex. These can have bittersweet endings, as opposed to the traditional romance happy ending, since first loves are often lost loves. (YA historical—Nancy Covert Smith, Louise Vernon; YA contemporary—Mary Downing Hahn, Kathryn Makris)

SCIENCE FICTION SUBCATEGORIES

Peter Heck, in his article "Doors to Other Worlds: Trends in Science Fiction and Fantasy," which appears in the 1996 edition of *Science Fiction and Fantasy Writer's Sourcebook* (Writer's Digest Books), identifies some science fiction trends that have distinct enough characteristics to be defined as categories. These distinctions are frequently the result of marketing decisions as much as literary ones, so understanding them is important in deciding where your novel idea belongs. We've supplied a brief description and the names of authors who write in each category. In those instances where the author writes in more than one category, we've included titles of appropriate representative works.

Hard science fiction. Based on the logical extrapolation of real science to the future. In these stories the scientific background (setting) may be as, or more, important than the characters. (Larry Niven)

Social science fiction. The focus is on how the characters react to their environments. This category includes social satire. (George Orwell's *1984* is a classic example.) (Margaret Atwood, *The Handmaid's Tale*; Ursula K. Le Guin, *The Left Hand of Darkness*; Marge Piercy, *Woman on the Edge of Time*)

Military science fiction. Stories about war that feature traditional military organization and tactics extrapolated into the future. (Jerry Pournelle, David Drake, Elizabeth Moon)

Cyberpunk. Characters in these stories are tough outsiders in a high-tech, generally near-future society where computers have produced major changes in the way that society functions. (William Gibson, Bruce Sterling, Pat Cadigan, Wilhelmina Baird)

Space opera. From the term "horse opera," describing a traditional good-guys-vs-bad-guys western, these stories put the emphasis on sweeping action and larger-than-life characters. The focus on action makes these stories especially appealing for film treatment. (The Star Wars series is one of the best examples, also Samuel R. Delany.)

Alternate history. Fantasy, sometimes with science fiction elements, that changes the accepted account of actual historical events or people to suggest an alternate view of history. (Ted Mooney, *Traffic and Laughter*; Ward Moore, *Bring the Jubilee*; Philip K. Dick, *The Man in the High Castle*)

Steampunk. A specific type of alternate history science fiction set in Victorian England in which characters have access to 20th-century technology. (William Gibson; Bruce Sterling, *The Difference Engine*)

New Age. A category of speculative fiction that deals with subjects such as astrology, psychic phenomena, spiritual healing, UFOs, mysticism and other aspects of the occult. (Walter Mosley, *Blue Light*; Neil Gaiman)

Science fantasy. Blend of traditional fantasy elements with scientific or pseudo-scientific support (genetic engineering, for example, to "explain" a traditional fantasy creature like the dragon). These stories are traditionally more character driven than hard science fiction. (Anne McCaffrey, Mercedes Lackey, Marion Zimmer Bradley)

Science fiction mystery. A cross-genre blending that can either be a more-or-less traditional science fiction story with a mystery as a key plot element, or a more-or-less traditional whodunit with science fiction elements. (Philip K. Dick, Lynn S. Hightower)

Science fiction romance. Another genre blend that may be a romance with science fiction elements (in which case it is more accurately placed as a subcategory within the romance genre) or a science fiction story with a strong romantic subplot. (Anne McCaffrey, Melanie Rawn, Kate Elliot)

Young Adult. Any subcategory of science fiction geared to a YA audience (12-18), but these are usually shorter novels with characters in the central roles who are the same age as (or slightly older than) the targeted reader. (Jane Yolen, Andre Norton)

FANTASY SUBCATEGORIES

Before we take a look at the individual fantasy categories, it should be noted that, for purposes of these supplements, we've treated fantasy as a genre distinct from science fiction. While these two are closely related, there are significant enough differences to warrant their separation for study purposes. We have included here those science fiction categories that have strong fantasy elements, or that have a significant amount of crossover (these categories appear in both the science fiction and the fantasy supplements), but "pure" science fiction categories are not included below. If you're not sure whether your novel is fantasy or science fiction, consider this definition by Orson Scott Card in *How to Write Science Fiction and Fantasy* (Writer's Digest Books):

"Here's a good, simple, semi-accurate rule of thumb: If the story is set in a universe that follows the same rules as ours, it's science fiction. If it's set in a universe that doesn't follow our rules, it's fantasy.

Or in other words, science fiction is about what could be but isn't; fantasy is about what couldn't be."

But even Card admits this rule is only "semi-accurate." He goes on to say that the real boundary between science fiction and fantasy is defined by how the impossible is achieved: "If you have people do some magic, impossible thing [like time travel] by stroking a talisman or praying to a tree, it's fantasy; if they do the same thing by pressing a button or climbing inside a machine, it's science fiction."

Peter Heck, in his article "Doors to Other Worlds: Trends in Science Fiction and Fantasy," which appears in the 1996 edition of the *Science Fiction and Fantasy Writer's Sourcebook* (Writer's Digest Books), does note some trends that have distinct enough characteristics to be defined as separate categories. These categories are frequently the result of marketing decisions as much as literary ones, so understanding them is important in deciding where your novel idea belongs. We've supplied a brief description and the names of authors who write in each category, so you can sample representative works.

Arthurian. Re-working of the legend of King Arthur and the Knights of the Round Table. (T.H. White, *The Once and Future King*; Marion Zimmer Bradley, *The Mists of Avalon*)

Contemporary (also called "urban") fantasy. Traditional fantasy elements (such as elves and magic) are incorporated into an otherwise recognizable modern setting. (Emma Bull, *War for the Oaks*; Mercedes Lackey, *The SERRAted Edge*; Terry Brooks, the Knight of the Word series)

Dark fantasy. Closely related to horror, but generally not as graphic. Characters in these stories are the "darker" fantasy types: vampires, witches, werewolves, demons, etc. (Anne Rice; Clive Barker, *Weaveworld*, *Imajica*; Fred Chappell)

Fantastic alternate history. Set in an alternate historical period (in which magic would not have been a common belief) where magic works, these stories frequently feature actual historical figures. (Orson Scott Card, *Alvin Maker*)

Game-related fantasy. Plots and characters are similar to high fantasy, but are based on a particular role-playing game. (Dungeons and Dragons; Magic: The Gathering; Dragonlance Chronicles; Forgotten Realms; Dark Sun)

Heroic fantasy. The fantasy equivalent to military science fiction, these are stories of war and its heroes and heroines. (Robert E. Howard, the Conan the Barbarian series; Elizabeth Moon, *Deed of Paksenarion*; Michael Moorcock, the Elric series)

High fantasy. Emphasis is on the fate of an entire race or nation, threatened by an ultimate evil. J.R.R. Tolkien's Lord of the Rings trilogy is a classic example. (Terry Brooks, David Eddings, Margaret Weis, Tracy Hickman)

Historical fantasy. The setting can be almost any era in which the belief in magic was strong; these are essentially historical novels where magic is a key element of the plot and/or setting. (Susan Schwartz, *Silk Road and Shadow*; Margaret Ball, *No Earthly Sunne*; Tim Powers, *The Anubis Gates*)

Juvenile/Young adult. Can be any type of fantasy, but geared to a juvenile (8-12) or YA audience (12-18); these are shorter novels with younger characters in central roles. (J.K. Rowling, Christopher Paolini, C.S. Lewis)

Science fantasy. A blend of traditional fantasy elements with scientific or pseudo-scientific support (genetic engineering, for example, to "explain" a traditional fantasy creature like the dragon). These stories are traditionally more character driven than hard science fiction. (Anne McCaffrey, Mercedes Lackey, Marion Zimmer Bradley)

HORROR SUBCATEGORIES

Subcategories in horror are less well defined than in other genres and are frequently the result of marketing decisions as much as literary ones. But being familiar with the terms used to describe different horror styles can be important in understanding how your own novel might be best presented to an agent or editor. What follows is a brief description of the most commonly used terms, along with names of authors and, where necessary, representative works.

Dark Fantasy. Sometimes used as a euphemistic term for horror in general, but also refers to a specific type of fantasy, usually less graphic than other horror subcategories, that features more ``traditional'' supernatural or mythical beings (vampires, werewolves, zombies, etc.) in either contemporary or historical settings. (Contemporary: Stephen King, *Salem's Lot*; Thomas Tessier, *The Nightwalker*. Historical: Brian Stableford, *The Empire of Fear*; Chelsea Quinn Yarbro, *Werewolves of London*.)

Hauntings. "Classic" stories of ghosts, poltergeists and spiritual possessions. The level of violence portrayed varies, but many writers in this category exploit the reader's natural fear of the unknown by hinting at the horror and letting the reader's imagination supply the details. (Peter Straub, *Ghost Story*; Richard Matheson, *Hell House*)

Juvenile/Young Adult. Can be any horror style, but with a protagonist who is the same age as, or slightly older than, the targeted reader. Stories for middle grades (eight to 12 years old) are scary, with monsters and violent acts that might best be described as "gross," but stories for young adults (12-18) may be more graphic. (R.L. Stine, Christopher Pike, Carol Gorman)

Psychological horror. Features a human monster with horrific, but not necessarily supernatural, aspects. (Thomas Harris, *The Silence of the Lambs*, *Hannibal*; Dean Koontz, *Whispers*)

Splatterpunk. Very graphic depiction of violence—often gratuitous—popularized in the 1980s, especially in film. (*Friday the 13th*, *Halloween*, *Nightmare on Elm Street*, etc.)

Supernatural/Occult. Similar to the dark fantasy, but may be more graphic in its depiction of violence. Stories feature satanic worship, demonic possession, or ultimate evil incarnate in an entity or supernatural being that may or may not have its roots in traditional mythology or folklore. (Ramsey Campbell; Robert McCammon; Ira Levin, *Rosemary's Baby*; William Peter Blatty, *The Exorcist*; Stephen King, *Pet Sematary*)

Technological horror. "Monsters" in these stories are the result of science run amok or technology turned to purposes of evil. (Dean Koontz, *Watchers*; Michael Crichton, *Jurassic Park*)

Professional Organizations

AGENTS' ORGANIZATIONS

Association of Authors' Agents (AAA), 20 John St., London WC1N 2DR, United Kingdom. (44)(20)7405-6774. E-mail: aaa@apwatt. Web site: www.agentsassoc.co.uk.

Association of Authors' Representatives (AAR), 676A 9th Ave., #312, New York NY 10036. (212)840-5777. E-mail: aarinc@mindspring.com. Web site: www.aar-online.org.

Association of Talent Agents (ATA), 9255 Sunset Blvd., Suite 930, Los Angeles CA 90069. (310)274-0628. Fax: (310)274-5063. E-mail: shellie@agentassociation.com. Web site: www.agentassociation.com.

WRITERS' ORGANIZATIONS

Academy of American Poets, 584 Broadway, Suite 604, New York NY 10012-5243. (212)274-0343. Fax: (212)274-9427. E-mail: academy@poets.org. Web site: www.poets.org.

American Crime Writers League (ACWL), 17367 Hilltop Ridge Dr., Eureka MO 63205. Web site: www.acwl.org.

American Medical Writers Association (AMWA), 40 W. Gude Dr., Suite 101, Rockville MD 20850-1192. (301)294-5303. Fax: (301)294-9006. E-mail: amwa@amwa.org. Web site: www.amwa.org.

American Screenwriters Association (ASA), 269 S. Beverly Dr., Suite 2600, Beverly Hills CA 90212-3807. (866)265-9091. E-mail: asa@goasa.com. Website: www.asascreenwriters.com.

American Translators Association (ATA), 225 Reinekers Lane, Suite 590, Alexandria VA 22314. (703)683-6100. Fax: (703)683-6122. E-mail: ata@atanet.org. Web site: www.atanet.org.

Education Writers Association (EWA), 2122 P St. NW, Suite 201, Washington DC 20037. (202)452-9830. Fax: (202)452-9837. E-mail: ewa@ewa.org. Web site: www.ewa.org.

Garden Writers Association (GWA), 10210 Leatherleaf Ct., Manassas VA 20111. (703)257-1032. Fax: (703)257-0213. Web site: www.gardenwriters.org.

Horror Writers Association (HWA), 244 5th Ave., Suite 2767, New York NY 10001. E-mail: hwa@horror.org. Web site: www.horror.org.

The International Women's Writing Guild (IWWG), P.O. Box 810, Gracie Station, New York

NY 10028-0082. (212)737-7536. Fax: (212)737-9469. E-mail: dirhahn@iwwg.org. Web site: www.iwwg.com.

Mystery Writers of America (MWA), 17 E. 47th St., 6th Floor, New York NY 10017. (212)888-8171. Fax: (212)888-8107. E-mail: mwa@mysterywriters.org. Web site: www.mysterywriters.org.

National Association of Science Writers (NASW), P.O. Box 890, Hedgesville WV 25427. (304)754-5077. Fax: (304)754-5076. E-mail: diane@nasw.org. Web site: www.nasw.org.

National Association of Women Writers (NAWW), 24165 IH-10 W., Suite 217-637, San Antonio TX 78257. Web site: www.naww.org.

Organization of Black Screenwriters (OBS). Web site: www.obswriter.com.

Outdoor Writers Association of America (OWAA), 121 Hickory St., Suite 1, Missoula MT 59801. (406)728-7434. Fax: (406)728-7445. E-mail: krhoades@owaa.org. Web site: www.owaa.org.

Poetry Society of America (PSA), 15 Gramercy Park, New York NY 10003. (212)254-9628. Web site: www.poetrysociety.org.

Poets & Writers, 72 Spring St., Suite 301, New York NY 10012. (212)226-3586. Fax: (212)226-3963. Web site: www.pw.org.

Romance Writers of America (RWA), 16000 Stuebner Airline Rd., Suite 140, Spring TX 77379. (832)717-5200. E-mail: info@rwanational.org. Web site: www.rwanational.org.

Science Fiction and Fantasy Writers of America (SFWA), P.O. Box 877, Chestertown MD 21620. E-mail: execdir@sfwa.org. Web site: www.sfwa.org.

Society of American Business Editors & Writers (SABEW), University of Missouri, School of Journalism, 385 McReynolds, Columbia MO 65211. (573)882-7862. Fax: (573)884-1372. E-mail: sabew@missouri.edu. Web site: www.sabew.org.

Society of American Travel Writers (SATW), 1500 Sunday Dr., Suite 102, Raleigh NC 27607. (919)861-5586. Fax: (919)787-4916. E-mail: satw@satw.org. Web site: www.satw.org.

Society of Children's Book Writers & Illustrators (SCBWI), 8271 Beverly Blvd., Los Angeles CA 90048. (323)782-1010. Fax: (323)782-1892. E-mail: scbwi@scbwi.org. Web site: www.scbwi.org.

Washington Independent Writers (WIW), 1001 Connecticut Ave. NW, Suite 701, Washington DC 20036. (202)775-5150. Fax: (202)775-5810. E-mail: info@washwriter.org. Web site: www.washwriter.org.

Western Writers of America (WWA). E-mail: wwa@unm.edu. Web site: www.westernwriters.org.

INDUSTRY ORGANIZATIONS

American Booksellers Association (ABA), 200 White Plains Rd., Tarrytown NY 10591. (914)591-2665. Fax: (914)591-2720. E-mail: info@bookweb.org. Web site: www.bookweb.org.

American Society of Journalists & Authors (ASJA), 1501 Broadway, Suite 302, New York NY 10036. (212)997-0947. Fax: (212)937-2315. E-mail: execdir@asja.org. Web site: www.asja.org.

Association for Women in Communications (AWC), 3337 Duke St., Alexandria VA 22314. (703)370-7436. Fax: (703)370-7437. E-mail: info@womcom.org. Web site: www.womcom.org.

Association of American Publishers (AAP), 71 5th Ave., 2nd Floor, New York NY 10003. (212)255-0200. Fax: (212)255-7007. Or, 50 F St. NW, Suite 400, Washington DC 20001. (202)347-3375. Fax: (202)347-3690. Web site: www.publishers.org.

The Association of Writers & Writing Programs (AWP), The Carty House, Mail stop 1E3, George Mason University, Fairfax VA 22030. (703)993-4301. Fax: (703)993-4302. E-mail: services@ awpwriter.org. Web site: www.awpwriter.org.

The Authors Guild, Inc., 31 E. 32nd St., 7th Floor, New York NY 10016. (212)563-5904. Fax: (212)564-5363. E-mail: staff@authorsguild.org. Web site: www.authorsguild.org.

Canadian Authors Association (CAA), Box 419, Campbellford ON K0L 1L0 Canada. (705)653-0323. Fax: (705)653-0593. E-mail: admin@canauthors.org. Web site: www.canauthors.org.

Christian Booksellers Association (CBA), P.O. Box 62000, Colorado Springs CO 80962-2000. (800)252-1950. Fax: (719)272-3510. E-mail: info@cbaonline.org. Web site: www.cbaonline.org.

The Dramatists Guild of America, 1501 Broadway, Suite 701, New York NY 10036. (212)398-9366. Fax: (212)944-0420. Web site: www.dramaguild.com.

National League of American Pen Women (NLAPW), 1300 17th St. NW, Washington DC 20036-1973. (202)785-1997. Fax: (202)452-8868. Website: www.americanpenwomen.org.

National Writers Association (NWA), 10940 S. Parker Rd., #508, Parker CO 80134. (303)841-0246. Fax: (303)841-2607. E-mail: anitaedits@aol.com. Web site: www.nationalwriters.com.

National Writers Union (NWU), 113 University Place, 6th Floor, New York NY 10003. (212)254-0279. Fax: (212)254-0673. E-mail: nwu@nwu.org. Web site: www.nwu.org.

PEN American Center, 588 Broadway, Suite 303, New York NY 10012-3225. (212)334-1660. Fax: (212)334-2181. E-mail: pen@pen.org. Web site: www.pen.org.

The Playwrights Guild of Canada (PGC), 54 Wolseley St., 2nd Floor, Toronto ON M5T 1A5 Canada. (416)703-0201. Fax: (416)703-0059. E-mail: info@playwrightsguild.ca. Web site: www. playwrightsguild.com.

Volunteer Lawyers for the Arts (VLA), One E. 53rd St., 6th Floor, New York NY 10022. (212)319-2787. Fax: (212)752-6575. Web site: www.vlany.org.

Women in Film (WIF), 8857 W. Olympic Blvd., Suite 201, Beverly Hills CA 90211. (310)657-5144. E-mail: info@wif.org. Web site: www.wif.org.

Women in the Arts Foundation (WIA), 32-35 30th St., D24, Long Island City NY 11106. (212)941-0130. E-mail: reginas@anny.org. Web site: www.anny.org/2/orgs/womeninarts/.

Women's National Book Association (WNBA), 2166 Broadway, #9-E, New York NY 10024. (212)208-4629. Web site: www.wnba-books.org.

Writers Guild of Alberta (WGA), 11759 Groat Rd., Edmonton AB T5M 3K6 Canada. (780)422-8174. Fax: (780)422-2663. E-mail: mail@writersguild.ab.ca. Web site: writersguild.ab.ca.

Writers Guild of America-East (WGA), 555 W. 57th St., Suite 1230, New York NY 10019. (212)767-7800. Fax: (212)582-1909. Web site: www.wgaeast.org.

Writers Guild of America-West (WGA), 7000 W. Third St., Los Angeles CA 90048. (323)951-4000. Fax: (323)782-4800. Web site: www.wga.org.

Writers Union of Canada (TWUC), 90 Richmond St. E., Suite 200, Toronto ON M5C 1P1 Canada. (416)703-8982. Fax: (416)504-9090. E-mail: info@writersunion.ca. Web site: www.writersunion. ca.

Resources

Literary Agents Category Index

Erotica

Ethnic

Experimental

Family

Family saga

Fantasy

Feminist

Agents Category Index

Horror

Humor

Juvenile

Mainstream

Military

New Age

Occult

Picture books

Police

Psychic

Satire

Science

Science fiction

Spiritual

Sports

Suspense

Thriller

Translation

Western

Westerns

Conference Index by Date

Our conference index organizes all conferences listed in this edition by the month in which they are held. If a conference bridges two months, you will find its name and page number under both monthly headings. If a conference occurs multiple times during the year (seasonally, for example), it will appear under each appropriate monthly heading. Turn to the listing's page number for exact dates and more detailed information.

Conference Index by Date

Category Index

Our category index makes it easy for you to identify publishers who are looking for a specific type of fiction. Publishers who are not listed under a fiction category either accept all types of fiction or have not indicated specific subject preferences. Also not appearing here are listings that need very specific types of fiction, e.g., "fiction about fly fishing only."

To use this index to find markets for your work, go to category title that best describes the type of fiction you write and look under either Magazines or Book Publishers (depending on whom you're targeting). Finally, read individual listings *carefully* to determine the publishers best suited to your work.

For a listing of agents and the types of fiction they represent, see the Literary Agents Category Index beginning on page 574.

Book Publishers

Adventure

Children's Juvenile

Comics/Graphic Novels

Erotica

Fantasy

Feminist

Horror

Humor Satire

Mainstream

Military/War

Mystery/Suspense

Psychic/Supernatural

Regional

Religious

Short Story Collections

Magazines
Adventure

Children's/Juvenile

Comics/Graphic Novels

Experimental

Family Saga

Feminist

Horror

Humor/Satire

Lesbian

Literary

Mainstream

Military/War

Mystery/Suspense

New Age

Psychic/Supernatural/Occult

Regional

Religious

Romance

Westerns

Young Adult/Teen

General Index

B

General Index